The final volume of *The New Cambridge Medieval History* covers the last century (interpreted broadly) of the traditional western Middle Ages. Often seen as a time of doubt, decline and division, the period is shown here as one of considerable innovation and development, much of which resulted from a conscious attempt by contemporaries to meet the growing demands of society and to find practical solutions to the social, religious and political problems which beset it.

The volume consists of four sections. Part I focuses on both the ideas and other considerations which guided men as they sought good government, and on the practical development of representation. Part II deals with aspects of social and economic development at a time of change and expansion. Part III discusses the importance of the life of the spirit: religion, education and the arts. Moving from the general to the particular, Part IV concerns itself with the history of the countries of Europe, emphasis being placed on the way that centralised (often monarchical) power developed, thus giving rise to the growth of the nation-states of the 'early modern' world.

The New Cambridge Medieval History

Volume VII *c.* 1415–*c.* 1500

Federigo da Montefeltro with his son, Guidobaldo, by Joos van Wassenhove, *c.* 1476,
Palazzo Ducale, Urbino

THE NEW
CAMBRIDGE
MEDIEVAL HISTORY

Volume VII c. 1415–c. 1500

EDITED BY

CHRISTOPHER ALLMAND

Professor of Medieval History
in the University of Liverpool

CAMBRIDGE
UNIVERSITY PRESS

PUBLISHED BY THE PRESS SYNDICATE OF THE UNIVERSITY OF CAMBRIDGE
The Pitt Building, Trumpington Street, Cambridge CB2 1RP, United Kingdom

CAMBRIDGE UNIVERSITY PRESS
The Edinburgh Building, Cambridge CB2 2RU, United Kingdom
40 West 20th Street, New York, NY 10011-4211, USA
10 Stamford Road, Oakleigh, Melbourne 3166, Australia

First published 1998

Printed in the United Kingdom at the University Press, Cambridge

Typeset in 10.5/12.5 Garamond   [SE]

A catalogue record for this book is available from the British Library

ISBN 0 521 38296 3 hardback

CONTENTS

vii

PLATES

Frontispiece
Federigo da Montefeltro with his son, Guidobaldo, by Joos van Wassenhove, *c.* 1476, Palazzo Ducale, Urbino (photo: SCALA)

between pages 490 and 491

1   Nuremberg, St Lorenz, interior of the choir, showing *The Annunciation* by Veit Stoss and the sacrament house (Bildarchiv Foto Marburg)

2   Jan van Eyck, *The Virgin of Chancellor Rolin*, *c.* 1435, Louvre, Paris (photo © RMN)

3   Jan and Hubert van Eyck, *The Adoration of the Lamb*, St Bavo's cathedral, Ghent, *c.* 1432 (photo © KIK/IRPA Brussels)

4   Rogier van der Weyden, *The Last Judgement*, Hôtel Dieu, Beaune, *c.* 1445 (photo J. Feuillie / © CNMHS)

5   Masaccio, *The Tribute Money*, Brancacci chapel, S. Maria del Carmine, *c.* 1427 (photo © Fratelli Alinari)

6   Gerolamo da Vicenza, *The Assumption and Coronation of the Virgin*, 1488, National Gallery, London (reproduced by permission of the Trustees)

7   Donatello, *The Feast of Herod*, bronze relief, baptistery, Siena cathedral (photo © Fratelli Alinari)

8   Dierec Bouts, *Portrait of a Man*, 1462, National Gallery, London (reproduced by permission of the Trustees)

9   Pisanello, marriage medal of Lionello d'Este, 1444, Victoria and Albert Museum, London (© The Board of Trustees)

10 Andrea Mantegna, *The Gonzaga Court*, Camera degli sposi, Mantua palace, 1474 (photo © Fratelli Alinari)

11 Donatello, equestrian statue of Gattamelata, Padua (photo © Fratelli Alinari)

12 Michelozzo di Bartolommeo, Palazzo Medici-Riccardi, Florence, begun 1444 (photo © Fratelli Alinari)

xi

MAPS

GENEALOGICAL TABLES

CONTRIBUTORS

CHRISTOPHER ALLMAND: Professor of Medieval History, University of Liverpool

JÁNOS BAK: Professor of Medieval Studies, Central European University, Budapest

ANTONY BLACK: Professor of the History of Political Thought, University of Dundee

ROBERT BLACK: Senior Lecturer in History, University of Leeds

WIM BLOCKMANS: Professor of History, State University of Leiden

ANTHONY BRYER: Senior Research Fellow, King's College, London: formerly Professor of Byzantine Studies, University of Birmingham

A.D. CARR: Reader in Welsh History, University of Wales, Bangor

BERNARD CHEVALIER: Professor Emeritus, University François-Rabelais, Tours

WENDY CHILDS: Reader in Medieval History, University of Leeds

PHILIPPE CONTAMINE: Professor of History, University of Paris IV

ART COSGROVE: President, University College, Dublin

PAUL CROSSLEY: Senior Lecturer, Courtauld Institute of Art, University of London

GARETH CURTIS: formerly Lecturer in Music, University of Manchester

MARIO DEL TREPPO: Professor of Medieval History, University of Naples 'Federico II'

BARRIE DOBSON: Professor of Medieval History, University of Cambridge

CHRISTOPHER DYER: Professor of Medieval Social History, University of Birmingham

FELIPE FERNÁNDEZ-ARMESTO: Faculty of Modern History, University of Oxford

JEAN-PHILIPPE GENET: Maître de Conférences, University of Paris I

ALEKSANDER GIEYSZTOR: Professor of Medieval History, University of Warsaw: formerly President of the Polish Academy of Sciences

ROSEMARY HORROX: Fellow of Fitzwilliam College, Cambridge

JOHN KLASSEN: Professor of History, Trinity Western University, Langley, British Colombia

NANCY SHIELDS KOLLMANN: Associate Professor of History, Stanford University

ANTHONY LUTTRELL: Formerly Assistant-Director and Librarian, British School at Rome

ANGUS MACKAY: Professor Emeritus, University of Edinburgh

DAVID MCKITTERICK: Librarian, Trinity College, Cambridge

MICHAEL MALLETT: Professor of History, University of Warwick

EDWARD POWELL: Formerly Fellow of Downing College, Cambridge

FRANCIS RAPP: Professor Emeritus, University of Strasburg

THOMAS RIIS: Professor of the History of Schleswig-Holstein, University of Kiel

ALAN RYDER: Professor Emeritus, University of Bristol

ROGER SABLONIER: Professor of Medieval History, University of Zurich

BERTRAND SCHNERB: Maître de Conférences, University of Paris IV

TOM SCOTT: Reader in History, University of Liverpool

ARMINDO DE SOUSA: Associate Professor, University of Oporto

MALCOLM VALE: Fellow of St John's College, Oxford

JACQUES VERGER: Professor of History, University of Paris XIII

JENNY WORMALD: Fellow of St Hilda's College, Oxford

ELIZABETH ZACHARIADOU: Professor at the Institute for Mediterranean Studies, Rethymnon

PREFACE

MUCH has happened in the development of historical study in the two generations which have elapsed since the tardy publication, in 1936, of the final volume of the original *Cambridge Medieval History*, to which the present volume is successor. More so than was the case sixty years ago, the historian today is a member of an ever-broadening international community, a development which is itself part of the greater internationalisation of society. Increasingly, the preoccupations of the historian take him beyond the boundaries, local, provincial or national, in which he normally works. Not only has he access to an ever-increasing number of books and periodicals which bring him knowledge and ideas from communities the world over. In an age of easier travel, he has opportunities to meet fellow specialists at conferences, whose published proceedings (if he cannot attend in person) he is often able to read, thus helping him keep up with current thinking and research. Furthermore, the results of his labours are given greater value by his conscious assimilation of the specialised knowledge of other disciplines (literature, art, philosophy for example) and other methodologies (such as those of the social scientist) which have given him a broader and better understanding of the past.

Such developments have greatly extended the horizons of modern historical scholarship. These have also been reflected in the way that much history is now taught, particularly in universities. The popularity of courses encompassing more than one of the traditional academic disciplines has forced teachers and researchers to look at their subjects or periods of interest within broader frameworks than might have been the case years ago. Add to this an awakening European consciousness and a growing willingness to consider the whole spectrum of European history, in both its unity and its diversity, as a field of comparison and contrast, and we have the conditions appropriate for the study of comparative history ready at hand.

The changes of approach can quickly be seen by comparing the contents of this volume with that published in 1936. Never mind the fact that this volume is

xvii

longer than its predecessor, and that the number of countries or states given a chapter to themselves has increased. More important is the fact that the number of chapters dealing with themes on a broadly European level has doubled. This underlines how the willingness and ability of historians to consider questions of this kind and in this way has greatly increased over the years. The decision to place the sixteen 'thematic' chapters (parts I, II and III) before, rather than after, those concerned with the development of the European states, the principal theme running through the fourth and final part of this *History*, is founded on the belief that both men and politics are part of a wider world picture which encompasses ideas, political, religious, cultural and artistic, as well as economic and social change and development. Before a subject or a period can be fully appreciated, something of its aspirations and culture must be understood. It is with this in mind, rather than with any intention of downgrading the individual political history of the states of Europe, that the more usual order of presenting history ('politics first, culture second') has been reversed.

Two concluding points may be made. The final century of the traditional Middle Ages has long suffered from being seen as a period of decay and decline which, in the eyes of some, inevitably required major changes to set the world 'on course' again. Such a view, however, has not unduly deterred a whole generation of researchers who have witnessed a significant shift of interest towards the late Middle Ages, and whose work has greatly enriched our understanding of fifteenth-century society. All over Europe, research has revealed an age of important, indeed dynamic, achievements, some of which are the outcome of earlier advances, others seeing their fulfilment only in the century to come. While the short-term, narrowly focused study can be of the greatest significance, the approach represented by this volume requires a willingness to see development in more than one field in terms of the *longue durée*.

It requires, too, that while each chapter (particularly those in part IV) should be separate and free-standing, each should also be regarded as part of an attempt to present Europe as a whole, rather than as a collection of individual entities. Here the approach by comparison and contrast, properly used, may be particularly fruitful. The ability to explain similar developments, like the skill in accounting for different ones, is something which may reasonably be asked of the historian. It is also a way of seeing what is both important and interesting in the history of Europe during a century which, far from being a dead end, was to complete what had been begun earlier and set in train what would be completed later.

ACKNOWLEDGEMENTS

THIS volume has been long in the making. Now that it is offered to the world, its Editor wishes to thank the contributors for their labours, their patience and understanding, as well as for coming to his rescue in times of difficulty. He is happy to acknowledge the help and advice of friends and colleagues freely and generously given at various times. Not least, he thanks the General Editors for their assistance at the planning stage of the venture. Members of the production team, most notably the volume's able copy-editor, Linda Randall, and its indexer, Meg Davies, have given much practical help in transforming a bulky typescript into an attractive volume. The calm encouragement consistently offered by William Davies, of the Cambridge University Press, has been greatly valued. It is acknowledged with particular gratitude. Anne Clough, Stephanie Dennison, Dr Stephen Rowell and Rosemarie Zamonski rendered valuable service with translations of several chapters submitted in languages other than that in which they finally appear.

ABBREVIATIONS

AB	*Annales de Bourgogne*
AHR	*American Historical Review*
AM	*Annales du Midi*
AN	*Annales de Normandie*
Annales ESC	*Annales: économies, sociétés, civilisations*
BBCS	*Bulletin of the Board of Celtic Studies*
BEC	*Bibliothèque de l'Ecole des Chartes*
BIHR	*Bulletin of the Institute of Historical Research*
BJRL	*Bulletin of the John Rylands Library*
BJRULM	*Bulletin of the John Rylands University Library of Manchester*
BL	British Library
BZ	*Byzantinische Zeitschrift*
DBI	*Dizionario biografico degli Italiani*
DOP	*Dumbarton Oaks Papers*
EconHR	*Economic History Review*
EETS	Early English Text Society
EHR	*English Historical Review*
HJ	*Historical Journal*
HZ	*Historische Zeitschrift*
IHS	*Irish Historical Studies*
JHI	*Journal of the History of Ideas*
JMedH	*Journal of Medieval History*
JModH	*Journal of Modern History*
JWCI	*Journal of the Warburg and Courtauld Institutes*
MA	*Le moyen âge*
NH	*Northern History*
NLWJ	*National Library of Wales Journal*
PBA	*Proceedings of the British Academy*
P&P	*Past & Present*

RH	*Revue historique*
RHS	Royal Historical Society
RQ	*Renaissance Quarterly*
RS	Rolls Series
SATF	Société des Anciens Textes Français
SHF	Société de l'Histoire de France
SHR	*Scottish Historical Review*
STS	Scottish Text Society
THSC	*Transactions of the Honourable Society of Cymmrodorion*
TRHS	*Transactions of the Royal Historical Society*
WHR	*Welsh History Review*

PART I

GOVERNMENT

CHAPTER I

POLITICS: THEORY AND PR.

Jean-Philippe Genet

EUROPE DOMINATED BY WAR

IN the summer of 1415 Henry V, king of England, invaded northern France. It might have been another of the lightning booty-raids of the previous century (the last had occurred in 1388), but once again an English force, as it withdrew, was overtaken by a French army in hot pursuit; once again, this time at Agincourt, the French suffered a disastrous defeat. The battle was to be the prelude to some forty years of warfare which brought both kingdoms in turn to the edge of the abyss. Yet the battle's importance is further highlighted by the realisation that it was one of a series which, within a period of a few years, was to spark off wars destined to become a characteristic of the new century. In 1410 Fernando, regent of Castile, had captured Antequera from the Moors of Granada, while in the same year the Teutonic knights had been routed at Grunwald (Tannenberg) by a Polish–Lithuanian coalition. In 1411 Sultan Süleyman eliminated his last dynastic rival at Kosmidion, thereby initiating the rebuilding of the Ottoman Empire, which Tamerlane's victory at the battle of Ankara, some ten years earlier, appeared to have permanently destroyed.

The list could be extended to form an unbroken line between the second phase of the Hundred Years War and the first of the Italian Wars, by way of the crusades against the Hussites and Charles the Bold's struggle against Louis XI, the Swiss, Lorraine and the Rhenish powers, quite apart from the civil conflicts in France, England and Castile. The Italian peninsula enjoyed relative peace only during the twenty or so years after the Peace of Lodi (1455), and between 1439 (the death of Albert II) and 1486 (Maximilian's partnership as ruler with his father, Frederick III of Habsburg) imperial power was unable to prevent internecine strife at the very heart of the Empire. In the east, two new powers, Muscovy and, above all, the Ottoman Empire, were putting eastern Europe to the sword.[1]

[1] Genet (1991).

age dominated by war, fifteenth-century thinkers were obsessed with
e, and sought ways and means to restore harmony to Europe, identified
ith Christianity,[2] which, after the defeat suffered at Nicopolis (1396) was
deemed in mortal danger from the advancing Turks. From Honoré Bouvet's
Arbre des batailles and Christine de Pisan's *Livre de la paix*, by way of humanistic
orations and treatises which punctuated the Italian Wars to one of the young
Erasmus's first compositions, such works *pro pace* proliferated until they
became a genre in their own right. The renewed outbreak of Anglo-French
hostilities had aroused the Council of Constance, and Sigismund, king of the
Romans, had undertaken a fruitless mission of peace (1416). Later in the
century, George of Poděbrady, king of Bohemia, with the help of the humanist, Antonio Marini, was to draw up a visionary 'plan for a universal peace',[3] in
fact merely a scheme for crushing the offensive of Pope Pius II (the humanist
Aeneas Sylvius Piccolomini) against the Czech Utraquists. This was the very
same Pius who succeeded in galvanising into action some of the faithful to
mount a crusade, a scheme aborted by his own death.[4]

CATEGORIES OF POLITICAL POWER

Europe comprised an involved network of rival and competitive states. In his
Mémoires (the earliest in a genre destined to achieve rapid popularity), Philippe
de Commynes, seeking to draw upon his personal experience in order to
understand how 'nations' prospered or declined, depicted a ruthless world of
warring princes, some wise, others foolish, surrounded by their counsellors,
armed only with their knowledge of politics. The consequence in the fifteenth
century was obvious; the annihilation of many minor powers, and thus the
formation of a 'simpler' political map of Europe.[5] In western Christendom the
great kingdoms, whose political organisation had in large measure progressed
beyond the merely feudal, finally achieved stability. This had been reached in
the British Isles (with the exception of Ireland), where the kingdom of
Scotland was cohesive enough to withstand the lengthy captivity of its
monarch, James I, and an almost endless succession of minors on the throne.
France, once the English attempt at conquest had failed and the Burgundian
state had collapsed, was left stronger and more united than she had ever been.
Once Brittany was incorporated, if not integrated, into the kingdom in 1491,
there was only one important principality left by the time of Louis XII's accession in 1498, that of the dukes of Bourbon, while the spoils from the houses of
Armagnac, Anjou (Anjou itself, Barrois, Provence) and Burgundy had enlarged
the kingdom. In Spain the union of the dynasties of Aragon and Castile

---

[2] Hay (1968).   [3] Messler (1973).   [4] Housley (1992).   [5] Tilly (1990).

allowed the new monarchy to absorb the Moorish kingdom of Granada, deemed so precious a political asset that it was speedily and brutally enhanced by the expulsion of the Jews (1492) and of the *mudejares* (1499). Thus the first 'modern states' had attained their majority.

The tendency to concentrate authority was a general one and could also be observed in those regions where other types of state pertained. At the end of the century the Italian peninsula was essentially divided into six regional states, only two of which, Savoy and Naples, had organisations comparable to those of the monarchies of western Europe. Florence, Milan and Venice were, at least to some extent, city-states, while during the fourteenth century the papal states had created a model principality which was astonishingly advanced. In the Empire, the promotion of dynastic marriages and the observance of rigid rules against the division of patrimony strengthened territorial principalities in, for example, Bavaria, Brandenburg, the Palatinate, Saxony and Württemberg. There the greatest successes were those recorded at the end of the century by the emperor-elect, Maximilian, who managed both to unite all the Habsburg territories and to realise his claims to a larger share of the Burgundian inheritance (Flanders, Artois, Franche-Comté and lands in the Low Countries). Maximilian, however, was always handicapped financially by the lack of a fiscal system comparable to that of the 'modern states': his status was that of supreme arbitrator in the conflicts and opposing interests of minor states. These were not simply a host of principalities; they included towns and leagues of towns, of nobles and of various communities, of which one at least, the Swiss Confederation, had achieved *de facto* independence.

On the fringes of the Empire, in Scandinavia, Hungary, Poland and, at the end of the century, even in Bohemia, yet another type of state was to be found, which might be termed 'extended', since, at times, monarchical power was embodied in a dynasty which transcended frontiers (Anjou, Luxemburg and Jagietto); monarchies, certainly, but where royal power was curtailed by a military nobility which was the real guardian of the nation's consciousness and made these states into 'noble republics'. There the towns, from the Hanseatic Bergen to the 'Saxon' towns of the Siebenburg, were often essentially 'foreign', populated by Jews and/or Germans, and there, too, the peasantry tended to retreat from liberty into a 'new' serfdom. The fact that the Jagietto family, through its different branches, extended its power from Poland and Lithuania to Hungary and Bohemia should not lead to a misunderstanding of the real nature of these states, which were sometimes powerful in military terms.

The costs of war were enormous and rising, and once field artillery had become indispensable, the cost was even further advanced. Spurred on by the vital necessity to generate an ever-increasing amount of capital, in the second half of the thirteenth century the growing 'modern states'[6] of western Europe had developed a means of raising money which guaranteed more abundant revenues than before:[7] national taxation, more or less by consent, amassed for warfare a growing percentage of their subjects' income and goods. From 1449 France was to be provided with a permanent professional army by this means.[8] This system of taxation allowed the 'modern states' to survive and prosper, despite cut-throat opposition. Taxation was the diversion of private means for the public good, and was plainly recognised as such; it was because the king protected his subjects' private assets that he could, in their own interest, ask them to contribute to their defence in time of need. As the revenues of these societies increased, so they functioned more effectively as states.[9]

It was in the 'modern states' of western Christendom that the 'internal' concentration of power developed most rapidly, since the relative efficiency of their state machinery, however modest, made it possible to compete success-fully both with those at the lower end of the power scale (the lords of the manor) and with those of middling authority (the semi-autonomous towns and principalities). Here judicial institutions, and therefore the law, played a determining role.[10] This development, which had reached different stages in every country (being far advanced in England, less so in France, much less so in the Iberian kingdoms), was more easily discernible in the 'modern states', yet was also taking place, if at a slower rate, among the territorial principalities of the Empire and in the Italian peninsula. Even so, a host of competing author-ities were left to perpetuate those seeking to legitimise and justify their very existence. These different levels of authority, superimposed one above the other, combined, with the co-existence of various types of state, to produce in Europe, in spite of the two-pronged impetus towards consolidation outlined above, an extremely complex and varied power structure.

THE ELEMENTS OF POLITICAL DIALOGUE

The 'modern states' of western Christendom were characterised by the provi-sion of substantial revenues derived from national taxation raised by consent. The *sine qua non* of this type of financial system was the existence, and the satis-factory functioning, of a certain level of dialogue between the prince and his subjects, in general by way of representative institutions. Dialogue, political intercourse between prince and subjects, was essential to the modern state, and indeed inseparable from it, since it made taxation possible by legalising it. The

[6] Genet (1990), pp. 261–81, and (1992); Blockmans (1993).
[7] Genet and Le Mené (1987); Bonney (1995).   [8] Contamine (1992), pp. 198–208.
[9] Black (1992), pp. 186–91, discussing Guenée (1991) and Reynolds (1984).
[10] Kaeuper (1988); Gouron and Rigaudière (1988); Krynen and Rigaudière (1992).

theoretical basis of this dialogue was borrowed from law, principally Roman law (the key concepts being necessity, consent and representation), from theology (political society, the *politia*, as a mystical body of which the king was head), and from classical philosophy (the very concept of the *res publica*, the *bien commun* or commonweal). In the practice of dialogue, however, none of these elements was serviceable in its original form. Thus, just as modern states had borrowed the theoretical foundations of political dialogue so, too, they borrowed the ways and means to put the theory into practice from institutions already in existence – the Church or towns, particularly Italian city-states which had already had to prove themselves as societies and bodies politic.

Both theory and practice needed adapting to the particular political society of each state on at least two levels. Though official parlance might well conjure up the vision of a collectivity aiming to include all adult males without discrimination, in practice dialogue was limited to a restricted political society which was actually consulted through representative institutions, the nobility and urban oligarchies,[11] but was dominated by the first whose outlook reflected the feudal and military ethic. On a different level, however, the dialogue was not restricted to these groups. The charters of manumission granted to the English rebels of 1381, the *ordonnances* which resulted from the demonstrations of the Parisian populace led by the butcher, Simon Caboche, in 1413, and the privileges granted by Mary of Burgundy in 1477 in response to the uprising by the people of Ghent[12] represented an enlargement of the political arena which already had a long history in the towns of Italy.

These trends were noted by contemporaries, who realised how rivalries were likely to lead to conflict. The tensions between the 'national' and the 'international' (Christendom, let us say) were recognised by theorists who, for example, devoted time to defining what an ambassador was in legal terms.[13] They were evident, too, in works aimed at a more general readership, witness the following conversation between an English and a French knight. To the Frenchman's remark that the Englishman was a sinner for waging an unjust war, the Englishman replied that he considered just 'everything commanded by the prince on the advice of his prelates and barons'. 'Then you are all sinners', retorted the Frenchman.[14] However, in an age when power was increasingly concentrated in the hands of the 'prince' (who might be an anointed king, a successful *condottiere* or a crafty *signore*), it needed a perceptive observer to note the differences between the societies and regimes which they governed. Fifteenth-century man marvelled at the rise and fall of 'princes', the theme of 'Fortune' enjoying an astonishing vogue. The character and magnificence of

---

[11] Contamine (1989); Bulst and Genet (1988).
[12] *L'ordonnance cabochienne*; Blockmans (1985).   [13] Arabeyre (1990).
[14] In Gerson, *Opera omnia*, IV, cols. 844–9, quoted by Guenée (1987), pp. 295–7.

princes, their virtues and vices, the degree of trust and loyalty they deserved, the defence, in the face of princely claims, of 'usages, customs and liberties' were the focus of much discussion. Modern state or not, it was the prince who polarised political opinions, dialogue and outlook.

THE SYMBOLISM OF POLITICS

Since the dialogue was public, and political society embraced groups whose level of culture was not high, any review of the history of political ideas and attitudes must avoid focusing too much on the 'great works' written for a circumscribed elite; as important is the study of their circulation and the intellectual milieu from which they derived.[15] The dissemination of a political message did not depend on words alone; coins, medals, seals, flags and emblems were ubiquitous and pregnant with meaning. Those celestial symbols, the French royal lilies which could be seen everywhere, were, because of their blue and gold hue (first in the hierarchy of colours), symbolic of the elect who could not be touched without sacrilege or *lèse majesté*.[16] Every king, every prince had his own 'political' church, starting with that housing the tombs of his dynasty: Westminster, Saint-Denis, the Charterhouses of Champmol, near Dijon, Miraflorès, Toledo cathedral and Batalha all testify to an identical concern. Complex iconographical schemes established therein a physical, visual, instantly perceptible link between a dynasty, its divine protectors and a whole gamut of religious and political principles.

Rites and ceremonies also played their part. Epitomising power, witnessed by an attentive audience, they became complex rituals, given tangible expression as dramatic presentations overlaid with symbolism. As both Joan of Arc and her contemporary, the Englishman, John, duke of Bedford, both fully realised, the anointing of the king of France gave legitimacy to his royalty in a visible and indisputable form. Royal progresses were occasions for celebrations. The ritual of the French king's *entrée* turned into a sort of Corpus Christi procession, when the king processed beneath a canopy exactly as did the Body of Christ, whose feast was one of the great liturgical inventions of the late Middle Ages which, what is more, had taken on civic, and therefore political, connotations.[17] In France the *lit de justice* became a more and more impressive occasion, providing opportunities for presenting the state in all its pomp, the monarch occupying centre stage.[18] Even the most complicated political theology, the concept of the king's two bodies, was demystified by being acted out in public. In a royal funeral cortège the monarch's mortal remains were accompa-

---

[15] Skinner (1978), pp. x–xi. [16] Beaune (1985), pp. 233–63; see Pastoureau (n.d.), pp. 22–4.
[17] Guenée and Lehoux (1968), pp. 15–18; Rubin (1991). [18] Hanley (1983); Vale (1974).

nied by a magnificent effigy to show that, although the king was dead, he was none the less immortal, since a king never died.[19] In all these great rituals, revolving around the king's person, the spectators' role was allotted to the people. Some of these ceremonies brought the prince into very close proximity with his subjects, even the lowliest of them: on important liturgical feast days the dukes of Brabant shared their meal with hundreds of the poor and, when in Brussels at Pentecost, with the city's weavers.[20] State and civil ritual was frequently combined, thus enabling the guilds of London to play a key role in English royal progresses and ceremonies. Such dramatic events stirred the emotions and memories, and gave to those participating the feeling of belonging to a single political society.

Things were different on the Italian peninsula.[21] There, princes, lacking the authority derived from feudal roots, had to turn to their advantage those festivals and ceremonies through which, in an insecure world, cities affirmed their identity. When the doge of Venice lit a candle on the high altar of St Mark's basilica on 25 April each year, he was demonstrating both the sacred nature of his office and the close ties between the city and its patron saint. All Italian cities had similar kinds of festivals at all levels of society, the carnival being a particularly flourishing ritual with its emphasis on 'the world turned upside down', hence on egalitarianism.

By introducing changes into the traditional processions in Florence, Lorenzo the Magnificent undermined the republican order by downgrading the position of the patricians, the pillars of society, as well as by encouraging the carnival's excesses. Since, in a non-feudal society, it was pointless to stress the 'contract' between the prince and his subjects, a different theme was emphasised: the mystery and secrecy surrounding his authority, the source of both his strength and wisdom, testimony and consequence of his wisdom. Hence was devised a subtle interplay between the *vita activa* and the *vita contemplativa*, a concept still in its infancy among the monarchies of western Europe. The object of Mantegna's carefully thought out symbolism in *The Gonzago Court*, painted in Mantua between 1465 and 1475 and undoubtedly based on a scheme taken from Pliny's *Panegyricus* to Trajan, was to show that the prince alone was the embodiment of good government, while at the same time he retained an enigmatic quality, the prerequisite of that government, which could not be revealed to his subjects.[22]

---

[19] Kantorowicz (1957), pp. 422–3.   [20] Uyttebrouck (1992).
[21] Muir (1981); Trexler (1980); see Klapisch-Zuber (1985).   [22] Arasse (1985).

TEXTS AND SPEECHES: POLITICAL THEORY AND PRACTICE

It would be a mistake to believe that only educated elites read and understood texts; in the same way the pictures, gestures and spoken words known to us are indicative of more than a mass oral culture. Some rituals showed evidence of erudition. The *entrée* of Charles VIII into Vienne in 1490 demonstrated how images and concepts taken from Italian humanism were being introduced: Hercules personified the French king liberating the garden of Atlas from a serpent resembling the dragon, 'that wishes to reside in Brittany'.[23] Conversely, other works had a popular appeal. Lollardy and Hussitism gave birth to a vernacular literature targeted less at converts themselves than at those responsible for their systematic instruction. In 1450, English rebels had at least two notaries draw up copies of their demands, and it is known that Sir John Fastolf sent a servant to obtain one. Even rebel princes conducted advance publicity in the form of letters and proclamations. Political propaganda was becoming a well-established practice, with its own techniques, of which one was the use of the written word. Political prophecy, often irrational, helped to stir up the debate about government; astrology was a princely enthusiasm, and the proliferation of mystics bearing supposedly divine messages, of whom Joan of Arc was the most remarkable, was a characteristic of this age.

Speeches, in particular sermons, could convey unequivocal declarations of political thought. At the start of an English parliamentary session, members were treated to a speech-sermon by the chancellor, usually an ecclesiastic,[24] while those attending the opening of the French estates general might hear allocutions from such distinguished persons as Jean Juvénal des Ursins.[25] Nor was the practice unknown whereby the *Reichstag* would be addressed, such as it was by the pope's representative, Nicholas of Cusa at Frankfurt in 1442.[26]

The 'political speeches' thus delivered, sometimes in the heat of debate, often expressed political ideas.[27] Some, such as those of Jean Gerson, were written down and circulated; a version of the address given by Jean Petit to justify the assassination of Louis of Orleans on behalf of John, duke of Burgundy, was later to be included in Enguerrand de Monstrelet's chronicle.[28] These, and many others, reveal close links with theoretical texts which, without being direct descendants of political ideas, bear witness to the vigour of their circulation. 'In the first place the sovereign people created kings by its vote', pronounced Philippe Pot, echoing 'a king exists by the will of the people' (*rex*

---

[23] Guenée and Lehoux (1968), pp. 295–306.   [24] Chrimes (1936).

[25] Juvénal des Ursins, *Ecrits politiques*, II, pp. 409–49.

[26] *Deutsche Reichstagsakten*, XV:2, pp. 639–46 and 874–6; XVI:2, pp. 407–32 and 539–43; see also Angermeier (1984); Isenmann (1990).   [27] Masselin, *Journal*, pp. 147–57.

[28] Guenée (1992).

est a populi voluntate) of John of Paris, while the traditional metaphor of the body politic proved ever-popular with those who wished to express ideas political and social in their meaning.[29]

This language, springing from many roots, showed great diversity. Political literature and political philosophy can be traced back to the 'rediscovery' of Aristotle in the late thirteenth century which provided theologians contemporary with the birth of the 'modern state' with the concepts and vocabulary necessary to describe and elaborate this new category of European experience, politics. Yet, while the influence of thinkers of that age, Thomas Aquinas and Giles of Rome, was still dominant, the language was not strong enough (with the exception of the word 'political', derived from Greek *polis*, so that the adjective finally eclipsed the Latin noun, *politia*)[30] to have engendered a framework of ideas common to all members of political society. In a Europe of varied political experiences, several political languages co-existed in parallel, their idioms employed by powerful groups, the Church and the universities on the one hand, the legal professions on the other. There was a third area where the desire to communicate with the public was paramount, and where men versed in law and theology were frequently found, that of literary genres proper in all their rich diversity. In none did political language enjoy genuine autonomy: since it occupied a subordinate position, it varied according to the area's main preoccupations. Each must be examined in turn to see how political ideas developed in relation to those preoccupations, special attention being paid to possible points of contact between them.[31]

THEOLOGY AND POLITICS

Clerics and ecclesiastics who had completed their university studies in the faculty of arts had become acquainted with the political works of Antiquity: Cicero, Plato and, after about 1265, Aristotle, whose complete *Politica* had become available, along, in the years to come, with many distinguished commentaries.[32] To the theologian, politics were but part of a series of more complex problems, and it was mainly through the questions in their biblical commentaries and the *Sentences* of Peter Lombard that their political thinking crystallised. It was mainly in moments of exceptional circumstances or crisis that the theologians produced their ideas. William of Ockham, for example, wrote as a direct consequence of his period of asylum at the court of Louis of Bavaria; the bull *Unam sanctam* and treatises of the genre *De potestate papae* were the product of claims and counter-claims to sovereignty on behalf of Papacy

---

[29] Juvénal des Ursins, *Ecrits politiques*, II, p. 444; Cusanus, *Concordantia*, III, p. 41.
[30] Rubinstein (1987).   [31] Carlyle and Carlyle (1903–36); Burns (1988); Ullmann (1974).
[32] Flüeler (1992a) and (1992b).

or monarchy,[33] while the Great Schism produced a huge literature of its own, much of it strongly political in character. The assassination of Louis of Orleans in 1407 had led theologians such as Gerson and Petit to tackle the problem of tyrannicide. In consequence of the rivalry between the Jagiellonians and the Teutonic Order, the Dominican, Johann Falkenberg, refused to admit that the Lithuanians' conversion to Catholicism was sincere, and so he came to perceive the Jagiellonian king as a tyrant to be overthrown; the same rivalry led the Pole, Paulus Vladimiri, to uphold the opposing view before the Council of Constance.[34] But their ideas cannot be understood simply as texts; the point of departure must be the core issues of contemporary theology,[35] since it was the attitudes adopted in these debates which determined the contributions of theologians to the political issues of the time. The origins of these debates largely go back to the late thirteenth and early fourteenth centuries.

When Aquinas had attempted to reconcile faith and reason, Greco-Arabic knowledge and Christian theology, his efforts had been rejected by many since they appeared to reduce divine omnipotence to a mechanical role in the history of the universe.[36] This rejection and a desire to redefine the divine *potentia absoluta* had made a different approach necessary, particularly to resolve two problems: on the one hand, that of knowledge (hence the distinction between 'realists' and 'nominalists') and, on the other, that of sin, free will and predestination.[37] Ockham is often linked with the intellectuals who frequented the court of Louis of Bavaria to oppose the Papacy,[38] and in particular with Marsilius of Padua (the author of *Defensor pacis*, 1324) although the latter had very different views. Two major concepts were reaffirmed in the Bavarian crucible. The first was the absolute autonomy of political over religious authority; since, in theory at least, the sovereign's power derived from the choice or will of the people, states and political organisms in general appeared completely natural; neither their law nor justice required legitimation, as they were based solely on the legitimacy, purely positive, of the state itself. Marsilius rejected the very principle of any spiritual authority whatsoever. The second idea was that it was the citizens/subjects who constituted the state, which was nothing other than the collectivity of its citizens. The concept of the political community (parallel to that of the Church) took as its origin the individuals who composed it and who had, formally or not, chosen a particular type of government.[39]

Ockham and Marsilius were read and imitated until the early sixteenth century. The author of the *Somnium Viridarii* (or *Songe du Verger*), written about

---

[33] Walther (1976); A. Black, below, ch. 3; on the tracts *De potestate papae*, see Miethke (1982) and (1991a).
[34] Belch (1965).   [35] Leff (1976); Ozment (1980).   [36] Leff (1968), p. 229.   [37] Stürner (1987).
[38] Lagarde (1956–70), v, pp. 281–9; McGrade (1974), pp. 37ff; see also Miethke (1969).
[39] Quillet (1970).

1374 at the behest of King Charles V, borrowed extensively from Marsilius, as did the eminent conciliar authors, Dietrich of Niem and the Franciscan Mathias Döring. The theories of Marsilius and Ockham rejecting papal sovereignty and supremacy, and leading, even in their most temperate form, to the conciliarist theses of moderate nominalists such as Pierre d'Ailly and Gerson, were unacceptable to the Papacy. This was the predominant theme of fifteenth-century political theology; its place, however, lies more appropriately in another chapter.[40]

The Papacy could not rely on Thomism to defend it. Although the Augustinian friar, James of Viterbo, used Thomist ideas to defend the Papacy,[41] he was overshadowed by the Dominican, John of Paris, who sided with Philip the Fair, deriving from Aquinas arguments useful to both supporters of the monarchical state and to conciliarists, as each engaged in combat with the Papacy. Others, some (including Giles of Rome) members of the Augustinian Order, rediscovered in the works of St Augustine arguments already employed, centuries before, in the struggle between Church and Empire. For them every *dominium* (the word covers a range of concepts from kingship to the simple ownership of property) was a divine gift created by an act of grace; as the fount of divine grace on earth, the pope was therefore the source of all earthly authority. If he had 'agreed' to reserve to princes the actual exercise of secular authority, there was nevertheless no doubt where his own authority stemmed from, nor about his right to exercise it. Furthermore, the Church was the community of Christians (the *corpus mysticum Christi*), all those individuals past, present and future who, in Heaven, formed one body with Christ, on earth the pope being to living Christians what Christ was in Heaven.

In Oxford Augustinianism took a new direction which, in a roundabout way, proved of fundamental importance for political doctrines. Did not upholding the absolute power of God, it was asked, imply belief in the predestination of man, in the abolition both of his free will and of the action of an independent agency in the pursuit of salvation? For nominalists like Pierre d'Ailly the answer lay in a distinction between *potestas absoluta* and *potestas ordinata*. The latter functioned as the guiding light in the void, a sort of contract between God and man; man had no need to fear predestination, any more than a child, *a priori*, needed to fear parental authority, because naturally his parents loved him;[42] in this way some liberty was left to man.[43] For realists, matters were more complicated. The measured response of Duns Scotus[44] was followed by the determinism of Thomas Bradwardine, a Fellow of Merton College, Oxford, who was to become archbishop of Canterbury. In his *De causa Dei contra*

[40] A. Black, below, ch. 3, and (1970); McReady (1975); Hendrix (1976).
[41] James of Viterbo, *De regimine Christiano*.   [42] Wilks (1964); Oakley (1964); Courtenay (1971).
[43] Miethke (1991b).   [44] Vignaux (1934); Pannenberg (1954).

Pelagium he postulated that God, being perfect, could imply no contradiction, and that everything had a beginning, a first cause. If man, for example, unquestioningly had a will, then that human will was totally dependent on the will of God. Human action could never free itself from its first cause, which was divine will. From this a crucial problem arose: did God will sin, and was He himself liable to sin? Theologians would discuss this at length. For Bradwardine, the existence of sin was part of the design of the Creation and the Redemption. The logical conclusion was that since God contained no contradiction, the destiny of every man was wholly mapped out by God's will; only divine grace could save sinners. Bradwardine, united with Augustine in opposing the Pelagian heresy (total liberty of man and his independence of God), was venturing into the dangerous waters of predestination.[45]

The political implications of predestination are to be seen in another controversy which set the mendicant orders against another Oxford master, Richard Fitzralph. This respected theologian, the Anglo-Irish archbishop of Armagh, was on bad terms with the Franciscans. Since the mid-thirteenth century the mendicants had been at the nub of the crucial problem of evangelical poverty, which, in turn, governed the question of property.[46] With the founding of the Franciscan Order and through the founder's renown and canonisation, the doctrine which made Christ the absolute model for the Christian life had aroused great interest. Was not Christ the poorest of the poor? He had no personal possessions and no wish to exercise power; hence the voluntary 'evangelical' poverty of the Franciscans, who allowed themselves no possessions. Since this called into question the legitimacy of the Church's wealth, beginning with that of the Franciscans themselves, it was a dangerous and ambiguous doctrine. Popes, therefore, imposed the idea that Franciscan poverty stemmed not from a belief that it was compulsory to follow Christ's example, but rather from voluntary asceticism. As for their wealth, the pope would have the *proprietas* of it, the friars the *usus*. This compromise, first expounded by Nicholas III in 1279, was shot to pieces by John XXII in 1322 and 1323: forbidding all future debate, the pope decreed that Christ possessed both material possessions and *dominium*. In his *De pauperie salvatoris* (1356), Fitzralph posed the question anew in the light of the Augustinian theory of grace. The original *dominium*, he wrote, was divine, since it was conferred by divine grace; any man in a state of grace might enjoy it, as he had before the fall, when all things had been held in common, just as with Christ and the Apostles. The mendicants could neither claim this *dominium* as a prerogative, nor could they renounce it; they were not arbiters of the workings of divine grace, which depended on God alone; without grace they could not claim inordinate privi-

---

[45] Leff (1957); Oberman (1956); Genest (1992).   [46] Coleman, in Burns (1988).

leges, either in respect of *proprietas* (which, like the *usus* it engendered, was a human concern governed by positive law), or within the bosom of the Church, where, like others, they had to submit to the authority of the pope and the hierarchy.[47]

For another theologian, John Wyclif, Fitzralph did not go far enough. An Oxford scholar of great reputation, but one whose ecclesiastical career had stalled, Wyclif was a realist of extreme persuasion and a passionate devotee of Augustine.[48] By 1373, he was tackling political problems in five major works: *De dominio divino, De civili dominio, De officio regis, De ecclesia* and *De potestate papae*. Returning to the propositions of Bradwardine and Fitzralph, he posited that an individual in a state of sin had no right to *dominium*; conversely, in a state of grace man had *dominium* over all things, which he shared with others in a like state. If the legitimacy of having possessions and use of them depended on grace, and only on grace, civil property, on the contrary, depended solely on positive law. In short, there was a dual legality, one divine, dependent on grace and predestination, the other man-made, based on property and human law. No one could make presumptions about divine grace. Since, unlike other Augustinians, he recognised no papal prerogative, Wyclif denied the pope any right as arbiter of divine grace, preferring the censure of positive law for the 'material sinner'. His personal strictures were aimed chiefly at ecclesiastics who, by claiming to be *ex officio* arbiters of divine grace, had secured the core of the Church's power and wealth under false pretences. The pope and his Augustinian champions were denounced: the Papacy, irreparably corrupted by the Donation of Constantine (a mid-eighth-century grant of territorial authority made by the emperor to the pope, exposed as a forgery in the fifteenth century by the humanist Lorenzo Valla), was not the heir of St Peter. Was there a single reference to the pope in the Bible, the only reliable guide of Christ's message available to man, which Wyclif's disciples had translated? The Church must be restored to its true self by stripping it of its wealth and restoring clerics to their true calling, that of catechising and pastoral care, under the militant protection of the king, lords and magistracy. Thus Augustinianism was turned against the Papacy, whose most formidable weapon it had been.

These theories, and their implications, were well received by an important section of the English governing classes. John of Gaunt, duke of Lancaster, supported Wyclif, and members of the gentry who were intimates of the court protected those clerics and copyists who were spreading his doctrines. Until at least 1410, the idea was afloat in England of confiscating the Church's property. By and large, however, Wyclif and his Lollard followers were failures. The

[47] Walsh (1981).
[48] Robson (1961); Kenny (1985); McFarlane (1952); Kaminsky (1963); list of Wyclif's works in Thomson (1983).

rejection of all things subversive after the Peasants' Revolt of 1381 meant that Wyclif's doctrine of the eucharist, condemned by the Church, alarmed an aristocracy fearful of heresy. In the next generation or so, the movement, as such, fell apart.[49]

These ideas were to live on in Bohemia, where antagonism between clerics and German and Czech members of the University of Prague had created an explosive situation. The works of Fitzralph and Wyclif were well known: German teaching masters at the university were nominalists and the Czechs realists. The most popular of the reformers, Jan Hus, had read Wyclif; although he was to evolve his own theories, almost a quarter of Hus's treatise, *De Ecclesia*, was borrowed directly from Wyclif, while his definition of the Church, the community of all the predestined (*omnium predestinatorum universitas*) was Wycliffite.[50] This true Church was indeed the mystical body of Christ, but differed perceptibly from the Church Militant, that is the Church comprising all members alive at one moment, since the latter included, alongside the elect working out their salvation, those who would be damned. Christ remained the head of the elect of this Church Militant, but the head of the Roman Church was not the representative of Christ; at most he was only his servant. Furthermore, this Church was not universal, since there was also, for example, the Greek Church. Hus's ecumenical vision was important; it mattered little whether the predestined belonged to the Roman Church. Taking his stand on the five patriarchates which had existed in the early Church, Hus believed that the different forms assumed by the Church on earth were legitimate.[51] Furthermore, those, like St Peter, who had become vicars of Christ by reason of their virtue, had no power beyond the spiritual. They were subject to the civil authority; and their own authority, based on their right to teach the Scriptures, was limited.

Hussite theories had a great influence in Bohemia, Poland and eastern Europe.[52] Yet their greatest impact may have been felt elsewhere. Taking as their starting-point the Augustinian theology of divine *potentia absoluta*, of grace and predestination, Wyclif and Hus evolved an elaborate theory justifying the Church's submission to secular authority, and so laid the foundations of a new political order, that of the Reformation. Even orthodox princes of this period were likewise preparing this new order by negotiating concordats with the Papacy.[53] Indeed, once the Great Schism had ended (1417), it was in the interests of princes to negotiate, since the pope was now secure enough to show a readiness to concede to them a measure of control over their national

---

[49] McFarlane (1972), pp. 139–232; Thomson (1965); Hudson (1988).
[50] *Tractatus de ecclesia*; see Spinka (1966).   [51] Spinka (1966), pp. 388–9.   [52] Kaminsky (1964).
[53] Ozment (1980), pp. 182–90.

churches. Princes gradually withdrew their support from the council, consigning to oblivion theories which, springing from nominalist theses, had gradually propounded the idea that the totality of the Church had supremacy over its head on earth. The crisis over, the popes and their theologians met little meaningful opposition; they now reverted to the old Thomist and Augustinian theories which justified their *plenitudo potestatis* to be exercised over both council and princes.[54] The Papacy, having seemingly won the battle and under the illusion that it had safeguarded the essential, none the less failed to respond to Wyclif and Hus.

The notable work of Nicholas of Cusa, with its consensus theology intended to restore harmony within the Church, was orientated, however, more towards the past than the future.[55] This consensus did not result from the 'democratic' process but was the unanimous accord of all inspired by the Holy Spirit;[56] it was given effective action not by a representative body from within the community of the Church or the Empire, but by the pope and the emperor as the embodiments of that community. The Church did not constitute an isolated case; Cusa wanted to restore peace and harmony to the Empire, and to save the German nation by restoring to the emperor those imperial powers usurped by the princes. The emperor was the guardian of the common weal; yet, to attain authority, he had to link himself by oath to the princes, his electors, to the detriment of that common weal.[57] Cusa thus returned very clearly to contemporary politics, constructing a dualistic system whereby Church (the Papacy) and state (the Empire) coexisted in a parallel not a hierarchical relationship (the emperor being 'created' by the people through the agency of the electors) that generated universal harmony. This dualism of pope and emperor was also found, through a different analytical process, in Italian writers: in Antonio Roselli's *Monarchia*, in the writings of Piero da Monte[58] (although in the final analysis he recognised the pope's supreme authority in spiritual matters), and in those of Aeneas Sylvius Piccolomini.[59] Whereas Cusa valued harmony and concerted action above all else, the Italian writers merely juxtaposed two absolutisms.

LAW AND POLITICS

The theologians' star was in the descendant. Although devoting himself to theology, Cusa was a doctor of canon law; Roselli was a professor of law at Padua

[54] For instance St Antoninus, for whom see Congar (1970) and Torquemada, *Oratio synodalis de primatu*.
[55] Cusanus, *Concordantia*; see Sigmund (1963); Mohr (1958); Watanabe (1963).
[56] Watanabe (1963), p. 187.   [57] *Concordantia*, III, pp. 31–2.
[58] *De potestate romani pontificis et generalis concilii*; see Haller (1941).
[59] Text in Piccolomini, *Epistola de ortu*, pp. 50–100; see Widmer (1963).

(where da Monte had been a pupil) and, later, at Siena (where Aeneas Sylvius was his pupil). At the councils, it was the canonists (Francesco Zabarella at Constance, Nicholas de Tudeschis (Panormitanus) at Basle) who had over-shadowed the theologians in ecclesiological, inevitably political, debate. When theologians ridiculed the *idiotae politici*,[60] they were fighting a rear-guard action. Princes had made their choices, packing councils and administrations with jurists. Canonists,[61] inured to the discipline of Roman law and familiar with theological problems, found themselves, as it were, on the bank of a broad stream between theology and Roman law, and acted as 'ferrymen'.[62] They could do this since some theories were common to both disciplines; for instance, the idea of natural law[63] as the expression of divine law determined, for theologians, the vexed question of property and authority and, for jurists, that of the legitimacy of law and legislation.

Those who dismissed the theocratic concept of a God-given law adminis-tered by papal *plenitudo potestatis* were faced with a law human in origin, whether created by the prince alone (*lex animata*) or by more complex procedures, ranging from a parliamentary type of legislation (making the entire population into the *legislator humanus*[64] by means of a system of law making by consent) to the recognition of the normative value of custom, itself justified by tacit consent.[65] Such law, however, was legitimate only if it conformed to natural law which, being divine in origin, was quintessentially superior. For Baldus de Ubaldis, with Bartolus[66] the most influential of the great Italian jurists of the fourteenth century, the pope himself was subject to this law of nature, which could be deduced from the Bible. An English jurist, Sir John Fortescue, did not hesitate to invoke *lex naturae*, because it was superior to any human law, when arbitrating on the legitimacy of English claims to the French crown; 'natural law', he wrote, 'is superior in matters of custom and of the constitution' ('dig-nitate vero jus naturae prevalet consuetudini et constitutioni').[67]

Drawing upon the entire range of laws, jurists sought to settle such matters as the problem of sovereignty. Baldus devoted much attention to the Donation of Constantine, which seemed to contradict a principle of civil law, that a sove-reign could not alienate any part of his kingdom.[68] One of the reasons for this was the idea, fundamental to the concept of the state, that the kingdom or principality was a public body (using a Ciceronian concept,[69] Baldus termed it the *res publica* of the kingdom) which, therefore, never died: 'the body politic

---

[60] Krynen (1991).   [61] Ourliac and Gilles (1971).
[62] Paradisi (1973); Maffei (1966); Gilmore (1941).   [63] Oakley (1981).
[64] Marsilius of Padua's phrase; see Ullmann (1975), pp. 204–14, and (1961), pp. 283–6.
[65] Doe (1990).   [66] Canning (1987); Woolf (1913).
[67] Doe (1990); Fortescue, *Opusculum de natura legis nature*, bk I, ch. 5.
[68] Maffei (1964); Canning (1987), pp. 45 ff.   [69] Mager (1968) and (1984).

cannot die, and for this reason it is said that it has no heir, because it always lives on in itself' ('non enim potest respublica mori; et hac ratione dicitur quod respublica non habet heredem quia semper vivit in semetipsa').[70] Royal power was thus limited, since the ruler could undertake nothing that was detrimental to the public body, and the pledges made *sub nomine dignitatis* were binding upon his successors.[71] Another important point was the distinction between *de jure* sovereignty (that of the emperor) and that achieved *de facto* (by other kings, princes or *signori*). Baldus applied the latter to Giangaleazzo Visconti who, although a subject of the emperor who had sold him his ducal title in 1395, was none the less a *princeps*, endowed with *plenitudo potestatis*.[72] The rights of such a prince were derived from those of the emperor, the classic example of them being the list of feudal rights enumerated by Frederick Barbarossa at the Diet of Roncaglia in 1158. Baldus' commentary on the *Libri feudorum* was to be transposed to the French king's advantage by Bernard de Rouserge in his *Miranda de laudibus Francie* (1450);[73] combined with the principle of inalienability, there was here a formidable weapon wielded to great effect by members of the French *parlements* and the jurists of many princes.

Although, particularly when commenting on the *lex regia*, some stressed the essential role of popular consent in the legislative process and the popular source of royal authority, most jurists fostered the growth of absolutist ideas, even if enthusiasm for princely legislative power was tempered by the assertion that a prince must keep within the framework of Christian morality. Such was the case in France where Jean de Terrevermeille, a lawyer from Nîmes, campaigned for almost total submission to the true sovereign (in this case the dauphin, the future Charles VII).[74] The Hundred Years War and the accompanying civil strife had convinced French intellectuals that their country was suffering from a lack of government: Jean Juvénal des Ursins criticised his king for his 'passive tyranny . . . of inadequate power';[75] in order to preserve the French monarchy – on the whole the lesser evil – it was better to strengthen it. Even Gerson, who had constructed a 'democratic' model for the Church, became an apologist for absolutism: 'as St Paul says, all authority proceeds from God, and whoever opposes authority opposes divine ordinance' ('toute poissance, comme dit Saint Pol, est de Dieu, et qui resiste a poissance resiste a divine ordenance'), a truth all the more forceful since the French monarchy was more 'approved and honoured' by God than any other. Yet even in France not all theorists would have concurred.[76]

In England Fortescue gleaned from Aquinas a theory of *dominium politicum et*

---

[70] Baldus de Ubaldis, *Consiliorum . . . volumen tertium*, fol. 45v, quoted by Mager (1991).
[71] Kantorowicz (1957), pp. 397–401.   [72] Canning (1987), pp. 221ff.
[73] Arabeyre (1990), pp. 322–3.   [74] Krynen (1981) and (1993); Barbey (1983).
[75] Lewis (1993), p. 178.   [76] Gerson, *Oeuvres complètes*, VII(2), p. 1140; cf. Krynen (1981), pp. 322–6.

regale which he set out in his *Governance of England*, written in English, and his *De laudibus legum Anglie*, written in Latin, both works composed for the instruction of Edward, son and heir of Henry VI. In these he expounded the difference between a *dominium regale* such as France, whose king was virtually a tyrant, taxing his subjects without their consent and thus keeping them in a state of poverty, and a *dominium politicum et regale*, such as England, where the *politia* was effectively represented and participated actively in the governmental process. If the constitutional implications of this theory were limited – Fortescue emphasised the role of the royal council, not that of parliament –[77] its impact in legal terms was considerable, for it firmly linked civil law to the first type of regime, and English common law to the second. In England this notion was, by tradition, already strong enough for the suspicion that John Tiptoft, earl of Worcester, wanted to introduce Roman law, and hence tyranny, into England to feature among the reasons put forward for his execution.[78] Another jurist, Peter von Andlau, may be compared to Fortescue; while professing support for the style of rule *regaliter*, he showed enough interest in the form *politice* to expound significantly upon it, concentrating his attention on towns.[79]

Among jurists, as among theologians, most of the outstanding fifteenth-century debates were an extension of those of the previous century. No fifteenth-century jurist displayed the originality or enjoyed the eminence of a Bartolus or a Baldus. Paradoxically, one reason for this was the very success of jurists in every sphere of power. The legal literature of the time was very varied. There was a proliferation of legislation in which jurists played a prominent part (to the point that in England and Germany there was a desire to bar them from legislative institutions) and which was to be found in royal laws (from the French kings' *ordonnances* to English statutes), in regional or urban codifications (Iberian *fueros* or *cuadernos*, the *Stadtbuch* or *Gesetzbuch* of German towns), in the compilations of *decisiones*, where one court of justice (the pontifical *rota*, the *parlement* of Paris) was superior to others,[80] and in Year Books providing the legal decisions of English judges. Jurists devoted much of their time to the drawing up of *consilia*, the expert opinions which they presented for the attention of courts, either at the request of clients or of the courts themselves. These, sometimes collected and even printed, represent the core of German and Italian jurists' output.[81] In the fifteenth century law was more bound up with everyday practice, including where this impinged on politics, than it was

---

[77] McIllwain (1932); Burns (1985).

[78] Hazeltine (1942); but see also Farr (1974), pp. 102–9, on the *lex fisci*.

[79] Andlau, *De Imperio Romano-Germanico libri duo*; the parallel between Fortescue and Andlau is suggested by Burns (1992), p. 119.   [80] Wolf, in Coing (1973); Dolezalek *et al.*, in Coing (1973).

[81] Kisch (1970).

preoccupied with the theories sometimes found, in earlier times, in the *consilia*, but which were now often consigned to brief preambles or merely touched upon almost in passing, by English judges, for example.[82]

LITERATURE AND POLITICS

There was, however, much common ground between theologians and jurists. As educated professionals both had experience of a language which, because of its technical nature, was precise yet beyond the grasp of the uninitiated. They were obliged to abandon it when, like Gerson and Fortescue, they addressed those who were not colleagues. From this period onwards an enormous potential readership was being created: among princes themselves; among those who frequented their courts and staffed their administrations; and among sophisticated merchants and the members of urban oligarchies. The reading public was now becoming so extensive and diverse that politics insinuated itself easily into a variety of literary forms in both prose and verse. The mendicant orders pointed the way by creating a literary genre, the 'Mirror of Princes', the pre-eminent didactic treatise *ad statum*, the most accomplished being the *De regimine principum* of Giles of Rome (*c.* 1277–9) which had lost nothing of its topicality and its appeal by the fifteenth century, as the numerous surviving translations and adaptations prove.[83] Its influence was to be found in a number of other works, the *Regiment de la cosa publica* written by Francesc Eiximenis in 1385–6, the *Regement of princes* compiled by Thomas Hoccleve in 1412 or the anonymous *Tractatus de regimine principum ad regem Henricum sextum*, written a few years later for Henry VI of England.[84] John of Salisbury's *Policraticus*, composed in the twelfth century, was still popular on account of its handling of the question of tyrannicide and its use of classical sources (not all of them authentic) while the prolific textual progeny of the pseudo-Aristotelian *Secretum secretorum*, oriental rather than Greek in origin, were to be found everywhere.

The literary exploitation of the 'Mirror' genre was assured by genuine professional or semi-professional men of letters closely associated with princes and their administrations, the Benedictine monk, John Lydgate, providing the exception to prove the rule. Thomas Hoccleve was an English chancery clerk, while Juan de Mena was official historiographer to Juan II of Castile. Alain Chartier, a graduate of Paris (whose brother would one day be its bishop), was a royal secretary whose career was punctuated by diplomatic missions to many countries. His work enjoyed an impressive popularity, surpassing that of

---

[82] Doe (1990).   [83] Singer (1981).
[84] In *Four English political tracts of the later Middle Ages*, pp. 40–168.

Christine de Pisan, which was intended specifically for the princes of the court. Many manuscripts, some of their titles suggestive of contemporary issues and preoccupations, survive to this day.[85]

A 'Mirror' was concerned with what a prince needed to know in order to rule well. This allowed writers to enumerate the virtues – justice, temperance, generosity, prudence, the capacity to choose wise counsellors – to be cultivated by the prince and, by extension, by all whose calling or social status placed them in positions of command. Professional authors and court poets expanded its themes by providing it with a narrative framework. The uniformity of tone and language created by their mastery of the literary form permitted the introduction of subjects which they knew would interest their readers: from the *Secretum* onwards diet, advice on health and hygiene, physiognomy, astrology (Christine de Pisan's father had been astrologer to Charles V) all featured; moral health was dependent on physical health, and determined the political regime. These authors borrowed from the 'literature of the social orders' (of which Geoffrey Chaucer's *Canterbury Tales* was the masterpiece) to create a genre focused on the nobility, which was exploited particularly by Burgundian authors.[86] The works of Ovid, Valerius Maximus and Boccaccio were used to provide a dazzling sequence of stories, legends, histories and *exempla*. The whole might be contained within an allegorical framework (a vision or an imaginary quest) and could be dramatised through the use of dialogue and symbolic description. Above all, the device of personification breathed life into the most abstract of ideas; the text played on the reader's emotions while appealing to his intellect. In this way, so far removed from traditional debate and rhetoric, a relationship grew between author and reader which provided a vehicle for conveying political ideas, images and experience. Politics henceforth entered the sphere of individual experience.

This was the most significant innovation, the new role to be played by literature. Yet if political morality was being highjacked, the message itself was scarcely changing. In a political system in which human relationships were still the determining factor, the virtues (or vices) of those in power were crucial. Nobles, the leaders of society, must still practise the virtues which constitute true nobility and without which nothing is noble; so wrote Christine de Pisan in the early years of the century.[87] Other themes occurred frequently, among them peace, fame and fortune. The political ideas, however, were hardly original. What gave them force and interest was the literary form and language in which they were couched, as well as their introduction into actual power relationships by way of a complex game involving successive, sometimes contra-

---

[85] Chartier, *Poetical works, Œuvres latines, Le quadrilogue invectif* and *Le livre de l'espérance*; Rouy (1980); Walravens (1971).   [86] Vanderjagt (1981).

[87] Christine de Pisan, *Le livre du corps de policie*, p. 135.

dictory, dedications.[88] In spite of borrowings from Italian, this literature was most appreciated in the major courts of western Christendom, England, France and Burgundy. It was also found, though to a lesser extent, in Iberia, where John Gower's *Confessio amantis* was translated into Portuguese and Castilian, and where, in 1444, Juan de Mena presented his *Laberinto de fortuna* to Juan II. However, on the Italian peninsula and in Germany, where only the theme of the nobility's virtues and vices held any genuine appeal, the genre was almost unknown. While Chartier's best-known poem, *La belle dame sans mercy*, was translated into English, Castilian and Tuscan, his political works were rendered only into English.

Political literature was not confined simply to those texts which, it should be noted, were sometimes critical of the world as it was. At the end of the Middle Ages there already existed a body of texts, far removed from recognised literary genres and the world of professional authors, which has been labelled 'protest literature'.[89] Particularly numerous examples were to be found in England, still preserved in commonplace books and collections of personal notes. Often violent in tone, these texts, which criticised the avarice of tax collectors and the vices of the higher classes, were the tip of an iceberg destined to remain for ever submerged. Chronicles, however, might sometimes reflect their ideas, such as those circulating among the rebellious 'labourers' of 1381.[90] Finally, as heretical movements of the period sought to disseminate their messages, including their political messages, they rendered the erudite Latin texts of their learned predecessors into the vernacular, the Lollards issuing several English adaptations of Wyclif's political ideas.

In the meanwhile humanism spread rapidly into the Italian peninsula, where cities provided new opportunities in the sociological, political and cultural fields. The term humanist appeared only at the end of the fifteenth century to define someone devoting himself to *studia humanitatis*: history, moral philosophy, grammar, rhetoric and poetry, but not logic or the disciplines of the *quadrivium*, a syllabus profoundly different from that of the medieval university. Such a curriculum corresponded to a cultural reality rooted in the vigorous civic and economic life of Italian cities where, since the late thirteenth century, scribes (*dictatores*) had been teaching the sort of writing and epistolary style to future lawyers and businessmen. In reaction against the 'French' *ars dictaminis*, aimed above all at university students, these scribes turned instead to classical grammar. Since, however, social constraints forbade them discard the *ars dictaminis* which they were paid to teach and practise in the chanceries of Italian states, they initially reserved this new style for their poetry and letters. But the astonishing success of Petrarch was to assure it ultimate victory; at the begin-

---

[88] Gauvard (1973).   [89] Coleman (1981).   [90] Justice (1994).

ning of the fifteenth century, at least in Florence, the classical style finally prevailed, advancing from private to public use, from grammar to rhetoric.[91]

Did the style herald a new ideology? The idea has been formulated and the theory taken shape of a 'civic humanism',[92] fundamentally republican, and witnessing in a Florentine republic which, in 1402, miraculously repulsed the attack of Giangaleazzo Visconti of Milan, a reincarnation of the Rome of Antiquity. This view is regarded as having been expressed by Leonardo Bruni who, in his *Laudatio florentinae urbis* written in 1400,[93] praised his native city, its splendour, its constitution and its destiny. In the official correspondence of the Florentine chancery the chancellors, Coluccio Salutati and later Bruni himself, extolled republican values, starting with liberty, as against the tyranny and despotism of the Visconti. These were sentiments which had reverberations in another republic, Venice, since Bruni was to engage in polemic with Pier Paolo Vergerio who, in his *De republica veneta*, had claimed Venetian rule superior to all others.[94] This expression of the doctrine of a city's sovereignty or its popular foundations was scarcely new, being found in varying degrees in the works of Azo, Bartolus, Ptolemy of Lucca and even of Marsilius of Padua. But Bruni and Vergerio argued the respective merits of the Florentine and Venetian constitutions from the standpoint of Aristotle's definition of the best possible constitution; indeed Bruni had retranslated the *Politics* in their entirety. It was Aristotle, and Cicero likewise, who inspired the Florentine Matteo Palmieri to write *Della vita civile*, in which the author, who had held several governmental posts, paid tribute to the concord and consensus among the city's inhabitants, exhorting his fellow citizens to dedicate themselves to the service of their native city. The Florentines, Palmieri, Poggio and Bruni, all stressed the Aristotelian theme of the importance of law and justice in guaranteeing peace within the civic community. The only sign of innovation was that in Palmieri and da Monte traces of Platonic influence were already discernible; Plato's *Republic* had been translated by the Milanese, Pier Candido Decembrio, with the aid of Manuel Chrysoloras, while in Venice George of Trebizond was translating the *Laws*. It was not, however, until the end of the century that Plato's influence became predominant.

It should not be supposed that Italian humanism was tied inevitably to republicanism. Princely states, those despotisms reviled by Florentine humanists, recruited other humanists ready to defend them and to praise princely government in preference to the civic form. The letters of Giangaleazzo Visconti's secretary, Antonio Loschi (ironically a pupil of Salutati), balanced those of the Florentine chancellor, and Decembrio's *De laudibus Mediolanensis*

---

[91] Witt, in Rabil (1988). [92] Rabil (1988), pp. 140–74; Baron (1966).

[93] Dated 1402–3 by Baron (1968), *after* the Milanese defeat which it would therefore echo.

[94] Rubinstein (1979), esp. p. 210.

urbis panegyricus (1436) was the worthy counterpart of Bruni's *Laudatio*. Orations, such as Decembrio's eulogy of Filippo Maria Visconti, composed for specific occasions, praised these princes in extravagant terms,[95] painting the portrait of the ideal prince on the model of the 'Mirrors', and embroidering the theme of princely *virtù* introduced by Petrarch in his letter to Francesco Carrara. In his *De republica* Decembrio justified theoretically the Milanese system, doing for Milan what Vergerio and da Monte had done for Venice, and Bruni and Palmieri for Florence.[96]

Humanists were aware of the contradictions inherent in the ideas and values which their careers led them to defend. In Salutati, Bruni and Loschi there already existed the idea of the 'republic of letters' which united exponents of the new style in spite of their political commitments. An extraordinary text written between 1443 and 1450 showed a perceptive grasp of the situation. In his *Momus* Leon Battista Alberti recounted the myth of the god, Momus, exiled to earth for having criticised Jupiter. Momus broke into a torrent of abuse against the gods, who sent to earth Virtus, a goddess esteemed above all others, escorted by her children, to re-establish truth. Momus, disguised as ivy, took advantage of the fact that Virtus's daughter, Laus, used to adorn her hair with a leafy crown to violate her; a monster, Fama, was born of this union. From birth the monster could talk, and it proclaimed everywhere that Laus, Tropheus and Triumphus, Virtus's children, were merely the offspring of Casus and Fortuna, chance and fortune. The moral of this nihilistic and cynical philosophy was that only flattery and hypocrisy ensured success in politics. Merit and the traditional values were of little consequence; the most moral activity, on the whole, was the idleness of vagrants, the *errones*.[97] One could, of course, draw a different lesson from the fable; to succeed one must know how to convince, persuade and, if need be, even lie skilfully in order to turn chance to account. For humanists the only truth was that created by language; everything stemmed from words.

HISTORY AND POLITICS

There was one field where the stamp of humanism was to be rapidly in evidence, and that was history. By the fifteenth century the great monastic tradition of historical writing was largely moribund. History, like politics, was being transformed by literature; the success of Jean Froissart's work in aristocratic and bourgeois circles is testimony of this. Several new kinds of history were appearing: national history in France, England and Iberia, where reigns and

[95] Finzi (1991); Rubinstein (1991), pp. 31–4.   [96] Rabil (1988), pp. 235–63.
[97] Alberti, *Momo o del principe*, pp. 71–80, 121–9; Garin (1988), pp. 97–100, 103–9.

sovereigns provided the chronological framework; histories of cities in Germany and in the Italian peninsula; biographies; accounts of travels, of wars and of remarkable expeditions, sometimes written by one of the participants. Almost all languages and literary forms were represented.

In England national history was recounted in the many versions of the *Brut*, and by the *Chronicles of London*. In France derivatives of the official history compiled at Saint-Denis, the *Grandes chroniques de France*, fulfilled the same purpose. When a suitable occasion arose, such works were provided with supplements, sometimes written by the owners of manuscripts themselves. Although these histories thus became a patchwork of texts of diverse provenance and inspiration, when collected in one manuscript, they took on a certain homogeneity, enabling many readers to discover their past and find unity in a common destiny. Princes, aware of such developments, commissioned histories, some of them early attempts at propaganda. Problems of genealogy were just as crucial for the Wittelsbach as for the Yorkists and Lancastrians. It might be necessary to bring unity to an ailing principality, or to a kingdom under threat, by glorifying its past (sometimes, as in the case of Burgundy, more imaginative than real), or to circulate a favourable version of sensitive political events (such as the return of Edward IV to England in 1471). The need for history was there, as the number of manuscripts testifies, but at the same time the disparate quality of the techniques, genres and languages leaves an impression of chaos. Without a religious framework, history seemed to have lost its way.

Humanism brought a radically different approach. Ignored by the medieval university, history was at the heart of the curriculum of the *studia humanitatis*. What was history if not the praise of ancient Rome? History no longer tried to give the authorised version from the Christian viewpoint of universal history, but endeavoured to present, thanks to rhetoric, a convincing version of the fortunes of a political community or an individual; history became the narration of politics. Thus the *Historia florentini populi*, compiled from 1416 by Leonardo Bruni, by taking Livy as its model, established in dazzling style Florence's unbroken line of descent from the Roman republic. The work was translated into Italian in 1473 at the Commune's expense. It is noteworthy that, in addition to Bruni, two other Florentine chancellors, Poggio Bracciolini and Bartolomeo della Scala,[98] wrote histories of their city, while in Rome, too, Flavio Biondo hoped to restore the glory of ancient Rome with his *Roma instaurata*, his *Italia illustrata* and his *Roma triumphans*.

The medieval principle of compilation was now no longer acceptable. Truth was not the objective, since truth did not exist in itself but only through its expression, a point which national histories, written for rival powers, illustrate

---

[98] Wilcox (1969).

with startling clarity. Rejecting all claims to objectivity, humanists presented some of their works as commentaries, referring to Caesar as their model: Bartolomeo Facio's *De rebus gestis Alphonsi I commentarii* (1455) exerted a considerable influence, particularly on Sforza historiography.[99] However, whether it was a history on the model of Livy, or a commentary in the style of Caesar, the object and method were the same – the object was political, the method rhetorical. Humanists of Italian cities provided what was most lacking in the historiography of the modern states of western Christendom, uniformity of subject matter and of language. The first commissions followed quickly. In England, Humphrey of Gloucester secured the services of the humanist Tito Livio da Forlì to write the *Gesta* of his late brother, the king, Henry V. In Spain, the close ties between Aragon and Naples inspired Lorenzo Valla to write his *Historia de Ferdinando Aragoniae rege*. In Castile Alfonso de Palencia, who had studied on the Italian peninsula with George of Trebizond, became historiographer royal in succession to Juan de Mena. The first great national histories entirely remodelled on humanist lines were not written until the end of the century, but the movement had been launched.

This survey of areas of medieval culture, each one almost, if not quite, a separate compartment in itself, reveals the difficulty faced by men of the late Middle Ages in seeking to articulate the political reality they were experiencing. The language of theologians or of jurists was too technical to express the questions, doubts and anxieties of a society confronted with this new power of states, so nebulous that giving it a name proved as yet impossible, and assailed by the ever-renewed violence of war and its concomitant, political instability. A handful of scholars, a few great minds, went on producing remarkable works in virtually all fields. Did such works respond to the aspirations of the new readership composed of the power-wielding elites, whether they supported the state or opposed it, whether they resided in the kingdoms and principalities of western Christendom (nations already, or would-be nations) or in other political systems which the network of alliances and rivalries likewise dragged into war? The appetite of these elites to know and understand was sharpened by their education, which had given them the means of doing this, even if it had not enabled them to read texts both too technical and too dry.

In part, history compensated for this lack. Its success revealed the expectations of a society which, having failed to account for the brutal shocks inflicted by the present, sought at least to preserve and to arrange what remained of the past. That past, however, at least outside Italy, appeared as impossible to understand as the present. Vernacular poets and prose-writers, who were popular with the new public, were constrained by an imprecise vocabulary which

---

[99] Ianziti (1988).

scarcely transcended the moral clichés taken from earlier 'Mirrors'; their language was too unformed, and thus suffered from the opposite defect to that of the theologians and jurists.

It is true that adventurous spirits broke new ground: Fortescue sought to combine what he knew as a jurist with what he experienced as a politician in a penetrating analysis of the English and French systems, where he explained effectively both concepts and personal observation. At the end of the century Commynes was to go even further. Yet new ideas and new theories were few and far between; debates on conciliar thought were to die out; the political message of the heretics Wyclif and Hus was stifled. However, something fundamental was produced in the fifteenth century: a realisation of the importance and fascination of history, and the grasp of the main principles of political morality by the public at large. Humanism gave to history a human face and, from the starting point of classical Latin, forged a supple and precise language, just as capable of dealing rigorously with abstract concepts as of giving pleasure and arguing convincingly by means of a rejuvenated rhetoric. This language was to be the vehicle for a new flowering of ideas liberated from the constraints of theology and law. The fifteenth century was the age which saw political language burst into life, both in vernacular and in humanistic Latin – a cultural revolution, slow, not easily detected, but undoubtedly essential for the genesis of the modern state, and inseparable from its development and its self-expression.

CHAPTER 2

REPRESENTATION (SINCE THE THIRTEENTH CENTURY)

Wim Blockmans

POLITICAL representation, based on the mandate bestowed on elected and responsible delegates, and applied at regional and national levels, can be considered as one of the major contributions of the western Middle Ages to world history. Some representative institutions, such as the English parliament, which developed from the thirteenth century onwards have functioned without interruption until the present day. The names given to others, such as the Spanish *cortes*, the Polish *sejm*, the German *Reichstag*, the Norwegian *stendermote* or the Dutch *staten-generaal*, were applied to modern reformed institutions, obviously with the intention of justifying their new legitimacy. The connection of parliamentary with national history has therefore always been a very strong one, and has hampered attempts to explain the phenomenon on a general European basis. Where such endeavours have been undertaken, generally one national example, usually the English parliament, or a concept based on a more or less stabilised situation in the early modern period, has been too easily considered as the 'normal' pattern. Comparative history has largely remained a mere juxtaposing of national developments, with a strong emphasis on the large western states.

Very few attempts have been made to offer overall interpretations of the origins of representative phenomena. The most comprehensive and influential theory was formulated as long ago as 1931 by the German historian Otto Hintze. He identified the conditions necessary for the unique emergence of representative government in western Europe. In his view, political and social life in the west was moulded by the twin systems of feudalism and the Christian Church. The high clergy, the only intellectuals controlling the chanceries of the emerging states, could oppose limitations to lay authority by referring to general rules of Christian ethic. Germanic law, especially as it was formalised in feudalism, offered a second limitation to rule in its concept of reciprocal power relations. A ruler was always bound by mutual obligations and could be held to respect certain moral and legal standards. In particular, the immunity of ecclesiastical institutions, clergy and the inhabitants of lordships and cities formed the basis of the subjective public rights of privileged groups. Western states did not grow into a unified *imperium* but constituted weakly integrated parts of a loose global system which shared Christian values, represented by a universal and independent Church. The constant competition between states led to an intensification and a rationalisation of state systems; rulers referred to the tradition of Roman law and sought the active support of their citizens in the mobilisation of resources needed in the growing competition. The ecclesiastical model of conciliar representation was easily transferred to secular circumstances. Hintze saw the extension of monarchical authority over the representative institutions as a necessary condition for the development of representation: in his view 'municipal structures everywhere excluded representation by estates'. On the other hand, unlimited feudalism tended to dissolve the emerging states. Representative institutions could only develop and last within centralising states.[1]

Hintze's thought-provoking insights carry conviction, even if his widely shared vision of the necessity of monarchical centralisation for the proper development of representation is open to serious challenge. In our view, communes could very well create stable representative systems which dealt with a good deal of public administration. Another element in his theory, concerning the typology of the constitutions of estates, has now been refuted on both theoretical and empirical grounds.[2] In 1962 Antonio Marongiu published an extensive description of the Italian parliamentary system, which was reworked in its 1968 translation into 'a comparative study'. Besides a juxtaposing of the factual evolution in some major western countries, it offered penetrating insights into their general characteristics and ideology. However, the debate on the typology, the evolution of structures and functions of representation is still very much alive today.[3]

THE PROBLEM

Concepts and terminology

No existing study offers a comprehensive interpretation of the representative institutions of medieval Europe. Authors of earlier generations focused on particular types of institutions, excluding other forms of representation. They tended to consider these as 'ideal types' or true models with which all other

---

[1] Hintze (1931), pp. 4–14, 40–2.
[2] Hintze (1930); Moraw (1992), pp. 5–6; Blockmans (1978b) and (1992).
[3] Blockmans (1978b) and (1992); Töpfer (1980b), pp. 10–11; Krüger (1983); Blickle (1986); Moraw (1992).

instances had to be contrasted, such were the English parliament, the Iberian *cortes*, the French estates general and provincial three estates, the German *Stände*. This limitation imposed sharp classifications on the sources which, on the contrary, reveal a wide variety of representative activities in many countries, including France, the Iberian lands and the Empire. In England, Edward III for twenty years after 1336 discussed taxes on exported wool with merchants' assemblies; only some of their members were elected locally, others summoned in person.[4] In France, regional assemblies of towns, of notables, of the clergy co-existed with regional assemblies of three estates. Peasants were represented as a fourth estate in Scandinavia as well as in Frisia and the southern imperial and Swiss territories, such as Tirol, Vorarlberg, Sion and Chur. On the other hand, in the ecclesiastical territories such as Württemberg, where there existed few important monasteries, and where the chivalry considered itself dependent directly upon the king, they left the *Ehrbarkeit*, the honourable men, consisting of patricians and local officials, as the sole estate facing the bishop. We will see that various types of representative institutions co-existed in the same time and space; that the same problems were dealt with by all these assemblies; and that one type of assembly could be substituted for another in the course of a single decision-making process. Therefore, it is necessary to have an open attitude towards all forms of representation without preconceived classification.[5]

Further, we still need to have at our disposal more elementary data than we have about the actual activities of assemblies. Indeed, many more sources have to be published and analysed before we can assess the role of representative institutions generally. Thanks to the early bureaucratic organisation of the English monarchy and the exceptional continuity of its archives, the parliamentary rolls have long been published and studied; much, too, is known regarding the careers of members of parliament. The voluminous and ongoing publication on the German *Reichstag*, on the other hand, offers important information about the Empire, yet the concept of the representative institution itself remains unclear.[6] Most recent scholarship has shown that only from 1470 onwards did there really exist such a representative institution. The very extensive source publication which began in 1867 under the title *Deutsche Reichstagsakten* collected numerous sources from which were reconstructed assemblies which were in fact more or less extended court meetings, not representative assemblies as such. The ambition of nineteenth-century historians to reveal medieval precedents for the presumed democratic institutions of their time misled their reconstruction.[7] The problem was experienced more widely:

[4] Roskell *et al.* (1992), I, p. 119.
[5] Criticism in this sense: Dhondt (1950), pp. 295–306, and (1966), pp. 345–7; Bisson (1964), pp. 1–11; O'Callaghan (1989).   [6] Moraw (1992), pp. 10–19; Heinig (1990); Engel (1980), pp. 15–17.
[7] Moraw (1980) and (1992), pp. 15–24; Boockmann (1988), pp. 298–307.

later developments too often wrongly influenced the interpretation of medieval representative institutions.[8]

Marongiu correctly refuted the term *estates* (*Stände*, *états*) as an overall concept too specific for the great variety of representative phenomena under consideration. However, his alternative, parliaments, raises similar problems unless it is understood in its original meaning of a convention for discussion. Even then, confusion remains with the French institution, the *parlement* (which was a royal court of law), and with modern parliaments. Moreover, it would be a mistake to attach too much importance to the appearance in our sources of a particular name in relation to the origins and composition of that institution: estates general, *cortes*, *Reichstag* and many other forms of consultative representation had been functioning for a long time before people, who developed the practice because it was convenient, noticed that it was lasting. Only at that stage were names thought of. This chapter, however, deals with the wider concept of representation, which includes forms not covered by the above-mentioned terms. The wider definition of the subject will help us to understand differences and to detect similarities in time and space. It is for that reason that the more widely encompassing scholarly term, that of 'representative institutions', has been chosen. Since it is independent of specific historical features and their designation in contemporary sources, and does not refer to a specific modern concept, it will allow for a neutral description, not suggestive from the outset of any analogy with other times or places .

We should try now to go further in explaining (a) the reasons for chronological variations in the appearance, decline or disappearance of assemblies, and (b) their typological variation. We will have to identify the conditions under which the phenomenon of political representation functioned on a supra-local level in specific ways. Indeed, while representative institutions appeared in nearly every European region at some time or other, there were striking differences in chronology, duration and impact which considerably reduce the alleged generality of the phenomenon. Neither can one ignore the disappearance of regional representative institutions in northern Italy, the most advanced area of the time, or in central France, and their only very limited impact upon central and eastern Europe. Before it is possible to discuss these matters some further preliminary points have to be clarified.

Representatives and constituencies

Who was represented by whom? Representation means literally to make present an absent. This can occur in a private relationship on a one to one basis.

---

[8] Boockmann (1992a), p. 39.

A great feudal lord was summoned in person, in the context of his personal feudal contract with his suzerain, which obliged him to counsel and help. Only in case of inability to travel was he represented by a proctor. Thus he had to attend when summoned by his lord; refusal signified an open conflict between them. He was invited since he was an important vassal, which implied that he was a great landowner and thus in a position of power. The people living on his domain were not represented by him since they were dependent and therefore unable to express a political will. Thus, there was no representation in meetings of feudal lords only, even if they upheld the fiction of representing the 'whole people', as did the English nobility and the Hungarian and Polish magnates in the thirteenth century. The same applied to prelates insofar as they were summoned as vassals. In England and Wales, twenty-one diocesan bishops were summoned in person, as were twenty-five French archbishops and bishops until the estates general of 1468. They fiercely protested when, in 1483–4, a new electoral system eliminated personal summonses and only twenty-four of them were elected as representatives of the clergy in their particular *bailliage* or *sénéchaussée*.[9]

However, representation by clergy who held an office to which they had been elected and appointed was true representation. Sometimes, a chapter or monastery convened to decide who would represent the community in a political assembly. The practice of representation of a community formed by people in an identical juridical position applied further to privileged communes of an urban or rural character. As soon as corporate bodies enjoying formal rights through custom and privilege were recognised within a hierarchical society, they created the basis for the representation of their common interests vis-à-vis other bodies or *estates*. The word *estate*, derived from the Latin *status*, originally meant nothing more than a social and juridical position. In the *ancien régime*, the hierarchy of particularly privileged individuals, institutions and communes was considered as the main characteristic of society. Collectivities, rather than individuals, enjoyed liberties and rights. Towns and rural communes acquired customary rights or were granted privileges in different forms at different times. The plurality of such legal positions demanded agreements and working arrangements between each of them. One way of achieving these formally was negotiation in assemblies of estates in which corporate bodies were personified by proctors.[10]

The summons by King John of England in 1213 of 'four discreet knights' from the counties of England clearly referred to the representation of districts by elected representatives. In England, the courts of hundreds and counties naturally developed out of the Anglo-Saxon period into constituencies for

[9] Bulst (1992), p. 340.   [10] Monahan (1987), pp. 111–21.

political representatives, as is clearly seen in the first appearance of the knights of the shire in parliament in 1254. It was the early and systematic organisation of rural communities on a national scale, a consequence of the exceptional administrative centralisation achieved by the Norman kings, which made this advance possible. In Sweden, the hundred districts likewise formed the basis for national representation. Yet, in the English counties, the constituencies were not free to elect representatives of their own social status, as occurred in religious, urban or rural communes.

Representation is often seen as the consequence of action by a monarch. This was not necessarily always the case. In southern France, assemblies of urban representatives were regularly summoned or convened in their own right. In 1252, Dublin and Drogheda agreed on a confederation 'on common counsel among representatives of the towns'. In 1285, the confederation was extended with Cork, Limerick and Waterford, prescribing the triennial meeting of two or three burghers of each on the morrow of Trinity.[11] Elsewhere, as in Holland, Frisia, southern Germany and the Alpine regions, emancipated communes of free peasants gradually developed representative systems from the bottom up. Representation required a constituency, a corporate privileged community itself able to designate those mandated by it. The feeling of community, resting on common rights and interests, did not necessarily require a prince to provoke representative actions.

The political system

It is generally assumed that states or, before their stabilisation, countries or territories formed the system in which representative institutions operated. Hintze regarded the nature of a monarchical state, competitive, centralising and rationalising, as a necessary condition for the full development of a *Ständestaat*. This concept, difficult to translate into English, refers to a state in which the estates have a constitutional political role. In this perspective German historiography adopted the view of a dualistic system of the (territorial) prince and the estates. Even the most recent opinion holds that 'the prince and his court were not only the point of departure and antagonist of the system of estates, but the nodal point from which the fundamental development of the territories has to be understood'.[12] Although this viewpoint may be adequate for large parts of continental Europe, it certainly does not fit urbanised coastal areas, where territorial and monarchical states had much less influence. It can certainly not be considered a general rule that the monarch was the initiator and sole focus of representative activities, not even in the

[11] Monahan (1987), pp. 124–5.   [12] Moraw (1992), p. 9.

Empire. In some urban areas, other types of representation developed into regional urban leagues; in some of these associations of cities (*Einungen* or *hermandades*) or *Landfrieden* (territorial peace treaties) princes and nobles were included as well. Such systems could develop only thanks to negotiations and some form of representation. Regional urban leagues found unity in the German Hanse, which German historiography, in my view incorrectly, does not consider as another type of representative system. The Hanse cities had their own representative assemblies on different levels and acted towards the outside world in the name of their member towns. In a similar way, groups of coastal towns created regular contacts with other authorities in support of their citizens' trade. From the *consulado del mar* of Barcelona, dating from 1258, to the more conventional participation in the sealing of commercial treaties struck between princes, such as that carried out by Flemish cities during the thirteenth century, we can observe many examples of urban representatives operating in networks very different from those of the territorial state and its monarch. Apart from the networks of commercial cities, communities of free peasants, in particular of cattle breeders, proved able to represent their interests on their own initiative before trading partners or political competitors.

In contrast to prevailing German interpretation, and particularly that of Hintze, representation did not always develop within the framework of one particular territory, state or monarchy. Conversely, too, not all monarchical states developed representative institutions: the silver mines of Thuringia and Meissen allowed their princes a sufficient income not to have to appeal to their subjects until the fourteenth century, as did its grain revenues for the Teutonic Order in Prussia.[13] Moreover, monarchs were often reluctant to summon existing representative institutions. Thus the view that representative institutions had to be focused on the monarchical state and limited to its borders is too narrow for our purpose. In broadening our scope and including the wide variety of types of representative activities developed in different regions, we may be in a better position to understand their evolution and functions. Moreover, few states were stable entities during the later Middle Ages. Dynastic strategies and accidents often united or separated territories, thus changing the political system in which representative institutions had to operate. A dynastic union, such as that between the kingdoms of León and Castile in 1230, could lead to the unification of both incipient *cortes*, while in the neighbouring kingdom of Aragon, the constituent territories kept their individual assemblies. Only on some occasions did the kings of Aragon in the fifteenth century summon combined assemblies of the *cortes* of Aragon, Catalonia and Valencia. The dynastic union of Castile and Aragon, however,

---

[13] Folz (1965), p. 182; Boockmann (1992b).

never led to common meetings of their representative institutions. Both cases show the importance of the sense of community, as contrasting to the unifying action of the princes. In the fifteenth century, the king of France ruled over territories some of which had representative assemblies, others not. His integrative action explains this co-existence but the different institutional traditions had been ruled out by him. The state is therefore not the only suitable unit of analysis: it was not always the exclusive focus of political representation, constituting in itself a variable unity which did not necessarily produce representative institutions. This is why we should opt for an analytical framework of political systems, starting from the various representative activities themselves, rather than from the territories.

The analytical framework

If the state is thus rejected as the unit of our analysis, we have to turn to less stable and more varied political systems as these really functioned and were felt as communities by the people. Besides the large monarchical states, the later Middle Ages saw the continued existence of regional or territorial states ruled by a lay or clerical prince, independent cities with a more or less extended territory, and virtually autonomous rural territories. The last two categories, when located in close proximity to one another, often united in federations of which some lasted for years, decades and even centuries, just as monarchies did. Representative institutions evidently were expressions of the most powerful segments of those societies from which they emanated. They should therefore be considered in their wider social and political context.

The first factor to take into account is the strength of the ruling dynasty, a result of the continuity of undisputed and capable heirs. Furthermore, a dynasty's strength depended on its success in pursuing a matrimonial policy aimed at acquiring as many inheritances, rights or claims as possible. Its position, too, was determined by the availability of independent resources which enabled it to indulge in political action.

The second factor is the sheer physical scale of the political system. Representation is a matter of communication in which facilities for travel play an important role. Some systems simply proved too large to be really functional. Strong dynasties often crumbled under their own over-expansion. The Empire, even without Italy, Bohemia and other peripheral regions, was so extensive that it took up to one month to cross; a factor which delayed the dissemination of information and increased the costs of transport. In France, while regional assemblies were regularly held, they showed very little ambition to have the estates general summoned more frequently. In 1468, the representatives in Tours, having agreed in nine days to the king's wishes, observed 'qu'ils ne se peuvent pas si souvent rassembler' and acquiesced in all his further decisions on those matters – and many others as well.[14] Distances and scattered settlement prevented a real sense of community from arising at the level of the kingdom. For the same reasons, the general assembly of the German Hanse (*Hansetag*) was mostly poorly attended and thus ineffectual; even if connections by ship were easier than over land, the distance between London and Novgorod created too many obstacles. Representative institutions thus reached their highest intensity in relatively small areas, with a diameter of, say 250 to 300 kilometres, mostly along an important river or a stretch of coast with good harbours, thus enabling major cities, and commercial activities between them, to develop. Their advanced social integration maximised both the need and the material possibilities for frequent interaction. Thus a political system was not necessarily based on contiguous territory: it could also consist of a network of cities.

The third factor in our analytical framework, containing a whole set of variables, has to be the social and economic structure in the political system. Power, as the ultimate aim of all representation, depended on the numbers of people in each occupational category and on their share in the wealth they controlled, including the measure of personal freedom which they enjoyed. It is essential for our purpose to be aware of the nature and size of the resources which each contending group in a political system could mobilise. In the last instance, these material factors determined the opportunities of which the contenders could make a more or less efficacious use. In the field of commonplace political ideas, however, the vision of society as a body, a metaphor derived from Aristotle, helped to legitimise social inequalities. In the terminology of the Catalonian *brazos* (arms) of the *cortes*, the Italian *brachia, bracci* or *bras*, and the Flemish *leden, membres*, we find echoes of this anthropomorphic thinking.

The fourth factor concerns the position of the political system in its wider context. Vulnerability to external challenges, for instance, strongly influenced internal relations. Geographical location, such as exposure to external pressures or isolation and lack of opportunity to develop relations with others, played its role. Expansion on a commercial or military basis, or the need to mobilise defensive forces, were among the most frequent items on the political agenda of representative institutions.

The fifth, and last, factor we will have to consider can be labelled the weight of institutional traditions. In each situation of relatively open power relations, contenders seek legitimation for their actions, which helps them gain acceptance. The existence of a tradition of problem-solving by negotiation helped

[14] Bulst (1992), p. 49.

to channel conflicts into peaceful solutions and to prevent their escalation. New situations could be settled by stretching the existing rules. For example, the incapacity and abuse of power by the duke of Brabant John IV in 1420 furthered the elaboration of the century-old constitutional tradition; this helped to limit the bloodshed. The absence of a tradition of active representative institutions eased the shift of power towards the monarch or the nobility. In any event, the solution of problems was normally sought along the lines of existing procedures and institutions such as, for example, the German regional peace treaties (*Einungen, Landfrieden*) or similar types of negotiated agreements (and the application of the feudal notions of loyalty, counsel and help to communities of citizens and free peasants). Particular problematic situations often triggered off solutions which in the long run proved to be real innovations. A typical example is the new procedure to summon the French estates general by districts. The Beaujeu party in the royal council designed it in 1483 in order to strengthen its own position during the regency. The system eliminated the traditional personal summonses, and required instead pre-elections of three representatives, one from each estate, in the administrative districts. It was to last until 1789.[15]

MONARCHICAL CHALLENGES

The development of particular forms of representation depended on conditions which now require investigation. Once a practice had grown into a tradition which was regarded as a customary right, it could not easily be discarded and thus it influenced its further evolution. Essentially there were only two ways of launching the process of the institutionalisation of popular representation: either the prince or some groups from the people had to take the initiative. From the side of the subjects only the communes should interest us now; the (high) nobility would not create a real representative political system, nor would the clergy other than in ecclesiastical principalities, where they must be considered as rulers. To get an innovation going, some problems had to trigger off solutions. We shall distinguish between the prince's problems and those of the communes.

The problems of princes: recognition

In 1230 and 1231 the Emperor Frederick II was obliged to grant rights to the German princes and cities in order to keep the country quiet before his return to his beloved Sicily. Without the active support of the magnates, no ruler

---

[15] Bulst (1992), pp. 356–62.

could carry out all his essential functions. The first concern of every feudal lord was to ensure the loyalty of his vassals, even if he had to pay a price for it. The moment of accession to the throne, therefore, was always a crucial one for a prince, especially since many successions were disputed by rivals whose rights were often no less convincing than his own. In the case when several contenders had comparable rights, effective power usually proved decisive, while the securing of support from as many elements in the population as possible was of vital importance. Many successions caused problems because of the uncertainty regarding the rules of succession. Such rules might be different in other countries, which had its consequences, given the nobility's pan-European matrimonial relations. Many marriages were rendered invalid by the rules of canon law on kinship. So, not infrequently, succession fell upon children or women, whose position was generally vulnerable. Add to these situations involving physically or mentally weak heirs, and one has a catalogue of possibilities for intervention by hostile powers, who in their search for support often encouraged participation in political strife by wider segments of society.

A well-known case in which the disputed succession to the throne gave rise to broad consultation with powerful groups of society is that of King Alfonso IX in León in 1188, who summoned the 'archbishops, bishops, the religious orders, the counts and other nobles of his realm, together with the elected burghers from the different cities'. Before them, he swore to respect the *mores bonos*, the good customs and not 'to wage war, make peace or hold a solemn court without the counsel of the bishops, nobles and good men with whose counsel I have to reign'. In their turn, they all 'swore fealty in my council, to keep justice and to bring peace in my whole realm'.[16] Scholarship and national pride have hailed this assembly as the first ever in which elected representatives of cities participated actively. We should not, however, overestimate even exceptional events like this coronation ceremony. That of Alfonso VII as emperor of Spain in 1135 was embedded in a solemn assembly of dignitaries among whom a chronicle mentions the presence, as the last in the enumeration, of 'judges' who may well have been the same elected members of the town councils as in 1188. The haphazard survival of documents, as well as the terminology used by those who wrote them, present today's historians with difficulties. It has been argued recently that the famous act of 1188 must have been formulated at least in part during a court meeting in 1194 for which the participation of citizens cannot be proved.[17] Moreover, in 1187 in neighbouring Castile, a meeting of the king's court (*curia*) had been summoned to recognise Berenguela's right of succession. The *maiores* of fifty towns promised to guarantee the observance of her marriage contract with Conrad of

---

[16] Procter (1980), pp. 51–2, 138–43, 176–85; O'Callaghan (1989), pp. 79–93; Estepa Diez (1990), pp. 21–39.   [17] Estepa Diez (1990), pp. 23–7.

Hohenstaufen. So it is likely that the leaders of these towns had been summoned to the same *curia* in 1187 where the contract had been prepared.[18] Rather than highlighting one date, it should be noted that participation of representatives of the cities gradually assumed an increasingly significant role in the political life of Castile and León: in the latter kingdom they certainly participated in *cortes* (a term occurring only by 1250) in 1202 and 1208, in the former also in 1222. Meetings remained rare, and it was only after 1250 that assemblies reached an average frequency of one in two years.

Castile–León shows a long tradition of interference by the representative institutions in the recognition of the heir. They did not formally elect the king, but influenced the determination of the succession. However, their intervention was not always necessary: the succession of 1284 and 1332 occurred without them. In 1202, 'the whole Leónese kingdom' swore allegiance to Berenguela's recently born son, Fernando. In 1254, King Alfonso X summoned the archbishops, bishops, magnates and representatives of cities, fortresses and towns to pledge homage to his eldest daughter Berenguela; it was clearly stated then that the kingdom of Castile–León had to be kept undivided. During the conflict about primogeniture which arose from 1275 until 1282, the support of the *hermandades*, autonomous associations led by the cities and including bishops and abbots, proved to be essential. The *cortes* curtailed King Alfonso X's competence in favour of his son, Sancho, and formulated conditions and the right of resistance in the case of violation. The power of the *cortes* was demonstrated by their direct refutal of Pope Martin IV's interdict and excommunication of Sancho in 1283. During the successive minority crises in 1295–1301 and 1312–25 rival candidates had to concede far-reaching powers to the *cortes* or *hermandades*. Their claims were formulated in *cuadernos*, which provided effective control of the government. Violation of the agreement would lead to the choice of another regent. The *cortes* of Castile–León did not interfere with the recognition of the king in 1284 and 1332, but repeated minorities and rivalries gave them many opportunities to influence the making of decisions and obtain increasing privileges for themselves.[19]

In the neighbouring kingdom of Aragon a 'general court' was held in Lerida in 1214 to swear fidelity to the child-king Jaume. Among them were 'barons, knights, citizens and the men [vassals] of the castles and villages'. On this occasion Catalonia got its Statutes of the Peace revised in favour of the cities and some dissident nobility; the abolition of tolls was confirmed, and no taxes were to be levied on the cities during Jaume's minority.[20] In 1228 during a difficult period after a revolt and just before his divorce, King Jaume summoned another 'general court' in Daroca. The names of three bishops, dozens of

---

[18] O'Callaghan (1989), p. 82.   [19] O'Callaghan (1989), pp. 79–93.   [20] Bisson (1986), p. 59.

nobles, the 'citizens, burghers and wise men', more than 180 in all, are listed in a charter drawn up during this meeting. Homage and fealty to the king's young son was given by the delegates of the thirty cities and towns both personally and in the name of their communes.[21] 'General courts' with more than 100 participants, at which not only dynastic affairs but also matters of internal peace, law, politics, taxation and coinage were discussed, had been a tradition in Aragon at least since 1154. The participation of the cities and towns, which, during the twelfth century, had been dominated by the members of the *concejos*, now achieved a broader representative basis since the communes, cities, towns and villages were represented by two to fourteen deputies of varied status, craftsmen and herdsmen as well as the local notables. When the dynasty of Aragon became extinct in 1412, it was the *corts* of Aragon, Catalonia and Valencia–Majorca which, together, took the decision in favour of one of the claimants, Fernando, son of King Juan I of Castile.[22]

Recognition of the kings of Castile, León and Aragon by the representatives of their subjects – the magnates, high office holders, noblemen and representatives of the *corpora*, political bodies – was far from formal ceremony. Recognition was conditional: the representatives were invited to swear an oath of loyalty as vassals or pseudo-vassals (the cities). This implied that the assent could be withheld or revoked, just as in a feudal contract. An early example of this action is described in contemporary chronicles in Flanders in 1128. Count William had been inaugurated in 1127 under condition that he showed respect for the privileges of the land and particularly for those of the fast-growing cities. Within a year he had violated so many stipulations that citizens rebelled in Saint-Omer and Lille and a broad movement of opposition arose. In Ghent, the citizens had the following request addressed to the court in their name by a sympathetic nobleman:

Lord count, if you had wished to deal justly with our citizens, your burghers, and with us as their friends, you would not have imposed evil exactions upon us and acted with hostility toward us but, on the contrary, you would have defended us from our enemies and treated us honourably. But now you have acted contrary to law and in your own person you have broken the oaths that we swore in your name concerning the remission of the toll, the maintenance of peace and the other rights which the men of this land obtained from the counts of the land, your good predecessors ... and from yourself; you have violated your faith and done injury to ours since we took the oath to this effect together with you ... Let your court, if you please, be summoned at Ypres, which is located in the middle of your land, and let the barons from both sides, and our peers and all the responsible (*sapientiores*) men among the clergy and people, come together in peace and without arms, and let them judge, quietly and after due consideration,

---

[21] Bisson (1977), p. 118. Just one example from Lerida: 'Isti sunt probi homines Ylerdenses qui iuraverunt pro se et pro tota vniversitate Ylerde; Ego Raymundus Petri iuro et hominum fatio.'

[22] Bisson (1986), pp. 134–6.

without guile or evil intent. If in their opinion you can keep the countship in the future without violating the honour of the land, I agree that you should keep it. But if, in fact, you are unworthy of keeping it, that is, lawless and faithless, a deceiver and perjurer, give up the countship, relinquish it to us so that we can entrust it to someone suitable and with rightful claims to it. For we are the mediators between the king of France and you to guarantee that you undertake nothing important in the county without regard for the honour of the land and our counsel.[23]

This remarkably clear and early pronouncement of the principles of constitutional government under the control of the representatives of the three estates emanates from the feudal notions of contract: a vassal had the right of resistance if he was wrongly treated. The argument introduced the widening of this concept to all citizens; it was grounded on their mutually sworn fealty on the basis of law. The count, however, refused the proposal, rejected the homage previously done to him by the spokesman and challenged him to combat. His reaction refuted the notion of the countship as a public office subject to judgement by the 'wisest' representatives from the three estates, united in his council. The proposed meeting of the broad *curia*, the count's court, was never held, and arms finally decided in favour of the citizens. During the remainder of the twelfth century, successive counts did not repeat the same mistakes but granted new privileges to the cities; no mention is to be found of any effective assembly of the kind announced in 1128.[24]

The formal and conditional recognition of the ruler by the representatives of the three estates, not only the feudal vassals but also those of cities and often villages, can be found in several other regions. In the states of the Church, several assemblies were summoned from 1200 onwards in different provinces. In that year 'qualified representatives' of the communes of the Marches were invited to swear an oath of fealty to Innocent III, and to contribute to the settlement of peace and the defence of the land. On other occasions, the three estates were summoned for similar motives. This frequent interaction gave the opportunity of presenting grievances and petitions, but remained limited to the provincial level, which hampered a further concentration of power. Indeed, no pope ever summoned assemblies in Campania or in the city of Rome.

In Sicily, where the Emperor Frederick II had initiated the representation of cities, these played an active role in the transfer of allegiance to the house of Aragon. The 'better men' of cities and villages convened to swear an oath of fealty to King Pere I in 1282, and to hear him confirm the laws and customs of the time before the Angevin kings. In 1286, the coronation of King Jaume was the occasion to hold another assembly at which twenty-three *capitoli*, or constitutions, limiting arbitrary government were issued. In 1296, it was the

---

[23] Galbert of Bruges, *De multro*, p. 95.   [24] Dhondt (1950).

'counts, barons and *syndici*' (envoys of the cities) who transferred the kingdom to Frederic of Aragon of whom it was hoped that he would defend Sicily better than his brother against the rival Angevin monarchy. He swore to keep the constitutions of his predecessors since Norman times, not to abandon the country, nor to make war or peace without the general consent of the kingdom. He even promised to call annually, on All Saints' day, a general *curia* of the counts, the barons and suitable representatives of the cities. The purpose of these meetings would be the redress of grievances against royal officers, 'it being most just that the king be bound to observe his own laws'. In the fourteenth century, the disappearance of the fear of an Angevin reconquest and a series of weak kings seem to have removed the challenges to the estates which could not take advantage of their far-reaching privileges.[25]

When King Louis VIII of France took possession of Languedoc in 1226 after the so-called crusade against the heretics, he took care to receive the oaths of fealty from all the prelates, nobles and cities in the region. His commissioners travelled around to receive the oaths, sworn both privately and in public assemblies where the consuls and other townsmen represented their communes. The translation of the county of Toulouse to King Alfonso IX of León was formalised in 1249 in a series of assemblies in which different sectors of the territory rendered their oaths. The townsmen of Toulouse did so and heard their liberties confirmed. At least sixty-six nobles and notables, together with the consuls of fourteen communes, swore their oath of fealty on the basis of the royal rights agreed earlier during a second assembly, after which followed two other similar meetings for 'many barons and other nobles and other persons, both clerical and lay' in various districts. In Agen, the assembly 'composed of barons and knights of the diocese, consuls of Agen, and councils and burghers of regional bourgs, *castra*, and villages' refused to comply with the request of the commissioners to render fealty, referring to their liberties and customs and to conflicting rights to the throne. Indeed, in 1279 an assembly of prelates, deputies of the chapters, barons, knights, nobles, deputies of towns and villages was summoned to transfer the lordship to the proctor of King Edward I of England, who secured feudal recognition in person in 1286 in a general assembly as well as in local meetings. The whole episode shows the necessity for kings to obtain the assent of their new subjects in the form of regional assemblies which had their own rights which they clearly wanted to have respected.[26]

In the Empire, it was only during the difficulties of Louis of Bavaria with the pope in 1338–44 that the king sought the active support of all his subjects, including dozens of cities which he summoned twice.[27] Most cases of

[25] Marongiu (1968), pp. 109–19; Koenigsberger (1978), pp. 22–9.
[26] Bisson (1964), pp. 143–63, 234–45.   [27] Engel (1980), pp. 38–9.

participation concern peripheral territories. Ecclesiastical principalities, in particular, were liable to open disputes about succession, since each implied a totally new beginning. No wonder that in a prince bishopric such as Liège, one of those cities which had grown very early in economic importance and political autonomy, many a vacancy gave birth to an urban league, first in 1229 and again repeatedly during the next centuries. The development of representation was interwoven with particularly violent clashes between variable configurations of the bishop, the chapter, the patriciate, the nobility and the common people of the cities, often in coalitions with neighbouring princes. Unions were followed by renewed violence and peace treaties until the end of the fifteenth century.[28] Nobles and aldermen (*Ratsherren*) of the cities of Rostock and Wismar formed the regency councils during minorities in Mecklenburg in 1282 and 1329.[29] The peace treaty made on the occasion of the division of Pomerania in 1295 between two half-brothers granted the vassals and cities the right of resistance against any infringement upon their corporate privileges. This treaty was called into effect in 1319 when one of the two dukes came into conflict with his subjects. When, in 1326, the other duke died leaving only young children, vassals and cities participated in the regency council. In 1338–9 the vassals and cities refused to inaugurate King Louis' son as their duke. Such instances strengthened the corporate identity of the two main estates of the territories.[30]

In 1315, repeated dynastic problems in Bavaria led to the formation of a union (*Einung*) of nobles and cities, and in 1324 of a deputation from these estates (*Ausschuß*) that would decide in all political matters.[31] After the Emperor Charles IV had usurped the Brandenburg March in 1363, the estates at first refused to inaugurate him, and only yielded under military pressure. In the fifteenth century, the estates nevertheless constituted the obvious regents, on a par with the councillors, to govern the territories during the prolonged absences and minorities of the elector.[32] In 1413, the estates of Prussia – thirty-two knights and esquires and sixteen citizens – collaborated with the knights of the Teutonic Order to depose the powerful Master, Heinrich von Plauen, and swore fealty to his successor. Between 1410 and 1466, the estates played a decisive role in the transition of Prussia to the king of Poland. In 1454 the deputies of the nobility and the six major cities refused obedience to the Teutonic Order and turned to the king of Poland who incorporated Prussia under the stipulation of far-reaching rights of autonomy.[33]

The most interesting tradition in this respect is that of the duchy of Brabant. Between 1248 and 1430, problems of succession, usually resulting from the

[28] Töpfer (1980a), pp. 114–35.   [29] Engel (1980), pp. 46, 53.   [30] Benl (1992), pp. 123–6.
[31] Engel (1980), pp. 52–3.   [32] Heinrich (1992), pp. 145–8.   [33] Biskup (1992), pp. 85–9.

minority or gender of the heir or the extinction of the ruling line, manifested themselves on eight out of nine occasions. In all these cases, the representatives of the cities, sometimes acting together with the most prominent noblemen, negotiated written guarantees with their dying or future dukes. In 1267, barons, magnates and cities agreed with the duchess to replace her incapable son, Henry, by his younger brother, John I;[34] while in 1312, with the prospect of yet another minority looming, a regency council was formed in which burghers assumed an important role. A solemn act recognised the right of the subjects to refuse any service to the duke if and as long as he violated the privileges granted in the constitution. From this text grew a tradition of granting, on the occasion of the taking up of power by a new duke, of an updated constitutional act growing to over 100 articles, a tradition maintained in Brabant until 1794. The three estates, formed as a regular institution in the course of the fourteenth century, decided on the acceptance of the Burgundian dynasty around 1400. Strict conditions were formulated to ensure that the successor would rule the duchy in person and according to its customs and privileges. In 1420–1 they suspended Duke John IV because of his infringements of the law, chose his brother as the regent for as long as he did not comply, and thereafter imposed an extended control on his government. This was a case in which extraordinary dynastic discontinuity led to the development of a very strong constitutional tradition.[35]

A comparable situation occurred in Württemberg, where, in 1498, a particularly inept duke was denied the fidelity of the *Landtag* which proclaimed a constitution and exercised the government by regents during the five years of a minority.[36] Recognition of the powers of regency was withheld by the estates in Flanders between 1482 and 1492. In 1483, a regency council composed of members of the count's family and representatives of the estates was recognised and ruled effectively for some years, but the position of the ruler concerned, later destined to be the Emperor Maximilian I, made him rely upon military superiority to impose his authority.[37]

In Bohemia, the extinction of the Premysl dynasty in 1306 created opportunities for the estates to decide between the rival contenders, Henry of Carinthia and Rudolf of Habsburg. For the first time *barones, nobiles et cives*, magnates, lesser nobles and citizens all participated in the election and imposed their conditions, *Wahlkapitulationen*. In 1307 and 1310, this procedure was repeated. In the latter year, the unworthy Henry of Carinthia was deposed

---

[34] 'De consensu benevolo et voluntate communi Aleidis ducissae Brabatiae, Baronum, Magnatum et communium oppidorum Ducatus' (Van Uytven (1966), pp. 432–3).

[35] Van Uytven and Blockmans (1969); Van Uytven (1966) and (1985); Graffart and Uyttebrouck, 'Quelques documents inédits'. [36] Folz (1965), p. 190.

[37] Blockmans, 'Autocratie ou polyarchie'.

under pressure from the estates, who negotiated with the king of the Romans to obtain his guarantee of the freedom of the Bohemian kingdom and his agreement with the succession. The newly elected King John of Luxemburg had to grant extensive privileges, especially the reservation of all royal offices to members of the native nobility. Citizens, in practice a tiny patrician elite, had participated in these events, but were still too weak to secure their political position in the long run. In a formal sense only the magnates can be considered as a politically structured estate in the fourteenth century.

The alleged incapacity of King Wenceslas, who had been deposed and captured twice during a revolt of the magnates, activated the Bohemian estates. During the protracted crisis after his death in 1411, the estates in fact were the sole institution to represent the identity of the country. The royal cities, dominated by the three cities of Prague, and the religious fraternities of the Hussite reform movement for the first time took a lasting share in political life at the side of the nobles. Magnates and the aldermen of Prague called for the denial of obedience to the king of the Romans, Sigismund, who was described as 'a terrible and cruel enemy of the kingdom of Bohemia and of the Czech language'. In 1421 the *Landtag* rejected him as unworthy of the Bohemian crown, chose an alternative government, and started negotiations with the Polish and Lithuanian courts with a view to selecting a new king. In 1432, its representatives participated in the Council of Basle, and a year later a governor was chosen in its name. Sigismund was finally inaugurated in 1436 under a *Wahlkapitulation* formulated by the three estates, magnates, knights and (royal) cities, stipulating respect for their privileges and, most remarkably for the time, for freedom of religion. From 1437 onwards, successive interregnums allowed the estates to keep up their influence. In 1440, eighteen magnates and fourteen representatives of the knights and the cities elected the king who had to promise, among other things, to appoint only native officials and accept the participation of the estates in the choice of his councillors. King Mátyás Corvinus of Hungary profited from the vacancy of the throne in 1468 to invade Bohemia; it was the estates who opted instead for a Slav king, whom they found in the person of Vladislav Jagiełło. In the history of fifteenth-century Bohemia one is struck by the harmonising role played by the estates not only in social and territorial matters but even in the more delicate fields of religion and nationality.[38]

Royal elections also stimulated the development of representative institutions in Sweden. In 1448, sixty to seventy 'men of the realm', all lords, elected Karl Knutsson, who was then 'taken and judged' by the deputies of the provinces, representing 'the commonalty'. In 1458, King Christian had his son

[38] Kejr (1992), pp. 194–216; Smahel (1992), pp. 221–30; Eberhard (1987), pp. 345–8.

recognised as his successor by a 'council of the realm, lawspeakers, good men and the commonalty'. In 1464, however, Christian had to withdraw to Denmark and the exiled Karl renewed his claims by summoning 'the common Swedish realm, noblemen, townsmen and commonalty' representing six provinces. In the dynastic crisis which followed, popular representation was activated, not least by armed levies, whose members claimed the right to make decisions. In all meetings the presence of representatives from the provinces, and especially of peasants and miners from the central district, is apparent. The peasants gathered in the *härad*, the 'hundred' districts, where they elected their representatives. These again formed the *thing*, from which the 'twelve good men from each province, as indicated by the law of Sweden' were delegated, together with 'noblemen, miners, the burgomaster and the councillors of the town of Stockholm, and all the other townsmen here in the Realm' to recognise Prince Christian as the future king at midsummer 1499.[39]

Similar effects of the election and inauguration of monarchs upon the emergence of representative institutions are not found in every country. Notable exceptions are England, France, the Empire, Poland and Hungary. The reason is simple: dynastic continuity raised fewer problems in England and France during the late twelfth and thirteenth centuries, which made it possible to keep the decisions limited to the small circle of the royal house. In the Empire, the elective procedure came to be monopolised by the great princes, later the prince-electors, while in Poland and Hungary the magnates kept this prerogative within their estate, unchallenged by other important social groups. While the English parliament played an active role in the deposition of Kings Edward II in 1327 and Richard II in 1399, it seems rather to have been the puppet in the hands of rival magnates. The repeated use of the impeachment procedure against high officials, courtiers and royal justices in 1386, 1388, 1397 and 1399, and finally the articles *Objectus contra Regem*, summing up Richard II's alleged crimes and misdemeanours, leading to his deposition, rather reflect shifts of power originating outside parliament.[40] In other countries, recurrent dynastic problems created the opportunity for representative institutions to build up a constitutional tradition in which they exercised effective control not only on the choice of the monarch but, more importantly, on the limitations to his power. Under extreme circumstances, recognition of rulers was denied, suspended or revoked. Representative institutions determined the regency councils in early fourteenth-century Castile–León, Brabant and Pomerania; and they decided about the translation to another dynasty in Agen 1286, Sicily 1296, Prussia 1410–66 and Bohemia 1468. All this could lead to a sometimes violent redefinition of the divisions of power.

[39] Schück (1987), pp. 27–32; Lönnroth (1989), p. 89.   [40] Roskell *et al.* (1992), I, pp. 69–76.

The problems of princes: aid

A monarch's need for support did not remain limited to his recognition as the suzerain of loyal vessals. In his constant competition with rivals both within and outside his territories, he had to rely on the active military and financial support of his subjects. The scale of the military operations grew from occasional feudal bands to professional standing armies. The formidable increase in military expenditure could only be supported thanks to the economic growth of the time which was mainly produced by the commercialisation concentrated in expanding cities, towns and ports. The differentiation in society accompanying this process formed the basis for the widening composition of the consultative councils which monarchs had always formed at their side. When not only personal feudal service but more regular and more general military and financial support was required, all free subjects were in a position to have a say on the matter of extra-feudal demands. We can single out warfare as the determinant factor in the political process which led to the elimination of many independent territorial entities and thus to the formation of larger states. The character of warfare changed from compulsory feudal service of mainly heavily armed knights on horseback to large numbers of infantry consisting of militias from the communes and mercenaries using crossbows, pikes and, in the fifteenth century, firearms. The method of mobilisation had to turn from an appeal for loyal service owed to negotiations about the levy or payment of soldiers. In the later thirteenth century, kings legitimised their expansive claims on service and aid through the use of canonical doctrine, pretending to 'defend and preserve the kingdom in peace for the common utility of all', as did King Philip III of France.[41] The higher the level of commercialisation of an economy, the easier was the step towards a modern and thus potentially more effective army in which subjects themselves no longer had to serve, as long they paid for others to do so for them.

The first stage was the stretching to the limit of feudal obligation: longer service, farther from home, greater levies on fiefs. These were the abuses perpetrated in England in the reign of King John and formulated by the barons in the famous Magna Carta of 1215. Although this document certainly did not emanate from a representative assembly, since the barons could speak only in their own name as the king's vassals, many of its articles were nevertheless referred to later as a constitutional act enunciating essential principles, such as 'no taxation without consent':

[12.] No scutage or aid is to be levied in our realm except by the common counsel of our realm, unless it is for the ransom of our person, the knighting of our eldest son or

---

[41] Bisson (1964), p. 271.

the first marriage of our eldest daughter; and for these only a reasonable aid is to be levied. Aids from the city of London are to be treated likewise.[42]

Article 14 further specified the 'common counsel of the realm' as 'the archbishops, bishops, abbots, earls and greater barons summoned individually by our letters; and we shall also have summoned generally through our sheriffs and bailiffs all those who hold of us in chief or for a fixed date'. The separate mention of the city of London can only be understood as referring to an independent feudal status on a par with the tenants-in-chief, not as the representation of the commune. From 1254 consultations on the scale of the kingdom in matters of grants started to include knights representing the shires. Their representative activity rested upon the tradition of their role as speakers for the counties before the itinerant royal justices. Each of the thirty-seven counties returned two knights. The first record of the appearance of representative burgesses in a parliament for the whole realm dates from 1265, but it was only in the 1320s that these would become a permanent factor. In 1295, 114 cities and boroughs were represented. Later on, their number fluctuated between eighty and ninety; each of them sent two members, London four.[43] Thus, the English parliament grew from the gradual extensions of the king's council under the pressure of increasing financial and military needs. The Welsh and Gascon wars in the period (1268–95) brought a shift in the notion of defence of the realm as a national concern to be borne by all subjects. The estates heard together the king's demands in the solemn opening session of parliament. Cathedral and parochial clergy (the latter disappearing from parliament in 1322), barons, knights and burgesses deliberated separately and returned different answers. Only about the middle of the fourteenth century were the Commons to form a separate house of the communes of the knights and the burgesses elected to parliament. In 1343 knights of the shires and the representatives of the communes met in the 'painted chamber of Westminster palace'. In the course of the fourteenth century the corporate identity of the Commons grew.[44]

In his writ of summons for the so-called 'Model Parliament' in 1295, King Edward I had recognised that 'what concerns all has to be approved by all', which implied that new customs duties needed the assent of parliament. This famous quotation was in its origin a principle of Roman private law reproduced as a general principle by the late twelfth century by the Bolognese law school. In 1222 Pope Honorius III had applied it to an invitation to Christian princes and great ecclesiastical dignitaries, and in 1244 the Emperor Frederick II had quoted it in the summons of a great assembly of ecclesiastical and lay

---

[42] Holt (1965), pp. 320–1. [43] Roskell *et al.* (1992), I, p. 41; Wedgwood (1936–8), II, p. vii.

[44] Roskell *et al.* (1992), I, pp. 46–7.

princes, as Rudolf of Habsburg had to do in 1274. It had become a standard formula to legitimise inevitable political choices where broad support for difficult demands was needed. It eventually equally implied that the king was bound by law and had to recognise the interests of persons concerned.[45] In 1297, the barons disputed King Edward I's aggressive attack against Flanders as not being a matter of defence of the realm and opposed the notion of the 'common profit' to the king's argument of 'necessity', which implied an obligation on the commons. In practice, while the king's interpretation prevailed, at the same time it limited his right to demand his subjects' aid for defence. In the nine years of truce in the war with the Scots, between 1297 to 1306, no taxation was imposed; nor was it during the years of truce with France 1360–9. Neither was there any direct taxation in 1422–9 when the occupied territories in France were considered to have to pay for the war. Through the periods of intensive warfare in 1294–8 and the opening years of the Hundred Years War 1338–42, when taxation reached unprecedented peaks, parliament associated petitioning for the redress of grievances with the supply of money, thus considerably extending its competence in all spheres of government. Indirect taxation, especially that on exported wool, was introduced first in 1275; in 1354 the Commons granted it for the unaccustomed period of six years. The wool subsidy became a permanent crown revenue under the control of parliament which granted it only for short periods and negotiated the duration, the amount, the appropriation of supply, the nomination of special treasurers and the relative burden to be placed on native and foreign merchants.[46]

In the Iberian territories under the crown of Aragon, the clergy, the barons and the towns were regularly summoned from about 1280 onwards. In Aragon, the knights or *ricos hombres* were summoned separately as well, to be institutionalised as a fourth estate in 1389. The 1283 statute prescribed yearly summonses, which were reduced to a slower rhythm in the following years. Custody of privileges, preservation of justice and peace, the approval of statutes and the voting of taxes for properly justified purposes formed part of their regular activities. Extensive warfare against Castile made the Aragonese kings highly dependent on their *corts*. In 1359 Pere IV had to cede judicial supremacy to the *corts* of Catalonia in return for a subsidy. They formed what would later be labelled *diputació del general*, the permanent administrative committee. Lack of support from the *corts* of Aragon compelled the king to give up his Castilian war in 1429. So, the constant dynastic tendency towards expansion, combined with the existing difficulties of controlling Sardinia and Sicily, created a kind of condominium in which the kings were obliged to negotiate with their influential subjects.[47]

---

[45] Marongiu (1968), pp. 33–7; Monahan (1987), pp. 97–111.
[46] Harriss (1966), pp. 169–78; Foreville (1966), pp. 156–63; Ormrod (1991), pp. 182–3; Roskell *et al.* (1992), I, pp. 116–42.   [47] Bisson (1986), pp. 98–9, 118, 143.

From 1295 onwards, urgent requirements prompted King Philip IV of France to intensify his demands in the existing regional assemblies of Languedoc, using the legal argument 'right of state'.[48] In 1302 he extended the tradition of regional assemblies to the scale of the kingdom. The immediate problem for which he sought the support of as many groups of society as possible was his conflict with Pope Boniface VIII; again, in 1308, his action of dissolving the Order of the Templars was the occasion for consultation with the three estates of his realm, later called the estates general. The formidable influence of the Church explains the king's urgent search for support. The success of these two meetings led to a third in 1314, where a purely financial aid was demanded in order to compensate for the huge costs of the king's ongoing war against Flanders. During the first half of the fourteenth century, other assemblies were held in various forms, some regional, others meetings of particular orders.

The catastrophic losses of the first phase of the Hundred Years War provoked intensive activity among the estates general of the Pays d'Oil (northern France) from 1355 to 1359. As in England, the extraordinary demands of the monarchy provoked counter-claims from representatives. In 1355, monetary stability and the consent to taxes by representatives of the king's subjects were the main issues in France; in 1356 the control of the estates general over the choice of the royal councillors came to the fore. The experience proved dangerous for the monarchy. After sessions in 1369, in which the launching of a new campaign against the English was approved, kings preferred separate negotiations with the provincial estates, usually those of the Languedoc and the Languedoil. There can be no doubt that the long distances and the different fate of the North and the Midi during the war help to explain the divergent institutional evolution. Almost every year in the phase of intensive warfare 1421–39 King Charles VII summoned an assembly of the estates general, or of the estates of the western or eastern part of Languedoil separately, to demand aids. After the introduction of the *taille* in 1439–40, however, he no longer needed these troublesome partners. In the heart of the realm representative assemblies were held only during moments of crisis; then they disappeared completely. In the peripheral principalities such as Normandy, Artois, Dauphiné, Burgundy, and especially in Languedoc and Provence, the estates rested on a solid tradition preceding their incorporation into the monarchy. They continued to meet at most once a year and to defend their particular interests and privileges. When, during the minority crisis of 1484, the estates general were summoned once again, more than two-thirds of the delegates for the third estate and one fifth of the nobles were royal officials, whose

[48] Bisson (1964), pp. 282–3.

freedom of speech for the interests of subjects must have been curtailed as a result.[49]

Rudolf of Habsburg, king of the Romans, succeeded in strengthening his position by raising taxes agreed in assemblies of cities in 1284 and 1290.[50] Neither the type of assembly nor the general aids became a tradition in the Empire before the sixteenth century, probably because of the weakness of the central power and the relative strength of territorial princes and barons. Before the institutionalisation of clearly defined estates, Duke John I of Brabant must have negotiated with the corporate nobility, cities and abbeys in the years 1290–3, when he granted one privilege for the nobility as a whole, analogous privileges to eight major cities, and others to a series of abbeys exactly in the period when he obtained a substantial financial aid. A notable concession granted on this occasion both to the nobility and to individual cities was the right of resistance in case of violation of their privileges.[51] During the period of the minority of Duke John III (1312–20) when a regency council led by the cities held power, the duke's finances came fully under the control of the cities and knights. The accumulated debts of his predecessors had necessitated strong intervention by the subjects.[52] A comparable example would be observed in Bavaria in 1356, when a committee drawn from the estates levied taxes, participated in the election of councillors and in the legislation, and heard grievances. Similar rights were claimed in the *Lüneburger Saate* of 1392, when eight burghers obtained temporary control of the ducal finances, heard grievances and even received recognition of the right, should the need occur, to confiscate the domanial income and to resist the duke in arms.

Taxation was an important factor in the development of representative institution, but not a determining one. It is well known that, helped by the tragic state of the realm, the kings of France succeeded in introducing permanent indirect taxes exempt from the assent of the estates. In 1355 the *gabelle*, a salt tax, and ¹/₃₀th on the value of merchandise were accepted by the estates general. This system was extended to ¹/₂₀th in 1435, and, from 1440 onwards, the annual *taille* was levied by the king's officials. These taxes made the French king fairly independent of the estates. In Burgundy during the fifteenth century, the estates controlled the levy of the *fouage* or hearth tax, and reserved a budget for their own expenses. Yet all indirect taxes, introduced earlier by the French crown, escaped the interference of the estates.[53] In the duchy of Brittany, the estates were convoked, probably for the first time, in 1352 to agree on the extraordinary taxation to pay the ransom of Duke Charles of Blois – one of the three feudal cases mentioned in Magna Carta in which aid was due.

[49] Bulst (1987), pp. 313–16, 322–9.   [50] Engel (1980), p. 23.
[51] Van Uytven (1966), pp. 415–25, 432–5.   [52] Van Uytven and Blockmans (1969), pp. 404–5.
[53] Richard (1966), pp. 311–15.

In 1365 the costs of war necessitated the introduction of the *fouage* into the whole duchy, the tax being granted by the estates. No document, however, reveals any concern with the port dues which the duke levied. The overall impression of the function of the estates is essentially one of acquiescence, the spirit which led to their passive recognition of the duke's two daughters as his heiresses in 1486.[54]

However, assemblies of estates did not always develop overarching powers thanks to their control of taxation: in some cases taxation was in the hands of representative institutions of only one estate, often the representatives of cities and rural areas. In late thirteenth-century Languedoc, the increased burden of military levies and aids caused by royal wars against Foix and Gascony did not lead to the development of general assemblies of three estates. Matters were handled in local meetings and in assemblies of separate orders.[55] We have observed the same practice in contemporary Brabant, while in Flanders it was not until 1400 that the count, Philip the Bold, duke of Burgundy, introduced the assembly of three estates as an institution, although aids had been granted by assemblies of cities, sometimes including the rural districts, since the second half of the thirteenth century.[56]

One may conclude that taxes served as a trigger to fuller participation by representative institutions only if taxation came to be excessive or was mismanaged by government, particularly as a consequence of intensive and protracted warfare, and if no other means of surplus extraction were available. Under these conditions, subjects obtained control over the state's (sometimes even the ruler's) finances and secured far-reaching rights for themselves. We should bear in mind, however, that even on those occasions when cities and villages were represented, we are still dealing mainly with privileged elites using representative institutions to protect and expand their collective prerogatives.

COMMUNAL INTERESTS

Even if the initiatives and weaknesses of monarchs challenged the subjects to meet in representative assemblies and to respond by insisting on the rights and needs of their communities, this factor certainly does not explain all forms of representation. Not everything can be reduced to the reactions of subjects to their rulers. For their own purposes, monarchs mostly used pre-existing structures, notably their own enlarged *curia* or court, the regional judicial courts such as in the English hundreds and counties, and the assemblies of *bayles*, bailiffs and consuls in Languedoc. Since 1152, the common council of the city of

---

[54] Kerhervé (1987), I, pp. 139–44.   [55] Bisson (1964), pp. 271–81.
[56] Prevenier (1965), pp. 20–1.

Toulouse had been formally recognised as the representative institution to negotiate with the count.[57] Many communes did not wait for the initiatives of princes to solve their problems but created their own devices on a federative and deliberative basis, often against the encroachments of lay and clerical lords. Assemblies which had grown to fulfil one particular function could take on other functions on the initiative of either the lord or the communities themselves. Equally we have to bear in mind the chronology of events, particularly the relative timing of the growth and decline of the power of monarchs, nobles and burghers.

Much depended on the social and economic structure of a region, especially its level of commercialisation and urbanisation. Large cities evidently had much wider interests and more power than the typical *Kleinstädte* of central Europe. Major cities were located on coasts or great rivers; trade routes influenced their political sensitivities. In general, their common interests consisted in the safety of these routes, for travelling merchants and their goods; in the reliability of monetary exchanges and trade agreements, and in the regulation of internal markets. Cities, therefore, organised their own meetings spontaneously, just as they were convened separately on behalf of the prince. Even as members of the *corts*, Barcelona and Valencia each dominated the urban *brazo* of their region as to claim half of its votes. So it was the larger cities which took the lead, as they were the leaders in the hierarchy of market places. Even when cities participated in assemblies or estates, the domination of the major ones remained obvious: Ghent, Bruges and Ypres outweighed all the other towns of Flanders and thus took many decisions without further consultation.

In northern and central Italy, the predominance of the cities in society was most marked, with capital cities of 60,000 to 100,000 inhabitants and many large secondary towns. The monarchical power of the emperor was clearly too distant and too weak to outweigh them in the long run. The Lombard League – itself a union of cities with elected deputies – made peace with Frederick Barbarossa after a long conflict in 1183 on terms which respected the autonomy of the cities. After the military defeat of the second Lombard League in 1237, Frederick II was again unable to break the autonomy of the ever-growing cities. After his death, regional states came into being in which the largest cities dominated their *contadi*, the surrounding countryside and smaller towns. The oligarchy of the capital city ruled the state in its private interest, using administrative and legal means wherever possible, and military force where necessary. The autonomy of the communes was widely respected in the fourteenth and early fifteenth centuries. Assemblies of heads of households kept their elective rights for the local councils. However, representation on a supra-local level was

---

[57] Mundy (1954), pp. 32–40, 66–8.

absent in a system of local vicaries nominated by the capital city. The only forces which could threaten the ruling elite of the capital and its puppets in the dependent towns were either popular revolts or the rival regional states, with which bitter wars were fought without requiring representation to legitimise and facilitate extra taxation: more modern means of exploitation were available here.[58] Northern and central Italy constituted the most extreme case of excessive power held by one social category, namely the oligarchy of the major cities, effectively eliminating as political contenders the monarchical power as well as that of other social orders and classes. This opened the way for party strife to determine local political life. Parties were not based on the representation of communities enjoying the same rights, but on quasi-feudal vertical ties of protection and dependence. Elsewhere in Europe, however, some plurality of powers remained the rule, allowing many varieties of representation to flourish.

The towns of Castile from 1282 onwards regularly formed *hermandades*, autonomous associations, independent from the king's summons, for preservation of their privileges, if necessary against him. Their movement went far beyond taking positions during the disputes for royal power. The towns' associations in fact formed the vanguard in the *cortes* which, during the new minority from 1295 to 1301, claimed a place in the royal household and chancery, as well as a role in the collection of taxes and the custody of royal castles. In 1312, a *hermandad* of some towns in León claimed the education of the young king to be laid in the hands of good citizens, objected to unlawful taxation and the alienation of royal castles and cities; if violations of the *fueros*, the customary rights, were not redressed, the towns would elect another regent. Even if these claims overplayed the towns' unity, a broader *hermandad* was formed in 1315, including 180 towns from Castile (seventy-eight), León (forty-five), Estremadura, Toledo, Murcia and Andalusia. They would meet every year and control the royal revenue, which they effectively did for some years. This episode shows the towns' capacities to organise themselves on a federal basis for the preservation of their common interests during periods of dynastic crisis. It equally shows, however, that the lack of unity made these associations short-lived, since most minorities at some time came to an end.[59] More was required to make communal representative institutions last.

In thirteenth-century Flanders, five major cities, each with more than 30,000 inhabitants, and the largest one, Ghent, with probably over 60,000, played a role as a collective body. They are mentioned as early as 1209 as the (then still) 'six cities' in an act of King John of England concerning La Rochelle; in 1213 as

[58] Fasoli (1965), pp. 71–86; Koenigsberger (1978), pp. 22–4; Comparato (1980), pp. 149–85; Chittolini (1986), I, pp. 94–9.   [59] O'Callaghan (1989), pp. 53–5, 85–93.

a league, they sealed a treaty with the king, which showed their ability to act autonomously with a foreign country with which they had close commercial ties. From 1241, documents call them the *scabini Flandriae*, an acknowledgement of the collective action of the administrators either in relation to judicial conflicts between themselves or disputes in which only one was involved, and over matters such as trade fairs and the control of the currency, including the assay of the intrinsic value of coins. In all these matters, the countess acted only 'with the assent of the aldermen of [the major cities of] Flanders'.[60] Even when, in the fourteenth and fifteenth centuries, the county had lost two of its major cities, the system of intensive deliberations between the 'Three (or Four) Members of Flanders' continued to develop. And in 1384 the richest and largest of the rural districts, that around Bruges, became the fourth 'Member' on a quasi-definitive basis. The rural district of Bruges (*Brugse Vrije*) was administered by nobles and rich peasants, which permanently widened the social classes represented. This helped to stabilise the predominance of the system which lasted until the end of the *ancien régime*. During the most active period, in the first half of the fifteenth century, meetings of the 'Four Members' took between 350 and 450 meeting days per year, often in parallel sessions, sometimes at different places and with missions abroad. Within the county, their meetings lasted normally four to six days. They were largely informal, normally involved ten to fifteen participants and took place mostly on their own initiative. Long tradition and the continuously strong demographic and economic position of the 'Four Members' led to their domination of the representative system being accepted, both by the smaller communes and by the courts of Flanders. In practice, however, the most important matters, in particular fiscal ones, were often discussed in larger assemblies at the level of the county generally or in the four quarters separately, each headed by one of the 'Members'. Moreover, smaller cities and rural districts quite frequently appealed to the 'Four Members' for judicial or diplomatic support. In the cities, meetings of large councils including deputies of the crafts, and, in the rural districts, assemblies of freeholders had the last word on taxation. Participation by guilds in the administration was nowhere as advanced as in Ghent between 1370 and 1540, when twenty out of twenty-six aldermen were elected annually by and from the crafts. Until the middle of the fifteenth century the main concerns of the 'Four Members' were trade regulations, commercial litigation, coinage, fiscal policy and foreign relations. Later, taxation and defence were to become the major interests. Assemblies of three estates were created by the count in 1400, but these met less frequently than did the 'Four Members' who dominated them. Towards the end of the fifteenth century, however, the meet-

[60] Dhondt (1977), pp. 73–8; Wyffels (1967), pp. 1131–6.

ings of estates and of the estates general become more influential, as the government preferred collaboration with these more conservative bodies.

A not dissimilar pattern, with informal and autonomous meetings between representatives of the major cities, in this case dealing mainly with economic affairs, has also been observed in the neighbouring principalities of Brabant, Liège, Holland and Utrecht.[61] Their commercial orientation brought them into close contact with partners from as far as Spain and Prussia. The unification of the Low Countries under the dukes of Burgundy between 1427 and 1433 facilitated and encouraged regular meetings of representatives from the different principalities. The estates general are the best-known type of overall representation, but commercial towns, or those situated on the coast, had their special border-crossing meetings as well. The role which cities could play in determining the political agenda varied. Rural communes were not always politically passive. In Flanders, those belonging to the countryside around Bruges were permanently represented in the College of the 'Four Members' while the other districts equally participated in various types of assemblies, sometimes including those of the estates general. In the Low Countries, the prince always remained a real factor, even if, in fourteenth-century Flanders, the count had to be rescued three times by his suzerain, the king of France, from the might of the cities acting together. Similarly, the nobility was less integrated in the urban elites than in Italy, and thus continued to act more independently as an estate. Acting primarily on their own behalf the communes of free peasants in the Low Countries organised regional boards to protect the land against floods. They supervised the construction of dykes, canals and sluices, levied taxes for this purpose, and, for their maintenance, promulgated regulations enforceable at law. The whole system rested on the participation of the landholders who had a full say in all decisions and in the election of board members. Meetings of villages grouped together sent deputies to regional assemblies from which representatives could be mandated to negotiate with the government or with neighbouring cities.

Cities and towns in the regions of Languedoc met on the initiative of royal officers as well as on their own to legislate on the export of grain (1269–75) and on coinage (1212 with the nobility, in 1292 alone), to collect petitions, to regulate trade routes, to press a suit against the English 'great custom' on the Garonne (1285) and against the bishop of Cahors in relation to usury.[62] Analogous matters were raised by the Prussian cities and rural districts along the Vistula, the deputies of which regularly petitioned the Master of the Teutonic Order 'umbe meynes nutcz', for the common weal. Territorial ordi-

---

[61] Uyttebrouck (1975), I, pp. 429–69; Dhondt (1966), pp. 357–8; Kokken (1991), pp. 126–48, 216–76; Van den Hoven van Genderen (1987), pp. 60–145.

[62] Bisson (1964), pp. 127–30, 218–28, 242–3, 260–5, 281–8.

nances dealt with problems such as shipping rights on the Vistula (1375 and later); craft regulations in the cities (1408); weights and measures; coinage; prices; wages and interest rates after debasement (1420). The evidence of 1427 issued rulings not only on beer prices and on pre-emption in the countryside, but also on a series of matters clearly inspired by the Order concerning religious observance, the limitations of celebrations and sumptuary laws. These concerns announced increasing tensions which led to the rejection by the Master in 1434 of the cities' petitions on the abolition of licences for grain export and of the toll called *Pfundzoll*. The conflicts of interest appeared, too, in 1433 when the Knights and the cities criticised the war which the Order had launched against Poland. The tight organisation of the two Prussian estates, both as social and political unities, explains how they could challenge the Order, turn to the king of Poland and yet keep most of their liberties, including control of taxation. Between 1466 and 1519 they held, on average, four meetings a year and dispatched several diplomatic missions, mostly on their own initiative. The city councils remained sovereign in judicial matters, while the *Landesrat*, or territorial council, in which the three major cities (Danzig, Elbing, Torun) each had two representatives, was the highest court for the rural areas.[63]

The preservation of peace, law and order was a general concern of burghers. In Quercy, the bishop had levied a peace tax, or *comune*, with the consent of the nobility and the great towns from the very beginning of the thirteenth century onwards.[64] In the Empire, cities clustered in regional associations to secure peace, especially as a protection against particular feudal lords and knights. Representatives of all the cities of the league on the Rhine below Basle were summoned by King William in 1255 to deal with judicial matters concerning coinage and lost merchandise.[65] King Rudolf of Habsburg extended the peace policy to *Landfrieden*, territorial peace treaties he had negotiated in regional assemblies of cities alone or with the nobility. In 1278 seventeen cities were convened by a royal official to agree on the abolition of new tolls on the Rhine, measures for the security of navigation and the prosecution of breakers of the peace. Other regions followed suit.[66]

The German Hanse emanated from some of these regional associations. During the thirteenth and early fourteenth centuries, these were formally associations of merchants aimed at securing protection on long journeys, in the same vein as the contemporary Flemish Hanse of London and the union of the 'Seventeen Towns' trading at the fairs of Champagne. In this period, the distinction between city magistrates and the members of local merchants' guilds was still minimal.[67] In Flanders, the craft revolution of 1302 and the fol-

---

[63] Neitman (1992), pp. 60–76; Biskup (1992), pp. 89–94.   [64] Bisson (1964), pp. 124–6.
[65] 'Sollemnibus nuntiis omnium civitatum pacis federe coniunctarum de Basilea inferius' (Engel (1980), p. 15).   [66] Engel (1980), pp. 24–33; Boockmann (1992b), p. 123.   [67] Van Werveke (1958).

lowing years radically changed this situation and the magistracies took over the functions of the external representation of the community which the merchants' guilds had fulfilled earlier. In northern Germany, the transition to a league of cities occurred in 1356, when the regional hanses united to defend their common interests. The functional analogy between urban leagues, which allowed for the representation of cities in one territory, and the German Hanse has been neglected or refuted by historians[68] who have focused on territories and monarchies more than on representative functions. Yet, given the weakness or remoteness of monarchical powers, the Hanse cities felt more closely united by their links along trade routes, mainly those overseas. Their common interests in the protection and regulation of trade formed the most prominent item on the agenda of the frequent assemblies on a regional or general (*Hansetag*) level. Moreover, they conducted diplomatic missions and negotiations with all types of German and foreign authorities, including other representative institutions such as the 'Four Members' of Flanders. In this way, as in that of the other city leagues, their activities inevitably touched on matters of national and foreign policy up to the point of waging war and levying taxes. However, their seaward orientation and very extensive sphere of interest did not provoke them to build city-states, which made them vulnerable to the increasing encroachment by territorial states in the late fifteenth century.[69]

The Swiss Confederation shows the case of the formation of autonomous *Landschafte* or territories based on the autonomy of their constituent communes. In the fourteenth and fifteenth centuries, many rural communes were able to buy off seignorial rights, the emancipated peasants forming strong communes guaranteeing their collective rights. The major cities tended to expand their domination into the countryside, but had to leave intact forms of communal participation in decision making, especially in the political field. As rural communities often lived on cattle raising, they entertained close commercial contacts with the outside world. Conflicts were traditionally solved by arbitration on the basis of the stipulations in the *Einungen* (associations). Occasionally during the fourteenth century, and regularly later on, the *Tagsatzung*, the general assembly of the deputies from all full members of the *Eidgenossenschaft* or sworn union, became the political platform to mediate conflicts. It was evidently not always possible to reach agreements, but an attempt of the major cities to constitute a separate co-ordinative committee was outlawed in 1481. The relatively small size of the Swiss cities explains their inability to dominate their countryside as did the Italian ones, while their vulnerability to foreign aggression obliged them to keep some kind of unity. However, an agreement made in 1503 to submit all foreign treaties, personal indentures and contracts

---

[68] Moraw (1992), p. 6.
[69] Wernicke (1986), p. 190; Blockmans (1986), pp. 183–9, and (1992); Moraw (1994), pp. 119–21.

for military service to the approval of a majority of the *Tagsatzung* was never fully implemented.[70]

Among the points most frequently raised by cities in their petitions and grievances was the care for a stable currency. Even in Poland, where cities had effectively lost the right of giving assent to the aid, Cracow had a say in monetary affairs during the fifteenth century.[71] In some cases, the ruler's seignorage (or tax) on coinage was bought off by the representative institutions in order to avoid further debasements. The duke of Lüneburg sold his right in 1293 to the three estates whose deputies would further implement it. In 1307 the dukes of Bavaria sold their mints for a subsidy.[72] In 1345 the three estates of Brandenburg refuted the monetary reform projected by the margrave.[73] The 'Members' of Flanders and the cities of Brabant and Holland repeatedly granted aids in return for monetary stability. In nearly half the assemblies of the estates general of the Low Countries monetary problems featured on the agenda. In the first decades of the fifteenth century the 'Four Members' of Flanders were to be actively engaged in decisions regarding the physical aspects of the coinage, its value, and in aspects of the assaying of the metal used to make it.[74]

Another grievance raised by representatives, especially those of the cities, was the appointment of foreigners as government officials. A non-exhaustive list might include the following examples: Bohemia, 1310 and again 1437; Brandenburg and Prussia, 1345; Brabant, 1356; Utrecht, 1375; Normandy, 1381; Hungary, 1387; England, 1406; Pomerania, 1459.[75] It makes no sense trying to enumerate all the powers which representative institutions claimed with more or less lasting success. What matters is that, under their overall responsibility for the common weal, as well as the defence of privileges and customs, they could raise any kind of problem of internal and foreign policy since the latter always produced repercussions in the spheres of defence and taxation, and often that of trade as well. As an example, the Castilian *cortes*, and especially the cities, had a strong influence on legislation since many of the lists of grievances, submitted as petitions by one or another of the estates in the form of *cuadernos*, formed the basis of ordinances issued in the *cortes*. In 1261, they required redress of grievances before granting a tax. In 1268, the detailed list of prices and wages clearly reflected the concerns and competences of an urban committee.[76] It will be clear that large urban communes dealt primarily with

[70] Holenstein (1990), pp. 23–6; Bierbrauer (1991), pp. 99–102; Bütikofer (1991), pp. 104–6, 113–15.

[71] Russocki (1992), p. 173.   [72] Engel (1980), pp. 47, 52.   [73] Heinrich (1992), p. 145.

[74] Van Uytven and Blockmans (1969), pp. 408–9; Blockmans (1973), pp. 104–22; Bos-Rops (1993), p. 89.

[75] Heinrich (1992), pp. 144, 146; Biskup (1992), p. 86; Soule (1990), p. 109; Bak (1973), pp. 28–9; Kejr (1992), p. 214; Smahel (1992), pp. 229–30; Roskell *et al.* (1992), I, p. 88; Benl (1992), p. 134.

[76] O'Callaghan (1989), pp. 72–5, 121–2.

economic questions which were vital to them and concerned their specific interests. They were producing, buying and selling merchandise, which created types of problems very different to those familiar to noble councillors. These matters required an expedient, practical and effective response, such as only people trained in normal trade practices could give. This explains why monarchs, more interested in territory and honour than in overseas trade, were slow to get a grasp of the world of the cities which served as outlets to maritime trade.

PATHS OF DEVELOPMENT

Having rejected from the outset an exclusive attention to ideal types of representation, we have found in fact a great variety of institutions, of which some proved better equipped than others to survive into early modern times. This eventual survival was not the privilege of one particular type of institution: until the end of the *ancien régime*, federations of towns and villages, as well as regional and general estates and parliaments, *Landtage* or *Reichstage* with two, three or four chambers continued to function. It became apparent that, fundamentally, there existed two ways by which representation was initiated: on behalf of monarchies in need of political and material support; and as a spontaneous action of communities defending their collective interests.

Monarchical initiatives generally took place on a large scale which raised problems of integration and continuity, especially in large territories. Overstretched ambitions and discontinuity of dynasties offered opportunities for subjects to raise their claims. The stronger their own organisation, especially that of the large cities, the better they were equipped to obtain a lasting grasp on government. Much depended on the type of society and its level of organisation: densely populated and highly urbanised areas, as well as rural communes with assemblies of free peasants, were able to react more promptly than scattered populations of serfs. The latter, having no institutional outlets for their grievances, could only turn to revolt. However, in territories where the monarchy's problems such as repeatedly problematic successions to the throne or the Hundred Years War were recurrent or constant, such frequent challenges created opportunities for the development of effective representative institutions. Yet, even then, much depended on the capacity of the most powerful groups in the political system to organise lasting pressure in support of their concerns. This involved close communication, only achieved over limited distances and in a modern, commercialised economy. The monarchical model would reflect its origins in the extension of princely courts and the legitimation based on romano-canonical theories. However, it was seldom considered to be in the interest of a monarch to cede power to representatives. As soon as the

pressure on the government lessened, for example by the exploitation of independent resources or the introduction of permanent taxes, the frequency of
meetings decreased, so that they might not occur at all over a period of years.
The English parliament met on average more than once per year during the
fourteenth and the first half of the fifteenth centuries. After 1450, however,
when the Hundred Years War had come to an end, the frequency of meetings
decreased drastically to only twenty sessions until 1510, and none at all during
seven years in 1497–1504. Such irregularity of course had a deleterious effect
on the efficacity of parliament.[77]

The royal privilege of summoning and dissolving representative institutions,
and of stopping the payment of wages and allowances, rendered the assemblies vulnerable to tactical manoeuvring. The French estates general were thus
summoned only in times of extreme crisis and dissolved as soon as solutions
had been reached. The monarchy clearly feared to lose control, having in mind
the Parisian revolts which originated in the sessions of the estates general in
1355 and 1413. Sessions therefore were afterwards held outside the capital.[78]
The systematic study of the careers and social background of representatives
has revealed more refined methods by which representative institutions lost a
good deal of their autonomous influence. Prosopographical research of the
French estates general of 1484 showed that royal officials numbered up to 84 of
the 269 representatives, nearly one third. They constituted 63 per cent of all
members of the third estate and nearly 22 per cent of the nobility. The latter
estate was further closely linked to the monarchy by honorary titles such as that
of royal councillor (which was the case of forty among the eighty-three noble
representatives) or by royal pensions. Only twenty-one urban officials (less
than 8 per cent) participated, and again three of them were afterwards honoured by a royal or seignorial office. Only 13 per cent of the latter held a university degree, most in law, while this was the case for 70 per cent of the royal
officials acting as representatives and 93 per cent of the members of chapters.
In this respect, the use of Latin obviously favoured the university graduates. In
1484, even more than in 1468, royal officials and clients acted as a supra-
regional power elite, linking local and regional interests with the court. The
autonomy of cities, and of the estates in general, clearly got lost in the extension of networks of power brokers.[79]

Similar observations could be made about the English parliament, for which
the most extensive prosopographical research has been carried through. From
1445 onwards, it was no longer required that electors should return local representatives, which led to an invasion of borough seats by members of the gentry

---

[77] Powicke and Fryde (1961), pp. 512–34.   [78] Bulst (1992), p. 372.
[79] Bulst (1992), pp. 338–67.

and other outsiders. Members of parliament increasingly used their election to obtain positions and offices for themselves and for their clients, or to further other private interests by means of petitions. In 1420, the Commons tried in vain to prevent the king from agreeing to private petitions without their consent, which left many possibilities open to private arrangements, even against the common weal.[80] More than 81 per cent of the about 700 knights of the shire returned from 1439 to 1509 were county justices of the peace. Half of the sheriffs were elected to parliament at some stage of their lives; while hundreds of members of parliament have been identified as escheators (the king's agent in feudal death duties), collectors, controllers or surveyors of customs, commanders of royal castles or holders of other royal or county appointments. Many such appointments were arranged while parliament was in session, which leads to the conclusion that hope of patronage was a strong incentive to obtain election to parliament. On the other hand, this attitude undermined the autonomy of the representative institution. Prosopographical research has further shown, for France as well as for England, the absence of clear-cut social divisions between the estates or houses. The share of university degrees may have been somewhat lower than in the French estates general – one out of five English members of parliament around 1420 – probably the result of the differences in the legal systems, but the tendency to erode the action of representative institutions from within by extending royal patronage helps to explain the general loss of political impact of the institutions, if not of their members.[81]

In the other model of representation, the communal one, representation was from the bottom up, largely on an informal basis, in most cases at least partially autonomous from monarchical power. Urban and rural communes organised the defence of their interests when these differed fundamentally from, or were opposed to, those of the great landowners. They formed associations of communes which negotiated on the basis of free participation. While external threats lasted, their collaboration became more institutionalised and gradually performed a wide range of tasks of government, especially those connected with trade, in a more efficient way than the monarch's bureaucracy might have done it. This proved most effective on a relatively small scale where frequent interaction and community of interests were widely perceived and accepted. Long-distance trade was a common incentive for the formation of urban leagues and similar representative institutions. Less dependent upon monarchical initiatives, the communal forms of representation were therefore less vulnerable to patronage, and continued to function in their own way as long as

---

[80] Roskell *et al.* (1992), I, pp. 43–5, 63–7, 101–3.
[81] Roskell *et al.* (1992), I, p. 171; Wedgwood (1936–8), II, pp. xvii–xlvii.

their economic basis remained firm. Yet, in confrontation with intensive external pressures, their lack of centralisation and cohesion became a disadvantage. Sometimes the leagues became incorporated as members of (eventually composite) assemblies of estates presided over by the monarch and his officials, and thus shifted in the direction of the monarchical model. In this way Hanseatic cities participated in the representative institutions of different territories. Where monarchs were distant, representation could very well develop in various, partially overlapping, forms outside monarchical territories. However, the process of state formation in the later Middle Ages made princely power more omnipresent and less dependent on the consent of subjects.

Plurality of powers in a political system, and the need for holders of opposing interests to find compromises, were necessary preconditions for the emergence and continuity of representative institutions. Regional variations in timing, types and evolution were essentially determined by the interaction between downward and upward organisational initiatives. The monarchical and communal models of representation met at some point in their evolution. Cities could only play a prominent role in areas of high urbanisation. As states grew more powerful in the later Middle Ages, they tended to incorporate hitherto independent cities, especially by integrating their ruling elites. The capital accumulation and monetarised economy of the cities offered immense competitive advantages to princes. They started with loans from individual merchants, and finally tried to impose continuous indirect taxation on trade, which ensured them a regular and easy income without having to face the unpleasant demands of subjects. None the less the communal model was to prove its strength in later centuries, even when the cities had to play their role in the framework of assemblies of estates.

Fundamental weaknesses of the medieval representative institutions were their lack of continuity in the monarchical model, and their lack of unity in both models. The sense of community in all sections of society remained far behind the means of centralisation at the disposal of princes. This enabled princes to play off estates and corporate participants one against another. As representatives realised that more could be achieved through the making of particular arrangements than through collective action, so their institutions began to lose effectiveness. Two reasons thus explain the decline of many of them in the second half of the fifteenth century: relative or even absolute loss of power, and the incorporation of local and regional elites in the state apparatus.

Conversely, a monarch was incapable of creating any enduring representative institution if this did not already rest on existing, politically well-organised, local and regional communities. Not would he even try to do so if he had at his disposal sufficient means to reach his goals independently, something which each late medieval prince constantly strove to achieve.

CHAPTER 3

POPES AND COUNCILS

Antony Black

ONE may distinguish three levels in the story of popes and councils in the fifteenth century: the political, or diplomatic and institutional; the doctrinal, or ideological; and the cultural, relating to the longer-term development of Europe and her peoples.

I

When the Council of Pisa opened on 25 March 1409, long years of patient diplomacy by churchmen and statesmen seemed at last to be bearing fruit. Since the schism of 1378 between Urban VI and Clement VII and their successors, rulers and clergy had opted for one 'allegiance' or the other, partly on grounds of domestic or inter-state politics. After more than a quarter of a century, with the 'Roman' Pope Gregory XII (Angelo Correr) and the 'Avignonese' Pope Benedict XIII (Pedro de Luna) showing no sign of willingness to give way or permit procedures for a mutual abdication, the French led the way by withdrawing their allegiance from Benedict in 1398. From then on the idea of resolving the schism by 'the way of the council' gathered momentum: the emergency, it was felt, was such that a general council could be called by special procedures, with powers to impose a solution on both claimants in the name of the whole Church. The council would ask both 'popes' to resign; if either or both did not, they would be tried for schism and implicit heresy; the council would then have authority to depose a pope found guilty of such crimes, and to make arrangements for the election of a new, undisputed pope. Supporters of the conciliar way also wanted the council to undertake a reform of the Church, especially of papal taxation and papal appointments to senior benefices.

Both popes refused to have anything to do with Pisa, and condemned it and its supporters; each held his own council, Benedict at Perpignan, Gregory at Cividale. Pisa had been convoked by a group of some fifteen cardinals drawn from both allegiances. Its strongest secular supporters were Charles VI of France and the Republic of Florence (which authorised Pisa as the venue); its other supporters included Henry IV of England, John, duke of Burgundy, the kings of Poland and Portugal, Milan and the Republic of Genoa. In Germany, which had for the most part originally supported Urban VI, there were various allegiances; the situation was complicated by rivalry for the royal–imperial crown between Wenceslas of Bohemia, who supported Pisa, and Rupert of Bavaria, who supported Gregory. Benedict's core of support lay in Castile and Aragon. The Republic of Venice was ambivalent. The situation in southern Italy was dominated by the unruly King Ladislas of Naples, who supported Benedict but was himself under challenge from Louis of Anjou.

Since it was clear that neither 'pope' would resign, the main business at Pisa was what to do with both claimants in order to achieve reunion. Despite some opposition from the representatives of King Rupert and of Poland and England, the French and others enabled the Council to pursue its cases against both claimants. Benedict and Gregory were declared heretical (23 April), condemned for refusing repentance (*contumacia*) (23 May), and deposed (5 June). On 26 June Peter Philarge, cardinal-archbishop of Milan, was elected pope and took the name Alexander V. Between 27 July and 7 August the Council issued rather vague reform decrees and stipulated that a further council should meet in three years.

The new 'Pisan' pope was supported by Charles of France, Florence, Savoy, the dukes of Bavaria and Austria, and Henry of England; Castile, Aragon and Scotland remained behind Benedict. A council summoned by Gregory to meet at Aquileia and attended by delegates of the Empire and Naples ended in confusion when Venice, on whose territory it was situated, withdrew from Gregory's allegiance. Gregory was forced to flee for protection first to Ladislas, then to Malatesta of Rimini. The aged Alexander meanwhile moved to Bologna, controlled by Baldassare Cossa; when he died in what some thought were suspicious circumstances, Cossa was elected pope in the Pisan line and took the name John XXIII (May 1410). Meanwhile, King Rupert had died and Sigismund of Luxemburg had been elected 'king of the Romans' (that is, king of Germany and emperor-elect), thus ending the imperial schism. He declared his adherence to John.

The ensuing military and political events had a decisive impact on church history. In May 1411 Louis of Anjou defeated Ladislas. In March 1412 John, who, despite appointing as cardinals such first-rate men as Francesco Zabarella, Pierre d'Ailly and Guillaume Fillastre, had the reputation of a bandit, duly convoked a council to meet in Rome under Ladislas's protection; representatives were sent by Sigismund, Charles VI, Naples and Florence. But Ladislas soon abandoned John and invaded the papal states (June 1413), causing John to flee for protection first to Florence, then to Sigismund, whose price was that the council be reconvened at Constance, a self-governing city immediately subject to the Empire. The point was that the sovereign on whose territory the council met could make it possible for it to complete its work. Sigismund proved to be the salvation of the conciliar way. On 30 October 1413 he announced on his own authority that the council would convene at Constance on 1 November 1414; he invited all three 'popes' and all secular rulers to attend. John added his own convocation in December; the following August, Ladislas died.

When the Council of Constance opened in November 1414, it had the support of the emperor-elect and a considerable number of German princes, of France, England, Burgundy, Poland, Hungary, Austria and Denmark. Benedict retained the adherence of Castile, Aragon and Scotland, all of whom refused to send representatives. But now that a council was actually assembling with such widespread support, ecclesiastical considerations and moral influence became important. This was by far the best-attended and best-supported – and the most 'representative' – council for a very long time, certainly since 1378. It was also the first time that such a reputable council had met under these circumstances; one may search in vain for a parallel in either medieval or ancient history.

The project of reunion through a council had been attracting strong support among the universities, especially Paris (the 'alma mater' of European theology), and the numerous clerics, including many senior prelates, who had been educated there. The University of Paris had played a prominent role at Pisa and Rome (1412); its delegation at Constance was led by the chancellor, Jean Gerson, a man of great moral and intellectual standing and the leading theologian of the day. For deliberating and voting, the Council was divided, along the lines of some universities, into four so-called 'nations' (English, French, German, Italian): the cardinals sometimes deliberated separately. These labels were imprecise: the 'English' nation included the Irish and Scots, the 'German' took in Poland, Bohemia, Hungary and Denmark. This system was adopted primarily because, had voting been conducted in the council as a whole (as in previous councils) the Italians, with their disproportionate number of 'mitres' (bishops and abbots) would have dominated it completely: it was in the nature of the enterprise that on this occasion there had to be international consensus. The exact numbers present are difficult to determine; the French nation once recorded over 100 votes (probably including many non-'mitres') and a total attendance of 400; but the total number of 'mitres' may never have exceeded 100. A further feature, and objective, of the system adopted was that secular rulers could directly influence members, many either representatives of secular domains or persons selected, under their ruler's eye, at local or national synods.

On the other hand, kings were advised by high ecclesiastics; they in turn had been appointed by, or with the consent of, the crown.

Sigismund and Gerson, with the support of the French, German and English nations (Robert Hallum, bishop of Salisbury, led the English delegation and worked closely with Sigismund), called upon all three contenders to resign immediately. John agreed to do so but only on condition that the others did the same (which was unlikely). The early months of 1415 were decisive: in March, John fled and was detained. On 6 April 1415 the Council issued the decree 'Haec Sancta' (formerly sometimes known as 'Sacrosancta') which stated that, as a universal council, it derived its authority 'immediately from Christ' and could exercise it even over popes 'in matters of faith, unity and reform'. Thus empowered, the Council brought John to trial and deposed him (29 May). In July Gregory finally agreed to 'convoke' the Council, and then resigned.

Sigismund now left Constance in order to negotiate with Castile, Aragon and Scotland, the supporters of Benedict who comprised the one substantial dissident group remaining. He insisted that during his absence the Council should confine itself to reform and do nothing about reunion – the trial of Benedict and election of a new pope. This was good political sense if those remaining European states were to be brought into agreement. But it proved a long absence – he did not return until January 1417 – and very costly in terms of conciliar harmony. Wrangles developed between the French and English, as one would expect given the state of war between their countries. Gerson, hitherto spiritual leader of the movement for conciliar reform, lost stature in a protracted debate about tyrannicide. Sigismund, nevertheless, achieved his goal when, in an agreement signed at Narbonne in December 1415 and ratified at Constance in February 1416, Castile and the rest withdrew their allegiance from Benedict. Yet the Aragonese delegation did not arrive until September 1416, when they formed a fifth, Spanish 'nation': the Castilians did not join them until March 1417. The way was at last open for the process against Benedict, who was duly condemned and deposed (June 1417).

Debate now centred upon reform and the election of a new pope. Reform provoked deep disagreements, and here the Council of Constance proved in the end ineffectual. Reform was linked to reunion: the secular powers had made reunion possible, but their influence depended on their ability to control their clergy, partly through the system of appointments. During the schism and in the run up to Pisa and Constance, secular rulers had formed their own ecclesiastical policies of allegiance to one claimant, or neutrality based on withdrawal from both. The king of France, in particular, with the declaration of 'Gallican liberties' (1408), had transferred important papal powers of taxation and appointment to de facto royal control. Appeals to church courts outside

France were forbidden, something which the English had achieved in the 1350s. Yet these very issues, along with pastoral absenteeism and the like, were at the heart of the reformers' programme. Thus, when the French demanded suppression of papal taxes, the Italians, as the main beneficiaries of the existing system, opposed this; the English and Germans declared it inopportune.

Now, after Benedict's deposition, the question arose whether first to elect a new pope or, alternatively, first to lay down reforms binding upon whoever might be elected. The latter course would clearly limit the central powers of the Papacy, and was more likely to achieve substantial reform. For a while the issue hung in the balance with the Italians, Spanish and now (paradoxically) French advocating election, while the English and Germans advocated reform first. In September 1417 Zabarella, seen by many as the ideal candidate for the Papacy, and Hallum, the mainstay of English support for Sigismund and reform, both died. The English changed their approach, taking a reluctant Sigismund with them: the papal election would come first. Even so the decree 'Frequens' was passed (9 October 1417). This was of the utmost importance for the future. It laid down that henceforth councils must meet at regular, stipulated intervals; before a council disbanded, the time and place of the next one must be decreed; and, in the case of a new papal schism, a council must immediately meet without any official convocation, and all rival contenders be 'ipso iure' suspended from office.

Dispute over the procedure for an election was resolved by constituting a special one-off electoral college of the cardinals with six representatives from each nation, which put the cardinals in a minority (so much were they distrusted). The election did not take long: Oddo Colonna emerged as Martin V (November). He was a scion of an old Roman family accustomed to ecclesiastical power, elected, no doubt, to make possible an early revival of an independent territorial base for the Papacy. On reform, a very general decree was passed obliging the pope to reform the Church and the Roman 'curia' with the help of the council and the 'nations'. In March 1418 reforms, dealing particularly with taxation and benefices, were introduced, not in the form of conciliar decrees binding on all, but rather as separate agreements (*concordata*) between the Papacy and the several 'nations'. Martin, unusually, did not confirm the council's acts as a whole but referred to what it had enacted 'in matters of faith in a conciliar way (*conciliariter*)', thus leaving the status of decrees like 'Haec Sancta' open to interpretation. The Council was dissolved in April 1418; in May, Martin issued a decree prohibiting appeals from pope to council even in matters of faith. From his viewpoint, nothing had changed.

The protracted schism and disruption of ecclesiastical government gave the reunited Papacy a honeymoon period. In accordance with the decree 'Frequens', a council was convened to meet at Pavia in 1423. But, after some months, the only significant delegation to have arrived was from the University of Paris, the homeland of conciliarist ideas; so Martin first transferred the council to Siena and then, on grounds of inadequate attendance, dissolved it (1424).

The next council was due to meet in 1431 at Basle, a self-governing city immediately subject to the Empire. Martin convoked it but died soon afterwards. He was succeeded by Gabriel Condulmaro from Venice, as Eugenius IV. He shared Martin's distrust of a council but found himself faced with an entirely new political situation. University men (*doctores*) from Paris and central Europe were again the first to arrive; most royal delegations and senior prelates did not appear until the spring or summer of 1432. This time, the Parisian delegation stood firm: when Eugenius decreed the Council's dissolution (December 1431), it replied by reaffirming the decree 'Haec Sancta' on the independent authority of councils, and in addition specifically asserting, in the decree 'De stabilimento concilii' (February 1432), that a council could only be transferred, prorogued or dissolved with its own consent. By the summer, with 'mitres' and representatives of the major European powers now attending in even larger numbers than at Constance, the papal legate, Giuliano Cesarini, advised Eugenius to recognise and participate in the Council. The main reasons for the massive and, to Eugenius in his Roman fastness, unexpected support for Basle were twofold. First, after the recent crushing victory of radical–Hussite forces over papal–imperial forces, followed by incursions and propaganda aimed at neighbouring German territories, Sigismund and the German princes hoped for a negotiated settlement, to include doctrinal issues, with the moderate Hussites who were willing to come to Basle. For this they needed the council. In the second place, advocates of thorough reform, including a transfer of papal powers to councils and some decentralisation, had in Eugenius and his court fresh evidence of the need for change.

This was their moment. The secular powers and senior prelates (not always distinct parties), although they supported the Council, were not in a position altogether to control it. This was because the *doctores*, led by Jean Beaupère and others from Paris, had transformed the organisation and procedures of the council before others had arrived. Instead of 'nations' pliant to secular control, there were now committees ('deputationes') based on subject areas, for faith, peace, reform and 'common affairs' (*communia*, meaning especially discipline and diplomacy). Another committee screened applicants for membership of the Council. Above all, every person admitted had an equal vote in the committees and general assembly, regardless of rank. Opponents of the system, which included secular rulers, complained that it gave a cook the same authority as an archbishop representing a monarch. This was an exaggeration: what it did, however, was to enshrine the voice of the intellectuals.

Disregarding Eugenius, the Council embarked on negotiations with the Hussites and on a comprehensive reform programme. Eugenius was suspended from office; the Council took over the functions of hearing appeals, deciding disputed elections, collecting certain taxes and distributing patronage formerly belonging to the pope. Such a step soon gave numerous individuals a vested interest in one side or the other. Sigismund and other rulers prevailed upon Eugenius to make peace with the Council (December 1433), but neither the papal court nor the conciliarists from the Universities took this very seriously. Each saw it as a fight to the death, in constitutional and ideological terms.

In the following years, from 1433 to 1436, the Council reached agreement with the moderate Hussites, thanks to whom 'Bohemia' ceased to pose a general threat. It also brought about peace negotiations between France and Burgundy (the Peace of Arras, 1435). Above all, it issued sweeping reform decrees, including the abolition of annates (June 1435) and replacement of papal powers of appointment with election by chapter (July 1433 and March 1436). Yet these very successes changed the political situation, rendering the Council offensive to some, unnecessary to others. Time, money and patronage worked quietly on the side of Eugenius and his greatly improved diplomatic corps. The conciliarist reformers, on the other hand, now under the leadership of the implacable Cardinal Louis Aleman, an old personal enemy of the pope, were the more intent on implementing their constitutional programme thoroughly. As the French archbishop Philippe de Coëtquis put it, 'this time we shall either take the Papacy away from the Italians or so clip its wings that it won't matter who has it'.[1] The French and Italians at Basle were said to regard one another with 'almost inborn hatred' ('odio quasi naturali').[2]

What finally destroyed the Council as an effective force was the further question of negotiation with the Greek Church. The Greek emperor and patriarch, desperate for Latin help against the Ottomans, were prepared to discuss theological differences but would not travel beyond the Alps. This was Eugenius's ace: a council in Italy would be more amenable to him. The conciliarists, although they realised this, ignored Greek sensitivities. Thus sincere churchmen, like Giuliano Cesarini and Nicholas of Cusa, were faced with a difficult choice. On 7 May 1437, amid uproar and threats of violence, two rival decrees were read out simultaneously in the cathedral: the majority proposed Basle, Avignon or Savoy as the meeting-place with the Greeks, the minority, including an actual majority of senior prelates, proposed transferring the council to Italy. (This meant that subsequent argument included the question of who was entitled to a full vote in councils.) Eugenius promptly recognised the minority

---

[1] Reported by Aeneas Silvius Piccolomini, *De rebus Basiliae gestis*, p. 188.

[2] Haller *et al.* (eds.), *Concilium Basiliense*, I, p. 435.

decree and transferred the council to Ferrara, and then, so as to avoid an outbreak of plague which soon afterwards reached Basle, to Florence.

In this confused situation, the opposed fortunes of Basle and Eugenius
largely depended upon the attitudes of the secular powers. Territorial control
mattered more and more. The Council itself spent much effort developing its
own power base in the Rhone valley (including Avignon), Savoy and the Swiss
Confederation, with Milan as an ally; it also had the support of Aragon and
Poland. Eugenius controlled the papal states and was supported by the
Republic of Florence, England and Burgundy. A great swathe of powers –
France, Castile, the emperor and most German princes – remained neutral. At
a German–imperial *Reichstag* held at Nuremberg in March 1438, the German
rulers formally adopted an Act of Neutrality, to which Castile also adhered. A
year later, in the *Acceptatio* of Mainz (26 March 1439), they adopted in general
terms the reform decrees from Basle, specifically the decree 'Frequens', and
the decrees on elections, and on provincial and diocesan synods; however, they
refused to commit themselves on the subject of papal or conciliar supremacy.
On the other hand, when Charles VII of France issued the Pragmatic Sanction
of Bourges (7 July 1438), giving legal effect in his own kingdom to most of
Basle's reforms – a momentous step, truly Marsilian in character, which
remained in force until 1516 – he also affirmed conciliar supremacy, though not
the legality of the recent acts of Basle.

From now on these neutral powers advocated 'a new, third council' to be
independent of both Basle and Eugenius. In terms of international diplomacy
there was some parallel with the situation before Pisa (1409). Negotiation and
debate were intense but increasingly fruitless, even though the *Reichstag* met
once or twice a year for several years, attended also by representatives of other
European powers. What emerged was a distinctively secularist attitude and
policy on church questions, a concern for reform, lay control and public order.

The majority at Basle proceeded as if unaware of this. In spring 1439, in the
face of protests not only from the Germans and French but from friendly
powers such as Aragon and Milan, the council proceeded to a yet more
unequivocal and provocative assertion of conciliar supremacy: a council is
superior to a pope unconditionally; a pope may not dissolve or transfer a
council without its own consent ('The Three Truths of Faith': 16 May).
Eugenius was declared heretical and deposed (25 June). Amadeus, retired duke
of Savoy, was elected pope as Felix V, with strictly limited powers. Eugenius
and his court understood diplomacy better; they also had the apparent achievement of unity with the Greek Church to their credit, after the Greek leaders
signed a decree of unity ('Laetentur Coeli': Florence, 6 July 1439). This contained a fulsome statement of the papal primacy. In September, Eugenius proceeded to condemn and depose from office all members of the Council of

Basle and their supporters. It was the papalists' handling of the neutral powers which was particularly deft. Although they never won an intellectual argument (and may have lost some), they knew how unimportant this was. They flattered their courtly audiences, they spoke the right political language, and above all they were prepared to negotiate on matters such as church finance and benefices ('to cede a little lest we lose all').[3] The key point, however, was that they could appear to meet requests for a 'new, third council' confident that the French and Germans would never agree on where it should be held.

Castile submitted to Eugenius in 1440; here one can detect the influence of ecclesiastics like Rodrigo Sanchez de Arevalo. Following the brief reign of Albert II, Sigismund's successor, the new emperor-elect and king of Germany was the young Habsburg, Frederick III, who was friendly towards the Papacy although he did not commit himself in public until 1444. The other leading German princes remained neutral; indeed, some were strongly inclined towards conciliarism and reform, if not towards all other aspects of the Basle programme. In 1443 Eugenius won over Alfonso V of Aragon by investing him as king of Naples. In the spring of 1446, after finally reaching agreement with Frederick, Eugenius lost patience and nearly ruined his case by deposing the archbishops of Cologne and Trier for their support of Basle. The *Reichstag* sat all summer. Matters were only settled when Eugenius died (February 1447), to be succeeded by Thomas Sarzana as Nicholas V, a seasoned diplomat. He drew up concordats with the emperor and the German princes, recognising ecclesiastical appointments made during the Neutrality, sharing out various revenues and rights of appointment between the Papacy and the rulers, and promising to convoke a new council within eighteen months. Only then did the German princes submit. The Papacy had to accept recognition from France without any hope of the Pragmatic Sanction's repeal. Poland accepted a *fait accompli*. The Council of Basle transferred itself to Lausanne and soon after dissolved itself (1449).

In the event, the defeat of the Council of Basle proved decisive for the western Church, for western Christendom and for European civilisation. But this was not apparent at the time. Most informed opinion continued to see a truly general and representative council as the best and, indeed, the only means by which the universally accepted need for church reform could be fulfilled. Partly for this reason, many continued to regard a council as in principle superior to a pope. This was notoriously the common opinion in the universities, which on this issue still tended to follow the lead of Paris. Perhaps the notion of such a council was becoming something of an ideal, detached from anything the efforts of prelates or princes were capable of achieving. Voices were

---

[3] Da Monte, *Briefsammlung*, pp. 73–4.

heard attacking the pope and clergy with an asperity that went deeper. Some turned to mysticism. It was amongst the Carthusians, the strictest of religious orders, that demands for a reform council and assertions of conciliar superiority were loudest in the 1450s.

These developments were especially acute in Germany, which now remained the fulcrum of conciliar aspirations, as it had already begun to be during the 1440s. Even at Constance, it had been said that immediate reform was the last hope for the clerical estate, especially in Germany. In that country, as Cusa's *De concordantia catholica* (1432–3) and the anonymous *Reformatio Sigismundi* (1439) made clear, reform of the Church was closely linked to reform of the Empire, which in turn involved strivings towards a renewed public order and, in some sense, national unity. The Emperor Frederick, crowned in Rome in 1452, gave no leadership in this matter. Instead, at a *Reichstag* at Frankfurt (1456), the princes drew up the 'Grievances (*gravamina*) of the German Nation', which included complaints about papal appointments to benefices and interference in elections, and about papal methods of raising money by taxation (expectatives, annates) and other means (indulgences).[4] One of the authors was Gregor Heimburg, a man who was not alone as a counsellor among princes in regarding the Papacy as an alien power. In fact, shortly afterwards he campaigned for the heretical king of Bohemia, George of Poděbrady. The aim of the *gravamina* was partly to get the reforms of Basle implemented; but they also demanded the regular holding of general councils and national councils as stipulated by the decree 'Frequens' and other decrees enacted at Basle. The princes aspired to the kind of ecclesiastical independence enjoyed by France and England. Their demands were repeated at a meeting of princes at Nuremberg in 1461. In response to this and similar moves by other rulers, Pope Pius II (1458–64: formerly Aeneas Sylvius Piccolomini, from Siena) renewed the condemnation of appeals from pope to general council in strong terms in the decree 'Execrabilis' (18 January 1460).

A few members of the Roman *curia*, especially men like Nicholas of Cusa and Pius II who were acquainted with Germany, were aware of the political as well as the spiritual need for reform. Cusa drew up an imaginative programme of 'reformatio generalis' for Pius, while the pope himself drafted a reform bull, 'Pastor Aeternus'. He died, however, before this could be published.

For much of the time the situation in Europe was masked by the apparent successes of papal diplomacy, the continued ineffectiveness both of reformers' pleas for a council, and of rulers' threats to call one as a means of bringing pressure on the Papacy in, for example, cases of disputed benefices. In Rome itself the trappings of power seemed intact as, under papal patronage, the city

---

[4] Text in Werminghoff (1910), pp. 113ff.

became a focus for the renaissance in architecture and the visual arts, which would culminate in the fateful plans for the rebuilding of St Peter's.

It was the eastern question, the need felt for yet another crusade following the dramatic advances made by the Ottoman Turks in the Balkans, Greece and the Aegean, culminating (symbolically, at least) in their capture of Constantinople in 1453, which prompted the next international assembly. This was, significantly, not an ecclesiastical council but a congress of princes (some indeed had advocated such an international 'council' or 'general parliament' of secular rulers as a solution to the quarrels between Eugenius and Basle). It was Pius II's brainchild, was convoked by him, and met at Mantua from September 1459 to January 1460. Even so, the pope dealt with the delegations not all together but separately. He expounded in his polished Latin the urgent need for a united effort on behalf of the Christian commonwealth (*respublica christiana*) against 'the common enemies' (the Turks). Pius II himself had started out as a fervent conciliarist and supporter of Basle, then gravitated into the service of the emperor-elect, Frederick III (whom he urged to assume joint leadership of Christendom alongside the restored Papacy), before finally entering upon a specifically ecclesiastical career. Despite his sense of which way the wind was blowing, he never lost a romantic flair, of which this project was another example. It is interesting to compare his policy towards Islam with that of two of his former fellow conciliarists. Both Cusa, now a reformist within the papal *curia*, and John of Segovia, the meek theologian who had reached a position of unexpected ascendancy at Basle only to end his days in enforced retirement in a remote region of Savoy, had embarked upon a study of the Koran as a prelude to engaging in theological debate, instead of armed conflict, with the victorious Muslims – much as they had with the Hussites at Basle.

The need for a crusade was added to reasons why a general council should be called; as such it featured regularly in the electoral pacts sworn by the cardinals before they elected one of their number as pope. At the time of the Christian Congress (*Christentag*) of Ratisbon (1471), it was argued that only through a council could the requisite money be raised.

The only serious, or at least half-serious, attempt to call a general council in defiance of the Papacy was undertaken by King Louis XII of France in combination with a group of dissident cardinals (1511). When Pope Julius II sought to deny domination of northern Italy to the French by dissolving the League of Cambrai and forming a new alliance against France with Spain and Venice, Louis responded by attacking Julius on the ecclesiastical front. The cardinals, arguing that Julius had infringed 'Frequens' and his pre-election oath by not having already summoned a council, and that this duty therefore devolved upon them, summoned the Council to meet at Pisa on 1 September. Part of the

Council's potential appeal lay in Julius's ruthless attempts to expand the papal states; it was supported on principle by the University of Paris, and was attended mainly by clergy from France, inspired by royal policy. The Emperor Maximilian, also a member of the League of Cambrai, supported the Council, but the German bishops did not. Even devoted reformers and conciliarists, like Giovanni Gozzadini in Julius's court, could see the Council as a political move. Julius dealt with it by convoking his own council to meet at Rome in April 1512 – the fifth Lateran Council. This was supported by Ferdinand of Spain, but was attended mostly by Italian bishops. Further promises of reform were made. In the meantime, the Council of Pisa went as far as renewing 'Haec Sancta' and suspending Julius, before Maximilian made peace. By now Louis no longer needed the council, which, after transferring itself to Lyons, dissolved itself. The reforms decreed at Rome were minimal. So it was that, right up to the start of the Lutheran Reformation and indeed beyond, pious German princes, like Eberhard of Württemberg and George of Saxony (many of whose clergy, incidentally, had participated in the Council of Basle), still looked to a general council for reform of the Church.

II

In the realm of ideas concerning popes and councils and their respective functions and authorities, there were considerable developments (particularly in the first half of the fifteenth century) amongst 'intellectuals' (*doctores*), those in power and, so far as can be known, wider public opinion. These were issues of both religious and political moment, and they concerned most thinking people (except, after about 1450, the Italian humanists). Ideas were set forth by professional theologians, jurists and other university men, in occasional speeches or treatises, by ambassadors speaking on behalf of sovereign princes and in official decrees issued by councils or popes. Such writings varied from the creative arguments and speculations of Gerson, Nicholas of Cusa (1401–64) and John of Segovia (1393–1458), to the impassioned rhetoric of Cardinal Louis Aleman, the icy calm of academic commentators on canon law like Francesco Zabarella (d. 1417) and Nicholas de Tudeschis (Panormitanus) (1386–1445), the elegant rhetoric of diplomats like Thomas Ebendorfer and Piero da Monte, the trite incantations of partisans and office-seekers, and the peremptory marshalling of argument and text by the authoritarian intellect of Cardinal Juan de Torquemada (1388–1468).

The supporters of some form of conciliar supremacy drew upon a tradition in canon law according to which a council could judge a pope if he fell into heresy, schism or other serious crime. They appealed to the practice of the early and patristic Church, when major religious questions were invariably settled by ecumenical councils – in the organisation of which the emperor also usually played a role. This stimulated some historical research and theories of historical development. More markedly original was Gerson's use of New Testament texts to prove that Christ deliberately gave his authority to the Apostles as a group; this was then transmitted by apostolic succession to present-day bishops, who, by assembling together, constituted a general council. The authority given to Peter and his successors, the popes, was secondary and inferior; at Basle some argued it was merely derivative, could be revoked by the council almost at will and, indeed, that it was the council which made the laws while the pope merely executed them according to conciliar wishes. This particularly suited the case for reform, which popes were manifestly unwilling to initiate and reluctant to carry out when initiated by others.

Another argument, put forward by some at Constance and many at Basle, was that final authority belonged to the Church *tout court*, as a collectivity, a corporation or mystical body, from which it was derived to the council as its representative. This rendered the role of bishops less essential and was used, especially at Basle, to justify the admission of deans, provosts, canons, monks, ordinary priests and even the occasional layman to a full and equal vote. Such an undifferentiated notion of a collective sovereignty was inspired and justified, first, by a diluted notion of popular sovereignty in the secular, and especially civic, sense, as expounded by Marsilius of Padua in his theory of the 'corporation of the citizens' (*universitas civium*) and 'corporation of believers' (*universitas fidelium*); secondly, by a branch of scholastic philosophy which drew a qualitative distinction between the whole as dynamic essence or 'form' and the mere disparate parts (here including the pope himself); and, above all, by the organic notion of society which was prevalent throughout medieval philosophy and folklore. It was significantly helped by a further argument from canon law, initiated by Zabarella at the time of the Council of Pisa (1408–9). He applied to the Church as a whole the collegiate authority exercised by cathedral chapters, which, on certain points, could over-ride the bishop: the 'college' (*universitas*) in this analogy was taken to be the prelates or the clergy generally – Zabarella and others were not precise here – who expressed their will through those attending the general council. This corporate view was connected to yet another idea, namely that in the Christian community authority was to be exercised in a fraternal manner; those in power were to act, in Christ's words, as the servants (*ministri*) of others. Christian decision making was supposed to be essentially corporate and fraternal; key decisions should be taken only after full discussion in an assembly, whose members would, it was said, develop mutual understanding and good will. In the council there should be 'one mind' and 'one will'.[5]

[5] Segovia and others in Black (1979), pp. 156–61.

The crucial point always remained that if necessary and in the last resort such a representative council could over-ride the otherwise normal authority of the pope, judge and sentence him if he persisted in error, and even depose him. In these ways conciliarists developed a theory of the intrinsic supremacy of a representative assembly that was far more explicit, and was argued in far more detail, than anything previously put forward on behalf of secular institutions.

Little effort was made to respond to all this theory on behalf of the Papacy until the 1430s. At first, the main papal argument was defensive, to restrict conciliar intervention to the minimum. Then some pro-papal authors and propagandists, like the Venetian Piero da Monte (a republican in secular affairs) and the fanatical Roderigo Sanchez de Arevalo (1404–70), Castilian ambassador and later curial official, expressed aggressively absolutist views on papal power in public speeches and tracts. But serious pro-papal thinkers, many of whom, including Torquemada, the most systematic of them all, came from the Dominican Order, always admitted that the pope's position as 'absolute' monarch did not mean that his powers were actually unlimited. Torquemada asserted that, if the pope refused to convoke a council when requested to do so by cardinals, prelates and secular rulers, he was to be treated as 'suspect of heresy and of doubtful legitimacy as pope', and the council might then be convoked by the cardinals, prelates or princes. He also gave a number of cases when, because the faith was in danger, the pope might not dissolve a council under pain of being suspected of heresy. If there were disagreement between pope and council on matters of faith, the pope was to be adhered to so long as he was defending previously defined doctrine; if he contradicted this, the previous definition should stand. When new doctrine is under discussion, 'more regularly one should stand by the judgement of the fathers of the whole council than that of the Roman pontiff'; but there could be no final decision until the pope and council were in agreement.[6] Compared with the fourteenth-century canonists the difference was that Torquemada was evasive or silent about what action could be taken against an erring pope. Amongst jurists themselves, on the contrary, the 'occasional' role of the council as judge of an erring, schismatic or criminous pope remained standard doctrine. This was expressed not only by the (for the most part) pro-conciliar Nicholas de Tudeschis, the most widely acknowledged authority on canon law, but much later by devoted servants of the renaissance Papacy at the turn of the century, notably Felinus Sandaeus (an auditor of the *Rota*) and Giovanni Antonio Sangiorgio (appointed cardinal by Alexander VI) – although the latter confined

---

[6] Torquemada, *Summa de ecclesia*, III.8, fols. 281v–2v; III.46, fol. 332v, on the possibility of the pope being *ipso jure* 'self-deposed'; III.64, fol. 353; III.69, fols. 356v–7r; Torquemada, *Commentarium*, p. 176a on d.19, c.8. See also *Summa de ecclesia*, II. 92, 101, 112.

this very strictly to the case of heresy, perhaps in view of his patron's life style.[7] In occasional speeches, however, even people like Torquemada ignored any limits on papal power.

Until the Council of Constance, the main question had been how to justify calling a council against the wishes of the pope(s) and then deposing the claimants who refused the council's stipulation that they step down. There were well-rehearsed legal arguments for judging a pope for heresy, schism or gross misconduct; and the general consensus among canonists was that a council was the forum in which such a pope should be tried and, if found guilty, deposed. The problem, at least before Constance, had been how to convoke a credible council against papal wishes. Here, too, canonist tradition was helpful, since respected jurists had for a long time affirmed an emergency right of convocation for the emperor or the bishops or the cardinals, or, more generally, for any of the three in default of the others. After Constance, however, many thought this whole question was settled by the decree 'Frequens'.

It was now, especially from about 1416 onwards, that the rather different question of the council's authority over an undisputed pope emerged as the major issue. The decree 'Haec Sancta', together with the contemporary experience of papal schisms and the evident need for reform of the Church, seemed to many to have resolved this whole question, too, in favour of the council. *Reformatio* meant two things: first, that clergy should live, and pope and prelates govern, according to canon law and the moral teaching of Christianity; secondly, that the constitution of the Church should be clarified or developed so as to ensure that reprehensible pastors, including the pope, could be dealt with effectively. This meant asserting and implementing conciliar authority over popes, and local synodal authority over the clergy generally. An increasing number of those who wanted the first came also to want the second, if only as a necessary means to the first. For many reformers, however, conciliar supremacy was a matter of principle.

At the time of Pisa and Constance, in order to justify this programme of reunion and reform, steps were taken which amounted to restating the very foundations of ecclesiology and political theory. D'Ailly and others argued, on the basis of natural philosophy, that the Church and any human society had the right and the ability to prevent schism – that is the disintegration of itself – by any means at its disposal. Therefore, a council could be convoked without papal consent. Zabarella argued, from the practice of ordinary corporations, that any association could judge and depose an erring ruler. This was for no less a reason than that power resided in the community (*universitas*, again), or, as 'philosophers' (Marsilius, in fact) put it in civic context, in 'the assembly of the

---

[7] Sandaeus, *Commentaria*, I, fols. 114v–15r on x.1.3.20; Sangiorgio, *Commentaria*, on d.40, c.6 (unpaginated); Decius, *Super decretalibus*, fols. 357v–8v, on x.1.6.4.

citizens or its weightier part'. Although what Zabarella meant was that the prelates of the Church could assemble of their own will and the council could judge a pope, the way he put it could be understood as a conceptual revolution in the understanding of the Church's power structure. Some did take it that way. Similarly, Gerson's argument for the collective superiority of the episcopate was sometimes couched in theological language as the superiority of the whole ('mystical') body of the Church. It was a very different way of viewing the Church from that found in the language of the papal 'principate', developed since the fourth century. In treatises written during Constance, both d'Ailly and Gerson stated that legitimate power and sovereignty (*iurisdictio* and *suprema potestas*) lay in one sense in the Church as a whole, in another sense in the council, and in a third sense in the pope.

In terms of volume, the heaviest crop of conciliar writings came in the 1430s, 1440s and 1450s. The great bulk of these expounded what amounted to a clarification of Gerson's view to bring it into line with Zabarella: power resides basically in 'the Church' as a corporation or body, and therefore also in the general council, but only derivatively and subordinately (*ministerialiter*) in the pope. This tied in with the view of the pope as the mere *executor* of conciliar decrees, as an accountable public servant.

One exception to this, however, was the most famous of all the conciliar theorists, Nicholas of Cusa (1401–64). A canon lawyer who had also studied philosophy, and eventually to become one of the most celebrated philosophical theologians of the later Middle Ages, he was especially noted for his *De docta ignorantia*; this exercised profound influence on renaissance thought in northern Europe. His *De concordantia catholica* was written early in his life, while he was at Basle representing an unsuccessful candidate for the prince-archbishopric of Trier; in fact he had been elected by the chapter, but this had been over-ruled by the pope. Cusa was typical of the period in that he was looking for a single principle which would shine out through the whole Church, indeed through all cosmology, and in the light of which all disputed constitutional issues could be settled. While later papalists found this in monarchy or monism, Cusa hit upon *consensus*. He understood this much more broadly than the juridical consent required in certain forms of decision making, and pre-eminently in ecclesiastical elections, although that was one place where the idea originated, and it was part of Cusa's genius to hit upon a principle which combined metaphysical range with legal precision. As *concordantia*, this principle permeates every corner of the universal hierarchy, and it must therefore be pre-eminently developed in the holy society of Christ's Church. This meant that, in principle, everyone ought to agree, and that, as Cusa put it, the more agreement there was, the more authority a law or decision had. But, being a good neoplatonist, he combined this with the idea of hierarchy: God had established certain offices in the Church. What these were and how much authority they had in respect of one another, Cusa answered by an original interpretation of church tradition and history, in which he tended to be more accurate than his contemporaries. Briefly, the pope with the synod (Cusa preferred Greek words) was superior to the pope alone; but the synod could not make a final authoritative judgement without papal consent. This was to a lesser degree true of the other four ancient patriarchates as well, which should also be included in a fully ecumenical council. It can be seen why, in 1436–7, Cusa should have preferred to stand with the pro-Eugenian minority which put unity with the Greek Church above other considerations. After attending the Council of Florence, Cusa developed in practical terms into a papalist, but remained a reformer. Parts of his *Concordantia*, notably the chapters on elections which (he said) depended upon divine and natural right, he never denied.

Other conciliar theorists at the time of the Council of Basle were less original. This cannot, however, be said of John of Segovia. He developed the neo-Gersonian view dominant at the Council, using the Bible and church history, the lore of corporations and city-states, and Aristotle's *Nicomachaean Ethics* and *Politics*. He combined political activity, as Aleman's right-hand man both in the Council and on diplomatic missions in Germany, with a volume of tracts, not to mention his enormous history of the Council, while maintaining his reputation as a gentle soul. Consequently (if one may quote Pope Gregory VII's use of a psalm) he died in exile; but not before he had started work on Islamic theology. Segovia was insistent that theology, that is the Bible and church fathers, rather than canon law, were the proper determinants of ecclesiology; and from these sources he drew some ideas, unusual for the time, on the fraternal nature of the Church and the Council. He used Aristotle to say that 'true' monarchy is not absolute but consultative and law-bound. He asserted in a variety of ways that fullness of power belongs to the Church and therefore to the council, to which the pope is subordinate and accountable.

Yet conciliar theory faltered at the same time and for the same reasons that the Council of Basle itself faltered: from 1437 onwards there were no clear indications why it, in particular, represented the Church at large. Segovia and others argued that the council represented the Church as its expression, its 'extension', because it contained wise and virtuous persons, and for other moral or metaphysical reasons. But they produced no concrete criteria by which anyone could assess the representative quality of this or that council, and so left the way open for the claims of the Council of Florence and, indeed, of the Papacy *per se*, which, in Cusa's later argument, represented the Church 'in a contracted way' just as the council did 'in an extended way'.[8] This was

---

[8] Cusanus, 'Epistola ad Rodericum', pp. 825–9.

presumably because such criteria as were available, such as the number of 'mitres' or the extent to which members were elected, might not have told particularly in Basle's favour.

From now on the theory of papal monarchy, along with the Papacy itself, staged a remarkable revival. Its exponents used all the old arguments, the Roman law idea of the unaccountable *princeps*, the monotheistic principle of cosmic unity, the scriptural and traditional texts ascribing authority to Peter and his successors. In one respect, their task was easy; if canon law and the jurists had mentioned occasional conciliar supremacy, they had far more to say about papal sovereignty (according to Bodin a century later, they understood sovereignty better than anyone). In order to refute conciliarism, these new papalists made their own contribution to the doctrine of monarchical sovereignty itself. Torquemada and others sharpened the distinction between jurisdiction and moral authority: even if the Apostles as a group or a council of wise men had greater moral authority, this did not give them jurisdictional superiority. They argued that there was no middle ground between monarchy and anarchy: social order required not any kind of government but one in which there was no appeal from the supreme hierarch and in which he might undertake any action required for the common good. Above all, they propounded a new theology of monarchy by making their interpretation of the neoplatonic notion of hierarchy a universal principle governing every natural system and social order; in both the natural and the supernatural spheres – the terrestrial and heavenly hierarchies – all power flowed from one to the rest, and therefore all laws and all legitimate jurisdiction must flow from the prince.

Part of the point was their audience. The kings and princes courted by papal diplomats and theologians from the later 1430s until the early 1450s had their own reasons for preferring monarchy to constitutionalism. When Eugenius IV, Torquemada and others argued that without a single leader society would fall into disorder, the point could be brought home vividly by pointing to the example of the Hussite rebellion: let princes beware lest the conciliarist notion of giving power to 'the people [*sic*]' give rise to 'many Bohemias'.[9] Within late feudal polities with complex jurisdictional rivalries, civic autonomies and parliamentarist assertions, it was convenient to have a principle which, as the papalists put it, made parliament depend upon convocation by the prince and reduced it to a purely advisory role. This entitled a monarch to make laws on his own authority, appoint his own subordinate officials as he pleased and intervene at any point in the hierarchy without being asked. The new theory entitled the monarch, if need be, to bypass inferiors; everyone was an immediate subject of the supreme hierarch. It was in fact exactly the same idea of absolute

[9] Raynaldus, *Annales*, xxviii, pp. 197, 199–200, 204–5 (Eugenius IV in 1436); Aeneas Sylvius Piccolomini, cit. Black (1970), p. 123.

personal rule, exercised against seignorial and bureaucratic oppression and for the welfare of subjects, that was so successfully preached – and to some extent practised – by the Ottomans of the middle and later fifteenth century. For example, a Turkish author of this period wrote, 'Without a sovereign men cannot live in harmony and may perish altogether. God has granted this authority to one person alone, and that person, for the perpetuation of good order, requires absolute obedience.' The roots of this doctrine lay in ancient Persia and the eastern Mediterranean, whence it had long since found its way into Roman imperial ideology, which in turn had influenced the early Papacy. Now it was being developed by men like Torquemada in a form in which it could be utilised by the absolutists of early modern Europe.[10] One may see here one model for 'the modern state'. Even so, the way both Torquemada and the Papacy in general emphasised the divinely appointed rights and status of the ruler was extraordinary.

On a more immediately practical level, the schism after 1437 could plausibly be blamed on the Council of Basle, which thus lost its appeal as the focus of unity. This was what tipped the balance. The papalists did not win the argument. Nor, as Segovia and others argued, did they win merely by bribery and deceit. The Council itself was becoming confused and out of touch; it lacked a serious overall policy. The Papacy won by default.

Hence the defeat of Basle was no watershed in constitutional thought. We have noted how the canonist doctrine of the occasional supremacy of council over pope continued unchanged. The view that a council was the normal superior of the pope was upheld by the influential theology faculty at Paris and in other universities. Public opinion generally, amongst intellectuals and in court circles, seems to have favoured the more moderate view that a council was the emergency superior of the pope in cases of heresy, schism and the urgent need for reform. This last made a new council highly desirable and indeed necessary: as time went on pro-conciliar treatises appeared in print.

Many people reverted from the extreme and now somewhat discredited notion of 'popular sovereignty' in the Church, as expounded at Basle, to the more moderate view associated with the Council of Constance and enshrined in the much-quoted decrees 'Haec Sancta' and 'Frequens'. One indicator of pious theological opinion can be found in the writings of Denis Rickel (1402–71), a famous Carthusian mystic who accompanied Cusa on his mission of reform to Germany in 1451–2. He wanted a 'middle way' between what the Council of Basle, on the one hand, and Pope Eugenius, on the other, stood for, and believed he could find this in the writings of Gerson and D'Ailly. His solution was that a council is superior in what 'Haec Sancta' had defined it as

---

[10] Torquemada, *Summa de ecclesia*, II. 65; Inalcik (1973), pp. 66–8.

superior in – faith, unity and reform – and a pope is superior in everything else; he sought to divide supreme jurisdiction according to subject matter. Significantly, he remarked that 'almost all *doctores* are agreed' that for heresy a pope may be deposed by a council.[11]

In the last conciliar enterprise before the Reformation (1511–12), the council's supremacy was vigorously upheld in the same terms as before by Jacques Almain and John Major from the University of Paris, and by several Italian authors. The most remarkable of these was the curial official, Giovanni Gozzadini, who adopted the more radical view that power resides fundamentally with the Church as a whole, of which the pope is 'chief minister'. The main opposition to this came from Cardinal Cajetan, a Dominican and the first serious theorist of papal monarchy since Torquemada. Insisting that this was a matter not for canonists but for theologians, he relied upon the Petrine commission to prove that, while the constitution of the Church could have been oligarchical or democratic, Christ had as a matter of fact chosen monarchy. Nevertheless, he admitted that a council could, in cases of papal heresy or schism, be called by others than the pope; and that, in the case of heresy, the pope could be deposed by a council. This was not 'subjection' but 'separation' by the Church of itself from the pope – election in reverse.[12] The most eloquent testimony to belief in conciliar authority came from Thomas More, writing in March 1534. While in one sense More died for the principle of papal authority, he thought a council the ultimate authority 'in the declaration of the truth' in which it 'ought to be taken for undoubtable': 'although I have for my own part such opinion of the pope's primacy as I have shown you, yet I never thought the pope above the general council'.[13]

III

A look at popes and councils in the longer perspective will show that the politics and ideology of this period had an effect in shaping European culture. One cannot prove conclusively that the ideas of either monarchical or of corporate sovereignty, to which this controversy gave such dramatic prominence, influenced any particular ruler or state. But their expression contributed to the language of public opinion and political thought, gave new currency and new refinement to these ideas, and also made some impression upon people's general views on what constituted a legitimate authority and a legitimate regime. It is noticeable that the analogy between an ecclesiastical council and estates or parliament was put forward more emphatically and confidently by

---

[11] Rickel, 'De auctoritate', 1, 32, p. 573b.
[12] Cajetan, 'De comparatione auctoritatis', ch. 20, p. 475.   [13] More, *Correspondence*, p. 499.

Almain and Major than it had been by D'Ailly and Gerson a century before, on the ground that both were expressions of a universal truth: power lies fundamentally with the community as a whole. It is obvious that this did not decide future constitutional history: however, that the *doctores*, who were supposed to know the truth better than anyone, were convinced of this was an important social fact. The same can be said for the parallel articulation of monarchical thought.

The conciliar struggle had an impact on diplomacy and international relations. The resolutions of the schisms between popes and later between pope and council engendered feverish diplomatic activity. On the one hand, these brought together sovereigns and clergy from all the European nations in a common effort. On the other hand, the outcome was achieved by a new method: direct negotiations between the Papacy and secular rulers, bypassing the clerical estate as an autonomous agency.

For once politics, ecclesiastical and international, were channelled into intellectual (legal and theological) debate among prelates and *doctores* – in the presence of secular rulers. And these princes rejected the use of force by any of the major contestants against others. There had been armed clashes in Italy after 1378; Eugenius occasionally urged rulers to persecute the supporters of Basle as heretics; the Council, on the other hand, adhered to the procedures of law. There were in fact no martyrs. This may be seen as a novel and 'enlightened' approach to ecclesiastical controversy. It meant that for a short space of time international relations were conducted in unusually ideological terms. The belief in persuasion by argument was a distinctive and, in the context, new approach to crisis management. The art of rhetoric was not explicitly developed; rather, the scholastic and juristic methods of textual citation and dialectic were applied to a practical political problem. The procedures for discussion in universities, where most participants had their training, were employed in the courts of kings, at the councils themselves (as was usual) and at national and semi-international assemblies such as the *Reichstag*. Behind this lay an outstanding faith in the power of the word. It was not dialectic or conversion that determined the outcome. Aeneas Sylvius expressed Italian 'realism' when he said that 'only a fool thinks that princes are moved by tomes and treatises'.[14] But this was to miss one point. After 1450 real ecclesiastical power – the ability to influence people and get things done – seemed temporarily in abeyance. In fact, the ability to exercise moral leadership had shifted towards anyone who could claim personal Christian charisma, and especially towards those who could combine this with a claim to wisdom or learning – the *doctores*, in other words, whose influence was further enhanced by the printed word. Someone

---

[14] Cit. Black (1970), p. 114.

with both these qualifications – a Savonarola, Erasmus or Luther – had very strong credentials.

On the other hand, the potential practical ability to reform the Church lay now with the secular rulers. One may see the conciliar movement as an attempt to recreate the *respublica christiana* and the Catholic clerical system, as this had existed since Constantine or even earlier, on a pattern different to that adopted under papal leadership since the eleventh century. Its failure meant that reform more or less had to come from outside that system itself; and some people began to perceive this. Throughout the crisis of 1378–1417, people acted on the assumption that the secular authorities had a key role to play; it was they, in collaboration with the senior clergy of their territories, who could effectively decide which pope was supported and whether a council was attended. The fact that Sigismund initially had to convoke the Council of Constance himself increased their status. The Councils of Pisa (1409) and Constance were preceded by national synods of clergy at which, under the royal eye, moneys, delegates and terms of reference were decided. In the crisis from 1437 to 1449, a council was no longer the forum in which matters were decided; now it was a question of direct negotiations between state rulers and the Papacy, on the one hand, or the Council of Basle, on the other. Court decisions were now all that mattered. This had an effect on the way in which church authority, and authority in general, were perceived. Some spokesmen for the emperor, princes and other kings, and even for the Papacy itself, began to speak of state rulers as representatives or 'heads' of the Church; Cusa with his theory of consent was the most explicit.[15] Things were clearer still by the time of the Council of Pisa–Lyons (1511–12) when the French monarchy, disowning its own creation, settled matters by a concordat (1516).

The relationship between Rome and Europe had changed. After 1450 large areas and some rulers were disaffected from or indifferent to Roman authority. The upshot was to be separate states – and Churches.

[15] Palacký *et al.* (eds.), *Monumenta*, III, p. 314 (declaration of neutrality, 1438); *Deutsche Reichstagsakten*, XVII, pp. 142, 145–6 (Cardinal Carvajal); and Cusa himself in *Deutsche Reichstagsakten*, XV, p. 874; XVI, pp. 428, 432; XVII, pp. 381, 384. See also Black (1970), pp. 97 n. 4, 109.

PART II

ECONOMIC AND SOCIAL
DEVELOPMENTS

CHAPTER 4

THE EUROPEAN NOBILITY

Philippe Contamine

MORE than any other social class or grouping (including the ecclesiastical one), the nobility of Europe at the end of the Middle Ages needs and deserves to be studied from a standpoint that is not merely socio-economic, but political and cultural, too. In this chapter Europe is deemed synonymous with Latin Christendom. None the less, this does not imply the assumption that contemporaries believed nobility to exist only within Latin Christendom. As proof of this, armorials compiled in France and elsewhere included, for example, the arms of the Grand Khan, the sultan of Babylon, the Grand Turk, and the king of Granada (these next to the arms of the Christian king of Armenia), while an author like Gilles le Bouvier, in his *Livre de la description des pays* (*c.* 1450), could refer in particular to the Turkish nobility. To a certain extent, then, the inhabitants of fifteenth-century Christendom regarded nobility as a universal social order.

Since there was not merely one European society, but many, each with its individual characteristics, the present approach must be comparative. In view of the enormous diversity among these societies, it is pertinent to ask whether comparisons are feasible and, above all, useful, enlightening and convincing. However, whereas doubts about the validity of this kind of approach may be understandable in the case of the peasantry (for example), the case of the nobility is different. For a start, then, two questions will be asked. Was there a European nobility? And, secondly, was there a European concept of that nobility?

Nobility here will be defined as a class which perceived itself and was perceived by others as occupying the apex of the social pyramid (in terms of prestige, power, wealth, way of life and standard of living) within societies which saw themselves as hierarchical and wished to be so. Furthermore, it was a class whose members were mostly recruited and replaced from generation to generation by birth and legitimate male lineage, a class essentially of inheritors whose special status was generally acknowledged. One of the main problems which immediately arises is that circumstances among the nobility tended to fluctuate within the period and the particular region under consideration; furthermore that, like the term 'clergy', the all-inclusive noun 'nobility' embraced individuals whose way of life, powers, prestige and wealth were subject to great diversity. Conforming to a practice widely shared by contemporaries, historians are accustomed, at the very least, to differentiating between the higher and lower nobility, and to comparing the two. Yet even this division is too cursory. A more precise picture would doubtless be painted if not simply two, but three or four levels could be envisaged. At the end of the fifteenth century, for example, the Castilian nobility was distinctly divided into three categories: the *titulos* (the *nobleza* proper), the *caballeros* and later the *hidalgos* (the *hidalguia*) and the *escuderos*.

I

Among the arguments in favour of a comparative approach is the one that contemporaries themselves sometimes resorted to such comparisons. It is well known that, at the end of his reign, Louis XI intended to transform the French nobility, taking as models its English and Italian counterparts: 'The chancellor proclaimed to us that the king's pleasure was that anyone wishing to engage in trade might do so within the kingdom, without forfeiting his nobility or other privileges, as was the custom on the Italian peninsula and in the kingdom of England.'[1]

The Castilian noble, Diego de Valera (c. 1412–88), a man with much experience of a variety of countries, wrote a treatise, *Espejo de verdadera nobleza* (1441), which was soon translated into French for the benefit of the Burgundian court. In the translation the author asks how long 'nobility dependent on heredity' is likely to survive. He reproduces the time-honoured answer of the celebrated Italian jurist, Bartolus of Sassoferrato (c. 1314–57): in the case of 'mere gentlemen', down to the fourth generation; as for those 'established in high offices and lordships, kings, dukes, counts, barons and others whose positions and lordships confer nobility upon them', they will survive as long as they retain the offices and lordships in question. Yet he also points out that Bartolus's theory no longer pertains because 'the custom has changed everywhere', declaring that an individual's nobility is now deemed all the greater when it can be traced to long-deceased ancestors.[2]

The author then comments on different countries. 'In Germany, nobility endures as long as nobles live honourably and without engaging in unseemly functions or professions.' On the Italian peninsula 'all descendants of legiti-

---

[1] Commynes, *Mémoires*, III, p. 345.   [2] Cited by Vanderjagt, *'Qui sa vertu anoblist'*, pp. 260–1.

mate nobility are noble as long as they are not reduced to poverty or demeaning customs through taking on unfitting positions, for then they are no longer considered noble'. Here Diego de Valera is in agreement with the contemporary Veronese, Bartolomeo Cipolla, who wrote that 'if an individual is reduced to poverty or engages in demeaning tasks, he cannot be called or be considered noble'. In France, on the contrary, according to de Valera, purely economic considerations do not enter into it: 'nobility endures as long as the nobleman lives an impeccable life, that is, a noble one, irrespective of wealth or poverty'. In Spain, particularly in Castile, even more latitude is allowed:

all these things are not so closely examined and considered, for although some are bastards legitimised by the prince, and have undertaken demeaning functions, or are not endowed with virtues and seemly customs as they should be, as long as they can show that their fathers and grandfathers were exempt from paying the *gabelle* to the prince, then they are considered to be of gentle birth, even though all these things are contrary to what is right and are forbidden by the laws of the kingdom, by which it is ordained and decreed that nobility is forfeit where there are disreputable manners, base occupations, and where nobility demeans itself.

For de Valera, this is a deplorable state of affairs. If only the laws were adhered to, 'nobles living in true nobility would be as highly esteemed as they ought to be'.

Diego de Valera also adopts an interesting comparative approach to heraldry. He begins by stressing that 'it behoves knights and nobles to wear their arms and carry pennants by which they and their kin may be identified'. These arms may indicate either ancestry or office, or a combination of the two, as in the case of the duke of Burgundy 'who bears by reason of his lineage the quartered arms of France with a bordure as mark of difference, and adds to them the arms of his principal dignities'. Having explained how arms can be adopted and worn in four different ways (by inheritance, grant by the prince, capture in war, personal initiative), de Valera returns to the subject of princely grants, remarking that 'this custom is universal, though practised chiefly in Germany, France and Italy'; he adds that 'this custom was formerly followed above all in Spain, and now is practised above all in your kingdom [that of Juan II] where there are individuals alive who were granted arms by your father, the late king Enrique [III] of blessed memory'. He notes that the custom of wearing a coat of arms in battle 'is practised more in France and England than elsewhere, for there any knight or noble, however poor, wears his coat of arms in battle'. Finally he observes that 'mainly in France and Germany' 'the bourgeoisie adopt arms as they please', but may display them only in their homes and parish churches, whereas 'nobles display their arms wherever they wish and on coats' (doubtless he has tournaments and jousts particularly in mind). All the same, according to de Valera, a bourgeois ennobled by the prince has the right to bear his arms everywhere, like nobles of ancient heritage.

Writing in 1441, the Paduan, Michele Savonarola, used a similar approach in order to compare 'military' chivalry, peculiar to the kingdom of Sicily and to Spain, with the 'civil' and ornamental chivalry to which aspired, through mere vanity, the urban patriciate of Tuscany even if it was connected to the *popolo*. These 'patricians' (adopting a word not in contemporary usage) betrayed no enthusiasm for things military; they engaged unblushingly in trade, agriculture and the mechanical arts, even though, just like authentic nobility, they had at their disposal horses, hounds, hawks and servants.[3]

In a chapter of his *Discourses . . . on Livy* Machiavelli was to reflect on the structures of states.[4] Having proposed as his definition of 'gentlemen' a leisured class without trade or profession that lived solely from revenues which came mainly from estates, and, stressing that those in possession of castles, rights of jurisdiction and subjects (in short, feudatories) posed the greatest threat to public order, he went on to consider the case of German towns where civic virtue and integrity, particularly fiscal integrity, held sway. Why was this so? According to Machiavelli it was because the inhabitants, having no knowledge of the outside world, were thus uncorrupted by it; because they were content with their lot; and because gentlemen were strictly excluded from their society. Such gentlemen were to be found in the kingdom of Naples, the papal states, the Romagna, and Lombardy; yet in the Italian republics – Florence, Lucca, Siena – they were few in number, and those few possessed no castles. But what of Venice, where only gentlemen could hold office? It was not a contradiction of Machiavelli's theory, since these Venetians were gentlemen in name rather than in reality, as their wealth derived from trade, and they had neither lands, nor castles, nor jurisdiction over subjects. Furthermore, their nobility was merely honorary; all Venetians understood the rules of the game, which consequently provoked no unrest. Only if it were dominated by a strong monarchy could a genuine noble class be compatible with social order. Similarly anyone wishing, for his own ends, to set up a principality or kingdom in an egalitarian society would be well advised to create nobles who, in return for the granting of castles, possessions and powers of jurisdiction, would render him service.

In the fifteenth century there were the acknowledged specialists in matters of nobility who were arbitrators, even judges, and at the same time acted as expert witnesses on various aspects of noble life. These were the heralds of arms (kings of arms, marshals of arms, pursuivants, who all formed part of a more or less official hierarchy) whose vocation and outlook were international. Their work was not simply the compilation of armorials. They travelled a great deal, from castle to castle, from court to court, from tournaments to jousts or

---

[3] Cited by Ventura (1964), pp. 291–2.
[4] Machiavelli, *Discourses on the first decade of Titus Livius*, bk I, ch. 55, in *Chief works*, trans. Gilbert (1965).

passages of arms, from weddings to chivalric festivals, from one diplomatic meeting to another, and (of course) from war to war. These heralds of arms could thus, with reason, lay claim to an extensive knowledge of noble circles, most particularly those of their own nation. Yet they also had the more or less avowed aim of gathering all nobles within the European sphere into the fold of a single model. Here can be glimpsed the origins of what would later become the *Almanach de Gotha*, guide to the exclusive society of nineteenth-century Europe.

Among these heralds (Toison d'Or, Navarre Herald, Richmond Herald, or Clément Prinsaut) Berry Herald merits attention since, in addition to his *Armorial* and his *Chroniques du roi Charles VII*, he also left a *Livre de la description des pays*, whose scope extends well beyond the limits of Latin Christendom. In this book are found numerous references to the nobility of different regions which the author reviews in turn. In Poitou, there is an 'abundance of nobles', while in Touraine there are 'great lords'. In the duchy of Bar 'fine nobility' is to be found, while Brittany has 'great lords, barons and gentlemen'. In his view, France has more nobles than any other two Christian kingdoms together. Other countries are also the object of the herald's curiosity; he may be more reliable on some than on others, as he comments briefly on their character-istics: the number of their subjects (county of Burgundy); their courageous conduct in war (Portugal); and their sense of courage and honour (Scotland). Beneath these conventional platitudes there is at least the notion that for any country it is a positive asset, above all an honour, to have a noble class that is numerous, courageous and well endowed with subjects, lordships and strong-holds.

If the European nobility presented a measure of unity, this resulted in considerable measure from a strong tendency to marry within itself, a characteristic particularly marked among princely and royal families. Amadeus VIII, duke of Savoy (1391–1451), provides a good example of the conse-quences of this. Among his sixteen great-great-grandparents were Theodore II Palaiologos, marquis of Montferrat, and Argentina Spinola (of a noble Genoese family); Louis I, duke of Bourbon, and Mary of Hainault; Charles of Valois and Mahaut of Châtillon (in Champagne); King Philip VI of Valois and Joan of Burgundy; John of Luxemburg, king of Bohemia, and Isabeau of Bohemia; and Count Bernard VI of Armagnac and Cécile of Rodez, giving him a broad and noble background covering France, the Italian peninsula and the Empire. As for Amadeus's own dynastic links, they extended as far as England in the person of Anne of Burgundy, wife of John, duke of Bedford; to Brittany through Francis, count of Montfort; to Navarre through Isabel of Navarre, wife of John IV, count of Armagnac; to Cyprus through John II, king of Cyprus; to the peninsula of Italy through Filippo Maria Visconti, duke of

Milan; to Bavaria through William of Bavaria; to Austria through Leopold IV, duke of Austria; and to the Low Countries through the person of Adolf IV of Cleves.

Chivalric orders and chivalric devices, which appeared in the second quarter of the fourteenth century, soon spread over a large part of western Christendom, a typical instance of cultural and institutional development over-riding linguistic, political and national frontiers. One of the main objectives evident in the statutes of these 'orders' or 'associations' ('fraternities' might be a better name for them) was to allow a prince, head of the order in question, to gather more easily about him, in his own service, the nobility of his states, domains and lordships, an aim most successfully achieved in the case of the order of the Golden Fleece ('Toison d'Or'), the only centralised and central-ising institution of a rather amorphous Burgundy. Nevertheless, in the case of a number of orders, such as that of the English Order of the Garter, the incorporation of a number of foreign members, besides furthering the diplo-matic and political ends of the order's sovereign, did add a significant interna-tional dimension to their character.

Nobles from different parts of western Christendom could also meet at the court. A treatise, written for presentation to Charles VII, urged the king to extend a welcome to both native and foreign nobles. Nobles met, of course, when engaged in war, the law of arms (*jus armorum*), in particular that part of it concerned with ransoms, helping to protect their relationship when they were on opposing sides. Generally speaking, courtly and chivalric principles applied without distinction, and above all to nobles of all countries whose social conventions bound them to an identical code of honour. The Prussian *Reise*, that cross-roads of western nobility, was more characteristic of the fourteenth than of the fifteenth century. Furthermore, the defeat of the crusading force at Nicopolis in 1396 left a permanent legacy: it wrecked Philippe de Mézières's plans to found the Order of the Passion, and Christian nobles of the fifteenth century had no opportunity, in spite of the Oath of the Pheasant (1454) and the admonitions of Pius II, to support a great crusade. Yet, on a perceptibly more modest scale, this did not prevent land or sea operations against the Turk giving nobles from different countries occasion to rub shoulders; while the Order of the Hospitallers of St John of Jerusalem, an order fully international in character, continued to function. Was it not, generally speaking, in the very nature of nobles to form as many different relationships as possible, to travel about freely, suitably armed with letters of recommendation and safe-conduct, even if only in their years of apprenticeship? The accounts of travellers reveal that within the European context nobles knew one another, or recognised their peers. They sensed that they belonged to the same social world, irrespective of the multitude of customs and linguistic barriers which might divide them, although it is worth noting that the higher a nobleman's rank, the more circumscribed his world was likely to become.

It goes without saying that the vocabulary relating to nobles and nobility varied from one language to another, but, if only through the medium of Latin, the whole of western Christendom at this juncture employed common terms for social concepts. This explains why *noblesse* in French echoed (if it did not exactly correspond to) the English word nobility, the Italian *nobiltà*, and the Spanish *nobleza*. It needs to be said, too, that in the fifteenth century the whole of western Christendom already knew, or adopted more generally than before, the traditional hierarchy of titles and offices that was Roman, Frankish or French in origin: duke, marquis, count, viscount, baron, knight, and squire. Translations from one language to another were suggested, for instance, in French/Flemish/English phrase books of the fourteenth century: 'duc'/'hertoghe'/'duke'; 'comte'/'grave'/'earl'; 'chevalier'/'ridder'/'knyghte'; 'écuyer'/'sciltknecht'/'squyer'; while the French 'grants seigneurs' was translated 'grote heeren' in Flemish and 'great lords' in English.

Texts, in some cases translations, spread far from their place of origin identical concepts of nobility and chivalry, and stimulated commentaries upon them. Such an example are the numerous translations made of *Le libre del orde de cauayleria* by the Catalan, Ramon Lull. In 1484, for example, 'at a requeste of a gentyl and noble esquyer', William Caxton printed his own translation, *The book of the ordre of chyualry*, for 'noble gentylmen that by their vertu entende to come & entre in to the noble ordre of chyualry'.[5] Earlier, Gilbert of the Haye, a Scotsman of letters, had translated the same work under the title *The buke of the ordre of knychthede*. In the same way Alain Chartier's *Bréviaire des nobles* was translated into English prose at the end of the fifteenth century as *The porteous of Cadzow*, while Christine de Pisan's *Livre des faits d'armes et de chevalerie* was also rendered into English.[6] The most striking example is perhaps that of the *Controversia de nobilitate*, written in Latin in 1428 by Buonaccorso da Montemagno, scion of a noble family of Pistoia, which was to be translated into Italian, French, German and English, the original, as well as the translations, being accorded the privilege of early printings, thereby ensuring their widespread dissemination.

II

The fact still remains – and Louis XI and Diego de Valera were not the only ones to be aware of it – that every European society had a distinct nobility with specific characteristics. The Polish nobility was not that of Germany, nor was

---

[5] Lull, *Ordre of chyualry* (trans. Caxton), p. 121.   [6] Pisan, *Book of fayttes of armes*.

that of France Italian. One might even question the very existence of a single, uniform nobility within the Empire or on the Italian peninsula.

The matter of actual numbers of nobles is fundamental, and must be considered first. It does not seem possible to suggest percentages, even approximate ones, for all the countries of Europe; available figures are incomplete and too imprecise to enable one to discern possible trends in this area in the fifteenth century. In France, at the end of the Middle Ages, the noble class, the 'peuple des nobles' as one contemporary termed it, from the princes of the blood to the most unpretentious squires and mere gentlemen, accounted for between 1.5 per cent and 2 per cent of the total population, although this masked considerable regional differences: Brittany, in particular, numbered some 9,000 noble families which, at a reckoning of five individuals per family, gives 45,000 souls, or some 3 per cent of a population of about 1,500,000. Proportions of 4 per cent cannot be discounted in Dauphiné and Savoy, for example, whereas elsewhere, in the region around Chartres, numbers would scarcely reach 1 per cent.

In England, a rather different picture emerges. About 1500, the nobility in the strict sense of the word ('peers of the realm' summoned to sit in parliament as 'lords temporal'), formed a group of sixty peers, in effect sixty families. Immediately below them were found the gentry (*generosi*) who, although claiming to belong both culturally and socially to the noble class in its broadest sense, by statutory definition were no longer deemed noble at the end of the fifteenth century. At a rough estimate this group comprised some 500 knights, about 800 esquires (constituting the squirearchy) and 5,000 gentlemen. Next in order descending the social scale were the yeomen, who cannot be included in the noble class, however loosely defined. Accordingly, it can be proposed that the noble class, in the broadest sense of the term, would have amounted to 30,000 individuals, which, assuming a total population of 2,500,000, is a proportion of only 1.2 per cent.

Castile, about the year 1500, had an estimated population of 5,000,000 people. According to contemporary sources nobles of all ranks (*grandes* and *titulos, caballeros, hidalgos, donzellos* and *escuderos*) would account for one sixth (16.6 per cent) of this total. Most historians consider this figure far too high: some suggest lowering it to 4 per cent; others, probably nearer the mark, to at least 10 per cent, that is 500,000 individuals or 100,000 families, with, as in France, strong regional variations, the Asturias, León and the region of Burgos providing more than half the *hidalgos*, who were uncommon in the dioceses of Cordova and Seville where, by contrast, town-dwelling *caballeros* were established. The proportion for the kingdom of Navarre may have risen to 15 per cent, while, somewhat unexpectedly, the proportion in Aragon may have been as low as 1.5 or 2 per cent.

In Scandinavia we have an example of a region where the nobility took a long time to become established, although, as it happens, the fifteenth century was an important phase in its evolution. Around 1500, in a country with a population of 300,000, there were some 300 noble families in Norway; making the noble families 0.5 per cent of the total population. In neighbouring Denmark, where such families numbered between 250 and 300 – of which a score or so belonged to the higher nobility – they constituted 0.25 per cent of a population of about 500,000. In short, these societies clearly were not essentially feudal in character; the well-to-do peasantry was more important.

Conversely in Poland, Hungary and Bohemia nobles were numerous: 2,000 noble families, it is claimed, in Bohemia; a population 5 per cent noble in Hungary; in Poland, not, as has been long accepted, 10–15 per cent noble, but rather between 3 and 5 per cent, yet a still far from negligible proportion of the population.

Finally, some 2,000 noble families have been identified in Scotland, constituting, at 10,000 individuals, some 5 per cent of the population, a significantly high proportion for a poor country, which would explain, among other things, the importance and persistence of emigration to France for military service.

The matter of percentages is of prime historical importance. A very small noble class may have meant a measure of affluence for the 'happy few', and less of a drain on production, particularly agricultural production, but more certainly it meant that noble dominance of society as a whole was weak, that noble brilliance was toned down. Conversely, a superfluity of nobles inevitably brought poverty in its wake. For, fundamental to the very concept of nobility, was the idea that it demanded, at the very least, a comfortable way of life.

The existence of noble classes of varying importance within different European societies is explained, first and foremost, by the long-term history of these societies, and, vitally, by its outcome. Being a noble in a parish of a hundred hearths with ten to fifteen other noble families was not the same as being the sole person with a claim to this status. In the latter case the noble was usually *the* lord (hence the use of 'de', 'von', or, in Poland, the suffix -ski or -cki), for whom a manorial pew might be reserved in the church whose stained-glass windows portrayed his armorial bearings.

III

More or less everywhere the titled nobility broke away, or stood apart from the mass of nobles: its members held high offices and were sometimes termed great lords or magnates. They numbered a few dozen families out of a few hundred or a few thousand ordinary nobles, perhaps between 1 per cent and 5 per cent of all nobles. Contemporary documents carefully listed the duchies and counties of the French kingdom, as well as their feudal status, but it must be said that the same individual might hold several of these great fiefs simultaneously and that 'sires', occasionally barons or viscounts, could themselves claim to belong to the high nobility (French examples include the families of La Trémoille, Chabannes, Estouteville and Rohan). In Castile, in 1474, there were forty-nine families termed *titulos* or *grandes* (dukes, marquises, counts, viscounts); they formed a unified body, were immensely wealthy, reasonably cultured, and exerted great influence on society, although far from posing a serious threat to the monarchy's political supremacy, which was constantly being strengthened. In fifteenth-century Scotland, from within the emerging nobility, and in opposition to the lairds, came the peers, dukes, earls and lords, who enjoyed the privilege of being individually summoned by the king to parliament. They numbered about sixty individuals (hence sixty families), as many as in England whose total population was some five or six times greater. In Hungary, the barons, who in 1430–40 held 40 per cent of the land, were about sixty in number and formed a class apart. In Portugal, where the first ducal title dates from 1415, the first marquisate from 1451, and the first barony from 1475 (all of them royal creations), the titled nobility numbered about thirty in the second half of the fifteenth century. In Poland, the powerful *communitas nobilium* (the celebrated *slazchta*) succeeded during the course of the century in reducing the power of urban societies politically and even economically, in winning control of the powers of the state, and in promulgating itself as the sole political group in Poland. Not only that. It also sought to prevent the institution of hereditary titles and the creation of a separate and exclusive aristocratic upper class. Poland, to use the accepted terminology, thus began to develop a 'republic' or a 'noble democracy'.

Poland, in point of fact, was an exceptional case. Generally speaking, the highest nobility had its clients, its loyal servants (the term used in Hungary was *familiaritates*) very many of whom were themselves nobles, or, in the case of England, gentlemen. In fact, in England bonds of a contractual nature (indentures) were formed between magnates and their retainers, the latter benefiting from the patronage of the former, whose livery they wore and from whom they received fees or annuities; they were also liable to interfere violently with the free functioning of justice. Hence the expression 'bastard feudalism', created by modern historians to describe this new type of bond between one man and another, which replaced the classic feudalism of the twelfth and thirteenth centuries. Such phenomena or tendencies, transcending institutional differences, were also to be found on the continent. Spanish grandees surrounded themselves with man-servants or *criados*, among them many bastards of noblemen. In France, the king, as well as princes and great lords, asked for and obtained without difficulty undemeaning service from middle-ranking or minor nobles (men, women, young people) who staffed their households as chamberlains, grooms and stewards, followed them in war and peace, and helped manage their estates. For a great many nobles, entry into the circle of a powerful individual was a step as natural as it was profitable.

Such clients could, in many cases, become 'bands', 'factions' and *alliances* that were active on the political scene. These developments appeared in many states and societies, if sometimes only intermittently. An example of aristocratic faction is provided by Olivier de la Marche who reports the occasion which occurred when, shortly before the war of the Public Weal broke out in 1465, those wishing to support Charles of France, Louis XI's brother, in alliance against the king, sent word of their commitment to a meeting allegedly held at Notre Dame, Paris. 'And those who had sent seals in secret wore a silk favour in their belts, by which they would recognise one another; and thus the alliance was made, the king knowing nothing about it, although there were more than 500 (princes, knights, squires and others) who were all staunch to this alliance.' In fact one of the foundation stones of the league of the Public Weal was precisely the discontent of a number of the kingdom's nobles who, under the protection of a few princes, wanted to resist the king's assaults upon their rights and privileges. Yet the sum total of these groups (whose cohesiveness is not always evident) is much smaller than the number of nobility as a whole (or, in the case of England, the number of knights, squires and gentlemen). It is clear that many mere gentlemen did not have a patron, and so were forced to rely upon their own resources, in consequence leading circumscribed and limited lives.

In every respect it would be an oversimplification to believe that political conflict hinged solely on the struggle between a king (or a prince) and his magnates seeking to preserve their 'feudal' privileges in defiance of a modern state in the making, and discovering their military arm in a lower nobility, itself wedded to the old order. Too often it is forgotten that kings (and princes) had their own noble clients who, because their means were usually more substantial and in the long term their chances of success consequently greater, were more numerous and firmer of purpose. It also happened that lesser nobles opposed those of higher rank by turning for support to the king. In Hungary, at the end of the century, Mátyás Corvinus made use of the lower nobility against the barons in order to destroy the system of *familiaritates*, to create a wholly royal army and, of course, to fight the Turks.

Over and above the vertical socio-political structures which have just been examined, others appeared which were essentially horizontal. As examples of this tendency we may note for instance, the anti-urban (or anti-prince) chivalric leagues ('Hörner', 'Falkner', 'St Georgsbund', 'Elephantenbund') native to Germany at the end of the Middle Ages, or, again, in the years about 1475, the nobles of Lorraine who, in order to cement their defensive alliance against the Burgundians, agreed to place their armorial shields in the choir of the collegiate church of St George at Nancy.

IV

As a hereditary class the nobility, for reasons which were both genetic and cultural, fell victim to the classic phenomenon of extinction of the line. Historians have sought to measure this either on a regional basis or by confining themselves to the better-documented though narrower world of the magnates. In the period 1300–1500 the proportion of English lords whose line became extinct was 27 per cent every quarter of a century (if one defines extinction as having only daughters, even if nephews are living). Of the 136 barons summoned to parliament in December 1299, only sixteen had male descendants in 1500. In Scotland, using the same terms of reference, the rate of extinction of families of dukes and earls in the fifteenth century varied from 17 per cent to 39 per cent (always calculated in spans of twenty-five years). Comparable figures have been suggested for the entire nobility of a few French regions, the most reliable study relating to the county of Forez.[7] In Germany, the trend was similar: of 138 noble Bavarian families qualified for tournaments (*Turnieradel*) known in 1440, only sixty-eight remained in 1500. In the district of Olpe in Westphalia, of the forty noble families known in the fourteenth century, only twenty survived in the fifteenth. This process of attrition was all the more unfortunate in that it affected a class which, by definition, was extremely preoccupied with the survival of its lineage, its estates, its name and its coat of arms. It is a well-known fact that all kinds of legal arrangements were preserved or initiated (including different versions of the law of primogeniture: *majoratus*, entailments) in order to ensure that families should continue to prosper. It is well known, too, that the nobility's matrimonial schemes bore witness to a keen vigilance on its part. In Spain a noble house united several families under the protection of the *pariente mayor* who, as head of the senior branch, controlled the *entierro* (family tomb), ecclesiastical patronage, as well as the principal seat, or *casa solar*. If, in spite of the obsession with survival peculiar to the noble mentality, levels of extinction were really as high as suggested above, many historians see this as overwhelming evidence that the class was in the grip of a serious crisis. This opinion is reinforced by the fact that although this must have led to a considerable transfer of riches, particularly in property – to whose profit? – there are no clear indications of a percentage decrease in the noble population between 1400 and 1500. It is likely, then, that

---

[7] Perroy (1962), p. 27.

there was a substantial influx of new members during these years, a situation which was bound to cause problems in a culture in which ancestry played so important a part.

This interpretation of the evidence, however, does require qualification, and the following points may be made. By studying individual families, demographers have been led to observe that within any group of people the incidence of family extinction is comparable, irrespective of social status. Secondly, is it not the characteristic of the ruling class (and the nobility had pretensions to be such a class) to exclude those of its members who fall below standard? Thirdly, the historian's habitual practice of omitting daughters from the equation doubles the rate of extinction. It should also be remembered that, in any event, this phenomenon was not exclusive to the fifteenth century: in terms of the nobility, the law of extinction seems to hold good for every era. Finally, in the light of specialised research, it appears highly unlikely that every twenty-five years between 25 per cent and 30 per cent of noble wealth (namely lordships) should have changed hands to the benefit of either favourably placed nobles (including the king or prince), or of the Church, or of non-nobles.

In any event, the important point is to understand how such extinction occurred. The example of the English and Scottish peerage shows that extinction could be widespread, even if the reasons were in no sense economic. It was not through poverty that a particular English earl's family disappeared; it can only have been the result of natural, genetic factors. After all, by this same criterion the line of France's kings died out in 1328, 1498 and 1515 – three times within two centuries.

Be that as it may, when the nobility is viewed as a whole, economic factors did come into play. Almost everywhere in Europe society looked upon an impoverished nobleman as an aberration; a noble, it was accepted, must have the means of maintaining his 'estate'. Moreover, a fact more pronounced in some countries than in others, nobility was incompatible, in reality or by law, with the practice of many professions. Nobles everywhere had to have landed revenue, a notoriously unreliable source of income, especially in this period. Here the spectre of *dérogeance* raises its head. For fiscal reasons this phenomenon was particularly severe and widespread in France. Strangely, the term has no equivalent in other European languages and is therefore untranslatable, although traces of the idea were to be found, in both attitudes of mind and in actual behaviour, more or less everywhere.

In England admission to the nobility was strictly controlled by the crown, but the same was not true in the case of the gentry, who were distinguished by the right to bear arms (a gentleman was, by definition, armigerous) and by the right to the titles 'sir', 'esquire' or 'gentleman' (the term 'gentilman' is said to have first come into use at the beginning of the fifteenth century to denote an 'estate' or 'rank' in society; its first appearance in a funerary description dates from the middle of the century).[8] To be a gentleman, or to be recognized as such, presupposed a certain wealth, above all from landed revenues (£10 per annum for a mere gentleman, £20 for an esquire, £40 for a knight) and, where appropriate, participation in a reputable profession, such as service of the king, a magnate, a bishop, or a town, service in the legal or even the medical profession, political or administrative responsibilities, large-scale commercial activities, but not direct working on the land or domestic tasks or craftsmen's trades. Those wishing to preserve or raise their social standing were well advised to practise their profession (even though a reputable one) only intermittently, or through an intermediary.

In the greater part of France (a case apart was the duchy of Brittany, where there was the concept of 'dormant' nobility, allowing a noble to suspend his noble status for as long as it took him to restore his fortunes by means of activities involving *dérogeance*) the main issue was whether nobility was compatible with trade, including participation in large-scale enterprise. A noble could, of course, sell his produce, or have it sold, cultivate his lands himself (if necessary putting his hand to the plough; the petty Breton squires of modern times are in this tradition), engage in various legal professions, take service under the king or prince, or invest capital in commercial ventures such as shipping or the leasing of livestock. Even so he could not be either an inn-keeper or a reputable tradesman. Clearly this limited money-making opportunities, with the result that living as a noble did not necessarily imply living off ample means. Studies focused on Burgundy, Auvergne, Bourbonnais, among other regions, at the end of the fifteenth century reveal the existence there of a whole army of very humble squires, the mirror image of the impoverished clergy mentioned in many sources. There was even the notion of shameful, or concealed poverty. Wills demonstrate how legacies were made in favour of 'poor young women, waiting to be married' who, without this chance windfall, risked remaining unmarried for ever. During the turmoil of the Hundred Years War many gentlemen had to resign themselves to taking up professions that were considered demeaning; problems then arose when they tried to retrieve their noble status and, in particular, their fiscal privileges.

In Italy the striking examples of Venice and Genoa reveal that nobility and commerce on the whole lived happily together. Even so there was a tendency, perhaps gathering momentum as the spirit of the Renaissance evolved, that made it advisable for those wishing to be regarded as being of the high nobility to distance themselves as far as possible from daily involvement in trade. For

[8] Morgan (1986), p. 33 n. 54.

his part, Bartolus had voiced the generally held sentiments when he wrote: 'Whoever engages in the mechanical arts cannot be a noble' ('Qui facit artes mechanicas, non potest esse nobilis').[9] On the other hand, the *caballeros quantosios* (or *de quantia* or *alardi*) of Spanish towns, although the ruling elite, could at the same time be cobblers or blacksmiths, inn-keepers or butchers, while innumerable impoverished *hidalgos* from rural areas, in receipt of poor relief (*escuderos pobres*), worked the land, were artisans or even, according to the well-known *topos* of later literature, became vagrants or beggars. In 1418, in the region of Murcia, *hidalgos* are known to have been doctors, tailors, furriers, cutlers and makers of carding combs.

The stricter the rules governing the inheritance of noble rank, the more widespread the incidence of biological extinction of the line. In France and Spain, in order to be considered noble, one required only a noble father and grandfather, whilst, during the turbulent fifteenth century, the odds on a noble's bastard acquiring noble status were high. By contrast, in the Empire the concept of a fourth degree of nobility involved a lengthy pedigree on both the maternal and paternal side.

For whatever reason, therefore (and the scale of the problem undoubtedly varied from region to region), the noble class was incapable of self-perpetuation by procreation alone. In every generation there was a short-fall. Yet, in spite of talk of crises, this was remedied without difficulty, even when the prospect of fiscal privileges to come played no part in the matter. This is a crucial point that completely contradicts the 'crisis' theory, despite the intellectual arguments in its support. It seems as though, in the eyes of society, the noble order was the one most worthy of envy. Perhaps it was envied now even more than it had been in the previous century, when the bourgeois and popular classes, especially on the Italian peninsula and in France, had certainly called into question its *raison d'être* through the doubts cast upon the usefulness of its social function. Such sentiments were to change in the fifteenth century, an era when candidates for the nobility were jostling forward in amply sufficient numbers. It was the task of the higher authorities (king, prince) to nurture and control this reaction, which affected society fairly broadly, and to turn it to advantage by means of, as appropriate, letters of ennoblement, patents of nobility, the creation of knights (hence the Castilian *caballeros de privilegio*) and grants of title and dignities. What was important for states was to stimulate, or simply reinforce, the idea among the nobility that it could, or should, be a class devoted to service – service that was naturally honourable and rewarding – in the civil as well as in the military sphere.

---

[9] Cited by Ventura (1964), p. 289.

V

Although the powerful attraction of the noble ideal was preserved, even strengthened, and the noble class showed a far greater adaptability than one would have supposed likely, and was in no way apathetic in the face of difficulties, historians should not be tempted to minimise these difficulties. Leaving aside eastern Europe, the seignorial system which traditionally under-pinned the nobility undeniably experienced a considerable jolt in the fifteenth century, while feudal structures were very often no more than feeble and out-dated relics. In spite of many regional variations and the mercurial economic climate, the fifteenth century could in no way pass for the golden age of landed revenues which, in fact, frequently fell catastrophically. Many nobles felt threatened by new elites who, because they used their legal, financial, adminis-trative or even military expertise to greater effect, were often regarded as com-petitors. Even where representative assemblies still existed (as they did in the majority of states) those institutions which brought nobles together were perhaps less vigorous in 1500 than they had been a century earlier.

However, some nobles did manage to find new sources of revenue (in the service of the state, for example), and eventually the economic situation picked up in their favour. Nobles also acquired at university, or elsewhere, the knowl-edge or expertise which would in future be indispensable for governing or managing men. The upper echelons of the Church did not escape their inva-sion: of the thirty-six Hungarian bishops appointed during the century, sixteen were of baronial and ten of noble origin. At least in the fields of war and diplo-macy, those twin pillars of the modern state, nobles maintained their dominant positions. In fifteenth-century Pisa, a few dozen families called noble provided the city with *condottieri*, castellans, *podestà* for the lands of the *contado*, as well as ambassadors and prelates. The Renaissance witnessed the flowering of courts and the exaltation of the courtier, an individual who naturally flourished in a noble environment, or rather in an aristocratic one. As for their rivals, histori-ans have been stressing how fervently 'outsiders' longed, sooner or later, to become 'insiders', to enter the magic circle by whatever means possible. Wealthy merchants from Burgos, proud of their genealogies and coats of arms, enamoured of fine weapons and wholeheartedly dedicated to the leisures of the chase, were not the only members of European society to be inspired by the example of the nobility. In France, the gradual creation of what would become the 'service nobility' (*noblesse de robe*) in the sixteenth century might be perceived as a threat to the traditional military nobility (*noblesse d'épée*); but it was also recognition of the traditional concepts of nobility: antiquity, wealth, private virtue and readiness to serve society. In the north of the Italian peninsula and in Tuscany, the ruling class combined in fairly eclectic fashion both *popolari* and *nobiles*. Christine de Pisan was thus able to define the Venetian patriciate as made up of 'ancient bourgeois families who claim that they are noble', a description worth comparing to her definition of the bourgeois as 'born of ancient families in cities; their names, surnames and arms are antique and they are the most important inhabitants in towns, with revenues; they inherit houses and estates, which are their sole source of income. In some places the oldest among them are called nobles when they have long enjoyed considerable status and reputation.'[10]

One portrait of nobility in this century paints it in a hundred different guises, fragmented, a mass of contradictions to the point where it would prove impossible to find common ground between a noble duke and a mere gentleman, between a Castilian *hidalgo*, a Scottish laird and a Prussian *Junker*, between a landowning Sicilian baron and a noble Venetian, or between a Franconian *Raubritter* and an English esquire, justice of the peace, or member of parliament. One is entitled to prefer, however, the vision of a noble society which, transcending obvious differences, not only derived from them its essence and its vitality, but also considered itself a single order, *una et eadem nobilitas*, within a society of orders (*Ständegesellschaft*).

Another portrait depicts this century as afflicted by the slow degeneration of an intellectually underdeveloped nobility, economically and demographically weakened, unsure of its own identity and vocation, threatened by states, businessmen and lawyers, reduced to means of self-defence now increasingly far-removed from the realities of the day (and only good enough for chivalric festivals); in short, a nobility on the verge of forfeiting for good its historic role. For this, one is entitled to substitute the vision of the world of the Renaissance, in which the relics of feudalism were gradually transforming themselves into nobility, when, for example, the *Herren* and *Ritter* of the Empire fused to form the *Adel*. In fact, the nobility of the *ancien régime* dates from the fifteenth century. In France, at least, it was to endure until the Revolution of 1789, whilst in the rest of Europe it would preserve its identity and its very essence at least until the First World War.

---

[10] Pisan, *Le livre du corps de policie*, p. 183.

CHAPTER 5

RURAL EUROPE

Christopher Dyer

THE European countryside in the fifteenth century was more sparsely populated than at any time since about 1150. This fact has dominated historical perceptions of the period. The 'demographic crisis' is seen as an all-pervading influence, having its origins around 1300 in fundamental problems of over-population, overextension of cultivation and ecological imbalances. The crisis began with the famines and plagues of the fourteenth century, and its effects persisted in some countries after 1500.[1] This chapter is based on the assumption that this view of a 'demographic crisis' helps our understanding of the fifteenth century, but that excessive dependence on it leads to a distorted and incomplete picture, and after examining the crisis we will turn to alternative interpretations, additions and modifications.

THE DEMOGRAPHIC CRISIS

The population of most European countries suffered a heavy death toll in the fourteenth century, and after 1400 epidemics of plague and other diseases continued to cause bouts of high mortality. These were less virulent and more localised than the initial Black Death of 1348–9, but evidence from Tuscany, England and the Low Countries suggests that most places experienced between eight and twelve serious epidemics in the fifteenth century. Relatively small numbers of children were recorded for each married couple; for example, in the Lyons region from a mean of 3.9 children mentioned in each will of the 1320s, the figure diminished to 1.9 in the 1420s.[2] Such statistics need to be treated with caution, though the general message of a shortage of children is repeated too consistently to be explained in terms of under-reporting. Small families could reflect simply another aspect of mortality, the vulnerability of infants and children to disease, but are likely to derive also from such

---

[1] Advocates of the 'demographic crisis' approach include: Abel (1980); Genicot (1966); Le Roy Ladurie (1974); Postan (1952) and (1966).   [2] Lorcin (1974), pp. 220–4, 504–5.

factors as changes in the age of marriage. At the lowest point of the population decline, which in many regions was reached at some point between 1420 and 1450, total numbers had been reduced to a half or two-thirds of those prevailing before the Black Death. So the population of the *contado* of Florence declined from about 300,000 in 1338 to 104,000 in 1427; Provence could muster about 400,000 people in 1315–16, but only 150,000 in 1471 (after a few decades of recovery). National population figures must be a matter of guesswork, but France has been said to have fallen from 18 million people in 1330 to below 10 million in 1450, and the English population can be estimated at about 6 million before 1348 and 2.5–3 million in the mid-fifteenth century.[3]

The desertion and shrinkage of settlements followed from the demographic crisis. Farms, hamlets and whole villages fell into ruin, and can sometimes now be traced on the ground from the archaeological evidence. In Germany from a total of 170,000 settlements known from before the Black Death more than 40,000 disappeared in the fourteenth and fifteenth centuries. 'Quotients' (percentages of villages deserted) varied from region to region, but reached as high a figure as 60–70 per cent in Brandenburg or the uplands of Swabia. Thousands of lost villages have been found in other European countries, with some quite high 'quotients', such as 38.4 per cent in Provence.[4] 'Quotients' of deserted farms varied in different parts of Sweden from 10 to 36 per cent, but in Scandinavia Norway bore the brunt of the recession – a half of its farms were abandoned, and these tended to be sited in high and remote places, with less fertile soils; the smaller, poorer and more recent settlements were most likely to lose their inhabitants.[5]

As the countryside was emptied of people and houses became ruined, so large areas of arable land fell out of cultivation. In the Parisian basin perhaps 60 per cent of the former cultivated area was no longer under the plough by the mid-fifteenth century. Sometimes this led to the loss of agricultural land, and it was invaded by scrub. But more often pasture replaced the corn-fields, and provided a profitable living for its occupants, who could obtain better prices for animal products than for cereals. In addition high labour costs were avoided as a single shepherd or herdsman could manage animals on an area of land that would, if under crops, have needed at least two full-time and a dozen part-time workers. In some places the change was carried out completely – the former territory of a village, like many in the midlands of England, became an enclosed pasture. Or, as in the war-devastated French province of Quercy, transhumant flocks from neighbouring regions occupied the now empty

---

[3] Herlihy and Klapisch-Zuber (1978), p. 172; Baratier (1961), p. 120; Le Roy Ladurie (1978), p. 117; Smith (1988), pp. 189–91.
[4] Abel (1955); *Villages désertés* (1965); Mayhew (1973), pp. 93–8; Rösener (1992), pp. 255–6; D'Archimbaud (1980), pp. 14–15.   [5] Gissel *et al.* (1981).

grasslands. More often a mixed farming system shifted its emphasis, so that a higher proportion of the land was used for grazing, and individual peasants acquired larger flocks and herds. In Languedoc peasant flocks of 200 sheep were commonly encountered in the fifteenth century.

These developments in farming amounted almost to a new ecological balance, reflected in the scientific evidence of pollen samples by a diminishing proportion of cereals and the weeds of cultivation, and increases in grass and tree pollen. Woodland, long in retreat before the axes of colonists, began to recover lost ground. In the German Seulingswald the area under trees increased by almost a third. The conservation of woods for timber and fuel, and other resources such as game, was relaxed for the first time for centuries – in 1401 the Grand Master of the Waters and Forests of France could proclaim 'Go into the forest, cut down trees, assart, make charcoal . . . hunt . . . rabbits, boars and other wild beasts.'[6]

Agriculture changed to meet the needs of a new diet. Before the fall in population, when the mass of people had to eat the cheapest sources of calories, cereal foods predominated: bread, often made of rye or barley rather than wheat; oat cakes in the uplands; many varieties of porridge based on oats, pulses or barley; and pasta in southern Europe. In the fifteenth century ordinary people – artisans, peasants, even labourers – consumed slices of meat in quantities previously enjoyed only by the aristocracy. Sicilian vineyard workers were given 1.2–1.6 kg per week; English harvest workers received 1 lb of meat for every 2 lb of bread; and even prisoners in Murcia (Castile) were allowed 40 g of meat each per day.[7] Cereals were still the mainstay of the diet, but the more expensive (and nutritious) wheat tended to replace barley and rye as the main bread grain, and a higher proportion of the cereal crop in northern Europe was brewed into ale or beer, or used to feed animals.

Over most of Europe trends in the rural economy reflected the scarcity of people. Grain prices moved from year to year depending mainly on the quality of the harvests, and also under such influences as variations in the currency and the disruptions of war: but an overall downward trend can usually be detected for the first three-quarters of the century. The amount of land under crops had diminished less than the numbers of consumers, so creating an excess of supply over demand. The prices of animal products, such as wool, hides, meat, cheese and butter, either increased, or declined less than grain prices. Wages often moved upwards, especially when calculated in terms of the amount of food that they would buy – workers were scarce, and their value was consequently enhanced. The price of manufactured goods tended to rise in

---

[6] Mayhew (1973), p. 100; Le Roy Ladurie (1969), pp. 122–3.
[7] Aymard and Bresc (1975), p. 594; Dyer (1989), pp. 151–60; Menjot (1984), p. 200.

relation to grain prices, so that for at least part of the period the effects of the 'price scissors' were felt; the nobility in particular found that the goods and services that they wished to buy became more expensive, in contrast to the sale price of the produce of their estates. Rents tended to decline. These were often so complicated, consisting of many different dues and payments, made in the form of cash, labour and goods, that changes are not easily detected. But champart rents, by which peasants, mainly in southern Europe, paid an agreed proportion of their produce, had at the peak of agricultural expansion in the thirteenth century amounted often to half or one third of the crop, were now commonly diminished to a quarter or even less. Cash rents which were fixed by bargaining between landlord and tenant, and which were therefore most likely to be subject to market forces (such as leasehold rents and entry fines), also declined. And payments fixed by custom, such as servile dues, were also reduced, or even abolished altogether after tussles between lords and tenants. Lords had to make concessions if no one would take a heavily burdened holding: in Germany vacant lands might be let under the *Ödrecht*, by which they were not liable to payments for a number of years. In that country and elsewhere the conditions of tenure improved for the peasant – formerly precarious tenancies became hereditary, and the number of years for which leases ran were extended.

These changes reduced the wealth and power of the noble and clerical landlords, and led to improvements in conditions for at least part of the peasantry. The lords suffered a drop in income in a number of ways: complete loss of rent and tithes from deserted holdings; reductions in rent reflecting their weaker bargaining power in relation to scarce tenants; and accumulations of arrears of rent as tenants could not or would not pay. Before the Black Death many lords had been directly involved in some form of agriculture, but by about 1400 the high costs of labour and low price of produce forced them to lease out their remaining demesnes and granges to farmers. Over many parts of Europe the nobility complained of impoverishment, and monasteries ran into debt. Nobles were forced, notably in France, to gain a higher proportion of their income from office holding. In Germany and other areas nobles are reported to have been reduced in number, so concentrating landed resources in fewer hands.

Peasants experienced some beneficial changes, such as reduced rents, and many former serfs gained their freedom. They had the opportunity to extend their holdings by acquiring land cheaply, and are found with two or three tenements previously occupied by separate families. If peasants are defined in terms of the small scale of their landholding, then we begin to doubt if individuals who accumulated forty hectares or more can really be described as peasants. The relaxation of population pressure helped the great majority (who certainly were peasants) with middle-sized holdings of two to twenty hectares of arable, by increasing their shares of common pasture, woodland and marshland. The smallholders (the definition varies from region to region, but certainly included those millions of households with less than two hectares) would have gained from the increase in wages, because they expected to obtain a proportion of their income by working for others. Doubts surround those middling or upper sections of the peasantry who had a surplus to sell, and who hired labour, because they would have experienced some of the problems of profitability encountered by the lords in their agricultural production. But these doubts should not be stressed too much. A high proportion of their crops went to feed the peasants' household, and a relatively small amount was sold, so they did not feel the full effect of falling prices. In general the demographic crisis caused a good deal of misery for those who were widowed, orphaned or forced from their homes and land, but it also led to a downward distribution of incomes and promoted geographical and social mobility.

The changing climate contributed to the crisis. The long cold period which is usually dated after about 1550 was apparently preceded by relatively cool and wet weather. On the uplands temperature changes could have encouraged the abandonment of farms, for example in Norway, and promoted the more general conversion of arable land to pasture. Weather patterns, while not as unstable as in the previous century, still led to a succession of bad harvest years, of which the most severe episode was the north European famine of 1437–9. Harvest failures did not just cause hardship for those deprived of food. They distorted the whole economy, as consumers transferred their expenditure from non-essential items to food, so causing a slump in commerce and unemployment in industry.

Man-made disasters also had their impact, notably the later phases of the Hundred Years War in France, the Hussite Wars in central Europe, various internecine conflicts in Germany and the internal disruptions in the Low Countries, especially over the disputed succession to the Burgundian lands in 1477–92. All of these can be shown to have destroyed farms, villages, crops and livestock, prevented cultivation and trade in agricultural produce and increased taxes and insecurity outside the immediate war zones. Perhaps such violence stemmed in part from the demographic crisis, as the nobility turned to war as a means of recouping their lost income from land. Military activities certainly contributed to the depth of the recession by compounding existing shortages of manpower and capital.

REGIONAL VARIATIONS

A Europe of ruined farms, grass-grown fields, nobles in financial trouble (with a compensatory improvement in peasant conditions), gives only one side of the picture. The varied experiences of different regions provoke doubts about whether the demographic crisis can be the sole explanation of the changes that we observe. We should be cautious of attributing so much importance to impersonal ecological forces.

First, the demography of Europe followed no uniform pattern. The plagues of the fourteenth century had a limited impact on parts of eastern Europe and in the Iberian peninsula, especially in Castile. In the case of the duchy of Wrocław the drop in population and the symptoms of agrarian crisis were delayed until 1425–80.[8] Castile suffered in some measure a fall in population before 1400, but in the early fifteenth century shows signs of growing numbers.

Secondly, in those countries which experienced the full impact of a fall in population by a half or more, recovery came at different times. In Sicily the population was growing by the 1450s, perhaps earlier, while in rural Tuscany expansion is apparent after 1460. French regions generally began to recover towards the middle of the century – from the 1430s in the Lyonnais, and the 1450s in Normandy. In Brabant a decisive upward movement is not apparent until after 1495, and the English population, though showing slight tendencies to growth from the 1470s, did not really expand until well into the sixteenth century, at a time when parts of France and Italy were near to regaining the population densities of the pre-Black Death era.[9] Movements in the size of population are very complex phenomena, depending in part on the incidence of epidemics, for which there is abundant evidence even in the period of population growth, and on the age of marriage, and rates of fertility within marriage, which were influenced by social customs and such economic factors as the availability of land and employment.

Some regions, thirdly, had special characteristics which help to explain their peculiar paths of development within this period. Parts of north-eastern Europe – now Poland and the Baltic states – are often cited as following a course opposite to that found in the west. Weak states, an underdeveloped urban sector and a powerful nobility meant that peasant conditions deteriorated, beginning the period of 'second serfdom', as tenants were restricted in their movement and forced to perform heavy labour services. In fact, the peasants of eastern Europe were being brought under serfdom for the first time (they had been encouraged to settle in new lands in the east with privileges and easy terms in earlier centuries). Enserfment took a long time, beginning in the later years of the fifteenth century, and was not completed until well after 1500. This cannot therefore be seen as an immediate response to any fall in population.[10]

---

[8] Hoffman (1989), pp. 273–374.
[9] Epstein (1992), pp. 33–68; Herlihy and Klapisch-Zuber (1978), pp. 181–2; Lorcin (1974), pp. 209–47; Bois (1984), pp. 49–77; Neveux (1980), pp. 165–6; Poos (1991), pp. 91–110.
[10] Blum (1957); Wunder (1983), pp. 265–72.

The greater nobles of Castile expanded their wealth and power; the monarchy at the end of the fourteenth century had been weakened by civil war, and made concessions of jurisdictional powers to a largely new generation of rising families. In contradiction of the landlords' withdrawal from agrarian life found elsewhere, the Castilian nobles' power over tenants and land grew on such a scale that the marquis of Villena's lordship, for example, extended over 25,000 square kilometres. They took an interest in the cultivation of demesnes, and owned a large proportion of the sheep in the great transhumance system, the *Mesta*, which by 1467 took flocks totalling 2.7 million across the country between summer and winter pastures. In northern Castile new villages were being founded in the second decade of the century, and there was some extension of arable.[11]

These examples have been taken from relatively thinly populated regions which could be regarded as escaping from the ecological problems resulting from 'overpopulation'. However, Sardinia is an example of a place which, though supporting meagre densities of people before 1348, still experienced all of the symptoms of crisis, making us doubt a direct relationship between excessive numbers before the plagues and the subsequent population decline and agrarian depression. The southern Low Countries ought to fit the conventional pattern, because here the densities of people were very high, yet they avoided the crash that in theory should have followed – very small holdings persisted and even proliferated in the early fifteenth century. Not many settlements were deserted in the long term, nor was there a universal reduction in rents. The large and numerous towns help to explain the resilience of a high-yielding agrarian system, based on intensive cultivation of small plots, involving large inputs of labour and manure, and the elimination or reduction of fallows.[12] A survival of smallholdings is found in other urbanised regions, such as parts of northern Italy, where there was some depression in the conditions of the peasantry who felt the uncertainties of short-term *mezzaddria* (sharecropping) contracts.

Districts specialising in pastoral agriculture, such as those in wooded, heathy or hilly landscapes, sometimes also diverge from the trends normally associated with the demographic crisis. An increasing emphasis on animal husbandry came easily to them, and contrary to the assumption that 'marginal' late colonised lands were always more vulnerable to depopulation, the dispersed settlements of the pastoral areas were obstinately long-lived, while lowland corn-growing villages often shrank and sometimes disappeared. The 'marginal' districts were especially receptive to rural industry, partly because their

---

[11] Vicens Vives (1964), pp. 241–57; Dufourcq and Gautier-Dalché (1976), pp. 234–5, 238–41.
[12] Day (1975); Van der Wee and Van Cauwenberghe (1978); Verhulst (1990), pp. 89–130.

resources included raw materials and fuel, and partly because pastoral farming left peasant men and women with spare time to work in crafts. The association of uplands and woodlands with industry is found everywhere, from the mining and metal-working districts of Iberia and Germany, to the cloth-making settlements of Yorkshire and Essex.

The examination of the varied history of different regions suggests that the 'demographic crisis' applies most appropriately to lowland arable farming regions. Even here we must doubt the idea of a cycle of demographic contraction and expansion as the sole explanation of change. Towards the end of the fifteenth century, as we have seen, population levels were recovering, sometimes rapidly. As a deterministic demographic theory would predict, many trends went into reverse: new settlements were founded (in Sweden, for example); arable lands were again extended at the expense of pasture (in the Auvergne); smallholdings multiplied (in Franconia); wages began to fall and grain prices to rise (in Normandy). Yet these tendencies are not found everywhere, nor did they apply to all aspects of rural life. Some of the changes of the late fourteenth and fifteenth centuries, like the rise of the *gros fermiers* of northern France or the yeomen of England, persisted: the large holdings survived and flourished in different circumstances after 1500. Some developments had been proceeding before 1348, and continued thereafter, like the long-term decay of the institutions of lordship and their replacement by more commercial forms of land management in north Italy, or the growth of rural industries everywhere. Clearly structural change was going on in the organisation of production, and the ordering of relationships between social groups, independent of the ups and downs of demography. These lead us to turn to developments in rural Europe which were not determined by population levels, but which sprang from other roots.

ALTERNATIVE EXPLANATIONS OF DEVELOPMENTS

The market

Fifteenth-century Europe had experienced centuries of commercialisation and urbanisation. In some regions (notably north Italy and the Low Countries) a third or more of the population lived in towns, and over most of the continent one in five people gained their main livelihood from industry or trade. Despite the mid-fifteenth-century trading slump, the 'bullion famine' and other troubles, a busy local and international trade in agricultural produce continued, and indeed in some cases shows signs of stimulation rather than depression. Although the numbers of potential customers fell, and the purchasing power of the nobility suffered, the survivors had surpluses to exchange. Peasants were consumers as well as producers; the increased demand for cheap and middle-quality woollen and linen cloth, and iron for tools and domestic implements, helps to explain the expanding rural industry of the period. Elderly peasants in Quercy would make agreements with their successors to hand over the holding, in exchange for a basic allowance (almost a pension), the details of which enable us to glimpse what contemporaries regarded as the necessities of life. In addition to bread grains, oil, salt, wine and pork, each old peasant would receive annually clothing worth £2 tournois (about twice the value of a pig).[13] Cumulative purchases on this scale by millions of peasants created a formidable market.

Production for sale, which enabled cultivators to pay rents in cash and buy manufactured goods, was often conducted on the largest scale on the lords' demesnes (increasingly in the hands of farmers), but also involved a high proportion of the peasantry. Responses to demand can be seen in the changing mix of crops – for example, in England the barley acreage grew in line with the increase in ale and beer drinking. In Germany vineyards expanded, and were planted in new regions because more people could afford wine. But the market could also encourage large-scale regional specialisation, such as extensive rye cultivation in north-east Europe, which supplied the towns of the Low Countries, allowing the peasants of that region to devote more land to industrial crops. During the fifteenth century grain exports from Danzig increasingly reflected the quality of the harvest in the Low Countries. Similarly Norway imported Baltic corn and concentrated on dairying and fishing.

The increased demand for meat, and especially beef, in the population centres of the Low Countries and the Rhineland promoted a large-scale international cattle trade. The animals were reared in Denmark, Hungary and Poland, and then travelled along well-established drove roads, via fairs and other points of sale to the urban butchers. Numbers of cattle exported annually from Denmark increased from 2,000 in 1423 to 13,000 in 1484–5.[14] In southern Europe specialisation in livestock encouraged the development of organisations to manage transhumance, not just the Spanish *mesta*, but also in Provence, Tuscany and southern Italy. Sicilian agriculture developed its specialisations, with the growing of corn (for export) in the west of the island, pastoralism in the uplands of the north-east, and wine production concentrated on the coast. Maltese cultivators found that they could profit best from the commercial economy by growing cotton and cumin for sale abroad, while wheat was imported.[15]

Towns influenced the countryside more directly when their inhabitants acquired land, as they did in growing numbers in the vicinity of cities as different as Lyons and Wrocław. Townspeople regarded land as a safe invest-

---

[13] Lartigaut (1978), p. 513.　　[14] Blanchard (1986).
[15] Epstein (1992), pp. 160–81; Wettinger (1982).

ment, and used it to grow both some food for their own consumption and raw materials for urban industries. Often they introduced no new techniques, but in the case of Valencia urban capital contributed to irrigation schemes and the development of a fertile agricultural region. Townsmen changed the rural economy more often by investing in rural industry, by building mills for fulling, iron working and paper making, and acting as entrepreneurs organising and exploiting the work of the artisan cloth-workers.

The peasants

Peasants accounted collectively for the bulk of agricultural production. They operated within constraints, but were not controlled entirely by their social and natural environment. They defended their interests and made difficult choices in adapting their farming to new circumstances. Reduction in rents and improvements in conditions of tenure and personal status did not automatically follow from the scarcity of people. Lords clung to their power and dues for as long as possible. Also lords and states were constantly developing new ways of acquiring income from the peasantry, and these were often resisted.

The fifteenth century saw rather fewer large-scale peasant rebellions than either in the preceding, or in the following, centuries, but peasants were still involved in numerous negotiations, law suits, petitions, confrontations and village agitations, the records of which enable us to see the issues that troubled them, and some of the ideas that lay behind their actions. Often they were concerned with the removal of old exactions which they regarded as burdensome and unjust. English peasants quietly but effectively refused to pay servile dues like tallage and collective fines, and secured reductions in their main annual rent payment, the 'assize' rents. The Catalan servile peasants, the *remences*, campaigned more publicly against the 'bad customs', by which lords could take a share of the goods of a peasant dying intestate or without legitimate heirs, confiscate a peasant's chattels if his wife committed adultery, fine a peasant whose house burned down, and exact a payment for guaranteeing the property settlement at a peasant's marriage. These customs went back two or three centuries, and had acquired a symbolic meaning as a badge of servile status. The crisis after the Black Death sharpened antagonism, as lords attempted to maintain the old dues, and specifically caused resentment by imposing them on peasants who had taken over vacant holdings. Encouraged by some vacillating support from the monarchy, the *remences* attempted to negotiate composition payments with the lords, and took part in civil war in 1462–72 and an uprising in 1484–5 before the bad customs were finally abolished in 1486.[16]

[16] Freedman (1991), pp. 154–202.

Rebellions against new exactions included the *Bundschuh* risings in Germany in 1439 and 1493 provoked by taxes and complaints of judicial abuses, the *Irmandada* of Galicia in 1467 against growing seignorial dues and bullying, and the revolt in Normandy of 1434–6 where the resentment against taxes was sharpened by the fact that they were imposed by English conquerors. In Majorca, the exploitation of peasant debts by urban money lenders provoked a long-running and sometimes violent campaign against the towns.[17]

Small-scale frictions between lord and peasant were especially characteristic of Germany, where in some regions attempts were made to impose new forms of serfdom, and to encroach on common rights in woods and pastures. Resistance came from village communities, led by the better-off peasants, the *probi homines*, who bargained with the lords over customs, the results being recorded in statements of rights and obligations, the *Weistümer*. The community could back up negotiations by such collective actions as offering money to buy areas of common land or to redeem lords' rights, and by refusing rents and services which were in dispute. In the east such resistance was led by the *schulz*, the official originally appointed by the lords to administer the village. We often see the growing formality of community organisations at this time; in the south-west of France the villages acquired consulates and assemblies like the towns, and paid their rents collectively.

All of this seemed to the lords like insolence and sedition. To quote a Bavarian monastery's court records, peasants 'held in contempt our orders and have also within the holiness of our monastery attacked us with rough coarse words and . . . threatening gestures'.[18] From the peasants' point of view they were gaining self-respect and the ability to stand up for themselves. We can see in their actions and utterances an alternative view of society, emphasising collective values, and advocating egalitarian ideas, like the rebels in the county of Forez in 1422–31 who looked back to the classless society of the time of Adam, and believed that the nobility should work. The Catalan peasants believed in an ancient state of freedom, arguing that the 'bad customs' had been imposed as a fixed-term punishment by Charlemagne. Peasants were encouraged in their confidence and independence of mind by improvements in their conditions and new opportunities; their undoubted successes led them to persist in resistance to authority.

Many peasants lived under weak lordship, or had no lord at all, and even those on whom lordship imposed considerable burdens were usually able to buy land, sell produce and generally exercise some choice in their agriculture. The size of holdings depended partly on peasant calculations of the most con-

---

[17] Dufourcq and Gautier-Dalché (1976), pp. 245, 258–9; Leguai (1982); Laube (1975).
[18] Toch (1991).

venient and efficient scale of production. In contrast with the large amounts of land (forty hectares or more) held by some yeomen and farmers in western England or northern France, middling holdings of ten to twenty hectares seem to have been most successful in Languedoc or Normandy, while smallholdings, as we have seen, continued to be viable in the Low Countries or parts of northern Italy. Historians have often assumed that large units of production were necessary for innovations in technology or increases in efficiency and market orientation. But this supposition is not supported by the ability of tenants of quite small holdings to change their methods. The shift in the balance between arable and pasture, use of intensive husbandry and crop specialisation were also adopted by middling or smallholding peasants.

Peasant society changed, but not uniformly. In parts of southern Europe, such as Languedoc and Tuscany, the labour shortage encouraged the formation of close and complex family units under a patriarchal head. In northern Europe the peasant family was weakened by the demographic crisis. This encouraged migration – on a small scale from village to village, but also over longer distances, leading to the repopulation of more productive land, like the Parisian region after it had suffered devastation from war.

For all of its apparent bargaining strength when dealing with outside authority, the village community suffered internally from divisions between wealthier and poorer peasants, and conflicts between individual interests and common welfare. Struggles broke out between the majority of villagers and those individuals who sought an unfair share of resources (by putting large numbers of animals on the common pasture) or who privatised their assets by enclosure or by cultivating their land in their own style. These problems were not usually resolved within our period, and it must be emphasised that in many ways – the 'poor tables' and almshouses provided for indigent villagers, for example – peasant communities seem to have increased their cohesiveness in the fifteenth century. In consequence they acted as a restraint on the more innovative, ambitious and selfish peasants.

Lords, towns and the state

Enterprise and initiative were by no means confined to the peasantry. The nobility, often depicted as in retreat in this period, in fact actively defended their position. In some cases this took the form of rear-guard actions to preserve their privileges, like those conducted by the Catalan nobles for most of the century. Historians remark sometimes on the apparent inertia of institutions, leading to the survival of archaic systems of lordship, but in such cases we should not underestimate the effort required to maintain rents and judicial power in the face of peasant obstruction. In Germany the nobility went on the offensive, especially in the south-west, by introducing new forms of personal serfdom. Peasants were tied to their holdings, being forced to pay heavy fines for permission to leave, or to find substitute tenants. Some lords insisted that permission was needed for a serf's marriage. Lordship was consolidated by making exchanges with neighbours, so that serfs who had left their lord's territory were brought back under control. Nowhere else in Europe was the seignorial reaction so co-ordinated, but there were efforts elsewhere to re-establish lords' rights, especially at the end of the century.

Lords had to make realistic judgements about their problems, but could still work in their own interests. The reconstruction of the post-war French countryside involved recreating estates, by attracting settlers with promises of large holdings at low rents. In the Paris region lords invested hundreds of pounds in building mills and ovens in order to profit again from the seignorial monopolies. In Tuscany lands continued to be consolidated into blocks, *poderi*, which were then leased out and yielded high rents from *mezzaddria* contracts.

Despite the widespread abandonment of direct production for the market, home farms still produced for lords' households (in northern Italy, for example), and some nobles ventured into profitable enterprises, like the large sheep flocks in Castile or, in Sicily, mills and aqueducts (at a cost of 8,000 florins on one estate) to set up sugar plantations.[19] English gentry in the late fifteenth century invested in hedges and fences when they enclosed village fields, but usually left the management of flocks and herds to graziers or butchers, who paid a great deal of money for the leases of these specialised farms.

The intervention of towns in their hinterlands represented a further pressure on the rural producers. Quite distinct from the purchase of land by individual townsmen, towns claimed rights over the surrounding country, whether by the city ruling its *contado*, as in northern Italy, or by claiming jurisdiction over individual *outburghers*, as in northern Europe. The city of Freiburg bought up woods, pastures and even whole villages for the sake of adding revenues to the public purse, and controlling the supply of resources such as fuel.[20] Towns everywhere were anxious to secure the cheapest possible food supplies for their inhabitants, and used various devices, such as declaring that the central urban market alone could handle the surplus production of the neighbourhood. By such interference in the market, and by individual townsmen obtaining rent charges from peasants to whom they had advanced loans, in areas of a relatively weak nobility, such as Holland, the towns assumed some of the extractive roles normally associated with lords.

Finally, the state intervened in rural society, again as an exploiter of the peasantry, notably in France where royal taxes rivalled and surpassed the burden of

[19] Epstein (1992), pp. 210–22.   [20] Scott (1986), pp. 31–46.

lords' rents. Rulers anxious to maintain revenues, or to avoid disorder, or both, might intervene to protect the peasants. The Catalan example has already been noted, and in Germany we find princes like the dukes of Bavaria or the dukes of Brunswick preventing some of the excesses of lords who attempted to impose personal serfdom. But the state always played an ambiguous role – as the Catalan example shows, the monarchy could oppose the interests of the nobility only with the greatest difficulty. Intervention often meant siding with the lords, by punishing rebellious tenants, legislating to limit wage increases, or attempting to curb the consumption of luxuries by peasants. Only on rare occasions can the state be seen promoting economic growth in the countryside, whether by quelling disorder, or by removing tolls and other obstacles to internal trade, or more directly, like the dukes of Milan, initiating drainage and irrigation schemes, building canals and encouraging new crops such as mulberry trees.

PRODUCTIVITY

Should the fifteenth century be regarded as a period of economic growth or decline? The debate is closely connected to the 'demographic crisis' interpretation: we must decide to emphasise either the overall drop in production, or the increases in the productivity and living standards of individuals. Advocates of 'economic decline' point to the lack of technical discoveries. We do find, however, that methods were, if not introduced for the first time, disseminated in this period. Industrial crops like flax, woad and madder; fodder crops such as turnips and rape; crops designed to provide for new consumption patterns, like sugar, oranges, saffron, hops and mulberry trees, were grown more extensively than before. New commercial vineyards developed in Spain in such districts as Jerez and Rioja; profits might be increased if land was flooded for fishponds (in Bavaria) and in East Anglia by the extension of rabbit warrens. Meadows were increasingly irrigated to give a better growth of hay, and scythes were more widely used instead of sickles as a harvest tool. Drainage of land in the Netherlands was assisted by the introduction for the first time of pumps operated by windmills. Rotations which had been devised in earlier centuries were spreading, especially in the Low Countries: either systems in which long fallows over a number of years alternated with periods of continuous cultivation, or more intensive sequences of crops without fallows, including more fodder crops. Above all, in almost every part of Europe, a new balance was established between the land cultivated as arable, and that used as pasture.

These adjustments and developments did not amount to an agricultural revolution. But instead of judging the century alongside the thirteenth or the eighteenth, and finding it wanting because of its lack of 'improvements', we ought to ask whether the peasants and farmers of the period were effective in their methods of production. Did they cater for their own needs and those of the consumers? Some very high grain yields could be achieved, such as eighteen hectolitres of wheat per hectare (twenty bushels per acre), or twelve times the seed sown, in the areas of intensive husbandry in northern France and the southern Low Countries.[21] Generally, however, yields were nearer to a half of these figures, and tended to decline, reflecting the shortage of labour, and the lack of stimulus from prices. High yields were perhaps not necessary. We cannot regard the century as an exceptionally hungry one. The severe famine of 1437–9 was not accompanied by a long succession of bad years. There were a number of subsistence crises and food riots in Castile, and the period saw hardship and reduced living standards in the Low Countries, but mostly grain could be bought quite cheaply. Agriculture supported a percentage of non-food producers (notably town dwellers) as high as at any time between *c.* 1300 and 1750. This can be attributed to many factors – stable weather, a quite efficient marketing system – but above all to the relative abundance of land, and the enhanced productivity per worker achieved by the reduced number of people employed in agriculture. In short, the agrarian system evolved to satisfy the needs of the society which depended on it.

CONCLUSION

The fifteenth-century countryside experienced a demographic crisis, and the landscape and the social structure changed in consequence. Yet this cannot explain all of the characteristics and developments of the period. The agrarian history of the different regions depended on their farming traditions, social organisation and economic opportunities. Beside the trends consequent on the falling population must be set the influence of the market, the interactions of lords and peasants, and the decision making of peasants, farmers, lords, townsmen and state officials.

[21] Tits-Dieuaide (1975), pp. 82–115; Derville (1987).

CHAPTER 6

URBAN EUROPE

Barrie Dobson

'A city is a multitude of men bound together by a certain bond of society.'[1] Any historian who approaches the towns and cities of fifteenth-century Europe in the hope of imposing a more precise and helpful definition than that offered by St Augustine is sooner or later doomed to disappointment. Even if, which has increasingly come to seem uncertain, an urban community ever provides an intelligible social construct for historical analysis in its own right, it is often painfully difficult to know how to discriminate between the smaller towns and larger villages of late medieval Christendom. Such problems of definition as well as the vagaries of record survival still make it impossible – and perhaps pointless – to try to estimate the total number of urban communities in late medieval Europe as a whole. Thus, although the total number of towns in fifteenth-century Germany has sometimes been estimated at as many as 3,000, by Italian, Flemish or even English standards most of those towns were very small indeed. More seriously still, recent research has demonstrated as never before that the political and economic fortunes of most fifteenth-century cities were endlessly volatile, rising and falling from decade to decade and even from year to year. 'The historian contemplating the economic evolution of this period has the impression that he is watching a relay-race, with the torch being taken over in turn by one town after another, and sometimes returning to its starting-point after one or two generations.'[2] Ironically enough, even the dramatic increase in the quantity of surviving original evidence produced by fifteenth-century towns and townsmen themselves, ranging from the unrivalled taxation records of Florence to the massive civic registers at Barcelona and the guild archives of many of the greater cloth-producing centres in the Low Countries, can sometimes add to these problems by making it more rather than less difficult to detect the most significant long-term urban trends.

Accordingly, and despite many attempts to do so, it has proved impossible to

---

[1] St Augustine, *De civitate dei*, 15.8, still the most common definition of a city in regular use during the fifteenth century: see, e.g., Giovanni Balbi's *Catholicon* (1286, printed at Mainz in 1460), s. v. *civis*. I owe this reference to Dr Peter Biller.   [2] Bautier (1971), p. 176.

Map 1   European towns in the late Middle Ages

make the towns of fifteenth-century Europe conform as a whole to the many and usually contradictory general hypotheses to which they have so often been subjected in recent years. How far were those towns the victims of sustained and continuous economic decline, of a less protracted demographic crisis followed perhaps by an *après-crise*, or of 'the great bullion famine of the fifteenth century'? Were their inhabitants essentially conservative in their attitudes, the incidental rather than deliberate beneficiaries of a supposed coincidence between 'hard times and investment in culture'? Or did the fifteenth century witness the rise of a distinctively bourgeois ideology of a genuinely new type? So insoluble, or at least unproven, are the many current theories of European urban development during the later Middle Ages that the historian of the fifteenth-century town must inevitably rely less upon certainties than upon impressions. Of the latter, not the least significant are the enthusiastic responses of innumerable modern tourists at their first encounters with the surviving medieval buildings of cities as different from one another as Florence and Toledo, as Bruges and Prague. The spectacular surviving historical monuments of these and other major late medieval towns still remain, obviously enough, the most tangible of all memorials to the fact that the fifteenth century witnessed not only a remarkable display of architectural creativity but also the culmination of 'the first – and perhaps only – age of the western city'.[3] In their very different ways, the house of Jacques Coeur at Bourges, the cloth halls of the Netherlands, the *Hallenkirche* of Germany and Brunelleschi's Foundling Hospital at Florence were the unrivalled products of that unique period when large numbers of wealthy townsmen throughout Europe felt themselves sufficiently free from external intervention to pursue their own aims in their own fashion.

Such corporate and individual freedom, never of course absolute and sometimes inherited from an even more emancipated fourteenth-century urban past, was at its most concentrated within the north Italian triangle formed by Venice, Genoa and Florence and, to a lesser degree, among the northern French and Netherlandish towns scattered between the rivers Seine and Rhine. Elsewhere in Christendom, among the *bonnes villes* of Valois France, the parliamentary boroughs of late medieval England and even the more or less 'free' cities of the German *Reich*, urban political initiatives often took the form of 'self-government at the king's command' and were therefore more limited or less sustained for that very reason. Even so, in these less propitious regions, too, several fifteenth-century towns were sufficiently large and self-possessed to create an urban society capable of articulating its own communal values in religious, ceremonial, literary and artistic form. Given the intense centrifugal-

[3] Holmes (1990), pp. 3–4.

ism and fragmentation inherent within the retailing and manufacturing processes fundamental to any large medieval town, such common civic purposes
were often harder to achieve than might be thought. Ironically enough, the
prospects of achieving a high degree of urban splendour and self-assuredness
were nearly always greatest in those towns dominated by a mercantile oligarchy
whose horizons stretched far beyond the local city walls. It is with these, most
interesting but in some ways most exceptional, major towns that the following
survey will naturally need to be primarily concerned.

THE ECONOMIC CONTEXT: DECLINE AND RECOVERY

As the civic councillors of Florence, Venice, Bruges and Barcelona were alike
aware, both urban self-expression and urban political power were always
dependent on a local economy prosperous enough to generate exceptional
wealth, albeit always unequally, among their citizens. To that extent, it is
appropriate enough that economic considerations have come to obsess most
modern historians of the fifteenth-century town. In particular, an ever-more
sophisticated concentration upon late medieval demographic problems has
begun to hold out some hope of discovering approximately how urbanised
pre Reformation Europe actually was. Admittedly, the more closely the original sources for most published population statistics are examined, the more
doubts arise as to the reliability of the data, not to mention the additional dis-
tortions necessarily created by the highly uneven prevalence of tax evasion, by
the vagaries of rural immigration and by extreme yearly variations in birth and
mortality rates. Those allowances duly made, it seems clear enough that the fifteenth century was generally not one of impressive demographic expansion
among the towns of Christendom, nor indeed in any region thereof. Of the
twenty-seven or so urban centres likely to have contained a resident population
of more than 40,000 in 1500, only five (Venice, Milan, Naples, Paris and probably Constantinople) seem to have sustained more than 100,000 inhabitants.
The other twenty-two largest European cities at that date also include few sur-
prises among their number: they tended to be concentrated either in Italy
(Florence, Genoa, Bologna, Brescia, Cremona, Rome, Naples and Palermo) or
the Iberian peninsula (Barcelona, Valencia, Cordova, Granada, Seville and
Lisbon). To these should be added a few major regional entrepots elsewhere,
namely in France (Lyons, Rouen and Toulouse), the German *Reich* (Cologne
and Augsburg), the Low Countries (Ghent and Antwerp) and even one
(London) in the kingdom of England.[4] There are, however, reasonable
grounds for supposing that nearly all of these major European towns still pos-

---

[4] Mols (1974), pp. 41–4.

sessed fewer inhabitants in 1500 than they had done on the eve of the first outbreak of the Black Death in 1348–9. It is accordingly hard to avoid the familiar
paradox that one of the most creative ages in the history of the European city
had been accompanied by a dramatic fall and then stagnation in the number of
the citizens themselves.

However, demographic analysis of late medieval towns has its well-known
dangers, above all if it suggests that there need be a direct correlation between
the size of a town's population and its economic productivity and influence. To
a limited extent the same reservation must inevitably apply to the scores of
middle-ranking regional urban centres – of perhaps a population of between
10,000 and 40,000 – which were usually of more direct significance to
members of the predominantly rural population of the period than the 'metropolitan' cities already mentioned. During the century and more after the Black
Death many of the almost innumerable small market towns of Europe continued to suffer severely from the contraction of the local population they served;
but the larger regional centres, like Breslau and Basle, Narbonne and Norwich,
were now able to compensate by providing their clients with more diversified
economic services, above all by offering a wider range of luxury or semi-luxury
goods for sale, than ever before. However, where successive outbreaks of
plague made the industrial activities of a particular town impossible to sustain
at their customary level, such comparative prosperity gradually ceased to exist.
No fifteenth-century town council could ever face with equanimity the decline
of its most important manufacturing crafts and their associated retailing facilities. In particular, most of the textile workers of western and central
European towns apparently found it progressively more difficult to maintain
their traditional production of woollen cloth at pre-Black Death levels. By
1400, Florence, Ghent and Ypres were already providing the best-known
examples of serious industrial decline for such a reason; but it is less often
appreciated that in the case of many other towns the decline of woollen manufacturing continued well into the fifteenth century. At Louvain in Brabant, for
instance, the number of cloths produced fell from over 2,000 pieces a year in
1400 to only 200 pieces in 1500. As a flourishing woollen textile industry was in
effect a *sine qua non* for the prosperity of nearly all late medieval urban communities, the instability of the market for manufactured cloths in the fifteenth
century presented many towns with their greatest economic problem. How far
the decline in the cloth production of well-established urban centres was compensated for by other manufacturing industries, notably perhaps by linen
weaving and the increasingly abundant 'new draperies', still remains a controversial issue. However, there seems little doubt that during the course of the
century the traditional woollen textile industries of England, the Netherlands
and Italy showed a marked tendency to migrate from the town to the rural

hinterland. By 1500 the poorer inhabitants of north European towns were often wearing clothing manufactured in the Polish, Silesian or Bohemian countryside.

In at least some fifteenth-century towns the erosion of their traditional manufacturing base could however be redressed, as will be seen, by industrial innovation in the field of such luxury commodities as merceries, arms and armour and other metal objects. More important still for many of the middle-ranking and smaller towns of Europe was their continued and now often much-expanded role as administrative centres. Here much the most dramatic if unique example is that afforded by the impact of successive popes on the city of Rome after Eugenius IV returned to more or less permanent residence there in 1443. Within fifty years from that date, a previously semi-derelict and chronically undeveloped city had become the undisputed 'civitas sacerdotalis et regia' of the known world, with a resident population of some 50,000 inhabitants. Elsewhere in Europe, however, the archbishops and bishops of Christendom – even at Cologne or Mainz – were now usually less important than their chapters in influencing the welfare of their cathedral cities. From Santiago to Salzburg and from Toledo to Trier, the material appetites of those chapters, and of the many other members of the cathedral clergy, often did much to protect urban communities from the complete disintegration of their economic position during the century after the Black Death. In even more cases the proximity of a large Benedictine monastery was so crucial to the welfare of its neighbouring town that the burgesses were utterly dependent for their own livelihood on supplying the monks with provisions and a local labour force. In such cases, as at the cathedral towns of Durham in northern England or of Roskilde in Denmark, the leading members of urban society tended to be neither merchants nor craftsmen but rather family dynasties of clerks or notaries who provided the cathedral chapter with secretarial and legal assistance.

Other cities, usually much less fortunately, owed their prominence in the fifteenth century to their role as garrison towns. Even in Italy the course of military operations was usually too erratic and unpredictable to warrant the creation of permanent new towns for purposes of war alone; but there were many European cities, like Carlisle in north-western England, which lived under the ever-present threat of armed assault and tended to be dominated by members of the local nobility and gentry for that reason. Much more remarkable were the effects of war and politics on the fortunes of Calais, in the more or less secure possession of the English crown throughout the fifteenth century and in many ways the most curious urban community anywhere in Europe during this period. Even at Calais, however, with its large if often transient population and its role as the centre of the English Company of the

Staple, political influence was not sufficient to guarantee genuine urban self-sufficiency and growth. Much more significant for the future was the evolution of princely 'capitals' in Germany and in eastern Europe. Charles IV's rapid success in developing a Bohemian political and cultural capital at Prague in the 1340s had an incalculable effect in stimulating the rulers of other central European principalities to do likewise. The University of Prague, for example, was the first university to be founded within the German *Reich* (1348): by the eve of the Reformation there were almost twenty universities east of the Rhine, all deliberately located by princes in their leading towns. Nor was such an increasingly obsessive search on the part of lay rulers for a permanent capital absent in western Europe, either; but it was in the east, and especially perhaps at Moscow under Ivan III (1462–1505), that it reached its greatest climax.

In fact, neither Prague, Vienna, Cracow nor Moscow was a novel urban creation of the fifteenth century. Indeed it can hardly be a coincidence that fewer 'new towns', in either the juridical or economic sense of that ambiguous phrase, seem to have been founded between 1400 and 1500 than at any time since at least the eleventh century. During the later Middle Ages the more peripheral parts of western Europe, like Ireland, Norway and Sweden (where there were only five towns with a population of as many as 1,000 inhabitants) were almost deurbanised. In most of Scandinavia the prospects for a genuinely effective urban network were in effect postponed until the seventeenth century. It seems equally clear that throughout the whole of eastern central Europe even the free royal towns of the region 'had failed to live up to their earlier promise'.[5] Similarly, the most striking feature of Scottish urban history in the fifteenth century was not at all a widespread urban renaissance but rather 'the continual rise of Edinburgh'.[6] Nor was Scotland untypical in this respect. As so many of the provincial towns of late medieval Europe continued to wrestle with the problems of a shrinking industrial base and of inadequate recruitment from the surrounding countryside, so the increased concentration of economic influence and political power within the walls of a few already 'over-mighty' cities is everywhere apparent. Thus in fifteenth-century Sweden the town of Stockholm contained a population of approximately 7,000 inhabitants, far greater than that of any other town in the country. The ever-increasing dominance of London, and of London merchants, within the kingdom of England provides a striking example of the same phenomenon; but so too – to compare small things with great – does the rise to greater ascendancy than ever before of the outstandingly wealthy family clans of the larger north Italian cities.

[5] Wolff (1977), pp. 306–11; Graham (1986–7); Sedlar (1994), pp. 126–39.
[6] Lynch *et al.* (1988), pp. 3–5.

Although many contemporary London, Parisian and Florentine observers often seem to have doubted the fact, it now seems clear enough that it was the most substantial of European cities before the Black Death which remained best placed to face the serious economic challenges of the fifteenth century. In particular, it was Genoa, Florence, Milan and Venice which emerged as the greatest residuary legatees of the demographic disasters which had engulfed their markets and themselves so often and so mercilessly. As the demand for basic foodstuffs declined throughout much of western Christendom, so the market for more luxurious manufactured goods and the commodities of inter-national trade – a market which only the largest commercial centres could fully satisfy – became even more significant than it had always been. Such was the opportunity seized, in dramatic and often spectacular fashion, by the already well-experienced Italian merchants of the age.[7] Despite the intermittently serious competition presented by the ports of Catalonia and southern France, to all intents and purposes the Mediterranean remained an 'Italian lake' until the crippling reverses suffered by the Venetians (including the loss of their strategic headquarters at Modon in the Morea) during the Turkish War of 1499–1503.[8] Nevertheless, the ability of the Venetian and Genoese merchants of the fifteenth century to withstand the ultimately inexorable pressure of the Ottoman Empire for so long is only one of many symptoms of a resilience which made them famous throughout Europe. Perhaps the collapse of the Medici bank at Florence in 1494, less than twenty years after the liquidation of its most important agencies at London, Bruges and Avignon, suggests that by then even the richest Italian cities were suffering from a lack of capital for intensive industrial and commercial investment. However, the Italian urban cloth industry still continued to flourish, even if its exports were primarily con-fined within the Mediterranean basin, to the kingdom of Naples, to Rome and not least to the Ottoman Empire itself. By 1489 the Florentine government was able to send to Egypt highly worked cloth and other luxury items of the sort which – ironically enough – had been the pride of Islam itself a century earlier.

Wherever technical expertise and technological initiative were at a premium, the workshops of northern Italian cities accordingly continued to impress – and often astound – visitors from elsewhere. During a period sometimes categorised as Europe's 'first age of iron', the reputation of Milanese arms and armour continued to withstand increasingly severe competition from Augsburg and other southern German towns: it is, for example, in a contempo-rary suit of arms of the highest Milanese workmanship that Richard Beauchamp, earl of Warwick, was represented in his celebrated life-size copper

---

[7] Sapori (1970); De Roover (1974); Heers (1961); Lane (1944).   [8] Lane (1987), pp. 146–73.

effigy of *c.* 1449.[9] Shipbuilding, like the production of arms, armour and artillery, was naturally among the most cost-intensive fields of entrepreneurial experiment in the major Italian cities of the period; but so too was investment in new ways of increasing energy itself. In 1416 an engineer from Rhodes applied to the city of Venice for a monopoly in the use of a new type of fulling mill, 'probably the first case of a patent granted to an inventor'.[10] In yet another and more neglected field of invention, recently described as being quite as significant as the mechanical loom or the steam engine, it was Florence which by the 1450s had become the undisputed 'optical capital of the world'. In 1462 the duke of Milan was already ordering expensive Florentine eyeglasses by the hundred to give as presents to his friends and courtiers.[11] At yet another extreme, the success of fifteenth-century Italian cities in applying reason as well as technical facility to that most fundamental of urban preoccupations, town defence, gradually revolutionised the art of war from the Mediterranean to the English Channel. Between 1485 and 1495 Ivan III of Moscow was already employing military architects from Bologna and elsewhere to rebuild the Kremlin as an enormous north Italian fortress erected in the heart of Russia.

Nowhere was the ascendancy of the north Italian merchant more remarkable, and to have greater long-term consequences, than in the sphere of trading and banking organisation. In a century when economic circumstances were often less than propitious for sustained commercial success, in their different ways the leading citizens of Venice, Genoa and Florence weathered a succession of crises by means of a sophisticated *pratica della mercatura* unrivalled north of the Alps. Above all, perhaps, north Italian businessmen found it possible to combine extreme complexity of commercial techniques (a wide variety of partnership contracts, the insurance of goods in transit, the use of monopolies, the ubiquity of credit arrangements) with an approach to trading sufficiently flexible and small scale to foster a genuinely entrepreneurial spirit. To take only the most famous example, during Cosimo de' Medici's period of political ascendancy (1434–64), the Medici bank in Florence became something of a central holding company with important subsidiary and almost autonomous branches dispersed throughout much of Europe. The Florentine mercantile companies accordingly pioneered the critical transition, fully visible by the fifteenth century, whereby the money changers of the most commercially active European towns developed into what amounted to directors of private banks. Not surprisingly, even north Italian bankers sometimes failed to cope satisfactorily with international exchange problems and the chronic, if intermittent, bullion shortages of the period.[12] Nevertheless, their financial

---

[9] Stone (1955), pp. 208–10.   [10] Ashtor (1989), pp. 28–30.
[11] Ilardi (1993), p. 513; cf. Eco (1986), pp. 64–5.
[12] Day (1987), pp. 1–54; De Roover (1948) and (1963), pp. 358–75; Munro (1972).

skills and their high degree of literacy ensured that in most respects they remained the unquestionable financial elite of late medieval European urban activity.

Certainly no citizens of fifteenth-century Christendom were more influential than these Italian merchants; and by 1500 they were settled in resident communities within at least twenty towns outside Italy itself, ranging from southern Germany (Augsburg, Ulm, Ravensburg, Nuremberg and Trent) and the Iberian peninsula (Barcelona, Valencia, Seville and Lisbon) to the most important commercial centres in north-west Europe (London, Paris, Rouen, Bruges and Antwerp). In these and the other major urban centres north of the Alps at the end of the century, patterns of urban development are usually much more mysterious than in Italy itself, still often impossible to explain, indeed, except in highly localised terms. Perhaps the most interesting, and most neglected, example of such uncertainties in Europe as a whole is provided by the obscurity which still tends to shroud the history of the very large number of substantial cities in Spain and Portugal. By the fifteenth century there are grounds for believing that over 15 per cent of the total population in the Iberian peninsula were town dwellers. Always a heavily urbanised region of Europe, the gradual reconquest of southern Spain from the Moors (culminating in the surrender of Granada in 1492) was accompanied by increased urban and demographic expansion. By the end of the fifteenth century, trade through the Iberian ports was almost exclusively in the hands of local merchants. Admittedly, Catalonia's previously important commercial relations with the eastern Mediterranean diminished in the years after 1450, partly because of fierce competition from the Genoese and partly because of periods of high mortality and political conflict in Barcelona. The most prosperous city in Aragon had accordingly now become Valencia, the site of a reborn silk industry with close links to Granada. Much more significant for the future was dramatic urban expansion along the Atlantic littoral, where Seville, Cadiz and Lisbon were already thriving ports before the great maritime discoveries of the 1490s. In 1503 Ferdinand V of Aragon had no difficulty in appreciating that Seville, the site of the largest Gothic church in the world, was also ideally suited to be the site of the Casa de Contratación: no European city was to have greater responsibility for the relations between the old and the new worlds.

More important for the fifteenth century, however, and long before the Genoese Christopher Columbus returned to the Spanish court in March 1493 with news of his great discovery, was the comparatively sudden emergence of long-established south German cities as the industrial giants of the European continent. One of the less predictable triumphs of business acumen in fifteenth-century Europe, the famous trading companies of Augsburg, Ravensburg and Nuremberg owed much of their success to their freedom from external intervention and even more to their proximity to the copper and silver mines of Slovakia, Hungary, Bohemia and the Tyrol. Accordingly, the metallurgical industries of Nuremberg in particular provided much of northern Europe with such invaluable commodities as body armour and crossbows, as compasses and hand mirrors.[13] Like nearly all business partnerships of the fifteenth century, the Great Company of Ravensburg (1380–1530), the Stromer of Nuremberg (1340–1490) and the Welser and Fugger of Augsburg traded in all the products for which a market existed. However, although their economic horizons were vast, the fortunes and very survival of these south German companies were dangerously dependent upon the continued existence of the urban family structures which had brought them into being. By contrast, German urban craftsmen, fortunate no doubt to be so often the inhabitants of imperial or 'free' cities, were even more fortunate in being able to profit from a growing demand throughout northern Europe for the products of the latest technology. It was such craftsmen, for example, who did more than their counterparts elsewhere to popularise the use of mechanical clocks as these were adopted with such enthusiasm by cathedrals and municipalities everywhere in the years before and after 1400.[14]

Such technological skill was a less notable feature of the northern German cities of the period; and, for that as well as more fundamental reasons, throughout the fifteenth century many towns within the Hanseatic League were hard put to maintain their cohesion and prosperity in a situation of gradually diminishing returns. Naval and political pressures from south, west and east gradually restricted the sphere of operations of north German merchants themselves; and in 1478 Ivan III's conquest of Novgorod (where in 1336 there had been as many as 160 Hanseatic traders settled within the Peterhof) deprived northern Europe of its most important outpost in the east.[15] However, it is a common error to write off the considerable economic power of the Hanseatic League long before it had actually begun to disintegrate. The diplomatic and naval reverses which they undoubtedly suffered often had the effect of reviving cohesion among those sixty or so Wendish towns on the southern Baltic coast which formed the core of the Hanseatic League. Despite the latter's notorious military and constitutional fragility (during the second half of the fifteenth century the League's general assembly or *Hansetag* only met once every six or seven years), from 1400 onwards it showed considerable tenacity in fighting what perhaps only in retrospect seems a losing battle. By means of an adroit combination of piracy on the one side and aggressive diplomacy on the other, English attempts to penetrate the Baltic were usually

---

[13] Ennen (1979), p. 183; Sprandel (1969).
[14] Bautier (1971), pp. 225–6; Le Goff (1980), pp. 35–6, 45–9.
[15] Dollinger (1970), pp. 294–5, 312.

held in check; and as late as 1449 nearly half the fleet trading for salt in the Bay of Bourgneuf was comprised of Hanseatic ships. Although never sizeable cities by Italian standards, towards the close of the fifteenth century Lübeck (always at the centre of the League's operations), Bremen and Hamburg were all benefiting from substantial immigration from the north German country-side and had resident populations of over 20,000.[16] Nevertheless, by the 1490s when Ivan III confiscated the goods of all Germans resident at the Peterhof, and Danzig was becoming an important port in its own right, the international power of the merchant oligarchies who ruled the Hanseatic towns was already in obvious decline.

By contrast, if there is any one development which did more than others to alter the patterns of urban development in northern Europe during the late fif-teenth century, the rapid growth and subsequent ascendancy of Dutch ship-ping is perhaps the most neglected but most influential of all. Increasingly more successful in handling the carrying trade across the North Sea than their English rivals, by the end of the century cheaply built ships from Holland and Zeeland dominated north Atlantic as well as Baltic waters. Although such intensive maritime activity rapidly began to transform the nature of urban life in the northern Netherlands, it did not necessarily create large new towns as such. As late as 1498, the town of Leyden, which owed its fortunes almost entirely to its woollen industry, was still much the largest town (14,240 inhabi-tants) in the whole of Holland and Zeeland.[17] Nevertheless, there is no doubt at all that the fifteenth century witnessed the progressive urbanisation of the northern Low Countries at the gradual expense of the once highly industrial-ised cities of Flanders (Ghent, Ypres, Douai and Lille) and Artois (Saint-Omer and Arras itself). Even Bruges, at the height of its influence as a commercial and banking centre as well as an entrepot for the sale of luxury goods during the first decades of the century, was soon to lose its primacy to Antwerp.[18] As late as the 1470s, both the English economy and English visual culture, too, were heavily dependent upon an extraordinary variety of expensive imports from Bruges, ranging from alum and dyestuffs to devotional paintings and highly accomplished illuminated manuscripts. During the next thirty years, however, Antwerp was not only to replace but to overshadow Bruges as the greatest international emporium northern Europe had yet seen.

The rise of Antwerp to great city status between the 1470s and the 1540s was generally regarded by contemporaries as the most dramatic urban phenome-non of their age. Quite how such a comparatively small Scheldt port, with a population of not much more than 5,000 at the beginning of the fifteenth

---

[16] Ennen (1979), p. 188; Du Boulay (1983), pp. 115, 164. [17] Brand (1992), pp. 18–19.
[18] Van Houtte (1966).

century, came to dominate the trading activities of all the important commercial nations in Europe is not in fact quite as easy to explain as is often assumed. As late as 1450, when the population of the town had risen to approximately 20,000, it would still have been impossible to predict its forthcoming economic 'take-off' as the greatest urban community in the Netherlands. In retrospect, however, it is clear that the burgesses of Antwerp were about to have both political and geographical advantages on their side. The progressive silting of the Zwin hindered maritime access to Bruges just at the time when the Brugeois themselves made the major political mistake of antagonising their overlords, the Valois dukes of Burgundy and their successor, the future Emperor Maximilian. By contrast, the previous limitations of Antwerp's position as a port (it was – and is – some ninety kilometres from the open sea) were ameliorated by a natural improvement of navigational conditions along the western Scheldt. It was for this reason above all that by 1500 the many neighbouring ports on and around the Rhine estuary, Middelburg, Bergen-op-Zoom, Veere and Arnemuiden, no longer offered a serious alternative to Antwerp as the commercial metropolis of northern Europe. More decisive still was the decision of the Portuguese royal factor to market the products of his countrymen's oceanic enterprises in Antwerp rather than Bruges. The first consignment of pepper and other oriental goods reached Antwerp from Lisbon in August 1501. By that date, moreover, Antwerp had already become the preferred centre of commercial interchange for English, south German and Portuguese merchants alike. To that extent, and despite its very considerable cloth and herring industries, the sudden prosperity of Antwerp was largely the result of forces and initiatives outside its own control. Although not in fact the 'capitalistic' or 'proto-modern' city so often eulogised by Henri Pirenne and others, Antwerp none the less experienced a phenomenal expansion in the years before and after 1500 which testifies to its ability to sponsor a new and exhilarating stage in the concentration of international trade.[19]

What the late Fernand Braudel once termed 'une meilleure organisation des activités urbaines' is similarly evident, although on a much smaller scale, within the kingdom of France as the latter began to recover from the disasters of the Hundred Years War.[20] It may be doubted whether Louis XI's exhortatory 'dialogues' with the merchants of his realm had any appreciable effect on the economic fortunes of French provincial towns; but at least the closing years of the fifteenth century were ones of considerable regional recovery, based on an expanding rural market for the urban goods produced or sold in the scores of small walled towns scattered throughout France. Above all, perhaps, this was

---

[19] Van der Wee (1963); Sortor (1993).
[20] Contamine *et al.* (1993), pp. 390–6; Chédeville *et al.* (1980), pp. 455–71.

the period when – at long last – the ports of the French kingdom began to play an appreciable role in European commerce. The growth of Marseilles, only now beginning to adopt a major role in Mediterranean trade, together with the increased prosperity of Bordeaux and Rouen, of Dieppe and Saint-Malo, all pointed the way towards Francis I's creation of the new royal port of Havre-de-Grace (Le Havre) in 1516 and Jacques Cartier's tentative foundation of a New France across the Atlantic eighteen years later. On the other hand, although most French provincial towns enhanced their role as administrative and social centres during the closing decades of the fifteenth century, it has been argued with some justice that the urban scene in France at the end of the Middle Ages was fraught with lost opportunities. 'The industrial revolution apparently ready to occur by 1540 did not in fact take place.'[21] According to their most learned historian, the development of the 'bonnes villes' of France from the late fifteenth century onwards is therefore essentially a case study in the 'trahisons des bourgeois' when confronted with the centralising appetites of a powerful state. As in England, where there were admittedly less valuable prizes to be won, the leading members of French urban society came to be increasingly preoccupied with the status that went with office under the crown and preferred to invest the profits of urban trade and manufactures in landed property. To that extent, the self-assured communities of townsmen who had constituted the *bonnes villes* of late medieval France were perhaps already divided against themselves and in a state of terminal decline. The *bourgeois gentilhomme* was about to replace the simple *bourgeois* as the more influential figure in the history of French art, culture and letters.

URBAN POLITICS AND SOCIETY: A CRISIS OF CONFIDENCE?

In the kingdom of France, about to become the greatest political power on the continent, the ruling elites of the *bonnes villes* were therefore increasingly conscious that they were no longer in control of their own destinies. Whether or not so bold, and melancholy, a thesis can be applied to western Europe as a whole, it is certainly hard to deny that after 1500 few urban oligarchies anywhere enjoyed the high degree of autonomy and self-confidence so comparatively common among many of their predecessors during the previous two centuries. Indeed, the political history of most fifteenth-century cities, as far as it can be traced amidst their many individual vicissitudes, is probably best interpreted in terms of the rise and fall of such self-confidence. The latter was naturally primarily determined less by the political initiatives of the citizens themselves than by the varying degrees of indifference, neglect or acquisitive-

[21] Chevalier (1982), pp. 151–71.

ness displayed towards them by their lords and monarchs. As it happened, the unique conjuncture – for half a century after the outbreak of the Great Schism in 1378 – of a divided Papacy, a disintegrating German *Reich* and a demoralised French monarchy had provided many of the major cities of that period with an opportunity for self-assertion they could hardly resist.[22] Here and there, however, as in Spain and much of northern Germany, urban liberties were strictly subjugated to the will of the prince at a quite early date in the fifteenth century. Within two generations of the enfeoffment of Frederick of Hohenzollern as margrave of Brandenburg in 1417 he and his successors had made a completely successful direct assault on the franchises of towns like Berlin and Frankfurt/Oder.[23] Not the least significant reason for the decline of the authority of the Hanseatic League by 1500 was the exhausting struggle forced upon so many north German towns by their local princes.

Elsewhere in fifteenth-century Europe, most notably in northern Italy and Flanders, the attempts of dukes and princes to impose their authority upon recalcitrant townsmen by armed force tended to be much more intermittent and indeed protracted. It was accordingly often possible, not least in much of Germany itself, for the citizens of many major towns to retain considerable practical independence, sometimes even including the legal right to resist their lord (*Widderstandsrecht*). By the second half of the fifteenth century delegates from such German towns also often played a leading role in the bewildering variety of representative estates which had come to characterise the government of so many principalities within the *Reich*. Given the urban patriciate's natural vested interest in reducing the miseries and economic dislocation caused by war, these assemblies sometimes achieved quite remarkable political successes. In 1492, for example, the estates of Württemberg intervened to reunite their duchy after a long period of fratricidal strife; and six years later they carried through a political revolution by deposing their duke for his alleged bad government. However, the limitations of German urban political and military power, even when towns associated themselves with one another in so-called leagues, were already becoming obvious by the end of the century. Only under very special circumstances, as in the extreme case of the town–country alliance against Habsburg oppression which eventually led to the creation of a fully-fledged Swiss Confederation in the early sixteenth century, was there any serious prospect that the towns of Bavaria, Swabia and elsewhere would forget their rivalries sufficiently to attain a common objective.

If the burghers of late medieval German towns have often seemed – to themselves and to posterity – more politically powerful than they actually were, by contrast the citizens of the urban communes of fifteenth-century Italy still

---

[22] Holmes (1990), pp. 4–6.   [23] Carsten (1943).

exercised greater influence outside their own walls than they sometimes supposed. Thanks to a high degree of literacy and the prevalence of a so-called 'notarial culture', large numbers of the inhabitants of the bigger Italian city-states were undoubtedly more 'politicised' than their counterparts elsewhere in Europe. Such political awareness could only be enhanced by the frequency of party divisions within the communities, by the existence of enduring political and military tensions between cities and by the gradual long-term process whereby in the years after 1400 nearly all the smaller city-states of northern Italy fell victim to the territorial appetites of the house of Savoy, of the duchy of Milan, of Genoa, of Florence and of the Republic of Venice. By the end of the century the territorial expansion of these powers, in many ways the logical extension of the Italian city's traditional obsessive quest for an economically adequate hinterland or *contado*, had extended the authority of Florence from Pisa to Pistoia and from Volterra to Cortona. Much more spectacular were Venetian acquisitions in the Lombard plain during the eighty years between 1404 and 1484: as these included cities as celebrated as Padua and Vicenza, as Brescia and Bergamo, they inevitably did much to transform the greatest sea-power of medieval Christendom into a land-based empire, too.[24]

Although an Italian townsman's loyalty to his own city usually remained – as today – little jeopardised by this process of apparent political centralisation, it was clear enough to contemporaries that supreme authority in northern Italy was becoming concentrated in fewer and fewer hands. Such a development seems equally apparent within the walls of most Italian cities themselves, especially in the case of the many late medieval communes which fell under the rule or so-called tyranny of hereditary rulers who presented themselves (on more or less dubious grounds) as defenders of their city against external aggression and as custodians of civic peace. A dramatic but not too untypical an example is the way in which Francesco Sforza, a *condottiere* general married to a bastard daughter of the Visconti family, imposed his authority on most aspects of public life at Milan after he became duke there in 1450. But it would be unwise to exaggerate either the autocracy or even the aggressiveness of the late medieval *signoria*. After Sforza and the Republic of Venice had come to terms at the Peace of Lodi in 1454, relations between the various north Italian city-states were normally conducted by means of energetic diplomacy rather than by war. In many ways Machiavelli, Guicciardini and others were correct to interpret the period before the long-threatened French invasion in 1494 as a golden age for political liberty in the Italian city. Genuinely radical popular movements were admittedly less common than they had been in the decades immediately before and after 1400; but the existence of a widely diffused civic consciousness, the survival of substantial local franchises and the proximity of a restless nobility continued to provide fifteenth-century Italian townsmen with an endlessly volatile sense of political excitement unmatched elsewhere in Europe.

Indeed, the emergence of a genuinely novel urban ideology, now usually known as 'civic humanism', within the city of Florence at the beginning of the century had been the outcome of exactly such political excitement. More precisely, and according to the most influential explanation of the origins of the Florentine 'renaissance', the sudden rise of Giangaleazzo Visconti to mastery over the whole of Lombardy during the 1380s not only confronted Tuscan cities with the prospect of a massive military onslaught but allegedly made several members of the Florentine ruling elite fear for the very survival of their city. As a consequence, Coluccio Salutati (1331–1406) and his exceptionally talented successors as chancellors of Florence responded by creating the most ingenious urban propaganda yet produced in medieval Christendom. On the basis of the highly dubious analogies which it was now possible to draw between early fifteenth-century Florence and Republican Rome, it became relatively easy to argue not only that republicanism was inherently superior to the rule of one prince, but also that the Florentine constitution had inherited the values and *virtù* advocated so eloquently by Cicero. Not only did Salutati, Leonardo Bruni and many other members of the Florentine intelligentsia extol the moral virtues of republican liberty in Ciceronian terms but they went on, by a logical progression, to advocate the fundamental importance of the *via activa* rather than the contemplative ideal in private as well as public life. In the words borrowed from Cicero himself which Vittorino da Feltre addressed to a Camaldolese monk later in the century, 'the whole glory of man lies in activity'.[25]

However, although the fifteenth-century Italian cities, and the early Florentine humanists in particular, were undoubtedly responsible for 'this enormous change in moral atttitudes', so profound an ideological upheaval rarely provided European towns with what one might call a coherent political agenda. Even in Florence itself the emergence of such a programme during the years before and after 1400 was as much the result of a unique and transient conjuncture of social and intellectual forces within the internal life of the city as of the fear of military aggression by the Visconti.[26] Sooner or later most substantial cities of late medieval Europe, not least in Italy itself after the French invasion of 1494, had to face the dangers of external intervention at the hands of an over-attentive prince. In few of these cases can it be said that the towns in question managed to develop a radical new urban ideology of

<hr />

[25] Baron (1955); Cicero, *De officiis*, I, vi; Woodward (1897), p. 82.
[26] See, e.g., Holmes (1969), p. 53.

opposition on the Florentine or indeed any other model. The German towns of the fifteenth century, for example, despite their considerable degree of practical independence and a series of long-standing myths to the contrary, 'lived in a state of immense, defensive conservatism'.[27] More revealing still, perhaps, the destructive impact of war and conquest on the city of Paris (under English control from 1420 to 1436) completely failed to produce a sophisticated literature of protest or complaint on the part of the so-called intellectual headquarters of medieval Christendom.[28] However well educated and culturally aware many fifteenth-century townsmen undoubtedly were, by 1500 Florentine 'civic humanism' would have seemed increasingly irrelevant to their practical political objectives. At the end of the century Italian Renaissance values had in any case already proved highly adaptable to the purposes of the princely court: and by a final irony the most distinctive ideological movement created within the orbit of the late medieval town had begun to subserve the purposes of kings and nobles rather than town councils. Perhaps only Venice continued to offer post-medieval Europe a significant memorial to the grandiose urban political ambitions it had now lost.

If not a paradigm for the future, what the fifteenth-century town does provide is the first serious opportunity in European history to probe the depths of urban society itself. It is in the field of economic and social analysis, despite the many intractable evidential problems which surround the subject, that recent research has done most to transform the traditional picture of the late medieval city. Not surprisingly, perhaps, the result has often been to make it less rather than more easy to generalise about conditions of life in late medieval towns than it was a generation ago. Some common denominators are, however, already clearly apparent, most obviously perhaps the extreme inequality of wealth in the case of all urban populations for which reasonably reliable statistics survive. Thus, according to the now famous Florentine *castato* of 1427, the richest 1 per cent of the population within Florence itself (about a hundred households) held over a quarter of the city's wealth; and in the very different town of Basle a few years later (1446), only 72 of 2,841 (or well under 3 per cent) of recorded heads of household were rich enough to be assessed for taxation purposes at more than 2,500 *gulden*.[29] Everywhere in western Europe it seems clear that great differences in wealth did indeed underlie the rough and ready distinctions so often made by contemporary burgesses between the *bonhomes* and the *menus communes*, or between the *potentes* and the

[27] Du Boulay (1983), p. 159; cf. Rörig (1967), pp. 181–7.
[28] Compare, e.g., *Journal d'un bourgeois de Paris, 1405–1449* with Leonardo Bruni's near contemporary *Historiarum Florentini populi libri XII*.
[29] Miskimin *et al.* (1977), p. 9; Miskimin (1975), pp. 149–55; Herlihy and Klapisch-Zuber (1978); cf. Schönberg (1879); Pounds (1994), pp. 277–8.

popolani. However crude and inadequate this bi-partite categorisation of urban society may now seem, it recurs so frequently in town archives from Lübeck to Lucca and Beverley to Bordeaux that it must often have been fundamental to the way in which fifteenth-century townsmen visualised their own social status and political power.[30]

Whether this perceived and persistent fracture within urban society necessarily led to political antagonism and violence inside the walls of a city is, however, a much more debatable matter. In some areas, notably Flanders and northern Italy, endemic class conflict undoubtedly did persist for many decades at a time, although it was generally less conspicuous in the late fifteenth century than it had been in the period of the Florentine Ciompi (1378) or the Parisian Maillotins (1382). Moreover, much of the evidence now available suggests that the 'commons' of many fifteenth-century towns, especially in France, England and Germany, were usually content with the government they received at the hands of their ruling elites. Although violence was always liable to erupt over such familiar issues as excessive taxation and disputes between craft guilds, most town councils were aware of the need to restore harmony at times of social conflict by judicial and other means. Those councils often found it more difficult, as does the modern historian, to form a precise impression of the elusive residents within town walls who were not citizens at all, often pauperised or near-pauperised immigrants commonly known as 'foreigns'. Rarely easy to identify except when they were guilty of violent crime or blatant prostitution, these *marginaux* probably presented no more of a threat to civic order than do the urban predators of modern New York. However, in many large late medieval cities, as in fifteenth-century Paris, such destitute immigrants did offer a genuinely alternative – but not necessarily revolutionary – urban society, while testifying to the surprising strength of the more or less completely unrecorded urban labour market.[31] Only comparatively small and well-regulated cities could hope to control that market and the sustained immigration from the rural hinterland upon which it depended. But then, as urban mortality can so often be shown to have exceeded that of the surrounding countryside, such immigration was nearly always to be welcomed despite the uncertainties and insecurities it might bring in its train. To that extent, it may well be argued that industrialisation was eventually to bring the European town not 'crisis' but stability in its wake, introducing discipline to a previously inherently unstable social order.

How far such instability was genuinely rationalised and ameliorated by the

---

[30] Waley (1969), pp. 182–97; Cohn (1980); Maschke (1967); Rotz (1976); Hilton and Aston (1984), pp. 138–41.

[31] Geremek (1986) and (1987); Gurevich (1988), pp. 176–225; and for the many totally destitute inhabitants of Tuscan towns in 1527, see Miskimin (1977), p. 11.

innumerable craft and other guilds which proliferated throughout all fifteenth-century towns remains one of the great unanswered – perhaps unanswerable – questions of urban history. If anything, within a context of great complexity and much regional variation, it seems most likely that the undoubted social and convivial attractions of a craft fraternity to a town's retailers and manufacturers were not usually matched by any commensurate degree of independent economic or political authority.[32] Increasingly harnessed to the purposes of the civic government as a whole, many guilds – like those of Bruges, Ghent and Lille – transferred their emphasis from craftsmanship to the control of labour and supplies. In any case, the influence which craft and other fraternities often undoubtedly enjoyed tended not to weaken but to strengthen the centrality of the concept and institution of the family within public as well as private life. Admittedly more or less every feature of the fifteenth-century town family or household is also controversial to a degree, not least its size. At Nuremberg in 1431, for example, there was an average of 5.3 members in each household at a time when the equivalent figure for the city of Florence was only 3.8, rising, however, to 4.89 in 1469, to 5.20 in 1480 and to no less than 5.66 in 1552.[33] Although these and similar statistics are uncomfortably dependent upon the reliability of tax figures and the definition of the household itself, they make it clear enough that in many fifteenth-century towns the size of urban families was in a state of endless flux as a result of changes in mortality rates and of the average age at marriage. To complicate the burgess's life-cycle further, much of the surviving evidence suggests that many townsmen of adequate means were first married at the age of approximately twenty-eight years to brides often a decade or so younger, thus creating a characteristic age imbalance within the structure of many urban families.[34]

Not that the residents of fifteenth-century towns would have expected consistency in such matters. They must certainly have been aware, for example, that most major towns probably included within their ranks, as at Florence in 1427, the phenomenon of the so-called 'two-tiered system of household', whereby the households of the richest inhabitants of the city were deliberately expanded to cater for more distant members of the family clan or *lignage* as well as for numerous servants.[35] Whether or not, as has been argued in the case of Italy, fifteenth-century European towns were often dominated by young rather than old men, it is now clear that their servants, too, played a much more

---

[32] The limitations of guild power within many fifteenth-century towns emerges in different ways from the recent studies of the subject by Black (1984), Swanson (1988) and S.A. Epstein (1991).

[33] Waley (1985), p. 247; Herlihy *et al.* (1967), pp. 173–84.

[34] Herlihy (1985), pp. 103–11, 157–9; Kowaleski (1988); for the probability of different urban life-cycles in northern Europe, see Goldberg (1986).

[35] Herlihy (1985), pp. 149–59; Lestocquoy (1952), pp. 86–114; Thrupp (1948), pp. 222–33.

important economic role in the support of their families and the urban economy than has usually been recognized. So too did their wives, daughters and (above all) their widows, especially during the acute periods of labour shortage that followed the plagues of the period. Not surprisingly, it was within the traditional female occupations of washing, cleaning, brewing and baking that women figure most prominently in urban records everywhere. The financial rewards of their industry were usually meagre; and when single women are visible in taxation records at all, as in fifteenth-century Sweden, they tend to appear at the bottom of the economic hierarchy. However, women naturally contributed greatly to family solidarity and, above all, to that obsessive concern with family survival which is the hall-mark of the richest members of all the most fully developed cities of the period. Whether among the *famiglia* of Tuscany, the *alberghi* (inns) of Genoa, the *paraiges* ('equals') of Metz, the bankers of Bruges or the *geschlechter* (families) of Germany, urban rule in the fifteenth century presents us with what was largely 'an economy of cousins'.[36]

When the Florentine merchant, Giovanni Rucellai, made his will in 1465, he instructed his executors that his magnificent palace should always remain (as it still is) the residence of his legitimate descendants. However, few wealthy citizens of fifteenth-century Europe devoted absolutely all of their resources to the welfare of their families, for they were equally well aware that their obligations to the Christian religion were certainly not to be denied. Even Giovanni Rucellai himself commissioned the rebuilding of the upper part of the façade of Santa Maria Novella by Leone Battista Alberti (1456–70) at his own expense.[37] Santa Maria Novella was – and is – the greatest Dominican church in Tuscany, a perpetual memorial to the critical role still being played by the mendicant orders in almost all major fifteenth-century towns. In northern Italy itself that role has always been obvious, not least because the influence of the friars on the Florentine laity was so critical in creating the intellectual ferment within which radical new modes of thought had begun to appear by 1400. Indeed, the great mendicant churches of the fifteenth century might sometimes do even more than cathedrals to suggest that cities were 'holy enclaves surrounded by a desacralised countryside'.[38] North of the Alps it is usually a little less easy, partly no doubt because of inadequate evidence, to prove that city religion had come to be organised 'around the mendicant orders rather than the parish church'.[39] However, the remarkable size and popularity of such now long demolished friars' churches as the London Greyfriars and Blackfriars, not to mention the fifteen friaries of Bruges, Ghent and Ypres,

[36] Bertelli (1978); Du Boulay (1983), p. 141; Chevalier (1982), pp. 197–210; Queller (1986).

[37] Preyer (1981); Hay and Law (1989), pp. 30, 34–6, 42–3.

[38] Holmes (1973), pp. 111–34, and (1986), pp. 45–88; Trexler (1980), p. 5.

[39] Holmes (1990), p. 18.

testify to the significant role still played by the mendicant orders in northern urban religious life.

It seems even more certain that during the course of the fifteenth century the parish churches of Christendom tended to become a much greater centre of attraction to townsmen than had always been the case. During a period of enhanced lay involvement in religious affairs, those churches could offer parishioners and their families a highly flexible and accessible focus for public display, religious devotion and personal commemoration. No doubt for that reason 'there is no period at which money was lavished so freely on English parish churches as in the fifteenth century'.[40] That generalisation, made with London, Bristol, York and Norwich specifically in mind, can safely be applied to many town churches in Europe ranging from (to take only two spectacular examples at random) the Marienkirche in Lübeck to the Igreza de Jesus at Setúbal in Portugal. As the site of the almost innumerable chantry chapels founded by the wealthier members of the urban patriciate, many of these city churches were not only a hive of diverse religious activity but were often highly responsive to lay intervention. In particular, and as so many European towns had become 'over-churched' by the fifteenth century, some exceptionally wealthy merchants (like Richard Whittington) were now provided with an opportunity to transform their modest local parish church into a chantry college, in some ways a curious revival of the early medieval *eigenkirchen*. Elsewhere, as in the case of St Lorenz in Nuremberg, an exceptionally large parish church might become a vast home of civic lay piety whose clergy were directly responsible to the city council itself.[41] Civic initiative in religious affairs is even more evident in the foundation of so many hospitals and almshouses throughout fifteenth-century Christendom; while most of the many confraternities which came to honeycomb the towns of the period were equally generated by the aspirations and values of urban society as a whole.

Whatever the private religious fears and anxieties, no doubt extremely varied, of the townsmen and townswomen of fifteenth-century Europe, there can be little doubt that this increasing involvement in ecclesiastical concerns gave them more rather than less self-assuredness in this world. It could indeed be argued that an increased confidence in 'lay professionalism', sometimes regarded as the fourteenth century's most important influence upon the development of Florence and the other Italian city-states of the early Renaissance, finally proved to be the greatest legacy of all major fifteenth-century towns to the future of Europe after 1500.[42] This was a legacy within which the learning of clerks, particularly the learning of university clerks,

---

[40] Thompson (1947), p. 128.
[41] Abulafia *et al.* (1992), pp. 3–22, 311–32; Du Boulay (1983), pp. 217–18.
[42] Mundy (1989), pp. 815–18.

played only a minor role; but a legacy in which the availability of notaries and scriveners was absolutely crucial. Ironically enough, the practical education received by late medieval townsmen and their wives is often the most mysterious thing about them; but that a vast extension of urban literacy underlies most of the developments outlined above is clear enough. So, too, is the greater degree of intellectual exhilaration experienced by the townsmen and townswomen who enjoyed that literacy in Florence or Venice as compared to those, in the Low Countries or northern France, whose grasp of written documents came later and less securely.[43] All in all, the original invention and early dissemination of printing (from Johan Gutenberg at Mainz in 1456 to Aldus Manutius at Venice before his death in 1515) therefore deserves its place as the most portentous of all urban achievements in a century when urban achievements have perhaps never been so varied and so impressive. The future history of the printing press is symbolically appropriate, too, of the way in which fifteenth-century cities were soon to lose control of their own initiatives. Christopher Columbus of Genoa and Desiderius Erasmus, 'Roterodamus', are most celebrated for the successes they achieved far away from their native cities. By a more fundamental paradox still, the Italian humanists who began by creating the most explosive new urban ideology in European history eventually helped to destroy that community of tastes and interests upon which a common civic mentality must ultimately rest. After 1500, historians who seek to discover a distinctively bourgeois culture within the continent of Europe will find that objective even more elusive to achieve.

[43] Murray (1986).

CHAPTER 7

COMMERCE AND TRADE

Wendy Childs

THE fifteenth century is generally seen as one of economic contraction until the late 1460s and then of expansion, although within it many short-term fluctuations took place. The commercial structure was flexible under these pressures: the trade network, tightly integrated, allowed specialisation; and the sophisticated level of organisation allowed adaptation to the increased need for cost effectiveness in the early period, and to increased opportunities at the end of the century.

ROUTES AND COMMODITIES

Trade took place at local, regional and international levels. Major international sea routes ran through the Baltic to the North Sea, with an offshoot to Iceland. The Hansard Kontors at Novgorod, Bergen, Bruges and London epitomise this great trading area, although the Hansards were not the only ones to sail it. Important routes ran along the Channel and Atlantic coasts, linking Bruges to Iberia. The north was also directly linked to the Mediterranean by regular fleets of Italian, Catalan and Basque vessels, and, later, by ships from England and the Low Countries. Equally important routes ran the length of the Mediterranean and into the Black Sea. Major land routes crossed Europe. The north was linked to the Mediterranean through France along the Rhone valley to Marseilles or over the western Alpine passes; through Germany, along the Rhine and over the St Bernard or St Gotthard passes; or further east over the Brenner. Major land routes also ran east–west, with Prague as one of the major junctions. Prague was linked to Bruges and Cologne via Frankfurt/Main, to Venice via Regensburg or Vienna, and to the mouth of the Danube and the Black Sea via Buda. A more northerly east–west route ran from Frankfurt/Main to Wrocław, and on via Lwów to the Black Sea, its terminus gradually retreating westwards – from Tana to the Crimea, and then to Belgorod (Akkerman) – as instability in the area grew. Other changes took place in the Atlantic. The route to Iceland grew busier and was dominated for a time by the English. More ships ventured

Map 2   European commerce and trade

to west Africa, to the Canaries, the Azores and Madeira. By the end of the century routes were open to the Americas and round Africa to Asia, although, as yet, they were commercially unimportant.

Besides major routes, many minor land, river and coastal routes existed, appropriate to regional and local trade. The multiplicity of routes allowed merchants to bypass war-zones or areas of increasing tolls, and to take advantage of improved roads, bridges and passes. Almost all had a seamless relevance to international trade, since along them flowed the produce, victuals and raw materials which sustained that trade directly, or which fed the people and industries of towns which organised and produced for it.

Luxury goods circulating on international routes were only the tip of the commercial iceberg. Semi-luxuries such as wine, raw materials such as alum, dyes, wool, iron, tin and copper, and necessities such as grain, timber, fish, salt and beer were carried in international as well as regional and local trade. Commodities were drawn from Europe, Asia and Africa, and to this extent fifteenth-century Europe was already a 'world economy', the epitome of which (until its replacement by Antwerp) was Bruges, where Baltic furs, Icelandic stockfish, English cloth, Polish grain, Iberian wine, Florentine silk and Indian spices could be purchased. But through many major towns, from Lisbon to Cracow, a wide selection of internationally produced goods flowed on into smaller provincial towns.

Merchants matched commodities to their markets: Italians bought English cloth differently for Tunis or Egypt, and Toulouse merchants ordered specific English reds for their customers. Producers responded to changing demands, as when fustian weaving spread in southern Germany, and developed new industries to satisfy those with surplus cash; two instances being the use of bronze for cannon, which stimulated the armaments trade, and the development of printing, which led to a speculative book trade. The desire of both merchants and producers to maintain profits in difficult times stimulated cheaper production through specialisation or increased use of new technology (the spinning wheel and blast furnace).

TRANSPORT

Transport, already well organised, regular and dependent on professional carriers, was steadily improved. On land better bridges, causeways and tunnels were constantly being built (in 1480 gunpowder was used to improve roads in the Tyrol), while at sea merchants looked for cheaper, faster, safer vessels, and improved port facilities (stone quays, cranes).

On land much was carried by pack animals and some by horse- and ox-carts, the largest of which could carry a ton in weight. Road surfaces were rough, and difficult in winter, but adequate for large amounts of goods to pass. Speed was governed as much by the stamina of men and animals as by the state of the roads. Over long distances land transport was more expensive than sea transport, but the relationship depended on the commodities, and the perceived risks at sea. In the late fourteenth century a Flemish correspondent wrote that dearer cloth could stand land costs to Italy while the cheaper could not; and in the mid-fifteenth century English wool sent overland to Venice was competitive with that sent in galleys.

Insofar as ships were easily adaptable to most cargoes, and commercial shipping was impressed for naval actions, it could be said that medieval ships were unspecialised, but this does not mean that all ships were much the same. In the Mediterranean the two extremes of oared galleys and round sailing ships were employed commercially, and elsewhere there was great variety of type and size. Galleys were effective war-ships, but expensive cargo ships: oars made them more manoeuvrable and added safety and speed, but large numbers of rowers increased costs and cut hold capacity. Commercially, therefore, they worked most profitably on routes with expensive light cargoes, as in the Levant and Black Sea, but still needed state subsidy. In Venice galleys of up to 250 tons burden were built by the state and their operation auctioned annually to merchants; they were also protected through extra tariffs not only on English wool brought overland, but also on cotton carried on competing sailing ships from Syria. The other extreme was to be found in Genoa, whose interests included bulk cargoes, notably alum. At first alum had been shipped from Asia Minor to Flanders on galleys, but soon cheaper sailing ships were used, which allowed other bulk goods – wines, olive oils and dried fruits – to be shipped northwards relatively cheaply. In the fifteenth century Genoa ran some of the largest sailing ships known to the medieval world, the 'carracks' which reached 800 to 1,000 tons burden. The essential difference between galleys and carracks is illustrated by Florence's new mid-fifteenth-century fleet. To obtain steady supplies of wool for its cloth industry, Florence chose the reliability of galleys, but without Levantine cargoes to finance the outward voyage these proved unprofitable. Elsewhere most sea-going vessels were sailing ships, varying in size, hull shape, hull structure, number of masts and rigging. Hansards ran large cogs to carry grain; ships in the Low Countries tended to be small and flatter-bottomed for access to shallow ports; and Iberians developed the caravel. A development common to Atlantic and Mediterranean nations was the three-masted fully rigged ship.

Shipping was a capitalised and professional enterprise. At one extreme, small ships were owned by one man, who might also be the master, but at the other were multiple ship-owners. The best known of these in England was William Canyngs of Bristol. In the 1470s he was said to own nine major vessels ranging from 140 to 900 tons and a ship's 'galyot' of 50 tons, to have 800 men working for him on his ships, and a further 100 as workmen, carpenters and masons. He was not alone; others in Bristol, Dartmouth or London owned several ships, either outright or in shares. Shares (which could be bought, sold, bequeathed and accumulated) were common and could be held as an investment by laymen and women who had no other interest in the sea. To maintain profits, owners ran ships all year round and tried to limit time in port by specifying loading times for those who chartered ships.

Fifteenth-century navigation skills were good. Ocean sailing was regular to Iceland, Madeira, the Azores and Canaries, and open-sea sailing within the Baltic and Mediterranean. Seamen used a boxed ship's compass, line and hourglass, and sounding lead. Professional pilots were available. Portolan charts were used by Mediterranean sailors, but northern sailors preferred written seabooks or rutters (*routiers*) which provided the information about tides, currents and soundings necessary in northern seas.

MERCANTILE ORGANISATION

Mercantile organisation was sophisticated enough to cope with geographically extended businesses of widely varying sizes, and, like shipowning, must be reckoned a capitalist activity: sleeping partners could invest spare capital, and one man could employ scores.

The Italians are known for using the most advanced company organisation and business techniques of their time. Initially developed to cope with extensive businesses and high risks in the twelfth and thirteenth centuries, techniques were constantly refined. Companies could be formally set up with a fixed number of partners and fixed capital, for fixed periods, and for prearranged interest rates and profit-sharing schemes. Overseas branches were run by junior partners or salaried employees. Money was moved internationally by letters of exchange, and at home local deposit banks made it possible to pay workers by the equivalent of a cheque system. Double-entry book keeping spread, and premium insurance was introduced. The greatest company of the century (although smaller than the Peruzzi company in the fourteenth century) was the Medici company, with a staff of nearly sixty at its eight banking branches.[1] Its founder, Giovanni di Bicci de' Medici, had run a prudent banking and wool shop business, with several Italian branches and one in Geneva. In 1420 his sons Cosimo and Lorenzo (who died in 1440) took over. They opened a second wool shop and a silk shop. Branches were opened in Bruges, Pisa, London and Avignon, and in the sixteen years between 1435 and

---

[1] De Roover (1963), pp. 72, 95.

1451 profits amounted to 290,791 florins.[2] Active and shrewd in both politics and business, Cosimo had expanded the company far beyond his father's ambitions. After his death in 1464, the business gradually declined, and in 1494 it was nearly bankrupt. It is noteworthy that the company's fastest rise came in what are reckoned the most difficult economic years of the century.

Not all Italian companies ran at this level. Many were modest businesses with few overseas branches. Nor were the techniques exclusive to Italians – the Catalans also developed a sophisticated banking organisation, and English, French and German merchants used letters of exchange. German and English merchants were also capable of sophisticated commercial co-operation, as is shown by the large group of northern German towns known as the Hanse and the English Staple Company. Of the four great Hansard overseas centres (*kontors*), three (Novgorod, Bergen and the London Steelyard) developed closed areas where merchants and factors had to reside. In the case of Bergen the organisation was particularly strict, to supervise large numbers of young men who were sent to learn business. In the fourth (Bruges), they lived scattered in the town, but were still strongly aware of their group identity. In Venice the Fondaco dei Tedeschi was a similarly enclosed environment, but there it was for all Germans not just Hansards, and was promoted by Venice in order to supervise German activity and limit competition in the Mediterranean. The co-operation of the northern Hanse towns extended to regular meetings, usually at Lübeck, to co-ordinate economic policy. This might entail political and military action, from embargoes to war, to protect trade. However, as the Hanse grew it became less cohesive. The interests of Cologne, trading southwards up the Rhine, differed markedly from those of Lübeck with its exceptionally strong interest in Scandinavia, which in turn differed from those of Danzig, which found that English trade best complemented its own eastern interests. In strained economic circumstances, the differences often showed.

The English Staple Company illustrates a different sort of trade organisation. At the beginning of the century the Staple ran along lines of a regulated company, passing ordinances to maintain high prices. Reorganisation after the partition legislation of 1429 turned it into something closer to a joint-stock company, in that it was agreed that a merchant's wool was graded and pooled with other wool of the same grade, and when all had been sold, so each merchant received his share of the proceeds. Associated bullion restrictions and political repercussions unfortunately hindered wool sales, and smaller merchants were driven out of business, unable to wait as long as the great merchants for returns on their exports. Regulations were, therefore, relaxed in the

---

[2] Giovanni had made profits of 151,820 florins in the twenty-three years to 1420; his sons made profits of 186,383 florins in the next fifteen years (De Roover (1963), pp. 47, 55, 70).

1440s, again allowing merchants to make their own deals, provided these complied with the company's minimum prices.

Trade within these co-operative groups was normally carried out through family firms of father and son, or one or two brothers, or through small partnerships normally set up for a single venture. Such businessmen were familiar with single-entry accounts, insurance, credit transactions. The English Grocers, for instance, did little inward trade and used letters of exchange to draft money home from sales in the Low Countries. Northern merchants were as aware as Italians of the need for up-to-date commercial news, and the letters of the Veckinchusens and of the Celys show constant discussion of trade conditions and political news. While their paperwork was less sophisticated than the most advanced Italian practices, it was adequate to run businesses in several places through servants and agents. They operated on a scale comparable to many lesser Italian partnerships, and used Italian bankers if necessary.

The Veckinchusen business illustrates the possibilities for medium-sized Hansard firms. The brothers Sivert and Hildebrand began in Reval, and benefited from family connections in the Hanse towns of Dorpat, Riga, Lübeck and Cologne, as well as in Bruges and Ghent. They moved westwards, and in the 1390s both were in Bruges. Sivert eventually settled in Lübeck, while Hildebrand, who also became a citizen of Lübeck, remained in Bruges. He sometimes travelled, but normally directed trade from Bruges, much of it on credit. The Veckinchusens primarily dealt in northern areas – along the Baltic coast, in Flanders, Frankfurt/Main and Cologne – but in 1407, with a capital of 5,000 marks, they also set up a 'Venice Society' to supply their northern markets.

The letters of the Cely family reveal similar business practices, although their geographical reach was smaller. Richard, his three sons and their cousin moved regularly between London and Calais, and visited Bruges, Bergen-op-Zoom and Antwerp. They similarly dealt for credit, and were familiar with transferring money by letter of exchange. They also branched out in a small way, buying their own ship and entering the Bordeaux wine trade. They were comfortably off and had interests similar to that of the country gentry from whom they bought their wool. Other English merchants ran businesses stretching to Danzig, Bruges, Iceland, Bordeaux and Iberia through factors and agents; some even sent their own wool to the Mediterranean through Italian factors.

Southern Germany, which offered extensive opportunities as Italian links grew with eastern Europe, also provides examples of large German companies in the Great Regensburg company and the Fugger company. The latter originated in the fustian industry of Augsburg, and developed in trade, finance and mining under a group of able brothers, especially Jacob Fugger. The firm collected papal taxes and lent to the Habsburg dukes and the Hungarian king.

Their loans were secured on silver and copper mines, which were made productive by further Fugger investment in new technology. They opened branches in Italy, the Low Countries, Germany, Silesia, Poland and Livonia and rose to immense wealth in the expansion of the early sixteenth century. However, the most spectacular personal rise in the fifteenth century was undoubtedly that of Jacques Coeur in France. Starting as a prosperous fur dealer in Bourges in the 1420s, in thirty years he built a widespread business and financial empire. He plunged into international trade in 1432 by buying two galleys and moving into the high-risk but profitable Levantine trade. He leased mines, and bought a paper mill. He owned property in Montpellier, Marseilles, Bourges and in the country. He was ennobled in 1440, and his loans helped the French king defeat the English in Normandy. Coeur's crash in 1451 was for political reasons (too fast a rise bred resentment), not commercial or financial ineptitude, and his fortune was alleged to be 1 million gold crowns (the equivalent of over £200,000 sterling at that time). As with Cosimo de' Medici, Coeur's fastest period of expansion came in what is reckoned the worst of the recession, but whereas Cosimo showed prudence and steady growth, Coeur appears to show exhilarating energy in seizing every opportunity offered, whatever the risk. Obviously, both styles could succeed even in difficult times.

INFRASTRUCTURE

Coeur's rise was extraordinary in that it occurred not only at a time usually seen as one of recession, but also in a country said to have been most hard hit by war. Yet what it illustrates is the essential soundness of the traditional European commercial structure. Merchants worked in well-known markets which, with energy, skill, foresight and a modicum of luck, could be harnessed to success. All large towns now had permanent wholesale and retail outlets. Sea and land transport operated all the year round, although certain commercial rhythms remained for seasonal goods such as wine, fish or wool clips. Fairs were less important than they had been in the thirteenth century, but survived alongside the permanent markets, giving opportunities to meet a number of customers and suppliers together, to see a broad supply of goods and to clear debts. The English wool Staplers regularly used the four main fairs in the Low Countries: the Easter and winter ('cold mart') fairs at Bergen-op-Zoom and the Whitsun (Sinxen) and autumn (Bammis) fairs in Antwerp. Major fairs, such as those at Frankfurt and Geneva, also developed at major junctions on the routes between the advanced west and expanding east. Fairs were worth manipulating, and Louis XI vigorously promoted Lyons as an alternative to Geneva, prompting the Medicis to move their branch from Geneva to Lyons by 1466.

As Louis's action shows, governments were keen to encourage trade, which they saw as a lever in diplomacy and, above all, as a source of revenue. The basic purpose of government was seen in the Middle Ages to be the provision of peace and internal order. Success in this alone benefited merchants, but the increasingly centralised governments of the late Middle Ages went further, and offered specific commercial protection through legislation and effective law courts. Not all government action was protective to all merchants. Governments might favour one interest or group above another, sometimes with formal charters of privileges, and consequently some of their actions were seen by some merchants as government interference. Not all mercantile legislation, therefore, was scrupulously observed. However, extra taxes and the manipulation of trade were, for many merchants, reasonably balanced by stability and the protection of courts.

Regular trade, backed by political stability, allowed commercial specialisation. The specialisation of shipping, based on the transport of particular goods, has been noted above. The specialisation of commodities was also an integral part of the European economy. Areas specialised because of natural resources, or because of human decisions to manipulate their environment. Thus around Bordeaux and in the Rhone valley vines were grown to the detriment of grain. Woad was grown in large quantities in Toulouse and provided a further profitable enterprise to merchants from Burgos, who shipped it alongside Biscay iron and the Mesta's wool, to become some of the richest merchants in Castile. Livestock specialisation included the activity of the Spanish Mesta, whose transhumance routes were protected by royal charters. Cereal specialisation is evident in the trade from eastern Europe, while in Madeira planters chose to turn from cereals to sugar, substantially undermining the former Mediterranean trade.[3] Human choice also developed industrial centres, whether of Flemish woollens, Augsburg fustian, Hainault linen or Florentine silk.

Widespread use of credit and the transfer of money by letter of exchange have already been noted. Reliable markets and transport allowed the development of banking, based on exchange. Lending for certain gain was prohibited by the Church, but lending in one currency and being paid in another always carried a certain element of risk and thus fell outside the Church's prohibition. Certain money markets were so predictable that the risk was small, and lending through letters of exchange (real and fictitious) became a regular part of business. It allowed companies like the Medici to become international bankers as well as commodity traders. Specie was still used in insecure markets (which included Russia as far as the Hansards were concerned), for final accounting, or where trade was in chronic imbalance (notably the Levant). Barter was also

---

[3] Rau and Macedo (1962), p. 14.

used in some peripheral markets, such as Iceland, or at times of shortage and glut.

MERCHANT STATUS AND WEALTH

Merchants might become very wealthy, but their status remained ambivalent. The Church taught that they could not avoid sin. Breach of contract (and therefore of oath), lying, cheating, avarice and adultery seemed inevitable portions of mercantile life, but deathbed penitence and restitution, and good works during life, might help. The aristocracy with wealth based in land and rents tended to look down on merchants, and even in Italian cities there was a recognition of an older nobility, conscious of having its origins in land and rents, and a newer one, based wholly on trade. None the less, mobility occurred: in England the de la Poles, dukes of Suffolk, had quite recent mercantile origins; lesser landed families might send younger sons to make their fortunes in commerce; and all over Europe merchants reached positions of influence in politics and courts. Although imprudent or unlucky merchants could fail, in the fifteenth century, as before, the appellation 'merchant' normally called forth an image of comfortable wealth and dignity.

Many merchants had surplus wealth for conspicuous consumption. Some became patrons of the arts and have left us more permanent signs of their passing than records of rich tables and wardrobes. Some focused on church memorials, among which William Canyngs's chantry in St Mary Redcliffe, Bristol, and the memorials of the Castro and Maluenda families in Burgos still testify to their taste and wealth. As in previous centuries, others contributed to major secular buildings: the wealth of London's fifteenth-century merchants provided a spacious guildhall, although one not so grand, perhaps, as those of the great towns of the Low Countries. Others poured their money into private palaces. Jacques Coeur's magnificent house in Bourges, built in the 1450s with an eye to family comfort, was ornate with sculptures inside and out. At about the same time Cosimo de' Medici, a great book-collector and patron of artists, was building his new palace in Florence. Outwardly austere, the palace must have been spectacular inside, as Cosimo commissioned work for it from Benozzo Gozzoli, Paolo Uccello, Donatello, and Rogier van der Weyden. After his death, the family continued its patronage, and in 1467 commissioned Hans Memling in Bruges to paint a Last Judgement to be sent to Florence. Below this level, merchants' houses of comfortable size survive in towns all over Europe.

DYNAMICS OF THE FIFTEENTH CENTURY

Already it will be clear that the commercial world of the fifteenth century was far from static. In each section above there is mention of change – not all in the same direction, and not all at the same pace. Much change would be expected over a century, as new competitors challenged old centres, as new styles appeared and as specific circumstances encouraged or hindered trade in particular places. However, historians also perceive general pressures on the economy, common to many areas, producing contraction in the early century and allowing expansion at the end. The evidence is both patchy and difficult to interpret, and, not surprisingly, the scale, duration and even the existence of the contraction have provoked much debate. Some historians have seen the contraction as severe and long enough to be called depression; a few already identify expansion after the severe problems of the late fourteenth century; but many prefer the more neutral term 'contraction', pointing to major differences in response, which make an overall picture of decline and malaise inappropriate. Much of eastern Europe, although economically less advanced than the west, was unaffected by contraction, and continued to expand throughout the century, and in the west, whenever immediate disasters receded, the economy began to recover, indicating resilience and a sound infrastructure. Some sectors of the economy and some areas did well, but whether they made up for decline elsewhere is often impossible to say. English cloth exports are an excellent example of expansion. They rose from 40,000 cloths a year at the beginning of the century to nearly 60,000 cloths a year in the 1440s and, after a slump to about 35,000 (still far higher than in mid-fourteenth century) in the 1450s, returned to 60,000 before the end of the century. In 1380 cloths sold in Toulouse were 80 per cent Flemish and Brabantine; in 1430 they were 80 per cent English. But, while English cloth output rose, English wool exports and the volume of Flemish cloth declined. An area of quick recovery or adjustment appears to be northern Italy, where Milan developed a major arms industry, Genoa advanced in western Mediterranean trade and Venice increased her share of Levantine trade. Certain junctions of trade routes continued to prosper because the remaining trade was concentrated in them (Venice, Bruges); others, especially in Germany, developed as trade increased between west and east (Frankfurt/Main, Augsburg, Nuremberg).

If there was a general contraction in western Europe, what caused it? While there is not yet a consensus on their precise effects, three problems are identified, which affected all Europe to some extent. How a locality responded depended on its resources and infrastructure, and on the conjunction of the problems in that area. Although it has been said that every expansion carries within it the seeds of its own destruction through saturation or exhaustion, the problems identified are to a large extent 'external' – demographic changes, bullion shortages and warfare.

Trade responded broadly to fluctuations in population. Population, and thus demand and production, were low at the beginning of the century.

Demographic decline had probably begun in the early fourteenth century, and was accelerated by plague after 1348. The great epidemics were over by 1400 but many towns continued to experience small outbreaks: Barcelona eleven times between 1396 and 1437; Paris eight times during the years 1414–39. Towns repaired numbers by immigration, encouraging a drift from country to town, and from marginal to better lands, leaving areas underpopulated. In many regions of western Europe the population declined by one third to one half, in some cases even more, and remained low. Inevitably such a decline in consumers and producers meant a contraction of demand and production and, thus, in the volume of trade, especially in necessities. However, low grain prices, normally indicating agricultural recession, are sometimes overestimated as an indicator of more general economic recession in this century. It is true that great agricultural producers who had relied on grain profits suffered, and that lesser men who now enlarged their tenancies or obtained them for the first time did so in a time when they could not benefit from rising prices. Yet, for those who had had nothing before, to be self-sufficient in food or to have a surplus, however small, released energy for extra earning and increased opportunities for spending. Moreover, landholders at all levels could move out of cereals to more profitable crops, shifting to livestock or market gardening near towns, or to cash crops, such as woad, madder or flax. Cabbages, garlic and onions became a steady import to England from the Low Countries; cattle were driven to Hamburg from Ribe in Denmark; in Spain the Mesta's flocks rose to 2.7 million sheep in 1467. While turning its own land to more profitable crops, western Europe could still enjoy cheap grain from eastern Europe. Thus, while the total volume of agricultural production and trade fell in the west, its value fell much less. Evidence concerning the textile trade is similarly complex. International 'mass' markets for cheap woollens exported from the Low Countries southwards in the thirteenth century disappeared in the fourteenth, and did not reappear in the early fifteenth. The lost volume was probably not made up by increased production elsewhere, but the increasing concentration on expensive woollen cloth in Flanders and Florence, and increasing amounts of fustian, linen, silk and velvet, meant that the value of the textile trade had similarly fallen far less than its volume, and in some regions might be greater. Moreover, an increasing demand for luxuries of all sorts, whether furs from Russia, paintings and tapestries from Flanders, silks, glass or jewellery from Italy, is clear in most of Europe.

Evidence of declining volume has, therefore, to be set against changing patterns of trade, and the precise effect of declining population provokes considerable differences of view between historians. Some emphasise the drop in the volume of trade, others the adaptability of the economy, although the two views are not incompatible. The emphasis tends to reflect the areas studied.

Historians of northern Europe and especially of England recognise the growth of conspicuous consumption and the luxury industries, but tend to emphasise a rising standard of living through higher wages and larger rural tenancies, and the continued widespread although moderate prosperity of merchants. In southern Europe, on the other hand, emphasis is placed on the high demand for luxuries and the increasing gap between rich and poor. This possibly reflects the more urban economy where urban oligarchies also more effectively controlled wages, and possibly also a poorer peasantry produced by the crop-sharing structure of the southern countryside.

The second problem, bullion shortage, although never ignored, was paid less attention a generation ago when the debate focused on the effects of population changes. Recently its impact has been better appreciated, and the worst shortage has been placed in the late 1450s and 1460s. Silver was lost through general wear and tear[4] and accidental loss. Some was taken out of circulation by hoarding, either as prudent saving or by keeping silver as plate, a practice likely to increase in a period of luxurious living. Fear, often the result of war, encouraged further hoarding, particularly if coinage was debased. Such hoarding contributed to yet further shortages of specie. Bullion also flowed eastwards, for northern furs and above all for eastern spices and luxuries. Eastern imports were increasingly offset by the export of manufactured goods, and of supplies such as olive oil and even dyes which had once come from the Levant, but the trade never balanced. While Europe's supply of silver was abundant this did not greatly matter, but when silver production declined at the turn of the fourteenth and fifteenth centuries, the outflow eastwards began to tell. Gold was an inappropriate substitute in local trade, although it might be substituted in the Levant trade if the gold–silver ratio was attractive.[5] Credit could only substitute for temporary shortages, since long-term tight money inevitably led to tight credit and higher interest rates. These rose about 2 per cent, and while 12 per cent on commercial loans was not particularly high, it was considerably higher than a century before,[6] and enough to help dampen demand. The bullion shortage was not uniform, depending on local resources and the flow of trade. England and Venice managed to keep stable currencies despite some problems. English fears of shortages were expressed in legislation against credit in international trade, and in the contemporary literary criticism of Venetian credit dealings in England,[7] but trade was sufficiently well balanced to tide the country over. Venice too had problems but, since much of the bullion sent to the Levant flowed through it, the shortage was partially hidden. Venice also benefited from modest supplies of silver from neighbour-

---

[4] Estimated as about 2.5 per cent a decade (Spufford (1988), p. 345 and note).

[5] Spufford (1988), p. 354.   [6] Spufford (1988), pp. 347–8.

[7] *Libelle* (written 1436), lines 396–455.

ing Bosnia and Serbia until the Turkish conquests there. Yet even in Venice in 1464 it was reported that the city was temporarily without silver coinage which had all been sent to Syria. A similarly acute crisis hit Valencia in 1451 when it was reported that two galleys could find no buyers whatsoever for their cargoes. Elsewhere shortages and war led to debasement. This caused less immediate damage to merchants than to those dependent on fixed rents for income. Unless merchants found themselves straddling a new debasement with an imbalance of letters of exchange or credit transactions, their gains eventually balanced losses – exports became more competitive, and consumers paid the higher import prices. None the less, although the intensity varied, bullion shortages were a substantial problem, especially in the 1450s and 1460s, and undoubtedly helped slow demand and undermine mercantile confidence. In the end shortages brought their own relief by encouraging prospecting and improved technology, and from the 1460s silver began to flow from new mines in Saxony and the Tyrol, and from reworked mines at Kutná Hora and Goslar.

War was the third major problem, but was intermittent and geographically patchy in its full effect. It had always haunted merchants. While some benefited from army victualling, the iron trade and armaments industries, most suffered, either directly from market closures, or indirectly from disrupted routes, impressed ships, increased piracy and brigandage, increased taxation and currency manipulations. In the fifteenth century states were better organised, better able to raise money and men and, thus, to wage war on a larger scale. Yet they could not control the forces they unleashed, and 'free companies' operated, especially in France and northern Italy. All over western Europe merchants had to cope with disrupted markets in the last stages of the Hundred Years War between England and France, whose kings allied variously with Portugal, Castile, Burgundy (whose duke inherited Flanders, then Brabant, Holland and Zeeland) and Genoa. At its end, England temporarily suffered by losing her semi-tied markets in Gascony, but the rest of France benefited from the cessation of war and its inevitable effects on French soil. Further south, rivalries between the Italian city-states led to almost continuous war. Venetian expansion on the mainland brought compulsory war loans between 1431 and 1441 estimated to have taken 28 per cent per annum of the assessed wealth of her citizens. Taxes recirculated through wages and payments for supplies, loans were eventually repaid or drew interest, but both hampered trade. In the north tensions between England and the Hanse led to the English seizure in 1449 of about sixty Hansard ships in the Channel, and to open war in 1468–72, a war which also exposed internal Hansard dissension when Cologne refused to follow Lübeck's lead. The Hussite wars disrupted Bohemian trade, and, further east, the expansion of the Ottoman Turks, to whom Constantinople fell in 1453, substantially disrupted Black Sea and Levant routes. Even there, trade did not cease, but risks and costs increased. Venice withstood these best, and ended the century as the dominant European power in the east, carrying perhaps two-thirds of Europe's Levantine trade, compared with one third at the beginning of the century.

It is not surprising that there are differences of opinion on the early fifteenth-century economy. It was complex, with many variables but few statistics, and the three general problems varied in intensity according to area and time. The population decline, which did not affect the east, was at its worst early in the century; the bullion shortage was most severe in mid-century, and war was intermittent. There is more agreement about the expansion which began sometime after mid-century, allowing western and eastern Europe to expand in tandem for the rest of the century. The exact date of the change might be rather fruitlessly debated, since, again, local circumstances slowed or speeded recovery, but by the late 1460s and 1470s the silver shortage had passed and in most areas the population was showing signs of growth. Bullion and population expansion together drove expansion. English cloth exports, having reached 60,000 cloths a year again in 1497–8, rose to 90,000 in 1507–8. Bordeaux, which had seen only 162 ships loading wine in 1448–9, received 310 in 1481, and 587 in 1509. Other fields of expansion included the new printing industry and book trade, the busy Baltic trade where the Øresund tolls show 795 ships to have passed in 1497, and 1,222 in 1503, and the ever-expanding exploration of west Africa and the Atlantic Islands, culminating in the 1490s in the discovery of America and the sea route to Asia. Even in expansion, some lost as others won. The Hansards lost control of Baltic and Scandinavian trade to increased Dutch and English competition, although trade through Hansard towns expanded; Bruges finally lost to Antwerp; the provincial towns of England lost to London; and the wealthy merchants of Burgos would soon lose to Seville. With hindsight we can see the opening of sea routes to America and Asia as symbols of a new era, with the commercial centre of gravity moving inexorably westwards towards the development of a truly 'world economy'. Yet the sea-going and mercantile skills which produced this new era were those already familiar, honed and refined during both the difficult early and the prosperous later years of the fifteenth century.

CHAPTER 8

WAR

Christopher Allmand

'WHAT a gratifying activity war is, for many are the splendid things heard and seen in the course of it, and many are the lessons to be learned from it.' Such was the chivalric language, used by Jean de Bueil, author of *Le Jouvencel*, in the mid-fifteenth century, to describe the feelings of those who participated in military activity.[1] War, however, was more than an opportunity for physical excitement or the chance to win reputation through deeds worthy of being recorded for the benefit of others. War was widely regarded as a way of securing peace and justice: 'he who desires peace, let him prepare for war',[2] Vegetius had written in the late fourth century, an approach echoed by Jean de Bueil when he wrote that 'when war is fought in a good cause, then it is fought for justice and the defence of right'[3] which might be legal, feudal, dynastic, in most cases 'historic' in some sense of that word. War was a last resort, a final, legitimate means of securing and maintaining justice. By the same token, victory was viewed as a sign from Heaven: God attributed victory to those whose cause was just.

Yet not all wars were waged in the name of justice as they often were in the kingdoms of northern Europe. Conflicts in northern Italy arose out of the need of city-states to protect their *contadi*, or surrounding districts, from which came men, foodstuffs and raw materials, and upon which local prosperity and survival depended; others were intended to defend or further commercial interests through the control of vital geophysical features such as ports and rivers; others still pitted men of ambition against those determined to deny them power. Thus Florence stood up against what was presented, in humanistic language, as the tyranny of Visconti Milan; later, it was in rivalry with Pisa over access to the sea down the river Arno; while its war against Lucca in 1429 was justified as achieving the security of the city and the sources of its wealth.

---

[1] 'C'est joyeuse chose que la guerre; on y voit beaucoup de bonnes choses, et y apprent moult de bien' (Bueil, *Jouvencel*, II, p. 20).

[2] 'Qui desiderat pacem, praeparet bellum' (*Epitoma rei militaris*, bk III, Preface).

[3] 'Quant elle est en bonne querelle, c'est justice, c'est deffendre droicture' (Bueil, *Jouvencel*, II, p. 20).

In the north-east of the peninsula the territorial ambitions of Venice brought it into conflict with others as it extended its dominion on to the mainland (*terraferma*), while it also sought to defend its commercial interests as these were threatened in the Adriatic Sea. The very nature of north Italian society, centred as it was upon manufacture, commerce and trade which needed extending and defending, dictated the purpose of war both within the peninsula and on the waters surrounding it. Lacking, as they did, the central authority of the great monarchies, the states of Italy all too readily resorted to war as a means of achieving their ambitions or protecting their interests.

Differences between religious and social systems lay behind wars fought mainly at the extremities of Europe. In the south-east, in what was regarded as both a holy war and an opportunity for territorial conquest, the Turkish army triumphed at Varna (1444) and again at Kosovo (1448), thus helping to keep the crusading light alive. The swearing of the Oath of the Pheasant at the Burgundian court at Lille in 1454, only a year after the fall of Constantinople, represented the enthusiasm for crusading still to be found in a number of European courts. Yet in practice it was only in the south-west that the war against Islam was successfully waged by the Spanish monarchs, who completed the reconquest of the kingdom of Granada from the Moors in 1492. As significant for the future, however, was the socio-religious conflict, with its strong nationalist overtones, which dominated the history of Bohemia during the first half of the century, a war in which the authority of the Church and what was seen as a threat of German domination were challenged by the Hussites who, seeking to create a new social order, engaged themselves in the most important 'people's' war of the period.

The nature of war was undoubtedly changing over much of Europe, although neither at a uniform pace nor in a uniform way. In terms of impact upon the future, the most decisive development was the move towards centralisation of military organisation and command which was to be achieved in many parts of Europe. In both England and France the long war between the two countries had already helped to bring about developments which were to be continued in the fifteenth century. The replacement of the feudal force by the paid army, symbolised by the indenture or contract, was by now almost complete.[4] Those acting on behalf of the crown could discipline armies, while they also ensured, through the regular muster, that numbers and acceptable standards of equipment were maintained.[5]

It was not only in the monarchies of northern Europe that the move

---

[4] For indentures, see Jones and Walker, 'Private indentures'. There were still feudal elements in the Hungarian army in 1459 (Borosy (1982)) and in the Burgundian army a few years later (Vaughan (1973), pp. 218–19).   [5] Rowe (1931).

towards centralisation, along with the development of institutions needed to achieve this, was carried out. The war fought on the mainland by Venice was to encourage such developments. The chain of command from the senate to the army was reorganised. The problem of how to establish and maintain a working link between the civil government and the captains (often mercenaries) was resolved by the appointment of *provveditori* who, as go-betweens with considerable experience behind them, were in an excellent position to interpret the ideas and wishes of one party to the other, while at the same time ensuring that the army remained subservient to the will of its Venetian paymasters. The growing reputation of Venetian arms at this period also owed much to the system of control which the long-serving *collaterali* exercised over both the personnel of the army and important aspects of military life, such as provisioning, without which no army could be successful.[6]

The marked tendency towards centralisation was to be found almost everywhere. In Burgundy a series of military ordinances published by Duke Charles between 1468 and 1473 stamped the ducal authority upon the personnel, organisation and command structure of the army. At a ceremony which may have inspired a similar one in Milan, captains appointed a year earlier surrendered their batons and their personal copies of the duke's military ordinances. As for the soldiers themselves, they were subject to exercises and drill carried out regularly with the intention of achieving a higher and more effective standard in the use of arms.[7] In Hungary, after King Sigismund had failed to impose change, János Hunyadi and, after him, Mátyás Corvinus built up armies which were the product of conscious reform, and which were intended to act (as were the castles constituting the system of border defence along the river Danube against the Turks) under royal control.[8] Here as, for example, in the kingdom of Naples, it was the active personal role played by the kings themselves which bound the various elements of the army together and made them act as one.[9]

Centralisation of military structures is one theme. Another is the establishment of permanent armies in many states during these years. The lead in this development was again taken by Venice which, in the early part of the century, set up a permanent force to be further developed in the succeeding generation. Continuity of development and organisation led to men being retained for periods which became longer and longer, while emphasis placed upon training and practice led to the creation of a national infantry. When, in 1454, the Peace

[6] Mallett and Hale (1984), pp. 102–13.

[7] Vaughan (1973), pp. 204–10, and (1975), pp. 127–8. As Vegetius had written: 'qui victoriam cupit, milites inbuat diligenter': 'he who wants victory, let him train soldiers diligently' (*Epitoma rei militaris*, bk III, Preface).   [8] Held (1977); Rázsó (1982); Fügedi (1982); Engel (1982).

[9] Ryder (1976), pp. 284–5.

of Lodi inaugurated a period of relative order in Italy, the size of armies could
have been reduced; yet the notion of the permanent force was accepted and
continued to operate in Italy even in time of relative tranquillity. The defeat at
the hands of the French in the 1490s was due less to lack of military capability
than to lack of political cohesion and effective structures born out of alliances
between states which did not yet trust one another.

In contrast to England, whose attempts to create a 'professional and
bureaucratically controlled army' were as yet largely unsuccessful,[10] France set
up an institutional and royal army between 1445 and 1450 based on the acceptance of a number of essential developments. In its origins this army (the *compagnies d'ordonnance*), which consisted largely of mounted units, was drawn from
men hand picked for their suitability; they were to be regularly paid and
inspected; and those so chosen were to recognise the authority of the king,
who alone had the right to recruit them, thereby rendering all other forces
illegal. In 1448, a fresh impetus was given to the infantry when the so-called
francs archers were established, each parish (later, every fifty households)
contributing one man who, undertaking to train regularly and to make himself
available when summoned, earned certain fiscal privileges. Following tradition,
leadership was still largely in the hands of men of noble background. None the
less, those who were not could still hope to make a career in the army, winning
promotion on the way. Not surprisingly, some who served in the king's new
army chose to have that service in this very professional corps recorded on
their tombstones. Even in death, it was something to be proud of.[11]

Venice and France were not alone in having permanent armies. Their
example influenced other parts of Italy, most notably the duchy of Milan, to a
lesser extent the kingdom of Naples, to follow suit, and their existence was in
practice sanctioned by the Peace of Lodi. Under Duke Charles, who saw
himself as a second Julius Caesar, Burgundy was to develop an army of which,
after 1471, the troops 'of the ordinance' (*de l'ordonnance*) were to form the
permanent core.[12] In Hungary, the efforts of Hunyadi and Corvinus created an
army which was a mixture of the traditional and the new;[13] while in Spain the
war against Granada in the closing decade of the century led to a series of
reforms (somewhat allied to the French model) which gave the monarchy
greater authority over the raising and control of forces and laid the foundations of the country's permanent army.[14]

At the centre of these changes was the soldier himself. What was his place in
the newly developing view of armies? How, indeed, was the army regarded by
those who did not belong to it? Traditionally, the soldier was feared and mis-

[10] Curry (1979).   [11] See Contamine (1964), p. 227, and (1972), plates 8, 9, 11 and 13.
[12] Vaughan (1973), ch. 6, and (1975), pp. 126–8.   [13] Engel (1982); Rázsó (1982).
[14] MacKay (1977), pp. 144–51; Ladero Quesada (1964); Stewart (1969).

trusted. He represented violence, so most preferred to have little to do with him. Could he be relied upon to fight when crises arose? Desertion, in particular by the mercenary of foreign origin, was not uncommon. In the Neapolitan kingdom securities in cash or land might be demanded from outsiders serving in the army; while in Venice a captain who deserted risked having a painted image of himself hung, upside down, on the wall of a public building.[15] In France, serious attempts had already been made in the previous century to give the soldier a better public image by presenting him as a servant of the king whose interests were those of a society at peace with itself.[16] In the fifteenth century the effort to do this continued. To be in the service of the crown was to be in the service of the public good, payment in coin (the *peccune publique*) being recognition of that service. Public service was regarded as both an honour and a responsibility for the good of others.

Yet, in spite of this, the tendency towards permanent armies did not meet with universal approval. While Robert Blondel saw the growth of such a force as a way of securing the defence of France against all its enemies, Jean Juvénal des Ursins considered the best way to counter the moral and physical dangers which soldiers presented to society was to put them to work on the task which they were best at: making war on others. To Thomas Basin, the army constituted a double tyranny: it was hugely expensive, and it was a threat to liberty. Why not, he suggested, go back to the old days when the defence of the kingdom had been in the hands of the nobility? That the soldier, widely regarded as the cause of disturbance, danger and destruction, should be the guardian of the public good was too paradoxical to win general acceptance. The reaction to change was mixed.[17]

A natural outcome of the growth of permanent armies was the extension, almost as a formality, of the length of service demanded by states such as Venice of those who served them.[18] In France, and not least in Brittany, the men who served for years brought a certain stability to the army.[19] They could also hope to aspire to positions of responsibility within it, a hope based on another change which, already widely debated in the previous century, was becoming a reality in the fifteenth: the advancement of men who, owing more to experience than to birth, were coming to be appreciated increasingly for the contribution which they could make to military success. The aristocratic view of war as a moment of individual opportunity was giving way to another: the fate of every state, large or small, depended upon the collective effort of those who fought on its behalf. The imperative to win, indeed to survive, was now

---

[15] On desertion, see Newhall (1940), pp. 150–4; Heymann (1955), p. 496 (10); Borosy (1982), p. 65; Mallett and Hale (1984), pp. 122–3.   [16] Allmand (1991).

[17] Solon (1972); Contamine (1992), pp. 205–8.   [18] Mallett (1973), p. 131.

[19] Jones (1985), p. 153.

taking over. The requirement to avoid the collective consequences of defeat thus led to societies choosing both soldiers and, in particular, leaders from among those who had good practical experience of war.[20]

Between the 'old-style' military hero (of Jean Froissart) and the 'new style' professional soldier (of Philippe de Commynes) lay the contracted mercenary leader, or *condottiere*, a familiar figure in Italian history (above all) since the thirteenth century. Here was the man who supplied the states of the peninsula with the leadership and the forces (in particular the specialist forces demanded by the times) which they could not always provide themselves. He and his men, who might be not only Italian but German, French, English or Spanish, were frequently the object of a love–hate relationship between themselves and their employers, since mercenaries, for all their skills, were often regarded as unreliable and cruel. Yet, in all this, the mercenary leader remained something of a star who attracted soldiers into his service and with whom states negotiated in the hope that he would defend their interests, although he faced risks if he were seen as acting against those of his employers. Francesco Bussone, son of a shepherd who rose to become count of Carmagnola, was executed by an assertive Venetian state for not obeying orders, dallying with the enemy and failing to 'deliver' results. Yet, for every Bussone there were others who advanced both their employers' interests and their own careers, and had their prowess recognised in different ways: titles and lands to enjoy in their lifetimes, state funerals after their deaths, in a few cases memorials such as statues in public places as evidence of their individuality put to good use in the service of the state which had employed them.[21] Such monuments often carried more than a hint of chivalric tradition, a chivalry which persisted in glorifying the individual who made his skills available to political masters in return for recognition and reward.

The fifteenth century was to witness a number of advances in the way that war was fought. For more than a century the general trend had been towards the growth in importance of the footsoldier. The ever-rising costs of war, in particular those involving the warhorse and the increasingly sophisticated armour needed to protect both him and his rider, were having a considerable effect upon the traditional constitution of armies. By the mid-fourteenth century (to go back no further) the cavalry was already suffering at the hands of massed archers who, at a distance of some 200 metres, could have a deadly effect upon it. Yet the day of the warhorse and his rider was far from over. In the favourable physical conditions of south-east Europe, they constituted the central arm of both Turkish and Hungarian armies. Further west, cavalry formed an essential part in the 're-formed' French and Burgundian armies of

[20] Allmand (1988), pp. 67–73.   [21] Mallett and Hale (1984), pp. 191–8.

the third quarter of the fifteenth century, continuing to play an important role both in battle and in the pursuit of those fleeing from the field.[22] The mercenary captains engaged by the states of the Italian peninsula were normally leaders of largely cavalry forces. The same leaders were usually represented mounted on powerful warhorses: the sections of Paolo Uccello's *The Battle of San Romano* (probably painted in mid-century) show a scene dominated by horses and their heavily armed riders. As for light cavalry, it was much in evidence in Spain,[23] while the stradiots employed in Italy were the most highly regarded in Europe. Those in the employ of Venice, who came from the far Adriatic coastlands and Greece, were armed with the short lance and bow, but their versatility enabled them to carry either the crossbow or, in due time, the handgun. What these troops lost in weight they more than made up in mobility. Constituting a relatively cheap force easily controlled by the Venetian administration, they were welcomed for their skill in countering the Turks in Dalmatia, Morea and Friuli; while their contribution to Venice's war against Ferrara in 1482 was only the first of their appearances in Italy in the conflicts of the years to come.[24]

Yet the trend in favour of the footsoldier continued. The Swiss army fought on foot, its pike squares famous all over Europe, its services employed by France, Burgundy and Venice, to name but three. The discipline of Swiss pikemen in the face of cavalry, as shown at Grandson in March 1476, will have erased all doubts regarding the future decisive role of heavy infantry.[25] The squares numbered some 7,000 men who stood in line about 100 metres long, some eighty to ninety men abreast, about seventy ranks deep. In the front ranks were pikes, behind them halberds with which the shocked cavalry troops were hooked off their horses. No mounted soldier had a chance against such numbers of pointed steel weapons which could, and did, move in highly disciplined formation, as at Marignano in September, 1515. Yet it was also at Marignano (on the following day) that the great Swiss weakness, the high vulnerability of dense formations (until that time a source of great strength) to firearms, showed itself when the French artillery made a devastating impression upon the ranks of the redoubtable squares.

Elsewhere, too, the footsoldier left his mark upon the art of war. According to Commynes, the Burgundian practice of knights dismounting in order to fight with the archers was learnt from the English whose archers still had a considerable reputation in the late fifteenth century.[26] In Bohemia, the characteristic style of making war, developed by Jan Žižka, was associated with the use of *wagenburgen*, mobile wagon fortresses made of carts intended pri-

---

[22] Vale (1981), pp. 127–8.   [23] MacKay (1977), p. 149; Macdonald (1948), pp. 36–40.
[24] Mallett and Hale (1984), pp. 47, 73.   [25] Hale (1957), p. 263.   [26] Commynes, *Mémoires*, I, p. 23.

marily as units of defence against cavalry, but which, tank-like, could be used aggressively to dislodge and drive back the enemy, as Žižka himself demonstrated at Kutná Hora in December, 1421. As the archer, the *wagenburg* (soon to be imitated by Hungarian peasants) and the pike square all showed, there were different ways of countering the awesome effectiveness of heavy cavalry.[27]

Žižka's forces also made good use of hand-held gunpowder weapons, already employed by Burgundian armies in the early years of the century. The hand culverin, which fired lead shot and used expensive gunpowder, was used by English armies in France by the 1430s.[28] Fitted with wooden stocks and used with a stand or tripod, it could be used with effect in defensive situations (fired from castle battlements, for instance): likewise it was employed in attack (at sieges, for example) as many defenders found to their cost. In its origins, the handgun was in rivalry with the crossbow, a weapon still susceptible to technical development such as the greatly increased power given it by being made entirely of steel. While crossbowmen still existed, there was no reason why their weapon should be superseded by the handgun. Although the army of Alfonso of Naples included more crossbowmen than handgunners,[29] the use of the gun on an increasing scale, both by the Burgundians in the reign of Charles the Bold and by the Swiss, is well attested by contemporary evidence, archival, literary and artistic. In 1490, the dependence of Venice on handgunners from Germany was recognised and a training programme initiated.[30] It did not do to lag behind others in such vital matters, in particular when the matchlock was about to help create something like a modern firearm.

Of greater immediate influence was the development of siege and field artillery. Developed for siege warfare in the second half of the fourteenth century, it was in the following century that the firearm (manufactured in many sizes) came into its own as a major influence upon the outcome of war. It was not, however, to be a constant development throughout Europe. Although used by Venice in the early years of the century, it was not until mid-century that artillery came to be employed by the republic in any serious way; much the same was true of the kingdom of Naples. In northern Europe, however, the situation developed differently. Urban communities (which could afford cannon) might have their own artillery, in particular for defensive purposes. This was the case in Germany, in the Low Countries and in France by the early years of the century. The war involving England, France and Burgundy, fought largely in the north and north-east of France, advanced considerably the use of heavy artillery in that part of Europe. From the time of the siege of Harfleur (1415) onwards,

---

[27] On Žižka, see Heymann (1955), pp. 295–6, 450–3; for a pictorial representation of a Hussite *wagenburg*, see Heymann (1955), pl. 3. For the immediate and longer-term influence of these wars in Germany, see Heymann (1955), p. 452; on Hungary, see Held (1982), p. 87.

[28] Vale (1976), p. 134.   [29] Ryder (1976), p. 282.   [30] Mallett and Hale (1984), p. 79.

English policy was to capture towns and military strongholds; much the same could be said of Burgundian war policy in the years both before and after that date. The use of both bombards, or heavy cannon, and a variety of smaller cannon which, fired horizontally from short range and aimed at the lower third of a wall, did much damage to stone defences, was an innovation developed, above all, in France. In Ireland, by contrast, where very different conditions prevailed, firearms did not appear until the closing years of the century.[31]

The first half of the century was a time of experimentation in the use of heavy artillery. Only over a period of some years were the true proportions of sulphur, charcoal and saltpetre developed for maximum effectiveness; only slowly were the problems of how to transport heavy artillery (first on four-wheeled carts pulled by large teams of horses or oxen, and then slung between two wheels, or, best of all, by water) resolved.[32] The ability to vary the angle of fire and, consequently, the range of an artillery piece was to be encouraged by the development of the trunnion; while the effectiveness of that fire was made all the greater by the use of iron, rather than stone or marble, cannon balls of uniform size produced from about the 1430s onwards. The first half of the century was thus an important period in the development of the effective use of cannon. Only in the second half, once initial problems had been overcome and the usefulness of artillery had been proved on the battlefields of Formigny (1450) and Castillon (1453), did it find favour in almost all parts of Europe. By the third quarter of the century, the special value of the new, lighter weapon on campaign having become fully apparent, most states had their artillery trains under the control of centrally appointed masters of the ordnance. In France, the special importance attributed to artillery may be recognised in the continuity of membership of its associated personnel, some of whom enjoyed careers lasting twenty years in the royal service. Furthermore, the crown emphasised the importance of the arm by establishing a monopoly in the provision of saltpetre and by spending large sums to provide the royal army with the cannon it required. Not surprisingly, it was the French artillery, the best in Europe, which most impressed Italians when the invasion of 1494 took place. By then, however, they had already begun to develop the architectural response to artillery, the angle bastion, which not only weakened the effect of a bombardment but enabled the defender to use his defences as a platform from which to counter attack. The traditional balance in favour of the besieged, threatened by advances in artillery technology which had overtaken those available to defenders, was, to some extent, being restored.[33]

---

[31] Eltis (1989); Salamagne (1993). On the rather different way of making war in Ireland, see Simms (1975).

[32] Contamine (1964), pp. 252, 256; Mallett (1981), p. 270; Sommé (1986); Vale (1976), p. 60.

[33] Hale (1965a); Vale (1982), pp. 188–90.

By the fifteenth century war at sea was beginning to assume genuine military significance, and the need to have ready access to vessels of either transportation or war was helping to shape diplomacy and influence the relationship between states. Building ships was expensive, and not all states needed to provide themselves with even a basic permanent naval force; the dukes of Burgundy and the kings of Naples were not alone in seeking to further their own war aims by sanctioning privateering by those who had a material interest in such activity. Overall, the century was to witness developments in naval warfare, and (in the Baltic, for instance) in the use made of ships built specifically for war.[34] The relief of the English garrison in Harfleur by a naval force which broke a blockade of the town by both land and sea (1416) demonstrated the importance of the naval arm, as did the use of ships in the dispute between Holland and the Hanseatic League (1438–41) which witnessed the technique of blocking the Baltic in what was a real trade war.[35] In this context the use made of rivers is also significant. These were coming to be recognised for what they were, cheap and often convenient methods of securing inland transport for men, provisions and heavy siege engines such as cannon. Access from the sea up the river Seine to Rouen made the siege of the Norman capital by the English (1418–19) easier and more likely to succeed; both the Turks and their Christian opponents used galleys on the lower Danube; while the Venetians, who controlled the mouths of both the Po and the Adige, and had ready access to shipyards, used river fleets, which included oared vessels as well as galleons (galleys with an upper-deck on which artillery could be placed and soldiers carried) on the main rivers of Lombardy.[36] Their significance lay not only in their considerable contribution to the state's military achievement; it underlined the fact that in certain states the organisation of the naval arm was now being more centrally controlled as part of a wider war effort. Alfonso of Naples had recognised the need for this; in Spain and England the long-term services of naval captains were retained through annuities paid by the crown.[37] At opposite ends of Europe, the spending of money on naval forces by James IV of Scotland and the sultans Mehemmed II and Bayazid was a reflection that the importance of the sea in both war and peace was now becoming widely recognised.[38]

The war aims of states could be furthered not only by direct conflict but also through negotiation and diplomacy, now increasingly appreciated as important adjuncts of war. In northern Europe the outlines of diplomatic procedure had

[34] See Richmond (1964), (1967) and (1971); Rose (1982); Mallett (1994), pp. 554–7; Contamine (1992), ch. 12; Paviot (1995).   [35] See below, pp. 684, 693.

[36] Allmand (1992b), pp. 230–1; Mallett and Hale (1984), pp. 96–100.

[37] Ryder (1976), ch. 9; MacKay (1977), p. 150; Allmand (1992b), p. 227.

[38] See below, pp. 519, 829.

been developed, particularly by the English, since the late thirteenth century.[39] Yet, in this century, it was in Italy that the most progress would be made. Long accustomed to fierce rivalries between states and to wars waged in defence of material interests, Italy, as it searched for peace, turned to maintaining a balance between those states. Not surprisingly, it was in that part of Europe, where there was the greatest need to set up effective links with neighbouring powers, to establish and maintain alliances, and to be well informed about the economic plans and intentions of others, that the first resident ambassadors (or spies, as some saw them) were to be found.[40] Likewise, it was with the aim of maintaining a balance in a competitive world which lacked a dominant authority that leagues, such as that created at Lodi in 1454, came into existence, their aim being to deter aggression through the threat of the exercise of collective power. The establishment of peace in 1454 brought relative stability to the peninsula during the next forty years, an achievement which led to such leagues becoming part of the European-wide diplomatic scene well on into the sixteenth century.

The rising cost of war fought in the interest of individual states led to the assumption of its expenses by those states. By 1450, a good warhorse could cost a French man-at-arms the equivalent of six months' wages or more, and a set of good plate armour what it would take him three months to earn;[41] not surprisingly, therefore, the expenses of war had to be met increasingly from the public purse. The provision of heavy artillery, the need to strengthen existing fortifications to counter the new weapon, not to speak of the growing requirements of naval forces, all underlined this point. War was now a huge drag on the prosperity of any community. Right across Europe, in the Ottoman state, in the Empire, as in the Iberian kingdoms, new taxes were raised to sustain the activities of war. Yet in Florence, where new levies had to be imposed in the 1420s, the state's revenue in the first half of the fifteenth century amounted to only about a third of what was required in time of war; the ten-year conflict between Spain and Granada probably cost the Spanish treasury something over half its annual revenue; while even in peacetime, at the very beginning of the sixteenth century, Venice was spending about a fifth of its wealth on the permanent army. Costs dictated both tactics and the use of particular troops. In favourable conditions the use of heavy cavalry could bring quick results, as did the tactics employed by the Swiss squares. These were 'high-risk' tactics of direct confrontation; the less well-off approached war more cautiously. The avoidance of the pitched battle in favour of the skirmish and pillaging, and the

---

[39] Cuttino (1985).   [40] Queller (1967); Mallett (1981).
[41] Vale (1981), p. 126, and (1982), p. 178, citing Contamine (1972), pp. 658–63.

manoeuvre which left the enemy morally and financially exhausted, often paid off, and so appealed to the less prosperous.[42]

War helped to stimulate the development of economies associated with it, in particular the provision of armaments and the materials which went into their making. Yew, much of it grown in Portugal, was used for bows, while oak was needed for shipbuilding. Large quantities of wood were required to feed the furnaces for the smelting of iron, much of which came from Spain and the southern Netherlands, used in the foundries where guns and cannons of all sizes were made. Such foundries were normally found in towns, the work of designing and making artillery pieces often being undertaken by men of other, associated skills such as clock making, which needed experience in the precise working of metals. Arms manufacturers came to the aid of towns, such as Malines and Tournai, whose traditional cloth trade was in decline.[43] Granted its origins, it is no coincidence that the development of the use of artillery for defensive purposes should have originated in towns, nor that the hegemony of the dukes of Burgundy over one of Europe's most densely urbanised areas should have been achieved at the end of a gun barrel. The high cost of individual artillery pieces led to cannon becoming the active instrument of state centralisation which, once achieved, would also be defended with the same army.

The century witnessed a significant development in the literature related to both the theory and the practice of war, which was much indebted to a tradition going back to classical times.[44] Far and away the most famous of those inherited from the past was Vegetius' *De re militari*, probably compiled in the late fourth century, whose influence would still be felt for some centuries to come. Freely 'modernised' in vernacular translations of the late thirteenth, fourteenth and fifteenth centuries, its appeal lay not in the support it might give to the personal virtues traditionally associated with the fighting man but rather in its rationalisation of war and its presentation of general principles which could lead to success. In a sense complementing the work of Vegetius, the *Stratagemata* of the first-century Roman writer, Frontinus, offered practical wisdom gleaned largely from the writings of ancient historians. This work was translated into French in 1439 (not long before military reforms were enacted by the French crown), and was published in a printed version first in 1487 and again in 1494 (on the second occasion with Vegetius, Aelian and others).[45] The mixture of the philosophical and the practical taught that victory depended on 'discipline', a term which could be interpreted as meaning a sense of 'teamwork' within the army; a readiness and ability to exploit opportunities both on

---

[42] Ryder (1976), p. 282. On the different attitudes of Italians and French to fighting, see Clough (1995), pp. 193–4.   [43] Gaier (1973).   [44] Vale (1981), ch. 1.
[45] See bibliography, *sub* Vegetius and Frontinus.

and off the battlefield, and, on the part of commanders, a willingness to learn from experience. All had this in common: they could be achieved by training. Bérault Stuart, who was to write his *Traité sur l'art de la guerre* in the first years of the sixteenth century, would underline the vital contribution of this practical characteristic to a successful outcome in war.[46]

When reporting the events of war at the end of the fourteenth century, Froissart had devoted much attention to individual *faits d'armes*; a hundred years later Commynes could almost ignore them. The intervening years had witnessed many changes in both attitudes to war and the manner of fighting it. Luigi da Porto ('a hundred against a hundred'), Baldassare Castiglione and others might prefer open combat and the chances it gave for personal valour to be seen and commented on.[47] Cannon might be given names (as many were) and be treated (with some care) as individuals,[48] rather as some of the machines depicted in Roberto Valturio's *De re militari* (written in mid-century and printed in Verona in 1472) were given animal characteristics as if to stress their individuality.[49] Yet neither took account of fundamental changes overtaking the waging of war, principally the constrictions being placed on the role of each soldier to act as an individual. However ingenious, neither the machines found in Valturio's work, nor those seen in the *Bellifortis* of Conrad Kyeser, written earlier in the century,[50] had much of a future before them; while that most chivalric and loyal of Frenchmen and latter-day Horatio, the Chevalier Bayard, would be killed by an arquebus in 1524. By the end of the fifteenth century it was increasingly appreciated that success in war depended less upon the brilliant feats of individuals than on the collective efforts of well-trained armies. Rather more in keeping with the times and with the arms now becoming available was the Greek treatise, *The Tactics*, compiled by Aelian in the first century (printed in a Latin version made by the humanist, Theodore Gaza, in Rome in 1487 with accompanying diagrams, such as had already been found in a fourteenth-century manuscript of the work), reflected a scientific approach to the art of war, to which the relative consistency of the printed page contributed a further dimension. Even more significant (it may be argued) than these 'reprints' from past ages were the recent works on war written by men who had up-to-date experience of it. Neither Bueil's *Jouvencel*, written in the 1460s and printed in Paris in 1493, nor the treatises of Robert de Balsac (d. 1503) and Bérault Stuart (d. 1508), relied heavily upon classical models. Rather, they mirrored their authors' experiences gained in the wars of their own times. Among the first practical works on war written since the late Roman era, they reflected an attempt to lift the subject into the realm of the practical, the specific and the

---

[46] Stuart, *Traité sur l'art de la guerre.*   [47] Cited in Clough (1993), p. 108.
[48] Vale (1976), pp. 63–4, 71–2.   [49] E.g., BL, Add. MS 24,945.   [50] Kyeser, *Bellifortis.*

scientific. Such writing represented a marked change of attitude.[51] While God might intervene, upon men fell the main responsibility for the outcome of wars, a point underlined by the diplomatic failure of the states of Italy to unite against the French in the closing years of the century. As if a symbol of the new thinking, Bérault Stuart's career included spells as a diplomat as well as longer ones as a soldier. Diplomacy represented a new expression of the ancients' teaching on preparedness; there was more to the making of war than what occurred on the battlefield. At the same time, the interest taken in Aelian's diagrams, the emphasis placed by both Balsac and Stuart upon experience (an idea which, before long, would lead to the founding of military academies for the training of officers)[52] and the insistence accorded to the role of good artillery as the weapon of the future all serve to underline the growing appreciation of human reason, inventiveness and ingenuity in the waging of war. Give no hostages to fortune, Vegetius had advised; fight the enemy only with the skills of the soldier. No longer was it sufficient to attribute defeat to Fortune or to divine displeasure. Men would need to know why it had occurred, in order to work out how the failure of yesterday might be turned into the victory of tomorrow.

[51] Contamine, 'The war literature of the late Middle Ages'.   [52] Hale (1976).

CHAPTER 9

EXPLORATION AND DISCOVERY

Felipe Fernández-Armesto

A cosmic observer, privileged to look down on the world of the fifteenth century from a commanding height, would have noticed a number of cultures and civilisations separated by great distances, poor communications and, in some cases, mutual ignorance or lack of interest. He might, however, have detected – in places, for the most part, outside Latin Christendom – some stirrings at the edges: the dilation of political frontiers or the beginnings of movements of expansion, of settlement, trade, conquest and proselytisation, which would make the world of the next few centuries an arena of imperial competition where expanding civilisations collided and where virtually all human communities were joined in conflict, commerce and contagion. The accomplishment of this enormous and conspicuous change depended on the creation of practical routes of access between previously isolated or barely-communicating groups of people.

In these pages, 'exploration' is understood to mean the identification, investigation and recording of such routes. The process came to be dominated by explorers from Latin Christendom. Yet our hypothetical observer, unless also endowed with foresight, would probably not have been able to predict such an outcome until the century was well advanced. Such sources of motivation as material exigency, scientific curiosity, missionary zeal, commercial spirit or wanton aggression were not peculiar to any one part of the world, and, compared with China and Islam, Latin Christendom was underequipped in the technical resources with which to undertake long journeys, to sustain life during them, to find directions in unfamiliar places, to record and communicate the information gathered.

Some otherwise promising cultures were subject to even greater technical limitations which perhaps inhibited or disqualified them from further big achievements in exploration. Among the Aztecs and their neighbours, for instance, as among the indigenous peoples of sub-Saharan Africa, there was no means of long-range navigation by sea; in Peru, no maps. The Polynesians, surrounded by the vast Pacific, may have attained the limits of the world accessible

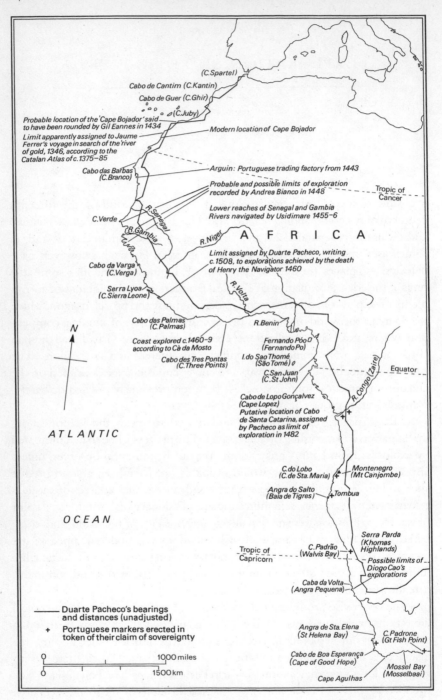

(C.Spartel)

Cabo de Cantim (C.Kantin)

Cabo de Guer (C.Ghir)

(C.Juby)

Probable location of the 'Cape Bojador' said
to have been rounded by Gil Eannes in 1434

Modern location of Cape Bojador

Limit apparently assigned to Jaume
Ferrer's voyage in search of the 'river
of gold, 1346, according to the
Catalan Atlas of c. 1375–85

Cabo das Barbas
(C.Branco)

Arguin: Portuguese trading factory from 1443

Tropic of
Cancer

Probable and possible limits of exploration
recorded by Andrea Bianco in 1448

R. Senegal

Lower reaches of Senegal and Gambia
Rivers navigated by Usidimare 1455–6

C.Verde

R.Gambia

R.Niger

A F R I C A

Cabo da Varga
(C.Verga)

Limit assigned by Duarte Pacheco, writing
c. 1508, to explorations achieved by the death
of Henry the Navigator 1460

Serra Lyoa
(C.Sierra Leone)

R.Volta

N

Cabo das Palmas
(C. Palmas)

R.Benin

Coast explored c.1460–9
according to Cà da Mosto

Fernando Póo
(Fernando Po)

Cabo des Tres Pontas
(C.Three Points)

I.do Sao Thomé
(São Tomé)

Equator

C.San Juan
(C. St John)

R. Congo (Zaire)

Cabo de Lopo Gonçalvez
(Cape Lopez)
Putative location of Cabo
de Santa Catarina, assigned
by Pacheco as limit of
exploration in 1482

A T L A N T I C

C.do Lobo
(C. de Sta. Maria)

Montenegro
(Mt Canjombe)

Angra do Salto
(Baía de Tigres)

Tombua

O C E A N

Serra Parda
(Khomas
Highlands)

Tropic of
Capricorn

C.Padrão
(Walvis Bay)

Possible limits of
Diogo Cao's
explorations

Caba da Volta
(Angra Pequena)

Duarte Pacheco's bearings
and distances (unadjusted)

+ Portuguese markers erected in
token of their claim of sovereignty

Angra de Sta.Elena
(St Helena Bay)

C.Padrone
(Gt Fish Point)

0   1000 miles

0   1500 km

Cabo de Boa Esperança
(Cape of Good Hope)

Mossel Bay
(Mosselbaai)

Cape Agulhas

Map 3   The extent of European discoveries on the west African coast

to them with the technology at their disposal. Yet the record of these societies from which routes were explored and recorded over vast distances – extending in the Peruvian case across thirty degrees of latitude and in the Polynesian case over thousands of miles of sea – shows how much can be achieved in defiance of technical insufficiency.

The best-equipped people, indeed, failed to fulfil their promise as explorers. Java, for instance, probably had by the late fourteenth century cartographical traditions and shipbuilding techniques at least as good as those of anywhere else, but all her shipping was absorbed by the demands of trade within a fairly restricted zone between south Asia and the far east. By the mid-fourteenth century, Arabic travel literature and pilgrims' guides covered the whole Islamic world and extended selectively beyond it, for instance, into Sardinia and China; and Arabic sailing directions of the second half of the fifteenth century covered the Indian Ocean from southern Africa to the South China Sea. Yet after the Arab commercial world had attained its desired limits in the Mediterranean and the far east, Islamic exploration further afield became fitful and slight. In particular, little attempt was made to imitate the achievements of Indian Ocean navigators in Atlantic waters, and mariners satiated with the profits of well-known routes showed no inclination to venture beyond the stormy latitudes which screen the Indian Ocean to the south. When the New World became an extension of Christendom and the Portuguese discovered an Atlantic highway to the east, the Ottoman sultans came, too late, to regret their failings.

Meanwhile, development of the exploring traditions of China was similarly arrested. The range of travel had long been limited to the reach of trade and diplomacy; but in China that meant including a huge swathe of the world, exceeding the length of the silk roads and the breadth of the Indian Ocean. Geographical scholars collated and mapped the information collected. In about 1220, for instance, a detailed account of the South China Sea and of countries of south-east Asia and India was produced, partly from personal observation, by a scholar and diplomat. A century later, passable maps of the Indian Ocean were made, perhaps including the coast of Africa to beyond the Cape of Good Hope.[1] Between 1405 and 1433, a series of tribute-gathering missions under the eunuch-admiral, Cheng Ho (Pinyin: Zheng He), consolidated knowledge of commercial routes and reported, from direct experience, on places as distant as Jiddah and Malindi. Yet for a combination of imperfectly understood reasons – which included the effects of the ebb and flow of factional conflicts, the hostility of the mandarin elite to eunuchs and traders

---

[1] Needham *et al.* (1961–   ), III, p. 352; Snow (1988), pp. 9–12; Norwich (1983), pp. 15–16; Fuchs (1953), p. 50; review, by J. Duyvendak, of Fuchs (ed.), *Mongol atlas*, in *T'oung Pao* 39 (1959), pp. 198–9.

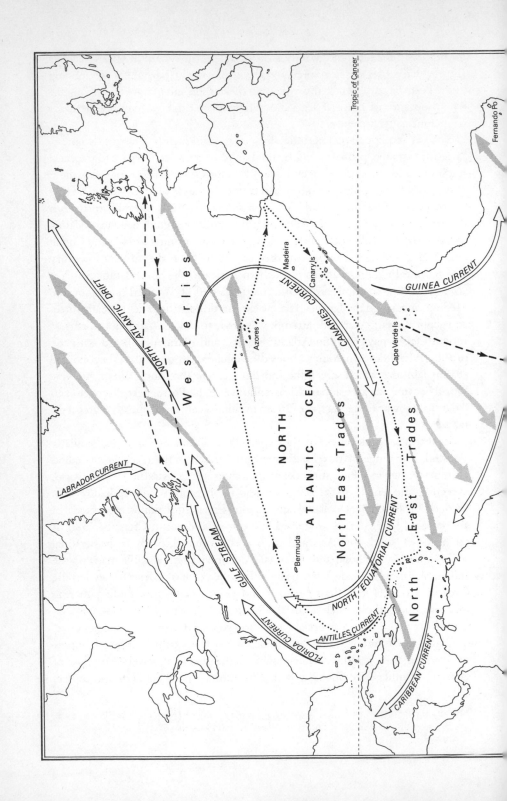

Tropic of Cancer

Fernando Po

GUINEA CURRENT

Madeira

Canary Is

CANARIES CURRENT

Cape Verde Is

NORTH ATLANTIC DRIFT

W e s t e r l i e s

North East Trades

NORTH   ATLANTIC   OCEAN

Azores

North   East   Trades

Bermuda

NORTH EQUATORIAL CURRENT

LABRADOR CURRENT

GULF STREAM

ANTILLES CURRENT

FLORIDA CURRENT

CARIBBEAN CURRENT

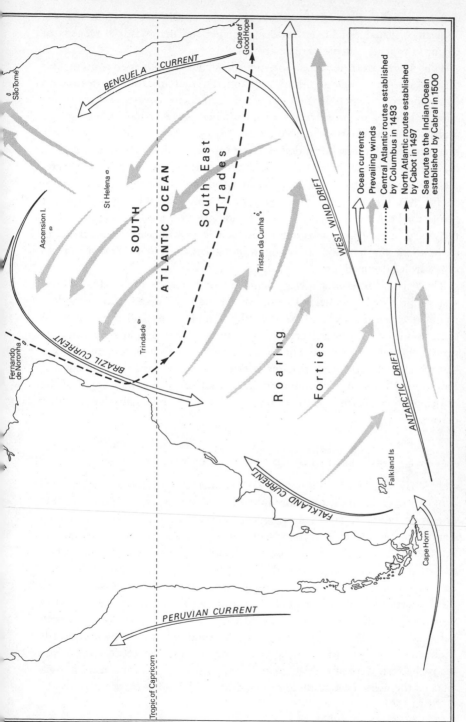

Map 4 Winds and currents facilitating the discoveries

Legend:

- Ocean currents
- Prevailing winds
- Central Atlantic routes established by Columbus in 1493
- North Atlantic routes established by Cabot in 1497
- Sea route to the Indian Ocean established by Cabral in 1500

Labels on map:

São Tomé

BENGUELA CURRENT

St Helena

Ascension I.

SOUTH

ATLANTIC OCEAN

South East Trades

Trindade

Tristan da Cunha

WEST WIND DRIFT

Fernando de Noronha

BRAZIL CURRENT

Roaring Forties

ANTARCTIC DRIFT

FALKLAND CURRENT

Falkland Is

Cape Horn

Cape of Good Hope

PERUVIAN CURRENT

Tropic of Capricorn

and the prohibitive cost of the ventures – this potentially imperial initiative was aborted. Naval shipbuilding was discontinued and many official records of Cheng Ho's achievements were destroyed.

Thus while more prosperous and proficient civilisations rested content with the exploitation of their traditional contacts, it was left to explorers from Latin Christendom to search for new resources, extend their reach and ultimately enmesh most of the world in their routes. Their biggest source of advantage was probably their starting-place on the edge of the Atlantic. In the age of sail, maritime route-finding depended on access to favourable winds and currents. Navigators from the Indian Ocean and western Pacific would not have found conditions favourable for long-range navigation outside the zone of monsoons, even had they wished to do so. The only navigable route eastwards across the Pacific was an effective dead end until trading-places developed on the west coast of America in colonial times. The ways out of the Indian Ocean to the south were laborious and dangerous and led, as far as was known, only to unrewarding destinations. .

The Atlantic, by contrast, was a highway to the rest of the world. Its wind systems provided potential links with the Pacific and Indian Oceans as well as routes between the Old and New Worlds. The location and exploitation of these routes was a labour, accomplished in the fifteenth and sixteenth centuries, which deserves its reputation as a revolutionary achievement in world history. Though there were episodes of interest or importance in other parts of the world, the story of exploration in the fifteenth century is very largely of the crossing of the Atlantic with routes that linked its shores and led to other oceans.

THE BACKGROUND IN LATIN CHRISTENDOM

This story should be understood against the background of the internal exploration of Latin Christendom in the late Middle Ages. The search for the origins of the vocations of European explorers can only be rewarded by taking a very long-term view and acknowledging that the process grew, cumulatively but slowly and unevenly, from modest beginnings. It can be traced, in a sense, to Latin Christendom's era of self-discovery in the late eleventh and twelfth centuries, when the riverbankers conquered the wild wood, in a vast project of the domestication of little-explored and underexploited environments, while observers and travellers turned inward to find and describe Europe's inner barbarians: the remote peoples of forest, bog and mountains, the imperfectly assimilated marchland-dwellers, whose evangelisation was sketchy, at best, and whose habitats were often blanks on the map. At about the same time, knowledge of the world beyond these recesses and thresholds was increased by the colonists and crusaders who extended the frontiers of Latin Christendom. Scholars in western Europe were acquainted with the vastness of the world by the experience of the crusades – reinforced, in the thirteenth and early fourteenth centuries, by the reports of merchants and missionaries who travelled the Mongol road as far as China or sailed, with indigenous shipping, on the Indian Ocean.

The map had to be pieced together gradually from a number of sources. Two of these went back to Roman times: the map of Roman roads preserved, among surviving medieval sources, in the fourteenth-century Peutinger Tables in Vienna; and local surveying techniques, the continuity of which is suggested by fragmentary survivals of maps made by the Roman *agrimensores* and their successors. The estate maps of wealthy monasteries could cover vast areas that were sometimes widely separated from one another. Estate management and the collective business of widespread religious orders generated itineraries – essentially, lists of stopping-places. Pilgrimages and royal progresses also yielded itineraries, which survive in map form in fairly large numbers from the thirteenth century. As their traditional, linear patterns were modified by the surveyors' tradition of rendering spatial relationships, so area maps evolved. The needs of warfare were an increasing stimulus to the development of techniques: the crusading propaganda of Marino Sanudo, for instance, was illustrated with maps of uncanny accuracy, made with the aid of a grid. In the fifteenth century, maps gradually became part of the regular equipment of field commanders. Maps like those made for Sanudo by Pietro Vesconte, covering areas not previously mapped by Christian hands, are documents of exploration, as are those derived from Nicholas of Cusa's fifteenth-century maps of Europe between the Baltic and the Black Sea, including regions only lately and imperfectly incorporated into Latin Christendom.

A similar evolution turned written sailing directions into marine charts during the thirteenth century. St Louis, voyaging to Tunis in 1270, had one, and the earliest surviving examples are of not much later date. Though the concept of scale was not applied with any rigour until well into the sixteenth century, as instruments for recording routes by land and sea the products of late medieval cartography became highly serviceable.

CARTOGRAPHY AND GEOGRAPHY

The mariner's occupation, according to Columbus, 'inclines all who follow it to wish to know the secrets of the world'.[2] Exploration and geographical speculation fed off each other and were both reflected in maps which strained at the

[2] Varela (ed.), *Cristóbal Colón*, p. 277: 'La mesma arte inclina a quien le prosigue a desear de saber los secretos d'este mundo.'

limits of geographical knowledge and aimed to include discoveries as they happened and conjectures as they arose. For it was not only the scope of maps that changed in the late Middle Ages but also their very nature. Until the thirteenth century – to judge from surviving examples – European world maps had been devotional objects, intended to evoke God's harmonious design in a schematic form, appropriate, for instance, for an altarpiece. By the fifteenth century, mapmakers were showing the same interest in geographical realism as Renaissance artists in naturalism. Mapmakers collated the reports of practical navigators, who set out, in some cases, to verify the cartographers' speculations. From 1339 onwards, the sea chart was a common medium for recording new Atlantic discoveries. Increasingly, this became the maps' explicit role. The Genoese maker of an unpublished map of 1403 recorded how he had checked the details of his work against the experience and information of seamen.[3] A famous map made in London by the Genoese Andrea Bianco in 1448 is expressly devoted to a record of the latest Atlantic discoveries of Portuguese navigators.

Marine and strategic charts were by their nature practical instruments and therefore susceptible to change and responsive to new information. The world map was encumbered with more tenacious traditions, derived from the genre's devotional origins. The convention of depicting the world as the *orbis terrarum*, a continuous landmass, surrounded by islands and ringed by a circumvallatory ocean, was maintained by some of the most up-to-date cartographers throughout the period: for instance by Henricus Martellus, who included the latest 'descriptionem Portugalensium' in a map probably made in Florence in 1489.[4] It remained usual to show the earthly paradise at the extreme orient and Jerusalem at least roughly in the middle of the world. Nevertheless, *mappae mundi* and globes were increasingly used to illustrate particular theoretical conceptions of the outlines of the world and the relative locations of places: most commonly, in the fifteenth century, those of Ptolemy, whose *Geography*, the text of which was translated into Latin early in the century, invited illustration to supply the want of original maps and to render the sometimes difficult language intelligible. Other examples from the fifteenth century include German maps which display unknown antipodean continents; the lost map made by Pietro Paolo Toscanelli of Florence, before 1474, to illustrate his theory of a navigably narrow Atlantic; and the Nuremberg globe of 1492, traditionally attributed to Martin Behaim, which seems designed, at least in part, to suggest the accessibility of the island of Cipangu, reported by Marco Polo.

Even in world maps – which gave their compilers a welcome chance to speculate about the fabled splendours of the Orient and the Indian Ocean – the

³ Kraus (1955), pp. 62–6.   ⁴ Nebenzahl (1990), p. 16; Vietor (1962).

greatest concentration of novelties was to be found in the fifteenth century in depictions of the Atlantic. This shows what a stimulus to the imagination Atlantic exploration was and how consciousness of an exciting and exploitable Atlantic space developed. To the mythical islands commonly assigned imaginary positions in fourteenth-century maps – those of Brendan, St Ursula and Brasil – a Venetian chart of 1424 added large and alluring islands, including 'Antillia', the latter identified with the island of 'Seven Cities', to which, in a legend not unlike that of St Ursula, Portuguese refugees from the Moors were held to have repaired in the eighth century.[5] These islands became standard in subsequent cartographical tradition and inspired voyages in search of them. As late as 1514, Portuguese official sailing directions gave courses to islands 'not yet discovered' and one of the most amusing forgeries of the sixteenth century is a spurious Spanish 'chronicle' of the conquest of St Brendan's Isle.[6] Attempts have been made to relate these mental wanderings to possible real finds, usually in connection with theories of pre-Columbian discoveries of America. But once one appreciates the genuine excitement aroused in the fifteenth century by the unlimited possibilities of the Atlantic, the fertility of speculation seems adequately explained.

Fresh discoveries were a direct stimulus: the Majorcan cartographers who first placed the Azores roughly in their correct position in maps of the 1430s also introduced new speculative islands into the tradition. Andrea Bianco was interested in the latest verifiable novelties, as his sea chart of 1448 shows, but in his world map of 1436 he scattered imaginary islands about the ocean and even in the 1448 chart he included some traditional isles, with an assurance that an 'authentic island'[7] lay 1,500 miles out in the equatorial Atlantic. Bianco seems to have felt that ancient certainties about geography had to be discarded. The same point was made implicitly a few years later by his collaborator, the acknowledged master of the Venetian cartographic school, Fra Mauro, who confessed in a note on his world map of 1448–60 – the fullest then devised – that his delineation must be imperfect, since the extent of the world was unknown.[8] The geographers of the fifteenth century were like prisoners-of-war who, unable to see their cell walls in the light of a tallow candle, could imagine themselves free.

The freedom of conjecture can be sensed in the speculations of academic geography as well as in the mapmakers' fancies. The dividing line between travel literature and academic work in this field or, within travel literature,

[5] Cortesao (1975).   [6] Benito Ruano (1978).

[7] Yule Oldham (1895), p. 222; Kamal, *Monumenta cartographica*, v, no. 1492: 'ixola otinticha'.

[8] Mauro, *Il mapamondo*, p. 62: 'Quest opera . . . non ha in si quel complimento che la doveria, perchè certo non è possibile a l'intellecto human senza qualche superna demostration verificar in tuto questa cosmographia.'

between *mirabilia* and genuine reportage, is, in the case of some works, hard to define. The Indian Ocean experiences of the Venetian merchant Nicolò Conti, between 1414 and 1437, were represented by Poggio Bracciolini who wrote them down, as a moral tale 'of the fickleness of fortune'[9] but they were full of facts which passed rapidly into geographical textbooks and scholarly maps. The *Travels* of 'Sir John Mandeville' are notorious, among fourteenth-century works, as the fabrication of an armchair traveller, but it is also a persuasive treatise, arguing for cosmographical propositions: the sphericity of the earth, the navigability of all oceans, the accessibility of all lands, the existence of an 'antipodean' world. Marco Polo, dismissed as a fable-monger by some, was justly appreciated by others as a true reporter of real observations. Columbus's indebtedness to these two last-named texts shows how such works could influence and inspire explorers.

Though historians' search for connections between the 'Renaissance' and the 'Age of Discovery' has sometimes been conducted with an air of desperation, it is also true that more learned texts, including rediscoveries from classical Antiquity, could also contribute to the atmosphere of speculation in which explorers' expeditions were launched. Notable cases from the fifteenth century are those of Ptolemy (fl. second century AD) and Strabo (d. 19 AD). Ptolemy's *Geography* became the most widely used geographical book of reference in Latin Christendom in the fifteenth century; it helped to inspire influential geographical treatises by Aeneas Sylvius Piccolomini and Pierre d'Ailly; it was read by Columbus and ransacked for points in support of his project; and it included speculations about the nature of the Indian Ocean which Portuguese expeditions in the 1490s may, in part, have been designed to test. Strabo was particularly important for the stimulus he gave to debate about the possible existence of the Antipodes; his text arrived in Italy in 1423; some of his ideas circulated widely from the time of the Council of Florence in 1439 (a great occasion for the exchange of cosmographical news as well as of ecclesiological debate); and a translation into Latin was in print by 1469. Though his references to the Antipodes[10] sound ironic, they seem to have helped to convince geographers of humanist inclinations or sympathies, before Columbus's voyage to the New World, that the tradition of an unknown continent or continents in the ocean was valid.

THE CULTURE OF EXPLORERS

To some extent, however, the explorers who enormously extended the coverage of the map in the fourteenth and fifteenth centuries must be seen as oper-

---

[9] Bracciolini, *De varietate fortunae*, pp. 153–77.   [10] *Geography of Strabo*, I, p. 243.

ating independently of the influence of academic geographers. Columbus was exceptional in his bookishness and in his taste for theoretical cosmography; and, even in his case, his academic interests seem to have developed rather in consequence than in anticipation of his vocation as an explorer.[11] Explorers did share a common culture, unique to Latin Christendom, which may help to explain the pre-eminence of parts of western Europe in this field; but its sources must be sought in other texts and other traditions, its ingredients discerned rather in patterns of behaviour than of thought. The task is not easy, because most explorers – those who were unsuccessful or unsung – probably remain unknown. The precarious nature of their memorials is obvious: few, outside the household of Dom Henrique of Portugal, had a chronicler to itemise their feats; fewer still had the skill in self-praise of a Columbus or a Vespucci; only one, Diogo Cão, engraved his deeds in stone. Many known by name are reported only or chiefly on maps: Lanzarotto Malocello, of Genoa, was recorded on the island in the Canaries which still bears a version of his name by a cartographer of 1339; in a mapmaker's note, Jaume Ferrer of Majorca was reported lost off the west African coast in 1346; of the Portuguese Diogo Silves, who may have established the true lie of the Azores in 1427, the sole memorial, on a Majorcan map, was accidentally blotted by ink spilled by George Sand. However, just as their efforts can be reconstructed, in part, from maps, so their common profile can be built up from a few surviving documents.

They came, to begin with, mainly from Genoa and Majorca and – later and increasingly – from Portugal, Andalusia and some maritime communities of northern Europe. They often had crusading experience or aspirations, like the Poitevin adventurer Gadifer de la Salle, who went to the Canaries in 1402, Joan de Mora, who was the king of Aragon's captain in Canarian waters in 1366, or Columbus, whose long-term destination was Jerusalem. Others had a background in piracy or privateering, like members of the retinue of the Infante Dom Henrique of Portugal (1394–1460), who were said to have raided Aragonese shipping in the 1430s, or crewmen from Andalusia who sailed in Columbus's wake in the 1490s and had formerly served, as privateers, against Portuguese vessels off the Guinea coast. Some of them were merchants, prospecting for offshore assets; more were penurious noblemen or would-be noblemen escaping from a society of restricted opportunity at home. They sought a 'river of gold' like Ferrer and la Salle;[12] or a route to spices, like the Vivaldi brothers whose galleys were lost in 1291 on their way 'ad partes Indiae per Oceanum';[13] or a rich fishery, like the Bristol merchants who loaded salt on

[11] Fernández-Armesto (1991a), pp. 23–44.
[12] Grosjean (1978), sheet III; Russell (1979), p. 19; Taylor (1928): 'Rio de oro.'
[13] *Monumenta Henricina*, I, pp. 201–6.

their quest for the fabled Isle of Brasil in 1481; or a source of slaves, like the Las Casas and Peraza families of Seville, who promoted a series of raids and conquests in the Canaries from 1393.

They sought to win fiefs or create kingdoms, like la Salle's partner, Jean de Béthencourt, who had himself proclaimed King of the Canaries in the streets of Seville, or the 'knights and squires' of Dom Henrique, who felt called by his horoscope to the accomplishment of great deeds. They came from a world steeped in the idealisation of adventure: the Perazas' squalid wars against stone-age aboriginals on the island of Gomera in the 1440s were celebrated in chivalric verse; the coat of arms of the Béthencourt family was charged with wild men in tribute to Jean's wild adversaries. They bore or appropriated story-book-names, like 'Gadifer' and 'Lancelot' or, in the case of an unsavoury thug who served Dom Henrique, 'Tristram of the Island'. They aspired to fame, yet have been forgotten.

Most of them shared, and strove to embody, the great aristocratic ethos of the late Middle Ages in the west, the 'code' of chivalry. Their role-models were the footloose princes who won themselves kingdoms by deeds of derring-do in popular romances of chivalry, which often had seaborne settings: figures like the medieval 'Brutus', who, when Troy was lost, found a realm in Albion, or Prince Amadis of Gaul, who battled with giants and won an enchanted island. Their spokesman was the Castilian knight, Count Pero Niño, whose chronicle, written by his standard-bearer in the second quarter of the fifteenth century, mixes history, romance and chivalric discourse: *El Victorial* celebrates a knight never vanquished in joust or war or love, whose greatest battles were fought at sea.[14] Columbus, whose life's trajectory startlingly resembled the plot of a chivalric romance of the sea, probably had similar role-models in mind. He arrogated to himself the prize for sighting land on his first Atlantic crossing, less, perhaps, out of naked greed than because his journey, though without precedent in fact, was precedented in literature: in a Spanish version of the medieval Alexander romance, Alexander makes his own discovery of Asia by sea and, the poet emphasises, was first, before all his seamen, to see it.[15]

The trajectory of fictional heroes of romances of the sea could be followed in real life. A suggestive case in point is that of Bartolomeu Perestrelo, the father of Columbus's wife. He was the younger son of a merchant of Piacenza, who made a fortune in Portugal, sufficient to enable him to place his children at court or in its vicinity. Bartolomeu entered the household of the Infante Dom Henrique, where service as a seafarer and coloniser won him the hereditary captaincy of the island of Porto Santo in 1446. This example, which Columbus

---

[14] Díez de Games, *El Victorial*, pp. 40–7, 86–96, 201.
[15] *Libro de Alexandre*, p. 182; Navarro González (1962), pp. 241–311.

had before his eyes, was typical of the experience of adventurers in other islands of the Atlantic. 'Tristram of the Island' in Madeira presided over a chivalric pantomime in which his vassals exchanged ritual kisses and inserted hands according to time-honoured convention. Columbus's fellow Genoese, Antonio da Noli, set up as ruler of Santiago in the Cape Verde Islands. The Peraza family ruled Gomera from a keep of stone and celebrated a chivalric self-perception. In 1499, Pedro Álvares da Caminha dreamed of building on his island of São Tomé in the Gulf of Guinea a city that would rival Rome. These self-cast romantic heroes were like pre-incarnations of Sancho Panza, begging the Don to make him governor of some island. Their spirit of seaborne knight-errantry contrasted with the landlubbers' complacency and contempt for the maritime life that dominated prevailing values in China, say, or the Maghrib.

FINANCE AND PATRONAGE

Yet even this intensity of commitment to adventure could not open new maritime routes without overcoming formidable material constraints. Availability of shipping was not usually an insuperable problem: explorers' expeditions were infrequent and small – normally requiring between one and three ships with crews of twenty to fifty men per ship – and could be supported, on the scale required in this period, from within the shipping stocks of many western Mediterranean and Atlantic ports. Few explorers, however, had the financial resources to pursue their vocation at their own expense or the power to protect any discoveries they might make against the depredations of interlopers. The progress of exploration, therefore, relied on powerful patrons and wealthy backers. Dom Henrique used exploration as a means of diverting to potentially profitable ends his large and unruly household; his role as a patron of explorers, which he probably shared with other royal princes, was later exercised by King João II. John Cabot had a pension from Henry VII and a royal commission to explore similar to that of Columbus. It took Columbus longer to find a noble or royal patron than to reach the New World: he is said in early sources to have approached at least two noble houses and perhaps as many as four or five sovereigns. Except in Portugal, royal financial contributions were generally modest: the patron's role was rather to confer legitimate title to the explorer's potential rewards or profits.

Even in Portugal, merchant-backers were essential, like the Flemings and Genoese who promoted voyages to the Atlantic islands, or Fernão Gomes who bought up Dom Henrique's rights to send expeditions along the African coast after the prince's death, or the Florentines who financed Vasco da Gama's mission to India, or the consortium of Azoreans and Englishmen who equipped north Atlantic voyages between 1501 and 1505. A large group of Bristol merchants, most of whom were engaged in the Icelandic trade and all of whom did business with Spain and Portugal, had combined in the 1480s and 1490s to finance the search for the Isle of Brasil. The Guerra brothers, hard-tack suppliers of Seville, were prominent among financiers of voyages in Columbus's wake. Columbus's own backers belonged to two groups, most of whose members had previously collaborated in raising money for conquest and colonisation in the Canary Islands: royal treasury officials combined with Genoese and Florentine merchants of Seville. The financial role of the crown was largely limited to pourboires for Columbus and the promise that his backers would be indemnified from the royal share of the profits of indulgences.

The viability of the explorers' enterprises is hard to assess. Dom Henrique's navigators found places where slaves could be got and gold traded cheaply, but he seems for a long time to have subsidised exploration from the profits of his interests in fisheries, soap and – perhaps – corsairing. He died in debt but Fernão Gomes, for one, recognised the profitability of his endeavours. Despite heavy losses in shipping and men, the route Vasco da Gama found to India proved instantly profitable, thanks largely to the price differentials that made pepper an extraordinarily valuable cargo. The same cannot be said, however, of the exploration of the north Atlantic, where voyagers persevered with extraordinary tenacity in the investigation of cloud-banks and ice-floes. Columbus's enterprise, though ultimately profitable, was jeopardised by paucity of returns. Anxiety to take home some evidence of potentially profitable trade or produce for his backers is a strong theme of the surviving version of his account of his first Atlantic crossing.

ARCHIPELAGOES OF THE EASTERN ATLANTIC

The explorations undertaken from Latin Christendom in the period with which we are concerned were chiefly directed along five new long-range routes. Since each in turn dominated a distinct but overlapping phase of the story they can conveniently be dealt with successively. First, the exploration of the principal archipelagoes of the eastern Atlantic, which began towards the end of the thirteenth century or early in the fourteenth and which, though well advanced by the 1380s, was only finally accomplished in the mid-fifteenth century; secondly, the search for routes across and around the Sahara, which made little progress before the fifteenth century, but which was prolonged until the entire coast of Africa had been explored to beyond the Cape of Good Hope by 1488; thirdly, the investigation of a new route into and across the north Atlantic, which can be documented in some detail from the 1450s; next, the discovery of routes back and forth across the ocean in central latitudes, made by Columbus in 1492–3; and, finally, the early exploration of the south Atlantic and the opening of a route to the Indian Ocean.

The first of these phases was the work of modest miracles of high medieval technology: the cog, the compass, the marine chart and primitive celestial navigation, done by making rough assessments of relative latitude on the open sea through observation of the height of the sun or Pole Star with the naked eye.[16] In the thirteenth century, when Mediterranean navigators overcame the intimidatingly adverse current that races through the Strait of Gibraltar and began to frequent the Atlantic in large numbers, some turned north to the lucrative and well-known markets of Flanders and England; others turned south into waters unsailed, as far as we know, for centuries, off the west coast of Africa. The record of only one such voyage has survived: the Vivaldi brothers' attempted circumnavigation of Africa in Genoese galleys in 1291. They were never heard of again, but it is likely that there were other journeys in the same direction. It was probably in the course of such journeys that the Canary Islands were discovered, 'memoria patrum' according to Petrarch, writing in the 1340s.[17] The first record of some of the Canaries, and perhaps of Madeira, occurs in a map of 1339. Records of voyages to the islands are prolific in the 1340s. One, which included references to Italian, Portuguese and Spanish participants, was copied by Boccaccio and dated 1341. From 1342, a series of voyages in vessels described as *cocas* or *coques* to 'islands newly found in parts of the west' was recorded in Majorcan documents.[18] Despite gaps in the archives, these can be shown to have had a more or less continuous history until the 1380s, though the nature of the enterprise was transformed in its course, as, from 1352 onwards, missionaries replaced merchants as its prime movers. Visits to the Azores and Madeira group can be inferred both from the nature of the wind system, which tends to impose a daring passage out into the ocean on traffic returning from the Canaries, and from cartographical evidence, which suggests that all but the two most westerly islands of the Azores may have been known to mapmakers of the 1380s.[19] In 1402 to 1405, the gold-hunting expedition of Béthencourt and La Salle contributed the first itinerary – transmitted in a form capable of being mapped – of an exploration by land, on the islands of Lanzarote and Fuerteventura. An exclusively Portuguese enterprise, intermittently pursued between 1427 and 1452, established the true relationship of the islands of the Azores to one another, enabled mapmakers to fix them in roughly their true positions, and added the two remotest islands, Flores and Corvo, to the known tally.

[16] Adam (1966), pp. 91–110; Verlinden (1978), pp. 105–31.   [17] Petrarch, *Le familiari*, i, p. 106.
[18] Rumeu de Armas (1986), pp. 35–7, 157–70: 'a les parts de les illes noveylment trobades envers les parts de occident'.   [19] Fernández-Armesto (1986).

ROUTES AROUND AND ACROSS THE SAHARA

Especially in its later stages, this enterprise has become inseparable from the name of the Infante Dom Henrique. His desire for an island-realm off the African coast belongs in the context of the long-standing desire among European markets and courts to improve access to the sources of the trans-Saharan gold trade. The search may have begun as early as the mid-thirteenth century, for a plausible legend dates a Genoese expedition to Safi in 1253. In 1283 Ramon Lull reported a journey towards the land of the Blacks from Ceuta.[20] The oasis of Sijilmassa is depicted along the trans-Saharan camel route that brought gold to Tlemcen in Giovanni di Carignano's map of the early fourteenth century. The auriferous reputation of the west African interior was reinforced by reports of the pilgrimage to Mecca in 1324 of the Mansa Musa of Mali, whose prodigality caused inflation in Egypt; but no fourteenth-century attempt to outflank the trans-Saharan routes, and open direct communications by sea, was successful. Beyond the range of the Canary current, in latitudes where fresh water was hard to find on shore, the natural hazards of navigation seem to have been too formidable.

The land route continued to attract occasional explorers. In 1413, Anselme d'Isalguier was reported to have returned to Toulouse from Gao with a harem of Black women, though how he could have got so far into the interior of Africa no one knows. In 1447 the Genoese Antonio Malfante got as far as Touat. In 1470 the Florentine Benedetto Dei claimed to have been to Timbuctoo and observed there a lively trade in European textiles. From the 1450s to the 1480s, Portuguese merchants made efforts to cut across country from Arguin, via Waddan, heading for the same destination: at least they seem to have succeeded in diverting some gold caravans to meet them. It was obvious, however, that the intractability of the land route demanded a seaborne approach.

Three developments gradually made such an approach viable: the emergence of a highly manoeuvrable type of ship, equipped with lateen sails for enhancing headway against the wind; improved methods of storing provisions for long journeys – the construction, in particular, of water casks which could keep their contents in potable form for periods extending to months rather than weeks; and the establishment, beginning in 1439, of way-stations in the Azores where ships could stop to victual on the long run back from the west African bulge, via the deep Atlantic, to find the homebound westerlies.

Traditionally, the status of a breakthrough in the enterprise has been assigned to the rounding of Cape Bojador in 1434 by one of Dom Henrique's

---

[20] Lull, *Libre de Evast e Blanquerna*, II, p. 191.

ships; but, to judge from surviving maps and sailing directions of the fifteenth and early sixteenth centuries, the cape known by that name in the vague and fluid toponymy of the time was the modern Cape Juby, which had certainly been rounded many times before.[21] 'The cape-by-cape depiction of the building of empire'[22] is in any case an heroic distortion, originating in the narrative technique of the chronicler Zurara, who wrote to glorify the deeds of fellow members of Dom Henrique's entourage. More significant were the achievements of expeditions led partly by Genoese navigators under Henrique's patronage in the mid-1450s, which reported the existence of the Cape Verde Islands, explored the lower reaches of the Gambia and Senegal rivers and established contact with outposts of the empire of Mali. These were genuinely unprecedented achievements in exploration. They produced, moreover, reports written by a Venetian participant, Alvise Da Mosto, whose observations of the people and environment of the Senegambia region were unsurpassed in vividness, among explorers' accounts, until the writings of Columbus.

After Henrique's death in 1460, explorers seem to have paused, presumably deterred by lack of patronage and the lee shores around the turn of Africa's bulge. In 1469, the initiative was revived by the grant of the right of exploration to Fernão Gomes. He commissioned voyages which added some 1,200 miles of coastline to the area navigated by Portuguese ships and extended the range of mapping to about the latitude of Cabo de Santa Caterina (2 degrees N.), the approximate limit of navigation with favourable currents on the outward voyage. Though his monopoly lasted only six years, on the face of it his explorations represented an astonishing rate of increase over the tentative efforts of Dom Henrique. But conditions were now more propitious. A way had been found through some of the most adverse of the sailing conditions that made the routes to and from Africa so arduous, and a route home, difficult but practicable, had been established via well-stocked ports. Moreover, the profitability of the enterprise had been enhanced by the discovery of further saleable products in the form of ivory and malaguetta 'pepper'.

The crown rescinded Fernão's monopoly in 1475, perhaps in order to confront Castilian interlopers on the Guinea coast. The navigation of west Africa now became the responsibility of the senior prince of the royal house, the Infante Dom João. Henceforth Portugal had an heir and, from his accession in 1481, a king committed to the further exploration and exploitation of Africa. He had a militant and organising mentality, forged in war against the Castilian corsairs. As 'Lord of Guinea' he boosted the prestige of African enterprise at home, centralised the control of commerce, built an emporium for the gold

---

[21] Mauny (1960); Campbell (1987), p. 141.   [22] Russell-Wood (1982), p. 20.

trade about 100 kilometres from the mouth of the river Volta and presided over an extraordinary turnover in baptisms and rebaptisms of rapidly apostasising African chiefs.[23] He was also the patron of heroic new feats of exploration, which dwarfed those of the eras of Dom Henrique and Fernão Gomes.

The voyages of Diogo Cão, who made contact with the kingdom of Kongo in 1482 and, having entered the river Zaire, established the shape of the coast to just beyond 22 degrees S. in 1485, were made with amazing tenacity in the face of adverse winds and currents. In the summer of 1487, Cão was followed by Bartolomeu Dias, who left Lisbon with three ships and a commission to find the ocean route round Africa. At first retracing Cão's coastbound route, he seems subsequently, with great daring, to have turned away from the coast, perhaps in about 27 or 28 degrees S., in search of a favourable wind. The result was a major contribution to knowledge of the wind-system of the south Atlantic, for Cão encountered westerlies which carried him to a landfall some 300 miles east of the Cape of Good Hope. The expedition seems to have been exceptionally well provisioned, suggesting that the detour into the open ocean was planned in advance.

The discovery of new sources of gold and slaves meant that the direct economic effects of west African exploration were potentially revolutionary. Yet in the sixteenth century the development of transatlantic and Indian Ocean trade largely left behind the west African world of dangerous shores, inhospitable climes, difficult access and relatively limited rewards. Exploration had, however, yielded great benefits for the growth of Latin Christendom's world-picture. The discovery of the south Atlantic wind-system was the key which unlocked access to the Indian and Pacific Oceans. The shape and southward reach of Africa had been established by empirical evidence after a long period of insufficiently informed debate. The African enterprise had, moreover, taken European seamen beyond the equator for the first time to a hemisphere where, out of sight of the Pole Star, an unfamiliar heaven made new demands of celestial navigators: this proved an enormous source of stimulation to the science and technology, as well as the prestige, of navigation. The early modern revolution in the methods, range and results of navigation was thus prepared and, to some extent, pre-figured, in the fifteenth-century African voyages.

ROUTES ACROSS THE NORTH ATLANTIC

In northern waters there was no great patron endowed with the means or tenacity of Dom Henrique or Dom João, no chronicler like Zurara to system-

---

[23] Russell (1986).

atise or romanticise the gropings of the explorers. This is surprising. The northern seas were full of romance. They were, for example, the setting of the peregrinations of St Brendan and the adventures of Amadis, of the voyages of conquest of the *Gesta Arthuri* and the armchair travels of the fourteenth-century friar, Nicholas of Lynne, who claimed to have visited the north pole five times.[24] Yet, perhaps because the results were disappointing, the real story of their exploration, compared with these engaging fantasies, is relatively unsung.

There was a route across the north Atlantic which might be called traditional: it led from Scandinavia, by way of easterly currents north of the Faroes to Iceland and Greenland. This route could be and was pursued as far as Newfoundland, at which point an adverse current inhibited further progress south, while prevailing westerlies were available to take ships homeward. The remains of a long-abandoned settlement or way-station at l'Anse-aux-Meadows in Newfoundland are consistent with Norse origins; these have been linked with the Icelandic saga tradition of the discovery of a land called Vinland at the end of the tenth century and its temporary settlement early in the eleventh. Until 1347, Icelandic annals continued to record journeys for trading or trapping to Markland, a name apparently applied to part of the north American mainland, north of Newfoundland. Thereafter, however, this island-hopper's route across the Atlantic dwindled in significance, owing in part, perhaps, to the colder weather which seems to have characterised northern latitudes for a while in the late Middle Ages. Communication ceased with settlements in Greenland and attempts to revive it early in the fifteenth century found that the colonists had died out or disappeared, although, if sixteenth-century traditions can be trusted, the attempt was renewed intermittently from Denmark in the last third of the century. If, as is often assumed, fishing or whaling expeditions from European ports continued to make voyages deep into the Atlantic, they are unrecorded.

The axis of penetration of the Atlantic shifted south in the fifteenth century to the zone of prevailing westerlies. This may seem paradoxical, yet it is a curious fact that, outside monsoonal climates, in the history of maritime exploration as a whole, most voyagers seem to have preferred to make their outwards journeys against the wind, presumably as an investment of present trouble in the hope of future return. The discovery of Flores and Corvo in 1452 marks the beginning of a series of such Atlantic voyages, which it may have helped to inspire. Between 1462 and 1487 at least eight Portuguese commissions survive for voyages from the Azores to discover new lands; some of these refer explicitly to the evidence of sea charts. Among the most general

[24] Taylor (1956a).

terms are those of Fernão Teles's grant, in 1474, of 'the Seven Cities or whatever islands he shall find'. In 1487, the Fleming Ferdinand von Olmen, also
sailing from the Azores under Portuguese auspices, was commissioned, in
terms strikingly similar to those of Columbus, for islands and mainland in the
ocean.[25]

Meanwhile, a similar project took shape in Bristol, where long experience in
the Iceland trade made navigators familiar with north Atlantic waters. What the
islands of 'Antillia' or 'the Seven Cities' were to Azorean ambitions, that of
'Brasil' was to the Bristolians. The origins of the legend of Brasil are obscure
but a putative island of that name appears, in various positions, on medieval
Atlantic charts. The beginnings of what seems to be a sustained programme of
exploration in search of it were noticed by the writer on chivalry, William
Worcestre, in a notebook of personal memoranda of 1480. On 15 July, he
records, a ship belonging to two well-known merchant families, who regularly
traded with both Iceland and the Iberian peninsula, set off 'usque ad insulam de
Brasylle in occidentali parte Hibernie'.[26] Bad weather forced them back in
September without success. The following year, another expedition with the
same objective was declared by a larger group of projectors. The continuation
or resumption of the search is suggested by the terms of a letter of 1498, in
which a Castilian ambassador assured his sovereigns that Bristolians annually
equipped expeditions in search of the Isle of Brasil and the Seven Cities.[27]

The context of this remark was the ambassador's desire to acquaint his
superiors with news of John Cabot, the Genoese navigator who had made
Bristol his base for a more ambitious project: the crossing of the Atlantic in an
attempt to reach China. Academic debate about the size of the globe and the
extent of the ocean had encouraged speculations about the accessibility of the
orient by way of the west. Paolo del Pozzo Toscanelli had proposed it in a letter
to a correspondent at the Portuguese court in 1474. The idea seems implicit in
the globe attributed to Martin Behaim. Columbus had attempted to put the
idea into effect along a relatively southerly latitude – and, therefore, across a
longer distance than would apply further north – in 1492. The Nuremberg
physician, Hieronymus Münzer, had appealed to the king of Portugal to
sponsor an attempt in 1493. Columbus's experiences seemed, to some, to
confirm the viability of the project: Columbus himself professed to believe
that he had got close to China and a published version of his report showed
traders in oriental garb visiting the lands he had discovered. The result of
Cabot's attempts, between 1496 and 1498, was the recording of a viable direct
route west, to and from Newfoundland, returning with the westerlies and

[25] Verlinden (1962) and (1970), pp. 181–95.   [26] Worcestre, *Itineraries*, pp. 308–9.
[27] *Calendar of state papers; Spanish, 1485–1509*, p. 177.

making use on the way out of a brief spring season of variable winds. It seems likely that the use of these winds was already known in Bristol, where Cabot's discovery was dismissed as of slight significance and identified with the Isle of Brasil;[28] nor did Cabot's exploits excite the imitators and emulators inspired by Columbus. The search for a route to Asia across the north Atlantic was not resumed until well into the sixteenth century.

THE CENTRAL TRANSATLANTIC ROUTE

Sailing conditions for transatlantic voyages were far superior further south, in the latitudes explored by Columbus. Yet, as he said of his own crossing in 1492, his route was one never, 'as far as we know', sailed before[29] and the presumption that he had been preceded by an 'unknown pilot', while often aired, has never been vindicated. Compared with documented attempts further north, Columbus's originality lay in his daring to sail with the wind at his back, to the consternation of some of his crew, until he made a landfall, with no certainty that he would find a means of return. This alone accounts for his unprecedented success. The assumption that he knew the wind-system thoroughly in advance is tempting but unjustified: he was a restless experimenter, a tireless advocate of an empirical epistemology, who, in the course of four Atlantic crossings, tried three routes out to his discoveries and three routes back. On his first crossing he adopted what seemed logically the shortest route between two points by trying to sail due west. If, as his language suggests, he steered by the compass, this would have meant in practice a route somewhat south of west, owing to magnetic variation; he contemplated returning the same way and even began on a more southerly course before turning in search of the familiar westerlies of the north Atlantic. After further experiments, the routes of his second voyage, in 1493, were established as the best: outward in the path of the northeast trade winds, along a diagonal from the Canary Islands to the Antilles, and back by climbing almost to the latitude of the Azores before turning due east. Indeed, apart from modifications made to the return route as a result of the discovery of the Gulf Stream in 1513, Columbus established what became the most favoured routes between Europe and most of the New World throughout the age of sail.

His reason for wanting to cross the Atlantic in the first place is a subject of unresolved debate. He appears at different times during the formulation of his plans to have contemplated a number of different objectives: the discovery of new islands, a search for the Antipodes and a short route to Asia. All these, as

---

[28] Gil and Varela (1984), p. 269.
[29] Varela (ed.), *Cristóbal Colón*, p. 16: 'por donde hasta oy no sabemos por cierta fe que aya passado nadie'.

we have seen, were matters of common speculation, discussed in academic geography and illustrated in cartography. By the time of his first crossing in 1492 Columbus's focus had narrowed to the quest for a short route to Asia: this, at least, is the only objective mentioned in what survives of his own account of the voyage. Still, this was perhaps as much his patrons' and backers' choice as his own, and Columbus's subsequent commitment to the view that his discoveries were indeed Asian, or close to Asia, should not be treated as evidence of what was in his mind earlier in his career. He seems to have been concerned not so much about what he would discover as whether, in a social sense, he would 'arrive'. For Columbus, the geographical nature of his objective was negotiable; what he insisted on was the chance to make a voyage and, if he found something exploitable, no matter exactly what, to claim the rewards of wealth and ennoblement to which the hero of a seaborne romance was entitled. His true objective was identified by the potential mutineers, on his first crossing, who are said in an early narrative source to have grumbled at the risk posed to their lives by Columbus's desire 'to make himself a lord'.[30]

There was nothing new in his methods or equipment. His methods of navigation, which he described as 'like prophetic vision',[31] were a mixture of the traditional and the intuitive. He relied on primitive celestial navigation and, probably to a lesser extent, on dead reckoning (which consists in plotting one's course by the compass and determining position by estimating speed). He resorted when necessary to such time-honoured expedients as following the flight of birds. He carried a quadrant or astrolabe, with which he impressed his men, but he never mastered the use of it. His fixings of latitude were made by timing the hours of sun and reading the corresponding latitude off a printed table.[32] His attempts to calculate longitude on shore by timing eclipses were, from a scientific point of view, valueless. He had an uncanny way of interpreting the weather – unsurpassed, in a shipmate's opinion, 'since Genoa was Genoa'[33] – and an enviable facility in the haven-finding art in unfamiliar seas. He was genuinely, passionately interested in technical innovations; but his achievements relied on technology which had been available literally for centuries.

By the time his exploring career came to an end, he had accumulated a dazzling record. As well as his major achievement – the discovery of a transatlantic link – he had observed and described the whole of the coast and part of the interior of Hispaniola, and parts of the Bahamas, Cuba, Jamaica, Puerto Rico, the Virgin Islands, the Lesser Antilles and Trinidad. He had crossed the Caribbean and explored the mainland coast of the New World from the Bay of

---

[30] Las Casas, *Historia de las Indias*, 1, p. 189: 'por hacerse gran señor'.
[31] Varela (ed.), *Cristobál Colón*, p. 325: 'a visión profética se asemeja esto'.
[32] Laguarda Trías (1974), pp. 13–17, 27–8; *Ymago mundi de Pierre d'Ailly*, 1, pp. 144–5, 159–63, plate facing p. 272.   [33] Gil and Varela (1984), p. 269: 'desde que Génova es Génova'.

Honduras almost to the Gulf of Urabá and from the mouth of the Orinoco to Margarita. He had recognised South America as an 'other world' and 'a very large continent, which hitherto has remained unknown',[34] though he misrepresented it as being close to or contiguous with Asia. He established an enduring transatlantic link, inaugurated a series of previously unimagined cultural contacts and initiated Spanish colonisation in the New World.

In terms strictly of exploration, he left little for other explorers to accomplish in the areas he touched. The terms of his royal commission granted him a monopoly of navigation to his discoveries; but, when he was out of favour at court from 1499 to 1502, imitators were authorised to follow his route from a small number of ports in and around the mouth of the Guadalquivir. They included collaborators and crew members of his own: Vicente Yáñez Pinzón, fellow traveller and brother of Columbus's co-commander on the first crossing, whose family, dominant in the shipping business of the port of Palos, had provided the ships and recruited men for Columbus; Alonso de Hojeda, on whom Columbus had relied heavily in the government of Hispaniola; Peralonso Niño and Juan de la Cosa, both of whom had accompanied at least one of Columbus's expedition; Cristóbal and Luis Guerra, who had supplied him with provisions; and Amerigo Vespucci, the business partner of one of Columbus's backers. Of leaders of expeditions in this direction in these years, only Rodrigo de Bastidas, Diego de Lepe and Luis Vélez de Mendoza came from outside Columbus's circle.

Between them they extended Columbus's achievement in two respects. Expeditions led by Hojeda and de la Cosa in 1499, Niño and the Guerra brothers in 1499–1500, and Bastidas and de la Cosa in 1501–2 followed the mainland coast of America along the section omitted by Columbus between Margarita and the Darién peninsula. Departing from Palos in November, 1499, Pinzón attempted a more original effect by aiming for a more southerly landfall than Columbus. Via the Cape Verde Islands, he crossed with the north-east trades on what was almost the most southward course possible, reaching the coast of what is now Brazil at a point he named Cabo de Consolación late in January, 1500. He then followed the coast northwards across the mouth of the Amazon as far as the area already familiar from Columbus's work. He can therefore be credited with the first recorded discovery of Brazil and a formidable addition to the information on the New World available at the Castilian court. In July, 1500, Vespucci recorded a claim to have preceded him to the mouth of the Amazon by approaching from the north on a detour from an expedition identifiable with Hojeda's; but, like most of the claims made by Vespucci, or on his behalf and under his name, this cannot be independently verified.

[34] Varela (ed.), *Cristobál Colón*, p. 238: 'esta es tierra firme grandíssima, de que hasta oy no se a sabido'.

EXPLORATION OF THE SOUTH ATLANTIC

Pinzón's route led into the south Atlantic, to a point on the Brazilian coast where, had he chosen to turn south instead of north, the current would have led him to beyond the Tropic of Capricorn and into the zone of the roaring forties. Luis Vélez de Mendoza, who followed hard on Pinzón's heels, did turn south but without getting much further. It was left to Vespucci, sailing in Pinzón's wake under Portuguese auspices in company with Gonçalo Coelho, in 1501–2, to trace the extent of the coast along the path of the current. He got at least as far as Rio de Janeiro – reached on New Year's Day, 1502 – and, by his own account, much further, though his reported southernmost reach of 50 degrees along the coast and 52 degrees after turning east into the open sea must be judged against the background both of his habit of exaggeration and of the poor record generally of navigators of the time in determining latitude. Vespucci was unstinting in self-praise and some of his other contemporaries were almost equally impressed with him. The rapid dissemination of an increasingly accurate picture of the Atlantic shore of south America in the early years of the sixteenth century probably owes much to his efforts and influence, and it was therefore not so great an error as is often suggested when the continent took its name from him.

Judged by its consequences, the exploration of the wind-system of the south Atlantic must be acknowledged to have been more important than the delineation of the ocean's coasts. Yet the sources available at present permit only a patchy and unsatisfactory reconstruction of the events. Between the return of Bartolomeu Dias in 1488 and the departure of Vasco da Gama, bound for the Indian Ocean in 1497, no voyages of exploration in those waters are known; the presumption that some part of the record is missing arises from the contrast between the tentative procedures of Dias and the boldness of da Gama. The former, after long, slow headway against the Benguela current, waited until a late stage before turning his prow out into the ocean to find the westerlies that carried him round the Cape. Da Gama, however, sailed exclusively with square-rigged vessels, demonstrating his intention of using following winds all the way. After his initial course to the Cape Verde Islands, he stood out to sea at about the latitude of Sierra Leone and steered a long course to the south and west, across the belt of south-east trade winds, before turning with the first favourable wind, probably around 30 degrees S. Even this proved insufficiently bold, for he made a landfall near the mouth of the Orange river and had then to work his way coastwise around the southern tip of Africa. If, as seems likely, his plan was to round the Cape of Good Hope without making land, he should have risked following an even wider arc into the south Atlantic and turning east below 35 degrees S. This was the course adopted in 1500 by the expedition of Pedro Álvares de Cabral, which, sent to follow up da Gama's achievement, sailed so far west on the outward voyage that a landfall was made on the Brazilian coast at about 17 degrees S. Nevertheless, it seems remarkable that, without benefit of any reconnaissance more thorough than that of Dias, Vasco da Gama should have undertaken this enormous voyage – probably by far the longest ever made on the open sea from Europe – of ninety-three days out of sight of land.

It is not even certain that he knew that this dangerous and laborious voyage would end by giving him access to the Indian Ocean. Late fifteenth-century maps in the Ptolemaic tradition showed that sea to be landlocked and barred to an approach from the south. Investigation of this problem was one of the objectives confided in 1487 to Pedro de Covilhã, whose mission to report on the spice routes of the Indian Ocean was financed by some of the same Florentine merchant houses that were investing in Portugal's exploration of the Atlantic. The surviving account of his exploits contains romantic episodes but there is no reason to doubt the claim that he investigated the routes between southern India and east Africa as far south as Sofala. Hearing of the death of a colleague who had been sent as Portuguese ambassador to the Negus of Abyssinia, he then decided to take up that post himself; he was found still living at the Negus's court by the next Portuguese embassy, which arrived in 1520. Meanwhile, however, he had despatched a report of his findings to Lisbon. While there is no evidence that it ever arrived, its existence raises the possibility that Vasco da Gama may have been guided by some such intelligence.[35] Though he entered the Indian Ocean by a novel route, once he had reached Sofala, da Gama did not engage in exploration but – like the many European merchants who had preceded him there in native shipping – merely followed the existing trade routes with the help of local pilots and guides, most notably a Gujerati Muslim who showed him the way from Malindi to Calicut.

Exploration was a means whereby the civilisation of Latin Christendom established access to and, in the longer run, command of a disproportionate share of the resources of the world. Explorers made a major contribution to the reversal of fortunes on a global scale. In the course of it, other civilisations, which in some cases had seemed better endowed and better equipped, became bystanders and ultimately victims of 'western' hegemony. The conquest of the Atlantic in the fifteenth century seems, in retrospect, a decisive step because of the way Atlantic routes led to previously isolated and underexploited lands, and connected with other oceans. Yet this great leap forward for Latin Christendom followed a period of demographic decline and, on most fronts, of contracting frontiers.

[35] Beckingham (1980), p. 310.

It may have helped to come from behind: in richer societies, there was less incentive to look for new sources of wealth; larger civilisations, more autarkic and more secure, could afford contempt for the rest of the world. Considered from one perspective, the endeavours of European explorers in this period resemble the efforts of 'developing' economies today, desperately drilling for offshore resources. On the other hand, as we have seen, the western rim of Latin Christendom had important advantages as a base for world exploration: an Atlantic-side position and a 'culture of explorers', whose vocation enjoyed higher prestige than in some potentially rival civilisations, reflected in the inspiration of literary role-models. The distribution of the technical prerequisites of long-distance travel should not, perhaps, be stressed too much: the achievement of Columbus shows that rudimentary and antiquated technology was adequate for revolutionary tasks. As for the new technology needed for African and south Atlantic exploration, the rule seems to have been *solvitur navigando*.

Unsurprisingly, the communities which produced the explorers and contributed the means were located, for the most part, in the western Mediterranean and on the Atlantic rim, especially in Genoa, Majorca, the Atlantic shores of the Iberian peninsula and, to a lesser extent, parts of England, France, Flanders and perhaps Denmark. Very broadly, it is fair to say that there was an overall displacement of the initiative, over the period as a whole, from other centres to Portugal and lower Andalusia, which enjoyed privileged access to the relatively productive central Atlantic and south Atlantic routes.

The conspicuous achievements of the 1490s raise a particular problem of interpretation. In a period of a few years, what came to be seen as decisive breakthroughs were made into the New World and the Indian Ocean. The voyages of Columbus and Vasco da Gama have often been highlighted as elements of what Adam Smith, for example, called 'the most important event in history',[36] which helped to transform a 'medieval' world into a 'modern' one. These terms are not very helpful, and the gradualist assumptions of recent historiography have happily compelled us to see events in the contexts of long, grinding processes of change. Nevertheless, the pace of processes varies and change sometimes occurs with bewildering rapidity. The story of European exploration is a long one, but the concentrated speed and power of the episodes of the fifteenth century, and of the 1490s in particular, still demand to be acknowledged.

As well as influencing what might be called the balance of world power, the explorers of this period had a major effect on the received picture of the world thanks to the increasing exchange of information between explorers and car-

---

[36] Smith, *Wealth of nations*, p. 590.

tographers. An agreed world map is a common resource of mankind: ours has been pieced together slowly, over a long period, mainly in the last 500 years. Whereas previous civilisations derived their images of the world from dogmas of cosmology, from inductive reasoning, from revelation, from inherited tradition or from the elaboration of theory, we owe today's largely to the practical contributions – often gathered at hazard in hostile environments and reported over vast distances – of the empirical observers whom we call explorers.

PART III

SPIRITUAL, CULTURAL AND
ARTISTIC LIFE

CHAPTER 10

RELIGIOUS BELIEF AND PRACTICE

Francis Rapp

THE religious history of the fifteenth century was dominated by the Great Schism. While the immediate repercussions of that schism were prolonged by the conciliar crisis until 1448, its long-term effects would be apparent until the end of the century. For Christian intellectuals there was no anxiety more pressing than repair of the damage caused by these misfortunes and the forearming of the Church against the repetition of a similar catastrophe. This preoccupation was the initial inspiration behind *reformatio in capite*. Even before the restoration of papal power had nullified those measures agreed by the fathers of the Councils of Constance and Basle, the importance of *reformatio in membris* had been recognised. Every prelate, every superior of a religious community was expected to regularise the organisation he headed, be it a diocese, a congregation or merely a monastery. It was not only the clergy, both regular and secular, whose faults stood in urgent need of correction; the appeal for endeavour was addressed to all Christian people. It was essential, furthermore, to point out to the faithful the path they should follow. The religious education of the laity had never occupied so high a place among the priorities of those clergy who took their duties seriously.

Zeal in the cause of education was the force which motivated Jean Gerson (1363–1429). The learning and moral authority of this Parisian master were greatly admired during his lifetime, and continued to be so long after his death. The theological doctrines he professed were in accordance with his pastoral vocation: man could attain salvation if he used God-given strength to set out in the right direction; the pressing need was to explain this, and to instil an understanding of the rules to be observed on the journey. The proven success of nominalism in the universities facilitated the spread of those ideas in which Pelagian tendencies were apparent. Quite a few adherents of the *via moderna* were responsive to Gerson's recommendations; not satisfied simply to devote themselves to *theologia speculativa*, they took pains to try to communicate their knowledge. Gabriel Biel will suffice as one example: his *Expositio canonis Missae* affected a vast number of readers – Martin Luther was merely the most famous of them.

Advocates of the *devotio moderna* were responding to the same desire to educate and mould Christians which inspired Gerson and his emulators. The Brethren of the Common Life were bent upon selecting edifying texts, on devising others, and on seeing that both were read by as many people as possible. They were, too, shrewd pedagogues, more concerned with developing the intelligence of their pupils than with simply filling their heads with information. Their school at Deventer quickly earned a reputation for efficiency which was amply deserved. The search for ways of awakening adolescent minds was at this same time a focus of attention for various Italian humanists, in particular Vittorino da Feltre and Guarino da Verona. Their concerns coincided with those of Gerson, who was wondering how to 'lead the very young towards Christ'. Without doubt they were all responding to the ever-broadening horizons of western society, with its desire to learn about and better understand the world. Reading was becoming more and more of a necessity, and in some regions the level of literacy reached 10 per cent. The proliferation of Latin schools heralded the flowering of Protestant gymnasia and Jesuit colleges in the sixteenth century. It was a matter of urgency to stabilise the bands of wandering scholars; it was necessary, too, to prepare future students so that they could benefit from a university education.

Universities were attracting more and more young men. Indeed, the network of these establishments had become considerably more tight-knit. A high proportion of the young who attended university subsequently entered a religious order. Furthermore, it was no longer exceptional at the end of the fifteenth century to find that one in three clerics, sometimes more, had spent several semesters in a faculty, although the overwhelming majority had studied liberal arts only. The colleges created to educate future priests, for example the Collegium Georgianum founded in Ingolstadt in 1494, were merely prototypes of the seminaries whose foundation in every diocese would later be required by the Council of Trent. However, the mendicant orders remained practically the only ones to equip their members with knowledge and training that had been properly thought out and methodically administered in the *studia generalia* or *particularia*. As far as theology was concerned, the secular clergy were often reduced to self-education; the books which bishops recommended for purchase, for instance the *Manipulus curatorum* of Guy de Montrocher, or the *Pupilla oculi*, written in Oxford in 1385 and still sought after in Strasburg in 1514, contained a large proportion of what the parish clergy might have the opportunity to learn.

An *Ars praedicandi* sometimes featured prominently in the modest libraries available to the least disadvantaged rectors and vicars. Such compositions set out the fundamental rules of preaching, and explained their simplest application. Preparation for preaching was not merely a matter of memorising a set of principles taken from a primer. Collections of *exempla* provided edifying stories suitable for sprinkling into the sermon like cherries into the cake, in order to illustrate the argument being developed, and to retain the attention of listeners more eager for anecdote than inclined to follow the subtleties of logical reasoning. It was convenient to resort to models: the *Summa praedicantium* by the English Dominican, John Bromyard, constituted a precious tool, and in Germanic countries Jean de Werden's sermons, collected together under the alluring title *Dormi secure*, were presented for easy use for priests whose education was below standard. Printed books reduced the price of texts to very low levels, and brought them within reach of meagre incomes. Collections of sermons rolled off the presses in their thousands, and circulated through the length and breadth of the Christian world. For instance, those written by the Hungarian Franciscan, Pelbartus of Temeswar, were printed in Alsace; the fact that they were continually reissued is testimony of their success. Ever-increasing numbers made use of such works. The study of preachers in the areas of France to the north of the Loire has identified more than 1,600 of them in the fifteenth century, of whom 1,000 belonged to the period 1450 to 1500, as against fewer than 350 in the second half of the fourteenth century.[1]

The majority of priests capable of preaching and eager to do so effectively lived in towns, and thus their normal congregations represented only a small proportion of the total Christian population. Country areas, however, were not entirely neglected by preachers. Priests ministering to rural parishes who had done some studying were becoming less of an exception; those capable of putting a sermon together, with books at their disposal to facilitate the task, could be found more and more frequently. Educated or not, rectors and vicars were expected to set out the fundamental truths of the faith at the Sunday Mass. Joan of Arc's answers to her judges prove that an intelligent, though illiterate, young woman could make good use of this. Municipal authorities were not uninterested in preaching. In many cities in southern Germany, as in Switzerland, they encouraged the establishment of 'preacherships', whose holders were required to have a doctorate or, at least, a degree. Their task was to preach regularly on Sundays and feast days. In England, in spite of restrictive measures taken after 1407 through fear of Wyclifite influences – measures severely criticised by Thomas Gascoigne – pulpits were erected in many churches as well as in cemeteries, where crowds could assemble more easily. French towns turned for preference to the mendicant orders: church wardens or town councillors commissioned from them cycles of sermons for Advent

[1] Martin (1988).

and Lent. Financial accounts give us an idea of how frequently they preached compared to the secular clergy. Between 1440 and 1520, 220 different preachers spoke 11,000 times in Amiens, an average of 137 times a year.[2] The far more modest reckoning for Romorantin, though noticeably lower, still reveals on average a pattern of almost forty sermons a year. What is more, these figures only include those whose remuneration justified an entry in the records. Probably the only preachers to be paid were those called upon to perform on special occasions – at festivals, or at times of crisis or exceptional solemnity.

Organisers of these 'show-piece' sermons sought the participation of personalities with a well-established reputation for eloquence. Preaching was a 'socially recognised' profession requiring its members to respect 'clearly defined conditions of practice', including a scale of fees.[3] Star performers came at the top of the scale. In France, the most valued of these 'stars' were among the Franciscans and Dominicans, for example Guillaume Josseaume, Olivier Maillard and Jean Clérée. It was the mendicants, in particular the Franciscan Observants, who practised the art of stirring a crowd with the most fire and skill. The example of the Dominican Vincent Ferrer who, from 1399 to 1419, travelled enormous distances exhorting the masses to repent, was followed by others: Bernardino of Siena, John of Capistrano and Giacomo delle Marche are merely among the most famous of these virtuosi of prophetic preaching. To make their listeners receptive to their message and to prolong the effect of their exhortations, they employed all the resources of a stage production. The impact of their impassioned preaching was so powerful that they inspired spectacular decisions in those who heard them. Thus the *rogo della vanità* consumed in flames objects which, turning Christians away from the straight and narrow path, were leading them into sin. That a solitary friar, Savonarola, fostered, albeit briefly, a climate of austerity in Florence, a centre of wealth and refinement, is testimony that the words of a popular orator, consumed by a passionate desire to convert, did not fall on stony ground. North of the Alps, the surges of religious fervour unleashed by similar preaching campaigns were less frequent than in Italy. None the less, the success enjoyed by the Carmelite, Thomas Connecte, and the Franciscan, Brother Richard, proves that the French were not always unresponsive to such eloquence.

Orators were more readily listened to the more they larded their sermons with references to matters of topical concern, particularly those likely to arouse anxiety or indignation. The principal objective of the preacher was to move his audience; to achieve this, he resorted to a dramatic style, so that sermons took on a theatrical character. References to images alluding to suffering and death were numerous. The systematic use of allegories was

---

[2] Martin (1988), p. 152.   [3] Martin (1988), p. 188.

designed to make the most important elements in the sermon easier to memorise, since touching the emotions of the congregation was not the sole objective; there was, above all, the intention to instruct. In fact, preaching was 'a catechism before its time'.[4] It taught the right way to believe so as to live a better life; by emphasising the Incarnation and Passion, manifestations of God's love for man, it encouraged him to mend his ways so that divine generosity should not lack a response.

A sermon's efficacy was measured by the number of confessions it provoked, and the famous Observant preachers were always accompanied by priests ready at all times to hear penitents. The confession of sins was not the only part of the proceedings; before giving absolution the confessor questioned the penitent in order to give him a better understanding of the nature and gravity of his failings. It was thus essential for the confessor himself to be sufficiently well educated to do this. The *Sommes de confesseur* was written to enlighten him but, until printing had lowered the cost, it was more or less a waste of time to recommend its purchase. For the same reason models for the examination of conscience, meant for the faithful, only became widely available after 1470, and then particularly in Germany. Qualified confessors were able to ensure that assiduous penitents did not lack spiritual guides. St Antoninus of Florence wrote the *Opera a ben vivere* for two of his female devotees, both of the Florentine aristocracy. Having a spiritual director was, in effect though not by right, the preserve of the privileged few. Mostly the faithful were content to fulfil their Easter duties, and the parish priest to whom they confessed on this occasion was but poorly equipped to instruct them.

Those who had an opportunity to develop their religious life by reading were, likewise, an elite. The books recommended were of a rich variety. The most common were collections of prayers, almost always co-ordinated to the sequences of canonical hours. Their tone varied according to temperament: in England, the predominant note was sweetness expressed in rhymed verse, though for all that there was no lack of theological muscle; in the Low Countries, the influence of the *Devotio Moderna* was perceptible; in Germany, the same tradition was integrated into the tradition of mysticism. The Bible was not presented solely in the guise of sacred history. Translations made its full text available to lay people. Printing took over the copyists' workshops and flooded the market with religious books in the vernacular. Production, however, outpaced the market; progress in education was slower than in technology, and reading remained a means of spiritual education for but a small minority of Christians.

Iconography, however, could appeal to everyone. Statues and pictures

[4] Martin (1988), p. 295.

proliferated, assuming many different shapes and sizes: monumental groups such as Breton calvaries, portable altarpieces, illuminations and wood-engravings intended to sustain the piety of the devout in the privacy of their rooms. The image could come to life: processions of *tableaux vivants* in England, as in Italy; theatrical productions in France and the Germanic countries. Large towns mustered troops of actors and participants who, against complicated back-drops, presented mystery plays which accredited theologians had packed with learning. The image-makers were fostering emotion even more than education. Gazing at these creations, Christians were moved by the sight of the Infant Jesus playing on his mother's knee; their hearts were touched by the Pietà; and patron saints reassured them by their presence. But, all the while, the *danse macabre* urged them not to forget the end of all earthly things.

The doctrine brought by the Church to Christian people was a rich one, but its teaching was not without its defects; it was unsystematic and was administered very patchily. Even if a few intellectuals had appreciated the vital necessity of ensuring that children should receive religious instruction, the catechism, as it was to be created by the Catholic and Protestant faiths in the sixteenth century, did not yet exist. None the less, Gerson and Joan of Arc show that, even in rural areas, parents (upon whom the responsibility of instructing their children largely fell) could fulfil the task with excellent results.

At the beginning of the fifteenth century a ruling of the Inquisition listed the actions characteristic of a 'good and faithful Christian': he attended church, made offerings, went to confession, extended a welcome to mendicants. The list was not exhaustive, and other compilers might have drawn up this list of priorities in a different way. Theological debates on the relationship between grace and good works need not detain us, as these questions scarcely affected the mass of the faithful who were blind to, and ignorant of, the subtle analyses of scholars.

The Catholic belongs to a complex society which cannot function without priests; they are, above all, dispensers of the sacraments. Normally they administer baptism, a rite sometimes carried out in a somewhat perfunctory fashion. Parents were anxious for their children to be baptised: how else can one explain the popularity of those sanctuaries where the Virgin Mary resuscitated stillborn infants for as long as it took to sprinkle water over them? All the faithful were baptised, but those who went on to be confirmed were often relatively few in number, since opportunities for contact with a bishop (who, alone, could confirm) were quite rare. As for extreme unction, it was a source of fear rather than of comfort and, because they tended to postpone it, the sick often died without its succour. Holy orders were of concern only to clerics. As regards matrimony, the religious and civil authorities vied with each other in stressing its importance. The amount of time consumed in ecclesiastical courts by disputes concerning lawful marriages proves that canonical recommendations were not a dead letter, although many, for lack of adequate means to put things on a proper legal footing, lived in concubinage.

The sacraments we have just dealt with, normally administered but once, mark decisive stages in a Christian's life. The same is not true of confession and communion, which restore and strengthen with grace. The Church ordains that they should be received at least once a year. We cannot know to what extent the faithful fulfilled their Easter duties. It was easier to shirk them in large cities than in villages, where the priest's flock was small enough for him to know and supervise everybody. According to church wardens' records, the vast majority of the faithful confined themselves to this obligatory communion; the relatively low number of hosts consumed being evidence of this. If people came to the communion table but seldom, it was not necessarily a sign of lukewarm piety: awe and reverence kept them at a distance. Ecclesiastical teaching and ceremonial did not scruple to stress that God was actually present in the guise of bread and wine, and these lessons were not without consequence. They instilled in the faithful a respect which expressed itself in the veneration they lavished on the reserved Sacrament. In large churches they constructed tabernacles as tall as houses to preserve it. They fell on their knees when a priest passed by carrying the Last Sacrament to the dying. All possible ceremonial was employed when the Blessed Sacrament was carried solemnly through the streets or round the bounds of a parish. The feast of Corpus Christi was no longer the unique occasion for religious processions which were now requested so frequently by parishioners that some clergy were driven to complain. The monstrance exposed the Bread of Life to be adored by the devout, who were eager at least to look upon it. In order to share in the spiritual benefits produced by the bloodless re-enactment of the Sacrifice of Redemption, it was not absolutely necessary to communicate during Mass; nor was it even essential to be present. Thus foundations of chantries, intended to ensure the regular re-enactment of these rites in perpetuity, were just as numerous after 1400 as they had been before. Even so, the custom of preordaining large numbers of Masses, to be said or sung as soon as possible after a testator's death, was already widespread. Such Masses were usually requiems; Purgatory was more than ever a gnawing anxiety. The practice of confession, obligatory since 1215, and vigorously recommended by the mendicants, had drawn the attention of penitents to the punishment which forgiveness of sin did not cancel out, but which had to be undergone, if not in this life, then in the next.

Theological doctrine gave to the pope, and to a lesser degree to the bishops, the power to commute such punishment. With the benefit of this mitigation and as reward for a pious deed, believers were assured of a shorter period in Purgatory, which they might even avoid altogether. So urgent did the desire to influence their fate in the after-life become, that the faithful obtained from the hierarchy an increase in the number of these indulgences. The plenary indulgence, in origin tied to the crusades, had subsequently, through the creation of jubilees, been made obtainable every twenty-five years to those making the pilgrimage to Rome. More and more often it was granted to patrons of sanctuaries which, for a few weeks, enjoyed the status of Roman basilicas during Holy Years. These graces were dispensed so prodigally that the term inflation would not be out of place to describe their increase, particularly since offerings represented considerable sums of money, and their allocation and transfer gave rise to large-scale financial operations.

Indulgences only remitted punishment. By failing to obtain absolution of a mortal sin before dying, the deceased risked condemnation to eternal hell-fire. Sudden death, then, was a formidable danger, since it prevented those whom it despatched from confessing their sins in time. The fervent Christian prepared himself for his final conflict down to the last detail; if he had not lived a good life, he should at least do everything in his power to die well. Jean Gerson and Nicholas of Dinkelsbühl each composed an *Ars moriendi* of which summaries were offered to readers in many works of piety.

The activities here illustrated are merely the most important and the most performed. They represent but a part of the body of rites created by almost a millennium of preaching and devotion. Prayers, offerings and blessings punctuated rhythmically each passing day, the cycle of the seasons and the stages of life. Localities where intimations of the supernatural had been experienced long ago in pagan times had often been Christianised and transformed into places of pilgrimage. Time and space bore the imprint of a religion which, at the close of the Middle Ages, had become truly omnipresent.

True piety was more than the simple multiplication of religious observances. Many preachers put their congregations on their guard against false certainties which would result from the mere performance of the actions prescribed or recommended by the Church. In order to be of some account these actions needed to be an expression of sentiments and intentions exemplifying the spirit of the Gospel. The rosary, whose popularity was evident throughout the fifteenth century, far from being reduced to a mechanical recitation of 'Our Fathers' and 'Hail Marys', should be an invitation to the devout to meditate upon the mysteries of the Redemption. A method of praying akin to that formulated by the founders of the *devotio moderna* percolated through the Christian community from the Confraternities of the Rosary. In the same period, some authors were urging the faithful to turn pilgrimages into a form of itinerant retreat, and to transform their daily lives into a kind of spiritual pilgrimage. Opportunities for reading, which the development of printing opened up to the educated elite, expanded still further the realm of personal prayer, which was thus stimulated by meditation upon devotional texts. In 1476 a bourgeois woman from Swabia voraciously read the entire Bible between the middle of Lent and Easter.

At the end of the Middle Ages, just as Gothic art was adorning the clean lines of architecture with characteristic flamboyant decoration, so piety was creating a plethora of supererogatory devotions around the basic acts of Christian worship. The fundamental truths were not changed in the fifteenth century; neither were they mutilated. But the rites performed and the words spoken by clerics and faithful, because they were a reflection of their feelings, conferred on the religious life of the period its particular flavour. It is worth devoting some attention to these themes which recur like leitmotifs in the various forms of worship, both private and public.

Above all else, emphasis was placed on the act of Redemption, manifestation of God's love for the human race. Authors and preachers, particularly the mendicants, sought to communicate to the entire population what the outstanding spiritual leaders, in particular St Bernard, had said as a result of their meditations upon the mystery. God Incarnate, the trials and tribulations of His hidden life, the torments of His Passion and Death on Calvary were constantly invoked. They were presented as so many entreaties to respond, initially through compassion for Christ and then through a desire to imitate Him, to the Son of God, made man in order to expiate the sin of Adam. Holy Week, especially Good Friday, remained the focal point of the liturgical year, but commemoration of the sufferings endured by the Saviour was now extended to every week, the last three days of which provided the opportunity to relive in spirit the drama of the Redemption. Pamphlets entitled *Orloges de la Passion* linked to each hour of the day one of the sorrows suffered by Christ and His Mother; Vespers evoked Mary's grief as she took upon her knee the lifeless body of her Son. For this reason Germans gave to the 'Pietà' the name 'Vesperbild'. Like time, space was overshadowed more and more by the Cross. Scenes most likely to play on the emotions of the faithful were depicted inside churches and in the enclosures surrounding them, in frescoes on walls, in stained glass, in altarpieces. In cemeteries could be seen Christ on the Mount of Olives. Crosses were erected at crossroads. Stones marking the stations of the *via dolorosa* signposted roads leading to places of pilgrimage. Finally, thanks to wood-engraving, pictures of the suffering Redeemer could be placed inside even the humblest of dwellings.

Image-makers – painters and sculptors – put the resources of their talents and craft at the service of this multi-faceted religion. During this period, particularly north of the Alps, art was seeking to convey feelings and states of being. The minute attention to detail given by Flemish masters, who founded numerous schools, prompted artists to portray as accurately as possible individuals, costume, interiors and countryside; these were qualities likely to capture the attention and to act on the emotions, which were precisely the objectives of religious pedagogy. Familiarity, it is true, deadened feelings; reviving them entailed endless exaggeration of the horrifying scenes intended to arouse them. Torments became more and more subtle and even bloodier. In the mystical winepress, Christ was crushed implacably by the screw-driven weight. The Man of Sorrows, bowed down with grief, was portrayed on the summit of Golgotha a few minutes before being nailed to the Cross – a plea to the faithful to remember the moral anguish which had overwhelmed their Saviour. 'The stench of blood' seemed more pungent when mingled with 'the scent of roses'.[5] Scenes of childhood were placed alongside scenes of the Passion, the serenity of the one highlighting the cruelty of the other. The Infant Jesus played with the wood of His Cross and pricked Himself on the thorns of His crown.

From Bethlehem to Calvary the Virgin Mary accompanied her Son. She was never portrayed without Him. Whoever venerated her, of necessity worshipped Christ whom she cradled in her arms as a baby, or supported on her knees as a bloodless corpse. The mysteries of the Redemption were those the faithful were urged to meditate upon while reciting their rosary beads, the most popular form of the Marian cult. The 'Hail Mary', recited 150 times, which equalled the number of the psalms, recalled the beginning of the story, the Annunciation, which occupied an outstanding position in fifteenth-century devotion. Jeanne de France, the rejected wife of Louis XII, named the order which she founded the 'Annonciade'. In the debate over the conception of Mary, which brought theologians into conflict, those who believed in the Immaculate Conception, such as the Franciscans and scholars as celebrated as Gerson, were no doubt following the path which the ordinary believers would have taken had they participated in the controversy. Nothing was too good for the mother of God.

'Mary, Refuge of Sinners', 'Notre Dame de Bon Secours', 'Maria Hilf' were prayers constantly used to invoke the most heedful of intercessors and the advocate most readily heard by the Sovereign Judge. There was an almost boundless proliferation of places attracting pilgrims because Mary's benevolence had manifested itself there in miracles. At the end of the fifteenth century these usually modest sanctuaries were so numerous in certain areas that, wherever one was, it did not take more than a day's walk to reach one. The filial trust inspired by Mary was extended to her relatives: her mother, Anne, was Jesus' grandmother: could the petitions she presented ever be rejected? Certainly, few intercessors were more frequently invoked. During the troubles

5 Huizinga (1955), p. 26.

of the schism, Gerson was responsible for bringing Joseph out of the background: Christ's foster-father would surely not permit the Church, his spouse, to perish. Gradually the Holy Family came to form a kind of portrait around the Virgin and Child. That family's patrimony was the Holy Land. Only the rich and important were able to make the journey there, but in a certain sense the land came to meet its children: the legend of angels bringing the 'Santa Casa' of Nazareth to Loreto is full of significance.

Petitions were addressed to a host of other intercessors. Each had his special quality or attributes: Leonard took care of prisoners, Anthony of those suffering from gangrene, Roch or Sebastian looked after plague victims, while Barbara and Christopher warded off sudden death. In 1445 a shepherd of Franconia had a revelation of the appropriate assistance which fourteen Apotropaics, reputed to have powers of averting a specific malady, could offer, each member of the group excelling in a particular therapy. The cult enjoyed by the 11,000 virgins or the 10,000 martyrs proves that the help of powerful forces was sought. Yet, at the same time, individuals established a privileged relationship with a particular saint, their patron.

Saints usually considered as protectors gave an example to follow, since their lives demonstrated that true love of God comes through love of neighbour. Charity remained the first duty of the Christian, even if states, kingdoms and towns did discover that poverty, a social evil, made poor relief a political necessity. The range of charitable institutions expanded still further and became more varied; licensed establishments took in epileptics, the insane, those afflicted with venereal disease. Orphans, the aged without means, girls without dowries, none was forgotten. The poor man, soon to be shut up in a workhouse, was as yet perceived as Christ who dispensed grace in exchange for alms. Wills made possible the posthumous accomplishment of deeds left undone or badly done during a lifetime. There existed a strong feeling of solidarity between the living and the dead. Confraternities, for the most part mutual aid societies, often took the place of families in having anniversary services said for those, so numerous in towns, without relatives. The preachers of indulgences most readily heard were those whose 'pardons' were applicable to the 'poor souls'. In parishes of modest means the Fraternity of the Holy Ghost looked after the living, while the Purgatory alms-bowl collected offerings to say prayers for the departed. Christian society formed a body whose institutions reached into the after-life.

What was the response of Christian people to such devotions? Did they practise them assiduously? Was there uniformity? Neither the present state of knowledge nor the nature of the evidence permits a clear-cut answer. Sermons evoke with some vehemence the laity's indifference, even hostility, either concealed or avowed; but then eloquence and exaggeration go hand in hand. Does this mean that no account should be taken of such polemics? That would be a mistake, for caricatures only exaggerate faults, they do not invent them. Other sources – reports of pastoral visits, decisions of ecclesiastical courts, financial accounts of churches, hospices and fraternities – all yield facts and figures recorded by administrators. There are, though, not enough of them to provide the necessary information for a complete picture to be painted; between the finished areas there are large, blank spaces.

Nevertheless, we may risk at least a sketch. Refusal to obey the Church's laws was first and foremost the action of a heretic. The fifteenth century had begun with a conflagration: Bohemia, already smouldering because of the execution of Jan Hus (1415), burst into flames as soon as Sigismund made to occupy it. For almost fifteen years all the forms which religious controversy could take flourished there. The victory of orthodoxy in 1436 was not a crushing one; the defeated did not embrace their conquerors' faith with sincerity. In spite of being dispersed, Hussite communities were not eradicated; scattered elements survived in secret, like the Lollards to whom they were closely related through their Wyclifite associations. Waldensian cells were likewise scattered over a large part of Europe; in order to survive, their members feigned submission to orthodoxy, except when they took refuge from persecution, insecure as it often was, in Alpine valleys. After 1450 these heretics in both thought and deed were increasingly isolated, but aspects of their doctrines had spread widely about them, and tended to make popular anti-clericalism more radical. It was not necessarily the principles of the official Church which were questioned; complaints about priests, especially the mendicants, were more concerned with the imperfections of their way of life than with their beliefs. These criticisms were due, at least in part, to the abuse of ecclesiastical censures; excommunications for debt continually renewed and swelled the band of recalcitrant Christians who resigned themselves to not seeking absolution, since they lacked the funds to put things right.

Insofar as we can estimate the frequency and regularity of religious practice, we can establish that the majority of the faithful did carry out the prescriptions of the Church, year in, year out. Their number fluctuated to some extent, irregular practice constantly modifying the picture; those no longer bothering to attend Mass would be replaced by others who had returned to the fold. A troop of fervent Catholics, perhaps one in ten of those baptised, the vanguard of the main force which was content simply to fulfil its Easter duties, left behind the laggards and the insubordinate, and received communion out of devotion on important feast days. There is no need to take into account the founding of chantries, or even requiem Masses, which were ordered in large numbers. Money was needed for these pious works, and it was not through lack of it that the poor were wanting in zeal.

In the end, was the generosity of the rich not simply a means of parading their wealth and maintaining their rank? Religious history cannot be based on statistical history alone. What motives prompted Christians to obey the Church's precepts and increase supererogatory practices? Examined in this light, the documents at our disposal are very difficult to interpret: how can one make a window into men's souls, unmask the hypocrite, and accurately recognise the signs of genuine piety? There can be no doubt that there were men and women who took the demands of the Gospel seriously. Individuals whose exceptional virtues have been acknowledged were surrounded by emulators seeking to live up to their models. Francesca Romana, for example, was able to assemble enough women to found a congregation of lay sisters, and the Brethren of the Common Life found buyers for the edifying volumes they had themselves copied and bound in order to sell at a profit. The Alsatian humanist, Jakob Wimpfeling, an embittered man, was for once over optimistic when he went so far as to say that people of very humble background were reading the Bible, the *Imitation of Christ* and the *Lives of the Fathers*.

An amazing contrast is discernible between the fervent approach of what was doubtless a narrow elite and the irresponsibility of the masses. Relationships with things religious often bore the hallmark of a familiarity which the ecclesiastical authorities of the fifteenth century deemed reprehensible. They had great difficulty banning from churches masquerades such as the Feast of the Donkey. Oaths, a fashion which, in various forms, swept over the whole of Europe, were in origin ejaculatory prayers turned upside down; they requested damnation, not salvation, and scoffed at everything which was normally venerated – the body or limbs of Christ, for example. Blasphemy by repetition, however, became a habit, and came to notify nothing more than indifference to God's law.

Yet this indifference was likely to be badly shaken by fear and anxiety. In distress, men sought contact with the spiritual. Without doubt they mostly had an 'objectivist' concept of religion, which tended to turn it into a collection of outward and visible actions; by multiplying these works, would they not be building an impregnable fortress against danger? 'Hail Marys' were reeled off by the hundred, Masses ordered by the dozen, and, in the absence of a plenary indulgence, a man might try to obtain a pardon worth thousands of days, weeks or years. Many expected that the performance of rites would elicit an immediate response, and their prayers turned into incantations. Some objects were considered to be charged with benevolent power, and in case of need one had only to look upon them to intercept the mysterious beams. A glance at the image of St Christopher was a guarantee against sudden death; pilgrims to Aachen who, swamped by the crowd, were unable to see the exposed relics, fixed a small mirror to their headgear. In such cases, Christianity was little more than a veneer applied to the immemorial beliefs of paganism. Unusual phenomena were readily seen as manifestations, good or bad, of celestial moods. The surprising was taken for the marvellous, and the marvellous promoted to the miraculous. Prelates tried to control the passion for places where, according to rumour, the sacred had made an appearance: the bishop of Saint-Papoul had a pond filled in because peasants were drawing their water with reverence on the pretext that an ox had knelt down at the edge of it. But not all cases were as simple. For decades scholars and the authorities argued about the hosts of Wilsnack, in northern Germany; some recognised the validity of the veneration accorded by crowds of pilgrims, believing that divine intervention had preserved the consecrated Bread from fire, while their opponents denied the authenticity of the facts reported by promoters of this new devotion. Such flagrant disagreement inevitably cast doubts in people's minds.

Echoing the views of Gerson and of Nicholas of Cusa, many in the universities condemned the profusion of those rites, exorcisms and pilgrimages which people were inclined to fulfil in a superstitious way. In some mountain regions the clergy strove to combat ignorance and cure dissension by religious instruction, which sometimes produced unforeseen results. Practices once tolerated were now forbidden. There was discrepancy between the peasant way of life and the biblical concept expounded by preachers. Old customs died hard; those unable to turn away from them felt guilty. Clerics wondered whether it was not a case of the devil blocking the path of true religion. Some inquisitors elaborated an entire theory from isolated circumstances; healers and their clients were not simply ignorant people, but apostates, whom Satan had turned into disciples. Sorcerers were the new heretics, taking over from Cathars and Waldensians; to fight them was a matter of urgency. The papal bull, *Summis desiderantes* of 1484, and the inquisitor's manual, *Malleus maleficarum*, of 1486, elevated these views to the level of official doctrine. In the Alps where, to eradicate Waldensianism, preaching had often been methodically carried out, fear of satanism first appeared at the end of the fourteenth century, before being found in the Rhine valley, where the authors of *Malleus* observed it and drew up their theories about it. In France, both the trial of Joan of Arc (1431) and the 'Vauderie' (burning of 'sorcerers') of Arras (1459–65) mark the development of a scourge which would reveal its utter maleficence in the sixteenth century. This machinery of repression, once set in motion, quickly gathered momentum, and actually caused the spread of those very ideas which it was meant to crush.

The preceding pages constitute a rapid sketch of what would comprise the subject matter of an elaborate painting; in this case, however, only those characteristics common to the whole of western Europe have been considered. A detailed study would require a canvas of bewildering diversity. The characteristic flavour of Christian life in some countries did not escape the notice of fifteenth-century travellers: Italians were struck by the fervour of Germans, who did not scruple to criticise Latin levity. Religion played a part in defining national identities: in this respect the Czechs, whose pride had been wounded by the condemnation of Hus, foreshadowed the devotion of Germans to Luther, who presented himself as the champion of their honour. Social environment provided just as many variations in religious behaviour as did nations. People in urban centres, where cultural levels rose more rapidly than in country areas, responded more easily to the exhortation to give Christianity a truly spiritual dimension; in towns, books, almost always indispensable for meditation, were less rare. There was no uniformity, either, among the peasantry, which was not totally impervious to influences from urban communities. Villagers with regular contact with town dwellers did not inhabit the same intellectual sphere as the people of a high mountain valley cut off from the world. Nor should we forget the differences influenced by gender. Already in the fifteenth century men did not wish to appear bigoted. Women receive communion more often and gave more generously; wills, foundation charters and the registers of confraternities bear witness to this. These remarks, which need qualification and correction, are in no way exhaustive. The history of religious sentiment is a vineyard where men may labour long. There remains one final question to which, once again, no definitive answer is possible. Did religious vitality vary in intensity over the course of the century? Given the present state of knowledge, any attempt to plot on a graph the highs and lows of the religious barometer would inevitably be doomed to failure. It does seem, however, that piety did not suffer permanent weakness; as some features declined, so others took their place. Devotion grew until it became, by the beginning of the sixteenth century, the 'appetite for the divine' noted by Lucien Febvre, an appetite which he considered to be one of the causes of the Reformation.

CHAPTER 11

SCHOOLS AND UNIVERSITIES

Jacques Verger

AT least until the crisis of the Great Schism, the salient features in the history of schools and universities of medieval Christendom were progress and, on the whole, continuity. By contrast, the advent of the fifteenth century ushered in an era of change. There was still progress, certainly: new foundations, a continually expanding body of teaching masters and students, a social demand that was increasingly vigorous. At the same time, however, institutions were being transformed and becoming secularised; traditional autonomy was in rapid retreat before new state pressures; the curriculum itself became the focus of unprecedented criticism, both implied and outspoken. This chapter, then, will be devoted essentially to a consideration of the old and the new, of tradition and innovation.

GROWTH AND CHANGE IN THE SCHOLASTIC AND UNIVERSITY SYSTEMS

Naturally, these systems continued to be based in large measure on structures inherited from the thirteenth and fourteenth centuries. By about 1400, in the case of universities, there existed around thirty functioning *studia generalia* endowed with imperial and papal privileges which clearly defined their status. Of these *studia generalia* only three ceased to exist during the course of the century.[1] The rest varied greatly in importance: the oldest (Bologna, Paris, Oxford, Salamanca) remained the most prestigious, the only ones capable of becoming luminaries on the international stage and of attracting really significant numbers

---

[1] The following *studia generalia* were functioning in 1400: Angers, Avignon, Bologna, Buda, Cahors, Cambridge, Cologne, Cracow, Erfurt, Florence, Heidelberg, Huesca, Lérida, Lisbon, Montpellier, Naples, Orange, Orleans, Oxford, Padua, Paris, Perugia, Perpignan, Piacenza, Prague, Salamanca, Siena, *Studium Curiae*, Toulouse, Valladolid, Vienna. The *studium generale* of Treviso had without doubt disappeared before 1400. It does not seem that the *studia* of Salerno, Verona and Lucca can be considered as genuine *studia generalia*. The Universities of Buda (*c.* 1460), Piacenza (transferred to Pavia in 1412) and Florence (transferred to Pisa in 1472) disappeared from the above list in the course of the fifteenth century (Ridder-Symoens (1992), I, pp. 62–5).

of students – it has been calculated that by about 1450 there were likely to have been almost 2,000 students at Oxford, with twice as many in Paris.[2]

Universities of more recent foundation were of an altogether inferior standard. In some cases, particularly among the small legal universities in Mediterranean countries, they were antiquated institutions lacking vitality, attracting merely a few hundred local students (sometimes but a few score, as at Cahors or Orange in France), and at the mercy of all the hazards of the prevailing situation such as war and epidemic. However, of these newer universities others seemed to enjoy a period of ascendancy in the fifteenth century, though sometimes after difficult beginnings: not overburdened by traditional structures, they were able to engage celebrated lecturers and to offer courses of study which, influenced to a greater or lesser degree by humanism, broke new ground. Hence they expanded their catchment areas and competed openly with the older institutions. For instance in England, Cambridge doubled in strength (from 700 to almost 1,400) and so, having lagged behind Oxford for centuries, gradually made up leeway.[3] The earliest Germanic universities (Vienna, Heidelberg, Cologne) took advantage of declining Parisian influence in the Empire, itself a consequence of the Great Schism. Prague, and subsequently Cracow, made their mark as important centres of intellectual life in central Europe. On the Italian peninsula the relative stagnation of studies at Bologna allowed a few enterprising universities (Padua, Perugia, Siena) to attract in their turn a by no means negligible complement of students from beyond the Alps no less than from the peninsula.

This overall picture of development, together with the increasing desire of princes to acquire for their own purposes both national and regional universities, explains the increase in new university foundations during the fifteenth century – and this in spite of all the difficulties of the period. Between 1400 and 1500 there were thirty-four of them (in addition to four whose university status is open to debate and four reopenings of defunct universities). In effect the number of European universities more than doubled in the course of one century.[4]

---

[2] Aston (1979); Favier (1974), pp. 68–76.   [3] Aston *et al.* (1980).

[4] The following *studia generalia* were founded during the fifteenth century: Würzburg (1402; disappears after 1413); Turin (1404); Leipzig (1409); Aix-en-Provence (1409); St Andrews (1411); Rostock (1419); Dole (1422); Louvain (1425); Poitiers (1431); Caen (1432); Bordeaux (1441); Catania (1444); Barcelona (1450); Glasgow (1451); Valence (1452); Trier (1454); Greifswald (1456); Freiburg/Breisgau (1457); Basle (1459); Ingolstadt (1459); Nantes (1460); Bourges (1464); Poszony (1465; disappears after 1492); Saragossa (1474); Copenhagen (1475); Mainz (1476); Tübingen (1476); Uppsala (1477); Palma de Majorca (1483); Sigüenza (1489); Aberdeen (1495); Frankfurt/Oder (1498); Alcalà (1499); Valencia (1500). The *studia generalia* of Pisa (after 1406), Pavia (1412), Ferrara (1430) and Rome (the *studium urbis*, 1431, later joined to the *studium curiae*: see Adorni (1992), pp. 416–21) all reopened. It is doubtful whether the *studia* of Parma (1412), Gerona (1446), Venice (College of Medicine, 1470) and Genoa (1471) can be classified as universities (Ridder-Symoens (1992), I, pp. 62–5).

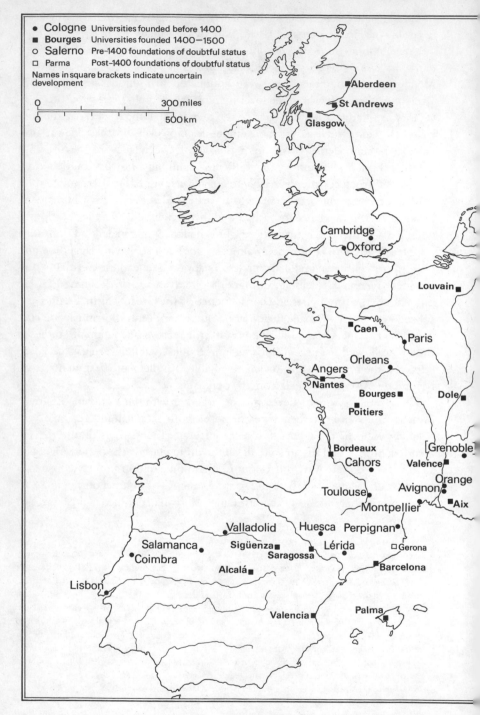

● Cologne Universities founded before 1400
■ Bourges Universities founded 1400–1500
○ Salerno Pre-1400 foundations of doubtful status
□ Parma   Post-1400 foundations of doubtful status

Names in square brackets indicate uncertain development

0 ——————————— 300 miles
0 ——————————— 500 km

Aberdeen
St Andrews
Glasgow

Cambridge
Oxford

Louvain

Caen
Paris

Orleans
Angers
Nantes
Bourges
Poitiers
Dole

Bordeaux
Cahors
[Grenoble
Valence
Toulouse
Orange
Avignon
Montpellier
Aix
Perpignan
Valladolid
Huesca
Salamanca
Sigüenza
Lérida
Gerona
Coimbra
Saragossa
Alcalá
Barcelona
Lisbon
Palma
Valencia

Map 5   The universities of Europe in 1400 and 1500

Uppsala

N

Copenhagen

Greifswald
Rostock

Frankfurt/Oder

Leipzig
Cologne
• Erfurt
Mainz [Würzburg] • Prague
Trier • Heidelberg
Tübingen Cracow
Ingolstadt
Freiburg/Breisgau Vienna
Basle [Poszony]
[Buda]

Padua
Pavia Verona ○ Venice
Turin [Piacenza] ■ Ferrara
Genoa □ Parma • Bologna
[Florence]
Pisa Siena
Perugia

Rome

Naples
Salerno

Catania

While it is true that few of these new foundations ended in total failure
(though there were some still-born schemes), most, at least before 1500,
never rose above middling importance. A dearth of celebrated lecturers,
catchment areas and spheres of influence that were essentially regional, and
small student bodies, at best a few hundred strong, were common to all.
Some very quickly stagnated; others, by contrast (one thinks of Caen and
Bourges in France, of Louvain, of the new German or Scottish universities),
enjoyed a period of fruitful development. The geographical distribution of
these new foundations is a point to bear in mind. They were not to be found
either in England or, except on the fringes (Turin, Catania), on the Italian
peninsula, where demand must have been satisfied by the existing system.
Seven *studia generalia* were founded in the second half of the century on the
Iberian peninsula; all, though, were doomed to remain mediocre, with the
exception of Alcalá, which became the bridge-head of humanism in the
Spain of the Catholic monarchs. The eight new universities created in fifteenth-century France, soon to be frequently linked with provincial *parlements*,
were in towns (for instance, Poitiers, Nantes, Bourges) that were asserting
their authority as regional capitals. It was, however, in central and northern
Europe (Germany, Scotland, Scandinavia) that the university movement
attained its greatest intensity. The foundations there, financed and promoted
by princes and towns, were an obvious manifestation of the vitality of these
'emergent countries' at the end of the Middle Ages and also testimony of
their desire for full integration into a European culture whose predominant
centres had previously been on the Italian peninsula, in France and in
England.

The vitality of universities in the fifteenth century is not to be measured
solely in terms of this wave of new foundations. One must also remember that
in the period some old universities were endowed with new faculties, particularly of theology (Avignon in 1413, Montpellier in 1421, Lérida in 1430,
Valladolid in 1436). Above all, the fifteenth century witnessed, in institutions
previously accustomed to uncertainty in the supply of material necessities, an
increase in the number of suitable buildings and of libraries. It witnessed, too,
the foundation of numerous university colleges: the concept was, of course, an
old one, but the social and cultural role of colleges, a point to which we will
return, was strengthened, and with it grew the size of the buildings housing
them, thus imposing their presence on the urban environment. Although
college foundations were somewhat fewer than in the fourteenth century in
Paris (twelve instead of thirty-seven) and in England (nine as against twelve),
they were on occasion lavish (All Souls and Magdalen at Oxford, King's and
Queens' at Cambridge); above all their numbers increased in the new universities in the countries that comprised the Empire (twenty-seven colleges

founded in the fifteenth century), in central Europe (three), in Scotland (three) and on the Iberian peninsula (six).

Universities formed the top tier of educational establishments in Europe during this period: it was in contemporary eyes the most prestigious, and remains for us the best known. The other tiers, which lacked the benefit of either royal or papal privileges, inhabited a world where diversity not consistency was the rule. Recruitment of masters was determined by fluctuating criteria; numbers of pupils, like their social origins, remain largely a mystery to us; the dearth of archival material prevents the recovery of facts about the financing and administration of such establishments; information is imperfect on the instruction actually provided, though no doubt it was a simplified counterpart of university courses.

First, there were the traditional ecclesiastical schools, to be found in large numbers in the vicinity of cathedrals, main collegiate churches and urban monasteries. Although primarily intended for young clerics or monks, they were able to accept external lay students as well; sometimes they were flanked by small colleges that served as lodgings for poor students. The importance of these traditional establishments should not be underestimated: St Paul's cathedral school in London was the most important one in the city;[5] while in 1469 the school of the old Benedictine monastery of St Giles in Nuremberg numbered an impressive 230 pupils.[6] The education meted out in such ecclesiastical establishments, usually under the responsibility of the chancellor or precentor, was of different kinds: there was the simple choir school for choristers; there were lessons in grammar, and there were, too, courses on philosophy, theology and sometimes canon law intended principally for future priests.

Even more numerous throughout western Europe were the institutions that may be classified under the general headings of 'small schools', 'Latin schools', 'grammar schools'. Their level varied enormously: priests might give lessons to a few of the parish children; elsewhere schoolmasters – sometimes priests, sometimes merely tonsured clerics or even laymen – set themselves up in a private capacity and entered into agreements with families to teach their children, on occasion taking them as boarders. Other schools were financed by religious foundations (one finds many examples in England) or by municipal grants; even so they were seldom entirely free of charge.

Numbers of pupils in a particular school might be as many as several hundred, but in most cases did not exceed a few score. Although several 'schoolmistresses' are known,[7] for example in Paris, pupils were mainly boys, usually aged between nine and fifteen. The background and qualifications of

---

[5] Orme (1973), pp. 194–223. [6] Miner (1987).

[7] The list of school-masters and school-mistresses in Paris having given an oath before the precentor of the cathedral is published in *Chartularium Universitatis Parisiensis*, III, no. 1713.

teachers were extremely varied, and the control in theory exercised over them by the ecclesiastical or municipal authorities was often nebulous. Only a minority of these masters possessed a university qualification (Master of Arts or Master of Grammar). Teaching was focused primarily on 'grammar', that is the study of Latin (reading and writing) to a more or less advanced level, supplemented by rudimentary arithmetic. It is difficult to judge to what extent the vernacular featured in this education. The clientele of schools might come from relatively humble backgrounds and include sons of artisans or peasants. As for the nobility and patriciate, they frequently preferred the solutions afforded by private tutoring.

Without doubt it was in the fourteenth century that the number of grammar schools started to increase appreciably in a number of western countries. This expansion continued in the fifteenth century, by which time it was not uncommon to find such schools not only in sizeable towns, but even in small market towns and in villages. In the second half of the fourteenth century in England, at least seventy-two localities are recorded as having a school; in the second half of the fifteenth century the figure rose to eighty-five.[8]

One must be careful, however, not to paint too rosy a picture. In the fifteenth century all towns on the Italian peninsula, even small and average-sized ones, financed one or several municipal schools, but north of the Alps it was a different story. Even if there, too, most important towns had several schools, it was far from being the norm in less significant localities. In the diocese of Châlons-sur-Marne in Champagne only thirty-seven parishes out of 300 are certified as having had a school during the fifteenth century.[9] Furthermore, many schools appear to have existed only intermittently, and their standard frequently must have been third-rate. Most were not destined to rise above an elementary level, and rare indeed were schools capable of imparting a sound grasp of Latin and of preparing pupils for possible study at university. The majority of the male population, and more particularly the female, was therefore condemned to illiteracy, and the invention of printing was to make only a very gradual impact on elementary education.

This education, it must be said, was not as yet attracting the attention of either princes or the Church. Schoolmasters, unlike doctors of the universities, did not enjoy a high social standing – even early humanists scarcely referred to them except to denounce their brutality or ignorance. The responsibility for primary education devolved upon municipalities and families, whose financial capacities were limited. The fifteenth century did, however, produce some interesting innovations in education and witnessed outside, or on the fringes

---

[8] Orme (1973), pp. 291–325.   [9] Guilbert (1982).

of, traditional milieux (cathedrals, monasteries, universities) the appearance of reputable establishments receptive to new ideas.

Not to be considered here are the *studia* of the mendicant orders which had been in existence since the thirteenth century and where those orders' future lectors and preachers received what was virtually a university education. It is possible that sometimes secular students were accepted. In the universities themselves some colleges, following a movement of fourteenth-century origin, continued to develop their own courses in competition with the faculties, particularly of arts; increasingly autonomous, these colleges *de plein exercice* (that is to say providing a complete course) were thus able to open their doors to such humanist disciplines as Greek and rhetoric; for example, the Sorbonne in the 1460s, and Magdalen College, Oxford, in the closing years of the century.

During the fifteenth century some university colleges initiated grammar courses in annexes, so that future students could be better prepared. In like manner grammar schools in Oxford and Cambridge enjoyed an excellent reputation, because although they remained external to the universities, they were supervised and fostered by them.

Other institutions were completely independent of the universities. On the Italian peninsula in particular, where as early as the beginning of the century humanists such as Pier Paolo Vergerio and Leonardo Bruni had stressed the importance of deficiencies in education, and where arts faculties offered only limited possibilities, new grammar schools and schools of philosophy of a high standard were founded in some towns. So, in Venice, a city lacking a university, the fifteenth century saw the birth of the Rialto school (philosophy) and the School of San Marco (*studia humanitatis*) for young patricians destined for state service. Mention must also be made of the 'humanist colleges' (*contubernia*) set up at the instigation of communes or princes by Gasparino Barzizza in Padua (1408), by Guarino da Verona first in Verona (1420) and later Ferrara (1436) and by Vittorino da Feltre in Mantua (1423). These institutions, whose clientele was fairly aristocratic, were characterised both by the broad-minded discipline to which pupils were subject and by curricula imbued with new ideas (the importance of rhetoric, direct access to classical texts, the study of Greek).

Outside the Italian peninsula a few similar initiatives can be found; although infinitely fewer in number and less innovatory, they did express an identical awareness of the deficiencies of traditional education in arts faculties. In England the colleges founded by Bishop William of Wykeham at Winchester (1382) and by Henry VI at Eton (1440) were designed to give future Oxford and Cambridge students a solid grounding in grammar. The school of Sélestat in Alsace (1450) likewise was a nursery for teaching masters of grammar and rhetoric in the Rhineland universities (Basle, Freiburg).

As regards scholastic reform the most important movement beyond the Italian peninsula in the fifteenth century was that of the Brethren of the Common Life. This religious reform movement (the *devotio moderna*) was born in the Low Countries at the end of the fourteenth century and soon adopted as one of its fundamental objectives the creation of grammar schools able to provide for pupils both a stable environment and effective teaching. The atmosphere was austere and very religious, but the educational principles (streaming of pupils into classes according to ability; direct approach to the text of the Bible and the church fathers), which echoed humanistic ideas, proved to be of immense importance in the future. The principal school of the Brethren in the fifteenth century was at Deventer in Gelderland, where Nicholas of Cusa, Erasmus and Rudolf Agricola were students. From there the movement spread rapidly. The Brethren opened a large school in Louvain adjacent to the university, and at the end of the century Jan Standonck, by reforming the college of Montaigu (1490), even introduced the principles of this educational system to Paris. Standonck subsequently settled in Louvain, where in 1499 he set up his *domus pauperum* within the university itself.

Medieval schools and universities had abandoned to apprenticeship what might be termed vocational training; the usual milieux for this were families, merchants' shops and, for the sons of the nobility, princely courts. During the fifteenth century one does, however, find here and there, and in embryonic form, the rudiments of vocational training, probably an indication of a rise in cultural expectations even among craftsmen, scribes and legal practitioners, for whom a university education seemed out of reach or inappropriate. One finds a few 'masters of the abacus' referred to on the Italian peninsula, particularly in Tuscany – they taught the basics of arithmetic and accountancy to the sons of merchants. In London the Inns of Chancery and Inns of Court, which date from the fourteenth century, achieved full maturity in the fifteenth: they were essentially private schools, where chancery and common law practice was taught. They trained, in a more practical way than university civil law faculties, a significant proportion of the administrative and judicial personnel of the monarchy. They enjoyed genuine prestige, and jurists of the calibre of Sir John Fortescue emerged from them.

THE CURRICULA

If one moves on from the educational system itself to the courses and curricula offered, one finds a similar mixture of sound, but occasionally hidebound, traditions, and innovations still in need of perfecting.

Obviously we are best informed about universities – they have left an abundance of detailed statutes, syllabuses and manuscripts used in teaching. In essence education remained faithful to its roots, which are to be found in the twelfth and thirteenth centuries, themselves heirs in large measure of the earlier Middle Ages and late Antiquity. The classification of knowledge, the hierarchy and division of disciplines, which was mirrored in the hierarchy and division of faculties, the list of ancient and modern authorities, all remained those of an earlier age.

The teaching of grammar was based on Donatus and Priscian, on occasion complemented by Evrard de Béthune and Alexandre de Villedieu. Aristotle continued to reign supreme in the study of logic and philosophy, not so much in the form of a coherent body of doctrine, but rather as a sort of universal vocabulary imposing on all and sundry its terminology, intellectual categories and the concepts, either implicit or explicit, of its psychology, physics and cosmology.

Likewise, in the superior faculties, teaching methods as well as curricula were in direct line of descent from those of previous centuries. The gloss and the question were still the two basic intellectual procedures, of which the *lectio* and the disputation were the practical application. Scholasticism, that strict, even inflexible combining of authority with reason, which operated within the imperious framework of the syllogism, reigned supreme over nascent intellectual curiosity. It was Aristotle's *Organon*, sometimes improved upon by Peter of Spain's *Summulae* (of the thirteenth century), that was thought to provide everyone with the master-key to the definition and explanation of all knowledge.

As for the actual subject matter of this knowledge, it was still thought to be enshrined in a sacrosanct list of authorities: in the faculty of medicine, Galen and his Arab commentators; in the faculties of civil and canon law, the *Corpus iuris civilis* (i.e. the codification of Justinian, sometimes in the thirteenth century modestly complemented by the *Libri feudorum*) and the *Corpus iuris canonici* (definitively concluded at the beginning of the fourteenth century by the incorporation of John XXII's *Extravagantes*); and in theology, the Bible and four *Books of Sentences* of Peter Lombard. The list of 'authorised' modern commentators, whose treatises, summaries and apparatus complemented the authorities themselves and constituted a more or less indispensable means of access to them, was a little more flexible: doctors of the Salernitan and Montpellier schools, glossators and commentators of Bologna, Parisian logicians and theologians; almost all of them, though, dated back to the twelfth and thirteenth centuries, or at best to the first decades of the fourteenth.

Yet it would be a mistake to conclude on the basis of the strength of this traditional apparatus that at the end of the Middle Ages university teaching was atrophied and utterly opposed to progress. In philosophy and theology, for instance, the revival which had started in the fourteenth century around what one may term (to use a convenient, if controversial, word) 'nominalism' continued to have an impact on numerous arts and theology faculties – in Paris and Oxford naturally, but also in the new German universities, particularly Tübingen, where Gabriel Biel taught between 1484 and 1495. This *via moderna* had its opponents in the advocates of the *via antiqua*, who were themselves split into Thomists and Scotists. Lively debates sprang from this antagonism. Some universities (Heidelberg, Freiburg, Ingolstadt) organised the co-existence of both schools of thought – students could choose their degree course in one or the other. Elsewhere hostilities broke out: 'nominalist' authors were banned in Paris from 1474 to 1481, but by the end of the century the 'modernists' had regained the ascendancy. All this goes to show that university life in the fifteenth century had not necessarily sunk into arid eclecticism and routine. In the same way Averroism, which formerly had been banned in Paris, maintained its standing in various universities on the Italian peninsula, especially at Padua where Pietro Pomponazzi (1462–1525) taught.

Law and medical faculties, too, enjoyed in the fifteenth century a late flowering of scholasticism. On the Italian peninsula the jurist Paolo di Castro and the canon lawyer Nicholas de Tudeschis finished the standard work begun by the fourteenth-century commentators. Output in the medical field continued unabated: ninety-seven authors of medical treatises have been identified in fifteenth-century France, scarcely fewer than in the fourteenth (107); among them several reveal decided originality, Jacques Despars in Paris, for example, and Jacques Angeli in Montpellier.[10] However, this comparative vigour was far from being ubiquitous and, it must be stressed, remained confined by the strait-jacket of the scholastic method, which conspicuously limited its scope. The fifteenth century, however, was to break new ground by casting doubts upon these traditional constraints.

One should not overstate the case. The success enjoyed by education, the obvious signs of which have been indicated above (the founding of new schools and universities, the general increase in student numbers), shows that those with political powers and, more broadly, society's dominant classes still had faith in it. We will return to this point. Criticisms were frequently merely implied: the historian believes he can detect them, observing as he does the increasing number of flaws in the system; one cannot be certain that contemporaries were as clearly aware of them. These flaws are, however, indisputable, and it does appear that they became worse during the course of the century. Degree courses became disorganised; whereas many students left university without even obtaining the first degree, others achieved one without completing the requisite length of study as prescribed by statute. In consequence of this, and because of the absenteeism endemic among teaching staff, curricula

[10] Jacquart (1981), pp. 199–205.

were often only partially covered, and the practice of disputation fell into disuse. Examination fees and costs escalated, yet examiners were frequently accused of culpable bias towards wealthy candidates. In some cases the qualifications awarded no longer appeared to accredit any genuine study whatsoever.[11]

The causes of these abuses were manifold, but it seems evident that all testified, among other things, to a failure on the part of courses offered to adapt to the actual aspirations of students. In short they appear as evidence of the intellectual dissatisfaction felt towards the existing system by many students and even teaching masters (including some who were gaining advantages from it on a social level).

As well as these significant reactions, the fifteenth century also witnessed the expression of formal criticisms of scholastic and university institutions. Those of religious reformers and popular preachers were relatively traditional: they denounced the arrogance of teaching doctors, the greed of jurists, the pointless subtleties of a too-theoretical theology. Princely counsellors, from their more political standpoint, condemned the disorderly behaviour attributed to students, at the same time deprecating the undue length of courses and their excessively theoretical nature. Lastly, humanists deplored the barbarity of scholastic Latin and the neglect of Greek, the contempt of universities for classical texts and the humanities, and their indifference towards the moral education of their students. As an example one thinks of the sarcastic remarks which Lorenzo Valla, who had been invited to the University of Pavia in 1431 as professor in rhetoric, directed at his colleagues of the superior faculties – remarks soon resulting in his expulsion.

Various individuals proposed reforms. In Paris as early as 1400 the chancellor, Jean Gerson, drew up a plan of reform for the faculty of theology.[12] Committees of the Council of Basle examined several schemes of a similar nature. In France, Charles VII's counsellors were continually urging the king at the end of the Hundred Years War not to neglect, in his task of re-organising the kingdom, the reform of the university.

Actual attempts at reform did occur. In France, for instance, it was rare for a university to escape: Angers underwent two reforms, in 1398 and 1494; Toulouse had two series of reform statutes, between 1394 and 1425 and between 1470 and 1499; in Orleans and Paris two 'general reforms' were imposed, in 1447 and 1452 respectively; at Avignon, however, a similar attempt in 1459 remained a dead letter.[13] Mention should also be made of the reform of Bologna University by the cardinal-legate, Bessarion, in the 1450s.[14] These

---

[11] Verger (1977) and (1986a).   [12] Jean Gerson, *Œuvres*, II, pp. 23–8.   [13] Verger (1976a).
[14] Nasalli Rocca (1930).

various attempts were, however, of limited scope. The reformers, principally preoccupied with the problems of university privileges and public order, and hamstrung by conservatism among teaching staff, achieved only minor adjustments to degree courses and syllabuses.

It would be wrong to conclude that there were no genuine innovations in the educational sphere in fifteenth-century western Christendom. There were, but they were limited, localised, and often occurred in institutions and areas of marginal importance. The pillars of the system – the old universities and superior faculties – did not exactly welcome them.

Some of the vehicles of educational revival have already been mentioned. The schools of the Brethren of the Common Life, the Italian humanists' *contubernia*, some university colleges (at least as far as optional courses were concerned) introduced new concepts of the master–pupil relationship. For the tedious repetition, year in year out, of the same *lectiones*, often but irregularly delivered, they substituted, above all in the teaching of grammar and the arts, a system of graded classes, where pupils were streamed according to their age and standard. The pleasure of free discussion in small groups replaced, or rather complemented, inflexible formal lectures or scholastic disputations. Apart from drilling in the prescribed syllabus, more emphasis was now placed on moral and religious education. In some institutions authorised games began to feature; some schools put on plays.

New ideas surfaced in the curricula. Here the superior faculties were the sector least affected: conservatism among the doctors and political constraints had the combined effect of preserving old syllabuses and stifling innovation. The latter scarcely found a toe-hold, except in the informal fringe activities of those small groups sympathetic to fresh ideas. Arts faculties, which were more diversified and less structured, were far more accommodating, as were some non-university establishments and others in the process of breaking away. In these cases educational revival went hand in hand with the realisation that what today would be labelled 'secondary' education was a specialised area, totally different from the university field proper, that is to say the superior faculties.

Clearly this development was a gradual process and was not to reach its full potential until the sixteenth century. The first signs, however, were already visible in the fifteenth. Italian universities seemed the most progressive: after 1450 practically all arts faculties on the peninsula offered a complete cycle of *studia humanitatis*. North of the Alps, too, there was an increase, at least spasmodically, in courses in rhetoric, Greek and Hebrew, often thanks to Italian teaching masters, or teaching masters educated on the peninsula. Indeed, the humanists' *peregrinatio academica* was then gathering momentum, and many were those from north of the Alps who journeyed to the Italian peninsula, especially Padua, to be initiated into the new ideas.

A few examples will suffice. In 1458 Lilio Tifernate started a Greek course in Paris; a little later on the Savoyard Guillaume Fichet added lessons in rhetoric within the Sorbonne college itself to the fairly traditional courses he gave as a theology regent. In Cambridge it was the Franciscan Lorenzo Traversagni di Savona who inaugurated a course of study in humanistic rhetoric. Yet the new German, Hungarian and Polish universities were those most receptive to Italian influences, thanks to courses subsidised by the patronage of princes and prelates. In 1447 Aeneas Sylvius Piccolomini (the future Pope Pius II) gave courses on classical poetry in Vienna; after him came the humanist astronomers, Georg Peurbach and Johannes Müller (Regiomontanus), later to be found at the Hungarian University of Pozsony. From 1440 onwards Gregory of Sanok and other lecturers educated in Padua fostered the humanistic environment at Cracow from which Copernicus would emerge – he studied arts there from 1491 to 1495.

Progress was not confined to courses in the humanities. Linked to them, philosophy, the sciences (mathematics and astronomy), law, theology and biblical exegesis began in their turn to bow to the philological demands brought into favour by the humanistic revival of grammar and rhetoric. Angelo Poliziano (1454–94) embarked on a new edition of the *Corpus iuris civilis*, while giving distinguished courses on Greek poetry in Florence. In Paris Jacques Lefèvre d'Etaples (*c.* 1450–1537) undertook humanistic editions of Aristotle and the Bible. New texts, new doctrines too. From the beginning of the century Jean Gerson had been preaching mystical theology in reaction to the dry-as-dust excesses of scholasticism – it found a sympathetic response among humanists; John Doket, destined to become provost of King's College, introduced Florentine neoplatonist doctrines (Leonardo Bruni, Marsilio Ficino) to Cambridge by way of his commentary on the *Phaedo* (*c.* 1470).

One final question needs to be asked. How far did the invention and spread of printing influence university and scholastic education before 1500? In truth, though the university libraries of France and the Italian peninsula seem to have been stagnating in the fifteenth century, German and English universities and colleges did not wait for the arrival of the printed book: even before 1450, frequently thanks to princely generosity, they enlarged considerably their collections of manuscripts, including classical texts or recent works of Italian humanists. One of the best examples is Erfurt, where in 1433 a former rector, Amplonius Ratingk, bequeathed his magnificent library of 637 volumes to the college he had recently founded (the university itself already possessed more than 800). University towns usually did not lack either manuscripts or the necessary means to produce copies at relatively modest expense. While early printers were not exactly scornful of university and scholastic clients, they did prefer to set up business in large, commercial towns without universities

(Nuremberg, Augsburg, Milan, Venice, Lyons, London). Though not entirely neglected, university towns were in the second division: the first workshop in Paris was established near the Sorbonne in 1470; Louvain had one in 1473, Cracow in 1479, whereas Cambridge, for example, had to wait until 1520. The textbooks produced by these early presses were above all elementary grammar books with some classical authors and manuals by Italian humanists; they were therefore aimed principally at pupils of pre-university schools and those attending arts faculties. It was only more gradually that the 'authorities' and *summae* in use in the superior faculties had the distinction of getting into print. It cannot be claimed that before 1500 printing genuinely revolutionised the conventions of university teaching.

INSTITUTIONS AND THE AUTHORITIES

It seems to have been generally accepted that scholastic and university institutions altered little in the fifteenth century. Church schools clearly remained under the direct control of the establishments to which they belonged – monasteries, convents, cathedrals or collegiate churches. Urban schools were usually governed by the contract drawn up between a commune and the teachers it had recruited. The situation in universities, however, was more complex. Officially they remained the same as the thirteenth-century foundations, autonomous bodies of academics and/or students, with the same constituent parts – 'nations' and faculties – and the same elected officers – rectors, deans, proctors. University autonomy relied on a body of privileges granted by ecclesiastical and lay authorities, guaranteed ultimately by the Papacy. Statutes drawn up by the universities themselves regulated their internal administration and discipline.

New universities of the fifteenth century adopted statutes modelled, more or less faithfully, on those of older universities. In the kingdom of Aragon, Lérida (itself inspired by Bologna) was the most popular prototype; in Germany and central Europe, Paris furnished the pattern, although with considerable modifications. New French provincial universities adopted statutes that mingled elements from various sources (Paris, Bologna, Montpellier, Toulouse).[15] In Scotland the statutes of St Andrews were modelled on those of Orleans and Angers and in their turn were copied in Glasgow. It should be added that the last decade of the fifteenth century did witness the birth of an original system, that of the 'university college' or, if preferred, the college endowed with the right to confer university degrees: it was found in Spain at Sigüenza (1489) and Alcalá (1499) and in Scotland at Aberdeen (1494–1505).

[15] Verger (1995a).

Yet, behind this relatively immutable façade, considerable changes were taking place. It was not that university autonomy and privileges had become meaningless: masters and students were devoted to both, above all in the oldest and most prestigious establishments, such as Paris and Oxford. Masters and students fought to defend their traditional freedoms, above all by strikes, and they managed to preserve a not inconsiderable part of them. They were able to remain more or less in control of the organisation of courses and examinations, and to preserve crucial elements in the guarantees which conferred on them a privileged personal status with protection from military requisitions, taxes and local secular courts. They were, however, powerless to prevent challenge to the actual principle of university autonomy, that is to say challenge to the right of the *studia generalia* to act without any control save that of the Papacy (which was remote and sympathetic), thereby corporately escaping the constraints of the political and economic system which princes were imposing on their states. By the end of the Middle Ages such constraints were being strengthened in every sphere, political power was increasingly intolerant of corporate autonomy and its officials were able to interfere in the internal affairs of universities knowing they would be supported.

At the same time it needs to be said that some universities were by reason of their intellectual capacity aspiring to a direct political role; this merely served to precipitate the tightening of external control. Faced with a variety of serious problems the kings of France had traditionally tended to seek the opinion and support of Paris University. The crisis of the Great Schism, followed by the Councils of Constance and Basle, in which they participated in large numbers, reinforced the belief of Parisian teaching masters that, by assuming the mantle of a faltering authority (in this case that of the Papacy), they could be directly involved in the actual exercise of power. Thus, during the first decades of the fifteenth century the University of Paris, through its chancellor, Jean Gerson (see his speech *Vivat rex* of 1405), offered its services to the king;[16] it took part in the representative assemblies, while later it was to support the Anglo-Burgundian regime and press vigorously for the conviction of Joan of Arc. Such political involvement was rash and would, after 1436, earn the undying rancour of Charles VII. One might quote other examples: Prague University would be one of the protagonists in the Hussite revolt, on the side of the moderate 'Calixtins';[17] Oxford's long-standing tolerance towards Wyclif and his Lollard heirs would expose that university to a purge at the beginning of the fifteenth century, when Lollardy had become the ideological basis of a movement perceived as subversive by the Lancastrian kings.

In a broader sense it is the general evolution of political institutions at the

[16] Jean Gerson, *Œuvres*, VII/1, pp. 1137–85.   [17] Kaminsky (1972).

end of the Middle Ages that explains why states everywhere, whether principalities or urban republics, sought to reduce the autonomy of the old universities to a level they found acceptable, and to endow new ones, which they themselves had created, with liberties that were strictly limited and supervised.

What form did such assumption of control take? As shown, it in no way precluded princely interest in, and respect for, the institutions themselves or for the men who made them function. The latter's personal status was guaranteed; they were not begrudged honours and favours; career prospects were good, even posts in princely circles being open to them. In the fifteenth century, towns and sovereigns conceded substantial financial support to promote universities. Considerable sums were devoted both to new foundations and old institutions for the establishment or enlargement of colleges, the erection of university buildings (previously an almost unheard-of occurrence), the endowment of student scholarships or salaried lectureships, the stocking of libraries. The understanding is that this munificence was commensurate with the university's willingness to accept a greater degree of control. However, in established universities things did not always go smoothly, and princes sometimes had to impose a 'general reform' on the uncooperative in order to bring statutes and privileges into line with the requirements of the new political order. The university reforms previously discussed were practically all achieved through the exertion of political power. The great reform of Paris, for example, was officially promulgated in 1452 by a papal legate, but had in fact been prepared by a body of royal commissioners appointed by the government of Charles VII. Its avowed aim was to restore order to an institution whose repeated strikes, critical spirit and corporate arrogance were particularly irritating to the king.

The state's desire for control was brought to bear even on the actual content of courses with regard to the strictness of their orthodoxy. At Oxford Thomas Arundel, archbishop of Canterbury, acting in the king's name as much as his own, hunted out suspected Lollards. In Paris in 1474 Louis XI approved the temporary expulsion of all 'nominalists'.

Above all governments were sensitive to the issue of university privileges. There was no thought of abolishing them, but rather of supervising them strictly by subjecting them to the authority of the state's officials and ordinary courts. In France, in the 1440s, the *parlements* of Paris and of Toulouse had their jurisdiction over universities confirmed and extended. At about the same time the office of chancellor at Oxford and Cambridge ceased to be held by a regent elected from among his peers; it passed into the hands of court prelates, intimates of the king. In cities of the Italian peninsula designated officials – *trattatores* or *reformatores studii*, 'Savi dello studio' – were in charge of implementing the policy of the commune vis-à-vis its university. On the other hand the ancient weapon of the strike or secession, which had been the principal means of resistance of the *studia generalia*, everywhere fell into disuse.

Furthermore, princes wanted the right to oversee recruitment in institutions where previously the rule had been election or co-option of lecturers and the unrestricted registration of students regardless of their social and geographical origins. The institution of salaried lectureships (or of ecclesiastical prebends reserved for lecturers) allowed the authorities to intervene directly in the recruitment of teachers. As for student enrolment, it was to become subject to various rules and regulations. The communes and *signorie* on the Italian peninsula sought to insist on their subjects attending the local university; thus in 1407 Padua became the official university of the Venetian state. In theory foreign students were still welcome, but the schism and general warfare, together with an overall intensification of nationalist sentiments, meant that the threat of expulsion hung over them constantly. In 1470 Louis XI expelled from Paris Burgundian students who were subjects of Charles the Bold, and in 1474 he decreed that in future a French rector would be mandatory. At the same time the authenticity of students was more closely monitored. Public authorities, tired of seeing spurious or perpetual students claiming, by reason of university clerical status, those fiscal and judicial privileges to which they had no right, enforced stricter registration procedures and a maximum duration of study. Louis XII was to do precisely this in Paris in 1499.

There is no doubt that these measures did not as yet constitute coherent practice, but they did reveal an obvious shift in attitudes. The increased mastery of external authorities over universities (and the corresponding decline of ecclesiastical control) was in fact a response to fairly high social expectations, particularly from groups of officials and administrators who entrusted to universities their children's education. Some of the university men at least seem to have found their own interests mirrored in this development.

It would be a mistake to overemphasise the contrast between the almost ideal situation pertaining in the thirteenth century (recruitment that was not restricted by social and geographical factors, autonomous and democratic administration of institutions, enthusiasm for study) and the decadence at the end of the Middle Ages. Apart from the fact that such an ideal situation doubtless never existed, the comparison would at best involve the oldest universities, while scarcely making sense in terms of the more numerous recent foundations. It remains true that the general political climate of the fifteenth century exerted its influence on both the internal administration and the way of life of the universities. Hierarchical and authoritarian features were everywhere strengthened. 'Student power' on the Bolognese model, where it existed, like community spirit, was in retreat before the increasing weight of political power, as also before the enhanced authority of the teaching doctors, who proved more tractable partners for princes. General assemblies were replaced by restrictive commissions. University life style was transformed so that magisterial authority and the influence of the hierarchies became more obvious. The decline of disputation in favour of *lectiones*, the increasing opulence of dress and facilities, the cost and lavishness of ceremonies, especially the conferring of degrees, had the cumulative effect of more clearly demonstrating the growing integration of universities into the controlling political order. This was where at the end of the Middle Ages the true 'aristocratisation' of universities lay, rather than in a hypothetical narrowing of social recruitment. This aristocratisation went hand in hand with a more pronounced local character. It is true that some old centres (Paris, Bologna) and new ones (Cracow, Louvain) retained sufficient prestige to attract students from a distance, although in limited numbers. Furthermore, the pull exerted by Italian humanists syphoned off growing numbers of students from all parts of Europe to the *studia generalia* of the peninsula (Padua, Ferrara, Perugia, Siena). Everywhere else, however, in consequence of the increase in the numbers of new universities, 'regionalisation' of recruitment became entrenched, an obvious sign of closer integration into the local social and political framework. Municipal elites and local bodies of officials tightened their grip on such institutions with greater ease. As 'living in' became the rule (in colleges, halls and all kinds of hostels) – something, for example, which the Paris reform of 1452 tried to impose – it proved an excellent way of stamping out certain aspects of traditional university life that could not fit in any more with the new social and political order.

SCHOOLS, UNIVERSITIES AND SOCIETY

Medieval schools and universities never developed on the periphery of society, since it was society's needs and expectations which in large measure dictated the evolution of educational institutions in the fifteenth century, as in the preceding ones. This does not mean that purely intellectual considerations were without influence. There is every reason to believe that society's demand for competent literates and university graduates continued to grow. Superimposed on the already strong demand from those countries where universities had existed since the thirteenth century was that from areas previously marginal, but now benefiting from newly founded schools and universities.

The Church remained a prodigious consumer. Only traditional monasticism remained aloof, while the mendicant orders continued to give a solid intellectual grounding to a significant proportion of their members, thanks to the dual network of their internal *studia* and of their university *studia*, whose numbers increased through the creation of new faculties of theology. After preparatory studies in arts and philosophy, mendicants studied essentially theology. In many areas, above all in Mediterranean Europe, they more or less held the monopoly in this latter discipline, which prepared them for their roles as preachers or inquisitors. Among the secular clergy, on the other hand, canon lawyers vastly outnumbered theologians. There were, too, many clerics who possessed only a master's degree in arts. Be that as it may, one finds that in many areas the proportion of graduates in the secular clergy as a whole attained a previously unheard-of level in the fifteenth century. In England seventy-two out of seventy-nine bishops identified for the period 1399–1485 had studied in a university and one in an Inn of Court.[18] The same applied to canons: in fifteenth-century York, 80 per cent of the resident canons of the minster were graduates. As for France, at least in the north, the figures were comparable: the proportion of graduates among canons of Laon, which between 1270 and 1378 had been 43 per cent, by 1409 had doubled to 86 per cent (though of these almost half were mere masters of arts).[19] Elsewhere progress may have been slower, but everywhere it was apparent. In the Danish chapter of Roskilde, for example, the proportion of former students rose from 55 per cent between 1367 and 1430 to 78 per cent between 1431 and 1493, while the percentage of graduates, above all in arts, it is true, increased from 19 to 45.4.[20] At the end of the century the number of graduates in many places was so large that some were unable to obtain a canonry, and were forced to make do merely with a parish.

If an ecclesiastical career remained the most usual prospect for young men who had studied at school or university, demand from the lay sector made spectacular strides in the fifteenth century, although one needs to remember that during this period many secular posts could still be filled by clerics, at least by those in minor orders; one sees this in England, for instance. Generally speaking, lay graduates did not belong to princely councils, which remained the prerogative of the higher nobility. Chancelleries and sovereign courts of justice on the contrary – the king's bench, the *parlement* of Paris, for example – from the early 1400s were largely in the hands of lay graduates. Even where this was not yet the case, the numbers of graduates grew very rapidly during the century: at the Council of Brabant, the duchy's supreme court, they rose from 40 per cent to 70 per cent.[21] Even more numerous were the posts available in the local machinery of princely administrations which supported a satellite community of attorneys and lawyers. Here, law graduates might carve out for themselves a comfortable niche. At the end of the century, however, graduates had become

---

[18] Rosenthal (1970). [19] Millet (1982), pp. 87–100. [20] Mornet (1983).
[21] Ridder-Symoens (1981).

so plentiful, in the *bailliages* near,Paris, for instance, that some doctors or licenti-
ates were obliged, at the start of their careers at least, to accept subordinate
posts, which in preceding generations had been filled by individuals without a
university education.

Increasing numbers of towns, as well as the more or less independent city-
states of the Italian peninsula and of Germany, and the *bonnes villes* integrated
into the national monarchies of France, England and Spain were drawing upon
the services of university-educated doctors and jurists. In some cases
(Barcelona, Montpellier, Nuremberg), the persistent mistrust of the merchant
patriciate restricted them to essentially vocational positions; elsewhere, they
gained access in the end to the actual management of municipal affairs. Such
promotion was obviously accompanied by significant social changes: bourgeois men of commerce began to send their sons to university and to marry
their daughters to graduates. Private practice likewise offered opportunities to
university graduates in law or medicine. Mere masters of arts, if they did not
remain in the ranks of the clergy, could at least become school-masters.

Finally one needs to add that studying for its own sake, or at any rate studying without instant vocational prospects, was not unknown in the fifteenth
century and perhaps enjoyed a certain revival. A more widespread desire for
access to the world of literacy which printing, by producing an abundance of
'popular' books, would assuage in the second half of the century was one of
the factors, among urban populations (even in artisan circles) and the nobility,
conspiring to propel a growing number of young people into schools. Other
influences were new demands, even from the laity, stimulated by the religious
reform movements (to read the Bible), and the reputation, whether it was
enjoyed for cultural or merely fashionable reasons, of Italian humanism. If the
response of the tradition-loving faculties to these kinds of expectations was
somewhat inadequate, the new schools (schools of the Brethren of the
Common Life, humanist *contubernia*) were certainly more efficient, and this was
one of the principal factors behind their success. In consequence of the new
peregrinatio academica (precursor of the Grand Tour of more recent times) young
English, German and Scandinavian nobles were beginning to venture to the
Italian peninsula for a rapid excursion round the principal *studia*. This, too, was
symptomatic of such cultural interests.

Given such conditions, in spite of a widespread demographic depression
until 1450 at least, the definite increase, in both relative and real terms, in the
numbers of people receiving education during the fifteenth century is easily
explained; and this despite the 'misfortunes of the period'. If some of the old
university centres (such as Paris, Montpellier and Toulouse) were perhaps
undergoing a period of stagnation, elsewhere progress was evident: the total
strength of Oxford and Cambridge in the period 1400–1500 rose from around

2,000 to around 3,000. It was in Germany that the advance was most spectacular: about 1480, 2,500 new German students registered each year, that is five times more than a hundred years before.[22]

Statistics alone are not enough. The progress they reveal provokes two main points. First, it must be remembered that, in spite of everything, only a small, essentially male, proportion of the population was involved. It is particularly noteworthy that although 'learning' was becoming increasingly important to them, many occupations remained outside the scholastic system, either through disdain or lack of awareness, and were thus limited to vocational apprenticeship or family associations – one thinks of the training of artists and architects, the beginnings of civil engineering (mines, metallurgy) and of military engineering (artillery, fortifications), or the principles of trading and shipping. Even occupations more closely related to scholastic disciplines were not really provided for by universities, which were satisfied with exercising a certain amount of jurisdictional control over them. Barbers and surgeons, notaries and scribes (soon to be replaced by printers) continued to be trained as apprentices. On a totally different level, in some bourgeois and noble circles, above all on the Italian peninsula, new types of learned associations (academies) sprang up, making it possible to economise on a traditional university education.

Secondly, one needs to enquire into the social and cultural significance of the enlarged scholastic and graduate population. Although some contemporary treatises complained of the overproduction of graduates – the first appearance of a theme destined to enjoy a long life – it would be wrong to claim that the expansion in numbers of those receiving education had reached a crisis point. While some graduates may have experienced early difficulties in their chosen careers, there was no glut of graduates. Although the shortcomings of universities, as considered above, reflected a certain lack of relevance in the courses offered, degrees none the less retained their value as social currency. One needs to substitute for the understandable, yet illusory, theory of a depreciation of knowledge and men of learning the notion of a 'general rise in the cultural level'. This seems better to take into account those developments to be found in the fifteenth century and beyond.

For all that, should one be hailing the birth of a modern meritocracy? In spite of the declining benefits of papal patronage, the spiralling costs of study and the restrictive rules adopted in some places, education was still a means of social mobility. Well-known individual cases can be quoted: Gerson, son of Ardennes peasants, and Nicholas of Cusa, son of a Moselle boatman. One recalls that almost 20 per cent of German university students in the fifteenth century were classed as *pauperes*; it is true that many never progressed beyond

[22] Schwinges (1986).

the arts faculty and, in consequence, the lower ranks of the secular clergy. Nowhere did the nobility monopolise educational institutions: its numbers in these were proportionally no higher than they were in society at large. At the beginning of the fifteenth century nobles accounted for scarcely 5 per cent of the population of universities in the south of France;[23] between 1380 and 1500 the figure at New College, Oxford, was less than 13 per cent, and most of those were gentry.[24]

Yet it is clear that the majority of students came from broad social strata of the middle rank, essentially rural in England, decidedly urban on the Italian peninsula and in the Empire – sons of farmers, artisans, tradesmen, reaping the benefits of a mobility that one might term 'oblique' or horizontal. Access to study provided the passport from the world of shops or trade to that of the clergy and to administrative posts that no doubt guaranteed more security and prestige. From the outset they had had financial means and personal relationships (kinship, friendship, protectors) and were thus able to accomplish without too much difficulty this change in occupation, sometimes compounded by a geographical move, which study and qualifications rendered possible. In succeeding generations one sees the formation of genuine graduate dynasties: places reserved in the best colleges, reductions in examination fees, books handed down from father to son, or from uncle to nephew; all these fostered the creation of castes or sub-castes of judges, lawyers, teachers, whose culture and learning were handed down as a family tradition and a hereditary commodity.

Certainly at the end of the fifteenth century there was no question of a glut of graduates. However, the schools and universities which developed at the end of the Middle Ages, rather than provoking widespread social mobility, seem above all to have allowed society to adapt to the changing political and economic situation of the age. This does not mean – no doubt fortunately for the history of western culture – that all the consequences, both short and long term, of the surge in education and learning had been foreseen and controlled.

[23] Verger (1976b).   [24] Lytle (1978).

CHAPTER 12

HUMANISM

Robert Black

A discussion of Renaissance humanism must begin with Burckhardt, whose *The civilization of the Renaissance in Italy* has set the terms of debate and analysis from the time of its publication in 1860 up to the most recent scholarship. Burckhardt's interpretation of humanism was not particularly novel, but he stated his views with powerful simplicity and systematic logic. No scholar can now accept Burckhardt's thesis as a whole, but it must be conceded that he raised the crucial historical issues concerning humanism.

For Burckhardt, the Renaissance was not fundamentally about the revival of Antiquity: 'the essence of the phenomena might still have been the same without the classical revival', which had 'been one-sidedly chosen as the name to sum up the whole period'.[1] In Burckhardt's view, instead, the 'characteristic stamp'[2] of the Renaissance was a new spirit of individualism. What was reborn in Italy from the mid-thirteenth to the early sixteenth century was not classicism but rather man himself.

In the Middle Ages both sides of human consciousness – that which was turned within as that which was turned without – lay dreaming or half awake beneath a common veil. The veil was woven of faith, illusion and childish prepossession, through which the world and history were seen clad in strange hues. Man was conscious of himself only as a member of a race, people, part, family or corporation – only through some general category. In Italy this veil first melted into air; an *objective* treatment and consideration of the state and of all the things of this world became possible. The *subjective* side at the same time asserted itself with corresponding emphasis; man became a spiritual *individual*, and recognized himself as such.[3]

With typical consistency, Burckhardt painted a portrait of the humanists in which the colours and contours of his subjects were not academic or scholarly but anthropological: superficially the humanists might have been 'mediators between their own age and a venerated antiquity',[4] but their essential definition

---

[1] Burckhardt (1990), p. 120. [2] Burckhardt (1990), p. 230. [3] Burckhardt (1990), p. 98.
[4] Burckhardt (1990), p. 135.

was human and personal: 'malicious self-conceit', 'abominable profligacy', 'irreligion', 'licentious excess'. It was not their devotion to Antiquity which in the sixteenth century resulted in their fall from grace, according to Burckhardt, but rather they were 'the most striking examples and victims of an unbridled subjectivity'.[5]

Burckhardt thus powerfully articulated several fundamental problems about Renaissance humanism which ever since have preoccupied scholarship. Was humanism essentially concerned with reviving the culture of classical Antiquity, or did it represent something more fundamental – a change in the very nature of man, in his view of himself, or at least a new philosophy of man? And what was the relation of humanism to the preceding historical period, to the Middle Ages? Did it represent a decisive break from previous cultural traditions, or is it more appropriate to speak of continuity and evolution rather than of revolution?

Burckhardt's thesis dominated the interpretation of humanism for at least half a century after the publication of *The civilization*. His definition of humanism and the Renaissance in human, not in scholarly or literary, terms was adopted by influential figures such as Symonds, Villari, Goetz, Taine and Müntz.[6] Burckhardt had posited a political explanation of the origins of Renaissance individualism, which in his view was the product of the egoistic and amoral political world of the Italian city-states;[7] this particular facet of the Burckhardtian synthesis was soon challenged by a succession of writers, such as Renan, Thode, Gebhart and most eruditely by Burdach, who saw the origins of the Renaissance in the religious world of medieval spirituality.[8] Yet despite their disagreement over the sources of the Renaissance, these early revisionists still carried on with Burckhardt's anthropological approach to the nature of humanism. Similarly Burckhardtian in conception was much of the so-called 'revolt of the medievalists' which gained momentum particularly in the first half of this century; their continued emphasis on the precocious discovery of the world and of man, on a 'truly Renaissance spirit', individualism, sensuality, rationalism, realism are all obviously Burckhardtian categories of analysis.[9] Even the attempt to deny to the Renaissance the status of a genuine new historical period, devaluing it instead as the decaying after-life of the Middle Ages – a type of *histoire des mentalités* most famous in the writings of Huizinga[10] – is

---

[5] Burckhardt (1990), pp. 177–9.

[6] Ferguson (1948), pp. 198–213, 226–7, 245–50; Symonds (1875–86); Villari (1877–82); Goetz (1907) and (1914); Taine (1866); Müntz (1889–95).   [7] Burckhardt (1990), pp. 19–98.

[8] Ferguson (1948), pp. 297–311; Renan (1884); Thode (1885); Gebhart (1879); Burdach (1893), (1910) and (1913).   [9] Ferguson (1948), pp. 333–41.

[10] Ferguson (1948), pp. 373–6; Huizinga (1990).

still painting with a Burckhardtian brush. Despite all this revisionism, more-over, it is important to remember that Burckhardt has continued to have his unabashed champions well into the twentieth century, not least two of the most famous German refugees in modern American academic life – Ernst Cassirer and Hans Baron. Individualism is a central theme of Cassirer's study of the philosophy of humanism; moreover, his emphasis on the inter-relation of the elements of a culture and an historical period – 'society, state, religion, church, art, science' – is pre-eminently Burckhardtian in conception.[11] It might seem paradoxical to connect Baron, who of course highlighted the republican strand of humanism, with Burckhardt, who saw despotism as the determining political influence in Renaissance Italy; nevertheless, Baron's preoccupation with a sharp contrast between the Middle Ages and the Renaissance ('a funda-mental transformation in *Weltanschauung*'),[12] with the emergence of modern secular and lay values, with the decline of medieval concepts such as Guelphism and Empire, not to mention his denigration of pure classicism and his attempts to link together the various strands of cultural history (political and historical thought, artistic realism, positive valuation of wealth) – all these features of his interpretation of early Italian humanism are solidly within the Burckhardtian tradition.[13]

However, it is particularly in the Italian scholarly tradition – most notably in the field of the history of philosophy – that Burckhardt has continued to enjoy the most powerful resonance. This is in one sense ironic, since Renaissance philosophy was egregiously ignored in *The civilization*.[14] Yet Burckhardt had declared that 'Every period of civilization which forms a complete and consis-tent whole manifests itself not only in political life, in religion, art and science, but also sets its characteristic stamp on social life',[15] and it has been irrefutably demonstrated by Gombrich that Burckhardt derived this concept of the spirit of the age from the idealist historical philosophy of Hegel.[16] Bertrando Spaventa introduced Hegelian idealism into Italian philosophical circles in the 1860s,[17] and his approach was a determining influence on the two giants of Italian philosophy in the early twentieth century – Croce and Gentile. Croce gave little detailed attention to humanism, although his support for a Hegelian literary historian such as De Sanctis and his implicit criticisms of a pro-Catholic revisionist such as Toffanin added weight to the Burckhardtian tradi-tion in Italy.[18] It was above all Gentile who developed an Hegelian/idealist interpretation of Renaissance humanism in Italy: the Middle Ages had deval-ued man and life in this world; Italian humanism, by contrast, restored the

---

[11] Ferguson (1948), pp. 218–20; Cassirer (1963).   [12] Baron (1958), p. 28.
[13] Baron (1938) and (1966).   [14] Kristeller (1961), p. 30.   [15] Burckhardt (1990), p. 230.
[16] Gombrich (1969).   [17] Spaventa (1867) and (1908); Ferguson (1948), p. 222.
[18] De Sanctis (1930); Croce (1941); Ferguson (1948), pp. 240–1, 350.

dignity of man, the potential of the human mind and the value of earthly existence. Gentile thus effectively bolstered the Burckhardtian view of
Renaissance Italians as 'the first born among the sons of modern Europe'.[19]
This Burckhardtian/Hegelian approach continues to find powerful support in
contemporary Italian philosophical circles. Indeed, the leading Italian post-war
Renaissance scholar, Eugenio Garin, was Gentile's protégé; it is not surprising
that he has emphasised a coherent outlook in Renaissance humanism, which
he sees as a new philosophy of man, in sharp contrast to medieval devaluation
of humanity.[20] It also comes as no surprise that Garin has embraced many of
Baron's views, including his 'civic humanism';[21] indeed, Garin finds Burckhardt
himself particularly sympathetic:

Humanism consisted in a renewed confidence in man and his possibilities and in an
appreciation of man's activity in every possible sense . . . Burckhardt's old and vigorous
conception which linked the reaffirmation of man with the reaffirmation of the world,
the reaffirmation of the spirit with the reaffirmation of nature, ought to be connected
without fear of rhetoric to the old notion that the Renaissance succeeded in bringing
about a new harmony. This ideal of the harmony and the measure of a complete man
runs . . . through those centuries.[22]

It is also ironic that the most effective and powerful challenge to the
Burckhardtian approach to the Renaissance and humanism has come from
another of Gentile's protégés from the 1930s. It is no exaggeration to say that
Paul Oskar Kristeller has revolutionised the study and interpretation of
Renaissance humanism in the last fifty years. This is not only because of his
now completed vast, six-volume catalogue of unpublished humanist manuscript collections, *Iter italicum*, a work which has rightly concentrated scholarly
attention on the study of unpublished primary sources in intellectual history,[23]
but also because of his fundamental repudiation of Burckhardt's thesis that
Renaissance humanism represented a new philosophy of man. In the single
most influential article on Renaissance humanism written this century,[24]
Kristeller refuted the interpretation of 'humanism as the new philosophy of
the Renaissance, which arose in opposition to scholasticism, the old philosophy of the Middle Ages', declaring 'that the Italian humanists on the whole
were neither good nor bad philosophers, but no philosophers at all'.[25] Instead,
he saw Renaissance humanism as a literary movement, focusing on grammatical and rhetorical studies; the excursions of humanists into the realm of
philosophy were often erratic, amateurish and superficial. Humanism could
not have replaced scholasticism as the new philosophy of the Renaissance for
the simple reason that scholasticism and Aristotelian philosophy continued to

[19] Ferguson (1948), pp. 222–3, 240–3, 350; Gentile (1912), (1931) and (1968).
[20] Garin (1965).   [21] Garin (1965) and (1969).   [22] Garin (1965), p. 221.
[23] Kristeller (1963–97).   [24] Kristeller (1979b), pp. 85–105.   [25] Kristeller (1979b), pp. 90–1.

thrive in Italy until the mid-seventeenth century. Because humanism was not a philosophical movement, it could not, for Kristeller, represent a new vision of man:

If we think or hear of such a topic as 'renaissance concepts of man,' we are immediately reminded of a view of the Renaissance period that is widespread and has often been repeated: the Renaissance, according to this view, had a special interest in, and concern with, man and his problems. Very often, and in my view mistakenly, this notion is associated with the phenomenon called Renaissance humanism, and in stressing the difference which distinguishes the Renaissance from the period preceding it, it has been pointedly asserted that the thought of the Renaissance was man-centered, whereas medieval thought was God-centered.[26]

For Kristeller, the essential focus of Renaissance humanism was precisely what Burckhardt had rejected: the revival of Antiquity. In undermining one foundation stone of the Burckhardtian edifice – the anthropological definition of humanism – Kristeller did not ignore the other central tenet of Burckhardt's thesis; besides stressing the importance of humanism's new classicism, Kristeller also emphasised its great debt to the Middle Ages: to the French medieval grammatical tradition of classical studies, to the Byzantine heritage of Greek scholarship and, above all, to the Italian medieval rhetorical tradition of *ars dictaminis*.[27]

The great merit of Kristeller's interpretation of Renaissance humanism – indeed the key to its lasting appeal – is his philological study of primary sources; unlike some of his German and Italian predecessors and contemporaries, his studies have not been preconditioned by adherence to an anachronistic philosophical school or methodology. Discarding modern meanings whereby 'almost any kind of concern with human values is called "humanistic"',[28] Kristeller returned to contemporary usage of the late fifteenth century when the term *humanista* was invented to designate teacher of the humanities on the analogy of such medieval university labels as *legista, jurista, canonista* or *artista*.[29] Although the term humanism was a nineteenth-century coinage, Kristeller connected *humanista* with a defined group of subjects, the *studia humanitatis*,[30] which in the late 1430s had been equated by the future Pope Nicholas V, in planning a library for Cosimo de' Medici, with grammar, rhetoric, poetry, history and moral philosophy.[31] Moreover, Kristeller cited a number of fifteenth-century texts by Bruni, Ficino, Antonio Benivieni, Alamanno Rinuccini and Pontano[32] (to whom can now be added Salutati, Barzizza and Traversari),[33] not to mention the above library canon, in which it

---

[26] Kristeller (1979a), p. 167.   [27] Kristeller (1964), pp. 147–65.   [28] Kristeller (1979a), p. 21.
[29] Kristeller (1979b), p. 99.   [30] Kristeller (1979b), p. 98.
[31] Kristeller (1979a), p. 282 n. 60; Kohl (1992), p. 186.
[32] Kristeller (1979a), pp. 282–3, nn. 60 and 62.   [33] Kohl (1992), pp. 191, 192, 195, 196 and 199.

is clear that the *studia humanitatis* were regarded as a literary programme, focused on grammar and rhetoric and clearly distinguished from philosophical, mathematical, medical, scientific and theological studies. Kristeller finally indicated how the phrase *studia humanitatis* was revived by fourteenth-century humanists[34] (in fact first by Salutati in 1369) on the basis of Ciceronian usage (in his oration *Pro Archia*)[35] to mean a literary or liberal education. All this suggested that humanism was a self-conscious cultural and literary movement which extended back at least to the days of Petrarch's discovery of *Pro Archia* in 1333.

Subsequent scholarship has continued to confirm the philological accuracy of Kristeller's definition of humanism. A recent collection of usages of the term *studia humanitatis* from 1369 to 1425, with selected examples to 1467, substantiates its meaning as a literary and cultural programme, albeit not always precisely spelled out.[36] Here it is perhaps worth pointing out that the ancients too had some difficulty with Cicero's meaning, to the extent that Gellius offered this gloss on the meaning of *humanitas*:

Those who have spoken Latin and have used the language correctly do not give to the word *humanitas* the meaning which it is commonly thought to have, namely, what the Greeks call φιλανθρωπία, signifying a kind of friendly spirit and good-feeling towards all men without distinction; but they gave to *humanitas* about the force of the Greek παιδεία; that is what we call ... education and training in the liberal arts ... That it is in this sense that our earlier writers have used the word, and in particular Marcus Varro and Marcus Tullius, almost all the literature shows.[37]

The correct antique meaning of humanism in the sense of *paideia*, not philanthropy, was universally adopted by fifteenth-century writers when using the phrase *studia humanitatis*, indicating the philological soundness of Kristeller's definition, as well as the anachronism inherent in associating humanism with humane values or a new philosophy of man. Moreover, a number of texts in which leading figures such as Bruni and Poggio speak of the *studia humanitatis* as their particular specialism ('nostra studia', 'nos omnes qui prosequimur studia hec humanitatis', 'nostra studia humanitatis')[38] confirm humanism as a self-conscious movement, with a genuine *esprit de corps*. Finally, although it has been doubted that the *studia humanitatis* were associated at first with the five disciplines of grammar, rhetoric, poetry, history and moral philosophy,[39] it needs to be pointed out that Petrarch himself identified these as his particular areas of interest. In his list of favourite books, published by Ullman,[40] Petrarch wrote, 'My specially prized books. To the others I usually resort not as a deserter as a scout.'[41] Besides the actual titles, this list is significant as indicating

---

34 Kristeller (1979b), p. 98.   35 Kohl (1992), pp. 187–8.   36 Kohl (1992).
37 Aulus Gellius, *Attic nights*, bk XIII, ch. 17.   38 Kohl (1992), pp. 192, 193, 200.   39 Kohl (1992).
40 Ullman (1955), pp. 117–37.   41 Ullman (1955), p. 118.

how Petrarch defined his particular area of academic specialism. The scholastic, philosophical disciplines are limited to one volume each, and dialectic is given only a grudging place: 'Tractat(us) (et) n(ichi)l ult(ra)'. The rest of the list falls under the headings 'Moral(ia)', 'Recth(orica)', 'ystor(ica)' (with its usual subsection 'ex(empl)a'), 'Poet(ica)' and 'Gram(matica)'.[42] It does not need to be emphasised that these are the five divisions of the *studia humanitatis* as found first in Parentucelli's canon and then with increasing frequency in the second half of the fifteenth century.

Kristeller's work with thousands upon thousands of humanist manuscripts has made him wary of generalising on the basis of a few texts, or of highlighting one or several famous humanist texts, in the Burckhardtian or idealist fashion, at the expense of numerous less well-known or even unpublished works.

Renaissance thought, he writes, when seen in its entire range, say, from 1350 to 1600, presents a very complex picture. Different schools and thinkers expressed a great variety of views, on problems related to the conception of man as on others, and it would be extremely difficult if not impossible to reduce all of them to a single common denominator.[43]

Although he himself, writing in 1979, still acknowledged that 'there is at least a core of truth in the view that Renaissance thought was more "human" and more secular, although not necessarily less religious, than medieval thought and that it was more concerned with human problems',[44] older as well as recent research has made it impossible to make even this small concession to the Burckhardtian tradition. In the first place, it has been established that the Renaissance emphasis on man was consciously borrowed from classical, biblical, patristic and medieval authors;[45] there was no lack of medieval authors (for example Honorius of Autun, Peter Damian or Hugh of St Victor) who used arguments (such as God's choice of man for the Incarnation, the creation of man in His likeness or man as the binding force of the universe) later favoured by Renaissance proponents of the dignity of man.[46] Moreover, there was no consensus among Renaissance humanists whether to lament the misery of the human condition or applaud the dignity of man. Famous treatises exalting human dignity by Facio[47] and Manetti[48] have of course been spotlighted, whereas the alternative view, as developed for example in Poggio's *De miseria humanae conditionis*, has been passed over in silence.[49] Indeed, human misery versus dignity had been conceived as a type of *paragone* (rhetorical arguments on both sides of a question) in the classic medieval treatment by Innocent III,

[42] Ullman (1955), p. 122.   [43] Kristeller (1979a), p. 167.   [44] Kristeller (1979a), pp. 167–8.
[45] Garin (1938); Trinkaus (1940), pp. 64–79, (1970), pp. 179–90, and (1983), pp. 343–63; Buck (1960); Kraye (1988), p. 306.   [46] Kraye (1988), pp. 309, 311.   [47] Facio, *De humanae vitae felicitate*.
[48] Manetti, *De dignitate et excellentia hominis*.   [49] Garin (1965), pp. 56–60.

who had failed to deliver his promised treatise on the dignity of man to complement his *De miseria humane conditionis*; in fact, Poggio 'not only borrowed Innocent's title but also elaborated many of the themes he had discussed',[50] highlighting there (as well as in *De varietate fortunae*) the frailty, the miserable destiny and the stupidity of mankind.[51] Indeed, it would be hard to find a more dismal portrait of the human race than in the youthful *Intercoenales*, as well as in the more mature *Teogenius* and *Momus* written by the so-called 'universal man of the early Renaissance',[52] Leon Battista Alberti.[53] Another important fact is that the anti-intellectualism and fideism of much humanist moral philosophy represented a serious limitation of man's potential. Petrarch's *Secretum* taught knowledge alone could not achieve Christian virtue, which could be gained through will and experience only with grace.[54] For Valla in his *Collatio Novi Testamenti* and *Adnotationes in Novum Testamentum*, theological understanding was enhanced by philology, but, as he also argues in *De libero arbitrio*, ultimately human free will and predestination were concepts that had to be accepted as acts of faith.[55] Similarly, in his *De vero falsoque bono*, Valla makes no effort to sustain the conclusions of religion through rational philosophy; in portraying the after-life, he seeks the help of faith and imagination, not knowledge.[56] Another fact which is frequently overlooked is the relation which would develop between humanism and the Reformation in the early sixteenth century. It would be impossible to go further than Luther and Calvin in denying human potential and dignity; according to the former, for example, 'If we believe Christ redeemed mankind by his blood, we are forced to admit that man had been entirely lost',[57] a view strongly supported by the latter: 'Wherever you turn, you understand you are nothing except squalor, vice, sickness, crime, and so worthy of every kind of loathing; all help, all salvation and dignity must be expected from God.'[58] The older view that this Reformation anthropology was rejected by Renaissance humanism, speaking through Erasmus,[59] is no longer acceptable; scholarship has demonstrated that countless reformers had been and continued to be humanists, and indeed it was largely by their efforts that the Reformation was able to spread throughout Europe.[60]

As a general definition of humanism, the anthropology of Burckhardt and

---

[50] Kraye (1988), pp. 306–7; Bracciolini, *Opera*; Trinkaus (1970), pp. 258–70.   [51] Vasoli (1988), p. 64; Bracciolini, *Opera*.

[52] Gadol (1969).   [53] Alberti, *Opera inedita, Momus o del principe* and *Opere volgari*; Vasoli (1988), p. 64.

[54] Petrarch, *Prose*; Trinkaus (1988), p. 330.

[55] Valla, *In Latinam Novi Testamenti, De libero arbitrio* and *Collatio Novi Testamenti*; Trinkaus (1988), p. 342; Lorch (1988), p. 334.   [56] Valla, *De vero falsoque bono*; Kristeller (1964), p. 33.

[57] *De servo arbitrio*, cited by Kraye (1988), p. 314 n. 78.   [58] See Kraye (1988), p. 314 n. 81.

[59] Phillips (1949).   [60] Spitz (1975), pp. 371–436, and (1988), pp. 380–411.

his innumerable successors must be discarded; indeed, attempts to reduce humanism to some kind of philosophical formula, to attribute to it a universal philosophical content or doctrine, will always fail. Just as scholasticism can never be defined in terms of a given body of propositions or views,[61] so humanism did not represent one overall intellectual theme or perspective. It is often said that humanism implied a new historical consciousness which was lacking in the Middle Ages,[62] and it is true that much revolutionary philological work of the humanists rested on new historical insights about texts, manuscript affiliations and translations. However, it is a fact that many humanists, as chancellors, secretaries or teachers of grammar and rhetoric, did not engage in original or significant philological activity. Moreover, the proposition that the Middle Ages lacked a sense of history, which then characterised the activity of Renaissance humanists, is patently false.[63] In some areas, for example, in ecclesiology, medieval authors had a powerfully developed sense of historical change and periodisation; such a view ignores the graphic historical contrast between the primitive and the contemporary Church drawn by writers such as St Bernard, Ptolemy of Lucca, Dante or Marsilius of Padua.[64] Similarly, it would be hard to find an approach less historical, yet one more powerfully supported by Renaissance humanists, than the ancient theology – the view that a body of mystical doctrines were transmitted to Moses and Hermes Trismegistus and then preserved miraculously unchanged through the Egyptians, Persians, Greeks, Romans, church fathers and medieval Byzantines to reach the contemporary world of fifteenth- and sixteenth-century Europe.[65] These types of generalisation – just like Panofsky's famous but equally false formula of the union of form and content in the Renaissance[66] (who would seriously argue that clothing classically modelled figures in antique garb was a characteristic of fifteenth- or sixteenth-century art?) – are simply variations on the Hegelian theme of the spirit of the age; no one will ever identify the 'characteristic stamp' of the Renaissance, because it exists only in the minds of Hegel, Burckhardt and their followers, not in historical reality. Not even antipathy to scholasticism was entirely characteristic of humanism; the attacks by Petrarch, Bruni, Valla or Erasmus are famous, but it should also be pointed out that Poggio praised and admired Aquinas,[67] and that his successor as Florentine chancellor, Benedetto Accolti, in contrast to the previous generation of humanists, showed a renewed interest in scholasticism and in natural, speculative and metaphysical philosophy, finding many scholastics to praise, while rejecting Cicero, who had been assigned the highest rank among philosophers by his Florentine predecessors; moreover, these views are shared by a

---

[61] Kristeller (1979a), p. 99.   [62] E.g. Burke (1969).   [63] Kelley (1988), pp. 236–7.
[64] Black (1995).   [65] Walker (1972); Yates (1964).   [66] Panofsky (1960).
[67] Bracciolini, *Lettere*, I, p. 16; Kraye (1988), p. 327 n. 144; Camporeale (1972).

number of Accolti's contemporaries, including Alamanno Rinuccini, Donato
Acciaiuoli and Ficino.[68]

Kristeller's definition of humanism as *studia humanitatis* tells us how humanists themselves described their particular field of learning, but of course the
nature of every historical phenomenon is not clearly articulated by contemporaries, if only because for them its essential features were so obvious as to
require no explanation. In the case of humanism, any moderately informed
researcher can detect the presence of a humanist text simply through its Latin;
by attempting to show his readers that he is affiliating himself, however imperfectly, with the Latin style of the ancients as opposed to the moderns (or
medievals in modern parlance), a writer is making an implicit declaration of his
affinity with the humanist movement. A humanist is thus someone who acts
like other humanists; this is how contemporaries would have identified humanism, and such a definition, stripped of historicist paraphernalia, will work
equally well for us. To take the limiting case, consider Machiavelli, who, because
of his unconventional and hardly humanitarian views, not to mention his
exclusively vernacular literary production, has frequently been denied the
status of humanist.[69] But by education, beginning scholarly and literary activity,
early latinate epistolography and classicised orthography Machiavelli showed
all the traits of a humanist, and, by appointing him as successor to other
humanist types such as Alessandro Braccesi as second chancellor, his
Florentine contemporaries obviously regarded him as a qualified humanist.[70]
When in the dedication of *The Prince* he pointed to his 'continual reading of the
ancients',[71] he was identifying himself in a way that his contemporaries could
never have misunderstood.

The *studia humanitatis* developed out of medieval traditions of grammar and
rhetoric; the activities of the Paduan, Aretine and Bolognese pre-humanists, as
well as of Petrarch himself, all have roots in Italian *ars dictaminis* as well as in the
classicism of northern Europe, particularly France.[72] Nevertheless, the
mixture of elements was unprecedented: medieval French grammatical studies
did not have a preponderant rhetorical emphasis, whereas the *ars dictaminis* had
had little direct connection with the reading and imitation of classical authors.
Although the origins of humanism have been intensively investigated, no
entirely satisfactory explanation for the change of direction taken by Italian
grammatical and rhetorical studies at the end of the thirteenth century has
emerged. Various hypotheses have been advanced: for example, almost all the
pre-humanists had a legal background which put them in immediate contact

---

[68] Accolti, *Dialogus*, Black (1985), pp. 211–14; Field (1988), p. 5.   [69] E.g. Stephens (1986), p. 49.
[70] Black (1990), pp. 72–8.   [71] Machiavelli, *Il principe e discorsi*, p. 13.
[72] Kristeller (1964), pp. 147–65; Witt (1982), (1983) and (1988).

with the antique heritage through ancient legal texts and compilations;[73] alternatively, the actual change instigated by the first pre-humanist, Lovato Lovati, has been reduced to the imitation of classical verse, which in turn has been explained by the lack of a medieval Italian tradition of Latin poetry, so that Lovato encountered fewer obstacles in imitating ancient metrical models.[74] All this is enlightening and doubtless provides valuable contexts for this fundamental change of taste; and yet it is impossible in the end to provide a complete historical explanation for the birth of humanism, precisely because this classical literary taste, implying the absolute superiority of ancient models in both grammar and rhetoric, was unprecedented in the Middle Ages. Ultimately, any fundamental change of style in the arts is inexplicable. Context and circumstances can fill in the background of why the Greeks in the fifth century BC made the decisive move from hieratic to naturalistic art; of why Giotto moved beyond the expressionism of Cimabue to genuine illusionism; of why Masaccio turned his back on the International Gothic to found a new monumental *gravitas*; of why Donatello rediscovered the human anatomy; of why Leonardo invented the High Renaissance style. But in the end we come up against genius and trend setting. Thus it is with Lovato, Mussato and Geri d'Arezzo: their new feeling for ancient literary style was their own creation.

If the ultimate origins of humanism are beyond the realm of historical research, more can be said of its achievements by the end of the fifteenth century. Many humanists were highly skilful or even professional scribes and copyists, and they launched a reform of script which has lasted to the present day.[75] Rejecting the Gothic bookhand which had come to dominate Europe in the thirteenth and fourteenth centuries, they created humanist script, believed to be an imitation of ancient Roman handwriting but in fact based on the script of the Carolingian revival which had been used both north and south of the Alps up to the early thirteenth century. The humanists also reformed cursive writing, distancing themselves from Gothic chancery hands and creating what has come to be known as Italic script. These were great and lasting achievements, but, in terms of their own aim of reviving *littera antiqua*, they were not fully successful. The humanists' idea of palaeographic chronology was primitive; their identification of Caroline with ancient Roman script must seem about as quaint as the widely held belief in the fifteenth century that the Florentine Baptistry was the Roman temple of Mars. Moreover, their imitation even of Caroline script was hardly a complete success: the characteristic rotundity of humanist bookhand is an adaptation of the round Gothic script of the fourteenth century; the humanists never realised that the Caroline 't' had been

[73] Weiss (1969a).   [74] Witt (1988).   [75] Ullman (1960); de la Mare (1973).

a low letter like the 'c', rising above the half-line level only in the course of the thirteenth century; they also never understood that Caroline copyists wrote usually above the first ruled line of the manuscript, not below as in Gothic manuscripts; they also preferred the more square page layout of Gothic manuscripts to the more normal oblong shape of Caroline codices. These are only some of the criteria according to which modern palaeographers distinguish humanist manuscripts from their Caroline precursors, and they demonstrate the limitations of the humanist reform of script; moreover, it must be remembered that Italic script is a hybrid creation, based on Gothic chancery cursive with elements adapted from Caroline writing, the likes of which never existed in the pre-Gothic period, much less in Antiquity.

In their central aspiration, the revival of the Latin language, humanist success was inevitably incomplete. The humanists wished to restore 'to light the ancient elegance of style which was lost and dead',[76] but modern scholarship has often been too much influenced by their own claims; in fact, the 'vocabulary, spelling, syntax of early humanist Latin, and even of certain late Quattrocento authors, have numerous features without parallel in classical Latin, but which are found in medieval Latin'.[77] The fifteenth-century controversy over neologisms demonstrates the extent to which coinages, just as in the Middle Ages, were still taking place; rare words, not really characteristic of classical Latin, were turned into normal usage by fifteenth-century humanists, desperate to widen the restricted classical vocabulary. Especially significant was the humanist failure to distinguish in practice between the language of classical poetry and prose, although certain critics (such as Valla[78] or Cortesi[79]) made theoretical objections to a practice which was founded in medieval habits. In some cases, it is even difficult to determine whether the unclassical practices of the humanists were the result of direct influence of the vernacular or were based on traditional practices, developed in late ancient Latin and compounded in the Middle Ages, particularly by the *ars dictaminis*. In fact, the concept of Latinity itself inherited from the Middle Ages died only a slow death in the fifteenth century. The medieval view (as stated characteristically by Dante in *De vulgari eloquentia*)[80] was that there had been two languages in Antiquity, the vernacular and Latin – the former learned and spoken naturally, the latter invented by the great authors as an artifice for their works of literature and philosophy and subsequently acquired at school. This view (upheld by early humanists such as Petrarch[81] and Bruni) was finally challenged in the mid-

---

[76] Solerti (ed.), *Le vite*, p. 290, trans. in Ross and McLaughlin (eds.), *The portable Renaissance reader*, p. 128.
[77] Rizzo (1986), p. 388.   [78] Valla, *Elegantiarum latinae linguae libri sex*, I, 17, p. 22; Rizzo (1986), p. 388.
[79] Cortesi, *De hominibus doctis*, p. 123.
[80] Dante Alighieri, *De vulgari eloquentia*, I, i, 3; Rizzo (1986), pp. 402–3.   [81] Rizzo (1990).

fifteenth century by such figures as Biondo, Alberti, Poggio, Guarino and Filelfo, who maintained that there was only one language in ancient Rome and that the medieval vernaculars developed from Latin as it was corrupted by the barbarian invasions. This dispute had vast importance not only for the birth of vernacular grammar but also for the humanists' attitude to the revival of Latin. On the one hand, if all languages were natural – Latin as well as the vernacular – then they all had a rational structure; it is no accident that the first grammar of the Italian language by Alberti emerged from this changed view of the history of Latin. On the other hand, as long as it was believed that the ancient Romans were in an analogous position to the moderns, then the revival of Latin was not an insurmountable task: if the Romans had had to learn Latin artificially, there was no reason why the moderns could not do the same. It was only necessary to clear away the corruption caused by the Middle Ages and to arm oneself with all possible purified texts; it is no accident that the most fervent upholder of the traditional, medieval concept of Latinity was Valla, whose *Elegantiae* were premised on the belief that there had been an ancient vernacular and that true Latin was universal and eternal, only to be rediscovered and purified. However, when it came to be taken for granted by the end of the fifteenth century (for example by Poliziano) that Latin was a natural language, humanists realised that they could never again step into the ancients' shoes. Many now felt they had to resort to extreme measures, abandoning the eclectic imitation typical of the early Quattrocento, and slavishly following just one model – hence the Ciceronianism prominent at the turn of the sixteenth century.[82] The humanists finally realised that their fundamental goal was an impossibility: as Silvia Rizzo has aphoristically put it, 'Latin became a dead language only when it was realised that it had been a living language.'[83]

The return to antique rhetoric was a fundamental goal of the Renaissance humanists, and here they faced fewer problems than in the revival of classical Latin; eloquence had had to be learned by the ancient Romans too, who bequeathed to posterity a number of excellent textbooks, including the pseudo-Ciceronian *Rhetorica ad Herennium*, Cicero's genuine *De inventione* and Quintilian's comprehensive *Institutiones oratoriae*. Rhetoric had been practised during the Middle Ages by means of the *ars dictaminis*, a debased derivative of the classical art, which itself continued to be studied and taught on a theoretical and academic level, although not put to practical use, by medieval commentators on the two Ciceronian textbooks. The early signs of humanism can be seen in the commentaries by a number of Bolognese *dictatores* on the *Ad Herennium* and *De inventione* at the turn of the fourteenth century. Cicero's

---

[82] Rizzo (1986) and (1990); Tavoni (1984).   [83] Rizzo (1990), p. 32.

orations had been neglected in the Middle Ages, and the classical emphasis of
early humanism was enhanced by the recovery of almost all of Cicero's orations between the 1330s and the 1420s, as well as of full texts of his other
rhetorical works, not to mention Quintilian's *Institutiones*, works which had
been either unknown, little used or available only in corrupt versions during
the Middle Ages. By the early fifteenth century, the humanists had largely
turned their backs on the *ars dictaminis*, reuniting classical rhetorical theory and
practice, not only by commenting on the ancient manuals, but also by using
them as guides to rhetorical practice, which was also now based on the imitation of the Ciceronian orations – something which had never taken place in the
Middle Ages. Moreover, the humanists began to gloss Cicero's *Orations*, even
before the recovery of Asconius Pedianus' ancient commentary; here they
diverged somewhat from ancient practice, going beyond purely philological
annotation to a discussion of rhetorical structure, reflecting their new concern
to imitate ancient models.

All this was far beyond the achievement of the Middle Ages, and yet even in
rhetoric the humanists were unable to put the medieval heritage fully behind
them. As in the Middle Ages, the *Rhetorica ad Herennium* remained the most
widely used textbook. The humanists added little in the way of new theoretical
works, preferring to compose epitomes of the antique art; the only significant
new large-scale rhetorical treatise to have been composed by the end of the fifteenth century was George of Trebizond's *Rhetoricorum libri V*.[84] More significant was the inability of the humanists to revive classical rhetoric as it had been
practised in the days of Cicero. The ancient treatises had divided rhetoric into
three genres, judicial, deliberative and epideictic, but in later Antiquity and the
Middle Ages, the first two, representing the oratory of the law courts and of
public debate, had fallen into disuse, leaving only the rhetoric of praise and
blame, as practised for example in speeches at weddings and funerals, university functions or on formal civic occasions. Although the humanists continued to give theoretical attention to judicial and deliberative oratory, the social
functions of rhetoric remained unchanged from the early days of the Italian
communes in the thirteenth century, with the result that the humanists have
bequeathed an exiguous oratorical literature apart from *epideixis*. Even more
notable was the continued humanist emphasis on letter writing, which had
been the principal focus of the *ars dictaminis*. The recovery of Cicero's letters in
the fourteenth century provided new models for epistolography; putting aside
the invented or contemporary letters used by the *dictatores*, the humanists could
now let Cicero show the way, not only in epistolary imitation but also in publishing their own letter collections. However, they never succeeded or possibly

---

[84] George of Trebizond, *Rhetoricum libri quinque*.

never even attempted to tip the balance of rhetorical literature again in favour of the oration; the numerous humanist treatises on epistolography written during the fifteenth century show that their over-riding interest was to supplant the *ars dictaminis*, not to restore to rhetoric its principal classical function of oratory.[85]

History, as one of the five disciplines of the *studia humanitatis*, was a principal concern of the humanists, who not only assiduously studied the ancient Roman histories but also wrote histories of their own, usually of the post-classical period, where their models were especially Livy and Sallust. The latter had been widely read and even imitated in the Middle Ages,[86] whereas the former had been copied and read[87] but had not served as a model. In this sense, Leonardo Bruni, with his *History of the Florentine people*, was an innovator, writing the first post-antique history explicitly imitating Livy; similarly Livian was the inspiration of a second great pioneer of humanist historiography, Flavio Biondo, who recounted the aftermath of the fall of the Roman Empire *ab inclinato imperio* just as Livy had written of the rise of Rome *ab urbe condita*. It has sometimes been argued that the achievement of early humanist historians went beyond formal classical imitation to philological research.[88] This is certainly true of sections concerning the foundations of cities and states; Bruni for example subjected his classical sources to critical analysis to prove that Florence had been founded not under Julius Caesar but rather under the Republic.[89] This was a kind of research closely related to the humanists' philological study of classical texts, and so it is not surprising that they applied their new critical techniques to this aspect of historiography. It has also been maintained that they carried this kind of philological critique of sources over into the main body of their historical works. However, it is doubtful that early humanists adopted new critical working methods for the writing of post-classical history. Not only did Bruni,[90] Biondo[91] and Accolti[92] fail to synthesise or compare the material in their sources; they also invented extensive passages in their histories. They adhered to the time-honoured medieval method of following one main chronicle, whose account was elaborated and embellished with additional material according to the requirements of classical imitation. Bruni's occasional use of archival documents here seems to have had the same purpose as older chronicles used by Biondo and Accolti: to supplement, not to

[85] Kristeller (1979a); Monfasani (1988).   [86] Smalley (1974).   [87] Billanovich (1951).
[88] Santini (1910), pp. 50ff; Fueter (1911), pp. 106ff; Ullman (1955), pp. 321–44; Fubini (1966), p. 546; Cochrane (1981).   [89] Bruni, *Historiarum florentini populi libri XII.*
[90] Bruni, *Historiarum florentini populi libri XII.*
[91] Biondo, *Historiarum ab inclinato Romano imperio decades III.*
[92] Accolti, *De bello a christianis contra barbaros gesto.*

displace or check, the account of the main chronicle source. History was regarded as a branch of rhetoric, where truth was defined not as absolute fidelity to sources but rather as verisimilitude or probability.[93] The adoption of more critical methods of historiography came much later for humanist historians under the influence of changed attitudes to the rules of history. In the earlier Renaissance, humanist historians followed Cicero's views, as stated in *De oratore*, that history required no special theoretical study, but in the wake of the debate at the very end of the fifteenth century over how to achieve a truly classical style, it began to be argued that, in addition to imitation, rules were needed.[94] This idea was immediately applied to history, with a succession of new and lengthy *artes historicae* emerging from the turn of the sixteenth century. A number of historians, including the Florentine chancellor Bartolomeo Scala, became unsure how to write history in the absence of rules and in this changed critical climate; others, such as Tristano Calco,[95] became highly critical of the achievements of their predecessors and began to rethink historical method afresh. The new *artes historicae* which emerged discussed not only style but also historical method and truth, often ranking types of historical sources in order of reliability. This new climate affected the historical outlook and method of the greatest humanist historian, Francesco Guicciardini,[96] whose scrupulous research methods could not have been further removed from the rhetorical practices of the early historians such as Bruni or Biondo.[97]

As grammar teachers, one of their principal professional activities, it has been asserted that the 'humanists of the fifteenth century changed the Latin curriculum, a major academic revolution', 'one of the few in the history of Western education, in the relatively short time of about fifty years – 1400 to 1450'.[98] It is true that humanist educators attacked the curriculum of their medieval predecessors; however, the reality is that the changes they effected in the classroom were often far more complex and gradual than is believed by some modern scholars, misled by the humanists' exaggerated tendency to self-advertisement.

The grammar curriculum in the Middle Ages and the Renaissance was divided into two relatively distinct phases: elementary education, which consisted of learning to read and write; and secondary education, in which Latin was learned properly, including both prose composition and the study of literature. As far as elementary education is concerned, the basic textbook in Italian schools both before and after the coming of humanism was a treatise on the parts of speech, attributed to the Roman grammarian Donatus but actually a

---

[93] Black (1981) and (1985).   [94] Cortesi, *De hominibus doctis*; Pontano, *I dialoghi*.
[95] Calco, *Historiae patriae*.   [96] Guicciardini, *Storia d'Italia*.   [97] Black (1987).
[98] Grendler (1989), pp. 140–1, 404. See also Garin (1953), (1957) and (1967) and (ed.) *Il pensiero pedagogico*.

compilation of material mainly from Priscian, which is conventionally known as *Ianua* by modern scholars after the first word of its verse introduction. There was complete continuity here between the Middle Ages and humanism, not only in textual but also in methodological terms: from the beginning of the fourteenth century the learning of *Ianua* was divided into two stages, first reading phonetically without meaning, then re-reading and memorising the text with meaning.[99] Accompanying *Ianua* as further reading material were a collection of verses preceded by an introduction and collection of moral aphorisms, the *Disticha Catonis*, a late ancient text which continued in heavy use throughout the sixteenth century and even received a commentary from Erasmus.[100] Learning *Ianua* meant memorising the basic Latin forms, so that the pupil, having left elementary school, was now in a position to learn Latin syntax, culminating in prose composition and letter writing. This was accomplished through *Regulae grammaticales*, a generic name for treatises written by medieval grammarians such as Goro d'Arezzo, Filippo di Naddo of Florence or Francesco da Buti of Pisa, just as by humanist teachers such as Guarino Veronese, Gaspare da Verona or Perotti. Again the most prominent feature of this genre of schoolbook, from Filippo di Naddo to Perotti, is continuity: the medieval concept of governance, developed in northern France during the twelfth century, was used without change to teach the relation between the parts of the sentence; mnemonic verses were employed to fix rules in the pupil's memory; medieval grammatical terminology was omnipresent; completely unclassical syntactical rules of thumb (such as the ubiquitous analysis of grammatical function according to word order (*a parte ante* and *a parte post*)) remained in constant use; invented sentences rather than quotations from classical authors continued to provide normal examples of grammatical usage.[101] The claim that humanists such as Guarino pioneered the abbreviated grammar textbook is unfounded, given that such works were already in circulation in the thirteenth (e.g. the *Regule* of Theobald of Siena)[102] and fourteenth centuries (e.g. the *Regule parve* of Goro d'Arezzo).[103] Even the supposed new departure of Perotti in ending his treatise with a section on epistolography is in fact traditional practice: many manuscripts of Francesco da Buti's *Regule* also end with a treatise on letter writing.[104]

Matching continuity in formal grammar at this school level was continuity in reading matter. For school purposes in both the Middle Ages and the Renaissance, the Latin authors were divided into two groups: the *auctores minores*, a cycle of late ancient and medieval texts, mainly in verse; and the *auc-*

---

[99] Black (1991a) and (1991b); Schmitt (1969).   [100] Grendler (1989), pp. 197ff; Avesani (1967), pp. 24–5.   [101] Percival (1972), (1975), (1976), (1978), (1981) and (1988).   [102] Black (forthcoming).
[103] Marchesi (1910).   [104] Black (1996), p. 113.

tores maiores, mainly the Roman poets but also a few prose writers.[105] Despite the harangues against them by the humanists, the minor authors continued to be read at school throughout the fifteenth century in Italy, as is attested by many manuscript copies which either originated or were actively glossed throughout the Quattrocento in Italy;[106] even Pietro Crinito, Poliziano's disciple, continued to teach Henry of Settimello's *Elegies*.[107] The most intensively read school text in the fourteenth and fifteenth century was Boethius' *Consolation of philosophy*, a work which often stood at the threshold between the minor and major authors. It is true that this text, like the minor authors, suffered a decline with the rise of the printing press at the end of the Quattrocento; nevertheless, manuscript copies, as in the case of the minor authors, continue to show intensive school use until the end of the century.[108]

The Roman classics had been read at school in Italy throughout the Middle Ages, as is clear again from the study of surviving manuscript schoolbooks. However, they were subject to significant changes of fashion and interest, and here the humanists did often play a significant role. The grammar curriculum in twelfth-century Italian schools finished with a study of the poets Vergil, Lucan, Ovid, Juvenal, Persius, Horace, Terence and Statius, as well as of prose texts by Cicero and Sallust's two histories. In the thirteenth century some authors such as Vergil, Persius and Cicero (apart from the suppositions *Ad Herennium* and the genuine *De inventione*, which were commented on as part of the study of rhetoric) seem to have dropped out of the curriculum with the rise of new, particularly northern European school texts such as Geoffrey de Vinsauf's *Poetria novella*, Alexandre de Villedieu's *Doctrinale*[109] and Evrard de Béthune's *Graecismus*.[110] In the course of the fourteenth century, a number of classical texts, including Seneca's *Tragedies* and Valerius Maximus' *Facta et dicta*, first entered the curriculum,[111] possibly under the partial influence of pre-humanists such as Lovato. However, the most significant curricular change was the recovery of Cicero, not to mention Vergil and Persius, for the schoolroom at the turn of the fifteenth century. Cicero's shorter moral treatises (*De amicitia*, *De senectute*, *Paradoxa stoicorum* and *De officiis*) had had a place in the twelfth-century Italian curriculum, and after nearly two centuries of neglect they once more became widely studied at school in the fifteenth century. Moreover, Cicero's letters, unknown in the Middle Ages, now became widely adopted as stylistic models in fifteenth-century Italian schools, although they were never subjected to philological commentary in the schoolroom like other classical texts.[112]

[105] Avesani (1965).   [106] Black (forthcoming).   [107] Ricciardi (1990), p. 265.
[108] Black and Pomaro (forthcoming).
[109] Alexandre de Villedieu, *Das Doctrinale des Alexander de Villa-Dei*.
[110] Evrard de Béthune, *Graecismus*; Black (forthcoming); Alessio (1986).
[111] Black (forthcoming).   [112] Black (1996).

As far as the classical authors are concerned, therefore, the picture is complex: neither revolution nor evolution is an adequate description, but continuity does describe the prevalent use of verse grammars from the thirteenth to the end of the fifteenth century. No classical grammar was written in verse, but it was found in the Middle Ages that versification was an essential method of prodding the memory of schoolboys. Works such as *Doctrinale* and *Graecismus* continued in constant use in Italy throughout the fifteenth century,[113] and when Lorenzo Valla, himself a grammar teacher, wanted to replace the *Doctrinale*, he began to compose a thoroughly unclassical verse grammar himself.[114] Similarly, there was continuity in methods used to teach the authors in the grammar schools from the Middle Ages to the end of the fifteenth century. Humanist teachers such as Guarino may have declared that their aim was to turn their pupils into better men,[115] but the reality of pedagogic practice was far more mundane: the study of hundreds of manuscript schoolbooks and their glosses in Florentine libraries dating from the twelfth to the end of the fifteenth century has confirmed the view that the overwhelming fare of humanist as well as of medieval grammar schools was simple philology (history, mythology, grammar, simple rhetoric, figures of speech, geography, paraphrase), not moral philosophy.[116]

In fact, if there was a pedagogic revolution in the Italian classroom, it took place not at the turn of the fifteenth but rather of the fourteenth century. It was at this point that the vernacular began to be used extensively as a pedagogic tool to teach Latin, not only to clarify vocabulary but also as a means to teach Latin prose composition; previously pupils had been taught to write in Latin through the medium of Latin, but at the beginning of the fourteenth century, possibly first in Bologna and then in Tuscany, Latin prose composition began to be taught by the use of *themata*, or passages to translate from the vernacular into Latin.[117] This practice continued throughout the fifteenth and sixteenth centuries, and was even used by a humanist such as Poliziano to instruct his pupil, the young Piero di Lorenzo de' Medici.[118] A complementary change in the curriculum, which seems to have taken place at the turn of the fourteenth century as well, and which also represented a concession to the growing numbers who wanted to make use of educational skills in a culture increasingly dominated by the vernacular language, was the abbreviation of the *Ianua* text to allow the minimum treatment of Latin grammar and the maximum amount of practice in reading skills. The text was still taught in Latin, often now by specialist elementary school teachers (*doctores puerorum* as distinct from *doctores grammatice*) with knowledge of Latin hardly extending beyond the texts taught,

---

[113] Black (1991c) and (1991d). [114] Rizzo and De Nonno (1997).
[115] Grafton and Jardine (1986). [116] Black (forthcoming); see also Grafton and Jardine (1986).
[117] Black (1997). [118] Poliziano, *Prose volgari inedite e poesie latine e greche edite e inedite*, pp. 17–41.

in preparation for abacus or arithmetic schools, where the language of instruction would be the vernacular, and for eventual entry into the world of business and commerce, also exclusively conducted in the vernacular.[119] It hardly needs to be pointed out that this new and significant role for the vernacular and for its culture in education had nothing to do with Italian humanism.

Poetry, in the medieval and Renaissance tradition, primarily meant the study of the ancient poets and so, in terms of the curriculum, was subsumed usually under the discipline of grammar. Some consideration remains due, therefore, to *moralia* or moral philosophy, the final constituent of the *studia humanitatis*, which, in a typical humanist assertion, were claimed to 'perfect and adorn man';[120] the humanists castigated their scholastic rivals for arid learning and for failing to inspire virtue in mankind[121] and yet there was little novel in the humanist contribution to ethics.[122] Humanist moral philosophy was overwhelmingly based on ancient ethics, much of which had been extensively studied in the Middle Ages. The main sources of Aristotelian *moralia* were all translated into Latin and received commentaries at universities during the thirteenth century; moreover, Stoic ethics, as expounded by Seneca and Cicero, had been a characteristic ingredient of medieval moral thought. These two traditions provided the core of most humanist moral philosophy too, although in the fifteenth century there was some attempt by humanists to revive philosophical sources weakly represented in the Middle Ages. These included, in the first place, Platonism, which however failed to stimulate a synthesis of ethics, unlike Aristotelianism, partly because Plato's writings were themselves, unlike Aristotle's, unsystematic and partly because most Renaissance Platonists, like their ancient, medieval and Byzantine forerunners, were more interested in cosmology and metaphysics than in ethics; even the Platonic doctrines of the contemplative life and the theory of love, ostensibly part of ethics, tended to form the backdrop to spiritualism, mysticism and metaphysical speculation in the hands of fifteenth-century Platonists. In the Middle Ages, Epicureanism had been even less known and understood than Platonism, although it had been handled with surprising subtlety by Abelard and Aquinas,[123] and the sympathetic treatment of Epicurus by Lucretius and Diogenes Laertius gradually came to the attention of humanists. His ethics, which propounded intellectual pleasure as the goal of life, convinced Cosma Raimondi and even appealed to Filelfo,[124] but his unfavourable treatment at the hands of Cicero prejudiced most humanists; even Lorenzo Valla, who preferred Epicureanism to Stoicism, in the end conventionally advocated Christian morality above all other systems.[125]

[119] Black (1991a) and (1991b).   [120] Bruni, *Epistolarum libri VIII*, II, p. 49.
[121] Gray (1963).   [122] Kristeller (1965); Kraye (1988).   [123] Kraye (1988), p. 376.
[124] Kraye (1988), p. 382.   [125] Kraye (1988), p. 322.

Humanist political thought, strictly speaking a division of moral philosophy,[126] has particularly preoccupied modern scholarship. According to Baron's theory of 'civic humanism', Bruni and his followers initiated the republican strain of thought which became a feature of some – though by no means all[127] – Renaissance political thought.[128] However, it is now clear that a fully developed republican ideology existed in the Italian communes long before Bruni, whose political ideas were only one phase of a long tradition, inaugurated by the growth of the communes and their struggle against the Empire and tyranny. The early communes produced such outspoken republicans as the author of the *Fet des Romans*, Rolandino of Padua and Brunetto Latini, and the translation and assimilation of Aristotle's *Politics* encouraged republican overtones in the political thought of Aquinas and Marsilius and inspired the militant and categorical republicanism of Ptolemy of Lucca.[129] The classical texts at the disposal of medieval civic republicans had been limited largely to Aristotle, Sallust[130] and Cicero's *De officiis*, a text which probably underwent a decline of influence in the course of the later thirteenth and earlier fourteenth centuries, as attested by sharply falling manuscript circulation of the Ciceronian moral treatises[131] possibly caused by the rise of Aristotelian scholasticism. Bruni's original contribution to republicanism was to restore its Ciceronian foundations – a process which had already been begun by his mentor Salutati, who had directly cited *De officiis* when advocating political equality.[132] Followers of 'civic humanism' have also overstated Bruni's commitment to the merits of the active over the contemplative life. It is true that he went further than many of his predecessors in championing active citizenship, but like previous thinkers he did not see the question in black and white terms, as is clear from one of his most significant assessments of the problem, the *Isagogicon moralis disciplinae*, where he states: 'Each of these ways of life has its own qualities worthy of praise and commendation.'[133] This kind of qualified judgement has its source in the tenth book of Aristotle's *Nicomachean ethics*, an analysis which Bruni approached even more closely at the end of his life in a letter of 1441;[134] Bruni's vacillations and qualifications echo the complex analysis of the problem found in the writings of his mentor, Salutati, as well as in the thought of Aquinas, who actually went very far in justifying the active life. Bruni has claim to some originality in the energy with which he puts the arguments for the active life, but the overall pattern of his political thought on this question is a development of Aristotelian thinking, along the lines already established by Aquinas and Salutati.[135]

[126] Kraye (1988), pp. 303–6.
[127] Kristeller (1965), pp. 46–7; Trinkaus (1970), pp. 282–3; Rice (1958), p. 49.
[128] Baron (1966); Witt (1971) and (1976).   [129] Davis (1974); Skinner (1978); Rubinstein (1982).
[130] Skinner (1990).   [131] Black (1996).   [132] De Rosa (1980), pp. 118, 120.
[133] Bruni, *Humanistisch-philosophische Schriften*, p. 39.
[134] Bruni, *Epistolarum libri VIII*, II, pp. 134ff.   [135] Kristeller (1984) and (1985).

The contrast between Middle Ages and Renaissance – the cornerstone of the Baronian school – is particularly out of place in studying the political thought of the Italian communes, whose actual history showed notable continuity between the fourteenth and fifteenth centuries; more fruitful has been the approach which attempts to relate the political ideas of humanism to the ambitions of particular regimes, political groupings and diplomatic needs, regardless of meta-historical concepts. It is clear, for example, that an emphasis on both equality and elitism are simultaneous features of the political thought of Salutati in the years after the defeat of the anti-oligarchic regime in Florence in 1382. It would be easy to accuse the Florentine chancellor here of inconsistency and insincerity, but this would ignore the close connection of Salutati's political ideas with the facts of Florentine political life. After 1382, in fact, the Florentine constitution was able to accommodate the ambitions of the wider political class to hold public office and yet at the same time enable a restricted oligarchy to retain a tight grip over real political power. This balance was achieved by qualifying ever-larger numbers of citizens for the highest public offices, while giving preferential treatment to the oligarchs through the use of constitutional manipulations such as the *borsellino* and the *accoppiatori*.[136] Such practices not only account for Salutati's emphasis simultaneously on democracy and elitism, but also explain Bruni's definition of political liberty as the equal hope of winning office in his *Oratio* for Nanni Strozzi of 1428,[137] a view which reflected the realities of the Florentine political world between 1382 and 1434, when 'many were elected to offices but few to government'.[138] Similarly, Salutati's advocacy of monarchy as the best form of government in *De tyranno*[139] was interpreted by Baron as 'political quietism',[140] reflecting his allegedly residual medieval and conservative belief in world empire as opposed to the truly Renaissance republicanism of his pupil, Bruni, whose views in the *Laudatio Florentinae urbis*[141] were supposedly more in tune with the needs of Florentine liberty in the struggle against Milanese tyranny. However, it is now clear that in fact Salutati's monarchism was more closely related to Florentine diplomatic interests than Bruni's generic republicanism; Salutati was actually upholding the inviolate imperial majesty of Florence's ally, the Emperor-Elect Rupert of the Palatinate, whose dignity had been debased by the sale of the imperial duchy of Milan to Florence's enemy, Giangaleazzo Visconti.[142] A less schematic approach explains Italian political thought much more sensitively than Baron's formula of a conflict between Florentine liberty and Milanese tyranny, when in historical fact both were imperial powers involved in a

---

[136] Najemy (1982), pp. 263–300.　　[137] Bruni, *Oratio in funere Nannis Strozae*, p. 3.
[138] Cavalcanti, *Istorie*, p. 20.
[139] Salutati, *Il trattato 'De tyranno'*.　　[140] Baron (1966), p. 163.
[141] Bruni, *Laudatio florentinae urbis*.　　[142] De Rosa (1980), pp. xiii, 164–5; Black (1986).

struggle to establish their respective territorial empires by extinguishing the political liberty of their neighbours.

It has been necessary to emphasise the limits of humanist achievements in order to dispel the notion – rooted in Burckhardt and ultimately in Hegel – that humanism somehow represented a new period in intellectual history. The fact is that change in the central disciplines of the *studia humanitatis* was irregular and uneven, alternately limited or facilitated by many distinct inherent traditions and differing external circumstances. Indeed, just because the humanists fell short of effecting intellectual revolutions in grammar, rhetoric, history and moral/political philosophy does not mean that in other areas they did not achieve a more decisive break with the medieval past. In Latin scholarship, the fifteenth-century humanists, with their discovery or rediscovery of texts either seldom read or completely unknown in the Middle Ages, virtually completed the corpus of the Latin classics such as is known today; as far as scholarship of Tacitus, Lucretius, Catullus, Propertius or Cicero's letters is concerned, therefore, humanism represented a decisive break with the Middle Ages.[143] Similarly, the notion of the public library was a creation of the Renaissance. Before the invention of printing, humanists such as Petrarch became acutely aware that the process of preservation and dissemination through copying inevitably implied textual deterioration; the foundation of public libraries in Florence, Rome, Venice, Urbino and Cesena during the fifteenth century was therefore intended to provide scholars with authoritative versions in order to counteract the further corruption of texts.[144] The procedures of textual criticism were vastly improved by the humanists. Few medieval scholars went beyond collation of manuscripts to secure a superior text, but the humanists now engaged in sometimes successful and even inspired conjectural emendation. Moreover, Poliziano inaugurated the ranking of manuscripts according to age, and his efforts perhaps even anticipate modern stemmatics; in this sense, the humanists were the remote ancestors of modern classical philologists.[145] Another important new contribution was antiquarianism; in the Middle Ages, classical artefacts had been prized mainly because they were precious, not because they were ancient. Petrarch, in contrast, began to collect ancient objects because they evoked for him the lost world of classical Antiquity; his antiquarian efforts remained largely romantic, but his humanist successors Poggio and Biondo actually did begin the critical study of ancient remains, providing the distant foundations of modern archaeology.[146]

Without doubt, however, the greatest single achievement of the fifteenth-

---

[143] Sabbadini (1905–14).   [144] Ullman and Stadter (1972).   [145] Grafton (1977).
[146] Weiss (1969b).

century humanists was the revival of Greek, an endeavour with few precedents in the western Middle Ages. There had been no tradition of Greek scholarship in the medieval west, few Greek manuscripts in western libraries, no place in the school or university curriculum for the Greek language. The Latin translations from the Greek were limited to a few authors and to a restricted range of disciplines; with rare exceptions, leading medieval scholars had no Greek.[147] The precedent for the humanists' Greek revival came from Byzantium, where the study of classical Greek language and literature had continued throughout the Middle Ages.[148] Although Petrarch and Boccaccio had engaged Greek teachers, the renewal really began only with Chrysoloras, called to teach Greek in Florence at the end of the fourteenth century; his pupils formed the first extensive circle of western Greek scholars since Antiquity, inaugurating the study of Greek as a major activity both of education and scholarship.[149] Most important here were the copying and dissemination of Greek manuscripts in the west and, above all, the translation of the classics of Greek literature, philosophy and science into Latin, including the retranslation in a less literal manner of authors such as Aristotle who had been available in the Middle Ages.[150] It remains the greatest achievement of Renaissance humanism that almost all classical Greek literature became available to the west, both in editions of the original texts and in Latin translations.

The most original aspect of humanist Greek scholarship in the fifteenth century was undertaken by Valla with his philological study of the New Testament; indeed, to subject the Bible itself to critical textual analysis was a genuine innovation in western history, without precedent either in Antiquity or the Middle Ages. Valla compared the Vulgate with the Greek text, bringing to bear all the philological knowledge of the ancient languages accumulated by the humanists – a revolutionary step as Jerome's translation had been revered as divinely inspired and authoritative for more than a millennium. Erasmus regarded himself as the continuator of Valla's work, which also profoundly influenced Luther's interpretation and general approach to the Scriptures, and yet in his own century Valla's biblical criticism remained an aberration, unpublished and without impact until Erasmus's edition of 1505.[151] In fact, despite its vast importance for future history, the Greek revival remained in the fifteenth century a limited enterprise. Many important humanists never learned Greek, a language which very few were capable of writing proficiently (Filelfo's letters and Poliziano's verse were exceptional). Many Greek authors were hardly appreciated or known, even in Latin translation, and it is almost bizarre that a spurious text such as the pseudonymous letters of Phalaris was far more widely

---

[147] Berschin (1988).   [148] Geanakopolos (1966).   [149] Thomson (1966); Cammelli (1941–54).
[150] Schmitt (1983).   [151] Valla, *In Latinam Novi Testamenti*, and *Collatio Novi Testamenti*; Bentley (1983).

circulated in translation than Homer. The taste for Greek literature in the fifteenth century tended to be Hellenistic, rather than classical, which is not really
surprising, in view of the fact that the Roman authors with which humanists
were most familiar had been the direct heirs not of classical, but rather of
Hellenistic Greece. Despite the Greek revival, Antiquity in the fifteenth
century on balance still meant largely Roman Antiquity.

In one way, the humanist movement, as developed by Petrarch and many of his
successors, represented, in negative terms a narrowing, more positively a deepening, of knowledge. This can be seen, for example, in Petrarch's list of
favourite books. Petrarch's interests are almost exclusively in the *studia humanitatis*; the ancient and medieval heritage in science, philosophy (apart from
ethics) and theology are virtually put to one side. Even his favourite, Augustine,
author of more than a hundred works of theology and philosophy, is represented by a mere four titles – *The city of God*, *The confessions* and two devotional
works,[152] demonstrating a notable deviation from the medieval view of
Augustine as a philosophical and theological authority and suggesting that he
had become a figure of more personal and moral inspiration.[153] On the other
hand, the classical works listed constituted a specialist collection, including
works and authors (e.g. *De oratore*, Cicero's orations, Livy) far removed from the
mainstays of the medieval literary canon; indeed, Petrarch's library was later to
include many recondite works almost unknown in the Middle Ages.[154]

Of course, not all humanists shared Petrarch's distaste for metaphysics and
speculative philosophy; his most notable immediate successor, Salutati, had a
wide knowledge of scholastic philosophy, including the latest trends in
nominalism and Scotism.[155] Although a number of other humanists, such as
Manetti, devoted many years, after their grounding in the *studia humanitatis*, to
the study of philosophy and theology,[156] it is clear that there was no intrinsic
connection between the humanist and scholastic disciplines; attempts to
connect Petrarch's or Valla's emphasis on will rather than intellect with
developments in late medieval nominalism showing similar tendencies have
revealed only links of the most generic nature, demonstrating at best that such
voluntaristic colourings were a common currency in much late medieval
thought from mysticism, pietism and devotionalism to nominalism and
humanism.[157] Nevertheless, the philosophical and speculative poverty of the
studia humanitatis worried a number of fifteenth-century humanists. Alamanno
Rinuccini, for example, criticised the generation of humanists before the 1450s
for taking no more than a small sip from the cup of philosophy, thinking it was

---

[152] Ullman (1955), p. 123.   [153] Kristeller (1956), pp. 355–72.   [154] Ullman (1955).
[155] Witt (1983); Trinkaus (1970).   [156] Vespasiano da Bisticci, *Le vite* II, pp. 520ff.
[157] Trinkaus (1970) and (1988); D'Amico (1988).

more than enough to have dabbled in ethics.[158] The most powerful (and amusing) assertion of this view came from Giovanni Pico in his famous letter to Ermolao Barbaro of 1485, when he ridiculed humanism as mere playing with words, in contrast to the sublime study of philosophy.[159]

Salutati's formulation of the *studia humanitatis* as a prelude to the *studia divinitatis*[160] was repeated in so many words by Pico in his famous *Oration*, a text only incidentally and initially concerned with the dignity of man; in fact its actual purpose was to underpin the traditional hierarchy of learning from grammar and rhetoric to dialectic and philosophy and finally to theology (the subject of Pico's 900 theses which the oration was meant to justify) as the queen of the sciences.[161] If the overall shape of knowledge remained so traditional in the fifteenth century, then it was inevitable that the programme of learning envisaged in the *studia humanitatis* would eventually come to be regarded as incomplete. It is against this background that the great Platonic revival of the fifteenth century must be considered. Attempts have been made to see this landmark in the history of thought in political terms, particularly with reference to Florence, where the new emphasis on the contemplative life propounded by Platonists such as Landino and Ficino have been related to growing Medicean hegemony and to the narrowing possibilities for real political participation;[162] however, this thesis has now been decisively refuted by the simple fact, overlooked by scholars keen to invert Baron's 'civic humanism', that the turn to speculative philosophy in Florence actually began in the mid-1450s, a time when Medicean control in Florence was near to collapse.[163] Another equally unsuccessful explanation has focused on the lectures of Argyropoulos, who, having begun teaching in Florence in the mid-1450s, supposedly championed Plato over Aristotle; many scholars have subscribed to this thesis, first propounded by Garin,[164] evidently without a close reading of Argyropoulos's actual writings, where it is clear that he was an Aristotelian who regarded Plato as a crude forerunner of his greater pupil.[165] Nevertheless, the role of Argyropoulos was decisive for the origins of a philosophical culture in Florence, if not for Platonism itself. The Byzantine learned tradition, of which he was a notable product, extended beyond rhetoric, grammar and literature to philosophy, science, mathematics and theology; there were almost no Byzantine scholars without developed interests in some of these areas.[166] When Argyropoulos came to Florence, it was natural for him to range beyond the narrow limits of *studia humanitatis* and to criticise humanists such as Bruni for their ignorance of philosophy, for their insistence that philosophy and elo-

---

[158] Field (1988), p. 5.   [159] Breen (1952).   [160] Salutati, *Epistolario*, IV, p. 216.
[161] Pico, *De hominis dignitate*.   [162] Brown (1986); Garin (1965).   [163] Field (1988).
[164] Garin (1954), (1958), (1961), (1965) and (1975); Holmes (1969); Geanakoplos (1988).
[165] Field (1988).   [166] Geanakoplos (1988).

quence were necessarily linked and for their disdain of speculation.[167] Some seeds of this favourable attitude to speculative philosophy may have been sewn at the University of Florence by Marsuppini, who seems to have himself ranged more widely than usual in his lectures in the humanities, and there are other important preliminary figures such as the scholastics Lorenzo Pisano and Niccolò Tignosi, Ficino's teacher;[168] moreover, the undoubted growing elitism of Florentine society in the later fifteenth century provided a receptive clientele for Ficino's 'special esoteric form of Christianity'.[169] Nevertheless, the seeds of the new philosophical culture of later Medicean Florence, with the essential critical attitude to humanism which underlay Ficino's and Pico's Platonism, must have come from Argyropoulos and the Byzantine tradition which he represented.

Fifteenth-century humanism was overwhelmingly an Italian phenomenon, but it has long been recognised that the Renaissance began to cross the Alps well before the turn of the sixteenth century.[170] Patriotic scholars earlier this century were keen to find indigenous roots for northern humanism, but their attempts were largely in vain.[171] Recent research, for example, has demonstrated that the Dutch *devotio moderna* was a devotional, not an educational, movement, which only coincidentally shared a distaste for scholastic theology with some (but not all) Italian humanists.[172] Moreover, humanism, like scholasticism, had its roots in the earlier medieval study of the liberal arts; while in Italy this ultimately led to a more intensive study of the classical Latin authors beginning at the end of the thirteenth century, in northern Europe the tendency was to direct the grammatical/rhetorical aspects of the curriculum as much as possible to the eventual study of logic, philosophy and theology. Nevertheless, the Latin classics were never completely abandoned in the north, and there were moments – for example among a few English friars at Oxford and Cambridge in the second quarter of the fourteenth century – of more intensive classical study.[173] However, these English mendicants, whose interest in the classics was mainly directed towards preaching, shared none of the Italian humanists' rejection of medieval learning, and the same can be said of a number of classically minded French clergy of the fourteenth century.[174]

Humanism was imported from Italy to the north. At first there were a few native scholars who, although influenced by Italian humanists, did not quite manage to establish the movement firmly across the Alps. Such, for example, were Jean de Montreuil, secretary of the French king and friend of Bruni and

---

[167] Seigel (1969).   [168] Field (1988).   [169] Hankins (1990), I, p. 287.
[170] A good brief summary of recent research is found in Nauert (1995), pp. 95–123.
[171] Mestwerdt (1917); Hyma (1965).   [172] Post (1968).   [173] Smalley (1960).
[174] Simone (1969).

Niccoli,[175] or the earlier imperial chancellor, Johannes von Neumarkt, correspondent of Petrarch's.[176] In fifteenth-century England, the brief residence of
Poggio led to no lasting results, while the great patron, Humphrey, duke of
Gloucester, who engaged Italian secretaries, collected a huge library of classical and humanist texts and numbered Italian humanists among his correspon-
dents, nevertheless failed to establish an indigenous English humanist
movement: in the mid-fifteenth century, English humanism was limited to men
such as Tiptoft, Grey, Flemyng or Free, all of whom acquired their humanist
inclinations while studying in Italy and who never managed to establish a solid
institutional basis at home.[177]

In the fifteenth century, humanism made its greatest inroads north of the
Alps in the Germanic regions of the continent. An early figure of note was
Peter Luder, another Guarino pupil, who taught the *studia humanitatis* at
Heidelberg, Ulm, Erfurt and Leipzig.[178] Much more significant was Rudolf
Agricola, who spent more than a decade in Italy, mainly in Pavia and Ferrara;
his treatise on dialectic, albeit uninfluential until its publication in the early six-
teenth century, became a landmark in the humanist reform of logic, emphasis-
ing probability and persuasion rather than certainty, and placing Cicero and
Quintilian above Aristotle as authorities.[179] Particularly important for the
establishment of the movement in Germany and the Netherlands was the
foundation of humanist grammar schools, the most renowned of which was St
Lebwin's in Deventer, headed by Alexander Hegius, whose pupils included the
German mystical humanist Mutianus Rufus and Erasmus himself. Hegius was
an archetypal transitional figure: he used the traditional medieval verse
grammar, the *Doctrinale*, but possibly also introduced the study of Greek and
criticised the use of medieval, logically orientated speculative grammar in
favour of the simplified grammatical methods current in Italy.[180]

By the close of the fifteenth century, there were humanists – some indigenous, some Italian trained – throughout Germany. A number were conservative, such as Jakob Wimpfeling, an outspoken nationalist, who, like Hegius,
called for a simplification of grammar and supported the teaching of some
pagan authors such as Cicero and Vergil, while banning others, including Ovid
and Catullus; after some dithering, Wimpheling upheld the value of scholastic
learning. A figure of greater significance, albeit strictly conservative in religion,
was Johann Reuchlin, who made three long visits to Italy, where he came into
contact with Lorenzo de' Medici, Ficino, Pico and Ermolao Barbaro; well
before the end of the century, following the path of his idol Pico, he began to

---

[175] Simone (1969).   [176] Hoffmeister (1977).   [177] Weiss (1941).   [178] Bernstein (1983).
[179] Mack (1993); Ong (1958); Monfasani (1990); Akkerman and Vanderjagt (1988).
[180] Post (1968); IJsewijn (1975); Cameron (1990).

study Hebrew, of which he published the first usable grammar in 1506, so becoming the first northern scholar of the three ancient languages. From Ficino and Pico he adopted the Ancient Theology, and he also took up the latter's view that the Cabala embodied a hidden wisdom revealed directly by God to Moses; his own cabalistic works provided an essential link between Florentine occultism and later developments in northern Europe. More iconoclastic than either Wimpfeling or Reuchlin was Conrad Celtis, an outstanding Latin poet, who on an Italian trip met Battista, son of Guarino, Ficino and Pomponio Leto; on his return he founded humanist societies or academies, possibly inspired by the example of Florentine and Roman academies, in various German cities including Ingolstadt, Heidelberg and Vienna. Equally important was the patronage he gained while teaching poetry in Vienna at the close of the century, from the emperor, Maximilian. A fervent German patriot, Celtis published a student edition of Tacitus' *Germania* in 1500, which helped to link humanism with frustrated German nationalism.[181]

By the end of the century humanism was fairly well rooted in Germany, with numerous local groups, humanist schools and a firm, if subordinate, position in the university curriculum, not to mention several outstanding indigenous representatives. The movement's progress in France was more marginal. In the fifteenth century, the Parisian colleges of Navarre and Montaigu remained strictly conservative. An Italian humanist, Gregorio Tifernate, had been appointed to a professorship of Greek in the mid-fifteenth century, and the scholastic philosopher Guillaume Fichet had lectured on classical authors, as well as establishing France's first printing press, whose output included a number of classical and humanist texts, as well as work by Fichet himself. But it was not until Robert Gaguin that France had its first genuine humanist. After several Italian visits, not only did he gather round himself a modest classical academy, but he also published vernacular versions of Livy and Caesar as well as his own history of Frankish origins in 1498. Particularly significant was his encouragement of the youthful Erasmus, whose first two publications appeared in works by Gaguin. Another important late fifteenth-century development was a scheme to replace medieval translations of Aristotle with those by Italian humanists. The great personality here was Jacques Lefèvre d'Etaples. Inspired by Ermolao Barbaro, he aimed to paraphrase essential ideas from Aristotle's metaphysics and natural philosophy, deliberately leaving to one side the accumulated tradition of scholastic commentary. After several Italian visits on which he met both Ficino and Pico, Lefèvre took up Platonism and Hermeticism; significant for French national sympathies was his publica-

---

[181] Spitz (1957) and (1963); Hoffmeister (1977); Strauss (1972); Bernstein (1983); Karant-Nunn (1990); Heath (1971); Overfield (1984); Nauert (1973), (1986) and (1990).

tion of the late ancient neoplatonic mystic, Dionysius the Areopagite, errone-
ously identified with a convert of St Paul's and also with France's patron saint,
Denis. Despite these important inroads, nevertheless, it is clear that by the end
of the century humanism had made greater progress in the Netherlands or
Germany than in France, where there is little convincing evidence of influence
on grammar school education.[182]

The picture is not dissimilar in the rest of western Europe. Spanish humanism produced only one figure of note in the fifteenth century, Antonio de
Nebrija, educated at Bologna and the author of perhaps the most successful
humanist Latin grammar, a work which soon achieved a notable circulation
throughout Europe, including Italy.[183] In England, the claims for humanism
have tended to be exaggerated, mainly owing to the misunderstood affiliations
of John Colet. Recent research has demonstrated that, although he visited Italy
and admired the Florentine Platonists, his educational reforms demonstrated
antipathy to most classical literature, which had little place in his curriculum for
St Paul's school, which was only given a genuine humanist direction by its first
high master, William Lily.[184] Other figures of some note were Thomas Linacre,
a physician who had studied with Demetrius Chalcondyles and Poliziano,
whose other pupil, William Grocyn, gave the first established lectures in Greek
at Oxford before the end of the century. Particularly significant for future
developments was Erasmus's brief stay in England in 1499. Recent research
has suggested that the English universities, although dominated of course by
the traditional scholastic syllabus, allowed greater scope for the development
of humanism than had previously been assumed. At Oxford, Cornelio Vitelli,
a minor Italian humanist, taught grammar at New College in the 1480s, while
also tutoring privately in Greek; Magdalen College school, founded before the
end of the century, also stressed from the start the reading of classical authors.
Greater early progress was made at Cambridge; Lorenzo Traversagni taught
rhetoric and moral philosophy there between 1472 and 1482, while another
Italian humanist, Auberino, taught classical authors, together with John Fisher,
later bishop of Rochester. Most notable was a statute of 1488, reinforced in
1495, establishing a public lectureship at Cambridge on 'humanity'.[185]

While the achievements of ultramontane humanists in the fifteenth century are
thus limited, their Italian counterparts had certainly accomplished great things;
nevertheless, in its core areas humanism preserved many traditional features

---

[182] Simone (1969); Gundersheimer (1969); Levi (1970); Lefèvre d'Etaples, *The prefatory epistles*; Renaudet
(1953).   [183] Lawrance (1990).   [184] Gleason (1989).
[185] Cobban (1988); McConica (1986); Leader (1988).

and showed marked continuity with medieval learning. Many of its genuine innovations, such as textual criticism or the revival of Greek, were esoteric pursuits, not even practised and certainly not mastered by the majority of humanists. The query remains, therefore, why humanism was so successful as a cultural movement: if it shared so much in common with medieval learning, what was the secret of its undoubted appeal not only in Italy but eventually throughout Europe? This fundamental question is never asked, much less answered, by Kristeller; pointing to the continuity and development of traditional Aristotelian studies throughout the Renaissance, as well as emphasising humanism's literary rather than philosophical focus, provides only a negative response: humanism's success could not have been due to its alleged appeal as the new philosophy of the Renaissance, because in fact it offered no genuine philosophical alternative to scholasticism. Hanna Gray goes further and asks why the humanists 'failed to recognize, indeed disclaimed, continuity with medieval practice', questioning why they should have been so highly valued by their 'particular age'. Her answer focuses on 'the subjective consciousness of novelty': the humanists succeeded because they were convinced, and were able to convince the world at large, that their studies – particularly the pursuit of eloquence – offered a surer path than scholasticism to virtue and the good life.[186] Gombrich similarly stresses the subjective appeal of humanism, its one-upmanship: like a fashion, it succeeded by giving its adherents a sense of superiority.[187]

These kinds of interpretations are the inevitable response to the 'revolt of the medievalists' – whose ranks Kristeller must to some extent join: if humanism was not objectively so different from medieval learning, then its appeal must have been subjective. There is doubtless much to recommend this approach, and yet it could hardly be the whole story. Humanism swept Italian society in the Quattrocento, to be followed by overwhelming success throughout Europe in the sixteenth century. It became impossible to get a job as a schoolmaster, private tutor or public servant without humanist credentials. Hard-headed Florentine businessmen paid large sums of money to humanist teachers to educate their children, to booksellers to fill their libraries with classical and humanist texts, to dealers and agents to adorn their palaces with enormously expensive antiquities. Was this no more than just fashion, and indeed a fashion which was to last for centuries? Surely they must have expected something more tangible than just virtue or one-upmanship for all the money, effort and time spent.

One solution to this problem focuses on the 'civic' world of late fourteenth- and fifteenth-century Italy, suggesting that humanism's success was due to its

---

[186] Gray (1963).   [187] Gombrich (1967).

practical political lessons. Scholasticism, it is argued, offered only intellectual knowledge; humanism, in contrast, taught men how to make hard political and moral decisions in the real world. Humanism appealed because Italian citizens found its lessons to be of greater practical use than those offered by the scholastics.[188] This view not only accepts literally the humanists' own claims for their wares, but also is far removed from the realities of Italian political life. In fact, humanist treatises, like their Ciceronian or Senecan models, offered few, if any, lessons in political reality; their moral platitudes and banalities could hardly have helped any Italian politician faced with decisions about war or peace, alliances, factional conflict, taxation or government of subject territories. This kind of interpretation in fact depicts the ideal political world 'of republics and principalities which have never been seen or known to exist', so scathingly ridiculed by Machiavelli in chapter 15 of *The Prince*. Evidently misleading has been the discovery that some debates of the Florentine deliberative council, the *Pratica*, contained more elaborate speeches, more citations from classical authors and more references to history in the 1410s;[189] however, these changes coincided with new chancery personnel in Florence, and may have represented bureaucratic elaboration, known to have occurred at other times in the fifteenth century, rather than an actual different style of debating.[190] More importantly, the records in the Florentine archives demonstrate that humanist moralising hardly concerns the speakers; at issue instead were the real problems of political life and even survival. Humanism appealed far beyond republican Florence or Venice: to suggest that in a time of growing elitism and loss of political liberty there was still scope for significant civic participation in the vestigial communal institutions of Milan, Mantua, Ferrara or in the host of subject cities such as Padua, Vicenza, Arezzo or Pisa is inappropriate; subjects in such cities were only too aware of the fact that they had lost their liberty and any kind of meaningfully active political life. Humanist educators promised to teach morals and create worthy citizens; the fact that they made no attempt to live up to these claims in the actual classroom must fundamentally undermine the thesis that humanism succeeded because of the practical benefits offered to society. No republican or 'civic' interpretation can adequately explain humanism's triumph for the simple reason that in the age of humanism civic and republican life were rapidly becoming anachronisms.

One historian has written that 'the acceptability of the new culture as the common currency of elite society rather than as the hobby of a few eccentrics depended on the conclusion by hard-headed Florentine oligarchs that humanistic studies were useful to a ruling class'.[191] The truth of this statement

---

[188] Nauert (1995).   [189] Brucker (1977) and (1979).   [190] Black (1985) and (1986).
[191] Nauert (1995), p. 33.

depends on the definition of the word 'useful'. If useful means teaching practical or even relatively more practical lessons for everyday political and social life, then it is patently false. If, however, 'useful' means fulfilling the interests of the ruling class, then we have at last arrived at the reason for humanism's success. For centuries Italy had been a snobbish, elitist society; even the Florentines, who stopped short of establishing a constitutionally privileged and exclusive aristocracy as in Venice, had never allowed rapid and extreme fluctuations of wealth, characteristic of the medieval Italian economy, to level the gradations of the social hierarchy. Traditionally, a classical education meant nothing to the Italian upper classes. What they wanted for their children was enough literacy and numeracy to carry on the family business, to maintain and improve the family's patrimony: for them, in Alberti's words, 'it is enough to know how to write your name, and to know how to add up how much money you are owed'.[192] It was along these lines that one patrician Florentine, Bernardo Manetti, provided for the education of his son:

At a young age, he sent him, according to the custom of the city, to learn to read and write. When, in a brief time, the boy had mastered the learning necessary to become a merchant, his father took him away from elementary school and sent him to arithmetic [abacus] school, where in a few months he similarly learned enough to work as a merchant. At the age of ten he went into a bank.[193]

Another Florentine, a member of an ancient Florentine family of illustrious feudal descent, Messer Andrea de' Pazzi, gave his son Piero little encouragement to pursue his education:

Being the son of Messer Andrea and a young man of handsome appearance, devoted to the delights and pleasures of the world, Piero gave little thought to the study of Latin letters: indeed, his father was a merchant and like those who have little education themselves, he had scant regard for learning nor did he think that his son would show much inclination in that direction.[194]

Similar were the views of one famous humanist's father, a man who was, 'in accordance with the custom of the city, more given to earning than to learning', and who therefore refused to sanction his son's classical studies.[195]

The Italian (and European) idea of a gentleman, however, was redefined by the circle of patricians who had originally gathered round Salutati and who became even more influential after his death. For such men as Palla Strozzi, Niccolò Niccoli, Roberto Rossi, Antonio Corbinelli and Agnolo Pandolfini, classical learning was an essential ingredient of gentility, a necessary qualification for membership of the social elite – a view which they derived from the study of the ancients themselves. The classical texts which provide the most

---

[192] Alberti, *Opere volgari*, I, p. 68.   [193] Vespasiano da Bisticci, *Le vite*, II p. 519.
[194] Vespasiano da Bisticci, *Le vite*, II, p. 309.   [195] Vespasiano da Bisticci, *Le vite*, II, p. 519.

compelling portrait of the ideal Roman gentleman – Cicero's *Orator* and *De oratore* and Quintilian's *Institutiones* – were either studied for the first time or with renewed vigour at the turn of the fifteenth century; from such sources the Florentine avant-garde was confirmed in its view that no one should command a high social position, no one could rightfully call himself a gentleman, no one was qualified to rule, without a classical education. Such ideas were the core of the first and most influential of all humanist educational treatises, Vergerio's *De ingenuis moribus*,[196] written *c.* 1402 in the wake of the author's stay in Florence and of his association with Salutati's circle as a pupil of Chrysoloras. Vergerio's work aimed to guide the education of society's leaders, whether citizens, princes or courtiers; it established classical learning as an essential qualification to merit or retain political power and social leadership. This new humanist ideal of education could be associated with any leader or elite, republican or monarchical, and therefore was adaptable throughout Italy and ultimately throughout Europe. The greatest humanist teacher, Guarino, who frequented Chrysoloras's lessons too, later teaching in Florence from 1410 to 1414, was also soon advertising the humanist claims to educate society's rulers, as in this letter to a *podestà* of Bologna in 1419:

I understand that when civil disorder recently aroused the people of Bologna to armed conflict you showed the bravery and eloquence of a soldier as well as you had previously meted out a judge's just sentence . . . You therefore owe no small thanks to the Muses with whom you have been on intimate terms since your boyhood, and by whom you were brought up. They taught you how to carry out your tasks in society. Hence you are living proof that the Muses rule not only musical instruments but also public affairs.[197]

The crucial change from the traditional medieval to the Renaissance ideal of education is revealed with great clarity by Alberti:

And who does not know that the first thing useful for children are Latin letters? And this is so important that someone unlettered, however much a gentleman, will be considered nothing but a country bumpkin. And I should like to see young noblemen with a book in hand more frequently than with a hawk . . . If there is anything which goes beautifully with gentility or which gives the greatest distinction to human life or adds grace, authority and name to a family, it is surely letters, without which no one can be reputed to possess gentility.[198]

Humanism succeeded because it persuaded Italian and ultimately European society that without its lessons no one was fit to rule or lead. The common misconception about this educational revolution is that it involved a change in

[196] Vergerio, *De ingenuis moribus et liberalibus adolescentiae studiis.*
[197] Grafton and Jardine (1986), p. 2; Guarino Veronese, *Epistolario*, I, p. 263.
[198] Alberti, *Opere volgari*, I, pp. 68, 70; Black (1992).

substance, in curriculum, as well as in ideology.[199] A change in the practical benefits of education never could nor did occur; better Latinity could never mean superior morality or greater political expertise. A change in curriculum only developed very gradually, slowly in the fifteenth century and then more quickly in the sixteenth. But the change in ideology was rapid and decisive.

What then was the appeal to the upper classes of this humanist educational programme? Italian society, since the rise of the communes, if not before, was always in flux; in an economy where wealth and prominence depended not just on land but also so much on commercial and industrial fortunes, on local as well as far-flung international and overseas trading adventures, families and individuals rose and fell with amazing rapidity. In this world, society was always on the look out for better definitions of social and political acceptability. This was particularly true in communal Italy during the fourteenth and fifteenth centuries, when traditional definitions of nobility had been devalued by association with mercenaries and with politically ostracised groups such as the Florentine magnates. Humanism's particular definition had the best of all possible seals of approval – it was endorsed by the ancients. The crucial texts by Cicero and Quintilian had been little known in the Middle Ages; moreover, Cicero's moral philosophical works in general had suffered a serious decline during the preceding century and a half. It is here that the subjectivity stressed by Gombrich or Gray comes into play. It did not matter that the equation between Latinity, virtue, social leadership and political power did not really add up. It suited everyone – humanists as well as the social elite. Nor could anyone say that a humanist education was empty, for its products emerged as outstanding Latin and ultimately Greek scholars. No one questioned the equation between a classical education and moral and political virtue: if it was good enough for Antiquity, it was surely good enough for the Renaissance.

---

[199] Grendler (1989); Nauert (1995); see Black (1991c).

CHAPTER 13

MANUSCRIPTS AND BOOKS

Malcolm Vale

THE production of books and manuscripts in the fifteenth century saw the culmination of tendencies which had begun during the latter part of the thirteenth century. The most significant of these were the increasing dominance of lay workshops over the *scriptoria* of religious houses; the rise of a commercialised book trade; and the emergence of veritable publishing houses in the major centres of European book production. The period none the less witnessed something of a revival in the copying of liturgical and devotional books by religious communities. It was also to see an invasion of the market by books produced by the new process of printing with movable type, and the eclipse of those book producers and dealers who did not adapt to the new techniques.

To satisfy the increasing demands of literate lay people, as well as the clergy, a more sophisticated organisation of the book trade was required. The single scribe, working alone, was still to be found, but he formed only one element in the complex process of book production. A structure dominated by entrepreneurs and middlemen was emerging and 'in the [later] Middle Ages true publishing houses existed, in the modern sense of the word'.[1] The best known of these were to be found in the Low Countries and in northern Italy, but there were comparable establishments in England, France and Germany. A distinction has been drawn between the *officine* (publishing house or shop) and the *atelier* (workshop) in both northern and southern Europe. The relationship of publisher and bookseller to scribe and illuminator varied from one centre to another. It is also important to distinguish between 'mere books' and elaborately illuminated manuscripts, produced on the finest sheepskin or goatskin parchment. The latter have tended to be more durable, while the cheaper, everyday books, normally written on paper, are far less likely to have survived. Any quantitative estimate of books in circulation at any given time is thus fraught with difficulties.

---

[1] Delaissé *et al.* (1959), p. 12.

An increasing use of paper in book production was evident fro
fourteenth century onwards. Although rag paper had already bee
for archival and documentary purposes since the later thirteenth ce
ary, theological, devotional and scientific texts on paper began to appear i.
profusion only after *c.* 1400. Paper had been imported from China via Italy,
where the first European paper mills were set up, the finest paper being made
at Fabriano. By *c.* 1390 the Stromer of Nuremberg had established a paper mill,
and manufacture of the material soon spread over northern Europe. Paper was
a cheaper medium than parchment and this enabled book producers to market
larger quantities of relatively inexpensive books. There were some limitations
upon its use, however: at Florence, the material most commonly employed for
commercially produced illuminated books was parchment until well into the
1460s. Parchment provided a better medium for manuscript painters, and was
far better suited to the production of *de luxe* editions for affluent patrons and
clients. Book prices therefore tended to fall. Florentine prices in the late 1450s
ranged from about fifty florins for large, lavishly illuminated liturgical books on
parchment to two to three florins for paper editions of classical and humanistic
texts. Even so, books were not an exceptionally cheap commodity: it cost eighteen to twenty florins to keep a young Florentine apprentice for a year. But the
paper book, often consisting of unbound quires, had little second-hand value
and the allusions in English wills to boxes or chests of unspecified books probably referred to items of this kind.

The fifteenth century also saw an unprecedented demand for illustrated
books at many social levels. These ranged from the lavishly decorated illuminated volumes commissioned for princes, nobles and wealthy patricians to the
rapiaria or commonplace books, often containing miscellaneous assortments
of devotional texts with woodcut illustrations, produced for humbler
members of the literate laity. The most popular works were already reproduced
by mechanical means before the introduction of movable type: a dialogue
between a ploughman and Death (*Der Ackermann aus Böhmen, c.* 1400) was the
first German illustrated book to be chosen for woodcut reproduction by
Albrecht Pfister in 1460. A similar process was experienced by the illustrated
aid to meditation known as the *Biblia pauperum*: a series of block-book versions
replaced the hand-illustrated texts which had previously circulated. These were
read by both clergy and laity in the middle levels of urban society and reflected
the popularity of devotional books in which Old Testament prefigurations of
New Testament events and doctrines were depicted in graphic form. Yet the
hand-illustrated book retained its vogue among the upper classes. The mid-
and later fifteenth-century German *Hausbücher*, mainly of Rhenish origin, and
Geschlechtsbücher (commonplace books recording family history and depicting
scenes from urban and courtly life) enjoyed great popularity. So too did the

Tournament books assembled for both individuals and fraternities in the German towns. These celebrated their participation in jousts and tourneys, represented by the vividly illustrated volumes made for the electors of Saxony and for patricians such as Marx Walther of Augsburg (*c.* 1480–1520).

The manufacture and sale of books was only loosely controlled by guilds and corporations. Those involved in the processes of book production were necessarily concentrated in towns, and were therefore not exempt from the differentiation and division of labour common to all medieval urbanised industries. The stationers, scribes and illuminators were distinct from the panel painters. But the booksellers, illuminators and binders of Bruges first grouped themselves together and were recognised as a guild dedicated to St John the Evangelist only in 1457. At Florence, the *cartolai* – book producers and dealers in book materials – were already members of the guild of Medici e Speziali by that date. These men dealt in the raw materials of book production, while the more enterprising among them also acted as middlemen in the processes of copying and illumination. Supervision and regulation was always difficult, because the manufacture of books involved the services of craftsmen who were often very mobile. The early career of Johann Gutenberg of Mainz bore witness to that fact. Similarly, one of the most influential of Netherlandish illuminators – William Vrelant – moved from Utrecht to join the illuminators' guild at Bruges (which totalled fifty-two members) by 1454, bringing Dutch methods and styles of book illustration with him.

Within each publishing or manufacturing business, division of labour was strictly observed. The preparation and ruling of parchment, copying of text, initial decoration, illumination and binding were all separate tasks. Unbound quires or *cahiers* could be sent out for illumination to a painter working in another town, such as Jean Tavernier of Oudenaarde, who worked upon manuscripts sent to him from Lille, Brussels and elsewhere (*c.* 1450–60). In Florence, most manuscripts were produced on commission for clients by the *cartolai*, who also employed independent scribes and illuminators working outside their shops, normally on a piece-work basis. Attempts were sometimes made to introduce a 'closed shop': a series of ordinances appeared in Bruges between 1427 and 1457 designed to regulate the import of pictures, mainly from Utrecht, unless they were bound into manuscripts produced in the city. In 1447 friction between the painters and scriveners led the councillors (*échevins*) of the city to resolve that manuscript illuminators were to work only in watercolours, reserving the use of gold, silver and oil to the painters' corporation of St Luke. Such restrictions were always very difficult to enforce and the evidence of surviving manuscripts suggests that they were frequently broken.

The tendency towards the establishment of publishing houses, which has already been noted, was especially marked in the Low Countries and at

Florence. Master Jean Wauquelin and his successor Jacquemart Pilavaine set up publishing businesses at Mons between 1440 and 1460, as did David Aubert at Brussels, Bruges and Ghent between 1460 and 1480. They adopted very similar procedures and methods to those followed at a later date by Colard Mansion and William Caxton, including the selection, promotion and translation of popular texts. Similar patterns can be seen in northern Italy. At Florence the *cartolaio* Vespasiano da Bisticci (*c.* 1422–98) emerged as a true bookseller in the modern sense, learning his trade from his predecessors Niccoli (d. 1437) and Traversari (d. 1439). The special conditions of Florentine intellectual life created a demand for both *de luxe* and more humdrum manuscript books. Vespasiano enjoyed the patronage of Cosimo de' Medici, to whom he supplied books for the monastic library of San Marco and for the newly created library at the Badia of Fiesole. He also accepted specific commissions from foreign clients such as Jean Jouffroy, bishop of Arras, in 1460–1, and from Federigo da Montefeltro, duke of Urbino, between *c.* 1465 and 1482. But Vespasiano also dealt in new books: 'he very boldly set out to exploit the potential market for uncommissioned books'.[2] He displayed new books in his shop, trying to anticipate and shape demand. He was unrivalled in Florence – and probably elsewhere – as an entrepreneur, and only one other Florentine *cartolaio*, Zanobi di Mariano, attempted to emulate him. Vespasiano was to enjoy a relatively brief, though very influential, hegemony over the Florentine book trade. The introduction of printing after 1465 led to intense competition, overproduction of humanistic texts and a dramatic fall in demand. In 1478 his shop was closed down for lack of business. He had refused to adapt to the new methods.

Such disdain for the new processes was not shared by German entrepreneurs. A well-established system of manuscript production absorbed new techniques and it has been said that 'clearly, there was a wide German network of families or people working in Nuremberg, Mainz, Strasburg, [and] Bamberg... as rivals but also as friends, interested in producing... the consumer goods of communication',[3] that is, parchment, paper, bookbindings and woodcuts. The major European centres of book production held their own against competition as demand rose. A major incentive had always been given to the book trade by the presence of universities, or by groups of scholars and visitors attracted by certain masters or intellectual trends, to Paris or Louvain, or to Florence during the Church Council of Florence–Ferrara (1438–9) and the congress of Mantua (1459). The foundation of many new universities during the fifteenth century also stimulated book production, although most scholars still engaged in the more economical method of copying texts for themselves.

The primary means of support for manuscript illumination still lay in the

[2] Garzelli and de la Mare (1985), p. 404.   [3] Du Boulay (1983), p. 16.

princely court. The influence of rulers and courtiers determined much of the content and style of manuscripts produced for a wider readership throughout this period. The *de luxe* market continued to be dominated by them, and they were emulated by wealthy patricians and burghers. Princely libraries were fundamental to the formation of taste and to the choice of manuscripts for reproduction made by entrepreneurs such as Vespasiano da Bisticci or William Caxton. Habits of book collecting formed in the fourteenth century were perpetuated, and the French royal library of Charles VI held about 1,000 volumes by 1420. The French royal collection was exceptional in northern Europe: alone among northern princes, Philip the Good of Burgundy managed to increase his library from about 250 volumes to over 900 between 1420 and 1467. His splendid collection was rivalled by that of Federigo da Montefeltro at Urbino, which also comprised over 900 books when it was completed in 1482. About one half of the Urbino library had been purchased from, and through, Vespasiano da Bisticci, who (not without an air of self-congratulation) described it as 'the most complete library anywhere'. Although the famous statement that it contained no printed books was untrue, for Federigo certainly possessed a printed Origen, dated 1481, and a few other incunables, these formed a tiny minority of his essentially manuscript collection.

To possess a library of 100 manuscripts or more was a notable feat for a non-princely owner by the end of the fifteenth century. In 1518, Francis I of France's book collection numbered only 254 volumes, for the earlier royal collection had been dispersed in the 1420s to John, duke of Bedford and others. Over 150 of these books derived from the library of the fifteenth-century Burgundian nobleman and courtier Louis de Bruges, lord of Gruuthuse (d. 1492). Gruuthuse's collection was a formative influence upon the commissioning of lavishly illuminated manuscripts from Bruges and Ghent by Edward IV of England. The possession of even a small number of books became a *sine qua non* of the educated noble or gentleman. At the courts of Burgundy, Anjou–Provence, Milan, Urbino, Castile, Aragon, Hungary, Bohemia and elsewhere, patronage of secular literature inflated the levels of book production. Vernacular books began to rival Latin texts, despite humanist efforts to promote classical languages, and were far more widely diffused by the later fifteenth century. The acceptance of vernaculars as languages of courtly literature in England, the northern Low Countries, Germany, Italy and Spain enabled greater inroads to be made into the primacy of French and Latin as media of culture and civilisation. Diffusion of manuscripts took place through dedication or presentation to potential royal and aristocratic patrons, followed by multiple copying of the texts. Volumes produced for royal or princely libraries were often reproduced on a large scale: for example, Jean Wauquelin supplied a paper copy of the *Chroniques de Hainaut*, of which he had produced a sumptuous manuscript for Philip the Good, to a *bourgeois* named Brassot in August 1448. A similar practice was adopted by Colard Mansion and William Caxton whereby copies were made of books in the Burgundian ducal collection and in the Gruuthuse library. Book-ownership was expressed heraldically and the passage of books from one collection to another at this time can be traced by the overpainting of coats of arms and devices upon change of proprietorship. There was much exchange, transference and borrowing of books among court circles and this led to a certain uniformity of style, such as that of the 'Master of Mary of Burgundy', which was widespread in the Low Countries during the latter part of the century.

The most important development in the style and format of illuminated books during this period stemmed from the emergence of a closer relationship between manuscript painting and the art of the panel painter. This tendency had already begun in the fourteenth century, and the work of the Limburg brothers for Jean, duke of Berry (d. 1416), exemplified this trend. It became increasingly common for the full-page miniatures in a *de luxe* manuscript to draw upon the techniques of panel painting, especially in the use of light, shade and perspective. The innovations of Hubert and Jan van Eyck (d. 1441) were soon applied to the illuminated book. It has been claimed that the so-called Turin–Milan Hours, stemming from the circle of the counts of Hainault–Holland, was a work of the van Eycks, although the attribution and dating of this partially destroyed manuscript is disputed. The illuminations in the book depict scenes of remarkable realism, in which landscapes, sea shores and domestic interiors are represented with the attention to detail and close observation of nature which was a hallmark of 'Eyckian' art. These innovations enabled manuscript painters to produce more faithful likenesses of the owners of books – especially of Books of Hours, where they often appear in adoration of the Virgin and Child with attendant saints – and to render doctrinal truths and devotional images more vivid and immediate. The lessons taught by the van Eycks, and by Rogier van der Weyden (d. 1464), permeated European manuscript painting. In Italy, their influence was most strongly felt at Venice and Naples, while the Italian ambitions of René of Anjou, titular king of Naples and Sicily, brought Italian manuscripts into France. These began to adopt Netherlandish features – such as greater concentration on landscape painting and portraiture – and the work of René's own painter, 'Master Barthélémy', a relative of Jan van Eyck, was an amalgam of Italian and Netherlandish styles.

The illuminated book was not, however, filled entirely with large, full-page pictures. Its border decoration, initial letters and script were also works of considerable artistry and invention. Study of the borders of both Netherlandish and Italian manuscripts has enabled attributions to specific scribes and workshops to be made. The elaborate use of foliage, acanthus and other compositional devices allowed the artist to indulge in fantasy, *grotesquerie* and heraldic allusion. Scribal hands naturally differed from one individual and region to another, but the Gothic *bastarda* and *rotunda* scripts perfected in the Low Countries were widely admired and copied. Even in Florence, choirbooks were written in large, well-formed Gothic *rotunda* hands, which were easier to read during services than the more cursive script of the humanists and their scribes. By the later fifteenth century, the illuminated book had become a form of art-work in which a number of hands were often involved. There was also a vigorous export trade in books: the great library formed by Mátyás Corvinus, king of Hungary (1459–90), was largely stocked with manuscripts purchased from Florentine dealers, while Carlos of Aragon, prince of Viana, bought both Netherlandish and Italian manuscripts which exerted their influence upon Catalan and Aragonese artists. The pages of illuminated books now served as 'windows' on to the natural world, reflecting the advances made in portraiture and landscape painting in the Burgundian Low Countries.

Religious sentiment, however, still remained a vital spur to book production. The demand for liturgical, theological and devotional texts was keen. Beginning with their Books of Hours, the laity had then helped to create a market for devotional treatises, homilies, manuals of the Christian life and of the pious manner of dying (*ars moriendi*), mystical writings and vernacular Bibles. These formed the core of many – if not most – book collections and reflected a spreading lay literacy and desire to be better informed in matters of doctrine and belief. The popularity of devotional books such as Thomas Kempis's *Imitation of Christ* (*De imitacione Christi et contemptu omnium vanitatum mundi*), completed in 1441, was well illustrated by its translation into other, more accessible, languages. Dutch versions soon appeared, and four different French translations are known, including one which was probably the work of Nicholas Finet, canon of Cambrai, almoner to Margaret of York, duchess of Burgundy. Court and aristocratic circles were thus kept acquainted with contemporary currents of religious sentiment and devotional practice through such books, some of which had their origins in the movement known as the *devotio moderna*.

The *devotio* also played a significant part in book production itself. One of the primary tasks of the houses founded by Gerhard Groote and his followers, such as Florent Radewijns (*c.* 1350–1400) at Deventer, Zwolle, Windesheim and elsewhere in the Low Countries, Westphalia and the Rhineland, was the copying, illuminating and binding of books. By 1450, there were nineteen houses of Brethren and Sisters of the Common Life, and manuscripts survive from some of them. The house at Zwolle was a prolific centre of book production and the *Lives* of its members by Jakob van Trier, together with Kempis's own *Chronicle* of the canons regular of Mount St Agnes, supply a fascinating picture of the community's work. The first prior of Mount St Agnes, Jan van Kempen (1399–1408), was a distinguished scribe and illuminator, while Henrik Mande (*c.* 1360–1431), an early member of the Windesheim convent, had been a scribe and secretary in the service of William IV, count of Hainault and Holland, before his conversion to the *devotio*. He wrote and decorated at least fourteen manuscripts during his early years at Windesheim. William Vorniken, second prior of Mount St Agnes (1408–25), caused 'a good store of books to be written for the choir and the library . . . and with his own hand he illuminated many books'.[4] Yet the communities did not only produce books for their own use: Egbert van Lingen, sub-prior of Zwolle, illuminated books 'that were written for sale'.[5] There can be no doubt that the houses of the Brethren were among the most important producers of liturgical and devotional books at this time. Their work was to some extent paralleled in Italy by the production of liturgical manuscripts and choirbooks by the members of Florentine and Venetian convents, for use in other churches, and by the activity of Carthusian monks in northern Europe. The Carthusians, as an eremitic order, devoted some of their ample time to the composition and copying of books, and houses such as the English foundations at Mountgrace and Syon inherited the role of the monastic *scriptoria* of earlier periods.

In their task of rendering the invisible world of the Spirit visible to human eyes, the manuscript illuminators of the fifteenth century followed the advances made by both panel and fresco painters. In the Low Countries, tangible objects and humdrum scenes of everyday life were infused with significance, emotion and Christian symbolism: 'the artist prefers his experience of men as he knows them to the inventive figuration of a world he has not observed'.[6] In Italy, the classicising and idealising tendencies of humanism imparted a special character to manuscript illumination, but northern influences were also clearly apparent. France derived much from the neighbouring Low Countries, but the introduction of Italianate forms and styles in the work of Jean Fouquet of Tours (*c.* 1420–80), and through the court of René of Anjou in Provence, gave French illumination a greater eclecticism. Spanish book production, in Castile, Aragon and Catalonia, absorbed and imitated both Netherlandish and Italian models, while the German lands looked mainly to Flanders and to the Rhineland for their inspiration. England supported indigenous book producers and illuminators, largely influenced by Netherlandish styles. But throughout western Europe, the number of manuscripts and books

[4] Thomas Kempis (1906), p. 46.   [5] Thomas Kempis (1906), p. 74.   [6] Delaissé (1968), p. 90.

in circulation had grown substantially by 1500. There was a ready demand for books from a wider readership, and entrepreneurs existed to satisfy their needs. Later fifteenth-century Europe was therefore well prepared for the introduction of new techniques for the mass-production and dissemination of the written word.

CHAPTER 14

THE BEGINNING OF PRINTING

David McKitterick

Of all the changes witnessed by the fifteenth century, it is arguable that none has had so profound an effect as the invention of printing. For more than two thousand years, much of Europe had depended on the written word for at least some aspects of its activities, while the history of Christendom was (as it still remains) defined by a central religious written text, the Bible. In such a context, the advent of printing heralded changes that have rightly been described as revolutionary. But like all revolutions, the invention of printing, its subsequent course, its effects and the ways in which it was exploited, raise issues that have little to do with the more immediate circumstances of invention: the application of metallurgical, chemical, calligraphic and engraving skills to the production of a printed page.

The concept of multiple copies, identical in text and in format, was not new. In the ninth century, the monastery of Tours, among others, had specialised in the production of Bibles, exporting them to centres throughout the Carolingian Empire. In the thirteenth century, the needs of universities at Paris, Bologna and Oxford for identical teaching texts had been met by the so-called *pecia* system, whereby authorised copies of parts of books were lent out for copying – a process that, because it enabled several people to copy out the same book simultaneously, added considerably to speed of production as well as reducing (if far from eliminating) the opportunities for inaccuracy. In thirteenth-century Paris, the production of small Bibles, for private use, was organised on an unprecedented scale and with much consequent uniformity. In the Low Countries, in the fifteenth century, the Windesheim congregation, and the Brethren of the Common Life, were committed to the production of manuscript devotional books in quantities sufficient for an increasingly interested lay public inspired by the *devotio moderna* movement encouraging private piety. In northern Italy, humanist demands for classical texts were met by stationers able to command an organised workforce of scribes, decorators and illuminators. These were all activities relating to the production of books. For less expensive parts of the market, and particularly to meet a widespread demand for religious images, printed images from woodcuts had been in circulation since at least the late fourteenth century: to judge by the surviving examples (not in themselves altogether satisfactory evidence), production and demand for such pictures were concentrated mostly in Bavaria, Swabia, Austria and Bohemia, and in the Low Countries in the north.

Each of these different kinds of literature had one feature in common: they were all defined not only by their content, but also by the existence of a market, be it in a religious or educational context. If we consider the range and nature of the books and other publications from the earliest presses, here, too, organised communities played an essential part, whether in the monastic world, popular religious cults, administration or university or other educational circles. In a market used to manuscripts, where the investment of time and materials meant that speculative production was strictly limited, one of the most forceful differences introduced by printing was the enormous increase in investment in raw materials. This was quite separate from the initial outlay for metals to make type-moulds or type. For the so-called Gutenberg, or forty-two-line, Bible alone, the major project towards which Gutenberg's efforts in Mainz are assumed to have been directed perhaps even from the first, sufficient paper was required for probably 120–50 copies, quite apart from the vellum required for perhaps 35–40 copies printed on that material – each copy requiring about 320 sheets. All the other principal publications associated with Gutenberg's press in the early 1450s were quite short, requiring correspondingly little capital investment in materials on which to print. Gutenberg's own concern at the cost of materials is reflected in the design of the forty-two-line Bible, a book which, though magnificent and highly visible in itself (as usually required for lectern Bibles), is in some respects noticeably compact in its layout and avoidance of wasted space. In other words, investment, materials and design combined to meet the underlying assumption of printing: that books could, if produced in sufficient quantity, be manufactured more cheaply.

There is some evidence to suggest that the decision to embark on such an expensive undertaking as a lectern Bible was itself prompted by a movement for monastic reform. The forty-two-line Bible, like its immediate successors printed elsewhere, was certainly not intended for general private use, though some copies are known to have been owned by individuals. On the evidence of binding and decoration, each of which would have been added locally, near or even at a copy's final destination, rather than necessarily in Mainz, copies seem to have found their way within a few years over much of Germany, including east to Leipzig and north to the port of Lübeck, as well as to Bruges and London. So, almost from the first, the principle was demonstrated: that large books, produced in quantity, could only be absorbed in a widespread market.

Likewise, many of the other of the earliest books printed at Mainz, Strasburg and Bamberg were on a scale that demonstrated that large books, handsomely produced, need not be as expensive as manuscripts of corresponding size. Of the two psalters printed by Johann Fust and Peter Schoeffer, in 1457 and 1459, the second was for specifically Benedictine houses, the first for more general use in and around Mainz. It may be assumed that Durandus's *Rationale* (1459) on religious ceremonies, and Pope Clement V's *Constitutiones* (1460), both printed by Fust and Schoeffer, were produced in response to the needs of similar customers. In Strasburg, the first books were also large folios, addressed to a market in which the organised needs of the Church figured most powerfully. Between the appearance of the forty-two-line Bible in *c.* 1454, and 1470, nine editions of the Vulgate were printed, in Mainz, Strasburg, Bamberg and Basle, all of them in folio.

This emphasis on an institutional market was limited, however, by its very definition: libraries and communities do not need to buy the same text very often. Gutenberg had printed shorter texts for secular needs, schoolbooks as well as indulgences, in the 1450s. In Bamberg, Albrecht Pfister turned his attention, albeit briefly, to vernacular German literature. And with the work of Ulrich Zel, the first printer in Cologne, where he seems to have been established by 1464, there was a sharp change of emphasis to works in Latin. His first work consisted in quarto editions of works for which sales could be expected to be to individuals, as well as to institutions: Antoninus 'of Florence's' *Summa confessionum*, Cicero, Jean Gerson, John Chrysostom and St Augustine.

Documentary sources, and close examination of surviving copies of books, have revealed a great deal of the background and financial and practical details of the beginnings of printing at Mainz in the 1450s; but it is only by considering the kind of books first printed, their size, design, likely readership, market and those who encouraged their production, that an understanding can be reached respecting the reasons for so much effort and money being invested in inventions and skills offering a future that can never have looked quite certain. The group gathered about Gutenberg does not seem to have been alone in attempts to discover a way of producing multiple copies; others were at work in Avignon, and perhaps elsewhere. But the invention was Gutenberg's. In practice, it consisted of several quite separate components, uniting metal working, calligraphy and chemistry. Though it is not clear in what order these came during the decade and more preceding the appearance of the first printed sheets in the early 1450s, it will be convenient to take them thus.

First, then, is type. Although it is possible to cut words in wood, and to print from that (as had been done in the far east for at least six centuries), such a process is slow, and requires great expenditure of effort even for short texts. The earliest known woodcut pictures in the west date from the late fourteenth century; and though most surviving blockbooks date from the late fifteenth, or even the early sixteenth, century, woodcuts bearing words survive from the first quarter of the fifteenth. By inventing the means to compose words from individual letters, Gutenberg created a flexible and adaptable method of producing a printing surface that, once used, could be dismounted and reassembled for some quite different purpose. Investment was thus not limited to a single publication. The method he developed in the 1440s and early 1450s remained the same in principle until the advent of photocomposition in the mid-twentieth century. Each character was engraved in relief on the end of a piece of soft steel, to create a punch. This punch was then struck into a small bar of copper, to make a matrix. After this matrix had been trimmed to ensure that its sides were square and regular, it was placed in a mould that could be adjusted according to the different widths of letters in the alphabet – 'i' being much narrower than 'm', for example. It is this type-mould that lies at the technical heart of Gutenberg's invention, and that is likely to have given most trouble as he adapted other existing skills such as punch-cutting and the knowledge of different properties of metals. Molten type metal, with a low melting point and consisting of an alloy of lead, tin and a hardening agent, was then poured into the mould, and a character, or sort, was cast. Each sort – be it an individual letter or number, or a ligatured group of letters – was cast separately.

A fount of type, at its simplest, consists of the letters of the alphabet, upper and lower case (capitals and small letters), numerals, punctuation and spaces. But the styles of formal script current in Germany in the mid-fifteenth century did not lend themselves to such separate analysis. Instead, they depended on a large number of contractions, linked letters ('ligatures') and diacritical marks, as well as a different range of punctuation from that in modern use. It has been calculated that the fount of type used in Gutenberg's masterpiece, the forty-two-line Bible, consisted of perhaps as many as 270 different sorts. Even this, however, represented a considerable feat of analysis and simplification in face of the assumption that a printed book should resemble a manuscript so far as possible in its layout, design of letters and qualities of legibility, which itself depended on familiarity. It is reasonable to suppose that the skills of Peter Schoeffer, one of Gutenberg's principal partners, and a professional scribe, were critical to this aspect of the invention.

Thirdly, a new kind of ink was required: one that could be applied to a non-porous metal surface (rather than, as for handwriting, to the porous surface of paper or vellum, or the treated end of a quill), and one that would retain its colour evenly when spread out. The oil-based inks used in the first Mainz press were composed of carbon, copper, lead and sulphur, the metal content being, in retrospect, unusually high. Though we know least of all about the earliest printing presses, it seems probable that the first ones were adaptations of existing mechanisms such as those for pressing grapes or olives. Certainly the main capital outlay for the fifteenth-century printer was not a press, which could be run up by a local carpenter and blacksmith. The principal expense was type, which during the first years of printing seems to have been cast usually by the printers themselves. Type-founding as a separate business seems to have become established only in the 1470s, in a development that crucially affected the appearance of books, since it meant that many different printers might share the same design of type.

Equally important, and essential to the concept of producing large quantities of books, was paper. Most books were printed on paper, though vellum remained in use for special copies, or for particular heavily used publications such as schoolbooks, or parts of books such as the canon of the Mass. Printing required paper in unprecedented quantities, and the cost of books was very largely made up of the cost of paper. Writing in 1492, Johannes Trithemius, the humanist Benedictine abbot of Sponheim, wrote in his tract *De laude scriptorum* of the distinction between the manuscript and the printed book, and singled out in particular the fact that the latter was on paper – a property that, in his view, would lead to its eventual destruction, whereas manuscripts, on vellum, would last much longer. By the mid-fifteenth century, the paper trade in western Europe was well established. Paper making had been introduced into the west in the twelfth century, and mills were built across Europe from Spain to northern Germany. The principal areas, all of them dependent on clean running water, a constant supply of rag and either steady local demand or the means to reach a market, were in northern Italy, Champagne, the Ile de France and south-west France. But in Germany, the first documented mill was established at Nuremberg only at the end of the fourteenth century – barely fifty years before Gutenberg began the course of experiment that was to lead to the invention of printing. The first in the Low Countries, near Lille, dates from about the same time. In Switzerland, the first mill was founded in 1433, at Basle, and the area soon became a major source of supply for rapidly growing demand. Not all areas were in a position to produce their own paper. There was no paper mill in England until the 1490s.

The development and spread of printing depended on a similar mixture of enterprise, speculation, investment, transport and, ultimately, market. An active international trade in printed books was established with remarkable speed, and it forms a pattern often independent of the spread of the new presses. The first twenty years of printing saw presses introduced not only in the major Rhineland cities of Mainz, Strasburg (1460), Cologne (1464) and Basle (*c.* 1467), but also further east, in Bamberg (before 1460) and Nuremberg (1470) on the Main, and Augsburg (1468). By 1470, there were presses as far north as Cologne and as far south as Rome. But in central Europe they were to be found only as far east as Bamberg and as far west as Basle. The single exception was Paris, where in 1470 the former rector of the Sorbonne, Guillaume Fichet, encouraged the establishment of a press with distinctive humanist overtones under the guidance of three men, Michael Friburger, Ulrich Gering and Martin Crantz, whose background and choice of publications give them a claim to be counted as the first secular learned press. Within ten years, presses had been set up from Budapest and Cracow to Seville and Salamanca, from Lübeck and Rostock on the Baltic to Naples and Cosenza on the Mediterranean, and printing had become well established in London, with smaller concerns, albeit briefly, at St Albans and Oxford. The concentration on a north–south corridor, from the Low Countries, through the valleys of the Rhine and upper Danube to the northern parts of Italy, remained noticeable. Only by 1500 could it be said that the spread of printing bore a serious relationship to the general distribution of population.

The reasons for this are complicated by geography, trade routes, population structure, literacy, local initiatives and, increasingly, the needs of education and administration. There is no evidence that printing was affected by changes in the size of population, which in the second part of the fifteenth century seems to have changed little. In general, printing was slow to take root in university towns; and where it did, as at Paris and Cologne, the earliest printers either showed little interest in local teaching needs, or moved on to other themes once a patron's initial enthusiasm waned. Firm connections between presses and universities were established only from the 1470s, and then, predominantly, in the higher faculties rather than at beginners' levels. Printing and publishing, dependent on capital and on communications, thrived and became established only in towns with good trade connections. But it is noticeable how many small towns, and even villages, had, by the end of the century, witnessed attempts to introduce the new skill, as a result of the wish of local magnates, lay or ecclesiastical, to extend their patronage. Few of these small presses survived more than a few years before their workmen moved on or sought alternative employment.

As part of this migration of the new skills, printers might travel great distances before settling. In Italy, the skill was introduced by Germans trained in the north; there were already powerful trade and cultural links with German-speaking Europe, into which printing was readily fitted. At Subiaco, the first printers, Conrad Sweynheim and Arnold Pannartz, came from the dioceses of Mainz and Cologne respectively: Sweynheim had probably been trained in the printing house of Fust and Schoeffer, moving south following the sack of Mainz in 1462. The first printers in Venice, the brothers Johannes and Vindelinus de Spira, were from Speier. At Foligno, Johann Neumeister, from Mainz, established a short-lived press in 1470, the same year as Johann Reinhart set up another, equally short-lived, in nearby Trevi: indeed,

'Moguntini calligraphi' – not necessarily printers – had been recorded at Foligno even in 1463. Elsewhere in Europe, the first printers in Paris were from Switzerland. The first at Lyons, Guillaume le Roy, came from Liège, and his professional connections seem to have been formed in Cologne and the Lower Rhine. In Seville, though the first printers (in 1477) were, unusually, native-speaking Spaniards, other printers came from Germany; Meinhart Ungut had worked previously in Naples, and the firm of 'Compañeros Alemanes' also had links with Italy, perhaps Venice. In England, William Caxton was unusual in that he was a native, having learned the craft in Cologne and printed in Bruges before bringing it to England and setting up his press at Westminster in 1476. The next press to be founded in England, a short-lived one at Oxford, was run by Theoderic Rood, who came from Cologne in 1478.

As this process implies, many of the early printers were peripatetic, as is shown by the careers of Germans who went to work in southern Europe. The effect of such migration was to be seen not simply in the establishment of presses, only some of which lasted, but also in the setting up of a local printing industry in towns across Europe. It simultaneously created a network of rela-tionships defined by the new medium of print, on a scale never matched by the manuscript trade. In northern Italy, many small presses, often private or semi-private affairs dependent upon the interest and investment of a single patron, lasted for only very brief periods, since peripatetic printers were common. Henricus de Colonia, whose father came originally from Dalen, near Cologne, worked in Brescia, Bologna, Modena, Siena, Lucca, Nozzano and Urbino in the last quarter of the century, always for short periods and returning to some places several times. Dionysius Bertochus, from Bologna, worked in Reggio Emilia, Vicenza, Treviso, Venice, Bologna and Modena over much the same period. Like all but a few printers, these men mixed printing with other forms of livelihood. Indeed, to judge by their output and by the expressions used in legal documents to describe their activities, printing was only a minor part of their lives. For example, Gerardus de Lisa moved south from Ghent, and by 1462 was a schoolmaster at Treviso. In 1471 he printed the first edition of a pseudo-Augustine *Manuale*. But in Treviso he was working in the shadow of the much more powerful printers and booksellers of Venice, where he removed in 1477–8, before moving on briefly to print in Udine and Cividale and then coming back to Treviso. He died, precentor of the cathedral, at Aquileia in 1499, having been by turn schoolmaster, bookseller, printer, choir-master, musician and debt collector.

But while the printing trade was characterised in some respects, especially until the 1480s, by émigré Germans, who were displaced by native speakers often rather haphazardly, and in other respects by craftsmen who moved press and type from place to place in search of a livelihood, the trade became domi-

nated by a few major firms organised internationally. This tendency was
encouraged by successive crises in the trade in the 1470s and 1480s, crises
brought on by overproduction of some texts and the consequent failure in a
collapsing market to realise adequate returns from investment. In Venice,
Nicolas Jenson, a Frenchman from near Troyes, established a new press in
1470 at a time when there was but one printing house in the city, and its powerful founder, Johannes de Spira, had died only recently. His early output was
dominated by classical Latin texts, including luxurious editions of which some
copies were printed on vellum and were clearly intended for illumination. This
policy helped him through the trade crisis of 1473; but he also met it by soon
afterwards forming a partnership with a group of German capitalists. This
powerful syndicate quickly proved successful, and soon came to dominate the
Venetian trade and therefore much of that in Europe. The group's hold on the
trade was confirmed by joining with Johannes de Colonia and Johannes
Manthen, successors to Vindelinus de Spira.

Other major and successful concerns remained dominated by members of a
single family. None of this kind was more successful than the Kobergers, in
Nuremberg. Though the city, a critical point in the exchange of manufactured
goods with cattle from the more thinly populated regions to the east, gained a
printing press for the first time only in or a little before 1470, the Kobergers'
systematic and rapid advance as scholarly publishers, taking full advantage of
local skills in metalwork and other arts, meant that for half a century the city
was also one of the most important publishing centres in Europe. Anton
Koberger, born in Nuremberg, set up his press in 1470 or 1471, and employed
as editors men such as Hans Amerbach (later a successful printer on his own
account at Basle) and Johann Beckenhaub, who had worked formerly at
Strasburg. His circle also included the humanists Willibald Pirckheimer,
Conrad Celtis and Hartmann Schedel, author of the most celebrated of all the
books to come from the Koberger printing house, the so-called *Nuremberg
Chronicle* of 1493. Books from the press became renowned for their lavish
woodcut illustration, and Michael Wolgemut, to whom Dürer was apprenticed
in 1486, was responsible with Wilhelm Pleydenwurff for some of the most
elaborate. By the 1490s, Koberger owned twenty-four presses, and employed
about a hundred apprentices. He had branches at Lyons, Paris and Toulouse,
agents in Milan and Venice, Lübeck and Antwerp, and had trading links with
England and Spain. The size of Koberger's organisation was unique for its
time; but it demonstrated on a European scale what was already apparent in
much smaller organisations. The manuscript book, and the trade in manuscripts, were far from extinct; but the potential ability of printing to reach out
to new markets and new kinds of readers, and draw readers together on an
unprecedented scale, was established irrevocably.

The potential of printing technology, linked to the exploitation of paper, was rapidly recognised for its religious, scholarly and social value. But it was not universally welcomed, and its effects were not always to the advancement of knowledge. In Venice, the Dominican scribe, Filippo de Strata, attacked the new printed books for the licence they gave to immorality and profanity. In Florence, the stationer, or *cartolaio*, Vespasiano da Bisticci continued to supply manuscripts on a scale that suggests the market was by no means restricted to the very wealthiest. Not surprisingly, those in the existing book trades who had most to lose were also those most vocal against the new art. These were extreme positions. But in Italy, France, Flanders and the Netherlands, the second half of the fifteenth century produced two or three generations of mature and talented illuminators, whose careers span the introduction of printed books and the gradual establishment of a market that looked to the printed, rather than the manuscript, word. Printing did not displace the manuscript book until, for some purposes, well after the end even of the sixteenth century. For the wealthiest, manuscripts of chosen texts, whether illuminated or, most commonly, decorated in established traditions, remained *de rigueur*. Federigo da Montefeltro, duke of Urbino, was said to have eschewed printed books. In Hungary, King Mátyás Corvinus (d. 1490) drew on the work of Italian scribes and illuminators to create a library humanist in its context and conservative in its preference (albeit by no means exclusive) for manuscripts. In England, illuminated manuscripts continued to be commissioned for the royal library. In the Burgundian duchy, the death of Charles the Bold in 1477 brought to a conclusion a period that had been able to look confidently to the ducal court for support in the production of elaborate and magnificent manuscripts. But the traditions and skills gathered in Flanders remained alive, not only to meet the commissions of a new generation of wealthy men such as Raphael de Marcatellis in Ghent (d. 1508) and Louis de Bruges, lord of Gruuthuse (d. 1492), but also to provide more modest books for the innumerable customers, many of them abroad, who expected their prayer books still to be in manuscript.

As the advantages of printed texts were accepted, so those who had met the demands for manuscripts either turned to other employment, or found places in the printing trade, or continued to supply decorative contexts to the printed word. In Bruges, Colard Mansion, a former scribe whose ornate typeface closely resembles the *lettre bâtarde* of high-quality Burgundian books, produced lavish editions of Boccaccio (1476) and Boethius (1477) where spaces were left for large illustrations to be added separately. Those in the Boethius were intended to be added by hand; but some copies of the Boccaccio were provided with engravings at these points, thus making it the first printed book to be illustrated with engravings rather than woodcuts. In Paris, Antoine Vérard specialised in books that combined printed text with illuminations commissioned at what must have been sometimes considerable expense. At Venice, in the 1470s, full advantage was often taken of the generous margins provided by, among others, Nicolas Jenson, to receive decoration as desired either from individual artists or from workshops, sometimes working in collaboration with the printer rather than a stationer. But amidst all this activity, much of it of a transitional nature as the book trade and readers alike came to terms with printing, the great majority of books were plain, or rubricated in the simplest possible way, and printed in such a manner as to make the most of the space offered by the size of sheets of paper. Just as most manuscripts had been quite plain, so were most printed books.

Printing and manuscripts marched side by side, the two techniques often appearing in the same volumes. By the later part of the fifteenth century, printed engravings from copper plates were well established as illustrations to manuscript prayer books. Until well into the sixteenth century, it was common practice for owners of manuscript and printed texts to arrange for them to be bound up together irrespective of their means of production. In sum, not only did printed and manuscript books exist side by side, but the two media were frequently combined in a single book. Printers left space for initial letters and other textual features to be filled in by hand, and there are many examples of manuscripts copied from printed texts. The printing revolution took shape only gradually.

The process was slower for some forms of text than for others. The technical difficulties associated with casting Greek type, with its ligatures, breathings and accents, as well as the cognate requirements of investment, scholarship, linguistic skills and market, were major factors in the tardy appearance of most of the major literature in ancient Greek. Even in England, despite Caxton's notable achievement as an advocate of printing major English literary texts, including editions of Malory (1485) and Chaucer (1476 and 1483), much vernacular literature remained unprinted until well into the sixteenth century. In all areas where there were presses, the introduction of printing as a means of disseminating vernaculars, whether for imaginative literature, for government, for legislation, for religious purposes or for practical instruction, had the effect of accelerating tendencies towards linguistic stabilisation. In England, the Low Countries and Spain, the earliest printers' attention to the vernacular was encouraged partly by the fact that by the time presses were introduced there, the European book trade was already well supplied with most of the standard classical and other Latin texts that formed the mainstay of literate activity. And throughout western Europe, for practical skills such as cookery and everyday medicine, it is probable that the number of printed texts remained outweighed by private manuscript compilations. But in all subjects, the success of the printing press is not necessarily to be measured by the dates of the first editions of much used works: for so long as there were sufficient manuscripts of a work in circulation, there was no need of a printed edition. This may partly explain the tardy responses of universities to the new skill, mentioned earlier.

It will be seen that different kinds of customers expected different things from printing. The printed book might bring uniformity and lower prices; but these were not always qualities either expected or appreciated. For classical texts, the introduction of printing, not of itself a guarantee of accuracy or authority, meant that the textual traditions of humanist manuscripts tended to be perpetuated, sometimes in glaring inaccuracy. Moreover, as was the case with Ovid, the textual authority quickly accorded to the *editio princeps* (Bologna 1471) actually drove out the better, if still inadequate, text published at about the same time in Rome. Whatever the benefits of printing, it was an acute disappointment for some, even in the fifteenth century, that inadequate and inaccurate texts were rushed to publication, and disseminated to an uncontrolled reading public. For many classical texts, the earlier and more accurate manuscripts were not introduced into the printed tradition for at least another generation or more of hard work by scholars. But printing also brought a new degree of competition, and increasingly so as different editions of the same text were put on to the market. It stimulated a new need to advertise. In 1470, for example, Peter Schoeffer warned customers against buying copies of Jerome's letters, as he was shortly to publish a superior edition, properly collated with sources in monastic and cathedral libraries.

Printed texts, because of their number, were less likely to be lost. But what was printed could also be forgotten or degraded, and not only in classical texts. Woodcut illustrations provided a means of circulating exactly repeated pictorial statements, whether in botany, medicine, engineering, astronomy or portraiture. But as these images were in turn copied, without recourse to an original, so crucial details could be coarsened. In these circumstances, printed editions actually encouraged a decline in knowledge, correctable only by aggressive marketing of major new editions. Botanical illustration suffered particularly in this way. In cartography, the map in Bernard von Breydenbach's great illustrated account *Peregrinatio in terram sanctam* (Mainz 1486) shows clearly the two forks at the north end of the Red Sea; but this was ignored by subsequent cartographers, and was not again included in printed maps until the seventeenth century. Greenland was included in a map of 1482, published at Ulm, but not in any others during the fifteenth century. The Caspian Sea, accurately depicted oriented north–south on Venetian maps, was usually shown oriented east–west until as late as 1721.

Whatever the textual achievements and limitations, the introduction of printing heralded wider fundamental and irrevocable change. Verbal communication, formerly mostly the prerogative of speech and the pen, was given a new guise, with the potential to reach diverse and scattered audiences far more rapidly than had hitherto been either feasible or even envisaged. Printed matter such as popular literature, books of instruction, almanacs and works of religion became, even for the semi-literate, part of everyday life, thanks to lower unit costs and the ready manufacture of hundreds, and even thousands, of copies. In scholarly work, the labour of editing was not merely transformed by the existence of printed editions to act as near-uniform standards for collating manuscripts scattered across Europe. Widespread publication in print also lent a new urgency to discussion. The effect on classical scholarship was tumultuous, as printing ushered in a century and more of fundamental reassessment. The same considerations applied in the Church, the indulgences printed by Gutenberg only hinting at the change of scale that might be achieved; they gave no inkling of the manner whereby religious and other debate was to be transformed. The ability of the press to accelerate the dispersal of laws and regulations, to promote instruction, education, scientific exchange, medicine or opinion, helped also to provoke responses that could be more rapidly shared. The printing press, the first agent of mass communication, was also the means to, as well as the cause of, an unprecedented acceleration in social intercourse, one of the defining characteristics of the early modern world.

CHAPTER 15

ARCHITECTURE AND PAINTING

Paul Crossley

FEW epochs in the history of art occupy so central a position in western achievement yet so strongly resist the neat distinctions of period and categorisation as the fifteenth century. Suspended between two pan-European artistic styles (a Parisian-centred Gothic and a Roman-based High Renaissance and Early Baroque), and straddling two historical epochs ('the late Middle Ages' and 'the Renaissance'), the arts of fifteenth-century Christendom, known variously as 'late medieval', 'early Renaissance', 'late Gothic', even 'florid' and 'flamboyant', present a confusing and extraordinarily heterogeneous picture. The period saw one of the most profound changes in visual language in the history of western art, from the late Gothic formalities of the so-called International Style of *c.* 1400, to the accomplished naturalism of Leonardo da Vinci and Michelangelo. In a Europe fragmented by complex political units and sharpening differences in vernacular languages, the fifteenth century is remarkable for an acute diversity of artistic styles. And cutting across these divergences of tradition and experience is the fundamental split between the neo-classical language of Quattrocento Italy and a vigorous Gothic style north of the Alps which went on resisting antique forms well into the sixteenth century. The ambivalences in that north–south divide add their own complications to any definition of fifteenth-century art as a whole. Burckhardt's classic attempt to distinguish the Italian Renaissance from the Middle Ages and the 'Gothic north' remained successful so long as it stayed within the stylistic categories of artistic language and pointed to the decisive revival of antique forms. But when it moved into more dubious historical categories, such as 'The Development of the Individual' and 'The Discovery of the World and of Man', it prepared the way for Huizinga's false contrast between a 'waning' fifteenth-century northern culture – its essentially late medieval art coloured by courtly aestheticism and morbidity – and an optimistic, individualistic and progressive Italian Renaissance. These confident polarities have long been undermined by our awareness of the fruitful exchanges between Italian Renaissance art and contemporary Netherlandish painting, and by our perception of the continuities between medieval and Renaissance culture, both in the periodic revivals of Antiquity throughout the Middle Ages (Erwin Panofsky's 'renascences'), and in the persistence of medieval habits of mind among even the most progressive of Renaissance artists and patrons.

In his biography of Andrea Mantegna, Vasari defined the art of the later Quattrocento with an observation that could apply to the whole century: 'at that time accomplished artists were setting themselves to the intelligent investigation and zealous imitation of the truths of Nature'. The fifteenth century established a new relationship between 'art' and 'life' which served to undermine the distinctions between both. Art transformed the face of fifteenth-century Europe. It marked the critical stages of life, from baptism to death; it articulated the public life of cities as fountains, crosses and street statues, and, less permanently, as the fantastic machinery of outdoor theatricals (plate 6); it broke out from its old, elite setting in church and castle, to decorate the houses of the bourgeoisie with diptychs and devotional panels; it cluttered churches with fonts, pulpits, sacrament houses, tombs and colossal altarpieces (plates 1, 3, 17, 21); it established new, more popular, genres of graphic illustration and printing. In turn, as life permeated into all branches of art, so art began to explore, with a new accuracy and logic, the diversity of the world. Artists developed a more analytical, more strictly scientific attitude to nature, and fashioned more sophisticated tools for its expression. The new reality these painters recorded belonged, of course, to many categories other than nature. The overt goal of fifteenth-century painters and theorists towards 'naturalism' and mimesis was profoundly modified by the complex of techniques, values and beliefs – many of them still imbued with medieval conventions – which they brought, often half-acknowledged, to the act of representation. Nevertheless, the most profound changes in fifteenth-century art seem to have been triggered by new techniques of rendering optical reality. The simultaneous discovery, at the beginning of the century, of a systematic linear perspective in Florence, and of the full possibilities of oil painting and aerial perspective in Flanders, launched European art from the two schools – the Italian and the Flemish – which were to dominate it for the next 200 years.

FLANDERS AND THE NORTH

In northern Europe, where the break with the medieval past centred not on the revival of Antiquity but on the creation of a new language for representing the natural (and supernatural) world, the most profound changes were bound to come from the most mimetic of media, manuscript and panel painting, and to leave architecture, and to a lesser extent sculpture, unaltered until the mid-sixteenth century. Not that architecture in the north lost its vitality – on the contrary, it underwent fundamental changes of function and emphasis, and displayed astonishing virtuosity in the handling of decorative linear patterns, particularly in vaults and window tracery. The fifteenth century saw the demise of the 'great church' (with some pretentious exceptions in the Low Countries and Spain) and the promotion of more secular and communal genres: the proliferation of the parish church and the chantry chapel, the transformation of the castle into the palace, and – particularly in urbanised Flanders – the emergence of the town hall as a colossal, ostentatiously decorated accent designed to match, even surpass, the city's principal churches (e.g. Brussels, 1444–54). It was in these new contexts, not in the old cathedrals, that the flamboyant imagination of late Gothic architects flourished most freely. The two most influential buildings in Germany in the late fifteenth century were both palaces – the Albrechtsburg in Meissen (begun 1471) and the Vladislav Hall in Prague castle (begun 1490). The high points of Spanish late Gothic are to be found in a distinctly Iberian type of polygonal funerary chapel, combining complex decorative vaulting and sumptuous exhibitions of heraldry (e.g. Constable's chapel, Burgos cathedral, begun soon after 1482). And in the box-like simplicities of the English Perpendicular parish church, and in the open vistas of the German hall church (plate 1), architects evolved a type of spatially diffuse and decoratively neutral auditorium suitable for sermons, municipal processions and the eye-catching display of a new class of micro-architectural furnishings – font covers, Easter sepulchres, and sacrament houses. Stylistically, however, northern architects proceeded as if Alberti and Brunelleschi had never existed. None of them deviated essentially from the archetypes laid down for them in the later fourteenth century.

Sculpture, with its inherent three-dimensionality and its classical associations, seems at first sight to be the most promising medium of artistic change in the north, especially since the new century saw two great workshops at either end of Europe – the Parler family in the cathedrals of Prague and Vienna and Claus Sluter's school centred on the duke of Burgundy's Charterhouse at Champmol, near Dijon – simultaneously evolve a style of extraordinary solidity and psychological intensity, achieved through penetrating portraiture and virtuoso displays of three-dimensional drapery. Yet stylistically the influence of Sluter (d. 1406) on panel painting was confined to the grisaille 'imitation sculpture' on the exteriors of Flemish altarpieces, while his impact on later sculpture was rapidly eclipsed by the physical expansiveness, the spaciousness and the style of narrative, of the Flemish painters themselves. Most late Gothic sculptors – in Germany, Tudor England and particularly Spain (where almost all were Flemish émigrés) – were content to elaborate the conventions of Flemish art of the first half of the century. Indeed the practice of polychroming figures and incorporating panel paintings into carved altarpieces meant that sculptors were never to be fully free from a fruitful tension with painters and painting until the very end of the century, when Tilman Riemenschneider and Veit Stoss introduced southern Germany to a new mode of monochrome carving. Sluter's real impact was felt in changes in workshop practice. The over-powering physical presence of his architecture-defying figures prepared the way for the most critical change in northern sculpture during the fifteenth century: its emancipation from architecture. Freed from its old position in church portals, sculpture could now be conceived as a semi-independent work of art, usually in wood rather than stone, and standing in, but not attached to, its architectural setting. Sculptors consequently moved from the mason's lodge (where they had been grouped with *lathomi, cementarii, tailleurs de pierre*) to inde-pendent workshops in the cities, where (as *ymagier tailleurs*) they responded to new kinds of patron and commission (usually single devotional figures or altar retables ordered by individual citizens or urban corporations) and developed new professional structures, with their own guild regulations.

The first decisive steps towards an art aimed at a new fidelity to nature were made in the first decades of the century by a triumvirate of panel painters – Robert Campin, Jan van Eyck and Rogier van der Weyden – working for the burgesses of Bruges, Brussels and Tournai, and for the immensely wealthy dukes of Burgundy in Flanders. Their new style, which marks a shift in political and artistic power from France to the Low Countries, became the lingua franca of northern European painting, metalwork, sculpture and tapestry, and excited the admiration of Italian *cognoscenti* from Naples to Venice. One of the qualities the Italians most admired – and which humanists like Bartolommeo Fazio found brilliantly exemplified in the art of Jan van Eyck (*c.* 1390–1441) – was the splendour of Flemish oil painting technique, not, as Vasari thought, invented by van Eyck, but certainly manipulated by him to create seemingly miraculous illusions of reality. Oil permitted the softest transitions of modelling and ensured an astonishing precision of detail. It created the subtlest effects of diffuse light in aerial perspectives and cast shadows, and it illuminated even the darkest passages by its rich but transparent glazes of colour. Jan van Eyck's semi-magical mastery of the medium (Vasari called him an alchemist) conjured up a new and almost palpable world, where the paint itself – particularly in the rendering of light, textures and materials – acts almost as a constituent element of what it represents. With self-effacing, almost imperceptible mastery the arti-fice of van Eyck's art seems to merge with the very laws and substance of nature. To the traditionally 'northern' subject matter of portraiture and land-scape – themes already handled with exquisite naturalism in fourteenth-century French and Netherlandish book painting – van Eyck brought a minute and pitiless observation. Like his lost *Map of the World*, praised by Fazio for depicting all regions of the earth accurately and at measurable distances, van Eyck's landscapes, the first atmospherically convincing panoramas in western art, recede in immaculate detail into a radiant horizon (plate 2), or advance forward as if to envelop the spectator (plate 3). Beside this macroscopic sense of enlargement lies a microscopic fascination for minutely executed details, both polarities (or 'infinities' as Panofsky called them) part of a single continuum.

Van Eyck's magical accumulations of minutiae are, however, as much 'ideal' as 'real'. They not only reduplicate nature, but reconstruct it with a new clarity and meaning. Italian humanists admired Flemish painting not just for its technical brilliance but its peculiar piety; it was *pietissimo* and *devoto*; it moved the spectator to empathise with its figures. In other words, it allowed traditional medieval pieties to resurface and regroup within the new medium. Into the illusionistic rendering of sacred materials and objects – the marbled columns, stained glass and bejewelled crown of, for example, *The Virgin of Chancellor Rolin (c.* 1435) (plate 2) – van Eyck compresses the old anagogical resonance of the treasures themselves; the translucency of the oil medium, like the reflections of a mirror, seems to distill the magical luminosity of the gold backgrounds of medieval panel painting and filter it through every aspect of the picture. And by a similar process of diffusion, the formal symbolism that once centred on isolated holy objects is now diversified, unobtrusively but pervasively, into nature as a whole. At the heart of the peculiar unreality of all van Eyck's (and most Flemish) religious painting is a sense of the holiness of all creation – a quiet and pervasive sanctity much admired by the Italians, and nowhere more apparent than in Hubert and Jan van Eyck's great altarpiece, *The Adoration of the Lamb (c.* 1432) (plate 3), a work already revered in the sixteenth century as the masterpiece of the founders of Flemish art. Here, in a vision of transfigured nature, the vast theological programmes associated hitherto with Gothic cathedral sculpture are infused with the sensuous naturalism and suggestive symbolism of van Eyck's new conception of humanity.

Van Eyck's conquest of the 'outer' phenomenal world, a largely static and emotionless world built up by detached observation and pervaded in its entirety by an all-inclusive, almost pantheistic significance, is matched by Rogier van der Weyden's (1399–1464) mastery of the 'inner' landscape of intense personal emotion. Van der Weyden concentrates primarily on human action and spiritual insight. The boundaries between painting and audience are dissolved less by van Eyck's trompe l'œil naturalism than by a new and engaging language of expression, maintaining van Eyck's tangibility, but purifying it with a new monumentality and linear energy. Van der Weyden's innovations directly address the meditative imagination, in the inclusion of half-length

donor figures in small diptychs of the Virgin, or the portrayal of contemporaries as *dramatis personae* in biblical events (Charles the Bold as one of the Magi
in the so-called *Columba Altarpiece*, Munich, Alte Pinakothek). New types of
figure composition, allied to an unprecedented mastery in the portrayal of varieties of emotion through gesture or facial expression, give van der Weyden's
paintings an intense and immediate power. The Prado *Deposition* (*c.* 1440) – half
Descent from the Cross, half Lamentation – compresses, almost painfully, a
novel ensemble of grief-stricken and unstable figures into the narrow confines
of what is a fictive version of the box or *corpus* of a contemporary wooden
altarpiece. His most ambitious composition, *The Last Judgement* altarpiece (plate
4), painted for Nicholas Rolin's hospital at Beaune in about 1445, deploys all
van der Weyden's powers of psychological insight and dramatic expressiveness
to prepare the sick for contrition and the Good Death. It presents a vision of
apocalyptic contrasts. The narrow spaces below are crowded with the damned,
each marked out by vivid and varied expressions of horror, each driven into
hell not by demons (van der Weyden's is one of the first Last Judgements
without them) but by a sharpened sense of their own guilt. Towering above
them, in almost surreal contrast, are the monumental and schematic figures of
the Court of Heaven, situated not in any 'real' space, but quietly silhouetted
against a supernatural background of blazing gold.

The contrasting sensibilities of van der Weyden and van Eyck established
the two poles within which Netherlandish painting operated to the end of the
century. Dierec Bouts (*c.* 1415–75) combined van Eyck's interest in spatial
construction and atmospheric effects with van der Weyden's feeling for
individualised faces and monumental figures (plate 8). Hugo van der Goes (*c.*
1435–82), the most faithful exponent of van der Weyden's emotionalism,
brought together a mastery of systematic perspective with a highly individual
sensitivity to portraiture, and a preference for unexpected dislocations of scale
(*Portinari Triptych*, 1475). Outside the Netherlands – in France, Spain and
Germany – in sculpture as well as in painting, van der Weyden's simple,
immediate, and therefore memorable, language found an echo in artists as disparate as Schongauer, Konrad Witz (plate 16) and the anonymous master of
the *Pietà* from Villeneuve-lès-Avignon (1454). The relatively conservative
nature of northern painting in the second half of the century may owe something to the training and production methods of the guild system, with its
emphasis on long apprenticeships, with its system of judging 'masterpieces' by
existing masters, and with the growth of large workshops composed of
journeymen mass-producing their master's style. Certainly, northern art, with
the notable exception of Jean Fouquet (1420–81), remained largely impervious
to the contemporary revolution in Italian painting.

ITALY

Humanism – or, more strictly, the *studia humanitatis* – was never an exclusively Italian phenomenon, but the first attempts to link the revival of classical litera-ture and learning with the revival of classical art and architecture took place in Florence at the beginning of the century, under the auspices of three artists whose careers typified the new categories of the 'fine' arts: Brunelleschi the architect (1377–1446), Donatello the sculptor (*c.* 1386–1466) and Masaccio the painter (1401–*c.* 1428). Florentine republicanism may have hastened the integration, for the heady sense of liberty that pervaded the city in 1402 after the death of its most dangerous enemy, Giangaleazzo Visconti, was articulated by its historian, Leonardo Bruni (*c.* 1370–1444) precisely in terms of Florence's unique classical past: 'of all peoples the Florentines appreciate liberty most and are the greatest enemies of tyrants . . . your founder is the Roman people, con-queror and lord of all the world' (*History of Florence, c.* 1430).[1] Brunelleschi's, Ghiberti's and Donatello's first steps in the creation of a new style *all' anticha* took place in the traditional setting of Florence's greatest monuments of civic corporate patronage – the cathedral, Orsanmichele, and the baptistery – and were driven by the familiar Florentine device of competitions between artists, set up and adjudicated by city guilds. Just as Florentine humanists recognised that the Latin of the ancients had been given literary dignity by the Tuscan vulgate of Dante and Petrarch, so Florentine artists – doubtless impressed by the myth that the culture of Rome had been providentially transposed to Florence during the Middle Ages – cast their revival of antique forms in a medieval, Tuscan mould. The monumental and emotionally powerful figures of Masaccio's Brancacci chapel at S. Maria del Carmine (*c.* 1427) (plate 5), which give to Renaissance painting a new weight and eloquence, owe a general debt to the statuesque solidity of Giotto, and to the passionate idiom of Giovanni Pisano's Trecento sculpture – itself based on classical models. The first true recreation of classical contraposto in Donatello's *St Mark* in Orsanmichele (1410) would have been inconceivable without the precocious revival of antique figure styles by Tuscan Trecento sculptors. Brunelleschi's first-hand knowledge of Roman ruins and his ingenious use of Roman constructional techniques in his monumental dome of Florence cathedral (1420–36) doubtless contributed to his heroic reputation as the one man who brought about the revival of classical architecture, but the general tone of his Florentine buildings – from the Foundling Hospital of 1419 to the Pazzi chapel of *c.* 1440 – is more Tuscan than Roman. Despite the new purity of their volumes and the mathematical clarity of their proportions, they recall the deli-

[1] Leonardo Bruni, *Historiarum florentini populi libri XII*, trans. D. Acciaiuoli, 3 vols., Florence (1855–60).

cate arcades and marble incrustations of Florentine Romanesque rather than
the scale and weight of imperial Rome. Brunelleschi's other, equally influential,
achievement, the invention of a systematic and mathematical linear perspective, may also have grown out of his direct experience of Florentine architecture, since the geometrical grid which single-point perspective imposes on
pictorial space (for which Alberti used the urban term 'pavement') finds its
closest analogy in the techniques used by surveyors and architects (among
them perhaps Brunelleschi himself) to measure real urban spaces. Significantly,
Brunelleschi chose to demonstrate his new invention with two (now lost) perspectival views of the two most significant urbanistic developments of
Trecento Florence, symbolic of the secular and ecclesiastical poles of its civic
life: the baptistery in the cathedral square and the Palazzo Vecchio in the Piazza
della Signoria. Such links between mathematical space and the ordered but
familiar ambience of the city were later made explicit in the townscapes of
Carpaccio, where Venice itself becomes the panoramic setting for the rituals of
its religious history and civic life. The unity between the ordered vistas of the
street and the ideal spaces of art must have been even more literally obvious in
the overlaps of image and civic spectacle provided by the outdoor theatricals
staged by any Italian city's guilds and confraternities. In painting, as in life, perspective provided at once a window on to a mathematically ordered world, and
a lucid stage for dramatic action, for *istoria*. In his treatise on painting, *De pictura*
(*c.* 1435), Leon Battista Alberti (1404–72) presented the first systematic
formulation of Brunelleschi's perspective, in the belief that the painter's
central duty was to uncover the principle of harmony (*concinnitas*) manifest in
the mathematical laws of proportion (*mesura*) and perspective which govern
creation. The painter, in other words, acted like a scientist (Alberti was
described by Cristoforo Landino in the 1480s as a 'natural scientist'), concerned not just with the imitation of the outward phenomena of nature (*natura
naturata*) – of primary interest to Flemish painters – but with the understanding
of the creative forces which lie within it (*natura naturans*). But if Alberti's
painter must align his art to the science of geometry and optics, he must also
obey the precepts of classical rhetoric. Like the poet, he must depict a heroic
narrative (*istoria*); he must apply the literary discipline of composition (*compositio*) to figures, limbs and planes, to ensure a pleasing variety (*varietas*) of action
and colour; he must add light, shadow and atmospheric effects to produce a
sense of projection (*rilievo*); and finally, he must suggest mental states through
gesture and facial expression (*vivacità* and *prontezza*).

Alberti's *De pictura*, like his other two treatises on sculpture and architecture,
De statua and *De architectura*, seems to be addressed more to the informed
humanist patron of the arts than to practising artists; but they articulated the
interests and practices of the leading Florentine artists of the early
Quattrocento, and fixed them, as *exempla*, for later generations. Masaccio's

Tribute Money in the Brancacci chapel (plate 5), or Donatello's bronze reliefs for the baptistery at Siena (*c.* 1425) (plate 7) set a dramatic *istoria*, composed around the complementary virtues of *varietà* and *compositio* (and Landino praised Donatello as 'mirabile in compositione et in varietà'), within a masterly delineation of classical architecture arranged in perfect perspective. And just as Masaccio was praised by Landino for his *rilievo* – which makes him 'the great imitator of nature' – so Donatello was praised at his funeral for 'putting nature into marble' – a reference which could include all the genres of sculpture which he revitalised, from the tomb, the free standing nude figure (*David*, Bargello, Florence) and the equestrian statue (plate 11), to his extraordinarily virtuoso low relief carvings (*rilievo stiacciato*) (e.g. *The Ascension*, Victoria and Albert Museum, London, *c.* 1428) that convey effects of atmosphere and soft light usually associated with painting. But 'nature' here was no doubt also a reminder of the peculiar *vivacità*, the psychological and nervous power, which infuses all his work, from the early *St George* in Orsanmichele (*c.* 1416) to his late reliefs on the pulpit of S. Lorenzo in Florence (1460–6) (plate 21).

Whatever the particular influence of Alberti's treatises, their identification of the fine arts with rhetoric and mathematics, and thus with the liberal arts, introduced a new distinction in western art between art and craft, and thus, at least theoretically, elevated the artist from a rude *mechanicus* to a man of letters. Of course, only the most eminent artists could maintain these pretensions, but the first biography of an artist, Manetti's *Life of Brunelleschi*, and Ghiberti's *Commentaries*, which contained the first collection of the lives of antique and modern masters, with the earliest known artist's autobiography, suggest that the leading Italian artists did so with some literary style. Their exceptional status marked them off from their leading contemporaries north of the Alps. When the young Dürer of Nuremberg arrived in Venice in 1494 he was struck by the divide: 'here I am a gentleman, at home I am a parasite'.

MEMORIALS

It was inevitable that a period which laid such emphasis on individual talent and virtue, on fame and *umanità*, should devote so much of its creative energies to the problem of commemoration. Portraits had uses that went beyond matters of individual prestige. They could act as accurate records of a future spouse, or as exotic curiosities (Gentile Bellini's portrait of the Sultan Mehemmed II) (plate 24). But their usual purpose was to convey, with decorum and vivacity, what Vespasiano da Bisticci called, in his *Lives*, *umanità* – the sitter's interests, personality and likeness. In the north, particularly in Flanders, portraiture extended its social range from the kings, princes and high ecclesiastics of the fourteenth century to a clientele of wealthy townspeople. To these serious and sober citizens Robert Campin, Jan van Eyck and Rogier van der Weyden gave an extraordinary presence, submitting them to intense scrutiny, turning them to a three-quarter face pose to the viewer, restricting their format to head and shoulders (to concentrate thereby on face and sometimes hands) and suggesting personality and achievement by such devices as held letters, chains of office or details of costume. In the second half of the century, first in the Netherlands and then elsewhere, this closed format could be broken into by descriptive or symbolic backgrounds, most notably the 'window portrait' – pioneered by Dierec Bouts in *Portrait of a Man* (1462) (plate 8) – where the sitter now interacts, visually, and at times symbolically, with the wider world behind him, and, by implication, with the viewer in front of him.

In Italy the humanists' notion of *umanità* was coloured by their nostalgia for Antiquity and their own scholarly priorities. Vespasiano da Bisticci's *Lives* devotes its longest section to scholars, as if greatness lay not in rank but in virtue and wisdom. The Quattrocento sanctioned all kinds of personal commemoration, not just for holiness or birth, but for political, military, literary and artistic achievement. No artefact encapsulated this democracy of fame more neatly than the portrait medallion, inspired by antique coins, but made into a virtually new and independent art form by Antonio Pisanello (1395–1455). With a strongly characterised profile portrait on the front and an allegorical device alluding delicately and often abstrusely to the subject's virtues on the reverse, the medal immortalised a broad section of Italian society, from princes and ecclesiastics to a prominent category of teachers and philosophers (plate 9). Its quasi-heraldic profile portrait probably accounts for the persistence of the profile portrait in Italy through much of the period (see Giovanni da Oriolo's portrait of Lionello d'Este, London, National Gallery, *c.* 1447) until it finally gave way, in the hands of Botticelli and Antonella da Messina, to the Netherlandish format of the three-quarter pose, or even a (rarer) frontal presentation.

The spatial settings of group portraiture encouraged a much more expansive relationship between sitter and surroundings. Beginning with the tradition of the donor portrait, promoted from a diminutive and marginal accent (Ghent altarpiece) to a full-size, if still secondary, witness to the main events, the group portrait in Florence emerged as a dominant force in Ghirlandaio's almost ostentatiously prominent depictions of Lorenzo de' Medici, his family and household, in the Sassetti chapel in S. Trinità (*c.* 1480). Henceforward, it was easy to jettison the sacred setting altogether, and devote whole fresco cycles to the lives of great men (Pinturicchio's *Life of Pius II* in the Piccolomini Library in Siena cathedral, 1502–8). In Mantegna's *The Gonzaga Court* in the ducal palace at Mantua (complete 1474) any attempt at a religious or secular *istoria* was abandoned, and the Gonzaga family are intimately presented to us as the painter knew them (plate 10). Grouped informally against an illusionistic background of terrace and sky – the precursor of the fictive loggias and land-scapes of sixteenth-century villas – the Gonzaga court has become the exclusive subject of art.

Dürer's definition of the second aim of painting, to preserve the appearance of men after their deaths, had been the task of sculpture far longer than painting, and in Italy the revival of the most distinguished commemorative genres of Antiquity – the portrait bust and the bronze equestrian statue – provided some of the most incisive portraiture of the century. The earliest busts, such as Mino da Fiesole's *Piero de' Medici* (Florence, Museo Nazionale, 1453), combine the Roman format with echoes of medieval reliquary busts; while Donatello's bronze equestrian statue of Gattamelata in Padua (1445–50) (plate 11) revives a tradition that goes back, through the fourteenth-century Scaligeri riders in Verona, to the bronze horses of St Mark's and the Marcus Aurelius in the Roman forum. These had been monuments to princes and emperors; Gattamelata was merely the successful captain-general of the Venetian Republic, raised, in the spirit of Petrach's *Trionfi*, 'pro insigni fama ipsius', above the square in front of the church of St Anthony, as a commemoration of individual heroism and of the ideals of Roman civic life. Revivals of antique genres were matched by wholly new types of memorial. In contrast to the *magnificenza* of Gattamelata and its imitators (Verocchio's *Bartolomeo Colleoni*, Venice, 1480–8), Leonardo Bruni's tomb in S. Croce in Florence (*c.* 1445–50), the first of a progeny of classical wall tombs extending to Spain, England and Poland, presents an idealised portrait of the great humanist, crowned with laurels, a book in his hand. Intellect, not rank, is his claim to immortality. Poised between the emblems of classical learning beneath him (the eagles of Zeus, the winged genii) and the Madonna with angels above, Bruni serves as an *examplum virtutis* of humanist learning and Christian hope.

The restraint of Bruni's tomb found no echo in the proud triumphal-arch-like monuments of the Venetian doges, or the megalomaniac visions of Filarete for the tomb of Giangaleazzo Sforza. Tomb sculpture could always degenerate into ostentation. To such monuments of *vanitas* as the tomb of the Infante Alfonso in the Cartujade Miraflores in Burgos (1489–93), with its Spanish format of a kneeling figure of the deceased enframed by a suffocating decor, or the lavish micro-architectural canopies crowning the effigies of English tombs (Bishop Beaufort's in Winchester cathedral, *c.* 1447) the fifteenth century counterposed an horrific emblem of *humilitas*: the image of the decomposing corpse, or *transi*, laid beneath the splendour of the clothed effigy as a gruesome reminder of death. The popularity in northern Europe of this and other didactic–moralistic themes, such as The Three Living and The Three Dead, or The Dance of Death, is not simply a reflection of the cultural morbidity and pessimism that haunted the plague-torn Europe of the later

Middle Ages. The appearance of a *transi* in the most rational and enlightened of contexts, Masaccio's *Holy Trinity* in S. Maria Novella in Florence (*c.* 1427), underlines the function of the tomb, not simply as the vehicle of fame, but as the reminder of salvation.

SECULAR PLEASURES

Fifteenth-century art was dominated by the culture of courts: the Sforza in Milan, the d'Este in Ferrara, the Gonzaga in Mantua, the Montefeltro in Urbino, the Medici in Florence and – most admired of all – the court of Philip the Good of Burgundy in the Netherlands. Their most prestigious monuments were their palaces. Michelozzo's Palazzo Medici-Riccardi in Florence (plate 12), begun for Cosimo de' Medici in 1444, combining an elegantly classical interior loggia with a massive exterior monumentality, set the pattern for all Florentine palaces of the Quattrocento, and established the Italian town *palazzo* as the largest and socially most important type of town house in Europe. By comparison all town houses north of the Alps, even Jacques Coeur's palace in Bourges (1443–51), seem meretricious and uncoordinated. Behind their intimidating and defendable façades, the household acquired a secular decoration attuned to the decorum of public and private life. The main rooms, decorated with costly and fashionable Netherlandish tapestries, and with large fresco and panel paintings whose flat and decorative style clearly sought to imitate them, displayed a rapidly enlarging range of secular subjects: the rural diversions of courtly life (the hunt, the Labours of the Month), the adventures of classical heroes (the duke of Burgundy's castle at Hesdin, with its painted history of the Golden Fleece, was enlivened by a 'machinerie' that imitated the lightning, thunder and rain called up by Medea) and – no doubt inspired by Petrarch's *Trionfi* – themes of triumph and victory, with a strong patriotic message. Paolo Uccello's three large panels of the *Battle of San Romano*, painted for the Medici palace in the 1450s – their busy surface patterns blending impressively with the Medici's prized tapestry of the duke of Burgundy hunting, which was kept in the same room – celebrated the Florentines' victory over the Sienese. Such displays of civic virtue relate the allegorical cycles of the fifteenth-century palace to the edifying personifications of justice and good government in contemporary town halls (e.g. Rogier van der Weyden's lost figures of Justice in the Brussels town hall, 1439–49). The elaborate furnishings of these Florentine rooms – the beds, the *deschi da parto* (ceremonial birth plates) and particularly the *cassoni* (marriage chests) (plate 13) – displayed a variety of classical and devotional themes. The outer surfaces of the *cassoni* often showed moralising classical narratives, while the inner face of the back panel (*spalliera*) – for example the exhausted, post-coital Mars in Botticelli's

Venus and Mars (London, National Gallery, *c.* 1485) – indulged in erotic references, part lewd joke, part lucky charm.

From the public spaces of the *camera* the humanist prince (or princess) could retreat to the privacy of the *studiolo*, a study, a picture gallery, and a treasury of *objets d'art*. In his palace at Urbino (1476) – a building whose mathematical clarity and restrained elegance so charmed Baldassare Castiglione that he used it as a setting for *The Courtier* – Duke Federigo da Montefeltro created a *studiolo* as evocatively personal as his laudatory biography in Vespasiano da Bisticci's *Lives* (plate 14). Lined with trompe l'œil intarsia panelling (representing fictive cupboards with the duke's books, armour and musical instruments), crowned originally with enthroned figures of the liberal arts, and containing a portrait of the seated duke armoured but reading, Federigo presents himself as both successful soldier and enlightened patron, in a setting that recalls the pleasures of connoisseurship, and evokes – in the scientific perspectives of the intarsia – the orderly discipline of the intellectual life.

Such *studioli* – replete with the bric-a-brac of coins, gems, and *objets trouvés* that clutter the backgrounds of Quattrocento images of scholar saints in their studies (e.g. Botticelli's *The Vision of Saint Augustine*, Ognissanti church, Florence, *c.* 1480) – usually contained prized bronze figurines, an antique genre revived in the middle of the century by Antico and Antonio del Pollaiuolo, and the epitome of a secular, and frankly hedonistic, taste. The muscular energy of Pollaiuolo's *Hercules* bronzes (*c.* 1470s) (plate 15) or the witty contortions of Riccio's nudes and animals transformed into bronze table lamps have little meaning beyond their technical brilliance. They exhibit a quality prized throughout fifteenth-century Europe: conspicuous skill, a mixture of *facilità* (fluency of technique) and *difficoltà* (making the difficult look easy). This sharpened awareness of artistic individuality is expressed in the growing premium put on artistic skill over the artist's raw materials (a fact which may explain the migration of trained goldsmiths, like Brunelleschi, Pollaiuolo, Botticelli and Ghirlandaio, to painting and architecture); it underlies the common practice of paying an artist for both materials and skill, and the insistence in contracts on the direct participation of the master rather than his journeyman; it may also explain the popularity of the new medium of engraving, which, in the hands of Pollaiuolo, Mantegna and especially Dürer, could demonstrate artistic virtuosity (made more conspicuous by prominent signatures) to a mass audience. But its principal impact is registered in the single most striking change in the appearance of Quattrocento painting: the rejection of the 'materialist' gold backgrounds of medieval art in favour of aerial and linear perspectives. Alberti recommended that any remaining gold or precious objects within the picture should be painted 'with plain colours', thus bringing the craftsman 'more admiration and praise'. Skill could triumph not only over materials but also over subject matter. In her negotiations in 1502 with Giovanni Bellini over the delivery and subject matter of a 'Nativity', Isabella d'Este was concerned less with the proprieties of subject matter than with the fact that the *istoria* came from Bellini himself.

SACRED IMAGERY

This cultivation of purely aesthetic values and interests, allied to a proliferation of new kinds of secular art in northern Europe and Italy, cannot obscure the fact that fifteenth-century art remained predominantly religious. To the ortho-dox definition of the threefold purpose of religious images – as instructions for the illiterate, as aids to memorising scripture and sacred history and as stimuli to meditation – the urban mysticism of the fifteenth century, ultimately Franciscan and Dominican in inspiration, added its own emphasis on visualisa-tion. Seeing, so closely associated with believing, had its own sacramental value. The institution of the feast of Corpus Christi placed an emphasis on lay visual participation with the consecrated host that led directly to new types of eucharistic display, such as the elaborate metalwork monstrance, and the spec-tacular sacrament house, which appeared in Germany and the Netherlands in the form of a monumental Gothic pinnacle (St Lorenz, Nuremberg, 1493–6) (plate 1). The sermon and the illustrated devotional handbook, the main-springs of fifteenth-century piety, instructed meditation as visualisation, and left their traces in religious imagery. The varied emotions experienced by the Virgin at the Annunciation were laid out by the preachers as successive spiritual and mental conditions, simultaneously re-experienced in the pious imagina-tion, and registered in the repertory of gesture and feeling found in numerous Quattrocento Annunciations, particularly those of Fra Angelico (*c.* 1387–1455), the only Italian artist of the century to be singled out by both Vasari and Landino for his *devoto*. The Italian *Garden of Prayer* recommends its readers to set the events of the Passion in their own city, and enact them imagi-natively with actors of their own acquaintance – an injunction rarely followed in Italian painting, which provided only a generalised framework within which the viewer could supply his own detail and action, but much more literally obeyed in the north, where Netherlandish artists (notably Robert Campin and his workshop) introduced a new type of Virgin and Child image, placed in an upper-middle-class domestic interior, and where Konrad Witz set his *Miraculous Draught of Fishes* (Geneva, 1444) on his own lake of Geneva (plate 16).

The private and sentimental character of this piety corresponds to the pro-liferation of small devotional works of art for private use in home or chapel, usually depicting the Virgin or the sufferings of Christ: mass-produced crucifixes, the Man of Sorrows, diptychs of the suffering Virgin and Christ crowned with thorns, St Veronica's *sudarium*, small panel paintings with prayers on their shutters (the counterparts to the fashionable illuminated Book of Hours), and in Florence Madonna images mass-produced by specialist *madonnieri* (as Vasari snootily called them), the most charming and humane in cheap white-glazed terracotta by the della Robbia family. At the opposite end of this devotional continuum stood the altar retable, the supreme focus of religious emotion and communal identity. The van Eycks' Ghent altarpiece (whose monumentality belies the notion that Flemish art is miniature) effectively translated the format, the scale and the theological universality of the Gothic cathedral portal into the interior of the church, and enlivened its narratives by a new, persuasive naturalism. But it was in southern Germany, in the last quarter of the century, at a time when Germany gained its international reputation for what Agrippa of Nettesheim called 'its piety and its craftsmen', that the altar retable acquired its most expansive form. Composed of a large central *corpus* with sculpted figures, flanked by painted or sculpted wings, and crowned by a high superstructure of Gothic tracery – the whole carved in easily worked limewood (though often gilded and painted with an hallucinatory brilliance) – the German altar-piece brought together all the technical and aesthetic possibilities of micro-architecture, sculpture and painting in a majestic *Gesamtkunstwerk* unprecedented in Europe since the High Gothic cathedral. Almost all were commissioned by a small, wealthy urban patriciate, or by clerics from the same patrician background. The largest of them, like Veit Stoss's giant for St Mary's in Cracow (1477–89) (plate 17), were high altars that proclaimed the identity of the whole community; smaller commissions decorated the chantry chapels of religious confraternities. Their arrays of saints, presented in the intimate and familiar style of a *sacra conversazione*, and each invoked as a specialist protector and prophylactic, voiced the intense need of individual laymen and their confraternities for spiritual insurance. The popular success of these giant prayer machines laid them open to charges of ostentation and idolatry. For radical reformers like Zwingli, Sebastian Franke or Savonarola, fifteenth-century religion had become so implicated in imagery that reform also entailed destruction.

NATURE INTO ART

Alberti's scientific and rational conception of nature did not prevent patrons and artists in later Quattrocento Italy from admiring paintings for their more obvious charms of naturalism, pleasing design and skill. Landino, after all, had praised Masaccio as 'a good imitator of nature', and when a knowledge of the prestigious Flemish 'ad olio' technique began to reach Ferrara and Venice in the middle of the century it was eagerly adopted by northern Italian painters like Cosimo Tura (before 1431–95) and Antonella da Messina (d. 1479), and, later, by Florentine artists such as Antonio del Pollaiuolo (*c.* 1432–91), both as a direct and rapid method of working, and as a technique which could transform the opacity of fresco and tempera – the equivalent of painted sculpture – into real textures, reflective surfaces and effects of landscape distance unprecedented in the art of Masaccio and his contemporaries. And in Giovanni Bellini (*c.* 1427–1516), the greatest Venetian painter of his day, 'still the supreme master' as Dürer called him in 1506, the perspectival rigour and sculptural *rilievo* of Masaccio was combined with Netherlandish oil technique to elevate light – a colour-saturated light as translucent and vibrant as Venetian glassware – to the primary and immanent element of all creation (plate 18).

Bellini's empathetic and poetic response to nature stands in marked contrast to Alberti's search for the laws of mathematical harmony that structure the world and our perception of it. All three of his treatises centre round problems of optics, mathematics and perspective. *De pictura* was the first proper formulation of Brunelleschi's single-point perspective. *De statua* tested the Polyklitan and Vitruvian proportions of the human body against empirical observation and created a new scientific canon of proportion – a canon extended by Dürer and Leonardo, and given scientific, anatomical depth by the first artists' dissections of corpses by Michelangelo and Leonardo in the early sixteenth century. In turn, Pollaiuolo's various renderings of the *Labours of Hercules* (plate 15) amount to a manifesto of his ambition to become, in Leonardo's words, 'an anatomical painter', for they achieved a new level of naturalism in the depiction of the male nude body in varieties of violent action. *De re aedificatoria* centred around the proper ordering of city life, in terms of functional decorum, and of mathematical beauty, for (borrowing Protagoras) man is the mean and measure of all things, and (borrowing Vitruvius) the proportions of the human body can be best identified in buildings and parts of buildings. Alberti's neo-Stoic aesthetics merged with a neoplatonic cosmology which saw human proportion as a microcosm of the musical and heavenly harmonies which order all creation. The observation of the Franciscan mathematician, Luca Pacioli, friend of Piero della Francesca in Urbino and Leonardo in Milan, that the human body 'contained all the ratios by which God reveals the innermost secrets of nature', is the counterpart of Vitruvius's diagram (drawn by Francesco di Giorgio and by Leonardo) of a man with extended arms and legs placed in a square or circle. The geometric lucidity of much Quattrocento church architecture (from Alberti's unfinished Tempio Malatestiano in Rimini to Leonardo's drawings of centralised churches), and particularly its emphasis on the dome and the circle, crystallises this cosmic–corporeal harmony. In contrast to the real, medieval, untidiness of most Quattrocento cities, the ideal townscapes painted at Urbino for Federigo da Montefeltro, with their rigorous perspectives and perfectly proportioned façades, remain the purest reflections of Alberti's ideal of civic–cosmic order (plate 19).

Piero della Francesca (*c.* 1420–90), who worked for some time in Urbino, distilled this clear and dignified world into figural art. For Piero, mathematics offered the key to understanding much of what the later Quattrocento meant by 'nature'. His textbook, *De abaco*, provided merchants with a mundane tool for the calculation of cubic capacity. His treatise on perspective, *De prospectiva pingendi*, offered mathematicians (like his pupil Pacioli) the most theoretically precise definition of spatial projection. And for artists, that treatise underlined the specifically mathematical value of *commensuratione* (the proportional relations of figures in space according to perspectival rules) as a central skill in painting. But in the last resort, the 'truth' of painting, for Piero and for most of his contemporaries, went beyond mathematical exactitude. In his understated colour harmonies, and his solemnly natural figures – all enveloped in a crystalline daylight – mathematics is subsumed into the symbolic, the epic and even the rustic (plate 20).

Leonardo da Vinci's (1452–1519) single-minded identification of art with knowledge – demanding from the artist both an encyclopaedic grasp of nature and a mastery of the theoretical rules for its proper representation – extended Piero's investigations into a complete cosmology. Overstepping the traditional boundaries between the various arts and the scientific disciplines, Leonardo's art (particularly his drawing, which he elevated into a new tool of research) became at once the instrument of knowledge and the summit of all theory: 'Painting . . . compels the mind of the painter to transform itself into the mind of nature itself and to translate between nature and art, setting out, with nature, the causes of nature's phenomena regulated by nature's laws.' The consequences of this obsession with process and impersonal principle are evident in Leonardo's output. Because intellectual mastery far outweighed technical realisation, the work of art often remained unfinished once its theoretical (essential) problems were solved. And as the artist uncovered nature's secrets, so he came closer to the mind of God himself. Alberti had already called the artist *alter deus*. Dürer characterised artistic activity as 'creating just as God did', and in 1500 – in a spirit that hovered between self-glorification and the *Imitatio Christi* – he painted a self-portrait in the startlingly frontal and hieratic pose reserved for kings and for Christ (Munich, Alte Pinakothek). Leonardo elevated the painter to 'signor e dio'. In this deification of the artist lay the germ of the post-Romantic worship of artistic genius. What separated Leonardo from his contemporaries was his denial of the didactic value of history, and particularly of Antiquity, at the very moment when Botticelli and the young Michelangelo were reappraising the lessons of the Tuscan and antique past for the creation of a new culture. Against Leonardo's Aristotelian fascination with the multiplicity of creation must be placed the neoplatonic belief – shared by many Florentine artists of Lorenzo the Magnificent's circle in the final decades of the century – in the powers of artistic *invenzione*, and in the kinship, not between art and science, but between artist and poet.

ANTIQUITY

In reality, humanists saw no dichotomy between Antiquity and Nature. For Alberti, as much as for Leonardo Bruni or Machiavelli, Antiquity offered dynamic *exempla* not just for imitation, but for the understanding of physical and human nature – particularly its more complex and elusive aspects. Behind the fantastic monsters and quasi-vegetal ornaments that overload the backgrounds of many late Quattrocento paintings (e.g. Filippino Lippi's *Expulsion of the Dragon* in the Strozzi chapel of S. Maria Novella in Florence, finished 1502) lies the grotesque, late Antique style of wall decoration unearthed in the 1480s by the excavations in the Domus Aurea, the Colosseum and Hadrian's Villa. Behind the increasing interest shown by late fifteenth-century artists in emotional characterisation, evident principally in an intensification of movement, of hair, drapery and gesture, lies not only the highly charged emotionalism of Flemish painting, but the antique 'pathos formula' (as Warburg called it) of Dionysiac ecstasy and pain. Andrea del Castagno's *David* (Washington, National Gallery, *c.* 1450) is a transfigured Niobe; the harsh pathos of Donatello's last works, with their Maenad-like gestures of grief, and their Dionysiac putti, convert the classical rhetoric of orgiastic release into a language of profound Christian emotion (plate 21).

Such transformations raised problems of decorum, what Leonardo defined as 'the suitability of action, clothing, and situation'. Ghirlandaio's use of figures with fluttering drapery seems confined to girls of lower social status. Social superiority was evidently expressed in dignified and barely perceptible movement. Similarly, the charade mood of many Quattrocento depictions of classical themes, particularly in *cassoni* and *deschi da parte*, where classical history is enacted in contemporary costume, attracted a number of fifteenth-century critics, among them Filarete, who argued that 'figures of Caesar or Hannibal ... should be done according to their quality and their nature'. To fashion a new antique style for classical subject matter was the principal achievement of Andrea Mantegna (1431–1506), whose upbringing among the flourishing humanists of Padua University gave a profoundly antiquarian flavour to every aspect of his art. His heroic evocations of the *gravitas* of Rome, particularly evident in his cycle of *The Life of St James* in the lost Eremitani in Padua (*c.* 1450) (plate 22), display a scholarly knowledge of Roman architecture, armour and epigraphy, and a special sensitivity to Roman sculpture, not only in the rendering of sculptural detail, but in a pervasive stoniness of texture (already noted by Vasari) which gives to all his objects, animate as well as inanimate, the appearance of the hardest Roman marble. Similarly, his painted simulations of ancient relief sculpture in stone or gilt bronze (London, National Gallery, *c.* 1490) imply a knowledge of antique cameos and precious stones which he may have seen in Isabella d'Este's *studiolo*. The ambience of connoisseurship also colours his highly finished drawings and his engravings, both bought as collector's items, the latter securing his position as one of the most influential artists in Europe.

Mantegna's creation of a classicising style corresponded to a growing interest in large-scale depictions of pagan subjects, usually classical mythologies, in the last decades of the century. The first such cycle, Pollaiuolo's lost *Labours of Hercules* (begun *c.* 1460) for the Palazzo Medici, identified the Medici family with the virtues of the Florentine Republic and its classical guardian, Hercules Florentinus. But many of the surviving paintings, notably Botticelli's *Birth of Venus* and *Primavera* (plate 23) (Florence, Uffizi, both *c.* 1480), evoke an obscure cluster of erotic, philosophical and poetic associations. Both paintings were made for the young Pierfrancesco Medici, perhaps for his wedding in 1482; both were conceived as decorations for private apartments and – particularly the *Primavera* – as inexpensive substitutes for tapestries. Like Mantegna's *Parnassus* (Paris, Louvre, *c.* 1500) they combined the charms of 'soft-core *all' antica* erotica' with more serious and uplifting meanings. Any attempt to disentangle their layers of association will never be wholly successful, since ambiguity is essential to their purpose. There can be little doubt that the compiler of their 'programmes' – as distinct from Botticelli himself – had in mind Poliziano's *Giostra* (1476–8), and various classical *ekphrases* of Aphrodite, and that he sought to translate this sexually erotic mythology into a moral allegory of Christian *caritas* through references to the chivalrous love poetry of Provence, of the German Minnesinger and of Dante's *dolce stil nuovo*. Equally decisive may have been the influence of the circle of Florentine neoplatonists, led by Pierfrancesco's spiritual mentor, Marsilio Ficino. Ficino's famous letter to Pierfrancesco in 1478, on the power of Venus to convey the highest virtues of humanity, is couched in the form of a horoscope, and typifies a deep preoccupation in Quattrocento Italy with astrology as a medium of cosmic order and a direct channel of divine intervention in human affairs. Hence the resurrection of the ancient Gods in much secular Renaissance art – in the conventional (medieval) form of zodiacal calendars; in diagrams of the human body as microcosm; in extended cycles of mythological divinities (chapel of the Palazzo Pubblico in Siena); in astrological ceilings (Old Sacristy, S. Lorenzo, Florence); and finally in complete astrological systems (Cosimo Tura's and Francesco Cossa's frescoes in the Palazzo Schifanoia in Ferrara). To Ficino,

Botticelli's Venuses, like amulets, had the power to charm and uplift, to initiate her devotees in the virtues of culture and refinement. In his neo-platonic belief in the fusion of heaven and earth, Venus represented both *amor divinus* and *amor humanus*, two poles that defined the endless struggle between man's lower and higher nature. Pierfrancesco may not have been aware of all the implications of these meanings, but his teachers were; and to open up secular painting of this kind to such elevated associations is consciously to equate it with the functions of religious art. Like sacred imagery, the power of this new mythological genre lay in its rich obscurities, in its veils of metaphor and symbol, which both reveal and conceal the highest truths. To retrace this maze of meaning was, for the humanist, a mark of the initiate, a matching exercise in *difficoltà*. For us, however, the charm of these poignant evocations of a lost Antiquity may lie less in their intellectual sophistications than in the poetic *invenzione* which gave them life.

CHAPTER 16

MUSIC

Gareth Curtis

ALL the evidence we have decrees that music permeated every walk of fifteenth-century life, from popular and aristocratic entertainment to religious
and civic ritual. The range of types involved must have been formidable – vernacular music reflecting the activities and preoccupations of the common
people, including also music for popular religious worship and popular drama;
the 'official' music of the Church, especially the unaccompanied plainchant
melodies supposedly hallowed by the pen of Pope Gregory the Great, and
passed down through subsequent generations; music for all manner of festive
occasions, ranging from the most functional of fanfares to the specially
commissioned major work; music for the fifteenth-century nobleman, often
designed less to help him while away the hours than to demonstrate the splendour of his establishment, the refinement of his taste and the personal piety
with which he lavished resources on his chapel. Music was sung or performed
on instruments, executed by individuals or groups, played by ear, improvised or
read from notation; as a branch of the *quadrivium*, it even became a cerebral
pursuit, in which sound might give way entirely to philosophical and
mathematical speculation.

Yet translating such an overview into tangible repertories which can be
explored and characterised can be a problematic, even an impossible, task. This
is not merely a matter of the loss of sources. First, it is clear that then, as now,
the bulk of the material, as ephemeral as the situations which prompted it, was
not considered worth preserving. Doubtless, in its widest sense, musical
entertainment probably took in not only singers and instrumentalists, but 'oral
poets and tellers of tales (often to a musical accompaniment), fools, jugglers,
acrobats and dancers; actors, mimes and mimics; conjurors, puppeteers and
exhibitors of performing animals'.[1] Second, a wide range of music had little or
no written tradition; that of the common people is an obvious but by no means

---

[1] Southworth (1989), p. 3; though specifically about minstrelsy in England, much of the material is
broadly applicable.

the only case. Third, and more subtly, much music depended so overwhelmingly on the individualism of the performer and the moment of performance that it was unnecessary to write it out. Indeed, to have done so would have lent false authority to a single version of something which was by nature semi-improvised, and was thus created anew on each occasion. Clearly, one would expect this to have been true in the cases of dance music and the singing of narrative poetry. In practice, however, it is likely to have applied to the entire range of activities which lay within the province of this kind of professional performer, the minstrel.

In practice, the minstrel's position was not specially enviable. For the most part, pay and social status were low, though it appears that certain categories were more highly regarded than others – trumpeters tended to be near the top of the hierarchy, for example, presumably because they made a vital contribution to more formal occasions. That said, and ephemeral as minstrel music essentially was, we should not assume that it or those who performed it could never achieve any distinction. Indeed, whether residents or itinerants who were just expected to attend on ceremonial occasions, those minstrels who were fortunate enough to acquire court employment might achieve considerable personal reputation. Thus, in a familiar passage from *Le champion des dames* (*c.* 1440), Martin le Franc refers to a pair of blind performers at the Burgundian court whose gifts were such that Guillaume Dufay (1397?–1474) and Gilles Binchois (*c.* 1400–60), two of the most eminent composers of the day, were said to have been struck with shame and envy.[2] Again, itinerants with court connections could command superior wages as they travelled the circuit around civic festivities and the homes of likely patrons; there was always the possibility of generous additional gifts both for them and for their colleagues who remained at court throughout the year.[3]

Though of some historical interest, it is potentially misleading and possibly just poetic licence that Martin le Franc should have chosen to compare minstrels with the two best-known Franco-Flemish composers of the day. In practice, the minstrel and the 'clerk' musician (one who was trained to read and, in some cases, to write music) occupied quite different places in fifteenth-century musical life – and, indeed, quite different social strata. Specifically, the clerk musician had little to do with the ephemeral world of the minstrel, but sang music which, for the most part, was composed in the sense of actually being written out. In general, he was one of a team of singers, and therefore unlikely

[2] Widely quoted in music histories; see Fallows (1987b), pp. 205–8, for additional critical commentary.

[3] It is a curious paradox that, despite his lowly status in practice, the minstrel might also be seen as part of a tradition whose highest exponents were King David and the angels – see the article 'Menestral' in Carter (1961). For further information and bibliography on minstrelsy in general, see the article 'Minstrel' in *New Grove* (1980).

to come under the spotlight as an individual performer. Furthermore, although he might happen to sing and write secular songs, his official duties were usually those of a chaplain; hence he belonged to a cathedral or other such establishment, or to a court chapel.[4]

No doubt much well-crafted entertainment flowed from the activities of the high-class minstrel; however, it was the clerk musician whose repertory was such that it had to be written down. Yet, in attempting to enter his world, we must realise that music was rarely copied for its own sake; there was normally a very particular reason for doing so. This was not necessarily, as one might assume, because it had the status of art in the sense that a given piece was regarded as an object of aesthetic contemplation – though, as we shall see later, this was a concept not entirely alien to the fifteenth century.[5] Rather, it was far more likely to be its function which demanded its preservation. As the Catholic liturgy had developed and, over the centuries, spread across much of Europe, so it had become virtually inseparable from the plainchant to which it was sung. Consequently, texts and their associated music gained an almost scriptural authority, and were therefore necessarily copied throughout the considerable sphere of influence of the Roman Church. In practice, therefore, much of this repertory became remarkably international, despite numerous local melodic variants and more extensive variations deriving from regional liturgical uses. This plainchant was, of course, the essential written-out repertory of the clerk musician.

The varying degrees to which liturgy might be overlaid by music and ritual action remind us that plainchant was not merely functional, but in a crucial sense decorative, too. So, for example, while prayers and readings tended merely to be intoned (i.e. sung mainly on a single note but with a short recurring melodic formula at the beginning and end of each phrase), other parts of the text were sung in a less austere and more distinctively melodic manner. It is also clear that the grander liturgical occasions were reflected in a more highly decorated melodic style: hence, on the greatest feast days, specially florid chants were sung in order to signal and celebrate the solemnity of the occasion.

This general principle, that level of adornment reflects importance of occa-

---

[4] The fact that a clerk musician was viewed as a singer does not preclude the possibility that he also played instruments, which raises the difficult matter of whether the type of music he performed involved instruments or not. Until the late 1970s, it was widely assumed that it did – or at least that the secular repertory did. At present, however, the general consensus is that instruments were at the very least unnecessary for accompanying songs, and that in sacred music they were positively undesirable, especially in the Mass – which is not, of course, to say that they were never used. Perhaps the safest position is that instruments were mainly the province of the minstrel, even if they could hardly have been exclusively so. The one significant exception is the organ, for which a small written repertory survives, consisting mainly of arrangements of polyphonic music.

[5] See below, pp. 327–8.

sion, provides a significant clue as to why sacred texts came to be set to polyphony, that is, music in independent vocal parts, the repertory which we most readily associate with the clerk musician. Simply, polyphony was a possible further layer of decoration which might be plain, even austere, or quite the opposite. Thus, at the most basic level, the polyphonic setting of a given text might be little more than simple harmonisation of its normal plainsong; indeed, large numbers of such settings survive in fifteenth-century sources, in particular of texts from the Office and the Proper of the Mass.[6] At the other end of the spectrum, a piece of polyphony might draw on all the ingenuity at its composer's disposal and, of course, require considerable reading and technical skills on the part of the performers.[7]

Here, of course, we are talking about the highest endeavours of the clerk musician, which presents a convenient opportunity to examine some of the more conspicuous features of his compositional activities. What is particularly striking about the most ambitious music of the earlier part of the fifteenth century is that it seems to have been normal practice to begin with the construction of a ground plan which then served as the framework upon which the composer hung the text and built the details of the polyphony. So, for example, in the isorhythmic motet, a genre which largely originated in the fourteenth and continued in use until the mid-fifteenth century, the composer's musical starting-point was a piece of plainchant, upon which he imposed a repeating rhythmic pattern, and which he placed in a foundation voice called the tenor.[8] Above and possibly below this tenor, he successively added further vocal parts, which might also involve a degree of rhythmic predetermination; also, different sections might constitute melodic variants of each other (isomelism), and succeeding repeats of the underlying plainchant might be presented in progressively shorter note-values (half-length, third-length, etc.), giving an impression of gathering momentum. Very commonly, as a further layer of complexity, some of these melodic lines carried different texts, either on the same subject, or with one commenting on the other.[9] Such additional elaboration was a matter of choice and local tradition; however, it was a conspicuous and universal feature of the genre that a complex edifice

---

[6] There is also ample evidence that singers were trained to improvise in this manner – see, for example, the article 'Faburden' in *New Grove* (1980).

[7] Traditionally, it has been polyphony which has attracted most attention from musicologists, and a substantial amount of the repertory is available in modern editions. Those in print by the late 1970s (together with extensive bibliographies) can be traced through composer articles in *New Grove* (1980). Those wishing to go beyond the select bibliography provided here can supplement it from recent histories like Strohm (1993).   [8] Cf. Latin *tenere* = to hold.

[9] All these characteristics are exhibited, at least to some degree, in the most widely copied isorhythmic motet of the fifteenth century, *Veni sancte spiritus/Veni creator* by John Dunstable (*c.* 1390–1453). This and his other works are published in *Musica Britannica*, VIII.

should have been built by successively superimposing further independent melodic lines over an initial foundation voice part. By contrast, most later music was created more as a series of events spaced in time.

During the 1430s and 1440s, the traditionally rather learned and esoteric iso-rhythmic motet was eclipsed as most prestigious genre by the so-called cyclic Mass, grouped settings of texts from the Ordinary of the Mass (generally the *Kyrie, Gloria, Credo, Sanctus* and *Agnus Dei*). At first, one of the most common compositional procedures here was to start by arranging a given segment of plainsong (usually extracted from the Office) over a preordained plan which was more or less reproduced across the five movements. As with the isorhythmic motet, the remaining vocal parts were then composed upon this foundation.[10]

Such music was, of course, heavily dependent on compositional decisions made at the beginning of the creative process; certainly, by the time a piece of chant had been selected for an isorhythmic motet and the chosen rhythmic pattern applied to it, the overall structure and much of the musical detail had been largely predetermined. That creative process therefore became one of progressive elaboration of what might be quite a rigorous architectural scheme; indeed, within some traditions, it was even acceptable for the under-lying musical structure to run counter to that of the words. It was, for example, commonplace in the English Mass repertory for the tripartite *Kyrie* text to be divided across two musical sections simply because a ground plan of two roughly equal segments had become a conventional part of the tradition.

That said, from early in the century, there had also run, in parallel, a tradition of smaller-scale settings, commonly of extra-liturgical votive texts, where the form of the words seemed to drive that of the music rather than vice versa. Presumably, these must have begun as a more modest part of the clerk musi-cian's trade. However, by the mid-century, the predominant trend was for this more text-oriented approach to be adopted also into more prestigious genres and, by the late Masses of Dufay[11] and other similar works from the 1450s onwards, it had become normal for the form of the words to determine the shape of the musical foundation.[12]

---

[10] This applies, for example, to the first English Mass cycles, such as those by John Dunstable and Leonel Power (*c.* 1380–1445), which probably date back to the late 1420s or early to mid-1430s. By the middle of the century, material from a motet or secular song might be used as the basis for a Mass cycle rather than a piece of chant, though this remained a predominantly continental feature.

[11] For example, the Masses *Ecce ancilla Domini* and *Ave regina celorum*. These and the remainder of Dufay's large surviving output are published as *Corpus mensurabilis musicae*, I.

[12] This was particularly obvious in a growing tradition of Mass settings in which the composer deliber-ately cultivated complex technical devices – see, for example, the many Masses from the last third of the fifteenth century based on the song *L'homme armé*, in which composers seem to have vied with each other in search of ever greater ingenuity; also the extraordinary contrivances explored by Johannes Ockeghem (*c.* 1410–97), for example in the *Missa prolationum*.

The smaller-scale music also tended to be composed rather differently, with simpler vocal parts conceived together rather than as successively super-imposed layers. Indeed, as the fifteenth century continued, the trend ran steadily towards this new simultaneously composed style, even in increasingly complex polyphony. Certainly, by the end of the century, the layered manner of composition was rapidly becoming obsolete in favour of a style in which a given piece was divided into sub-sections, each of which was built from a short, pithy musical idea which was passed around the voices in imitation. With this came a distinct move towards the 'series of events spaced in time' men-tioned above, the potential for varying tension from one moment to the next, and therefore the possibility of more obvious expressiveness. Even in the early part of the century, it is instructive to compare the rather inscrutable world of the isorhythmic motet and the early Mass cycle with the more communicative manner of smaller-scale music of the time.[13] Though many composers remained equivocal over 'expressing the sense of the words', there was an unmistakable general move towards a more deliberately eloquent type of text-setting, especially in the last third of the fifteenth century. Perhaps the most notable products of this trend were the later motets of Josquin Desprez (c. 1440–1521), in which the composer not only shows an impressive ability to match musical type to text, but also cultivates a clarity of word declamation which was taken as the ideal for sixteenth-century sacred polyphony.

By now, it will be clear that complex polyphonic sacred music was far from essential to the liturgy – indeed, most people would never have heard anything other than chant or the most basic polyphony unless they had contact with a large church or cathedral or with the court of a prince or other nobleman. Rather, the driving force leading to the establishment of a group of clerk musi-cians competent to sing complex polyphony and the provision of music for such a group was only likely to come from ecclesiastical, royal or other kind of aristocratic patronage; indeed, the quality of a person's household chapel was an important indication of his status.[14] Accordingly, some noblemen went to considerable lengths to attract high-quality musicians to their courts. Thus, among the best employed by Philip the Good of Burgundy were Binchois and the Englishman Robert Morton (c. 1430–after 1472); while his son retained an

---

[13] Ironically, as the Marian antiphon grew in consequence in England, so it tended to return to the older method of composing. Indeed, in contrast to what happened on the continental mainland, the most ambitious English music (that of the Eton Choirbook, for example – see below) moved towards superimposing an ever greater number of vocal parts (commonly six rather than the previous three or four) which had become progressively more florid. Incidentally, this extension of old-fashioned practices rather than development of new ones explains the rapidly waning influence of English music in the second half of the fifteenth century.

[14] Doubtless this is one of various explanations for the unmistakable trend in the fifteenth century from polyphony sung by three or four soloists towards the use of a small chorus.

excellent chapel first as count of Charolais and then as duke of Burgundy, with Antoine Busnois (*c.* 1430–92) as his most distinguished resident composer. Remarkable, too, were the Sforza court in Milan during the 1470s, which boasted not only Josquin, but also significant lesser figures like Gaspar van Weerbeke (*c.* 1440–1518), Johannes Martini (*c.* 1440–97 or 1498), Loyset Compère (*c.* 1445–1518) and Alexander Agricola (*c.* 1446–1506); and the d'Este court in Ferrara which at various times employed Josquin, Martini and Jacob Obrecht (*c.* 1450–1505). During times when the Papacy was not under political pressure and the pope was interested in music, the papal chapel also attracted important musicians, most of them Franco-Flemish. Dufay, Jean Pullois (d. 1478) and Josquin each spent several years in the papal chapel. In England, the best composers were traditionally drawn to the Chapel Royal or to the chapel of some royal personage close to the monarch.

In the circumstances, one would expect many of the clerk musician's most impressive pieces to have been written for important state, even internationally significant, occasions. So, for example, Dufay's isorhythmic motets *Supremum est mortalibus bonum* and *Nuper rosarum flores* celebrated respectively King Sigismund's entry into Rome in May 1433 and the dedication of Florence cathedral in 1436, while his Mass *Ave regina celorum* was probably composed for the dedication of Cambrai cathedral in 1472.[15] The texts of the motets were often distinctly topical, even polemical on occasions, and celebratory work might involve more or less transparent compliments to the parties involved. Josquin, for instance, based his Mass *Hercule Dux Ferrarie* on a musically encrypted version of the name Ercole d'Este. It is also clear, however, that an appreciable amount of sacred music was written to provide repertory for the various choral foundations which, though endowed by noble or ecclesiastical patrons, remained largely independent of the courts. These establishments were a particularly common feature in England, and usually – as, for example, with Oxford and Cambridge colleges founded at the time – had educational extensions. Although nowadays regarded as primarily educational institutions, the original foundations of such colleges and some schools (Eton College, for example) were often more concerned that sacred polyphonic music should be performed, commonly votive antiphons in honour of the Virgin Mary.[16]

Though polyphonic sacred music remained the exception rather than the norm during the fifteenth century, and almost exclusively the province of the nobility and of the richest churches and foundations, its use clearly underwent an exponential increase. Thus the needs of different religious and secular

[15] Fallows (1987a), pp. 34, 45 and 79.
[16] For an extended survey of choral establishments in England, see Harrison (1963), especially chs. I and IV, and Bowers (1975a). The only surviving collection of such pieces is the Eton Choirbook (Eton College MS 178), whose contents are published as *Musica Britannica*, X–XII.

establishments for repertory must have provided increasing stimulus to a market in music. In some cases, it may have been possible to meet this demand locally: so, for example, the two largest English manuscripts of mainly fifteenth-century music, the Old Hall Manuscript and the Eton Choirbook, contain works by what may be rather narrow circles of composers.[17] Often, however, establishments must have looked further afield to supplement local repertory, and here it seems likely that transmission involved a variety of processes.

Doubtless, music was often passed on through various types of direct contact. So, for example, a group of five English Mass settings appear in a Burgundian manuscript dating from about the time of the marriage of Charles the Bold and Margaret of York in 1468.[18] Whether or not actual copies of these works arrived with Margaret of York's entourage is hardly the point: the fact is that cultural contact between the English and Burgundian courts was such that music could flow from the former to the latter, and there must have been countless similar circumstances in which cultural artefacts could be transmitted.[19] In some cases, direct contact might even be between composers. It seems likely, for example, that Ockeghem, first chaplain to the French king and foremost composer at that court, passed on music, presumably including some of his own, to Cambrai cathedral when he twice visited Dufay in the early 1460s.[20]

Precise details of how and why music was transmitted from place to place is all too rarely available. As to the mechanics of the process, it is likely that music was passed around in so-called fascicle manuscripts, individual or small connected groups of unbound gatherings containing one or two substantial works or a handful of smaller pieces.[21] These fascicles were then either bound into larger volumes, or their contents copied into larger collections. There is also evidence, particularly in the Low Countries and from the last years of the century, of manuscript workshops;[22] these seem to have fulfilled commissions, either using repertory specified by whoever was responsible for the commission, or else drawing on whatever stock of appropriate music was available.

---

[17] Certainly, their contents are almost exclusively English, the only exceptions being a handful of French pieces in the Old Hall MS (London, BL, Add. MS 57950); for the Old Hall music, see *Corpus mensurabilis musicae*, XLVI.

[18] Brussels, Bibliothèque Royale Albert 1er, MS 5557; the works are published in *Early English church music*, XXXIV. For a wider picture of political and cultural contact which took place at this time between the English and Burgundian courts, see Armstrong (1983), especially pp. 409ff on manuscripts.

[19] Strohm (1990) explores the thesis that Bruges was one of the most important centres for cultural contact.   [20] Fallows (1987a), p. 74.   [21] Hamm (1962), *passim*.

[22] The best known of these is that of Pierre Alamire who, between the late 1490s and the 1530s and together with at least two associates, copied many music manuscripts of which over fifty survive.

Products of this type were often presentation manuscripts which, perhaps in most cases, were not intended for normal use. As one might expect, those that were copied for the singers frequently had a well-defined purpose: so, for example, a given source might contain music for the Mass or for the Office. Surprisingly, there are also manuscripts which contain seemingly random musical collections; one explanation, which is obvious but not without its problems, is that these were repositories of repertory from which performing manuscripts could be compiled.[23]

Whatever the problems involved in answering specific questions of transmission, there is no doubt that music did travel; indeed, many styles became international within a remarkably short space of time. It is significant, for example, how widely distributed is the spiky, rather dissonant, style which seems to have originated in late fourteenth-century France; the smoother style which grew out of it just after the turn of the century also seems to have taken over quickly across most of Catholic Europe. For a while after that, perhaps rather surprisingly, the most critical stylistic developments in fifteenth-century sacred music were initiated in England. Indeed, the English manner (the so-called *contenance angloise*) was described as the *fons et origo* of a new and highly favoured type of music, its best-known proponent being John Dunstable.[24] However, while his works and those by other English composers of his and the following generation were widely copied and imitated by continental musicians from the 1430s until around the middle of the century, the rather discursive feel of the style eventually fell out of favour. Subsequently, it was the Franco-Flemish composers of the later part of the century who tightened it up, in particular curtailing its long flowing lines in order to make the words more audible. The resulting so-called Franco-Flemish style became the new norm, as with earlier styles rapidly spreading throughout Catholic Europe.

Of all the genres available to the late medieval clerk musician, the courtly secular song is the one which perhaps comes closest to the *objet d'art* whose beauty is to be contemplated for its own sake rather than in terms of some external function. Subject matter was highly stylised – even esoteric, as with some unusual work from the court of the Avignon popes, which combined highly arcane texts with self-conscious musical ingenuity.[25] In general, however, the trend during the fifteenth century was towards something rather less mannered, with texts more straightforwardly reliant on the language and symbols of the courtly love tradition. As convention decreed, text and music were connected according to the long established tradition of the *formes fixes*,

---

[23] The most extensive of these wide-ranging collections are the so-called Trent Codices, which contain, including duplicates, over 1,800 pieces composed over the period 1425–70.

[24] By Johannes Tinctoris in his treatise *Proportionale musices* (c. 1476); for the passage in question, see Strunk (1950), p. 195.   [25] This repertory is published in *Corpus mensurabilis musicae*, LIII.

with the *rondeau* becoming the most favoured type. What emerged – and, indeed, dominated courtly secular song for most of the rest of the century – was the elegant and subtle manner of what is still called the Burgundian song, though in practice the term is used more in a generic than a literal sense, since many of its proponents had little or no association with the Burgundian court.

Attention should be drawn here to the existence of several specially beautiful presentation manuscripts of the song repertory, of which one of the most remarkable was that known as the *Chansonnier cordiforme*,[26] because of its heart shape, and the fact that, when open, it appears as two hearts joined. It has to be said, however, that taste for such conceits, indeed for the rituals of courtly love in general, declined steadily towards the end of the fifteenth century. Accordingly, the Burgundian song gave way to a new, less rigidly structured type which eventually developed into the tuneful and dance-like French *chanson* and Italian *frottola* of the early sixteenth century.

In general, non-courtly vernacular song of the period was rarely written out in such a way that it has survived the passage of time. Though traces survive from across Europe, the most familiar repertory to have been preserved in any quantity is the English carol, a verse and refrain genre whose precise function remains something of a mystery.[27] From the early part of the century, subject matter varies from the devotional (*Ther is no rose of swych vertu*) to the political and patriotic (*Owre Kynge went forth*, otherwise known as the Agincourt Song), and this variety remains until the demise of the genre in the early sixteenth century. Range of musical style is also surprisingly wide – despite a general tendency towards a tuneful, semi-popular manner, there are also a number of far more refined and sophisticated pieces, especially among the more austere devotional carols of the later years of the century.

Fundamentally, the clerk musician was a servant whose employment prospects lay most obviously at court or in the Church. However, he was unlikely to be employed simply as a musician, even though it was his musical abilities which had first attracted his patron's attention. So, for example, a cathedral musician of some standing was likely to hold a number of benefices in addition to his 'official' post. As was pointed out earlier, even clerk musicians at court were normally chaplains; they, too, might hold such benefices as their employer could, by his influence, acquire for them.

Servants or not, some clerk musicians seem to have led remarkably varied lives and even achieved notable social status – here it is instructive to consider the career of Dufay, quite the best documented of any composer before 1500, and one which, though probably more diverse than many, cannot have been

---

[26] Paris, Bibliothèque nationale, Collection Rothschild, MS 2973.

[27] The carol repertory is published in *Musica Britannica*, IV and XXXVI; see R.L. Greene (1977) on the literary aspects of the genre.

entirely untypical.[28] Born in the late 1390s, he received musical and presumably a more general education at Cambrai cathedral, an institution with which he retained links throughout his life, even though he disappears from its records for some time after 1414. His whereabouts over the next few years are uncertain, though he may have been a member of Pierre d'Ailly's household at the Council of Constance (1414–18), certainly had associations with the Malatesta of Rimini and Pesaro in the early 1420s and seems likely to have lived in Laon in the mid-1420s. By 1427, he was in the entourage of Cardinal Louis Aleman, then papal legate at Bologna, and he probably became a priest early the following year. Although documentation for these early years is very thin, it does not appear that Dufay's activities were purely musical, despite the significant reputation which he was acquiring as a composer of both sacred and secular work. It is also clear that, whatever remuneration he received from a succession of influential patrons during these years, he, like most other church musicians of any consequence, also relied to some extent on benefices.

Dufay spent most of the period 1428–37 as a papal singer, with a short interlude at the court of Savoy, apparently because, for a variety of political and financial reasons, the papal choir had to be considerably run down in 1433. One may judge something of his standing at the time by the important commissions he received;[29] for much of the period, too, he appears in documents as master of the papal chapel, though it is unclear what this meant in practice. His activities cannot have been exclusively musical, however; it is clear, for example, that he had achieved a degree in canon law by 1436 at the latest.

For all his reputation, a composer like Dufay was far from immune to political events. Thus, following the deposition of Pope Eugenius IV by the anti-Pope Felix V in 1438, he found himself forced to choose between the generous patronage of Cambrai cathedral, beholden to Duke Philip the Good of Burgundy and supporter of Eugenius, and the less predictable sponsorship of the new anti-pope who, as Duke Amadeus VIII of Savoy, had employed him in 1433. Calculating that Cambrai was the safer alternative, he returned there in 1439 to a position whose initial nature is unclear for lack of documentation. However, he soon became master of the cathedral's *petits vicaires*, held various administrative posts and was responsible for a thorough overhaul of the cathedral's music books, both of polyphony and plainchant. He also seems to have had close connections with the Burgundian court, being described variously in accounts as *cappellanus*, *cantor* and even *familiaris* to the duke.

One might have expected Dufay, widely regarded as the greatest living com-

---

[28] For a thorough account of Dufay's life, of which the following is a summary, see Fallows (1987a), pp. 7–85.   [29] See above, p. 325.

poser, but now in his forties, to have settled down quietly in Cambrai for the rest of his life. However, for reasons which are unclear, he seems to have spent most of the 1450s elsewhere, perhaps associated with the Savoyard court. By 1458, however, he had returned again to Cambrai, where he remained until his death. Despite his advanced age, it is clear that he was still composing during these last years, and that he maintained a wide range of contacts, among them Charles the Bold of Burgundy. His social standing was evidently such that he was entrusted with entertaining Pierre de Ranchicourt, bishop of Arras, when he visited Cambrai in 1472 to dedicate the cathedral.

No doubt other clerk musicians led more or less colourful lives – though Binchois was perhaps exceptional in spending some time as a soldier, possibly in the service of William de la Pole, earl of Suffolk, as part of the English force occupying northern France. John Dunstable was regarded as remarkable not only as a composer, but also as a mathematician and astronomer; in addition, he was for a while granted rights over certain lands in northern France, and was accorded the title *armiger*, suggesting a status which few musicians could have expected to achieve.[30] None the less, a number of features stand out as commonplace. First, the careers of many composers were international, in some cases involving much travel; it was particularly common, for instance, for Franco-Flemish musicians to spend at least part of their careers in Italy. Second, an ambitious and able composer might cultivate the patronage of a wide range of ecclesiastical and secular authorities. Certainly, he would want the relative financial security of benefices, which might be acquired through the good offices of either of these; and in consequence he would very probably be in some grade of holy orders. Third, as we have seen, his employment was not necessarily limited to musical duties.

The topic of musical education has been left until a late stage in this survey because it opens up broader questions as to what music was, not merely in the conventional sense of organised sounds, but also within the wider sphere of philosophical thought. True, the initial training of the clerk musician was straightforward in nature. A boy who showed promise would be taught, perhaps from quite a tender age, under the auspices of a cathedral, college or other institution set up specifically to perform sacred music. Here he learnt the chant repertory and, depending on the institution, he might also learn to sing, read and improvise polyphony to whatever level of sophistication was required. Though evidence is far from clear, continued education of more gifted individuals is likely to have been by a process akin to apprenticeship.

[30] English composers may more often have achieved a higher social status, especially the Gentlemen of the Chapel Royal; see, for example, Bowers (1975b) on Leonel Power who also styled himself *armiger* towards the end of his life. For the land interests of Dunstable, Power and some other English composers, see Wathey (1989), pp. 197ff.

Presumably traditions which made little or no use of the written note relied still more on such apprenticeship. We have evidence, too, that both nobility and courtiers might aspire to musical skills as a sign of social accomplishment, acquired probably under the individual tutelage of a resident minstrel or clerk musician; though few are likely to have gone to the lengths of Charles the Bold of Burgundy who is said to have written songs and a motet, possibly under the guidance of Dufay.[31]

It is not surprising, then, that many treatises should have survived which deal with a range of practical aspects of music: notation, and the composition and improvisation of counterpoint, for example.[32] However, there also survives a considerable number of more abstract and academic treatises, reminding us that musical education was not concerned entirely with practice. Perceived at its highest level, music was a component of the *quadrivium*, the basis of all medieval and Renaissance university learning.[33] Its study stretched from the philosophical *musica mundi* (the harmony of the universe) and *musica humana* (the harmony of the ideally attuned human being) down to the audible *musica instrumentalis*. The last mentioned was, in turn, divided into higher and lower levels – respectively the abstract *musica speculativa*, which was essentially a mathematical account of musical theory, and *musica practica*, music as composed and performed.

The basis for academic study of music and the ultimate source for most of the speculative treatises was Boethius' treatise *De institutione musica*, a largely mathematical document whose tone, widely echoed by later pedagogues, is captured in his notably dogmatic conclusion to Book I:

there are three classes of those who are engaged in the musical art. The first class consists of those who perform on instruments, the second of those who compose songs, and the third of those who judge instrumental performance and song. But those of the class which is dependent upon instruments and who spend their entire effort there . . . are excluded from comprehension of musical knowledge . . . None of them makes use of reason; rather, they are totally lacking in thought. The second class of those practising music is that of the poets, a class led to song not so much by thought and reason as by a certain natural instinct. For this reason this class, too, is separated from music. The third class is that which acquires an ability for judging, so that it can carefully weigh rhythms and melodies and the composition as whole. This class, since it is totally grounded in reason and thought, will rightly be esteemed as musical. That person is a musician who exhibits the faculty of forming judgements according to speculation or

---

[31] Fallows (1987a), p. 73; see also below, pp. 444–5.

[32] Most of the more important treatises are to be found in Coussemaker (ed.), *Scriptorum de musica medii aevi*, and the series *Corpus scriptorum de musica*.

[33] Carpenter (1958) remains the classic study of music in the universities of the period. See also Gushee (1973) on different types of speculative treatise and a critique of some of Carpenter's ideas.

reason relative and appropriate to music concerning modes and rhythms, the genera of songs, consonances . . . as well as concerning the songs of the poets.[34]

It may be no coincidence that Boethius chose to divide his musicians into three types; one is reminded, for instance, of the division Plato made in his *Republic*, much as one would not wish to take the parallel any further. Certainly Boethius draws much of his authority from classical philosophers, notably Plato and the neoplatonic movements, Aristotle, Ptolemy and, inevitably, the followers of Pythagoras. Yet for all his mathematical rationalism, we find that number in music (as indeed elsewhere) could never be separated from moral associations, and this feature of his thinking is clearly implicit in that of his later medieval and early Renaissance disciples. As with the other elements of the *quadrivium*, one of the most central concepts is ratio, since mathematics, geometry, astronomy and music represent proportion respectively in number, on a surface, in space and in sound. Of the different types of ratio which exist, the multiple (2:1, 3:1, etc.), being the simplest, attains the highest form of perfection, with more complex relationships being correspondingly less perfect. This carried an obvious acoustical significance, since multiple and other simple ratios relate to the most perfect consonances.[35] However, the moral connotations of simple proportion were such that they did not merely relate to the superiority of consonance over dissonance; simple proportion meant consonance in all its perceived manifestations, and was therefore seen to partake of the harmonious perfection of God's creation.

Neither, in practice, were such considerations an entirely academic matter. Certainly, it does not take any great leap of faith to imagine that even the modestly regarded *musica practica* might raise itself within the broader intellectual framework if it could in some way emulate this perfection; indeed, one might positively expect the most ambitious music to do so as a sign of its aspirations. It is not surprising, therefore, that the use of proportions is fairly commonplace, if far from universal, in such works – for example, the lengths of subsections in isorhythmic motets were very often cast in one or other of the ratios 3:2:1 or 6:4:3.[36] Yet practice was far more complex than might be anticipated. In particular, it appears that such proportions as were used did not necessarily preserve the simplicity which the Boethian view would suggest was morally ideal. Indeed, it is obvious that composers were often interested far

---

[34] Boethius, *Fundamentals of music*, p. 51.

[35] The theoretician's 'instrument' was the monochord, a single string whose length could be varied, and thereby produce different note pitches. Essentially, lengths which are in simple proportion to each other produce notes which are most consonant – thus, the ratio 2:1 produces the octave, 3:2 the fifth, and so on.

[36] Despite the possibility of additional complexities, proportions and significant numbers (see below) were almost always based on the lengths of sub-sections of a given piece.

less in simple proportions than in significant numbers, chosen for either their arithmetical elegance or their symbolic meaning.[37] As one might expect from a mathematician, Dunstable's music is especially rich in the use of both proportion and numbers with arithmetical or symbolic significance; indeed, in some cases, his usage looks to have been notably arcane, taking in Greek *gematria*, amongst a wealth of ingenious mathematical devices.[38]

Here, of course, we encounter a highly esoteric art in which layers of decoration were contained within a superstructure which was not random, but which added further dimensions of symbolic meaning of which God was no doubt aware, but listeners and singers alike were oblivious. It represents medieval *musica practica* at its most uncompromisingly erudite, one might say in its most occult, form. Significantly, we have also moved into an area about which both Boethius and the medieval musical theorists were largely silent – one which must surely have been considered a more advanced level of study than the *quadrivium*. Ultimately, though, it belongs to a manner of thinking which did not accord with changes of taste which were taking place in the fifteenth century. True, a few composers, most of them English, cultivated proportion and significant numbers until as late as the 1520s; however, only patchy evidence has so far been found for such techniques in continental music after the isorhythmic motet fell out of favour. Yet again, we see that crucial move away from the characteristically medieval 'edifice with decorative overlay'. The more pragmatic style which we have seen to take its place, and the trend towards the 'series of events spaced in time', had altogether different connotations, looking forward, ultimately, to that greater preoccupation with text which is associated with Renaissance values.

---

[37] Arithmetically elegant numbers would include, for example, triangular and square numbers; in the shadowy world of numerology, almost any number can have some significance – as an obvious example, 33 represents the number of years Christ spent on earth.

[38] Trowell (1978). Such usage can hardly have been limited to music; see Peck (1980) for examples in medieval English literature.

PART IV

THE DEVELOPMENT OF EUROPEAN STATES

CHAPTER 17

GERMANY AND THE EMPIRE

Tom Scott

TO speak of 'Germany' in the fifteenth century is an anachronism. Until late in the century the sources invariably refer to the 'German lands'; even the seemingly singular *Deutschland*, which became current in the sixteenth century, may in fact derive from a plural form. But what made these lands German? Recourse to geography, or ethnicity, or language quickly reveals more contradictions than congruences. To take the most obvious example: in the west the Rhine from Roman times had separated Germania from Gallia, but in the mid-fourteenth century the Strasburg chronicler Fritsche Closener could note that the archbishop of Trier possessed political authority in that part of Gallia which lay 'on German soil' (*in tutschem lande*). In the early sixteenth century Alsatian humanists became locked in a bitter controversy over the historical roots of German identity west of the Rhine, in which Thomas Murner (1475–*c.* 1527) derided as naive the contention of Jakob Wimpfeling (1450–1528) that Alsace had always been both geographically and politically 'German' since the days of the Roman Empire. On occasion, it is true, writers chose to distinguish Alemannia (west of the Rhine) from Germania proper, but at other times the terms Alemannia, Theutonia and Germania were used interchangeably. Further afield, the German lands east of the Elbe were, in ethnic terms, by the very fact of colonisation admixed with Slavs. In the north-west, the Frisians settled along the North Sea coast, though within the German lands, were not strictly speaking German, whereas by the close of the Middle Ages their neighbours to the west, the northern provinces of the Netherlands, were gradually ceasing to be reckoned part of the German lands, even though they were indubitably Germanic. Linguistically, the evidence at first sight seems less ambiguous. Throughout the fifteenth century the 'German tongue' was used to stamp a linguistic community set apart from foreign (*welsch*) speakers. But that community was itself divided by the late thirteenth century into distinct areas of Low and High German, not always mutually comprehensible. Within the Low German area a standard form of speech evolved, as the Lübeck dialect came to

Map 6   Germany and the Empire

Boundary of Empire in the fifteenth century
MAINZ Ecclesiastical principalities
HESSE Secular principalities
•**Bremen** Cities
Kingdom of Bohemia
Swiss Confederation
Teutonic Order

predominate on account of its diffusion through the Hanseatic League. But to the south, even the invention of printing by moveable type failed to achieve more than an approximation of the various High German dialects before 1500: that only came about in the course of the next century as Luther's German Bible made its impact. Nevertheless, 'tongue' (*Gezünge*) comes closest to marking a German identity in this period; in the reform plans of the 1450s 'tongue' was regularly used to translate the Latin *natio*.

By the end of the century, indeed, the singular 'German nation' had displaced the plural 'German lands'. That shift, however, owed more to the artifice of high politics than to any organic growth of a popular national consciousness. Demands after mid-century by the three ecclesiastical prince-electors for independence from Rome and its exorbitant taxation of the German clergy were presented as the *gravamina et turbaciones provinciarum et nacionis Almaniae*. That particular sense of German nationhood had been amplified after 1400 by attempts to heal the Great Schism. Not only did the calling of two General Councils on German soil (Constance 1414–18, and Basle 1431–9) help bring the category of *nationes*, once used to categorise university students but then extended to distinguish those attending the councils, into wider political discourse: it reaffirmed also the sacred mission of the Germans to protect Christendom and preserve Christian unity. That spiritual task, traditionally expressed in the struggle to convert the heathen, took on a new urgency by the fifteenth century, as the Germans bore the brunt of combating heresy in Bohemia and repulsing Ottoman advances in the Balkans. Such responsibility derived ultimately from the doctrine of the *translatio imperii*, symbolised in Charlemagne's coronation, so that German nationhood from the outset was indissolubly linked to and defined by the sacred character and function of the Empire. By the mid-fifteenth century these two elements were fusing into a new entity, the 'Holy Roman Empire of the German Nation', although the term itself was not officially recorded until 1492. Yet the equation of a once universal Empire with a specific national identity was bound to have practical political consequences as well.

The campaigns against the Hussites were launched as European crusades with papal sanction, but their military organisations and financial burden drew members of the Empire into closer and more frequent consultation. From the exigencies of the Hussite wars stemmed the first imperial quota list (*Matrikel*) of military contributions (1422) and the earliest attempt to impose a general poll tax on all inhabitants of the Empire (1427). The intensification of political and constitutional life was attended by myriad proposals for imperial reform which, though seldom more than blueprints, fuelled public debate among the estates of the Empire and so helped create a national public opinion with a sense of common fate and shared purpose. 'Nation' was thus applied to the political nation, the estates of the Empire. When Maximilian (*r.* 1493–1519) appealed to the 'German nation' at the Diet of Worms in 1495, the king was not invoking an imaginary *Volk* but addressing his constitutional counterparts (or adversaries). None the less, Maximilian was more than willing to harness the humanists' preoccupation with German history as propaganda for his own imperial schemes. The rediscovery of a copy of Tacitus' *Germania* in the abbey of Hersfeld in 1455 and its subsequent printing in Nuremberg lent credence to the notion of a German fatherland of heroic antiquity. At the hands of the arch-humanist Conrad Celtis (1459–1508), who planned to bring out an illustrated edition of *Germania*, such a belief could soar to extravagant nationalist enthusiasm or plummet into polemical racism. If the German nation had taken on the mantle of the Roman Empire, as one pamphleteer in 1500 could boast, the substance of the Empire might appear to have shrunk to a purely German kingdom. Efforts to preserve the title *rex Romanorum* in the face of *rex Germaniae* or *rex Alemanniae* were indeed finally abandoned: the monarchy had become not only German but identified with a territory (whatever its bounds) rather than with the community of Latin Christendom. Earlier, it is true, Fritsche Closener had used the formula *Deutscher Kaiser*, but his understanding was still that of an emperor of Germanic race or of the Germans, not the ruler of 'Germany'. By the fifteenth century, however, *regnum* and *imperium* (once both translated as *Reich*) began to pull apart. *Regnum* came to mean the increasingly institutionalised (German) *Reich*, whose members participated in a constitutional dualism with the monarchy, whereas *imperium* was upheld as a general affirmation of imperial authority over subjects within and without Germany who owed feudal allegiance to the emperor.

Notionally, the frontiers of the Empire still remained those of the high Middle Ages, reaching well beyond the 'German lands'. In the west they encompassed the Arelate, the ancient kingdom of Burgundy stretching from the Jura to the Mediterranean. By the end of the fourteenth century, however, Provence had been lost to the house of Anjou and the Dauphiné to France, while in 1378 the Emperor Charles IV had conferred the imperial vicariate over the kingdom of Arles upon the dauphin, later Charles VI. As part of his *arrondissement* of the western borders of the Empire with France, Charles IV at least succeeded in bringing the county of Savoy under imperial sovereignty in 1361. But pressure from France, all the greater once it had gained Provence from Anjou in 1481, finally induced the dukes (raised from counts in 1416) to remove their residence from Chambéry to Turin in Piedmont in 1536; by then the house of Savoy had long since ceased to play a part in imperial affairs. Burgundy in the narrower sense, that is, the duchy and county (Franche-Comté), straddled the Franco-imperial border. On the death of Charles the Bold, the last duke of Burgundy, in 1477 his inheritance should have passed in its entirety to Maximilian, by virtue of his marriage to Charles's daughter Maria, but France laid claim to the duchy, which had been held as an appanage of the French crown. Imperial sovereignty over Franche-Comté and the other Burgundian lands lying within the Empire – Luxemburg and the Low Countries – was not finally recognised until the Treaty of Senlis in 1493; by its provisions France even had to cede francophone Flanders and Artois to the Empire. After the death of the Emperor Charles V, however, the Burgundian inheritance fell to the Spanish Habsburg dynasty, but during his lifetime Luxemburg, although linguistically and ethnically in part a 'German land', was no longer ruled as part of the *Reich*, while Franche-Comté, though adjacent to the Outer Austrian territories in Alsace which were ultimately accountable to Innsbruck, was administered as part of the Spanish Netherlands. Between the two lay Lorraine, but its dukes, although imperial vassals, effectively detached themselves from the Empire in the wake of Charles the Bold's failure to conquer the duchy, and aligned themselves to the French crown.

Well before the fifteenth century many Swiss communes, both rural and urban, had declared themselves independent of their feudal overlords, in particular the Habsburgs, and were refusing to acknowledge imperial obligations. The Habsburgs' accession to the imperial throne in 1438, far from arresting the whittling away of their possessions in eastern Switzerland, brought a local struggle between feudal lordship and communal autonomy into the arena of high politics. The threat from Burgundy in the 1470s led to a brief *rapprochement* with Archduke Sigismund, the Habsburg ruler of Tirol and Outer Austria, yet by the terms of the Perpetual Accord (*Ewige Richtung*), concluded on 11 June 1474, Sigismund was obliged to renounce all Habsburg claims within Switzerland. Out of that agreement grew the Lower Union, a defensive league of lords and cities on the Upper Rhine, whose alliance with the Confederates in the League of Constance inflicted three defeats in quick succession upon the Burgundian forces. When Maximilian tried to revive the Lower Union in 1493, however, as the vehicle of his imperial-dynastic designs in the west, he failed: the readiness of the Swiss to co-operate with the monarchy was never more than temporary. The Swiss (or Swabian) War of 1499, fought almost as a civil war by the south German and Austrian nobility against the 'republican' Swiss, confirmed their undimmed mutual distrust. Its outcome, a sweeping victory for the confederates, sealed their separation from the Empire in fact if not in law. Yet the Swiss had no desire to leave the Empire in its manifestation as *imperium*, a juridical corporation embodying a universal salvific purpose. What they rejected was any attempt at integration into the more state-like configuration of the *regnum* with its financial and constitutional obligations. Beyond the Alps, imperial power in Italy had long been more shadow than substance. Apart from the broken-backed campaign against Milan by the anti-king Rupert of the Palatinate in 1401–2, no German monarch of the fifteenth century made any concerted effort to reassert imperial rights in Lombardy or Tuscany until the Italian Wars after 1494 ushered in a struggle for European hegemony between Habsburg and Valois. Apart from the powerful bishopric of Trent, only the patriarchate of Aquileia and the county of Görz (Gorizia) on the Adriatic held loyal to the Empire. Venetian claims upon Trent and Görz were rebuffed, until Maximilian inherited the county in 1500 and was able to incorporate it into his Habsburg patrimony.

The eastern frontier of the Empire in the fifteenth century was at least clearly established. It took in the eastern Austrian lands (Carniola on the Adriatic, Styria and Upper Austria), the kingdom of Bohemia with the neighbouring Luxemburg possessions of the margraviate of Bohemia and the Silesian and Lusatian duchies, and the territories of Brandenburg and Pomerania. Yet at the same time it was undoubtedly the most troubled border of the Empire for much of the century. Heresy, dynastic rivalries and the Turkish menace absorbed the energies of the three emperors who spanned the century – the Luxemburg Sigismund (*r.* 1410–37), and his Habsburg successors, his son-in-law, the short-lived Albert II (*r.* 1438–9), and the exceptionally long-lived Frederick III (*r.* 1440–93). The Hussite movement in Bohemia severed that kingdom from the Empire for much of the century; its virtual independence was underscored by the election of a 'national' king, George of Poděbrady (*r.* 1458–71). To the south, Styria and the Austrian duchies came under repeated attack from another 'national' king, Mátyás Corvinus of Hungary (*r.* 1458–90), forcing Frederick at one stage to flee his capital Vienna in 1485. Behind the complex manoeuvrings over the crowns of Bohemia and Hungary can, however, be discerned a wider struggle for political hegemony in the Balkans, of which the Habsburgs – against all the odds – were the ultimate beneficiaries. The cornerstone of their success was laid by the Emperor Frederick III in the Treaty of Bratislava (Preßburg) on 7 November 1491, which recognised Maximilian as pretender to both thrones if their ruler, Vladislav, from the Polish house of Jagiełło, should die without heirs. When, after several dynastic vicissitudes, Maximilian's grandson, Archduke Ferdinand of Austria, was finally able to make good these claims in 1526, the outcome was not, as might be expected, the augmentation of the *Reich*, but rather the creation of a separate Austro-Hungarian Empire ruled patrimonially by the house of Habsburg.

In the north, the limits of the Empire were naturally defined by the North Sea and the Baltic, but between them lay the Danish peninsula where feudal and territorial claims straddled the imperial frontier, just as in Burgundy. Traditionally, the county of Holstein marked the boundary with Denmark, but from 1386 its rulers, the counts of Schauenburg, also held the duchy of

Schleswig immediately to the north as a Danish fief. On their extinction in 1460 both Schleswig and Holstein fell to King Christian I of Denmark (r. 1448–81), yet in terms of feudal law Holstein (elevated to a duchy in 1474) remained under imperial sovereignty. Within its northern frontiers, but quite remote from imperial authority for much of the Middle Ages, lay Dithmarschen and Frisia. These coastal communities had developed a strong sense of local independence in a manner reminiscent of the Swiss. Dithmarschen, which could look back on a long struggle against its titular overlord, the archbishop of Bremen, was given in fee to the crown of Denmark by Frederick III, but managed to regain its autonomy in 1500, only to be absorbed into Holstein in 1559. Frisia, on the other hand, was the object of determined efforts by the Emperor Sigismund to reassert imperial authority. An imperial charter of protection in 1417 was followed more significantly in the 1420s by a series of fiscal demands, designed to document Frisia's participation in the *Reich* as a political nation. It was only at the end of the century, however, that Maximilian saw fit to appoint an imperial governor for Frisia, Duke Albert the Brave of Saxony. In the north the Empire also embraced one distant fief, Livonia, which had passed to the Teutonic Order in the fourteenth century. The Teutonic Knights rounded off their jurisdiction in the Gulf of Finland by buying Estonia from the Danish crown in 1346. These territories, corresponding to the present republics of Estonia and Latvia, were geographically remote from the Empire, but could easily be reached by sea across the Baltic. Indeed, Riga and Reval (Tallinn) had been founded as German colonies at the beginning of the thirteenth century, and subsequently became leading members of the Hanseatic League. Between Livonia and the duchies of Brandenburg and Pomerania lay Prussia, the heartland of the Teutonic Order, which lay outside the Empire. However, both by recruitment and by religious mission the Order was closely allied to the universal monarchy of the Empire; though not of the *regnum*, it was certainly of the *imperium*. That link was indeed invoked after his accession by Frederick III, who issued summonses to the High Master to attend imperial diets. After mid-century, however, the emasculating conditions of the Second Peace of Thorn (Toruń) obliged the Order to submit to Polish sovereignty (though neither Frederick nor Maximilian ever recognised the claim), thus effectively severing its connection to the *imperium*. Certain towns in the Prussian Union (the political opponent of the Order) – Thorn, Danzig (Gdańsk) and Elbing (Elblag) – still found themselves pressed to pay imperial taxes: Danzig indeed brushed aside Polish protests at this affront to its authority by declaring that it belonged directly to the Empire (*on mittel zum heyligen Reich gehörig*).

To 'belong to the Empire' meant to acknowledge its monarchical authority: the Empire derived its reality not from territoriality but from the particular character of the monarchy and its links with the Papacy. Before the papal coronation of the emperor, however, lay the election and coronation of the king of the Romans by the German prince-electors. By the fifteenth century the fact of election and coronation as king in Germany outweighed the expectation of coronation as emperor. Frederick III was the last emperor to be crowned in Rome by the pope. His son, by contrast, in a delicious twist, simply proclaimed himself 'elected Roman emperor' in Trent in 1508, with neither coronation nor anointing. While the need for election had been a source of weakness for the medieval German monarchy, both Charles IV (*r.* 1346–78) for Wenceslas in 1376, and Frederick III for Maximilian in 1486, persuaded the electoral princes to co-elect their sons during their own lifetimes, thereby ensuring an undisputed succession; much earlier the Capetians had used exactly the same device to establish their dynastic authority in France. Moreover, as the Habsburgs were ostensibly to demonstrate, a dynasty powerful or rich enough could buy or bribe its succession to the Roman crown and so reduce election to a formality. In any case, the seven electors – the three prince-archbishops of Mainz, Cologne and Trier, and the four secular princes, the Count Palatine, the margrave of Brandenburg, the duke of Saxony and the king of Bohemia – had no right to depose the king-emperor, as the terms of the Emperor Charles IV's Golden Bull of 1356, which remained the constitutional foundation of the Empire until 1806, made clear. By the fifteenth century both depositions and double elections had in fact become rare. Rupert of the Palatinate (*r.* 1400–10) was the last anti-king; 1410 saw the last double election. These are pointers to the growing consolidation of the Empire, in which other constitutional forces sought to participate in the *Reich* as the political nation alongside the electors and so curb their often autocratic exercise of power. Plans to depose Frederick III – on account of his alleged neglect of the *Binnenreich* (the Empire excluding his dynastic lands) – foundered precisely because a recognised constitutional framework was firmly in place by mid-century.

The increasingly consolidated *Reich*, though it might have lamented the monarch's failings and baulked at his extravagances, dared not throw into question the institution of the monarchy as such, for its members derived their own legitimacy from its feudal character. However weak the king might be, fiefs, privileges and patents of nobility were by right his alone to bestow; the crown was seen as the dispenser of justice and patronage, rather than as the source of political power. And yet the monarch could still command political allegiance, in an Empire dominated by the high aristocracy, in his capacity as supreme liege lord. A startling instance occurred as late as 1487, when Frederick III brought the proceedings of the Diet of Nuremberg to an abrupt close by declaring that the decisions of the royal council (*Hoftag*) took precedence over the deliberations of the *Reichstag*, and went on to demand that his vassals there assembled, in accordance with their oaths of fealty, follow him to war without delay against Mátyás Corvinus of Hungary. That, admittedly, was the last fling of a monarch wedded to a monistic view of his sovereignty which brooked no form of constitutional dualism; it underscores, nevertheless, the essentially personal and feudal, rather than institutional, character of the German monarchy, whose authority, therefore, depended heavily upon the king's presence. Prolonged absences from the *Binnenreich* – Sigismund's absorption with the affairs of his Hungarian crown lands, Frederick III's sedentary preoccupation with the difficulties of his Austrian duchies – could not help but erode that authority. On the death of Sigismund there were already plans to appoint an imperial vicar to oversee the *Reich* if the monarch would not do so. Frederick III's concentration on Danubian affairs was so pronounced that it grew increasingly hard to raise support from the *Reich* for policies which appeared to serve dynastic rather than imperial interests. The Ottoman menace was indeed a concern of the Empire as a whole, but Frederick's claims upon the crown of Hungary could less obviously be justified on the grounds of imperial necessity. When, at the end of the century, Maximilian invoked a sense of imperial destiny in his repeated attempts to gain subsidies for his campaigns in Italy, the blank refusal of the estates in almost every instance to comply showed how divergent the perceptions of imperial necessity had become.

Although the peripheral nature of the monarchy for much of the century (until the age of Maximilian, at any rate) undoubtedly weakened the emperors' personal authority, they could still expect to make their presence felt in those areas of the Empire which had close ties to the monarchy as an impersonal dignity. Those who were placed directly under the Empire (*reichsunmittelbar*) – for example, the imperial abbeys, counts, knights and cities – were part of the 'king's body' and clung to the monarchy as a guarantee of independence and a source of protection against the princes' aspiration to subjugate them to their territorial jurisdiction. These 'immediate' subjects of the Empire were often concentrated on old crown lands which had been administered through bailiwicks (*Landvogteien*), notably those in Swabia and Alsace. By the fifteenth century the cities, in particular, had succeeded in emancipating themselves from the jurisdiction of the bailiffs, but their loyalty to the crown remained intact. During the Hussite wars, for instance, several imperial cities and convents in Swabia responded willingly to Sigismund's appeal for troops, but insisted that they would serve under the bailiff only in his capacity as imperial military commander. Broadly speaking, the regions of royal influence were spread across central and southern Germany, particularly Franconia, southern Hesse, the Middle and Upper Rhine, and parts of Swabia. In the Wetterau north of Frankfurt/Main, for instance, lay a congeries of diminutive estates held by imperial courts, who formed a union of mutual protection in the early fifteenth century. The imperial knights, whose corporate identity was recognised in a privilege from Sigismund in 1422, were concentrated in Franconia along the Main and its tributaries, in the Kraichgau between Rhine and Neckar, and throughout much of Swabia, where many imperial abbeys were also situated. The imperial and free cities, numbering around sixty-eight in 1500,[1] were mainly located along the Middle and Upper Rhine (in Alsace, ten alone in the league of the Decapolis), above Lake Constance, in northern Württemberg and in Franconia. These regions may therefore be described as being 'near to the king' (*königsnah*).[2] From them (as well as from their dynastic lands) the monarchs drew their courtiers and officials; to them, especially to the cities, they turned for troops and taxes. These were predominantly regions of fragmented lordship: where the greater princes were consolidating their own territories – a process in full swing during the fifteenth century – the royal writ scarcely ran. Such areas encompassed not only the geographically remote north, but also the one large and powerful principality of the south, Bavaria. Between areas 'near to' and 'distant from' the crown lay others with fewer personal ties to the monarchy while none the less remaining potentially open to royal influence. The Upper Rhine is the leading example, for there, apart from the imperial cities (some of them in truth little more than villages), royal rights were vested in the bailiwick of Lower Alsace, but it remain pawned to the Palatinate for most of the century. These regional variations in royal influence diminished, however, in the course of the century, as the consolidation of the *Reich*, evident above all in the establishment of quota lists for imperial contributions, gradually placed all its members, near and far, on an equal footing in their dealings with the monarch.

The growing dualism of the Empire, expressed in the formula 'König und Reich', is reflected most vividly in the supersession of the looser usage 'members' (*Glieder*) of the Empire by the term estates (*Reichsstände*) towards the end of the fifteenth century. Though the estates saw themselves as individuals rather than representatives, the shift towards a corporate identity had been foreshadowed in the development of curial deliberation and decision making by the electors at the start of the century. All the members of the Empire shared a duty to defend it, but the Golden Bull of 1356 had imposed a particular responsibility upon the electors to safeguard its integrity and to further the

---

[1] The imperial cities were originally those directly under the king, usually on old crown land, or else those in which the king had rights of stewardship; the free cities were the former residential cities of bishops and archbishops. By the fifteenth century this distinction had largely been elided. The number of imperial cities listed in the *Reichsmatrikel* of 1521 stood at eighty-five, but that figure no longer corresponded to political reality.

[2] This term, coined by Peter Moraw, has now passed into general scholarly usage.

commonweal. Royal incompetence or absence encouraged the electors to make the most of that responsibility. It was a league of the electors (*Kurverein*) which had deposed King Wenceslas (*r.* 1378–1400) in 1399, leading to the installation of Rupert of the Palatinate as anti-king. During his reign Sigismund tried to bring the electors to heel by granting the electoral vote of the margraviate of Brandenburg to his ally, Frederick VI of Hohenzollern (*r.* 1415/17–40), burgrave of Nuremberg, in 1415, and thereafter by conferring the Saxon electoral dignity, on the extinction of the Ascanian dukes in 1423, to the margraves of Meißen from the house of Wettin. In neither, alas, did he find a reliable partner; rather, the electors banded together once more against the crown in the Bingen *Kurverein* of 1424. The search for a corporate identity and purpose in these years can also be observed in the electors' organisation of imperial armies to fight the Hussites, as well as in the decision, taken collectively, to declare themselves neutral in the name of the Empire in the conflict between Pope Eugenius IV and the Council of Basle, which had set Germany at loggerheads during the short reign of Albert II in 1438. Frederick III's separate negotiations with Eugenius, however, exposed the deep political divisions within the electoral college, which the stance of neutrality had been designed to conceal. After mid-century the position of the electors, although constitutionally impregnable, was further undermined by the relative decline of the three western ecclesiastical prince-electors, as well as by the rise of the secular territorial princes as rival players on the imperial stage.

That stage was provided by the king's diets, which were the outgrowth of the court assemblies (*Hoftage*) of the king's major vassals. Early in the century it looked for a time as if the electors might usurp the royal prerogative, for they began to summon diets of their own accord, initially in 1394 when Wenceslas was held prisoner by his Bohemian subjects. Thereafter the 1420s and 1430s saw the heyday of 'diets without the king' (*königslose Tage*), convoked at the behest of papal legates to combat the Hussites while Sigismund was otherwise engaged in his Hungarian lands. Such diets, of course, had no standing in imperial law; nevertheless, they demonstrated the need for a forum in which the political nation could articulate its will without depending on a summons to the royal council at the monarch's pleasure. Even those diets which were summoned by royal writ met for much of the century in the monarch's absence, although in theory his presence was still regarded as essential to their legitimacy. Not surprisingly, therefore, the participants came to see themselves as independent of the monarch, as constitutional players in their own right. As a consequence, what had once been the 'king's diet' became known from the 1470s as the imperial diet (*Reichstag*), that is, the assembly of the *Reich*, though the term only entered official parlance in the recess of the great reforming Diet of Worms in 1495. More significant than nomenclature, perhaps, was the principle, adumbrated at the Diets of Vienna in 1460 and again at Nuremberg in 1481, that the emperor had no choice but to summon all the estates of the Empire if the *Reichstag* were to be held competent to discharge imperial business.

Yet the *Reichstag* was very far removed from a parliament. The monarchs avoided attending the diets (pleading dynastic emergency or shortage of money) precisely in order that their presence be not construed as lending weight to the proceedings. For their part, the estates' attendance was at best patchy. Of the estates, only the electors could exert real influence in the diets until after mid-century. The secular territorial princes who were not electors, by contrast, distrusted the diets almost as much as the monarchs, for they feared that their influence would be marginalised in an assembly attuned to those whose *raison d'être* was defined by their imperial status – the electors, and the immediate nobles and cities. Not until 1487 did the secular princes appear as a corporate body, a *curia*, alongside the electors. Beneath the princes, the imperial and free cities, because they were regarded as part of the 'king's body', had little chance of raising a distinctive voice. They had no separate vote in the *Reichstag* (that was only conceded in 1648); instead, they were expected to fall in with the princes' decisions. In one notable instance, Frederick III ordered the imperial cities in 1471 to abandon their attempts to link financial contributions to a guarantee of public peace and to adjust their response to that of the estates with full voting rights. The cities hardly helped their cause, moreover, by insisting that their emissaries refer all proposals back for approval (*Hintersichbringen*). Despite their reluctance to commit themselves politically, the cities none the less were able to develop constitutional activity of their own within the penumbra of the imperial diets. Separate urban diets (*Städtetage*) are recorded from 1471. These met before the full diets to co-ordinate policy: their impetus derived from the extraordinary burden of taxation necessary to fight the Turkish wars, which fell disproportionately upon the cities. The very profusion of urban diets – thirty-one in the first twenty years of their existence – is testimony to incessant political activity by the estates of the *Reich*, though earlier Aeneas Sylvius Piccolomini (1405–65), Frederick III's secretary and later Pope Pius II, had mocked that one diet merely begot the next. The effectiveness of the *Reichstag* was certainly impaired by the fact that majority voting was unknown until 1497, when the legal fiction was introduced that a summons to the diet of itself constituted acceptance of its ultimate decisions, regardless of whether the member actually attended. What power the *Reichstag* had lay essentially in its passive right to withhold men and money; it never arrogated to itself prerogatives which lay with the monarch and his court, above all the dispensation of justice as the highest court in the land. The *Reichstag*, therefore, was but one element of the institutionalised dualism of the Empire, in which the *Reich*, the political nation, was ranged alongside the monarchy vested latterly in the Habsburg dynasty, a distinction neatly illustrated by the fact that the estates of the Austrian crown lands did not sit in the imperial diet.

The dualism of the Empire is reflected in the two issues which remained running sores throughout the century: on the one hand, the need for the kings to establish a dynastic power base (*Hausmacht*) strong enough to enable them to rule effectively as emperors; on the other, the concern of members of the *Reich* to establish public order and the rule of law within Germany. For the former, foreign policy, not least relations with the Papacy, claimed primacy; for the latter, domestic politics were paramount. On neither count were the omens favourable as the century began.

The Wittelsbach Rupert was elected (anti-) king in Rhens on 21 August 1400 by the four Rhenish electors alone (the three prince-archbishops of Mainz, Cologne and Trier, and his own vote as elector Palatine). Throughout his brief reign he was rejected by the three eastern electors (Saxony, Brandenburg and naturally by Wenceslas himself as king of Bohemia). The Palatine territories in the west controlled the Middle Rhine and its important toll-stations, but around half the lands were held as imperial mortgages and thus subject to reversion. Rupert's only major gain was the reconquest of the Upper Palatinate around Amberg and Sulzbach, pawned by the Wittelsbachs to the Luxemburgs, with its extensive reserves of iron ore, which may have yielded as much in revenue to his exchequer as the Rhine tolls; certainly, wealthy merchants from Nuremberg and Regensburg helped finance Rupert's ill-fated campaign in Italy in the prospect of gaining lucrative mining concessions from the king. The campaign was intended to demonstrate Rupert's commitment to the welfare of the Empire (and therefore his rightful claim to be king) by ousting the upstart Giangaleazzo Visconti of Milan (r. 1395–1402), whose elevation to a dukedom – and prince of the Empire – by Wenceslas had provoked outrage and contributed significantly to the latter's deposition. Thereafter Rupert hoped to win recognition from the Roman pope, Boniface IX (r. 1389–1404), whom he supported against the rival Avignonese pope with French backing, Benedict XIII (r. 1394–1417), as a prelude to bringing the Great Schism to an end. But Rupert was beaten back at Brescia (21 October 1401), and his meagre forces retreated in disarray over the Alps. Boniface's belated recognition of Rupert (in the *Approbation* of 1 October 1403) was an empty gesture, couched, moreover, in language which sought to revive earlier papal pretensions to interfere in royal elections.

On his return, Rupert broached the subject of a public peace in several diets, but quickly ran up against the hostility of the very prince who had been most instrumental in his election, the archbishop of Mainz, John II of Nassau (r. 1397–1419). As arch-chancellor of the Empire, John was slighted by the king's refusal to grant him any real say in the running of the chancery; moreover, he suspected Rupert of pursuing territorial ambitions under the cover of his newly won crown. John of Nassau was able to put together a formidable coalition, the League of Marbach (14 September 1405), including seventeen imperial cities in the south (who were opposed to Rupert's fiscal demands), with the purpose of hobbling the king's power. The rivalry of Mainz and the Palatinate – which lasted throughout the century – serves to illustrate exactly why the issue of public peace was so intractable in late medieval Germany. As territorial neighbours of roughly equal standing when the century began neither could hope to dominate the other (though the Palatinate certainly tried), yet both had to remain constantly alert to any infringement of their sovereignty, which provoked feuding and reprisals. Rupert was driven on to the defensive by the League of Marbach, unable to discharge his imperial duties. In local conflicts he was powerless to intervene, most notably in the wars between Appenzell and the imperial abbey of St Gallen, which raged from 1401 to 1408, sucking in the Swabian nobility and the cities along Lake Constance. Although Rupert was finally able to mediate a peace at Constance (4 April 1408), the victorious Appenzellers had already allied in the 'League above the Lake' in 1405, which prompted the Swabian lords to form their own knightly association of the Shield of St George two years later. Such unions for mutual protection (*Einungen*) were the only recourse if imperial authority was too weak or too distant to maintain the peace. At the same time, however, the profusion of regional alliances of self-help ran the danger of raising the feud to a new and corporate level. In foreign affairs, too, Rupert was reduced to the role of onlooker. He watched helplessly as the cardinals of both observances convoked a Council at Pisa in 1409 on their own initiative, while he maintained his support for the Roman pope, then Gregory XII (*r.* 1406–15). However justified his suspicions of the cardinals as partisans of the French crown, Rupert found himself isolated as his opponents, not least Wenceslas himself, hurried to recognise the authority of Pisa. The Council declared both existing popes deposed and elected in their stead Alexander V (*r.* 1409–10), but the refusal of the Roman and Avignonese popes to withdraw left Christendom briefly blessed with three pontiffs. Rupert struggled to uphold the Gregorian obedience, but died on 18 May 1410 as he was preparing for a showdown with Mainz, which had raised the stakes in their princely rivalry by recognising Alexander.

The succession of Sigismund, the last Luxemburg to wear the Roman crown, heralded the most turbulent generation of foreign politics in the fifteenth century. They consumed the monarch's attention to such a degree that Sigismund spent little more than two years of his twenty-seven-year reign in Germany itself. The emperor was beset on all sides by conflicts actual or potential. As king of Hungary he faced aggression along his eastern and southern borders from the Turks (who had routed the crusader armies at Nicopolis on the Lower Danube in 1396), rivalry with the Venetians over access to the Adriatic (which embroiled him in Italian politics), and possible Polish claims to the Magyar throne (through the last Angevin princess, Jadwiga (Hedwig)). In Bohemia, where royal authority was increasingly paralysed by the Hussite rebellion, Sigismund could only make good his inheritance after Wenceslas's death in 1419, but at his coronation in Prague in 1420 the estates were only prepared to recognise him as king of Bohemia, not as king of the Romans, though he was accepted in the neighbouring Luxemburg territories of Moravia, Silesia and Lusatia. In the *Binnenreich* his dynastic power was nugatory. The duchy of Luxemburg itself was ruled by his niece, Elizabeth of Görlitz, widow of Anthony of Brabant, until, in spite of the Estates, she ceded it to Philip the Good, who took it irrevocably under Burgundian control. The remaining inheritance, the margraviate of Brandenburg, a remote and unruly territory, Sigismund was to confer upon Frederick of Hohenzollern, who had served the Palatine cause under Rupert but who switched his allegiance to the house of Luxemburg on Rupert's death. Sigismund's election was itself a bizarre affair. One elector, the duke of Saxony, still held true to Wenceslas, but a majority of the electors chose Sigismund's cousin, Jost of Moravia, ruler of Brandenburg and therewith holder of an electoral vote. Quite illegally Sigismund claimed this vote by proxy for himself, so that for a few months of high farce there were three claimants to the Roman crown, all from the same family. Jost's early death on 18 January 1411, and Wenceslas's infirmity, however, spared the Empire from a possible catastrophe of intrigue and civil war; even so, Sigismund was unable to attend his coronation in Aachen until 1414. Within eight weeks of Rupert's death another crisis struck, when the army of the Teutonic Order was routed by King Władysław of Poland (*r.* 1386–1434) at the battle of Grunwald (Tannenberg) on 15 July 1410. Not only the *imperium* but also Sigismund's position as king of Hungary was threatened by this defeat, for his brother-in-law Władysław (who as grand prince of Lithuania had married Jadwiga and accepted the Polish crown on his conversion to Christianity) nursed a claim to the Magyar throne himself. In the subsequent (First) Peace of Thorn (1 February 1411) the Teutonic Order received more favourable terms than it deserved – aside from substantial ransoms, it only had to surrender Samogitia lying between Livonia and Prussia – and in the following year Sigismund reached an accommodation with Władysław designed to secure Polish attendance at a General Council of the Church.

Sigismund was quick to spy the benefits which would accrue to the *imperium* by revivifying royal rights of stewardship over the Church in order to promote the cause of reform. Unlike his predecessor, however, he had no qualms about defying the Papacy by placing himself at the head of the conciliar movement.

The Pisan Pope John XXIII (*r.* 1410–15) bowed to pressure from Sigismund by summoning a Council to Constance, which he was obliged to attend in person (the only anti-pope to do so). John's deposition in 1415 and the election two years later of Oddo Colonna as Martin V (*r.* 1417–31) restored the unity of western Christendom and marked the high point in the Church's attempts at reform from within: first, by the declaration that decisions of a General Council were binding on all Christians, the pope included (in the decree 'Haec Sancta' of 6 April 1415), and then by the provision for regular assemblies to carry forward reform (in the decree 'Frequens' of 9 October 1417). The Council at Constance represented a remarkable affirmation of Sigismund's authority as emperor and guardian of the Church. In terms of the *Reich*, however, Sigismund's triumph was altogether more equivocal. By assembling on German soil the Council certainly demonstrated the emperor's ability to mobilise a region 'near to' the crown in his interest, and its outcome went some way to counteracting the preponderant influence of French and Italians over the Papacy. But the Council had also burnt Jan Hus as a heretic (6 July 1415), which not only transformed a localised movement for religious renewal into a quasi-national revolution, but thereby estranged Bohemia from the Empire and vitiated any hope of effective rule by Sigismund in his kingdom for the next twenty years. Meanwhile, Sigismund, by declaring forfeit the western Habsburg lands of Archduke Frederick IV of Tirol (*r.* 1406–39) for abetting the deposed anti-Pope John XXIII, opened the prospect of restoring royal rights in southern Germany and northern Switzerland: for a time, the Austrian towns in Swabia and on the Upper Rhine were placed directly under the Empire. But in the end Sigismund was too weak to prevent the escheat being reversed; Frederick regained control of his lands north of the Rhine, but the Habsburg lordships to the south passed irretrievably into the hands of the Swiss.

Sigismund's further forays into European politics enjoyed moderate success at best. He did contrive to hinder the formation of a pan-Slavic alliance of Poland–Lithuania with Bohemia by investing the Lithuanian Grand Prince Vytautas (Vitold) with a royal title of his own in 1429, despite having been incommoded in the early 1420s by the dynastic schemes of his chosen lieutenant, Frederick of Hohenzollern, who had married his second son to the Polish heiress, Jadwiga. By contrast, his intervention in the turbid waters of French politics during the civil wars and the ascendancy of Joan of Arc was inept. Sigismund's attempts to play France, Burgundy and England off against one another brought no diplomatic advantage; rather, they failed to prevent the annexation of imperial fiefs by Duke Philip the Good of Burgundy (*r.* 1419–67), who between 1429 and 1433 acquired Brabant, Limburg, Hainault, Namur, Holland and Zeeland. A despairing effort to raise an army against

Burgundy in 1437 petered out in a brief sortie into the duchy of Limburg. This feeble response to Burgundian expansion exposed the deficiencies of the Empire's military organisation, which the Hussite campaigns had done nothing to improve. Sigismund himself only took part in the first crusade in 1420; the mounting of the four subsequent campaigns, which culminated in ignominious defeat at Domažlice (Taus) on 14 August 1431, devolved by default upon the electors, whose *Kurverein* of Bingen (17 January 1424) was designed to present a united front against the Hussites, who were at that time raiding into Saxony, Franconia and Lower Bavaria. But the electoral college was rent by internal divisions, not least the continuing hostility between Mainz and the elector Palatine, Louis III (*r.* 1410–36), who objected to Sigismund's provocative nomination in 1422 of its new archbishop, Conrad of Dhaun (*r.* 1419–34) as imperial vicar in his absence, an office which Louis with some justice regarded as a Palatine prerogative. As a result, the Hussite campaigns were *ad hoc* affairs; launched somewhat archaically as crusades, they brought no advance in military organisation or technique. Out of them there never developed an imperial standing army – in marked contrast to France where in these years Charles VII (*r.* 1422–61) created standing companies of cavalry in response to the excesses of the mercenary bands of *écorcheurs*. The contribution of the Hussite wars to the consolidation of the *Reich* lay elsewhere: in the establishment of quota lists, and in the plans for a general imperial poll tax, to be paid by all Christians over the age of fifteen, and by all Jews. These financial reforms (though not implemented) marked the first faltering steps on the long path to the Common Penny, the universal tax agreed at the Diet of Worms in 1495.

The weakness of royal authority in the *regnum* under Sigismund is graphically revealed in his plans to promote justice and the public peace. The king's own high court (*Hofgericht*) was too distant to be effective, for it accompanied the monarch on his itinerary; the electors and major princes had, in any case, long since secured exemption from citation before it. Instead, Sigismund chose to encourage plaintiffs to have recourse to the welter of private courts of appeal, known as the *Veme*, which had spread from their origins as the courts of free counts in Westphalia. Because their sessions were held in secret, these courts rapidly acquired a sinister reputation; in truth, the danger lay much more in their proliferation, which resulted in conflicting and apparently arbitrary judgements. The *Veme* became the target of growing hostility from princes and cities alike. Its courts declined from the 1430s, as their function was taken over by the royal chamber court (*Kammergericht*) which was acquiring institutional identity at the end of Sigismund's reign. Its development must largely be credited to the king's treasurer, Konrad von Weinsberg, who deployed it in the first instance to retrieve alienated imperial fiefs and mortgages in Swabia and Alsace. This policy of 'revindication', as it was termed, was only one aspect of a wider determination by Sigismund to reassert sovereignty over the immediate lands and subjects of the Empire. On the one hand, he put an end to the mortgaging of imperial cities (although their revenues were still on occasion pawned); on the other, he selected the imperial knights to act as agents of royal power in regions 'near to' the crown, most notably in 1430, when he sought to bring about a grand alliance of the Swabian knights of the Shield of St George, the Franconian lesser nobility and the Bavarian League of the Unicorn. These attempts to create a bulwark against the expanding territorial principalities, it must be said, were no more successful than Sigismund's greater use of out-lawry (*Acht*) earlier in his reign against overmighty subjects such as Frederick of Tirol. The issue of public peace was not addressed in detail by Sigismund until 1434, when he set forth a programme of sixteen articles which took up earlier proposals to divide the Empire into four circles for the administration of justice. Because these circles would have impinged upon the princes' territo-rial jurisdiction, the scheme fell by the wayside. Counterproposals advanced by the princes three years later at the Diet of Cheb (Eger), which took territorial sovereignty as their starting-point, incurred in turn royal displeasure. Both emperor and princes had their attention distracted by the wranglings of the Council of Basle, which by renewing the struggle between conciliar and papal authority brought to the surface the old tensions between the secular and eccle-siastical princes in Germany and the monarchy. Before these issues could be resolved, Sigismund died at Znojmo (Znaim) in southern Bohemia on 9 December 1437.

Although Sigismund had nominated his son-in-law, Duke Albert of Upper and Lower Austria, as his successor, his election was by no means a foregone conclusion. The ageing Frederick I of Brandenburg, as the elector of the great-est stature, had some hopes of the crown, while the western electors, led by the archbishop of Cologne, toyed with the idea of offering the throne to Philip the Good of Burgundy. Albert's election owed as much in the end to the likelihood that the difficulties of his Hungarian and Bohemian inheritance would prevent him from interfering too closely in the affairs of the *Binnenreich* as it did to his undoubted personal qualities after the vainglorious and erratic Sigismund. And so it proved. Albert was elected by the Hungarian magnates and crowned at Székesfehévár (Stuhlweißenburg) on 1 January 1438, but had immediately to deal with a massive Turkish irruption across the Danube; in Bohemia, by con-trast, his election was disputed by a minority who pinned their hopes on a Polish king. These problems in the crown lands were to plague his successor for the rest of the century. During his twenty months on the throne Albert never visited the interior of the Empire. He sent instead his Bohemian chan-cellor, Kaspar Schlick, to listen to the electors' proposals for imperial reform at a diet in Nuremberg, but in the negotiations it is significant that Albert's own dynastic lands, including the Austrian duchies, were not on the agenda. Before any agreement could be reached, Albert died on 27 October 1439 of dysentery contracted while fighting the Turks in Serbia.

The unanimous election of his cousin Frederick, ruler of the remote provinces of Styria, Carinthia and Carniola, as king of the Romans pointedly underscored the electors' desire to place a safe distance between themselves and the monarchy, notwithstanding their constant lament that the emperors wilfully neglected the affairs of the *Binnenreich*. In that they succeeded, for Frederick devoted only a small part of his fifty-three-year reign to western affairs. How divergent the respective spheres of activity of dynasty and *regnum* became in those years is illustrated by the establishment of separate royal chanceries, one for the Austrian crown lands, the other an imperial chancery for the remaining territories of the *Reich*. Frederick's claims to the Bohemian and Magyar crowns were complicated by the posthumous birth of a son, Ladislas, to Albert's widow three weeks after Frederick's election. For the next twelve years the emperor kept Ladislas a ward at his court (a prisoner in all but name) to be used as a pawn in the intricate quadrille of Danubian politics. But his primary concern was the strengthening of his shaky grasp on Austria itself. The partition of the Austrian lands into two lines, albertine and leopoldine, in 1379 had been followed in 1411 by the division of the latter into Styrian and Tirolean branches. Frederick was faced, therefore, with claims on all sides, which had already given rise to virtual civil war between the rival branches. He could administer the albertine lands – the duchies of Upper and Lower Austria – *pro tempore* as Ladislas's guardian, but in the leopoldine lands he had to contend with the ambitions of his younger brother, Albert IV, upon whom he was obliged to confer the governance of the Outer Austrian lands (*Vorderösterreich*) in 1446. Nor were his relations with the Austrian estates any easier. Within a year of his accession he was confronted with an uprising in Vienna over his plans to offload King Albert's debts on to the estates of the duchy. In 1452, the estates, resentful of a Styrian who, they believed, had abandoned them to anarchy, laid siege to Frederick in his residence of Wiener Neustadt (then part of Styria). Nine years later the populace, egged on by Duke Albert, again besieged Frederick in Vienna. Only the deaths of Ladislas Posthumous in 1457 and Duke Albert in 1463 allowed Frederick to assume control of the Austrian heartlands. Even then, Tirol and the outer lands remained under the rule of the hapless Archduke Sigismund, until he was finally pensioned off in 1490. These domestic difficulties are essential to the proper understanding of a monarch whose motives and policies have often been regarded as elusive and ambiguous. That the dynastic consolidation of the house of Austria informed all his thinking is incontestable, even if his penchant for the grandiose motto *Austriae est imperare orbi universo* in the cabbalistic monogram *AEIOU* should be put down to a personal conceit. Yet Frederick did not marry – the precondition of any dynastic policy – until 1452, when he was already thirty-six. His bride Eleanor, from the Portuguese royal house of Avis, brought him no visible advantage except a rich dowry; the marriage, moreover, had been contracted after Frederick had rejected more promising alliances with France, Savoy and Luxemburg. By contrast, to blame Frederick for his neglect of the Empire (discounting the two-faced attitude of the electors) misses the point that his reign fell into several distinct phases, in only one of which, from 1452 to 1471, can he be said to have retreated entirely into his Styrian homeland. Yet that withdrawal is all the more perplexing since Frederick, newly wed, had just been crowned emperor in Rome by Nicholas V. Up to 1452 Frederick was certainly active in imperial affairs, even if he failed to visit the *Binnenreich* after 1444.

Frederick, who by temperament took a lofty view of his sovereignty, sensed that his imperial authority would be better served by an accommodation with the Papacy than by espousing the conciliarist cause, which was by then increasingly discredited and on the wane. Despite their declared neutrality, the majority of the electors inclined towards the anti-pope favoured by the conciliarists at Basle, Felix V (*r.* 1439–49), who, as the former Count Amadeus of Savoy, was a fellow prince of the Empire, but cautiously Frederick nudged them towards acceptance of Eugenius IV. Negotiations reached a successful conclusion under Nicholas V (*r.* 1447–55) in the Concordat of Vienna in 1448, which in time was accepted by all the estates of the Empire and remained in force until 1806. Though its terms were much more favourable to the *curia* than the equivalent Pragmatic Sanction of Bourges for France in 1438 – papal provisions were not abolished, while the clergy in most sees continued to pay annates and first fruits to Rome – the Concordat confirmed Frederick's right of nomination to the bishoprics of his Austrian lands, agreed three years earlier, and paved the way for the secular princes to exercise the same prerogative in their own territories. Frederick had turned the vexed issue of Church–state relations skilfully to his advantage: the Concordat had been achieved without the direct involvement of the estates; it prepared the ground for his investiture as emperor four years later; and it saw his secretary and trusted adviser during the negotiations, Aeneas Sylvius Piccolomini, subsequently elected pope as Pius II (*r.* 1458–64). Where the Concordat failed, however, was in initiating any thoroughgoing reform of the Church in the German lands; ordinary layfolk chafed at the feudal power of the ecclesiastical princes, who in turn continued to nurse their own grievances against Rome.

Frederick's freedom to attend to the affairs of the *Reich* was bedevilled from the outset by a chronic lack of money. The Emperor Sigismund had earlier complained that his income from the royal domain (*Reichsgut*) amounted to a mere 13,000 guilders (fl.) a year, but he at least was the reigning monarch of a rich kingdom, Hungary. Frederick had no such resources – though his accommodation with Eugenius IV had brought him the assurance of papal coronation and a payment of 100,000 fl. in 1446. In his own duchies he promoted iron and lead mining in the Carinthian Alps and the brine-pits at Aussee, but the much vaster regalian revenues from the Tirolean mines were never at his disposal during his lifetime. Frederick's income from the *Reichsgut* is difficult to estimate. He continued Sigismund's policy of revindication and redeemed many of the pawned revenues of the imperial cities. At the same time, he embarked on a calculated policy of fiscalisation, charging, for instance, much higher fees to the cities for the renewal of their liberties, and granting additional privileges only against a share of the revenue. But income from the imperial cities and taxes on the Jews – in effect, the only royal revenues left in Germany – were often pledged to his own councillors, or else promised to creditors. The remuneration of the hereditary imperial marshal, Heinrich von Pappenheim, alone is reckoned to have consumed a good part of the regular income from the crown domain. Offices of state were often farmed to their incumbents: Kaspar Schlick paid 10,000 fl. per annum for the chancery, but even then still had to agree a division of the spoils from chancery business with the emperor himself. As his reign wore on, Frederick became increasingly dependent on irregular sources of income. He sold feudal titles, patents of nobility, judicial rights and administrative offices on a grand scale. He granted exemption from military service in return for hefty payments: in 1470, for example, Frankfurt/Main offered 2,500 fl. to avoid raising a contingent against the elector Palatine, but Frederick demanded 8,000 fl. (in the end he received only 1,500 fl., described as a 'loan'). He was even willing to cancel proclamations of outlawry if the price was right. By these various means Frederick acquired considerable wealth during his reign, but he also lost it. Much of the revenue stuck to the hands of his officials, and the rest was consumed by the campaigns against Charles the Bold of Burgundy and Mátyás Corvinus of Hungary. It is doubtful whether Frederick's annual income ever matched that of the richer German princes – the electors Palatine or the dukes of Bavaria–Landshut – let alone the French crown or the Burgundian dukes. Fiscalisation, however, exacted its own high price: the greed and corruption of his councillors, and Frederick's shameless profiteering, harmed both the standing of the monarchy and the prestige of justice.

Yet in the opening years of his reign Frederick had been far from indifferent to public order and the commonweal in Germany. At a diet in Frankfurt in 1442 he put forward comprehensive plans for an imperial peace ordinance, known as the *Reformacio Friderici*, which would transcend the regional peace treaties policed by the *Einungen*. In its enforcement the imperial cities were to be accorded an advisory role, which they promptly used to lay claim to full membership of the estates (*Reichsstandschaft*), though without success. The failure of this initiative lay in the emperor's unwillingness to contemplate any institutionalised form of law enforcement, which would derogate from his authority as the fountainhead of justice. When the electors put forward a counterproposal in mid-century for an imperial council (*Reichsrat*) to act as a permanent court of appeal, along the lines of the Parisian *parlement* or the papal rota, to be financed by imperial taxation, Frederick's only response was to declare yet another Perpetual Peace (*Ewiger Landfriede*), which he enshrined in imperial law in 1465. The logic of his own conception of royal justice led Frederick instead to a much more drastic proclamation of public peace two years later, whereby law-breakers would be held guilty of *lèse-majesté*, with the automatic penalty of outlawry and confiscation of property. The implications of this measure were so far-reaching, however (if enforced, it would have put in jeopardy the princes' consolidation of their territorial power), that Frederick was obliged to rescind the decree in 1471. Thereafter, the preservation of public peace reverted to regional responsibility, most markedly in the attempts by the Swabian estates, counselled by the emperor's closest adviser, Count Haug von Werdenberg, to check Bavarian expansion, which culminated in the formation of the Swabian League of princes, prelates, knights and cities in 1488.

The Swabian League was significant because for the first time it brought (somewhat uneasily, it is true) princes and cities together in a common defensive alliance; the lawlessness in the Empire, which had reached a new height in mid-century, turned largely on rivalry between princes and cities. In those struggles the princes were not always the aggressors. The attempts by the archbishop of Cologne, Dietrich of Moers (*r.* 1414–63), to assert his territorial authority throughout north-west Germany had begun with the installation of several of his brothers in the neighbouring sees of Paderborn, Münster and Osnabrück, but his expansionist drive only led to open war when the territorial town of Soest in Westphalia defied his jurisdiction in 1443. The ensuring feud lasted until 1449, exhausting both parties, when Soest passed to the duchy of Cleves. But that did not prevent Dietrich from embarking on another, equally futile, campaign to retain control of the see of Münster after his brother's death in 1450, which again ended in defeat for Cologne and the establishment of Cleves's authority over the bishopric. Meanwhile, southern Germany was seized by a conflict between Albert Achilles of Brandenburg (*r.* 1437–86) and the city of Nuremberg, whose rural territory separated the margravial lands of Ansbach and Bayreuth. The powerful cities of Franconia and Swabia were a thorn in the princes' flesh because of their readiness to grant burgher's rights

to the lords' feudal subjects; the cities, in turn, complained of interference in
their trade, highway robbery and excessive tolls. Already in 1466 thirty-one
cities in the south had formed a league of mutual assistance, but the so-called
Second Cities' War (1448–53) exposed their inability to sustain a united front:
they were, after all, commercial rivals themselves. After mid-century it was the
territorial ambitions of powerful Wittelsbach princes such as Duke Louis the
Rich of Bavaria–Landshut (r. 1450–79) and Elector Frederick the Victorious of
the Palatinate (r. 1451–70) which most threatened the fragile political stability
of the Empire. Indeed, the emperor declared Frederick an outlaw and his electoral dignity forfeit in 1471, though the edict was never carried out. But
however serious the rivalry between principalities, that did not preclude the
effective enforcement of law and order within individual territories, as elector
Frederick II of Hohenzollern (r. 1440–70) demonstrated in his quelling of the
fractious nobility of the margraviate of Brandenburg after 1440.

The emperor's neglect of the *Binnenreich* in the two decades after 1450 had
given rise to several schemes for his deposition. As an alternative, the councillor of the archbishop of Mainz, Dr Martin Mair (or Mayr) (c. 1420–80), proposed in 1457 that Frederick the Victorious of the Palatinate be elected Roman
king, an act which was quite improper except in the case of the monarch's son.
In the dynastic lands, however, the emperor's policies bore some fruit. After
Ladislas Posthumous's death, Frederick had been able to secure his royal title to
the crown of Hungary by the Treaty of Wiener Neustadt (17 August 1463),
which further promised him succession to the throne, should Mátyás Corvinus
die without legitimate issue. But in 1471 the balance of power in central
Europe tilted decisively away from the emperor, as the Turks invaded his
homeland of Styria, and Corvinus occupied the eastern provinces of the
crown of Bohemia. Frederick felt compelled in his extremity to summon
support in person from the estates gathered at the Diets of Regensburg and
Augsburg. Simultaneously, the emperor was confronted in the west by the
naked aggression of Charles the Bold of Burgundy (r. 1467–77) against the
bishopric of Liège, the duchy of Guelders and the county of Zutphen. It was
entirely in keeping with his character that Frederick chose at first to avert the
danger by intricate negotiations, not force of arms, in which he dangled before
Charles the bait of the Roman crown, or else the creation of an independent
kingdom of Burgundy as an imperial fief, in return for the marriage of
Maximilian to Charles's daughter, Maria. But once the negotiations had stalled
at Trier in 1473, Frederick displayed unsuspected energy by raising a feudal
host of 40,000 men to relieve the Burgundian siege of Neuß, west of Cologne,
having publicly declared that Burgundy was threatening the 'Holy Empire and
the German Nation'. The power of the emperor to mobilise the patriotism of
the political nation when its immediate interests were at stake had been tri-

umphantly reaffirmed – but the victory was fleeting, for Frederick failed to convert that enthusiasm into practical support against the much more distant Corvinus, whose open warfare against Austria itself after 1477 forced the emperor to flee his homelands, leaving him isolated and destitute in the east. The initiative passed to Maximilian, whose struggle to secure his inheritance in the west finally vindicated the old emperor's dynastic vision by creating a Habsburg Burgundian–Austrian empire of truly European stature.

The question of public authority in the Empire exercised contemporaries throughout the fifteenth century. In addressing the issue of imperial reform clerics, jurists and political writers held up a mirror to the age in countless tracts and manifestos. Yet in that mirror was reflected more often a typically Renaissance fascination with utopian models of state building than any real understanding of what the constitutional dualism of 'König und Reich' implied. Schemes for imperial circles governed by imperial vicars can be traced from the anonymous author of the *Reformation of Emperor Sigismund* (1439) through the *De concordantia catholica* (1433) of Cardinal Nicholas of Cusa (1401–64) back to proposals put forward in 1417 by the Palatine jurist, Dr Job Vener (1370–1447), and even earlier to the late fourteenth century. In a similar vein, the administration of justice was to reach down into the localities in a pyramid of courts whose tiers expanded in symmetrical progression. These administrative blueprints were essentially schemes for better government, not clarions of social rebellion. Only the *Reformation of Emperor Sigismund* (possibly composed by a cleric attending the Council of Basle) went further by demanding the secularisation of the ecclesiastical principalities, the prohibition of capitalist practices and the abolition of serfdom. It lay unheeded, however, until its first printing in 1476, though a spate of editions thereafter suggests that it had struck a popular chord among the German populace at large. The abiding concern of such visionary writings, from the *Reformation of Emperor Sigismund* through the welter of prophetic literature after mid-century to the extraordinary *Booklet of One Hundred Chapters* of the so-called Revolutionary of the Upper Rhine around 1500,[3] was the strengthening of the monarchy: a new emperor would arise to sweep away the arrogant and selfish princes and prelates, and so restore prosperity and peace to the German nation. It took a more sober voice to appreciate that the problem of political authority lay elsewhere: not in a simple antithesis between monarch and political nation, but in the competing claims of different estates within the *Reich* for political representation – and, it may be added, of different regions competing for centrality. At the start of the century, reform proposals had concentrated on the appropriate relationship between the king–emperor and the electors; by mid-

---

[3] For the likely authorship of this tract, see Lauterbach (1989).

century, however, Martin Mair had recognised that the Empire could not be ruled without the involvement of the territorial princes as a whole. In his scheme for a general imperial tax in 1458 he acknowledged that its success would depend on the four main dynasties of the Empire – Habsburg, Wittelsbach, Hohenzollern and Wettin, who ruled both electoral and non-electoral lands – acting in concert. The absence of the three ecclesiastical electors from his scenario shows how far their influence had dwindled in the course of the century.

In the consolidation of the greater secular principalities fifteenth-century Germany displayed some of the constitutional and political features which elsewhere in Europe marked the emergence of nation-states. But that consolidation was rarely the outflow of deliberately 'territorial' thinking, based on the purchase or conquest of land; rather, the princes pursued the much more traditionally dynastic aim of augmenting their patrimony through enfeoffments, marriage and inheritance treaties, and also mortgages. To take one example: the minor landgraviate of Hesse advanced during the century to a major principality by bringing the county of Ziegenhain, which had separated Upper and Lower Hesse, into feudal dependence in 1450, and by gaining the county of Katzenelnbogen, which controlled strategic toll-stations on the Rhine, by inheritance in 1479. The princes continued to regard their assorted lands as a patrimony, to which all male heirs had a claim. Partitions were frequent, and primogeniture seldom prevailed before the sixteenth century. Yet it was less the fact than the circumstances of partition which weakened the principalities. In the south, Bavaria, which had been divided until 1445 into four, then three, was ruled thereafter by the two Wittelsbach lines of Landshut and Munich. But that did not prevent the duchy of Bavaria–Landshut, a territory rich in agriculture, from playing a vigorous part in imperial affairs, situated as it was on the borders of the Habsburg lands and regions 'near to' the crown. The venerable Welf (or Guelph) dukes of Brunswick in the north, by contrast, saw their lands crumble into fragments through repeated partitions, which left only Lüneburg, the senior line and imperial vassal, of any consequence; furthermore, Brunswick was too remote from the heart of the *Reich* to wield much political influence. Partition, in any case, did not need to disturb existing administrative practices or impede co-operation between the joint lines over matters of mutual concern. In Saxony, for instance, the establishment of separate central and local administrations, each with its own exchequer, after the civil wars of mid-century remained in place in both the albertine and ernestine duchies after the partition of the Wettin lands in 1485. A joint diet of both houses, moreover, was convoked at Naumburg in 1499 to hear grievances against the Saxon bishops and consider proposals for church reform. Although primogeniture had been established in only one German territory before 1500 – in Württemberg, by the Treaty of Münsingen which reunited the Stuttgart and Urach lines in 1482 – princes sought by other means to keep their territories intact. In 1473 Margrave Albert Achilles regulated his succession in the *Dispositio Achillea* in such a way that the margraviate of Brandenburg, to which the electoral dignity attached, should remain undivided in the hands of his eldest son, while Ansbach and Bayreuth were to fall by lot to his two younger sons; formally, indeed, primogeniture did not become binding in Brandenburg until 1599. In the Palatinate (which as an electorate should have been impartible according to the Golden Bull of 1356), Frederick the Victorious was driven to a more desperate device. In the *Arrogation* of 13 January 1452 he declared himself elector regent by adopting his nephew Philip, the heir to the title, who was still a minor, while undertaking to remain single and without issue himself – a constitutional conjuring trick which was accepted by the other electors but steadfastly rejected by the emperor, who sought to depose him.

Partition, of course, bore no threat to the ecclesiastical territories, which knew no principle of dynastic succession. Though the machinations of Dietrich of Moers in Cologne indicate that the principle was not absolute, the ecclesiastical princes succumbed in the longer term to *de facto* mediatisation, whereby secular territorial rulers, in an extension of their own dynastic policy, installed their kin or leading councillors in neighbouring sees. The classic example is the Palatinate, where the chancellor, Matthias von Rammung, was appointed bishop of Speyer in 1464, and his successor, Johann von Dalberg, became bishop of Worms in 1483: both men retained their secular offices! In Cologne, Frederick the Victorious secured his younger brother Rupert as archbishop in 1463 after the demise of Dietrich of Moers. Far from restoring its fortunes, however, Rupert plunged the archbishopric into turmoil by inviting Charles the Bold to intervene against his rebellious cathedral chapter, which led to the fateful siege of Neuß in 1474–5. In the case of the other two ecclesiastical electorates, the sprawling primatial see of Mainz had been weakened by the intrigues of the counts of Nassau earlier in the century; thereafter it spent vast sums defending its territories against secular predators (chiefly Hesse and the Palatinate), until by mid-century it was all but bankrupt (as was Cologne). The engagement of its famous archbishop, Berthold of Henneberg (r. 1484–1504), in the cause of imperial reform at the end of the century may well have sprung from the need to retrieve or conceal the collapse of Mainz's power. The third ecclesiastical electorate, Trier, enjoyed a much calmer passage through the century, but was too small and too exposed to Burgundian influence to make much impact in imperial politics. The episcopal territories in general were handicapped, moreover, by their elective character. Conflicts between bishops and their chapters could capsize into wider political instability, as the numerous episcopal feuds (*Stiftsfehden*) of the century testify. In sum, while the absence of partition saved the ecclesiastical territories from sinking into insignificance, the lack of a dynastic policy prevented them at the same time from augmenting their power in open competition with the secular princes. The Teutonic Order suffered a rather different fate. With Lithuania's conversion to Christianity, the Knights had lost their *raison d'être*; increasingly the Order became a refuge for the younger sons of noble families in the south and south-west of the Empire. The defeat at Grunwald cost the Order vast sums in ransom money, which could only be raised with the help of the estates. But the mentality of the Knights, backward-looking and exclusive, made it difficult to frame a constitution which would grant a political voice to the native nobility and towns. The thirteen years' war between the Knights and the estates, which ended in 1466 with the Second Peace of Thorn, brought the Order under Polish sway and led to the division of its territory into two unconnected halves, 'western' Prussia, the original homeland, and Livonia, which was governed by an independent High Master. After the secularisation of the Prussian territory in 1525, the office of Teutonic High Master was assumed by the German Master, the superior of the German Knights of the Order who led a separate existence within the Empire, organised into twelve bailiwicks.

However, the political disintegration of the Teutonic Order in the fifteenth century should not obscure its pioneering achievements in book keeping and estate management, without which territorial consolidation was hardly possible. The Order's Great Rent Book (compiled between 1414 and 1422, and again from 1437 to 1438) may have been an epitaph to vanished rents and abandoned holdings, but its scope and accuracy were unprecedented. Soon there followed in many German territories, notably Saxony and Bavaria, the institution of the office of receiver-general of domanial revenues (*Rentmeister*), though the establishment of a treasury (*Kammer*) usually came later. The princes' attention during the century broadened, moreover, from the narrowly fiscal and financial – taxes, tolls, mines and coinage – to wider issues of public welfare, enshrined in economic and social legislation, known in contemporary parlance as 'good police' (*gute Polizei*). By 1500, thirteen territories had promulgated ordinances to improve the administration of justice and to promote the commonweal, and many more followed in the next century.[4] Such ordinances presupposed, in turn, a network of officials in the localities and at the centre of government capable of supervising and enforcing their provisions. The development of territorial bureaucracies staffed by salaried officials is indeed a hallmark of the age, but it needs to be remembered that such clerks were at the

---

[4] Ordinances were issued for Thuringia (1446), Lower Hesse (1455), Bavaria–Landshut (1474), the Rhine Palatinate (1475), Saxony (1482 and 1488), Tirol (1487), Liège (1487), Baden (1495), Württemberg (1495), Upper Hesse (1497), Nassau (1498) and Bavaria–Munich (1500).

bottom of the pecking order at the princes' court; the written records which they began to generate in such profusion must not be taken as a true reflection of the exercise of power, which still flowed through verbal instructions by the prince to his closest aristocratic councillors expressed in confidential audiences. Nevertheless, the rise of professional bureaucrats, many of bourgeois origin, and often trained in codified civil law ('Roman law') rather than German customary law, is unmistakable. To provide such trained men for their chanceries the princes founded universities within their territories: between 1380 and 1480 twelve high schools were established in the Empire (in relation to population a figure exceeded only by Scotland in this period), and several more were attempted.[5] It was only in the mid-fifteenth century, however, that civil, as opposed to canon, law came to dominate the curriculum.

The concentration of princely power was matched in many cases by the growth of territorial estates, who were often the stoutest defenders of territorial integrity against mortgages and partitions. In the ecclesiastical principalities the estates were usually dominated by the powerful and aristocratic chapters. In Cologne, for example, in the aftermath of Dietrich of Moers's misrule, the chapter even managed to set up a permanent territorial council in which it held an equal share of power with the archbishop in the governance of the territory (hence Rupert of the Palatinate's assault on his chapter in the 1470s). In the secular principalities the composition and competence of the estates varied greatly. Where the prince could rely on his own revenues, whether from domains and tolls (as in the Palatinate) or from regalian rights (as in Saxony), he could frequently dispense with the need to summon the estates to vote taxes: in such cases the estates remained politically weak. Temporary opportunities to assert their influence could present themselves during minorities or partitions, but on the restoration of unity and firm rule the estates' power receded, as in Hesse under Landgrave Philip the Magnanimous (r. 1518–67) after his long minority. In Bavaria, where the nobles' estate had dominated the ducal council in the years of partition, the nobles saw their influence wane, as the reunited duchy after 1503 created a strong central administration which over-rode their rights of feudal jurisdiction in the localities. In Württemberg, by contrast, the gross misrule of Duke Ulrich (r. 1503–19; 1534–50) roused the estates to active political participation, which was formally recognised in the Treaty of Tübingen (8 July 1514).

---

[5] Universities were founded in Heidelberg in 1386 (for the Palatinate), in Cologne in 1388 (by the city), in Erfurt in 1392 (for Thuringia), in Rostock in 1419 (for Mecklenburg), in Louvain in 1425 (for Brabant), in Trier in 1454 (for the prince-electorate), in Greifswald in 1456 (for Pomerania-Wolgast), in Freiburg im Breisgau in 1457 (for Outer Austria), in Basle in 1459 (by the city), in Ingolstadt in 1459/1472 (for Bavaria–Landshut), in Tübingen in 1476 (for Württemberg–Stuttgart) and in Mainz in 1476 (for the prince-electorate). On the universities founded in Europe at this time, see above, pp. 220–1.

Württemberg was one of several German territories, situated mainly in the south, where towns and peasants were fully represented in the estates. The commons' estate (*Landschaft*) in Württemberg was based on the administrative division of the duchy into districts (*Ämter*) which comprised a small town and its surrounding countryside, though only the urban notables, rather than the commons at large, had an effective say in the territorial diets. Elsewhere the commons formed a political estate in the ecclesiastical principality of Salzburg (where the *Landschaft* rebelled against the archbishop in 1462), in the margraviate of Baden (where the third estate comprised only peasants), and in the Austrian county of Tirol (where there were four estates in all, with the towns and rural commons each constituting a separate estate). It is no accident that commons' membership of the territorial estates was concentrated in southern Germany, for there the rural commune (*Gemeinde*) as a political association was most highly developed. Indeed, in the course of the fifteenth century many rural communes in the south were actively seeking to extend their authority by taking control of parish administration as well. These communal rights were fixed in custumals (*Weistümer*), in which dues claimed by the feudal lords but denied by the peasants were excluded. Where custumals were rare, as in much of northern and eastern Germany, the village as a political community was weak, and the *Landschaft* absent (except, of course, in Frisia and Dithmarschen). In the smaller principalities of the south, such as the monastic territories which lay strewn across Swabia, peasants by the end of the century had in some cases succeeded – after years of resistance to feudal obligations – in negotiating treaties of lordship (*Herrschaftsverträge*) with their overlords, which made considerable concessions to communal demands. In the fragmented and diminutive jurisdictions which characterised much of southern Germany there was, however, no territorial framework in which the commons could express their will as a *Landschaft*. Accordingly, in those instances they looked instead to the looser forms of corporative–confederal association which were the hallmark of the Swiss Confederation. That may serve as a pertinent reminder that the constitutional dualism of monarch and estates which marked the political consolidation of the Empire in the fifteenth century was not the only road down which Germany might have travelled into modern times.

CHAPTER 18

HUS, THE HUSSITES AND BOHEMIA

John Klassen

AT the beginning of the fifteenth century the king and nobility of Bohemia were in competition to fulfil what each saw as the interests of the kingdom. By 1405 the nobility had halted the efforts towards centralisation being pursued by Wenceslas IV, and largely controlled the country's government. Soon afterwards Jan Hus and others began to call for reform of the Church and religious life. Followers of Hus also worked to include all social groups within the political community, which was to be broadened to include institutions giving the commons of both town and country their place. Imbued with a particular understanding of the Christian faith and of the laws of God, all levels of Bohemian society would be identified by a common faith and by a common, Czech language. Tradition, however, was to prove too strong for them. By 1434, the nobility had defeated the radicals, and by the end of the century it once again dominated the country. Calls for popular sovereignty had been silenced.

SOCIETY

Along with Moravia, Silesia and Upper and Lower Lusatia, the kingdom of Bohemia was one of five provinces united under the crown of St Wenceslas. The population of these lands consisted of a mixture of Czechs, Germans, Poles, Lusatian Serbs and Jews. In Bohemia, by the beginning of the fifteenth century, the Czech language was used by noble courts and town councils to record business, by chroniclers to describe the past and by religious writers to inspire the faithful. The Czech language came increasingly into its own during the revolution as theologians used it to express delicate turns of phrase and abstract concepts. Others were to use it to arouse people to fight for reform and revolution, and to create a national consciousness among the common people. At the beginning of the century, most Germans lived in the border regions, although in some interior towns, such as Kutná Hora, government

367

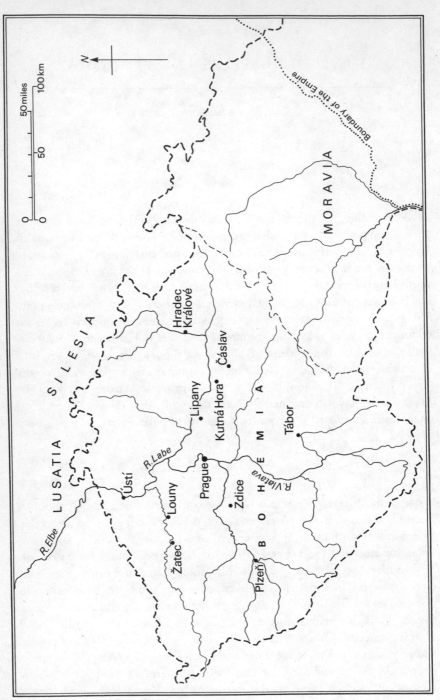

Map 7   Bohemia

remained in German hands even though Czechs made up the majority of the population. In Prague, some crafts and trades followed ethnic lines, but both groups were about equally represented in the important textile trade. The government in Old Town Prague was in German hands, although this caused no resentment until 1408 when it frustrated the efforts of Hus and his friends to reform the Church.

The fundamental fact of economic life was its subsistent character. Bohemia had been spared the worst effects of the Black Death in the mid-fourteenth century and the calamitous drop in population which had so often followed. None the less, destructive waves of the plague did hit Bohemia in 1380, 1395 and 1413–15, resulting in overall population decline between 1380 and 1420. In particular, this was to hurt agricultural producers whose prices did not rise at the rate of their labour costs. A drop in consumption also affected commerce and artisanal production.[1] The struggles for power within the royal family, as well as between king and archbishop and king and nobility, also harmed the economy. When the German princes deposed Wenceslas as head of the German Empire in 1400, the imperial court left Prague and no longer patronised its entrepreneurs and artisans. Growth in the economy depended mainly on internal trade, since few Czech products were exported. Prague and lesser towns such as Plzeň produced cloth for domestic markets: Prague exported some military weapons and some hides left Plzeň for foreign countries. To pay for what they imported, Czechs sold the silver mined at Kutná Hora; they also deliberately debased the Prague *groschen*, whose value, in the first two decades of the century, declined by 20 per cent by comparison with the currency of neighbouring Hungary. Debasement of the *heller*, the coin in which most day-labourers and peasants were paid, was even more rapid. To make matters worse, in the decades before the revolution, tax burdens on royal and ecclesiastical estates rose relentlessly. In 1418, one of the worst years for taxation, residents of New Town Prague were asked seven times for contributions.

Those clergy with prebends were among the wealthiest people, but there were also many poor priests. Before the revolution, the Church owned about 28 per cent of the land overall. Prelates such as the canons of St Vitus enjoyed an annual income of some 18,000 *groschen*, or almost fifty *groschen* a day, in strong contrast with the single *groschen* owed to the holder of an altar or with the two or three *groschen* earned by the skilled labourer. Furthermore, among the clergy, only some 4,000 of the 20,000 who sought ordination between 1395 and 1416 found a parish or other living.[2] The clergy were encountered in many aspects of daily life, both as spiritual guides and as secular lords. By the fourteenth century, lay religious groups such as the Waldensians were active in

---

[1] Maur (1989), p. 40. [2] Šmahel (1985), p. 23.

southern Bohemia, Hradec Králové, Prague and Žatec, and would supply recruits for the Hussite cause.

The nobility's domination of political life depended on its military skills and experience and on the ownership of land and castles, these symbolising the power which it exercised over the countryside and its population. Nobles and members of the gentry exercised right of patronage to some 60 per cent of the country's parish churches, a figure which reflected their share of landowner-ship. Nobles ranged in wealth from the Rožmberks, whose extensive domains in the south rivalled those of the king, to the Švamberks, pressured by urban and royal expansion near Plzeň. Yet they were far from being a united group, as was shown by a great baronial landowner, Čeněk of Vartemberk, who helped the Hussite movement in a crucial way between 1415 and 1419 by leading a public protest against the execution of Jan Hus by the Council of Constance, and by organising the defence and ordination of Hussite clergy.

Because they owned land and could formally register it, members of the gentry (*vladykové* or *zemané*) were part of the ruling community. They also fought in war. At the beginning of the fifteenth century there were about 2,000 such families in Bohemia. Together they formed two groups: the upper group, called *rytíři* (*milites*) or knights and esquires, and the lower group called *panoše* (*clientes, armigeri*) or mere gentlemen. While a few built themselves small castles, many lived in simple farms which scarcely raised them above their tenants. Study of the gentry from 1395 to 1410 shows that close on 80 per cent had rental incomes between 120 and 600 *groschen*, paid by three to five peasant fami-lies. Since 600 *groschen* was about subsistence level, these gentry families needed to find other incomes.[3] Some augmented their livelihoods by serving powerful lords; others simply reverted to robbery. While some gentry entered the circles of power as individuals because king, baron or Church needed their particular skill, by the beginning of the fifteenth century the baronage was increasingly restricting access to its group. In response, the lesser nobility was to develop a sense of its own political identity.

The political experience and prestige gained by the lesser nobility was to contribute to the success of the radicals between 1420 and 1434. Jan Žižka's brilliant military innovations, the success of his revolutionary armies and his leadership in seeking a politically realistic settlement are well known. He was not alone: Nicholas of Hus constituted an example of a man prepared to risk worldly achievements for the sake of Hussite ideals. A member of an impover-ished family, he had a successful career as burgrave in a castle belonging to the canons of the Vyšehrad chapter. By joining the radicals, however, he turned his back on all that. In July 1419 he made his experience available to the radicals

---

[3] Polívka (1985), pp. 154–7.

when he successfully negotiated on behalf of a crowd which had gathered to ask the king for the right of children to be given communion.

Peasant society included great variations of wealth which differed according to region. By the beginning of the century most labour services had disappeared, and many peasants paid their rent in money, freeing them to work their own lands and sell surpluses for profit. Generally speaking, the wealthiest 4 to 5 per cent worked some 20 to 25 per cent of the land. Most peasants held modest-sized holdings, and there seems to have been no great hunger for land. In the late fourteenth century an entire village was deserted in the estate of Chynov, near Tabor, later to be the centre of radical peasants.[4] Nevertheless, in their struggle for existence peasants as a group were confronted by uncertainties, humiliations and mistreatment. When promised a new dignity, they joined the Hussite call for a new Church and a new society. These former servants and cottars served with radical enthusiasm and self-confidence in Taborite armies, fighting side by side with bailiffs, stewards and even gentry with whom they were brothers in faith. Back in the village, however, little changed. Here they were again dependants, owing rents and obeisance to their lords who, in some cases, were the officials of Tabor itself. Throughout the century of war, peasants also faced the added burden of supplying the permanent armies of the revolution from the hard-earned produce of their land. The urban author of the *Old Czech Annalist* described vividly how prices had increased in the 1460s. Just as the peasants prepared to harvest, soldiers came and burned the crops; as peasants began to plough, so soldiers prevented them from doing so. It was soldiers, too, who repeatedly ordered peasants to pay levies in the name of the country's competing authorities.[5]

In royal cities and towns wealthy burghers held the status that the nobility enjoyed throughout the country. Townspeople had considerable freedom to govern themselves, although the king could intervene and appoint magistrates if he wished. Urban revenues came mainly from trade, industry and the interest arising from debts and rents. The people used their wealth to buy land in the countryside, something which the nobility viewed as a threat. The wealthy elite monopolised the politically powerful positions on the town councils. Their piety was reflected in the support which they gave to Czech-language preachers, to the production of vernacular translations of the Bible and to the provision of hospitals, public baths and other material aid for the poor. Their patronage played an important role in helping the reform effort get under way in the late fourteenth and early fifteenth centuries.

In smaller towns a majority of residents lived off agriculture and rents from

[4] Šmahel (1993), I, esp. pp. 426–32.
[5] Šimek (ed.), *Staré Letopisy České z Vratislavského Rukopisu*, p. 146.

their holdings, while artisan manufacturers and tradesmen earned their living by meeting local needs. Tariff records show a healthy local trade in goods ranging from grain and cattle to iron and pottery. The poor and propertyless, exempted from taxation, could not participate in the public lives of their communities. Both peasants and urban commoners heeded the Hussite call to a life based on apostolic models of prayer, sexual purity and generosity. Preachers gave the laity the right to decide whether their priests were morally qualified or not. When the revolution broke out in 1419, commoners played an essential political and military role in preventing King Sigismund from taking the throne.

POLITICS

As the kings of the Luxemburg dynasty in the fourteenth century had tried to develop monarchical power on the basis of feudal ties with the landowning classes, so they had built a separate set of royal institutions alongside those already in existence. Royal government had jurisdiction over ecclesiastical lands, royal towns and estates, including those held as fiefs of the crown. Here the king was sovereign and absolute ruler; disputes regarding property in these categories were heard in royal courts. But in the government of the country supreme power lay in the high court (*zemsky soud*). This met four times a year and had jurisdiction over all free landholders, barons, knights and gentry; even the king could be cited before it. At the head of the country's government was a committee of four chief officials whose membership rotated among the old baronial families. The chief burgrave presided over the court in the king's absence, and summoned armies needed to keep the peace. The chief chamberlain issued summonses, arranged judicial investigations, conducted hearings and pronounced the verdicts of the court. The chief judge named the juries and supervised the court's proceedings with an eye to traditional legal formalities. The chief notary recorded the court's actions. The same prominent families claimed the right to govern the twelve districts into which the country's administration was divided.

At the beginning of the fifteenth century the nobility was putting the finishing touches to its successful struggle with King Wenceslas in which it had seen itself acting on behalf of the whole community. The nobles had contested the monarch's power from 1394 to 1405, accusing him of threatening their allodial property, of opening his council to foreigners and of permitting men amenable to bribery to serve in the royal court to the detriment of the interests of long-standing noble families, to whom the king's policies were destructive of the welfare of the realm. So, in their pact of 1394, they had claimed to seek the good of the country, to promote and effect true justice within it, and always to stand by it together, so as to keep zealously as our goal the welfare of the country . . . If anyone should try in any way to oppress any one of us or of our men, against the custom of the land or against the law defined by the lords of the country's court, we promise to help our fellows faithfully.[6]

For the nobles, the national good meant that they controlled the government. Among the twenty-one demands of 1394, to which the king acquiesced in 1405, six concerned the filling of governmental offices. Article fifteen was representative; it read:

The office of the burgrave of Prague is to be held by a native lord as of old, and he shall be placed in this office with the counsel of the lords . . . The same goes for the other offices that the lords have held from of old; to all such offices a noble-born lord is to be named.[7]

Wenceslas was also required to stop appointing gentry and townsmen to his high council. The lords further demanded that traditional procedures in the running of the courts be restored, that the law, according to ancient custom, be applied and that royal officials should not interfere in the government of regional districts. To them, tradition and custom once again meant noble control. In 1405 the king, for the good of the whole country as he put it, finally agreed to these demands. Henceforth the barons had to approve any appointment to the royal council. A ruling against the king in a property dispute in December 1405 underlined clearly the king's position in the realm as merely the first among equals. Shortly after the baronial victory, Czechs became preoccupied with issues of religious reform. In that process, the baronage came under pressure from Hussite reformers to revise fundamentally and to extend its understanding of the national community along lines of language and religious belief so as to include all social groups.

JAN HUS: TEACHING AND ACTIVITIES

The fifteenth century was marked by the Hussite revolution which grew out of an attempt to reform the religious lives of the people. Hus was primarily concerned with the reform of religious life both in the individual and in the Church. His skills as a university teacher and preacher to the people helped him capture the imagination and loyalty of his fellow Czechs. After his death in 1415 they took up his cause, attempting to weld the national will around his memory. He and his followers emphasised personal morality, care of neighbour and reform of the clergy by the secular government. They called for the creation of a community whose regulations and pattern of life, both political

---

[6] Palacký, *Archiv Česky čili staré písemné památky ceské i moravské*, I, p. 52.   [7] Palacký, p. 57.

and ecclesiastical, would be based on the law of God. At the same time their rhetoric assumed a strong national character.

The substance of Hus's programme was summed up in his tract *De ecclesia*, which, written in 1413, was strongly influenced by the ideas of the Englishman John Wyclif. Hus defined the church as the congregation of those living under the rule of Christ. Everyone was a member of the Church by virtue of baptism administered just after birth. However, not everyone in Christendom was faithful to the way set out by Christ. The Church, then, according to Hus, included both the sheep chosen for salvation and the goats whose damnation was foreknown. The faith of those predestined to follow Christian love might only emerge later, and so the identity of each could not be positively known. Nevertheless, an indication of faith could be inferred from men's actions. Hus taught that true Christians should be judged by their fruits.

Hus preached a standard Catholic piety. People needed to recognise themselves as sinners before they could know God. They must renounce the world, with its possessions, pleasures and dignities. He assured them that they were saved by God's prior grace, and that a living faith was adorned by good works leading to the supreme love of God. The word of God should be preached freely because it enlightened reason, regulated desires, eliminated sin and engendered God's grace. He recommended that the rich give their wealth to the poor, and spoke against elaborate burials and a multitude of masses for the dead.[8] Judging from the actions of propertied residents of the Catholic town of Plzeň, who reduced their gifts to the clergy for funeral rites and replaced them with gifts for the poor, his preaching won widespread support.

Hus gave the laity the choice whether or not to obey priests, saying that they should acknowledge only those priests who lived holy lives. The prelates who lived barren spiritual lives in luxury and pomp, devoured the alms of the poor, accumulated benefices and, as in the case of the pope, allowed himself to be adored on bended knee and to have his feet kissed were unworthy of their calling. As his predecessors of the late fourteenth century had done, Hus also stressed that, in the face of general poverty, the Church's wealth and affluent life style was a mark of sin and faithlessness. He criticised the Church's elaborate ceremonies, its pictures and vestments, and its use of chalices, bells, organs and singing which, he claimed, diverted people from God. Lay men and women were urged to admonish priests on the basis of Holy Scripture, and if a priest refused to accept correction, people need not believe him. Christ had appointed Peter 'captain and shepherd' of the Church because of his qualities, and only virtuous popes could be elected. In essence such ideas made the

[8] Spinka (1966), p. 217.

people sovereign, and represented the foundation upon which the Hussites assumed the right to choose their own king and Tabor built its republic.

Hus also taught that the Church's authority was limited to the spiritual realm. The power of the keys given to Peter was for spiritual purposes, for discerning sins, not for juridical or monarchical rule. Coercive governmental powers belonged exclusively to the secular lord and king. At first Hus believed that if he spelled out the scriptural life of faith to his fellow clergy, they would voluntarily reform. The Bohemian Church, however, declined his invitation. Hus took up Wyclif's idea that the king and the nobility should reform the Church and deprive it by force of its secular dominion and property. The Church should be subject to the sovereign lay ruler. Not surprisingly, Hus's attack on the ecclesiastical hierarchy, including the Papacy, made his reform unacceptable at the Council of Constance.

The controversies surrounding the reformers and their encouragement to the laity to emulate the apostolic Church stimulated reading of the Scriptures. Like Wyclif, Hus wanted common people to have access to the Bible, and so he advocated both Czech and German translations, albeit in the face of ecclesiastical opposition. In the previous century, parts of the Bible had been rendered into Czech for monastic women who wished to follow the lectionary. Then, in 1381, a wealthy Prague burgher had underwritten a translation of a German Bible, and a partial translation had resulted. It seems that in 1392 Matthew of Janov had a translation of the Czech Bible which the consistory confiscated. It was in an effort to satisfy a hunger for the Scriptures that Hus published the Czech, St Mikulovský Bible, containing the New Testament, the Psalms and the Wisdom literature in 1406. The *Orthographia Bohemica*, attributed to Hus, was published no later than 1412, predating the *Orthographia Gallica* by at least eight years. This text guided Czech writers of theological and moral discourses, as well as poets and story tellers. Hus's rural ministry among the common people called for the whole Bible in Czech and for the simplified orthography in which cumbersome compounds, such as 'cz', were replaced by 'č', making the book less expensive and more accessible to the public. František Bartoš assumed that Hus published a fully revised Czech Bible in 1413–14.[9]

Hus also opened the door for women to participate publicly in national life. His affirmation of women is best reflected in his tract of 1412, 'Recognising the true way to salvation', also known as 'The Daughter', in which he chose woman to represent humanity in a generic sense. In the opening chapter, on creation, Hus reminded his readers that, as women, they were made in the image of God, and that they could act with dignity and courage, fearing no

---

[9] Bartoš (1947), pp. 250–5; Kejř (1984), pp. 123–6.

man.[10] Women responded to his call. Female patrons placed reformers into parishes; women preached and wrote tracts. In July 1420 women figured decisively in a key battle fighting off an attack on Prague. In the following year a group of women occupied the city hall and forced a change of policy, placing Prague back in the moderate camp. However, their gains were short. After 1421, Czech men reverted to the principle of masculine privilege, and the body politic remained an arena reserved for males.

After 1407 Hus and his followers stepped up their attack on ecclesiastical property and indulgences, and life in Bohemia became increasingly coloured by ethnic rivalry. The struggle between the mostly Czech reformers and their German opponents reached its first crisis that year. The Czechs found that they were hindered in their efforts because the powerful and remunerative offices in the university were in the hands of their foreign opponents. King Wenceslas's wish for a representative at the Council of Pisa, which had been convened to heal the schism in the Church, helped the Czechs. As Archbishop Zbyněk would not send a representative, in January 1409, through the Kutná Hora decree, Wenceslas gave control of the university's administration to the Czech masters and students, who subsequently authorised a delegation to go to Pisa.

During these debates over church life, the reformers appealed to national and ethnic identity to which they gave a religious dimension. In 1409, Jerome of Prague described his nation (*nacio*) not as the territorial community of the university nations, but as a Czech-language community, a political group whose members spoke Czech, both of whose parents were Czech, and who supported the religion of the Bohemian-Wycliffite reform movement. His Czech community, or nation, retained the three estates, nobility, clergy and commons, with respective sub-gradations. He gave predominant place to orthodox belief, persons of other tongues not being *per se* excluded if they supported reform. Another reformer, the lawyer John of Jesenice, fuelled the conflict when he argued that the king had the right to raise the native sons of the kingdom to the top positions in royal and ecclesiastical offices because they sought the kingdom's welfare, while foreigners did not.[11]

In 1410 tension between the archbishop and Hus increased as King Wenceslas appropriated ecclesiastical estates. Although the king, Queen Sophia, several lords and the city council supported Hus, the Papacy summoned him to the *curia*. In 1411, when he did not go, the pope pronounced an anathema over Hus and an interdict over most of Prague. In the following year, the king changed sides and supported the Church in the controversy over

[10] Molnár, 'Dcerka- O Poznání česty pravé k spasení', pp. 164–5.
[11] Šmahel (1969), pp. 163–78; Kaminsky (1967), pp. 68–9.

indulgences. In the autumn, Hus left Prague for the south of the country where he preached and wrote in Czech, preparing broad social support for reform in this region. In late 1414, in response to Emperor Sigismund's request, and armed with statements from the king and his court, from the high courts representing the baronage and even from the inquisitor himself clearing him of heresy, Hus travelled to the Council of Constance to defend his cause. About the same time Jakoubek of Stříbro gave wine to the laity during communion in several churches in Prague. The chalice thus became the symbol of the Hussite movement and of its rebellion against the Church. This irregular liturgical practice did not help Hus's case at Constance, and he was executed on 6 July 1415.

Hus's cause stimulated the nobility to include religion in their area of jurisdiction. From 1415 to the death of King Wenceslas in 1419 the nobles headed the national effort to reform the Church. In the name of the Czech crown they issued a protest against the burning of Hus. Speaking on behalf of the Czech language and all true or poor Czechs, whatever their faith, they accused those Czech Catholics who joined the common front of foreigners of betraying the Czech crown and language. The Council's execution of Hus, they asserted, was an insult to the most Christian Czech kingdom. To underline their words, they formed a league to defend one another and their clergy against any attack from abroad. These leagues, one for the defence of Hussite priests, the other for Catholics, were designed to retain noble control over the social order. The Hussite league, augmented by a regional association of gentry in 1417, gave protection and assurance to preachers of reform, who ranged from radicals wanting to reduce the use of elaborate ceremonies and vestments of the liturgy to the moderates who hoped to find acceptance within European Christendom for communion in both kinds and a reform of the most blatant clerical abuses. The protection and patronage of the Hussite nobility were particularly important from 1417 to 1419 when the Church launched a drive to suppress reform. King and archbishop vacillated in the face of the nobility, and so a 'live and let live' attitude prevailed until Wenceslas's death in 1419. However, Sigismund, the heir apparent, constituted a test to such religious toleration. Committed to the suppression of Hussitism, he was, as such, unacceptable to the country's rulers. Consequently, he had to wait until 1436 to secure his throne.

Sigismund's stance forced the Hussites to face the question of what type of government they wanted. Some, despairing of secular rule, placed their hope in the imminent return of Christ and his kingdom. When Christ did not return on the predicted day, most of these joined other radicals in fortified settlements such as Tabor in southern Bohemia, Hradec Králové in the east, or New Town Prague. For purposes of maintaining public order in the country there were basically two groups among the Hussites: (i) the moderate coalition of nobles, university masters and municipal officials led by Prague, and (ii) the radicals, led by the gentry and the university-trained priests whose political dynamic depended on the energy of the urban commons and the peasantry. The means favoured by the moderates to establish national order were the diets, of which some twenty were called between 1419 and 1435, which established governing councils for the country. The radicals sent representatives to the diets but, when their programmes were not adopted, they concentrated on organising local communities under the protection of their field armies.

To the radicals, the moderates appeared as traitors because they negotiated away castles as well as religious principles in a vain hope that Sigismund and the Church would accept Hussite reforms. The radicals also disliked what they regarded as the indulgent life style of the moderates, their elaborate liturgies and vestments and their refusal to give communion to infants. To the moderates, the radicals disrupted the social order with their attacks on monasteries and churches, and through their destruction of property. Both groups saw themselves as providing social order. The moderates hoped the way was through negotiation with the king, compromise being implicit. The radicals declared that the welfare of the realm required a total religious cleansing of the individual, and tended to separate themselves into their own communities in which they tried to establish religious purity.

HUSSITES AND NATIONAL DIETS: 1419–36

Between 1419 and 1436 the diets were primarily concerned with forging national unity, with questions of social order, the conditions under which to accept Sigismund as king, and the nature of the agreement with the Catholic Church to the fore. Before 1419 the king or his representative had called the diet, and sometimes the meeting of the high court took on the character of a deliberative assembly. After 1419 there was neither a king to convene a diet nor a set order of procedures. During the revolution, in order to be effective, resolutions had to be accepted almost unanimously, which was possible only if one or more of the extreme parties was absent. The Catholic barons often refused to attend, and sometimes the leading Hussite barons, too, were absent. Enforcement of decisions depended upon who controlled what territory. In effect this meant that resolutions of the diets were applied only in Hussite territories, and even there only partially. Historians of Hussitism are not in agreement as to whether some sessions should be called official diets or only strategy meetings of one party. None the less, diets claimed country-wide jurisdiction, and it was out of them that national government emerged in the 1430s.

At the beginning of the revolution the most significant change in government was the reduced role of the barons. The religious convictions of the townspeople and of the gentry, along with the economic power emanating from Prague, encouraged them to play a more self-confident and influential role in the polity. Royal towns claimed legal equality with the nobility. They took the initiative in convening diets according to the needs of the moment, and helped set the agenda. At some diets even the common people were represented.

The first diet of the revolution recognised urban power and was determined to give Czechs the dominant position within the realm. The session of August 1419, attended by all factions, issued a number of demands which, in some ways, simply continued traditional requirements made of rulers since the coming to power of the Luxemburg dynasty. But the diet also reflected growing national self-confidence, in particular the interests of the urban population now literate in Czech. In 1413 the king had decreed that half the town councillors in Old Town Prague were to be Czech, the other half German. The diet of 1419 excluded Germans from office where Czechs were able to govern. Whereas in the previous century Charles IV had proposed that the Czech language be an option in government, the diet of 1419 demanded that court actions be carried out only in Czech. In church, Latin was no longer to be exclusively the language of sacred rituals. The diet resolved that Czech should be allowed in worship, which included singing and the reading of the epistles, and stated that, in general, Czechs should have the first voice throughout the kingdom. In expressing Prague's concerns, the diet, including the nobles, spoke for a national community in which, for the first time, the common people had some say.

The foreign armies which entered Bohemia hoping to extirpate heresy and reap material benefits inflamed national feeling among the Czechs. In March 1420 Sigismund decided to take his crown by force. To assist him, Pope Martin V issued a bull declaring a crusade against Bohemia. The Hussites responded with propaganda designed to rouse the people to resist. They attacked the king's moral character and religious faith in order to destroy any aura of majesty which he might enjoy among the people. They also appealed to national feeling. In April 1420 a Hussite manifesto described the German crusaders as natural enemies of the Czech language. The radicals called the Czechs to fight first for God's law, then against the age-old enemy of their language. In addition, they evoked the memory of valiant Czech fathers and of the glorious patron, St Wenceslas, all lovers of their country, to inspire the people to free their most Christian kingdom from oppression. As Prague intellectuals groped for ways to exalt their national feeling, so they exalted their own city, describing it as the first-born of the Czech crown, personifying the nation and the state. A spokesman for the towns asserted this political self-importance when he censured the nobility's all too rapid and irregular coronation of King Sigismund in 1420. The nobles, he claimed, had no right to crown him, 'because you did not have the consent of the capital city, nor of many other Czech towns and communities; you simply did what you wanted, placing a crown on him and declaring him king in a blacksmith's shop'.[12]

Prague's leadership was evident at the Čáslav diet held in June 1421, at which both Hussites and Catholics were present, and which issued a list of grievances and a declaration of unrelenting war against King Sigismund. The fragile national unity among Hussites was expressed in the Four Articles: communion in both kinds (bread and wine), free preaching of the word of God, limits to priestly property and the purgation of public sins. The diet established a twenty-member council of the kingdom. Five of its members were to be nobles, eight or nine were gentry (although Žižka and Chval of Machovice represented Tabor, and in that sense the common people) and seven were townspeople. Several of the diet's official statements ranked Prague, rather than the barons, as heading the national community. What was particularly revolutionary was the voice that the commons of both Old and New Town Prague received on the national council. The diet held at Zdice on 28 October 1424 also gave the commons representation on a governing council.[13]

Despite gains by the commons, the three-tiered social structure remained deeply ingrained in the minds of most people. This mentality, characterised by distinctions of estate, facilitated the effort of nobles to regain control of the country's government. The Diet of St Gall, which met in Prague in November 1423 and took a moderate stand towards Sigismund, marked the decline of Prague and the return to influence of the nobility. In order of precedence Prague was now placed third, after the archbishop and the lords. The twelve-member governing council which it established was made up of six lords from each religious camp. Three of the Hussite lords were allies of Prague, but the city itself was not represented, its activity being confined to issuing safe-conducts and providing notarial and secretarial services. However, the conservative politics of the diet of 1423 hardly reflected the realities of power. Žižka's armies had won major battles against the royalists, and the diet could not address the question of Sigismund's succession or reconciliation with the Church without reference to Žižka and to the radicals.[14] The conservatives who wanted a return to Europe's ecclesiastical and political order had to wait until after the defeat of the radicals in 1434.

Towards the end of the 1420s internal divisions among the Hussites, a general war-weariness and, a little later, a seeming willingness to negotiate

---

[12] Daňhelka (ed.), *Husitské Skladby Budyšínského Rukopsiu*, p. 66.

[13] Hlaváček (1956), p. 80; Tomek (1899), pp. 158–64; Heymann (1954).

[14] Hlaváček (1956), pp. 85–90; Šmahel (1990), p. 365.

shown by the Council of Basle facilitated the efforts of the nobility in the moderate Hussite camp. At a diet in late 1433, poorly attended by the gentry and the towns, the nobility prepared itself for government by first appointing Aleš Vřešťovský as the country's regent. Although a nobleman, he was acceptable to a wide range of Hussites since he had fought alongside Žižka and had helped found one of the radical brotherhoods in eastern Bohemia. Barons such as Menhart of Hradec, who drifted between the Catholic and Hussite parties, wanted him in power because of his status as a noble. Aleš was to keep order with twelve assistants, mostly barons and gentry. The diet gave legitimacy to the nobles' move to restore order to the polity. Meanwhile the radical field armies, dispirited after a long siege of Catholic Plzeň and squabbling among themselves, lost a number of allies from among the gentry. This gave the conservative townspeople, the nobility and the gentry their opportunity. In 1434 they defeated the radical armies at Lipany, and then began implementing their resolutions. Henceforth the more conservative Hussites became the spokesmen of their cause in Bohemia.

The diet of March 1435 reflected the gains of the revolution as well as its programme in its most moderate form. The Bohemian estates, the towns, gentry and nobility, now drafted the requirements to be submitted to King Sigismund. The fact that the nobility made separate demands from the towns reflected its refusal to accept these fully into the national polity. All three estates called for freedom to receive communion in both kinds, and required that foreigners be excluded from public office. The gentry claimed regional representation on the high court for both knights and esquires, asserting that the baronial monopoly had created serious difficulties for them. Prague stipulated that the city's sub-chamberlain should be a Praguer of the Hussite faith. The towns, too, demanded representation on the high court, as well as the right of approval of the king's choice of military captain, and exemption from extraordinary taxation. They wanted, too, to be able to decide property disputes involving exiled citizens, and insisted that no German should be appointed as a city councillor. The cities further distinguished themselves with religious demands which included the right to resistance should they be hampered in exercising their faith.[15] The demands of the gentry and towns were unprecedented. Whereas the barons' demands were consistent with a long tradition, the gentry and towns expressed a new sense of self-confidence as they sought to exploit the gains of the revolution. The requests were granted by Sigismund on 20 July 1436 at an elaborate ceremony at which he was accepted as king.

Prague's struggle for autonomy and for the country's political voice continued through the fifteenth century, success coming only after Catholic and

[15] Tomek (1899), pp. 668–770; Hlaváček (1956), pp. 98–100; Šmahel (1990), pp. 487–8.

Hussite towns had patched up their political differences. After the quarrel between Mátyás Corvinus of Hungary, the Catholic choice for king of Bohemia, and Vladislav (son of King Casimir of Poland), the choice of the Utraquists (as Hussites were known in the late fifteenth century) had been resolved in 1479, Vladislav supported the attempt by Catholic lords to reintroduce Catholicism. But by means of a spirited revolt, the people of Prague prevented the effort to recatholicise their city. One of the outcomes of Prague's success was that nobles began to identify more with other nobles, and townsmen sought the interests of other townsmen, even when they did not share the same confession. Catholic and Hussite lords co-operated in the Peace of 1485, in which each group agreed to allow the other to live in peace. After 1487, the gentry acquired the right to sit on both royal and high courts, and the upper and lower nobility turned their combined attention to curbing the claims of the towns. The result was the Vladislav constitution of 1500 which excluded the towns from representation in the diet. In response, the cities also created a general confederation of Catholics and Utraquists in order to protect their political rights. It took the cities until 1517 to gain representation on the country's diet. But the noble estates still dominated as they determined the composition of the royal council and courts and, by 1500, they required council members and officials to take the oath of loyalty to the diet as well as to the king. The nobility's narrow base contained the seeds of the eventual submission of the estates to the centralising might of the Habsburgs.

The impact of the revolution was most dramatic in its redistribution of property. It is estimated that between 30 and 40 per cent of productive land changed hands. The Church was reduced to the role of a minor property owner, and the crown lost, too, as Sigismund, in 1436 and 1437, reimbursed his allies and confirmed many Hussites in their new holdings. Both Catholic and Hussite nobles gained land, but a minority of noble families secured the lion's share of ecclesiastical property. This redistribution of property led to major upheavals as the estates of individual gentry and the new nobility came to exceed those of many of the old families. For example, Nicholas Trčka of Lípa, once a member of an insignificant gentry family, acquired an immense estate which, by 1450, comprised nine castles and manors, fourteen towns and over 320 villages. The estates of most gentry, however, continued to be too small for their owners to live off the rents. Yet the shift of property owning from the Church was a significant factor in the nobility's drive to power.

TABOR

During the 1420s a significant portion of the Czech people lived outside the jurisdiction of the country's government, and offered an alternative approach to the ordering of society. The radicals, attempting to apply ideas of a strict personal morality, believed that the welfare of the country required a total religious cleansing of the individual which went much deeper than the moderates felt necessary. At a meeting held near Plzeň in September 1419 in preparation for political action they put it thus:

Accordingly all of us, with one will, . . . ask God that we be purged of all that is evil and damaging to the soul, and be developed in all that is good . . . And so, dearest ones, we ask and beg you for God and your salvation to join us all on Saturday at The Crosses . . . for godly unity on behalf of the freedom of the Law of God and for the salutary benefit and honourable welfare of the whole realm, in order that offences and manifest scandals and dissensions be ended and removed, with the help of God, king, lords, knights, esquires, and the whole Christian community.[16]

The moral and religious vision of these people was at the same time a political programme for the whole country. The radicals (or Taborites, as their contemporaries referred to those who, in 1419, gathered on a hill, dubbed Mount Tabor, in southern Bohemia) none the less failed to organise their nation around their ideas of religious and national reform, a failure which they recognised late that year when Prague and the moderate nobles negotiated with Sigismund and dismantled their defences. At the same time the royalists plundered the property of the Hussites, drove out their priests and killed their brothers and sisters. Some radicals, or Chiliasts, interpreted this as the activity of the anti-Christ, concluding that the wrath of God would soon be upon the earth, followed by the early return of Jesus. Rejecting all existing social and political forms, they proclaimed it time for the faithful to leave their livelihoods, seek refuge in five cities and prepare to defend themselves with the sword against the enemies of God. For a brief time those who fled to the five cities imitated apostolic practices and pooled their resources, their priests setting up chests and distributing goods to the needy. Their leaders exhorted them to await the advent of Christ, and to make way for the coming millenial kingdom by destroying his enemies. Wenceslas, a tavern keeper in Prague, and Martin Húska, operating in southern Bohemia, explained that the elect of God would then possess all their enemies' goods, and freely administer their estates and villages. Gold and silver would be freely available; rents paid to lords would be abolished, as would be all forms of subjection. The elect would freely and peaceably possess their villages, fish ponds, meadows, forests and the domains of former lords. All persons of high rank were to be chopped down as pieces of wood. Women would give birth without pain and would no longer suffer the grief of the death of children.[17] Even those who repudiated Chiliasm were influenced by its egalitarian vision of social peace.

---

[16] Palacký, *Archiv Česky čili staré písemné památky ceské i moravské*, III, pp. 205–6; Kaminsky (1967), p. 300.
[17] Kaminsky (1967), pp. 310–60.

There were several towns, from Hradec Králové in the east to Žatec in the north-west and Písek in the south, to which radicals fled. Tabor, the name given to the deserted fortress of Hradiště near the town of Ústí, was in many ways the most important. Both here and in other radical towns the leadership knew that a stable and ordered society involved rules and laws which must be enforced. These men and women formed social, political, economic and military organisations enlivened by ideals of human equality while restrained by tradition and the material realities of life. They viewed as threats some of the alternative approaches to social organisation found in their midst. One such was that of Peter Chelčický who argued that to use force, either against enemies or in order to organise a society and force people to behave in a Christian manner, was incompatible with biblical teaching. Chelčický held that no lord could ask a peasant to do labour which he himself was unwilling to perform. He rejected the three-tiered social structure, and called for a community organically unified by its faith in Christ, whose members treated one another as loving equals. Chelčický also went furthest in subverting the centuries-old prejudice that women were inferior beings. In an undated sermon for Christmas day, after noting the current negative feminine stereotype, he reminded his listeners that both sexes were capable of vice and virtue, and that courage and strength were not preserves of the male.[18]

A second danger came from the free spirit Pikartism of Martin Húska which can be seen as a muted continuation of Chiliasm. Húska believed that God would work real changes in men and women so that their behaviour would be such that there would be no need for law. He taught that Christ was not present in the eucharistic elements, and that this Christian celebration acquired its real meaning when the faithful feasted around supper tables in small groups, performing acts of kindness to one another following the example of Christ. Since He was present in their actions, ordinary people were transformed into something better, something which would exist at the consummation of the age. A small breakaway group, led by Peter Kaníš, practised ritual nudism, and their enemies accused them of gathering for sexual love feasts. Perceived as undermining the wider Hussite cause, they were exterminated by Jan Žižka in April 1421.

Tabor's participation in the efforts to establish national government depended on whether its view of a reformed Church was taken seriously. Its representatives participated at the diet held at Čáslav in 1421, and two of its military captains, Jan Žižka and Chval of Machovice, were named to the twenty-strong governing council. In 1426, however, Tabor opposed the decision of its allies to establish a government on a regional, rather than on a

---

[18] Smetanka (ed.), *Petra Chelčického. Postilla*, I, p. 66.

confessional basis, in order to co-operate with the central government in its attempt to reach agreement with King Sigismund.[19]

Nevertheless, Tabor co-operated with others to create at least a modicum of social peace. For most of the revolution, up to 1434, Tabor was part of a federation of allies, including gentry and towns largely from southern and eastern Bohemia, and including the towns of Žatec and Louny in the north-west. Ties with allied lords were quite free as Tabor's captains entered into agreements with nobles who provided military security for a number of out-lying posts. Ideological agreement was voluntary, and the lord could enter the service of a Catholic once he had fulfilled the terms of his agreement with Tabor. Such nobles were useful allies. They brought armed retinues into battle; they served as administrators of castles conquered by the peasant field armies; and they built up independent retinues. However, the commitment of impor-tant nobles such as Nicholas Sokol of Lamberk, John Smil of Křemž and Přibík of Klenová could easily evaporate. None of these fought on the side of the radical brotherhoods when these were defeated by conservative forces at Lipany in May 1434. Many of the captains who had gained property with the help of peasant armies were later to desert the commoners in order to enter the Hussite aristocracy.

When they established their settlement on the plateau of the deserted fortress, Taborite settlers thought of themselves as breaking decisively with the old Babylon and as being uncontaminated by the past. However, the first set-tlers looked after their own interests and took the best plots for themselves, showing the kind of greed denounced by reformers. None the less this new settlement represented a social revolution of sorts because some who, before the revolution, had owned small dwellings, now found themselves living on the prestigious town square.[20] Furthermore, the founding of Tabor was an act of popular sovereignty and spontaneous free will in that these radical Hussites recognised no human lord, in either the religious or the political sphere. They tried to act with the autonomy of the resurrected Church as they saw it described in the Bible. Individual Taborites lived out that freedom in their worship. Sermons, the simple liturgy and hymns were all in their own Czech language. In discussion groups people offered informed opinions on public life based on their own reading or on the many sermons or expositions which they had heard. As an urban centre, not subject to any lord, Tabor resisted calling itself a town, preferring the more egalitarian form of 'commons'. When refer-ring to themselves as 'We, the commons (*obec*) of the Taborites' they meant a society of people with the same faith and goals, brothers and sisters as partners in self-government, privileges and rights. To the older idea of the urban

---

[19] Šmahel (1990), pp. 337, 379.   [20] Kaminsky (1967), p. 385; Šmahel (1988), pp. 256–63.

corporation they added the notion of the common faith. Howard Kaminsky described the form of democracy there as 'the leader acting with the people, in a sort of resonance that cannot be fixed in the routine of institutions'.[21] In the early days women may have participated in the community's self-government, although they probably did not have voting rights.

The highest organ of civil government was the assembly of all citizens to which the council of elders was responsible. This 'Great Commons' made important decisions, such as in 1450 when it had to decide how to respond to the demand for submission from George of Poděbrady, the leader of moderate Hussitism. Normally the 'Commons' met once a year to elect twenty-four elders, from whom twelve were selected to serve on the town council. The 'Great Commons' approved taxes and the budget, and discussed matters of war and peace. By the end of the 1420s they elected a ruler (*vladař*) who, in time of war, led the forces of Tabor and its allies. The elders had direct responsibility for the non-military matters of the region. After 1432 the town council was elected regularly for one year, the chair rotating with each member holding it for four weeks. The judge was elected at the same time as the council. He supervised the property market within the town walls, as well as agreements over debts, and the sale of property of those dying intestate. With the help of bailiffs he looked after policing and fire safety needs. Appeals from his decisions could be heard by the council.

Despite its egalitarian rhetoric, leadership of the radical federation remained substantially in the hands of nobles. The new rulers in each town sought first and foremost to consolidate their own position at the expense of the urban classes in the county as a whole. Only rarely did members of those classes represent Tabor or serve as military captains. This inclination towards tradition was reflected in a dispute in 1427 when the Taborite council of elders, acting as arbiters, supported the hereditary judge against the autonomy of the town council of Pelhřimov.[22]

The lines of authority and jurisdiction between the civil, spiritual and military life of Tabor's community were blurred before the charter of King Sigismund clarified them in 1437. Although committed to equality between brothers and sisters, two informal elites, one clerical, the other military, dominated. The Taborite priest, better educated and more articulate, carried great influence; he was at once agitator, organiser, councillor and warrior, giving the commune a theocratic character. By the mid-1420s two military leaders were appointed, one responsible for the home army, the other, resident in a nearby fortress, leading the troops further afield. For many years Prokop the Shaven, a

[21] Kaminsky (1967), pp. 484–9; Šmahel (1990), pp. 355, 581–4.
[22] Šmahel (1990), pp. 385–90.

priest and military captain, dominated the federation of radical forces. Yet, in a serious crisis, even he had to submit to his soldiers. In deteriorating military circumstances, during the futile siege of Catholic Plzeň, they criticised his policies and choice of captains, and in 1433 they deposed and briefly imprisoned him.

After his accession in 1437, King Sigismund granted Tabor the status of a royal town, and it entered the normal framework of late medieval politics. It could elect its own council, and rights of appeal from urban and local courts could be made before the king or his representative. The royal judge or advocate was subject to the town council. Tabor was to be free of all royal taxes, except for a small, twice-yearly, payment of 300 *groschen*. It was to remain a free town until integrated under the government of the country by George of Poděbrady in 1448.

Because the radicals wanted a general renewal of the Church in the whole of Europe, they made little use of national arguments in the early stages of the revolution. However, their practices and experience enhanced a Czech identity in their midst. They introduced Czech as the language of worship so that the believer could better communicate with God. It was fundamentally important to Tabor's leaders that their children could read the Bible and sing. By 1446 a separate building had been built for the school. Girls and boys were taught reading, writing, arithmetic, Latin and other subjects from the seven liberal arts. The language of instruction was Czech.

As Tabor became more isolated, it saw itself as alone representing the Czech people, as its support of Kolda of Žampach in 1441 illustrates. Kolda, a lord, had disturbed the peace, and the government, with the help of German-speaking Silesia, had taken action against him. The government saw itself as keeping the peace in the crown lands to which the Silesians belonged; they were not foreigners, simply subjects of the crown. It was as a fellow Czech, however, that Tabor supported Kolda. In a letter of 27 May 1441 Tabor complained of the destruction done, in particular, by Silesian elements in the government's armies. For the sake of the Czech tongue they were helping their friend Kolda against Czech lords and their German allies: 'let the good people see who it is that loves the Czech and Slav languages, who stands for the promotion of the praise of God and for the spread of the Czech language; is it we or is it those who want to counsel and help foreigners?'[23] The patriotic tone of their complaint reflects the distance the radicals had come since their early hopes for a redeemed Europe.

[23] Palacký, *Archiv Česky čili staré písemné památky ceské i moravské*, I, pp. 368–9.

BOHEMIA IN EUROPE

King Sigismund's rule was short and contentious. At his death in 1437 Bohemia's internal political development was vulnerable to interference from neighbouring territories. Nor was the power of the Papacy yet spent; in co-operation with dissatisfied subjects and with ambitious neighbours, it could seriously undermine the position of the ruler of a heretical state. The challenges for anyone trying to rule Bohemia were threefold: to satisfy the minimal demands of the Hussite community; to establish internal political order; and to secure the country against threats from its immediate neighbours.

Rivals of the Bohemian king could easily exploit the unsettled religious situation. On his accession in 1436 Sigismund had confirmed the Compacts, a watered-down version of the Four Articles. Originally the Articles had called for the giving of the wine to the laity in communion, for freedom to preach, for the clergy to renounce pomp, avarice and secular lordship, and for the cessation of public sin. In 1436 Sigismund added the important reservation that only those who had practised communion in both kinds up to that time might continue to do so. Sigismund also endorsed the diet's election of the Hussite, John Rokycana, as archbishop. The king's action was important for the moderates, but neither the Council of Basle, the pope nor the returning Catholic clergy would recognise Rokycana. As a result, differences between Catholics and Hussites continued to thwart the organisation of a single Bohemian Church.

In 1440, however, the Catholics of Bohemia joined the Hussites in drawing up a Letter of Peace affirming the Compacts, and indicating that no candidate other than Rokycana could be seriously considered. Negotiations with the Council and the pope failed, but the Hussite cause in Bohemia was furthered by the capture of Prague by George of Poděbrady in September 1448, an event which allowed Rokycana to enter and assume leadership over the Church. However, he and his church wanted papal confirmation without which he could not ordain priests. Hussite hopes were not fulfilled. In 1458 Pope Pius II appointed Wenceslas Krumlov as administrator of the archdiocese of Prague, dashing Rokycana's expectations. Later, on 31 March 1462, Pius proclaimed the Compacts null and void. However, the two faiths at least partially respected royal decrees to live in peace. When Vladislav became king in 1471 he confirmed freedom of worship for the Hussites. In the agreement made at Kutná Hora in 1485, Catholics and Hussites promised to be content with the parishes under their control, and to abstain from polemics against one another. The freedom to worship according to Catholic or Hussite rites was guaranteed to all social classes. But no archbishop would be appointed to Prague until 1561.

Rivals of the king also took advantage of the unsettled dynastic issue. King

Sigismund died in December 1437, but left no male heir. His son-in-law was Albert of Austria, but he died soon afterwards, leaving an infant son, Ladislav. Political forces in Bohemia were divided between Catholics, led by Ulrich of Rožmberk and Menhart of Hradec, and the Hussites, led first by Hynek Ptáček of Pirkštejn and, after 1444, by George of Poděbrady. The Hussites wanted recognition of the chalice by a legitimate ruler. To this end they persuaded Frederick III of Austria, the guardian of Ladislav, to send the minor heir-apparent to Prague and establish stable government. In the heir's absence, George wanted a governor or administrator. From 1444 to 1448 George prepared himself for that position by marrying the Catholic, Kunhuta of Šternberk, and by removing his rival, Menhart of Hradec, from the royal castles of Vyšehrad and Hradčany. In June 1450 George defeated the league of Strakonice formed by his opponents in the southern and south-western parts of the country. On 27 April 1452 a diet named George as governor to work with Ladislav for two years. In October 1453 Czechs celebrated Ladislav's accession to the throne.

In 1458, after Ladislav's death, both Catholic and Hussite estates accepted election as the most appropriate way of resolving the problem of succession. The general population was involved in the choice, albeit not directly. The Hussite archbishop-elect, Rokycana, sent his priests and chaplains into towns and castles and into the houses of ordinary citizens to influence opinion on behalf of George, a native son. Their propaganda stressed the age-old strife between Germans and Slavs. It described Germans as natural lovers of violence, treacherous and deceitful, with the Elbe Slavs among their victims. Czech history was a warning not to accept a German king.[24] The decisive session of the diet opened on 2 March 1458 in the town hall of Old Town Prague. The large square between Týn church and the town hall was filled. After ancient documents had been examined, it was decided that the assembled lords, knights and representatives of royal towns were entitled to proceed to an election. The Catholic lords met separately and persuaded their most conservative members to accept a Hussite king. No formal vote was needed, and the Catholic, Zdeněk of Šternberk, indicated the choice of the estates by announcing 'May the Lord Governor be our king'; he then knelt before George of Poděbrady. The assembled electors signalled their approval. George walked amidst the crowds to Týn church, where clergy and students sang the 'Te Deum'; from there to the royal residence his procession marched singing the ancient hymn honouring St Wenceslas. In the following year the Emperor, Frederick III, proclaimed George king and imperial elector.[25]

---

[24] Šmahel (1970), pp. 146–9.
[25] Odložilík (1965), pp. 93, 103; Heymann (1965), pp. 153–60.

As king of a country branded heretical, George was vulnerable to papal politics. In December 1466 Pope Paul II declared George a heretic. Since they did not need to obey George, his baronial subjects used the opportunity to elect Mátyás Corvinus of Hungary as king. He was loyal to Rome and unhappy about raiding Hussite armies. However, since the crown and regalia were in George's hands at Karlštejn, there could be no coronation, and as neither the German princes nor Casimir of Poland supported Mátyás, George remained in power. However, he had to abandon any thought of designating his son as his heir, and of thus establishing a native dynasty. After his death in March 1471, the diet voted to invite Vladislav of Poland to be king. Vladislav granted the ancient privileges and freedoms of the kingdom, including the Compacts, and was crowned on 22 August 1471. In 1477 he was confirmed as king by Frederick III, and in 1490 the estates of Moravia, Silesia and the Lusatias united with Bohemia so that the lands of the Crown of St Wenceslas once again had a single ruler.[26]

George's diplomatic efforts in the Empire, and his contribution to Europe's welfare, helped him ward off some of the Papacy's attacks. Overall, his court was a lively centre of diplomacy. In 1460 he supported efforts to reform the Empire and prepare for its defence against the Turks. He also undertook to mediate between the Wittelsbachs and Albrecht Achilles and the margrave of Brandenburg, through which he gained respect and friends. From his court came the plan for European co-operation, the work of Antonio Marini. This proposed league had at its core a supreme assembly. Among other things it was to decide what weapons were to be used against the Turks, the roles of ground and naval forces, the appointment of commanders, the control of supplies and the establishment of hospitals. It proposed a common currency for all Europe, as well as a common fund.[27] The league foundered because no European prince would seriously consider surrendering his autonomy.

Hussites were given a mixed reception when travelling abroad. At the Council of Basle, in 1433, the popularity of the Hussites compelled the Council's protector and the city's magistrates to threaten death and loss of property to all who attended a Hussite service or engaged with them in discussion of theological issues. Hussite leaders were requested to forbid their people to preach while on visits to nearby villages. None the less, George of Poděbrady was able to block papal efforts to isolate his country from Europe, and Czechs who travelled abroad during his reign felt at ease there. Yet Hussite Bohemia remained an island in a sea; outsiders regarded the heretical Czechs as defective, their country one which needed to be put straight. Czech travellers reported that while a German inn-keeper's wife cursed all Czechs as heretics,

---

[26] Odložilik (1965), pp. 220–1, 271–2.   [27] Heymann (1964).

some French, who expected them to be primitive, were surprised at how politely Czechs dined.[28]

Fifteenth-century Bohemian life was deeply marked by Hussite efforts at religious reform. In the 1420s, the most radical adherents held sway militarily, and threatened to eradicate the office of kingship and any other country-wide governing institution. For a time, the Hussites were poised to weld national feeling to the notion of popular self-government, expressed in secular terms in Prague and in religious terms in Tabor. Tradition, and the desire for a Church and a king accepted by Europe as legitimate, proved too strong for this early form of democracy to establish itself. As a result, the nobles seized the advantage. They set up temporary governmental offices, defeated the radicals on the battlefield and sponsored negotiations for the return of the monarch. As leading arbiters, they laid down the rules and the requirements to both the king and the other estates. The roots of decay among the radical Hussites, popular disillusionment with them, and their military defeat, prevented them from creating a national solidarity. But the victorious nobility was no more successful. It refused to lead a socially broad commonwealth, and its narrow view of the national community, as represented by the nobility alone, effectively cut short Czech experiments with national sovereignty in the fifteenth century.

[28] Šmahel (1970), pp. 174–6; Šmahel (1990), p. 433.

FRANCE AT THE END OF THE
HUNDRED YEARS WAR (*c.* 1420–1461)

Malcolm Vale

IN 1521, Francis I of France visited Dijon, where he was shown the skull of John the Fearless, duke of Burgundy. The Carthusian monk who accompanied the king was alleged to have said 'my lord, that's the hole through which the English entered France'. He was referring to the wounds sustained by the duke from the axe-blows which felled him on the bridge at Montereau in September 1419. The shadow of that assassination fell over much of the succeeding period, which saw a profound crisis of Valois monarchy in the face of English invasion and French civil war. John the Fearless's death was clearly a product of the internal strife which had plagued the higher echelons of French society since the murder of Louis of Orleans by his Burgundian enemies in 1407. Henry V's successes were partly based upon his ability to exploit the internal divisions of the French nobility to his own ends. The Valois monarchy's very survival was for a time thrown into question and it was not until the late 1430s and 1440s that positive signs of recovery were clearly visible.

In the aftermath of Henry V's invasions of Normandy in 1415 and 1417 the kingship of Charles VI had suffered a series of severe setbacks. The king's intermittent madness had allowed the factions associated with the houses of Orleans and Burgundy to wage war around the throne and had led to Burgundian supremacy in 1418–19. The Dauphin Charles was forced to flee from Paris in 1418, taking his supporters with him, and this group was to form a long-standing source of support for the embattled Valois monarchy. It included civil servants, lawyers, churchmen and nobles, among whom the Jouvenel des Ursins, the Harcourt, the Cousinot and the Tancarville were prominent. The systematic reduction of Normandy to English obedience between 1417 and 1419 drove the higher nobility of the duchy into exile with the dauphin. Paris was in Anglo-Burgundian hands, supplied from Normandy by means of the Seine, and the so-called 'Armagnacs', or Orleanists, were subjected to physical violence, dispossession and confiscation of their property. The most assertive of the Parisian merchants and tradesmen supported the

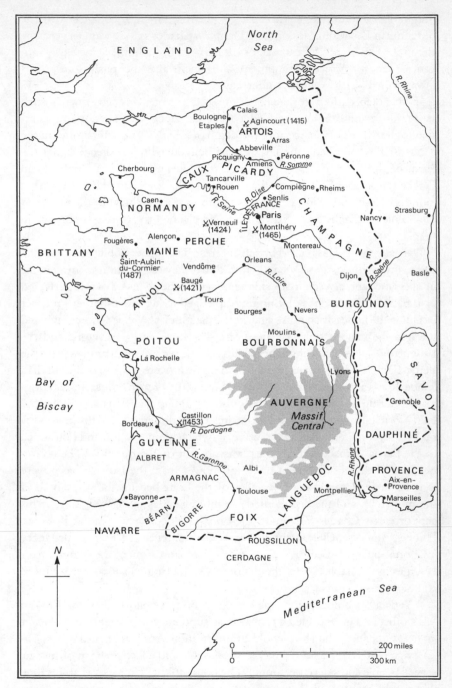

Map 8   France

Burgundian interest, largely because of their commercial contacts with the Burgundian Low Countries, and the Dauphin Charles's cause was at a very low ebb in the city. Henry V's campaigns of 1419–22 brought the Seine valley into Lancastrian (or Anglo-Burgundian) allegiance, and the push southwards towards the Loire was already under way.

In May 1420, oaths were taken by some of the greatest French princes – such as Burgundy and Brittany – to pledge their allegiance to a Lancastrian succession to the throne of France after the death of Charles VI. All territories in the hands of the 'so-called dauphin' were to be reduced to obedience under the terms of the Treaty of Troyes. A Lancastrian dual monarchy of England and France was in effect created on the deaths of Charles VI and Henry V within months of each other in 1422. It was the most serious threat to the power of the Valois monarchy since Edward III had claimed the throne of France in 1340.

Dynastic rivalry was fuelled by self-interest. The higher nobility of France – and many of the lesser seigneurs – found that they might profit from a choice of allegiance and played off one side against the other. This was a role perfected by Philip the Good, duke of Burgundy, pledged to avenge his father's murder by aiding the Lancastrian cause against the dauphinists. Valois power gravitated towards the regions south of the Loire – Poitou, Berry, Auvergne and the Languedoc – while the central heartlands of the old Capetian monarchy in the Ile-de-France, Champagne, Perche and Picardy were in Anglo-Burgundian hands. It was a reversal of the process whereby the French monarchy had originally built up its authority under Louis VII, Philip Augustus and Philip the Fair. Normandy and Aquitaine lay outside Valois dominion, and the possibility of a recreation of the Angevin empire, in which Maine, Anjou and Poitou fell to the Lancastrians and their allies, was not out of the question. The consequences of this displacement of Valois power from the Parisian basin were long-lasting and important. The valley of the Loire became the stronghold of the monarchy, and the disinherited Dauphin Charles (acclaimed king by his supporters as Charles VII on 30 October 1422) spent his time at Bourges, Poitiers, Amboise, Chinon and Tours. While the regent of France for Henry VI, John, duke of Bedford, ruled from Paris and Rouen, the 'kingdom of Bourges' was established by the dauphinists, drawing its support from more southerly possessions.

A separate administration was set up at Bourges and Poitiers by Charles VII's officers. This included a *parlement*, as supreme court of appeal, a *chambre des comptes*, chancery and household administration. Analysis of the Poitiers *parlement*'s records has suggested that it was a viable and effective organ of justice, served by able and skilled personnel. The household of Charles VII at this time was not the shabby and penurious institution of historical caricature, as access to the resources of southern France, and to the commercial and maritime networks created by the port at La Rochelle, enabled the court to survive with some degree of credibility. Grants of taxation on a regular basis from the estates of Languedoc ensured the funding of the regime, and frequent (though illicit) trafficking with the 'enemy' on the frontiers brought considerable benefits to the regions under Valois rule.

A significant diplomatic gain was made in 1425, when the allegiance of the great southern house of Foix was secured by Charles VII in return for the grant of contested territories, including the long-disputed *comté* of Bigorre. After Henry V's death, Lancastrian diplomacy had failed to win the greater southern families and ecclesiastics to its side. With the exception of the house of Armagnac, the allegiance of the great families of the Languedoc tended towards the Valois cause, while the important towns of the Toulousain, the Albigeois and the *sénéchaussées* of Beaucaire-Nîmes and Carcassonne also acknowledged Charles VII as 'true heir and king of France'. Charles was also aided by the house of Anjou's support in his time of greatest need.

The death of Henry V in August 1422 delivered a severe blow to the Lancastrian war effort. Lancastrian military supremacy had been virtually unchallenged before that date, with the exception of the defeat and death of Henry's brother Clarence at Baugé on 22 March 1421. This was, however, only a temporary setback, and the great victory over the dauphinists and their Scots allies at Verneuil on 17 August 1424 demonstrated the continuing strength of Lancastrian arms. Normandy was now secure, and the extension of the *pays de conquête* began in earnest. To annex regions such as Champagne to the dual monarchy's dominions was not too difficult a task: the problem lay with areas further south which formed the point of entry to dauphinist strongholds south of the Loire. The estates of Normandy were prepared to underwrite the Lancastrian regime with subsidies (at least until 1428) and Burgundian aid was an essential prerequisite for the conquest and occupation of northern France. But outside Normandy and the Burgundian sphere of influence the Valois cause was doggedly espoused by power groups allied to the Orleanist or Armagnac factions. Hatred of the Burgundians and their allies was as powerful an incentive to resist the Lancastrian war effort as any sense of nascent French nationalism. Pressing forward to besiege Orleans in 1428 Anglo-Burgundian forces encountered resistance of a kind to which they were unaccustomed.

'The seige of Orleance [was] takyn in hand God knoweth by what avys', wrote the duke of Bedford in 1434. Despite the self-justificatory tone of his memorandum on the subject, Bedford's observation may represent a more realistic view of the limitations of Lancastrian power in France than that held by some of his contemporaries. Without whole-hearted Burgundian support (which was lacking in 1428–9) the expedition against Orleans was unlikely to succeed. The appearance of 'a disciple and leme of the fende called the Pucelle, that used fals enchantement and sorcerie' (as Bedford described Joan of Arc in 1434) brought the Lancastrian monarchy up against a species of ideological warfare which was unprecedented in the course of the Hundred Years War.[1] To elevate the conflict into a religious war was no easy task, and it was a measure of Joan's success that the credibility of the Valois monarchy was so rapidly enhanced. For her mission was essentially a symbolic and ideological one: Charles's coronation and sacral unction at Rheims on 17 July 1429 vastly outweighed the military benefits of her short career. To have raised the siege of Orleans was a notable achievement, for which Charles's captains were largely responsible; but to have secured the elevated status of a properly crowned and anointed sovereign for the dauphin dealt a profound body-blow to both the moral and tangible authority of the Lancastrian crown of France.

After the coronation at Rheims, as Joan herself acknowledged, her mission was at an end. The events of 1430–1 demonstrated that she had outlived her usefulness. The leading members of Charles's own entourage – Regnault de Chartres, archbishop of Rheims, Georges de la Trémouïlle, Robert le Maçon and Raoul de Gaucourt – were all too ready to deny her support once the journey to Rheims had been accomplished. Captured by the Burgundians at Compiègne in May 1430, sold by her captor – Louis of Luxemburg – to the English administration, she was delivered (at the request of the University of Paris) into the hands of the Inquisition. Her divinely inspired vocation had not won any significant victories for her dauphin after Orleans, and Normandy remained firmly in Lancastrian hands. Hence her trial took place at Rouen, where a tribunal (overwhelmingly French in composition) presided over by Pierre Cauchon, bishop of Beauvais, condemned her to death as a relapsed heretic on 30 May 1431. The trial revealed the extent of active collaboration between the Anglo-Burgundian regime, the University of Paris and the clergy of northern France at this time. But Joan's achievement – apart from the outstanding example of devotion, courage and fortitude which she gave to future generations – lay largely in the moral sphere. The hastily prepared coronation ceremony which the child Henry VI underwent at Paris on 16 December 1431 exemplified the fact that the Valois monarchy had received consecration by the time-honoured and proper means at Rheims. This propaganda victory was to play its part in the gradual process by which the disaffected were won over to the cause of Charles VII.

Although the Lancastrian position in Normandy remained secure, the same could not be said for relations between England and Burgundy. Philip the Good had many reasons for complaint about the manner in which the

---

[1] *Proceedings and ordinances of the Privy Council of England*, ed. N.H. Nicolas, 7 vols., London (1834–7), IV, p. 223.

Lancastrian regime in France had behaved towards him: he had not received a lieutenancy in the kingdom of France; appeals from his Flemish lands still went to the *parlement* of Paris; the marital affairs of both Humphrey, duke of Gloucester, and Bedford himself, after the death of his first wife (Philip's sister, Anne of Burgundy), did not promote Burgundian aims; and the refusal of the regent to grant the *comté* of Champagne to him progressively alienated Philip from Henry VI's cause. By 1432 it seems that he had resolved to detach himself from the Anglo-Burgundian alliance. This was to be fatal to the survival of the Lancastrian dual monarchy. Some Englishmen, such as Cardinal Henry Beaufort and Sir John Fastolf, tried in their different ways to salvage the Burgundian alliance, but incentives to reach a reconciliation with his father's murderers became too strong for Philip and his counsellors to resist by 1435. Handsome bribes were offered to the chancellor Nicolas Rolin and other prominent Burgundian courtiers by Charles VII's government in July 1435. Favourable legal opinion which justified a revocation of the Treaty of Troyes was secured by Philip from the masters of Bologna University and a reconciliation with Charles VII was finally reached at Arras in September 1435. Although the Burgundian *volte-face* of that year has been dismissed by some historians as a less significant action than had been previously supposed, it undermined the foundations of Lancastrian power in northern France. Burgundy was no longer the ally essential to the fulfilment of Henry V's war aims: a reorientation of both English and Burgundian ambitions was henceforward inevitable. Philip the Good had already distanced himself from French politics and was accumulating extensive territories in the Low Countries; Henry VI's government found itself increasingly forced to fall back upon Normandy and Maine, and this was reflected in the events which followed the fateful meeting at Arras.

The beginnings of Valois recovery soon became evident. Paris was regained in April 1436, and Lancastrian power in northern France steadily became confined to Normandy and its marches. Another setback had already been experienced by the death of Bedford in 1435. But the war continued, despite the moral victories of the Valois cause. Burgundian efforts to capture Calais in July 1436 were thwarted by Gloucester's forces, and the vested interests of English captains in Normandy and Maine were all the more fiercely defended under the threat of dispossession. Valois successes were therefore largely diplomatic rather than military at this stage. The turning-point in the diplomatic history of the Hundred Years War at this time fell during the period between the Arras conference of 1435 and the Anglo-French negotiations at Gravelines in 1439. The first indications that the Lancastrian government might be prepared to renounce Henry VI's title to the throne of France in exchange for substantial territorial gains appeared at that date. This was a reversion to an older formula of English claims which long predated Henry V's reign. Cardinal Beaufort continued to underwrite the English war effort with his loans, but was concerned to improve the territorial position in both Normandy and Guyenne, partly as a bargaining counter in negotiations. The issue of the crown of France, however, proved divisive within the Lancastrian council: Gloucester accused Beaufort and his supporters of betraying Henry V's war aims. Factional strife around the feckless and incompetent Henry VI tended to reproduce the political conditions previously suffered in France under Charles VI. Charles VII could only benefit from the disintegration of his increasingly implausible rival's authority both in England and in Lancastrian France.

Yet the process of recovery was very gradual. Charles VII, though demonstrating considerable political acumen, was unable to control his own magnates. The ambitions of self-seeking courtiers such as Jean Louvet or Georges de la Trémouïlle which had bedevilled his early years now gave way to a revival in the power of the princes and higher nobles. The return to France in 1440 of Charles, duke of Orleans, imprisoned in England since his capture at Agincourt in 1415, simply provided a focus for magnate resistance and the outbreak of the so-called Praguerie, or noble rebellion, in 1440 ensued. There was little evidence at this time that the greater magnates felt inspired to drive the English out of France, as Joan of Arc had urged them to do. Burgundy supported the Praguerie, and plotted against Charles VII, lending little support to the Valois war effort against the English. Orleans and Anjou pursued their own ends, turning towards Italy, where both houses possessed territorial claims, in the mid-1440s. Bourbon's participation in the Praguerie was in part determined by the unwelcome intervention of royal officials within his lands, especially by the royal *baillis* of Montferrand. Unless very substantial concessions were made to them, the higher nobility were reluctant to further Charles VII's campaigns against Lancastrian France, in either the north or the south of the kingdom.

Charles VII successfully put down the Praguerie, but to win the nobility's confidence involved more than mere repression. The lure of territorial gain could always be offered. To recover Normandy, Maine and Guyenne necessitated the grant of captured lands to faithful supporters of the Valois cause. But the picture was clouded by the confiscations of the period 1417–35. Were those who held titles to confiscated lands in 1429 (the date of the edict of Compiègne which regulated confiscation and dispossession) to be restored to them and in what state were those lands to be returned? How were long-standing pillars of the Valois monarchy, many of whom had lost all their lands and movable goods to the Anglo-Burgundians, to be rewarded? Such questions exercised the minds of Charles VII's counsellors and the lawyers who served the regime. However, an advantage enjoyed by his government in this respect was increasing financial stability. As the Lancastrian war effort became embroiled in what has been called the 'vicious spiral of Lancastrian insolvency' Valois fortunes tended to improve. One reason for this was the ability of Charles VII's government to raise taxation. The inhabitants of many provinces, especially those on the frontiers of war, were apparently prepared to underwrite the Valois regime in order to be free of the worst excesses of the soldiery – or so they hoped. Some localities were prepared to be directly taxed through the apparatus of royal *élus* who levied and collected the revenues. In others, the estates were prepared to vote grants of taxation – the *taille*, the *aides* and the *gabelle* – to enable Charles to raise a more disciplined army and to rid the countryside of roving bands of *écorcheurs* and of the garrisons of freelances who subjected them to ransoms and protection money. In 1439 a royal ordinance decreed that the crown possessed a monopoly in the raising of troops – a significant act which, although very difficult to enforce, attempted to outlaw private armies and freebooting bands. Valois efforts to reduce military excesses contrasted with the increasing difficulties experienced by the Lancastrian administration in Normandy and Maine. Peasant revolts in the *pays de Caux* and disaffection throughout the southern parts of the duchy were a response to the problem of brigandage and the exploitation of the countryside by unpaid English garrisons.

Charles VII's military reforms have secured a prominent place in historical textbooks. Between 1445 and 1448 a force of 12,000 mounted troops was created, known as the companies of *grande* and *petite ordonnance*. Each company of this army consisted of 100 *lances*, or units of six men, headed by a heavily armoured man-at-arms. There were twenty of these companies, providing both a field army and a garrison force for the crown. They were never intended, at their inception, to be a permanent standing army. Their purpose was to reduce military disorder and to drive the English from France. In 1448 a militia of *francs-archers*, raised by levy upon all hearths in the kingdom, was formed to provide infantry. Other groups of men-at-arms, not recruited to the companies, were declared to be illicitly raised and were to be disbanded. It was easier to enact such edicts than to enforce them. The models for this new army – although many of its members were already professional soldiers, some being 'nothing more than old *écorcheurs*' – were derived from both English and Italian example. Above all, the practice of muster and review, perfected by Henry V's and Bedford's military administration in Normandy between 1417 and 1424, and regular pay mediated through civilian pay clerks, was adopted by the French standing army. Companies were regularly inspected to ensure that they were up to strength, properly equipped and not defrauded of their wages by their captains, who let them live off the country. The relationship between military disorder and civil unrest was clearly perceived by Charles VII's treasurers for wars and other financial officials, some of whom had previously served the Lancastrian regime in occupied Normandy. A tendency towards greater stability of personnel in the companies serving the French crown has been detected at this time, and careers in the service of a given captain became longer. An elementary *esprit de corps* appears to have been born and, by making the crown the sole paymaster of the troops, magnate influence upon the behaviour of the companies was much diminished. The risk of private armies being formed from the *compagnies d'ordonnance* was low under Charles VII. Yet their cost was high: Philippe de Commynes estimated that Charles raised about 1,800,000 francs a year. Over 50 per cent of this sum was spent on the army. But it absorbed an element which had plagued the provinces of France and provided occupation for men who had formerly terrorised the countryside. By establishing permanent garrisons, some measure of control – exercised through the *prévôt des maréchaux* and his archers – was established over a volatile and disorderly body of soldiery.

The creation of the standing army had been preceded by a period in which positive gains were made by Charles VII's forces, especially in the southern territories of the Lancastrians. Between 1441 and 1443, the king had taken the initiative in Guyenne and recovered important strongholds such as Dax and La Réole from Anglo-Gascon forces. The abortive negotiations for a marriage between Henry VI and the count of Armagnac's daughter (1442) reflected the decline of Lancastrian authority in this region. Defections by some members of the Gascon nobility, who had traditionally supported the English cause – especially in the Landes – undermined the regime and the negotiation of a truce at Tours in May 1444 gave both sides in the conflict a breathing space in which to retrench and consolidate their positions. A major problem encountered by the Valois war effort now lay in the strength of regional and localised resistance. In the north, the entrenched interests held by certain English captains in Normandy and Maine hampered all efforts to dislodge them; in the south, the traditional resistance of the Gascons to Valois authority, particularly at Bordeaux and Bayonne, and its attendant taxation, was an even more formidable obstacle to the annexation of territory to the crown. In Normandy and Maine, the landed interest of English knights and nobles was dominant, and led to the refusal of men such as Matthew Gough and Fulk Eyton to surrender the *comté* of Maine to the French crown as a result of the treaty made with Charles VII by Henry VI's lieutenant, the duke of Suffolk, in March 1445. In Guyenne, economic connections with England and a very long-standing loyalty to the English crown rendered the position very different from that which prevailed in relatively recently occupied Normandy. Yet in both regions, the continuance of the war spelt economic dislocation and a certain degree of devastation. Normandy experienced greater damage: the destruction of mills, the wasting of standing crops and burning of villages were frequent occurrences even during periods when full-scale campaigns were not in progress. The random and sporadic effects of brigandage and looting by unpaid English troops, or by Normans professing to be in the service of Charles VII, were keenly felt in the duchy. Yet Thomas Basin's famous picture of a totally devastated province, in which no cultivation took place and no animal population was to be found, was clearly exaggerated. The effects of war could be very severe indeed, but they were very localised and intermittent. It was only after 1449, when large expeditionary forces were launched by Charles VII against Normandy, that the level of economic damage rose to intolerable heights. Even then, it lasted for a relatively short time, for the capacity of medieval armies to cause enduring damage was limited.

It can be argued that the 1440s was a decisive decade in which the balance of political, diplomatic and military power shifted in favour of Valois France. In March 1449, the taking of the Breton frontier fortress of Fougères by François de Surienne, an Aragonese mercenary in English pay, broke the truce negotiated at Tours five years previously. Urged on by a powerful Breton faction at his court, Charles VII decided upon the reconquest of Normandy. The war was resumed on 31 July 1449. Within fifteen months, all of Henry's V's and Bedford's conquests in Normandy and Lancastrian France fell to Valois arms. The way had been prepared during the previous decade. Charles VII had been aided by the failure of the Italian ambitions of great magnates such as Charles of Orleans and René of Anjou. The crises of the years between 1442 and 1449 which opened up opportunities for the prosecution of their territorial claims in the peninsula – using French troops – were now at an end. There was nothing to stop the French crown from moving into Normandy except the stubborn resistance of English captains and the ever-present problem of finance. The latter question was to some extent solved by the exercise of *force majeure*: in July 1451 the vast assets of Jacques Coeur, Charles VII's *argentier*, responsible for the supply and provisioning of his household, were confiscated by crown agents. Jacques Coeur had risen from humble origins to dominate the credit finance of the kingdom, lending huge sums to the crown. Arrested on trumped-up charges of treason, his fortune contributed directly to the recovery of Normandy and Guyenne. His assets totalled some 3,500 florins (the Medici *Bottega di Sieta* had about 5,000 florins) and his plate was melted down to strike coin so that the troops in Guyenne might be paid in July 1453. Taxation from the estates of both Languedoil and Languedoc also contributed to the financing of the last phase of the war and the magnates were content to serve the crown, for they benefited from substantial concessions of royal taxation levied within their own lordships. A combination of effective siege artillery, deployed by the brothers Bureau, bribery, ruse, incitement of the local population and buying off of English garrisons won Normandy for Charles VII by

August 1450, when Cherbourg – the last remaining bastion of resistance – fell to French troops.

In Guyenne, the French succeeded in taking Bordeaux, Bayonne and the remainder of the duchy by August 1451, largely by means of sieges. The major strongpoints, both towns and seignorial castles, surrendered either after bombardment by the heavy artillery of the Bureau brothers, or as a result of negotiated agreements to surrender. Aid from England did not arrive to succour the loyal inhabitants of the duchy. Yet the terms imposed by Charles VII were generous and Gascon liberties and immunities were to be respected. The position was abruptly changed, however, by the rising of a group of Gascons, some of them exiles in England, others representing the mercantile and shipowning community at Bordeaux, against French occupation. In this instance, help from England appeared in the person of John Talbot, earl of Shrewsbury, who, with an expeditionary force 'for the keeping of the seas', descended upon Bordeaux in October 1452. The coastal regions of the duchy were temporarily recovered for Henry VI but this reversal of Valois fortunes was not to endure. Talbot was not reinforced from England, and a French expeditionary force, consisting of a field army as well as a siege train, defeated and killed him at Castillon on 17 July 1453. Bordeaux held out until 19 October, when it capitulated to the French for the second time. Heavy penalties were then levied by Charles VII's government upon the recalcitrant Gascons. These were not to be lifted until Louis XI's reign, when the king granted the duchy its own sovereign court – the *parlement* of Bordeaux – in 1462, and set in motion a process for the canonisation of the saintly and pro-English archbishop of Bordeaux, Pey Berland. With the establishment of a delegated appellate jurisdiction for the duchy in 1454–5 – the *Grands Jours* – Guyenne was to be gradually, but thoroughly, brought into line with French judicial and administrative practices. French taxation was imposed upon the region; its yields were soon visible in the accounts of the constables of Bordeaux. Gascon privileges in the wine trade with England were revoked and a period of economic hardship set in for Bordeaux and Bayonne.

This picture of the onward march of Valois victory was somewhat tarnished by two related problems: the role of the Dauphin Louis, and the attitude of Philip the Good of Burgundy to Charles VII's successes. Since taking up residence in the Dauphiné in 1446, the dauphin had intrigued against his father. In 1456, he fled to the Burgundian lands, where he was harboured by Philip the Good at Brussels and Genappe. Burgundy had taken no part in the campaigns against Normandy and Guyenne between 1449 and 1453. A state of 'cold war' has been discerned between France and Burgundy at this time, represented by Charles VII's favouring of Flemish dissidence from the Burgundian regime. Had his armies not been campaigning in Guyenne in the summer of 1453, there was a distinct possibility that they might have supported the Ghenters in their bitter war with Philip the Good. Charles's agents had created instability within the Burgundian lands by encouraging Flemish appellants at the *parlement* of Paris, while the harbouring of the dauphin, against his father's will, carried the risk of treason charges being levelled against Burgundy. A critical point was reached in October 1458 when Jean, duke of Alençon, was tried for *lèse-majesté* before Charles VII and the *parlement* at Vendôme. Philip the Good was not present at the trial, and Chastellain reported that men feared that he would not be exempt from a similar prosecution. In the event, intermediaries such as Jean, count of Nevers, worked to prevent a further escalation of Franco-Burgundian tension and the storm did not break until after the accession of Louis XI.

An assessment of the state of the French kingdom at the death of Charles VII in 1461 must take account both of striking achievements and deep-seated uncertainties. The war with the English had in effect been won. Although there were apprehensions about a further revival of English war aims (as occurred, for instance, in 1475) the disturbed political condition of Lancastrian and Yorkist England militated against a concerted policy of intervention in France. Calais remained the sole English possession on the European continent. Charles VII's title to the French throne was secure. The civil war among the French nobility had been largely quelled. The crown had subdued the count of Armagnac by coercion (in 1445), the duke of Alençon by indictment for treason (in 1458) and the duke of Brittany by compromise over his homage to the monarchy (in 1446 and 1450). Factional conflict, exemplified by the Armagnac/Orleans–Burgundian feud, had ceased to tear the higher nobility of France apart. Charles VII's servants could legitimately claim that a form of social and political peace had been restored to French society. The recovery of Normandy, Maine and Lancastrian France, and the annexation of Guyenne, brought economic as well as prestigious gains to the crown. In 1461 Guyenne yielded 30,000 *livres tournois* in *aides*, and 70,000 *livres tournois* in *taille*. Both taxes were innovations introduced after the French conquest. In the autumn of 1452, the Norman estates already considered taxes to be excessive and petitioned for a restoration of ancient privileges and institutions. Herein lay the danger of over-zealous activity by French royal officers in recently recovered provinces. But such measures were the price to be paid for peace and for integration into the kingdom of France. The English occupation of Normandy had 'witnessed a revival of local patriotism and local institutions which helped to create an institutional dimension to local sentiment'.[2]

---

[2] Allmand (1983), p. 304.

Similarly, enquiries launched by the crown into regional customs, in the wake of the great judicial ordinance of Montils-lès-Tours in 1454, could lead to a recrudescence of regional sentiment and a heightened awareness of ancient privileges.

In 1461, the problem of regionalism was to some extent compounded by the continuing power of the higher nobility. Regional sentiment could join forces with seignorial, or princely, independence to arrest the territorial consolidation of the kingdom. At the very top, uncertainty over the future attitudes and behaviour of the Dauphin Louis, estranged from his father and from many members of the group who governed France, caused disquiet. The close association of Louis with Burgundy also gave rise to fears of a Burgundian *coup* which would displace the old and loyal servants of the Valois monarchy from their places in the sun under Charles VII. Burgundy formed a potential focus of opposition for the discontented and disaffected. Philip the Good had achieved an independent status as ruler of most of the Low Countries. The war with the English had in fact prevented Charles VII's government from effectively tackling the problem of Burgundian expansionism and state building. Valois resources had been stretched to their limits by the war effort and by the need to provide ample rewards to both nobles and *bonnes villes* for their support against the Lancastrians. The need to compensate the faithful for their losses also taxed the patience and ingenuity of Charles VII's officers and lawyers, although they often profited from cases of dispossession and resettlement. The fortunes of the great dynasties of Parisian *parlementaires* – the d'Orgement or the Cousinot – were in part made in the aftermath of war. Many purchased estates in the region of the capital and elsewhere, often from impoverished petty nobles, while the *parlement*'s fundamental role in administering the land settlement reinforced an existing tendency towards a rise in the status of its members. 'To be a king's counsellor or even an advocate at the *parlement* was to *vivre noblement*. The notion of a *noblesse de robe* was established.'[3] The principle of resignation from office in favour of a named relative, and of covert venality, began to entrench itself within the ranks of the legal, as well as the financial, bureaucracy. This was soon to pose problems of control by the monarchy of its own legal apparatus.

The burgeoning of the lawyers and financiers in the crown's service was illustrated in many ways. Upward social mobility lay in office holding, lubricated by access to liquid capital. In the aftermath of the war, fortunes could be made (and lost) through the accumulation of legal and financial offices. The law was a safer avenue of social ascent than finance. Jacques Coeur's fate was a salutary warning to merchants and financiers who sought to promote them-

---

[3] Autrand (1981), p. 261.

selves and their families through lending to the crown and the nobility. Legal fortunes were perhaps harder to make, but the volume of legal business thrown up by the war – above all in civil litigation and property disputes – ensured a steady source of income for the counsellors and advocates of the Paris and provincial *parlements*. The temptation to invest in land and to set themselves up as *seigneurs* – around Paris, in the Toulousain or in the Bordelais – appealed greatly to these men. Their legal profits served to guarantee solvency and thereby offset the tendency for land-locked fortunes to yield low returns. The collapse of the senior branches of a family such as the Ysalguier of Toulouse, who had risen as creditors of the monarchy in the fourteenth century, stemmed from the shifting of all their assets from trade and commerce to land. Diminishing returns conspired with the effects of war damage to render them unable to meet the expenses of 'living nobly' and of providing adequate dowries for their daughters to maintain their position in Toulousain society.

In the prevailing economic climate, marked by what has been called a 'bullion famine' in the mid-fifteenth century, the need to maintain and increase liquidity was all-important. Mercantile fortunes had often to be channelled through office holding if steady social ascent was to be sustained. It was in this way that the great commercial fortune of Giovanni Arnolfini, Lucchese merchant residing at Bruges (d. 1472), patron of Jan van Eyck, descended to his nephew, Marc Cename, lord of Luzarches and *élu* of Paris. Arnolfini had lent money to the dauphin, Louis, during his Burgundian exile and was created *conseiller sur le fait des finances* by Louis, as king, in 1462. A balance between office holding, landownership and the accumulation of liquid capital was thus essential for the survival of a recently ennobled family among the ranks of the nobility.

The revival of the Valois monarchy under Charles VII was also expressed through the arts. In danger of eclipse by the brilliant court culture of Burgundy, the court and household of France displayed a marked tendency to patronise the visual arts and literature with renewed emphasis during the 1440s. Around the king was an entourage, castigated by moralists such as Thomas Basin for its corruption and jobbery, which included Jean Juvénal and Guillaume Jouvenel des Ursins, Etienne Chevalier, Laurent Girárd and Simon de Varie. All these servants of the crown are known to have patronised the arts: Jean Juvénal des Ursins, archbishop of Rheims, was himself a chronicler and a distinguished writer of exhortatory treatises. Lesser men, such as the Norman notary Noël de Fribois, produced propagandist histories, celebrating the victories of Charles VII and vehemently arguing for the legitimacy and moral supremacy of Valois kingship over its rivals. Fribois's *Chronique abrégée* (1459) contained the memorable assertion that 'whenever I come to something concerning the English, I cannot control my pen'.[4] Others were less passionate in their detestation of the ancient enemy. A voluminous literature of panegyric emerged from the circle around Charles VII in the 1440s and 1450s: Thomas Basin's discordant voice of resistance and protest was exceptional. A chorus of near-unanimous eulogy praised Charles VII, the *roi très-victorieux*, after 1453, and the court (now permanently located in the towns and castles of the Loire valley) was presented as a focus of loyalty and centre of patronage.

Those responsible for presenting an image of Charles VII's kingship were assisted in their task by the visual arts. Efforts to exalt the dignity of the monarchy at royal entries into the *bonnes villes*, and at other royal ceremonies, such as plenary sessions of the *parlement*, were recorded by artists. The work of the painter Jean Fouquet, born in Tours (*c.* 1420–80), forms an invaluable iconographical source for the milieu which surrounded Charles VII. The king himself was portrayed by Fouquet in ceremonial contexts – at the trial of the duke of Alençon at Vendôme in 1458, sitting in majesty surrounded by higher clergy, secular nobles, members of the *parlement* and royal officers, or as the eldest of the Magi performing their homage to the infant Christ in the Hours of Etienne Chevalier (*c.* 1452–5). The king's unprepossessing features were transcended by the dignity of his office and Fouquet's art exemplified the contrast between the king's mortal body and the immortality of the sovereignty of France. Among Fouquet's patrons, the civil servants were well represented. Guillaume Jouvenel des Ursins, chancellor of France, commissioned a splendid portrait, depicting him in a rich furred robe in front of a gilded, Italianate architectural background. Etienne Chevalier, treasurer of France, invested his profits of office in a lavishly illustrated Book of Hours, noteworthy for its use of Italianate motifs. Laurent Girard, an officer in the *Chambre des Comptes*, owned the Boccaccio manuscript, now at Munich, in which the Alençon trial forms a topical frontispiece recalling the fall from grace of great men. Simon de Varie, brother of Guillaume de Varie, factor of Jacques Coeur, commissioned a recently discovered Book of Hours (1455) from Fouquet in which this financial official (ennobled in 1448) is represented kneeling, in full armour, before the Virgin and Child on the *Obsecro te* page, with his heraldic achievements prominently displayed beside him. New nobility was thus expressed visually – even vulgarly – and the predilection of his civil servant patrons for Fouquet's style, with its gestures towards a novel Italianism, was perhaps indicative of an *arriviste* mentality. The illuminated manuscripts and panel paintings produced for Charles VII's courtiers and officers demonstrated that the shift in art patronage from northern France (particularly from Paris)

---

[4] See BL, Add. MS 13961, fol. 58v: 'Toutes foiz que je suis en matiere qui touche les Anglois, je ne puis contenir ma plume' (cited in Lewis (1965), p. 3, and (1985), p. 195).

towards the Low Countries after 1420 had been partially reversed. The dominance of artists from Touraine after 1445, however, meant that Parisian production never again achieved its previous levels of quantity or excellence.

France in 1461 was not yet a united monarchical state. The monarchy was simply not powerful enough to create the institutionally centralised organism beloved of nineteenth-century historians. It could be argued that this was not in any case the primary purpose of the crown in the later fifteenth century. Dynastic loyalty and a recognition of the crown's theoretical sovereignty was as much as could be expected from many of the kingdom's inhabitants. Divided by law, language and custom, France was not a 'nation' in the modern sense in 1461. Despite the encroachment of northern French upon southern dialects, linguistic uniformity was not established, either in law or government, until Francis I's edict of Villers-Cotterets in 1539. The strength of regionalism had led to a widespread devolution of royal authority: poor communications alone militated against effective government from the centre. With the creation of provincial *parlements*, a further phase in the decentralisation of justice and administration began, from which strongly regionalist corporate bodies were to emerge. The mould from which the *ancien régime* was to be cast was in part created as a direct consequence of the war with the English. The taxation system, the standing army, which to a large degree justified the taxes, the system of justice and the greatly reduced role of representative assemblies were already evident by the death of Charles VII. The gradual and difficult progress towards absolutism had begun.

THE RECOVERY OF FRANCE, 1450–1520

Bernard Chevalier

HOW is one to define the revival of France after her decisive victory over England in 1453? The current view is familiar enough. France witnessed not only the recovery of lost territory but also a crucial advance towards territorial cohesion and monarchical absolutism. This approach, which owes its inspiration to a view of history based on the glorification of the nation-state, is not without its points. Yet it requires re-examination in the light of recent investigation and reinterpretation. In the past half-century the perspectives of French historians and others regarding the history of that country have altered considerably. No longer may we see the end of the reign of Louis XI (1483) or even that of Charles VIII (1498) as marking the end of the 'fifteenth' century or, indeed, the end of the Middle Ages. This long span of years cannot be left in the relative obscurity 'between two worlds', medieval and modern, into which it has tended to fall in the past. While the wars undertaken in Italy must have an interest of their own, they should also be seen as part of a wider movement to create the unity of France in the face of the power of the great feudal principalities. The role of Louis XII, in particular, needs re-emphasising.

Nor is the time-scale alone worth reviewing. The perspective, too, requires reconsideration. The position of the great nobility is now better understood, while the recovery of France after the war against England is no longer seen as an inevitable royal victory but rather the story of how a fragile monarchy (for that is what it was in the mid-fifteenth century) overcame the power of the princely polyarchy. How that was achieved will be described in this chapter. It involved the use of, and the encouragement given to, institutions, military, financial and legal; the establishment of links between the crown and local societies, urban and rural; the development of political ideas and doctrines, and the expression of those ideas (particularly the ideas of power) through the language of signs and symbolism. Finally, it demanded a particular vision of the past, deeply influenced by humanism, upon which the present could be built. History and tradition, much of it myth, were to be transformed into political assets helping to create a sense of national identity in the present.

INTEGRALITY OF THE MONARCHY

The issues

Charles VII had managed to maintain the precarious balance between royal sovereignty and princely polyarchy which had been struck after the defeat of the Praguerie in 1440. This sovereignty was exercised throughout the kingdom, in theory a territory whose eastern boundaries were defined by four rivers (the Escaut, the Meuse, the Saône and the Rhone), seen as so many natural frontiers until, before long, the Rhine was to relieve them of this role. In practice, however, it was only over some two-thirds of this territory that the king was able to further royal policy unchallenged. None the less, he could rely upon an established doctrine of unity under the crown which, from the reign of Louis XII, would be summarised in the adage 'One God, one king, one faith, one law' ('Un Dieu, un roi, une foi, une loi'). On his side the king had a formidable weapon in his arsenal, one which had been tested against the duke of Alençon in 1458: trial for high treason which was at once felony, *lèse-majesté* and sacrilege.

In the remaining third of the kingdom, however, royal authority had to come to terms with the existence of principalities which, far from being relics of a long-dead feudal past, were genuine, well-organised states. Some (Burgundy, Bourbon, Anjou, Orleans and Alençon) were ruled over by individuals of royal descent. Others were in the hands of princes who, through marriage alliances, came near to being so, whether within the kingdom (Brittany, Foix-Béarn, Armagnac and Albret) or outside it (Lorraine and Savoy). Such princes could thus claim a share of the prerogatives attendant upon royal blood, that mystical symbol which, in the fifteenth century, denoted an aptitude for governing the kingdom. Louis XI himself thought no differently: indeed, his final advice to his son was to conduct himself 'according to the counsel, opinions and government of our next of kin and kindred lords' ('par le conseil, advis et gouvernement de noz parens et seigneurs de nostre sang').[1] Thus the doctrine of government under the king had to come to terms with one in which the highest nobility participated, a system which the League of Nevers had clearly expounded in 1442, and which may have shown the influence of parliamentary government on the English model, particularly in the appeal to the estates general which it encouraged.

However, almost all the princes also held fiefs outside the kingdom, while some had claims to thrones: Burgundy in the Low Countries; Bourbon in Dombes; Anjou in Provence as well as the throne of Naples; Orleans in Asti, with the anticipation of the duchy of Milan; Foix in Navarre, his wife's

[1] *Ordonnances des rois de France de la troisième race*, XIX, p. 56.

kingdom. These might provide useful opportunities for the king to operate outside the country in support of princes of the blood; at the same time they constituted a considerable danger for the monarchy should it become weak. Indeed, the princes, all capable of negotiating as equals with their counterparts throughout Christendom, were risking the dismemberment of the kingdom, which could thus have become the mirror-image of the Empire. Any support for the princes' cause was thus enough to make the king's supporters suspicious; for them, royal authority appeared all the more sacrosanct in that its defence was synonymous with the protection of their own interests.

Life-and-death struggle between king and princes, 1465–83

Yet, somewhat ironically, on 22 July 1461 there succeeded to the throne in the person of Louis XI the very man who had assumed the leadership of the insurgent princes. Before long he managed to antagonise everybody by the inconsistencies of his actions: his former allies, the princes, by his arrogant insistence on the crown's privileges; his father's old retainers, devoted monarchists, by harrying them with the peevishness of a former rebel; and others whom he alarmed by the breadth of his projected reforms. The result was a serious uprising in March 1465, led by the princes under the pretext of defending the 'Public Weal' (the 'Bien Public') or, to put it differently, aristocratic self-interest. The league was organised by three dukes: Burgundy (through his heir, Charles), Bourbon and Brittany. It set against the king his younger brother, Charles, the heir presumptive, and it fielded forces capable of holding him in check on the ground: witness the indecisive battle of Montlhéry fought on 15 July 1465. Indeed Louis XI was only saved from disaster by the loyalty of the *bonnes villes* (towns enjoying both wealth and the means of defending themselves, as well as the right to be represented in the estates), by the enforced neutrality of the English king (another candidate for the French throne), and by his own almost abject surrender.

This unresolved crisis was to inaugurate a period of ruthless struggle between the king and his opponents. Far from being the 'universal spider' of Jean Meschinot's over-celebrated phrase, entangling the enemy in the web of his intrigues, more often than not during this period Louis lived in fear of being overthrown or assassinated, a terror which was to lead to the execution of, among others, the constable, Saint-Pol, in 1475, and that of the duke of Nemours in 1477. The princes, for their part, were no less fearful, both for their positions, should they fail to maintain a united front, and for their lives, should they show their hands too soon.

The years 1465 to 1477 thus constituted a period of high political tension. Shortly after having installed Charles as duke of Normandy, and regardless of a solemn undertaking made to him, Louis XI evicted his brother who, packed off to Guyenne, conveniently died in 1472. The king was also able to hold in check the princes, who lacked any kind of unity of purpose. None the less, Charles the Bold, duke of Burgundy, had grown impatient of so many plots and displays of bad faith. When, too sure of himself, Louis came to Péronne in October 1468 thinking that he could win over the duke of Burgundy, he was compelled to make major concessions. The political situation was once again in the melting pot.

Political bargaining and shows of force allowed Louis to maintain a precarious balance between himself and the princes; he also appealed to public opinion, such as when he took the initiative by calling the estates general in 1468. These difficult years were further characterised by wars which, however brief, proved fatal to the count of Armagnac, ruinous to the duke of Brittany and fruitless for the duke of Burgundy. At last, in 1475, a covert coalition was formed among the king's opponents. This has not been accorded the significance it deserves for it could have been more dangerous than that of 1465, given the presence among the conspirators of the constable of France and the part played by England in it all. Yet, once again, the procrastination of the plotters retrieved the situation, and Louis was thus in a position to buy peace with Edward IV at Picquigny (29 August 1475) and to inflict his terrible justice upon the other conspirators. As for Charles the Bold, he had abandoned his allies in favour of war against the Rhenish towns, Austria, Switzerland and the duke of Lorraine, thus turning himself into the 'grave-digger of his dynasty',[2] a further stroke of luck for the king who had little to do with it all.

The tragic death of the duke of Burgundy outside the walls of Nancy on 5 January 1477 was to deliver Louis from danger. But it also presented him with a difficult choice: should he offer peace to Mary, Charles's daughter and heir and his own godchild, or should he brazenly try to crush the house of Burgundy by force and, with it, all its potential allies in the kingdom? He opted for the second choice, one which would bring him the duchy of Burgundy, but at the cost of a long war along France's north-eastern frontiers with Maximilian of Habsburg, whom Mary had married as a means of escaping potential disaster. In the end a settlement proved inevitable, and was negotiated in unfavourable circumstances. The Treaty of Arras (23 December 1482) provided for the marriage of the infant dauphin, Charles, to Margaret, young daughter of Mary and Maximilian, whose dowry comprised a part of her Burgundian inheritance (Artois and Franche-Comté). As for the policy of systematic intimidation employed against the princes, it had resulted in the neutralisation of the house of Orleans through the enforced marriage, in 1476, of Duke Louis to Jeanne,

[2] Contamine (1977).

one of Louis's daughters, who was probably barren. In 1481 it had also caused the patrimony of the house of Anjou to fall into the king's hands; this brought him the duchy of Anjou, the county of Maine, as well as Provence, Barrois and rights, still to be enforced, to the kingdom of Naples.

Conflict within the aristocracy: European conflict, 1483–91

Despite these successes, and contrary to some opinion, when Louis XI died on 31 August 1483, the contest between the monarchy and the principalities had not yet run its course. Certainly the new king, Charles VIII, being very young, was no longer perceived as the target; the problem was who would rule on his behalf? His sister, Anne, had entered the lists along with her husband, Pierre de Beaujeu, who became duke of Bourbon in 1488. In so doing, the princely couple never for a moment lost sight of the particular interests of their own house. Indeed, at the end of her life Anne even advised her son-in-law, the constable, Bourbon, to ally himself with the emperor, head of the house of Burgundy, against the French king. For the moment, though, the Beaujeu cause and that of the monarchy were one and the same; as usual, the adversary was the heir presumptive, Louis, duke of Orleans, who, backed by the majority of the other princes, laid claim to the regency. Conflict was now to divide the aristocracy itself.

In 1484 confrontation unfolded first before the estates general which decided in favour of Beaujeu, and then on the battlefield. In the name of the 'Public Weal' the conspirators continued to advocate struggle against a tyrannical government and action to reform the kingdom. In the following year the 'Guerre Folle' occurred. The uprising was swiftly subdued, but its lesson for the rebels was plain: as a result of Louis XI's policy of building up his army, no princely coalition would in future be capable of effective resistance. Members of such a coalition were dependent on the army of Brittany, a virtually independent state, and even more on foreign assistance, which was certainly offered, for Louis XI's power politics had left a legacy. For his part, Maximilian of Habsburg always considered it vital to defend the integrality of his children's rights to the Burgundian inheritance. When, in 1487, Louis of Orleans fled to Brittany, a bitter war had already broken out again on the northern front. Close at hand, at Calais, the king of England was an ever-present threat; while, at the southern end of the kingdom, Spain was manoeuvring to obtain the restoration of Roussillon, ill-gotten by Louis XI in 1462. For the Beaujeu, this was the signal to pursue afresh the ruthless struggle to crush the duke of Orleans and to destroy for good the house of Brittany whose head, Francis II, had but two daughters as his heirs. The victory of Saint-Aubin-du-Cormier (23 July 1488) was decisive; the duke of Orleans was taken prisoner, the Breton army broken. However, it had also been necessary to fight against Castilian, English and German contingents which had come to their aid. Power politics within the kingdom was leading to a foreign war against a triple coalition which was strengthened by the marriage of Anne, heiress to the duchy of Brittany, to Maximilian of Habsburg, now a widower. In 1489 and 1490, the French king's army was victorious in almost the whole of Brittany: Alain d'Albret, one of the conspirators of 1485, surrendered Nantes, and Rennes was forced to capitulate. Finally, in order to extricate herself honourably from a desperate situation, the young duchess Anne was driven to break with Maximilian and marry the king of France (6 December 1491). The Beaujeu had crushed their rivals, but not the triple coalition of England, Spain and the house of Austria. Thus the war continued.

Change of course, 1491–1520

On assuming the royal authority, however, the young Charles VIII was to view developments differently. Now a grown man, he chose to abandon the former 'royal' policy of uncompromising insistence on the rights of the crown and the defence of the kingdom's unity at the cost of weakening the princes and their foreign allies. On 28 June 1491 he took the initiative himself, setting free his cousin, Louis of Orleans, thus effecting a reconciliation between them. This event, often insufficiently appreciated, was a genuine *coup d'état*.[3] Rejecting the vindictive policies of both his father and his sister, Charles strove to unite the nobility of France around the throne. He should, therefore, have married Margaret of Austria, daughter of Maximilian and grand-daughter of Charles the Bold, in order to secure peace with the house of Burgundy. Instead he agreed, although without enthusiasm, to the Breton marriage thrust upon him, while making every effort to ensure the end of power politics by making treaties with England (Etaples, 3 November 1492), with Spain which, at last, regained Roussillon (Barcelona, 19 January 1493) and with Maximilian (Senlis, 23 May 1493), returning to him both his daughter and her dowry, Artois and Franche-Comté.

The young king had in mind a different policy which might be termed both 'aristocratic' and 'imperial'. It consisted of Charles setting himself up as heir to the house of Anjou by laying claim to Naples and even to Jerusalem, and dragging the flower of the aristocracy headlong into a 'war of magnificence', that is to say not a domestic war but one undertaken 'to make conquests in distant and foreign countries or to fight for the catholic faith' ('conquerir en loingtaing et estrange païs ou soy combatre pour la foy catholique deffendre ou eslargir').[4]

---

[3] Labande-Mailfert (1975), p. 95.   [4] *Débat des hérauts d'armes*, p. 12.

The accession to the throne, in 1498, of his successor, Louis of Orleans, showed even more clearly the two different paths open to the French monarchy at that time, for, once again, it was the former rebel leader of the aristocratic party who became king under the title of Louis XII. First, after divorcing Jeanne de France, he married his predecessor's widow, Anne of Brittany. Was this a definite step in favour of furthering a 'royal' policy? Probably not, for the king's actions between 1501 and 1506 reflect his hesitation and doubts as to which road, 'aristocratic' or 'imperial', to follow. Accordingly, he retained under his control his county of Blois, and set off to make good his claim first to his duchy of Milan, and then to the kingdom of Naples. From 1501 he was to promise all these, as well as Brittany, together with the hand of his daughter, Claude, to Charles (the future emperor, Charles V), heir to the house of Burgundy. Such a settlement would have had unfortunate effects upon the unity of France, but was doubtless beneficial in terms of bringing peace to Europe. However, he was also secretly contemplating the marriage of this same Claude to his cousin, Francis of Angoulême, heir to the throne, so as to ensure the unity of his own house and the perpetual union of France and Brittany. The Treaty of Blois of 1504, which clearly had the support of the queen, Anne, approved the first outcome, but in the end, in 1506, it was the second which, with the backing of the estates general, was to prevail.

Under these circumstances Francis I, who became king in 1515, should have remained faithful to a 'royal' policy. On the contrary, he believed it possible to renew the 'war of magnificence' in Italy. Yet, very shortly afterwards, intent upon fostering the interests of his own dynasty as much as those of the kingdom, he decided to confiscate the lands of Charles, head of the house of Bourbon, whom he had created constable. Outraged, Bourbon made an alliance in 1523 with the emperor, head of the house of Burgundy. Although he had visions of a new 'Public Weal', none would lend him support, not even the count of Albret who had been badly treated by the crown which had not helped him regain his trans-Pyrenean kingdom of Navarre, lost to Castile in 1512. Times had changed. Henceforth, the aristocracy would believe that its best chance of self-preservation lay within the bosom of the monarchy.

RENAISSANCE, OR CONSOLIDATION OF THE STATE

If the monarchical state found it necessary to suppress the principalities, the reason lay in its claim to a monopoly of public power in matters of defence, justice, finance and spiritual authority. Can it be said to have realised that claim?

Monopoly of the armed forces

Fundamental to the new institutions was the distinction between the ordinary, war-time provision, the professional army, and the extraordinary provision, which relied chiefly on service by the nobility. In 1461 the professional army consisted essentially of the royal guard, French and Scots, and the *compagnies des gens d'armes de l'ordonnance*, that is 7,000 heavy cavalry, gentlemen for the most part, permanently maintained at the king's expense. It also included artillery, although its four companies were to be organised in the reign of Louis XI. The Achilles heel of this mobile emergency force, usually stationed on the frontiers, was the infantry. The reserve force of the *francs-archers*, mobilised in case of need, proved so unsatisfactory over the years that, in 1480, the king decided to replace it with a permanent body of 14,000 men, a most costly experiment which Louis's successors abandoned in favour of a levy of volunteers (*aventuriers*) and of Swiss mercenaries, employed as the need arose. In spite of the plan drawn up by Marshal de Gié in 1504, the infantry remained in the 'extraordinary' category.

The infantry was also responsible for the defence of the country's territory, but not for that of royal castles, maintained by old retainers (*mortes payes*). The fortifications and defences of the *bonnes villes* were left entirely in the hands of their inhabitants; the levy of nobles, in the form of the *arrière ban*, was frequently used, but could provide no more than a meagre territorial reserve of poorly equipped horsemen.

Only the king possessed an effective military force since, in theory, princes were not allowed to levy men. For all that, private wars did not die out: witness the conflict waged in the Midi from 1483 to 1512 by the two branches of the house of Foix. As for the *aventuriers*, they became completely uncontrollable between campaigns, and posed a constant threat to law and order, particularly about 1520. Command of the *compagnies d'ordonnance* themselves was distributed as a favour to chosen members of the aristocracy; the men remained in the service of their captains, who were in sole charge of recruitment. In short, the royal monopoly in matters of the use of force was still very precarious. None the less, the professional army was relatively inexpensive. Apart from the period 1472 to 1483, when Louis XI forced an extravagant arms race on his Burgundian and Breton enemies, the army was only one and a half times greater in 1520 than it had been at the death of Charles VII (1461), although the resources of the kingdom had more than doubled in the meantime.

The king as dispenser of justice

The bedrock of the state, however, was not military might but the upholding of justice by which 'kings rule, while kingdoms, principalities and monarchies are maintained' ('les roys regnent, les royaumes, principautés et monarchies sont entretenues').[5] This prime attribute promoted the comparison between the king and Christ as the 'sun of justice', a device which became part of royal iconography in the time of Charles VIII.[6] This was justice which the king was expected to dispense himself through his council, under the leadership of the chancellor. Such was the importance attributed to it that, in 1497, the *grand conseil* was detached to become a genuine, specialised court of justice. Whether justice was dispensed by the king in person or, as was more usual, through delegation, it was important that it should be well administered, based as it was on laws that were constant and readily understood. Hence the decision was taken in 1454 to draw up and record all local customs, a long and exacting labour which came to fruition only in the period 1506–15. At the same time there was an increase in the number of *grandes ordonnances* aimed at the reform of justice (ten were issued between 1490 and 1539), while the reign of Louis XII saw the first printed collections of *ordonnances*, forerunners of a codification of French law.

None the less, the king did not possess a judicial monopoly, and in no way aspired to one. Clergy remained answerable to their own courts; they were not put on trial, not even for treason, as the cases concerning Cardinal Jean Balue (1469) and Georges d'Amboise (1487) were to show. In the vast majority of cases trials were conducted by seignorial judges who administered justice that was prompt and inexpensive, though it was not guaranteed in law. Exactly the opposite can be said of the royal courts in the *bailliages* and *sénéchaussées*. As courts of appeal, they received more and more cases of first instance. Their proliferation (there were some 323 in existence in 1515, excluding those in Provence and Brittany) demonstrates even better than the *parlements* the existence of a network of royal courts so tight-knit that no litigant would be more than a day's walk away from one. It was in this manner that the king fulfilled his role as dispenser of justice.

The financial state

The royal fiscal system had been reconstructed after the recapture of Paris in 1436. It was still based on the fundamental distinction between the ordinary finances, the receipt from the domain which the sovereign received by right and without question, and the extraordinary revenues, otherwise known as taxation, whose collection relied upon compulsion by the state and, perforce, upon the consent of his subjects. There were thus two systems, each with its separate parallel administration; in both, the sanctioning of expenditure –

---

[5] *Ordonnances des rois de France de la troisième race*, XX, p. 386.   [6] Scheller (1981–2).

guaranteed either by the treasurers of France or by the *généraux des finances* – functioned independently of collection and overall administration. However, the two systems were not of equal importance, since the ordinary finances amounted to scarcely more than 2 per cent of total state revenue, while extraordinary finances were obtained by direct taxation, the *taille* and (to the extent of a third) by indirect taxation such as the *aides* on the sale of articles and the *gabelle* raised on salt.

None now questioned the principle of taxation, even if regions with their own estates, such as Languedoc, reserved the right to discuss the amount to be raised, while the princes acknowledged the crown's monopoly of its use. In 1512, for instance, Jean d'Albret, although king of Navarre, dared not levy, without authorisation, in his French possessions the subsidy intended for the reconquest of his lost kingdom. This right to tax without opposition was indeed the hallmark of the monarchical state's absolute power. Even so, the royal financial system was a long way from being as coherent as is often alleged, a fact proved by the distinction maintained between ordinary and extraordinary finances. The fundamental concept behind the system was not as yet the idea of public contribution, but still that of a tax granted in return for the royal gift which had created the corresponding obligation. For the king, generosity was not a weakness but a virtue, after justice the most important for which he was esteemed. He was obliged to dispense grace and favour, either by giving alms, annuities and wages raised from his domain, or by paying out at his discretion many pensions, two-thirds of which went to persons of middle rank – the total, between 1460 and 1520, invariably accounting for 35 per cent of gross expenditure. The king was doing precisely the same when he distributed positions of command in the *compagnies de gens d'armes* or those responsibilities and offices which brought to their holders wages, pensions and special payments. In this sphere the introduction, in 1523, of venality through the sale of offices under the guise of loans was a way of securing a sensible financial return for this practice.

Traditionally, the king's largesse called, in return, for service: service under arms from the nobles, fulfilment of their duties from office holders, prayers from the clergy. This was not true of the *pauvre peuple*, who paid the *taille*, but received nothing; for them, the king's gift was embodied in the rigorous discipline of the *gens d'armes* who, thanks to the enforced taxation of the poor, were regularly paid. From this tradition it followed that any other use made of extraordinary finances, especially the payment of pensions, was not generosity but wanton extravagance berated by moralists and theorists from Guillaume Budé to Claude de Seyssel. It was a moral rather than a political issue, to the extent that genuine fiscal reform, such as the merging of the ordinary and extraordinary revenues under the umbrella of the *trésor de l'epargne* in 1523, turned out to be almost ineffective in practice.

Hence, in spite of appearances, the system lacked true efficiency. In order to pay for the enormous military expenses of the last ten years of his reign, Louis XI had logically doubled the taxation of his father's day, increasing it to a sum roughly corresponding to 140 tons of silver. The increase was deemed a breach of right rather than an excessive burden, with the result that the estates general enforced a return to the 1461 level. The state was still so flexible that it could withstand this halving of its livelihood without faltering. In real terms the levy of about 60 tons of pure silver was not to be surpassed before the 1520s. In other words, in this era of renewed prosperity the state was becoming relatively poorer. Meeting current expenses with difficulty, it was compelled, in order to finance the war, to resort either to borrowing or to depredation, in Italy, for example. To make ends meet, the *généraux des finances* were obliged to fall back upon financial stratagems and negotiate loans, taken out in their own names, from foreign bankers of Lyons. The first issue of annuities (*rentes*) in 1522 showed that there was at last a readiness to take the plunge and resort to public credit.

Throne and altar

One of the reasons for the continuation of old practices of this kind was that royal absolutism, if it ever existed, was above all 'mystical'.[7] The king was, indeed, 'Most Christian', an ancient form of words which entered diplomatic parlance from 1469 by way of Pope Pius II, and which no one turned to better account than did Louis XI. Consecration with the holy oil and the miracle-working power that flowed from the sacred ampulla (*sainte ampoule*) established kings as latter-day Davids. This sacred character, ostentatiously proclaimed by Louis in 1479 in his confrontation with the pope, was a royal monopoly, and the most important one of all. It is what gave the king the authority to set himself up as head of the Gallican Church, over which he exercised fully both his sovereign rights within the kingdom as well as his rights as God's lieutenant. Here was the mainspring of Louis XI's ecclesiastical policy after 1461 when, in a fit of temper, he abolished the Pragmatic Sanction. In its place was introduced the regime of the concordat, but one to which neither the whole-heartedly Gallican *parlement* nor the Holy See ever adapted satisfactorily. It was, however, to allow Louis and his successors to settle clerical affairs harmoni-ously with the pope on a case by case basis, as far as possible accommodating the interests of both parties, and taking into account, too, the pastoral needs of the day. The genuine concordat, that of 1516, merely formalised practices already well established.

[7] Lot and Fawtier (1958), p. 46.

The king had in his gift numerous benefices which he bestowed upon his favourites; this was another kind of largesse, and by no means the least important. Thus at the estates of 1484 mischievous tongues could vilify those whom they called Louis's bishops. For his part, Louis XII used this kind of patronage to bestow favours on his Italian clients. All in all, between 1470 and 1520, 78 per cent of bishoprics were held by members of the king's council or those connected to them. It is clear that the fusion of service of the Church and that of the secular state was increasing, not diminishing.

Having said that, it should not be imagined that the will of the king always succeeded in brushing aside local candidates (witness the difficult but successful election of François d'Estaing to the see of Rodez in 1501–4), or that royal bishops, for example Louis d'Amboise in Albi or Etienne de Poncher in Paris, were unsatisfactory bishops. The assemblies of clergy convened by the king as a means of exerting diplomatic pressure on the Holy See proved most attentive towards reform of the Church in 1478 and 1479, above all in 1493, and again in 1510 and 1511, while the estates of 1484 were also much concerned with the matter. The Gallican Church performed its role as a moral guardian of the state more often than it may appear. Claude de Seyssel was not exaggerating when he wrote 'Since he lives according to the law and the Christian religion, the king may not engage in tyranny. And if he should do so, every prelate or other religious of good character who has the advantage of the people at heart, has the right to remonstrate with him and reprimand him' ('Vivant le roi selon la loi et religion chrétienne, ne peut faire choses tyranniques. Et s'il en fait quelqu'une, il est loisible à un chacun prélat ou autre religieux bien vivant, ayant bon estime envers le peuple, le lui remontrer et l'incréper').[8] The restitution of Roussillon, ordered by the dying Louis XI and carried out by Charles VIII, or the protest raised by Jan Standonck against Louis XII's divorce, are examples of this. The Church of France, however much under the sway of the Most Christian king, was far from being merely a cog in the wheels of state.

A decentralised state

'Mystical' absolutism thus found itself limited by its very nature; its secular form, too, incorporated many other restrictions. In spite of the theory long accepted by historians, the revitalised post-1450 monarchy cannot be perceived as a centralised state manned by a hierarchical body of officers dedicated to its service. On the contrary, the gradual elimination of the principalities and the centralisation of power in the person of the king enforced a decentralisation in

---

[8] Seyssel, *Monarchie de France*, p. 116.

geographical and institutional terms which respected the strength of provincial particularism.

The size of the kingdom, unequalled in western Christendom, enforced it, too. Even after the creation of the royal postal system by Louis XI, it still normally took four weeks to cross France from north to south or from east to west. This alone would have justified setting up, as happened between 1450 and 1520, the ten *gouvernements* entrusted to *lieutenants généraux* endowed with sweeping powers. The function of these important individuals was, above all, to take the place of the princes in regions in which it no longer seemed appropriate to establish apanages. Such governors, recruited, particularly after 1483, from among the king's relations, helped to give the royal estate the appearance of a monarchy strongly tempered by aristocracy.

It is against this background, too, that the increase in the number of sovereign courts must be viewed. Even if it was impossible to split up decision-making bodies such as the *conseil du roi*, the *chancellerie* or the college of the *généraux des finances*, the same was not true of the administrative machinery. It was a way of stealing a march on Parisian supremacy and of upholding the prestige of provincial capitals in spite of the downfall of their princes. After 1450, *parlements* in Bordeaux, Grenoble, Dijon, Rouen and Aix-en-Provence joined those of Paris and Toulouse; *cours des aides*, like the one at Montpellier, were created in Rouen, Dijon and Grenoble, while Louis XII maintained a *chambre des comptes* at Blois. The regions thus singled out were precisely those whose provincial estates had retained their vitality.

Local autonomy, however, did not chiefly function at this exalted level, but rather on the smaller scale of the *châtellenie*, seat of rural power, or of the *bonne ville*, focal point of a small region six or seven leagues in radius, normally the seat of important financial and judicial authorities, a religious centre and a busy market place. A community with municipal institutions, that is a mayor and magistrates, the town enjoyed complete military autonomy, substantial financial resources, and a freedom of administration whose only restraint was the existence of urban lordships. The central authority, of which the town was the local instrument, was exercised by an elite body of public officers and officers of the law who stemmed from the local oligarchy; they wielded this power with an independence that was safeguarded by their wealth and the fixed tenure of their posts. From the same breeding ground came members of the new sovereign provincial courts and deputies, both to the provincial estates, which had in general been abandoned by churchmen and nobility, and to the various assemblies convened to draw up customs or to decide upon monetary and commercial questions. If, in 1515, 5,000 public officers were enough to administer the vast French kingdom, it was because state intervention in local affairs was reduced to a minimum. The renascent monarchy was in no sense a bureaucracy.

The strength of local autonomy, as much as the size of the kingdom, explains also the rarity of estates general. Since discussions normally took place within the separate regions, only the settling of exceptional affairs, such as the refusal to allow any dismemberment of the kingdom in 1468, the organisation of the pseudo-regency in 1484 and the marriage of Claude de France to Francis of Angoulême in 1506, required general meetings. It is probable that the aristocratic party, had it been successful, would not have been able either to modify this state of affairs or to transform the estates general into parliamentary assemblies along English lines.

SOCIAL FORCES

Economic recovery

France's new found strength after the war with England was sustained by an economic revival, a European phenomenon of which the state was the beneficiary, not the creator. At the time all the indicators, demographic, agricultural and commercial, were rising, thus creating a 'process of steady growth which, without doubt, reached its peak under Louis XII'.[9] Was this genuine growth, or merely a return to the level already reached at the beginning of the fourteenth century? The point is debatable, but as centuries go, growth was certainly the chief characteristic of the 'wonderful sixteenth century' which began about 1460.

To consider the demographic upturn first. Despite the considerable progress made by research in this field, it is difficult to pinpoint accurately stages in its development. However, three periods may be discerned: a definite revival from 1450 to 1470, a spectacular boom between 1470 and 1500 and, after that date, a steadier advance until the first check in the 1520s. In short, this was a population returning to the level of 15 million, and achieving unparalleled influence in western Europe.

In agricultural matters the line on the graph unmistakably follows that for population growth, except that the recovery of land abandoned during the period of stagnation in general preceded the spectacular demographic surge. Production increased rapidly, particularly that of cereals which, according to the yield of the tithe, doubled between 1450 and 1500. Later there was to be a slowing down of this process, but agricultural revenues continued to increase thanks to prices which were starting to rise. After 1520, the frequent recurrence of shortages showed that the Malthusian ceiling had been reached. All in all,

---

[9] Le Roy Ladurie and Morineau (1977), I, pt 2, p. 992.

although the rise achieved in wages was sustained, it was cultivation by peasant families that was the first to profit from the state's lack of financial appetite and favourable economic circumstances; small landowners and the nobility also reaped the benefits of these conditions.

The revival of trade did not follow quite the same pattern. First to recover was widespread merchant activity, the sort that supplied the weekly markets and small seasonal fairs. The network of these was re-established and increased; 13 per cent of royal letters patent addressed to towns, both large and small, in the fifteenth century concerned new fairs. Large-scale maritime commerce and long-distance trade picked up later and more slowly. The fairs at Lyons set up by Louis XI to rival those of Geneva became important only after 1465, the Channel and Atlantic ports after 1475; but Marseilles, acting for the Languedoc, now in full decline, not before the end of the century. A complete recovery of large-scale trade was not seen until the first two decades of the sixteenth century.

Rural communities

The rural lordship, 'the unique legal and stable framework of the recovery',[10] took full advantage of this favourable economic situation. For example, the revenues of the county of Tancarville, in Normandy, doubled between 1450 and 1520.[11] There were, broadly speaking, two kinds of lordship. First, the countless small ones, reduced to their principal dwelling place and farm (*métairie*) which enjoyed a number of traditional rights; these were owned largely by the lowest ranks of the nobility (*écuyers*) who remained, in their way of life, very close to the peasantry, unable to keep up appearances at musters of the *arrière-ban*, yet very proud of their noble blood. In particular after 1450, these lordships were those which came into the hands of the bourgeoisie from the neighbouring towns.

Lordships of importance were those which administered justice (*haute justice*) and, even more so, those bearing a title, beginning with the *châtellenies*, 'the best possible investment for a noble servant of the king',[12] not on account of their profits, which scarcely ever topped 4 or 5 per cent, but for the honour and security which they provided. From his fortified *château* the lord ensured that justice prevailed on his estates; he maintained law and order, policed markets and guaranteed the authenticity of contracts. For country people, the *châtellenie* was, as a rule, the only place where administrative and judicial authority was exercised.

The state did not interfere with these lordships, but it did overshadow them

[10] Neveux (1985), p. 62.   [11] Bois (1976), p. 232; Eng. trans., p. 257.   [12] Olland (1980), p. 530.

as the supreme court of appeal, and circumvented them in the matter of tax collection and in the recruitment of *francs-archers*. In these cases, it dealt directly with the parish whose nature was thereby altered, becoming a secular district and an organised community of inhabitants, as it already was in an ecclesiastical guise. Henceforth, in every village, an elite grew up, recruiting from among its members attorneys, seignorial officers, tax assessors and farmers, and collectors of the *taille*. With the state in support, this elite, forming a kind of French 'yeomanry' which had been reinvigorated by the economic recovery, was capable of providing a counterbalance to the ecclesiastical and seignorial authorities. In this way, albeit diffidently, the peasantry gained access to political existence and experience.

Towns and trade

As regards the merchant economy, the role played by the state with its partner, the bourgeoisie ('the class that manages the nation'),[13] had long been crucial. Louis XI has been hailed as the king of the merchant class, a view which, today, appears far-fetched. It is undeniably true, however, that economic thinking was gradually asserting itself; it can be traced by analysing the themes in certain *ordonnances* from the time of Louis XI to Chancellor Duprat's speech to the towns in 1517. Such thinking inspired numerous measures taken with a view to opening up the kingdom to large-scale trade: for instance, customs protection was employed to reserve the production of silk goods, and other profitable articles, for the manufacturing merchants of the kingdom. Other measures, too, were designed to produce a favourable exchange rate: the export of precious metals was banned and the use of foreign currency forbidden. All this, however, constituted neither a body of doctrine nor a coherent economic policy.

The truth was that, in important commercial affairs, the French kingdom was dominated by forces outside its boundaries. The success of the new fairs at Lyons, both before and after their brief eclipse between 1484 and 1494, the annexation of Marseilles in 1481 and the revived vitality of Paris and the Channel ports renewed the significance of the axis formed by the Rhone, Saône and Seine to the detriment of the hopes once nurtured by Bourges and Tours. However, on closer inspection, the hub of this activity is revealed as having been either the Bank of Lyons, controlled by Italians or Germans, or the trade carried by Castilians and Portuguese in and out of the western ports. The backwardness of France at the capitalist level was clear. That is perhaps why Louis XII and Francis I were so intent upon dominating Milan and Genoa,

---

[13] Imbart de La Tour (1948), p. 414.

since the other financial capitals, with Antwerp top of the list, were completely beyond their grasp.

At no time during these years were there, in France, great businessmen capable of exerting weighty influence upon the state. The successors of Jacques Coeur were but pale imitations, merely indispensable intermediaries between the treasury and the Bank of Lyons. There was unbroken continuity from Jean de Beaune to his son, Jacques, who became lord of Semblançay. They were not businessmen, but the first 'financiers' in the history of the monarchy, whose authority rested largely on the penury of the state. The downfall of such men in 1523, followed by the execution of Semblançay in 1527, changed nothing, except that it opened the door a little wider to the Italians.

The strength of French merchants was not to be found at this level, but rather in the 'silent trade' which gave such a boost to the work of artisans. This was one reason for the robust health of the urban economy, which was able to alleviate in part the first signs of weakness in rural areas during the 1520s. Merchants grew in number, but not in political importance, owing to a lack of a national market and to a decline of their position on the social scale.[14] Other than in Lyons, they were not pre-eminent among urban elites, being over-shadowed by royal officers and lawyers. In the same way there was a sense of hierarchy among the 300 or so *bonnes villes* which, for the most part, held sway within the small cell of which each formed the nucleus. It was, though, thanks to this local ascendancy, largely political in nature, that the state was able to act out its predatory role to the detriment of the country's rural districts.

Social dynamism: political society

It should come as no surprise that, in a renascent France, it was not the spirit of enterprise, but service to the king or Church which opened the door to rapid social advance. Royal favour was the prize sought by the ambitious. It gave access to the court, an artificial environment long vilified by moralists, yet exerting a fascination which nothing could obscure. The panegyrist of the *Chevalier sans reproche* shows the young Louis de la Trémoïlle disregarding the traditional warnings of his father, and setting out for the court of Louis XI. Two separate establishments were to be found in this place of blandishment: the royal household and the council, the one being where those close to the king and, after Anne of Brittany, to the queen might be found; the other consti-tuting those responsible for the day-to-day government and administration of the kingdom. It was an ill-defined milieu, but one which, for a long time, had

---

[14] Chaunu and Gascon (1977), p. 233.

spawned the sovereign courts, already constituting genuine bodies of civil servants. It is still misleading to try to compare the old nobility (*noblesse d'épée*) with the new (*noblesse de robe*), the aristocracy of the court with the parvenus of the council. In the *Dialogue de noblesse*, Symphorien Champier most aptly wrote: 'We have three types of nobility: the first is theological and spiritual, the second is a product of nature, the third is political and civil' ('Nous avons trois manières de noblesse: la première est théologique et spirituelle, la seconde naturelle, la troisième polictique et civile').[15] In other words, the nobility was ever the breeding ground that nurtured the governing elite of the country,[16] whether a man belonged to it by birth or destiny. Even under Louis XI, the princes always made up a quarter of the complement of the council, the nobility, taken together, providing two-thirds.

Within the multitude of nobles, the 'political and civil' appeared as an oligarchic structure. Recruited by recommendation dependent upon the whims of clientage, it functioned within a closed circuit, thanks both to its ability to secure secular and ecclesiastical offices and to the king's largesse, which yielded prodigious fortunes to its members.[17] Yet this nobility did not constitute a wholly united body, being divided from those born to serve in the royal council or by the particular outlook of those who were to man the sovereign courts.

If the apex of the political nobility's world was the court, then its base was rooted in the depths of civil society. There, in the heart of the *châtellenies* or the *bonnes villes*, it was possible to acquire a modicum of local power, and thence place a network of associations which allowed a man to obtain the king's favour. It was, however, a precarious situation, since disgrace could strike at any moment, bringing with it secular excommunication. Hence it was vitally necessary for members of the serving oligarchy, whatever their background, to reinforce their position by the acquisition of rich lordships which conferred stability and power, or of ecclesiastical benefices and offices in the sovereign courts which procured similar guarantees. The system worked well once the war between the king and the princes was over, and once loss of the king's good graces was no longer synonymous with losing one's life, at least if one were well born. Although convicted of *lèse-majesté* in 1504, Pierre de Rohan, marshal of Gié, was able to enjoy his estates in honourable retirement, whereas some twenty years later the financier, Semblançay, ended up on the gallows.

NATIONAL CONSCIOUSNESS AND IMPERIAL VISION

In order to see the growth of a national consciousness, nurtured by a long history and now enriched by the ideas of a rediscovered humanism, one must

---

[15] Harsgor (1980), IV, p. 2751.   [16] Contamine (1971), p. 156.   [17] Contamine (1978a), pp. 72–80.

take as one's vantage point the heart of this society, political in the broadest sense of the word. It was this growing consciousness that formed the link between the over-remoteness of the state and the various sections of local civil society.

The arts

National unity in the cultural sphere was not really of the kind that can be easily recognised in a French artistic school. Painters and sculptors, if they outgrew their reputations as local artists, worked for princely courts which supported them. Tours and Blois, Moulins and Aix-en-Provence were so many separate centres, while the Burgundian (i.e. Flemish) school was the most brilliant of them all. In the case of music, it was not so much a question of Burgundian supremacy as of a monopoly. The dominance of northern styles was to be little changed by the arrival, at the turn of the century, of a few Italian artists, whose presence was to exert even less influence on a blossoming of architecture unequalled in western Christendom, which took as its model the French *château*, that combination of stronghold and aristocratic abode which was the perfect expression of seignorial power regained. As an innovative style, it culminated on the banks of the Loire in the creations of the king and his greatest courtiers.

Literature, language and history

It is rather in works of literature that one must seek a national culture, principally in the art of the royal and princely courts, but also in that of the *grands rhétoriqueurs* so unjustly disparaged. This was an art divided among the various princely houses, among which that of Burgundy, with George Chastellain (d. 1475) and Jean Lemaire des Belges (d. 1524) was paramount. At the same time it was a form profoundly united by the subtle use of the raw material: the French language.

This was the language of the king, his court and his capital and, at the time under consideration, the language spoken on the banks of the Loire. Since the end of the fourteenth century it had won its place beside Latin as the language of culture; it was extolled by scholars for its 'Trojan' antiquity; and it was acknowledged by the whole of political society, both socially and geographically. By 1450 it had conquered the Rhone valley, by about 1490 Bas-Languedoc, in 1520 Bordeaux. There was no trace here of cultural imperialism, but evidence, instead, of a pride that was national as well as linguistic. To adopt the language of the king was to render oneself better able to serve him; it was also to acknowledge oneself as French.

The humanist *rhétoriqueurs* were not only the best propagandists for the nation's language, they were also pioneers in the history of its foundation. Court poets and pamphleteers who tailored their work to suit the occasion, they turned themselves as need arose into chroniclers or even historians in the classical manner. They were joined in this task by religious scholars of reputation, men such as Robert Gaguin, whose *Compendium* (1495) or short history of France enjoyed considerable success, and by notaries and secretaries of the royal chancery, such as Nicole Gilles, author of the *Annales et chroniques de France* (1492), for whom history was a tool of the trade. These men were much read by a widely based readership for whom the *Grandes chroniques de France* had constituted almost a bible.[18] It was not simply a matter of the written word; pictures, devices and symbolic representations, all products of the same ambience, circulated widely in the *bonnes villes* through the ceremonies of the royal *entrées*.[19] All these works helped disseminate, as if through a sort of Vulgate, a universal concept of the nature of monarchy and the glorious origins of the nation. The myth of Trojan origins had been attacked by scholars, but was revived by the discovery of the Gauls who, with their direct descent from Noah, were neither Roman nor Germanic. It was known that some of them had travelled in Italy and the east; it was they who arrived in Troy before returning with Francus to rejoin those compatriots who had remained in their native land. Everywhere they spread wisdom, knowledge and just laws, of which the Salic Law, attributed to the Merovingian king, Pharamund, became about 1500 the perfect symbol. After being baptised as Christians these Gauls, alongside the Frankish warriors, had been kept perfectly orthodox by a saintly dynasty whose symbolic figures were St Clovis, St Charlemagne and St Louis. The Most Christian kings were now the leaders of a new chosen people, destined by providence to safeguard the defence of the Church and the triumph of the intellect, as the *translatio studii*, the transfer of Greek knowledge to the Gallo-Franks, guaranteed for all humanists, from Robert Gaguin to Guillaume Budé, the superiority of their country over Italy.

Imperial vocation

This budding national consciousness incorporated an imperial vocation, a resurgence of the ancient concept of the holy and universal monarchy. Louis XI, who, in the face of the princes, needed to assert himself as emperor within the kingdom (*empereur dans son royaume*), was not the least of its devotees. He deliberately proclaimed his sacred mission to reform the Universal Church by

[18] 'presque une Bible' (Guenée (1971), p. 124; Eng. trans. p. 58).
[19] See above, p. 8.

convening a General Council, a threat which the Papacy would not take lightly, neither at the time of the Pazzi conspiracy (1478) nor when Alexander VI saw Charles VIII arrive in Rome at the end of 1494. The Italian faction of the Sacred College also took it seriously when, in 1503, it was faced with the candidature of Louis XII's principal counsellor, Georges d'Amboise, at two separate papal elections. So did Julius II when, at last, on 1 November 1511, the long-promised council (whose lack of success was to be purely the result of the defeat of French arms) opened at Pisa. It has been said, and not without good reason, that these were simply diplomatic intrigues. Yet it is difficult to attribute to political considerations alone initiatives first encouraged by kings whose spiritual devotion was hardly in doubt, and then pursued by bishops not all of whom were men totally lacking in religious sensitivities.

It was always in the context of Italian affairs that France flaunted this desire to reform the Church. Not without reason, for Italy, as well as being the country where the Roman pontiff had his seat, was also the 'garden of the empire' once glorified by Dante. The Italian Wars were not the exploits of monarchs wandering in a chivalric Utopia indifferent to national interests, but were inseparable from this national and imperial perception of Gallo-Frankish history. Concerns of princely houses, defence of ancient rights fiercely pursued, results of international politics, the wars reflected all these factors. Above all else, however, they were wars of magnificence pursued in accordance with France's imperial vocation. Louis XI had kept a close eye on Italian affairs, and had even gone so far as to set himself up as the guarantor of peace in the peninsula in the face of Neapolitan and papal hostility in 1478. He was unable to take matters further, however, owing to the vengeful policy he was pursuing against the house of Burgundy. Charles VIII, relieved of any such concerns and anxious to counter the glory won before Granada by the 'Catholic Monarchs', dedicated himself to the restoration of his princely rights and the fulfilment of his duties as Most Christian king in his kingdom of Naples and, hence, of Jerusalem too. The expedition was presented in good faith as the prelude to a crusade against the Turks, whatever Commynes might say. The vast number of messianic prophecies, associated in France with Jean Michel, but likewise in Italy and Spain,[20] put the finishing touches to the significance of the expedition. After the solemn entry of the king into Naples (12 May 1495), the league formed by the pope, Venice and Aragon put political realism back on the agenda, but the battle of Fornovo, fought on 6 July 1495, showed that France could also justify her claims to supremacy by armed force. Louis XII, not satisfied with avenging his predecessors as dukes of Orleans by evicting Ludovico Sforza from Milan and subsequently capturing him, retook

---

[20] See below, pp. 616–18.

Naples in conjunction with Ferdinand, king of Aragon (1500–1). At the same time he, in his turn, launched the last of the crusades as far as the island of Mytilene, making an alliance against the Turks with King Vladislav of Bohemia. If, after 1504, he lost Naples, Louis did successfully defend Lombardy (well remembered as once having been Cisalpine Gaul) against the rebellious Genoese in 1507 and the Venetians at Agnadello in 1509. The display of a complete range of imperial symbolism enlarged the significance of these campaigns. The closed imperial crown now bore the stamp of the arms of the king, who presented himself in Italy as the avenger of his Trojan ancestors (*ultus avos Trojae*). The title of father of the country (*pater patriae*), conferred on him in 1506 by the estates general, made him a new Augustus.[21] Even in Italy, iconography celebrated his triumphs in the classical style and portrayed him surrounded by the nine 'worthy' Roman emperors from Augustus to Justinian.[22] On this field of battle Louis had essentially only one true rival, equally of imperial stature, and that was the other Caesar, Pope Julius II, who, ironically, organised the Holy League against the Most Christian king in order to 'protect the Church' and to save Italy, land of the Empire, from the barbarian. Although defeated at Ravenna in 1512, Julius finally triumphed over his adversary. Novara in 1513 was Julius's posthumous victory, although Marignano in 1515 was to overshadow it. Once again, everything was in the melting pot.

It remains to consider whether, in the midst of these wars which no Frenchman ever denounced as futile, the Most Christian king was dreaming only of Italian conquest, of reforming the Holy See, of leading a crusade, or whether his true ambition was to win the imperial crown itself. Despite what has long been said, Charles VIII, during the whole of his campaign, carefully refrained from hinting that he wanted it. But after 1491 Maximilian of Habsburg (who was never able to receive it) constantly proclaimed the reverse to the whole of Germany, and thus to the whole of Europe. No French king replied to these insinuations, other than when, in 1501, Louis XII promised to do nothing to secure the Empire nor give the impression that he desired to be Emperor ('pour occasion que puissions avoir ou imaginer d'estre empereur').[23] It is enough to show that Francis I's enthusiastic response to invitations from Germany after 1516 was not a pipe-dream without precedent. On the contrary, it was the inevitable outcome of Maximilian's rash campaigns, and the result of a policy of hegemony of which the plans for crusades in 1517–18 and the Concordat of 1516 were the manifestations. In the eyes of the electors, Francis I as a candidate for the Empire had arguments on his side that compared not unfavourably with those of Charles, his rival, who was more Burgundian than German.

---

[21] See below, pp. 635–6.   [22] Scheller (1985).   [23] Zeller (1934), p. 499.

There is nothing to tell us whether the kingdom of France or Europe as a whole would have gained a great deal had Francis I been successful in 1519. Yet, as Jean Thénaud wrote about 1523, the facts demonstrate well enough the apogee reached by a renascent France and her sovereign, 'the most Christian and most Serene king and emperor of the sacred Gallican monarchy' ('le très chrétien et très sérénissime roy et empereur de la sacrée monarchie gallicane').[24]

[24] Jean Thénaud, *Le voyage d'outre-mer*, cited by Zeller (1934), p. 505.

CHAPTER 20

BURGUNDY

Bertrand Schnerb

ON 27 April 1404, Philip the Bold, duke of Burgundy, died in the town of Hal, south of Brussels. A contemporary, Christine de Pisan, described the event in terms of the ideal death which should be associated with a prince. On his deathbed the duke gave his three sons, John, Anthony and Philip, the benefit of his final thoughts, advised them to remain faithful to the crown of France and divided among them the lands which he had patiently assembled under his authority during his forty years of rule. This partitioning was to be subject to certain conditions, and would be fully effective only after two years. On his father's death his eldest son, John 'the Fearless', inherited the duchy of Burgundy and the county of Charolais: less than a year later, in March 1405, on the death of his mother, Marguerite de Male, he was to pick up the major part of his maternal inheritance, namely the counties of Flanders, Artois and Burgundy (Franche-Comté). His brother, Anthony, was not formally involved in the partitioning of Philip the Bold's legacy for, in 1403, Philip had arranged with Jeanne, duchess of Brabant (who had no heir), that he would succeed her; in 1404, he took over the regency of Brabant and, on Jeanne's death in 1406, he assumed the title of duke of Brabant. Philip the Bold's third son, also Philip, received the counties of Rethel and Nevers, which had formed part of his mother's bequest.

Such a procedure avoided the territorial break-up of Burgundian territory; the new duke held the most important lands bequeathed by his parents. As for Anthony's accession to Brabant, it would be seen as an example, achieved post-humously, of Philip the Bold's policy of expansion. Burgundian influence would now be felt within the Empire, where a network of alliances was already proving useful. The late duke's matrimonial policy had, in effect, led to the marriage of three Burgundian princesses to princes of the Empire: in 1385, Margaret of Burgundy had been espoused to William of Bavaria, heir to the counties of Hainault, Holland and Zeeland, whose sister, Margaret, had at the same time married the future John the Fearless. Some years later, in 1393,

Map 9   The Burgundian dominion

Catherine of Burgundy would marry Leopold IV of Habsburg, duke of Austria, while in 1401 Mary of Burgundy was to marry Amadeus VIII, count of Savoy.

None the less, the position of Duke John in 1404–5 was, in some respects, unsatisfactory, for although the extent of his territorial authority could not be denied, his financial position was far from sound. Ever since his father's time the whole matter of the duchy's finances had been closely linked to the role played by the duke of Burgundy at the heart of French affairs. Between 1395 and 1404, when the annual ducal revenue was in the order of 450,000 *livres tournois*, some 30 per cent of this came from gifts and pensions granted by the king of France, Charles VI, to his uncle of Burgundy. This figure reflected the dominant position occupied by the duke at the French court. On Philip's death, however, this source of revenue dried up immediately, and his son, John, could rely only on the resources of the two Burgundies (duchy and county) and, after March 1405, upon those of Flanders and Artois, respectively 12 and 43 per cent of the sums raised by his father between 1395 and 1404.[1] The new duke was immediately forced to borrow where he could, soliciting loans from government employees of every kind, from the towns of his principalities, from the richest of his subjects and, quite naturally, from his supporters, both merchants and financiers, such as the Lucchese, Dino Rapondi, and the Parisian, Guillaume Sanguin. The loss of influence felt by the duke of Burgundy at the heart of royal government in 1404 (all to the advantage of Louis of Orleans, the king's brother) and the financial effect caused by the loss of almost a third of the ducal revenues weighed heavily upon Burgundian policy as it sought new avenues to follow.

REGIONAL AND 'CENTRAL' INSTITUTIONS

Heir to an important group of principalities, the new duke of Burgundy also took charge of the administrative and judicial institutions upon which ducal government relied. Seen in the context of the entire ducal dominion, these institutions were neither united nor centralised. Their structures and functions differed in the two Burgundies and in the principalities of the north, although there already existed some 'central' institutions which bore the marks of belonging to a truly 'Burgundian state'.

Since the duke visited Burgundian lands but rarely and then only briefly, it became necessary for him to be represented either by his duchess (this was very much the case under John the Fearless, much of Margaret of Bavaria's time being spent in Dijon) or by a governor to whom were delegated powers of

[1] Nordberg (1964), pp. 27, 29, 31, 34–6; Van Nieuwenhuysen (1984), pp. 373–83.

administration and justice such as the duke would have exercised.[2] Along with this ducal representative, the essential agent of government in the two Burgundies was the ducal council which met at Dijon. Since 1386 this body had acted, above all, as a court of justice hearing appeals from within the duchy. Parallel to it were other courts of appeal, the most important being the *Grands Jours* held in Beaune which drew appeals from both the duchy and from the county of Charolais. This court heard only cases which came before it from that part of the duchy which lay within the kingdom of France and which, having been considered in Beaune, could still be heard before the king's *parlement* sitting in Paris. Since most of the duchy was a fief of the French crown, the duke's subjects could always appeal, in last resort, from ducal courts to Paris. This 'appeal to France', as it was called, was the most tangible evidence of royal sovereignty over Burgundy: the situation would not change until Charles the Bold became duke.

The administration of justice within the county of Burgundy (which was imperial territory) was very different. Here, justice was dispensed by a *parlement* whose seat was at Dole, and which acted as a sovereign court hearing appeals in last resort. In spite of this, the justice of the two Burgundies differed but little, if at all. The result was that efforts to achieve institutional unification worked well, the president of the *Grands Jours* of Beaune fulfilling the same function in the *parlement* at Dole.

In the principalities of the north, the administrative and judicial organisations differed, but the practices followed by the dukes meant that, although they lacked uniformity, they none the less moved more closely together. Thus, since 1386, there had existed in Lille a council which, acting as a judicial body, was broadly similar to that functioning in Dijon. The authority of the court of appeal extended over Flanders, to the lordship of Malines, even as far as Antwerp. The dukes' Flemish subjects complained of the institutions' markedly 'French' character, and when John the Fearless became count of Flanders he recognised the legitimacy of such complaints by transferring the council first to Oudenaarde (1405) and then to Ghent (1407), ordering that henceforth the Flemish language should have its proper place in its procedures. Those living in the kingdom of France, yet subject to the court, could appeal from its decisions to the *parlement* in Paris.

At the summit of the Burgundian system of administration and justice there existed institutions which can be called 'central', through which, in a certain sense, the unity of the government responsible for the different Burgundian principalities expressed itself. The ducal council (*grand conseil*), for instance, accompanied the duke on his travels, and included among its members rela-

---

[2] Richard (1957a).

tives, political allies and great officers of state; it was a body to which all who bore the title 'ducal councillor' (*conseiller de monseigneur le duc*) could be summoned. This council, centred on the court, differed from those which sat in Dijon and Lille; as the main organ of government, although one lacking specialised competence or powers, it could discuss all and any matters concerning the duke. At its head was the ducal chancellor, *de facto* head of all Burgundian justice and administration. Between 1405 and 1422 the position was in the hands of Jean de Saulx, lord of Courtivron, who was replaced by Jean de Thoisy, bishop of Tournai. In 1422, Thoisy gave way to Nicolas Rolin, a figure of great importance who was to be retained in this post for almost forty years.

The tendency towards 'bi-polarity', with two capitals, one in Dijon, the other in Lille, which affected both administration and justice, could also be observed in the organisation of ducal financial affairs. Since 1386, as the result of a conscious decision taken by Philip the Bold, the two ducal institutions had worked in strict symmetry. For both groups of principalities which formed the Burgundian state there were created, in addition to local institutions, two regional receivers' offices, one for the counties of Flanders and Artois, the other for the duchy and county of Burgundy. Similarly, there also existed two *chambres des comptes*, one, sitting in Lille, exercising control over the northern principalities, the other in Dijon, having jurisdiction over the two Burgundies and Charolais. At a regional level, the authority of these institutions extended over the accounts of all receivers, over the management of all ducal estates and over the preservation of all financial and estate records. In addition, each had other rights of jurisdiction, just as, at a higher level, the king's *chambre des comptes* in Paris exercised such rights.[3]

Parallel to this regional organisation there existed financial bodies which followed the dukes on their travels. The general office for ducal receipts (*recette générale de toutes les finances*) which, in spite of its name, also concerned itself with expenditure and was far from exercising control over the entire ducal system of finances, and the *chambre aux deniers*, which was more particularly concerned with the expenses of the household, were two such. The accounts of these 'central' bodies were first overseen by the *chambre des comptes* at Dijon and later, after 1420, by that at Lille.[4]

The various outlets drew funds from a variety of forms of revenue. In addition to revenues from their lands, which were particularly profitable in Flanders, the dukes of Burgundy benefited from a complex system of taxation. In Burgundy, the late fourteenth century had witnessed the creation of an

[3] Andt (1924); Cauchies (1995), pp. 50–1.
[4] Mollat (1958); Vaughan (1962), pp. 113–50, and (1966), pp. 103–29; Cauchies (1995), pp. 48–51, 63–4.

elaborate system which consisted of three kinds of indirect taxation (a tax of one twentieth, or twelve *deniers* in the *livre*, on all transactions; an eighth, or thirty *deniers* in the *livre*, raised on wine; and the *gabelle*, or salt tax, raised as in France) in addition to a direct hearth tax (*fouage*). This last was voted by the estates of Burgundy, and had to be specially requested by the duke.[5] In Artois taxes (*aides*) were agreed by the estates, and in Flanders by the 'Four Members', Ghent, Bruges, Ypres and the 'Franc' of Bruges.[6] The raising of taxes was thus preceded by negotiation between the duke and the representative institutions of his principalities. How much taxes produced depended on the level of persuasion which could be achieved by those acting on behalf of the duke, as well as on his own popularity and the level of prosperity enjoyed by those who paid. During the rule of John the Fearless (1404–19) the known total paid in taxes by his northern principalities (Flanders, Artois, Lille, Douai and Orchies) amounted to more than 1,092,000 *livres tournois*, to which Flanders alone contributed 1,029,000 *livres*. In the same period the two Burgundies collected only 129,500 *livres* between them.[7]

The existence of such institutions, judicial, financial as well as fiscal, often reflections of royal institutions, sometimes provoked opposition, even rebellion. If the two Burgundies never witnessed revolt during this century, the same could not be said of the principalities in the north. In Flanders, in particular, the dukes met considerable, even violent, opposition from the towns. John the Fearless did not have to make war in the same way as his father had done against Ghent and its allies between 1382 and 1385, and he tried to meet the demands made by the 'Four Members' on behalf of his Flemish subjects; none the less, Duke John had to make serious efforts to persuade the towns of Flanders not to rise in revolt. This aspect of his work cannot be ignored, in particular the intervention against Liège in 1408. In this case, the duke's first aim (shared with his brother-in-law, William of Bavaria, count of Hainault) was to bring help to the prince-bishop, John of Bavaria, William's brother, who was resisting a revolt in Liège. For the duke of Burgundy, it was a matter of preserving a valuable piece in a network of regional alliances, and of making a show of force which would stifle any inclination to rebellion among his own subjects. Such an episode must not be seen in a single perspective. Yet, to understand its significance more fully, it must be observed in a much wider context.

A EUROPEAN POWER

Ever since the end of the fourteenth century the position of the duke of Burgundy was such that action by him, whether political, military or diplo-

---

[5] Dubois (1987a) and (1987b).   [6] Prevenier (1961).   [7] Vaughan (1966), pp. 110–11.

matic, had repercussions across the length and breadth of Euro
first of all, a French prince: Philip the Bold and, after him, John
and Philip the Good, all had ambitions to play a major role in the a
French kingdom. During this period, and above all during the first
century, the dominant political problem was to be the conflict with

On the death of his father in 1404, Duke John wanted to regain the influence
which the former had exercised at the seat of government as the result of the
illness of the French king, Charles VI. His first attempts to do this led him into
confrontation with Louis, duke of Orleans, brother of the king. The two were
playing for high stakes: whoever controlled the decision-making body controlled the royal finances. John's aim was to become once again the beneficiary
of gifts from the crown. He also needed to influence diplomatic policy for, as
duke of Burgundy, and in complete contrast to the duke of Orleans, he was an
advocate of a negotiated solution to the English problem, preferable, in his
view, to the state of war which, after long periods of truce, dominated Anglo-
French relations. The duke was, in this sense, the supporter of his Flemish subjects and, in particular, of the 'Four Members' who, as trading partners of the
English, sought to secure the safety of the seas.

The struggle for power was to lead to the assassination of the duke of
Orleans (23 November 1407), a crime organised by Duke John. This murder of
the king's brother, committed in the very heart of Paris, was to lead to civil war
which continued for the next twenty-eight years.[8] At first, the duke of
Burgundy was able to take advantage of the situation. Thanks to the support of
a group of members of the University of Paris, led by the theologian, Jean
Petit, author of a justification of tyrannicide, Duke John organised an intense
campaign of propaganda to justify his action. With the support of the university and of a part of Parisian society, helped by a strong military hand and
encouraged by the victory achieved over the rebels of Liège in 1408, John was
able to silence any opposition and take power. But after 1410 that opposition
began to crystallise around the person of Charles of Orleans, son of the late
duke, and his father-in-law, Bernard, count of Armagnac. Their quarrel soon
entered an active stage, punctuated by truces which few respected. In 1413,
after the Cabochians, the duke's most active supporters in the capital who were
led by the guilds and, notably, by the butchers, had compromised his popularity
through their excessive violence, John lost both Paris and his hold on power.
He would regain neither before May 1418.

In the meanwhile, as the result of English military intervention in 1415 in
support of the claim to the French crown, the situation had become more confused than ever. Having crushed the French army at Agincourt (25 October

---

[8] Autrand (1986), pp. 349–421; Guenée (1992).

1415) and set out to conquer Normandy two years later, the English king, Henry V, was now a threat both to the 'Burgundians' and their rivals, the 'Armagnacs'. These, however, found the differences between them too great to allow them to unite against the growing danger from England, in spite of the attempts by Duke John to convince the dauphin (the future Charles VII), leader of the opposing party, to join in common cause against the English invader. It may be noted that John's own attitude was not entirely unequivocal for he was, at the same time, negotiating with the English. Finally, at a meeting with the dauphin at Montereau on 10 September 1419, Duke John was murdered by his rival's Armagnac councillors, thus avenging the death of Louis of Orleans a dozen years earlier.

This event had important results for Anglo-Burgundian relations. The new duke, Philip the Good, and his councillors, taking account of the situation thus created and strongly influenced by economic considerations, decided to enter into negotiations with the English. An Anglo-Burgundian agreement was made in December 1419 followed, on 21 May 1420, by the Treaty of Troyes. The French royal government, now controlled by the Burgundians, as well as Duke Philip himself, accepted the creation of a double monarchy of France and England, to be ruled by Henry V and his heirs to be born of his marriage to Catherine, daughter of Charles VI and sister of the dauphin. This treaty was to dominate Burgundian policy for the next fifteen years.[9]

The successive deaths of Henry V and Charles VI (August and October 1422) and the minority of the young Henry VI did not allow Duke Philip to gain control of the government, as the regency of the kingdom of France came into the hands of John, duke of Bedford, uncle of Henry VI. The fact is not unimportant, as the duke of Burgundy slowly began to distance himself from the government of France in a way which contrasted with the policy followed by both his father and grandfather. Without acting against the terms agreed at Troyes, Philip followed a policy which was independent of them. Thus he never lost contact with Charles VII who, faced with an 'English France' ruled by the duke of Bedford, still controlled half the kingdom; in September 1424 he even went so far as to arrange a truce with him. Elsewhere, his policy of expansion into the Low Countries brought him up against the ambitions of Bedford's brother, Humphrey, duke of Gloucester. This confrontation undoubtedly helped to sour Anglo-Burgundian relations within France itself. Duke Philip was mainly intent upon securing control over Picardy, keeping open the routes leading from his territories to Paris as well as those, running through Champagne, which gave him access between the territories in the north and the two Burgundies in the south. It was only these three

[9] Bonenfant (1958).

objectives which could justify Burgundian military aid to the English in their own war against the dauphin and his supporters.

From 1429–30, the reversal of the military situation, to the advantage of Charles VII (finally crowned king of France in July 1429), prompted Duke Philip to consider breaking the Anglo-Burgundian alliance. Discussions undertaken by the chancellor, Nicolas Rolin, with representatives of Charles VII in 1432 were to lead to a reconciliation at Arras in 1435 which marked the official end of the civil strife which had begun in 1407. In exchange for territorial concessions agreed by Charles VII, the Burgundians abandoned their allies, the English, to join the French who were able to retake Paris in the spring of 1436. A major military operation, organised by Burgundy, to besiege Calais failed. Further setbacks were experienced at the hands of the English in Picardy and Flanders, and through a revolt in Bruges (1436–7). As a result, Duke Philip took part in negotiations with the English at Gravelines in 1438 in order to safeguard the economic interests of Flanders and, in 1439, he even offered to try to negotiate a lasting peace between France and England.[10]

By the beginning of the 1440s, therefore, the duke of Burgundy had managed, without great loss, to put himself on the periphery of the Anglo-French conflict. By now he ruled a group of principalities to whose number he was constantly adding and which, in geopolitical terms, constituted a vital element within the very heart of western Europe. On the French side, the duke had secured important territorial concessions at Arras in 1435: Charles VII had confirmed the cession of three important lordships in Picardy, Roye, Péronne and Montdidier which had originally been ceded to Duke John in 1418; in addition, the king now pledged to Duke Philip the county of Ponthieu and the 'Somme towns' (Saint-Quentin, Corbie, Doullens, Amiens and Abbeville) which he could buy back for 400,000 *écus*. In addition, in the region of the duchy of Burgundy itself, Charles VII now ceded the towns of Bar-sur-Seine, Auxerre and Mâcon.

Turning in a more easterly direction, Burgundian expansion into imperial territory was achieved in several stages and through diverse means in the years 1420–40. Duke Philip began by negotiating the purchase of the county of Namur in 1421; the count, Jean III, surrendered this territory in exchange for a life interest and the sum of 132,000 *écus*. In fulfilment of this agreement, the county duly became Burgundian in 1429. The next stage was to prove more difficult. In 1425 war broke out between Philip the Good and his cousin, Jacqueline of Bavaria, heiress to the counties of Hainault, Holland and Zeeland, who enjoyed the support of Humphrey, duke of Gloucester. It took three years of war to bring the countess to terms; in July 1428, by the Treaty of

---

[10] Thielemans (1966), pp. 49–163.

Delft, she made the duke of Burgundy her heir before finally abandoning all her rights to him in April 1433. In the meanwhile Philip had succeeded in seizing the duchy of Brabant following the deaths of his cousins, Jean IV in 1427 and Philippe de Saint-Pol in 1430: having no children, this last bequeathed his inheritance upon Duke Philip. In spite of some reluctance on the part of the estates of Brabant, who showed considerable hostility to him, Philip finally made his formal entry (*joyeuse entrée*) into Brussels in October 1430. Thus, within a matter of twelve years, he had secured control over what may be called the Burgundian Low Countries, termed, in contemporary language, 'the lands on this side' ('les pays de par deça'). The process was completed with difficulty with the acquisition of the duchy of Luxemburg which the duchess, Elizabeth of Görlitz, ceded to Duke Philip in 1441, but which he had to secure by force of arms two years later when he encountered the opposition of the duchy's subjects and the claims of William, duke of Saxony.

The development of the Burgundian state within imperial lands was not achieved without causing anxieties within the lands concerned. Sigismund of Luxemburg, king of the Romans and then, in 1433, emperor, had witnessed with increasing hostility the bringing together, under Burgundian control, of the counties of Hainault, Holland and Zeeland and the duchy of Brabant, followed, in 1431, by military intervention in the war of succession over Lorraine in which René of Anjou was opposed by Antoine, count of Vaudémont. Sigismund had lodged a vigorous protest against the accession of Philip the Good to the duchy of Brabant in October 1430, while in 1434, in the matter of Lorraine, he had given a judgement against the count of Vaudémont whom Burgundy was supporting. In the same year Sigismund declared war against Duke Philip over Brabant, hoping that King Charles VII would help him defeat a common enemy. But the emperor was to be disappointed both by his failure to secure help from the imperial princes and by the reconciliation of France and Burgundy at Arras in 1435. Sigismund's death in 1437 put an end to the strong hostility of the empire to the growing strength of Burgundy. None the less it is undeniable that, in its dealings with the Empire, Burgundian diplomacy had few successes. It is true that, within Germany itself, Philip the Good benefited from a network of alliances, of which his brother-in-law, Adolf I of Cleves, Albert, duke of Austria, and his Bavarian cousins were the mainstays; but the king of the Romans, Frederick III of Habsburg, who was to become emperor in 1452, while never taking major steps against Burgundy, never gave satisfaction to its ambitions. Even if, between 1445 and 1448, relations were better than in years past, Frederick III continued to uphold the claims of the duke of Saxony to Luxemburg. The proposal that all, or at least some, Burgundian lands within the Empire should be raised to the rank of a kingdom never came to anything.

In 1454 Philip undertook a great tour which took him to Regensburg where the *Reichstag* was meeting. However, not even the organisation of sumptuous feasts could win the duke any support, nor could he persuade those present to commit themselves to the organisation of a crusade against the Turks. The Turkish 'question' was, indeed, one of the major issues of the day. At the Burgundian court, the fall of Constantinople had rekindled the idea of a crusade, an idea which found much favour among the Burgundian nobility. Since the time of Philip the Bold all the dukes of Burgundy had regarded their presence on all the 'fronts' of Christendom as part of their calling. In 1396, the future John the Fearless had played an active role in a great anti-Turkish expedition which had ended in disaster at Nicopolis, but one from which, paradoxically, the prestige of the house of Burgundy had emerged with great credit. On his part, Duke Philip the Good always showed interest in the Levant. Certain of his servants, notably Guillebert de Lannoy and Bertrandon de la Broquière, had, after their travels in the area, drawn up reports of their voyages for their master to read. Burgundian foreign policy was influenced by this factor. Christian states concerned with the struggle against Islam sought out the support of the dukes of Burgundy; such was the case of the kingdom of Castile, neighbour of the Moorish kingdom of Granada. During the 1440s a Burgundian naval presence in the eastern Mediterranean and the Black Sea was a reflection of Philip the Good's active commitment to the idea of a crusade.[11]

When Constantinople fell in May 1453, the duke of Burgundy could not react immediately, for he was already involved in a war against the city of Ghent. But early in the following year, at a great feast dedicated to the Pheasant held at Lille, Philip the Good and several members of the high nobility from his lands solemnly undertook to go on crusade against the Turks, enemies of the Christian faith.[12] The enterprise, however, never took place. Apart from a modest naval expedition under Antoine, Bastard of Burgundy, which went no further than north Africa, the difficulties of organising the project, political problems and the deterioration of the duke's health conspired together to prevent him carrying out the crusading venture which he had hoped to fulfil.

SOCIETY, CULTURE AND ECONOMY

The court of Burgundy was both an organ of government and a manifestation of prestige.[13] It was a court governed by a strict awareness of the values of hierarchy. Close to the duke were members of the high nobility, whose most prestigious representatives were members of the ducal family: at the time of Philip the Good these were the duchess, Isabel of Portugal, the heir (who bore

---

[11] Paviot (1995), pp. 105–51.   [12] Lafortune-Martel (1984).   [13] Paravicini (1991).

the title of count of Charolais), Jean de Bourgogne, count of Etampes, Adolf I, duke of Cleves and, after his death in 1448, his son, Jean I, and Adolf's brother, the lord of Ravenstein. To this group were added the duke's illegitimate children, among whom the bastards of Burgundy, Corneille and Antoine, deserve mention. After these ducal relatives came the aristocracy. Under Philip the Good the representatives of certain great families from Picardy, Flanders, and Hainault, notably the families of Croy, Lannoy and Lalaing, played an important role in the ducal entourage. As members of the ducal council, they also took over important administrative and military functions. The first among them, Antoine, lord of Croy, already councillor and ducal chamberlain, acquired further responsibilities, being either in turn or simultaneously governor or captain-general of both Namur and of the duchy of Luxemburg, and governor of the county of Boulogne. Representatives of the high nobility of the two Burgundies also held important positions at court and in administration: for instance, Pierre de Bauffremont, lord of Charny, acted as governor of Burgundy, while Thibault IX, lord of Neufchâtel, was marshal of Burgundy from 1443 to 1469.[14]

The cream of this nobility was united in membership of the Order of the Golden Fleece, founded by Philip the Good in January 1430 on the occasion of his marriage to Isabel of Portugal. In founding this order of chivalry, the duke had three intentions in mind: to strengthen the links uniting him to the representatives of the aristocracy who formed its membership; to bring together in a single institution members of the nobility from all Burgundian territories; and to enhance the prestige of the founder-prince who acted as the Order's sovereign. The founding of this order, placed under the double protection of a pagan hero (Jason) and a biblical one (Gideon), may also be seen in the perspective of the crusading ideal and the attraction of the east. Above all, however, it was a political instrument in the hands of the duke of Burgundy. Very soon, indeed, its growing prestige began to give it diplomatic leverage, for if, in 1430, only ducal subjects and vassals had been admitted to membership, it was not long before the order's collar was bestowed upon princes who were in no sense connected with Burgundy: John V, duke of Brittany, Charles, duke of Orleans, and Alfonso V, king of Aragon.[15]

It must not be thought that the court of Burgundy was constituted only out of members of the aristocracy. An elite representing both legal and financial institutions also asserted itself, forming a strongly coherent group whose members, often united through family ties, were looking for promotion and advancement, largely through marriage, to the ranks of the old nobility. At the

---

[14] On Bauffremont, see Caron (1987), pp. 315 ff.
[15] For a list of the knights of the Order, see De Smedt (1994).

centre of this group was Nicolas Rolin. Born into a bourgeois family from Autun, in the duchy of Burgundy, he began his legal career in the *parlement* in Paris. Having entered the service of John the Fearless, he became, under Philip the Good, first a councillor and then, in 1422, ducal chancellor. Between that date and his disgrace in 1456, he was closely involved in all aspects of government, becoming, after the duke himself, the second most important person in the Burgundian state: in 1444, the mayor of Dijon could write of him: 'It is he who organises everything, and through whose hands, more than ever before, everything passes.' The social success experienced by Rolin serves as a pattern. At the height of his career he could count on an annual revenue of 25,000 *livres tournois*, of which 4,000 *livres* came from a ducal pension. His rise to nobility was achieved by a succession of stages. In 1412 he had married Guigone de Salins, who came from a noble family of the county of Burgundy; by the 1420s he was already 'living nobly' (*vivant noblement*), purchasing a number of lordships; from 1424 he took on the title of knight and deemed himself noble. All his children were regarded as noble, and pursued careers corresponding to that state: Antoine Rolin, lord of Aymeries, became ducal chamberlain and *grand bailli* and captain-general of the county of Hainault; his brother, Jean, doctor in both laws, entered the Church and became successively ducal councillor, bishop of Chalon-sur-Saône in 1431, bishop of Autun five years later and cardinal in 1449.[16] His career, indeed, underlines the role played by members of the high clergy within the echelons of the court: Jean Chevrot, bishop of Tournai, was president of the ducal council, while Jean Germain, bishop of Chalon, was chancellor of the Golden Fleece, and was succeeded in that post by Guillaume Fillastre, bishop of Tournai.

It has already been noted that the ducal household played a crucial role at the centre of the court. Ever since the second half of the fourteenth century the household of the dukes had been modelled upon that of the king of France. It consisted of six offices whose functions had been domestic in origin. Now its members were organised according to a strict hierarchy. Added to their number were the ducal confessor, the members of the chapel and its clergy, musicians, kings-of-arms (the most prestigious being 'Toison d'Or'), heralds and pursuivants, falconers, huntsmen and many others. The daily expenses of this household were under the control of a special office, the *chambre aux deniers*.

For members of the nobility, integration into the household with a title did not necessarily mean the effective exercise of a household function near the duke, but only an honorific position implying a salary and a variety of other benefits. The household fulfilled not only a domestic function; its size (some

---

[16] On Nicolas Rolin, see Berger (1971); Bartier (1955); Kamp (1993).

700–800 people were in constant attendance upon Philip the Good) and its style of living reflected the duke's prestige. From early on, too, it served an important military function. The process which would culminate under Charles the Bold had originated at the beginning of the fifteenth century with the creation of a permanent corps of archers and, every so often, the appointment of a marshal of the household.

Under Philip the Good and Charles the Bold the Burgundian court was one of the most brilliant in Europe. The feasts and ceremonies marking both political events, such as diplomatic meetings, treaties, undertakings to go on crusade, as well as important domestic events, provided an opportunity to reflect, in the visual language of the day, the wealth and power of the duke.[17] Such ostentation was intended to impress all who witnessed it, to reassure supporters and intimidate rivals: rather than reflecting a vulgar display of wealth, it was a genuine instrument of political propaganda. In the same order of things can be seen aspects of princely patronage which gave the Burgundian court a cultural brilliance almost without equal. Painters and sculptors worked on a number of princely projects. So the names of certain sculptors (*imagiers*) such as Jean de Marville, Claus Sluter and Jean de la Huerta, along with painters such as Melchior Broederlam,[18] are closely associated with the artistic embellishment of the Chartreuse de Champmol, near Dijon, where the first three dukes of Burgundy were laid to rest, and where the painter Colart de Laon and the tapestry-worker Nicolas Bataille also worked. Rogier van der Weyden was commissioned to paint portraits of Philip the Good and Charles the Bold (as count of Charolais) and of the 'Grand Bâtard', Antoine, while the services of Jan van Eyck were retained on his appointment as a member of the ducal chamber. Following upon such examples, several high-ranking members of the court patronised these artists and their workshops: thus Nicolas Rolin commissioned from van der Weyden the altarpiece of the Last Judgement for the chapel of the Hotel-Dieu which he founded at Beaune in 1443; he also had van Eyck paint a portrait of him at prayer before the Virgin and Child which he then gave to the cathedral at Autun. Van Eyck also painted Baudouin de Lannoy, governor of Lille and knight of the Golden Fleece, while Jean Chevrot, bishop of Tournai and ducal councillor, commissioned the altarpiece of the seven sacraments from van der Weyden, who also painted portraits of Philippe de Croy, lord of Sempy, and of Jean III Gros, secretary of Charles the Bold.[19]

Music was also given great prominence at the Burgundian court. It should not be forgotten that Philip the Good retained the services of the composer Gilles Binchois (d. 1460), who came from Hainault, and who was responsible

---

[17] Lafortune-Martel (1984); Caron (1994).

[18] David (1951); Camp (1990); *Actes des journées internationales Claus Sluter* (1992).

[19] De Patoul and Van Schoute (1994), pp. 144–79. See plates 2 and 4.

for writing not only religious music for the ducal chapel but secular music, too, for performance at the prince's feasts and entertainments.[20]

However, in the context of this princely culture a special place must be reserved for literature. Philip the Good and Charles the Bold were not alone in their love of books and book collecting. Antoine, bastard of Burgundy, Jean de Bourgogne, count of Etampes, Jean, lord of Créquy, Hugues de Lannoy, Louis de Bruges, lord of Gruuthuse, and Jean, bastard of Wavrin, are all known to have possessed fine libraries stocked with manuscripts of high artistic quality. This cultivated environment encouraged a broad range of literary types.[21] Works of fiction concerned with a historical figure, such as the 'Livre des conquêtes et faits d'Alexandre le Grand' or 'Girart de Roussillon', both the work of Jean Wauquelin, were very popular at the court. The intentions of the authors of this genre were, while telling the story of a notable person, to provide their aristocratic readers with tales exalting the chivalric ethos. Flattery of the prince's tastes was not forgotten; attracted by the idea of an enterprise in the east, Philip the Good likened himself to Alexander. As for Girart de Roussillon, twelve times conqueror of Charles the Bald, he was to become the symbol of the struggle of the dukes of Burgundy against the Crown of France. The tastes of those at court, however, were not monopolised by epic literature: a collection of stories, such as the 'Cent nouvelles nouvelles', much influenced by Boccaccio, reflects a liking for literature of a lighter sort and an attraction towards humour of a more bawdy kind.

Of an altogether different genre, many didactic treatises were to be found in the ducal libraries. These covered, for example, the hunt, medicine and astrology. The art of war had its place: several copies of the 'De re militari' of Vegetius, a classic which had already been translated several times, were owned by Philip the Good and Charles the Bold. Other works, recently written with the duke in mind, could also be found in these libraries: the 'Livre du seigneur de l'Isle-Adam pour Gaige de Bataille' was the work of a famous Burgundian captain of that name who was also a knight of the Golden Fleece; while the treatise, 'La toison d'or', had been written by Guillaume Fillastre, chancellor of the Order. Above all we should note works with a historic character. It should be stressed that, from the early years of the fifteenth century, great emphasis had been placed in all Burgundian historical literature emanating from the court upon the need to convey a clear ideological message. A work such as the 'Geste des ducs de Bourgogne', written under the influence of the civil conflict and thus bitterly hostile to the house of Orleans, is one of the earliest examples of the genre. Following this, the Picard chronicler, Enguerrand de Monstrelet, although not formally linked to the Burgundian court, but close to the house of

---

[20] Marix (1939).   [21] Doutrepont (1909); Régnier-Bohler (1995); Martens (1992).

Luxemburg-St-Pol, showed himself to be an admirer of John the Fearless and Philip the Good. The tendency was reinforced by the appointment of the first official 'historiographer' in 1455: both Georges Chastellain (d. 1475) and Jean Molinet (d. 1507), who successively fulfilled this function, conveyed a positively Burgundian view of history. Their example was to be followed by Olivier de la Marche, whose 'Mémoires' were dedicated to Philippe le Beau, son of Mary of Burgundy and Maximilian of Habsburg.

This court culture was naturally but a reflection of the tastes of an elite constituted from the aristocracy which formed the upper echelons of the state, an elite which itself was only a part of those classes which dominated society. In the Burgundian lands, the nobility consisted of only 1 or 2 per cent of the population, the clergy numbering no more than 1 per cent. The remaining 97 per cent was characterised by a marked diversity in its structures. At the social level, the great differences which existed between the various territories ruled by the dukes of Burgundy make it difficult to compare the society in the Burgundian Low Countries with that of the duchy and county. In the lands of the north, urban life assumed a great importance since, in the final quarter of the fifteenth century, a third (34 per cent) of their inhabitants were town dwellers, while Bruges, Ghent and Antwerp each had more than 20,000 inhabitants. In Burgundy, by contrast, society was very largely rural; Dijon, the duchy's biggest town, had only some 13,000 inhabitants in 1474.[22]

Yet, even in the north, one cannot speak of a homogeneous society. In the towns the urban patriciate found itself at different stages of its development. In Flanders, its power had been much eroded by the craft guilds, whilst in Brabant it still preserved a large part of its prerogatives in the economic and political domain. Ducal agents and servants also formed part of the elites within the towns. In a number of them, where they exercised administrative functions, they could be important. Such was the case at Lille, centre of the *chambre des comptes*, seat of the governor of Lille, Douai and Orchies, of the local judicial organisations, and of two ducal residences.[23] Alongside these representatives of ducal power was a bourgeoisie which dominated all economic activity, merchants trading in wine or cloth, brokers and senior members of the manufacturing guilds which dealt in furs, skins and beer.

The artisan world was itself very diverse. With their internal hierarchies, the guilds were well structured and influential. They accounted for a substantial part of urban activity; in Ghent, for instance, in the second half of the fourteenth century, there were fifty-three guilds, among which were those dealing in wool, leather, metals, food and building. Yet, however large or numerous,

---

[22] Prevenier and Blockmans (1986), pp. 30, 43–5, 391–2; Humbert (1961), pp. 20–3.
[23] Fourquin (1970), pp. 219–34.

such organisations did not include all workers, as those without formal qualification were excluded from their membership. So it was that, in the fifteenth century, some guilds, above all those representing trades in decline, were obliged to close down. This phenomenon, also found outside the Low Countries, reflected a determination to reserve membership of such guilds to a strictly professional group; this was reflected in the rise of charges levied at the time of entry, and by the tendency to reserve access to membership to the sons of the masters of the trade. Of the 264 new masters admitted into the guild of brewers in Ghent between 1450 and 1479, 249 were sons of practising masters. However, it should also be recognised that during the same period artisanal activity, particularly in the production of cloth and beer, greatly increased in those small urban centres and rural areas where the guilds had no influence.[24]

In Burgundy, urban society had another function. In a town such as Dijon (as in Lille) where ducal employees had an important role to play, a bourgeois elite, whose wealth stemmed from trade in wine, cloth and cereals, constituted the dominant political and economic class. Artisans were organised into guilds, but there none the less existed close links between the ducal capital and its rural hinterland, links emphasised by the pressure of a large group of wine growers who lived in the town.[25] In rural Burgundy, where the lordship based on land-ownership of the traditional type continued to exist in order to provide a structure into which rural society could fit, the peasantry was very diversified. Certain communities were 'free' ('franches'), others were not ('serves'). The Burgundian serf, liable to all forms of taxation ('taillable haut et bas'), was subject to merchet and mortmain. Attempts had been made since the mid-fourteenth century to improve the lot of the serf, but in the fifteenth his status had scarcely changed. Yet that status, particularly in a period when the effects of population decline, economic crisis and war were being felt, presented a threat to traditional lordship. The granting of freedom and an improvement in status were to come as society climbed out of the period of crisis. This point was made clear when, in December 1454, Guillaume de Bauffremont and Jeanne de Villersexel, his wife, granted a charter to their tenants at Sombernon to help them in their process of recovery; they were said to have suffered great hardship in the wars and disasters which had struck Burgundy in the past, and, in particular, at the time of the passing of the *écorcheurs*, or raiding mercenaries, ten years earlier.[26]

Differences perceptible at a social level reappear at the economic one. Standing astride great trade routes or at places where such routes met, the territories ruled by the dukes assumed a role of vital importance in the international

---

[24] Prevenier and Blockmans (1986), pp. 156–70.   [25] Gras (1987), pp. 87–92.

[26] *Chartes de communes*, II, pp. 593–7.

trade of the period. In the northern principalities, Bruges was one such centre; another was Antwerp, whose role increased rapidly during these years. Likewise, the Burgundies were at the cross-roads of two great axes of communication: those of the rivers Saône–Rhone and Yonne–Seine, those of roads towards Paris to the north, Lyons to the south, Lausanne, Geneva and the Alpine passes leading into Italy in the south-east, towards Basle and the Rhine valley to the east.

Such a privileged position in nature greatly helped the export trade. Naturally, the products concerned differed from region to region. Burgundy was renowned for its wines, and that which came from Beaune could be sold at a high price in the great urban markets. The dukes themselves were not afraid to publicise its qualities. In 1395, Philip the Bold announced that his lands produced the very best wines in the kingdom of France 'for the benefit and good of human kind', while in 1459 Philip the Good claimed to be lord of the finest wines in Christendom ('seigneur des meilleurs vins de la Chrétienté'). Salt, too, the product of Burgundian salt works (principally at Salins), was sent to the two Burgundies, while large quantities were exported, mainly towards Geneva, Lausanne, Basle, Berne and Freiburg.[27]

The nature of products exported from the north was very different, a reflection of the different economic structures of the two groups of principalities ruled by the dukes of Burgundy. Any evocation of the economy of the Low Countries at this period leads to thoughts of textiles and to the production of cloth in Flanders and Brabant. It must be noted, however, that during the fifteenth century the cloth industry, developed long ago in the great urban centres, went into decline. A Brabantine town such as Louvain which, about 1350, produced 756,000 ells every year, could only produce 26,600 ells in 1476, the size of the population (around 18,000) having scarcely fallen in the meantime. Certain well-established centres felt the effects of such a decline very strongly: in 1311, Ypres had 1,500 looms functioning in the town; in 1502, the number had sunk to 100, while the population fell from 20,000–30,000 to some 9,500 inhabitants during much the same period. During these years, the production of both woollen and linen cloth moved either into the country or into the small towns, the movement being encouraged by those who sought to avoid the imposition of craft regulations still being applied in the large towns.[28]

The decline in urban cloth manufacture was compensated for by the development of other activities. During this century the Burgundian Low Countries greatly increased the exports of an iron industry created around the mines in the region of Namur and Liège, and in Limburg; salt and herrings from the coasts of Holland, Zeeland and Flanders were also exported in quan-

[27] Dubois (1978).   [28] Prevenier and Blockmans (1986), pp. 45, 79.

tity. A traffic in luxury goods also grew up, in particular in tapestries from Arras, Lille and Brussels, the last two centres experiencing a great increase in production in the second half of the century.

In all this activity the role accorded to Bruges proved vital. The town, meeting-place of two major commercial networks (one from the Mediterranean, the other from the Baltic), was a financial centre, a place of trade and a giant storage house. Its activity was truly international; colonies of foreign merchants had their centres and their trading facilities there, enjoying privileges accorded by the dukes. So the Venetians, Florentines and Genoese each had their 'consulate' there, while the Castilians, the Portuguese and, above all, the 'Oosterlingen', or Hansards, had similar facilities. The German Hansa was, in effect, the principal trading partner of the Burgundian Low Countries, and Bruges, along with London, Bergen and Novgorod, was one of their main trading posts. Most of the products (cereals, wood, furs, wax, honey and amber) which came from the Baltic passed through Bruges, while those products on their way to the Baltic (luxury goods, salt, wine from the Atlantic ports, textiles) did the same. This trade continued to expand until about 1470: it amounted to 212,000 marks (of Lübeck) in 1369, 651,000 marks in 1419 and 1,332,000 marks in 1467. Thereafter came a decline, particularly after the 1480s, as the role of Bruges was gradually taken over by Antwerp.[29]

During the fifteenth century Bruges was also one of Europe's great financial centres where commercial transactions, credit and the exchange of currencies were developed on a large scale. It was in the house at Bruges belonging to a family of brokers, van der Buerse, that the first exchange in Europe was organised. The development of banking activities attracted financiers from abroad, in particular from Italy. The Rapondi, merchants and bankers from Lucca, had extended their activities to Bruges in the second half of the fourteenth century, putting both their money and their experience at the service of the house of Burgundy. The same was to be true of the Medici, who had one of their principal offices at Bruges.

The dynamism of the Burgundian territories, the place which they occupied at the heart of western Europe and the importance of their economic activities combined to give contemporaries an impression of incomparable prosperity. In a famous passage in his *Mémoires*, Philippe de Commynes, describing the Burgundian principalities at the end of the rule of Philip the Good, could write that his lands came nearer to being the promised land than did any others. For this reason, the dramatic fall of the house of Burgundy, when it happened, was an event all the more worthy of comment.

[29] Dollinger (1970).

CHARLES THE BOLD AND THE BURGUNDIAN STATE

Did Charles the Bold create the Burgundian state, or did he dig its grave? During the twelve years stretching from 1465, when he took over as his father's lieutenant, to 1477, when he met his death in battle, Charles subjected the lands under his rule to extensive institutional reform. At the same time, the rapid evolution of new structures brought this state first to its apogee and then to its destruction.[30]

Charles, son of Philip the Good and Isabel of Portugal, had always been interested in matters of politics, his intervention in affairs of state leading him into direct confrontation with his father. This was not simply the result of a generation gap. In the 1460s and, in particular, from the accession of Louis XI as king of France (1461), Charles feared a French policy aimed at the dismantling of the Burgundian defensive system in Picardy. In 1463–4 a crisis occurred, provoked by the repurchase, negotiated by Louis XI, of the 'Somme towns' ceded to Burgundy by the Treaty of Arras of 1435. To Charles, then count of Charolais, this was a major political error committed by his father, now well advanced in years and ill advised by members of the Croy family who favoured the king of France. The crisis over, the services of that family were dispensed with, and Philip the Good ceded the reality of power to his son, who chose to intervene actively in France by adhering to the 'League of the Public Good'. This league brought together those French princes (Charles de France, the king's brother, François II, duke of Brittany, Jean II, duke of Bourbon, and others) who were concerned by the new king's first political acts. In October 1465, by the terms of the Treaty of Conflans, Louis XI, compelled to negotiate with the members of the League, restored the 'Somme towns' to Duke Charles.

This first confrontation underlined the importance of the control of Picardy to both the French and the Burgundians. The matter was always to remain one of Duke Charles's main preoccupations. Another important matter, one which concerned the maintenance of the internal cohesion of the Burgundian state, was the degree of control to be exercised over the towns. The problem of Liège soon came to the fore. Ever since the time of John the Fearless, this episcopal principality had been within the zone of Burgundian influence, which the towns, notably Liège and Dinant, rejected. Between 1465 and 1468, Duke Charles organised four campaigns against the people of Liège, sacking first Dinant and then Liège and, from 1467, imposing the authority of a ducal lieutenant-general, Guy de Brimeu, lord of Humbercourt. The episcopal principality became simply a Burgundian protectorate.[31]

---

[30] Contamine (1992b).   [31] *Liège et Bourgogne* (1972).

Once he had become duke of Burgundy on his father's death (15 June 1467), Charles faced the opposition of towns within his own territories. His predecessors had had considerable experience of urban uprisings: Philip the Bold had led a war against Flanders between 1382 and 1385, while Philip the Good had only with difficulty regained control first of Bruges in 1437 and then of Ghent in 1453. From the autumn of 1467 Charles was confronted by far-reaching demands from Ghent, Antwerp and Malines, all related to the defence of urban privileges which had been ignored by the house of Burgundy since the acquisition of its lands in the Low Countries. The new duke had to come to terms, but gradually his institutional reforms and the imposition of a heavy fiscal burden led to opposition by the towns. Yet, in spite of the difficulties which characterised the start of his rule, Duke Charles threw himself resolutely into the political enterprise which was to lead to the creation of a centralised and independent Burgundian state. This was in no sense an easy task, for a successful outcome required the breaking down of local particularism, keeping the king of France at arm's length, achieving significant territorial expansion in imperial territory, while at the same time bringing about widespread and fundamental reforms of an institutional nature within the lands which he had inherited.

Charles the Bold's first ambition was to break the juridical bond which bound his lands in the kingdom to the crown of France. An opportunity to achieve this occurred in October, 1468. On the occasion of his interview with Louis XI at Péronne, Charles took advantage of an uprising in Liège allegedly provoked by French agents to demand from the king, then at his mercy, a treaty specifying that the Burgundian lands would, in future, no longer be subject to the authority of the *parlement* in Paris. This was a direct challenge to the royal authority and, once free of his opponent's control, Louis would denounce the terms of the Treaty of Péronne, whose terms Duke Charles none the less used to prohibit 'appeals to France'.

The struggle for independence was to lead to armed conflict punctuated by periods of truce. During these years Charles the Bold experienced great difficulties in protecting his frontiers in Picardy, Burgundy, Charolais and Mâconnais. Several important towns were lost, notably Amiens, retaken by the French in 1471, but in September 1475 he was able to bring a measure of peace to the situation by an agreement made at Soleuvre which enforced a truce which was maintained until 1477.

In Burgundian thinking, policy towards France was always associated with that to be pursued towards England, whose civil troubles were closely followed in both France and Burgundy. In the conflict confronting Lancaster and York, the French crown, while pursuing a policy of realism, preferred to lend its support to Lancaster, mainly on account of its links with the house of Anjou.

So it was that Duke Charles, while being equally prudent, none the less gave diplomatic and financial support to the house of York. In 1468, at Bruges, he married Margaret of York, sister of Edward IV, the occasion being an opportunity for sumptuous celebrations. In October 1470, he welcomed his royal brother-in-law, expelled from his own kingdom, and gave him hospitality at The Hague before providing him with money, men and ships to help him regain his English kingdom. Edward's successful venture provided Charles the Bold with a trump card which he tried to use to good effect in his struggle against the king of France. In July 1474, through the Treaty of London, he made an alliance directed against France which, however, he was not able to follow to its conclusion. Taken up by his policy in the Empire, he could not give military support to Edward IV when, in July 1475, the large English army landed in France. Disappointed by this, Edward abandoned his Burgundian ally, secured an agreement with Louis XI at Picquigny (29 August) and then sailed for home.

The setback for Charles the Bold may only be explained by the scale of the enterprise he was undertaking in the Empire. Not only was he attempting to secure his independence of France; he was pursuing an ambitious policy towards the east, a policy characterised by intense diplomatic activity and by a movement aimed at territorial expansion. To the links already uniting the house of Burgundy to certain German princes (those of Bavaria and Cleves, for instance) who were traditional allies were added attempts to secure alliances with the kings of Bohemia and Hungary and the duke of Austria. Charles did not hide his ambitions in the Empire: to achieve them he chose the road of expansionism. By the Treaty of Saint-Omer (1469) he acquired Upper Alsace, the Sundgau and the Breisgau from the duke of Austria as a pledge for 50,000 Rhenish florins. In 1473, under pretext of a conflict which was tearing apart the ducal family of Guelders, he took over that duchy. In the same year he arranged a meeting with the Emperor Frederick III at Trier. This meeting should have marked the high point of Burgundian policy vis-à-vis the Empire, for Duke Charles hoped to negotiate the title of 'king of the Romans' or, at least, an imperial vicariate and the up-grading of his ducal territories into royal ones. But nothing came of the meeting. Frederick was anxious to keep the imperial dignity within his family, and it is very likely that the advance of the house of Burgundy into the Empire was already worrying a number of German princes and imperial cities, notably in the valley of the Rhine. Although he proposed a marriage between Mary, his sole heir, and Maximilian, son of the Emperor, Charles found his ambitions thwarted. All that he secured was the imperial investiture to the duchy of Guelders, after which Frederick left Trier in haste.

This diplomatic setback failed to stop Charles, who was in the process of creating a new state. The year 1473 marked the high point of his reforming activity. Malines was chosen as the capital of the Burgundian Low Countries. In June, his council (the 'Grand Conseil'), granted official status in 1446 but hitherto itinerant, was established there. This was soon followed by the creation of a *parlement* to act as sovereign court for all the Low Countries.[32] In December 1473, the ordinance of Thionville completed the process of reorganisation by abolishing the two *chambres des comptes* in Brussels and Lille in favour of a single one in Malines.

The judicial and financial institutions were not the only ones to be reformed: a complete shakeup of military institutions was also planned. Up to that moment, the Burgundian state had only had access to an army composed of feudal contingents and companies of volunteers and mercenaries. According to this tradition the soldiers were summoned and disbanded as need arose: permanent forces were rare. Such a military system, however, while adequate for the needs of John the Fearless and Philip the Good, failed to meet the needs and ambitions of Duke Charles, for it could not rival the French royal army with its *compagnies d'ordonnance*. Charles thus decided to give his state an army similar to the French one. Three military ordinances, issued at Abbeville in 1471, Bohain in 1472 and Saint-Maximin-de-Trèves in 1473, established the details of this development. In theory, the army was to number twenty *compagnies d'ordonnance*, each with 900 soldiers.[33]

To pay for these reforms, the duke was obliged to develop the taxation system. From the duchy's earliest days to the end of the rule of Philip the Good, its dukes had been obliged to negotiate annually the rate of taxation with the estates, both in the two Burgundies and in the north.[34] Charles the Bold, on the other hand, tried to secure taxes for periods of several years and from his principalities as a whole. In May 1470, he requested 120,000 crowns for three years from his northern principalities, but negotiated separately with the estates of each. In March 1473 he chose to do things differently; calling the estates of all the lands in the north to meet him together in Brussels, he secured from them taxation worth 500,000 *écus* per year for six years. In the following October the estates of the two Burgundies, Charolais, Mâconnais and Auxerrois granted taxation to the annual value of 100,000 *livres* for six years. This was clearly the first step towards the institution of permanent taxation which Duke Charles was not to have time to put into force.

So, by the beginning of 1474, the Burgundian state appeared to have come into being, at least at the level of the creation of judicial, financial and military institutions. That state was a great European power, and its prince was held in great respect. Yet, at that very moment, it began to fall apart. The crisis started in

[32] On the institutions at Malines, see Van Rompaey (1973).
[33] On the military affairs and the reforms of Charles the Bold, see Brusten (1954) and (1976); Vaughan (1973), pp. 197–229, and (1975), pp. 123–61.   [34] Vaughan (1970), p. 262.

the region of the Rhine. Burgundian expansionism in Upper Alsace, in the direction of Mulhouse and Basle, posed a direct threat to the political and economic interests of the Swiss Confederation and its allies, and was causing concern in the Rhineland towns, notably in Strasburg. Tension rose in the region and soon led to confrontation. In the spring of 1474, a broad anti-Burgundian alliance, the League of Constance, uniting the Swiss, some of the Rhenish towns and the duke of Austria, came into being. This diplomatic development was followed by a general uprising in Burgundian lands in the region of the Upper Rhine, and then by an armed confrontation with the Swiss who attacked Franche-Comté, which led to a Burgundian defeat at Héricourt in November 1474.

At that moment Charles could attempt neither the reconquest of Upper Alsace nor a counter-attack against the Swiss, since he was engaged in military activity in the archiepiscopal principality of Cologne. This undertaking has been seen as a response to the setback suffered at his meeting with the emperor at Trier. Having determined to assert himself in the Empire, Duke Charles decided that the use of force was necessary. He came to the rescue of his ally, the archbishop of Cologne, against whom his subjects, helped by the landgrave of Hesse, were in revolt. Duke Charles decided to besiege the town of Neuss, the very centre of the revolt. The enterprise was a failure; for more than ten months, from 29 July 1474 to 13 June 1475, the Burgundians pursued a fruitless siege. After an attempt by the emperor to relieve the town, Charles negotiated his departure and retired to Luxemburg.

He then turned his attention to Lorraine. Ever since the beginning of the century successive dukes of Burgundy had been interested in the duchy which linked the south of Luxemburg to the north of the county of Burgundy. It thus held a strategic position in the internal links of the Burgundian state, its importance ever increasing as the dukes gradually abandoned France to turn towards the Empire. At the beginning of the century Charles, duke of Lorraine, had wisely remained on good terms with the Burgundians. But on his death (1431) the accession of René, brother-in-law of King Charles VII and a member of the house of Anjou, to both the duchies of Lorraine and Bar had created considerable tensions which had led to Burgundian military intervention (battle of Bulgnéville, July 1431).[35] As a result, the Angevin dukes of Lorraine had allied themselves to Burgundy until that alliance was broken by Duke René II in 1475. In a period of crisis, as the Swiss, notably those from Berne and Freiburg, threatened not only Burgundian territories but the duchy of Savoy, too, Charles the Bold could not allow the north–south axis of his principalities to be cut. He thus over-ran the duchy of Lorraine and, after a brief siege, captured the town of Nancy in November 1475.

[35] Schnerb (1993).

He now had his sights on the Vaud. The people of Berne had invaded the region, held by two Burgundian allies, Yolande, duchess of Savoy, and Jacques de Savoy, count of Romont. Charles the Bold immediately intervened but, to the general surprise, suffered two defeats, the first at Grandson on 2 March 1476, the second at Morat on 22 June. After this second defeat, the Burgundian state fell into a crisis from which it never recovered. The system of alliances crumbled when Milan and Savoy abandoned it. The demands for money submitted by ducal representatives both in the two Burgundies and in the northern lands were greeted with reticence, even outright refusal. To complete the process, the duchy of Lorraine rose in revolt against Burgundian domination. It was while attempting to regain control of Nancy and to keep open the road which, passing through Lorraine, united the northern and southern areas of his dominions, that, on 5 January 1477, Charles the Bold was killed in battle outside the town fighting against a coalition uniting forces from Lorraine, Alsace and Switzerland.

RUIN AND SURVIVAL OF BURGUNDY

The death of the duke led to the collapse of the political edifice which he had created. In the weeks following Louis XI, disregarding the agreement made at Soleuvre, ordered his soldiers into the two Burgundies, Picardy, Artois and part of Hainault. The government of Burgundy was now personified by Mary, daughter and sole heir of the late duke, and by Margaret of York, his third wife and now his widow. In the short term they were obliged to face rebellion in the north. The estates general forced Mary to grant them a 'Grand Privilège', limiting her own powers and causing a general restoration of rights and customs previously abolished. They also sought the abolition of the new centralising institutions based on Malines, seen as symbols of princely authoritarianism. In April 1477 the people of Ghent, rising in rebellion, went further by executing two of the late duke's closest collaborators, his chancellor, Guillaume Hugonet, and the lord of Humbercourt.

Margaret of York and Mary of Burgundy saw that the only way of rescuing what survived of the Burgundian inheritance lay through an alliance with the house of Habsburg. In August 1477 Mary married Maximilian, son of the Emperor Frederick III. It would be Maximilian's task to resist French attempts to settle the Burgundian 'matter'. In this respect, Louis XI failed to achieve all his ambitions. The Treaties of Arras (1482) and Senlis (1493) brought about only a partial break-up of Burgundian territory. If Louis XI, and then Charles VIII, were able to secure the duchy of Burgundy and Picardy, the Habsburgs, heirs to the rights of the house of Burgundy, maintained control over Franche-Comté and most of the Low Countries. This new geopolitical settlement was to have important consequences for the history of Europe in the sixteenth and seventeenth centuries.

Writing to the members of the *chambre des comptes* at Dijon in January 1477, during the crisis of the French invasion, the Duchess Mary urged them 'always to keep faithful to their belief in Burgundy'. Such an exhortation suggests that a sense of belonging to a historic Burgundy had developed during the fifteenth century within the context of Franco-Burgundian confrontation. The ideological origin of this sense is to be found in the wish of the dukes to discover historical examples with which to support the political ambitions being opposed by the exercise of French royal sovereignty. Under Philip the Good there circulated within court circles a literature which extolled the memory of the ancient kingdoms which had formerly occupied those areas now part of the duke's principalities: the sixth-century Burgundian kingdom ruled by Gondebaud; Lotharingia; and the kingdom of Arles.[36] However, it is unlikely that the recalling of such names had much influence beyond the narrow circle of the politically aware who lived close to the duke. Among his subjects, the sense of being 'Burgundian' developed late and unevenly in the ducal territories as a whole. It was first to be observed as the growth of loyalty to a princely dynasty which knew how to make effective use of propaganda. Then, as the result of armed conflict between 'Burgundians' and 'French', there developed a hatred of the enemy within the territories ruled by the duke. Thus there came into existence those two elements – devotion to the prince and rejection of a foreign enemy – which are essential for the creation of national identity.

After the death of Charles the Bold, the loyalty owed to the house of Burgundy was redirected to the house of Habsburg, heir to the political ambitions of the Valois dukes. The period of crisis and disarray which followed the events of 1477 was ripe for the development of a sentiment which fed upon a feeling of nostalgia for a glorious past and which was expressed through a political literature written by men such as Olivier de la Marche and Jean Molinet. By their attitude and the very words which they uttered, the princes, too, acted as propagandists for this ideology. Welcomed into Cambrai in June 1493 with the traditional cries of 'Noël! Noël!', Margaret of Austria, daughter of Maximilian of Habsburg and Mary of Burgundy, replied 'Rather, cry "Long live Burgundy."'

[36] Lacaze (1971).

LANCASTRIAN ENGLAND

Edward Powell

IN the name of the Father, Son and Holy Ghost, I, Henry of Lancaster, challenge this realm of England and the Crown with all the members and the appurtenances, as that I am descended by right line of the blood coming from the good lord King Henry Third, and through that right that God of his grace has sent me with help of my kin and of my friends to recover it, the which realm was in point to be undone for default of governance and undoing of the good laws.[1]

With these words, on 30 September 1399, Henry Bolingbroke claimed the throne of England from his cousin Richard II. Since his return from disinheritance and exile in July 1399 Henry had acted swiftly and ruthlessly to out-manoeuvre Richard himself and to divide and neutralise his supporters. It was a breathtakingly audacious coup and, the deposition of Edward II not withstanding, an unprecedented one. After two hundred years during which the throne of England had passed uninterrupted from father to son (or grandson), Henry's usurpation marked a radical departure which foreshadowed a century of dynastic instability. Before 1500 three more kings, Edward IV, Richard III and Henry VII, were to seize the throne by force, in disregard for the traditional principle of primogeniture. Another, Henry V, was to claim the throne of France in a similar way: under the Treaty of Troyes of 1420 he became the heir of Charles VI, and the Dauphin Charles was disinherited.

The usurpation of 1399 provided a precedent and a model which exercised a profound influence over the politics and government of fifteenth-century England. The dubious title of the Lancastrians diluted the hereditary principle and thus widened the field of potential claimants to the crown. Henry IV's reliance on the support of a few powerful magnates, notably the Percy family, made him beholden to a faction and threatened the stability of his rule from the outset. The Percies' dissatisfaction with the rewards they received from their role as 'kingmakers' led to their rebellions in 1403 and 1405, just as, sixty

---

[1] *Rotuli parliamentorum*, III, pp. 422–3.

years later, Edward IV's determination to assert his independence led to the disaffection and rebellion of Richard Neville, earl of Warwick. The enforced abdication of Richard II on the grounds, *inter alia*, of breach of his coronation oath and lack of good governance gave added prominence in the following century to the king's obligations to enforce the law, defend the realm and maintain sound finances, at a time when royal government faced great difficulties in those areas.

The Lancastrian era, from Henry IV's usurpation until Henry VI's deposition in 1461, was dominated by three interwoven themes: warfare, service and finance. Henry IV's accession in 1399 and his survival of the years of rebellion which followed rested ultimately on armed force, and the legitimacy of the Lancastrian dynasty came to be particularly bound up with military success or failure. The battle of Agincourt in 1415 consolidated the stability of the dynasty, whereas the fall of France between 1449 and 1453 irreparably weakened Henry VI's rule. Military success helped foster political stability, but both were dependent on the quality of service the king could command from the nobility and gentry. Henry IV relied on a comparatively narrow group of trusted Lancastrian servants. Henry V's qualities of leadership and his victories in France won him the unqualified support of political society as a whole; whereas the dominance of a small household clique during Henry VI's adult rule bred faction and division, and helped prepare the ground for the open hostilities of the Wars of the Roses. Inadequate financial resources and the dependence on parliament for taxation caused intractable problems for the Lancastrian kings, which even Henry V was able only to defer, rather than resolve. A crushing burden of debt crippled Henry VI's government and severely hampered the war effort as Lancastrian France crumbled and then disintegrated in the 1440s.

The themes of warfare, service and finance come to the fore from the very outset of Henry IV's reign. Not only did Henry have to combat repeated internal revolt to retain his throne, but, until 1407 at least, he faced a full-scale rebellion in Wales led by Owain Glyn Dŵr, intermittent war against the Scots, and threats to Gascony and Calais from the kingdom of France. His survival was due in no small part to the loyalty and ability of his Lancastrian servants, both in the military and political spheres. Warfare and service were costly items, however, particularly for a king as insecure as Henry IV. The series of military emergencies and Henry's need to buy support early in the reign soon created serious financial problems, and he faced prolonged struggles with successive parliaments over taxation and royal finances.

Henry's military success enabled him to seize and retain the throne. His abilities as a military leader and strategist were crucial not just to his success in 1399 but also to his defeat of the Percy rebellion in 1403, the most serious challenge of the reign. On both occasions he moved decisively to divide his opponents geographically before they could muster against him in force. He was also well served by able captains in several different theatres of war, for example Prince Henry in Wales, Ralph Neville, earl of Westmorland, in the north and John Beaufort, earl of Somerset, in Calais.

Service was one of the most contentious issues of the reign. As a usurper Henry IV came to the throne as the head of a faction, with a narrow base of committed support amongst the nobility. Under his rule the Lancastrian affinity never entirely lost its factional character. The king made lavish grants of retainer to bolster his regime early in the reign, but the core of his support came from the Lancastrian following established before 1399. Henry filled the royal household with trusted Lancastrian knights and esquires, among them John Norbury, John Tiptoft, Thomas Erpingham and Hugh Waterton. Such men were unusually prominent in all aspects of royal government, particularly in the first half of the reign, before the parliamentary crisis of 1406 and the establishment of the magnate council.

Henry IV's dependence on the knights of his household was accentuated by the depletion of the higher nobility, caused largely by forfeitures and rebellion during the political crises between 1398 and 1405. Only after 1407 did a new generation of magnates begin to emerge, several of them closely associated with the prince of Wales. In the crucial middle years of the reign the circle of adult magnates on whom the king could rely was very restricted. They included Ralph Neville, earl of Westmorland, and the king's Beaufort half-brothers: John, earl of Somerset, Sir Thomas and Henry, bishop of Winchester. Neville was the Beauforts' brother-in-law through his second wife Joan; thus the Beaufort–Neville connection lay at the heart of the Lancastrian political establishment from the beginning. The eventual breakdown of that connection in the early 1450s was to signal the disintegration of that establishment.

The heavy costs of warfare and service, and the lack of effective controls at the exchequer, led Henry IV into acute financial problems, which soon made it impossible for him to keep his promise, made at the beginning of the reign, to 'live of his own' and do without parliamentary taxation. In fact the king had to turn repeatedly to parliament for tax grants, and in response faced a growing barrage of criticism, culminating in the 'Long Parliament' of 1406. The basis of criticism in the House of Commons was the king's failure adequately to defend the realm and suppress rebellion, in spite of heavy taxation; his inability to maintain public order and do justice; and his failure to manage royal finances. The Commons demanded the appointment of the royal council in parliament, the reform of royal administration (in particular the application of crown revenues to the expenses of the household), the appropriation of taxation to specific military needs and the appointment of special treasurers to oversee the disbursement of taxation.

In the parliament of 1406 these demands were conceded. A new, largely aristocratic council was appointed under the leadership of the prince of Wales, and its members swore to adhere to the articles of reform put forward by the Commons. Exercising control of government expenditure, the council curtailed the king's spending on the household and committed itself to a policy of 'bone governance', aimed at securing the defences of the realm, restoring the crown's financial credibility and regaining the confidence of parliament.

Initially Prince Henry's involvement in the council was only nominal, and it was led by the chancellor, Archbishop Thomas Arundel. After suppressing the Glyn Dŵr rebellion in Wales, however, the prince was free to spend more time at Westminster, and from 1407 his presence was increasingly felt in central government. His abilities and obvious impatience to rule, compounded by Henry IV's debilitating bouts of illness, spawned rumours of the king's abdication. Indeed during 1410–11, as head of the council, Prince Henry was effectively the ruler of the kingdom, until a dispute with his father over military intervention in the civil war in France enabled the old king to reassert his authority.

Henry IV's entire adult life, first as magnate, then as king, was shaped by political crisis. His principal achievement was to ensure the survival of the Lancastrian dynasty. The effort broke his health, however, and his usurpation prolonged and exacerbated the bitter aristocratic faction of Richard II's reign. Political and military instability translated directly into financial insecurity, and his impoverishment led to humiliation at the hands of parliament. Nevertheless, Henry IV was a well-served king. His own family, notably the prince of Wales, proved particularly able; and several of his most trusted retainers, such as Tiptoft and Erpingham, went on to serve his son and grandson with equal distinction, providing an important thread of continuity within Lancastrian government.

Henry V ascended the throne in March 1413 better prepared for kingship than any English monarch since Edward I. Although only twenty-six at his accession he already had ten years of military experience and five of active involvement in government. Henry was thus a known quantity, with strong credentials as a ruler and an established network of relationships with leading magnates and royal administrators. This helps to explain the confidence and purposefulness with which he assumed power: there was no sense of youthful impetuosity such as characterised the early adult years of Edward III or Richard II.

Indeed, as king, Henry V was merely picking up where he had left off at the end of his period as head of the council during 1410–11. In that sense there is a strong degree of continuity between the first two years of Henry V's reign and the closing years of his father's. In the parliament of May 1413 the Commons pointedly drew attention to Henry IV's failure to fulfil his repeated promises to restore 'bone governance', and raised several matters of 'unfinished business' from the old reign, including the defence of Calais and Gascony, the safe-keeping of the sea, the settlement of Wales following the Glyn Dŵr rebellion and the restoration of public order.

On the other hand Henry V was determined to put an end to the aristocratic faction, financial and administrative mismanagement and widespread lawless-ness which had prevailed since 1399. Most pressing was the reconciliation of the Lancastrian dynasty with the noble families which had suffered loss and dis-inheritance as a result of the rebellions against Henry IV: notably the Hollands, Mowbrays, Montagues and Percies. Here Henry V was lucky in that the heirs of these houses, like much of the nobility in 1413, were young men of about his own age and untainted by personal involvement in revolt. Henry allowed them a partial recovery of the lands and titles forfeited by their ancestors, making it clear that further restoration was dependent upon continuing active service, above all in war.

In the first two years of his reign Henry V also devoted considerable time and energy to restoring the financial health of the crown and enforcing public order. Royal creditworthiness was swiftly re-established by the imposition of strict controls at the exchequer over the assignment of income, and by the vigorous exploitation of all available sources of revenue. The effectiveness of these measures helped to create a virtuous circle of solvency by increasing par-liament's confidence in the king and its willingness to grant taxes, so that in preparation for the Agincourt campaign Henry was able to amass a war-chest of over £130,000 in cash.[2] Just as vigorous was the king's campaign to curb public disorder, which had been particularly widespread in the Welsh Marches and the midlands. During 1414 the court of king's bench was sent from Westminster to hold visitations in Leicestershire, Staffordshire and Shropshire. Thousands of offenders were indicted and summoned before king's bench, including many powerful Lancastrian supporters whose misdeeds Henry IV had chosen to ignore.

Nevertheless, despite Henry V's best efforts, a shadow of uncertainty still hung over the dynasty until 1415. There were fears of a Ricardian rising sup-ported by the Scots, and in 1414 the Lollard Sir John Oldcastle, a former member of Henry V's household who had fallen out with the king over his heretical beliefs, attempted unsuccessfully to raise a rebellion of his sect to overthrow the lay and ecclesiastical establishment of the realm. Finally the earl

[2] Harriss (1985), p. 164.

of Cambridge's abortive plot of July 1415, which was revealed to the king by its supposed beneficiary Edmund Mortimer, earl of March, demonstrated that, on the eve of the Agincourt campaign, the legitimacy of the dynasty was still not universally accepted amongst the nobility.

II

Henry V's expedition to Normandy in 1415 took place in circumstances unusually propitious to English success. The insanity of Charles VI of France led to a struggle for power among the French princes which had degenerated into civil war between the Armagnac and Burgundian factions. Henry's main diplomatic aim was to exploit those divisions in order to attain his own military objectives, and the success of the Agincourt campaign and the conquest of Normandy between 1417 and 1419 was certainly facilitated by the inability of the French to present a united front against him. The neutrality of John the Fearless, duke of Burgundy, towards the English invasions was a particularly important factor.

The battle of Agincourt on 25 October 1415 was nonetheless an astonishing triumph for Henry V and marked a decisive turning-point in the Hundred Years War: without it the conquest of Normandy and the Treaty of Troyes would have been inconceivable. Not only was it a shattering military blow, resulting in the death or capture of most of the Armagnac leadership; its psychological effect on the political nation in England was incalculable. A tide of exultation swept the country, epitomised by Henry's reception in London in November 1415, and by the contemporary *Agincourt Carol*, a paean of nationalistic fervour.[3] After half a century of military failure and political instability, England could celebrate a victory to compare with Crécy and Poitiers. In the euphoric aftermath of the victory the issue of Lancastrian legitimacy was buried for a generation. The Commons loosened the purse-strings of national taxation: on top of the double subsidy granted in 1414, the Commons uncomplainingly voted six and one third subsidies between 1415 and 1419. In addition the parliament of November 1415 granted Henry the wool subsidy for life.

Most significantly, Agincourt, and the capture of Harfleur which preceded it, opened the way to further conquests in France. A naval victory in 1416 consolidated the Harfleur beachhead, and in August 1417 Henry set about the systematic conquest of Normandy. The ruling Armagnac faction in France was unable to offer effective resistance to the invasion, being more preoccupied by the duke of Burgundy's encirclement of Paris. After eighteen months of virtually continuous warfare, including numerous sieges and two winter cam-

---

[3] *Historical poems*, ed. Robbins, p. 91.

paigns, Henry had subjugated Normandy. Rouen, the capital of the duchy, fell, after a protracted siege, in January 1419.

Throughout the months of campaigning Henry continued diplomatic negotiations with both the Armagnacs (now nominally led by the Dauphin Charles) and the Burgundians. In spite of his successes he was well aware that the large-scale military operations conducted between 1417 and 1419 could not be sustained indefinitely. He sought a treaty with one of the warring factions which would perpetuate France's internal divisions and consolidate his territorial position. The extent of his gains, however, and the scale of his demands – which in 1419 constituted the duchies of Normandy and Aquitaine in full sovereignty and the marriage of Charles VI's daughter Catherine – made such a treaty unobtainable. They presented such a threat to the integrity of the kingdom that neither the Armagnacs nor the Burgundians could accept them for fear of losing all political credibility and support. Indeed, after the failure of negotiations between Henry, John the Fearless and Queen Isabeau at Mculan in June 1419, there was even the prospect that the two factions might sink their differences in order to repel the invader.

The situation was dramatically transformed by the murder of John the Fearless by the dauphin's men at Montereau in September 1419. The diplomatic stalemate was broken, and within a few weeks Henry concluded a firm alliance with Philip, the new duke of Burgundy. His diplomatic demands now increased accordingly, amounting to nothing less than the throne of France itself.

The Treaty of Troyes of May 1420 saw the acceptance of all Henry's demands by Burgundy, Queen Isabeau and the invalid Charles VI. Henry was declared 'Heir of France' and embraced by Charles as his son and successor; a status reinforced by his marriage to Princess Catherine. The Dauphin Charles was declared disinherited and banished from France. In December 1420 Henry V entered Paris in triumph to witness the ratification of the treaty by the French estates general.

Troyes has been a source of great controversy among historians. On the one hand it represents the high point of English success in the Hundred Years War. The establishment of a dual monarchy was an achievement which had eluded even Edward III. On the other hand, far from achieving a final peace as Henry claimed, it involved an open-ended commitment by the Lancastrians to a continuing war of conquest and attrition against dauphinist France which was far beyond their resources, even allowing for the Burgundian alliance. On this analysis the seeds of Lancastrian decline were sown by Henry V's over-reaching opportunism at Troyes.

Certainly the task which Henry V had set himself proved beyond his physical resources. The years of relentless campaigning, summer and winter, had taken their toll, and barely two years after Troyes, in August 1422, Henry died of dysentery at the age of thirty-six. He left as heir his nine-month-old son Henry VI, who on the death of his grandfather Charles VI in October 1422 also inherited the throne of France.

The task facing the minority council after 1422 was simple but awesome: to secure and consolidate Henry V's achievements until the infant king came of age. The abandonment or renegotiation of Troyes was inconceivable while Henry VI remained a minor, and the council thus enjoyed very little flexibility of policy. At first this was by no means a disadvantage. The momentum of victory was maintained, and the upholding of the dual monarchy provided a single over-riding objective which lent cohesion and unity of purpose to the Lancastrian establishment. With the setbacks of the later 1420s and 1430s, however, Troyes became an increasing burden, devouring the meagre resources of the English crown.

Henry V's elder surviving brother, John, duke of Bedford, assumed responsibility for Lancastrian France, and became regent of France on Charles VI's death. To the younger, Humphrey, duke of Gloucester, Henry V had committed the guardianship of his infant son. Gloucester attempted to claim powers of regency in England by virtue of this position, but this was firmly resisted by the leading magnates, and government was vested in a council named in parliament, nominally headed by Gloucester as protector. The council was staffed by many of the most able and long-standing Lancastrian servants, for example Henry V's Beaufort uncles, Richard Beauchamp, earl of Warwick and Sir John Tiptoft.

The council's over-riding preoccupation was the prosecution of the war in France and the maintenance of the Burgundian alliance. Bedford, his rule based on Paris, had several experienced captains under his command who had served with Henry V – notably Salisbury, Suffolk and Talbot. Initially, they enjoyed considerable success: victory at the battle of Verneuil in 1424 secured the borders of Normandy and took the war into Maine and Anjou. From the outset, however, the war effort was hampered by lack of funds from England. The country was drained after several years of unprecedented taxation under Henry V, and following the Treaty of Troyes the Commons expected Lancastrian France to pay for itself. In consequence, no parliamentary subsidies were granted between 1422 and 1429, and royal finances inevitably slid back into deficit.

In the mid-1420s the cohesion of the minority government was threatened by the duke of Gloucester's pursuit of his wife's inheritance in the Low Countries, which diverted resources from France and unsettled relations with Burgundy. Excluded from an active role in France, and denied what he considered to be his rightful position in England, Gloucester gave further vent to his disappointments in bitter quarrels with Bishop Beaufort, whose wealth and political connections made him a powerful figure on the minority council. Bedford was twice obliged to return to England to resolve disputes between Gloucester and Beaufort.

The conquest of France was brought to an abrupt halt at the siege of Orleans in May 1429. For so long demoralised by English successes, Charles VII's supporters, inspired by the arrival of the visionary Joan of Arc, forced the English to raise the siege and abandon their bridgeheads on the Loire, inflicting successive defeats at Jargeau and Patay. Two of the commanders at Orleans, Suffolk and Talbot, were captured. French troops swept northwards to the east of Paris, and in July 1429 Charles VII was crowned king of France at Rheims.

The spring and summer of 1429 marked a turning-point in the war. The defeats at Orleans and Patay put an end to any realistic prospect that the Lancastrians could conquer France and inflict a final defeat on Charles VII. Now Bedford's energies were devoted to a military holding operation. Control over Paris and its environs was formally handed over to the duke of Burgundy, leaving Bedford free to concentrate on the defence of Normandy.

The propaganda coup achieved by Charles VII's coronation required an immediate riposte. In November 1429 Henry VI was crowned at Westminster, and the following year, assisted by a double subsidy from parliament, he led an expedition to France. In December 1431, after much delay because of the precarious military situation, the ten-year-old Henry VI was crowned king of France at Notre Dame.

The early 1430s saw a modest revival in English fortunes in France, but the government's options continued to be restricted by lack of finance. In 1433 the financial statement of the Treasurer Ralph, Lord Cromwell showed accumulated debts of over £160,000, against annual income, without parliamentary subsidies, of less than £60,000. Disputes arose between Bedford and Gloucester over the best target for available funds: Gloucester advocated the reinforcement of Calais, Bedford the defence of Normandy.

Military and financial reality forced the minority government into negotiation with Charles VII, and the period between 1430 and 1435 saw intense diplomatic activity between England, France and Burgundy. Under cover of negotiations for a general peace the duke of Burgundy, disenchanted with the English alliance, edged towards a rapprochement with Charles VII. The English negotiating position was inevitably inflexible, since during his minority Henry VI could not be committed to a final peace which would overturn the Treaty of Troyes. The peace conference at Arras in 1435 broke down over French insistence, as a prerequisite of any settlement, upon the abandonment of English claims to the throne of France. A few days later a Franco-

Burgundian alliance was signed, and the duke of Burgundy renounced his allegiance to Henry VI.

Arras signified the collapse of the dual monarchy constructed by Henry V at Troyes. It was followed within a year by the loss of Paris and the contraction of Lancastrian power to Henry V's original conquest, the duchy of Normandy. These events, compounded by the death of the Regent Bedford less than a month after Arras, probably hastened the end of the minority. Just as, in 1429–31, the government responded to military crisis by Henry VI's coronations, so now it sought to reaffirm royal authority. On 13 November 1437, a month short of his sixteenth birthday, Henry VI formally assumed his powers as king.

III

It was Henry VI's tragedy that he took after his mother rather than his father. Passive, pliant, indecisive and mentally fragile, Henry VI was dominated by those around him. Facing a situation at home and abroad which required all Henry V's abilities, Henry VI showed not the slightest aptitude for warfare or government. His main interests were spiritual and educational – his collegiate foundations at Eton and Cambridge and the new university at Caen. Described as a 'dangerous compound of forcefulness and weakness',[4] Henry's forays into diplomatic negotiations with the French were invariably disastrous. Nevertheless, the impression of forcefulness was perhaps an illusory one, created by the nature of the office rather than the man. In the fifteenth century the king's will remained the first mover in government, and in its absence it had to be manufactured.[5]

The character of government under Henry VI reflected the king's personality (or lack of it). The conciliar regime of the minority soon fell away, to be replaced by the rule of a narrow clique based on the royal household, led by William de la Pole, earl (later duke) of Suffolk, who had been steward of the household since 1433. The king's pliability and lack of interest in government meant that the normal flow of power was reversed. Instead of the king ruling through his household, the household ruled through the king, a situation not seen in England since the reign of Edward II.

The king's coming of age prompted a scramble for patronage, the main beneficiaries of which were inevitably members of his household. The young king's generosity in granting petitions was so profligate that in 1444 an attempt was made to set up an advisory body to monitor petitions and prevent inappropriate alienations. This appears to have had no more than a temporary effect.

---

[4] Wolffe (1981), p. 133.   [5] Watts (1996).

An example of the indiscriminate nature of Henry VI's patronage was the grant to the earl of Devon in 1441 of the stewardship of the duchy of Cornwall, an office already held by Devon's enemy Sir William Bonville. The double grant needlessly increased tension between the two magnates and caused consternation and confusion at the centre, necessitating lengthy council sessions to defuse the problem.

The financial consequences of such mismanagement, on top of the heavy burdens of Lancastrian France, were disastrous. The commitment to a policy of 'bone governance' involving tight financial controls, which had been the keystone of Henry V's success, went by the board. In the early 1440s the regime was kept afloat only by the enormous sums lent by Cardinal Henry Beaufort, which gave the Beauforts a disproportionate influence over policy.

The king's majority sparked off fundamental debate over the direction of policy towards France, which had been in suspense since 1422. The pacific Henry VI favoured peaceful negotiation leading towards a final settlement. In 1440, as a token of good will, he unilaterally freed Charles duke of Orleans (captured at Agincourt), whose release Henry V had considered such an important diplomatic asset that he had forbidden it until his son was of age. Gloucester, Henry V's last surviving brother, furiously opposed Orleans's release, and championed a policy of vigorous military action to counter the reverses of the previous decade. Elder statesmen such as Cardinal Beaufort and the treasurer, Lord Cromwell, recognised the precariousness of royal finances and of the military situation in France, acknowledging the need for negotiations to win time for recovery. Henry VI's title as king of France remained non-negotiable, however. Even the suspension of his use of the title, proposed at the Gravelines peace conference of 1439, was unacceptable.

Meanwhile the military situation in both Normandy and Gascony continued to deteriorate for want of money, men and royal concern. After the death of Richard Beauchamp, earl of Warwick, the king's lieutenant in France, in 1439 Normandy was left without a supreme commander until the despatch of Richard duke of York as king's lieutenant in 1441. Shortly before York's arrival the royal council in Normandy sent Henry VI a bitter complaint, lamenting what they saw as the king's abandonment of the duchy. The defence of Gascony was similarly neglected, and only the French invasion of 1442 and panic-stricken appeals from Bordeaux prompted some reaction at Westminster. Temporarily abandoning his peace policy Henry resolved upon a great expedition under the command of his cousin John Beaufort, duke of Somerset. Unfortunately, as Treasurer Cromwell made clear, the resources were not available for campaigns in both Normandy and Gascony. Instead the objective was for Somerset to relieve the pressure on the two duchies by marching into the Loire valley and bringing Charles VII to battle – a plan substantially determined by Somerset's desire to consolidate his own territorial interests in Maine and Anjou. In the event the 1443 expedition was a costly anti-climax, and Somerset died in disfavour the following year.

Negotiations resumed at the peace conference at Tours in 1444, the English delegation being led by Suffolk. The weakness of the English position was painfully apparent, and the valuable diplomatic asset of Henry VI's marriage was traded for a mere two-year truce with France. Furthermore, Henry's bride Margaret, daughter of René, duke of Anjou, proved at first little more than a vehicle for Charles VII to exert pressure on Henry VI to surrender the English-held county of Maine. The king secretly agreed to the surrender shortly after his wedding in 1445, but the proposal caused uproar when it became known, and was finally effected only in 1448. Once again, Charles VII had won a major concession at no significant cost to himself.

During the periods of truce after 1444 Henry VI's government showed no sense of urgency in restoring the crumbling defences of Normandy. York was recalled after the expiry of his term of office as lieutenant in 1445, and his successor, Edmund Beaufort, duke of Somerset, did not arrive in the duchy until March 1448. With the acute financial problems of the late 1440s, the funds were simply not available to maintain adequate garrisons in Normandy. By contrast, Charles VII exploited the truces to carry out a fundamental and far-reaching reorganisation of his army.

Confusion and indecision abroad were matched by profligacy and misman-agement at home. The crown's indebtedness had grown to such an extent that by the late 1440s it was effectively bankrupt. In 1449 the cost of meeting the crown's debts and current charges was estimated at £372,000 (as against the proceeds from a single parliamentary subsidy of only about £30,000). In spite of this financial crisis, however, Henry VI continued with the lavish dispensa-tion of patronage. The Lancastrian affinity and the establishment of the household swelled to unprecedented numbers. The provinces were dominated by household men who exploited their power to manipulate the law and local government. Suffolk's retainers, Thomas Tuddenham and John Heydon in East Anglia, and James Fiennes, Lord Say and Sele in Kent, provided the most notorious examples of such exploitation.

The nadir of Henry VI's rule during the 1440s was reached with the arrest on suspicion of treason of the king's uncle Humphrey, duke of Gloucester, in 1447, an event so traumatic and humiliating for the duke that the shock of it killed him. The suspicions were almost certainly baseless, but Gloucester's vocal opposition to Henry's peace policy had fostered the king's mistrust, which was clearly played on by the Suffolk clique in order to destroy the duke, whom they feared as the only magnate with the standing to oppose them. The arrest, at Bury St Edmunds, was dramatic and unexpected: most of

Gloucester's retinue was arrested with him. Gloucester's estates were dispersed with unseemly haste, some of the grants being dated on the very day of his death.

The crisis of the Lancastrian monarchy was inevitably precipitated by events in France. The trigger was the capture and sack of the Breton border fortress of Fougères, with the connivance of the dukes of Suffolk and Somerset, in March 1449. The duke of Brittany appealed for aid to Charles VII, to whom he had paid homage in 1446. This provided Charles with the pretext to reopen the war, and at the end of July 1449 the reconquest of Normandy began. The defending forces, under Somerset's command, were totally unprepared for the invasion, and French armies advanced through Normandy virtually unopposed. The most humiliating moment in this military catastrophe was the surrender by Somerset of Rouen, in October, without even a token siege. Rouen was the capital of the duchy, and had held out for six months against Henry V in 1418. Its loss was to bulk large in the charges brought by York against Somerset as their feud gathered momentum in 1452. Harfleur fell in January 1450, and an inadequate relieving force under Sir Thomas Kyriell was defeated at Formigny in April. Caen was lost in June, and Cherbourg, the last stronghold held by the English, on 12 August 1450.

In the long term it is clear that the loss of Normandy was a fatal blow to the house of Lancaster. The military collapse revealed the scale of paralysis, confusion and incompetence which had gripped royal government since 1437. The immediate target of popular and parliamentary fury was not Henry VI himself, however, but his court. In January 1450 Adam Moleyns, keeper of the privy seal, was murdered at Portsmouth by troops on their way to Normandy. The following month parliament commenced impeachment proceedings against Suffolk. As the king's chief minister during the 1440s the duke was held responsible for all the diplomatic and military failures of the decade, from the release of Charles of Orleans to the surrender of Maine and the loss of Normandy. All were now seen as part of a treasonable conspiracy by Suffolk to overthrow Henry VI, and, with French help, to place on the throne his own son John, who had been betrothed to Margaret, daughter and heiress of John Beaufort, duke of Somerset. Henry, showing the loyalty to his servants which was one of his few redeeming features as king, cut short impeachment proceedings and banished Suffolk for five years. This was, however, insufficient to save the disgraced favourite, for on his way into exile in May 1450 Suffolk was murdered by seamen on a ship in the Channel. His headless body was found on Dover beach.

Within weeks of Suffolk's murder rebellion swept across Kent and much of the south-east, sparked off by the disastrous news from Normandy and the oppressiveness of the king's household men. The rising in Kent, led by Jack Cade, began comparatively peacefully as a mass demonstration demanding the removal of the 'false traitors' around the king and the restoration of substantial aristocratic counsel. Henry responded ineptly with a show of arms, and then fled to the midlands when the rapacity and indiscipline of his forces inflamed rather than forestalled the rebellion. The Cade rebels advanced on London early in July and pillaged the city for three days from their base in Southwark; they captured and executed the Treasurer Lord Say, who was particularly hated as a royal favourite and extortionate Kentish landowner. The rebels dispersed after the grant of a general pardon on 7 July, but unrest continued throughout the south-east during the summer and autumn.

One of the complaints of the Cade rebels was against the 'covetise' or greed of the king's household men, who had enriched themselves at the expense of the crown and the realm. This was a leading theme of the reaction against Henry VI's regime, appearing also in the charges against Suffolk and later in York's articles against Somerset in 1452. In parliament it took the form of demands for the annulment of all grants made by the king or in his name since his accession: resumption, rather than further taxation, was the Commons' immediate response to the calamitous financial situation. The first act of resumption was passed in 1450, but was so qualified by exemptions as to be largely ineffective. A second resumption was, however, passed in the parliament of 1451, which for a time allowed revenues from crown lands to be assigned in the traditional way to the expenses of the royal household.

The crisis entered a new phase in August 1450 with the return of Richard, duke of York, from Ireland, where he had been serving as king's lieutenant. By virtue of his exclusion from the inner circle of Henry VI's counsels during the 1440s, the logic of events now drove York willy-nilly into opposition to the court. York was untainted with responsibility for the failures of the regime. In the febrile atmosphere of 1450 his blood, wealth and status as a possible heir to the throne made him an object of seditious rumour. One of Jack Cade's aliases was John Mortimer, a possible reference to the Mortimer claim to the throne now represented by Richard duke of York, and the rebels found it necessary to deny that they intended to make York king in Henry's place.

York's avowed intention in returning to England without the king's permission was to protect his honour and defend his name from any imputation of treason. With the death of Suffolk, Somerset's humiliation in Normandy and the collapse of the regime's credibility, he might also have been expecting to return to a leading role in government. Instead, he found that Somerset, far from being disgraced, had succeeded Suffolk in the king's favour, and had been named constable of England. This was doubly intolerable for York inasmuch as Somerset's abandonment of Rouen in 1449 called into question his own honour under the law of arms as captain of the city, although absent in Ireland at its fall.[6]

Following his return, York sought to claim a place in government, and to oust Somerset from power and bring charges against him for the loss of Normandy. Late in 1450 he pressed his case on Henry VI in personal encounters, written bills (which were widely publicised) and, in November, in parliament, where York's chamberlain, Sir William Oldhall, was elected speaker. The duke associated himself with the bitter complaints of the Commons against Henry VI's household, and the demands for justice to be done against the 'traitors' round the king. The political atmosphere remained highly unstable. Several magnates brought large retinues to London for the parliament, and sporadic unrest continued in Kent and the south-east. In December Somerset narrowly escaped assassination and had to be placed in the Tower for his own protection.

The king and the court remained hostile to York and intensely suspicious of his motives. Henry VI repudiated York's proffered counsel and rejected his offers of assistance in restoring order and justice. In parliament a petition for the banishment of some thirty members of the royal household, headed by Somerset, met a cool response from the king; while the proposal from York's councillor, Thomas Young, for the recognition of York's title as heir to the as yet childless Henry VI was answered by the prompt dissolution of the parliamentary session in June 1451.

1450 was potentially a revolutionary year. What was at stake was not Henry VI's throne, but the structure and personnel of his regime as it had developed since 1437. York was clearly the magnate best placed to profit from the collapse of that regime and to sweep it away, yet in the event it survived, and the duke was left isolated and dangerously exposed. Paradoxically it seems as if York's challenge may have rallied the demoralised household, providing a focus against which it could regroup behind Somerset. York's failure to seize the moment in 1450 was in large part the result of his inability to carry a significant section of the nobility with him: the magnates were not sufficiently convinced of the justice of York's charges against Somerset. The survival of the regime, however, may ultimately have cost Henry VI his throne: if York had successfully challenged Somerset and purged the household in 1450, the polarisation of national politics which led to the first battle of St Albans in 1455 might have been avoided, and thus the descent into dynastic rivalry and civil war.

With the initial crisis past, the years 1451–2 saw a modest revival in royal authority, despite continuing losses in France. The king, with uncharacteristic energy, embarked on a series of punitive judicial visitations around the south

[6] Jones (1989), pp. 285–307.

and midlands. As Somerset consolidated his power, York felt his position increasingly threatened. The arrest of Gloucester, less than five years before, was an obvious reminder of the risks of opposing the court. In the autumn of 1451 York further incurred the king's displeasure by his intervention in the dispute in the south-west between Lord Bonville and the earl of Devon. With a miscalculation born of desperation York risked an armed demonstration to force his will on the king, which barely stopped short of open rebellion. At Dartford in March 1452 a royal army supported by most of the leading nobility faced down York's forces. The duke was compelled to make a humiliating submission. The king dismissed the articles which he had presented against Somerset, and he was made to take an oath of loyalty to Henry, swearing not to attempt anything against the crown, and to attend the king when summoned.

Events in the summer of 1453 rescued York from the political margins. The defeat of the expeditionary force in Gascony at the battle of Castillon in July extinguished any realistic hope of the recovery by the English crown of its territories in south-western France, over-run by Charles VII's forces in 1451. A few weeks after Castillon Henry VI suffered a mental collapse from which he did not emerge until the beginning of 1455. York could not be excluded from the magnate councils which were convened to respond to this unforeseen crisis. Once admitted he soon became dominant: Somerset was committed to the Tower in November 1453, and following the death of the chancellor, Archbishop John Kemp, in March 1454, York was named protector and chief councillor.

The escalation of violent magnate disputes was no less important than the king's madness for the revival of York's fortunes. The most serious of these was the Neville–Percy dispute in the north, which broke out into armed confrontation in August 1453, when forces led by Thomas Percy, Lord Egremont, ambushed a Neville wedding party at Heworth Moor in Yorkshire. Richard Neville, earl of Warwick, was also in dispute with Somerset over the lordship of Glamorgan, while the young duke of Exeter, Henry Holland, was prosecuting a bitter feud against the long-standing Lancastrian servant, Lord Cromwell.

The proliferation of such disputes reflected the king's signal failure to contain and resolve conflict amongst his nobility. Their significance ran still wider, however, for they foreshadowed the break-up of the nobility into factions. The cohesion amongst the leading magnates, long sustained by the common purpose of defending Lancastrian France, began to disintegrate. Most important was the rift between Somerset and the Nevilles, which facilitated the alliance between the latter and York. The Neville–Beaufort connection had been the backbone of Lancastrian magnate support since the reign of Henry IV, and its demise marked an important step in the fall of the house of Lancaster.

During his brief Protectorate York sought to restore public order and to reduce the size and expense of the royal household. Richard Neville, earl of Salisbury, was appointed chancellor, and with the support of Cromwell and the Nevilles, York led a judicial visitation to Yorkshire to discipline followers of Exeter and the Percies. Exeter himself, who openly defied York's authority, was imprisoned in Salisbury's castle at Pontefract. York, however, failed to bring charges against Somerset, and although he took over the captaincy of Calais from the latter, he was unable to establish his authority there before Henry VI's recovery early in 1455.

Henry VI's return to sanity abruptly ended York's pre-eminence and restored his enemies to power. Somerset was quickly released and declared free of any suspicion of treason. Salisbury, having been forced to release Exeter, resigned the chancellorship in March. A magnate council summoned to meet at Leicester in May, ostensibly to provide for the king's safety, was probably designed to compel the Yorkist lords into submission. They responded with force. At St Albans they attacked the court on its way to Leicester; Somerset and the Percy earl of Northumberland were murdered and the king was seized.

At the battle of St Albans York 'had finally achieved by force of arms in half an hour what in politics had painfully eluded him for the last five years: the elimination of his chief political rival . . . and control of the king's person'.[7] The advantages he gained were comparatively short-lived, however, and they were won at the price of abandoning the traditional constraints against violence in the king's presence. The decline of respect for the king's person – he was slightly wounded at St Albans – revealed the decrease in his own personal authority. Henry became a passive repository of royal charisma, bestowing legitimacy on whichever faction controlled him. More fundamentally, the battle of St Albans witnessed the collapse of any semblance of normal political discourse, initiating as it did a string of aristocratic blood-feuds.

Having gained custody of the king, York now controlled government for about a year after St Albans. Henry VI suffered a mental relapse in November 1455 (from which he appears never to have fully recovered) and York was for a short period re-elected protector. In the summer of 1456, however, Queen Margaret withdrew the king away from Westminster to the Lancastrian strongholds in the midlands. The queen, as mother of the infant Edward, prince of Wales (born on 13 October 1453 during Henry VI's first bout of insanity), now assumed leadership of the Lancastrian and household faction. Like Richard II after 1388 she sought to rebuild royal authority on a regional basis, using in particular the duchy of Lancaster estates, the principality of Wales and the earldom of Chester. Her intention was to accumulate sufficient military

---

[7] Wolffe (1981), p. 294.

resources to overwhelm the Yorkist lords and prevent a recurrence of St Albans. The withdrawal from London nevertheless marked a further stage in the process of political fragmentation.

By the summer of 1459 Queen Margaret and her allies felt strong enough for a confrontation with the Yorkists. In May loyal Lancastrians were summoned to Leicester for military service, and the following month a great council was held at Coventry. York, Salisbury and Warwick received summonses to this council but failed to appear. Their non-appearance provided the pretext for military action. In October a royal army encountered a Yorkist force near Ludlow: the latter broke up in confusion, the soldiers refusing to oppose the king in the field. York fled to Ireland, and his son Edward, earl of March, escaped with the Nevilles to Calais, where Warwick was captain. Parliament was immediately summoned to Coventry, where the attainder of the Yorkist lords was proclaimed and their estates confiscated.

The queen's triumph lasted less than a year. Calais, with its garrison of professional soldiers, was an ideal base from which to launch a counter-attack. In June 1460 Salisbury, Warwick and March landed in Kent and occupied London. A few days later Warwick and March defeated a royal force at Northampton and captured the king. The rebel lords continued to stress their loyalty to Henry VI, but on York's return from Ireland in September he soon made clear his intent to claim the royal title. He apparently expected to sweep to the throne on a tide of popular acclaim: events proved that he had miscalculated. The magnates and prelates would not countenance a deposition. Henry VI, for all his failings, was not a tyrant like Richard II, nor was he childless. An awkward compromise, the Act of Accord, was agreed which owed much to the Treaty of Troyes: Henry was to remain as king but York was named as his heir, thus disinheriting Prince Edward.

The leading Lancastrians were not a party to this abortive settlement. The queen and the prince took refuge in Scotland, while Exeter, Northumberland and Somerset defied the regime in the north. In December 1460 they took their revenge for St Albans, inflicting a crushing defeat on the Yorkists at Wakefield in which York and Salisbury were both killed.

The death of York finally broke the impasse which had paralysed national politics since the crisis of 1450. March, York's heir, now considered himself absolved from any allegiance to Henry VI. The triumphant Lancastrians saw victory within their grasp and advanced south. At St Albans in February 1461 they defeated Warwick's forces, and the road to London lay open before them. At this critical moment the queen hesitated fatally. Instead of pressing home her advantage she withdrew her forces once more to the midlands, abandoning the capital to the Yorkists. Warwick and March re-entered London, and on 4 March 1461 York's heir went through a form of coronation and claimed the throne as Edward IV. Three weeks later, at the battle of Towton, the new king inflicted a decisive defeat on the Lancastrians and the reign of Henry VI was effectively at an end.

The disintegration and collapse of Henry VI's regime reveal again the significance for the history of the Lancastrian monarchy of the themes of warfare, service and finance identified at the beginning of this chapter. In all three areas, Henry VI showed himself to be completely unsuited to kingship. His most significant failure was military. The victories of Henry V, culminating in the Treaty of Troyes, linked the fortunes of the Lancastrian dynasty inextricably to continued military success in France. Remarkably, and uniquely among medieval English kings, Henry VI never took an active part in any military campaign. Nor did he ever visit his French realms as an adult. Without his leadership, and despite the efforts of his military captains, the Lancastrian cause in France ultimately went by default. The marked decline in aristocratic and gentry participation in the last phases of the Hundred Years War was clearly attributable in part to Henry VI's own example.

Henry VI's failure to provide military and political leadership rendered him incapable of commanding the quality of service from the nobility and gentry necessary for stable and effective government. His effective abdication of the king's political role to surrogates such as Suffolk and Somerset meant that the exercise of royal power was distorted through the prism of sectional magnate interests. It was in this context that the aristocratic divisions which made possible the Wars of the Roses were generated. Henry IV had relied for his survival on the Lancastrian affinity; Henry V transcended his father's limited support to create a genuinely national following. Under Henry VI the duchy of Lancaster again became the power base of a faction, whose members exploited royal authority for their own advantage.

The crisis in the crown's finances was closely linked to Henry VI's failure to provide military and political leadership. The parliamentary taxation necessary to finance adequately the war in France could only have been negotiated by an active warrior king, and strict financial controls were necessary to make the most of the crown's limited resources. Henry VI's inability to maximise war taxation was compounded by the profligacy with which he dispensed patronage. The cumulative result was a deficit by 1450 tantamount to bankruptcy, which crippled royal policy and rendered illusory any prospect of the recovery of Lancastrian France.

Henry VI's misrule had far-reaching effects which long outlasted his reign. The political instability engendered in the decade between 1450 and 1460 was so profound, and the divisions amongst the nobility so bitter, that they took more than a generation to eradicate. The Wars of the Roses, and the Tudor settlement which followed, led to permanent changes in English political society. Royal authority emerged considerably enhanced from the crisis (as it had in France under Charles VII). The forfeitures and redistribution of estates which accompanied the changes of dynasty undermined traditional loyalties to regional magnate houses, and fostered more direct links between the crown and the gentry in the provinces. Finally, the traumatic memory of instability and civil war remained lodged in the collective consciousness of the nation, and helped to shape the political culture of sixteenth-century England.

CHAPTER 21(b)

YORKIST AND EARLY TUDOR
ENGLAND

Rosemary Horrox

I

EDWARD IV dated the start of his reign from 4 March 1461, the day he was acclaimed by the Londoners and took his seat on the throne in Westminster Hall. But his claim to be king of England received its real confirmation three weeks later, on 29 March, when he led the Yorkists to victory at Towton. This was the largest battle of the Wars of the Roses, and the decisiveness of its outcome forced the acknowledgement of Edward's title by all but the most committed Lancastrians. There were, however, aspects of the situation which were less comfortable for the new king. The deposition of Henry VI was the first to draw its validity from a trial of military strength. Both previous depositions – of Edward II and Richard II – had rested on a much broader political consensus. A military verdict was necessary in 1461 precisely because there was no general agreement that Henry should go. Edward IV was also the first king to have his predecessor still at large when he assumed the title. Henry VI and his wife had remained at York while Towton was fought and had fled to Scotland on hearing the news of their army's defeat.

Edward IV thus faced, in a particularly acute form, the need to establish himself as the rightful and effective ruler of England. The early years of his reign saw almost continuous military involvement in the north of England, where the Lancastrians could call on Scottish support, and more sporadic activity in Wales and elsewhere. It was not until the Yorkist victory of Hexham in 1464, followed by the surrender of the Northumbrian castles still held by the Lancastrians, that Edward's military hold on his realm could be considered entirely secure – a hold recognised by a truce agreed with Scotland in June.

This confrontational approach was not typical of the early years of Edward's reign. From the outset the new king showed himself consistently willing to take former Lancastrians into favour and make use of their services. Given the narrowness of Edward's power base such a policy made good

477

practical sense; but it also marked a deliberate attempt to restore political life to normality after the factionalism of the previous decade, and as such was one expression of Edward's self-identification as the redeemer of an oppressed people. The policy produced some dramatic failures, including Sir Ralph Percy, the Lancastrian commander of Dunstanborough, who was allowed to retain the command when the Yorkists took the castle in 1461, only to open his gates to the Lancastrians in the following year. But in general men were as eager to support the *de facto* king as he was to have their backing, and it is some measure of Edward's success that when Henry VI was finally betrayed and captured in July 1465 it was in Lancashire, the hereditary heartland of his dynasty.

Alongside Edward's search for domestic security went the need to secure recognition for his dynasty in Europe. In the context of the 1460s the most immediate opening for England on to the European stage was the growing tension between France, on the one hand, and the duchies of Brittany and Burgundy on the other, caused by the manifest desire of Louis XI to draw them more firmly under French control. It was by no means obvious where Edward's own interests lay in this conflict. France was the old enemy, but Charles, count of Charolais, the heir (and already effective ruler) of the duchy of Burgundy, had Lancastrian sympathies, as had Francis II, the duke of Brittany. There were also obvious diplomatic advantages for England in delaying a decision. The need of both sides to acquire English backing, or at least deny it to their opponents, gave Edward a European importance which he would otherwise hardly have merited, and which would inevitably be diminished when he committed himself. Once it had become clear that Edward had chosen to back Burgundy, Charles was able to drive a hard bargain in the negotiations of 1467–8.

The Burgundian alliance was formalised in the marriage of Duke Charles to Edward's sister Margaret – the only one of the Yorkist royal family to make a 'dynastic' marriage. Discussions of possible European brides for Edward and his brother George, duke of Clarence, had been a feature of earlier diplomacy, but nothing had come of them. Edward, indeed, had taken himself out of the running by his marriage, on 1 May 1464, to an English widow, Elizabeth Grey (née Woodville). The marriage was kept secret until the following autumn, a tacit admission that Edward himself was aware of the awkwardness of the situation.

Edward's action was undoubtedly an error of judgement, and many commentators have seen the Woodville marriage as the great mistake of his reign. Socially, the king had married beneath himself. Elizabeth's father was a modest landowner, who had been made Earl Rivers in recognition of his marriage to Jacquetta of Luxemburg, the widow of Henry V's brother, John, duke of Bedford. In spite of this European dimension, which may have helped to nudge Edward towards a Burgundian alliance, an important diplomatic opportunity had been lost. Edward's marriage removed a valuable bargaining counter just as English pretensions to European power were coming to fruition. Worse, the king's delay in admitting the marriage – which left his ambassadors negotiating a French match which had now become impossible – exposed the regime to charges of bungling and bad faith.

The impact of the marriage on domestic politics is less straightforward. Elizabeth brought a large, and largely unmarried, family into the royal circle: two sons by her first husband, as well as five brothers and six sisters. Within eighteen months Edward had found aristocratic husbands for all the queen's sisters. This series of marriages is unlikely to have been prompted only by the king's infatuation with his new wife. Edward, with his usual pragmatism, was seizing the opportunity to ally his dynasty more securely with the English nobility – an interpretation strengthened by the fact that he showed much less interest in finding brides for his wife's male kin. The marriages consolidated links with existing allies of the house of York, such as the Herberts and Bourgchiers, but also forged new alliances with the Staffords and FitzAlans. This is not to say that the advantages were all on the king's side. By the mid-1460s his dynasty was sufficiently well established for marriage into the extended royal family to confer welcome prestige and influence, and the grants which accompanied several of the marriages should probably be seen not as Edward buying grudging acquiescence, but as the first fruits of an alliance valued by both sides.[1]

Not everyone, however, could be persuaded to view the Woodvilles in so positive a light. The king's marriage signalled a turning-point in Edward's relations with his erstwhile ally, Richard Neville, earl of Warwick. To at least one contemporary observer, the earl had been the key player on the duke of York's behalf in the critical months of 1460.[2] Warwick had then emerged not only as the public voice of Yorkist negotiation but also, it seems, as a powerfully persuasive voice in the political deals going on behind the scenes. It is doubtful whether Edward IV ever relied on his cousin as thoroughly as the duke of York had done in those months, but the regime's early insecurity meant that any change did not become immediately apparent. With hindsight, Edward's marriage, and the creation of an extended royal family which followed it, provide the first clear indication that Warwick's pre-eminence was being eroded.

This may well have been less obvious at the time and the earl's immediate response was not overtly hostile. He was one of two noblemen, the king's brother Clarence being the other, who escorted Elizabeth Woodville on her

---

[1] For a more critical interpretation than that offered here, see Hicks (1979).
[2] Johnson (1988), p. 214.

first public appearance as queen; and he was later to stand godfather to her first child. Significantly, Warwick also made a bid for his own niche within the royal family by floating the possibility of a marriage between one of his daughters and Clarence, who was at this point still the king's heir male. Edward's response was unwelcoming, and in the course of the next few years relations between the two men cooled as it became increasingly obvious that Warwick's influence was waning.

The political tensions which this induced are reflected in the stirrings of Lancastrian activity noticeable in the late 1460s. None of this activity amounted to very much, but it suggests that opposition to Edward IV was coming to seem viable again, and also that contemporaries were well aware of where the blame for that lay. It was claimed in both England and France that Warwick had a hand in the unrest, and although this was probably no more than wishful thinking on the part of the conspirators, that in itself is testimony to the importance being attached to the earl's disaffection.

That disaffection finally erupted into open conflict in 1469. In the early summer there was a major rising in the north-east of England. It was fuelled by a range of local grievances, but the 'Robin of Redesdale' who headed it was one of Warwick's retainers and the unrest served to draw the king north just as the earl's own schemes came to fruition. On 11 July Clarence married Warwick's eldest daughter, Isabel, at Calais. On the following day the two men issued a manifesto, couched as a list of popular grievances which they had resolved to bring to the king's attention 'for the honour and profit of our said sovereign lord and the common weal of all this his realm'. The complaints were targeted at named associates of the king, including several members of the extended royal family which Edward had created in the mid-1460s. They were accused of forcing up taxes, to make good the financial shortfall their own rapacity had caused, and of maintaining wrongdoers so that the law could not be enforced. The two nobles called for the offenders to be punished and for the king to be better counselled in future.[3]

The tone of the manifesto was in many ways reminiscent of the criticisms which York had levelled against the circle around Henry VI in the 1450s. Like York, the two lords argued that the cure for misgovernment was a greater royal reliance on the advice of the princes of the blood. Like York, too, they found that this was not something which could be imposed on the king; and the events of 1469–70 offer a speeded-up replay of the dilemmas which had confronted Duke Richard between 1450 and 1460.

At first their resort to force seemed to give Clarence and Warwick all they could have wanted. The defeat of the royal army at Edgecote on 26 July was

---

[3] Warkworth, *Chronicle*, pp. 47–50.

followed by a series of executions which cold-bloodedly removed several of Edward's closest associates. The king himself fell into the rebels' hands and was taken by Warwick to the Neville stronghold of Middleham in Wensleydale. But although the rebels had succeeded in destroying one power structure, they found themselves unable to create another to take its place. Their failure was spelt out by an upsurge of violent disorder as men realised that royal authority was in abeyance. At the beginning of September Warwick tacitly admitted defeat by calling on the king's help to repress a Lancastrian rising in the north – the Nevilles' own sphere of influence. When Edward then summoned his supporters to accompany him back to London the earl was in no position to resist.

Once back in charge the king seemed willing, as at the beginning of his reign, to trade forgiveness of past disloyalty for future service. He was careful to emphasise that Warwick and Clarence were 'his best friends' and that their grievances would be taken seriously.[4] But the two men must have feared that Edward was merely biding his time until he could have his revenge – a reading of the situation which was current among the king's own servants and which received some confirmation early in 1470 when Edward restored Henry Percy to the earldom of Northumberland.

The last Percy earl had died fighting for Lancaster at Towton, in 1461, and the ensuing forfeiture of his estates had left the way clear for the Neville domination of the north. By restoring the Percies – the obvious counter-weights to the Nevilles – Edward was signalling an intention to limit that domination. Both Clarence and Warwick were required to give up their shares of the forfeited Percy estates. The real loser, however, was Warwick's younger brother John, who had become earl of Northumberland in 1464. As a loyal supporter of Edward IV, John, unlike Warwick and Clarence, was compensated for his losses, but compensated in a way which wrote off his existing interests. His new title of Marquess Montagu represented nominal promotion but carried none of the local authority of the earldom he had lost, while the land he received in exchange lay predominantly in the south-west – confronting him with the task of building a new power base in an area where he had no inherited interests.

There is no reason to believe that Edward IV wanted to diminish John Neville's power. The land which he was given had formed the core of the Courtenay earldom of Devon, and had most recently been held by the king's close associate, Humphrey Stafford, whose death after Edgecote had freed it for redistribution. Its size and coherence made it a suitable endowment for a new marquess, and it may also be that Edward had some idea of using Neville

---

[4] *Paston letters*, I, p. 410.

as a replacement for Stafford as his representative in the region, just as he used his brother Gloucester to replace another of the rebels' victims, William Herbert, earl of Pembroke, in Wales. But the episode is symptomatic of Edward's tendency to manipulate landed interests for his own advantage, apparently unaware of – or unconcerned by – the resentment that might arouse in the people who found themselves unceremoniously shifted. Although Edward was to show himself in other respects a very shrewd man-manager, there was a streak of calculating ruthlessness in him which was to emerge more strongly in the 1470s and which could sometimes, as in this case, backfire.

John Neville did not immediately make his resentment felt, although his brother and Clarence were soon to move back into opposition. In the spring of 1470 the two men utilised unrest in Lincolnshire to stir up renewed rebellion, with the aim (according to the official version of events) of setting Clarence on the throne. This version has been disputed, with a few writers going so far as to claim that the rebels' aims were exaggerated by Edward to justify an attack on Warwick and Clarence.[5] But if the deposition of Edward IV was not already their intention, it was soon to become so. When the rising collapsed the two men fled to France, where Warwick announced his intention of allying with the exiled Lancastrians to restore Henry VI to the throne. Whatever their position in spring, by summer they had been pushed down the same slippery slope as York: deposition now seemed the only way out of the vicious circle of disloyalty and mistrust.

In September 1470, Warwick and Clarence, with French support, landed in the West Country. This time John Neville backed them, and turned the troops which he had been raising in Edward's name against the king. Edward, caught unawares by the defection of his former ally, escaped to the Low Countries, leaving Clarence and Warwick to retrieve Henry VI from the Tower and reinstate him as king of England.

Edward's arrival in Burgundian territory was a considerable embarrassment for his brother-in-law, Duke Charles. As part of the price Warwick had paid for French backing, the new regime in England was committed to support a French invasion of Burgundy. Charles's initial reaction was to keep Edward at a distance – both literally and figuratively – to avoid giving any cause of offence to the new Anglo–French alliance. It was only when Louis XI declared war on Burgundy in December 1470 that the duke abandoned his neutrality and agreed to support a Yorkist invasion of England.

That invasion took place in March 1471. Edward IV, now reconciled with Clarence, defeated Warwick at the battle of Barnet and then went on to over-

---

[5] Ross (1974), appendix V; Holland (1988), pp. 849–69.

come a Lancastrian army at Tewkesbury three weeks later. As in 1461, Edward's claim to the throne had been vindicated by battle. But there was one major difference. Prince Edward of Lancaster died in the rout at Tewkesbury. As long as he had been alive, and beyond Edward IV's reach, the Yorkists had had every reason to keep the imprisoned Henry VI alive: there were obvious advantages in having the Lancastrian claimant in safe custody. With the prince's death, that argument lost its force, and Henry VI was killed on the night of Edward IV's victorious return to London, Yorkist claims that he died of 'pure displeasure and melancholy' probably then, as now, commanding little credence.[6]

II

Edward IV's overthrow and restoration were seen by contemporaries as dramatic evidence of the arbitrary revolution of Fortune's wheel. For later writers this instability was, rather, a sign that royal authority had been profoundly compromised and had not yet been effectively reasserted. But what happened in 1469–71 hardly sustains this interpretation. Although Warwick and Clarence ran through the whole gamut of opposition much more quickly than Richard, duke of York, had done, they had even less success than York in persuading men to oppose the king. Warwick found it difficult to mobilise his retainers in 1469 and 1470, and those of his followers who combined service to him with service to the crown (a 'double allegiance' which is sometimes assumed to be detrimental to royal authority) tended on the whole to stay loyal to the king. The lesson of 1469–71 (and of the Wars of the Roses in general) is the importance attached to effective royal authority. The violent resort to self-help which accompanied dislocation at the centre generally rallied support for the king – as Edward IV found in 1469.

What the period does show, however, is the specific danger posed by a rival royal claimant, whose mere existence could make opposition respectable. Clarence's claim to the throne was treasonable; Warwick's support for Henry VI, by definition, was not. With both Lancastrian claimants out of the way, the 1470s do have a very different 'feel' about them compared with the 1460s. To put it rather crudely, Edward now had room to make mistakes, and his domestic policies show him to have become unassailable. Contemporaries recognised as much, and the early 1470s brought the reconciliation of most of those Lancastrians, like Sir Richard Tunstall, who had remained in opposition throughout the 1460s. The handful of exceptions included the Lancastrian half blood – now represented by Jasper Tudor and his nephew Henry – and a few

[6] *Historie of the arrivall of Edward IV,* p. 38.

men who knew that they had no hope of regaining their land under York, such as John de Vere, earl of Oxford, whose estates had been used to endow Edward's younger brother Richard, duke of Gloucester. Oxford secured French backing for a rebellion in 1473, but, like the other flurries of unrest around this time, it came to nothing.

The clearest evidence of Edward's authority is his successful manipulation of property descents: most famously in his virtual disinheriting of the Mowbray heirs to endow his second son. The integrity of inheritance was a subject about which landowners, understandably, were normally extremely sensitive – his disinheritance of Bolingbroke in 1399 had cost Richard II his throne – and it is testimony to Edward's authority that such interventions met no significant opposition. Many of the tenurial readjustments were enshrined in parliamentary acts: one sign of the extreme docility of Yorkist parliaments.

Such readjustments were not only directed at endowing the royal family. Edward used the same tactics to redesign the political map of England by edging out men who had no place in his plans. William Herbert II, whose father had been Edward's right-hand man in Wales in the 1460s, was made to exchange his earldom of Pembroke for land in the south-west. His father's role was taken instead by a group of lesser royal servants associated with the council established for the prince of Wales at Ludlow.

Herbert was a nonentity. But Edward was also able to destroy his own brother, Clarence. By the time of the duke's execution for treason in 1478, his power had been deliberately eroded – in part by demonstrating that he no longer enjoyed royal support; in part by taking back some of his land. Edward achieved the latter through a parliamentary act of resumption, and it is characteristic of him that a measure which under Henry VI had been seen as an unacceptable restriction on the royal prerogative should become, in his hands, a valuable weapon in the royal armoury. Edward used regular acts of resumption not only to rethink his patronage (as in Clarence's case), but to make patronage go further at no cost to himself, since each grant of exemption from such an act was a further exercise of patronage.

Edward's manipulation of landed influence was designed to create power as well as destroy it. Throughout his reign he encouraged the formation of regional power bases for his most trusted supporters, including his brother, Gloucester (who was effectively put in charge of the north of England in the 1470s), and his chamberlain, William, Lord Hastings (who took over Clarence's influence in the north midlands). For many subsequent commentators this policy was a disaster: the wanton diminution of royal authority by a king who should have known better. But this assumes that the power which Edward delegated was thereby lost to him, which was not the case. As the career of Clarence shows, what Edward made, he could break. Even without such dramatic royal intervention, a former royal ally who tried to turn his power against the king was likely to find (as Warwick did) that he could not carry all his men with him.

The role of the noblemen who exercised influence on the king's behalf over whole regions differed only in degree from that of the smaller landowners who acted for the king at a local level. Under both Yorkist kings, the relationship of such men to the crown was generally formalised by their membership of the royal household – a body which formed the essential bridge between central authority and local government. When the king's commands were carried out by men who were simultaneously his servants and landowners in the area concerned, royal government could be presented as an act of co-operation rather than aggression.

That co-operation should not be taken as a sign of royal weakness. For Edward IV, delegation was not a diminution, still less a negation, of his authority. On the contrary, allowing influence to his servants affirmed his role as the source of power. This explains both his readiness to sanction the development of power bases by his allies and his cynical disregard for the existing interests of others. Both traits were in evidence throughout his reign. Edward's expulsion in 1470 did not force a change of style; nor were his opponents seeking such a thing. Their grievances were personal rather than structural.

The same could be said of Edward IV's own attitude to kingship. In sharp contrast to Henry VII, Edward took no interest in setting up institutional power structures. His most impressive achievements remained dependent on him. His re-ordering of the political map rested on a series of personal relationships. The council of the prince of Wales was the most 'institutional' of his local arrangements, but it would inevitably dissolve on the king's death, when his heir ceased to be prince of Wales.

The same criticism can be levelled against Edward's development of the chamber as a financial agency under his direct control. Under this system, the receivers of the crown lands (most of whom were household servants) paid their revenues directly into the chamber, where they were available for the king's immediate use. This gave far more flexibility than exchequer practice, which was based on the assignment of future revenue. It was also highly efficient. Coupled with a concerted effort to maximise the yield from prerogative sources such as wardships and vacant temporalities – which were also paid directly into the chamber – it enabled Edward to build up the cash reserves which, at the end of his reign, paid for a year's campaigning in Scotland before he had to ask parliament for money. But when Edward's directing authority was removed, the chamber organisation collapsed, and the exchequer had to pick up the pieces.

Edward IV evidently found the direct exercise of power very congenial. His recorded pronouncements catch the voice of a king absolutely confident of his authority in his dealings with his subjects. Significantly, one of the things which most impressed contemporaries was his marvellous memory for people – the *sine qua non* of personal monarchy, and an attribute which had been signally lacking in Henry VI.

When Edward died on 9 April 1483 he was the undisputed master of England. Within three months of his death his twelve-year-old heir, Edward V, had been deposed, and the duke of Gloucester had taken the throne as Richard III. The deposition of a minor was unprecedented, and it has been argued that the explanation must lie in the previous reign. Edward's willingness to build up the power of his associates has been blamed for creating factional conflict within his court – and for giving the protagonists the power to translate their animosities into violent action once his own controlling hand was removed. On this argument, the young Edward V was the victim of long-standing hostility to the Woodvilles, with whom he was so closely linked that their political eclipse could only be made permanent by his deposition.[7]

There is, however, very little evidence of factional conflict on this scale, either before or after Edward's death. In the course of the 1470s the Woodvilles had been largely assimilated into the political world, helped by less aggressive royal patronage on their behalf. Contemporaries clearly felt deep anxiety about how the political balance would be affected by Edward's death, and this inevitably had a bearing on the situation as it unfolded between April and June; but it is Gloucester who emerged as the real driving force in those months. At the end of April he took possession of the young king and declared himself Protector. Less than two months later he announced that his brother's marriage had been bigamous, its offspring illegitimate, and that he was the rightful heir to the throne. He was crowned on 6 July.

The underlying justification for Richard's action, emphasised in his public pronouncements, was that he was the man who could ensure the safe continuance of his brother's regime. This tacit recognition of the vulnerability of Edward's achievements in the hands of a child probably led the political community to welcome Gloucester's assumption of the Protectorate, even if (as seems likely) it represented a departure from the dead king's own wishes. But it was not an argument which could validate something as radical as a deposition. Although Richard was careful to practise what he preached, and the early months of his reign were characterised by almost total continuity with his brother's regime, opposition to him began immediately. A plan to rescue Edward V and his brother was uncovered in July, and in October rebellion erupted throughout southern England.

---

[7] As argued by Ross (1981) and Ives (1968).

The rebellion reveals how totally Richard's usurpation had destabilised politics. Most of those involved were former servants of Edward IV. Some, notably the Woodvilles, had been removed from power by Richard and their opposition was predictable, but many had been continued in favour and had no material reason for disaffection. The rising also drew in a handful of former Lancastrians who had lost land in the previous reign and who now – for the first time in over a decade – saw rebellion as a viable strategy. The rebels' initial aim was the restoration of Edward V, and it was probably in response to the July conspiracy that Richard ordered his nephews' death. Any setback to the rebels' plans was short-lived. By September a new rival to Richard had emerged in the person of Henry Tudor, the son of Margaret Beaufort and Henry VI's half-brother, Edmund Tudor. That his dynastic claims could be taken seriously at all, let alone by Yorkists, reveals better than anything the profound dislocation brought about by Richard's usurpation.

The rebellion posed a major threat to the new regime, and Richard was fortunate that internal tensions led to its collapse before it could gather momentum. Its failure brought the king a few months of unchallenged rule, during which he presided over a notably acquiescent parliament. But the lack of a military resolution meant that opposition had been postponed, rather than overcome. The rebellion also brought Richard new problems. As in the early 1460s, there was now an acknowledged rival beyond the king's reach. Henry Tudor had made good his escape to Brittany, and Richard immediately commenced negotiations for his surrender. By the summer of 1484 these were close to success, but Henry was warned and managed to escape to France.

The rebellion had also demonstrated Richard's weakness in the southern counties, where the network of household men created by Edward IV had been fatally compromised. With no time, and little inclination, to build up a following among the local gentry who had escaped involvement, Richard used the land and office forfeited by the rebels to 'plant' his own servants (many of whom were from the north of England) in the areas affected by the rebellion. Although this gave him a ready-made household presence in the southern counties, the imposition of outsiders triggered fierce local resentment, and laid Richard open to accusations of ruling in the interests of a clique.

In the summer of 1484 there was further unrest in the south. None of it amounted to very much, but it added to a sense that the regime was vulnerable. By late autumn men hitherto prepared to back Richard were reconsidering their allegiance, and there were defections in England and, more worryingly, among the Calais garrison. Yorkist support for Henry Tudor had been encouraged by his promise, made at Christmas 1483, to marry Edward IV's daughter, Elizabeth. Richard paid tribute to the force of the move by considering marriage to her himself, after the death of his first wife early in 1485.

But the main boost to Tudor's credibility was his flight to France in 1484. Unlike Brittany, France had the resources and the motive to back military action against Richard III. England and France had been in a state of near war since the spring of 1483. In December 1482 France and Burgundy had finally reached agreement at the Treaty of Arras, after it had become apparent that England was not prepared to help Burgundy against France. The agreement allowed Louis XI to abandon the terms of the Treaty of Picquigny, agreed with Edward after an English army had invaded France in 1475. This diplomatic setback enraged Edward IV, and when he died in April 1483 he was actively planning the dispatch of an expeditionary force to Brittany. Although the scheme had to be abandoned, France evidently feared that Richard planned to reactivate it, and Tudor accordingly offered a useful means of distracting him.

Tudor invaded in August 1485, and met the king's army just south of Market Bosworth (Leics) on 22 August. Richard's forces, weakened by treachery, were defeated and the king himself killed in a battle traditionally regarded as one of the turning-points of English history. The verdict of Bosworth on Richard III is, however, far from clear. The composition of the royal forces demonstrates the extent to which Richard was still reliant on the men who had helped to bring him to power in 1483, but his was the larger army and he came very close to victory; while Henry Tudor only arrived at the battlefield at all thanks to French and Scottish backing. If men did not much want to fight for Richard III, they were clearly no more enthusiastic about Tudor; and perhaps the one incontrovertible lesson of the battle is that after a generation of war men were no longer willing to risk their lives and livelihoods.

Yet Richard should have been able to call on wider support after two years as king (as Henry VII demonstrated at the battle of Stoke in 1487) and his failure to do so suggests real disenchantment with him and his regime. There were immediate reasons for this unpopularity, notably the affront to local sensibilities caused by the 'plantation' of northerners in the south. Even more fundamental was the perception that it had been Richard who, after the stability of Edward IV's last years, had triggered the return to political conflict – and had done so, moreover, for what could (with whatever justice) be seen as essentially selfish motives. Richard's strategy for preserving the stable government of his brother was indistinguishable, in practice, from a desire to preserve his own pre-eminence in the Yorkist polity.

III

Richard III's brief reign had demonstrated the vulnerability of political stability. But this should not be taken as evidence of some fundamental weakness in the late medieval polity. What happened in 1483 was unique: the result of the conjunction of a child king and an individual prepared to step right outside the boundaries of normal political behaviour. What is significant is not that order could be subverted, but that most contemporaries desperately wanted to mini-mise the risk of that happening. Edward IV's reign had already demonstrated the readiness of men to support the *de facto* king as a bulwark against continuing disorder. Had Richard won at Bosworth he would almost certainly have bene-fited from the same attitude. As it was, Henry VII was the beneficiary. Once he had defeated Richard III, the only alternative to another generation of civil war was for men to rally round and support him.

This explains the paradox which lies at the root of Henry's regime. Viewed objectively, the new king was vulnerable – in spite of the divine sanction implied by his victory at Bosworth. In 1485 he was an unknown quantity, whose title to the throne was virtually non-existent. There was no shortage of Yorkist claimants, notably Clarence's son, Edward, earl of Warwick, whose title had been better than Richard's own, and whom Henry took the precaution of securing before his own entry into London. There were also the de la Poles, the sons of Richard's sister, Elizabeth, duchess of Suffolk; and there was the ques-tion mark over the fate of Edward IV's sons. Although few contemporaries seem to have doubted that Richard had had them killed, the absence of proof was to leave the way open for pretenders.

Henry's own sense of vulnerability seems never to have left him, and a number of his policies can be interpreted as a quest for security. The most famous example is his use of bonds to ensure the good behaviour of his leading subjects. The tactic was not new. Both Yorkist kings had used it exten-sively, but usually only in special cases: Edward in his tenurial manipulations and Richard in dealing with men he seriously mistrusted. Under Henry VII it became almost routine.

The king's drive to amass treasure can be seen in a similar light. Henry clearly agreed with Sir John Fortescue's dictum that kings, if they are to be powerful, must be wealthier than their subjects.[8] But suggestions of vulnerability seem misplaced given how little opposition such policies generated. Henry's bluff was never called, and he has accordingly acquired a reputation as a 'strong' king: the man who drew the teeth of the overmighty subjects whose ambitions had triggered the Wars of the Roses. This traditional reading of the situation is misleading. Henry succeeded because his leading subjects wanted him to succeed; he did not govern in despite of them.

The challenges to Henry VII make this clear. Unrest and rumours of unrest were persistent and unsettling; but overt opposition commanded little signifi-cant support within England. Bosworth, predictably enough, was followed by

[8] Fortescue, *Governance*, pp. 128–30.

trouble in the north, the Ricardian heartland, yet by 20 October Henry had abandoned plans to lead a force against the rebels, announcing that they 'have withdrawn themselves and be severally departed, sore abashed and rebuked'.[9] In the following spring a northern rising planned by Francis, Viscount Lovell, generated little local enthusiasm; while the attempt of his fellow conspirator, Humphrey Stafford of Grafton (Worcs), to raise support within the lands of the imprisoned earl of Warwick was an almost total failure.

Lovell's failure gave Henry only a brief breathing space. By the beginning of 1487, if not earlier, the king was aware of renewed conspiracy. This time his opponents had provided themselves with a figurehead: a young man called Lambert Simnel, who had been coached to impersonate the earl of Warwick. Henry promptly paraded the real earl through London, but this did nothing to halt the conspiracy. Most of those involved were again unreconciled Ricardians, like Lovell and Thomas Broughton of Furness (Lancs), but they were now joined by John, earl of Lincoln, the eldest of Richard III's de la Pole nephews. Lincoln had been received into favour after Bosworth, and Henry had trusted him sufficiently to put him in charge of the enquiry into Stafford's treason. His defection was thus a personal blow to Henry, but it made little practical difference to the rebels' strength. Such credibility as they enjoyed derived from foreign, rather than domestic, backing. Margaret of York, the dowager duchess of Burgundy, supplied financial support and 2,000 German mercenaries. Additional military help, and a jumping-off point for invasion, were provided by Gerald, earl of Kildare, who had decided that the restoration of the Yorkists offered the best chance of preserving his pre-eminence in Irish affairs.

Henry VII, by contrast, had been steadily extending his domestic support. From the outset of his reign he had sought to win over Richard's followers. On 11 October 1485 he had announced the availability of royal pardon to all the inhabitants of the northern counties who had fought against him at Bosworth, with just eight named exceptions.[10] Many former Ricardians, including the linchpin of the Middleham retinue, Sir John Conyers, were even welcomed into the royal household. As Richard's reign had demonstrated, such continuity could prove more apparent than real, but in this case it appears to have been genuine enough. When Henry confronted the rebels at Stoke, near Newark (Notts), on 16 June 1487, he did so with the military backing of several former Ricardians.

Stoke was a decisive victory for the king. Lincoln was killed and Lovell disappeared. Simnel fell into Henry's hands, and was found a menial place in the

---

[9] Hughes and Larkin (eds.) *Tudor royal proclamations*, I, p. 5.

[10] Hughes and Larkin (eds.), *Tudor royal proclamations*, I, pp. 3–4.

Plate 1   Nuremberg, St Lorenz, interior of the choir, showing *The Annunciation* by Veit Stoss and the sacrament house

Plate 2 Jan van Eyck, *The Virgin of Chancellor Rolin*, c. 1435

Plate 3 Jan and Hubert van Eyck, *The Adoration of the Lamb*, St Bavo's cathedral, Ghent, *c.* 1432

Plate 4 Rogier van der Weyden, *The Last Judgement*, Hôtel Dieu, Beaune, *c.* 1445

Plate 5 Masaccio, *The Tribute Money*, Brancacci chapel, S. Maria del Carmine, *c.* 1427

Plate 6   Gerolamo da Vicenza, *The Assumption and Coronation of the Virgin*, 1488

Plate 7   Donatello, *Feast of Herod*, bronze relief, baptistery, Siena cathedral

Plate 8   Dierec Bouts, *Portrait of a Man*, 1462

Plate 9   Pisanello, marriage medal of Lionello d'Este, 1444

Plate 10   Andrea Mantegna, *The Gonzaga Court*, Mantua palace, *Camera degli Sposi*, 1474

Plate 11   Donatello, equestrian statue of Gattamelata, Padua

Plate 12   Michelozzo di Bartolommeo, Palazzo Medici-Riccardi, Florence, begun 1444

Plate 13   Zano di Domenico, Jacopo del Sellaio and Biagi d'Antonio, *cassone* with a tournament Scene

Plate 14   *Studiolo* of Federigo da Montefeltro, Palazzo Ducale, Urbino

Plate 15   Antonio del Pollaiuolo, *Hercules and Antaeus*, bronze

Plate 16 Konrad Witz, *The Miraculous Draught of Fishes*

Plate 17 Veit Stoss, high altar, St Mary's church, Cracow, 1477–89

Plate 18   Giovanni Bellini, *The Virgin and Child with Saints and Angels*, S. Giobbe altarpiece

Plate 19   Circle of Piero della Francesca, *An Ideal Townscape*

Plate 20   Piero della Francesca, *The Baptism of Christ*

Plate 21 Donatello, *Lamentation over the Dead Christ*, bronze relief, S. Lorenz, Florence

Plate 22 Andrea Mantegna, *St James on his Way to Martyrdom*, for the cycle *The Life of St James the Great*, church of the Eremitani, Padua, now destroyed

Plate 23   Sandro Botticelli, *Primavera*

Plate 24   Gentile Bellini, *Sultan Mehemmed II*

royal household. The battle is traditionally seen as the last of the Wars of the Roses, but it did not mark the end of the challenges to Henry's regime. There may have been a Ricardian dimension to the northern rising of 1489 in which the earl of Northumberland was murdered, although the immediate cause of the unrest was opposition to royal taxation, and it had no political consequences beyond forcing Henry to find an alternative to the Percies in the north-east.

In 1491 a new pretender appeared in Ireland, this time claiming to be Richard, duke of York, the younger of the two sons of Edward IV. The claimant, Perkin Warbeck, seems to have received a cool response, and was soon looking elsewhere for backing. Over the next few years he was passed around the courts of Europe as a useful diplomatic weapon against England. His first patron, in 1492, was Charles VIII of France, at a time when Henry VII was preparing to send military aid to Brittany. On 3 November, however, the two kings agreed the Treaty of Etaples, which included a promise that neither would support the enemies of the other. Warbeck then moved to the Low Countries, where he received the enthusiastic backing of Margaret of York. He was also taken up by Maximilian, the heir of the Emperor Frederick III, and Maximilian's son, Philippe, the ruler of the Low Countries in right of his mother Mary, the only daughter of Duke Charles of Burgundy.

The extent of Warbeck's support within England is much less clear. Henry VII apparently believed that it was considerable, and 1494 brought a crop of executions and attainders for treasonable correspondence with the pretender. On the evidence of the attainders the conspiracy was within the Tudor establishment, rather than representing a flare up of Ricardian sympathies. Some of the accused were former Ricardians, but (like George Neville, who had supported Henry at Stoke) they had all transferred their service to the king. The loyalty of others to the Tudor dynasty went back to Bosworth, and the most eminent victim was the king's step-uncle William Stanley, whose intervention at Bosworth had given Henry his victory.

It is hard to know whether the attainders provide an accurate list of the disaffected, or are simply an index of Henry's anxieties. What is clear is that if there had indeed been support for Warbeck at this level, the king's actions destroyed it. When the pretender, with Burgundian backing, landed in Kent in July 1495 he received no local support and was forced to flee. Nor was his next invasion, from Scotland in September 1496, any more successful. It was important only because the levying of taxation early in 1497 to meet the costs of a planned invasion of Scotland triggered a major rebellion in the south-west. The Cornish rebels met no opposition on their march to London, until they were defeated at Blackheath by royal forces under Lord Daubeney.

The Cornish rising has generally been seen as the first of the popular risings which, in the following reigns, were to become an increasingly common way of expressing fiscal dissent. But it now seems that the rising commanded signifi-cant 'political' support throughout the south-west – or, at least, that Henry believed it did. As so often in this reign, there is a tension here between the apparent vulnerability of the regime, which could make rebellion seem viable, and the success with which Henry enforced punitive measures against those believed to have been involved.

In spite of the reassessment of the rising, it is difficult to see Blackheath, rather than Stoke, as the last battle of the Wars of the Roses. The rebels (conventionally) denied that they were criticising the king, far less aiming to remove him. The rising was independent of Warbeck's efforts, and when the pretender landed in the south-west in September 1497, to try to exploit the unrest, he again met no support, and this time was captured and imprisoned. In 1499 he was executed on a charge of conspiring to escape from the Tower of London in company with the earl of Warwick, who was executed for the same offence, his attempt to escape from royal custody being construed as treason.

The 'conspiracy' was almost certainly a contrivance to secure Warwick's death. Henry was negotiating a Spanish marriage for his heir, Arthur, and the survival of so dangerous a claimant to the throne was a stumbling block. But if Henry hoped that Warwick's death would end dynastic rivalry he was to be dis-appointed. The mantle of Yorkist claimant passed to Edmund de la Pole, who, with his younger brother, Richard, fled to Maximilian's court in the summer of 1501. Henry immediately began attempts to regain possession of Edmund, but was unsuccessful until 1506 when Maximilian's son, Philippe, was storm-driven on to the English coast and, in return for generous hospitality from Henry, was persuaded to hand over Edmund.

The convoluted history of opposition to Henry says rather more about the king's position on the international stage than about his domestic security. The willingness of European powers to back the pretenders is a sign that Henry's involvement in Europe was not only defensive. In the early years of his reign the king could not afford to take an independent stand, contenting himself with negotiating a series of short-term truces; but by 1488 he was beginning to pursue a more active policy.

Henry's activities initially centred on the fate of Brittany, where the death of Francis II in 1488 left the duchy in the hands of his daughter, Anne. In spite of the debt which he owed to Charles VIII for helping him to secure his throne, Henry pledged himself to protect the autonomy of Brittany against France, and in February 1489 Anne accepted that protection in the Treaty of Redon. Over the next year and a half Henry constructed a series of alliances for mutual security against France. In September 1490 he reached agreement with Maximilian and with Spain, the latter in the Treaty of Medina del Campo, which also paved the way for a marriage alliance between England and Spain.

Henry, an unknown, and probably underestimated, force in European affairs, had emerged as a shrewd and forceful diplomat. But this was not enough to halt French expansion into Brittany, and by the end of 1491 Charles had captured Rennes and married Anne of Brittany. It was at this point that Charles, faced by the threat of English military reprisals, began to support Warbeck – just as he had earlier tried to tie Richard III's hands by supporting Tudor. Henry was not distracted, but his efforts to rebuild English influence in Brittany foundered on lack of Breton enthusiasm, and by the end of 1493 the two powers had agreed the Treaty of Etaples.

The treaty was a triumph for Henry VII. As well as withdrawing his support from Warbeck, Charles agreed to pay the arrears of the pension due to the English crown under the 1475 Treaty of Picquigny (repudiated by Louis XI), and to repay the costs of England's involvement in Brittany. The favourable terms owed less to English military pressure, which was ineffectual, than to Charles's anxiety to settle affairs on his borders before launching an invasion of northern Italy. But this in itself was confirmation of Henry's ability to turn the European situation to his own advantage, something which was to characterise foreign affairs for the rest of the reign. England never really held the balance of power in western Europe, but Henry's skilful opportunism produced a very respectable appearance of its doing so.

In domestic affairs, too, Henry proved himself an extremely efficient ruler. His great strength was as a consolidator and formaliser of what, under the Yorkists, had tended to be fairly informal power structures. Henry evidently liked orderly administrative processes, and since these are more likely to generate surviving records than informal structures, he has in the past often been seen as an innovator. In fact he was not. Very little of what he did was new – and this is not a criticism. Contemporaries did not expect kings to be radical new brooms.

The clearest example is provided by chamber finance. The chamber's financial operations had collapsed in 1483. They did so again in 1485, and this time took rather longer to revive fully. But when Henry did turn his attention to the chamber his contribution was a more defined administrative structure. This is not to say that Henry relinquished direct control – on the contrary, he personally vetted all the accounts – but when he died in 1509 the chamber had sufficient institutional identity to survive him.

It would be wrong, however, to see Henry as a mere tidier-up of other people's bright ideas. Under his leadership the chamber spear-headed a drive to maximise royal revenue which, although based on Yorkist precedents, was far more effective than anything the Yorkists had managed. A major contribution was made by Henry's exploitation of his prerogative rights. It seems to have been Richard III who first appointed a local commission to pursue concealed royal rights, an *ad hoc* approach which Henry followed until the very end of his reign, when he appointed a surveyor of the king's prerogative. But the degree of formalisation is less important than Henry's unprecedented success in raising money from this source. That this was a personal, rather than a bureaucratic, achievement is emphasised by the fact that although his son, Henry VIII, kept the chamber organisation, he spent its reserves. Henry VII's skill as an administrator was a facet of personal monarchy, not a negation of it – and, as in any personal monarchy, his achievements were accordingly vulnerable to change.

Henry VII's preference for refining existing models is also apparent in the wider political arena. This is not the traditional interpretation of his reign. Many writers have argued that the king's response to more than a generation of civil war was to initiate a radical readjustment of the arena in which political life functioned, with the seat of power being shifted to the centre (to the court) and away from the localities. In practical terms this meant making more use of men whose power derived largely from the king himself: the lawyers and bureaucrats among the king's councillors, and the gentry of the royal household. At the same time the king aimed to limit the autonomous power of the nobility at the peripheries, while welcoming them as ornaments of his court.

This interpretation rests on an unrealistically sharp dichotomy between centre and periphery. But, more important, there is no evidence that the reign did bring a structural shift in the balance of power between the three main players in the political arena: the king, nobility and gentry. This is not to deny all change, merely to suggest that it was circumstantial rather than fundamental. The balance between the three powers was never static, and the changes within Henry's reign were well within the system's tolerance.

Henry was not waging a campaign to limit the local power of the nobility. The number of noblemen had been dwindling over the last decades, and Henry, like Edward IV, made most of his new creations at the lowest level of the peerage, creating barons rather than dukes and earls. But this probably reflects Henry's sense of what nobility properly entailed, rather than any desire to diminish the importance of the aristocracy. Henry, far from being the grey bureaucrat of popular imagination, had a highly developed respect for the aristocratic and chivalric virtues. In this context it is significant that he was never prepared to ennoble his financial adviser, Reynold Bray, although Bray's landed possessions could have sustained the elevation.

Henry continued to look to the nobility as his chief representatives in local affairs. None of them enjoyed the degree of power which Edward IV had entrusted to Gloucester, but this is an unfair comparison. Gloucester's power had been exceptional, and under Henry VII the local influence of men like

Thomas, earl of Derby, or Robert, Lord Willoughby de Broke, was analogous to that enjoyed by other noble associates of Edward IV. Henry may have been less willing to allow his nobles a free hand, but he made no sustained attempt to undermine their authority as the natural leaders of local society.

In any late medieval reign the household was the natural complement of the nobility, rather than a substitute for it. Both acted as a bridge between the king and the localities; where they differed was in the type of task which could appropriately be asked of them. It was the gentry of the household, rather than the nobility, who were responsible for the minutiae of royal government at a local level. This state of affairs did not change under Henry VII. The household did not eclipse the nobility. Nor was there any adjustment in the balance of power between the household's central role (its attendance upon the person of the king) and its role in local affairs. Henry's creation, in *c.* 1495, of an inner privy chamber distinct from the chamber, and staffed by socially less eminent figures, says something about the king's more reclusive style of monarchy. Unlike Edward IV, Henry seems to have disliked being accessible to the wider political community. But the reform should not be taken as a deliberate attempt to play down the importance of the local landed interests represented in the household by the upper levels of the chamber.

If Henry VII's reign brought no radical departures it was because it did not need to. Contrary to what historians once assumed, Henry was not struggling with the problem of rebuilding royal power after its usurpation by overmighty subjects. The unrest of the previous decades had made the political community more, not less, willing to endorse royal authority. But, equally, this did not mean that Henry had carte-blanche to indulge in autocratic centralisation. Medieval government did not work like that. A successful king, and Henry VII was certainly that, was one who could persuade his subjects to lend a hand when needed, and that demanded the recognition of independent local influence. Henry may have been more inclined than his immediate predecessors to rely on sticks rather than carrots in that process of persuasion, but that does not constitute a shift in the balance of power. In this, as in other things, Henry VII was adjusting means, not redefining ends.

CHAPTER 22(a)

IRELAND

Art Cosgrove

RICHARD II was unusual, indeed unique, among medieval English monarchs in making two visits to Ireland in the course of his reign. Within Ireland, the results of royal intervention were disappointing. Before the end of 1399 the acting chief governor of Ireland reported to the English administration that the 'Irish enemies' were 'strong and arrogant and of great power', that they were aided in their assaults on the king's loyal subjects by 'English rebels' with the result that 'the law cannot be executed and no officer dares to attempt to execute it'; for there were no soldiers and no resources to pay soldiers to protect the king's subjects against these attacks.[1]

Ultimately, the king's expeditions achieved little, but Richard II had at least attempted to go beyond the normal objective of military containment and to formulate proposals for a more lasting political settlement. He could not but be aware of the ethnic division within Ireland which, as we have seen, could lead the administration in Dublin to categorise even its foes on the basis of their real or supposed descent as 'English rebels' (opponents of English stock) or 'Irish enemies' (hostile Gaelic Irish). This cleavage between the posterity of the settlers of the twelfth and thirteenth centuries and the progeny of the older indigenous population, between, as the Irish annalists put it, the foreigners (*Gaill*) and the natives (*Gaedhil*) had been accorded statutory recognition in the legislation passed by the Irish parliament at Kilkenny in 1366. The Statute of Kilkenny, having noted in its preamble that the abandonment of English social, legal and cultural mores could lead to political disaffection, sought to protect the colonial population (the English-Irish or Anglo-Irish)[2] from further contamination through the adoption of customs and habits taken from the 'Irish enemies' (the Gaelic Irish). Hence it insisted that the colonial population should use English language and law, dress in English clothing and ride

---

[1] *Roll of the proceedings . . . King's Council*, pp. 261–9.
[2] Cosgrove (1990), pp. 104–6; Frame (1993), pp. 83–104.

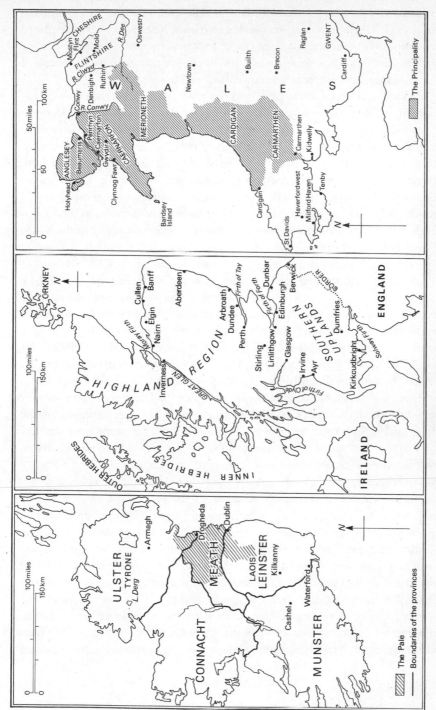

Map 10 The Celtic world

Wales map (right panel):

CHESHIRE
Mostyn
Flint
Mold
Oswestry
FLINTSHIRE
R.Clwyd
R.Dee
Ruthin
Denbigh
Conwy
R.Conwy
Newtown
Builth
Brecon
Raglan
GWENT
Cardiff
WALES
Penrhyn
Caernarfon
CAERNARFON
MERIONETH
CARDIGAN
CARMARTHEN
Carmarthen
Kidwelly
Beaumaris
Gwydir
Holyhead
ANGLESEY
Clynnog Fawr
Haverfordwest
Tenby
Bardsey
Island
Cardigan
Milford Haven
St Davids
N

100 km
50 miles
50

The Principality

Scotland map (centre panel):

ORKNEY
N
OUTER HEBRIDES
INNER HEBRIDES
HIGHLAND REGION
GREAT GLEN
Moray Firth
Inverness
Nairn
Elgin
Cullen
Banff
Aberdeen
Arbroath
Dundee
Perth
Firth of Tay
Stirling
Linlithgow
Firth of Forth
Edinburgh
Dunbar
Berwick
BORDER
Glasgow
Firth of Clyde
Irvine
Ayr
SOUTHERN UPLANDS
Dumfries
Solway Firth
Kirkcudbright
IRELAND
ENGLAND

100 miles
150 km

Ireland map (left panel):

ULSTER
Armagh
TYRONE
L. Derg
CONNACHT
Drogheda
MEATH
Dublin
LEINSTER
LAOIS
Kilkenny
Waterford
Cashel
MUNSTER
N

100 miles
150 km

The Pale
Boundaries of the provinces

horses after the English fashion, with saddle and stirrups. To prevent the erosion of 'Englishness' among the Anglo-Irish severe limitations were placed on contacts between them and the Gaelic Irish and, in particular, intermarriage between the two ethnic groups was formally prohibited, an unusual example of a ban on marriage between two avowedly Christian groups.

Richard II seems to have envisaged the reversal of this policy of segregation. In the submissions made to the king in 1395 many Gaelic lords undertook to attend the king's council or parliament when summoned to do so, an indication that Richard II wished, by introducing the Gaelic aristocracy to institutions from which they had hitherto been precluded, to comprehend both ethnic groups within the lordship's governmental framework. It had always been open to individual Gaelic Irish to secure charters of denization which would allow them to have the same legal status and entitlements as the Anglo-Irish. In 1395 Richard II was poised to extend equality of status to the whole Gaelic Irish community or, at least, to those who wished to have it, thus giving substance to an ordinance of 1331 which had proclaimed such an extension of English law[3] and making loyalty, rather than ethnic origin, the yardstick by which a subject's fidelity could be measured. Opposition from within both groups frustrated the king's plans to make equality of treatment the basis of an enduring settlement, and the re-enactment of the Statute of Kilkenny in 1402 marked the triumph of older official policies. Not until the reign of Henry VIII would another serious effort be made to bring the leaders of Gaelic Ireland within the ambit of English governmental structures.

There is little doubt that the colonial settlement had declined in size, security and revenue since its peak in the thirteenth century. Inflated estimates of the Irish lordship's former profitability fuelled Richard II's ambition to extend royal authority over the whole island so that it might again become a source of revenue for the crown. After 1399 it became even clearer that Irish revenues were totally insufficient to mount any campaign to extend the colonial settlement; indeed, they were hardly adequate to the task of preserving it. Any advance in Ireland must therefore be financed from England, where there was a general reluctance to sanction large-scale expenditure on Ireland. The Commons in the English parliament of 1406 complained, with some justification, that the money spent on war in Ireland had brought little improvement in the situation. It was their view that in Ireland, as in other disturbed areas, such as the Welsh borders, defence needs should be met by local magnates and local resources.[4] The reopening of the French war in 1415 reinforced Ireland's low position on the scale of English priorities, a point tellingly illustrated in financial terms by the sums allocated to various areas in 1421 when Calais received

---

[3] Murphy (1967), pp. 116–38.   [4] *Rotuli parliamentorum*, III, p. 573, no. 33; p. 577, no. 40; p. 610, no. 17.

£19,100, the defence of the Scottish borders £9,500 and Ireland a mere £1,666.[5] The complaints about lack of resources and dire predictions of the consequences which emanated from Ireland lost force through repetition and may simply have confirmed the English administration's assessment of the intractability of the problems of the lordship. Certainly there was no support for the view advanced by the earl of Ormond in the 1430s that, if what was spent on one or two years' warfare in France was applied to Ireland, a conquest of the whole country could be made.[6] Naturally preoccupied with the Anglo-French conflict, the government regarded Ireland as an undoubtedly subordinate theatre of war which offered little prospect of profit or glory.

In keeping with the view that Irish problems should be the responsibility of Irish resources, the English government enforced Absentee Acts which required those holding lands in Ireland either to reside there and defend them or to provide for their protection. Lower down the social scale, depopulation in England caused by successive outbreaks of plague had combined with disturbed conditions within Ireland to encourage emigration from the lordship to avail of the beckoning opportunities across the Irish Sea. In 1394 Richard II ordered back to Ireland all Irish-born residents in England reflecting the opinion advanced by one chronicler that 'such a great number of Irish had come to England to earn money that that region was devoid of men and women. The result was that the pure Irish, the enemies of the English-Irish, devastated the part of the island which obeyed the English king without resistance.'[7] That the order was enforced is clear from the fact that over 500 Irish-born residents paid fines to the crown for the right to remain in England. In September 1413 the desire to replenish the colonial population and to secure quiet and peace within the realm of England resulted in a proclamation that all Irish-born residents, with some specified exceptions, were to return home by Christmas Day 1413.[8] Similar repatriation orders were issued in 1431, 1432 and 1439, and these were paralleled within Ireland by statutes which attempted to curb emigration without licence from the administration in Dublin. The comment of Archbishop John Swayne of Armagh in 1428 – 'there is mo gone out of the lande of the kyngis lege pepyll than be in'[9] – would suggest that neither set of measures was effective in bolstering the colonial population, and schemes for recolonisation briefly espoused under Richard II were not to be considered again until the sixteenth century.

For those charged with the responsibility of governing Ireland lack of financial rather than human resources was normally a more pressing problem, either because of the inadequacy of their stipend or their inability to gain payment of

---

[5] Wylie and Waugh (1929), III, pp. 274–5.   [6] *Libelle*, p. 39.   [7] *Ypodigma*, p. 367.   [8] *Statutes of the realm*, II, p. 173.   [9] *Reg. Swayne*, p. 108.

it. Rule of Ireland was usually entrusted to the king's lieutenant with power to serve the office by deputy and, more often than not, it was the deputy who actually presided over the administration in Dublin.[10] In cases of emergency where the lieutenancy or deputyship was vacated by the death or departure of the holder, or where the appointment lapsed owing to the death of the king, a temporary chief governor, termed 'justiciar', was appointed to head the administration until new arrangements were made. In the second half of the fourteenth century lieutenants had been granted at least £6,000–£7,000 per annum from England. By 1408 the annual grant had been scaled down to 7,000 marks (£4,666), and on Henry V's accession the allotment to the Irish lieutenant, now Sir John Stanley, was further reduced to 4,000 marks (£2,666) for the first year and 3,000 marks (£2,000) per annum thereafter. All subsequent appointees to the lieutenancy under the Lancastrian kings were granted similar sums, and by 1453 these figures seemed to be established as the fixed rate for the job. However, if the lieutenant was an absentee, even the payment of his full salary might bring little financial benefit to the lordship since neither deputy lieutenants nor justiciars had direct access to such revenues. Deputies tended to make their own financial arrangements with lieutenants, but the indications are that they were expected to defray most of their expenses from local resources. Justiciars traditionally received a salary of £500 per annum and, on occasion, were also provided with a small defence force of twelve men-at-arms and sixty archers, but both the salary and the cost of the force had to be derived from Irish revenues. On many occasions, therefore, effective defence of the colonial settlement depended upon the chief governor's ability to tap local resources.[11]

In the first half of the fifteenth century there were ten appointees to the Irish lieutenancy. Nine of these were English men varying in rank from the king's son, Thomas of Lancaster, duke of Clarence, to knights like Sir John Stanley or Sir John Grey. The exception was the Anglo-Irish magnate, James Butler, fourth earl of Ormond. His first appointment in February 1420 was motivated, in part at least, by the belief that he could exploit local resources more effectively and thus decrease dependence upon the English exchequer. In contrast to his English predecessors, Sir John Stanley and John Talbot, Lord Furnival, who had left behind many unpaid debts, Ormond gave a firm undertaking to the Irish parliament in 1421 that he would make due payment for anything he required. Indeed, he went further and pledged the rents from certain of his lands as satisfaction for any debts outstanding at the end of his term of office. The same parliament formally thanked the lieutenant because 'he abolished a bad, most heinous and unbearable custom called coigne',[12] a reference

---

[10] Moody *et al.* (1984), pp. 475–7.   [11] Matthew (1984), pp. 97–115.
[12] *Statutes and ordinances*, p. 573.

to the forced billeting of troops upon the countryside, a practice to which previous chief governors had resorted because of the inadequacy of their financial support. Ormond's renunciation of this method of supporting an army was clearly welcomed by the Anglo-Irish community, but it did not lead to the abolition of 'coyne' or 'coyne and livery' which persisted into the sixteenth century, when it was aptly described as 'takeing horsse meate and mannes meate of the kinges poore subgettes by compulsion, for nought, withoute any peny paying therefor'.[13]

Ormond also differed from English lieutenants in his relationship with the Gaelic Irish, particularly with the learned classes who enjoyed a quasi-clerical status and immunity in Gaelic society. Stanley's blatant disregard of this status in his attacks upon the bards in 1414 resulted ultimately in his own death, in the view of one annalist. For the master-poets reacted to his onslaught with such powerfully venomous verses that he died within five weeks of their composition. Talbot, his successor, continued the assaults upon the poetic order, perhaps in an attempt to demonstrate by his own survival the inefficacy of such poetic tirades. Against Ormond, however, no such charges were made. As a member of a long-established Anglo-Irish aristocratic family, his attitudes towards Gaelic culture and society were markedly different. His father's skill in the Irish language had enabled him to act as an interpreter between Richard II and Gaelic Irish leaders in 1395. Ormond employed a Gaelic legal expert (*brehon*) in his own territories and was himself a recipient of laudatory verses from a Gaelic poet. His enemies even charged him with having Gaelic Irishmen illegally elected to parliament as knights of the shire.[14]

Smaller than its English counterpart, the Irish parliament also differed in its composition since it included among its elected representatives proctors from the diocesan clergy who, in England, were now comprised within the provincial convocations of Canterbury and York. As the main forum for the expression of opinion by the Anglo-Irish community, it often petitioned the English crown for greater royal intervention in Ireland with predictions of dire consequences if such was not forthcoming.[15] The parliament contained no representatives of the Gaelic Irish community with the exception of occasional Gaelic Irish bishops who could attend by reason of their office. Hence the charge of illegality against Ormond, itself an outcome of the long-running feud between the earl and John Talbot.

Shortly after Talbot's arrival in Ireland in 1414 a quarrel broke out between himself and Ormond, which was to continue for almost thirty years and led to the disruptive growth of two factions within the colony. The divisions caused by the dispute within the administration and the community as a whole

[13] *State papers . . . Henry VIII*, II, p. 12.   [14] Simms (1989a), pp. 177–97.
[15] Cosgrove (1983), pp. 34–6.

contributed to the decline of the colonial settlement, a decline now frequently delineated in territorial terms. In the 1420s Archbishop Swayne of Armagh maintained that the territory under the effective control of the Dublin administration amounted to little more than one shire. The author of the gloomy report to the king in 1435 reckoned that within the four counties of Dublin, Meath, Louth and Kildare there was only an area thirty miles in length and twenty miles in breadth where it was safe to go in response to royal instructions; and the same point was made in a more succinct way by the *Libelle of Englyshe polycye* when it claimed that

> oure grounde there is a lytell cornere
> To all Yrelande in treue comparisone.[16]

The concept of a geographically defined limitation on English authority, an 'English Pale', had already emerged, though the earliest official use of the term occurs only in 1495 when the Irish parliament ordered 'diches to be made about the Inglishe pale'.[17]

The contrast between the Pale and the rest of the country should not be overemphasised. There remained many areas of English language and loyalty outside the Pale. Almost all the major towns fall into this category, but most had now to rely on their own resources to provide for their defence as the administration in Dublin could not assist them. For example, travel between Waterford and Dublin had become so hazardous that the mayor of Waterford was exempted from the requirement to take the oath of loyalty to the crown at Dublin, and in 1448 the administration formally acknowledged Waterford's military isolation by authorising the city to organise its own defence forces. By permitting these to march against any rebels 'with standards displayed', the government in Dublin was effectively licensing private warfare by the city against its enemies.[18] In other parts of the country, too, the growing influence of Gaelic customs and traditions could be resisted. A recent study of the Kilkenny/Tipperary region has distinguished between areas which were conquered but not colonised and those districts which had been densely settled. In the former, 'Gaelicisation' proceeded apace either through the recovery of lands by indigenous families or the adoption of a Gaelic way of life by a thinly spread settler group. In the latter, however, there was strong and successful resistance by the settler community to the threats to their lands and their traditions, and they continued to resolve their disputes not by *brehon* or Gaelic Irish law but by reference to the hundred or manor courts.[19] Beyond the Pale the colonial settlement had certainly fragmented but it had not disappeared. Hopes for its revival still centred on intervention by the English king. If he could not

---

[16] *Reg Swayne*, p. 108; Betham (1830), p. 361; *Libelle*, p. 37, lines 726–7.
[17] Conway (1932), pp. 127, 215.   [18] Lydon (1979), pp. 5–15.   [19] Empey (1988), pp. 457–62.

come himself, then he should send some great lord from England. The appointment of Richard, duke of York, as lieutenant in 1447 seemed an answer to that plea, and the extent of the welcome he received when he came to Ireland in 1449 was a measure of the optimism that he might restore the fortunes of the colony after the decline of the previous half-century.

York was an obvious potential focus of the opposition to Suffolk, Henry VI's chief counsellor, and it is not surprising that contemporary chroniclers interpreted his nomination to the Irish lieutenancy as banishment or exile, 'on the malicious advice of the duke of Suffolk'.[20] It was not, however, until July 1449 that York came to Ireland. The initial submission of many Gaelic Irish leaders so impressed one of York's followers that he expressed the view in the autumn of 1449 that 'with the myght of Jesus ere twelvemonth come to an end the wildest Yrishman in Yrland shall be swore English'.[21] By the following spring the renewal of hostilities by Gaelic Irish lords combined with the delays in paying York's stipulated salary to dissipate such euphoria. In June 1450, in a letter to his brother-in-law, the earl of Salisbury, York stressed his dire need of ready cash. If he did not receive his promised salary, then he would be unable to retain Ireland in the royal obedience and would be forced to return home; for he would not have it said that Ireland had been lost through his negligence. The latter protestation is an indication of York's concern that he should not be held responsible for surrendering territory in Ireland at a time when Henry VI's government faced mounting criticism because of its abandonment of former English possessions in France. Suffolk paid the supreme penalty for failure when he was murdered on his way into exile in April 1450, and the government's continuing unpopularity was underlined by the rebellion of Jack Cade in the summer of that year. One of the rebels' demands was that York should be recalled from Ireland, and there were even rumours that York would replace Henry VI on the English throne. There is no evidence to link York directly with the Cade rising, but it was inevitable that he should be suspected of some involvement with it. The rebellion was speedily quelled and Cade himself killed, but knowledge that accusations of treason were being made against him may have been one of the factors that determined York to leave an unpromising situation in Ireland towards the end of August 1450.

York's sojourn in Ireland had brought little benefit to the colonial settlement; but it did consolidate a link between Anglo-Ireland and the Yorkist cause which was to last for over forty years and exercise a sporadic but occasionally crucial influence on the course of relations between England and Ireland. One link that did not survive was that between York and the earls of Ormond. Shortly before his departure from Ireland, York reached an agreement with the

<hr/>

[20] Johnson (1988), p. 70; 'Benet's chronicle', p. 195.   [21] Curtis (1932), p. 168.

earl of Ormond whereby the latter pledged himself to York's service in return for an annual payment of 100 marks. And it was Ormond whom York chose to act as deputy lieutenant during his absence from Ireland. The death of Ormond in August 1452 not only removed a dominant figure from the Irish political scene but also conferred the title on his absentee son, James Butler. He had married Eleanor Beaufort, daughter of York's leading opponent, the duke of Somerset, and had been raised to the ranks of the English nobility by his creation as earl of Wiltshire in 1449. Unlike his father, the new earl of Ormond and Wiltshire was firmly attached to the faction which supported the king, the Lancastrians, and the deepening divisions between them and Yorkist supporters was reflected in Ireland in the appointment of Ormond to replace York as lieutenant in the spring of 1453. York disputed Ormond's appointment and in February 1454 the confusion caused was such that it was decided that the sums of money assigned to Ireland should be paid to the treasurer of England until it had been legally determined 'who is and ought to be lieutenant'. In the following April, York, now protector of England during the king's insanity, was able to have the dispute resolved in his favour.[22]

The deteriorating situation in England, which saw the antagonism between Lancastrian and Yorkist factions erupt into open warfare at the battle of St Albans in May 1455, allowed York little opportunity to intervene in Ireland, despite pleas to do so. When York did return to Ireland he came, not as a saviour, but as a refugee from military and political defeat in England in the autumn of 1459. His eldest son, Edward, earl of March, and his chief supporter, the earl of Warwick, may also have intended to come to Ireland but eventually ended up in Calais.[23] Thus in 1459–60 while Henry VI retained control in England, both 'English Pales' – in Ireland and France – were in the hands of his opponents.

In November 1459 the English parliament attainted York of treason and all his offices, including the lieutenancy of Ireland, were stripped from him. But the Irish parliament summoned by York to Drogheda in February 1460 confirmed York's tenure of the lieutenancy and made it a treasonable offence for anyone to challenge his authority. The parliament then proceeded to a definition of its own powers. It was claimed that Ireland was and always had been a distinct entity and that it was not bound by laws made in England unless they were accepted by parliament in Ireland. Further it was asserted as a consequence of the fact that Ireland was 'corporate of itself' (*corporate de luy mesme*) that no one could be summoned to answer charges outside Ireland unless such a summons was made in proper form, namely under the great seal of Ireland.[24]

---

[22] Wood (1928), pp. 156–7.   [23] Johnson (1988), p. 195.

[24] *Statute rolls of . . . Henry the sixth*, pp. 644–6.

At one level these measures can be seen simply as legal devices to safeguard York's position inside Ireland. The claim that Ireland was bound only by the laws accepted by its own parliament meant that the English legislation convicting York of treason could be considered inapplicable in Ireland. The concurrent enactment invalidating all writs summoning people to answer charges outside Ireland unless they were endorsed by the Dublin administration legalised York's own refusal to obey such a writ ordering his arrest. The measures gave a legal veneer to clearly treasonable behaviour while stopping short of openly rejecting the crown's authority over Ireland.

Yet the legislation also reflected a body of opinion within Anglo-Ireland which sought greater autonomy for the colonial settlement. A subsequent act of the same parliament establishing a distinct Irish coinage reinforced the point. The justification for the measure was that the land of Ireland, though it was under the obedience of the realm of England, was separated from that realm and from all its statutes, except those that were freely accepted by Irish parliamentary assemblies.[25] More generally the enactments can be seen as the outcome of the growing consciousness among the Anglo-Irish of the distinctiveness of their own traditions and institutions and of the difference between themselves, 'English by blood', and those born in England, 'English by birth'. For those Anglo-Irish going to England the difference was underlined by sporadic repatriation orders, restrictions on the right of entry to the universities and the Inns of Court and, most tellingly, by the formal classification of the Irish-born as foreigners in 1440 to bring them within the scope of the poll tax imposed on aliens. The protests from the Dublin administration, ultimately successful, against this categorisation included the plaintive request that the colonial population in Ireland should have 'suche fredomes . . . lyke unto English men borne within his said noble roaume'.[26]

Nevertheless, the immediate beneficiary of the legislation was the duke of York, whose position within Ireland was secure enough to allow Warwick to visit him there in the spring of 1460 to concert plans for the overthrow of Henry VI. The government in England seems to have attempted to counteract York's influence by enlisting Gaelic Irish aid. Parliamentary measures against four men, accused of having brought letters from England inciting the Gaelic Irish to rise against York, tend to confirm the veracity of a charge made in a Yorkist propaganda manifesto that Henry VI had been persuaded 'to wryte letters under his privy seale unto his Yrisshe enemyes, which never kyng of England did heretofore, whereby they may have comfort to entre in to the conquest of the sayd londe'.[27]

[25] *Statute rolls of . . . Henry the sixth*, pp. 664–5.
[26] National Library of Ireland (Dublin), MS 4 (Harris Collectanea), p. 337b.
[27] *English chronicle*, p. 87.

If true, the accusation suggests that Henry VI's government, in the peculiar circumstances obtaining in 1460, was prepared to sacrifice control of Ireland in order to retain its grip on England. However, York's position was never seriously threatened in the period prior to his departure to England in the autumn of 1460. There the situation had been radically altered in his favour by Warwick's successful invasion from Calais and his defeat of the Lancastrian army on 10 July at the battle of Northampton. In October a compromise was reached whereby Henry VI was to retain the throne for his life but was to be succeeded by York and his heirs. This unsatisfactory settlement pleased neither side, hostilities were resumed and York himself was killed in battle at Wakefield in December 1460. But the Yorkist cause did not die with him, and victory at the battle of Towton in the following March ensured the succession to the throne of York's eldest son as Edward IV.

The victory of Edward IV ended the possibility of a continuing confrontation between a Lancastrian England and a predominantly Yorkist Anglo–Ireland. Yet the events of 1460 had clearly demonstrated how Ireland could be used as a base from which a defeated English faction could launch a counter-offensive. The lesson was not lost on recalcitrant supporters of the Lancastrian cause.

One of the casualties of the Yorkist triumph was the earl of Ormond and Wiltshire, executed after the battle of Towton. His brothers, Sir John, the claimant to the earldom, and Thomas Butler, were both convicted of treason in November 1461 and thus forfeited all their lands, including their large Irish possessions, to the crown. Sir John Butler's invasion of Ireland in 1462 was an attempt both to regain his own inheritance and to mount an effective Lancastrian challenge to Edward IV himself. The administration in Dublin had insufficient resources to counter the threat and it was Thomas Fitzgerald, soon to be seventh earl of Desmond, who inflicted a decisive defeat on Butler forces at the battle of Piltown, near Carrick-on-Suir. His reward was appointment as deputy lieutenant of Ireland in the spring of 1463.

Of the three great comital families in late medieval Ireland, Kildare, Ormond and Desmond, the Fitzgeralds of Desmond were most closely linked with the Gaelic Irish. Almost a century had elapsed since an earl of Desmond had occupied the office of chief governor, and the selection of the seventh earl was a new and, to some at least, hazardous departure. Desmond's capacity to quell a potentially dangerous Lancastrian resurgence in Ireland relieved Edward IV of the trouble and expense involved in personal intervention, but there were obvious risks in entrusting the rule of Ireland to one who had such close connections with the Gaelic Irish. In a personal letter to the earl at the time of his appointment the king warned him that he must govern Ireland in accordance with its traditional laws and statutes and specifically enjoined him to stamp out 'that dampnable and unlawful extortion and oppression . . . called coyne and liverie'.[28] At the same time Edward IV also wrote to other members of the Irish council urging them to control any possible waywardness on Desmond's part.

Opposition to Desmond's rule soon surfaced within the Pale. There were accusations that he had extorted coyne and livery in County Meath, and that he was under the influence of rebels and traitors, and clashes between his followers and those of the English-born bishop of Meath, William Sherwood, resulted in nine deaths. Desmond survived a summons to England in the summer of 1464 and retained the deputyship, but a change of chief governor, mooted in 1465, was finally implemented in 1467 with the appointment as deputy of John Tiptoft, earl of Worcester, one of the king's most trusted agents. Within four months of his arrival in Ireland, Worcester had a bill passed through the Irish parliament charging Desmond, Kildare and Edward Plunkett, a member of a prominent Meath family, with treason. When Desmond came to Drogheda to answer the accusation, he was arrested, kept in custody over the week-end and on Monday, 15 February, summarily beheaded.

The main consequence of the execution was the complete alienation of the Desmond family from the administration in Dublin. Sixteen years after the event, Richard III attempted to regain the loyalty of the executed earl's son, James, the eighth earl, by admitting that the death of his father had been a mistake. Appealing to James to let bygones be bygones, he urged him to abandon Gaelic Irish ways and to renew his allegiance to the crown; he even sent him items of English apparel which would enable him to dress in the English fashion and abandon the wearing of Gaelic Irish clothing. There is little evidence that the appeal had any effect. As late as 1533 the earl of Ossory could remark that the earls of Desmond 'have suche a cankerid malicious rebellion rotid in theym, evyr sithens the putting to execucion of oon Thomas, erle of Desmond at Droghedaa, that they ben asferr seperated from the knowlege of any duetie of alegeaunce . . . as a Turke is to beleve in Christ'.[29]

One of the factors in the downfall of the seventh earl of Desmond was his relationship with the Gaelic Irish, the 'Irish enemies' in a rigorous interpretation of the official government policy of segregation laid down in 1366. An unflattering stereotype of the Gaelic Irish already existed in England, drawn mainly from the twelfth-century writings of Gerald of Wales. His works remained popular throughout the Middle Ages and were often drawn upon by other writers thus giving wider currency to a depiction of the Gaelic Irish as lazy, backward, irreligious, immoral and barbarous.[30] Outside observers also

[28] Public Record Office (London), E28/89 (30 March, 3 Edward IV).
[29] *State Papers . . . Henry VIII*, II, pp. 229–30.   [30] Gillingham (1987), pp. 16–22.

distinguished between the two ethnic groups within Ireland. In the country, according to one chronicler, there were

two races speaking two languages; the one speak bastard English and dwell in the good towns, cities, castles and fortresses of the country and in the seaports ...; the other are a wild people who speak a strange language ... and dwell always in the woods and on the mountains of the country, and have many chiefs among themselves of whom the most powerful go barefoot and without breeches and ride horses without saddles.[31]

The term 'wild Irish' (*sylvestres Hibernici*) was increasingly used from the late fourteenth century onwards to describe the Gaelic population and distinguish them from the Anglo-Irish. In London in 1401 an Augustinian friar from Ireland suffered temporary imprisonment on the charge that he was 'un wilde Irisshman', and in 1422 it was claimed that many crimes in Oxford and the surrounding counties were committed by students from Ireland 'of whom some were lieges of the king, but others were enemies to him and his kingdom called wylde Irishmen'.

Geographically and culturally Gaelic Ireland certainly lay outside the mainstream of western Europe, the edge of the known world until the discoveries of Columbus. It had little to attract visitors from outside – with the exception of the famous pilgrimage centre in Donegal, the Purgatory of St Patrick. Those who entered the cave or pit on an island in the middle of Lough Derg were supposed to be able to get in touch with the dead. The Catalonian knight, Ramon de Perellós, made the long journey from Avignon to Ireland in the autumn of 1397 in hope of discovering the fate in the next world of his recently deceased king, Joan I of Aragon. On his way back from St Patrick's Purgatory, where he claimed he had succeeded in contacting King Joan, Perellós spent Christmas with the leading Gaelic Irish lord in Ulster, Niall O'Neill. Many of the customs and practices he encountered struck him as strange. He noted the predominantly pastoral nature of Gaelic Irish society in the north with its concentration on cattle as a source of wealth and the tendency of those looking after the herds to move with them from one pasture to another. Milk and butter figured prominently in the general diet of the people with beef as a food for special occasions, and at Christmas O'Neill gave alms to the poor in the form of ox-meat. Dress, too, attracted Perellós's attention. Cloaks or Irish mantles were worn by men and women from all classes of society. The great lords favoured a hooded version covering a tunic cut very low at the neck; they wore neither breeches nor sandals and put their spurs upon their bare heels when riding in the usual Irish fashion, mounted upon a cushion rather than a saddle. The Catalonian knight clearly found Gaelic Irish society very different from that to which he was accustomed. Yet he also

---

[31] *Chronique de la traison et mort*, pp. 28, 171.

recounted how in conversation with Niall O'Neill (in Latin, through an interpreter), 'it appeared to me from his words that they consider their own customs to be better than ours and more advantageous than any others in the whole world'.[32]

The distinctive character of Gaelic Irish society was obvious and the division between Gaelic and Anglo-Irish, *Gaedhil* and *Gaill*, was an enduring feature throughout the later Middle Ages. Mutual antagonisms persisted, well illustrated by two coincidental events in 1421. One of the petitions to the king from the Irish parliament of that year was that he should request the pope to launch a crusade against the Gaelic Irish on the grounds that their leaders had broken the oaths of allegiance given to Richard II and had not paid to the Papacy the money pledged as a penalty for default.[33] Around the same time the Gaelic Irish archbishop of Cashel, Richard O'Hedian, was charged by one of his own suffragans that he 'made very much of the Irish, that he loved none of the English nation, and that he bestowed no benefice upon any English man, and that he counselled other bishops not to give the least benefice to any of them'.[34]

The latter incident is an illustration of the effects of ethnic rivalries upon the Church. Within the archdiocese of Armagh the division between the two 'nations' was formally recognised in the later Middle Ages by the partition of the diocese into a northern section among the Gaelic Irish (*inter Hibernicos*), and a southern part lying within the Pale among the Anglo-Irish (*inter Anglicos*). Houses among a number of religious orders were segregated along ethnic lines, in accordance with one of the provisions of the 1366 Statute of Kilkenny. That same statute's ban on marriage between the two 'nations' could not always be enforced but that opposition to intermarriage was not confined to the legislators is made clear by the record of a marriage case in the Armagh ecclesiastical court in 1448. Mabina Huns sought a nullification of her marriage to John Brogeam on the grounds that John, at the time of his contract with Mabina, was already validly married to a Gaelic Irish woman called Katherine. In evidence it was stated that John, an Anglo-Irishman, had married Katherine in a clandestine ceremony in 1436. Many of his friends were displeased by the marriage since they believed that it was not fitting that 'the son of a good father should take as his wife such a Gaelic Irish woman (*talem Hibernicam*)'. Some persisted in their efforts to rescue John from what they clearly regarded as a most unsuitable match. After nine years they succeeded and went on to arrange a marriage between John and Mabina, which was celebrated in the parish church

[32] Carpenter (1988), p. 111.
[33] *Statute rolls ... of Henry the sixth*, pp. 564–7. The petitioners were echoing a similar request made ninety years earlier in 1331. See Watt (1956), pp. 14, 20.
[34] Henry of Marlborough, *Chronicle* (1809 edn), p. 30.

of Stackallen in County Meath, and witnesses claimed that Katherine was still
alive at the time of the second match.[35]

Yet the rivalries and antagonisms between the two groups should not be
overstressed. The very fact of proximity made compromise and some assimilation inevitable. A revealing injunction was laid down by the parliament of 1447
to cope with the problem that similarity in dress between Gaelic and Anglo-
Irish on the Pale borders made identification difficult. Any man who wished to
be accounted of English descent was to shave his upper lip at least once every
two weeks so that he would not have a moustache. Those who failed to comply
with the order were liable to be treated as 'Irish enemies'. In 1463 a petition
from four Munster towns to remove the legal barriers to trade with the Gaelic
Irish claimed that 'the profit of every market, city and town in this land
depends principally on the resort of Irish people bringing their merchandise to
the said cities and towns'. And a recent study of trade in Ireland has concluded
that while the island may have been composed of two 'nations' in the political
sense, economically it was one.[36] The ecclesiastical diocese and province of
Armagh were divided but the archbishops could and did rise above ethnic rivalries and achieve 'a remarkable *modus vivendi* between the *ecclesia inter Anglicos* and
the *ecclesia inter Hibernicos*'.[37] Repeated bans on the reception of Gaelic Irish into
Dublin and the wearing of Gaelic Irish dress within the city show that not even
the capital of the Anglo-Irish colony was immune from Gaelic influence. The
relationships between the two groups were much too complex to allow them to
be reduced to a simple formula of consistent antipathy and estrangement.

The most striking feature of Ireland outside the Pale and the English towns
was its political fragmentation. Its extent may have been exaggerated by the
writer of a report on the state of Ireland *c.* 1515 which claimed that Ireland was
divided into ninety separate 'countries', fifty-eight ruled by Gaelic Irish lords,
thirty-two by leaders of English descent. Nevertheless, the exercise of power
was localised and a number of lords conducted their affairs with only sporadic
reference to the administration in Dublin. Alliances were formed and hostilities undertaken on the basis of local advantage rather than ethnic origin. In the
north, the persistent struggle for control of Ulster between the O'Neills of
Tyrone and the O'Donnells involved occasional incursions of Scottish troops
from the western isles, and the northern part of the Pale usually had to pay a
substantial 'black rent' or bribe to the O'Neills to prevent attacks by them. In
the west, branches of the O'Connors vied for supremacy with the Gaelicised
Burkes (formerly de Burghs) of north and south Connacht. The domination of

---

[35] Public Record Office of Northern Ireland (Belfast), Reg. Prene, fol. 54r–v; Trinity College, Dublin,
MS 557, vol. V, pp. 213–15.

[36] *Statute rolls . . . of Edward the fourth*, pp. 139–41; O'Neill (1987), p. 130.   [37] Watt (1989), p. 54.

the south-west by the earldom of Desmond was occasionally challenged by the McCarthys and O'Briens, and the Ormond lordship, straddling the border between Munster and Leinster, was weakened by the absenteeism of the earl between 1452 and 1461, the forfeiture of the earldom after Edward IV's victory at Towton and, to a lesser extent, by the continuing non-residence of the earls after the restoration of the title in 1477. The claim to the kingship of Leinster had been revived by the McMurroughs, and other families like the O'Connors of Offaly or the O'Mores of Laois were also powerful enough to extract black rents from the Pale as the price of their non-aggression.

A chief governor from England who wished to enforce royal authority beyond the Pale could do so only with the support of a substantial and expensive military force. An Anglo-Irish magnate, on the other hand, could use local resources and familiarity with the complex politics of the area to exercise a far greater influence at much less cost to the crown. It is not surprising, therefore, that in the half-century after 1470 Englishmen occupied the office of chief governor for only five years and that for most of the other forty-five the administration in Dublin was headed by the earls of Kildare, natural leaders of the Anglo-Irish community in the absence of the earls of Ormond and the alienation of the earls of Desmond.

In 1478 Gearóid Mór Fitzgerald succeeded his father as eighth earl of Kildare and chief governor of Ireland. Having successfully resisted the challenge of a rival appointee, he was confirmed in office as deputy lieutenant by Edward IV in 1479 and was to remain as the king's chief representative in Ireland for all but four of the remaining thirty-four years of his life. Combining the delegated royal authority with his own widespread contacts and influence in Gaelic Ireland, Kildare achieved an unparalleled political dominance within the country, one previously approached only by the fourth earl of Ormond. In part his ascendancy depended upon the willingness of Edward IV and Richard III to allow him a good deal of latitude within Ireland. The new Tudor king, Henry VII, seemed equally willing to continue him in office, but the accession of a king of Lancastrian descent evoked a recrudescence of the Yorkist sympathies so apparent in 1460 among the Anglo-Irish aristocracy. When the Yorkist pretender, Lambert Simnel, arrived in Ireland in 1487 he was welcomed as Edward, earl of Warwick, the legitimate Yorkist aspirant to the throne, crowned king as Edward VI in Christ Church Cathedral, Dublin and formally recognised as such by a parliamentary assembly summoned by Kildare. And the earl's brother, Thomas Fitzgerald, was among those who perished in the vain attempt to place Simnel on the English throne at the battle of Stoke in June 1487.

Though Kildare had prudently remained at home in the summer of 1487, his lack of direct involvement in the military struggle could not detract from his openly treasonable behaviour towards Henry VII. Yet, such was the weakness of the Tudor king's position that he could not afford to confront him, and it was only in June 1488 that a special royal commissioner, Sir Richard Edgecombe, was despatched to Ireland to obtain firm guarantees of future loyalty from the Anglo-Irish lords. In line with the bonds and recognisances which Henry VII had extracted from members of the English aristocracy, Edgecombe demanded that Kildare and the other Anglo-Irish leaders take an oath of loyalty to Henry VII with the attached stipulation that failure to observe it would result in the automatic forfeiture of their lands to the crown. In defiantly rejecting this demand, Kildare and his followers stated that, rather than accept such an oath, 'they wuld become Irish every of them'.[38] The threat to 'go native', effectively to follow the example of the earls of Desmond, may have been a hollow one, but Edgecombe could not ignore it. In the end he had to be content with simple oaths of loyalty sworn on a consecrated host.

It was the arrival in Ireland in 1491 of a second Yorkist pretender, Perkin Warbeck, which finally spurred Henry VII to more decisive action. Kildare was not directly linked to the conspiracy to replace Henry VII with the supposed younger son of Edward IV, but his failure to act against those who were involved led to his dismissal from office in June 1492. And in the autumn of 1494 the king finally assigned the rule of Ireland to one of his own most trusted servants, Sir Edward Poynings.

Poynings spent just over a year in Ireland as deputy lieutenant. At the outset a quarrel between himself and the earl of Kildare led to the latter's arrest and subsequent imprisonment in London on a charge of treason. In the summer of 1495 his army forced the departure from Ireland of Perkin Warbeck who had reappeared to lay siege to Waterford. In the interim Poynings held a parliament which significantly strengthened royal control over the Irish administration. Specifically rejected was the assertion made in 1460 that residents in Ireland could not be summoned out of the country by writs issued in England. All royal commandments from England were to be obeyed, notwithstanding any pretended privilege claimed in 1460. In the act, which became known sub-sequently as Poynings' Law, it was laid down that in future no parliament was to be held in Ireland without the king's explicit permission, and any legislation to be enacted must first be inspected and approved by the king and council in England. The basic objective of the act was to ensure that no Irish parliament could pass measures which were contrary to the interests of the English king as had happened in 1487 when parliamentary recognition was accorded to Lambert Simnel as King Edward VI.

Poynings had succeeded in dissipating the Yorkist threat from Ireland, but at

---

[38] Harris, 'The voyage of Sir Richard Edgecombe', I, p. 65.

a cost which was not covered by the increased revenues generated from within Ireland. The maintenance of an English chief governor and army in Ireland was still a temporary expedient rather than consistent policy. In 1496 the charge of treason against Kildare was dropped and he was restored to office. Loyalty to the Yorkist cause had ceased to be a factor in Anglo-Irish relations. Kildare and Anglo-Ireland had accepted that the Tudor dynasty had come to stay.

For the rest of Henry VII's reign Kildare remained as chief governor of Ireland, and if the policy of delegating royal authority to a great Anglo-Irish magnate had its dangers, it also allowed postponement of any serious consideration of alternative methods of governing the lordship.

CHAPTER 22(b)

SCOTLAND: 1406–1513

Jenny Wormald

FIFTEENTH-century Scotland was a very violent society.[1] It was also a very fragmented one. Neither of these things make it particularly unusual. External threats and internal rivalries bedevilled fifteenth-century European monarchs, papal and secular; and the Scottish Highland–Lowland divide, much exaggerated in any case by the rival schools of tartan romanticists and searchers for excessive disorder, did not notably differentiate Scotland from the France of the independent lordships and great appanages or the Empire of multifarious German principalities. Nevertheless, a period which begins in 1406 with the death of a lamentable king, Robert III, and ends in 1513 with the death of one of the most outstandingly successful ones, the 'glore of princelie governyng',[2] James IV, does mark Scotland out. For the end of every reign, whether it had been a failure or a success, produced the same outcome: another collapse of royal authority, another dismal decline into faction-ridden minority. Whether at the hands of their subjects, a faulty cannon or the English, the early deaths of the Stewart kings, their consistent inability to survive to see their sons grow up, created a problem which could not be put down to the instability caused by competing claimants – from rival popes to rival kings for the thrones of France, England or Castile – or by power-hungry princes and magnates. It marked a visible and enduring flaw in the senior line of the royal house of Stewart itself.

If one problem about fifteenth-century Scotland, was the recurrent minorities which were unparalleled in any European kingdom, another, which has perplexed historians of late as well as early medieval Scotland, is its paucity of literary remains. One only has to contrast Scotland with Ireland to see in stark

---

[1] Of recent years, studies of fifteenth-century Scotland have greatly changed. Thanks to work in many areas of research, the old two-dimensional view of endemic power struggles and uncontrolled discord has gone, to be replaced by new questioning from which Scotland no longer emerges as a smaller-scale version of England, but as a society with its own distinctive features.

[2] Lindsay, 'Testament of the Papyngo', p. 71, line 504.

terms the difference; even the Welsh in the early period outdid the Scots. The poverty of institutional records, compared to the increasingly lavish out-pouring of French and English clerks, is a rather different issue, relating more specifically to the way in which government was expected to work. But the comparatively small corpus of literary works poses a very perplexing problem. As fifteenth-century Scotland was manifestly not a backward and unsuccessful society, there has been a tendency among historians and literary scholars to concentrate on highlighting what there was, rather than asking why there was not more; and anyone ruminating on its poets from James I to Robert Henryson and William Dunbar, or its chroniclers like Andrew of Wyntoun and the great Walter Bower, may wonder about the idea of paucity. Yet after Bower completed his work in the late 1440s, there was nothing but the most patchy of chronicles until the writing of narrative history was taken up again in the second decade of the sixteenth century. Moreover, in seeking to understand the *mentalité* of fifteenth-century Scotland, historians have naturally empha sised the nationalism of Wyntoun and Bower, and their late fourteenth-century predecessor, Fordun, chroniclers who extolled the courage and valour of the Scots who fought off the threat from their imperialist and mighty neigh-bour, and the great epic poets, Barbour, writing in the 1370s, and Blind Hary, a century later. And to that apparently determined literary Scottishness can be added the work of William Elphinstone, late fifteenth-century bishop of Aberdeen, and one of the most inspiring and charismatic of them all, who, replacing the Sarum Use with a new Scottish liturgy, and reviving the cult of Scottish saints, raised the number in the calendar from a mere handful to over seventy. At first sight, it appears impressive. But what does it actually amount to?

Surely we are faced here with a very curious phenomenon: the kingdom of Scotland failed profoundly to create a corpus of material which would dis-tinguish and enhance the nation. From the end of the thirteenth century, the Wars of Independence offered wonderful material for patriotic writing – and inspiring employment for the inhabitants of monastic scriptoria. Yet no monastery ever built up a tradition of chronicle writing. Melrose and Holyrood had produced one each before the fourteenth century, but neither was specif-ically a history of Scotland. We are then faced with the puzzle that success against the English, which was certainly a matter for pride, was not a matter for literary record until the 1370s and the writing of the first of the two great epics, Barbour's *Brus*, and the 1380s when John of Fordun, having gone on an extended tour of Britain to find material for his history, established the myth that the wicked Edward I had removed all Scottish chronicle evidence. Edward I was no doubt guilty of a great deal, but not of this particular crime. It was the Scots who were silent about Scottish history.

It is just possible that in the early and mid-fifteenth century, Andrew of Wyntoun, prior of Lochleven, and Walter Bower, abbot of Inchcolm, may have intended to establish a tradition of the writing of national history, building on the work of Barbour; their work, however, was not followed up. There was an abridged version of the *Scotichronicon*, the *Liber Pluscardensis* written in the 1460s, whose name associates it with the abbey of Pluscarden, but which was more probably produced at Dunfermline. And in the 1470s, the second great epic of the Wars of Independence, the *Wallace*, was produced by Blind Hary. In their own right, these works are impressive. Barbour's famous lines, beginning 'A! Fredome is a noble thing', ring down to us. Fordun and Wyntoun had a clear sense of their mission to show Scotland's importance as a free kingdom in the wider context of the history of Christendom. Bower's memorable colophon 'Non Scotus est Christe cui liber non placet iste' certainly gives point to the idea of national history.[3] And Hary's *Wallace*, less historical, more mythical than the other works, still extols and raises to a new level of heroic legend one of the great heroes of the Wars of Independence. But can one create, out of five authors spread over a century, a 'Scottish' interest in nationhood and national identity?

The problem is only compounded when one considers the patronage of these works; for one certainly cannot identify royal interest. Barbour did receive a pension in 1378 from Robert II, grandson of the great Robert Brus, which may have been for the writing of the *Brus*. Robert, first of the Stewart kings and one of the most dismal of the line, undoubtedly needed all the help he could get; but that was a personal interest. And the patrons of Wyntoun, Bower and Hary were not kings at all, but members of the lesser nobility: Sir John Wemyss of Kincaldrum, Sir David Stewart of Rosyth and, in the case of Hary, Sir William Wallace of Craigie and Sir James Liddale of Halkerston. In the later fifteenth century, when evidence for the copying of manuscripts begins to pile up, we find a Fifeshire vicar commissioning the *Brus*, and a group of lairds and clerics buying their *Scotichronicon*. James III, on the other hand, possessed a splendid copy of Vergil, and commissioned the *Travels of Sir John Mandeville*. We do not know if he read his Vergil; but he evidently preferred the racy light relief of the *Travels* to the glories of Scotland's history. As the first king since Alexander III in the thirteenth century to pursue a policy of firm peace with England, Scottish heroes in the fight against the long-standing enemy and tales of the wicked Edward I were perhaps not entirely to his taste. Nevertheless, it is a little surprising that the hard-won independence and achievements of his kingdom were apparently of so little interest to him, or to his less Anglophile ancestors and successor.

---

[3] Barbour, *Brus*, II, p. 9, line 225; *Scotichronicon*, VIII, p. 340.

The patronage and purchase of the 'nationalist' works therefore show a few writers satisfying some of the members of the lower nobility. But the problem does not end there. Barbour may, at least in part, have been writing to shore up the faltering beginnings of Stewart rule, just as Blind Hary may have composed his work to remind the pro-English James III that England was indeed the enemy. And if Bower is best remembered for extolling his nation's history, he was in fact as interested in the failures as in the successes of the nation's kings. It is therefore possible to see in the patriotic works a concern not so much for national achievement as for kingship. This prompts the conclusion that a distinctly curious feature of Scottish society was its casual and confident sense of its success, a sense which required no fuss and panoply, but was, apparently, taken for granted. It also suggests another line of enquiry. Switching the focus from 'nationhood' to 'kingship' brings us to that focal point of Scottish society, the monarchy. And here, lack of propaganda and image making becomes a very specific issue.

What is striking about the fifteenth-century kings is their almost consistent failure to indulge in any sort of ideological underpinning. They did nothing to encourage a concept of national identity, and certainly nothing to link such a concept to themselves. Nor did they attempt to bind their subjects to a monarchy which was either ancient or divinely ordained. They did nothing for their sacerdotal image: there was no Scottish 'Royal Touch'. Nor did they invoke ancient ancestry. In the late sixteenth century, George Buchanan boasted with pride that the two oldest monarchies in Europe were those of Denmark and Scotland, but it was not a theme whose value was recognised by the Stewart kings. Barbour apparently composed an ancestry for them, the *Stewartis Orygenale*, a work now lost, and curious in that it traced them back to the Trojans, when every self-respecting Scotsman knew that his origins lay in ancient Greece and Egypt, the Greeks being the conquerors of the Trojans who had ultimately found their way to England. The problems which beset the Stewart kings might well have encouraged them to underwrite their kingship with stirring and prestigious myth. Instead, they emphasised the fact that their origins were all too recent, and anything but heroic. As one Jacobus Seneschallus (James Stewart) succeeded another, so the reality was restated: that the origins of the royal house of Stewart lay in a family who had been household stewards, initially to the counts of Dol in Brittany. To this day the prince of Wales numbers among his titles 'Steward of Scotland', a reminder of the propaganda his ancestors did use; the stewards of the household had become stewards of the kingdom. But even that was casual and sporadic; and it had nothing to do with an ideology of kingship which stressed either antiquity or divinity.

These are not the only examples of the perplexing indifference of the

monarchy to the propagandist techniques of more mighty kings. The 'nationalist' writers, with their emphasis on kingship, take us into the field of *specula
principis*. Here again, the crown held itself aloof. That may appear to be understandable; do kings want to be lectured? Yet the normal answer seems to be yes,
if only for the propaganda value of appearing to aspire to an ideal. Thus the
late medieval kings of Scotland stand in marked contrast to their English
counterparts, every one of whom, from Edward III to Edward IV, received at
least one book of advice to princes. In Scotland, such works were certainly in
circulation. But although James I had some fairly lofty things to say about the
impartial justice he would offer, as a cloak for the ruthless establishment of his
authority after eighteen years' imprisonment in England, and for the equally
ruthless acquisition of his subjects' lands, it was not he who encouraged Bower
to write about the just king, even though Bower was prepared to praise his rule.
Gilbert Hay's mid-fifteenth-century *Buke of the governance of princes*, a translation
of the pseudo-Aristotelian *Secretum secretorum*, was written for William Sinclair,
earl of Orkney. The highly critical *Thre prestis of Peblis* and *Lancelot of the laik* –
both written in the mid-fifteenth century – were not 'royal' works. Nor were
Robert Henryson's *Morall fabillis*, with their comments on kingship. Despite the
reference to 'My soverane Lord, sen thou hes gevin me leif' in the anonymous
poem *The harp*, which was attached to *Liber Pluscardensis*, the most recent discussion rejects the idea that it was in fact a work commissioned by James II.
And Book VII of John Ireland's *Meroure of wyssdome*, described as 'the closest
approximation to a true *speculum*', being written for James IV, has been shown
to borrow so massively from Gerson as to 'erode somewhat its evidential value
. . . for the indigenous history of political ideas in late medieval Scotland',
important though it was.[4] Once again, the monarchy emerges as unusual; not
until James VI wrote *Basilikon doron* for his son Henry did it come into line.
Meanwhile other, lesser patrons did their best to show their kings how to rule
wisely. There is no evidence that their kings paid much attention.

Strenuous efforts have been made to show that, even if they were not concerned with *specula principis* as such, there was at least a flourishing and vibrant
court culture. Indeed there was – for some of the time. But it is very difficult to
show the crown as a literary patron, certainly before 1488; and in any case there
was, for long periods, no court, during the years of absentee or minority kingship. When adult kings ruled, they did indeed put up a reasonable show. A
major criticism of James I, for example, was that taxation raised for his English
ransom went instead on luxuries for the court. In 1448, Jacques de Lalain and
two companions came to Scotland from that model of court life, Burgundy, to
fight against Sir James Douglas and two other Scottish knights in a tourney in

---

[4] *Liber Pluscardensis*, I, p. 382; Mapstone (1991), pp. 413–14; Mason (1987a), p. 135; Burns (1990), p. 170.

the presence of James II, who knighted them, and presided with pomp and ceremony, even if the actual fighting degenerated into an unchivalric brawl. We know less about James III, since the old legend of his cultural and artistic tastes, exemplified by his 'low-born favourites', was laid convincingly to rest;[5] even that architectural glory, the Great Hall of Stirling, was not his work, but that of his son James IV, who followed up the legacy of his great-grand-father and grandfather at Linlithgow and Falklands by building at both Stirling and Holyrood. But James III was no exception to another Stewart enthusiasm: guns, that supreme status symbol which had proved fatal to James II at the siege of Roxburgh in 1460. And to that interest, James IV added another, ships. He spent vast sums on a navy which was not to be used for the benefit of the Scottish crown, being sent to France in 1513. The greatest ship, the *Great Michael*, was a source of immense pride to its builder, and the envy of his brother of England, Henry VIII, whose *Henri Grace à Dieu* was constructed to the same scale.

Their courts were naturally a centre for scholars and writers. They were not devoid of literature; indeed, James I himself was almost certainly a poet, author of the *Kingis quair*. But only James IV clearly emerges as the king who most visibly sought to rival his fellow monarchs in the range of his patronage and court display. His marriage to Margaret Tudor in 1503 was made the occasion for all the splendour of a royal entry into the capital, thus enabling the Scottish ruler belatedly to catch up with a fashion already familiar in western Europe, adopted in France and England, for example, by the end of the fourteenth century. And it was in James's reign that 'court poetry' at last clearly emerges, notably in the person of the brilliant William Dunbar. Accident and good luck that may have been; but as with his ships, so with his poetry in this period did the Scottish king and his court outshine England, provoking the embittered and savage anti-Scottish satire of that failed court poet, John Skelton. Before that, we catch only glimpses of the cultural life of the court. And in terms of what kings themselves encouraged, the prevailing impression is of an interest in the symbols of power.

In any event, the obvious criteria for successful kingdoms, a strong monarchy – even if personified by some less than strong monarchs – presiding over a people encouraged by royal propaganda, outside threat, or both, to identify with the nation's divinely ordained king, do not readily apply to Scotland. Of course no country in fifteenth-century Europe achieved the ideal. The point about the Scots, and particularly the Scottish kings, is how little they tried. It was not that the Scots did not take immense pride in themselves; 'fier comme un écossais' was a phrase bandied about by the early sixteenth century. But the

[5] Macdougall, in Brown (1977), pp. 17–32; Macdougall (1982), esp. ch. 12.

source of that pride was astonishingly prosaic and low-key, significantly lacking any firm ideological concept or base. When pushed, they could produce one. The Scottish origin myth erupted into full-grown form, without any obvious earlier development, under pressure from Edward I; it was simply lifted, when needed, from the Irish *Lebor Gabal Erenn*, and given enchanting pictorial representation a century and a half later in the delightful illustration in a Fordun manuscript of the 1440s, showing Scota and Gathelos sailing to Scotland, wearing highly fashionable Burgundian hats. The claim that Scotland was an independent kingdom, free from English overlordship, produced one of the most moving of all medieval conceptions of the community of the realm, the *Declaration of Arbroath* in 1320. But these were the crisis moments. In general, both the crown and the 'nation' had remarkably little to say about themselves; and even opponents of kings were amazingly casual about self-justification, in each case to a degree which, when compared with England, France, Aragon or Castile, raises perplexing questions about fifteenth-century Scotland, and at the same time offers a clue to understanding.

Inevitably, historians of Scotland have tried to demonstrate the success of the kingdom in terms of contemporary experience. That has involved straining to extract 'modern' fashion out of very limited evidence. A better starting-point is a much earlier model, the relationship between centre and periphery in early medieval England. Subjects, as James VI and I was later to remind his exasperated and faithful English Commons, were bound by love to support their monarch. In the seventh century, that meant that they fed him. In the 'centre', the area of the normal royal circuit, they did this by hospitality; they killed the necessary cow, and gave the king dinner. In the periphery, the same rule operated, but the king was much less often seen. And in the outlying areas, the subjected kingdoms, they sent the cow to the king. Thus those at the centre actually met the king, great lord and great patron; the dinner was the chance to advise, to bargain and seek reward. Those in the periphery had much less opportunity, but were correspondingly less burdened. And in the outlying areas, grudging acquiescence at best, resentment at worst, were what accompanied the cow which the king took from them; but refusal might bring the king in person – and then not as patron, but in force.[6]

It may seem a little odd to invoke an early medieval model for late medieval Scotland. But to what was becoming an increasingly exceptional degree, effective Scottish kingship was still peripatetic kingship. Every part of that three-tier model does have its parallel in Scotland, with the Highlands and borders representing not only the geographically far-flung, but also the least politically integrated areas of the kingdom, where royal control might indeed

---

[6] Charles-Edwards, in Basset (1989), pp. 28–33.

mean kings arriving with armies at their backs, as James I did, provocatively, against Alexander Macdonald, lord of the Isles, in 1428, and James IV in a series of expeditions to the western seaboard in the 1490s, in the course of which the lordship itself – sub-kingdom or semi-independent Celtic province, like late medieval Brittany – was suppressed. Such actions did not resolve the 'Highland problem'. To a very real extent, an overactive crown began to create the 'Highland problem' which was to be fully in evidence by the end of the sixteenth century. It started with intermittent military attacks on the structure of Highland society, and went on to attempt to transfer power from the Macdonalds to the rising families of Campbell and Gordon; it established lieutenancies, held by the earls of Argyll in the west and Huntly in the north-east, these increasingly powerful magnates who crossed the boundaries of Highland and Lowland and might therefore bring the Highlands under closer royal control. But even by 1513, despite Fordun's famous division of Scotland into two peoples, the wild (Highland) and domesticated (Lowland) Scots, and anti-Gaelic jokes, notably by Richard Holland in the mid-fifteenth century *Buke of the Howlat*, and then Dunbar in the *Flyting of Dunbar and Kennedy*, the differences and antagonism between Highland and Lowland society were by no means as clear-cut as they were later to become. The justice of the feud, for example, was not a barbaric survival among the Gaelic clans, but a workable and effective Scottish system, based as much on obligations of Lowland kinship and lordship as Highland; and the language of that justice drew on both Celtic and English terms. 'Assythment', the word for compensation given in settlement of feud, is middle English, but 'slains', used to describe the letter given by the aggrieved party acknowledging the assythment, is Celtic *slainte*, a legal guarantee or indemnification. Similar duality occurs in the language and procedures of the courts. And that perfectly well-known Scots word 'tocher' (dowry) was the Gaelic word used in the Middle Ages to translate *maritagium*. James IV himself, according to the Spanish ambassador Pedro d'Ayala, spoke at least some Gaelic, although we do not know whether this meant more than a few basic phrases. And his lieutenant, Archibald earl of Argyll, and his son Colin, were patrons of Gaelic literature, and may have had bardic training. This is a century before James VI, in his desire to show the English how congenial the Scots were, came to see Highland society *per se* as a distinct and unwanted embarrassment; even then, not all his contemporaries agreed with him, and historians should be wary of taking his word for it as a general comment on Highland/Lowland relations. The real point, in the fifteenth century, was an expansionist crown bent on extending its control, and using the ancient language of the sword, sometimes wielded personally by the king, and sometimes through royal commissions; for the Scottish crown invoked language as violent as the most violent of its feuding subjects, and issued letters of fire and sword.

Less dramatically, the justice of the eyre, last attempted in England in the 1330s, continued in Scotland in the fifteenth century and throughout the sixteenth as well; and the really successful eyres were those 'driven', in the periphery as well as the remotest areas, by kings. That is a clue to the respective fates of the static James III (1460–88) and the peripatetic James IV (1488–1513). The attempt of the first to remain in Edinburgh and run government from there was a significant reason for his failure. The second travelled his kingdom regularly and restlessly, dragging councillors and justices after him; and there is no doubt of the popularity and success of this energetic and charismatic man. Both kings died violent deaths. James III was killed in battle against rebellious subjects. James IV made the one serious mistake of his life when in 1513 he offered battle to the English; for English armies defeated Scottish ones, except on the one occasion when it really mattered, Bannockburn in 1314, and wise kings usually found other ways of dealing with English imperialists than by fighting them. Yet when this king was hacked down in the rain and mud of Flodden in 1513, he was at the head of an army generally agreed to be unusually large, and drawn from all parts of his kingdom: a testimony – if ultimately a tragic one – to the success of his kingship.

By that time, Edinburgh was the undisputed capital of Scotland. This trite and obvious statement, in terms of London or Paris, or that most spectacularly successful of all medieval centres of centralising power, Rome, becomes neither trite nor obvious in the context of Scotland. Despite the fact that it was undoubtedly the largest town in late medieval Scotland, Edinburgh achieved its position as capital remarkably late. James I, in the thirteen years of his personal rule (1424–37), preferred Perth; all but two of his parliaments and general councils were held there, the exceptions being one at Stirling, the other in Edinburgh. The fact that he was murdered there may have created a certain disenchantment in the mind of his successor; even so, James II's parliaments were divided between Edinburgh (thirteen), Stirling (nine) and Perth itself (six). Only in the reign of James III did Edinburgh become for the first time the undoubted seat of the king's government; and although James IV did not reverse the process as far as parliament and the supreme civil court, the Session, were concerned (though the court had been peripatetic for the first half-century after it came into being in 1425), he took personal royal government and criminal justice back into the localities. That is one reason why the early medieval model works for a society flourishing 800 years later. It has nothing to do with being socially or culturally backward. Rather, it is because the most effective of its kings saw a value in thinking of the 'centre' in terms of the royal circuit, in their efforts to impose their rule. In Scotland, there had simply not yet developed, to anything like the extent it had done in England, the separation of the person of the king and the king's government, so that the institutions of government and justice – the exchequer, for example, which remained an event held wherever convenient – were far less tied to the 'capital', whether the king was there or not. It was a style of kingship which worked – in this kingdom.

It was not, however, a style which has made it easy for historians. Scholars infinitely prefer monarchs like Henry VII, who kept and signed their account books, to casual kings like James III, who died leaving an unquantified 'treasure' stuffed into black boxes, one of which he was careless enough to take on to the battlefield at Sauchieburn, where it was picked up by his victorious opponents who promptly went off to look for more. There is no evidence about how he amassed it, or how much he amassed. But there is surely here another echo from the past. Otto I has been described as doing 'as much justice as he dared, but it was never cheap'; thus when those in the north heard in 952 that he was returning from Italy, everyone settled with his adversary as soon as possible, so that he would find nothing to judge.[7] In fifteenth-century Scotland, the justice of the feud survived because of its effectiveness in containing violence in the localities, and because the crown, recognising its value, co-operated with the kin and the lord who enforced settlements and compensations by giving remissions where the injured party pronounced itself satisfied. But to leave it there understates the strenuously interventionist power of the Stewart kings. For fifteenth-century Scotsmen could not, like tenth-century Saxons, settle to avoid the king's justice; they settled – and paid the king. This gives point to the terse little entry in the exchequer rolls for 1435 which records payment for six pounds of wax for sealing remissions – remissions in the reign of James I, that king whose propaganda about impartial justice was believed by later historians to equal reality. In 1473–4, the crown got almost £13,000 for remissions, prompting the question whether it was from this kind of source that James got his treasure, and suggesting why his parliaments were so particularly critical of his sale of remissions, collected by the king who did little else to fulfil his judicial role. Undoubtedly it was a profitable business; compositions – including remissions – brought James IV £29,000 in 1507 and £31,000 in 1511. Royal justice was not the justice that is blind or anything like it. It was personal, often violent, and regularly profitable. Small wonder, then, that contemporary writers, like Bower and the author of *The Harp*, howled for impartial justice. Small wonder that kings on the make did not commission their works.

The subject of the Scottish feud has, however, a wider aspect. The crown did not simply reinforce the justice of the feud and extract its cut. It was also the regular instigator of the great political feuds: James I against his Stewart

[7] Leyser (1979), p. 35.

relatives; James II and the Black Douglases; James III and a good number of the political nation, at one time or another; James IV and the lord of the Isles, and, intermittently, the earl of Angus. And as well as these conflicts, there was also the crown against a series of lesser men, the Erskine claimants to the earldom of Mar in the reigns of James I and II, the Crichtons and the Gordons with their claim to the earldom of Moray in the early 1450s. The Stewart kings were supreme manipulators of the balance of power in the state, creating as well as resolving conflict.

Two ultimately got it badly wrong. James I destroyed his chances of playing off the two sides of the great Stewart kin-group, the descendants of the two marriages of Robert II, when he brought down his closest relatives, Albany Stewarts, in 1425. When he went on to threaten the other side, notably in rendering its head, the aged Walter, earl of Atholl, insecure in his own possessions, he sealed his fate; in 1437 he was the victim of a *coup d'état* in which Atholl made common cause with partisans of the Albany Stewarts, clearly intending to seize power for himself, at least as lieutenant for the six-year-old James II. The inefficiency of the conspirators was astonishing. They murdered James I before bothering to secure the person of James II; and they failed to kill the queen, the redoubtable Joan Beaufort, who escaped 'yn hir kirtell', to exact terrible revenge.[8] James III consistently attacked and undermined powerful men without ensuring the counterbalancing support of others. His arbitrary dismissal of his long-serving chancellor, Colin, earl of Argyll, in February 1488, was the catalyst for the successful coalition which fought and killed him at Sauchieburn in June. They did not repeat the mistake of Atholl and his associaties; this time the heir to the throne was in the hands of the king's opponents, and at the nominal head of their army.

Yet these kings had had a long run of arbitrary rule before they were finally brought down, challenged because of their immense strength, not because of weakness. The challenge was political, violent and personal. The Stewart dynasty as such was not threatened. Nor was any real effort made to justify these events. James I was apparently described as a tyrant at the moment of his squalid death in a privy; James III's opponents felt obliged to fight when the king broke his agreement with them, and the new regime of James IV managed to put together a little propaganda about the dead king threatening to bring in the English. But it was pathetic stuff compared to the 'vox populi, vox Dei', which thundered out in justification for what happened to Edward II of England, or the rationale later surrounding the usurpation of Henry IV. Only with the deposition of Mary in 1567 did the Scots produce a political theory to reinforce their action, and then only because they had to justify it to an out-

8 Brown (1992).

sider. They never saw the need, as the English did, to explain to themselves the resolution of that most complex of political problems, rule which had become unacceptable. In its abnormal moments, just as in its normal ones, Scottish political reactions were simpler, more uncluttered and direct.

The same was true the other way round. James II's destruction of the mighty family of Douglas, whose estates and titles sprawled across Scotland, from the south-west to the north-east, was violent and bloody. He personally killed the eighth earl, William, and defeated his heir, James, in battle; and he did so with comparative ease, because he understood the nature of political faction, the way to appeal to those for whom Douglas power was a frustration or a threat. It was no accident that at the murder in Stirling castle in February 1452, those with the king, taking part in the killing, were a group of southern lairds who had every reason to resent the total domination of the Douglases in that part of the country. Nor is it surprising that the lavish royal patronage of the parliament of 1452 – some of it later withdrawn – persuaded men that a king determined on destruction was a better bet for their support than the object of his vengeance, so that the Douglases were left without allies when the final trial of strength came in 1455, at the battle of Arkinholm. In the law of the political jungle of fifteenth-century Scotland, the Scottish Lion – true to his heraldic device – reigned supreme.

Indeed, the nature of Scottish political society highlights sharply an issue obscured by more 'developed' societies: that in the end, successful rule is a political and not a constitutional matter. By comparison with their French and English counterparts (though not, for example, with Scandinavian or German ones), Scottish institutions of government can be, and have often been, regarded as 'weak' and 'backward'. But that moves the debate from the politically effective to the constitutionally and bureaucratically advanced. Even James I showed a certain caution in his demands for parliamentary taxation. It was a Scottish parliament in 1455 which told an acquisitive king, flush with the material benefits of the fall of the Douglases, that certain named lands, lordships and castles must be annexed to the crown, and never alienated by it. In 1473, another parliament bluntly told another king, James III, that he should forget his ideas of gaining glory by foreign military adventuring, but stay at home and win fame by the justice he offered his subjects; they failed on the second point, but won the first. And James IV's evident desire, after 1495, to do without parliament as far as possible is hardly testimony to its political weakness. Nor can it be claimed that the council, increasingly professionalised in the reigns of James III and IV, lacked political energy and will. These bodies sought to restrain their kings, and sometimes succeeded. Crucially, what they did not do was to hedge Scottish kings and Scottish government about with constitutional constraints.

In a very real sense, therefore, there were no formal limitations on royal power in Scotland. The only one which was utterly unchallengeable was death. Perhaps, therefore, the sombre power of the picture of the death of a Scottish king in James IV's *Book of Hours* is a very appropriate image, not in the sense in which older Scottish historians might have used it, to symbolise the weakness of the crown against that outworn concept, overmighty magnates, but as the one thing which actually did curtail the power of a Scottish king. And death came, violently and early, to all the fifteenth-century Scottish kings. There was political irony as well as political consequences in this. For an instinct for survival in a small kingdom, potentially and sometimes actually under threat from its more powerful neighbour, had led the Scots to state, at a very early stage, the concept that the king never died. It was there in the twelfth century, as the monarchy struggled out of the past of the tanist (the selected and named successor to the king) into the future of primogeniture. Doubts over the succession and the huge fright of the Wars of Independence produced the entailing of the crown, in 1281, 1284, 1318 and 1371. And from 1329, when the five-year-old David II succeeded his father Robert Bruce, the crown never did die, for the regnal year of each new king was dated from the day of his father's death – a practice not begun in England until 1483. For immediately political reasons, the political nation of Scotland gave its monarchy a permanence and a dynastic security which the monarchies of late medieval England and France might have envied.

But the ability to go to the political heart of that fundamental matter, succession to the throne, did not save the Scots from having the worst record of minorities in late medieval Europe. This was, indeed, a major factor in determining the nature of Scottish society. Historians have tended to accept the truth of the famous biblical text, 'Woe unto thee, o land, when thy king is a child.' In Scotland, the minorities were a saving grace.

Inevitably, they produced faction fighting; the first task for each king, as he came of age, was to get rid of the dominant faction, Albany Stewarts, Livingstones, Boyds. It gave them little trouble. They could tap the resentment created by an imbalance of power, just as James II did, more dramatically, when bringing down the Douglases, themselves beneficiaries of his minority as well as excessively powerful in their own right. And, paradoxically, the minorities enhanced the power of adult kings. If they created faction, they also diminished it; for their lamentable habit of dying young meant the absence of faction round an heir to the throne old enough to provide a serious counterpoise to the king. Whatever the intentions of his murderers, in a conspiracy which happened fast, James I's heir was not himself a rival; the only king who seriously – and briefly – suffered from the problem of the heir was James III. And if Stewart kings failed to live long, they had the immeasurable advantage of having been kings from youth; most were barely aware of a time when they had not worn the crown. The full significance of this in terms of the confidence it gave them can only be guessed at; not until the reign of James VI did a monarch speak of the profound effect of having been a 'cradle king'.

Moreover, it only took the experience of one 'minority' – the absence of James I, in English hands from 1406 to 1424 – to produce the expedient of the Act of Revocation, which every king passed thereafter when he came of age. Nothing more clearly shows the power of the crown, and the acceptance of that power by the aristocracy, than this amazing 'deal' by which kings revoked all grants made in their name during minority. The 'deal' certainly included the expectation that they would regrant what they had revoked; but they did not need to do so, and it was therefore the magnates, rather than the crown, who could be rendered insecure by the advent of minority. Yet that potential insecurity was far outweighed by the advantages of recurrent minorities. They, and they alone, provided a breathing-space from royal rule which was always harsh, even if occasionally leavened with the charisma of a James IV.

Thus fifteenth-century Scotland provides us with the paradox of exceedingly tough and effective kings ruling a decentralised kingdom, in which to an increasingly unusual degree local power could be exercised without challenge. It is, therefore, peculiarly appropriate that in European terms there are comparatively few records of central government, but an unrivalled wealth of documentation of local lordship, in the bonds of maintenance and manrent which articulated relationships between lords and their men from the mid-fifteenth century. These bonds clearly restated the concept hidden beneath the complexities of feudal lordship that such relationships depended on personal protection, loyalty and service, and not material reward. They could therefore simply give written expression to existing affinities, and as such became increasingly commonplace. But initially there were two particular motives for committing these agreements to parchment. One was that the families built up by the crown, like the Gordon earls of Huntly and the Hay earls of Erroll, in the shake-up of power after the fall of the Douglases, saw advantage to themselves in asserting their new superiority over former social equals by entering into these bonds. The other was to end feud, by establishing formal relationships between men as a symbol that reconciliation had been achieved. They were not therefore the product of a peaceful society, but of a violent one. Yet their intention was pacific. They were used to enhance established local power. There was no direct material advantage to those who made bonds of manrent and therefore no strong motive to seek more than one lord, even among those who made them under a degree of compulsion. Fifteenth-century Scottish lordship was therefore both simpler and more stable than its 'bastard feudal' counterparts. Affinities did indeed support their lords in their feuds. Equally, men could invoke the help of their lord in the resolution of their own. And it was an integral part of the concept of personal justice and arbitration that the feuds and disputes of men of equal status should be resolved by informal tribunals of their peers. The violence endemic in late medieval society, when men pursued their ambitions, their claims to land, by the sword as well as through patronage and the law, was not thereby eradicated. But it was local, and it was contained.

The existence of these bonds tells us much about the working of power in the localities, and the means of control. But it was not only the minorities which explain the survival of decentralisation and the power of lords and heads of kin, which depended far more on their position in their localities than any royal commission. In another way, Scotland was unique: it was not a country at war. In an age dominated by military glory, or humiliation, both of which had a direct connection with domestic success or failure, this again initially appears to be a sign of Scottish weakness. No doubt had fifteenth-century Scotsmen stopped to think about it, the fact that once the English had turned their attention to France, no one else was in the least interested in them, would have seemed humiliating. They did not, of course, think about it. The Hundred Years War gave plenty of opportunity for military adventure, with the additional bonus of allowing them to fight in France against their greatest enemy. In 1421, they won at Baugé. Three years later, the battle of Verneuil showed the full horrors of the risk; the earls of Buchan and Douglas were only the most notable among the heavy Scottish losses. But there were rewards. A grateful Charles VII gave the duchy of Touraine and county of Longueville to the earls of Douglas, and created the prestigious Scots Guard in 1445; ironically, the inhabitants of this nation at peace, not famed for much in Europe, habitually beaten in battle when – and wherever – they fought the English, were highly regarded for their courage and fighting skills. They got, on the cheap, the reputation which other countries sought at enormous cost.

That was not their only gain from this paradox. It led to the supreme achievement of being, unlike so many contemporary kingdoms, a state which never over-reached itself, in terms of overstraining the resources of the kingdom. Endemic warfare produced the regular taxation, the burgeoning administrative growth, of England and France. Scotland was burdened by neither. Scottish kings, during their adult rule, were as able to disturb their subjects, intervene, force their will, as any other monarch – and better at it than some. But they disturbed fewer people. Those closest to the crown might suffer as individuals. But it did not bear down on lesser people in the kingdom at large, or need to send its officials and tax collectors into reluctant and resentful localities, because it was not constantly on the search for men and money to support its wars. The effect of this, combined with the recurrent absence of direct royal rule, was to allow the concept of the community of the realm, called into conscious being by the succession crisis and threat from Edward I in the 1290s, to survive. At its most inspiring, it found expression in the Declaration of Arbroath; it found expression also in the law of treason, for in sharp contrast to the emphasis in the English act of 1352, where treason was defined as an attack on the person of the king, his wife and heir, in Scotland – as in France – treason was against king and 'kynrik', king and realm. This gives us a rare insight into a normally unrecorded phenomenon: that awareness of the source of authority was diffused, spreading out from the king to the kingdom, to the benefit of both; political tensions were not exclusively confined within the orbit of the crown. More prosaically, Scotland was, by absolute standards, a poor country. Yet in its own terms, it was a thriving one. It could satisfy its basic needs; the upper echelons of society could afford their luxuries; but the production of backbreaking surplus to meet royal ambition was not required.

Only for a brief moment, in the early 1470s, did James III threaten to disturb the resulting stability and equilibrium by proposing to lead armies into Brittany, Saintonge and Gueldres. He was the one Stewart king to dream the dreams which led Edward III in the 1330s to envisage an empire stretching from the Pentland Firth to the Pyrenees, Henry V to rule France and England, or Charles VIII to show off his artillery train in conquest in the Italian peninsula. But James's ambition was small scale and unsupported. Intelligent Scottish kings had other ways of making their presence felt.

They were not actually important at the council tables of Europe. This mattered less, however, than their ability to act, for home consumption, as though they were. James II's intervention in the dispute between Charles VII and his son Louis in 1459, and his efforts to reconcile France and Burgundy; James IV's role in stage-managing the treaty between France and Denmark in 1499, and his sustained attempt to bring together the great powers of western Europe in a campaign against the Turk, all showed a confidence in their international position far greater than the reality of that position warranted, and had the obvious benefit of adding the aura of strength in Europe to strength at home. Their marriage alliances showed the same purpose. Apart from David II's first marriage, every king between 1307 and 1406 married into Scottish noble families. No king thereafter stooped so low. In his particular circumstances – which may have included love – James I married an English noblewoman; but his daughters were married to the French dauphin, the duke of Brittany, the duke of Austria and the son of the lord of Campveere, while James II married Mary of Gueldres. This southwards look was balanced, in the case of James III, by his marriage to Margaret of Denmark, for diplomatically and economically Scotland's links with Scandinavia were as important as those with France and the Low Countries, not least because the full extent of the Scottish kingdom, already enhanced by the annexation of the western isles from Norway, was achieved by the incorporation of Orkney and Shetland as a result of that marriage. Dealings with a Papacy struggling to reassert its prestige and authority after the Great Schism displayed the same aggressive confidence. Indeed, Scotland got its first university, St Andrews, in 1412, by supporting the anti-Pope Benedict XIII for just long enough, after he had lost all other allies, to get his approval for the foundation before abandoning him. And Scotland was the first kingdom to receive formal recognition of the right of the crown to nominate to the greater benefices; the Indult granted to James III in 1487 anticipated those subsequently given to Ferdinand and Isabel, and Francis I. No doubt Scotland had this distinction because the Papacy was more willing to give to the less important kingdom; but that was hardly a relevant consideration to the Scots.

This, surely, is what success was all about. The duke of Milan might tartly refuse to marry his daughter to James III's heir, rather than send that daughter 'so far off as Scotland would be'.[9] Commynes could incorporate a dismissive little section on the violence of Scottish society, exemplified by the downfall of James III, into his much more interesting account of the death-throes of Yorkist kingship. But the Scots' perception of themselves as Europeans, and important Europeans at that, was very real. An unknown group of visitors left a record of that perception, inscribing on the wall of the catacomb of San Callisto 'MCCCCLXVII quidam Scoti hic fuerunt'. Rome itself was familiar territory, to clerics seeking benefices and laymen and women divorce, and to the Scottish lawyers who had enough business coming from home to live there; indeed, Scotland's legal system, based mainly on Roman law, itself tied it into Europe. Two further universities, Glasgow and Aberdeen, were founded in the fifteenth century; but Scottish scholars continued to pour abroad to Paris, Louvain, Cologne, Montpellier and other places, for their higher degrees. Diplomatic negotiations widened trading links. Not only kings but many of their subjects knew a very simple truth: they lived on the fringes of Europe, and their only chance of being taken seriously was to spend time and energy on loud demands for attention. That is why an internalised ideological image of kingship was of so little importance to the Scottish crown. That is why the Scots so significantly failed to beat the nationalist drum. For such drum-beating is essentially inward-looking, even a cover-up for weakness. It was not that which primarily concerned the Scots, nor even their strenuous maintenance of their independence within the British Isles. What did can still be seen today, in the early sixteenth-century heraldic ceiling of St Machar's cathedral,

---

[9] *Calendar of state papers . . . Milan,* I, p. 198.

Aberdeen. Dedicated to a Celtic saint, the cathedral displays the arms of the burgh and university of Aberdeen, the bishops and nobles of Scotland, the king, the principal princes and dukes of Europe, the Holy Roman Emperor and the pope. It was a very comprehensive vision, and an all-embracing self-image.

WALES

A.D. Carr

THE revolt of Owain Glyn Dŵr, which had begun some three months before the fifteenth century opened, belongs really to the history of the fourteenth century; the next chapter in the history of Wales begins as the revolt drew to a close and the comment that 'modern Wales begins in 1410' has in it a measure of truth.[1] The revolt can justly be described as the most important event between Edward I's conquest of Gwynedd in 1282 and the first Act of Union of 1536 and the description of it as 'the massive protest of a conquered people' and as the completion of the Edwardian conquest places it firmly in its historical context.[2] Its end marks a significant point in the history of medieval and early modern Wales and is a reminder that the traditional bench-mark of 1485 is, in many ways, irrelevant in Welsh terms, even if that year did see the triumph of a dynasty of Welsh extraction and the accession to the English throne of the great-grandson of a man who had been in rebellion with Glyn Dŵr. The ending of the revolt marks the beginning of a change in the attitudes and perceptions of the Welsh political nation; the vision of the restoration of an ancient independence was replaced by the urge to work within a wider political dimension.

The end of the revolt was a gradual process. As early as 1406 some communities had submitted and the last great raid into Shropshire was defeated in 1410. Owain himself may have died in 1415, but his son Maredudd tried to carry on the fight, parts of north Wales being far from pacified during the second decade of the century. It was feared that the fugitive Lollard leader, Sir John Oldcastle, was in league with Maredudd and there was talk of a possible Scottish landing in support of them. It may not be without significance that Oldcastle was captured in Powys in 1417 and the revolt really only ended when Maredudd ab Owain accepted a royal pardon in 1421. There were surprisingly few reprisals; individuals made their peace from an early stage and communi-

---

[1] Williams (1959), p. 183.   [2] Davies (1987), p. 462.

ties were able to purchase forgiveness. After his accession in 1413 Henry V, anxious to embark on a campaign in France and concerned about the possibility of a Lollard rising, combined firmness with conciliation, going so far as to offer a pardon to Owain himself. Arrears were cancelled, an enquiry into the revolt and its consequences held and money was earmarked for the replacement of livestock to help communities in north Wales get back on their feet.

Against this conciliatory response, however, must be set the penal legislation rushed through parliament in 1401 and 1402. Although these statutes have been accurately described as racist, it may be fair to add the rider that they were essentially a panic reaction and many of them were a repetition of a series of ordinances promulgated by Edward I in the 1290s.[3] Once the revolt was over and men had made their peace they were usually a dead letter. The plain truth was that both the king and the marcher lords needed the leaders of the native community; neither Principality nor lordship could function without their cooperation, particularly at the local level. Some were formally granted denizenship or English legal status, but most men of substance returned to favour without much trouble; the men who governed at the local level after the revolt tended to be those who had done so before. The penal statutes were not, however, always ignored; they could be used to further personal rivalries, as in 1433, when Owain Glyn Dŵr's son-in-law, Sir John Scudamore, was dismissed from all his offices through the machinations of Edmund Beaufort. From time to time during the century the statutes were confirmed, while English burgesses regularly called for their enforcement.

Not all Welshmen joined Glyn Dŵr. Many remained loyal to the crown or to their lords and allegiances were often dictated by the rivalries of local politics. Some joined the revolt but had the foresight to make their peace before most of their fellows and profited as a result. The short-term economic consequences were disastrous; it had been a war of attrition, won in the end by the superior resources of the English crown. Neither side had shown any mercy, even to the Church, for cathedrals and abbeys were among the victims. Many towns and their property had been prime targets and even Carmarthen, the administrative headquarters of the southern Principality, had been sacked. Yet, despite the havoc wrought by Glyn Dŵr, much of the physical damage was soon repaired. And the long-term consequences should not be exaggerated; account rolls record the flight of bondmen, depopulated communities and arable land let for grazing, but the roots of this decline lay in the years before 1400. Its causes were, in reality, among the causes of the revolt itself.

Wales in the fifteenth century was not a coherent political or administrative unit; it never had been. There was not even any precise territorial definition.

---

[3] *Statutes of Wales*, pp. 31–6; *Record of Caernarvon*, pp. 131–2.

The south and east were made up of those marcher lordships which were the result of Norman invasion and conquest in the eleventh and twelfth centuries; the rest of the country, shired and in the possession of the crown since the thirteenth century, formed the Principality. Most marcher lordships had changed hands on several occasions and some concentration of ownership had already begun. Several were in the possession of the duchy of Lancaster and had therefore passed to the crown in 1399; the process of concentration continued in the fifteenth century, and in 1425 Richard Plantagenet, duke of York, inherited the great Mortimer complex of lordships with an annual value of nearly £3,000 on the death of his mother. On the accession of York's son to the throne as Edward IV in 1461 these lands all became permanently attached to the crown. Other families with extensive interests in the March were the FitzAlans, earls of Arundel, and the Staffords, who became dukes of Buckingham. By 1485, a substantial part of the March was in the direct possession of the crown, but this did not lead to any practical strengthening of royal government since each lordship retained its identity and its autonomy.

The main aims of royal government under Henry V were to bring about financial and economic recovery and to restore the revenue to something approaching its level before the revolt, and the same was true of marcher administration; for those magnates who were marcher lords the revenue from their Welsh lands formed a substantial part of their income. In the short term the various administrations were not unsuccessful but this was not to endure. There may have been a measure of recovery from the immediate effects of the rebellion but the underlying problems, which went back well into the fourteenth century, were less easily solved; indeed, under the existing system of government they may well have been insoluble.

The death of Henry V in 1422 removed a strong and active ruler and the minority of Henry VI saw a gradual increase in magnate power in the Principality. Effective government depended on the careful exercise of patronage and in the royal lands a great deal of this was available. Henry V had taken much care in making appointments but towards the end of the minority an increasing number of local offices in north Wales, hitherto the preserve of the leaders of the native community, were being granted to members of the royal household, and with the assumption of personal rule by Henry VI in 1437 the floodgates were opened. By 1450 the north was dominated by the king's household, particularly by those of its members who came from Cheshire; in south Wales the household did not profit in the same way, partly because of the influence of such magnates as Edmund Beaufort and the duke of York, but the choice of officials came increasingly to reflect the power and influence of factions at the centre and the use of patronage was more and more the result of external political factors. An active prince entrusted with the royal lands in

Wales might have made a difference but after 1413 no prince of Wales was of full age. Nor was the March much better; seignorial income was declining steadily and several lordships were bedevilled by long minorities. Magnate lords were generally absentees who came to depend increasingly on local deputies. There were sporadic attempts to impose some kind of administrative order but there could be no substitute for constant supervision by a vigorous resident lord.

The deputies of absentee officials were drawn from the leaders of the native community. Given effective supervision there would have been nothing wrong in this, but the problem was that under Henry VI the government of the realm, faced with a war in France that it could not win and beset by factional rivalries, could not supervise the periphery. Many parts of Wales fell more and more under the control of local landowners; the most blatant example was the Carmarthenshire gentleman, Gruffydd ap Nicholas, who, with the aid of his sons, during the 1440s and 1450s, ruled the south-west, ostensibly in the name of Henry VI but in reality as his personal satrapy. He had enjoyed the patronage of Edmund Beaufort and Humphrey, duke of Gloucester, but by the time Gloucester fell from power and died in 1447 he no longer needed a patron. He was able to ignore the authorities almost completely at a time when tensions at the centre were leading inexorably to civil war. He was the most prominent of these local potentates, but there were many others like him; in the south-east the outstanding Welsh leader was the Gwent knight, Sir William ap Thomas of Raglan, who held various offices in the Principality and the March. No such figure emerged in the north; here the grip of the royal household, under the supervision of its controller, Sir Thomas Stanley, was secure and was strengthened by marriage alliances with local notables.

It was the Yorkist victory in 1461 and the consequent accession of Edward IV that led to a new initiative to deal with the problem of the government of Wales. Edward's key supporter there was Sir William Herbert of Raglan, the son of Sir William ap Thomas. By 1468 most of Wales was under his direct control and the poet Lewis Glyn Cothi described him as 'King Edward's master-lock'.[4] Raised to the peerage in 1461, he was created earl of Pembroke in 1468. From now on the king would leave his lands and interests in Wales in the care of a trusted servant who was one of the most powerful men in the realm. Herbert's rapid rise had made him many enemies, particularly the earl of Warwick, who also had interests in Wales, and Warwick's change of allegiance in 1469 led to Herbert's defeat at Banbury and subsequent execution. His place in Wales was taken by the king's younger brother, Richard, duke of Gloucester, but when Edward recovered the throne in 1471 he made his young son,

---

[4] *Gwaith Lewis Glyn Cothi*, p. 4: 'Unclo'r King Edward yw'r Herbard hwn.'

Edward, prince of Wales and sent him to Ludlow with a council to advise him
and rule in his name. After Edward IV's death in 1483 Gloucester, first as protector of the young Edward V and then as king himself, tried to continue his
brother's policy by entrusting Wales to the duke of Buckingham, but within a
few months of Richard's seizure of the throne Buckingham had led an
unsuccessful revolt and been executed.

The reign of Henry VI has often been seen as a period of particular violence
and disorder in Wales; the most graphic picture is that drawn by Sir John Wynn
of Gwydir, writing at the end of the sixteenth century. He depicted north
Wales as a society in which men had had to take the law into their own hands to
survive because the whole mechanism of public order had broken down.[5]
There is similar evidence from other parts of the country; in the Stafford lordship of Caus in 1454 a Welsh mercenary was employed to protect the tenants
and in Flintshire a fairly high level of violence is reflected in the records of the
justiciar of Chester's sessions. Perhaps the worst example of disorder was the
county of Merioneth in the Principality, where order and royal government
seem to have collapsed entirely during the 1450s; the county, described by one
historian as 'ungoverned and ungovernable', had ceased to yield any revenue at
all.[6]

The 1440s and 1450s were certainly decades of violence and lawlessness and
this has tended to be blamed on the Glyn Dŵr revolt. But it is simplistic to talk
of anarchy and a complete collapse of order and government; there was just as
much disorder in many parts of England at this time. Among the reasons for
the lack of public order in Wales was the absence of magnate officials in the
Principality and of magnate lords in the March. They operated through
deputies, who tended to be drawn from leading local families with local interests and ambitions, and who were only too ready to use office to further their
ends. But the behaviour of the leaders of the native community must not be
dismissed solely as gratuitous lawlessness and the pursuit of personal ambition. Very often local rivalry was part of a quest for stability and for a dominance which only one protagonist could enjoy. And the various administrative
units were not completely self-contained; even in the fourteenth century there
had been arrangements between lordships for extradition of fugitives, hot
pursuit and the punishment of captured felons, and there were also formal
agreements for the settlement of disputes.

The texts of several of these from the fifteenth century survive and there are
also references in accounts to the traditional Welsh method of negotiation
between different jurisdictions, namely the Day of the March or meeting of
representatives on the common border. One practice which has often been

---

[5] *Gwydir Family*, pp. 33–58.   [6] Griffiths (1972b), p. 155.

seen as a contributory factor to the decline of public order in the southern counties and lordships was that of redeeming or dissolving the Great Sessions; an announcement that such sessions would be held would be followed by negotiations which would lead to the crown or the lord agreeing to accept a lump sum equivalent to the anticipated profits. In the lordship of Brecon in 1418–19, for example, the sessions were redeemed for 2,000 marks and in Carmarthenshire between 1422 and 1485 only twelve out of fifty-two sessions ran their full course. But redemption had more to do with revenue than with buying off justice; in both Principality and March there was already a hierarchy of courts which went on being held and this practice was, in effect, a form of taxation at a time when the traditional sources of seignorial income were yielding less and less.

There were various discussions of Welsh problems in the 1440s and 1450s but nothing positive was done by the crown to solve them; with royal authority in the state it was in under Henry VI, it was difficult to contain or control the activities of such men as Gruffydd ap Nicholas. It was only with the rise of William Herbert that there was a powerful royal representative actually resident in Wales; in these circumstances effective local rule and authority fell naturally into the hands of the leaders of the native community and it was these men who formed the Welsh political nation. Their power and influence rested on traditional leadership, the tenure of local office, descent and kinship links and, increasingly, landed wealth and economic power. They could be described as a squirearchy or as gentry, but the Welsh term *uchelwyr* is probably more accurate. The support of this class had been crucial for Owain Glyn Dŵr; now they gradually gained control of the levers of power in both Principality and March, and although few were to emulate Gruffydd ap Nicholas in creating personal fiefdoms, many prospered, often beyond the confines of Wales. The outstanding example is William Herbert, but there are many others. The Dwnn family from Kidwelly played a prominent part in the south-west. Henry Dwnn had been an active supporter of Owain Glyn Dŵr; his grandson Gruffydd, involved as a very young man in the revolt, was to have a distinguished record of military service in France, and one of Gruffydd's sons, John, held various offices at court in addition to Wales. He was knighted in 1471 and acquired extensive lands in England as well as being sent on diplomatic missions by Henry VII. He commissioned a triptych, now in the National Gallery, from no less a painter than Hans Memlinc. Such men, together with William Griffith of Penrhyn in north Wales, were the outstanding members of their class; but there were scores of other landowners of ancient lineage and local influence without whom there would have been no government at all.

Judicious marriages lay behind the rise of many Welsh landed families; perhaps the outstanding example is the great house of Mostyn in Flintshire which, during the fourteenth and fifteenth centuries, built up an extensive estate throughout north Wales by four successive marriages to heiresses. Alliances were carefully planned and, as the fifteenth century progressed, families who dominated particular regions came to look further afield when choosing partners for their sons and daughters, so that such marriages could involve more than one generation or more than one child. Marriage often meant land; this was the period when the process of estate building, which had begun for some families in the fourteenth century, gathered momentum. A recently discovered cartulary lists the lands in Gwynedd which William Griffith had purchased and which made him the greatest landed proprietor in north-west Wales; he also purchased land to provide an inheritance for one of his illegitimate sons.[7] Other emergent estates included Peniarth in Merioneth, Clenennau in southern Caernarfonshire and Rhydodyn in Carmarthenshire; indeed, the same process may be seen in operation all over Wales as what had been hereditary land was being snapped up by enterprising neighbours. Some free tenants were drawing ahead of their fellows and would in time join the ranks of the gentry; others, who already enjoyed local power and influence, were adding substantially to their holdings. Hundreds of deeds in collections of family papers bear witness to this process.

These were the social and political leaders of the native community, and their economic power was increasing. They were also the nourishers and custodians of the native cultural tradition. The century between 1450 and 1550 is one of the great periods of Welsh poetry and the work of the professional poets revolved around the *uchelwyr*. Some, indeed, were poets themselves, since every gentleman was expected to have at least an acquaintance with the strict metres of Welsh poetry. In the middle of the century Gruffydd ap Nicholas, a prominent patron, presided over an *eisteddfod* at Carmarthen which revised the traditional metres. The output of poetry from this period comes from all over Wales and the poets travelled widely, visiting their patrons in their houses. This was the age of poets like Guto'r Glyn, Lewis Glyn Cothi, Gutun Owain, Dafydd Nanmor, Dafydd ab Edmwnd and Tudur Aled; many of these came themselves from the ranks of the *uchelwyr* and they served a long and rigorous apprenticeship. Their art was based on patronage; they praised the patron's lineage, generosity and courage; they sought gifts from him; and they mourned his death. They gave expression to the social values of the society in which they lived. Within a strict metrical framework they produced great poetry and their work sheds light on contemporary social and political attitudes.

Another integral part of native culture was Welsh law. The introduction of English legal procedure in the Principality at the conquest did not mean the

---

[7] University of Wales, Bangor, Dept of Manuscripts, Penrhyn Further Additional MSS (uncatalogued).

eclipse of native jurisprudence, particularly in the southern counties and the March, and the legal texts written in the fifteenth century are practical rather than antiquarian in their emphasis. There are examples in contemporary judicial records of the use of Welsh procedure; it survived in both criminal and civil actions and it was at its strongest in the field of real property. The Welsh procedure known as conveyance in *tir prid*, which had evolved as a way around the inalienability of hereditary Welsh land, played an important part in the growth of landed estates, as the deeds in so many collections of family papers reveal. Until 1536 the law of Hywel Dda had its distinct place in Welsh life, and no Welsh gentleman, particularly in the March or the southern counties, could afford to be ignorant of its provisions.

The long-term effects of the mid-fourteenth-century plague had been exacerbated by the revolt and these effects showed themselves particularly in the position of the bondmen. These formed a minority in the population but they bore the heaviest burden of dues and services, although most of the latter had by now been commuted to cash payments. By the fifteenth century bond status had, in the Principality at least, become a means of raising revenue. The bondman had been subject to various restrictions, but these could now be easily circumvented on payment of a fine. Some deeds record the sale of bondmen, but what was probably conveyed was the land where the bondman's holding was situated and possibly the right to his labour. Nor did bond status necessarily mean poverty; in 1481–2 a bondman from Anglesey had goods valued at £26 18s 4d, had married his daughters to free men and had himself married the daughter of one of the leaders of the local community.[8] On the other hand there were many free tenants who can only be described as indigent. But bond townships in the Principality had yielded a substantial portion of the crown's revenue from Wales and since the late fourteenth century these had been a wasting asset. Bondmen were leaving; in the northern counties, some townships had been completely depopulated and their arable lands had to be let for grazing. The return of fugitive bondmen was suggested after the revolt, but this would have been a pointless exercise. The income had to be replaced by grants negotiated with the native community.

At the upper levels of society, among the *uchelwyr*, there was no lack of visible wealth; indeed, the patronage of poets was itself a form of conspicuous consumption. The poets describe a world of tables groaning under imported delicacies, of fine houses and of increasing domestic comfort; in the early years of the century the poet Siôn Cent, a severe critic of his age and society, summarised the values of this class when he asked what would avail their houses, wine-cellars, horses and hounds and trips to England when no man

---

[8] Public Record Office (London), SC6/1155/6, m. 11a.

could expect more than seven feet of earth.[9] These men were confident and comfortable, a fact reflected in the many houses which survive, built of stone in the north and west and timber in the east. Below these men a class of substantial tenants was emerging; the whole pattern of land tenure had changed. In what was essentially an upland economy there was much poverty but also wealth; the fact that wine from Spain and spices from the east could find their way to the tables of squires in Cardiganshire or Anglesey bears witness to this. Increasing prosperity was also reflected in the rebuilding and embellishment of churches, especially in the north-east, possibly the most flourishing part of Wales. Although the finest churches there, like Wrexham, Mold and Gresford, owed much to the generosity of the Stanleys and Margaret Beaufort, the double-nave churches of the Vale of Clwyd and, elsewhere in Wales, churches like Clynnog Fawr, Holyhead, Tenby and St John's, Cardiff, are further evidence of recovery.

The main products of Wales were cloth and cattle. The export of wool had been replaced to a large extent by cloth and this was reflected in the existence of many fulling mills; depopulation had led to more land being given over to grazing, and this led in turn to a greater emphasis on sheep farming. The most highly organised cloth industry was in the town of Ruthin; the Grey family, lords of Ruthin, were among the most capable and efficient of the marcher lords. Large quantities of cattle were exported on the hoof to England and even some poets had experience of droving.[10] The mineral wealth of Wales, in the form of lead, coal and slate, was already being exploited on a small scale, and woods and forests played a significant part in the economy. But the concept of a full-time industrial labour force had not emerged; industrial workers and most craftsmen were usually smallholders as well, with a continuing stake in the soil. The principal exports of Wales were wool, hides and cloth; the main imports were wine, salt, iron and luxury goods. Every coastal and estuarine town was a port but the most important ones were Beaumaris in the north and Carmarthen, Haverfordwest and Tenby in the south-west; they traded with Brittany, Spain and Portugal, as well as with England, Scotland and Ireland. Towns were essentially market and service centres, with the possible exception of Wrexham, which was the largest and most flourishing town in north Wales and a centre of metal working. The other leading towns which were regional commercial centres included Cardiff, Brecon, Carmarthen, Denbigh and Newtown; other towns had a more local catchment area, while some were little more than villages. Prosperous burgesses of English stock continued to buy land. The Conwy burgess Bartholomew de Bolde built up a substantial estate by the patient accumulation of small pieces of Welsh heredi-

---

[9] *Cywyddau Iolo Goch ac Eraill*, pp. 288–92.   [10] *Gwaith Guto'r Glyn*, pp. 84–6.

tary land in the lower Conwy valley, while in Beaumaris William Bulkeley from Cheshire bought up burgages in the town and then extended his activities into rural Anglesey. His eldest son married the only daughter and heiress of Bartholomew de Bolde and the Bulkeleys of Beaumaris thus became a major power in north Wales; within a generation they had become part of the fabric of Anglesey society and were receiving the plaudits of the poets.

The fifteenth century was not generally an age of intense religious devotion. The rebuilding and extension of churches were as much an expression of civic pride or of aristocratic or seignorial generosity as of piety. For most of the century no Welshmen were appointed to bishoprics and few to cathedral dignities; able and ambitious Welsh churchmen had to make their careers in England, usually as canon lawyers. Among the parish clergy were to be found prosperous members of *uchelwr* families; these men were patrons of the poets and their way of life, as reflected in contemporary poetry, was highly secular. But most of the clergy were not far removed, in means or education, from the mass of their parishioners. Many monasteries were facing increasing economic difficulties and their estates were coming more and more under the control of leading local gentry, many of whom, in the next century, were to reap a rich harvest at the Dissolution. There is little or no evidence of Lollard activity in Wales after the capture of Sir John Oldcastle, but there is no evidence either of any intellectual ferment or intense spiritual life; the Church functioned, but it cannot be described as militant or triumphant. For most of the Welsh, popular religion was a matter of usage and habit. Pilgrimage centres like St David's and Bardsey retained their popularity, while some ventured further afield, particularly to Santiago de Compostella. There is a substantial body of religious poetry, but it is rarely of great intensity or devotion. Of education we know little. Some of the monasteries may have maintained schools; there were grammar schools at Oswestry and Haverfordwest, while Sir John Wynn referred to his great-grandfather having been put to school at Caernarfon to learn reading, writing, English and Latin.[11] In 1406 Owain Glyn Dŵr had sought the establishment by the pope of two universities, one in the north and one in the south, but Wales was to have no such institution until the nineteenth century. Nevertheless, many of the deeds and other documents which survive from the fifteenth century are evidence of lay literacy and most of the *uchelwyr* and many burgesses must have been literate, as were the poets.

Welsh soldiers, who had played an active part in the French wars in the fourteenth century, continued to do so. Many saw service in France under Henry V and his son and they included some who had followed Owain Glyn Dŵr a few years earlier. Welsh participation continued throughout the wars

[11] *Gwydir Family*, p. 50.

and some captains had distinguished careers, among them Sir Richard Gethin of Builth, Gruffydd Dwnn and Matthew Gough, as well as the young William Herbert. Many of them, particularly Gough, were rewarded for their services with lands in Normandy, although these riches evaporated when the French recovered the province in 1450. The poets at home were well aware of their patrons' exploits across the Channel and there are many references in their work; indeed Guto'r Glyn was himself a soldier in France. The French wars have often been seen as a source of wealth for their leading participants, but no Welsh family seems to have gained financially or territorially. What military service did bring, however, were patronage and useful contacts. Men like Gethin and Herbert came back from France with a far wider circle of acquaintance, and they had often come to the attention of leading commanders; this could be extremely valuable in the future, since a highly placed patron could make or break a political or military career. The other consequence of service in France was the availability of a large pool of military experience which was to benefit both sides when the English civil war broke out in 1455.

These wars in England brought Wales into the mainstream of English politics and its leaders on to the English political stage. William Herbert's father had been a prominent figure in the affairs of south-east Wales, but Herbert was a great deal more. Both factions had a Welsh power base; the Principality, being crown territory, was largely Lancastrian, as were the duchy of Lancaster lordships like Monmouth and Kidwelly. The former Mortimer lordships were obviously Yorkist, but there were exceptions on both sides; loyalties might often be dictated by local power struggles or even by the sides taken during the Glyn Dŵr revolt. And allegiance might often be the result of personal convenience; Gruffydd ap Nicholas claimed to be loyal to the house of Lancaster but this only persisted as long as weak royal government left him in control. When Edmund Tudor was sent to south Wales by Margaret of Anjou in 1456, hostilities soon followed. The other marcher lords went their own way; the Staffords were Lancastrians, while the lord of Glamorgan was the earl of Warwick, who was guided entirely by self-interest. The Stanley family in Cheshire and north Wales also looked to its own advantage. But if the foci of dynastic and political loyalties in England were the houses of Lancaster and York, in Wales they were in practice Jasper Tudor and William Herbert, both of whom held at different times the title of earl of Pembroke.

Following the Yorkist victory at Mortimer's Cross in 1461, Jasper Tudor fled to Ireland, while Herbert mopped up Lancastrian resistance in Wales. Like most contemporary commanders, Herbert was ruthless, and he and his men were much feared in England; however, the fact that he was Welsh meant that he was admired by his compatriots, and Guto'r Glyn called on him to unite

Wales and expel the English.[12] Both he and Jasper made extensive use of the poets for propaganda purposes. This may suggest that the poets were nothing more than time-servers who sang for their paymasters; but their loyalties were to Wales, rather than to York or Lancaster, and many of them sang to patrons on both sides. The death of Herbert after his defeat at Banbury in 1469, along with that of many of his Welsh followers, was mourned by the poets as a national disaster.

Edward IV's crushing victory at Tewkesbury in 1471 was, perhaps, the most significant battle in Welsh terms; it meant the extinction of the direct Lancastrian line and for the rest of his life Edward's position was unchallenged. Jasper and his nephew, Henry Tudor, found asylum in Brittany. But their position had changed dramatically. Jasper had been the leader of the Lancastrian party in Wales and no more than that. Now, however, the young Henry was the nearest Lancastrian claimant to the throne. His mother Margaret Beaufort was the great-grand-daughter of John of Gaunt, while on his father's side he was descended from the leading lineage in north Wales. The Tudors were the stock of Ednyfed Fychan, the seneschal of the princes of Gwynedd in the first half of the thirteenth century. After the Edwardian conquest the family had been the effective leaders of the native community in the Principality. Their support of Glyn Dŵr had brought their dominance to an end, but one of them, Maredudd ap Tudur ap Goronwy, had a son, Owain. Maredudd disappears from the record without trace after the revolt but Owain, after service in France, found his way to court and eventually married Henry V's widow, Catherine de Valois. They had three sons, Edmund, Jasper and Owen, the last of whom became a monk at Westminster. Henry VI showed much favour to his other half-brothers, making Edmund earl of Richmond and Jasper earl of Pembroke. Now, with the virtual elimination of the house of Lancaster, it was Henry who emerged as its candidate, and during the years of exile Jasper maintained contact with Lancastrian supporters in Wales and built up a party for the future. While Edward IV lived, there was little that could be done but in 1483 the king died suddenly and was succeeded by his young son, Edward V. His younger brother Richard, duke of Gloucester, was entrusted with the regency; the rest of the story is well known.

The seizure of the throne by Gloucester and the disappearance of his nephews changed the political situation completely. It was followed by Buckingham's abortive revolt; but the duke was unpopular in Wales and little support was forthcoming from there. The circumstances of Richard III's accession created hostility and suspicion, and high prices following two bad harvests made matters worse. All this breathed new life into the Lancastrian

---

[12] *Gwaith Guto'r Glyn*, pp. 129–31.

cause, and Henry Tudor's position changed overnight. Jasper's years of intrigue in Wales now began to bear fruit and the poets pleaded Henry's cause. There was in Wales a long tradition of vaticinatory poetry, calling on the *mab darogan*, or son of prophecy, to arise and redeem his people. Now the poets were singing in this vein, calling on Henry as the messianic leader who would lead the Welsh to victory. An ancient tradition, going back to the tenth century, was being harnessed to a particular cause, with implications for England as well as for Wales. In keeping with the zoomorphic imagery of the vaticinatory tradition Henry was hailed as the Swallow and the Bull. This poetry was not an atavistic Celtic response; it was contemporary political propaganda expressed in a traditional form. As Henry was praised, so was Richard damned, and some poets accused him of the murder of his nephews;[13] at the same time much of this poetry contained an anti-English tone, hailing the *mab darogan* as the instrument of Welsh vengeance. Opponents of Richard were now making their way to Brittany. After an abortive expedition in the autumn of 1483 Henry landed at Mill Bay on Milford Haven early in August 1485; on his march through Wales he was joined by many with whom Jasper had been in communication, particularly Rhys ap Thomas of Dinefwr, the grandson of Gruffydd ap Nicholas, and now the dominant figure in the south-west. The invaders advanced through Wales and the midlands and, at Bosworth, Richard III was defeated and killed. Henry Tudor, the impecunious exile, became King Henry VII; the intervention of his stepfather, Lord Stanley, and Stanley's brother, Sir William, was decisive.

The effect of Bosworth on the Welsh imagination was electrifying, and this is reflected in the reaction of the poets. Their feeling was that the son of prophecy had come to his people and that Llywelyn ap Gruffydd, the last native prince, had been avenged, since a Welshman now wore the crown of London. Many Welshmen went to England in search of their fortunes and Bosworth, where Henry had fought under the banner of the red dragon, was seen as a Welsh victory. The question of how Welsh Henry really was is an open one; only one of his four grandparents was Welsh but, having spent some of the formative years of his childhood in the Herbert household at Raglan, it is possible that he did speak the language and he seems to have enjoyed Welsh poetry. The red dragon of Wales became one of the supporters of the royal arms and he named his eldest son Arthur. It is easy to dismiss such gestures as cosmetic but Henry Tudor does seem to have been very aware of his Welsh ancestry, and he knew how great was his debt to many of his Welsh supporters. Those who had stood by him were now rewarded; Jasper, to whom he owed everything, became duke of Bedford and was entrusted with the oversight of Wales and

[13] Williams (1986), pp. 23–4.

the Marches, although without the authority given by Edward IV to William Herbert or by Richard III to Buckingham. Rhys ap Thomas was also well rewarded and in 1496 he became justiciar of south Wales.

Once Henry was king there was some bardic complaint about the lack of attention given to Wales, but this did not reflect the attitude of the leaders of the community. Their position and influence had not been affected and they knew very well that Henry's priorities were to restore stability and remain on the throne. For them it was enough that he was there, and there was to be no lack of Welsh support in putting down the risings which occurred from time to time. In 1486 there was a Yorkist insurrection in the lordship of Brecon and the rebels captured Brecon castle; they were suppressed by Sir Rhys ap Thomas, who had been knighted at Bosworth. Henry's determination to maintain peace and order was shown in 1495 when Sir William Stanley, who had been instrumental in securing his victory at Bosworth and whose brother was his stepfather, was executed for his involvement in the conspiracy of Perkin Warbeck. In 1507 Sir Rhys ap Thomas held a great tournament at Carew castle which symbolised the reconciliation of England and Wales, and to poets throughout the sixteenth century Henry VII was the liberator. The Elizabethan antiquary, George Owen, described him as the 'Moyses that delyvered us from bondage'.[14] Welshmen began again to be appointed to Welsh bishoprics and loyalty was rewarded at every level of the administration.

By 1485 most of the March was in the possession of the crown, the main exceptions being the Buckingham lordships in the south-east and those of the Stanleys in the north-east. But Henry did not undertake a drastic reorganisation of Welsh government; what he did was to follow the example of Edward IV and try to make the existing system work, at the same time strengthening the position of the crown. The surviving lords were obliged to enter into indentures or formal agreements with the king to maintain order. However, the problem of the multiplicity of jurisdictions remained; although much of the March was in the king's possession, each lordship was autonomous and there was no central machinery. Henry again imitated Edward IV in sending his eldest son to Ludlow with a council; this council was retained after Arthur's death in 1502 and from it was eventually derived the council in the Marches of Wales. But the king tended to depend on individuals rather than institutions to control Wales, and in this a significant part was played by Sir Rhys ap Thomas.

The problems of governing Wales were as much financial as administrative. The financial difficulties had a long history, going back to the second half of the fourteenth century. In 1490 steps were taken in north Wales to recover as much revenue as possible; the chamberlain was dismissed and royal servants

---

[14] Owen, *Description of Penbrokshire*, III, p. 37.

brought in. The resulting pressure on the community was such that it may have led in 1498 to a revolt in the county of Merioneth. A force of soldiers had to restore order and the community paid a heavy fine. There were similar problems in the March. In 1496 accumulated arrears of over £2,000 had to be written off in the Stafford lordship of Brecon; mounting arrears were one of the worst problems lords had to face. Henry's response to the problems of north Wales was the granting of a series of charters to the Principality in 1504 and 1507 and to various marcher lordships between 1505 and 1509; these emancipated bondmen and abolished partible succession to land and a number of traditional dues.

These charters were not the result of spontaneous royal generosity to deliver the people of north Wales from 'miserable servitude'; they were bought by the recipients. There was some doubt as to their validity, but before the matter could be resolved Henry died in 1509. His son, Henry VIII, had little direct interest in Wales and in the first part of his reign he made no changes. He depended on Cardinal Wolsey and Wolsey depended on the traditional leaders in Wales. The key man in the south continued to be Sir Rhys ap Thomas and he remained so until his death in 1525; a similar part was played in north Wales by the third William Griffith of Penrhyn. Griffith ruled with a very heavy hand, arguing that the problems of governing north Wales were such that he had no choice. In the March two prominent figures remained. One of these was Charles Somerset, the illegitimate son of Henry Beaufort, third duke of Somerset. He had been among those who landed with Henry Tudor in 1485 and he married William Herbert's grand-daughter. The other marcher lord was Buckingham, rich, arrogant and unpopular. Buckingham had been on friendly terms with the king, but he offended Wolsey and his overbearing ways added to Henry's suspicion of a man who was a close enough relative to have an interest in the succession, should the king leave no heir. He was accused of treason and in 1521 he was tried and executed. In a sense the fall of Buckingham marked the end of an era. The age of the marcher magnate was over and practically the whole of the March was now in the king's hands. It was for Thomas Cromwell to put an end to the anomaly of Wales once and for all; the union legislation of 1536 and 1543 did not so much unite Wales with England as unite Wales within itself.

THE NORTHERN ITALIAN STATES

Michael Mallett

In many respects Italy in the fifteenth century was becoming a more coherent political area and it is hard to confine discussion to the northern part of the peninsula, without reference to the pope or to the king of Naples. The inter-relationships between increasingly powerful and organised states are a key part of the history of the period. Even the tensions and fears that seemed to grow in the second half of the century as outside powers, France, the Spanish king-doms, the emperor, and above all the Ottomans, gathered their strength, were felt by all the Italian states. Thus, while this chapter will focus on the Milanese, Venetian and Florentine states and the smaller satellites around them, the wider Italy, increasingly sharing the same experiences, expectations and fears, cannot be excluded.

A main cause of uncertainty, and even gloom, both amongst contempo-raries and amongst recent historians, has been the economic condition of the Italian states. An 'economic depression of the Renaissance', following the demographic disasters of the fourteenth century and lasting through much of the fifteenth century has been seen as accompanying, and indeed possibly contributing to, the extraordinary cultural flowering of Italy in this period.[1] An atmosphere of cautious economic pessimism is thought to have resulted from a steep decline in Genoese trading activity, an apparent dramatic collapse in Florentine woollen cloth production and a lowering of levels of investment in banks. These are issues which have been much debated without any very clear consensus emerging. There have undoubtedly been exaggerations in the depressionist arguments; Genoa's retreat from the eastern Mediterranean was matched by renewed advantage for Venice. Venice's sense of economic well-being in the 1420s is expressed in the famous death-bed oration of Doge Tommaso Mocenigo, and all the evidence points to an expansion of economic

---

[1] The debate aroused by Lopez (1953) and Lopez and Miskimin (1962) has never been satisfactorily resolved. Despite the adverse responses of many, led by Cipolla (1963) and Goldthwaite (1980), ch. 1, the idea of prolonged depression lingers on. For the latest analyses of the problem, see Brown (1989) and Aymard (1991).

Map 11   Italy

activity in the Republic in the first half of the fifteenth century. Genoa itself was finding new outlets for economic enterprise in the western Mediterranean, and in seeking to develop interests in the Iberian peninsula created a new rivalry with Aragon. Florence's woollen cloth industry moved towards a more luxurious and profitable product, and a growing interest in the manufacture of fine silk also helped to offset any fall in the level of output. At the same time the occupation of Pisa in 1406 and Livorno in 1421 opened the way to the sea, and the creation of a maritime enterprise which took the Florentines into competition with the Venetians in the ports of the Levant and northern Europe. Milan and many of the cities of Lombardy benefited from links over the Alps with the expanding economies of the south German cities in the first half of the fifteenth century.

All this suggests that too gloomy a view of the economies of the northern Italian states in the late fourteenth and early fifteenth centuries is unjustified. There was undoubtedly rising competitiveness, but this stemmed as much from the expansion of the states and of economic opportunities as it did from restraints in traditional areas.

There are, however, two further points to be made about the economic context. In the first half of the fifteenth century the Italian state system emerged with the expansion of Florence and Venice into regional states, and the establishment of the Aragonese dynasty in Naples. The extension of central control implicit in these developments created new economic strength. Florence undoubtedly benefited from the subjection to its rule of Arezzo, Prato and Pisa even if the emergence of a coherent regional economy was scarcely perceptible. The main purpose of Venetian expansion was to gain political control over the trade routes of north-eastern Italy and to encourage the flow of traffic to and from Venice on the landward side. Milan's periodic control over Genoa drew Milanese merchants into the commercial world of the western Mediterranean. There was an inevitable drift of resources and manpower towards these new capital cities, and towards the centres of the smaller states, Turin, Mantua, Ferrara, which stimulated their economies.

At the same time it has to be said that the costs of government and of defence tended to spiral and always to outrun the resources. The real problem for fifteenth century Italy lay not so much in reduced economic activity as in vastly increased demands on the resources available. Rising levels of taxation and borrowing, increasing expenditure on state enterprises, both military and cultural, eroded the instinctive capitalistic interests of individual entrepreneurs and distorted the economies of the Italian states. In Florence the costs of war in the first half of the fifteenth century were more than three times the normal revenue of the state. Attempts to spread this burden over the expanded state were frustrated both by the centralising tendencies in the economy and by a real lack of centralised power. There has been a tendency to exaggerate the growth of the Renaissance state in Italy in the fifteenth century. Whether they were princely states like Milan, or republican states like Venice and Florence, the Italian states lacked the resources, and indeed the will, to centralise power effectively. Compromises with localism abounded and this will be one of the main themes of this chapter.

In the early fifteenth century the hegemonic aspirations of first the Visconti and then Ladislas of Naples appeared to be the controlling factors in Italian politics. Giangaleazzo Visconti, having received the title of duke of Milan from the emperor in 1395, aimed at control of Tuscany through the subjection of Pisa, Siena and Bologna. His sudden death in 1402 brought relief to beleaguered Florence, and, together with the similar death of Ladislas in 1414 as he was pushing Angevin–Neapolitan power northwards towards Tuscany, gave the Florentines some justification for thinking that God and good fortune were on their side. A deep-rooted civic pride and republican patriotism was given a new impetus by these events and by the subsequent temporary decline of Milanese and Neapolitan power. In the duchy of Milan centrifugal forces took over; the ambitions of Giangaleazzo's *condottieri*, linked to the continuing yearnings for autonomy of the Lombard cities, led to a collapse of Visconti centralisation. Giovanni Maria Visconti was just beginning to make some headway in restoring order when he was assassinated in 1412. His young brother, Filippo Maria, started a more sustained revival of Visconti authority by marrying Beatrice Tenda, the widow of his father's most powerful *condottiere*, Facino Cane. At this moment the death of Ladislas led to a renewal of Angevin–Aragonese rivalry in Naples and the temporary removal of hegemonic threats from the south.

The vacuum created in northern Italy by the weakening of Visconti power provided the opportunity for Florence and Venice to expand and arm themselves more effectively against future threats. Florence's occupation of Pisa in 1406, and subsequent extension of control of the Tuscan coastline with the purchase of Livorno from Genoa in 1421, was a key moment in the life of the Republic. Venice's extension of its previously limited foothold in the Italian *terraferma* by the destruction of the Carrara *signoria* and the occupation of Verona, Vicenza and Padua in 1404–5, and large parts of Friuli by 1420, gave an entirely new dimension to the political and economic interests of the Serenissima. In both cases military force had been a significant factor in the expansion, although there was also a strong element of smaller communities surrendering themselves to the influence and protection of the larger states. However, more importantly, the greatly enlarged states now needed more permanent and more effective defensive systems. There was already a growing tendency in the late fourteenth century for links between the states and the mercenary captains to be strengthened and permanent nuclei of troops to be established. After 1406 Florence's first preoccupation was the fortifications of Pisa, while Venice quickly deployed large permanent forces to defend its newly gained territories. The defence of far-flung frontiers imposed very different military, and subsequently fiscal and organisational, problems than a reliance on the walls of the city and the waters of the Venetian lagoon.

In this move towards increasingly permanent and expensive defence commitments, Venice had considerable advantage over Florence. Expenditure on permanent naval defence was already a part of Venetian government policy and the normal income of the state was substantially larger than that of Florence. But perhaps more significant was the immediate situation in the early decades of the fifteenth century, in which while in northern Italy the move towards standing military arrangements was clear-cut, in the south the opportunities for captains to secure lucrative temporary employment in the highly volatile political situation remained the dominant factor. Florence, on the frontier between north and south, found it both more difficult to retain the services of captains and easier to dispense with them, knowing that it would be possible to recruit when necessary. It was Italy from Umbria southwards which was in the third decade of the fifteenth century the battleground for the two great schools of *condottieri*, the Sforzeschi and Bracceschi, from which the traditions of late medieval Italian warfare grew. To the north of this line the stable military power of Milan and Venice was steadily growing.

Of the three main states of northern Italy it is Florence which has attracted most interest from historians in the first half of the fifteenth century. This is partly because of the dramatic and influential cultural changes which took place in the city, and partly because of greater dynamism and variety in the political scene than was apparent in either Milan or Venice. The two factors are not unrelated. The rapid expansion of the Florentine state to a position of dominance in Tuscany, leaving only Lucca and Siena independent, but with little prospect of territorial advancement, has already been discussed. This was undoubtedly a major factor in a growth of Florentine self-confidence and assertiveness. The successful defence of the Republic against the aggression of the 'tyrannical' rulers of Milan and Naples has also been identified as a source of self-congratulation and pride.[2] But most attention has been focused on internal political and social changes which gradually transformed Florence from a factious and volatile commune into a stable and coherently directed

[2] For the famous 'Baron thesis', see Baron (1966) and (1988). An initial intellectual historian's response came from Seigel (1966), but the broadening of the whole debate owes much to Holmes (1969) and Brucker (1977).

state. Traditionally, much of the credit or, in the eyes of some, blame for this change has been allotted to the Medici family, and 1434, the year of Cosimo de' Medici's return from brief exile in Venice, has been seen as a turning-point. But recently the three decades before 1434 have received more careful study and the basic continuities in Florentine history now tend to be emphasised.[3]

Florentine republicanism was edging gradually towards oligarchy in the later years of the fourteenth century. The checks to economic and demographic growth were a part of this, but it was also an acceptance of political and social realities. The regime which emerged in the aftermath of the Ciompi uprising in 1378, and the brief experiment in popular republicanism which followed it, was self-consciously oligarchic. While the republican values of liberty and wide participation in public affairs were still ostentatiously proclaimed, real power shifted towards an inner regime of some seventy senior politicians in each generation. The public offices, ranging from the Gonfalonier of Justice, the titular head of state, and his eight priors, appointed every two months by a process of drawing from bags filled with the names of eligible guildsmen (sortition), to judicial and fiscal officials dispatched throughout the expanding state, continued to be filled in the traditional way. Access to office remained a crucial part of civic life and a component of social status, alongside wealth, family connections and life style. But behind the scenes, manipulation of the lists of eligibles and the names which were actually placed in key sortition bags, increasing resort to special and carefully chosen emergency councils (*baliè*) to make decisions on particular issues, and continuous use of a permanent body of informed experienced advisers (the *pratica*) as the main forum for policy discussion, all tended to stabilise power in the hands of an inner elite dominated in the early years of the century by the Albizzi family. However, this was not yet an aristocratic elite; access to it, which to some extent depended on family links and traditions, was conditioned by experience in public affairs, wealth and neighbourhood influence. The members of such a regime not only sought ways to enhance their individual status, but collectively emphasised the importance of civic and republican values in order to create loyalty to the regime in the rest of the community. Cultural projects, whether the embellishment of public buildings, the patronage of particular works of art or the encouragement of the writing of patriotic histories and literary propaganda, were of great importance in this situation. They served to transmit the self-confidence and commitment of the elite to the whole city.

A growing concern for the wider state was also reflected in new taxation proposals instituted in 1427. The *Catasto* was a complete survey of all households in the state in terms both of human components and wealth on the basis

---

[3] Rubinstein (1966), pp. 1–29; Brucker (1977); Hale (1977), pp. 9–24; Kent (1978).

of which both taxes and forced loans could be applied. The emphasis was more on property than on business interests and it revealed the extent to which wealth was by this time concentrated in Florence. Two-thirds of the wealth in the state was held by Florentines who made up only one sixth of the population. The need for a more equitable taxation system had for long been a source of friction between the oligarchic regime and its critics; the wars of the late 1420s which made the new taxes necessary, and particularly the concern of the regime to continue the expansion of the state and absorb Lucca, added to the internal conflicts. At the heart of opposition to the Albizzi regime was the Medici family which, with its rapidly rising wealth, its links with the Church and papal banking, and a consciously populist attitude towards the problem of the distribution of power within the state, seemed to stand for traditional republican values. This contrast between an elitist and increasingly aristocratic tendency in Florentine society, and a strong yearning and support for a more egalitarian tradition was reflected in the cultural trends of the period. But it would be wrong to press the links between politics and culture too far. The Medici relied as much on effective manipulation of a political faction and the building up of support within the elite as they did on any popular appeal. The attempt by the regime to destroy them in 1433 failed because it was carried out inefficiently and was not ruthlessly followed up. Medici supporters were able to regroup and gain control of the key committees in the following year, and the recall of Cosimo from exile led to the creation of a more effective oligarchy.

The apparent change of direction for Venice in the early fifteenth century, with the creation of a regional state in Italy and a new commitment to mainland politics, was even greater than that for Florence. But in fact the change was less striking than it seemed; there was no sudden decline of interest in the eastern Mediterranean; the *stato di mar* was continuing to expand and trade with the Levant appeared to be booming in the 1420s; Venice at this stage seemed able easily to hold its own with the advancing Ottomans. On the other hand, the mainland interest was not new; the security of the river routes of Lombardy and the roads to the Alps and to Germany had been a preoccupation for more than a century. The lesson of the war of Chioggia (1378–81) was that an alliance between the commercial rival, Genoa, and increasingly powerful hinterland *signori*, like the Carrara, was an immense threat to both the security and the prosperity of Venice. The post-Chioggia generation of politicians, led by Carlo Zeno and Doge Michele Steno, was increasingly alert to events on the mainland and the dangers of expanding political power strangling Venice's flimsy influence.

Thus the decisive moves westwards in 1404–5 as far as Verona, and eastwards over Friuli in 1419–20, represented the more effective application of well-established policies. Inevitably, Venetian interests switched to some extent to the new mainland horizons; a new committee of *savi*, the *savi di terraferma*, was added in 1422 to the traditional *savi del consiglio* and *savi agli ordini* who steered business through the Senate and acted, along with the doge and the ducal councillors, as the heart of Venetian government. Posts became available to Venetian patricians as captains and *podestà* in mainland subject cities, and as bishops of mainland dioceses; a tendency to acquire mainland estates gradually accelerated. A factional interest within the ruling class which focused on mainland issues and international relations within Italy became apparent.

But these changes, obvious in the long run, came about slowly. Venice, while insisting on clear dominance over its new subject cities and on maintaining a distinction between the Venetian patriciate and the ruling elites of those cities, had little interest in organising the day-to-day affairs of the mainland state. The institutions of cities of Roman origin, like Padua and Verona, were quite different to those of the Venetian Republic, and much of their administration and that of their hinterlands was left in the hands of the local elites. A small number of Venetian officials became responsible for security, good order and equitable justice; the new provinces were expected to pay the costs of their own administration and defence, but not to contribute significantly to central state funds. Venice, unlike Florence, was little concerned with economic exploitation or close supervision of the new state. As a result the links between the *terraferma* and Venice were fewer and created less impact than might be expected.[4]

Nevertheless Venice was not the unchanging, balanced, harmonious society portrayed in the famous 'myth of Venice'. The myth was already well-established by the early fifteenth century, and compared to Florence Venetian society was indeed less competitive and more stable. The creation of a fixed political class through the so-called 'serrata' (the closing of the Great Council) started in the late thirteenth century, and the traditions of public service and the subordination of private interests to a collective good were now already well established. By 1432, 732 government posts a year were available to members of the patriciate, including membership of the main policy-making body, the Senate. The five new *savi di terraferma* and the new rectors of the *terraferma* cities were but a small proportion of these office holders. But in Venice all these appointments were elected and not drawn by lot; there was a far greater emphasis on continuity and proven experience in Venetian office holding than there was in Florence, and this created a more formal elitism.

---

[4] Cozzi and Knapton (1986) have helped significantly to pull together the strands of the history of Venice's relationship with the *terraferma* state in the fourteenth and fifteenth centuries. However, debate over Venetian attitudes towards the subject provinces continues; see Ventura (1964); Bertelli *et al.* (1979), pp. 167–92; Cracco and Knapton (1983); Grubb (1988); Law (1992); Viggiano (1993).

Venice was a consciously aristocratic society headed by the doge, elected for life, whose formal authority was tightly prescribed, but whose informal influence was immeasurable. Thus, while lip-service was paid to the principles of equality, and even anonymity, within the patriciate, in practice there were marked gradations of influence, status and wealth. Deliberate avoidance of public office, vote-rigging in elections, factionalism in politics, were all part of the Venetian scene. The fact that significant political office could only be achieved by senior mature men of proven experience meant that there was always division between the older politicians and the young patricians crowding into the Great Council at the age of twenty-five or even younger. This split, known as that between *giovani* and *vecchi*, tended to emerge over almost any controversial issue, particularly in foreign policy. It was exemplified in the 1420s when Francesco Foscari (1373–1457) was elected doge at the unusually young age of forty-nine. Foscari with his commitment to *terraferma* affairs and intervention in Italian politics represented a faction of young politicians who rejected the conservative, cautious, defence of maritime interest, policies of the senior politicians of the time. At almost the same moment Antonio and Marin Contarini challenged another orthodoxy with their building of the flamboyant Ca' d'Oro palace on the Grand Canal. Here was a society in which tradition was being constantly challenged in the fifteenth century as Venice was gradually drawn into the mainstream of Italian political and cultural development.

The great commercial rival of Venice in the previous centuries, Genoa, was experiencing very different fortunes in this period. To a large extent eclipsed by Venice in the struggle for dominance of eastern Mediterranean markets, the merchant families of Genoa were engaged in creating new commercial contacts in the western basin. The strong emphasis on external commerce at the expense of internal unity and growth was primarily the result of the physical and political barriers to the expansion of a Genoese state on the Ligurian coastline. The institutions of the state remained weak in the face of the great clans which dominated Genoese society and its economy. The one centralising institution, which on occasions acted almost as the state, was the Banco di S. Giorgio, a sort of super guild of merchant and banking families. But the very presence of the Banco as a focus of the economic activities of the Genoese elite seemed to impede the development of any socio-political coherence in the city, or any major role in Italian political affairs.

The second quarter of the century was dominated by wars; wars fought not so much for hegemony in Italy, as for living and breathing space. The starting-point of these wars was the recovery of Visconti power in Milan. Filippo Maria Visconti had gradually rebuilt the integrated duchy of his father. In 1421 he occupied Genoa and reclaimed Brescia from the control of Pandolfo Malatesta. He was thus in a position to challenge the mercantile powers and had moved forward to a common frontier with the new Venetian state in the centre of the Lombard plain. Filippo Maria had achieved this revival with the help of a single dominant military captain, Francesco Bussone, count of Carmagnola, and of the Milanese financiers, like the Borromeo family. Now, in 1424, like his father, he sought to extend Visconti influence south-eastwards towards Bologna and the Romagna. Florence, fearful and jealous of its own influence in the Romagna, opposed the move but was defeated at Zagonara.

The new power of Visconti Milan quickly produced an alliance of northern states to contain it. Carmagnola, dissatisfied with the rewards offered him by the suspicious Filippo Maria Visconti, turned to Venice and stimulated the already wakening concern of the Foscari regime. By the end of 1425 an anti-Visconti alliance had been forged between Venice and Florence. This was joined in the following year by the duchy of Savoy, Milan's western neighbour, where Amadeus VIII had succeeded in creating a substantial state on both sides of the Alps by uniting Savoy and Piedmont, winning an outlet to the Mediterranean with the occupation of Nice, and gaining in 1416 the title of duke from the emperor.

The coalition proved too strong for Milan. In the wars that followed, Venice gained Brescia and Bergamo and moved its western frontiers up to the line of the Adda. Carmagnola won a crushing victory at Maclodio (1427), while Amadeus VIII, through the intervention of the emperor, secured a redrawing of his frontier with Milan to include the acquisition of Vercelli by Savoy as the price for his withdrawal from the coalition. Florence alone gained little advantage; its attempts to occupy Lucca as a preliminary to encroaching on the Milanese position in the Lunigiana were frustrated by Milanese armies coming to the aid of the little Tuscan republic. At this point there emerged the figure of Francesco Sforza who was to dominate the northern Italian scene for the next thirty-five years. Francesco was the son of Muzio Attendolo Sforza and succeeded his father as the leader of the Sforzeschi military companies. The military opportunities in northern Italy soon attracted back many of the captains who had been occupied in the south in the first half of the 1420s, and by the end of the decade Francesco Sforza had become the chief captain of Filippo Maria Visconti. To ensure his loyalty the duke offered his natural daughter and heiress, Bianca Maria, to the captain as bride, and encouraged him to create a satellite state in the Marches. With Sforza, and to a lesser extent Niccolò Piccinino who was now consistently linked to the Visconti cause, Filippo Maria had the military strength he needed to turn the tide against him. This was even more the case when, in 1432, the government of Venice lost patience with Carmagnola's imperious ways and suspect fidelity, and executed him.

At this point much hinged on the ambitions of Francesco Sforza. His consistent loyalty to the Visconti would have secured for them military predominance and led probably to the recovery of some of the territory in Lombardy to which Milan attached so much importance. But Filippo Maria was not a man who encouraged and inspired consistent loyalty, nor was Sforza a man prepared to wait to take the political limelight. His base in the Marches gave him the possibility of intervening in central and southern Italian affairs, and left little time for furthering Milanese interests in the north. But the dramatic victory of the Genoese fleet over the Aragonese at Ponza (1435) gave a new advantage to Filippo Maria as overlord of Genoa. He used it to forge an understanding with Alfonso of Aragon linked to an alliance with Savoy. Despite the revolt of Genoa from Milanese rule which followed, Filippo Maria now seemed to be poised to reassert Milanese predominance in northern Italy. The threat reactivated the Venetian–Florentine alliance with papal support, and Francesco Sforza, fearful that a more confident Filippo Maria would repudiate his marriage agreement, joined the allies as their captain-general.

For three years (1438–41) war raged over the land between Brescia and Verona, and in the Romagna. Despite a long siege the Milanese failed to take Brescia, and with dramatic marches and counter-marches Sforza and Gattamelata were able to save Verona for Venice. A Milanese attempt to break out into the Romagna was frustrated by a Florentine–papal victory at Anghiari (1440). By 1441 Filippo Maria Visconti was ready to come to terms with his son-in-law, and the peace of Cavriana was accompanied by the formal celebration of the marriage of Sforza and Bianca Maria. But the rivalries stimulated by the disputed lands in central Lombardy, still held by Venice, and by the quest for influence in the Romagna, persisted; nor were Francesco Sforza's suspicions of his father-in-law assuaged.

When Filippo Maria Visconti died on 13 August 1447 confusion reigned. There were persistent rumours that he had left a will bequeathing his state to Alfonso of Aragon following the understanding forged after Ponza. At the same time Francesco Sforza had in the last weeks finally rejoined Milanese service and was already on his way to Milan. Florence and Venice feared the possibility of an Aragonese take over even more than that of a Sforza succession. But at this point an alliance of Milanese aristocracy and popular feeling stood out against all the foreign influences at work and set up an Ambrosian Republic. Sforza, not wishing to impose himself by force on Milan, was content to wait, took command of the army of the Republic and defeated the Venetians at Caravaggio (1448). His patience was rewarded; the business interests in Milan soon perceived that the Republic was too weak to give the security that they needed; Cosimo de' Medici, for similar reasons and increasingly fearful of Venetian power, finally broke the long-term alliance between

Florence and Venice, and supported Sforza's bid to claim the duchy. On 26 February 1450 Francesco Sforza was invited to enter Milan and take control.

The next four years saw a culmination of the wars which had beset Italy since the beginning of the century. The fighting itself was perhaps less intense than in some previous moments, but the implications of political confrontation and rivalry, and the costs of constant preparedness, were now fully apparent. Florence and Pope Nicholas V continued to support Francesco Sforza and his new regime in Milan; Venice and Alfonso V, now firmly established in Naples, came together as unlikely allies. Venice had opposed the Sforza take over in Milan to the end, fearing that it would inevitably lead to a more determined effort to recover the lost territories in central Lombardy. Initially, this clearly was one of Francesco Sforza's intentions; in 1451 he succeeded in winning over Bartolomeo Colleoni, one of Venice's leading military captains, and two years later Milanese and Florentine diplomats persuaded Charles VII to support an Angevin bid to topple the Aragonese in Naples by sending troops to Italy to help the triple alliance. Meanwhile a Neapolitan army was operating in southwest Tuscany as an indication of the new-found intentions of Alfonso V to extend his influence into northern Italy.

By 1453, however, the pace of the war was slackening and an almost universal interest in peace became apparent. Francesco Sforza had failed to persuade the Emperor Frederick III to invest him with the title of duke of Milan during his coronation journey to Rome in 1452, and this validation now became a more important objective of Sforza policy than territorial expansion. The fall of Constantinople to the Turks sent a tremor round Europe, but particularly disturbed Nicholas V and Venice who both saw peace in Italy as an essential preliminary to a Christian riposte. All the states were financially exhausted and none more so than Florence, compelled to defend itself from the Neapolitan threat from the south as well as provide subsidies for its allies. The spectre of large-scale foreign intervention in Italy was raised by the presence of French troops in Lombardy. All these factors were at work in creating the basis for at least a temporary cessation of the fighting. Peace talks started in Rome in November 1453 under the aegis of Pope Nicholas V, but it was practical realities in the spring of 1454 that actually led to peace. The potential costs of renewed mobilisation, Venetian success in once more drawing Colleoni on to its side and a real threat that Charles VII was preparing to change sides and join Venice in a dismemberment of the Milanese state led to the Peace of Lodi agreed between the northern states on 9 April 1454. Venice gained Crema and recognised Francesco Sforza as duke of Milan. The end of fighting was followed by a gradually expanding series of negotiations to organise the peace which produced, by January 1455, the so-called *lega italica* – the Italian League.

A territorial status quo was recognised and mutual obligations amongst the major Italian states to assist one another in the event of attack were reinforced by an endorsement of certain levels of standing military forces. Each of the powers nominated its adherents and allies amongst the minor states and lordships thus theoretically drawing them into the protective net – but at the same time clearly identifying politically dangerous overlaps in spheres of influence. The agreement was signed for twenty-five years and undoubtedly contained an element of Italian states seeking to draw together in the face of external threat – whether Ottoman or French. But the internal rivalries could not be ended so easily nor the power balance regulated so artificially.

One of the key figures in the creation of the more settled political order in Italy in the mid-1450s was Cosimo de' Medici. By his personal financial support, and the influence which he exercised in providing Florentine diplomatic support, Cosimo had done much to ensure the success of Francesco Sforza in taking over in Milan. In doing so he created a Florentine–Milanese entente that was to last for most of the rest of the century. This in itself says much about the changes which had taken place in Florence since the heady days of the early Quattrocento; republican Florence was now firmly allied with ducal Milan.

A part of this change was the expanded Florentine state. New physical horizons meant new institutions and new responsibilities; senior Florentine politicians were likely to spend more time holding office outside the city, patronage networks widened, economic opportunities expanded and diversified. But these were adjustments that were slow to change fundamental political attitudes. The continued dominance of Florence and the Florentine political elite within the territorial state ensured that attitudes towards that state changed only slowly. The main preoccupations and interests of the elite remained focused on the political and familial life of the city itself. However, it was within that narrow political elite that expansion had its limited effect. It served, in a sense, to provide more space for the elite whether as merchants and economic entrepreneurs, as office holders, or as landowners. It enabled some to extend their personal influence; it released others of the tension of traditional rivalries and suspicions; it provided a new identity of interest for the Florentine elite.

At the same time real changes were taking place within Florentine society as a whole. Florence was no longer a boom city; there were plenty of opportunities for economic success but they lay in the production of high-quality wool and silk cloth with a limited and skilled workforce and heavy investment of capital in raw materials and unsold products, and in the careful calculation of risk in the economic and financial fields. Large-scale immigration was discouraged from the 1380s onwards; social mobility tended to decline; respect for wealth became increasingly respect for old, established wealth; a commitment to participate in public affairs had become a major component of social status, but increasingly it was high political office and major cultural benefactions that gained esteem. The gaps between social groups were widening, the barriers rising; dowry inflation was both contributing to and resulting from this situation. In brief, the elitist trend in Florence was accelerating through the middle years of the century; and this is the background to the growing ascendancy of the Medici.

The other fundamental factor which conditioned the style of Florentine politics by the mid-fifteenth century was the general acceptance by the political class of the need for greater continuity and greater expertise in the conduct of public affairs. The expanded state, the growing role of fiscalism, the pressures of external relations, all pointed in this direction. A greater emphasis on secrecy, smaller and more informal councils, the continuous presence of experienced politicians at the heart of the regime, were the signs of an inevitable change of political style. They fostered oligarchy as well as being instruments of oligarchy. Continuity of leadership was an essential part of this pattern of development.

From the moment of his return from exile in 1434 Cosimo de' Medici became the acknowledged leader of the regime. The exiling of more than seventy political opponents stifled faction and a relatively coherent oligarchy was able, in a time of prolonged external crisis in the 1430s and 1440s, to exploit already time-honoured devices for the focusing of political authority within an apparently republican system. Distortion of the traditional constitutional practices took two main forms. On the one hand the initial scrutiny and sortition processes which qualified citizens for public office and distributed office were subjected to much closer control by permanent *accoppiatori* whose role it was not only to ensure that the names of the politically suspect were excluded, but that high offices were filled, when necessary, by appropriately qualified candidates. The other device employed was extensive use of the traditional mechanism of creating a specially selected council with wide powers (*balìa*) to deal with an emergency situation. The war years between 1434 and 1454 were dominated by government by *balìa*, and the membership of the inner political elite can be confidently defined by examining the lists of the successive *balìe* that were created in these years. When, after 1454, political emergency could no longer be used to justify the *balìe*, the regime turned to the creation of new permanent councils, the Council of One Hundred in 1458 and the Council of Seventy in 1480, to provide the same cores of assured support within a formal constitutional framework. The Council of Seventy with its membership for a five-year term, renewable, and its powerful sub-committees for external and domestic affairs, represented a complete absorption of oligarchic trends into constitutional forms.

The role of the successive heads of the Medici family in these constitutional developments remains a matter of debate.[5] It has been argued that Cosimo, Piero and Lorenzo de' Medici were aiming at establishing the family permanently at the heart of Florentine politics and society and were engaged in preparing the way for princely power; that the constitutional changes were engineered by them personally for this purpose; and that any sense of unanimity and collaboration that emerged was with a Medici faction rather than a Florentine elite. On the other hand it can be suggested that Medici ascendancy in the fifteenth century was essentially an alliance between the family and a reasonably broad cross-section of the Florentine elite; that, for example, the Council of Seventy was not just a caucus of Medici sycophants but a real expression of oligarchic solidarity; and that Medici influence depended more on a wide range of patronal activity than on specific political mechanisms. Cosimo de' Medici was clearly accepted as the first among equals by a generation of experienced politicians who had grown up with him and shared the difficult years of the 1430s and 1440s. Lorenzo, on the other hand, succeeded to leadership of the family as a man of twenty surrounded by the leaders of his grandfather's generation. That he was able to establish a precedence and authority which seemed to exceed that of Cosimo was perhaps as much due to the changing nature of the times as it was to his own undoubted skills and personality. In a world increasingly dominated by princes, Lorenzo was bound to be seen by some as a prince and to behave in some respects like a prince; but it is the restraints imposed on this tendency both by the circumstances of Florence and by his own political intelligence which are the more interesting phenomena.

The social transitions taking place in Florence in the second half of the fifteenth century were not peculiar to that city. Throughout northern and central Italy the same tendency towards elitism was apparent. To some extent this was a question of expanded frontiers and consolidation of power, but much criticism has been levelled, in recent years, at the idea of the 'Renaissance state' in Italy as a centralising construct. The example of Milan under the Sforza dukes has been much explored.[6] Here the focus on Milan as a capital city undoubtedly increased in the second half of the fifteenth century; new public buildings, powerful ducal officials such as Cicco Simonetta, refurbished constitutional mechanisms like the *consiglio segreto*, all seemed to reflect the growing authority of the duke and at the same time the essential alliance between the dukes and a Milanese elite. But in reality ducal power was not just a matter of the creation

---

[5] Gutkind (1938); Rubinstein (1966); Hale (1977), pp. 24–75; Hook (1984); Ames-Lewis (1992); Brown (1992); Garfagnini (1992) and (1994).

[6] Jones (1965); Chittolini (1979); Capitani *et al.* (1981); Frangioni (1987); Mainoni (1988).

of central facilities and mechanisms; it depended on a series of compromises with persistent traditions of local self-government. Ducal decree did normally take precedence over municipal statute but usually after a process of negotiation; the duke did appoint the *podestà* in Lombard cities, but his choice was usually a local magnate; new taxes and new tax levels were decreed in Milan, but the ultimate distribution of the fiscal burden was decided at local level based on local custom and local knowledge. The authority of the duke depended on creating alliances and loyalties throughout the state. Many ducal officials came from outside Milan, the old feudatories were crucial allies and a process of refeudalisation helped to widen the circle of the elite. The new feudalism did not carry the overtones of judicial and jurisdictional authority associated with traditional forms, but it conferred wealth through lands and local influence on favoured *condottieri*, bureaucrats and merchant bankers. It was part of a clientage network which was an essential feature of princely rule in fifteenth-century Italy.

Similar reservations have to be expressed about the authority of the dukes of Savoy and other princes in this period. The duchy of Savoy, divided as it was by the Alps into westward-facing Savoy and eastward-facing Piedmont, presented particular problems of control. The dukes deliberately refrained from establishing a fixed capital, moving their court when seasonally possible between Chambéry, Thonon, Pinerolo and Turin after it had been inherited from the Acaia branch of the family in 1418. The death of Amadeus VIII in 1451, followed as it was by a succession of less effective and more short-lived reigns, led to a period of stasis in the development of ducal authority. Local privilege and the authority of traditional elites were given a prolonged reprieve. The smaller princely states like Mantua and Ferrara were somewhat different cases. Here the ruling families of the Gonzaga and the Este were becoming gradually more entrenched and accepted. Giovan Francesco Gonzaga acquired the imperial title of marquis of Mantua in 1433, and his successors in the sixteenth century became dukes. Borso d'Este was made duke of Modena by Frederick III in 1452, and gained the title of duke of Ferrara from the pope in 1471. These were important confirmations of authority, but the true basis of the authority lay in the creation of an effective and supportive elite, in a reasonable regard for a wider public opinion and the principles of good government, and in maintaining substantial wealth, as much through military contracts and landed income as through taxes. The court became the focus of power in these small states, but the emphasis was on real power exercised collectively rather than on the much-publicised authority of the prince.

In Venice the principles of collective responsibility and the sharing of power within a relatively narrow political elite were well established and the constitution had evolved in this direction. Nevertheless, by the mid-fifteenth century the pressures for a narrowing of the elite and for more effective and confidential decision-making processes were also apparent here. A gradual widening of the competence of the Council of Ten to include foreign policy and defence issues, and a growing emphasis on the day-to-day running of affairs by the *collegio*, were characteristic of the second half of the century. The doge was a member of both these groups, but so were the six ducal councillors, elected from among the most senior politicians in the city. Personal influence becomes more effective in a smaller caucus and it increasingly becomes possible to attribute policies and decisions to the influence of particular individuals, as with Francesco Foscari and *terraferma* expansion, Cristoforo Moro and the war with the Turks (1463–79), Francesco Michiel and the war of Ferrara (1482–4). Two of these were doges, Michiel was never more than a *savio di terraferma*. But despite these glimpses of personal political roles, the system continued to function as a collective one, even if an inner political elite was gradually identifying itself.

The political tendencies of this period were reflected in the life styles and culture of the new elites. Leisure and the pursuits of leisure became a major preoccupation of men who had already detached themselves sufficiently from professional or commercial activity to take on the greater commitment to public affairs. Country living, villas and *villeggiatura* played a growing role in this life style. For the Florentine elite the maintenance of a country property had always been a significant part of the way of life. However, in the second half of the fifteenth century the villa became not just a simple place for summer retreat and a source of cheap provisions, but an object of pride and prestige, a place of entertainment and a focus of political influence. Horses, hunting dogs, falcons and even prize herds of cattle became objects of everyday concern and a part of elite iconography. The rebuilding and decoration of villas increasingly occupied the time of architects and artists. It became necessary for the busy politician to have not only a country villa, but also a second property close to the city for weekend enjoyment. Ambassadors in Florence began to bemoan the fact that political decisions were delayed by the absence of all the key committee members at their villas. But this was as much a reflection of a new urgency in decision making as of a changing life style of the elite.

For the Venetian elite such a trend was a novelty, only beginning in this period. But in a sense the Venetian political class had less need of a distinctive life style; membership of the Great Council was by now the traditional mark of distinction, but the emergence of elitist trends within the patriciate was beginning to encourage new cultural traits.

It has been argued that the social and political trends of the second half of the fifteenth century encouraged a switch of intellectual interest away from the societal ideas of early humanism, heavily influenced by Aristotle, towards the

more introverted, individualistic emphases of Platonism. While there is a hint
of this in the intellectual enthusiasms of the circle who met around Marsilio
Ficino in Florence, it is not an idea that should be pressed too far. What distinguished the elites of the later fifteenth century was a growing respect for and
involvement in learning and humanistic interests of all sorts, in building up
libraries, in sponsoring editions of classical texts and the work of early printers,
in philosophical debate. Humanism was ceasing to be an avant-garde movement in the strictest sense of the word, and becoming the emblem of the political and social elites. It moved to court and into the universities; it pervaded the
programmes of the new fresco cycles of villas and palaces. Those fresco cycles
themselves became representations of an increasingly narrow social world;
Botticelli's banquet scenes and nativities, the court cycles of Mantegna and
Cossa, the processions and miracles of Gentile Bellini and Carpaccio, all focus
on an elite society.

The corollary to this emergence of class and cultural division within the
individual societies of Renaissance Italy was a tendency for the elites to seek
links with each other. Exiled members of a ruling elite were welcomed in
neighbouring states; intermarriage became more common; lists of godparents
of children of the elites reflected a growing Italian emphasis. Travel became a
more frequent feature of the life style of the elites, and this was in large part
due to a dramatic increase in diplomatic activity in the second half of the fifteenth century. As external affairs played an expanding role in political debate,
diplomatic experience and external personal contacts became of crucial
importance to aspiring politicians. Information, exchanged through letters and
dispatches, was becoming a much-valued commodity and the gathering of it a
main function of the burgeoning clientage networks. Led by humanist chancellors and secretaries, the emphasis of rhetoric switched from oratory to correspondence as the audience became more extensive and dispersed.[7]

The years 1454 to 1494 have often been described as the period of the 'balance
of power'. Insofar as this title suggests that external affairs were the main preoccupation of the Italian states it still has some validity. It was not the constructive balance conferred by the Italian league and the far-sighted efforts of a
few Italian political leaders, which has sometimes been suggested. Nor was it a
balance which seemed to be leading towards greater unity of interest and
purpose amongst the states. There were contemporaries who spoke of the
need for a single leader in Italy as did the Florentine politician and diplomat

---

[7] Over the last twenty years a renewed interest in the so-called 'origins of modern diplomacy' has been
apparent in the historical writing, stimulated by the publication of the Milanese ambassadorial dispatches (Kendall and Ilardi, 1970–81) and the letters of Lorenzo de' Medici (Medici, 1977–   ). See
also Mattingly (1955); Pillinini (1970); Ilardi (1986); Garfagnini (1992), Fubini (1994), pp. 185–360.

Angelo Acciaiuoli in a letter to Francesco Sforza in 1447: 'I have said to you on other occasions that it was necessary for you to create a *signore* in Italy who would be powerful enough to protect you from all others.'[8] But there was little chance of any such unity; harmony and serenity were not the keynotes of the period, but rather suspicion, self-interest and opportunism. The need for balance, for some degree of mutual support and protection, for caution, was accepted by all the Italian states, crippled by the long wars and fearful of the growing strength of external powers. But this acceptance was reflected in the emergence of a series of opposed and balanced leagues rather than in any long-term adherence to the concept of a general Italian League.[9]

The rising pressures from outside Italy were obvious. Following the fall of Constantinople (1453) an expansion westwards of Ottoman power under Mehemmed the Conqueror seemed inevitable. Venice fought a lonely war for sixteen years (1463–79) to protect its empire and its trading interests. Negropont, and many lives and ships, were lost; attempts to hold back the advancing Turks in Dalmatia and the Morea largely failed; Turkish horsemen invaded Friuli and ravaged the countryside to within sight from the bell towers of Venice itself. In 1480 the blow fell on Otranto and it was the turn of Naples to suffer. The death of the great sultan in the following year did, indeed, relieve the pressure, but not the fear.

Meanwhile the end of the Hundred Years War (1453) led to a renewal of French interest in Italy. In 1458 Charles VII won the support of the Genoese and established his lieutenant in the city. He actively promoted Angevin claims to Naples and Orleanist claims to Milan. The style of Louis XI was somewhat different; he had little time for the ambitions of his princely subjects and preferred to advance his own role as broker and arbiter in Italian politics. He surrounded himself with expert advisers on Italian affairs and with fawning diplomats from the Italian states. French ambassadors intervened, often in a peremptory manner, in every Italian crisis.

These pressures did little to create unity in Italy. Venice and Naples shared an apprehension about the Turks – but little else. Venice's problems in the eastern Mediterranean were seen by the other Italian states as a merciful diversion of feared resources. Milan and Naples shared a fear of French intervention and a suspicion of French motives, but Angevin and Orleanist claims were rarely concerted in this period. Florence and the Papacy, on the other hand, tended to be pro-French, as did Venice. All were prepared to intrigue with France in their

---

[8] 'Che altre volte io ve ho dicto queste parole che ad vuy era necessario fare uno signore in Italia il quale fusse sì grande chi ve defendesse da ogni altro.' Quoted in *Gli Sforza a Milano* (1982), p. 247.

[9] The prolonged debate about the nature of Italian inter-state politics in the period 1454–94, summed up by Pillinini (1970), needs to be substantially reassessed in the light of the immense amount of new information provided by the editors of the Lorenzo de' Medici letters (Medici, 1977–   ).

own interests, or indeed intrigue with Charles the Bold of Burgundy in order to divert French attention. Meanwhile, a Spanish interest in the affairs of the peninsula gradually revived with the union of the Spanish crowns and the active European policies of Ferdinand of Aragon.

Nevertheless, the crux of continued Italian disunity lay within the states themselves. For the new Sforza dynasty in Milan the key issues were achievement of imperial recognition and consolidation of the regime within the duchy. Frederick III's determination to withhold recognition from Francesco Sforza and his successors was a last flicker of active imperial interest in Italy, and it contributed to the continued instability of the Sforza. The duchy, which could have been the solid bulwark against French intervention and the leader of a strong and permanent coalition against possible Venetian imperialism, was riven with uncertainty. The Sforza dukes focused on the local issues: control of Genoa, won at huge cost in 1461 and lost again in 1478; superiority over Savoy, won with the exclusion of the latter from the Italian League in 1454, but lost in 1468, when Venice insisted on Savoy's inclusion in the renewal of the League; intrigue along the southern frontiers, in the Lunigiana, in Bologna and in the Romagna. These were all issues which created suspicion and enmity in Italy. The Aragonese kings of Naples resented and feared Milanese control of Genoa; the Florentines contested Milanese pretensions in the Lunigiana and the Romagna; Venice was suspicious and alert. But Venice remained largely on the defensive throughout this period. Its preoccupation lay with the advance of the Turks, with its eastern Mediterranean empire and the routes of trade and food supplies, and to a lesser extent with its relations with the Austrians and Hungarians beyond the Alps. As long as Bartolomeo Colleoni held sway as permanent captain-general in his base at Malpaga there was little to fear from Milan, but the Po routes, Ferrara and the Romagna remained of great interest to Venice. Ravenna was already in its hands and the acquisition of the salt pans of Cervia in 1463 added to the fears of its neighbours and the confidence of some of its politicians.

Florence, militarily the weakest of the major Italian states, depended more than any other on peace and the support of alliances. It shared a long frontier with the papal states and this generated a particular suspicion of the temporal aspirations of popes and their nepots. It depended largely on alliance with Milan for its military security and the maintenance of the Medici regime. A growing subservience to France and an erratic hostility to Venice were the results of policies which were largely aimed at preserving commercial prosperity.

At this point the analysis requires that the two halves of Italy should be brought together. The general Italian League did at first serve most interests. Following the temporary aberration of Calixtus III's attempt to overthrow the

Aragonese dynasty in Naples, Pius II, Francesco Sforza and Cosimo de' Medici worked to maintain that dynasty against its Angevin rivals. But by the mid-1460s and 'succession' crises in both Florence and Milan, it was becoming apparent that the natural alliance systems were Milan, Florence and Naples on one side, and Venice and the Papacy on the other. This created the natural counterbalance to Venetian strength and papal instability, although the Milan–Florence–Naples axis was also subject to considerable internal tensions and suspicions. There was a major realignment in 1474 when Florentine suspicions of Sixtus IV's policies were fuelled by Neapolitan support for the pope's eviction of Niccolò Vitelli from Città di Castello. This, together with Venice's urgent need of help against the Turks, led to a league of the northern powers and eventually to the alignments of the Pazzi War (1478–80). In this war Florence was largely defended against papal–Neapolitan attack by Milanese and Venetian troops. But the tensions in the alliance were very apparent and in late 1479 Milan and Florence were looking for peace without any reference to Venice. Similarly King Ferrante of Naples was seeking to distance himself again from the pope who opposed the growing Neapolitan influence in southern Tuscany, one of the main results of the war. This was the background to Lorenzo de' Medici's famous journey to Naples which culminated in peace and a new alliance system along the, by now, traditional lines.

The Milan–Florence–Naples axis survived for the remainder of this period. It succeeded in halting Venice's attack on Ferrara (1482–4), aided by a volte-face on the part of Sixtus IV who abandoned his alliance with Venice in the face of pressure from the axis and from Ferdinand of Aragon. It was successful in preventing the overthrow of the Aragonese dynasty in Naples by the revolt of the Neapolitan barons, supported by the pope (1485–6).

One of the causes of the more settled political atmosphere in Italy by the second half of the 1480s was the ascendancy which Lorenzo de' Medici succeeded in establishing over Innocent VIII, with the marriage of his daughter Maddalena, to the pope's son, Franceschetto Cibo, and the elevation of his son, Giovanni, to the cardinalate. The new prestige and influence which Lorenzo personally derived from this entente, and the new political alignment of four of the five major Italian powers, gave these last years before 1492, and the deaths of both Lorenzo and Innocent VIII in that year, the appearance of serenity and prosperity so persuasively argued by Guicciardini in the opening chapters of his *Storia d'Italia*.

But it was not just the appearance of external solidarity that was misleading in the 1490s. By this time many of the regimes themselves were in difficulties. To talk of rising popular unrest is always a difficult generalisation to sustain, particularly when more efficient policing was one of the policies of the oligarchic regimes and this in itself both constrained unrest and further identified it. But in Florence and Venice in particular there is clear evidence of a sort of political disillusionment with oligarchy, a yearning for the more traditional, open politics. This manifested itself to some extent in political debate, but more clearly in private correspondence, diaries and memoirs. An undercurrent of resentment of the Medici regime and of the growing authority of the Council of Ten in Venice can be clearly charted although it had relatively little impact on the surface of politics.

What was more apparent, and not always easy to separate from anti-oligarchic feelings, was the resentment of traditional elite groups excluded from the new regimes. The position of Ludovico Sforza, despite his growing authority as regent for his nephew, Giangaleazzo, after 1480, was threatened not just by the traditionally anti-Sforza Milanese Guelphs, but increasingly by leading Ghibelline magnates on whose support Ludovico had relied. The estrangement of a figure like Gian Giacomo Trivulzio was an indication of the increasingly personal nature of the Sforza regime and its consequent fragility. The example of the Neapolitan barons, in outright revolt in 1485 because of heavy tax burdens and exclusion from involvement in government, is the most obvious one of this phenomenon.

Exile was the standard solution to such problems, and this was frequently employed by the regimes of the later years of the century. Fieschi and Adorno exiles from Genoa, Noveschi exiles from Siena, Sanseverino exiles from Naples, Acciaiuoli exiles from Florence, plotted and intrigued against the regimes which had ousted them, creating internal tensions as well as external pressures. The concentration of Neapolitan exiles in France by the late 1480s when the new king of France, Charles VIII, had inherited the Angevin claims, was particularly ominous.

Such opposition would have been a good deal less dangerous had the regimes been stronger in financial terms. But the 1480s were difficult, if not hard, times. The Pazzi War and the War of Ferrara left considerable legacies of debt. King Ferrante of Naples owed huge sums to Florentine bankers, and Italian banking as a whole was in difficulties in this decade. The trading conditions on which banking depended were unfavourable; a decline in the supply of English wool because of restraints imposed by the English crown on exports unbalanced the trade with the north, while the growth of Turkish naval power undoubtedly threatened east Mediterranean trading interests. Florence abandoned its attempts to run a state monopoly galley system in 1480 and enthusiasm in Venice for the trade of the galleys was beginning to decline. At the same time there seemed to be an increase in rural poverty as population and prices rose, and wealth moved towards the towns. These trends had little to do with any ongoing 'economic depression of the Renaissance'; they were associated with overall growth in economic activity and rising competition.

But the real problem was less economic constraint than the inability of Italian regimes to contemplate the large-scale taxation necessary to give them financial stability. With relatively little progress made towards the internal organisation and cohesion of the northern Italian states, a high tax policy was both impractical and dangerous. With wealth moving towards the major cities and the hands of the elites, loans, even forced loans, were a more acceptable recourse than taxation, and governments weakly bowed to this postponement of the problem. Fiscal policy therefore inevitably exacerbated social antagonisms and further discouraged the growth of any real unity in the states.

There was also evidence of rising religious and spiritual ferment in northern Italy. This was particularly apparent in Florence where a lay piety trend linked up with dislike of the increasingly ostentatious life style of the Medici elite and a resentment of the spiritual failings of the Church. Anti-papalism and anti-clericalism also gathered strength in Florence at this time because of the long political confrontation with Sixtus IV. Inevitably the Church in country areas suffered from being associated with the central regime of the state, as Florentine, Venetian and Sforza bishops assumed diocesan responsibilities over the subject areas.

Much has been written about the French invasion of 1494 and the subsequent 'crisis of Italy'. Enough has been said already to indicate that neither the invasion nor the 'crisis' were entirely unpredictable. Certainly the deaths of Lorenzo de' Medici in April, 1492, Innocent VIII later in the same summer and King Ferrante of Naples in early 1494 had their consequences. Mutual suspicions within the main Italian League noticeably hardened as Naples and Florence intrigued against the new pope, Alexander VI, whose election had been supported by Milan and whose natural affiliations lay with Spain. Ludovico Sforza's clear intention permanently to dispossess Giangaleazzo and his Neapolitan bride, Isabella, the grand-daughter of King Ferrante, made collaboration between Milan and Naples increasingly unlikely as her father succeeded her grandfather on the throne. Piero de' Medici inherited a new and dangerous situation which would have been beyond the political skills of his father to control.

But Charles VIII's decision to invade Italy was not primarily the result of appeals by Italian princes, or even of a perception of the disunity of Italy; it was part of an emerging power struggle in Europe. Nor was the striking and immediate success of the invasion the result of crushing military strength on one side or anachronistic and effete soldiery on the other. The Italian states had indeed learnt to rely too much on diplomacy in the years since 1454, but their armies were large and well equipped. There was, of course, no general Italian League ready to oppose Charles VIII but that was no longer even a gleam in the eyes of Italian politicians. More immediate and damaging were the profound divisions within the existing alliance system, and particularly the complete breach between Milan and Naples. However, the real failure, and indeed the real crisis for Italy, was the failure to create effective centralised states with coherent elites and a will to survive. It is striking that the efforts of Italian diplomats, politicians and soldiers were undermined by the surrender of key subject cities like Pisa in 1494 and Verona in 1509, and betrayal by factions and individuals of the elites. While many of the essential mechanisms of state building and interstate relations had been developed in Italy in the fifteenth century, the development of harmonious societies for those states had been compromised and neglected.

CHAPTER 23(b)

THE PAPAL STATES AND THE KINGDOM OF NAPLES

Alan Ryder

HALF the territory of Italy, but far less of its wealth and population, lay within the kingdom of Naples and the papal states, for much of the land – mountain, marsh and arid plain – defied habitation or exploitation. Devastated by plague in the fourteenth century, the population touched its nadir around the start of the fifteenth, then began a slow overall growth through the next hundred years despite recurrent epidemics and famine. Six general visitations of plague (1422–5, 1436–9, 1447–51, 1477–9, 1485–7, 1493) and a five-year cycle of crop failure inflicted appalling casualties: Viterbo lost 6,600 of its 10,000 inhabitants at the outset of the century and had not recovered fifty years later; 14,000 are said to have perished in Bologna alone in 1447, and 75,000 over the whole kingdom in 1493. Malaria infesting the marshlands created by sedimentation of rivers on the western coasts took its own steady toll of life to add to the victims of occasional disasters such as the earthquake which struck the south in December 1456 killing some 30,000 people.

Relatively few reached an advanced age: Pozzuoli in 1489 had 77.5 per cent of its citizens under thirty years of age, 45.5 per cent under fifteen, figures not without significance for the fiscal health of government. How slowly the population recovered may be measured by the census figures for the kingdom: excluding Naples, they showed only 254,000 hearths in 1500 against 230,000 in 1450. Nor was this increase evenly distributed. Rural depopulation went hand in hand with rapid urban growth, especially in the larger cities. In the province of Rome a quarter of the villages had disappeared between the onset of the Black Death and 1416, most of them for good. Great landowners everywhere seized the opportunity to occupy abandoned farmland which became incorporated in their latifundia – large, backward, thinly peopled estates devoted overwhelmingly to a pastoral economy which produced wool for export and meat for the cities. Only in a few climatically favoured regions – Puglia above all – did they grow sufficient grain to furnish a significant export. Urban development, by contrast, attracted immigrants, often from far afield. Rome, peculiarly open

571

thanks to the multi-national character of its government, absorbed waves of Genoese, Tuscans, Lombards and, above all, Neapolitans, balking only at an influx of Corsican peasants in 1485. Towns and cities generally welcomed the newcomers to fill their empty quarters and coffers. Most grew at a slowly accelerating pace, and some to a great size by contemporary standards. Rome, the administrative and devotional centre of an international religion as well as a regional centre of government, expanded its population during the century from under 20,000 to some 50,000, but continued to share its importance, as the popes did their temporal power, with other great cities of the papal states, such as Ferrara which grew to 30,000 or Bologna which regained its pre-plague level of 50,000. Ancient universities helped attract men to Bologna and Perugia, whereas that of Rome had withered away until Martin V gave it modest new life. In the kingdom, by contrast, the old capital, Naples, reasserted its primacy to such a degree that its population reached 150,000, whereas other cities remained relatively stunted; one as important as Salerno, for example, boasted fewer than 5,000 inhabitants. Programmes designed to boost industry and commerce in these capitals failed to change their character as centres of conspicuous consumption sucking in the surplus wealth of their regions. However, they could boast some of the most inspired urban development of the century whether in public utilities or architectural splendour. Inevitably, many other cities which had earlier enjoyed some prosperity saw it slip away: those on the northern Adriatic coast suffered markedly, Rimini and Fano from the silting of their harbours, others from Venetian hostility. Only Ancona prospered.

In such an overwhelmingly agricultural economy native traders found themselves confined to a secondary, short-distance role. Those from Salerno, for example, would not venture out of the Tyrrhenian Sea, nor those from Trani and Barletta beyond the Adriatic. Powerful economies on its land borders had a similar inhibiting influence on the papal state. Long-distance and substantial transactions, whether in merchandise or money, therefore lay in the hands of foreigners – Florentines, Genoese, Venetians, Catalans and Ragusans – throughout the century. Ferrara and the Romagna might, indeed, be said to have passed into a Venetian economic orbit, while Florence gained an increasing ascendancy over Perugia and Bologna.

In contrast to its passive commercial role, the kingdom developed an active naval power thanks to the revival of the Neapolitan shipyards and arsenal by its Aragonese rulers. Used in conjunction with land forces, the galley fleets constructed there made Naples a power to be reckoned with in central Italy throughout the century. The Papacy enjoyed no such advantage, its naval endeavours being directed solely to crusading ends which were mainly served by hiring vessels at Ancona.

Politically the region in 1415 was a kaleidoscopic patchwork subject to a papal suzerainty that had lost all substance through a century of exile, schism and conciliar challenge. In Naples the Angevin rulers had fared little better: dynastic feuds and incompetent monarchs had allowed the formidable state apparatus created by Normans, Hohenstaufen and early Angevins to decay to a point where, like papal suzerainty, it existed in little more than name. A phantom recovery under King Ladislas (1386–1414) owed everything to his military flair and to papal disarray, nothing to regeneration of his state. Everywhere power had consequently passed to local magnates and oligarchies determined to resist any reimposition of central authority. Technical distinctions can be drawn between the feudal nobility of Naples and the proprietary landowners of the papal states, but all shared a common aristocratic ethos and often, as with the Orsini family of Rome, ramified throughout the south. Some – most notably the Este of Ferrara, the Malatesta of Rimini and the Montefeltro of Urbino – had under the guise of papal vicariates achieved *de facto* hereditary rule and independence; much the same might be said of Giovanni Antonio del Balzo Orsini, Prince of Taranto, whom no king dared tax or call to account. Others nursing the same ambition pursued it with a ruthlessness that imperilled the fabric of state and society.

After the death of Ladislas their prospects looked bright, for those who commanded any form of force or authority had a free hand. None took grimmer advantage than the *condottiere* Braccio da Montone; with the most battle-hardened army in Italy at his command and the helpless acquiescence of Pope John XXIII he made himself master of his native Perugia, then went on to carve out a large domain in the heart of the papal states. Muzio Attendolo Sforza, his erstwhile comrade in arms, chose to seek his territorial fortune in the service of Queen Giovanna II, Ladislas's ageing, weak-willed sister and successor who had become the prey of baronial factions.

European diplomacy orchestrated by the Emperor Sigismund was meanwhile labouring at the Council of Constance to impose a settlement on the schismatic factions of western Christendom. It finally emerged in the form of Cardinal Oddo Colonna who became Pope Martin V on 11 November 1417. Sprung from the clan which had dominated a great swath of Roman countryside and city throughout the Middle Ages, Martin determined to establish his court in that native stronghold lest he remain a captive of conciliar forces. But the road to Rome, he soon discovered, was long and painful, for none of those wielding power in papal lands, save his own kin, had cause to welcome a master cloaked in greater authority than any seen in those parts for a century. With no army and an empty treasury, Martin had little choice but to negotiate his passage, yielding what those who stood in his path might demand. What they asked – the *signori* who had established their sway over the towns of the

Romagna, Umbria and the March of Ancona – was recognition of their *de facto* independence as papal vicars bridled only by a modest annual tribute. Titles proved another useful currency: that of duke of Spoleto won the services of Guidantonio da Montefeltro against Braccio who none the less extracted from Martin the vicariate of Perugia and virtual licence to conquer at will.

On 29 September 1420 Martin finally entered Rome amid tumultuous rejoicing. Since all ranks of society expected the return of a papal court to resurrect the city from the miserable insignificance into which it had fallen, Martin had little difficulty in imposing municipal statutes that gave him control of key appointments, including those of senator and treasurer, and in directing a substantial portion of Roman revenues to the office of his own chamberlain. The Colonna, backed by clients and allies, gave him the muscle needed to enforce his will. The embellished family palace in Rome became his headquarters; relatives were manoeuvred into every available estate and office; one niece married the lord of Urbino, another a Malatesta. In the *curia*, Italians quickly achieved a preponderance that was to become entrenched from the greatest dignity to the least. Only the Orsini and their friends stood implacably hostile, convinced that Colonna triumph must presage Orsini ruin. Thus securely installed as *signore* of Rome, Martin continued to deal cautiously with his territorial vassals, and with the Church at large, for the shadow of conciliar authority hung over him still. Nor had he the resources for an adventurous territorial policy. By 1426, remnants of former papal revenues assiduously garnered were yielding an income of 170,000 florins, perhaps only a half of their pre-schism level, and now derived in equal parts from ecclesiastical function and territorial dominion, the last of which had earlier contributed relatively little.

Martin's sure-footed performance within the papal territories was matched by similar adroitness in his dealings with Naples. While ready to recognise the childless Giovanna in return for lavish territorial gifts to his brother Giordano, he became persuaded that Rome's long-term interests would best be served by backing French claims, represented by Louis III of Provence, to the succession. Louis, supported by Sforza's army, duly invaded the kingdom in 1420 to enforce his title. Against that threat the queen and Sergianni Caracciolo (her lover and the power behind the throne) appealed to Alfonso, the young king of Aragon and Sicily, who, in that summer of 1420, was battling to secure his dominion over Sardinia and Corsica. After some hesitation he accepted what he chose to represent as a call to rescue a damsel in distress; in reality he had staked his reputation on winning the kingdom of Naples, and so bringing to a triumphant conclusion the adventure launched by his ancestors at the time of the Sicilian Vespers. Around these foreign banners the Neapolitan nobility rallied into opposing factions: Sforza, the Colonna and former partisans of Anjou supported Louis; Braccio and the Orsini, led by the prince of Taranto, predictably joined the other camp. In the ensuing conflict, with neither party strong enough to prevail, the crown lost all authority. What turned the scales was an irreconcilable contradiction between Alfonso's pretensions as heir apparent and Caracciolo's resolve to remain master of the queen. Exacerbated by xenophobic mistrust of Alfonso's Spanish entourage, their enmity escalated during the summer of 1423 into open hostilities culminating in the sack of Naples by a Catalan fleet. In October 1423 the frustrated king returned to Spain furiously resentful against a pope whom he regarded as the architect of his humiliation. Martin, by contrast, had the satisfaction of seeing Giovanna recognise the Angevin prince as her heir, and – a still greater joy – Braccio fall in battle. Perugia thereupon passed into the hands of a noble oligarchy hardly more subject to papal control than the defunct warlord, but decidedly less dangerous.

The influence which a pope might exercise upon the Neapolitan succession was denied him in respect of his own throne. The more autocratically he wielded power in his lifetime – and all subsequent attempts by the cardinals to curtail it by means of articles sworn on election proved futile – the more violent was the reaction when his death returned authority to the College of Cardinals. This cosmopolitan body of talented men, working in the interest of secular patrons as well as of their own ambitions, defied all efforts at long-term manipulation. The doubling of their number over the century only increased the range of interests at play by bringing in the great families of Italy: Medici, Sforza, Gonzaga, Farnese. Moreover, the comparative brevity of papal reigns ensured that most cardinals outlived several popes. From Martin V to Alexander VI these reigns averaged only some nine years, a stark contrast to Naples, where Alfonso and his son reigned for sixty years, or to Ferrara, ruled for a century by Niccolò d'Este and three sons. When Martin died in February 1431 it was an anti-Colonna coalition engineered in the conclave by the Orsini that brought about the election of Cardinal Condulmer, a Venetian patrician who styled himself Eugenius IV. Their further manipulation of this 'capricious and stubborn man' to undo the Colonna loosed such carnage and devastation upon Rome and the surrounding countryside that on 29 May 1434 a popular rising forced Eugenius to flee in fear of his life. Thus menaced in the very heart of his state, he had been compelled to abandon almost every effective claim upon the service of papal vassals, and to yield the March of Ancona to Francesco Sforza, son of the old *condottiere*, who had conquered that province in the style of Braccio. With the Council of Basle simultaneously challenging the very foundation of his authority, a new descent into schismatic disintegration looked imminent. Although Giovanni Vitelleschi, a cardinal turned *condottiere*, did regain possession of Rome late in 1434, the chief beneficiaries of this success were the Orsini; Eugenius himself dared not return.

To the south Alfonso's ambitions posed another threat. Ever since 1427 disaffected Neapolitan nobles led by the prince of Taranto had been trying to coax him back. In the summer of 1432 he reached Sicily with a large fleet, patently awaiting the opportune moment to launch himself upon Naples, and meanwhile bombarding Eugenius with demands for recognition of his claims to its throne. When first Louis of Anjou and then Queen Giovanna died within a few weeks of each other early in 1435 the way seemed clear, despite Giovanna's last-minute nomination of Louis's brother, René, as heir, for that prince lay captive in the hands of the duke of Burgundy. Alfonso, now self-proclaimed king of Naples, had to reckon instead with resolute opposition from the Genoese who feared that their trading life-lines might be severed should their Catalan rivals gain the kingdom. A first, seemingly decisive, trial of strength saw a Genoese fleet annihilate Alfonso's superior force in a battle fought off the island of Ponza on 4 August 1435. No naval encounter of that century had a more dramatic outcome: Alfonso, two of his brothers and his whole entourage, Spanish and Italian, found themselves prisoners of the Genoese and ultimately of Filippo Maria Visconti, Milanese overlord of the Republic.

By an extraordinary exercise of personality and persuasion Alfonso contrived to turn disaster to account by converting Visconti from captor to accomplice in a grandiose design for the subjection of Italy: all north of a line bisecting the papal states would be in the province of Milan, to the south the will of Aragon should hold sway. Even though this deal with the arch-enemy goaded Genoa into rebellion against Milan, Alfonso, free once more, renewed his Neapolitan campaign in January 1436 in a far stronger position than ever before. His opponents lacked an effective leader, despite the arrival of René's spirited wife Isabel; nor could they match the financial resources he was able to draw from Aragon, Sicily and Sardinia, his other kingdoms. With the port of Gaeta, second only to Naples itself, as his base, he began a methodical subjugation of the kingdom concentrating first on the Terra di Lavoro, the richest and most populous province. That it took more than six years to complete the conquest was due partly to an insufficiency of men and money (any European state would have found it well nigh impossible to amass the resources needed for definitive success in so large an enterprise), still more to persistent intervention by Genoa and the pope. Half-guest, half-hostage in Francophile Florence since 1434, Eugenius could not abandon the Angevin cause; nor did Alfonso encourage him to do so as, in league with Milan, he threatened to give his allegiance to the anti-Pope Felix (elected by the Council of Basle in 1439). But papal finances, woefully reduced by the collapse of Eugenius's authority, could not hope to sustain a war in the kingdom. The fearsome Cardinal Vitelleschi, dispatched there at the head of an army in 1436 and again in 1437, achieved some passing triumphs only to find his supplies cut off when Eugenius had to devote his limited resources into hosting his Byzantine guests at the Council of Florence.

Into the pope's place stepped René of Anjou. Having spent everything on ransoming himself from Burgundy, he arrived in Naples as a pensioner of the Genoese with little to offer his followers but an agreeable personality. That quality failed to stem a tide of defections when barons and towns, sensing the ebb of Angevin fortune, began to grasp Alfonso's ready promises of pardon, office, title and cash. Only Genoa and the *condottieri* families of Sforza and Caldora, both with huge estates in the kingdom at stake, stood firm. By the spring of 1442 René was isolated, under siege in Naples; even Genoa now began to despair. On 2 June the Aragonese forces broke in and the capital was theirs; a victory over Antonio Caldora and Giovanni Sforza on 28 June completed their triumph.

Pope Eugenius had then to accept that no power, Italian or foreign, would challenge Alfonso's victory, and that, unless he came to terms, he risked the king defecting to the anti-Pope Felix V and invading the papal states. A peace was accordingly patched up at the border town of Terracina in June 1443. Brokered by the pope's chamberlain, Cardinal Ludovico da Treviso, who had assumed Vitelleschi's mantle as terror of the papal court but with a pro-Aragonese stance, it recognised the title of Alfonso and his illegitimate son Ferrante to the Neapolitan crown, granted Alfonso the papal territories of Benevento and Terracina for life and reduced the tribute due to the Papacy to a token white palfrey. A joint operation to expel Sforza from the March of Ancona, where he threatened Alfonso's hold on the Abruzzi provinces, was dressed up as a service to Eugenius against a disobedient vassal.

Most Italians would have joined the king's Spanish subjects in wishing him a speedy departure from Italy once Naples had been won. He disappointed them all by remaining there for the rest of his life, partly to escape fruitless entanglement in Iberian conflicts, partly because he never felt entirely confident of his hold upon the kingdom, and partly for the growing attraction of congenial political and cultural surroundings. Until Alfonso's death in 1458 Naples thus became the political and administrative centre of an Aragonese empire that dominated the western Mediterranean. The central councils and regulatory organs of the Aragonese state, complete with their Spanish personnel, which had accompanied him to Italy in 1432, now functioned alongside, but separate from, the established machinery of Neapolitan government where natives held almost every office. In order to convince those who wielded power in the kingdom – the landowning aristocracy – that their interest lay with his dynasty, Alfonso confirmed their authority over their estates and those who lived on them, indulged them with a lavish creation of titles, flattered them with titular offices and consultation in parliaments and enmeshed the greatest – the Orsini and Ruffo – in marriages to his children. At the same time he reinforced the crown's hold upon them, a hold almost obliterated by thirty years of turmoil, by forbidding them to keep armed retainers, reforming central and provincial administration, securing an adequate revenue estimated in 1444 at 830,000 ducats and reacting decisively against any show of resistance. After he had stamped on a rebellion in 1444 no one risked further open defiance. He endeavoured also to create bonds between his new kingdom and his other realms: bonds of economic self-interest based upon a proto-mercantilist vision of a trading community; familial bonds growing from the settlement of Spanish nobles and officials, led by his own children, among the Neapolitan nobility. And Alfonso himself, though remaining a Spaniard in personality, exhibited the traits of an Italian prince, fostering a court culture that in its art, building, music, poetry and humanist enterprise fused Italian and Spanish elements into an achievement that rivalled those of Tuscany and the north. Naples, his capital, doggedly loyal to Anjou until 1442, changed in sympathy as it prospered at the centre of Alfonso's empire: its university reopened, its port was rebuilt and its roads paved, while nobles built mansions and the king refashioned the old fortress of Castelnuovo to new standards of magnificence.

With so formidable a neighbour, the pope had no choice but to follow a policy of complaisance that gave Alfonso an informal protectorate over the papal states, yet not without benefit to himself for it secured Eugenius in possession of Rome (to which he returned in September 1442), and drew the teeth of the Council of Basle and its anti-pope. Filippo Maria Visconti, duke of Milan, held meanwhile, albeit erratically, to his Aragonese alliance, but Florence and Venice, dismayed by this northward spread of Alfonso's influence, struggled to check or reverse it. Time and again they rescued Francesco Sforza from final defeat in the March of Ancona until in December 1446 the king in person led an army towards Rome resolved to expel all rivals from the lands of the Church. He camped at Tivoli in January 1447 too late to browbeat Eugenius further – the pope died on 23 February – but well placed to secure another malleable occupant of the papal throne.

The new pope, Nicholas V, emerged from within the curial system: a prelate well versed in papal government but without the backing of great family or fortune; a man of humanist and peaceable inclinations. His even-handed distribution of lands among the Colonna and Orsini brought peace to the Roman countryside. The problem of the March of Ancona solved itself when Sforza renounced his titles there in order to press his claims to Milan following the death of Filippo Maria Visconti, his father-in-law. Other *signori* and oligarchs enjoyed untroubled possession under Nicholas who reaped some benefit from this unaccustomed stability in more regular tribute payments, reorganised transhumance tolls, and from the pockets of thousands of pilgrims who flocked to Rome in 1450 when he proclaimed a jubilee to celebrate reconciliation with the schismatics of Basle. Prosperity visibly returned to the city so that when, in January 1453, Stefano Porcari, a member of the old municipal elite, tried to raise Rome against papal rule he found no response. Romans old and new, high and low, were bound by self-interest to that power symbolised by Nicholas's new Vatican with its state apartments, refashioned basilica and fortifications; there now lay the fixed centre of the Catholic world.

Sforza's departure for Milan left Alfonso uncontested arbiter of the papal states as Florence and Venice concentrated their attention on the fate of the Visconti dominions. The moment had come, he reckoned, to fall upon Florence and force it to accept Aragonese encroachment upon the coastlands north and south of Elba. Twice he fought the Republic using papal territory as his base. In 1447–8 he took command himself with Milan as his ally; on the second occasion (1452–4), in league with Venice, he gave command to his son, Ferrante. Both campaigns ended in humiliation: a precipitate retreat from Piombino in 1448, and betrayal when Venice negotiated the Peace of Lodi behind his back in 1454. Although he managed to hold on to a few coastal bases, the strength of Aragon and Naples combined had clearly run against effective countervailing combinations backed by France and Anjou; from the resulting rough equilibrium emerged the Italian League. On its flanks, however, Alfonso still found freedom to pursue his designs for the subjection of Genoa and lands on the eastern shores of the Adriatic.

When Alfonso Borgia, former president of Alfonso's council and then his henchman in Rome, was elected Pope Calixtus III in April 1455, the seal appeared set on Aragonese domination of the Papacy. Spaniards swarmed into Rome in numbers sufficient to upset those growing used to an Italian near monopoly of curial offices; two Borgia nephews received cardinals' hats in an unprecedentedly blatant exercise of nepotism, and another became captain-general of the papal armies. Alfonso confidently looked forward to compliance in everything from the grant of vicariates to annulment of his marriage to a barren wife. Europe, Italy and he were therefore all astounded to see Calixtus turn violently against his old master. They clashed almost immediately over Calixtus's refusal to confirm the Aragonese succession in Naples; within a year they had become open, bitter enemies as Alfonso retaliated by sabotaging the pope's projects for a crusade against the Turks.

In this wreck of the understanding between Rome and Naples both states were to suffer. The blows fell first on the Roman lands where, by mobilising the Colonna against Alfonso's Orsini allies, Calixtus ended a promising decade of order. The wider Romagna suffered the depredations of Jacopo Piccinino, an unemployed *condottiere* to whom the king gave every encouragement, and in 1457 Alfonso launched both Piccinino and Federigo da Montefeltro against his detested foe, Sigismondo Malatesta of Rimini, with scant regard for claims of papal suzerainty. Blank refusal of every request from Naples was all Calixtus could oppose to this onslaught until Alfonso's death (27 June 1458) put the fate of the kingdom momentarily in papal hands and severed its bonds with the crown of Aragon which passed to Alfonso's brother, Joan. Ignoring Neapolitan recognition of Ferrante, he declared Naples a lapsed fief, perhaps under the senile delusion that his nephew, Pedro Luis, might reign there. The true beneficiary proved to be John of Anjou, René's son, who landed near Naples in November 1459, once again with Genoese backing, to reopen the contest for the throne. For Calixtus this was posthumous revenge; he had died in August 1458. But his anti-Aragonese vendetta was not sustained by his successor Pius II, a career diplomat and writer of encyclopaedic range from Siena, who had been much impressed by Alfonso on a visit to Naples and understood the danger that turmoil in the kingdom posed for his own state. A papal legate was accordingly despatched to crown Ferrante in February 1459, despite strident protests from France.

The fires of civil war stoked by Calixtus, Anjou and Neapolitan magnates looking for a more tractable ruler none the less took hold during that summer, and it would be four years before Ferrante could extinguish them. Throughout, Pius maintained steadfast support, resisting French pressure, mobilising the Italian League, and contributing troops paid by his own treasury. He had good cause to persevere, for a backlash of war swept from Naples over the papal states. Piccinino, Sigismondo Malatesta and the count of Anguillara, with Angevin support, rampaged through the March of Ancona to the gates of Rome inciting disorder within its walls. Only with the collapse of the Neapolitan rebellion in 1463 did peace return.

A common struggle had re-established the understanding between pope and king which was given a new dynastic twist by the marriage of Antonio Piccolomini, Pius's nephew, to Ferrante's illegitimate daughter, Maria. All this warfare, however, had cost Pius great sums at the same time that he was endeavouring, like Calixtus, to lead Europe by example into a crusade. There came providentially to his rescue the rich alum deposits discovered in 1461 north-west of Rome at Tolfa, profits from which in time boosted papal revenues by some 20 per cent. Yet still more was needed, so in 1463 there appeared a new fiscal device that was to be adopted time and again by Pius's successors – the curial office created specifically for sale; whose holders were in effect purchasing a life annuity. Pius began on an heroic scale with a College of seventy abbreviators, clerks responsible for the drafting of papal bulls. All the proceeds, along with the profits from alum, went into a special crusading account as earnest of the pledge that he had given at the Congress of Mantua in 1459. However, this had no more effect upon international indifference than did his final despairing journey to Ancona, the designated port of departure, where he died on 15 August 1464.

Ferrante meanwhile went about the business of consolidating his throne on foundations less grandiose than those that had supported his father. Although many Spaniards established in the baronage and bureaucracy continued in his service, large numbers returned to their native land, their places being filled by Italians of proven fidelity, conspicuous among whom were the principal secretaries, Antonello Petrucci and Giovanni Pontano. To redress a gross imbalance between baronial and royal demesne Ferrante bestowed land forfeited by rebellion, including the huge estates of the prince of Taranto, upon his numerous progeny and relatives by marriage. A reduction in the rates of direct taxation, granted as a gesture of good will at the outset of his reign, was offset by increased revenue from a rising volume of trade. Alfonso's mercantile enthusiasm had left its mark on his son. Road-building schemes and a drive against baronial abuse of tolls and markets in a background of domestic peace brought a modest prosperity to ports and fairs. A rising output of wool and silk fuelled the export of those raw materials. Projects to develop quality textile production in Naples, on the other hand, made little headway against a regional decline, but the capital continued to flourish as the provincial nobility with royal encouragement moved to build themselves palaces there. As external buttresses to his throne Ferrante relied principally upon Sforza Milan and Aragon, both states, like Naples, menaced by French ambitions. With both he contracted marriage alliances. The Italian League, although never entirely effective in a crisis, offered some guarantee against Florentine and Venetian hostility. In the papal states the need of many *signori* to find a reliable paymaster ensured a measure of influence, most importantly through Federigo da Montefeltro of Urbino who, after the fall of the Malatesta, emerged as the greatest *condottiere* prince of that region. Unlike his father, however, Ferrante seldom held the initiative in his dealings with the Papacy, but had to follow the shifts of policy resulting from the play of Roman politics. Both he and the Church had the good fortune to see the tiara pass in 1464 to the Venetian, Paul II. Admittedly Paul, a nephew of Eugenius IV, was vain and worldly but his character had an open, pleasant aspect uncommon in fifteenth-century popes, and he was not plagued by consuming ambitions. Moves to buttress his territorial base by executing claims upon the lands of old adversaries, first the Roman barons of Anguillara, then the residual Malatesta possessions, did arouse Ferrante's suspicions to the extent that, in 1469, he sent troops to Rimini to support Roberto Malatesta against Paul. But when Milan and Florence, too, declared for Roberto, and Venice declined to intervene, Paul backed away from confrontation. A battle over alum ended by contrast in a papal victory. In order to safeguard his revenue from the Neapolitan mines at Agnano, Ferrante intrigued against Paul's operations, backed by the Medici, to secure ownership of Tolfa. He failed both there and in a subsequent scheme to tie papal and Neapolitan interests together in a consortium. By 1472 production from the Tolfa mines had so far outstripped that of their southern partners that the arrangement collapsed.

An expanding revenue, no longer mortgaged to war or crusading, enabled Paul to resume the building in Rome which had been neglected since Nicholas V. (Pius II had invested all his architectural enthusiasm in transforming his native village into a model Renaissance town.) Work concentrated on Paul's private residence, the palazzo of St Mark, rather than the Vatican, with spin-off benefits to the adjacent old centre of Rome, the Capitol. The pope could also afford to dispense with the abbreviators, a move which precipitated a conflict with the 'Roman Academy', a community of humanists led by Pomponio Leto, a professor of the university, that had proliferated in the papal bureaucracy since the days of Nicholas; many of them had invested in the new offices. Yet economy alone did not motivate Paul; a desire to curtail the influence of Sienese introduced into the *curia* under Pius II is also evident, as it was in the pope's restoration of the Medici as papal bankers in place of the Sienese Spannocchi. Humanists who indulged in pagan and republican posturings were inviting trouble from an ecclesiastical autocrat; yet Paul was no enemy to their true concerns, for he patronised scholars generously, encouraged the introduction of printing in Rome (1468) three years before Ferrante brought it to Naples, and began building the Vatican library.

How moderately Paul had governed the Church and its lands became evident when they fell into the very different hands of his successor, the Genoese, Francesco della Rovere, Sixtus IV. A Franciscan of humble origins, Sixtus owed his tiara to anti-Venetian settlement in the Sacred College and Italy at large. He discovered no constructive purpose for the power that was now his but employed it rather in the unashamed aggrandisement of his family. Six close relatives were packed into the Sacred College within seven years, others into positions of temporal glory; Giovanni della Rovere, a nephew, married the duke of Urbino's daughter (1474); another, Leonardo, in 1472 became both prefect of Rome and husband of a daughter, albeit an illegitimate one, of Ferrante; the king's niece married Antonio Basso della Rovere in 1479, while yet another nephew, Girolamo, the greediest of them all, was given a Sforza bride. To this unscrupulous gang the Papacy afforded an ideal instrument for achieving the goal of every parvenu Italian in that century – temporal dominion; and they knew that time was against them, Sixtus being already fifty-five years old when elected. Instead of obstructing their designs, as he had those of Paul II, Ferrante unwisely chose to back them in the belief that he would thereby make himself an indispensable ally to petty princelings, increase his influence in the papal states and win concessions from Rome, as indeed he did when Sixtus waived for life the tribute due for Naples and created the king's son, Giovanni, a cardinal in December 1477. Milan and Urbino, too, fell in with the della Rovere, a stance that earned Federigo de Montefeltro his ducal title in 1474. Florence proved less accommodating. Quarrels with the Medici over alum contracts and Imola led to Lorenzo losing the papal account to a Genoese banker, management of Tolfa to the rival Pazzi, and in 1478 to the murder of Giuliano de' Medici; Lorenzo narrowly escaped the same fate. Whether or not the della Rovere were directly implicated in the crime hardly matters, for they seized upon the subsequent mob murder of the archbishop of Pisa and imprisonment of Cardinal Raffaello Riario (a great-nephew of Sixtus) as justification for war upon Florence. Ferrante joined them because Medicean Florence remained in his judgement an irreconcilable foe of his dynasty. Moreover, he desired to demonstrate to Italy, and to his own subjects, how fifteen years of internal peace and reorganisation had strengthened the crown's military capabilities.

A Neapolitan army led by Alfonso, duke of Calabria, the king's eldest son, combined with the forces of Urbino, quickly justified Ferrante's confidence with a string of victories that by the end of 1479 had Florence at bay. Then doubts began to arise as to the wisdom of engineering too great a papal triumph; from doubt came secret negotiations, and then Lorenzo's astonishing venture to Naples in December 1479 in search of peace. There followed a diplomatic somersault as dramatic as that accomplished by King Alfonso in 1435: Ferrante and Lorenzo sealed not only a peace but an understanding that lasted the rest of their lives. A furious Sixtus had to rest content with booty far below his expectations, the main prize being Forlì which he bestowed as a vicariate on Girolamo Riario.

For a brief time Ferrante appeared as the arbiter of Italy, only to find himself suing for its aid when, in August 1480, a Turkish invasion force, long feared yet largely discounted, stormed the Adriatic port of Otranto. The Neapolitan army had to abandon Tuscany to confront the Turks, and most of the gains of war were sacrificed for promises of Milanese, Florentine and papal assistance. In the event the duke of Calabria's military competence and the death of Sultan Mehemmed II led to the expulsion of the Turks in August 1481 without any significant outside aid; papal galleys and Hungarian troops appeared very late in the day. But Ferrante's enemies were resolved that the triumphant Christian hero should not reappear as cock of the walk in central Italy. With Sixtus's blessing the Venetians fell upon the king's ally, Duke Ercole of Ferrara, and the kingdom's Adriatic coast, where they occupied Gallipoli; they worked, too, upon the discontents of a baronage alarmed by the advance of royal authority. Reacting energetically, Ferrante sent Duke Alfonso against Rome, hoping to cudgel Sixtus into neutrality, and his brother Federico to confront Venice in the Adriatic. The odds, however, had turned against him. When Alfonso suffered a heavy defeat outside Rome, only pressure from Milan, now controlled by an erstwhile protégé, Ludovico Sforza ('Il Moro'), on whom Ferrante had bestowed the dukedom of Bari, managed to detach the pope from Venice. Late in 1483, as Neapolitan finances began to crumple under the strain of continual warfare, it became impossible to pay the armies engaged against the Venetians, and thereafter Ferrante had no choice but to accept a peace (7 August 1484) that was largely the work of his Milanese ally. It rescued Ferrara, and made Venice surrender most of its conquests, but left Naples exhausted. For Pope Sixtus, the outcome of six barren years of fighting was still more calamitous. Legend has it that news that his schemes had come to naught precipitated his death on 12 August. Certainly this was a fitting moment to terminate a career dedicated to a megalomaniac concept of the papal office which was destined unfortunately to resurface in the pontificate of Giuliano della Rovere as Julius II.

Like many another despot, Sixtus embellished his capital with fine monuments that caught the full flowering of Renaissance genius in art and architecture. In August 1483 great crowds flocked to wonder at the new Sistine Chapel. Botticelli, Perugino, Ghirlandaio, Pinturicchio, Melozzo and Rosselli all served him in the pursuit of magnificence and fame. Many wealthy cardinals competed in swelling the flood of patronage. But let it not be forgotten that this century saw more destruction of the antique in Rome than building of the new. Elsewhere in the lands of the Church, every *signore*, from the greatest – Montefeltro, Este, Malatesta, Bentivogli – to the least, devoted money and enthusiasm to rebuilding and beautifying their own surroundings. All the arts blossomed in a blaze of courtly competition. And the cost to the Papacy paled beside the sums poured into war and the extravagant life style of the della Rovere family. Need for money drove Sixtus to revive the College of Abbreviators in 1478, and then to float the Colleges of Sollecitatori (1482) and Notari (1483). He also found a fruitful source of largely unsolicited business in a swelling volume of petitions from all corners of Europe for papal dispensations; the office of the datary, which collected the fees, assumed a new prominence in the *curia*. On the other hand, an attempt to stimulate the pilgrim trade by reducing the interval between jubilees to twenty-five years did not live up to expectations in 1475 when flooding of the Tiber drove visitors away.

The conclave to elect Sixtus's successor met in an atmosphere of violence provoked by the late pope's onslaught on the Colonna, who had been drawn into alliance with Naples, and by his longer-running campaign against communal autonomy in Rome. The horse-trading between these hostile interests and those of the della Rovere clan, desperate to retain some grip on power, settled upon an ineffective Genoese cardinal, Giovanni-Battista Cibo, who, as Pope Innocent VIII, behaved as the creature of Giuliano della Rovere. While Romans looked in vain for the promised restoration of their liberties, the Colonna gained a free hand against the Orsini, and there ensued a reign of lawlessness unparalleled since the days of Eugenius. Soon the turmoil of Rome became caught up in a greater upheaval, the second barons' revolt which convulsed the kingdom of Naples in 1485. A steep increase in taxation made necessary by war debts, dislike of Ferrante's authoritarian style of government, apprehension at the prospect of being ruled by the still sterner figure of his son, Alfonso, and, in some, fear of retribution for treasonable dealings with Venice, gathered into a widespread mood of disaffection which yielded to neither threats nor concessions from the crown. It found in Cardinal della Rovere a champion who, while labouring to enlist France and Venice for the cause, cast the whole weight of papal influence against Ferrante, and gave the signal for the outbreak of rebellion on 26 September 1485. Although the king initially fell into despair, his position was substantially more favourable than in 1459. No French invader materialised, Florence remained staunch, Milan followed, while Venice shuffled; Ferdinand the Catholic sent Sicilian troops and Spanish galleys to support his cousin. Most crucially, the internal balance of forces favoured the king decisively from the beginning, a measure of the shift of power effected over two decades. Consequently the duke of Calabria was able, with Orsini support, to fall upon Rome, defeat Innocent's forces and extract a peace treaty (11 August 1486). This left the rebels helpless before a king who speedily and ruthlessly plucked out those judged most disloyal and dangerous, among them Petrucci, his chief secretary, the princes of Altamura and Bisignano and the dukes of Nardo and Melfi. Most disappeared into the dungeons of Castelnuovo to become the subject of grisly legends. In the aftermath the Aragonese succession in Naples seemed internally secure, but for five years more Innocent pursued his quarrel, rejecting Ferrante's proffered tokens of tribute, and threatening him with France. Only in 1492 did Lorenzo de' Medici, shortly before his death, succeed in bringing them to an agreement that ratified the Aragonese succession.

While this futile contest absorbed all Innocent's resources he had no choice but to yield on every other front. The Orsini returned to favour and, with the Colonna, reimposed their domination upon the Roman countryside. Medici influence made a spectacular comeback with a cardinal's hat for Lorenzo's thirteen-year-old son, Giovanni, and two marriages: his daughter, Maddalena, to the pope's son, his son, Piero, to an Orsini. Elsewhere, too, in his states the pope submitted his authority to Florentine interest, as in Perugia where in 1488 the Baglioni made themselves sole masters. A similar upheaval in Bologna led the Bentivogli to tie their fortunes more closely to Milan. Thus had papal authority come to count for nothing in the greater cities. In the light of that retreat, repeated on a smaller scale throughout the lands of the Church, it is unsurprising to find that Innocent financed himself by selling yet more offices including another college and twenty-four apostolic secretaryships, with the explicit provision that no duties whatsoever attached to them.

A pontificate which, by general consent, had been disastrous ended with Innocent's death on 25 July 1492, but with little prospect of improvement because, after several unsuccessful bids, the turn had come of Rodrigo Borgia, nephew of Calixtus III, to ascend the papal throne as Alexander VI. Thirty-six years a cardinal and only one less as vice-chancellor of the Church had made him the most influential figure in the *curia*, and one identified with most of the excesses that had disfigured papal government over those years. Three sons, a daughter and a flock of nephews, all fired by della Rovere example, stood ready to carve their fortunes from the Church. Six of them became cardinals. Memories of an earlier generation of Borgia ambition did not reassure Ferrante, now well advanced into old age; nor did Alexander's dependence upon Cardinal Ascanio Sforza, Ludovico il Moro's brother, because Neapolitan relations with Milan had soured since 1488 when the king's grand-daughter, Isabel, married to the titular duke of Milan, had tried to prise Ludovico's hands off her husband and his state. An immediate clash of wills developed over a mischief-making sale arranged by della Rovere of some estates near Rome belonging to Innocent's son. They were bought by Virginio Orsini, relative of the Medici and captain-general of the Neapolitan army. Milan and Venice promptly lined up behind Alexander's protests, threatening to resolve the matter by force. Ferrante, however, refused to be drawn, and by the summer of 1493 had produced a solution that satisfied honour on both sides; moreover, he managed to trump the marriage of the pope's daughter, Lucrezia, to a minor Sforza with a suitably endowed match between her brother, Goffredo, and his own illegitimate grand-daughter.

As one Spanish dynasty tightened its grip on Rome and the papal *curia*, the other in Naples was nearing the end of a long reign. For long enemies, they now found themselves driven together by a common peril. Cardinal della Rovere, Alexander's doughtiest opponent, had withdrawn to France in despair after failing to block the appointment of hostile cardinals, including two Borgias, in September 1493. At the French court he joined with Neapolitan refugees from Ferrante's vengeance in urging Charles VIII to pursue the title to Naples that he had recently inherited from the Angevins. Knowing what was afoot, Ferrante had begun to prepare his defences. Those on land he entrusted to the formidable duke of Calabria, those at sea to his second son Federico, while his agents laboured in every court to turn the diplomatic tide. Should an invasion come, he felt confident his sons would fight with 'hands, feet and every limb', and would again beat the French who were widely reckoned inferior to Italians in fighting qualities. In that belief he died on 25 January 1494. He was deceived; in little more than a year his sons were in flight and Charles entered Naples unopposed. But the deeper transformation wrought in the kingdom by fifty years of Aragonese rule was not so readily undone, nor would the dynasty led by Ferdinand 'the Catholic' yield possession to France. In Naples and in Rome the way had been prepared for a long-lasting Spanish domination.

CHAPTER 24(a)

ARAGON

Mario Del Treppo

THE COMPROMISE OF CASPE

The death of King Martí (31 May 1410) led to a crisis within the states of the crown of Aragon. It was resolved in a radical fashion which has been the cause of debate ever since. Martí's death brought to an end the dynasty founded with the marriage of the *infanta* Petronilla of Aragon to Ramon Berenguer, count of Barcelona, which had reigned uninterruptedly since 1137. The demise of the line was caused by Martí's lack of legitimate heirs, after the death of his son, Martí (July 1409), during the military campaign in Sardinia, although, through Martí, the king did have an illegitimate grandson, the young Frederic, count of Luna. Martí I's fondness for Frederic did not blind him to the problem of his illegitimacy, especially since there were other claimants to the crown whose rights were beyond dispute. The strongest of these was Jaume, count of Urgel, who had been appointed first lieutenant and later governor-general by the king himself, who thus almost appeared to be naming him his heir, giving rise to constitutional questions among the Aragonese. On his father's side, Urgel was descended from a junior line of the family of Alfons IV 'the Benign'. A member of the powerful Catalan family, he was disliked by the minor aristocracy and was strongly opposed by the patrician class of Barcelona. Louis of Anjou, duke of Calabria, and Fernando 'de Antequera', the *infante* of Castile, were more closely related to Martí, but through the maternal line, Violante, the mother of Louis, being the daughter of King Joan I, Martí's elder brother and his immediate predecessor, while Fernando's mother, Elionor, was Martí's sister and wife of Juan I of Castile.

Given the nature of the problem Martí I, a scrupulous observer of constitutional traditions, made strenuous efforts to involve the kingdom in the discussion, requesting the *corts* to send him delegates with whom he could discuss the question. He also sought the advice of legal experts on such basic problems as the limits of his decision-making powers on this matter, and the extent to which

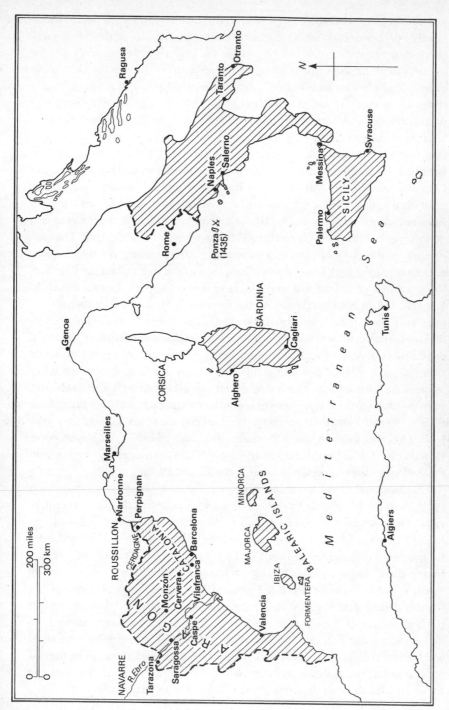

Map 12   The Aragonese dominion

kinship lines were considered legally valid. But the delegates' slow deliberations failed to produce solutions, so that to the captious, insinuating deathbed question put by Ferrer de Gualbes, a councillor and leader of a delegation from the city of Barcelona, as to whether the king agreed that his thrones should now be inherited by whoever had the best claim by the *via de justicia*, Martí's affirmative reply was as a feeble 'hoc', repeated in Catalan. On the day following the king's death, arrangements were put in hand to resolve the question of the succession in the best-qualified and largest forum available: a general *cort* of the three principal states in the crown of Aragon: Aragon itself, with Valencia and Catalonia. But the fierce conflicts between the noble factions – Urrea and Luna in Aragon, Centelles and Vilaragut in Valencia – brought the plans to nothing. Another solution was therefore sought, that of agreements between selected commissions and delegations nominated by the assemblies which, in the interregnum period, had become the only recognised form of authority in the land. The candidates to the throne, however, stepped up the pressure on these representatives. Along with foreign candidates, such as the French and the Castilian, the count of Urgel in particular even went so far as to apply military pressure. In January 1412, in Alcañiz, faced with the internal divisions of the other assemblies and their paralysing obstructionism, the Aragonese assembly firmly declared Aragon to be 'superior to the other kingdoms and lands of the royal crown of Aragon' ('cabeça de los otros regnos e tierras de la real Corona de Aragón'), and decided that, in the absence of any agreement from the other assemblies, it would now proceed to declare alone. As a result, the Aragonese *corts* submitted to the Catalan assembly a list of nine people, three for each of the three states in the kingdom, to whom the choice of the new sovereign should be entrusted. This solution was enthusiastically endorsed by the Aragonese pope, Benedict XIII, who hoped that strong support from the monarchy would regain for the Papacy the obedience lost during the Great Schism.

The commission met in the castle of Caspe, in Aragon, and, after examining the titles of all the candidates to the crown, pronounced its decision on 24 June 1412. The successor to Martí I would be Fernando, the *infante* of Castile, by right of his close blood ties with the late king and by the rights inherited from his mother, the daughter of Pere IV 'the Ceremonious'. The role of Vincent Ferrer, the Dominican friar and one of the *compromisarios*, was decisive in the election, but Bernard de Gualbes, mayor of Barcelona and spokesman of the Catalan middle classes, also voted for Fernando, who gathered six votes against the one and a half for the count of Urgel. The Aragonese *compromisario* who had voted for the duke of Gandia and the count of Urgel was later forced to admit that Fernando was the candidate best suited for the throne, given the disorder and public paralysis resulting from the long interregnum, thus refuting future Catalan theories that the decision had been forced on their state.

The Compromise of Caspe cannot be reduced to a mere matter of the rights of succession limited, furthermore, to the kingdom of Aragon alone. The decision had far-reaching repercussions. During the two-year interregnum, there was great activity in the constitutional bodies of all the 'states' of the kingdom, and considerable emotional involvement by the populace, the latter planting the seeds of the deep tensions which would later emerge. This does not mean that what followed was a fully fledged election in the modern sense which laid the basis for a people's self-determination.[1] None the less, it was a form of election and was seen as such by the legal experts of the time. In a difficult situation the Aragonese ruling class, unlike its Catalan counterpart, was able to produce and follow a political plan. The indecision of the Catalans ('claudicació de Catalunya', as it has been defined)[2] had ethico-political origins, and was not simply the result of a socio-economic crisis.[3] Catalonia was not, in effect, forced to submit to any injustices; she had merely to adapt to a solution proposed by others and which met the requirements of the hour. Fernando de Antequera was a member of a powerful baronial clan with far-reaching ambitions which had recently acquired the throne of Castile. He represented all the demographic, military and economic potential of a country which, far better than the old sea-trading Catalonia, was able to meet the challenge of a new and different type of power politics.

POLITICO-CONSTITUTIONAL STRUCTURE OF THE CROWN OF ARAGON

The original structure of the kingdom of Aragon is clear from the events described above. The kingdom is perhaps better described as the 'crown of Aragon', a term already in current use long before Jerónimo Zurita first introduced it into historiography in 1562. By 'crown of Aragon' we mean all the kingdoms and lands (*regnes e terres, vassals e sotmesos*) over which the kings of Aragon ruled. In the language of the chanceries and in the titles on royal diplomas they were normally listed in order of institutional hierarchy after Aragon, whose pre-eminence was historical in origin. The concept of the 'crown of Aragon' developed from the original *casal d'Aragó*; the alternative, *reial corona d'Aragó*, was a later logical and historical development connected with the emergence of a stronger concept of regality, to which the solemn coronation in Saragossa cathedral contributed in the second half of the fourteenth century. As royal authority established itself throughout the land, this finally produced the more geo-political term, the 'crown of Aragon'.[4]

---

[1] See Menéndez Pidal (1964), pp. clxiii–clxiv. [2] See Soldevila (1971), pp. 111ff.
[3] See Vicens Vives (1956), pp. 17ff.
[4] According to Queen Maria before the Monzón *corts* in 1435: 'tots los regnes e terres de la corona d'Arago de ça mar' (*Parlaments*, p. 164).

The juridico-institutional aspect of this institution is currently the subject of renewed interest and discussion among historians. Historical writing now defines the entity as a confederation, a term unacceptable to those who consider it a modern concept, and believe that the only tie holding all the parties together was the ruling house, meaning that the crown of Aragon was nothing more than a personal union. It could be objected that the legal concept of such a union suggests a link between the kingdoms of Aragon, Valencia and the principality of Catalonia which is too weak and inadequate to describe even the strong ties which did, in effect, unite them. What we have here, on the contrary, not originally but certainly from the end of the thirteenth century, is a real union with federal overtones guaranteed not so much by the person of the sovereign – who, given the period's general conception of the state as a personal estate, could be, and was, a source of weakness – but rather by the will of his subjects as expressed in the representative assemblies which imposed on the king the inalienable rights of his dominions. The co-ordinating factor, in what has been called 'a form of political co-ordination',[5] was not the king alone but rather that institution common to all the states of the crown, the royal household in its governing role, where the selection of functionaries from the various member states did not merely depend on the personal choice of the sovereign or on the influence of factions at court, but was, to a certain extent, already institutionalised. This meant that Aragon, Valencia and Catalonia each secured one of the three positions of major-domo, and one of the three vice-chancellorships, each position carrying responsibility for its own 'state'. As has been pointed out, the *corts* of the different kingdoms kept close watch on the central household as a governing body so that the king could not alter its function or composition, or in any way damage the delicate balance of power within it.[6] The modern definition of a confederation as the sharing of sovereignty between member states and a central governing body does basically fit the crown of Aragon, even though there was no cession of sovereignty by the member states to the central governing body. Likewise, the sources of sovereignty and authority remained, on the one hand, the king, on the other, the *corts*.[7]

Each member state in the confederation retained not only its own institutions, laws, customs, privileges and original political identity, it preserved its

---

[5] Lalinde Abadía (1978), p. 105.

[6] Immediately after Fernando I's eleçtion, the *corts* of Tortosa sent a delegation to persuade him 'en lo que tocaba a la ordenanza y regimiento de la casa real, para que en todo se conformase a las reglas y costumbres con que se governaron por los reyes sus predecesores' (Zurita, *Anales*, XI, p. 90).

[7] In 1412 the general council of the kingdom of Majorca was firm on this point: 'lo dit regne de Mallorques, qui de dret e justicia no menor potestat e auctoritat ha e haver deu en los dits afers [the king's succession] que cascum dels dits regnes e principat' (*Cortes... de Cataluña*, IX, p. 364).

own language, too: Catalan in the principality, the Balearic Islands and Valencia (although with local variations in the last two), Aragonese, linguistically similar to Castilian, in Aragon.

Each state's representative assembly was called periodically to discuss, in the first instance, its domestic problems (*del bon stat i reforma de la terra*). If foreign policy was discussed at all, the horizons adopted tended to be limited. The Aragonese *corts* seem to have been interested only in frontier problems with Castile, while the Catalans, who had a more open and dynamic approach, were concerned with Mediterranean matters. In 1435, however, all three assemblies of Aragon, Valencia and Catalonia met in a general *cort* at Monzón to consider the problem of the imprisonment and ransom of the king who had fallen into the hands of the Genoese during the naval battle of Ponza.

The three states had different socio-economic backgrounds. With its agricultural economy and a mainly feudal nobility, Aragon was the least developed. Its *corts*, for instance, had four rather than the more normal three divisions, the nobility being represented by two groups, the *ricos hombres*, or magnates, and the *caballeros*. Valencia and Catalonia, by contrast, were more advanced, maritime societies, with powerful urban aristocracies whose interests lay in commercial speculation, exchange and insurance.

The customs barriers between the states, introduced in the second half of the fourteenth century for fiscal rather than protectionist reasons, did not affect the economically homogeneous or politically defined regions. This was because the crown of Aragon in its turn was part of a much wider economic area: Aragon, along with Valencia and the Balearics, was part of the wool-, rice- and saffron-producing area controlled by Italian business, while Catalonia, with its industrial centres in Barcelona and Perpignan, was the centre of a different economic system extending throughout the Mediterranean and controlled by Catalan merchants.

During the fifteenth century the institutions of all three states underwent the same form of development. First, the 'deputation' (*diputació*) as an institution came into being. This was the permanent delegation of the *corts*, first found in Catalonia as the *diputació del general* or *generalitat*, which later emerged in Aragon and Valencia. Operating between one sitting of the *cort* and the next, it soon became an autonomous institution (Catalonia after 1413, Valencia after 1418 and Aragon after 1436), independent of both *corts* and sovereign. Supported by a complex bureaucracy, the *diputacions* had one (as in Catalonia) or two members for each social grouping. Their mandates ran for three years, and they were empowered to co-opt their successors. Originally administrative and financial institutions with the power to impose taxes (the *generalitats*) and to manage the public deficit which more or less grew up with them, the *diputacions* eventually developed into full political bodies. As guarantors of the freedoms, customs and privileges of each state, they thus became a focus for national identity. This developed in Valencia[8] and Aragon[9] during the course of the fifteenth century, and followed the birth of a general consciousness of the *nació catalana* in Catalonia. The institutional differences and strong national feelings were not, however, sufficient to compromise unity under the crown.

During the course of the century the kings of the new house, Fernando I and Alfonso V, shared a common conception of power with their predecessors of the house of Barcelona, Pere IV and Martí I, both continuing the work of bringing the institutions into line with the political realities of the time. Fernando and Alfonso introduced two policies which, while apparently contradictory, in reality converged to give a better-defined role to both the central and regional organs of government, and to improve co-ordination between them. On the one hand they strengthened the centralised authority of the state, above all by extending the general competence of certain, in particular financial, authorities (the treasurer-general, the auditor-general, the conservator-general of the royal patrimony) to include the entire crown of Aragon. At the same time these same functions submitted to a process of decentralisation. Typical are the changes made to the functions of the auditor, originally the court official responsible for the management of the accounts. In 1419, at the insistence of the population of the city of Valencia, an auditor was appointed with responsibility for that state, and some time later another (first referred to in 1446) was nominated to Aragon, so that the duties of the original court official were reduced to cover Catalonia alone. As a result of these changes, an auditor-general was created, higher in rank than the others, to represent the central authority.

As the royal household and the apparatus of central government became more complex, they tended to be counterbalanced by a strengthening of the individual powers of the three states. Part of this process was the increasingly frequent delegation of authority by the sovereign to viceroys, governors and lieutenants, especially lieutenants-general, usually close friends or relatives, to be the king's personal representatives at the head of any state which he found himself temporarily unable to govern in person. It was thanks to this remarkably flexible system that the crown of Aragon survived the serious crisis which rocked it during the course of the century, and that these crises had no effect on the recent foreign conquests of Sicily and Naples, territories which, after a

---

[8] 'Car com [Valencia] sia vengut e eixit, per la major partida, de Catalunya, e li sia al costat, emperò no es nomena poble català, ans per especial privilegi ha propri nom e es nomena poble valencià' (Eiximenis, *Regiment*, p. 35).

[9] In Aragon one spokesman of the national conscience and of the country's historical past was the Cistercian monk Gauberte Fabricio de Vagad, who, appointed 'royal chronicler of the kingdom of Aragon' by King Joan II in 1466, wrote the *Crónica de Aragón*, published in Saragossa in 1499.

period of merely personal union with the crown, became fully fledged members of it.

The victor of Caspe, Fernando de Antequera, soon made clear his intention of continuing the Mediterranean policy of his Catalan predecessors. He immediately secured investiture of the kingdoms of Sicily and Sardinia from the antipope, Benedict XIII, since, during the interregnum, there had been a real risk that they might be lost to the crown. Similarly, he made sure of his title to the kingdom of Corsica, which had never been totally subdued. He then began to settle the problems of those regions with determination. He pacified Sicily and modernised its administration, side-stepping the island's persistent requests for a king of its own by sending his son, Juan of Peñafiel, as viceroy. In Sardinia he stopped the viscount of Narbonne in his attempt to take over Alghero, and prevented a general insurrection by reaching agreement with the marquis of Oristano, thus not only keeping the island under Aragonese control but boosting its depleted population with a new wave of Catalonian and Aragonese immigrants. Fernando's ambitions, however, extended further to the newly acquired Naples, his diplomatic efforts being aimed at creating a climate favourable to an enlargement of Aragonese dominion in the Mediterranean. He thus toyed with the idea of a marriage between his son, Joan, and Giovanna II of Anjou-Durazzo, queen of Naples. These projects, along with his defence of Catalonian trading interests in Egypt and on the Barbary Coast, were the most valuable part of the inheritance which he bequeathed to his son, Alfonso V 'the Magnanimous'. Even under Alfonso, this policy, termed 'road of the islands' (*ruta de las islas*) by modern Spanish historians, in conjunction with Catalan commercial expansion in the direction of the great spice emporia (*ruta de las especias*), was no crude alternative to those traditional Trastámaran interests in Castile which sought to establish their dominion throughout the entire Iberian peninsula. Within Iberia itself, even after his election to the throne of Aragon, Fernando I did not step down as regent of Castile, ruling in the name of his brother, Enrique III. Fernando's second son, Juan, was created duke of Peñafiel in Castile, and his other sons, Enrique, Sancho and Pedro, were placed at the head of the powerful military orders of Santiago, Calatrava and Alcántara respectively. The marriages of his children, too, were arranged to consolidate Aragonese power. In what has been termed the marriage policy of the *infantes* of Aragon, Alfonso, his first son, married María, *infanta* of Castile, in 1415, while his daughter, María, became the wife of the future Juan II of Castile three years later.

After 1442, following the conquest of Naples by Alfonso V, who had succeeded his father in 1416, the policy of Mediterranean expansion so dear to Catalan hearts finally became more important than expansion in the Iberian peninsula. Alfonso's extremely personal view of Mediterranean and Italian policy was inspired by the myth of humanistic glory, which caused him to act more and more as a *rex Italicus*. This, however, did not prevent his policies from offering significant benefits to Catalans who, within the 'realm', acquired financial positions previously reserved for Florentine merchants and bankers. Although, even at the beginning of his reign, Alfonso had established that, on his death, the kingdom of Naples would be separated from his other possessions and given to his illegitimate son, Ferrante (Ferdinando), while the rest of his inheritance would pass to his brother, Joan (II), this should not be taken as an admission on his part that, without constant and expensive controls, the new conquests could not be maintained.

Alfonso's sweeping vision of the Mediterranean situation led to a plan for the economic integration of all territories of the crown of Aragon: those close to home were to undergo industrial development, while those further away (Sicily, Sardinia and Naples) were to have their agricultural potential developed. An enlarged national (Catalan) fleet would encourage trade between all the regions (*mutua e reciproca contractació e comerci*), while protectionist laws would help keep Florentine merchants and Italian vessels out of this huge market. With the Peace of Lodi and membership of the Italian League in 1455, Alfonso was obliged to suspend his policy against the Florentines, who had already been expelled from his kingdoms. Their return to Naples, however, in no way affected the position of Catalans in the commercial and banking fields as, even under Ferrante, they retained direct control of the 'realm's' financial institutions.

PACTISM : THEORY AND PRACTICE

The conquest of Naples gave the crown of Aragon which, previously, had had no fixed seat of government, a fixed capital which had profound constitutional implications. With the establishment of the capital in Naples and the permanent absence of the king, who no longer set foot in Spain after 1432, the kingdoms entered a period of great political debate. The physical absence of the sovereign broke with tradition, and was a painful rupture of that mystical union between sovereign and people which had become almost tangible whenever the king presided over the *corts* he had summoned. This was known as 'pactism', at once political ideology, collective mental concept and practice whose historical development in all three states of the crown had resulted in the same basic form with, sometimes, significant regional variations. In Catalonia, 'pactism' was essentially feudal in character, being based on the fealty and duties of *auxilium* and *consilium* owed to the lord and sovereign. In Aragon, it was more straightforwardly political, founded on the balance of power existing between the sovereign and a strong nobility, and on the former's ability to control the latter's aspirations. In Valencia, on the other hand, 'pactism' was basically an economic contract.[10] Such differences notwithstanding, in all parts of the kingdom the political and legal principle governing relations between the king and his subjects was an agreement going beyond a mere theory of political philosophy to become the true expression of an identity and traditions which were to be defended and cherished, as legal documents of the time demonstrate.

The death of Martí I without heirs and the 'election' of a successor, however, suddenly meant that the parameters of 'pactism' could be altered, limiting the powers of the monarchy. In his *Recort historial*, written in 1476, Gabriel Turell pointed out with satisfaction that as Fernando I had been elected to the throne (*rey ab pactes elegit*) he was therefore obliged to keep his pre-coronation promise to respect the rights of the 'nation' (*tengut servar les libertats*).[11] The 'pactist' offensive against the Castilian dynasty began in Barcelona in 1412–13 with the frequently asserted claim that royal decisions which did not fall within the bounds of what the Catalonian deputies described as 'the contracted and agreed law' (*ley paccionada*) had no legal force. The offensive was stepped up against Alfonso V both because of the new forms of government which he introduced and because of his absences from the country. Furthermore, between 1449 and 1453, the *corts* of Perpignan sought to place restraints upon the exercise of royal authority by preventing the king from appointing his own chief officials (the vice-chancellor and the head of chancery), removing the administrative role of the *diputació* from royal control and, finally, obstructing the king's efforts to redeem the royal patrimony, already greatly reduced in size. Such proposals, which undermined the constitution and were an intolerable affront to the monarchy's dignity, were firmly rejected by Alfonso who, in response, seized the opportunity to replace the increasingly rigid 'pactist' system of privileges, rights and franchises with a form of government which better suited the generally felt need for an improved system of justice and security. This enlightened step, which met requirements felt even by his critics, was defined by Alfonso himself as *potestat absoluta*. Yet, apart from Felip de Malla (1370–1431), who declared that it was better for the *res publica* to be protected by a good prince than by a good legal system, no Catalan or Valencian legal expert, including Jaume Callís (1370–1434) and Pere Belluga (1390–1436), both royal servants with a training

---

[10] 'He leges in Curia factae, si detur per populum pecunia, ut assolet fieri, transeunt in contractum. Et haec sunt leges pacionatae' (Pere Belluga, *Speculum principum*, 2, 4, fol. 7a); see the comments in Vallet de Goytisolo (1980), pp. 80, 126. [11] Turell, *Recort*, p. 199.

in Roman law, was prepared to lend his support to changes, in the absolutist sense, to the 'pactist' system which, in spite of its evident inadequacies, all continued to uphold.

CRISES AND CIVIL WAR IN CATALONIA

The constitutional crisis coincided with an economic and social one. In Barcelona, Catalonia's largest and richest city, rising tensions produced two factions which competed for control of the city's administration: the conservative *biga*, supporting 'pactism' and opposed to any form of royal centralisation of power, and representing the interests of the urban oligarchy (the *ciutadans honrats*), the traditional source of power in Barcelona; and the *busca*, composed of merchants, professionals and artisans (*mercaders*, *artistes* and *menestrals*) who demanded protectionist policies to counter the economic crisis, along with a devaluation of the silver *croat* and reform of the council of one hundred, the influential body which governed Barcelona independently of the royal authority.

In the Catalonian countryside, far more sensitive than that of Aragon to the possibilities of achieving a general rise in living standards through the development of an economy based on maritime trade, the serfs (a quarter of the population) were becoming disillusioned by a legal system which allowed feudal lords to impose heavy burdens on them under what the country's constitution called the *jus maletractandi*. These agricultural vassals (named *remences* after the term *redemtione, redimentia*, meaning the price they had to pay to secure their freedom from the soil) won the support of Alfonso who recognised their claims and set up a number of public tribunals to settle the innumerable differences that arose between them and their masters.

On the death of Alfonso in 1458, all these tensions came to a head. A large anti-monarchist group opposed to his successor, Joan II, was formed by those, including the nobility, the clergy and the upper middle classes, whose interests were under threat. Joan had been the executor of his brother's absolutist policies which he planned to continue. This meant that he did not intend to recognise as heir to the throne, or name as his lieutenant, Carlos of Viana, his son by his first marriage to Blanche of Navarre, as he had polarised dangerous opposition to the king wherever he went, from Navarre to Sicily and Naples. Joan underestimated Carlos's popularity in Catalonia and made a false move when he had him arrested on 2 December 1460. This led to a revolt which set off a decade of civil war. The Catalan *corts* and the *biga* aligned themselves with the prince. The assembly was called upon to judge the king who was alleged to have violated the laws of the land, and a new constitutional body, the *consell representant le principat de Cathalunya*, was set up which proclaimed Carlos heir to the principality. At this point King Joan decided to give in, freed his son and, on 21 June 1461, sealed the Agreement of Vilafranca.

Rather than being the conclusive triumph of 'pactism' over royal authoritarianism, this agreement reflected a radical alteration in the basic concept of 'pactism'. Under its terms, every political demand made by the Catalan oligarchy since the time of Pere IV (d. 1387) was met: an independent government for Catalonia under the king's eldest son who became his lieutenant for life; the separation and independence of the legal system from the executive; total control over the crown's civil servants; and the banning of the king from entry into the lands of the principality without the express permission of all the constitutional bodies. This was revolution by the privileged classes who were aspiring to full realisation of that vision of 'pactism' which they had only glimpsed, years before, at Caspe.

On the sudden death of Carlos, however (September 1461), Joan II persuaded the *generalitat* to bestow the lieutenancy on Ferdinand, his son by his second wife, Juana Enriquez. There was, however, the possibility that the army of the *generalitat* would march on Gerona where the queen and her son were living, and seek not only to repress a rising of the *remences* but also to kidnap the royal personages. Joan, therefore, decided to seek military aid from Louis XI, king of France, who in return demanded 200,000 ducats, linked to the income of Roussillon and Cerdagne on the Pyrenean border. When the payment was not made, the two provinces passed into French hands. Juana Enriquez and her son were freed by the French, but when the king of Aragon led his troops into Catalonia, violating the Agreement of Vilafranca, the *generalitat* declared him a public enemy, in effect deposing him by declaring the throne of Catalonia vacant. They then offered the crown of Catalonia, but not that of Aragon, to Enrique IV, king of Castile. Intense diplomatic negotiations, begun to avert the danger of escalating the conflict, were to culminate in the Treaty of Bayonne (August 1463). Called in to judge the Catalan question, Louis XI persuaded Enrique IV to abandon the rebels and, instead, put forward Castile's ally, Pedro, constable of Portugal, as candidate for the throne. Pedro quickly won the support of the rebels, who played up his connection with the count of Urgel, his uncle and one of the claimants at Caspe. The Portuguese candidature was also the result of international political intrigue and the convergence of Castilian and Portuguese interests in the Mediterranean which, hitherto, had fallen within the Catalan sphere of influence. In his war against the constable of Portugal, Joan II was able to rely on the support of the other states of the crown of Aragon: Aragon, Valencia, Majorca and Sicily, which had been prudently sitting on the fence since the beginning of the conflict. On the constable's death in June 1466, the war took a sudden and unexpected twist when the extremist wing of the rebels took the politically and economically radical decision to elect René of Anjou, lord of Provence and Lorraine, to the throne, giving a sudden boost to France's Mediterranean aspirations. From Joan II's point of view, the war became one aimed increasingly at liberating Catalonia from French occupation, and in this sense may only be said to have ended with the Treaty of Barcelona (1493), through which Ferdinand 'the Catholic' managed to extract the two provinces from the French king, Charles VIII, in exchange for a free hand in Italy. However, the civil war had in effect ended in 1472 with Joan II's entry into Barcelona, while the capitulation at Pedralbes in October closed this painful episode with a general act of clemency to the defeated rebels, the king swearing once more to uphold all the Catalan constitutions with the exception of the Agreement of Vilafranca.

THE CASTILIAN MARRIAGE OF FERDINAND 'THE CATHOLIC'

The war had strengthened Joan II in his conviction that the future of Aragon lay in Castile, potentially much stronger than Aragon–Catalonia. Castile, however, was exhausted by decades of internecine fighting between opposing noble factions, a festering sore in the side of the Trastámaran dynasty. Joan encouraged a revival of the old Aragonese party, so as to weaken his personal enemy, Enrique IV, and also to exploit the struggle for the succession which was bound to follow Enrique's death. On the death of his heir, Alfonso (June 1468), Enrique IV was forced to admit the illegitimacy of the *infanta*, Juana 'la Beltraneja', the fruit of one of his wife's extra-marital affairs, and to proclaim as his new heir his half-sister, Isabel. This proclamation made it clear whom Ferdinand, Joan's heir, should marry. His suit was supported in Castile by one of the noble factions (the archbishop of Toledo, the marquis of Villena and others) who hoped that the young prince of Aragon would be a strong *condottiero* whom they could bend to their cause. Other factions were hostile, but the Princess Isabel, the main interested party, openly stated her wish to marry Ferdinand. Given Enrique IV's opposition to the idea of such a marriage, Isabel's diplomatic strategies were extremely dangerous. Yet the marriage contract signed at Cervera established that the future sovereigns would take all decisions jointly, and that all decrees would bear both their signatures. However, *de jure*, the sole sovereign regnant would be Isabel. In several clauses added as a protocol at Aragonese insistence, it was established that Ferdinand would exercise the highest responsibilities in Castile, but that he would respect the rights and privileges of his Castilian subjects who alone would enjoy positions of public office in their country. Ferdinand, therefore, was relegated to the rank of consort and, furthermore, was obliged to put himself militarily at the disposal of Castile which he could not leave without permission. The marriage was celebrated at Valladolid on 18 October 1469 and when Enrique IV died in December 1474, Isabel had herself proclaimed queen and legitimate holder of the title to the kingdom of Castile. The problem of Ferdinand's legal and constitutional position then arose once more. The Edict of Segovia (15 January 1475) referred to the queen as 'the lady Isabel, queen of Castile, with Ferdinand her true husband', a mode of address not appreciated by her spouse who had been king of Sicily since 1468, and was heir to the throne of Aragon. He therefore asked to be associated with the title of king. While, legally, the decision was merely expressing on paper the intention of the Cervera agreement by naming Isabel as the holder of the title to the crown and the line through whom that title should pass, Ferdinand's position had changed (a fact which he mentioned with great satisfaction to his father) as his consort had delegated wide powers to him, enabling him to carry out the same functions as the queen. In 1481 Ferdinand conferred similar powers on his wife within the crown of Aragon.

INSTITUTIONAL REFORM AND ECONOMIC RECOVERY

When Joan II died in 1479, Ferdinand ascended the throne of Aragon, and set about resolving the problems of his inheritance. For some time the *remença* peasants had been in revolt against their masters in the Catalan countryside. In 1484–5 there was a further, widely supported, uprising, in which some royal cities were sacked. Afterwards the peasants split into two groups, one led by Pere Joan Sala, which supported total freedom for the *remences* and the abolition of all feudal measures, the other, constituting the majority and led by Francesc Verntallat, which sought a peaceful solution to the problem, and therefore advocated the sincere reformist views of the monarchy. After Sala's arrest and death (1485), and following painstaking negotiations, the Sentence of Guadalupe was proclaimed by the king on 21 April 1486. In this instance Ferdinand was not acting as a judge called in by the two parties to a conflict but rather as the sovereign whose existence had been proved to be vital to the solution of Catalonia's tortuous problems. The Sentence legally abolished the *remences* as a class, along with their servile obligations, known as the *mals usos*. As freemen, they were permitted to exercise the use of their holdings, provided that they paid rent. The lands expropriated during the years of upheaval were returned to the nobility, who were compensated for the rents and services lost. The revenues and rents proper to a feudal system, which there was no intention of abolishing, remained in place. In the Aragonese countryside, on the other hand, where the balance of powers was different, and where the peasants had lacked real revolutionary zeal, the repressive feudal system remained in place, to be endorsed by Ferdinand in the Sentence of Celada in 1497.

Institutional and administrative reform on a wide scale was also pursued. In

1484, taking advantage of the war of Granada and the problems concerning the liberation of Roussillon, the king called a meeting of the *corts* at Tarazona and secured approval for a number of sweeping fiscal reforms, including the method of levying the new direct taxes (*sisas*). Their purpose, the pursuit of war in Granada rather than the defence of the kingdom, was, however, a breach of the Aragonese *fuero*, and could have led to the king's excommunication. Ferdinand avoided this, however, by obtaining a bull from Pope Innocent VIII dispensing him from the requirement that *sisas* should only be levied in defence of the kingdom, an implicit recognition of his right to impose new taxes and dispose of the revenues as he saw fit.

Part of the new general policy was the plan to create some basic form of public policing in Aragon, similar to the Castilian *hermandad*, to replace the old inefficient municipal juntas dominated by the local oligarchic consortia. All towns and cities in the kingdom were obliged to join a *hermandad* for five years. It carried out the policing of rural areas which suffered from chronic banditry and noble gang war. Each *hermandad* numbered 150 lances and was supported from taxes levied by itself. Its principal officers were royal nominees chosen from candidates proposed, for example, by the city of Saragossa. The king thus obtained a fiscal and military body totally beyond the control of the constitutional authorities. Although approved in 1487, the *hermandad* was suspended in 1495 when the great Aragonese families of Urrea, Luna and Alagón, among others, who had refused to join it, undertook the financial maintenance of a new military order for the king in exchange for his suppression of the *hermandad*.

The reform of Saragossa's municipal council in 1487 is also connected with Aragonese *hermandad* plans. The members of the council consented to a system whereby, instead of being appointed through a random selection process, they would be directly nominated by Ferdinand for three-year terms. At the same time, the procurators of the *corts* granted him the right to nominate the members of the kingdom's *diputació*.

The profound economic crisis in Catalonia meant that its institutional deadlock had to be broken by a radical reform of the principal self-governing bodies: the *diputació del general* and the council of one hundred. Only the king could carry out this reform, as the ecclesiastical and patrician branches of bodies dominating the *corts* were insensitive to the problem. As a result the king and the city of Barcelona were drawn together in the realisation that the *corts* would never reform the *generalitat*, which was mainly responsible for running up the huge public debt. The reform plans were drawn up by the chief councillor (*conseller en cap*) of the city, the energetic Pere Conomines (1483), who had been one of the leaders of Catalan resistance to Joan II, but was now putting into operation Ferdinand's reorganisation of the system. The plans themselves were based on the reduction of the public debt (the *censals*, or documents of credit issued by the *generalitat*), a salary cut for state officials, and the imposition of taxes on the clergy.

In 1488, at the instigation of the guilds of Barcelona, the king enacted the reform of the *diputació*, suspending the legislation governing the election of deputies and, without protest (for such was the level of corruption and disorder at the time), began appointing the deputies, including their president, the Castilian Juan Payo, abbot of Poblet. He followed this up with a series of protectionist measures which set off the economic recovery (the *redreç*): these included the reintroduction of the Catalan monopoly on coral fishing in Sardinia; the enlargement of the network of Catalan merchant consulates in the Mediterranean; the extension to Catalans of the privileges enjoyed by Castilians in Bruges; provisions against Genoese and Provençal merchants; and the protection of Catalan cloth exports to Sicily and Naples. Thanks to these measures the crisis was certainly averted. Barcelona, however, did not regain the pre-eminence she had enjoyed before the civil war. That position was now assumed by Valencia, evidence of whose economic growth and strength lay in the loans she was able to make to the crown and the reports of visitors who commented favourably on the splendours of the city.

It took longer to reform the government of Barcelona, where the gravity of the situation could be seen in the repeated, occasionally contradictory, interventions of the sovereign. As a result of the privileges granted to it by Alfonso V in 1455, the city was ruled by a government (*consellería*) composed of five councillors elected annually by the council of one hundred: two by the *ciutadans honrats* and one each by the *mercaders*, *artistes* and *menestrals*. Each *consellería* also had the right to nominate half the members of the council, each of whose mandates ran for two years. Finally, the government of Barcelona was in the hands of a restricted oligarchy made up of some fifteen families from the patrician class and their allies, the great merchants. As this group was unable to make decisions which accorded with the perceived general interest, it was deeply resented by the other social classes. In 1490 the king suspended the elections of the councillors and personally appointed a new *consellería*, presided over by Jaume Destorrent, and made up of members of the groups favouring royal intervention in the city's affairs. Led by an open-minded, effective president, the new government was able to approve and enact all the measures of the *redreç*, but its excesses and abuses of power finally reached the attention of the king, who dissolved it in 1493, introducing a system of election by lottery (*insaculació*) in its place.

ARAGON WITHIN THE SPANISH MONARCHY

Although the institutional reforms introduced by Ferdinand involved some deep-seated changes to the administration of the hereditary states of the crown of Aragon, they were not based on some Castilian plan to impose a new and radically different form of government run along modern absolutist lines. To this extent there was no innovation, but rather a restoration of the monarchy's lost dignity and authority. At the same time, the changes reintroduced a climate of legality and justice, compromised by a half-century of 'pactist' excesses and provocation by the various parties. The reforms were now introduced as and when opportunities arose (in the state of Valencia there was a greater centralising trend, since there was less resistance to the powers of the crown) and, on the whole, the overwhelming desire for an overhaul of the system by some strong and respected authority caused the innovations to be generally accepted.

However, the introduction, in 1494, of the *consejo supremo de Aragón* was a novelty. Its first president, Alfonso de la Caballeria, who stemmed from a Jewish family that had long ago converted to Christianity, was a strong supporter of the monarchy. The *consejo*, composed of the vice-chancellor, the treasurer-general of Aragon and the regents of the chanceries of Aragon, Valencia and Catalonia, was the governing body common to all the states of the crown of Aragon which, in this way, managed to retain its pluralistic and federal character within the dual monarchy of the Catholic sovereigns, a monarchy based exclusively on personal and dynastic ties.

It would be a mistake to imagine that the continuing separation of Castilian and Aragonese institutions was indicative of Ferdinand's belief that the problem of the dual monarchy would only be solved by its dissolution. It would be equally wrong to consider that evidence of this pessimism lay in his renunciation of his title to the throne of Castile on Isabel's death (1504), in his second marriage to Germaine de Foix, niece of the king of France, in 1506, or in their naming of their son, who died only a few months old, as heir to the throne of Aragon alone. Ferdinand never doubted the validity of the union of the two crowns expressed in the Edict of Segovia and repeated in Isabel's will. His rule was dominated by this conviction, together with the belief that the epicentre and guiding light of the new monarchy had to be Castile. However, this does not alter the fact that from the point of view of foreign policy the Catholic monarchs were guided by Aragonese interests whose traditional points of focus were the Mediterranean and Italy, in pursuit of which Ferdinand used Castile's military and economic might. After the death of Alfonso 'the Magnanimous', Naples had become an independent state under the bastard line of the house of Aragon (Ferrante, or Ferdinando, 1458–94) and was treated as an Aragonese protectorate in expectation of its eventual reabsorption into the crown's territories. This occurred in 1503, following the complicated international situation brought about by the French invasion of Italy in 1494, and thanks to the great military skill of Gonzalo Fernández de Córdoba. However, when the *gran capitán* and Philip, Ferdinand's son-in-law and king of Castile, made it clear that they considered Naples a Castilian appendage, Ferdinand acted decisively, travelling to Naples in 1506 and moving the *gran capitán* to another base. His aim was to demonstrate that the kingdom of Naples, the culmination of Alfonso V's (his uncle's) expansionist dreams, was an Aragonese, not a Spanish or Castilian possession. His speech before the *corts* at Monzón in 1510 also aroused the enthusiasm of the Aragonese and Catalans when he declared his aims of expansion into the Mediterranean and North Africa, where Algiers and Tripoli had already fallen into Spanish hands, and the struggle against Islam gave hope of further conquests to follow.

Seen from the outside, Ferdinand's policies appear to continue the uniform approach typical of the policies of Ferdinand and Isabel. This led many of the king's contemporaries to assume that the unification of the Spanish monarchies had already been achieved, and to a tendency to call the 'Catholic Monarchs' by the titles of king and queen of Spain, titles which they themselves never adopted. Machiavelli and Guicciardini also followed this trend. But Guicciardini, who had a better understanding than Machiavelli of the domestic policies of countries on the Iberian peninsula, when considering the year 1506 in his *Storia d'Italia*, gave Ferdinand the title 'king of Aragon', and ceased calling him 'king of Spain', on the basis that following Isabel's death and the passing of the validity of her will, the purely personal union of the two crowns was terminated. The kingdom of Aragon, although joined to that of Castile, could not lose its identity through total merger into a new kingdom of Spain. On the contrary, the states of Aragon and Catalonia were destined to retain their original political and institutional character within the wider Spanish kingdom until 1714.

CASTILE AND NAVARRE

Angus MacKay

BOTH at the time and subsequently, the history of fifteenth-century Castile seemed to be one of cosmic chaos, a period of almost constant anarchy until Isabel 'the Catholic' and her husband, Ferdinand of Aragon, restored law and order in the 1480s. Observers reacted to the violence and disorder with expressions of weary incomprehension or with reflections on men's innate greed and disloyalty. On 11 August 1465, for example, the urban chronicler, Garci Sánchez, noted in disbelief that when two men of the Saavedra lineage in Seville quarrelled with others of the Ponce de León faction, several thousands took to the streets, the Saavedra house was sacked and Fernando Arias de Saavedra himself escaped only by fleeing across the rooftops of his district. Nobody but the Devil, he observed three years later, was capable of understanding such feuds between factions (*bandos*). According to the chronicler Fernán Pérez de Guzmán, matters were not much better at the royal court. Politics there, he reflected, were characterised by endless imprisonments, expulsions and confiscations of wealth 'for the praiseworthy custom of the Castilians has reached such a point that men will consent to the imprisonment and death of a friend or relative in order to have a share in the booty'.[1] Foreigners, likewise, painted a dismal picture. In 1466 the Bohemian noble Leo of Rozmital travelled widely through the kingdom, and two of his companions described their experiences. The Basque country was 'wretched', its people 'murderous', the inns 'evil beyond measure' and the priests were married and unlearned. Further south they had to cross tracts of wilderness and mountainous territory, and when they visited one of the two rival royal courts, that of Enrique IV, they observed that the king 'eats and drinks and is clothed and worships in the heathen manner and is an enemy of Christians'.[2] But then Enrique has always been the leading contender for the title of Spain's worst king.

What sense is to be made of this? While it is possible to concentrate on spe-

---

[1] Pérez de Guzmán, *Generaciones*, p. 47.
[2] See the short section on Castile in *The travels of Leo of Rozmital*, pp. 78ff.

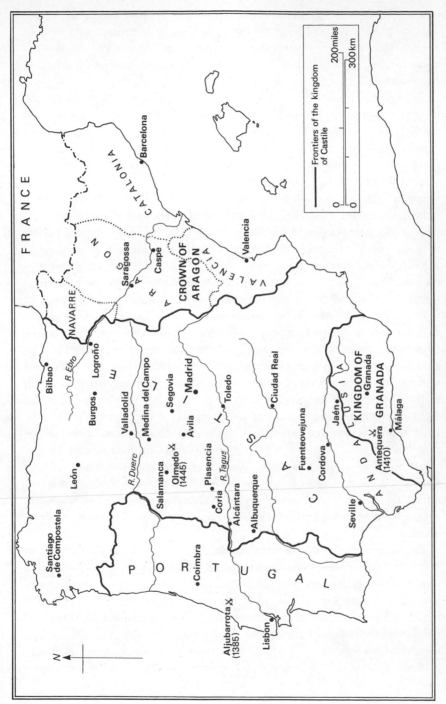

Map 13   Castile and Navarre

The map shows:

FRANCE

CATALONIA
Barcelona

NAVARRE
Saragossa
Caspe
CROWN OF ARAGON
VALENCIA
Valencia

R. Ebro
Logroño
Bilbao
Burgos
Valladolid
Medina del Campo
Segovia
Ávila
Madrid
Toledo
Ciudad Real
León
R. Duero
Salamanca
Olmedo (1445)
Plasencia
Coria   R. Tagus
Alcántara
Albuquerque
Fuenteovejuna
Cordova
Seville
Jaén
ANDALUSIA
Granada
KINGDOM OF GRANADA
Antequera (1410)
Málaga

Santiago de Compostela
Coimbra
PORTUGAL
Aljubarrota (1385)
Lisbon

Frontiers of the kingdom of Castile

200 miles
300 km

N

cific aspects in order to find part explanations, the historian is forced to look at the large picture. Can anything other than mindless anarchy be detected? Were the 'Catholic Monarchs' (*Reyes católicos*) geniuses who replaced chaos with law and order, or did they build on the work of their predecessors, however imperfect that work had been?

To begin with, it may well be asked how violent and senseless were episodes of apparent anarchy? In 1458, in the hill-top town of Alcaraz, violence had reached such a stage that Enrique IV commissioned a special enquiry to be carried out by the royal *corregidor*, Pedro de Silva, and one of his military commanders and royal councillors, Gonzalo Carrillo. The commissioners examined some twenty people, all inhabitants of Alcaraz and eye-witnesses of the events. Eighty-four pages recorded their evidence. The witnesses identified individuals, located the events in specific streets and houses and even gave renderings of direct speech which they overheard during the disturbances. The violence had split the oligarchical lineages of the town, and the riots and fighting which took place on the night of 10 January were viewed with great seriousness. There had been an uprising, 'delinquents' and 'evil-doers' had armed themselves to the teeth, and both sides had tried to secure control of strategic tower-houses and churches. Numerous people named in inordinate detail had rushed to provide armed support for the lineages of either side. As far as the royal commissioners were concerned, the affair was one of the utmost gravity, a classic case of urban anarchy, armed conflict and bloodshed. Yet the detailed evidence of these witnesses, observing the same events, emphasises certain features. Whatever their political allegiances, and wherever they went on the night in question, the same anarchy was described in similar ways. In fact, the royal commissioners went out of their way to ask the right sort of questions, so that the answers of any one witness could be cross-checked against the evidence of others in order to determine in detail what had happened, and who was responsible for this or that particular incident. The remarkable fact is that during the uprising in Albacete not a single person was killed or wounded, although one man was trapped, disarmed and then allowed to escape 'dishevelled'.

The same remarkable conclusion could probably be made with respect to what was regarded as a major battle, that of Olmedo in 1445. One important victim, the *infante* Enrique, injured in the hand, died from his wounds several days later. And yet it would be wrong to conclude that violence did not lead to bloodshed for, as will be seen, some episodes of political unrest entailed horrific acts of cruelty. Distinctions must be made between different types of violence, and there must also be consideration of the way in which certain 'structural' factors affected the political activities of contemporaries.

Of the two kingdoms under scrutiny, Castile was overwhelmingly of greater significance, emerging as the dominant partner of the uneasily 'united' Spain established towards the end of the century, while the small realm of Navarre, retaining a precarious independence, was a mere pawn in the complicated events of the period. Any attempt to make sense of the turbulent history of the age, therefore, must perforce focus primarily on Castile, and this in turn requires consideration of two fundamental or structural features about this kingdom: its demography and its chronic monetary instability.

For a long time the kingdom of Castile had been growing in size, and that process was not yet over. The most striking expansion had taken place in the thirteenth century, and as late as 1492 it was to conquer the Muslim kingdom of Granada. Changes in the configurations of its frontiers, therefore, entailed important demographic consequences. During the thirteenth-century reconquest, after cities such as Cordova and Seville had fallen to the Christians in 1236 and 1248 respectively, the kingdom had doubled the size of its territory. Since, with minor exceptions, the defeated Muslim populations had not been assimilated by the Christians, the occupation of new territories entailed processes of repopulation and colonisation, these in turn giving rise to a shortage of manpower and a relative abundance of land. Unlike the rest of western Europe, land became available at a faster rate than it was needed, and this situation, aggravated by the Black Death and later endemic stages of plague, implied that, well into the fifteenth century, the arable economy of the kingdom was characterised by an almost total absence of demesne exploitation. Pastoralism and transhumance flourished and, at a time when colonists were still being attracted by the south, the great noble and ecclesiastical landlords had to compete for manpower by offering easy conditions of land tenure.

The problems resulting from this land:population ratio were aggravated by a history of monetary instability. Throughout the late Middle Ages debasements and devaluations had a catastrophic effect on the Castilian money of account, the *maravedí*, so much that it has been calculated that it lost more value than any other western European equivalent. Several factors may be adduced to explain this disastrous performance, and in terms of the political history of the period it is important to evaluate briefly their significance. Castile certainly did not escape the consequences of the bullion famine and liquidity crisis which affected the whole of western Europe during the late Middle Ages. The European famine was characterised by an inadequate stock of bullion due to a decline in silver mining, interruptions in the trans-Saharan gold trade from the western Sudan, and an unfavourable balance of trade with the Levant. Nevertheless, although Castile did not remain unaffected by the crisis, she did not suffer to the same extent as her European neighbours. Indeed, although Castilian bimetallic ratios and other sources of evidence confirm a relative

shortage of silver, they also confirm a relative abundance of gold, and emphasise the kingdom's strategic and intermediary position between the sources of
supply of both metals. Yet, despite these advantages, the money of account
lost value catastrophically, as may be seen by measuring its fortunes against relatively stable indicators. About 1300, for example, the Florentine gold florin
was worth just under 6 *maravedíes*; by 1500, the same florin was worth 375 *maravedíes*. The same result emerges from measuring the fortunes of the *maravedí* in
terms of silver: about 1300 a mark of fine silver was worth about 213 *maravedíes*;
by 1472 it had climbed to some 2,000 *maravedíes*. Expressing the same disaster in
different ways, we could say the *maravedí* fell in value from 1.08 grams of silver
to 0.115 grams, a fall of 98 per cent, during the period. Matters might not have
been so bad had the *maravedí* been subjected to controlled devaluation, but, in
fact, its history was marked by abrupt secret and open devaluations, sudden
attempts at monetary reforms and a marked contrast between the full-bodied
and relatively stable coins of silver and gold, on the one hand, and constantly
debased base-metal coins on the other.

Apart from episodes of bullion crises, what specific factors explained the
monetary chaos, and what were the consequences? Of course, the *maravedí*, or
money of account, did not exist as a coin; it was a device which made it possible to make sense of all the variations affecting the real coins in circulation.
On the other hand it was, in an accounting sense, all too real and ubiquitous,
since prices, wages, debts and salaries were almost invariably expressed in its
terms. The consequences for political activity were serious.

Take, for example, the so-called 'old' seignorial taxes or dues paid by the
inhabitants of the Tierra de Campos, to the north of the river Duero in Old
Castile, during the course of the late Middle Ages; the customary and fixed
payments such as *infurciones*, *fumadgas*, *martiniegas* and *yantares* recorded in the
famous fourteenth-century *Becerro de las Behetrías*. Many villages of this region
paid their lords 500 *maravedíes* per year in *martiniegas*, but whereas such a sum
would have been worth some twenty-eight Florentine florins in the mid-fourteenth century, a hundred years later its value had plummeted to below two
florins.

Yet, although these customary payments had dropped in value, they were
still worth having. The dues paid by one peasant or inhabitant, usually referred
to as a 'vassal' (*vasallo*), may have been insignificant, but in their hundreds their
value was considerable. When Juan II tried to buy the support of Pedro de
Acuña, in 1439, he promised him 1,000 'vassals', but on giving him the town of
Dueñas, worth only 600 'vassals', he had to admit that he still owed him another
400.

None the less, these old seignorial revenues paled into insignificance when
contrasted to the huge sums raised and spent from the proceeds of the new

royal taxes which had appeared and been shaped into a consolidated form during the second half of the fourteenth century. Of these, the most important was undoubtedly the 10 per cent sales tax (*alcabala*), which by the fifteenth century was a permanent imposition accounting for well over half the crown's regular revenue. Substantial sums were also netted through other regular taxes, such as the royal share of ecclesiastical tithes (*tercias*), customs duties (*diezmos* and *almojarifazgo*), the revenues raised from transhumance (*servicio* and *montazgo*), not to mention the extraordinary taxes frequently voted by a docile *cortes* (*pedidos* and *monedas*), the sums raised from papal indulgences or subsidies on the clergy and the tribute money (*parias*) paid by the Muslim rulers of Granada.

An important feature of most of the regular taxes is that they were farmed out or auctioned to individual financiers or groups of financiers, the highest bidders offering what was, in effect, the best price to the royal administration. As with others, the prices of the tax-farms tended to rise as debasements and devaluation took their toll on the money of account, with the result that royal revenue was, to some extent, protected against erosion. Even as late as 1458, for example, royal revenue was in real terms well defended against the full effects of devaluation, although it fell alarmingly during the second half of the reign of Enrique IV. It is this fact which explains one of the apparently puzzling features of the political history of the age, namely that the great nobles and their supporters did not normally seek open confrontation with the king, but tended, instead, to try to manoeuvre themselves into a position in which, by means of threats or provisional offers of support, they could obtain shares in the profits derived from royal fiscality.

There were important exceptions to this picture of a society whose nobility, including the urban nobility, were uninterested in a direct involvement in demesne exploitation, markets and economic activity. Regional variations in royal income derived from taxation, especially the amounts from the two most important sources, the sales tax (*alcabala*) accounting for about three-quarters of regular royal income, and customs duties for about an eighth, reflected, however imperfectly, differentials in terms of the volume of commercial transactions. The regions of greatest fiscal and commercial activity were south-western Andalusia, where Seville was the largest city in the kingdom, and northern Castile, whose coastal towns of shippers were linked to important centres of the interior such as Burgos, Valladolid and the famous fairs at Medina del Campo. In both these regions great nobles and urban patricians were attracted by the profits to be derived, directly or indirectly, from foreign markets. A flourishing export trade in olive oil and wine in the south, for instance, involved not only foreign merchants but great magnates like the duke of Medina Sidonia, whose officials also directly administered flourishing tunny fisheries (tunny was exported preserved in oil), and supervised the preparation of ships owned by the duke for voyages to England and the Canary Islands. Similarly, at a lower but eminently respectable social level, an urban oligarch of Seville like Fernán García de Santillán exported olive oil from his estates to Flanders. As for the urban oligarchs of Burgos they sent wool from the northern ports to Flanders, while from Seville, where they formed the largest colony of native merchants, they exported a wide variety of commodities, such as almonds, dyes, olive oil and leather. Evidently many of the nobles and oligarchs of south-west Andalusia were actively interested in the profits to be made from trade in primary products, an interest in economic matters reflected in other ways. The manufacture of soap, much of it exported to England, attracted their attention and gave rise to complicated dealings whereby they in effect bought shares in the enterprise. They were also certainly aware of the ways in which devaluation and inflation could erode the real value of their landed income, and so in many cases leases grew progressively shorter, allowing for the readjustment of rents with stipulations that these be paid in kind, the subsequent sales of the wheat and barley paid by tenants fetching market prices which matched (and, in some years, outstripped) the rate of inflation. In other regions of the kingdom, however, perpetual leases, fixed rents and rampant nominal inflation seriously eroded, or threatened to erode, the incomes which the nobility derived from lands.

The crisis in noble incomes provoked a variety of reactions, but the most important one, and the one with the most serious implications for the political history of the period, was the manner in which noble factions attempted to wrest wealth from the crown. The ways in which they attempted to do this largely depended on such factors as the age of the king, his ability as a ruler, the role of royal favourites, the power and influence of the king's closest relatives, and the machinations involving the composition and powers of the royal council.

A convenient starting-point for a consideration of the main events of the political history of the period is afforded by the death of King Enrique III on 25 December 1406. He had never enjoyed good health and, at his death, his son, Juan II, was not yet two years old. But Enrique had foreseen the problems likely to be posed by a long minority, and he had already arranged for the government of the kingdom to be entrusted to his wife, Catalina (Catherine) of Lancaster, to his brother, Fernando, and to the royal council. Fernando was undoubtedly the dominant personality during the minority, and he quickly gained a golden reputation. He refused to consider any pretensions to the throne, urged on his behalf by supporters, persuaded the leading nobles and churchmen to accept his young nephew as king and subsequently enhanced his reputation by waging war against the Moors, taking Antequera in 1410, and assiduously cultivating a mystique which combined the highest ideals of chivalry (he had already founded the Order of the Jar and the Griffin) with apparent loyalty to his nephew and a profound devotion to the Virgin Mary. This mystique paid off in a spectacular way. When Martí I, the childless king of the crown of Aragon, died in 1410, Fernando 'of Antequera' peddled his claims to the vacant throne and was elected to the succession by the Compromise of Caspe of 1412, taking care to stress that he was the Virgin's candidate and predestined to become king notwithstanding the election.

Of greater impact for the future, however, was the fact that Fernando not only retained his regency in Castile but that he concentrated on consolidating his family's powers in both kingdoms until his death in 1416. His eldest son, Alfonso 'the Magnanimous', succeeded his father and preceded his brother, the *infante*, Joan, as monarch of the crown of Aragon. But the latter succeeded to vast possessions in Castile and, despite marrying Blanche of Navarre, and thus also becoming king of Navarre after the death of Charles III 'the Noble' in 1425, for most of his life remained primarily interested in Castilian politics. In addition, moreover, Fernando had also obtained the mastership of the powerful military Order of Santiago for another son, the *infante* Enrique, as early as 1409, while his daughter, María of Aragon, was to become the wife of Juan II of Castile, while the latter's sister was married to Fernando's son, Alfonso.

When Juan II of Castile married María of Aragon in 1418, the Aragonese party, consisting of those who supported the *infantes* Juan and Enrique, already controlled considerable wealth within the kingdom and dominated the royal court. Their power, however, was to meet the resistance of a subtle and determined politician, Alvaro de Luna, the king's favourite and, indeed, virtually king in all but name.

Feared by many, despised as an upstart by his aristocratic opponents, this bastard from a relatively obscure background dominated the politics of Castile for over thirty years. Luna began his career at court as a mere squire to the young king, who soon fell under the spell of a man accomplished in all the courtly arts, who worked assiduously at improving his chivalrous image, earned a reputation as a graceful dancer and singer, wrote occasional poetry and, above all, organised glittering *fiestas* which, with their tournaments, 'inventions', complicated allegorical meanings and sumptuous banquets, were on a par with the better-known spectacles for which the court of Burgundy became renowned. It came to be widely felt that the favourite's hold over the king, who disliked the routine tasks of government and would not sign royal documents without Luna's approval, was excessive and, later in the century, was to take the form of an alleged attachment which had overtones of diabolism and magic.

The political history of Juan II's reign is most easily understood in terms of a struggle for power between a rather disunited Aragonese party and Luna, not forgetting the leading nobles who affected the balance of power by changing sides to their own advantage. When the young king came of age early in 1419, the *infante* Juan seemed to be the obvious leader of a governing oligarchy in Castile. Surprisingly, however, the real opposition to his power came from his brother, the *infante* Enrique. The ambitious master of Santiago aimed at gaining a personal base of power outside his order and, by organising a *coup d'état* at court in July 1420, he dislodged his brother from power, married the king's sister and obtained the vast estates of the marquisate of Villena as a dowry. Luna, who was to exploit the divisions among the *infantes* with varying success, worked to build up support for the crown, but did not feel strong enough to take decisive action until 1428. First, the *infante* Juan, now king of Navarre, was ordered to leave the kingdom; then Luna, who had skilfully converted a domestic crisis into a foreign war, crushed the *infante* Enrique, and took over the administration of the Order of Santiago; finally, when the truce of Majano ended hostilities in 1430, the *infantes* of Aragon were forbidden to live within the kingdom without royal permission.

Luna's powers now increased dramatically. His half-brother became archbishop of Toledo in 1434; his own control of the Order of Santiago was confirmed by the pope in 1436; his second marriage allied him to the influential Pimentel family, and he used the confiscated possessions of the Aragonese party to build up his personal support. But his successes provoked a reaction among nobles backed by the Aragonese party, and revolts ended in his defeat in 1440. Royal government was to be controlled by the king's council, Luna was sentenced to six years of exile from the court, and the Aragonese party had triumphed. But the nobility soon realised that they had replaced one despot with another. Above all, the king of Navarre, who had already demonstrated a close interest in economic matters by, for example, acquiring the military Order of Calatrava for his son, dropped all pretence of sharing power and purged the court and central administration. The inevitable reaction followed. Within a year the king escaped from his clutches, joined forces with Luna and other disaffected nobles and, in May 1445, won a decisive victory at the battle of Olmedo.

Yet, although the favourite's position seemed to be enhanced, his days were numbered. In the coming years he acquired the mastership of the Order of Santiago and the lands and title of the county of Albuquerque, in both cases arranging to renounce these bases of power directly to his son. Moreover, although there were signs of mounting opposition, with disaffected nobles joining the disgruntled heir to the throne, Luna dealt with these difficulties with skill. His real problems came from an unexpected quarter. In 1447, at Luna's suggestion, Juan II had married Isabel of Portugal, in part because the favourite thought that a Portuguese alliance would counter the influence of the

Aragonese party. The new queen, however, disliked Luna intensely, and he became isolated. Juan II who, despite his profligacy, had always displayed a streak of avariciousness, now began to assess the favourite's wealth and, after a trial of sorts, Luna was beheaded in Valladolid by royal command in June 1453, an execution which caused a sensation. Little more than a year later Juan himself died.

The reign of his successor, Enrique IV, was to be bedevilled by court intrigues and unsavoury scandals. The king's marriages and morals came to assume enormous significance, being used by his opponents as propaganda, ultimately deciding the legitimacy of Isabel 'the Catholic's' succession to the throne. In 1440, while still Prince of Asturias, Enrique had been married to Blanche of Navarre, daughter of the *infante* Juan, king first of Navarre and then of Aragon. The marriage, however, produced no children and was dissolved thirteen years later by canonical decree, on the grounds that it had not been consummated. Enrique was free to marry again, and the unfortunate Blanche was obliged to return to Navarre.

Two years later and now king, Enrique married Joana of Portugal. For six years the marriage remained fruitless, but in 1462 the queen gave birth to a daughter, later to be known as Juana 'la Beltraneja'. By the time that Enrique IV died, in 1474, a mixture of truth, propaganda and lies, coupled with the open assertion that Beltrán de la Cueva, a royal favourite, was the father of 'la Beltraneja', had completely obscured the problem of the succession to the throne.

Yet, down to 1463, Enrique IV had been held in considerable respect both at home and abroad. He obtained a papal bull empowering him to administer the military Orders of Santiago and Alcántara; he drew on the abilities of civil servants; and he shrewdly attempted to deflect noble opposition by preparing a campaign against Muslim Granada. Abroad, the Catalans, in rebellion against Joan II of Aragon, actually proclaimed Enrique as their king in 1462.

These successes, however, were more apparent than real. Increasingly, power at court was being wielded by one of the king's favourites, Juan Pacheco, marquis of Villena, whose personal ambitions and cynical amassing of royal privileges made bitter enemies among the nobility, particularly among the powerful family of Mendoza. Above all, the campaign against Granada was widely considered to have been nothing more than a misuse of *cruzada* revenues raised, with papal blessing, by a king who refused to launch attacks, preferring instead to play ineffectual war games or admire the presents and minstrels with which his Moorish opponents regaled him.

Already, by 1460, some of the nobility had formed a league of the 'public weal' (the term 'cosa publica' would be used shortly afterwards), and by 1463 Juan Pacheco, replaced at court by the new favourite, Beltrán de la Cueva, was using his undoubted talents to win powerful allies, the most notable being the archbishop of Toledo, Alfonso Carrillo, in order to put forward a reform programme. The king was accused of favouring infidels and heretics, manipulating the coinage and surrendering his powers to worthless favourites. Presented with a long list of grievances, Enrique IV was forced to agree to the setting up of a commission of reform, the results being contained in the comprehensive judgement (*sentencia*) of Medina del Campo of January 1465. Within a month, however, he had repudiated the findings of the commission, and in June the rebel nobility deposed his effigy in an extraordinary ritual ceremony known as the 'Farce of Avila' ('la Farsa de Avila') and proclaimed his young half-brother as Alfonso XII. With two kings and two royal administrations, the next three years were ones of general anarchy, the situation changing only with the unexpected death of the young king.

Alfonso's death posed two related problems, that of the succession, and that of arranging a marriage for his sister, the *infanta* Isabel. In September 1468 Enrique IV and Isabel negotiated an end to the civil war by the Agreement of Toros de Guisando, Isabel being recognised as heir to the throne. However, her marriage to Ferdinand of Aragon in October 1469, a marriage backed by Aragonese diplomacy and arranged against the king's wishes, prompted a renewal of Juana's claim to the succession.

On the death of Enrique IV in December 1474, Isabel immediately had herself proclaimed queen in Segovia, and during the following years of civil war and crisis, characterised by threats from supporters of Juana's claim and hostility from France and Portugal, she and Ferdinand used a mixture of military force, privileges and concessions, pardons and arbitrary measures, such as the confiscation of church plate, to consolidate their position. With the entry of the defeated Juana into a nunnery in Coimbra, the dynastic crisis was over.

The remaining years of the reign of the 'Catholic Monarchs' were ones of almost apocalyptic success, the events of 1492 usually being accorded greatest significance as marking the transition into a more 'modern' age. On 1 January Muslim Granada surrendered to the Christians; three months later, on 31 March, Ferdinand and Isabel decreed the expulsion of the Jews from their realms; while in October Columbus, who had been present at the surrender of Granada, 'discovered' America. In the context of the period in which they happened, these events appear thoroughly medieval; their full significance would emerge with time. The point may be illustrated by alluding to chronicle accounts of the circumstances of Ferdinand's death.

Shortly before his death on 25 January 1516, Ferdinand 'the Catholic' received a message from God passed on to him by a famous female visionary, Sor María de Santo Domingo, also known as the Beata de Barco de Avila, or the Beata de Piedrahita:

And while His Highness was in this place [Madrigalejo], his illness became much worse, and he was made to understand that he was very close to death. But he could hardly believe this because the truth is that he was much tempted by the enemy who, in order to prevent him from confessing or receiving the sacraments, persuaded him to believe that he would not die so soon. And the reason for this was that, when he was in Plasencia, one of the royal councillors who had come from the Beata told him that she was sending to tell him on behalf of God that he would not die until he had taken Jerusalem. For this reason, he would not see or send for Fray Martín de Matienzo, of the Order of Preachers, his confessor, even though the confessor himself tried several times to see him.[3]

Sor María, who delivered sermons-in-trance and suffered ecstatic crucifixions, had enthralled the royal court; even the great Cardinal Jiménez de Cisneros was a devotee. What did the message about Jerusalem mean?

King Ferdinand would certainly have understood the implications, related as they were to the apocalyptic legend of 'The Last Roman Emperor' who, at the end of time, would defeat the Muslims, conquer Jerusalem and renounce his world-empire directly to God at the Hill of the Skull, Golgotha. In Spain this tradition, suitably influenced by Joachimite ideas and prophecies attributed to St Isidore of Seville, produced a Spanish messianic king and world-emperor, known variously as the Hidden One (*Encubierto*), the Bat (*Murciélago*) and the New David. In the Spanish context, too, the Antichrist would make his appearance in Seville, and the eschatological battles at the end of time would take place in Andalusia, the messianic forces expelling the Muslims and taking Granada before crossing the sea, defeating all Islam and conquering the Holy City of Jerusalem as well as the rest of the world. The beginning of each new reign, therefore, aroused eschatological expectations. When would the Hidden One reveal himself?

The problem was that reality had to match eschatological expectations, and this coincidence was not achieved until after 1480. Suddenly, between that year and 1513, there was an explosion of exuberance as events made eschatology credible. As the successes of the 'Catholic Monarchs' multiplied so, too, did the prophetic texts, commentaries and even ballads which identified Ferdinand as the Bat (or as the *Encubierto*) who would conquer Jerusalem and the whole world. Nor was this the work of obscure fanatics, as the letter of revelation which Rodrigo Ponce de León, marquis of Cadiz, circulated to the great nobles of Castile in 1486 demonstrates. In it the marquis recounted what had been revealed to him by a mystic:

the illustrious, powerful and great prince, King Ferdinand . . . was born under the highest and most copious planet that any king or emperor ever was . . . There will be nothing in this world able to resist his might, because God has reserved total victory

[3] Galíndez de Carvajál, *Anales*, pp. 562–3.

and all glory to the rod, that is to say the Bat, because Ferdinand is the *Encubierto*. . . He will subdue all kingdoms from sea to sea; he will destroy all the Moors of Spain; and all renegades to the Faith will be completely and cruelly ruined because they are mockers and despisers of the Holy Catholic Faith. And not only will his Highness conquer the kingdom of Granada quickly, but he will subdue all Africa, and the kingdoms of Fez, Tunis, Morocco and Benemarin . . . Furthermore he will conquer the Holy House of Jerusalem . . . and become Emperor of Rome; . . . and he will be not only Emperor, but Monarch of the whole world.[4]

What had allegedly been revealed to the marquis was hardly new, and Ferdinand was simply being made to fit into a medieval tradition which was aptly summarised in a critical way some hundred years earlier by the wise tutor who warned his noble student, Pero Niño, about such prophecies, his advice being recorded, about 1448, in the chronicle *El Victorial*:

If you look at the matter carefully, you will see that a new Merlin appears at the accession of each new king. It is held that the new king will cross the seas, destroy all the Moors, conquer the Holy House [of Jerusalem], and become Emperor. So then we see that matters turn out as God disposes. Such prophecies were attributed to kings in the past, and they will be made about future kings as well.[5]

Pero Niño's tutor was right: even Enrique IV was cast in a messianic role! The difference in Ferdinand 'the Catholic's' case was that events and successes from 1480 seemed to contemporaries, including chroniclers, to make the messianic prophecies credible.

The project to take Jerusalem had other bizarre consequences. When Columbus sailed westwards and 'discovered' America, his destination was, in fact, Asia where he hoped to find support for a grand alliance which would encircle Islam and lead to the reconquest of Jerusalem. For it was in Asia or in Africa that the legendary Prester John, the liberator of the Holy Places, was to be found; it was in Asia, too, in Cathay, that the pro-Christian Great Khan of the Mongols resided. Earlier, in 1403, the Castilian, Ruy González de Clavijo, had been sent by Enrique III to the court of Tamerlane at Samarkand, and when Columbus departed he duly carried a letter of introduction to the Great Khan of the Mongols with him. In doing so, he was simply continuing crusading aspirations which were thoroughly medieval.

Continuity was also evident as far as ideas about the nature of kingship and monarchical power were concerned. The 'Catholic Monarchs', frequently credited with introducing new notions about enhanced royal authority, even 'absolutism', were simply building on the work of their predecessors, particularly Isabel's father, Juan II. Ably supported and advised by *letrados* (or graduates in law) as well as by Alvaro de Luna, Juan displayed an inordinate fondness

---

[4] *Historia de los hechos del marqués de Cádiz*, pp. 247–51.   [5] Díez de Games, *El Victorial*, p. 26.

for justifying his commands and policies, some of them extremely arbitrary, by simply claiming that he was acting 'as king and lord, not recognising a superior in temporal matters, and by virtue of my own will, certain knowledge and absolute royal power'. In so doing, he openly ignored the traditional view that the king was not above the law, and that the making or revising of laws was a matter for joint action by the king and the *cortes*. By using his absolute royal power (*poder real absoluto*) he simply enacted laws which he said were to be as valid 'as if they had been made in the *cortes*'. It is probably true that the practical day-to-day operation of this royal absolutism owed more to Luna than to his rather indolent master, but ultimately the policy worked in the monarchy's favour. Indeed, when Luna was at last brought to account, royal councillors, fearful of the outcome, informed the king that only he could proceed against Luna, so that the favourite received no trial and was beheaded by order of Juan II's personal *poder real absoluto*.

Nor did the *cortes* provide an effective check on arbitrary royal power. For most of the century its meetings could hardly be deemed to be representative in any meaningful sense. The participation of the nobility and clergy was usually limited to those who happened to be at court, and the representatives (*procuradores*) of the third estate, drawn from a limited number of some fifteen royal towns (two per town), were usually noble oligarchs who had their expenses paid by the crown. In practice, therefore, the *cortes* were small assemblies of some thirty representatives of the third estate together with court officials and members of the royal council. Moreover, their procedures were controlled by the king and his officials. There were no regular meetings, and the summoning and dissolution of assemblies were entirely dependent on the king. The representatives usually agreed to taxation, from which they were themselves largely exempt, and only then presented petitions to the king. Inevitably, since there was no redress of grievances before supply, the royal responses to petitions were often evasive and vague. In any case, few taxes still required consent, since the chief source of royal revenue, the *alcabala*, had escaped the control of the *cortes* from the late fourteenth century onwards.

Unlike the *cortes*, royal councils and other administrative institutions, particularly those concerned with finance (the *contradurías*), functioned regularly, were serviced by *letrados*, royal secretaries and chancery officials, and provided the basic framework of government inherited and expanded by the 'Catholic Monarchs'. The highest court of justice, or *audiencia*, for example, finally settled down in Valladolid from 1442 onwards, and *corregidores*, the famous and probably most disliked royal officials of regional or local administration, were already being used extensively by Juan II. *Corregidores* were not natives of the towns to which they were sent, and their intervention in urban government, usually bitterly resented, was supported by wide-reaching powers. Although the Catholic monarchs did not create such institutions and officials, they expanded their use to a considerable extent. For instance, they installed *corregidores* in all the principal royal towns, and they established additional *audiencias* in Ciudad Real (subsequently moved to Granada) and Santiago.

Compared with Castile, the small kingdom of Navarre in the fifteenth century presented a picture of limited resources coupled with considerable institutional sophistication and a pronounced insecurity arising from its position as a political pawn between Castile and France. The long reign of Charles III (1387–1425) was characterised by his absence and involvement in French politics; when, however, the succession passed to his daughter, Blanche, the fact that she was married to the *infante* Juan of Castile (Joan II of Aragon), meant that Navarre became involved in the internal conflicts of Castile. On Blanche's death in 1441 Joan of Aragon secured control of the kingdom, ignoring the claims of his son, Carlos, prince of Viana, who died in 1461 amid rumours of poison, and in 1455 he named as his successors his daughter, Leonor, and her husband, Gaston IV of Foix. But it was difficult for Castile to accept a situation in which the ruling house of Navarre held lands in France as well, and by 1494 Navarre had in effect become a Castilian protectorate, thus pointing the way to Ferdinand's assumption of the title of king of Navarre in 1512, and the incorporation of the kingdom in the crown of Castile in 1515.

For administrative purposes, above all as far as taxation was concerned, Navarre was organised into regions known as *merindades*, the royal financial administration betraying French rather than Castilian influences. By the fifteenth century a *camara de comptos* was already well established and charged with examining the accounts of the *recibidores* of the *merindades*, and of collectors (*peajeros*) of tolls on goods in transit. For long, the main source of royal revenue remained the *pechas*, which in theory were direct taxes related to the size and wealth of the tax-paying population, but in practice had become the fixed customary sums paid by each locality which, through time, lost their value in real terms. By the fifteenth century, therefore, it had become customary for the king regularly to request *ayudas* from the *cortes*. These were, in effect, hearth taxes, levied in accordance with information recorded in the *Libros de Fuegos*, which affected all the population and quickly replaced the *pechas* as the most important tax. In addition to these taxes the monarchy in Navarre frequently derived revenue, the so-called *provecho de la moneda*, through debasements of the royal coinage.

Although the tensions between Castilian monarchs and the great nobility monopolised the attention of court-orientated chroniclers, the evidence relating to political conflicts at a regional or local level tends, with important exceptions, to confirm the picture of relatively sophisticated order in the midst of apparent chaos. Political issues at court and in the localities were not, of course, divorced from one another. At the end of his chronicle about Alvaro de Luna, for example, Gonzalo Chacón provided an astonishingly detailed account of those important individuals in a lengthy list of towns who, in one way or another, supported Luna, an account so detailed that it must have been based on some sort of register. It revealed all those individuals, families and lineages who, metaphorically, 'lived with' Luna, 'lived with him and received money from him', 'had been raised up by him', 'were of his household', or even held money fiefs from him. It also revealed that Luna was fully aware how political affiliations worked out in practice.[6] He did not exercise his influence through the formal and theoretical frameworks of royal and urban government; instead, he endeavoured to know the right people and to win them over with money, offices, titles, promotions and matrimonial alliances. The extent of his power and influence may seem to have bordered on corruption, but in fact it was limited by a system of political balances at an urban level which was remarkably sophisticated and tended to provide stability.

Valladolid provides a good example of this. From Chacón's account it would appear that almost anyone of importance was indebted to the constable in one way or another, but in practice his influence could not penetrate right to the heart of a political system which was controlled by the two *bandos* of the Tovar and the Reoyo. These *bandos* of Castilian towns were remarkably similar to the *alberghi* of Genoa or the *consorterie* of Florence. Typically, a *bando* was a coalition of urban lineages which usually derived its name from the leading lineage or from the area of the town which it controlled. But it also included many who were not related by kinship links but by affinity. The Tovar *bando* of Valladolid, for instance, included the 'houses' or lineages of Fernán Sánches de Tovar, Gonzalo Díaz, Alonso Díaz, Castellanos and Mudarra, while the Reoyo *bando* also included five 'houses'. Each *bando*, therefore, included five lineages, and it was from the total of these that the officials of the oligarchy were chosen. But the surviving ordinances of the various 'houses' show that access to a lineage was not restricted to kin, and that others, knights, lawyers and men of substance, were admitted, and were eligible to serve in the offices allocated to the 'house'. The *bandos* and their related lineages were consequently to some extent flexible and 'open', and this enabled them to assimilate substantial outsiders capable of challenging the power structure of the town. Each *bando* controlled half the urban offices, and as these fell vacant they were allocated in turn to one of the five 'houses', the person assuming office being the oldest individual available in the lineage or, in the case of 'outsiders', the individual with the earliest date of entry to the 'house'. This complicated system had definite advantages, and even kings were prepared to institutionalise it, as happened in

---

[6] Gonzalo Chacón, *Crónica*, pp. 442–9.

Salamanca in 1390 and Bilbao in 1544. Moreover, even in those royal towns where such elaborate arrangements did not exist, power was still limited to, and shared by, two *bandos* which, although apparently opposed to each other, were quick to unite if a third party challenged their monopoly. Frequently, too, the conflicts between such *bandos* consisted of ritualised aggression which did not involve fighting or bloodshed.

Nevertheless, although the affinities of the *bandos* and lineages provided the normal pattern for the politics of Castilian towns, there was an awareness of alternative ways in which urban power could be organised, particularly that based on the concept of the *comunidad*. This was a sworn association of the heads of households (*vecinos*) which, in practice, tended to function only in times of crisis, that is when grave abuses were perceived to exist or when royal and urban authorities were failing in their duties. Episodes of unrest involving the *comunidad* of a town could be extremely violent, but a *comunidad* was normally well structured, and tended to follow certain traditional norms or rituals of behaviour. A *comunidad* perceived its violence as being entirely justified, acted as it felt the authorities should have been doing and often focused its collective activities openly and 'lawfully' on the main square of the town in question. A famous example of such an episode, celebrated in a play by Lope de Vega, was the uprising in Fuenteovejuna in 1476 when, on the night of 22 September, the people, led by their *alcaldes* and *regidores*, rose up as a *comunidad* and assassinated Fernán Gómez de Guzmán, the *comendador mayor* of the Order of Calatrava who dominated the town.

In some of these episodes of urban unrest Italian ideals about civic government were influential. In 1433, for example, there was a conspiracy to convert Seville into a commune along Italian lines, and this was followed thirty years later by another plot, fomented by the archbishop himself, to establish a republican city-state free from royal control. In this second case there were overtones of a spirit of civic humanism and contacts with Florence, while a rebellion in Malaga in 1516 aimed at establishing a *comunidad* modelled on that of Genoa.

Both at the royal court and in the towns political life was made even more complicated by the religious and social issues involving the presence of Jews or *conversos*, namely New Christians from a Jewish background. The twelfth and thirteenth centuries had been ones of relative tolerance or *convivencia*, a form of co-existence characterised by Christian respect for Jewish (and Islamic) culture. During the fourteenth century, however, *convivencia* was to give way to a rising tide of intolerance which culminated in widespread massacres in 1391. In that year a fanatical demagogue, Ferrant Martínes, archdeacon of Ecija, already well known to royal and ecclesiastical authorities, incited the mobs of Seville to attack the Jewish community. The killings spread rapidly to nearby towns, then to Cordova, Toledo, Valencia, Barcelona and Logroño. This was the great pogrom of 1391, and scarcely a Jewish community escaped massacres and looting. In Seville, for example, the Jewish community virtually ceased to exist. Terrified Jews now accepted conversion to Christianity in large numbers. As the number of *conversos* rose sharply, and additional conversions were to follow, for example after the preaching campaigns of Vincent Ferrer in the early fifteenth century and at the time of the expulsion of the Jews decreed in 1492, so such conversions had complicated consequences. There was, in the first place, a social problem. Jews could not hold offices in Church and state, although the same did not apply to *conversos*, so that during the first half of the fifteenth century a substantial number of *converso* families succeeded in obtaining important posts in the royal administration, urban oligarchies and in the ecclesiastical hierarchy. Many also married into Old Christian families, and the royal secretary, Fernán Diáz de Toledo, himself a *converso*, described in considerable detail how a large number of noble families had acquired *converso* relatives by mid-century. Such rapid political and social advancement provoked resentment and hostility. *Conversos* were accused of corruptly buying urban offices, of manipulating royal and municipal taxation to the detriment of Old Christians, and of being crypto-Jews. In fact the religious beliefs of the New Christians were inevitably complicated. For instance, the descendants of the celebrated convert and ex-rabbi of Burgos, Solomon Halevi, who, as Pablo de Santa María, became bishop of Burgos, were to produce outstanding churchmen of great learning and religious conviction, including bishops of Burgos, Coria and Plasencia. However, in addition to crypto-Jews and genuine Christians, large numbers of *conversos* appear to have been 'Averroists', that is they were basically irreligious, even atheists, while others still had only the haziest notion about the Christian doctrines they supposedly professed.

In 1449, therefore, the two principal disruptive elements in Castilian political life, noble intrigue and hostility towards the *conversos*, fused together to produce a serious rebellion in the city of Toledo. The troubles began as a popular rising against tax collectors and *conversos*, but almost immediately a nobleman, Pero Sarmiento, redirected the popular fury into a rebellion against Alvaro de Luna and the monarchy. Resentment against royal taxation, accusations of municipal corruption, the declining fortunes of the nobility and the economic hardships of artisans and peasants, hatred of the *conversos* and their success, and the widespread perception of them as heretics deliberately undermining the religious fabric of Christian society were inextricably linked together. Acting as the leader of the *comunidad* of Old Christians of Toledo, Sarmiento skilfully deployed arguments justifying rebellion in written manifestos and quasi-juridical documents. Although the rebellion failed, it led to a series of urban riots which culminated in a wave of massacres in Andalusian towns in 1473.

In almost all such cases there were no leaders of the calibre of Pero

Sarmiento to justify rioters who acted with extreme violence, and the resulting impression is one of senseless ferocity or 'blind furies', especially since descriptions of the events were penned by hostile observers. Indeed, it is difficult to account for such incidents as the way in which Miguel Lucas de Iranzo, lord of Jaen, was hacked to death by an enraged mob while he was at church attending Mass. Yet examination of some of the rites of violence involved in such incidents can provide valuable clues.

In the uprising of Toledo in 1449, the leader of the *conversos*, the wealthy tax-farmer, Juan de Ciudad, was killed, his body then being taken to the main square to be hanged upside down. In Toledo, again, in 1467, warfare broke out between the *comunidad* of Old Christians and that of the *conversos*. During the violent confrontations, on the night of 22 July, a leading *converso*, Fernando de la Torre, was caught attempting to flee the town, and his Old Christian enemies hanged him from the tower of a church, subsequently hanging his brother, as well. Their bodies were then cut down and taken to the main square to the accompaniment of a proclamation: 'This is the justice decreed by the *comunidad* of Toledo for those traitors and captains of the heretical *conversos*. Since they attacked the church, they are to be hanged head downwards by the feet. Whoever does this will pay the same penalty.' Accused of treason, both brothers were hanged in this ignominious fashion. But the violence had not yet ended; a 'collective' or 'participatory' mutilation of the naked corpses was to continue for several days. Once again, this was a case when the *comunidad* administered its own form of justice in which, as in Fuenteovejuna, everybody participated in one way or other in the city's main square. The violence associated with such gruesome executions, which would be re-enacted down to the revolt of the *comunidades* in 1520 and beyond, was not senseless. Such executions were a specific sign that the victims were guilty of crimes which threatened to turn the world upside down. In the cases cited, the alleged misdeeds of crypto-Jews were described as a form of treason which threatened the very fabric of Christianity itself.

Above all, in aping the actions of royal or urban officials, and by taking the law into their own hands, the rioters in the towns were implicitly indicating what they believed the authorities were failing to do. Both Juan II and Enrique IV were forced by circumstances to approve exclusion of *conversos* from the oligarchies of certain towns, but it was the 'Catholic Monarchs' who set up the Inquisition which punished those who had previously been the victims of popular violence, thus providing official 'texts' for the urban populace.

To a large extent the officials of the Inquisition were engaged in what may be described as semiological detective work. The Inquisition had no jurisdiction over Jews as such, only over baptised Christians, which in practice meant *conversos* suspected of crypto-Judaism. However, there was no easy way in which the inquisitors could gain access to the inner beliefs of *conversos*, and so they looked for signs of their externally enacted behaviour which might indicate heretical intentions. Did a suspected *converso* go to church? If so, how often and, once there, how did he behave? What did he do on Saturdays? What did he eat, or not eat, and what sort of clothes did he wear? Did he buy his meat from a Jewish or a Christian butcher? What did he do during the time of religious festivals? Was he circumcised? And where and how was he buried? *Conversos* were adept at apparently fulfilling Christian religious obligations while at the same time nullifying their actions by exploiting the polysemic possibilities of ritual observance. Inés López, for instance, did not go to church, and witnesses at her trial alleged that they had watched her closely and that she did not make the sign of the cross properly, confining herself to a token motion from the forehead to only one shoulder, and while invoking the name of the Father she never invoked that of the Son or the Holy Spirit. In his defence, a *converso* would argue that he had bought his meat from a Jewish butcher because the knives there were cleaner and sharper. *Conversos* did baptise their children, but on returning home would immediately 'de-christianise' them with an 'anti-ritual' which would efface the effects of the Christian sacrament. Similarly, or so it was alleged, *conversos* going to confession were rapidly despatched when priests found they had nothing to confess.

The predicament of the *conversos* also involved all manner of habits and customs which could be read as signs of a deliberate deviance and a reluctance to integrate properly. Moreover, awareness among the *conversos* of the tensions which existed between their outward performance of Christian rituals and their inner adherence to beliefs and customs which they could not express openly may have led some to use literature as a vehicle in which to encode attacks on the prevailing religious and social values which they despised. Fernando de Rojas was a *converso* whose masterpiece, the *Celestina*, contains much material, in the form of dialogue, asides and soliloquies, which may be interpreted as an attack on Old Christian values. Less ambiguously, Francisco Delicado, a *converso* and Catholic priest living in exile in Rome, wrote a novel, *La Lozana Andaluza*, between 1513 and 1524 (it was published in Venice in 1528) which depicted the activities and fate of the many New Christian girls of Andalusian and *converso* origins who fled the Inquisition in Spain to survive, as best they could, through a life of prostitution in the capital of Christendom. Appropriately, the heroine, Lozana, eventually acquires *sapientia* or 'fear of the Lord', adopts a new name, the typically Jewish one of Vellida, and leaves Rome (depicted as Babylon) just before its sack in 1527, an event which, in an epilogue, is depicted as a divine punishment.

Spain would shortly enjoy a Golden Age of territorial expansion and imperial rule. Habsburg Spain would be the dominant European, Catholic and world power, engaged in spreading its language and cultural values to other countries and continents, and championing the true religion against the dangerous threats posed by heretical Lutherans and Calvinists. However, although distinguished humanist scholars were in evidence, the intellectual leadership of Spain and its universities continued to be dominated by the theologians and Thomism. Humanists might study the Bible, but they could not challenge scholastic and religious orthodoxy. Even the publication of the six volumes of the famous Complutensian Polyglot Bible (1514–17), the project initiated by Cardinal Francisco Jiménez de Cisneros, had been made to conform to traditional and established authority notwithstanding the fact that philological knowledge indicated that mistranslations were involved.

Traditional religious orthodoxy in Spain was also reinforced by the fate of Christian humanism associated with Erasmus. Its impact was not so much due to humanism as to a desire for religious reform, following the precedents of such movements as the Observants, Franciscan mysticism and the *devotio moderna*. But when antipathy towards Erasmus surfaced in trials conducted by the Spanish Inquisition during the 1530s and later, the consequences for humanism were dire. So, too, were the effects of other measures designed to protect religious orthodoxy, such as the *Indices* of prohibited books produced by the Spanish Inquisition, and Philip II's decree of 1559 forbidding his subjects to study in foreign universities other than the four designated ones of Bologna, Rome, Naples and Coimbra.

Naturally, such measures could be circumvented, as the career of Juan Luis Vives (1492–1540) illustrates. Given a scholastic education in Spain, he became a humanist in Paris, went to the Low Countries in 1512 and became a friend and disciple of Erasmus. Among his many practical concerns, he was interested in the duty of public authorities to provide assistance for the poor. Perhaps a form of Erasmianism surfaced in Spain as well. The anonymous sixteenth-century account of the adventures and mishaps of its eponymous protagonist, *Lazarillo de Tormes*, certainly plunged its readers into a sub-world characterised by hypocrisy, hunger, greedy priests and the inevitable selling of indulgences to the gullible faithful by improper methods. Why did the author prefer to remain anonymous? Was he a crypto-Jew making an obvious attack upon Catholic hypocrisy? Or an Erasmian concerned with dubious religious attitudes and practices? While either is possible, it should not be forgotten that he may have been an early representative of the change which was soon to develop in the form of the Catholic or Counter-Reformation, a movement genuinely concerned with the socio-religious problems faced by the world of its day.

PORTUGAL

Armindo de Sousa

PORTUGAL comprises two large and very distinct geographical zones, a mountainous one in the north, a lowland one in the south, the dividing line being the river Tagus. From a climatic point of view, the country displays elements of both the Atlantic seaboard and the Mediterranean: high levels of rainfall in the northern regions and striking dryness in the south. Five rivers act as gateways to the ocean and the outside world: the Douro and Tagus, whose sources lie in Spain, and the Vouga, Mondego and Sado which rise in Portugal itself. The principal urban centres, Coimbra, Lisbon, Oporto and Silves, were riverside communities, as were many lesser settlements with a history of fishing, shipbuilding and maritime enterprise. Several inland towns acted as seats of bishoprics and as centres of administration, agriculture, manufacture and commerce.

The north had always been more highly populated than the south, and it was the northern region of Entre-Douro-e-Minho which had provided the population which had moved southwards in the twelfth and thirteenth centuries as the Moors were driven out. Later, in the fifteenth and sixteenth centuries, after the discovery of the Atlantic islands and Brazil, it was still from the same region that the largest numbers of settlers came. In the fourteenth century, on the eve of the Black Death, the population of Portugal probably stood at about 1.5 million, at a reasonable European average of some seventeen inhabitants per square kilometre. In 1348, however, this figure fell between a third and a half, at which level it was maintained, with slight modifications, until about 1460, when a recovery began. By the first quarter of the sixteenth century, the pre-Black Death figure had been restored.

The last hundred years of medieval Portugal did not, in fact, coincide strictly with the fifteenth century. Where, then, should the beginning of that 'century' be placed? In 1415, the year of the capture of Ceuta and of the start of Moroccan expansion? Since the fifteenth century marks the shift towards the seas and the new worlds, this date in Portuguese history would be appropriate

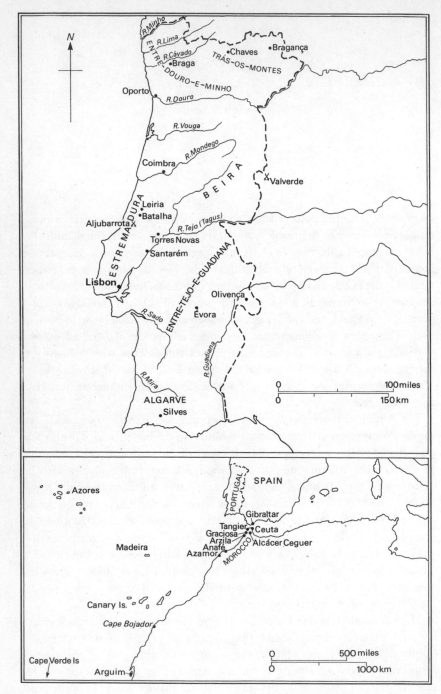

Map 14   Portugal (and the north-west coast of Africa)

enough, for it was through Ceuta that this progress was begun. In the Portuguese context, however, a more suitable starting date is 1385, the year which ushered in the second Portuguese dynasty, that of Avis (1385–1580). Indeed, 1385 was a year of myth making for the Portuguese. Linked to a wider historical chronology through the Hundred Years War, it signalled the final independence of the country. Portugal had already ruled itself for a long time, but it was in this year of crisis that she became a nation. The consciousness of Portuguese nationalism, *portuguesismo*, awoke with war: the battle of Aljubarrota (14 August 1385), elaborately reported by chroniclers and further exalted by myth, marked its birth. Although patriotic sentiment developed slowly over a period of time, it can be said that, by the time the dynasty of Avis began to rule, national awareness had emerged, among the popular classes, at least. The year 1385 thus becomes an appropriate date at which to start.

By that year Portugal was already a mature country. It had been independent of León and Castile for over two centuries, during which nine rulers had reigned, and its boundaries had been almost finally defined since 1297. Furthermore, it had its own language, well-recognised political, administrative and social structures, a defined economic direction, a developed system of education, established international diplomatic relations, all backed by an emerging national consciousness. Yet by 1385 this country, although mature, was undergoing a serious dynastic crisis. Dom Fernando, the last king of the founding dynasty, had died in 1383, leaving no male heir. His only daughter, Beatriz, wife of the Castilian king, and Leonor, his unpopular widow, were endangering independence. The urban masses, linked in a movement of social revolt not particular to Portugal alone, were skilfully manipulated by the burgesses, intellectual elite and discontented nobility in support of what amounted to a nationalist uprising in favour of a palace revolution to regain lost honour and avenge insult. The regent widow's lover, a detested foreign nobleman, was assassinated, and the assassin himself was declared a popular hero. With the queen's deposition and flight went the Afonsine dynasty, the first to rule Portugal.

All this occurred in Lisbon and its outskirts in December 1383. The coup, master-minded by members of the nobility, was soon transformed into a popular and nationwide revolution, affecting both Oporto in the north and the south in its entirety. The hero gradually learned to live up to his new role. He was to be styled 'ruler' ('regedor') of the realm, then 'ruler and defender' ('regedor e defensor'), and would finally be proclaimed king. Later he would earn the title of 'Messiah, unvanquished victor, father of the Portuguese' ('Messias, vencedor invicto, pai dos portugueses'); later still, after two and a half centuries, there were those who would call him a saint. Such was João I, bastard son of King Pedro, half-brother of King Fernando, master of the Order of

Avis, founder of the second Portuguese dynasty which, born of a union of Hispanic and English blood, was to be that of the future.

Between 1383 and 1495, the final century of medieval Portugal, there would be four reigns and one important regency. During about half the period under consideration, the reigns of João I and Duarte (1383–1438) were to witness the centralisation of monarchical power, the growth of the prestige and authority of the king and a consolidation of the state at the expense of landowners and municipal councils. Moreover, the expansion of Portuguese influence into Morocco and the Atlantic would be accelerated. The regency of the *infante*, Pedro (1438–48), would witness the continuation of these trends, now firmly encouraged from the centre and assisted by an alliance with the town councils, particularly with those with strong commercial interests. As a result, Moroccan expansion, associated with the nobility and costly in terms of lives and money, was to give way to an emphasis upon an Atlantic outthrust and the commercial possibilities thus opened up. However, the reign of Afonso V (1448–81), a man lacking a broad political vision, was to witness a setback in royal authority to the advantage of a revival of seignorial control by the great landowners and the Church; the crown would pay the price of the king's neglect of political issues. In reaction, during the reign of his successor, João II (1481–95), centralist government was to become almost absolute, as king and state merged together. The king's 'Indies Plan' was to be an indicator of the new directions towards which Portugal would now commit herself.

Of all the elements forming Portuguese political structures in the fifteenth century, the royal office was the most important. Long gone were the days when the monarch was seen as the equal of the nobility, superior to it only because of the extent of his patrimony. Since Afonso III (1248–79) such notions had been in decline. Partly through the influence of lawyers imbued with the Roman law which they had learned at Bologna, but mainly because of the growing interest in administration which accompanied the Christian reconquest of the south of the country, the transformation of the kingdom into a unified state had begun and would continue during the next hundred years. Towards this end fiscal, administrative, military, legislative and judicial measures had to be enacted. The most important of these were the confirmation of the grants of privileges to towns and villages, the creation of a national guild of archers, the institution of royal notaries public, the appointment of local magistrates, the transformation of royal councils into the *cortes* (or parliament), and the drawing up of laws aimed at avoiding the uncontrolled concentration of land owned by the Church. Thus, by the time that the Avis dynasty came to power, it could be said that the kingdom of Portugal was a unified state. By then it was already a political power enjoying stable geographical frontiers; it possessed permanent and impersonal secular institutions; and it was inhabited by a people who saw and understood the need for a supreme authority to which it was freely and loyally bound.

By 1385, then, the monarchy was a vital structural element within the state which, although still of limited capacity, was none the less growing. João I, Duarte, the *infante* Pedro and João II faced the challenge of strengthening and developing it. This would be achieved largely through the appropriation by the state of all powers of sovereignty: legislation, the execution of laws and policies, the introduction of direct and indirect taxation, decisions regarding war and peace, and the conclusion of treaties and alliances with foreign countries.

Thus, between 1385 and 1495 the state began to grow. Yet the monarchy did not have it all its own way. The exercise of its powers was still to be opposed by what remained of traditional feudal structures, the secular and ecclesiastical landlords and town councils which, however, were themselves in the throes of bitter conflict. The secular landlords had a history which went back to before the days of the emergence of nationality; they dominated the north, around Entre-Douro-e-Minho, where countless noble families found their ancestral roots. That was why the north tended to be conservative, dominated by the nobility, scarcely urbanised, the only exception to this being Oporto, a city symbolic of bourgeois virtue and autarkic independence. The south was different, being in character largely urban and municipal, the area from which, in due time, the *cortes* would draw its main support. It, too, had its landlords, both secular and ecclesiastical, who, rewarded with lands, had settled there among communities in order to defend the reconquest. But they were largely members of the military orders who did not share the mentalities of the seignorial nobility of the north who were tied to their ancient, hereditary estates. While the north sent few representatives to the *cortes*, the lords of the south, forced to adapt to their new surroundings, chose to express their influence through that institution.

In this period much secular land, from one end of the country to the other, was in the hands of the nobility. But not all was subject to the same legal and political authority. Some nobles held land exempt from royal control, since they possessed property with rights of private jurisdiction (*mero e misto imperio*); others had life tenures, some with the exercise of civil jurisdiction alone, others with both civil and criminal. The first form of tenure was passed from father to son, from reign to reign, kings being obliged to preserve the conditions of tenure unchanged through an oath sworn when they came to the throne; this happened until the time of João II, who refused to conform to precedent and turned all landlords into vassals. The second group, the lords of simple, life-long jurisdictions, could not bequeath their titles to their heirs; nor could they preserve them by right as king succeeded king. However, out of respect for their predecessors, newly crowned kings normally confirmed such titles and, in effect, permitted hereditary succession. Since the same applied to their jurisdictions, all lands with such rights tended to be held in perpetuity. There were only two ways of incorporating these into the crown: through the so-called Mental Law (*Lei Mental*) of 1434, which was applied whenever the titleholder died without leaving a male heir; or through confiscation from those judicially sentenced for the crimes of heresy or treason. Both methods were not infrequently used.

On lands of private jurisdiction no royal fiscal, military or judicial power was applied until the reign of João II. Until that time, royal judges, even those dealing with appeals, were regularly prevented from carrying out their duties, orders and verdicts from courts of high jurisdiction being totally ignored. As we can surmise from the records of the *cortes*, lords went to the extreme of imposing upon their subjects taxes disguised as loans, and of requiring that they be addressed as if they were royalty. Thus the crown's sovereign rights over these lands became non-existent. In such circumstances political power, expressed in the form of judicial and financial administration, was lost by the crown which could not control abuses. Thus secular lands with civil and criminal jurisdiction, and even the socio-political structures of the state, constituted real enclaves of power which competed with that of the king.

In the case of ecclesiastical lands the situation was worse, largely because of the confusion caused by the overlapping exercise of religious and civil authority. This was encouraged by bishops, abbots and other clergy who sought to further their extreme claims. Their abuses were the same as those of secular landlords, who were often related to them, but with the aggravating difference that they punished disobedient subjects, as well as overzealous royal and municipal officials, with interdicts and excommunications. There thus ensued this cynical paradox: churchmen used the threat of ecclesiastical censure against royal officers acting in the king's name, while at the same time demanding that the king, as a loyal member of the Church, should punish with his secular power those whose crime had been to obey him. Kings, however, did not usually agree to such demands. Duarte, for example, was categorical on the matter, arguing that, since prelates were so quick to turn to the secular power for justice, they ought first to comply with its law, disregard of which was punishable by the secular authority. But such a judgement, however logical, proved ineffectual as a warning to ecclesiastics. Yet, because of the frequency with which it was used, excommunication as a punishment, the private weapon of ecclesiastical landlords, became discredited by virtue of being used as an instrument of political pressure. Not even in the reign of Afonso V did it regain its former effectiveness.

Evidence shows that, in most parts of the country, private secular and ecclesiastical estates covered a greater area than those of the crown, the exception being the region of Entre-Tejo-e-Guadiana, where royal property exceeded half the total. In the region of Tras-os-Montes, however, crown lands amounted to little more than one quarter. As a result, royal power, measured in terms of territorial control, was less than that of the nobility and clergy combined. None the less, because those who might have opposed him were not themselves united, the king remained in effect the most important lord in the countryside.

The great estates found at the beginning of the Avis dynasty were the traditional ones, bishoprics, monasteries and the military orders whose lands were found in both town and countryside. Among the most important were those of Oporto and Braga, which João I secured for the crown in 1402, when all cities came to be recognised as belonging to the crown; only Braga, seat of the primate of Portugal, eventually had its former independence restored, reverting to archiepiscopal control in 1472. Of the great monastic estates, basically rural in nature, many were north of the river Tagus. In the case of the military orders, of which that of Santiago stands out, we note that they controlled 40 per cent of the lands and rents of Entre-Tejo-e-Guadiana, 19 per cent of Estremadura and 13 per cent of Beira. It is clear that the great abbeys and the four masterships of the military orders constituted seignorial potentates who, therefore, never ceased to attract the attention of the crown. Hence abbots' staffs and masters' swords were placed in the hands of the monarchy's most trusted servants. It comes as no great surprise that few dangers for the kings were born from these notionally powerful men. This succession of titleholders was kept well under control.

The same cannot be said, however, of the great secular lordships. Handed down from one generation to the next, they served to support persons ambitious for power who could threaten the prestige of kings and their freedom to rule. João I saw this in his constable, Nun'Alvares Pereira, the owner of riches the like of which Portugal had never seen. By marrying his son, Afonso, to the constable's sole heiress, the king solved his own problems but multiplied those of his successors, since this marriage created the house of Bragança which, accumulating great quantities of land, was to be the cause of misfortune for the regent Pedro and, eventually, a seat of conspiracy against João II. When this prince ascended the throne in 1481, there were two secular lordships which were excessively powerful and potentially dangerous: that of the house of Bragança, and that of the duke of Viseu e Beja. Their titleholders, Fernando and Diogo, that year stood in the *cortes* in opposition to the new king who, as everyone knew, was determined to rule with a strong hand. Their daring, or their wealth, was to cost them their lives.

A brief consideration of the town councils, a further element in the structure of the state, is called for. The powers of the municipalities during this period were limited, dependent as they were on the king and the private estates. As a result, they were open to the authority of powers outside their control: royal judges, non-elected magistrates and their officials and tax collectors. The ancient freedoms and exemptions once enjoyed by the towns, and witnessed to in their charters of government, in matters concerning lands, taxation, justice and military affairs were gradually being undermined. New charters were being imposed; indirect local taxes (*sisas*) were being appropriated to the crown; royal judges were extending the king's authority; weights and measures were being harmonised. Local autonomy was now increasingly restricted to matters of price-fixing, overseeing public works of a civil nature, judging minor crimes, drawing up lists of contributors to the extraordinary taxes (*pedidos*) and, in some councils, taking complaints and criticisms before the *cortes*. It is notable that it was in the *cortes* that the political power of municipalities flourished, and thus became a force in terms of the whole country. Although weak and divided at the local level, in the *cortes*, where they represented their communities and dared criticise kings and censure the nobility and clergy, the councils exerted real power capable of producing results. The reduction of their authority at the local level had the paradoxical effect of compelling the councils to seek group solidarity, which confirmed them as a political structure of the state, and the *cortes* as the institution in which they could exercise their influence most effectively. On several occasions, in 1433, 1439, 1459, 1472–73, 1477 and 1481–2, they acted in this way against the authority of landowners, clergy and crown in spite of their dependence, at a local level, upon each of these. Thus the effective political power of the councils as one of the state's structures was characterised by being a force for criticism and for acting as the conscience of the nation. As such, that power had to be respected.

The two reigns of João I and Duarte reveal coherent continuity, a result of the fact that Duarte was associated with his father's rule in the last third of the latter's very long reign. By 1412 he was linked with the politically most sensitive areas of administration, those of justice and finance. Thus administrative measures as important as those decided in the *cortes* of 1427, or the very significant agreement (*concordata*) reached with the clergy in that assembly, can be attributed equally to father and son. In the *cortes* of 1433, the first of Duarte's reign, it was made clear that the previous style of leadership would not be abandoned; there might be evolution and progress, but no great changes.

João I, elected to the throne after a troublesome interregnum, had found himself among candidates, notably Beatriz, daughter of King Fernando, and his half-brothers, João and Dinis, sons of King Pedro and Inês de Castro, with better claims than his. The *cortes* held at Coimbra, at which the supporters of Beatriz were not represented, divided into two camps. One, supported by the councils and lesser nobility, stood by João, Master of Avis. The other, reflecting the power of the higher nobility and, probably, the majority of churchmen, pre-ferred João or Dinis. The official speaker of the *cortes*, the jurist João das Regras, clearly affiliated to the first group, argued at great length the ineligibility of the Master's opponents, or at least the inconsistency of the fundamental motives for supporting them. His advocacy was decisive in assuaging legitimist scruples, but could not convince the followers of the *infantes*. Finally, after a month of indecision, the *cortes* unanimously elected the Master of Avis. Unanimity had seemingly been achieved. For years the new dynasty would be preoccupied with creating both within and without the kingdom an image of unblemished legiti-macy, both charismatic and nationalist, sanctioned by law, by the people and, above all, confirmed by God. The work of future chroniclers and propagan-dists, continuously encouraged by the Avis dynasty, is clear proof of this.

It was on 14 August 1385, a few months after taking the throne, that João I faced the most dangerous moment of his life: confrontation on the battlefield with the Castilian king who, for the second time, had invaded the country in person with the intention of pursuing his rights to the succession, married as he was to the only daughter of the late king, Fernando. The forces on that day were very unequal, the Castilians having the advantage. Yet whether it was because the Portuguese had time to prepare the field, or because their tactics disconcerted their opponents, or because the Castilians, perhaps already exhausted, underestimated their enemy, within a few hours the conflict had been resolved; João and his constable, Nun'Alvares Pereira, had secured the most resounding victory in the history of their country. Still to be seen today at Aljubarrota, there lies the tomb of the victor, one of the finest monuments of Portuguese architecture, the monastery of Santa Maria da Vitoria, better known as that of Batalha (Battle). Such a victory was soon proclaimed a miracle, divine confirmation of the election made at Coimbra and of the right of the dynasty to rule. God, always on the side of legitimacy, had descended upon the field of Aljubarrota; João das Regras had been right.

Epic language glorified the interpretation which would be made of the facts. Such is apparent from the epitaph of João I at Batalha, where only two great deeds were recorded: the battle of Aljubarrota, which saved Portugal and the dynasty, and the capture of Ceuta, which avenged the honour of Christianity and of Spain. Having been defeated, the king of Castile fled. Towns and vil-lages which had been loyal to him now quickly surrendered to the Portuguese victor. Once again Portugal had remained intact, her own king now firmly in control. Yet men would have to wait many years for a final peace: pacts nego-tiated in 1402 and 1411 were to be two important stages in this process.

João I was to go down in history as the 'king of good fame', this honorific reflecting dynastic propaganda as well as patriotic and political feelings. It is certain that such attitudes affected the people who, in 1451, eighteen years after his death, named him 'Father of the Portuguese'.[1] However, life was not easy during his reign. Until 1411 his people lived close to a state of continuous war; monetary inflation reached very high levels; according to the records of the *cortes* the people's traditional complaints against the privileged persisted and even increased; the extraordinary taxes (*pedidos*) not only became chronic but were introduced without consultation with the *cortes* and were employed for uses other than for national defence; and, finally, the indirect municipal taxes (*sisas*), highly criticised and regarded as tantamount to robbery, were appropriated to the crown as if they were legal rights. So the description of the king as being of 'good fame' is highly equivocal.

The reign of João I can be divided into two periods. The first lasted until 1411 or 1412, the second from then to 1433. The first was marked by the war with Castile, and by the consolidation of the country; the second by the war of Moroccan expansion and the beginnings of continuous Atlantic exploration. Running through these periods were administrative developments, with the king at the centre of them all.

From the time of the success at Aljubarrota until 1411 attempts were made to reconquer the towns and districts which had shown loyalty to Beatriz and the Castilian king, a task completed in 1388. Meanwhile, as raids and even a battle in enemy territory (Valverde) were taking place, the Portuguese were also strengthening international alliances, particularly the reinvigoration of the alliance with England established in 1373. In 1386 the Treaty of Windsor was sealed, an alliance which resulted in the integration of João I's own conflict into the wider Hundred Years War then dividing western Europe. Later, after many precarious truces had been made only to remain ignored by both contenders, the pact of 1402 was negotiated, declaring peace for ten years. Its terms would be observed and in 1411, at Segovia, final peace was agreed under conditions which brought hostilities between the two Iberian kingdoms to an end. João was now the unchallenged ruler of a country which had returned to its traditional borders dating from 1297. There was now time to consider overseas expansion.

There had been earlier forays into the Atlantic, but these had been spasmodic, almost accidental, and had met with little success. The first step towards systematic expansion was achieved by the conquest of Ceuta, in Morocco, in 1415. Alternative options for military assault, some in the peninsula (Granada and Gibraltar), others in Morocco and the Canary Islands, had already been considered. It is difficult to explain such a need to conquer. Economic, political, religious, social and historical reasons, many of which do not concern

---

[1] National Archives/Torre do Tombo, Lisbon, Suplemento de Cortes, maço 4, number 47.

Portugal alone, must have worked together to syncretise powerful ambitions. Yet, from an economic and strategic point of view, Ceuta proved to be a disaster, a real consumer of people, goods and money. Early on, voices representing the people, the bourgeoisie and even some members of the royal circle, protested against keeping Ceuta, or at least against the political attitude which it represented. Yet Ceuta represented honour and titles; it looked back to past crusades and forward to others still to come; and it served as a sign of monarchical prestige and of Portugal's good name in Rome and in all Christian lands. So Ceuta was retained and other strong points, equally symbolic, would be sought. Among the recommendations left by João to his successor was that Ceuta should continue to belong to the crown, and that Tangier should be added to it.

While Ceuta was becoming an extension of Portugal, the Atlantic was being travelled and discovered (in some parts rediscovered) to the west and to the south: Madeira (1419–21), the Azores (1427–32), the African coast as far as Cape Bojador, bordering the Mar Tenebroso (1422–33). The exploration was carried out largely by adventurers, encouraged by the man who, to this day, remains a puzzling figure, the *infante*, Henry, known as 'the Navigator'. The result was that, when João I died in 1433, Portugal had the bounds she has today, in addition to ruling the territory of Olivença, the Atlantic islands of Madeira and the Azores, as well as Ceuta in North Africa.

At home it was João's aim to increase the royal authority over the clergy, the nobility and the town councils, and to create an aura of prestige across all Europe. It would be wrong to say that the force behind the idea was state interest; rather it was the confirmation of the king and the new dynasty which was being sought. Many texts, propagandist in character, such as the epitaph at Batalha and the moral portrait of João recorded by his successor, Duarte, in his work, the *Loyal counsellor* (*Leal conselheiro*), demonstrate this.

In order to free himself from those who had helped to give him power, and to keep the clergy and the nobility under reasonable control, João sought the support of the municipalities in twenty-eight *cortes* which met between 1385 and 1430. On these occasions, for example, measures were taken with regard to wage regulations, the movement of the workforce, the administration of municipal councils, the scope of influence of royal and seigniorial officers, the rights and prerogatives of the privileged classes and the jurisdiction of churchmen. In addition, and in spite of the pope and the episcopate, an agreement (*concordata*) favourable to the monarchy and consisting of ninety-four chapters setting limits to ecclesiastical privileges was negotiated with the clergy at the *cortes* which met at Lisbon in 1427. In the *cortes*, too, the jurisdictions and rights, as well as the obligations of the nobility, were defined, mainly touching matters ranging from the payment of taxes to punishments for abuse of power over subjects. The Mental Law (*Lei Mental*), applied before it was ever published, clearly shows the degree of authority achieved by the king who had already placed under his close control the only other great estate competing with his own, that of the constable, Nun'Alvares Pereira. As for the municipal councils, associates with the king in the process of centralisation, they were to accept the authority of royal judges. Furthermore, as the needs of war demanded, indirect municipal taxes and traditional extraordinary taxes were also levied. The aim was to raise both sorts of levies as a normal part of royal revenue, one permanent and general, the other extraordinary, to be sought only at the king's discretion. The first aim was achieved; the second, while it proved successful in the case of the marriage of the *infantes*, Pedro and Duarte, was to continue to depend upon the approval of the *cortes*.

Lord of the realm, João I did not forget the importance of establishing links with the rest of western Europe, not specifically to prevent wars or to secure support, but because it was part of the notion of monarchy, and was necessary for the fame and prestige of the new dynasty. As the chronicler, Zurara, noted, it was important to belong to the princely club of Europe.[2] Thus through the safe and traditional process of marriage, Portugal and its dynasty came to be linked with Aragon, Burgundy and England; in the last case, ties already established by Philippa of Lancaster were further strengthened. Relations also improved with the Empire, with Hungary and with the Papacy, thanks to the exchanges of embassies and the prestige gained by the capture of Ceuta. It can thus be said that when João I died on 13 August 1433, there died a true king who had achieved much in spite of the opposition which he had met. Military successes had been won; independence had been finally achieved. The king merited the reputation which soon came to be accorded him by people and writers alike.

The man who had come to personify the growing spirit of national awareness was succeeded by Duarte, who ruled for five years. Little need be said about him since, as already noted, he had taken charge of important aspects of government some twenty years before inheriting the throne. Yet his achievement should not be under-rated. He continued existing policies, maintaining counsellors and high-ranking servants of the crown, as well as following already proven political policies, in such a way that there was a coherent development in the conduct of Moroccan business, in overseas expansion, in the process of royal centralisation and in the area of foreign relations. In the first *cortes* to meet (Leiria–Santarém, 1433) from which there survive 155 general proposals (*capitulos gerais*), Duarte showed himself to be a mature politician, attentive to the municipal councils, firm with the nobility, determined to

---

[2] Zurara (1978), ch. 144.

suppress the abuses of jurisdiction by the clergy. Two reasons have been invoked to belittle his personality and cast a shadow over his reign: the psychological depression which seized him when, as a young man, he was first brought into contact with government; and the failure of the expedition against Tangier. Neither should be held against him. The illness from which he suffered was effectively overcome. And, while the failure before Tangier, where the Portuguese suffered the embarrassment of 'going for wool and coming back shorn' was, indeed, something of a military humiliation, it is clear that Duarte was not only king in name, but acted as such, consulting groups within the nation, encouraging the seeking and giving of advice, and not being afraid of accepting responsibility for decisions taken.

Duarte died of the plague on 9 September 1438. Since his heir was a six-year-old boy, he naturally left the regency in his will to his widow. The decision, however, displeased the country, not only because it feared that the regent would place the independence and peace of the kingdom in danger through the influence exercised by her Aragonese brothers, then in rebellion against the king of Castile, but even more so because it believed that the government would be better placed in the hands of a man. Hence, in the *cortes* convened at Torres Novas at the end of 1438, a royal ordinance was approved by all members, applicable until the political majority of King Afonso V should be reached, according to which power would be shared between the queen-regent, the *infante*, Pedro, and a council of nine who would all meet specifically once a year for consultation. The solution, however, proved ineffective. Within seven months the co-regents had fallen out, and the cities of Lisbon and Oporto, determined to hand over the government to the *infante*, actively sought to achieve this in the *cortes* which met in Lisbon in December 1439. In this they succeeded. The ordinance of Torres Novas was revoked and, through popular pressure, the *infante*, Pedro, was declared 'protector and guardian' ('tutor e curador') of the king and 'ruler and defender' ('regedor e defensor') of the realm. Supported by certain internal forces and by promise of help from the *infantes* of Aragon, the queen-regent tried to resist. However, when all failed, she had no choice but to go into exile in Castile, where she died in 1445.

Pedro, brother of the late king, a man of wide experience and considerable learning, had for some time shown that he possessed ideas on how to run the country. The letter which he had written to Duarte from Bruges in 1425 or 1426 was the manifesto of a statesman, expressing advanced opinions on all kinds of matters.[3] In these he stressed the needs of the country above private or sectional interests. Yet it is one thing to offer advice from a distance, quite another to govern. The regent Pedro did, in fact, have to assume ambivalent positions.

---

[3] *Livro dos conselhos* (1982), pp. 27–39.

From the start Pedro was a man imprisoned between two groups, indeed between two epochs. On the one hand were the feudal landowners among whom he had been brought up; on the other, the urban bourgeoisie whose position in the developing world of the day his practical experience had taught him to appreciate. He had achieved his position as the result of action by the town councils, particularly that of Lisbon; in the circumstances he could have allowed political demagogy to take over. Yet he refused to let this happen, blocking all attempts to make a popular hero out of him, and refusing to become a *caudillo* against the clergy and the nobility. In the very *cortes* which, through popular pressure, conferred on him the regency of the kingdom and the tutelage of the king, he stressed that he would not prejudice the privileges of the landlords and nobility. His aim, as he made it known, was not to benefit particular groups, but to serve the country and all its estates. His government would have to find a balance between the older and the newly emerging world.

Historians are divided in their appraisal of the regency. For some it was a period in which royal centralisation not only progressed but even, by separating the person of the king from the exercise of power, assumed the form of state centralisation, foreshadowing the 'Caesarian' model which would be confirmed by João II four decades later. For others, precisely the opposite happened. By such, the regent Pedro is regarded as the inaugurator of a neo-seignorialism which would be well expressed during the reign of Afonso V. Both appraisals may be exaggerated. However, a consideration of the king's concern to give the country a coherent legal structure, of the way in which external politics were conducted, of the conduct of an expansionist movement decidedly biased towards Atlantic navigation to the detriment of exploits in Morocco, coupled to the attention bestowed upon merchants and burgesses in the *cortes* of 1446 in which Pedro was re-elected to the regency – all these and other indicators suggest that the first appraisal comes nearer the truth. Pedro's government witnessed two things: first, the continuation of royal centralisation which had been gradually established over the years, particularly since João I, against the interests of the clergy, the nobility and the councils; and, secondly, the confirmation of the state as the vehicle of direction and control of the interests of the common good (*res publica*), a term now beginning to appear with greater frequency.

As for the municipal councils, although their initial fervour of 1439 began to cool off, they never really cherished any other policy or leader, preferring to see what might be achieved by tactical opportunities. So while the crowd was to criticise Pedro after his downfall, the councils kept silent. Indeed, they suffered from the departure of the regent, for his rule was to be followed by a period of revival of secular and ecclesiastical seignorialism. The proposals of the cities and towns presented to the *cortes* between 1451 and 1475 are witness to this, as are those offered by the clergy in 1456, together with the respective replies which annulled decades of royal effort towards centralisation.[4] A reading of contemporary chronicles confirms this view. It is clear that, in the fifteenth century, councils did not agree with either nobility or clergy. So when the councils lost power, the law was used to the advantage of noble and clerical privilege, and the state bowed before a revival of feudalism.

Any study of Afonso V must take into account the facts of his childhood, for he was left fatherless at the age of six, and he became, in practice, motherless a year or so later. The conditions and circumstances of his formative years are, therefore, crucial. Probably the greatest political error of the regent, Pedro, should be sought in the way in which he allowed the young king, his nephew who also became his son-in-law, to be educated. It was an education for great deeds, but one pursued in defiance of reality and the pragmatism required for the proper handling of government. In 1455, when the last crusader pope, Calixtus III, ordered an expedition against the Turks, Afonso took up the cause with enthusiasm. He summoned the *cortes* in order to obtain money, formed regiments of soldiers, minted coin to pay for the cost of the enterprise, despatched ambassadors to other countries, reinforced garrisons to prevent unexpected attacks from the Moors, and at the same time easily obtained imperial edicts to raise tithes and to sell indulgences. At the crucial moment, however, the great international expedition never materialised. What was Afonso to do with his army? In 1457 the decision was taken to crusade in Morocco. In the following year Alcácer Ceguer was conquered. In 1463–4 another expedition against Tangier failed. In 1471 it became Arzila's turn. Ironically, in this same year, Tangier, now uninhabited, was occupied ingloriously. Anafé (now Casablanca) had also been conquered in 1469, but was soon abandoned because of its difficult position in the south. Here Afonso's African conquests ended. Shortly after the capture of Alcácer Ceguer, he gave himself the title of 'king of Portugal and the Algarves on this side and beyond the sea in Africa', a fine-sounding title, but one lacking real substance. Economically, financially and militarily this 'Africa' brought nothing. Much more would be gained from Arguin, Mina and all Guinea, regions of continental Africa in which 'the African', as Afonso was called, showed little interest.

The expansionist policies of Afonso V appeared to have forgotten the Atlantic and the peaceful commercial contacts with Black Africa stimulated by the regent, Pedro. If anything was achieved between 1448 and 1475 in terms of Atlantic expansion, it was due to the initiatives of individuals, mostly merchants, born out of recognition that navigation brought in profits. The wealthy Lisbon merchants, Fernão Gomes, for example, bid successfully at the auction

---

[4] Sousa (1983).

which enabled him to trade with Guinea, a step which made the advance of the discoveries to the south possible. Others, such as Martin Anes Bom-Viagem, won further monopolies. In effect, the discoveries were literally put up for public auction by Afonso, as if he were dealing with real estate to be allocated to the highest bidder. The representatives at the *cortes* which met at Coimbra–Évora in 1472–3 were to protest vigorously against such a way of acting. As a result the king, in 1475, handed over to Prince João oversight of a heavy responsibility, that of navigation and Atlantic commerce.

In that year, as Moroccan conquests were running smoothly, Afonso V halted them and initiated a new phase in foreign policy. He returned to the Iberian peninsula, cherishing the idea of becoming ruler of a united Spain and Portugal. It was an old ambition which had never been far from Castilian minds, but in Portugal it had inspired only one king, Fernando, a century before Afonso V. As on the first occasion, the project failed. The opportunity to fulfil a dream, planned, it seems, since 1465, occurred with the death of Enrique IV of Castile in December 1474. The late king, who had married a sister of the Portuguese monarch, had bequeathed the succession in his will to his only daughter, then aged eight, who, at the appropriate time, was to marry her uncle, Afonso V, who, in the meantime, would act as regent. To carry out these intentions, after taking counsel at Estremoz, convening the *cortes* at Évora, investing Prince João as his lieutenant in Portugal and securing support in Spain, Afonso invaded Castile in mid-1475. After many setbacks, he sought support in France; failing to secure it, he proposed to abdicate and become a hermit in the Holy Land. Persuaded to return home, he delegated many powers to his son, and eventually died in 1481. In many respects he had failed to recognise and come to terms with the changes which were taking place around him.

At home, Afonso pursued policies of protecting the Church and the nobility, as well as encouraging neo-seignorialism. The councils reacted persistently against such policies, in particular in the *cortes*; most notable were the complaints presented in 1459 and in 1472–3, and those laid before João II in 1481–2. By this time monarchical power was considerably weakened and diminished. João II summed it all up in one sentence. Ownership of the roads of Portugal, he stated, was all that his father had left him.

João acceded to the throne twice, once at the end of 1477 when his father abdicated while in France, and again in 1482 when his father died. Born in 1455, he was scarcely twenty when he began to govern the county as regent. Although young, he was clear minded, decisive and pragmatic, very different from his parent. When he took over government, it was as if Portuguese politics had suddenly jumped into a more modern world. The 'perfect prince', as he was later called, was a good military leader, a sound administrator, an able diplomat and the manager of a policy of expansionism both into north Africa and into the Atlantic. The 'Indies Plan' was probably his handiwork, along with the rounding of southern Africa and the negotiation of the Treaty of Tordesillas (1494). Vasco da Gama, who discovered the sea route to India, and Alvares Cabral, who discovered Brazil, were the crowning glories of the effort of the 'Discoveries' to which João gave consistent and systematic support. At the same time, the process of peaceful mercantile relations with Black Africa were resumed, the fortress of Mina was founded, and João II became the first European ruler to establish friendship and cultural relations with an African ruler, the king of the Congo. Yet, as a prince of the house of Avis, he also turned his attention to Morocco, and even cherished the idea of dominating the whole area commercially. This he failed to achieve, in spite of founding the town and fortress of Graciosa (soon abandoned) to the north of Arzila. But he did obtain Azamor, which would be an important name in the following reign.

In all endeavour abroad, even in Morocco, João preferred to achieve peaceful accords rather than to use force. None the less, force, on land or at sea, was always available for use, or as a weapon of dissuasion if required. When Spanish corsairs ventured to the south of Cape Bojador, an area declared by João to be 'marc clausum', they were systematically and unceremoniously sunk. Concerned with the transformation of his ships into a force to be reckoned with, he had sketched in his own hand a project according to which artillery used on land might function effectively on the decks of small caravels. Of this development the chronicler Garcia di Resende was to write:

to guard his coast with greater security and at less cost, [the king] devised and commended small caravels which carried great cannon . . . He was the first to invent this . . . Portuguese caravels were so feared on the sea for so long that no ships, no matter how large, would dare to confront them, until they discovered how the cannon were transported.[5]

In Portugal itself, João continued the policy of centralisation interrupted by his father, a policy which he took to unexpected extremes. Tactically supported by the councils, from whose energy he had learned to profit in the first *cortes* of his reign (1481–2), he revived the reforms, first proposed by the representatives of the commonalty ten years earlier, but which, in the meanwhile, had been put aside. These led him to decree that royal judges were to enter any jurisdiction, privileged or not; that all general confirmations of privileges and landownership were to be suspended until evidence of title had been worked out; and that charters were to be reviewed and brought up to date. All this was done after antagonising the duke of Bragança and other magnates who were obliged to take an oath in the style and according to the formula demanded of municipal governors, whereas the king, contrary to tradition, made it plain that

[5] Resende (1973), ch. 181.

he would take no such oath, because princes should not have to do this. In view of this action (and much else) João drew against himself the hatred of high churchmen and the great nobility. The result was a struggle to the death which would subside only after the public execution, in 1484, of the duke of Bragança and the assassination, carried out by the king in person, of the duke of Viseu e Beja, along with the execution of some lesser noblemen and the imprisonment of a number of churchmen. In this way, through administrative, judicial and, on occasion, arbitrary intervention, the neo-seignorialism of the reign of Afonso was destroyed. From now on, dispensing with the support of the councils, João II governed the country like an absolute lord. With him the Portuguese Middle Ages ended and the modern age, that of the country's great achievements, began.

CHAPTER 25

THE SWISS CONFEDERATION

Roger Sablonier

INTRODUCTION

THE system of alliances among imperial provinces and cities in the area
between the Alps, the Jura mountains and the Rhine, known as the Swiss
Confederation (Schweizerische Eidgenossenschaft), emerged about the year
1500 as a distinct political unit within the German Empire. The Confederation
as a whole occupied no clearly defined territory. However, by 1500, the northern limits of its sphere of influence ran more or less along the Rhine as far as
Lake Constance. In the east, its frontier with Graubünden was unclear; the
west of what is now Switzerland was largely under the dominion of Savoy;
south of the Alps, the hegemony of Milan persisted until shortly before 1500.
Within the Confederation of cantons, or *Orte* (the traditional name for
members enjoying full rights), with their widely differing structures and identities, each guarded its freedom of manoeuvre in both domestic and foreign politics, but, by 1500, did have a visible political cohesion.

The Confederation, at first just one of the numerous systems of alliances
existing within the German Empire, had not succeeded in giving itself a more
stable framework until after 1350, and then only hesitantly. Alongside the free
imperial cities of Berne and Zurich, the centres of political power within the
federation, the cities of Lucerne and Zug appear as early as the fourteenth
century as full members of the Confederation. Fribourg and Solothurn already
belonged to this circle well before the end of the fifteenth century, when their
membership, like that of Basle and Schaffhausen, became more binding.
Among the rural communes, important members of the alliance were the
valley communities and imperial districts in the alpine region of central
Switzerland; other rural members were Glarus and the hinterland of Zug. The
three forest cantons (*Waldstätte*) of central Switzerland, Uri, Schwyz and
Unterwalden, had formed a closer alliance towards the end of the thirteenth
century, and consequently are often found acting together.

By 1500 the subject hinterlands were also part of the Confederation. Some

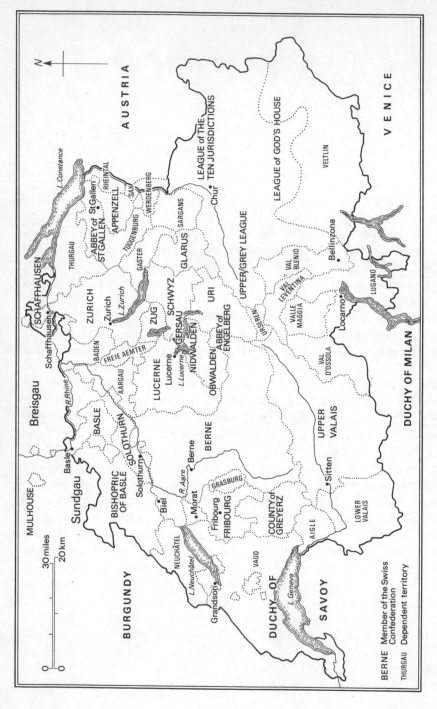

Map 15   The Swiss Confederation and it neighbouring territories, c. 1500

were ruled by a single city – Zurich, Berne or Lucerne; others, like Aargau and Thurgau in the Rhine valley and (in part) Ticino, were dominated and governed jointly, as mandated territories (*Gemeine Herrschaften*), by more than one of the *Orte*. Moreover, around the geographical and political area of the confederal *Orte* was a whole network of more or less close alliances among a wide variety of partners. Among these associated members (*Zugewandte Orte*) were the Three Leagues in Rhaetia, the Upper Valais, the abbot of St Gallen, the count of Greyerz and some individual towns such as Rottweil and Mulhouse.

Most treaties among the *Orte* were only bilateral. Some of them went back into the fourteenth century and assured mutual assistance and supervision. The oldest extant agreements between Uri, Schwyz and Unterwalden, dating from 1291 and 1315, were primarily concerned with keeping the peace and securing the privileged position of local elites; in this, they did not differ from other contemporary treaties. Only in modern times has the covenant of 1291, the *Bundesbrief*, been taken as the founding document of the Confederation. Much more significant, among the bilateral treaties, is the League of Zurich (*Zürcher Bund*) of 1351, by which the *Ort* of Zurich and the forest cantons promised one another aid against the Habsburg overlord. This became the pattern for other links between members of the Confederation.

Such bilateral treaties were regularly renewed, especially in the years immediately after 1450. By contrast, comprehensive alliances including many or all of the *Orte* were infrequent, thus highlighting the significance of the Compact of Stans (*Stanser Verkommnis*) of 1481. The lack of constitutional and conceptual unity within the league of confederate towns and provinces reflects the fact that very few such all-embracing institutions existed at all until much more recent times. Can we speak of the Confederation in 1500 as a 'state'? Only with the greatest reservations. Although the political elites may have had some notion of the Confederation as a self-governing political entity and even, in certain circumstances, some show of solidarity, the concept of 'state' has to be applied primarily to the individual territories.

How did this development of the state, unique in contemporary Europe, come into being? Our knowledge of political events is relatively good. The great merit of earlier Swiss historiography remains unquestioned, but the present generation of historians has assumed a certain critical distance from the nationalistic exuberance which led such writing to view the period as a time of 'great-power politics' and 'vigorous maintenance of independence'. Recently, horizons have been greatly extended by an increased awareness of the political and economic environment of the Confederation, and a comparison with circumstances in the rest of Europe. Discussions of the making of the modern state have become as prominent as the drive to relate political evolution to structural changes in the economic, social and cultural environment, and in mental outlooks. Given the serious gaps in our knowledge, however, such links are often hard to make. Only slowly have historians come to realise the implications of the fact that other political developments and traditions existed in late medieval Switzerland (or in what we now call Switzerland) alongside the Confederation itself. There is still need for research into political relationships in the west and south of the country; into small 'non-confederate' states such as the abbey of St Gallen; and generally into the history of the former dependent territories. There are thematic gaps as well. What follows will concentrate on the changes in the old patterns of political power and on the emergence of new structures within the urban and rural communities. The consolidation of the state within the confederate communes brought integration, but it also led to internal conflict. Finally, the European role played by Switzerland, largely through its mercenaries, and the rise of national consciousness will be examined. In all this, how unique can Switzerland claim to have been?

OVERLORD, EMPIRE AND NOBILITY

As the Middle Ages began to decline, the most significant development within the German monarchy was the rise of small independent territories. In Switzerland, this development was already in full swing in the fourteenth century. Among a multitude of competing rulers, nobles, ecclesiastics and cities, the leading duchies had already clearly emerged. Since about 1250 Savoy, to the west, had been striving successfully to create a modern, and to a large extent self-contained, territory which was efficiently governed, even after the shift of Savoyard interests towards Piedmont. In what is now southern Switzerland, the Visconti dukes of Milan had become the dominant influence. In the east and north, from their hereditary territories as far as the Swiss midlands, the Habsburgs, despite setbacks, still enjoyed remarkable success. In between, and for the time being, some middle-ranking domestic nobility – for example, the counts of Toggenburg, Greyerz and Neuenburg, and the lords of Hallwil and Landenberg (local families owing service to the Habsburgs) – held their ground well. A substantial share of the variegated number of small and middle-sized domains and of fragmented and scattered sovereign rights belonged to ecclesiastical rulers such as the bishops of Chur, Basle and Sitten. About 1370, the small states of the Confederation, whose territorial expansion had scarcely begun, were no more than isolated dots on the multi-coloured political map of what is now Switzerland.

The rise of the Confederation at the turn of the fifteenth century was influenced very significantly, though not exclusively, by events in the Austro-Habsburg sphere of influence. The political activity of the Habsburgs, over and above their imperial responsibilities, focused mainly on the possessions which they had inherited in the thirteenth century in what is now Austria. But in the years about 1360, in particular, and again after 1380, they strove, sometimes with great success, to extend and consolidate their power in the west. In 1363, for example, the Austrian Habsburgs gained possession of the Tyrol. Between 1375 and 1413 they took over almost all the territories of the counts of Montfort as well as those of the Werdenbergs in the Rhine valley, in particular the town and domain of Sargans.

The greatest contributor to this process was Duke Leopold III of Austria (1351–86), who turned his attention westwards after inheriting the Austrian Habsburg possessions in 1379, showing himself everywhere in his new territories as an ambitious, though not particularly skilful, local politician. His political clashes with the cities were further complicated by the ambiguity of his positions during the Great Schism. As a result, the cities to the south of the German Empire formed themselves into leagues which constituted a powerful opposition. Such leagues came into being in Swabia in 1376, in Alsace in 1379, and in the central Rhineland in 1381, while Zurich, Berne, Solothurn and Zug joined together with fifty-one other towns in the region to form the League of Constance in 1385. In the area of the river Aare, Leopold had to reckon with the imperial city of Berne, while in the alpine foothills he came up against the territorial and political interests of Lucerne. In 1386 localised conflicts over Lucerne's attempts to dominate her hinterland and the Entlebuch, where the Austrian duke also had rights, culminated in a threat of war on both sides. Leopold attempted a show of force with an army made up of nobles, mercenaries and contingents from the cities. It ended in disaster. At Sempach, on 3 July 1386, Leopold lost both battle and life when he met an army from Lucerne, reinforced by men from central Switzerland.

The defeat of the Austrian army of feudal nobles by the Swiss infantry has been set down as a remarkable event of military history. The great victory of Sempach, and the antagonists, Leopold and the legendary Arnold Winkelried, bulked large in Swiss historiography and national consciousness from the fifteenth century onwards. However, the impact of this single event on politically conducted territorial development should not be overestimated.[1] Dramatic clashes between opposing forces make up only a small part of the long series of changes which occurred in the years after 1380. Changes in social and economic structures played a part, as did military action in advancing political ends; so, too, did widespread, but initially submerged, unrest among the rural population. The difficulties faced by the cities in restricting the scope of the unrest among the rural population is revealed by the *Sempacherbrief*, a treaty

---

[1] Marchal (1986).

sealed in 1393 in which the confederate partners, acting under the pressure of events, agreed to suppress the waging of all feuds and wars uncontrolled and unsanctioned by their own governments.[2]

Only later did it become clear that the heavy blow to the prestige of the Austrian monarchy had also involved a real loss of power. At first it seemed that the peace agreed in 1389 between Duke Albert I (1349/50–95) and the Confederation (which was replaced by a treaty in 1394 and, in 1412, by a peace which was to last fifty years) had guaranteed the continuation of Habsburg power. However, the *de facto* absence of Austria from political and military affairs after 1395, which could not have been foreseen, had far-reaching consequences, especially for the lesser nobility which was politically and economically dependent on the Habsburgs. In fact, the sovereign's absence from politics was due much less to military misfortunes than to quarrels which divided the house of Habsburg after the death of Albert in 1395.

However, it was not long before an event occurred which really did weaken the position of the Austrian monarchy. This was the dispute between Sigismund of Luxemburg and Bohemia (1368–1437), crowned king of Germany in 1410, and his Habsburg rival. At the opening of the Council of Constance, Sigismund published a decree outlawing Frederick IV of Austria (1382/3–1439), who had received the Tyrol and the old western domains (*Vorlande*) as his portion of the 1400 inheritance. In 1415 the Confederation, headed by Berne, was summoned to make war on Sigismund's behalf; it seized the opportunity to occupy the Austrian Aargau with the minimum of military effort. Subsequently, the Confederation bought the Aargau as an imperial pledge, and thus legalised its *de facto* exercise of power. Only after 1440 did this lead in part to a new internal order within these territories, and the conquerors continued to quarrel over the captured lands for decades. While part of the land eventually became a common lordship of all the confederates, it was Berne, which acquired all Austria's rights in by far the largest part of the Aargau, which emerged as the real winner. In vain did Austria, for years to come, repeatedly demand the return of the Habsburg pledge. Not until 1474, in the peculiar political atmosphere engendered by the diplomatic manoeuvring prior to the Burgundian war, did Duke Sigmund finally renounce all former Austrian rights in the Confederation to the eight confederate *Orte*. This Austro-Swiss treaty (11 June 1474) is known as the Perpetual Accord (*Ewige Richtung*). Even this did not end the political and propagandist polemics over the legitimacy of confederate rule in the region, a fact which explains (among other things) why contemporary chroniclers placed such heavy emphasis on the enmity of the confederates towards their Habsburg rivals.

[2] Stettler (1985).

The events in the Aargau underline the importance of relations with the Empire for the ambitions of the political elite within the Confederation. They profited from Habsburg–Luxemburg rivalry then, as they had already done in the fourteenth century. Evidently Sigismund hoped to harness the Confederation to his own enterprises in Italy and against the Hussites; he was therefore more generous in granting it privileges than his predecessors, Charles IV (1316–78) and Wenceslas (1361–1419), had been. He also pursued a distinctly friendly policy towards the cities. For example, Wenceslas had granted Zurich the right to elect its own imperial governor (*Reichsvogt*) and through him to exercise high justice; in 1415 Sigismund converted the Austrian pledges into imperial fiefs, and in 1433 he sanctioned subinfeudation. At that time Zurich, temporarily at least, played the leading part in the Confederation's relationship with the Empire, although the city still felt a closer affinity with the towns on Lake Constance than with its confederates in central Switzerland. Moreover, during the years of the ecclesiastical council, Constance was to an extent the centre of the Empire's diplomacy. In this sense the relationship with the crown was of some importance, not only as the central source of legitimation but also, to the individual territories of the Confederation, as a political reality. Only at the end of the fifteenth century did such territories really begin to cut loose from the Empire.[3]

The overlord and the urban communes were keen competitors in their political pursuit of territorial aggrandisement and consolidation, but they did not compete only against one another. They shared the political aim, already pursued with considerable success throughout the fourteenth century, of ousting or controlling the lesser dynastic nobility. These nobles had traditionally based their independent rule on landed estates and bailiwicks, but by the end of the thirteenth century they were already demonstrably lacking in competitive power.[4] Only the minor regional nobility, such as the lords of Hallwil, Landenberg and Klingenberg, who had risen in the service of the overlord, were able to strengthen their position thanks to their lucrative careers. When, in the first half of the fifteenth century, the house of Habsburg ran into difficulties, this posed enormous problems for those who depended upon Austrian support. Whether through loss of political position and social standing, extinction of the family line or migration, they rapidly disappeared from the scene. A number were to find their way into non-noble groups within the political elite of the Confederation.

This elimination of the nobility is a specifically local development found in no other region of the Empire. In the disappearance of the traditional forms of aristocratic rule, political factors were of great importance. This can be

---

[3] Mommsen (1958).   [4] Sablonier (1979a).

shown through a comparison with the still intact position of the nobility under Savoyard rule.

There were also economic and social problems behind this disappearance of the nobility, problems which had nothing to do with the hostility towards the nobility of which the Confederation would be later accused. Their difficulties arose in part from the lack of profitable career opportunities in royal service.[5] Moreover, the income of the lesser nobility must have been sharply reduced by the crisis which undoubtedly afflicted the agricultural economy, particularly at the beginning of the century. Nor did the limited development of traditional feudal authority in the forest cantons help to maintain the influence of the nobility, whose ranks were also exposed to the burghers of the confederate cities who were all ready to step into their political shoes.[6]

URBAN AND RURAL COMMUNES

The transformation and decline of the political order built up by the Austrian dynasty and nobility were counterbalanced by the decisive progress in the constitution of urban territorial rule between 1370 and 1430. Compared with the situation in Savoy or Württemberg, the Habsburg overlordship was noticeably weak, and often failed to make its presence felt. The chief beneficiaries of this situation were the midland cities. Berne, Lucerne and Zurich were first in the rush for territories, while Solothurn and the Austrian city of Fribourg also took part, as did some smaller cities. Berne's traditionally good relations with her powerful neighbour, Savoy, enabled her to hold her own in the Aare region against political and territorial competition from the Habsburgs, particularly under Leopold III. Zurich's rapid succession of territorial acquisitions – the district of Greifensee (1402), the lordship of Grüningen (1408), the district of Regensberg with Bülach (1409) and, above all, the first acquisition of the lordship of Kyburg (1424) – led to the constitution of one of the largest territories in the Empire, after that of Berne.

This policy of territorial expansion was seldom pursued through military intervention. In some cases the mere threat of military force was enough; Berne and Zurich could count on getting mercenaries from central Switzerland. On the whole, however, the cities attained their aims by peaceful means, chiefly through money and skilful financial policy. They bought land and feudal rights, and often took noble ecclesiastical rulers, willing or not, under their 'protection' (*Burgrecht* or *Landrecht*), which led to rapid integration. Often against the will of their lords, the confederate cities also admitted people from the countryside into the urban citizenry, as 'external citizens' or

---

[5] Bickel (1978).   [6] Sablonier (1982).

Ausburger, a strategy for expansion that was employed throughout the Empire.

The success of this policy of acquisition was largely attributable to specific political circumstances, namely the weakness of the overlord's policy. However, it would have been unthinkable without the sharp increase in economic prosperity enjoyed by many cities in the first half of the fifteenth century. They profited directly and indirectly from the upsurge in trade over these years (Berne, for instance, did well out of the customs dues along the Aare), and from the increased commercial activity which can be seen, for example, in Fribourg from as early as 1350. Between 1430 and 1450 the volume of trade evidently dropped off, but the cities still managed to strengthen their leading role within the Swiss Confederation.

In the long run, the cities' territorial policy and bid for autonomy against the overlord's attempts to centralise rule were far more successful within the Confederation than in the neighbouring regions of Savoy and southern Germany. The same period saw a consolidation and expansion of the communal movement in the rural areas which is an even more strikingly exceptional element in the development of this region.

Of immediate interest here are the communes in the valleys of central Switzerland. The rural communes of Uri, Schwyz and Unterwalden, which had obtained exemption from all territorial jurisdiction save that of the king about the year 1300, developed a political autonomy which was unprecedented and astonishing. The reasons for this autonomy have been long and fiercely disputed among Swiss historians[7] and are still controversial. Were they the result of a singularly precocious and successful drive towards autonomy by a rural community, a resistance to the feudal order?[8] Or did local groups of the political elite in a very incompletely feudalised area succeed in establishing their own forms of organisation, based mainly upon parochial units and earlier institutions regulating common agricultural exploitation?[9] In any case, the long-term consequences of events during the so-called founding epoch (*Gründungszeit*, 1291–1315) in central Switzerland have often been greatly overestimated on the basis of fifteenth-century historiography.[10] Only after the middle of the fourteenth century, or even after 1370, can a decisive consolidation of these valley communities into a 'state' (*Land*) be observed, both from within and from without. Towards the end of the century this came to include Glarus, while the hinterland of Zug was able to preserve some elements of autonomy only by connecting itself with its eponymous town. At the same time the individual valley communities, especially Schwyz and Uri, engaged in the same active policy of territorial integration being pursued by the cities:

[7] Guenée (1971), pp. 292–6; Eng. trans. (1985), pp. 212–16.

[8] Blickle (1990), pp. 88–100.   [9] Sablonier (1990).   [10] Blickle (1990), pp. 27–8.

Schwyz in the rural district of Küssnacht, in the territory of the monastery of Einsiedeln and in the March, Uri in the Urseren valley. In the course of the fifteenth century territories subject to confederate control were added.

It is this development of communal autonomy in rural areas which gives the organisation of the late medieval Confederation its special place in modern constitutional history. Various aspects of this organisation represent a development towards statehood according to a 'model of communal solidarity' in a time of 'communalism', marked by attempts to 'construct a state on the principle of community, and the joining together of different communes'.[11] Throughout the fourteenth century and into the fifteenth, the rural communes of central Switzerland stood their ground against both the territorial claims of the overlord (although these were seldom pressed) and the much more menacing pressures of territorial aggrandisement and consolidation coming from their own urban confederates.

Not all the rural communes were by any means so successful in their striving towards independence, especially not in competition with the confederate cities. After 1380 Lucerne blatantly hindered the independence of the Weggis community and the Entlebuch, while Berne soon brought the valley of Hasli, exempt from all jurisdiction save that of the king, under its control; it was to do the same to the Saanen district (after 1403). In the subject hinterlands and the mandated territories, the confederate states took over the role of the former rulers, even if they justified and exercised their authority in different ways.

Another good example of these complicated procedures is to be found in eastern Switzerland. Here, at the beginning of the fifteenth century, the rural population of the Appenzell region was still striving unsuccessfully to free itself from the control of the abbot of St Gallen. With military help from Schwyz and the citizens of St Gallen, the Appenzellers had defeated two armies of mounted knights from southern Germany (in 1403 and 1405); but after a defeat in 1408 by the troops of the League of Knights and from Austria, the communal movement lost its way, and by the end of 1411 Appenzell, like the town of St Gallen a year later, was more or less obliged to accept confederate invitations to place itself under the protection of the Confederation (save Berne). The abbot's rights were acknowledged and, in 1421, the Confederation even strengthened them. In 1428, after fresh unrest, Count Frederick VII of Toggenburg staged a military invasion to restore order. The count who, by this time, had acquired, by pledge, almost all the Austrian possessions from Rheineck to Montafon, in addition to the lordship of Werdenberg from Sargans to the upper regions around the lake of Zurich, was among the major

---

[11] Blickle (1981), p. 114. On communalism in general, see Blickle (1985), pp. 165–204; on central Switzerland in particular, see Blickle (1990), pp. 93–111.

gainers from the conflict. Zurich, in open rivalry with Schwyz, also greatly increased its influence in the region at this time. Significantly, in 1436, when the peasants of Toggenburg asked the Confederation for support in their struggle for independence from the count, none was forthcoming.

The disturbances in the Appenzell were important not only for these shifts in political spheres of influence. The chronicle tradition, together with the founding of the league of nobles 'with the shield of St George' (*St Jörgenschild*) in neighbouring Swabia, proves that the nobility of this region had directed harsh polemics on the subject of class distinction against the peasantry – presumably in analogy to a phenomenon widespread in contemporary Europe.[12] The defeats in the Appenzell war, like that of Sempach in 1386, had caused profound disquiet among the knights and nobles of southern Germany. In their fear of the communal movement they successfully demanded that their enemies be excommunicated, stigmatising them as 'peasants' (according to the idea of the God-given three orders of society), although they must have known that many of them were townsfolk from St Gallen and other cities. 'The Swiss Confederation seemed a socially uniform union of "peasants" only to the lords' fearful and hostile eye.'[13] As a result, 'peasant' strivings towards autonomy in southern Germany attracted the catchphrase 'schweytzer werden' or 'turning Swiss'.[14]

We must be very careful to distinguish between the ambitions of the political elite and politically motivated social movements among the peasants. This is important because traditional constitutional history has tended to imply that the people of Appenzell or Schwyz, for example, were acting on behalf of a national state. Only if we distinguish among the different political groups can we explain why this region, like the whole of central and western Europe, was affected by growing unrest among the rural population at the end of the fourteenth century, and why the revolt of Appenzell sometimes took on the appearance of a peasants' revolt against the overlord. The events in the Appenzell also saw another fundamental aspect of the situation before 1450: that political solidarity among the confederate *Orte* against claims made by the overlord would endure only so long as it did not conflict with their particular plans for expansion. There can be no question of selfless support for 'communalism' as a principle from the Confederation's political elite; nor, for that matter, did they intend to support 'peasant' resistance within their own spheres of influence.

In the same context we can situate the development of rural communes in the Valais and Graubünden, which also affected the Confederation. In the

---

[12] Lutz (1990), pp. 129–213.   [13] The phrase is from Brady (1985), p. 32.
[14] Brady (1985).

Valais, the seven upper valley communities or *Zenden* (Sitten, Siders, Leuk, Raron, Visp, Brig and Goms) had wrested a degree of independence from the bishop of Sitten and from Savoy; in 1435 they decisively strengthened this position by creating their own governmental and judicial system. Similarly, in Graubünden, rural communities had joined together in leagues. This had begun in 1367, when the cathedral chapter, officials of the bishop's household, the citizens of Chur as well as the communes in Domleschg, Schams, Oberhalbstein, Bergell and the Lower and Upper Engadine banded together to form the nucleus of what would become the 'League of the House of God' (*Gotteshausbund*). A large number of lords and peasants from the upper Rhine valley joined in the 'Grey' or 'Upper' League (*Grauer* or *Oberer Bund*), which had been in the process of formation since 1395, up to its solemn confirmation in Truns in 1424. The 'League of the Ten Jurisdictions' (*Zehngerichtebund*) of 1436, centred on Davos, included only rural communities. On the basis of these Three Leagues, Graubünden (Grisons) embarked on an independent and original path of statehood with a strongly communal character. Both the Upper Valais and the Three Leagues would prove to be faithful partners of the Confederation.

With the exception of the League of the Ten Jurisdictions, it is clear that all fifteenth-century associations in both Graubünden and the Valais are to be understood as unions of mixed estate. Collaboration among the estates – especially the representation of the 'common man'[15] and the importance assigned to the interests of townfolk and peasants – was not spelt out as precisely as it was (for example) under ducal leadership in the Tyrol or in Savoy; nevertheless, Graubünden clearly differs on this point from the rural communities of central Switzerland. Such differences should be borne in mind when sweeping references are made to a widely disseminated and specifically 'alpine' form of communal statehood.

THE INNER CONSOLIDATION OF THE CONFEDERATE COMMUNES

From the end of the fourteenth century the drive towards political independence and territorial expansion in the cities and rural cantons (*Länder*) of the Confederation advanced alongside the beginnings of an institutional inner consolidation of the state. Within individual territories some of the conditions generated by specific developments in institutions and methods of government were to last until the nineteenth century.

We should first note the considerable constitutional differences between urban and rural cantons. From the beginning of the fifteenth century power in

---

[15] Blickle (1973) and (1981).

the cities was increasingly centralised in small councils (*Kleine Räte*), independent of existing craft guilds, involving a small group of eminent urban families and those co-opted by them. Their rule, in particular the administration of justice, customs, taxes and military forces, was refined and extended into all areas. This consolidation of government generally proceeded faster in the towns than in the rural communities. The political disparity between urban and rural areas within the Confederation in the closing years of the fifteenth century was heightened by this growing inequality. Among the rural political elite it nourished some fear of being unable to compete, politically or socially, with the towns.

Nevertheless, during the second half of the fourteenth century the rural *Orte* had formalised their assemblies (*Landsgemeinde*), circumscribed offices such as that of the *Landammann*, appointed their councils according to a definite juridical concept and produced written constitutions: in fact they had emerged as stable, lasting, structurally well organised political 'states'. It was first to these rural constitutions, rather than to the towns, that nineteenth-century historians turned to satisfy their modern ideas of a peaceful and democratic order. The widespread concept of a '*Landsgemeinde* democracy' was the outcome. This tradition is surely erroneous.[16] At this time the *Landsgemeinde* was basically far more concerned to publicise and make effective the claims of oligarchies than to encourage egalitarian co-operation among the 'people'; there was still no such thing as a sovereign people of citizens with equal rights. None the less, it is undeniable that under these circumstances political decisions could be more strongly influenced from below than they were in the towns, and that the political and social position of the rulers was legitimised and exhibited in a rather different way.

In spite of these differences, recent research into constitutional history[17] has rightly insisted on the essential structural similarities between the urban and rural communities. Both were communally organised republics, steered around 1490 by a ruling group which was still very unstable but in its structure fundamentally oligarchic. Towards the end of the century the political and social aims of these ruling groups became increasingly similar, in spite of their diverging political organisation. In the later fifteenth century they tended to become more aristocratic, a tendency which was to be institutionalised in the early modern period. To contemporaries from outside, the Confederation at least, and, by comparison with the elite of government elsewhere, the oligarchies of the Confederation, both rural and urban, were distinctive in respect of their origin, group consciousness and outward manifestation of power, these common characteristics becoming more evident after 1450.

[16] Peyer (1978). Hence Blickle (1990), pp. 93–111, prefers to speak of 'communal parliamentarianism'.
[17] Peyer (1978).

The process of state consolidation can only be partly characterised by the old-fashioned concept of a steady path to local domination through the build-up of comprehensive and undivided territorial and state controls over an ever more closely united group of subject regions. It is also inseparable from the development of new techniques of day-to-day government. Increased surveillance and control over its subjects, and a tighter grip on power by the ruling class, are important features of the 'early modern state'. A good example of this increase in governmental power, already well developed (by contrast with other parts of the region) before 1450, is found in Lucerne.[18] Following the practical example of the increasingly powerful Habsburg monarchy, Zurich, with Berne and Fribourg, which were in close contact with the highly developed ruling machinery of neighbouring Savoy, also strove to make its government more effective. Besides effective judicial control, the exaction of taxes and military service from newly acquired subjects were central concerns. Indeed, the attempt to impose military service (the so-called *Mannschaftsrecht*) was a primary assumption of those wishing to monopolise the legitimate exercise of power. A new and highly significant way of demonstrating the domination of the urban ruling class over its subjects was to administer an oath of allegiance.[19] It is interesting to note that no proper system of representation by estates was able to develop in the ruling towns.[20] The 'plebiscites' (the so-called *Ämteranfragen*), first introduced by Berne and later by other towns, did not constitute such a system. In the fifteenth century neither the urban nor the rural communes possessed a form of estate representation comparable with other European examples such as the Tyrol.

The tightening of territorial administration became manifest after 1450, particularly in the big city republics of Berne and Zürich. However, we should not overstress this process of concentration and consolidation of inner administrative structures during the fifteenth century, especially in comparison with contemporary royal states and principalities which were, to a greater or lesser extent, centralised. The institutional consolidation of individual territories, and the penetration and unification of state power which accompanied them, were long-drawn-out and precarious processes; even the great strides made in the sixteenth century did not quite complete them. The strength of local self-regulation was still structurally significant, as was the limited degree of administrative centralisation and the diversity of mechanisms for the exercise of state power, both *de facto* and *de jure*.

Nevertheless, in the late medieval Confederation there was no lack of indication that the political and social changes in the claims and practice of

---

[18] Gössi (1978); Marchal (1986).   [19] Schorer (1989); Holenstein (1991).
[20] Peyer (1978), pp. 43, 69.

government were beginning to have some effect. Witness, above all, the more or less chronic uprisings in the countryside which, under various forms and with various intensity, plagued the developing confederate oligarchies from the end of the fourteenth century. However, this widespread rural unrest must be related to economic and social developments. First, economic reasons may be presumed for the disturbances of the 1380s. Secondly, there are at least isolated indications that the Swiss midlands were affected by the widely known agrarian and demographic crises that marked the century 1350 to 1450. These difficulties, compounded in some regions by an upswing in the rural economy perceptible after the 1450s, may well have increased social tensions in the countryside. Thirdly, the increase in stock rearing in the alpine and pre-alpine regions of central Switzerland must have increased the potential for social conflict.[21] And fourthly, a further probable reason for the conflicts after 1470 was discontent with the amount of money that the governing class was receiving from mercenary contracts, and possibly the socially unjust division of the enormous booty gained from the war against Charles the Bold.

A persistently unruly area was the Bernese Oberland, where there had been resistance to the monastery of Interlaken in the fourteenth century and, later, much opposition to Berne by the 'Evil League' (*Böser Bund*) from 1445 to 1451. In 1447 political disputes around Fribourg led to another substantial peasant uprising. In many parts of the countryside around Zurich, peasant resistance was never completely stilled after the beginning of the fifteenth century, and in 1440–1 the district of Grüningen formally demanded a return to the (evidently much milder) domination of Austria. While the subjects of Wädenswil rebelled (and not for the last time) against the town's tax demands in 1467–8, the revolt against Hans Waldmann, burgomaster of Zurich, in 1489 gave drastic expression to the widespread rural opposition to the centralising policies of the urban oligarchies which rode roughshod over the special and individual rights of rural communities.[22] In Berne, in 1470–1, the question of competence to administer the countryside led to the 'quarrel of the Judicial Lords' (*Twingherrenstreit*), a serious dispute within the city's ruling class.[23] Overt peasant resistance also developed in the Entlebuch (the *Amstaldenhandel* or Amstalden affair of 1478), and in St Gallen in the attack on the monastery of Rorschach (*Rorschacher Klosterbruch*) in 1489–90; less violent, however, was the resistance to the oath in Thurgau in the 1470s. Peasant unrest prior to the Reformation was seen again in the unquiet years from 1513 to 1515 in the region of Berne; in the revolt of Köniz (*Könizer Handel*); in the hinterland of Lucerne (the so-called 'Onion War' or *Zwiebelnkrieg*); in the upper bailiwicks of Solothurn (the 'Gingerbread War' or *Lebkuchenkrieg*) and elsewhere.

---

[21] Sablonier (1990), pp. 154–66.   [22] Dietrich (1985).   [23] Schmid (1995).

In 1489 the Council of Berne urged the governing council of Zurich to put an end to the disturbances in its countryside as soon as possible. This example shows clearly that the internal consolidation of individual *Orte* was related to the wider matter of consolidating the whole confederate system of alliances. A common interest in internal law and order, and in mutual interdependence (both of which had been, to varying degrees, powerful motives as early as the fourteenth century), without doubt fostered the integration of the whole Confederation. That process must now be considered.

INTEGRATION AND CONFLICT WITHIN THE CONFEDERATION

Well into the modern period the Confederation remained a league of independent states; but in the fifteenth century it increasingly took on the look of a political entity. To this picture, however, must be added the bitter conflicts among the *Orte* themselves.

In 1500, the 'Confederation' as a system was still unstable, although from the outside the organisation, albeit assembled by chance, uncertain of its frontiers and as yet poorly equipped with common institutions, appeared as a politically autonomous entity. Inside, however, there existed only a loose, mostly bilateral network of treaties, in which only the three cantons of Uri, Schwyz and Unterwalden regularly acted together. There were a few inclusive treaties such as the 'Priests' Charter' (*Pfaffenbrief*) of 1370, the 'Charter of Sempach' (*Sempacherbrief*) of 1393, the Compact of Stans (1481) and the 'Treaty of the Pensions' (*Pensionenbrief*) of 1503. These, however, did not amount to anything like a common constitution.

Nevertheless, the fifteenth-century Confederation, viewed as a whole, did show signs of institutional consolidation. This is shown, for instance, in the numerous renewals of alliances between all parties in the 1450s. While the aim of such treaties was always to keep the peace, they also ensured mutual help and control, or protection, within a completely open and flexible system of mutual obligations and guarantees. Newly admitted into the Confederation as equal members were Fribourg and Solothurn (1481), Basle and Schaffhausen (1501) and Appenzell (1513). However, any distinction between confederates such as the abbot of St Gallen (granted *Burg-* and *Landrecht* in 1451) was still vague and rather coincidental.

At the institutional level, the Assembly of representatives of all *Orte* of the Confederation (*Tagsatzung*), which had met regularly since 1415, was certainly a force for integration, even though there was no representation of different estates, no clearly defined authority, and no delegate might speak without the leave of his superiors. But the common administration of the subject regions, especially Aargau and Thurgau, was of great importance, and dealings with the associate *zugewandte Orte* and treaty partners helped to keep the Confederation together even through internal disputes. Furthermore, joint deliberations over negotiations with neighbouring powers and the consequent conclusion of treaties (in particular contracts for the pay of mercenaries) became important, in particular during the years of disarray in Italy after 1495. Important in this connection, too, was the development of courts of arbitration and of mediators. Although unanimity seldom reigned in the Assembly, which showed little ability to deal with conflicts, it did attain a certain equilibrium. Unsteady as it was, it was none the less working towards some kind of integration.

However, differences in political and economic outlook within the Confederation remained significant throughout the fifteenth century. Berne had turned itself into the dominant political force in the Swiss midlands and, by reason of its traditionally close links with Savoy, looked chiefly westwards, towards the Upper Rhine valley and Alsace. Obviously, too, Berne had economic interests along the Aare and wished to keep open the trade route from Upper Germany to the west. The ambition of Zurich to gain greater hegemony in eastern Switzerland acquired greater political weight after 1400. Once again economic interests – control of the passes in Graubünden, still much more important than the St Gotthard route – should not be underestimated.

In fact, it was chiefly Milan that was concerned with securing the St Gotthard pass; and for the stockbreeders of central Switzerland the demand from the south was the decisive incentive to guard the route, rather than the interests of the north in securing a steady market. From an economic point of view the cantons of central Switzerland at this time are best described as Lombard alpine valleys.[24] From 1350 onwards, Uri and Unterwalden looked increasingly towards the Valais and Milan; the Valle Leventina, like the Urseren valley earlier, came within the sway of Uri. Lucerne succeeded, albeit on a small scale, in becoming the axis of trade between Upper Germany and Lombardy. In brief, the conditions and orientations of the confederate *Orte* differed from one another economically as well as politically. It is too early to talk of a well-defined Swiss commercial and economic domain in the fifteenth century.

Moreover, from time to time during the first decades of the century there were serious disputes among the confederates. This tendency showed itself early in the 'Raron affair' which, from 1415 to 1435, set Berne against central Switzerland over influence in the Valais. In 1436, when Count Frederick VII of Toggenburg died childless, the rivalry between Schwyz and Zurich for his inheritance led to an important political crisis. It was greatly intensified when, in 1438, the German Empire returned into Habsburg hands, completely transforming the political order in south-western Germany.

[24] Sablonier (1990); Vismara *et al.* (1990).

Characterised by sporadic outbreaks of violence, the 'Old Zurich War' or 'War of the Toggenburg Inheritance' lasted intermittently from 1436 to 1450. Older historians referred to a dramatic 'fratricidal war', but more recent research has clarified the actual objectives of Zurich and the complex relationship with events in a wider Europe. Zurich, a self-conscious and independent imperial city, was trying to come to an arrangement with Austria and with the imperial Habsburg government over power sharing in the whole of eastern Switzerland. The change in the political landscape brought about by the Treaty of Arras (1435), which led to a sharp increase in French and Burgundian pressure on the Upper Rhine and Alsace, may have played a part within the large framework; while, at a more local level, Zurich's well-founded fear of Schwyz's drive towards the north and the route to Graubünden was also important. The peace negotiations of 1450 brought Zurich back into the system of a balance of power within the Confederation.[25]

Even after 1450 there were still conflicts over integration and severe political divergences within the Confederation. To this context belongs the warlike raid of 1477 carried out 'under the banner of the boar' (*Saubannerzug*). This involved a band of young people who had been celebrating carnival in central Switzerland and who, to the terror of the oligarchies (particularly in the towns), went storming through the Confederation as far as Geneva. The campaign, over which the state had no control, triggered a serious conflict within the Confederation. Underlying it was a series of fundamental disagreements between the urban and rural oligarchies over the constitution of internal law and order, the binding force of joint resolutions, the centralising of the league, and the granting of full rights to the towns of Fribourg and Solothurn. These now emerged into the light of day, and for a time quite directly threatened the survival of alliances between urban and rural *Orte*.[26]

A compromise, the Compact of Stans, which later tradition endowed with strong religious connotations, was finally reached in 1481, but only through the intervention of a hermit, Niklaus von Flüe. In fact, many of its provisions, such as the banning of private war, reflect the efforts of the communal oligarchies to defend and secure their rule over the lower classes, over and above existing internal divergences. In this respect, as with the integration of Solothurn and Fribourg as full members, the urban oligarchies undoubtedly emerged the winners. Not surprisingly, the validity of the Compact of Stans was solemnly repudiated by Schwyz as early as 1489.[27]

Conflicts over integration should not be overemphasised; they continued to characterise the Confederation well into the modern period. Despite them, after 1450 the situation changed in a way which looked certain – from the

[25] Niederstätter (1995).   [26] Walder (1983).   [27] Walder (1994).

outside – to lead to increased unity: in the second half of the century the Confederation slowly grew into a major factor in European power politics. This was to be a distinguishing feature of the troubled late fifteenth century, a period in which the Confederation experienced both the heights of political power and the depths of internal conflict. It was as early as 1424 that the Assembly had been first formally requested by a foreign power – Florence – to supply a large army of mercenaries.[28] By the end of the century, the Confederation's reputation as a huge reservoir of highly skilled mercenaries had become a decisive and recurrent factor in its policies.

EUROPEAN POLITICS AND THE MERCENARY

By about 1460 the Confederates had risen to be the most important political powers between the Rhine and the Alps. By this time the claims of Austrian overlordship scarcely posed any real threat, and coming events were to reveal new political directions: the southwards thrust from central Switzerland; the conquest of the Austrian Thurgau in 1460; Berne's political and economic contacts northwards towards Basle, the Sundgau, Alsace and the Black Forest. 'This fifteenth-century Swiss federation, or at any rate a large part of it, was dynamic, expansionist and aggressive.'[29] This was certainly true of the 1460s and 1470s.

For the Confederation's political situation, even more important than the perceptible pressure for expansion from within were the shifts in the European scene, since every aspect of its political development was strongly dependent on changes in its wider environment. By 1465 or earlier, a rejuvenated France, now the greatest political power in the region, had come up against the ambitions of Charles the Bold, duke of Burgundy. Whereas the Sforzas of Milan had succeeded in consolidating their power, Savoy, rent by internal dissensions, had become weaker and weaker, and greedy eyes were being turned on it from France, Burgundy and, soon afterwards, from Berne. Trouble with Burgundy was soon affecting Austria's western dominions (the *Vorlande*), while the cities of the Upper Rhine and Alsace feared for their independence and became ever more open to the influence of the Confederation, in particular that of Berne.

The 1470s witnessed the fateful conflicts known in history as the Burgundian wars. These precipitated the fall of Charles the Bold and his state, thereby deeply affecting the subsequent course of European history. The policies of the emperor, Frederick III, and (intermittently) of Austria had favoured the expansion of Burgundian power along the Upper Rhine, but the cities of this area, especially Basle and Strasburg, rapidly stiffened their resistance. The situation was calmed to an extent by the so-called 'Perpetual Accord' (*Ewige*

---

[28] Contamine (1984), p. 136.   [29] Vaughan (1973), p. 264.

Richtung) between Austria and the Confederation signed in 1474. Berne, however, was enthusiastically in favour of war against Burgundy; recent research suggests that French bribery was not the deciding factor.[30] As a powerful imperial city, Berne closed ranks with the cities of the Upper Rhine, fearing for its profits from free trade in central Europe. Burgundy's growing influence on the Savoyard Vaud also aroused deep suspicion from 1472 onwards.

The ensuing events are well known. In 1476, confederate armies inflicted severe defeats upon Charles the Bold before Grandson and then, even more spectacularly, at Morat (Murten). In January 1477 a great number of confederate mercenaries were in the army which defeated Charles outside Nancy, a battle at which the duke himself was killed. Shortly before this, Berne had made incursions into the Savoyard Vaud (and the Bas-Valais), a first sign of her ambitions in this area which were fulfilled when she conquered it in 1536. But the real fruits of victory after Charles's fall were reaped by others: by Louis XI of France and by Maximilian, son of Frederick III, who was to marry Mary of Burgundy, and so prepared the rise of the Habsburgs (and, later, of the Netherlands) as a world power.

In 1499, local territorial and political disputes led to open war between the Confederation and Maximilian, allied with the Swabian League of south German lords and cities. This 'Swabian' or 'Swiss' war was fought out on various battlefields from Graubünden to the Sundgau, but was resolved before the year's end by the Peace of Basle. One of its direct consequences was the entry of Basle and Schaffhausen into the Confederation in 1501. This detached the two free imperial cities, which had previously enjoyed a high degree of independence, from the structural order uniting the cities of southern Germany. The old view of the Swabian war as a struggle for independence against the Empire is no longer tenable; events in the south of the Empire played only a secondary role in Maximilian's wide-ranging political ambitions. The association of the Confederation with the Empire continued to act as a fundamental basis of its legitimation, especially in view of the growing particularism of the Swiss union of communal states when contrasted to the other parts of the Empire. This special position had now become more evident at the constitutional level as well. In an almost paradoxical manner, the ideological weight of the Confederation's association with the Empire was coming to correspond to a progressive loosening of ties between them.

In the decade up to 1500, Italy had taken centre stage in European politics. The cast consisted of the French crown, ambitious to capture Milan and to oust the Aragonese from Naples; Maximilian, now defending former

---

[30] Gasser (1973); Esch (1988).

Habsburg claims in the name of the Empire; together with the papal states, Venice, Genoa and Savoy. The Confederation's political interests were involved particularly in the political destabilisation of the duchy of Milan, which was only hastened, not begun, by Louis XII's attack in 1499. In that same year another contract to supply France with mercenaries was signed. This involvement in the struggle between major powers in Italy and, above all, its ability to supply mercenaries, made the Confederation (or, often, particular *Orte*) into a political factor of some importance.

Confederate mercenaries had been serving in Italy since the fourteenth century, more frequently since the Burgundian wars. The fortunes of war between 1495 and 1503 brought the whole of today's southern Switzerland and, after 1500, the important county of Bellinzona, under the control of Uri. However, the renewed and massive incursions by confederate troops after 1512 had no lasting effect. Except for Uri's claims on Bellinzona, and at times beyond into the southern Ticino and the neighbouring valleys (Val d'Ossola, Valle Maggia and Val Blenio), the Confederation had scarcely any discernible political objectives. This is true even though confederate troops were more than once in a position to establish a temporary military protectorate over the duchy of Milan. At no time were the confederates in agreement over which side they should support; seldom had disputes and open contradictions been as much in evidence as now. Mercenaries and commanders pitched into the war where wages were highest and the booty richest.[31] In the upshot, the Confederation's political gains were extremely modest.

A number of factors explain the importance of the confederate mercenary. All the parties embroiled in Italy needed mercenaries, and, since the Burgundian wars, the military prestige of the Confederation had been high. Furthermore, this confederate military potential was subject to only a very modest degree of state control, and only in so far as the oligarchies' financial interests were involved. This is basically true of official mercenary contracts and pension agreements made with either particular *Orte* or with the Confederation as a whole, although it is in this context that important early stages of state supervision can be detected. The hire and broking of mercenaries had developed into an important business undertaking for many of the leading confederates, who profited both directly and indirectly.[32] It seems that military careerism and the mercenary business were a growth sector which closely paralleled the developing livestock trade to the south.[33] As regards the common mercenary, a real labour market for his services was to develop, probably involving a high proportion of poor people, most from the rural population, but including many from the towns. Since the Burgundian wars

---

[31] Esch (1990).   [32] Sablonier (1979b).
[33] On Fribourg, see Peyer (1975); on Obwalden, see Rogger (1989).

there had been a perceptible mobility among large sectors of the population, among whom were many rootless young people, a factor remarked upon by contemporaries, and which was connected with the rural uprisings described above.

By the turn of the century the mercenaries had become quite professional. It was becoming ever harder to put a brake either on the greedy business dealings of rulers or on the work-hungry and self-perpetuating zest for battle of the increasingly professional mercenaries; the state had great difficulty in directing them into at least partly controllable channels. This restless mobility was further increased by the multifarious contracts, broken as often as they were respected, which were signed (with France in particular) and by the unscrupulous and unrestrained dealings of the recruiting officers from France, the Empire, the Papacy and Milan.

Mercenary potential, and military strength and prestige, were generally not a state concern, even though mercenary contracts always involved an element of state intervention. Hence the bloody defeat of a confederate army before Marignano, near Milan, on 13–14 September 1515, although prominent in European military history, was not a 'national catastrophe'. It was, however, an incontrovertible demonstration of French military superiority. The defeat laid the psychological foundations for the acceptance of existing political realities. The peace terms of 1515–16, dictated by France to the confederates following their withdrawal from Milan, were simple. France strengthened her hold over the Confederation's mercenary potential by the contract of 1521. This was the temporary conclusion to a development which had been in progress since the mid-fifteenth century. Henceforward France, with her economic strength and her rank as Europe's foremost power, would be the Confederation's protector and partner *par excellence*.

External factors were thus important in maintaining cohesion among the diverse partners in the network of confederate alliances. It has already been stressed that the evolution towards nationhood within these territories, and the degree of cohesion in the entire confederate system at the end of the fifteenth century, should not be overestimated. State control, even over the Confederation's military potential, although so important in terms of foreign policy, was only in its infancy. The prohibition of individual acts of belligerency contained in the Compact of Stans (1481) and the *Pensionenbrief* (1503), which aimed at preventing private recruitment and payment (*Pensionen*), expresses no more than a tendency. Nevertheless, after the Italian wars the consolidated political oligarchies tightened their control over the mercenary business with startling rapidity.[34]

[34] Romer (1995).

What happened to the Confederation in the second half of the fifteenth century had a great deal to do with wars and mercenaries. Hence any survey of the political history of the confederate 'state' must take these factors into account. But there must be no idea that this unusual state of affairs was created by a group of *Zapoletes*, the efficient 'Venalians' of Thomas More's *Utopia*. The confederate oligarchies did make attempts at political and social integration in the fifteenth century, and these should be placed on a par with the fostering of trade and specialisation in stock rearing. And in the cultural domain we should not fail to mention at least the importance of Basle, of the great ecclesiastical councils which met at Constance and Basle, and of the humanist movement. One important aspect of the cultural outlook connected with the peculiarities of the development of the Swiss state now deserves consideration: the development of a particular tradition of state evolution.

STATE FORMATION AND NATIONAL CONSCIOUSNESS

The Confederation undoubtedly represents an exceptional case of state development within the territory of the German Empire, and even in late medieval Europe as a whole. By 1550, this uniqueness was clearly recognised from the outside. At a constitutional level, all separate territories – both urban and rural communes – have to be regarded as states, in spite of the many differences between them. They were communally organised republics with oligarchies of self-styled aristocrats – political, social and economic in origin. In contrast with the rest of Europe, with its central, sovereign authorities, the confederate alliance had no such power. Its political system was characterised by a very limited degree of state integration, as is shown clearly in the military domain and in the great importance of local, communal autonomy even in the subject regions. These institutional characteristics go hand in hand with the distinct character of the political elites: instead of an aristocracy of officials of noble or bourgeois birth in the employ of the sovereign, there were local, rural potentates and urban aristocratic councils who showed increasing social similarity, and whose political and social cohesion was steadily growing.

Overall, the growth of a common foreign policy was fostered less by internal consensus than by political developments in the wider European environment. The mercenary contracts with neighbouring powers were, in part, an expression of this tendency to act in concert. At the same time, a military career was a very good way to improve social status, and 'foreign' (mercenary) service long remained an important field of activity for members of the confederate upper classes, the distinguishing mark of a confederate oligarch. So important was this fact that it induced local rural potentates to make common cause with the ruling urban aristocracy in a far closer way than ever

happened in the monarchies. Careers like that of Hans Waldmann of Zurich –
ironmonger, notorious ruffian and guild-master who rose to be a sought-after
mercenary captain with a European reputation, burgomaster of Zurich and
the town's richest citizen – were certainly not the rule, but they throw a revealing light on the peculiar political culture of the Confederation about 1480.

A further vital contribution to the specific character of this political culture
was made by the construction and propagation of a unique and wholly individual tradition of statehood, an expression of the political self-consciousness of
the elites. Political opponents often alleged that this non-ducal, non-noble state
lacked legitimacy, for it exercised power in defiance of the God-given order of
estates. One aspect of this polemic was, initially, the well-known, graphic and
unflattering description of the confederates as 'Cow Swiss' (*Kuhschweizer*). This
referred not so much to their alleged immorality in the modern sense as to their
supposed identity as heretics. Confederate publicists retorted that it was legitimate to place power in the hands of the 'peasant', the 'pious, noble and pure
peasant' as he appeared in so-called historical folk songs; in any case, their military successes proved that they were a Chosen People. The idea of a legitimate
'peasant state' was part of a way of thinking which probably remained confined to the political elite;[35] it is hard to prove that it promoted solidarity among
the common people.[36]

On this level, alongside political propaganda, the rise of confederate historiography was also highly important.[37] It had to justify the existence of the
Confederation as a state. Not until shortly after 1470 were tales of the 'original'
freedom, legitimate resistance to wicked Habsburg bailiffs and the battles of
the Chosen People woven into the first mythical narrative of early confederate
history, the 'White Book of Sarnen'. The portrayal of William Tell and other
heroes echoed notions widely held among the population at large.

Too little is still known about the popular dissemination of these legends at
the beginning of the sixteenth century. The ties which bound together the
'common people' within the Confederation were almost certainly dependent
less on notions of history and conscious statehood than on shared forms of
social life, similar ideas about society and politics and the power of visible
symbols; apart from a few points, this, too, has received too little attention.[38]
Research into military history has indicated that among the common soldiers
from the Confederation a fierce rivalry with the German *Landsknechte* may have
fostered a certain popular solidarity. But in times of war the ordinary people
would have found much more meaning in the simple expressions of piety, such
as the special prayer 'with outstretched arms'[39] and the annual commemorative

---

[35] As Weishaupt (1991) believes.   [36] Marchal (1987a).   [37] Marchal (1987a) and (1992).
[38] Sieber-Lehmann (1995).   [39] Ochsenbein (1979).

services in honour of the fallen. Such traditions were already significant in the fifteenth century, and were to reach their zenith in the sixteenth.

The developments in culture and mentality towards the end of the fifteenth century are vitally important to any later understanding of the rise of the confederate state. The building of an independent tradition of statehood, subordinate to a wider process of construction of a specific political culture, must be seen as an important factor in the creation of a consciousness of political unity and communal uniqueness which became firmly anchored in the confederate mind.

Thus it was possible to talk about the construction of an independent political culture in the Confederation; and in the nineteenth century (in Switzerland, as elsewhere in Europe) such a concept could scarcely be understood other than as the birth of a 'nation'. In a country like Switzerland, lacking a common language or tradition, this meant a nation built on the will to freedom and on unique geographical and geopolitical circumstances. In the final analysis, it seemed to be a political destiny chosen by nature and by the people themselves. Since the eighteenth century, bourgeois and Enlightenment ideas of natural freedom and democracy had been particularly strongly associated with the 'mountain herdsmen' of the Alps. When this was coupled to a romantic and nationalistic harking back to medieval history, it was inevitable that Switzerland would soon be seen as the cradle of democracy and freedom in Europe. Not only was this the conscious message of liberal bourgeois historians in Switzerland itself; it was also the picture projected upon Switzerland from without.

Nineteenth- and twentieth-century notions of a medieval 'heroic age', which were strongly encouraged by national Swiss historians, contributed to a historical picture which found its way into socio-political discourse, and so strongly affected the national consciousness of wider sections of the population. Concepts drawn from this nationalistic and patriotic environment, and dating back to the time of nationalist upsurge, still have some influence on popular notions of the fifteenth century. Indeed, quite patently nationalistic admiration of the 'warlike strength' and 'glorious military achievement' of the early Confederation, and even the belief in the innate inclination of those 'peasants' towards 'freedom' and 'democracy' are still widespread – and not simply in ageing history books in Swiss schools. Against this background it is easier to explain the unusual prominence, unparalleled elsewhere in Europe, of the 'heroic age' of medieval history in modern Swiss state ideology. The so-called foundation of the Confederation in 1291, whose anniversary was first celebrated on a large scale in 1891, then in 1941 and again in 1991, is a metaphor of political discourse, not a figure of historical argumentation. To the historian it is clear, to the point of cliché, that the building of the Swiss state was a long-drawn-out, complex process in which the overthrow of the *ancien régime* in 1798, and the federal constitution of 1848, were incomparably more important than anything which happened in 1291.

In conclusion, we must turn away from these features of the emerging Swiss tradition and ask the fundamental question: what were the real reasons for the unique state development which began here in the late Middle Ages?

Without doubt there was an interplay of very varied factors, political, social and ideological; but these cannot be assembled systematically, since so much happened by chance. However, some political factors can be considered to have been particularly important. First and foremost, the often aimless and sadly discontinuous policy of the Habsburg monarchy. This left the field clear for the developing communes, a field in which the imperial free cities of Berne and Zurich operated with deliberate purposefulness. The assertion of political autonomy by the valley communities of central Switzerland was basically due to the fragmentary feudal penetration of the area, its southward facing economic orientation and its early integration into a supra-regional context. At all times, and particularly in the fifteenth century, the changing political relationships among the Confederation's nearest neighbours, especially the rivalry over the German crown, the French incursions eastwards after the end of the Hundred Years War and the fall of Burgundy, had a decisive influence. The peripheral location of the Confederation within the Empire was also an important factor. Because its statehood was not yet highly developed, the Confederation posed no threat to the great powers, and its military potential, which achieved enormous prestige after the Burgundian wars, was and remained for hire. It was the French who first realised the significance of this, so that the link with France, firmly established in 1521, was to remain a decisive political element of Swiss statehood.

CHAPTER 26

THE STATES OF SCANDINAVIA,
c. 1390–c. 1536

Thomas Riis

I

TOWARDS the end of the fourteenth century the Scandinavian countries were recovering from the effects of two crises. The earlier of these was at least partially caused by a deterioration of the climate, c. 1300. As a consequence of this farms and even villages, often those situated on less fertile soil, became deserted. This happened in Norway and in Denmark, whereas Sweden, colonised later, only felt the crisis after the middle of the fourteenth century. The Black Death (1349–50) struck the whole of Scandinavia except Iceland; in Norway, in particular, its effects were aggravated by subsequent epidemics, smallpox in 1359–60, plague in 1371. In both Norway and Denmark the results of the agrarian crisis – deserted farms and redundant peasants – were counterbalanced by the effects of the diseases. In certain regions, however, they were to create a lack of manpower.

Other effects were the formation of large estates belonging to the Church or to the aristocracy, and an increase of the share of animal husbandry in the rural economy. In certain parts of Norway the desertion of farms could be avoided by supplementing rural activities with fishing or forestry. At the end of the fifteenth century water-driven sawmills were founded at many river estuaries in southern and western Norway; this was to become a source of economic growth during the early modern centuries.

In Finland, at least in the south-west, agriculture was sufficiently developed to offer a living to the peasant and his family; nevertheless, the change in climate rendered difficult the cultivation of certain cereal crops. In the interior and in Ostrobothnia, a complex economy prevailed, combining agriculture with animal husbandry, fishing and the hunting of animals for their furs. In the east, burnbeating was widespread, and here, too, subsidiary sources of income (especially from furs) were important. Although the epidemics did not spare Finland, the complexity of her economy facilitated its adaptation to the new conditions which were to develop.

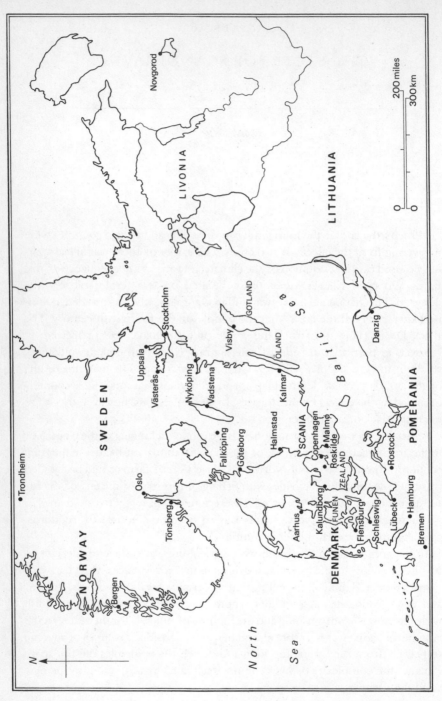

Map 16 Scandinavia and the Baltic

Sweden also suffered from the Black Death, but her agrarian crisis, with its desertion of farms, belongs to the century after the plague. It is difficult to see, however, whether this fact reveals a crisis of manpower (because of the epidemics) or whether it had independent causes. The response to the new conditions was a concentration on animal husbandry in regions less suitable for the growing of cereals, and the desertion of farms founded in the less fertile districts during the early medieval colonisation. Moreover, subsidiary activities such as fishing, hunting animals for furs and mining must have been important in the regions outside the fertile belt around the great lakes in central Sweden.

Iceland, the only Scandinavian country to remain untouched by the Black Death, none the less suffered severe outbursts of plague in 1402–4 and again in 1495. Such scanty evidence as survives indicates some desertion of marginally situated farms, a movement probably aggravated, but not caused, by the epidemics.

Denmark was the only country to have a fairly large number of towns, most of them being rather small. Although the advance of the Hanseatics after the middle of the thirteenth century had repelled Danish ships from long-distance trade and navigation, Norwegian traders still called at English ports in the late fourteenth century. During this century, Bergen became the centre of Norwegian foreign trade, but most of it was in the hands of others, Hanseatics, Englishmen and Scots. Nevertheless, after the union of the Norwegian and Danish crowns in 1380–1, the sea between southern Norway and Stralsund came to be regarded as one on which local ships and long-distance traders were active. Similarly, the eastern – and interior – parts of the Baltic formed a region where Hanseatic, Swedish and Finnish vessels undertook the transport of goods. In each it was the aim of the Hanseatics to obtain as large a share of the trade as possible and, consequently, it was often Scandinavian policy to support Dutchmen, Englishmen or Scots against their Hanseatic rivals.

II

In the political history of the Scandinavian countries – Denmark, Finland, Iceland and the states of the Scandinavian peninsula, Norway and Sweden – the long fifteenth century from c. 1390 to the Reformation forms a well-defined period. It began with the union of the Nordic crowns; it saw Sweden's attempts to break away from the Union and Denmark's endeavours to restore it, until it collapsed, once and for all, in the 1520s, while a few years later the old-established Church came to be supplanted by Protestantism of the Lutheran variety.

The years around 1390 saw the culmination of German immigration, especially in Denmark: during the fifteenth century Hanseatic political and economic influence in the Scandinavian countries was gradually repelled. Lübeck's involvement in the Danish civil war 1534–6 was a last, unsuccessful attempt to recover lost ground. In the cultural field the fifteenth century was increasingly marked by northern Germany, especially in the visual arts and in literature; the introduction of Protestantism in its German and not in its French, Calvinist, form is, in this respect, revealing.

On the death of King Oluf of Denmark and Norway (3 August 1387), his mother, Margrete, was elected regent of Denmark by the provincial assemblies (*landsting*) of Scania, Zealand and Funen. Apparently no such election took place in Jutland, but representatives of the region may have taken part in those of the other provinces. In Norway, Margrete's legal position was stronger: she was the queen mother, and in February 1388 the Norwegian council (*rigsråd*) declared that the other pretenders – the relatives of Margrete's sister, Ingeborg, wife of Duke Heinrich of Mecklenburg, their son Albrecht IV, and Heinrich's brother, Albrecht, king of Sweden – had forfeited their rights to the Norwegian throne. Consequently, the son of Margrete's niece, Erik of Pomerania, was accepted as heir apparent, and was confirmed as such in 1389.

To the Swedish throne Margrete had very slight claims. Her father-in-law had been deposed in 1363 and her husband, Håkon VI of Norway, had taken up his father's claim. When, in 1385, King Oluf came of age, he had resumed his father's claim to Sweden, adding to his title 'true heir to the kingdom of Sweden'.

Much more important was a group of aristocrats, executors of the will of the late seneschal, Bo Jonsson (d. 1386), who, holding his fiefs and estates, was opposing Albrecht's government. The king, using military force, tried to obtain control over the lands in question, but this led to an aristocratic revolt in the summer of 1387. Contacts were made with Margrete and Oluf, which must have continued after the latter's death. In March 1388 the executors recognised Margrete as regent of Sweden, and in the decisive battle at Åsle, near Falköping, Margrete's army defeated and captured Albrecht (24 February 1389).

The countries now governed by Margrete were very extensive. Besides Norway, Sweden and Denmark, they comprised the duchy of Schleswig, the Norwegian Atlantic islands of Greenland, Iceland, Orkney, Shetland and the Faroes; only part of Finland – to the west and south of a line from Zelenogorsk in the Carelian Isthmus to Raahe/Brahestad on the Bothnian Gulf – was clearly Swedish. The remaining territories of present-day Finland as well as the northern regions of the Scandinavian peninsula were inhabited by Lapps who were subject to very little governmental control. Excluding Greenland, Margrete's countries corresponded to an area twice that of present-day France; all, however, were very thinly populated.

III

Margrete's victory at Åsle had won for her most of Sweden. Only Stockholm, dominated by its strong German element, remained faithful to Albrecht and even organised a massacre of 'treacherous' Swedes (*Käpplingemorden*, spring 1389). Margrete appears to have made Albrecht's release dependent on his abdication. Consequently, his native land, Mecklenburg, declared its ports open to everybody who wanted to fight Denmark; Rostock and Wismar had to follow the duke's policy. Letters of marque were granted by the dukes or the cities to privateers, who took the name of *Vitalienbrüder*. The aim of this naval guerrilla warfare was to free Albrecht and to revictual Stockholm.

Attempts were made to resolve the problem by diplomatic means, and in June 1395 agreement was finally reached at Lindholm. Albrecht and his son were to be freed for a period of three years, during which time Stockholm would be held by a group of Hanseatic towns. When the three years had expired, Albrecht and his son, who were not obliged to renounce their claims to Sweden, would have three options. If they surrendered Stockholm to Margrete, they could have 'eternal' peace with her; if they paid a ransom of 60,000 marks of silver, they would be free to declare war on Margrete after a delay of one year; finally, if they agreed to re-enter captivity, this time span could be reduced to nine weeks.

In the meantime, Visby became an important base for the *Vitalienbrüder*, whose activities in the western Baltic were curtailed as a result of the Treaty of Lindholm. Having lost their last veneer of legality, they operated after 1395 in the North Sea – they had already made a raid on Bergen at Easter 1393 – and in the eastern Baltic. In order to pacify these waters, the Teutonic Order and the Prussian towns occupied Gotland in 1398, with the desired effect: by 1400 the *Vitalienbrüder* had disappeared from the Baltic. At the same time, the Hanseatic towns and Margrete cleared their respective parts of the North Sea of the remaining pirates.

According to the Treaty of Lindholm, Stockholm was to be returned to Sweden after three years, if Albrecht preferred to stay at liberty. It was equally important in another respect. Were Margrete to die before the three years had elapsed, Erik, her adopted son, would take over her rights. Already designated king of Norway in 1389, he was acclaimed in Denmark and Sweden in 1396. Margrete continued as regent for another year, until Erik came of age and was crowned at Kalmar in June 1397 at a ceremony recognised as valid by his three kingdoms. It was thus indicated that the Union was to be more than a union of crowns.

At the same time as Erik's official recognition as future king of Sweden and Denmark the foundations of the domestic policies of both kingdoms for the coming years were established by statute. The texts express concern for the personal security of the subjects. In Denmark, the construction of private fortresses was forbidden; while in Sweden, those built after Albrecht's accession to the throne (1363) were to be demolished, if Margrete or Erik desired it. Attempts were also made to reduce exemptions from taxation on land claimed by the Church or by men whose title to aristocracy could be legitimately challenged. Moreover, considerable areas of land were reclaimed for the crown by the scrutiny of title-deeds.

Two documents inform us about the negotiations held after Erik's coronation in order to organise the Union. The so-called 'Coronation charter' shows that Erik had been recognised in the three countries and crowned as their legal king. Consequently his subjects promised to do their duty towards their lord and ruler, as he was to do his duty towards them. Finally, Margrete received discharge for her administration.

The 'Coronation charter' provided few rules for the future government of the three kingdoms; only the coronation itself gave them the legal basis for any sense of unity. To remedy the situation, a group of Margrete's closest collaborators from the three countries drafted the 'Union charter', which, however, was never ratified. After Erik's death, the three countries were to elect one of his sons; however, if a king left no children, the 'councillors and men' of the three countries were to elect a new king. The right of succession was thus limited to the male children of the preceding king, which represents a compromise between the elaborate Norwegian rules of succession and the Swedish and Danish system of election within the royal family. Each country was to be governed according to its own laws both in home and foreign affairs; however, if one country got involved in war, the two others were to come to its assistance. Proscription in one country should be valid in the others as well. Moreover, the king should always have a few councillors from each country at his court, in case urgent decisions had to be taken. Finally, Margrete's possession of her dower and other estates was confirmed.

The queen realised the good use she could make of the Church and its personnel. To have a loyal collaborator appointed to a bishopric by papal provision meant, in most cases, the creation of a solid support of governmental policy within the decision-making body of the country in question. Thus Peder Jensen Lodehat, who had begun his career as Margrete's clerk, was appointed to the Swedish see of Växjö in 1380. In 1387 he took over the bishopric of Aarhus (Denmark), which, eight years later, he exchanged for the richest Danish diocese, Roskilde, where he served until his death in 1416. Economic reasons, too, told Margrete to collaborate with the Church. From it she could obtain loans, if money was urgently needed; in this respect, St Mary's church at Oslo and the cathedral of Roskilde served her as banks. The loans were often paid back either by cession of part of the *regalia* to the ecclesiastical creditors or by donations to the Church, thus adding a spiritual dimension to the prosaic settling of accounts.

In foreign affairs, the government of Margrete and Erik saw the main issues as the settlement of the succession and the restoration of the Union's territorial integrity. In 1406, Erik married Philippa, daughter of Henry IV of England. Her sister had married a son of Ruprecht, king of the Romans, and so became sister-in-law to Erik's sister, Catherina, when she married Ruprecht's younger son, the count palatine, Johann, in 1407.

Stockholm was returned to the Swedish government in 1398, but in the same year, Margrete and Erik lost Gotland to the Teutonic Order. In face of growing tension between Poland–Lithuania and the Teutonic Order, the latter became more inclined to a compromise with Margrete and Erik about the surrender of the island, and in November 1408 the last Prussian occupants left.

The Danish government had found a *modus vivendi* with the counts of Holstein, as in 1386 Gerhard VI had been enfeoffed with the duchy of Schleswig. At his death in 1404 he left his widow, Elizabeth, and three sons, all minors. Elizabeth needed money, which Margrete was ready to lend her against security in land. In this way the queen won control over large parts of the duchy, where the bishop of Schleswig was a staunch supporter of Margrete and Erik. In 1409 the pro-Holstein part of the aristocracy realised that the objective of Margrete and Erik was the acquisition of Schleswig for Denmark and consequently its separation from Holstein. In order to thwart these attempts they revolted, and war ensued. By negotiating a five-year truce (1411), Margrete succeeded in bringing the hostilities to an end; on Erik's behalf, she received the oath of allegiance from Flensburg, the largest town of the duchy, but she was to die of the plague only a few days later (28 October 1412).

IV

In many respects Erik's government continued that of Margrete. Their styles, however, differed. Whereas Margrete preferred political means and never dealt with more than one major issue at a time, Erik had an inclination for legal action and allowed himself to get involved in new problems before old ones had been resolved. In Sweden, the resumption of alienated crown lands had aroused the opposition of the Church. In September 1412 the bishops protested openly against laymen trying cases concerning ecclesiastical property. Soon after Margrete's death, Erik visited Sweden, where he realised the necessity of granting concessions to the opposition. Some of the most unpopular local administrators (*fogeder*) were dismissed, and new rules for the resumption of land made the local bishop the crown's representative.

Erik's concern about the crown's fiscal interests is most clearly seen in his urban policy. Several settlements obtained urban status during his reign, some having already done so before Margrete's death: in Denmark, Præstø 1403, Nysted 1409, and Landskrona was founded between 1410 and 1413. Here the developing urban economy was to provide opportunities for the mendicant friars who settled when the town was being built. Similar considerations lay behind the creation of towns at Vadstena (1400) and at Danish Maribo (1416) as support for the Bridgettine convents. In other cases, places of strategic importance were favoured: older settlements were moved closer to castles (Korsør 1425, Elsinore 1426); Malmø was fortified, as was Flensburg, when Margrete and Erik first won control over it in 1410.

More spectacular features were the collection of the Sound toll at Elsinore, perhaps transferred from Helsingborg (1429), and Erik's acquisition of Copenhagen from the bishop of Roskilde, after the death of Peder Jensen Lodehat in 1416. In Denmark, Erik's interest concentrated on towns close to the Sound and the Great Belt, both of them channels of international trade and shipping. The granting of urban status to certain settlements and the removal of others to more favourable sites were intended to offer better conditions to the urban economy and in its turn, through taxation, to the royal treasury. Likewise, the government claimed taxes from foreign craftsmen at Bergen (1415), and encouraged rural trade in some localities (1425), no doubt in the hope of seeing them develop into settlements which might achieve urban status.

At the same time, Norwegian trade with Iceland was dwindling, as Englishmen and Germans tried to take it over. In 1419 the *althing* accepted the presence of English merchants, provided they were active in both fishing and trade. Twelve years later, however, the *althing* felt foreign activities to be so intrusive that Englishmen and Germans were forbidden to stay in Iceland during the winter months. International price fluctuations made Icelandic trade profitable: during the fifteenth century the price of fish increased by 70 per cent, whereas that of imported grain fell by a third. Monasteries and the two Icelandic bishoprics played their part in increasing this prosperity, not least by trading with the English. Erik's government could not tolerate this state of affairs, and in 1425 sent a commissioner to Iceland in order to stop English trade.

By 1416 Erik and Philippa had been married for ten years and still had no family. Although, according to Norwegian law, Erik's uncle, Bugislaus VIII, was the heir to the throne, since Erik had been born in 1382, he could still expect to rule for many years to come. Consequently, from about 1416 he began to consider his cousin, Bugislaus IX of Stolp, a younger man, as his heir apparent.

In the summer of 1419 a treaty of alliance between Erik's union and that of Poland–Lithuania had been concluded and ratified. The Teutonic Order was seen as the contracting parties' mutual enemy, whose existence as a temporal power was to be eliminated. The treaty established three categories of territories which the Order would have to cede: those formerly taken from Poland or Lithuania, which were to be returned to them; those to which either party had a claim, and which were to belong to the country with the better title; other territories, which were perhaps to be ruled as a condominium. In practical terms, Prussia would belong to the first category, Estonia to the second (and would go to Denmark), whereas Curonia and Livonia would be jointly governed.

The projected co-operation against the Teutonic Order was completed by the plan of a marriage between Bugislaus IX and Princess Jadwiga (Hedwig), heir to the Polish–Lithuanian union. However, the scheme was thwarted by the *rapprochement* between Poland and Brandenburg and by the pressure exerted upon Erik by Sigismund, king of the Romans. As ruler over Germany, Sigismund could not accept the annihilation of the Teutonic Order as a secular state. But with the birth, in 1424, of a male heir to the Polish king, Jadwiga became less interesting in international relations.

At the same time, Erik tried to infiltrate Estonia and the northern part of Livonia, especially by winning allies among the clergy and the landed aristocracy. The towns very soon realised that their interests in Russian trade were better promoted by co-operation with Erik than with Lübeck and the other Wendic towns. This policy thus met with a certain success, but before the goal had been achieved, Erik allied himself with the Teutonic Order and the Hansa, no doubt in order to demonstrate his power to the Polish king, and to induce him to approve the plans for Jadwiga's marriage to Bugislaus. In this, however, he failed. The other north European powers realised the danger inherent in the projected union of unions, and succeeded in opposing it. After 1425 the Schleswig question increasingly occupied Erik's mind, and he was not able to continue his infiltration of Estonia. Thus he lost what he had won, without attaining the aim for which he had abandoned his efforts in Estonia.

From Margrete, Erik inherited the problem of Schleswig. By resorting to military force, the counts of Holstein could be considered guilty of high treason against Erik, and had consequently forfeited any right to the duchy. The Danish parliament (*danehof*) had not been summoned for many years when, in 1413, it met as the high court of parliament to hear the case of Schleswig. It adopted the royal point of view: as enemies of Erik, the counts had lost all their rights in Denmark. Belonging as it did to the Danish realm, the duchy of Schleswig could thus be confiscated. Two years later Erik had the verdict confirmed by his cousin Sigismund.

Although respecting the five-year truce concluded in 1411, the counts would not accept the verdict of 1413. Hostilities were reopened in 1416; in the following year Erik occupied the city of Schleswig, but could not take Gottorp castle. The Danes also captured Fehmarn in 1417, but they suffered a serious setback in the west, where the Frisians supported the counts of Holstein. For several years hostilities and truces succeeded each other, until, in 1421, the contending parties agreed to submit the issue to the arbitration of Sigismund, king of the Romans. After thorough legal investigations, Sigismund pronounced his verdict: Schleswig belonged to Denmark and to Erik, leaving the counts of Holstein with no rights as Schleswig was not to be considered a fief, but an integral part of Denmark (28 June 1424).

Two years later Erik began to execute Sigismund's verdict, asking the Hanseatic towns for military support. Fearing Erik's plans for domination of the Baltic, the Hanseatics offered mediation. In the summer of 1426 Erik opened hostilities, forcing the counts of Holstein to seek help from the Wendic towns, which, in September 1426, decided to enter the war against Denmark. Hanseatic vessels raided the coasts of southern Denmark in April and May 1427, but only in June did the Nordic navy reach full strength. A Hanseatic fleet was sent to the Sound in order to protect the westbound voyage of the convoy from Prussia as well as the entry into the Baltic of ships coming from western France. On the same day the united Nordic fleet threw back the Hanseatic fleet and captured the eastbound ships coming from France (11 July 1427). Events in 1428 confirmed that the Hanseatic fleet was only superior until Erik's navy reached full strength; furthermore, that privateering harmed Hanseatics and Scandinavians alike, as the spectacular pillaging of Bergen in the spring of 1429 was to show. Consequently, the coalition of Wendic towns and the counts of Holstein concentrated on military operations which resulted in the conquest of Aabenraa in north-eastern Schleswig.

This success showed the Wendic towns that if they could help the counts of Holstein to win control over Schleswig, they would themselves be in a better bargaining position in their negotiations with Erik. At Easter 1431 the coalition succeeded in taking Flensburg, whose castle, however, held out until September. Erik had now lost almost all of Schleswig, and he agreed to a truce with the counts and the Hanseatics (22 August 1432). Three years later, on 15 July 1435, a formal peace treaty was concluded at Vordingborg: Erik retained the parts of Schleswig under his control, as did Count Adolf VIII of Holstein. In 1440 Erik's successor, Christoffer III, recognised Adolf as duke of all Schleswig; the personal union of Holstein and Schleswig had thus been restored to what it had been in Margrete's early years.

Erik's unsuccessful and protracted war over Schleswig strained the resources of his kingdoms. In Sweden, in particular, the war effort was felt as burdensome, and, and, other than in Norway, it was not compensated for by the government protecting other national interests such as trade in northern Norway or fishing around Iceland. The war also hindered the exportation of important Swedish goods, such as iron and copper from Dalarna or furs from Norrland. The debasement of the currency only made matters worse.

There were, moreover, other reasons for opposition by the native aristocracy to Erik's government. Erik continued Margrete's policy of using foreigners in local government, sometimes as governors of lesser fiefs (*fogeder*), but above all as governors of fiefs with civil and often military powers as well (*lensmænd*). As the case of the brothers Thott shows clearly, a typical mid-fifteenth-century seignorial economy would draw more income from the fiefs (*len*) granted by the government than from private property. Thus barred from an important source of prosperity, the native aristocracy risked estrangement from King Erik.

Like most of his contemporaries Erik tried to influence the appointment of bishops through collaboration with the pope. The Great Schism having undermined the authority of the Papacy, the general council emerged as the leading ruling body of the Church. One of the issues between pope and princes on one side and the council fathers on the other was the appointment of bishops, who, in principle, were elected by cathedral chapters. At least since the thirteenth century the pope had interfered with such appointments, but in July 1433 the Council of Basle decided to adhere strictly to the rules for election of bishops as described in canon law. Already, in 1432, the chapter of Uppsala cathedral, in a deliberate attempt to exclude Erik from the election, had chosen a new archbishop, who immediately, and without seeking royal recommendation, travelled to Rome to secure papal confirmation. In the subsequent conflict over the issue the ideas were also to win support from other Swedish cathedral chapters. Erik was beginning to estrange himself from the Swedish Church, upon whose collaboration he, like Margrete, had relied.

Further opposition was increasing. In Dalarna, dissatisfaction with the local royal administrator (*foged*) Jens Eriksen (Jösse Eriksson) was growing; the squire, Engelbrekt Engelbrektsson, appeared as the leader of the opposition and travelled to Denmark in order to present its complaints to the king. Erik asked the Swedish *riksråd* to investigate the matter, and as a consequence the *foged* was dismissed. However, since he was not punished further, dissatisfaction grew, until it broke out in armed revolt (June 1434).

Having been informed of these events, Erik summoned the Swedish *riksråd* to Vadstena on 1 August in the hope that it would be able to come to terms with the insurgents. However, Engelbrekt forced the councillors to join him, and soon the Swedish aristocracy realised what benefits could be gained through alliance with the insurgents. Engelbrekt's military campaign in the autumn of 1434 won them several important castles; in January 1435, he was admitted to the *riksråd* and appointed commander in chief.

Although the insurgents accepted the Union of crowns, they maintained a national programme. Sweden was to be governed according to Swedish law; administrative posts (whether as *lensmand* or as *foged*) were to be filled only by Swedes, and a seneschal and a marshal for Sweden were to be appointed. In the subsequent negotiations with members of the Danish *rigsråd* a compromise was reached (May 1435); as a result the Danes began to consider Erik's administration in the same critical terms as their Swedish colleagues. An agreement between Erik and the Swedes was reached at Stockholm (14 October 1435), but Erik was slow in the execution of its terms. Early in 1436 this led the *riksråd* to withdraw its allegiance to Erik, entrusting the government to Engelbrekt and to the marshal, Karl Knutsson (Bonde). But the balance between the popular and the aristocratic parties in the revolt was soon overturned when Engelbrekt was murdered on 27 April 1436.

The significance of Engelbrekt's revolt lay in the formation of a Swedish political programme with distinct national features, which was to be taken up again and again for the coming ninety years.

Before his death, Engelbrekt had declared himself ready to support revolt in Norway under Amund Sigurdsson Bolt, whose insurgents appear to have been strongest in the spring of 1436. An accord was made in June promising the eviction of Danes from Norwegian local government. According to the final terms made on 18 February 1437, posts in local government were to be reserved for Norwegians; the Norwegian seal would be kept in Norway; a seneschal was to be appointed; and the currency was to be kept stable. Harald Gråtop's rebellion (summer 1438) was aimed at the remaining foreigners in the Norwegian administration, and at the aristocracy as well. It was easily crushed, but in 1439 Erik recognised Norwegian claims, appointing a seneschal and a chancellor for Norway.

Engelbrekt's death led to the success of the aristocratic party. Although the revolt's political programme was upheld, the aristocracy, unlike Engelbrekt, was committed to the Union under one king with carefully circumscribed powers. The ideas expressed in the rejected Union Charter of 1397 now took on a new lease of life.

After long and hard negotiations at Kalmar, during which Hanseatic envoys and members of the Danish *rigsråd* mediated, Erik and the Swedish council were at length reconciled (August 1436). The terms, however, constituted a surrender by Erik rather than an agreement between equals. The governmental practice which aimed at drawing the three realms closer to one another was now considered illegal, and no binding rules for administration of the Union were adopted. When the king returned to Denmark in the autumn of 1437 it soon became clear that he could not accept his new role. He was weary of the struggle over the constitution of the Union, and he desired to see his cousin, Bugislaus IX, as his successor. According to Norwegian law Bugislaus was now, after the death of his father, Bugislaus VIII, the heir to the throne, whereas the Swedish *riksråd* could be expected to accept nothing jeopardising their free choice. The Danish council had tacitly recognised Bugislaus when, after ten years of married life, Erik and Philippa still had no family, but its members now took the Swedish point of view. A last attempt to find a way out of the crisis was made in July 1438, when Swedish and Danish councillors met at Kalmar. The agreement recognised Erik as king, maintaining that the individual states should be governed according to their national laws. They were bound to assist one another in case of war, but the country seeking help had to pay for it, as had already been established by the failed Union Charter of 1397. Now it was widely recognised that the recent agreement prescribed consultation between the countries before the election of a new king. On that occasion, it was to be decided whether the states should be ruled by one or more kings (9 July 1438).

The participants at the meeting had probably discussed the necessity of finding another king in case the constitutional conflict resulted in Erik's deposition. To both Danes and Swedes Bugislaus was unacceptable, as he was descended from neither the Danish nor the Swedish royal family. On the other hand he was the next heir to Norway, despite the fact that he was not of royal Norwegian pedigree. This is why the Kalmar agreement of 1438 did not exclude the possibility of more than one king to rule over the three states. Were this to happen, the Union would have been replaced by a mere alliance. While Erik has often been seen as a supporter of legalistic form, in this case the Swedish and Danish councillors were no less so. Against Norwegian and Swedish statute law stood Danish common law; against the aim of preserving the Union stood the Danish and Swedish principle of election from members of the royal family. Legal considerations thus led to a stalemate, and any solution would have to be a political one.

Against this background the councillors assembled at Kalmar must have considered the possibility of electing the son of Erik's sister, Duke Christoffer of the Palatinate, who like Erik, but unlike Bugislaus, was descended from the Nordic royal families. On 27 October 1438 the Danish *rigsråd* invited Christoffer to assume the task of regent of Denmark in Erik's absence, and in the same month Karl Knutsson, marshal of Sweden and ringleader of the national faction in the *riksråd*, managed to secure appointment to the analogous post. Using all kinds of threats, Karl Knutsson tried to silence his political enemies, who, in turn, addressed themselves to Erik in Gotland. Strengthened by moral and material aid and by concerted action from Norway on Erik's behalf, they sought to achieve Karl Knutsson's overthrow.

Fear of Erik rallied the Swedes to the national cause, and the short civil war was soon over. Christoffer had offered his good offices to the Swedes, but although the Diet of Tälje deposed Erik in September 1439, it elected no successor. Karl Knutsson continued to rule the country as regent.

Having accepted the Danish invitation Christoffer met Danish bishops, councillors and members of the aristocracy at Lübeck in June 1439. The Wendic towns and Duke Adolf of Schleswig took part in the negotiations. Their outcome was the deposition of Erik, and the recognition by the Wendic towns and Adolf that a new king had to be elected.

Thus, at the end of 1439, each of the three countries was ruled in its own way. Sweden had deposed Erik and was ruled by Karl Knutsson as regent; Denmark had acted likewise, but had a princely regent; only Norway remained loyal to Erik, who had agreed to appoint a seneschal and a chancellor to govern the country in his absence.

V

The Wendic towns had accepted Erik's deposition by the Danish *rigsråd*; it was thus natural for the old king to seek support from their rivals in the Netherlands. In the winter of 1439–40 Erik concluded an alliance with the overlord of the Low Countries, Duke Philip of Burgundy. In return for help in his restoration he promised extensive trading privileges to the towns in the Netherlands and agreed to pledge the castles of Elsinore and Helsingborg to Philip. In view of this danger the Danes acclaimed Christoffer as king (9 April 1440). Less than a month later Christoffer enfeoffed Adolf VIII of Holstein with the entire duchy of Schleswig. In 1441 peace was concluded between the Wendic towns, the Netherlands, Duke Adolf and Denmark (Treaty of Copenhagen, 29 August 1441). Lübeck had not succeeded in keeping vessels from the Low Countries out of the Baltic.

In 1440 Hans Laxmand, archbishop of Lund, negotiated with the Swedish councillors on Christoffer's behalf. In return for the promise of Finland and Öland as fiefs, Karl Knutsson agreed to leave the government. He accordingly resigned in the autumn of 1440, and the Swedes declared themselves in favour of Christoffer; in September 1441 he was acclaimed and crowned at Uppsala. In June 1442 the Norwegian *rigsråd* accepted him as king of Norway. In July he was crowned at Oslo and finally also at Ribe, in Denmark (1 January 1443). The Union had been restored, but in a less centralised form than under Erik. Legally speaking, the only institutions covering the three kingdoms were now Christoffer as king and a few commonly observed practices such as the recognition in all countries of a sentence of outlawry imposed in any one of them.

As Christoffer was going to be absent from Norway for long periods, he set up a royal commission to deal with complaints regarding the administration of justice, with wide powers to redress wrongs. In Sweden, a similar commission with six members was established. Its task was mainly to supervise the granting of fiefs which were to be held on the king's behalf by the commission. In addition, a treasury for the king's Swedish revenue was set up. Yet the most far-reaching development was the new code for the rural districts, which was a revision of one now almost a century old. *Kristoffers landslag* was ready by 1442. It stressed Sweden's character of constitutional elective monarchy governed by king and *riksråd* and administered by native Swedes.

At Christoffer's Danish coronation at Ribe important ecclesiastical reforms were adopted: for example, the payment of tithes to bishops was introduced where it had not been practised. Yet, in reality, things continued much as before. Many monasteries needed reform; this is why the Danish archbishop and Christoffer issued a joint manifesto calling for monastic reform. Everybody except the peasants – prelates, aristocracy and burgesses – was asked for help in attaining this noble aim. In practice, it meant that many monasteries came under the administration of laymen, losing their economic independence. At the same time, parish churches lost theirs, as their finances came to be controlled by the bishop, and no longer by the parish alone. The reforms could have rendered ecclesiastical administration more efficient, if they had been carried out with probity. However, they proved to have far-reaching, but unforeseen, consequences. The concentration of economic power in the hands of the bishops made them vulnerable. Were they to be neutralised, it would be fairly easy to gain control over the Church, especially as monasteries and parishes had lost their autonomy. The Lutheran Reformers of the 1530s were well aware of these facts.

Christoffer's Danish government was important in another respect. It moved the financial administration from Kalundborg to Copenhagen, where the king preferred to stay. The connection between royal residence and permanent central administration in one of the biggest towns of the country justifies us in considering Copenhagen as the capital of Denmark from the 1440s.

King Christoffer's foreign policy had to deal with issues in two separate regions: the North Sea and the Baltic. Although the settings were different, the two were connected, as the Wendic towns and Christoffer had interests in both.

In 1442 Bergen's local government passed statutes limiting German influence, while at the same time the *rigsråd* granted trading licences to English merchants at Bergen. Similarly, in 1443–4 a number of towns in the Low Countries, among them Amsterdam, were allowed to trade with Norway. In order to satisfy the Wendic towns, Christoffer set up a commission to hear complaints and to propose means for their redress. Against the minority view that the

Hanseatics were indispensable for the provisioning of northern Norway, the majority prevailed. The position of the Hanseatic merchants was weakened and German craftsmen were not allowed to create an organisation corresponding to the German merchants' *kontor*. A Norwegian public quality control of fish for sale was established, and a German merchant could only claim half of his debtor's catch.

Christoffer accepted these proposals by the act of 4 December 1444, but appeared to contradict himself by confirming Hanseatic liberties in Norway in 1445. In so doing, he was playing for time: the privileges represented the exception, the act the rule. Christoffer's successor would be bound by the act and not by the privileges, and if Christoffer later felt strong enough to stand up to the Wendic towns, he would be free to revoke their privileges.

Baltic affairs were more complicated. Three main issues can be discerned: the traditional desire to control trade with Novgorod; the wish to recover Gotland, controlled by King Erik; and, above all, the aim of curtailing the Wendic towns' domination of the Baltic.

Lübeck and her Wendic allies maintained relations with Erik in order to wring concessions from Christoffer. In his turn Erik held out the possession of Gotland as a bait to the Teutonic Order in return for military assistance in his restoration.

Novgorod's trade with the west was flourishing, a considerable part of it being in non-Hanseatic hands, a fact which jeopardised the traditional transit trade of the Livonian towns. In the 1440s Novgorod's policy aimed at their eviction from its trade, because the republic sought an understanding with Lithuania. This could threaten the rule of the Teutonic Order in Livonia, while in Prussia the Order was under Polish pressure. Consequently, the Livonian Master sought support where it was to be had, namely in the Nordic countries.

In the autumn of 1444 Christoffer sent Karl Knutsson from Viborg with a force against Pskov, and promised the Teutonic Order in Livonia not to allow trade to Novgorod from his kingdoms. The engagement at the side of the Teutonic Order's Livonian branch against Novgorod remained a constant factor in Christoffer's foreign policy, and that mainly for three reasons: Estonia and Livonia were a traditional sphere of interest for Sweden–Finland and Denmark, as Erik's policy had shown; further, by supporting the Teutonic Order actively, Erik's offer of Gotland in return for military aid became less tempting; finally, Danzig, which belonged to the Order, was one of the major markets for Swedish exports.

The solution of the Gotland question by military means had probably been considered seriously in the summer of 1447. Preparations ensued, but before the invasion could take place, Christoffer died, probably on 5 January 1448, leaving no issue. In home affairs he had realised the necessity to respect the new constitutional rules, while in foreign affairs he had demonstrated a subtlety which recalled Queen Margrete. His handling of Norwegian trade privileges is eloquent proof of this.

VI

After Christoffer's death both the Danes and Swedes prepared for the election of a new king by electors from the three kingdoms. In Denmark, the *rigsråd* first asked Duke Adolf of Schleswig, who was descended from the three Nordic royal families. He declined the offer, however, proposing in his stead Christian of Oldenburg, son of his sister.

In June 1448 meetings of the councils of the three countries were held for the purpose of nominating candidates for the coming election. Duke Adolf introduced his nephew to the Danish *rigsråd*, to whose members he would be more acceptable were he to marry Christoffer's widow, Dorothea of Brandenburg. In Sweden and Norway certain factions were in favour of calling back the deposed king, Erik, but the idea had been rejected in Denmark. However, when it became clear that Christian was going to be a serious candidate, the Swedes elected Karl Knutsson; he was acclaimed on 29 June 1448, and crowned on the following day. Consequently, the Danish *rigsråd* proceeded with the election of Christian as king of Denmark; acclaimed at the *landsting,* he took up government at Copenhagen in the autumn of 1448.

Norway had nominated no candidate of her own before the elections in Sweden and Denmark, and the Norwegian *rigsråd* was divided between the adherents of Karl Knutsson and those of Christian. In February, 1449, the latter obtained the majority, not least because he had promised to grant a succession charter (*håndfæstning*). In July, Christian was elected at Marstrand by members of the Norwegian council, aristocracy, bourgeoisie and peasantry, although some councillors had already committed themselves to Karl Knutsson's cause. Before the end of September his Norwegian adherents offered him the throne, which he accepted. In November, he was crowned at Trondheim. Christian was prepared to evict him by force, and asked Lübeck and the Prussian towns to establish an embargo on trade with Sweden. At a meeting at Halmstad in May 1450, the Swedish negotiators left Norway to Christian; the Union was re-established as an alliance which was to develop into a union when one of the kings died. Later, the Treaty of Bergen attached Denmark and Norway to each other under one king, stipulating rules of succession (29 August 1450).

The island of Gotland remained a problem. The Swedes had never forgotten that Valdemar IV of Denmark had conquered the island in 1361. When one sovereign ruled over both Sweden and Denmark, the political status of the island was of slight interest. But which country was to take it over when Erik died?

The old king had favoured privateering based at Gotland to such an extent that the Hanseatics and the Teutonic Order determined to fit out armed vessels in order to protect shipping. Erik tried to win over the Teutonic Order by his proposal of pledging Gotland to it, but the Order lost all interest in the scheme when Karl Knutsson's forces invaded and occupied the island (except Visby and its castle) in the summer of 1448. The town was taken in December, and Erik agreed with the Swedes to surrender the castle on 20 April 1449.

In the meantime Erik had asked the Danish government for reinforcements, declaring that he held Gotland of the Danish crown. Christian sent him victuals and troops, and in April 1449, more arrived under the command of Oluf Axelsøn Thott, together with an offer of reconciliation with the Danish government. Erik would receive three castles in Denmark and a yearly pension in return for his surrender of Visborg castle and transfer of his rights to the realms to Christian. Erik accepted, but did not sail back to Denmark. He settled down in Pomerania, where he was to die in 1459.

In the spring of 1449 both Danes and Swedes sent troops to Gotland, trying at the same time to settle the question by diplomatic means. At the end of July, Christian arrived at Visby with a considerable force, compelling the Swedes to leave the island and to accept a truce. His work well done, Christian could now marry Dorothea and celebrate his coronation at Copenhagen (28 October 1449). The final settlement of the issue was to have taken place in the coming year, but was delayed until June 1451. At this meeting, at which both kings were present, neither party was willing to yield. In September, hostilities broke out in the form of a raid from Norway across the frontier into Värmland. Indeed, the war was to be characterised mainly by raids across the frontiers, combined with Danish privateering against Swedish trade in the Baltic. In 1453, a two-year truce was concluded; Karl Knutsson used the interval to increase his resources by a resumption directed against ecclesiastical property. In 1456, Karl Knutsson's situation deteriorated when Christian captured the castles of Älvsborg, near present-day Göteborg, and Borgholm on the island of Öland. As had happened twenty years earlier, the mining districts suffered from the hostilities, which prevented the exportation of their products, and in January 1457, Archbishop Jöns of Uppsala led a revolt against the king. The prelate, supported by Stockholm, by the mining districts, by the peasants in Dalarna and Uppland and by councillors from the provinces around Lake Mälar, forced Karl Knutsson to go into exile at Danzig. In March, the *riksråd* appointed Archbishop Jöns and the Danish-born Erik Axelsøn Thott (brother of Oluf, Christian's governor in Gotland) as regents of Sweden until a king could be elected. In June, Christian arrived at Stockholm and began negotiations with the council. Having promised to observe Swedish law, privileges and liberties, he was elected, and set out on his *Eriksgata* (journey during which a king-elect was acclaimed by the individual provinces). However, nobody had foreseen that Christian would be accompanied by his two-year-old son, Hans, whom he now had recognised as heir to the thrones by both the Norwegian and Swedish councils.

In order to obtain support from the Swedish clergy Christian had had to confirm the privileges of the Church. He had also been obliged to reconcile himself with the Norwegian prelates. In 1458, Christian found it necessary to confirm the *sættargjerd* of 1277, which defined the traditional liberties of the Norwegian Church. In his Norwegian *håndfæstning*, Karl Knutsson had promised to respect the *sættargjerd*, but Christian's charter of succession had contained no such clause. Only when these questions had been settled did the Norwegian council agree to accept Christian's elder son after his death.

On 4 December 1459, Adolf, duke of Schleswig and count of Holstein, died without issue. The aristocracy of Schleswig and Holstein, the *Ritterschaft*, declared itself in favour of choosing only one ruler for the two provinces. At a joint meeting with the Danish *rigsråd*, Christian was elected duke and count after his uncle (Ribe, 2 March 1460). Christian had to recognise Adolf's debt and to make financial arrangements with the other heirs, Christian's brothers and Count Otto of Holstein–Pinneberg. In 1479–80, the king enfeoffed his queen with Holstein, which had been raised into a duchy in 1474, and Schleswig; she was thus responsible for the payment of the entire debt. This task she accomplished by 1487, a year earlier than foreseen.

As king of Sweden Christian left castles in the hands of native or naturalised governors, but he saw to it that the influential Oxenstierna–Vasa faction did not obtain too much power. Nevertheless, among Christian's governors was Danish-born Erik Axelsøn Thott, who ruled important fiefs (*len*) in Sweden and Finland.

Christian's finances did not allow him to live off the ordinary income from the crown lands or off his customs revenues. He had to levy extraordinary taxes, not least in order to raise funds for payment to his creditors in Schleswig and Holstein. From a Swedish point of view this aim was considered by many as being as irrelevant as had been Erik's obsession with the Schleswig question a generation earlier. In 1463, a new tax was levied, but when the peasants of Uppland complained to their archbishop, he exempted them from payment. The fundamental question was thus being asked once again: who was to govern Sweden – the king or an aristocratic faction? Christian, deciding not to tolerate the prelate's behaviour, imprisoned him and captured his residential castle.

In January 1464 the archbishop's cousin, Bishop Kettil of Linköping, rebelled in order to bring about the release of the archbishop. The peasants of Uppland and Dalarna, as well as the inhabitants of the *len* governed by members of the Oxenstierna–Vasa faction, rallied to the archbishop's cause, and Christian's army was defeated by the Dalarna peasants commanded by Bishop Kettil. The insurgents decided to offer the crown to Karl Knutsson, if he would rule according to Swedish law. He accepted and returned to Sweden. He was soon to realise that he was governed by the same faction that had rebelled against him seven years before. After negotiations with Christian, he managed to have the archbishop set free, but when Karl Knutsson tried to liberate himself from the faction's embrace, it took to military action. Karl was defeated and forced to resign, but was allowed to keep his royal title and two Finnish *len* for his lifetime (January 1465).

The victory of the Oxenstierna–Vasa faction aroused opposition from another dynastic group uniting the Axelsønner (Thott), important landowners and politicians in both Denmark and Sweden and Karl Knutsson's relatives. Whereas the various aristocratic factions were prepared to accept a Danish king who would further their interests, the burgesses of Stockholm and the peasantry of Dalarna found the idea of an alien king intolerable. In November 1466, the nationalists invited Karl Knutsson to return to the throne; the Axelsønner had to support his cause, as they did not feel strong enough to resist Christian, the Oxenstierna–Vasa faction and the nationalists at the same time. The invitation to Karl was repeated in the autumn of 1467, and before the end of the year he was back in power. His interests were now bound to those of the Axelsønner, whereas Christian had to support the rival faction and, if possible, estrange the Axelsønner from Karl. The king of Sweden died in 1470, which led Christian to prepare a campaign in order to win back his lost kingdom. Karl's nephew, Sten Sture, had been elected *riksföreståndare*, and he and the *riksråd* negotiated without result with Christian. In the following summer Christian arrived in Stockholm with a fleet. An agreement was made which gave him clear advantages in the struggle for control over Sweden. Sten Sture and his cousin, Nils Sture, left the negotiations in order to mobilise support against Christian, who was acclaimed by the peasants of Uppland. In the decisive battle at Brunkeberg, near Stockholm (10 October 1471), Christian was defeated and left for Denmark.

Whereas the Oxenstierna–Vasa faction's field of interest was limited to Sweden–Finland, the Axelsønner were more comprehensive. Their father, Axel Pedersøn Thott, had governed Varberg castle on Erik's behalf, and he was the last governor to leave his cause (1441). His sons, among whom six became politically important, held together, always helping one another and keeping their family interests well to the fore. Their father had acquired estates in both

Sweden and Denmark, and his sons continued this policy. Three of them – Erik, Aage and Iver – married Swedish ladies, thus obtaining double nationality. All six sons endeavoured to acquire land near their fiefs, which were mainly situated near the principal routes of communication. Their entrepreneurial interests included agriculture, animal husbandry and trade; their commercial activities, in particular, widened their spheres of interest to most of the Baltic. That Gotland and Viborg castle were fiefs of extraordinary importance to the brothers can be a matter of no surprise: in 1449, King Erik surrendered Gotland to Oluf, whom Iver succeeded in 1464; Erik Axelsøn, on his part, governed Nyköping in Sweden and the Finnish castles of Tavastehus and Viborg. With two of the brothers in charge of Gotland and Viborg, Christian could delegate his intervention in Estonia–Livonia to them, thus continuing the Baltic policy of his predecessors.

The fact that the Axelsønner had interests in both Denmark and Sweden–Finland caused them to change their allegiance when it served their interests. Despite their collaboration with Christian during the early 1460s, the victory of the Oxenstierna–Vasa faction over the two rival kings in 1464–5 led the brothers into matrimonial alliances with Karl Knutsson, his daughter marrying the widower, Iver Axelsøn, and his nephew, Sten Sture, being engaged to Aage Axelsøn's daughter. The nationalistic programme advocated by an important part of Karl Knutsson's supporters obliged the Axelsønner to commit themselves more firmly to Karl Knutsson's cause. Christian's sequestration for their Danish fiefs 1467–8 had the same effect.

As king of Sweden for the third time Karl Knutsson had granted vast powers to Iver Axelsøn, who continued to rule over Gotland after his rupture with Christian. The Swedish castles should have been accessible to him on King Karl's behalf, but on the king's death (15 May 1470) his nephew, Sten Sture, was elected *riksföreståndare*, perhaps in order to hold together the coalition of aristocrats and nationalists. The Axelsønner were ready to invite Christian back to the Swedish throne, but on condition that he be reconciled with the brothers and restore them to their fiefs. When Christian finally arrived at Stockholm, he came with considerable force and made no concessions to the Axelsønner. In order to save at least their fiefs in Sweden–Finland, they had to espouse the Swedish cause once more.

After the victory won at Brunkeberg the Axelsønner played a leading role as governors of important castles. Erik and Laurens were in charge of Finnish castles, while Iver ruled over Gotland and held Stegeborg as fief. Moreover, in the early 1470s, they were to take charge of Swedish policy in the eastern Baltic, as they had done on Christian's behalf ten years earlier.

In 1474, the Swedish clergy declared that a legally elected *riksföreståndare* should be considered sacred, as if he were an anointed king. Strengthened by this moral support and by the effects of his policy of filling vacant fiefs with his own adherents, Sten Sture strove to render himself less dependent on the Axelsønner. Before his death, in 1481, Erik Axelsøn transferred his fief, Viborg castle, to his surviving brothers, Laurens and Iver, an arrangement which Sten Sture was not ready to recognise. The negotiations with the new Danish king, Christian's son, Hans, led Sten Sture to accommodation with Iver, now the sole surviving Axelsøn, after the death of Laurens in 1483. In his negotiations with Sten Sture (1483) Iver Axelsøn surrendered both his and his brother's fiefs in Finland, except for Raseburg, but obtained Öland in their place. Iver's influence had been limited to the central Baltic. Hans promised to restore Iver to Sølvitsborg castle, which his father had confiscated in 1467, but in return Iver was to renew the recognition, made in 1476, that he held Gotland as a fief of the Danish king and assist Hans in winning the Swedish crown.

The conditions for Iver's restoration to Sølvitsborg had not changed, and Iver attempted in vain to overthrow Sten Sture. Having pacified leading members of the *riksråd* by concessions, the *riksföreståndare* confiscated Iver Axelsøn's remaining fiefs except Gotland, to which Iver withdrew. When he felt unsafe there, he gave up the island to King Hans (1487) and settled down at his estate at Lillø; he died in the same year.

At the beginning of his reign Christian had tried to limit the Hansa merchants' influence at Bergen; at the same time he had endeavoured to prevent the English from sailing through the Sound. This measure hit the Prussian towns, but was condoned by Lübeck. Christian's aspirations to the Swedish throne told him not to estrange himself from Lübeck, and Icelandic interests urged him to show the English that any abuse committed by them in Iceland would cause retaliation elsewhere.

Complaints against the governor of Bergen castle, Olav Nilsson, led Christian to look into his administration in 1453, and as a result he was removed. As Christian needed Hanseatic support, or, at least, neutrality in the conflict with Sweden, he had to make concessions to the German merchants; among other things, Norwegian local government officials were to assist the Germans in the collection of debts. But Olav Nilsson, who had been restored to office, continued his policy of confrontation with the Hanseatics; on 1 September 1455, riots, led by the German merchants, broke out at Bergen. By the time they were over, Olav Nilsson and the bishop of Bergen had been killed and the monastery of Munkeliv burnt down. Although the secular government, which needed Hanseatic neutrality in the conflict with Sweden, did not punish the riots too severely, the Church demanded extensive reparations from the German community at Bergen.

As Karl Knutsson had friendly relations with Danzig, Christian saw his interest in an entente with Lübeck; this was to be a constant feature of international relations in the Baltic for the remaining part of the 1450s and 1460s.

Christian's relations with England dominated a considerable part of his government's foreign affairs in the same years. In 1456, Charles VII of France and Christian concluded an offensive and defensive alliance against England, and, through French mediation, negotiations between Scotland and the Nordic countries were taken up in 1460. James III's minority postponed the conclusion of a similarly motivated treaty until 1468, when it was decided that Christian's daughter, Margrete, should marry the king of Scots. The Northern Isles – Orkney and Shetland – were pledged as part of her dowry, but the Danish–Norwegian government, in spite of repeated attempts, never succeeded in redeeming them during the next two centuries.

VII

The battle of Brunkeberg (1471) was a turning-point in Scandinavian history. Although the Union was restored in 1497 and again in 1520, each time it lasted for only a few years. For the next century, Sweden–Finland was a power with mainly Baltic interests, whereas Denmark–Norway was concerned with the North Sea as well.

In both Nordic states the authority of central government increased considerably at the end of the fifteenth century. Administration was made more efficient by the keeping of registers with copies of outgoing letters, but above all, the increasing use of firearms gave governments a definite advantage over everybody else. Only they could afford artillery in considerable quantity and the castles of the aristocracy could not resist an attack with cannon. While elaborate systems of defence might protect their strongholds against peasant riots or feuding neighbours, they could not do so against governments determined to compel headstrong aristocrats to obedience. In Denmark–Norway this tendency was reinforced by the creation of a genuine navy comprising ships built for war, not merely merchant ships adapted for that purpose. Although a royal fighting ship is referred to as early as 1414, the wars against Sweden and Lübeck during the first decade of the sixteenth century made the government appreciate the need for a bigger navy. Since vessels could not be acquired abroad because of the wars, they had to be constructed within the kingdom.

By about 1500, many towns had a grammar school. This was the situation in Finland, Sweden, Norway and Denmark; in Iceland, schools were attached to the cathedrals and monasteries. Both states founded a university in the 1470s: Uppsala in 1477 and Copenhagen in 1479. From the 1480s, printers worked for the Nordic markets, some even establishing themselves in Denmark and Sweden. While their works were mainly liturgical books for individual dioceses, they also produced practical legal texts, historical works and fiction, an indication that literacy was spreading.

In both states governments encouraged the development of towns, not least for fiscal reasons. Swedish law had given German town dwellers separate representation on urban councils, but this was abolished in 1471. In Denmark, integration was likewise to be encouraged in 1475 and 1477 when the German merchants' guilds were abolished: Germans were welcome, but they would have to enter the Danish merchants' guilds, and they were not allowed to remain in the country during winter. Should they desire to do so, they would have to settle there for good, eventually marrying Danish women and paying taxes like everybody else. Related measures were taken in Iceland, which was subject to the competition of Englishmen, merchants of Hamburg and Lübeck merchants from Bergen. About 1480 the Icelandic assembly, the *althing*, reserved the right of residence during winter to those foreigners born in the countries under the king of Norway. The so-called Píning's verdict (1490) confirmed this decision. In the same year, however, a treaty was concluded with England, allowing English merchants to trade in Iceland and in any Norwegian town, but in Denmark only in certain localities in the Sound region. A few years later the treaty between James IV of Scotland, Hans of Denmark–Norway and their realms allowed the subjects of either king to trade freely in the other's dominions. Clearly, Hans's government wanted to counterbalance the Hanseatics without surrending to English influence, while at the same time securing supplies of foreign goods.

Christian I died in May 1481, but the succession of his elder son, Hans, proved difficult, although he had already been recognised as future king by both Norway and Sweden in 1458 and as future ruler of Schleswig–Holstein in 1466. In Denmark, where Hans had already been recognised as future king in Christian's lifetime, he was acclaimed in the spring of 1482.

Christian's rule had aroused criticism, which manifested itself after his death. The Norwegian council wanted a future king to be more firmly bound. Consequently, in the autumn of 1481, the Norwegian *rigsråd* made the mainly tactical move of taking up contacts with the Swedish *riksråd*, which led to a treaty of alliance in February 1482. In Sweden, however, the men in power became more sympathetic to the idea of union and offered to mediate between the Danes and Norwegians; in return, the latter were to participate in a meeting at Halmstad in January 1483, in order to elect a new king. However, when the delegates assembled, it was found that only Norwegians and Danes had been empowered to carry out an election. The Swedish attitude was rightly seen as an evasion of responsibility, so that the Norwegian delegates joined their Danish colleagues. Together they elected Hans, who accepted a rather restrictive charter (*håndfæstning*, the so-called *Halmstad reces*, or agreement) on 1

February 1483. Hans was crowned at Copenhagen at Whitsun 1483 and at Trondheim on 20 July of the same year.

In the preamble to the charter Hans promised to recognise its articles as the basis for his administration. If he did this, the Swedes would accept him as king, but, until then, its terms would be applicable in Norway and Denmark alone. The domestic affairs of each country were to be kept separate from those of the other realms, and the king was to regain control over lands and revenues belonging to the crown of Norway. Fiefs and castles were to be given only to members of the country's aristocracy, and neither the royal family nor the unfree estates were allowed to acquire 'free' land. In Norway no foreigner was to hold office in town government or to act as a judge appointed by the king (*lagmand*).

The most interesting clauses are those concerning the Norwegian economy. Minting was to be taken up again, but coins should have the same value as those struck in Denmark. All foreign merchants were to be allowed to visit Bergen and other Norwegian towns, but only if customs dues were paid; they were not authorised to interfere in the affairs of urban craftsmen, of the crown or the Church, nor to acquire rural property as security for loans. Clearly, the government wanted to keep not only agriculture and animal husbandry, but also sawmilling, which was expanding in the late fifteenth century, free of foreign capital. Merchants from the Low Countries were to be permitted to sail to Norway, as they had been accustomed to do. Finally, Hanseatic merchants were strictly forbidden to sail to Iceland, where Hans promised to appoint only native governors. In August 1483 it was decided to discuss Swedish adherence to the Union. The outcome of the ensuing meeting at Kalmar was a charter, the so-called *Kalmar reces* (7 September 1483) adopted by the Swedish participants alone. However, it contained some conditions for the election of Hans as king of Sweden, which, in several respects, restricted royal powers even more than the Halmstad agreement. Hans never sealed it.

Towards the end of the Middle Ages trade with the Low Countries, which depended on exports of corn from the Baltic region, became increasingly important. To the Nordic countries, trade with that area presented notable advantages: its merchants could offer the same goods as the Hanseatics, but they did not interfere in Scandinavian politics as did the Wendic towns. The foundation of Nya Lödöse (1474) in the Göteborg region was to attract ships and merchants from the Low Countries, exactly as did the foundation of Göteborg a century and a half later, while in Norway, they were played off against the Hanseatics in order to limit the latter's influence. Moreover, in the decades around 1500 Danish trade was changing direction. The Low Countries became ever more interesting as partners – the export of Danish cattle was specially important – with the consequence that the Hanseatics, above all Lübeck and the other Wendic towns, lost ground.

During the 1480s, Sten Sture's government pursued the traditional Swedish–Finnish policy of infiltration in Livonia. An agreement with Riga was concluded in 1485 directed against the Livonian branch of the Teutonic Order; the Swedish scheme was thwarted, however, when Riga made peace with its archbishop and with the Teutonic Order in 1491. In the previous year Sweden had begun to co-operate with Lübeck. The export of Swedish copper was thus secured through an agreement which was also profitable to the German town: in 1492, 25 per cent of its Baltic imports were of Swedish origin.

The Danish government realised the danger inherent in Sweden's friendly relations with Livonia, as these could jeopardise free trade with Russia. Hans, who had ruled over Gotland since 1487, concluded an alliance with Ivan III of Muscovy in 1493: he needed Russian support against Sweden, and Ivan wanted Danish assistance against Lithuania. To the dismay of the Hanseatics, Ivan closed the German settlement at Novgorod in 1494 (it was to be reopened twenty years later) and in the following years the Russians raided eastern Finland. Within Sweden, opposition to Sten Sture grew, as did the desire for peace with Russia and for a settlement with Denmark–Norway, even at the cost of accepting Hans as king.

By 1497 the political situation in Sweden had further deteriorated, and hostilities broke out between the *riksråd*, on one side, and Sten Sture and his popular followers on the other. At that moment Hans declared war on Sten Sture (13 March 1497), defeating the peasant levy of Dalarna near Stockholm. Sten Sture now recognised Hans, and in return was granted large fiefs: Nyköping and all Finland. On his part, Hans promised a general amnesty; he would also observe the stipulations of the Kalmar charter. On 26 November 1497, he was crowned as king of Sweden, while his son, Christian, was recognised as his successor in 1499.

In his determination to pacify Sten Sture, Hans had forgotten to remunerate the councillors – among them Svante Nilsson, who called himself Sture, but in reality belonged to the family Natt och Dag – who had supported his cause. Hans would soon regret this when it became apparent that the agreement which he had made with Sten Sture would not last. In 1500 the bishop of Linköping died, and, not without Sten Sture's assistance, Hemming Gad, former Swedish resident at Rome, was elected to the see. A staunch nationalist, Gad brought about the collaboration of Sten Sture and Svante Nilsson. On 1 August 1501, a confederation was established which meant the beginning of the revolt against Hans. The king was deposed, and Sten Sture once again assumed the post of *riksföreståndare*. Swedish dissatisfaction was further nourished by fear of Muscovy, which appeared to be co-operating against Sweden–Finland, whose eastern frontier was disputed by the Russians. The Swedish insurgents also found a certain support in Norway, where Knut

Alvsson had inherited a blood-feud with Henrik Krummedige, leader of the pro-Danish faction. Alvsson was to make common cause with the Swedish insurgents. His first incursion into Norway (autumn 1501) was driven back, but he returned in February 1502. Hans now sent his son, Christian, who had been acclaimed heir to the Norwegian throne in 1489, and he soon managed to halt the rebellion. Krummedige arranged a meeting with Alvsson, but, in spite of a safe-conduct granted to him, had him killed (18 August 1502).

In Sweden, Stockholm had fallen to the insurgents by October 1501; only the castle was held by Queen Christina. After a heroic defence she surrendered it in the spring of 1502, a few days before Hans came to her assistance, but in vain. Hans sailed back to Denmark; his queen was only released late in 1503, after Hanseatic mediation. Soon afterwards Sten Sture died (14 December 1503) to be succeeded by Svante Nilsson.

Hostilities were resumed in spring 1504; Kalmar castle was still held by the Danes, while the town had surrendered to Svante Nilsson. In June, a truce was concluded, the intention being to solve the differences at a meeting to be held at Kalmar in June 1505. Hans attended with members of the Danish and Norwegian *rigsråd*; representatives of the emperor, certain German princes; the king of Scots also appeared, but the Swedes did not. After two weeks of waiting a court was constituted by the Norwegian and Danish councillors, who found that Hans was Sweden's lawful king. The *Reichskammergericht* confirmed the verdict in October 1506, as did the emperor shortly afterwards, forbidding the subjects of the Empire to assist the Swedish leaders.

Despite this, Sweden was not entirely isolated, being invited by Poland to join an alliance with Livonia against Russia in May 1506. Yet, on 7 October, Lübeck promised not to support Sweden, and to work for Hans's restoration (agreement of Segeberg, confirmed in July 1507). In the late summer of 1507 Lübeck and other towns offered their mediation, forbidding Swedish ships to call at their ports. In the meanwhile, hostilities were to continue in 1508 and for most of 1509. Danish superiority at sea made coastal raids possible in Sweden and Finland. One such, Otte Rud's attack on Åbo (Turku) in August 1509, became renowned for its cruelty. In early 1509 Hans's Russian ally invaded Finland; the effects of the suspension of Swedish trade with the Hanseatics were multiplied by dearth in 1507–8, by a poor harvest in 1509 and by plague. Sweden was thus obliged to conclude the Peace of Copenhagen (August 1509) and to pay Denmark a yearly tribute until Hans or his son, Christian, became king of Sweden. In the meantime Öland and Kalmar were to be held by Denmark.

Lübeck, which had concluded a trade agreement with Sweden in September 1509, still felt that the Danish friendship towards merchants of the Low Countries threatened her vital interests. Consequently, when Sweden renounced the Peace of Copenhagen, Lübeck soon followed, declaring war on Denmark on 21 April 1510, and concluding a formal alliance with Sweden against Denmark in July of the same year. As Sweden made a simultaneous truce with Russia, Denmark–Norway now had to rely on the monarchy's own resources. When war broke out at the beginning of the sailing season 1510, Lübeck showed its superiority at sea. Hans lost Kalmar and Borgholm castle in Öland, but German and Swedish incursions into Danish territory were thrown back. Furthermore, an energetic programme of securing armaments and recruiting mercenaries abroad made the Danish navy in 1511 as efficient as that of the Wendic towns, and, early in the year, Prince Christian raided western Sweden from Norway. Lübeck tried to obtain peace by offering an annual tribute to Hans, who, in return, was to allow only a restricted number of vessels from the Low Countries to enter the Baltic each year. Declaring himself a partisan of the freedom of the Danish seas, Hans refused.

In the meantime, Svante Nilsson's war became ever less popular with the members of the *riksråd*. When he was asked to resign, he led a campaign rallying the people to his cause, but died suddenly on 2 January 1512. The party which favoured peace won over the *riksråd* to its views, and peace was concluded at Malmø on 23 April 1512. The treaty was in most respects a confirmation of the Treaty of Copenhagen; the decision concerning the rights of Hans and Prince Christian to Sweden was postponed until the coming year.

Svante Nilsson's son, Sten 'Sture', succeeded his father as *riksföreståndare* (against the candidacy of Erik Trolle) in July 1512. After his election he strove to circumvent his agreements with the *riksråd* on the pretext that his mandate had been given him not only by the council, but also by the people, probably a deliberate confusion of the distinct ceremonies of election and acclamation.

On 20 February 1513, Hans died at Aalborg, and was succeeded by his son, Christian, who had been elected heir to Denmark and acclaimed as such in 1487 (confirmed in 1497 and 1512), and had been recognised in Norway in 1489. At Hans's death, he had already ruled Norway with viceregal powers between 1506 and 1512. One of his first tasks as viceroy had been to confirm the privileges of foreign merchants at Bergen. In 1507 Lübeck had agreed to establish an embargo on trade with Sweden, and Christian had to be more accommodating with the Hanseatics. Merchants from the Netherlands lost their right to remain in Norway during the winter months, and the German craftsmen of Bergen were placed under the control of German merchants. Furthermore, the Hanseatic monopoly of trade north of Bergen was confirmed. Early in 1508 Christian abolished Rostock's privileges at Oslo and Tunsberg. The measure proved fruitful, as it stimulated the formation of a native trading class.

As viceroy Christian had shown that he could rule a country and that he expected loyal collaboration from both clergy and secular aristocracy. Not all found this achievement to their liking. Hoping that he would be more accommodating, certain members of the Danish *rigsråd* offered the throne to Christian's uncle, Frederik, who refused it. In June 1513, negotiations began at Copenhagen about Christian's *håndfæstning* and about Sweden's fulfilment of the Treaty of Malmø. A meeting in the following year was demanded in order to answer the question whether Sweden was prepared to accept Hans or Christian as king. The Swedish delegates, however, had not been empowered to recognise Christian as king of Sweden, so it was agreed to postpone the decision until June 1515 and to keep the peace between the realms until Easter 1516. In the meantime in Norway, the German establishment at Bergen maintained its monopoly of trade with northern Norway and Iceland against competition from Bremen and Hamburg. Christian's conciliatory attitude towards the Wendic towns was caused by his need for their support in order to obtain the Swedish crown. When he visited Norway in 1514 on the occasion of his coronation, Rostock sought the grant of new privileges from him. The burgesses of Oslo, and especially Tunsberg, however, were adamant: they wanted to keep the advantages acquired by them in 1508. Some months later, when Christian was negotiating an alliance with the duke of Mecklenburg about military aid to win Sweden, the duke made the grant of privileges to Rostock a condition of it: Christian was obliged to acquiesce, sacrificing the interests of the Norwegian burgesses to his Swedish undertaking.

The contents of Christian's *håndfæstning* were the subject of important negotiations between the prince (represented by the chancellor) and members of the Norwegian and Danish *rigsråd*. As had been the case in 1483, this *håndfæstning* applied to both Norway and Denmark. A series of demands had been submitted by the aristocracy, most of them intended to secure a respectable income for its members. Since land and fiefs were being concentrated in the hands of the highest ranks of the aristocracy, it could now be difficult for a gentry family to keep up with Rosencrantz and Guildenstern. Thus, as in 1483, fiefs and castles were reserved for members of the native aristocracy. In Norway, however, local conditions could necessitate exceptions. The Norwegians had desired that the same clause should be valid for both countries, but Christian had clearly wanted to keep open the possibility of appointing Danes to Norwegian fiefs. As in 1483, neither the royal family nor the unfree estates were allowed to acquire land from the aristocracy, who in return were prevented from acquiring crown lands. A new clause now allowed the clergy and the aristocracy to trade directly with foreign merchants, although the principle had already been recognised in Danish, Norwegian and Swedish common law. The monetary union between Norway and Denmark was maintained, but the currency was aligned to the Rhenish florin, liberating it from the monetary domination of Lübeck.

Regarding appointments to offices in the Church, the charter represented a compromise: the king was not allowed to exercise any pressure upon electors, and he was bound to respect the outcome of elections. On the other hand, he could be an ally for the native Churches against the practice of papal appointments to offices, frequently of persons belonging to the Roman *curia*. These seldom took up their posts; instead, they received the entire income from the office, paying only part of it to the vicar who acted for them.

Finally, the *håndfæstning* allowed the people to see to it that the constitution was respected if remonstrances from the *rigsråd* to the king proved to be of no avail. Hans's *håndfæstning* had contained a similar clause, but only as regards violations of the *habeas corpus* principle. Clearly, the experience of Hans's administration necessitated further guarantees against unconstitutional behaviour. The terms of this *håndfæstning* were sealed on 22 July 1513. Almost a year later, Christian was crowned king of Denmark, and on the same day (11 June 1514) he was married by proxy to Elizabeth, sister of Charles, later to become emperor. As the embargo against Sweden had proved, the backing of the emperor could still be useful. Charles and Elizabeth had been brought up in the Low Countries: Christian's marriage shows how important the connection with that area had become to both the Danish and, to a lesser extent, the Norwegian economy.

In 1512, Sten Sture had been elected *riksföreståndare* in Sweden. During the five years following his election he strove to increase his power, not least by seeking popular support for his policy against the *riksråd*, by augmenting the resources of his office, and by granting important fiefs, mainly to his political allies. Like his predecessors, he recognised the political force of the mining districts, especially in Dalarna, and of Stockholm, in both cases a consequence of their economic development.

In October 1514, the ageing archbishop of Uppsala resigned in favour of Gustav Trolle, son of Sten Sture's opponent in the election of 1512. No doubt the new archbishop was intended to reorganise the council's constitutional party in opposition to Sten Sture. Consecrated at Rome in 1515, he obtained on that occasion the right to be served by a force of 400 armed men. In addition, the pope confirmed him in the possession of Stäket (castle and fief), allowing him to lay interdict on those who tried to contest it. When Sten Sture maintained that the fief of Stäket belonged to the realm, the prelate would neither discuss the question nor swear fealty to the *riksföreståndare* for the fief. In the autumn of 1516 Sten Sture laid siege to the castle; not all members of the council approved this measure, but he succeeded in mobilising popular opinion against the archbishop, so that, in certain parts of the archdiocese, the peasants refused to pay their tithes.

In 1513 a new meeting of Danes, Norwegians and Swedes was fixed for June 1515, to apply the clauses of the treaty of Malmø. As the Swedes, who knew that their choice lay between the payment of tribute and the recognition of Christian as their king, demanded further negotiations with the evident aim of postponing a decision, the meeting agreed to prolong the truce until Easter 1517 and to fix a meeting for February of that year.

Christian used the delay to find support abroad. The Hanseatics promised to establish an embargo on trade with Sweden, if the country refused to carry out the treaty, and in 1516 Christian renewed the Russian alliance. Nor was Sten Sture idle: he tried to have Christian's title to the Swedish crown declared invalid by the pope, who suggested that the problem be resolved by a verdict. This Sten Sture refused, although he was willing to accept the idea of pontifical mediation.

In the summer of 1517 a Danish fleet raided the Swedish and Finnish coasts; it landed at Stockholm in order to relieve the besieged archbishop, but was defeated (13 August 1517). In November of the same year a diet met at Stockholm at which clergy and aristocracy, Stockholm's town government and representatives of the people, as well as Gustav Trolle, were present. At the meeting Archbishop Trolle, held responsible for the Danish attack and accused of high treason, was deposed on those grounds and his castle at Stäket was ordered to be demolished. Further, those present at the diet formed a confederacy, promising one another assistance, even at the Roman *curia*, in case of excommunication by the archbishop or his chapter (23 November 1517). In the following month Stäket was taken (to be subsequently demolished) and the archbishop resigned (to be held as Sten Sture's prisoner).

In 1518 Christian again made a seaborne attack on Stockholm, but was defeated. A truce was concluded, but was renounced by Christian, who took with him to Denmark six hostages left as security for a personal meeting with Sten Sture. In 1519, Christian's forces won back Öland and barred Sweden's access to the west, where a new fortress was constructed at Älvsborg.

The deposition of Archbishop Trolle led to legal action at the Roman *curia* on his behalf: Sten Sture and his adherents were ordered to seek ecclesiastical absolution from the excommunication incurred for the demolition of Stäket and the imprisonment of the archbishop. If they proved recalcitrant, interdict was to be laid over Sweden and assistance could, if necessary, be asked from the secular arm, that is, from Christian.

Early in January 1520, a Norwegian force marched into Dalsland and Värmland, while Otte Krumpen invaded Sweden from Halland with a large army. The main force met Sten Sture's troops on the frozen Lake Åsunden, where the Swedes were defeated and Sten Sture himself was wounded. The invading army arrived at Tiveden at the end of the month, overcoming the

Swedish resistance after fierce fighting; from there it marched on to Västerås. In the meantime Sten Sture had died from his wounds (February 1520).

His death opened the way for a compromise between his opponents in the *riksråd* and the leaders of Christian's army. After some two weeks' negotiations, Christian was recognised as king of Sweden; in return a general amnesty was granted. The new king was to govern Sweden with the assistance of the council and according to Swedish law; the castles were to be held of the *riksråd*, which was to help Christian to compel Stockholm to obedience, were the capital not to respect the agreement (*Uppsala dagtingan*, 6 March 1520, ratified by Christian on 31 March).

Commanded as it was by Sten Sture's widow, Christina Gyllenstierna, Stockholm did not agree. Moreover, a peasant army was gathering: it met the invading army on Good Friday (6 April) near Uppsala, where it was defeated after very hard fighting. In the coming weeks hostilities continued, while Christian prepared to sail to Stockholm with a fleet. It arrived in May, and siege was laid to the capital. It was September before Stockholm's defenders were ready to negotiate. Hemming Gad, once Sten Sture's close collaborator and Christian's hostage, had espoused Christian's cause; he managed to convince the defenders, who surrendered the capital on honourable terms (5 September). Two days later, Christian entered the Swedish capital.

VIII

The *riksråd*, convoked to meet on 30 October, declared on the following day that Christian was lawful heir to Sweden. On 4 November he was crowned at Stockholm.

When the festivities had lasted for some days, a complaint from the restored archbishop, Gustav Trolle, was produced. In it the prelate asked on behalf of himself, his predecessor and the bishop of Västerås that a number of notorious heretics – notably the late Sten Sture and his widow – should be punished for their crimes, in particular for the imprisonment of Trolle himself and the demolition of Stäket. During further negotiations Christina Gyllenstierna produced the confederation charter of 23 November 1517, but only the bishop of Linköping could prove that he had sealed it under pressure.

It was obvious that the confederates were heretics; not only had they fought against and deposed an archbishop, but they had promised each other to contest excommunication or interdict, that is the very authority of the Church. Furthermore, a proven violator of the Church incurred anathema, and according to Swedish law was liable to death, if he did not reconcile himself with the Church within a certain time. On the other hand, heresy, too, implied *ipso facto* anathema.

The definition of the confederates as notorious heretics dispensed Christian from keeping the promised amnesty; it would also allow him to confiscate property belonging to those convicted. Even persons who had collaborated with Christian (for example, Bishop Matthew of Strängnäs and Hemming Gad) were executed because they had agreed to the confederation. Nevertheless, Christina Gyllenstierna and her mother were pardoned, suffering only imprisonment rather than execution.

The total number of victims in the 'massacre of Stockholm' (*Stockholms Blodbad*) on 8 November and the following days was about eighty-two; others were executed later. Cruel as it was, the *Blodbad* was no lawless slaughter. Its illegality is to be sought elsewhere, because in some cases people were executed although their guilt had not been well established.

It is impossible to identify the instigator of the *Blodbad*: Christian must share responsibility with the bishops who were plaintiffs or served as experts. All four bishops in the latter group witnessed the experts' declaration with a seal and not merely their signet ring; in all likelihood they had been prepared in advance.

One of Christian's Swedish hostages, Gustav Vasa, had succeeded in escaping from his Danish captivity in 1519. After visiting Lübeck, he returned to Sweden in the spring of 1520; by the end of the year he was calling the people to revolt. In January 1521 he was elected commander of the region of Dalarna, defeating Gustav Trolle in Uppland, while the people of Dalarna beat back Christian's governor of Stockholm castle. The insurgents' victories showed that their movement had to be taken seriously. Aristocrats rallied to their cause, and in August, 1521, Gustav Vasa was elected *riksföreståndare*.

In 1522, the important castles of Kalmar, Stockholm and Älvsborg, as well as those in Finland, were still controlled by Christian's commanders. With Hanseatic naval assistance, Gustav Vasa now conquered the castles, and entered Stockholm after his election as king of Sweden on 6 June 1523.

In the meantime revolt had also broken out in Denmark; on 21 December a confederation was formed with the purpose of offering Duke Frederik of Schleswig–Holstein the throne. At the end of the year Lübeck agreed to furnish troops for an attack on Denmark in Duke Frederik's name. On 20 January 1523, the rebellion was formally proclaimed at the *landsting* at Viborg, and on 29 January Frederik accepted the Danish crown. He invaded Jutland and was acclaimed at Viborg on 26 March. In April, Funen surrendered without fighting, and on 13 April Christian and his family left for the Low Countries. During the coming months one commander after the other gave up his castle to Frederik, who now tried to win over to his side those loyal to Christian by a combination of pressure and bribery.

Copenhagen capitulated on 6 January 1524; in August 1523 Frederik had sealed his Danish *håndfæstning*, but was crowned only one year later. In Norway, the *rigsråd* revoked its allegiance to Christian, when it had ascertained Frederik's willingness to accept its claims; he was accordingly elected on 23 August 1524.

Why did Christian's rule collapse so quickly and at the moment when he seemed to be at the height of his power? No doubt his campaign to win Sweden had strained his finances to the utmost. Furthermore, when that country had been conquered, he alienated the Hanseatic towns with an audacious plan for a Nordic trading society. Its purpose was the collection of goods from all parts of the Nordic countries as well as from Russia; they should be offered for sale through the company's factory in western Europe (probably in the Low Countries) where the necessary goods for importation could be obtained. Lübeck's trade would thus be confined to the Baltic, and Swedish iron would no longer be taken to Danzig and re-exported on westbound ships. If Hanseatic international trade (outside the Baltic) were to survive, Christian's project had to be stopped. Consequently, the Hansa supported the Swedish revolt, and Lübeck took sides with Duke Frederik. For Lübeck, Christian's trading society was as dangerous as had been King Erik's alliance with Poland–Lithuania a century earlier.

Christian had carried out many reforms, notably two important statutes (1522) for the Danish towns and countryside respectively. All exports of cattle to Germany should pass through Ribe; similarly, corn from the Danish provinces was to be exported by way of Copenhagen, Elsinore, Landskrona or Malmø. Clearly, the intention was to make Denmark into a furnisher to the Netherlands, as the corn trade was to be concentrated along the international sailing route through the Sound. Moreover, urban government was remodelled and although the government had had to accommodate the aristocracy and the clergy for political reasons, many new laws changed the daily life of peasants and burgesses. Reforms were sometimes necessary, but too many enforced during a short period provoked a reaction and led to revolution. Consequently, Christian's statutes were abolished as soon as he went into exile in 1523.

IX

The overthrow of Christian, both in Sweden–Finland and in Denmark–Norway, had been carried out with Hanseatic assistance. In 1523 Gustav Vasa granted extensive privileges to Lübeck, Danzig and other Hanseatic towns which were exempted from paying customs in Sweden. Further, Swedish merchants were not allowed to trade beyond the Danish straits, these rules being complemented in 1526 by a Swedish–Prussian commercial treaty.

In 1531 Christian II invaded Norway with support from the Low Countries, which once more induced Frederik I to align himself with Lübeck. On 2 May 1532, the Danish–Norwegian government concluded an agreement with Lübeck valid for ten years. The Hanseatic town promised to aid Frederik in his war against Christian; in return Frederik undertook to attack vessels from the Low Countries in the Baltic, but only once Christian's forces in Norway had been beaten. By a provisional agreement with Frederik's forces (9 July 1532) Christian had ceded Norway, but obtained a safe-conduct to negotiations with Frederik. When Christian came to Copenhagen, relying on the safe-conduct, he was not allowed ashore, as the council had decided to keep him prisoner for life. At the end of July, he was sent to Sønderborg castle, where he was kept until 1549. He was then transferred to Kalundborg, where he lived in milder custody till his death in 1559.

Frederik's death in April 1533 complicated the situation because his Lutheran son, Duke Christian, was unacceptable to the still Catholic majority of the aristocracy. For the same reason, the interim government by the *rigsråd* would not lend support to Protestant Lübeck. Consequently, the latter's troops, commanded by Count Christoffer of Oldenburg, invaded Denmark in 1534 in order to restore Christian II, who still had followers in the bourgeoisie and among the peasants. In the ensuing civil war ('Grevens Fejde' or 'the Count's War', 1534–6) Duke Christian emerged the victor. He sealed his *håndfæstning* in 1536, and was crowned on 12 August 1537. The intervention in Denmark was to be Lübeck's last large-scale attempt at controlling Baltic trade and at dominating Nordic commercial policy.

Both Gustav Vasa and Frederik had to deal with the problem of the spread of Protestantism, which came in the German, Lutheran form. Using for their own purpose existing tendencies towards increased control of the Church by the government or by laymen in general, the two rulers steered a course between a benevolent neutrality (and sometimes even more than that) towards the Reformers, a prudent attitude towards the remaining Catholic majority of the people, and the desire of both for political and economic advantages to be gained from the subordination of the Church.

In Sweden–Finland, the turning-point came with the Diet of Västerås in 1527; in Denmark, with that of Copenhagen in 1536. Schleswig–Holstein had in many respects already adopted Lutheranism in 1528. In Norway and Iceland, resistance towards the Reformation meant, at least for some people, resistance against national subordination under Denmark. Christian III's *håndfæstning* (30 October 1536) abolished the Norwegian *rigsråd* since its majority had illegally seceded from the union with Denmark. In future, Norway was to be considered as a province of Denmark governed by the Danish *rigsråd*, a development in which the interests of the Danish aristocracy in Norwegian fiefs played a significant role. When Archbishop Olav Engelbrektson of Trondheim learnt that the Danish bishops had been imprisoned (12 August 1536) and that Lutheranism was being introduced as the official religion, he prepared for armed resistance, but was defeated and fled to the Low Countries, where he died in 1538.

Fifteenth-century Scandinavia shows the same tendencies towards the strengthening of princely authority which can be observed in other European countries. In the Nordic monarchies, however, these were reinforced by the victory of the Reformation. The Church disappeared as a political factor, and most of the spoils fell to the crown. In Finland and Sweden, burgesses and peasants were not excluded from political life at the diets, despite the fact that one of Gustav Vasa's first tasks was to eliminate the mining districts of Dalarna as a political factor. Since the time of Engelbrekt, too many revolts had begun there.

In Denmark–Norway neither peasants nor burgesses now had recognised political powers, and diets (assemblies of estates) were seldom convoked during the remaining part of the sixteenth century. Moreover, most towns were still small and generally unable to influence political decisions. The late medieval administrations had sought support from the bourgeoisie and the peasantry against clergy and aristocracy; for the century after the Reformation the aristocracy was allowed to share power with the king, until, in its turn, it was eliminated in the middle of the seventeenth century.

The fifteenth century is important in Scandinavian history because the instruments of government were modernised and the independence of the Church was eroded until it fell at the Lutheran Reformation (which can be seen as the culmination of German cultural influence); because wealth and political power were concentrated in the hands of the higher aristocracy to the detriment of the gentry; because Lübeck's dominating role in Scandinavian politics was curtailed in favour of the Low Countries; and, finally, because the fourteenth-century union of Sweden–Finland and Norway broke up, leaving Sweden and Finland alone and aligning Norway, Iceland and Holstein with Denmark. The composite monarchies thus formed were to last until the nineteenth century.

CHAPTER 27

HUNGARY: CROWN AND ESTATES

János Bak

The main feature of political history in fifteenth-century Hungary was the shift from monarchical to aristocratic power. Although in mid-century the lesser nobility displayed its strength at the diets (parliamentary assemblies) and in the second half an able and popular king made valiant efforts to recoup the power for the crown, by the end of the century baronial factions dominated the political scene. As ruler and nobles vied for power, the country was increasingly threatened by the mightiest outside power to attack Europe since the Mongols: the Ottoman Empire. The resources of the kingdom could not match those of the enemy. Over time Hungary failed to muster the necessary finances, organisation, military capabilities and diplomacy. The internal struggles further weakened the country's ability to defend the southern borderlands. The fall of Belgrade in 1521 and the disastrous defeat in the battle of Mohács (1526) meant the end of the independent kingdom of Hungary.

At the beginning of the fifteenth century, that kingdom still held sway over all the territories acquired in the preceding era. Beyond the entire Carpathian Basin, Hungarian sovereignty was acknowledged in most of Dalmatia. The dependent territories south of the river Sava and along the lower Danube (the banates) controlled a sufficiently wide 'glacis'. Several states in the northern Balkans, such as Serbia, Bosnia and Wallachia, were intermittently drawn into dependence by the kings of Hungary. The kingdom's territory was about 350,000 square kilometres with an approximate population of three and a half million. By mid-century, however, Dalmatia was lost to Venice, most of the banates and vassal states had fallen under Ottoman rule and even the southern regions of Hungary began to be ravaged and depopulated by recurrent Turkish raids. Conquests in the 1470s and 1480s in the north and west were temporary gains, more than counterbalanced by losses in the south. Simultaneously, the defence burdens and economic stagnation (due to the shifting of trade routes making Hungary the terminus of commerce controlled by foreigners) seriously depleted the country's resources. By 1500, the once rich and influential kingdom had become a poor country, fighting for its survival.

Map 17   Hungary in the late fifteenth century

THE REIGN OF SIGISMUND (1387–1437) AND HIS BARONS

The succession after the death of the Angevin King Louis I was anything but smooth. Having survived the disastrous defeat of the crusade at Nicopolis (1396) and loosened the fetters placed on him by his electors, the great lords, King Sigismund of Luxemburg maintained an, at times, tenuous hold on Hungary for decades. One baronial revolt followed another. In 1401 the king's former allies, led by Archbishop Kanizsai,[1] turned against him. Taking the king captive, an aristocratic council governed the country in the name of the 'Holy Crown of Hungary'. This constitutional construct, though ephemeral at the time, was to have a long life. Juxtaposing the medieval metaphor of the crown, meaning the fullness of monarchic power, with the community of the realm (calling it in the Latin form *corona regni* in contrast to the older *corona regis*) came to express the noble commonwealth's claim to sovereignty. In 1403 the same lords and a great number of lesser nobles supported Ladislas of Naples, son of the hapless Charles of Durazo (for a few weeks king of Hungary in 1385/6), in his short-lived bid for the Hungarian crown. However, Sigismund's followers quickly crushed the uprising and the king's position was not challenged further. While most of the rebels were pardoned, they never regained their commanding position. Since Boniface IX, the Roman pope, had backed the pretender, Ladislas, Sigismund took the opportunity to strengthen the crown's control over the Hungarian Church: in 1404, he issued a decree, the so-called *placetum regium*, by which he prohibited appeals to the Roman *curia* and barred the way of papal appointees (the *bullati*) to Hungarian sees and prebends.

Sigismund's establishment of the Order of the Dragon in 1408 marked the consolidation of his hold on the government of the kingdom. For the next thirty years Hungary was ruled by a new aristocracy, allied and devoted to a king who was usually absent. The twelve Hungarian Knights of the Dragon (the king and his queen and foreign potentates) between them held approximately half of the country's castles, most of which they had received from Sigismund. Only three of these families held any position in the Angevin era, and only one of them came from a major landholding clan. Their collective holdings were nearly equal to what remained in the hands of the king, who had lost the greater part of the royal domain during his fight for the throne. While fourteenth-century kings had been able to count on the income and military force of about 150 royal castles and their appurtenances, Sigismund began to stabilise his position with fewer than fifty. Thus, crown and aristocracy held a balance of power in the kingdom.

---

[1] Hungarian names will be given in their vernacular form. In the late Middle Ages, noblemen used names referring to their estates: e.g. Johannes de Kanizsa. The suffix -i is the Hungarian equivalent of this appellation, and was the form used by contemporaries.

DEFENCE AGAINST THE OTTOMAN EMPIRE

Sigismund was the first ruler of Hungary for whom the defence of the southern border became a central issue. With the defeat of the allied Balkan army at the battle of Kosovo (1389) the 'buffer zone' keeping the Ottomans far from Hungary's territory had collapsed. Nicopolis had shown that the long-outdated crusading idea would not serve in the confrontation with the sultan. However, for a short while the country could still count on a 'third force' against the Turks. Hungarian foreign policy was successful in winning the Serbian ruler, Stephan Lazarević, as a valuable ally. For several years Hrvoja of Bosnia and Mircea of Wallachia also acknowledged Sigismund's suzerainty. However, suspicions of Hungary's political aspirations and memories of her missionary zeal (against Bosnian 'heretics' and Orthodox Christians) hindered the consolidation of such alliances. Sigismund and his barons, aware of the need to protect the country's frontiers, began to build up a system of defences. Pipo Scolari, the Florentine financial counsellor who became commander of the southeastern border regions, and later the brothers Tallóci (of Ragusan origin) established a two-tiered chain of fortifications from the Transylvanian border to the Adriatic Sea with ample garrisons and a sizeable light cavalry settled around and between them. These troops consisted in a large part of South Slav lords and their retainers, who had been forced out of their country by the advancing Ottoman Empire, and were thus familiar with the enemy's warfare. The linchpin of the system was Belgrade, acquired by Hungary from the Serbian despot, Stephan, in 1427. To finance the building and upkeep of this system, Pipo and his successors were granted the income of several counties, the banates along the frontier, and the Transylvanian salt mines. (The salt monopoly was a large monetary source; in fact, soldiers were often directly paid in salt.) After 1403 counties and royal domains were no longer given to officers of the household as 'honours' (similar to service fiefs), but entrusted to military men, usually styled 'captains', with full powers.

In the 1430s the country was faced with challenges from both north and south, when the Hussites attacked northern Hungary (today's Slovakia). The threat of war on two fronts (aggravated by an ongoing struggle with Venice for Dalmatia) triggered a royal proposal for a new military ordinance that would remain the basis of defence for a long time. This, the so-called Siena Register, was drafted by Sigismund during his involuntary stay in Italy, on the way to his imperial coronation in 1432/3. Although not formally implemented by the diet of 1435, it reflects the distribution of wealth, prestige and power in the country. Consistent with tradition, seignorial troops (called *banderia*, meaning a force of 100–400 lances) were to be fielded by the two archbishops, the six or seven richest bishops, the palatine, the chief justices, the officers of the king's and the queen's household, the bans of Croatia, Slavonia and the border districts, the voivodes of Transylvania and the lords of Croatia and Dalmatia. In addition one or more royal *banderia* of up to 1,000 lances (partly paid by the king, partly supplied by his 'knights of the court') were to be deployed at the threatened borders. In the framework of the general levy, the seventy-two counties were to supply 50–300 mounted soldiers each, according to size and population. One of the two innovations was that some fifty noblemen, holders of the newly established great landed estates, were listed by name as commanders of 50–100 lances. Most of them came not from the leading families, but were rich middle-rank landowners who, in the course of the century, became 'banderial lords', forerunners of the formalised estate of magnates in early modern times. The other reform was the establishment of a local militia, based on taxable plots (*porta*), hence called *militia portalis*. Envisaged as early as at the Temesvár (Timişoara, Romania) diet of 1397 and decreed in 1435, this auxiliary military force was intended to augment the *banderia* of the great lords and prelates. The decree stipulated that all landowners (the lesser ones in groups) should arm and equip a soldier for every twenty (in later regulations thirty-three) tenant peasants and send them to war under command of the county's captain.

The Siena Register also points to the fact that barons, prelates and richer nobles had sizeable armed retinues, ready to follow the king's call. These troops consisted of those noble *familiares* who took service with more powerful lords. Thus the majority of Hungarian nobles, whilst not living like peasants (they still claimed exemption from taxation), none the less became the servitors of their more fortunate fellows. This arrangement did not infringe on the noble status and inalienable estate of the retainer, who remained 'the king's man', subject only to royal courts, except in matters regarding his contractual service. Retainers were rewarded with cash or other kinds of revenues, rarely with land, and served their seniors not only as armed companions but also as administrators of their estates and aides in public offices. Retainers followed their *domini* into higher royal service as well, and thus became, for example, judges and protonotaries (practical lawyers) of the central courts. While *familiaritas* somewhat resembled a western type of feudal relationship, it was less formal and less reciprocal than classical vassalage, and rarely lasted as long. On the other hand, it was not essentially different from the English practice of livery and maintenance.

SIGISMUND'S GOVERNMENT AND FINANCES

Even though the king spent most of the last decades of his reign abroad – especially after his election as emperor and his entanglement in the problems of the general council – he implemented a number of administrative reforms in Hungary. Between 1405 and 1435 Sigismund and his council issued a series of major laws, enhancing the status of cities (a reliable source of income for the treasury), regulating the administration of justice and revamping the defence of the realm. Although the central authority remained the informal royal council of barons and prelates, Sigismund co-opted lawyers, financial and military experts (the 'captains' of the defence system), lesser nobles and even burghers into it as 'special counsellors'. In addition, the central royal courts of justice became more professionalised. First the court of the master of the treasury (*magister tavarnicorum*), with jurisdiction over the seven most important cities, was augmented by burgher assessors. Then the benches of the 'personal royal presence' and of the 'special royal presence', two courts passing judgement in the king's name, mainly against violent nobles and usurpers of estates, were filled with men trained in law, although their chief justices remained barons. The predominance of customary law, even though the king issued a series of statutes (*decreta*), can be seen from the fact that university-trained jurists served only in the court of the chancellery; the real administrators of justice in most other courts were practically trained lawyers, well versed in the customs of the realm. Sigismund's decrees also enhanced the jurisdiction of county magistrates, elected representatives of the lesser landowners: they were granted the right to call judicial assemblies on their own and to proscribe criminals. Through these meetings, called 'proclaimed assemblies', the counties were able to keep the peace in the absence of the ruler or even – as during the interregnum and civil war of the mid-century – in a kingless country. Furthermore, the county was empowered to secure the free movement of tenant peasants and to curb their violent abduction by greater landowners to the detriment of the lesser nobility in times of labour shortage. The military ordinances also increased the rights of county magistrates, entrusting them with the conscription of the local militia, the selection of a commander for the county's levy, and meting out punishment to those reluctant to serve.

Sigismund was, however, less successful in meeting the crown's ever-growing financial needs. Shortage of income was, of course, a new feature of the age, common to all rulers of Europe, but this predicament was more unusual for Hungary, where the Angevins had been dispensers of fabulous amounts of gold and silver from the northern Hungarian and Transylvanian mines. However, the output of these seems to have decreased, and the continuously adverse balance of Hungary's foreign trade depleted the country's reserves. The king had to mortgage many of the remaining royal estates, in one of his financial straits giving as security to the kings of Poland sixteen rich (mainly German) towns of the region which is today northern Slovakia. (They would not be returned to Hungary until the First Partition of

Poland in 1772.) In contrast to his immediate predecessors, he turned again to the thirteenth-century practice of debasing the coinage (though not the Hungarian gold florin which never lost its value). By 1411 the silver penny was worth one third of its face value and the 'quarting' (farthing) issued in the 1430s triggered an uncontrollable fall in the value of money of change.

This 'inflation' was the main cause of a widespread uprising in Transylvania and eastern Hungary, the first major recorded rural revolt in the country. When in 1437 the bishop of Transylvania demanded the tithe in good money (after not having collected it in bad coin for many years), Magyar and Vlach (Romanian) peasants and lesser nobles, supported by a few towns, rose in arms in response, and the privileged groups of the region, Magyar nobles, free Székely warriors and Saxon (German) townsmen, established a 'union of three nations' (the Kápolna Union of 1437, confirmed as the Torda Union of 1438), excluding Hungarian and Romanian peasants and freemen. The peasants, who agreed to abide by the king's arbitration, were easily defeated by the lords, but the Union became the constitutional basis of Transylvania for centuries to come.

That Sigismund's reign was later remembered in Hungary in negative terms was probably due to the nobility preferring valiant forays and heroic campaigns to diplomacy and efficient defence. There was also an element of xenophobia that reviewed the king as a 'Czech pig', as he was apostrophised during an attack on his foreign entourage in 1401. In fact, he brought Hungary into European politics, gave her leading men a chance to participate in the great issues of the age (Kanizsai, for example, became Roman chancellor, and many lords attended the Council of Constance or received military experience in Italy), and tried to emulate his father, the Emperor Charles IV, by making his residences into cosmopolitan capitals. Sigismund's buildings in Pozsony (Bratislava) and Buda (the 'Fresh Palace'), the art commissioned by him and the visits to his court of important early humanists (such as Pier Paolo Vergerio) are just now beginning to be properly appreciated by historians. It is true that many of the reforms in urbanisation and in the more efficient administration of justice remained incomplete, mainly because of the treasury's poverty and the barons' resistance to innovation, but some of them, especially the system of southern defence, survived their sponsor for decades.

THE RISE OF THE NOBLE DIET

Even though Sigismund did his best to secure in advance the undisputed succession of his daughter, Elizabeth, and his son-in-law, the Habsburg Albert V, duke of Austria, the barons insisted that, as king, Albert (1437–9) sign an election pact, just as Sigismund had done fifty years earlier. This document, reflecting the leading men's dissatisfaction with most of Sigismund's reforms, stipulated the abolition of all 'novelties' (including new taxes) and confirmed the barons' intention to exclude 'foreign counsellors'. In the following year dynastic business kept the king (who became Albert II, Holy Roman Emperor) away from Hungary. During his absence increasing disaffection among the nobility with the royal council's government, combined with Turkish attacks on the border requiring the financial and military support of the counties, resulted in the calling of a diet. The 1439 meeting of the estates marks the beginning of the rise of what may be termed 'the commons' in Hungary. The county deputies virtually renegotiated the arrangements between king and barons, changing a fair number of articles (paragraphs of law) to their advantage. These issues ranged from matters of defence, to pardons for felons, to the marriages of the king's daughters. Where the election promises had bound the king to the assent of his council, the diet either freed him or stipulated the consent of the nobility. However, little of all this was implemented because of Albert's death in camp during an unsuccessful campaign against the Ottomans, only two years after his accession.

Having become aware, in 1439, of their corporate strength, the nobility insisted on their right to elect a ruler. Albert had only two daughters, but the queen was pregnant and her supporters were counting on the birth of a male heir. However, the 'soldier barons', who had acquired considerable power in the preceding decades and also enjoyed the support of the counties, thought that the country needed a military leader, preferably one who could bring troops and arms to the defence of the endangered realm. They elected the young King Władysław III of Poland (Wladislas I of Hungary, 1440–4). This election was the first in which no dynastic link connected the new ruler to his predecessor. Barely had Wladislas entered Hungary, having signed an election promise, than Elizabeth bore a son, Ladislas (called Posthumous, as Ladislas V, king of Hungary). Through a ruse she managed to have him crowned with the Holy Crown 'of St Stephen' in May 1440, and then retreated, with the venerated insignia, to the western border of the country. The nobles assembled at the coronation diet decided to solve the problem by enunciating a new legal maxim: they decreed that the 'force and power of coronation lies with the nobles representing the entire body of the realm'. (Nevertheless, hallowed tradition was strong enough to make them choose a crown from the reliquary of St Stephen to replace the one abducted by the queen.) Wladislas and his soldier barons soon defeated the queen's supporters and gained control of most of the country. Only the north-western parts, with the rich mining cities, remained in the hands of a Bohemian captain, Jan Jiškra of Brandýs. With the help of formerly Hussite Czech soldiers, Jiškra kept the territory – in the name of the Habsburg party – despite threats and armed confrontations, for almost two decades. While negotiating for peace, Elizabeth died and left the child king in the care of Emperor Frederick III, head of the house of Habsburg.

The four years of Wladislas's reign were taken up with defensive and offensive campaigns against the Ottomans. These were the years of the rise of János Hunyadi, victor in the decisive battle against the pro-Habsburg party, together with his mentor and fellow voivode and ban, Nicholas Ujlaki, later king of Bosnia. Hunyadi, whose family had come from Wallachia only a generation earlier, grew up in the entourage of Sigismund's barons and of the emperor himself. Through what may be termed military entrepreneurship he gradually amassed extensive properties, especially in the south-east and in Transylvania. With the fall of Serbia in 1439 the Ottoman Empire reached the border of Hungary. The defence system built up under Sigismund still protected the frontier, but the enemy now stood at the border. In the 1430s Ottoman raids reached deep inside Hungarian territory. The region between Drava and Sava (Slovania and Srem) became so depopulated that a number of noble counties ceased to exist. For example, the inhabitants of Keve along the Danube, once a rich city, had to leave their town and resettle in the vicinity of Pest. In 1441–2, Hunyadi, sensing the warlike mood in the country, launched successful attacks against the Ottoman bey of Smederevo and scored several victories in Transylvania and Wallachia as well. During 1443–4, in the so-called 'long campaign', Wladislas and Hunyadi led a Hungarian army, supported by allies from the Balkans, as far as the Rhodope mountains. Although no territory was regained, Hungarian troops, after decades of defence, were moving into enemy territory and instilled hope in the near-extinct resistance of Balkan people. In 1444, Hunyadi and the ruler of Serbia, Despot George Branković, who had fled to Hungary a few years before, secured a ten-year truce with the sultan allowing the return of Despot George to parts of Serbia. However, Wladislas, choosing to follow the prodding of the papal legate, Cardinal Giuliano Cesarini, and counting on Venetian help, broke the peace.[2] Once again a crusade was called; and once again, it led to a disastrous defeat. In the battle of Varna (10 November 1444) the king, the cardinal, most of the Polish knights and a good part of the army were killed on the battlefield. Hunyadi barely escaped with his life.

---

[2] The debate among historians about the background to this decision and the responsibility for it continues. P. Engel (in Bak and Király (1982), pp. 103–23) demonstrated the common interest of Hunyadi and Branković in securing peace in return for possessions passed on from the despot to Hunyadi. Military historians agree that by this time only a much wider coalition of European forces could have risked open confrontation with the Ottoman army with any hope of success (Szakály (1979), pp. 83–92).

INTERREGNUM AND HUNYADI'S REGENCY

For nearly a decade Hungary had no resident king. Negotiations with the Emperor Frederick III concerning the return of Ladislas (and of the Holy Crown) continued; finally, in 1453, after a joint action of the Austrian, Czech and Hungarian lords, they succeeded. In the meantime, however, the government of the realm was in the hands of the counties, the diet, its elected captains and – from 1446 to 1453 – János Hunyadi, as regent. Diets were now called virtually every year, many of them attended by the nobility, armed and in great numbers. From this time forward all nobles with more than ten tenants customarily came to the wide field across the Danube from Buda (where the barons met), the name of which, Rákos, became synonymous with the assembly. In the 1440s the cities were also regularly invited and participated in major decisions, such as the naming of four to six 'captains' for different regions to keep the peace and, in 1446, electing Hunyadi as regent. However, they soon found that their voice counted little among the masses of the nobles, and ceased to attend. The decrees passed in these years repeatedly affirm the concept according to which the assembled nobility – either in person (*viritim*) or through their delegates – constituted the 'body of the Holy Crown of Hungary'. Indeed, the notion of 'estates' in Hungary should be used in the singular: the nobility virtually alone, legally equal from magnate to the poorest one-plot nobleman, constituted the political nation. The prelates belonged to it as aristocrats; the lower clergy and the towns were in fact left out. The counties, based on decrees of the diets, were able to curb atrocities by powerful barons, to raze illegally built castles and to force chief officials to hand over and receive their commission from the estates. Hunyadi, still somewhat of a *homo novus*, built a successful alliance with the middle-rank nobility active in the counties, many of whom were his retainers. Not only were they the only effective power in the realm, but the regent needed them, at any rate until he was able to gain the support of the magnates. However, since his reputation among the nobility rested on heroic deeds, his defeat at the second battle at Kosovo in 1448 seriously damaged his standing, while also demonstrating that the sultan had final control over the Balkans. The Ottomans could prohibit the co-operation of the Albanian and Hercegovinian centres of anti-Turkish resistance with the advancing troops of Hunyadi and his allies. As a consequence Serbia and Bosnia, once again, sued for peace from the stronger side.

LADISLAS V POSTHUMOUS

In 1453, the young king was able to take up government in Hungary and Bohemia. Ladislas affirmed the nobles' privileges: the ideas of corporate autonomy were forgotten, the 'annulled' coronation of 1440 was accepted, the acts of both Queen Elizabeth and King Wladislas were cancelled. The central royal courts and the chancelleries were revitalised after many years of virtual legal vacuum. The trusted counsellor of Hunyadi, a champion of the lesser nobility, John Vitéz of Sredna, became secret chancellor; Hunyadi was made chief captain and perpetual count in charge of royal revenues. About the finances of the country around 1454 we have a unique and valuable document.[3] Designed as a proposal for reform, it records that the main revenues came from the salt and mining monopolies (100,000 to 150,000 gold florins) and the direct taxes on tenant peasants (the so-called portal dues, 40,000 florins); much less from customs duties (12,000 florins), urban taxes and payments from the Jews (11,000 florins), from other groups in royal service (such as the Saxon townsmen, the free Cuman and Székely warriors, who still paid partly in kind, 30,000 florins in coin) and lesser items (such as the profit from sturgeon caught in the Danube). The losses of income from the southern and Transylvanian regions, the result of Ottoman devastation, were significant enough to be noted as reasons for reducing demands on these previously lucrative areas. The treasury's total income amounted probably to half the hoped-for sum, leaving for the king's use hardly more than 25,000 florins. The crown's poverty seriously hampered the kingdom's defence capabilities. Considerable funds for the upkeep of castles and the payment of professional soldiers were needed even in so-called peacetime, when minor skirmishes were still everyday occurrences along the long southern border. The relatively low customs and urban income suggests a lag in commercial development. The preponderance of direct taxes on the peasantry, much of which finally came into the coffers of their landlords, theoretically in return for hiring soldiers, points to a still overwhelmingly seignorial, agrarian economy.

Hunyadi, in charge of the finances for defence, seems to have been able to make good use of the limited resources, but was, apparently, unable to muster sufficient forces, when, in 1453, Constantinople was facing the final Ottoman onslaught. Minor victories were still scored, but the Ottoman-controlled regions kept growing to the detriment of Hungary. Three years later, Sultan Mehemmed II, the Conqueror, challenged Hungary at the siege of Belgrade, defended by Hunyadi's brother-in-law, Michael Szilágyi. The crusade called by the pope, this time propagated by the charismatic preacher and inquisitor, John of Capistrano, mobilised thousands of peasants and townsmen in Hungary and the neighbouring countries. On 22 July 1456, Hunyadi, with the help of the crusaders, raised the siege. The relief of the fortress, the strategic key to the

---

[3] The text of this financial reform plan was probably drafted by Ulrich Eizinger, an Austrian councillor of the king. Having survived among the family archives, it was first published in 1852 and then re-edited by Bak (1987), pp. 380–4.

Hungarian Plain, became a legend in its own time and in fact secured peace for the kingdom for decades. However, unrest among the crusading poor, raising their voice against the lords' reaping the fruits of the victory, prohibited the pursuit of the enemy. The troops were sent home, and Hunyadi died a few weeks later in the epidemic that broke out in the camp. Capistrano, soon to be revered as a saint, followed him in October.

With the hero's death the latent conflicts between his followers and the king's party broke open. Hunyadi's elder son, Ladislas, was first inclined to hand over the supreme command his father had held, but when the king and his uncle, Ulrich von Cilli, the new captain in chief, came to Belgrade, Hunyadi's men killed Ulrich. As soon as the king regained his freedom of action, he had the Hunyadi sons arrested and Ladislas executed for treason. In response, their family, supported by its followers, openly rebelled. King Ladislas left for Prague, taking the younger son Mátyás with him, but died there a year later. Hungary was left without a ruler.

GAINS OF THE CROWN UNDER MÁTYÁS CORVINUS (1458–90)

The fame of the father, the army of the family and a deal with the leading families secured the unanimous acclamation of Mátyás Hunyadi, the first Hungarian magnate to become king of Hungary. In January 1458, the nobles assembled *en masse* on the frozen Danube and hailed the son of the great hero of anti-Ottoman wars. His uncle, Michael Szilágyi, assured the other barons that, as regent during Mátyás's minority, he would guard their interests. However, the young Hunyadi, betrothed to the daughter of George of Poděbrady, the elected king of Bohemia (also the first ruler of that country chosen from the local nobility), soon upset these plans. Even though his rule was not rendered legitimate by a coronation for six years (the Holy Crown was still in the hands of Frederick III), he dismissed Szilágyi and made his tutor, the old family friend, John Vitéz, archchancellor and later archbishop of Esztergom. The spurned Garai–Cilli group thereupon 'elected' the Emperor Frederick III, who claimed dynastic rights to Hungary, to be king. Years of negotiations were to follow; they finally ended with the emperor forsaking the crown (in consideration of the sum of 80,000 florins) but retaining a claim to Hungary for life while recognising Mátyás 'as his son', in return for the promise of Habsburg succession to Hungary should Mátyás die without an heir. Considering the age difference of thirty-odd years between the two men it seemed unlikely that the clause about succession would ever lead to Hungary becoming part of the Habsburg Empire.

The coronation in 1464 having strengthened the king's hand, he introduced a series of financial and administrative reforms. First he officially renamed the old portal tax as the 'tax of the royal treasury' (by which token all previous exemptions were cancelled) and made sure the moneys were more rigorously collected than before. The same was done with the customs duties (earlier called 'thirtieth', now rebaptised *vectigal coronae*). More important, Mátyás engaged a number of commoners, among them a very able merchant, the baptised Jew, John Ernuszt, later to become his chief treasurer, to farm the major revenues. Other burgher and lesser noble officers were also brought into the fiscal administration, which began to grow into a true bureaucracy. Systematic collection of regalia, regular imposition of extraordinary taxes, and revenue from the extensive Hunyadi domains increased the income of the treasury many times over. With the defeat or death of the opposing magnates, Mátyás obtained the chance to introduce political changes: during the years 1458–71, more than one third of baronial office holders were new men, promoted by the king. In the following decades this number rose to nearly half of the members of the royal council. Mátyás organised an inner council in which the old aristocracy was less preponderant and business was frequently transacted by the king and his *secretarii*, just as under Sigismund. Although the introduction of new seals was not as unequivocally connected to new chancelleries and offices as in some western monarchies, the use of the privy seal and the signet for important decisions suggests a considered move towards exploiting the royal prerogative and restricting the control of the baronial council.

As was expected of the son of Hunyadi, as soon as his hands were free from parrying domestic opposition, Mátyás embarked on anti-Ottoman campaigns. The results of János Hunyadi's campaigns were slowly vanishing. In 1458 Sultan Mehemmed II conquered Serbia and defeated Vlad of Wallachia, Hungary's vassal. The Ottomans now moved against Bosnia. Mátyás, unable to counter the main Ottoman forces, waited out his time and used the collapse of the Bosnian resistance to secure the northern part of the country, with the fortress of Jajce at its centre. The conquest of the citadel and its subsequent defence against repeated Ottoman attacks was an impressive military feat. The new banate of Jajce, established in 1464, withstood Ottoman attacks and secured the south-western flank of the Hungarian–Croatian border for almost seventy years. However, precisely because he was his father's son, Mátyás also knew that without significant outside help, Hungary could not do more than secure her own frontier against the most powerful military machine of the times. Hungarian diplomacy was very active in searching for support, but rarely successful. The most reliable allies were the Papacy and Venice. In the 1450s, several elaborate schemes were floated by Rome for an all-European army. The experts calculated, realistically, that some 200,000 soldiers, in co-operation with the Middle Eastern enemies of the sultan, could expel the Ottomans from Europe. What was unrealistic, however, was that popes and some politicians expected that countries not immediately threatened by the Turk would embark on such an enterprise. The new pope, Aeneas Sylvius Piccolomini (Pius II), well acquainted with the central European scene from the service at the Habsburg court, was a great champion of crusading ideas. Some money did come to Buda from Rome, but irregularly and mostly late; temporary alliances with Venice and Moldavia were established, but these did not allow more than defensive operations. The chances for a great war of coalition were as slim as those of concentrated counter-attack by Hungary's neighbours. Therefore, in 1465 Mátyás signed a truce on the basis of the status quo that secured the Hungarian lines of defence. In fact, between 1465 and 1520 no Ottoman imperial army appeared on the frontiers of Hungary: the Balkans were firmly in the hands of the sultan, and the empire was engaged in expansion elsewhere.

WARS OF CONQUEST VERSUS SOUTHERN DEFENCE

It has long been debated whether the king's decision to volunteer for a 'crusade' with papal sanction against the 'heretical' King George of Bohemia (whose daughter, Mátyás's first wife, had died in childbirth in 1464) and fight his wars in the north and west was motivated by his plan to establish a powerful empire that could successfully fight the Ottomans. His chancellery did not cease emphasising, with the best humanist rhetoric, that this was Mátyás's long-term design. The acquisition of Moravia, Silesia, Lusatia and, finally, sizeable parts of Austria might have added up to an agglomeration of resources nearly sufficient for the expulsion of the Ottomans from Europe. (The Habsburgs, centuries later, partially accomplished the task, albeit under different conditions.) But since 'the king's heart is in the hands of the Lord' (Prov. 21:1), the controversy will probably never be resolved.[4] What the records show is that in 1468 Mátyás attacked Bohemia, scoring in the next six years a series of military and diplomatic victories. Although the Catholic lords made him king of Bohemia in 1469, most of the kingdom remained in the hands of King George and, after his death in 1471, in those of Władysław Jagiełło (King Vladislav I of Bohemia). Hungarian armies resisted several Polish sieges in Silesia and secured that province for ten years for Hungary. In 1477 and in 1480, Mátyás's troops marched against Frederick III, and in 1485 he victoriously entered Vienna. Altogether, Mátyás spent twenty-three years at war on the northern and western front: by contrast, his activities against the Ottoman Turks

---

[4] Recent contributions to this debate are in volumes published, in Hungarian, to mark the quincentenary of the king's death. See, in particular, the articles by A. Kubinyi, J. Macek, G. Rázsó, and F. Szakály in Rázsó (1990). See also Bak (1991), Kubinyi (1991) and Maraosi (1991). Nehring (1989) emphasises the king's life-long concern to acquire equal standing with the established dynasties of Habsburg and Jagiełło.

(including the successful conquest of the fortress at Sabac on the Lower Danube, in 1476) took up only ten years at the most.

These military operations were made possible by Mátyás's most successful governmental reform, the establishment of a mercenary army. Beginning in 1462, with the hiring of the last remnants of the formerly Hussite Czech troops of Jiškra, and continuing with systematic recruitment of domestic and foreign professional soldiers, in the 1470s, Mátyás kept approximately 20,000 men at arms. The army was financed by the extraordinary war tax (called *subsidium*), four to five times higher than the regular portal levy, which the king collected almost every year. Such *subsidia* had been occasionally levied earlier under the threat of attacks from the Ottomans, but Mátyás made the war tax into a regular income of the crown. First he called diets to approve it (an innovation, for the noble diets of the 1440s did not insist on their right, in contrast to the European-wide practice, to approve taxation) in return for strengthening the power of the counties. Later the noble deputies found it cheaper to empower the king for years in advance, rather than spend weeks at the diet. With this special income, by the end of Mátyás's reign the treasury's income may have been in some years as high as 800,000 florins, a sum not very much lower than the budget of western European monarchies. Still, the country's own resources, although stretched to their limits, did not suffice to pay up to 600,000 florins for a standing army. Hence, the mercenaries (after Mátyás's death, called from their commander, the 'Black' Haugwitz, the 'Black Army') had to be steadily deployed in campaigns with opportunities to acquire booty. Last but not least, newly conquered territories had to finance the wars fought for acquiring and keeping them. (Contemporary opinion does not make it clear whether they did this or not. The sources are insufficient and Mátyás's hold on the conquered regions was too short to draw a reliable balance sheet.)

According to the description of the court historian, Antonio Bonfini, the muster of the 28,000 man army at Wiener Neustadt in 1487 was the most impressive military show he had ever seen. By that time Mátyás's troops were certainly equal to the best military forces of their time. The combination of foreign mercenaries, Hungarian *banderia* and the light cavalry (Hussars) of the noble levy and Hungarian professional soldiers, applying their traditional hit and run tactics, remained unbeaten in the northern and western theatres.

The shifting of Mátyás's foreign policy away from the south, combined with the efforts at reducing the aristocracy's influence in government, caused the growth of ever more serious opposition against him. While a revolt in Transylvania in 1467 was still easily quelled, in 1471, the king's closest supporters, Archbishop John Vitéz and his nephew Bishop and Ban Janus Pannonius, the acclaimed Neo-Latin poet, raised the flag of rebellion. They offered the throne to Prince Casimir of Poland, who entered the country with force.

Mátyás swiftly returned from Bohemia, arrested the conspirators, repelled the Polish pretender with ease, even winning over some of his troops for the new mercenary army. Janus Pannonius died while fleeing the irate king, while old Vitéz, humiliated and under house arrest, followed a few months later. The king's disappointment must have run deep. After 1471 foreign-born prelates, for example the Silesian Johannes Beckensloer, archbishop of Esztergom, and, after his defection to the Emperor Frederick, Friar Gabriele Rangoni from Verona and the Moravian John Filipec, became his trusted councillors.

Attempts at replacing the barons with Mátyás's own men seem to have also gained momentum after the conspiracy, yet the latter never outnumbered the magnates from the old families. Clearly, the military, economic and political preponderance of the great landowning clans could not be broken in a few decades. Conspicuously, the *homines novi* who were able to remain on the council and in national positions for more than short periods of office were only those, who, by marriage and land acquisition, managed to join the aristocracy and thus, in fact, changed sides from crown to baronage. While in the branches of the treasury and in the command of the mercenary army the king succeeded in having his appointees from the lesser nobility keep the leading positions, in the royal courts and the council the balance of power remained precarious. The reorganisation of the central courts of justice, now only formally presided over by magnates, but in fact staffed by jurists, combined with the issuing of an extensive law code (Mátyás's *Decretum Maius* of 1486, the first law to be published in print, in 1488) and the king's insistence on equity in the administration of justice, seem to have been particularly successful. A jingle about 'Dead is Mátyás – Justice is Lost' and anecdotes about the king's meting out punishment to cruel lords were recorded soon after his death, even before the loss of the country's independence made his reign appear the last 'golden age'. Strangely enough, the increased tax burden, deeply resented by contemporaries and denounced by mendicant preachers, was forgotten, while the results of a stronger control over local lords found their way into the 'collective memory'.

RENAISSANCE COURT AND ROYAL PATRONAGE

Mátyás's marriage in 1476 to Beatriz, daughter of the Aragonese king of Naples, brought about noticeable changes not so much in foreign and military affairs, which were western oriented in any case, but in the style of the court. Mátyás wished to match the fashionable courts of the princes of the small northern Italian states – mostly, like himself, descendants of *condottieri* – in pomp, artistic display and hospitality for scholars and poets. He may not have been fully successful in making his monarchy into a 'Renaissance state' in terms of an independent civil service, regular diplomacy and a less aristocratic social base, but he was a true Renaissance prince in utilising the political value of sponsorship for the arts, architecture and literature. Italian humanists were welcomed at his court, duly delivering the panegyrics expected from them. Buildings in Buda and in the summer residence of Visegrád along the Danube, started in a late Gothic style, acquired in the course of the years Renaissance marble decorations and sculptures at the hands of Dalmatian and Italian artists. Doubtless the most impressive achievement was the Corvinian Library, for which the king ordered manuscripts from the best workshops in Italy, establishing one such in Buda as well. By 1490 it may have contained as many as 2,500 volumes, mainly manuscripts (only a fraction of them survived the Ottoman occupation and the destruction of Buda). According to incomplete estimates, in the last decades of his reign, Mátyás spent up to 80,000 gold florins annually on artistic patronage. Plans for establishing a university in Pozsony (Bratislava) – after several failed trials at a *studium generale* in the preceding centuries – were progressing well, when the death of Janus Pannonius and the arrest of John Vitéz cut them, as well as many other humanist projects, short. The patronage of the new learning and arts remained limited in Mátyás's time: while the king and a few prelates embraced the fashionable trends, the rest of Hungary remained, as the hapless Janus had put it, a 'frozen land, a barbarian country'. However, the seeds had germinated and, under the Jagiellonians, humanist centres grew up in several episcopal towns and aristocratic courts.

The last years of Mátyás were devoted primarily to securing the succession of his sole heir, his natural son (from the Austrian burgher woman, Barbara Edelpeck), John Corvinus. Great parts of the enormous Hunyadi–Szilágyi family fortune were transferred to him, he was given the title of duke, and elaborate marriage plans were contemplated, the last including Bianca Sforza of Milan. In 1486 Mátyás issued new regulations for the office of the count palatine, the king's deputy, by which he hoped to leave a reliable baron in charge of the royal election. Many of the king's men were given comital positions to control the noble diet and bound by oaths to support the election of Corvinus. In the midst of these plans and of preparations for securing the Austrian conquest, the fifty-year-old king died unexpectedly in Vienna.

BARONIAL REACTION UNDER WLADISLAS II (1490–1516)

Mátyás's efforts were not sufficient to secure the succession: John Corvinus was only one of the candidates at the election diet, and not the most popular. The Emperor Maximilian raised claims based on the Habsburg–Hunyadi treaty; Vladislav, the Jagiełło king of Bohemia, and his brother, Jan Olbracht, could count on the support of various noble factions. The crucial post of count palatine happened to be vacant, and the lesser nobles placed at the head of counties by Mátyás did not support the son of their benefactor. Instead, the diet chose Vladislav of Bohemia (as Wladislas II of Hungary), apparently because, in the words of the lords, he promised to be a king 'whose braids they could hold in their hands'. When Corvinus and his party attempted a coup, they were defeated by Paul Kinizsi, the man his father had raised from common estate to become the famous commander of the southern defence. Wladislas signed an elaborate treaty repudiating the centralising reforms of his predecessor, agreed to marry Queen Beatriz (celebrated *pro forma*, the marriage was annulled ten years later) and was crowned in September 1490. John Corvinus, accepting his defeat, received the government of Slavonia and Croatia, where he led many successful campaigns against the Ottomans until his death in 1504. Maximilian and Jan Olbracht did not give up so easily; both marched with force deep into the country, before being finally repelled.

The victory of the barons over Mátyás's innovations did not mean that all the reforms of the treasury and the administration were to be abolished, but that the new offices and structures were to serve the interests of the barons and prelates of the council and not the central authority of the crown. One of the main promises of the new king, not to collect the extraordinary subsidy any more (though in fact disregarded within a few years), immediately lowered the country's defence capability. Other consequences included the loss of Mátyás's conquests and the demoralisation of the 'Black Army', which, neither paid nor deployed on campaigns which promised booty, looted the villages of southern Hungary. In 1492 this unruly company had to be dispersed by its own former commanders.

During the last decades of its existence as an independent kingdom, Hungary's main problem was to counter the increasing pressure on the southern border. The professional army disbanded, the defence was once again entrusted to the *banderia* of the barons and prelates and the local militia. The great landowners were now allowed to collect the subsidy themselves in return for mobilising their own troops. The lesser nobles, however, not receiving anything for joining the general levy and raising the *militia portalis*, were reluctant to do so. In 1498–1500 a series of decrees (partly lost) introduced a military reform: the subsidy of one florin or more per tenant household came to be split between the king and the estates. For their share, the magnates and the nobles of the counties had the duty to hire mercenaries according to the traditional quota of one soldier for every twenty tenants. The law of 1500 designated by name those who had the right and duty to have their own troops under their flag (thus updating the Siena Register and keeping it current, year by year).

The reforms of the system of recruitment seem to have had greater political than military significance. The list of 'banderial lords' made a definite distinction between magnates and the rest of the nobility, which was contrary to customary law. The county nobles were placated by receiving the right to send sixteen lesser noble jurors to the benches of the royal courts and, from 1500, into the royal council as well. From the mid-1490s the noble counties, or their different factions, sometimes supporting one baronial group, sometimes the other, appeared at the diet with their hired soldiers. Typically, those lesser barons who were omitted from the banderial list succeeded in rallying the county nobility and presenting themselves as spokesmen for the commoners. The king, ever more threatened by the armed baronial and noble factions, looked to other monarchs for support. In 1492 the Jagiello brothers agreed to support each other in case of rebellion, and there was also a gradual *rapprochement* between Wladislas and Maximilian. In response to the king's overtures to the Habsburgs and in support of the popular voivode of Transylvania, John Szapolyai (to become King John from 1526 to 1541), the diet of 1505 passed a decree against ever electing a 'foreign king', should Wladislas die without an heir. However, the birth of Louis (as Louis II, king of Hungary and Bohemia 1516–26) having taken the edge off this 'national' grumbling, the diet accepted the king's coronation oath in the name of his son and crowned the baby king of Hungary in 1508. Nevertheless, in 1506, a Jagiello–Habsburg family treaty was signed (renewed in 1515), sealed by a marriage arrangement between the children of Wladislas and Maximilian, confirming the latter's right to succession in Hungary.

LOSING THE BATTLE FOR SURVIVAL

Around the turn of the century, the ever changing networks of aristocratic party leaders and their noble followers in the triangular tug-of-war between crown, baronage and county nobility became so complicated that neither contemporary observers nor modern historians can disentangle the threads. There were years when both the king and nobility called a diet, and chief officers of the crown were deposed and reinstated under conditions as close to anarchy as those of the noble commonwealth in eighteenth-century Poland. In the meantime, the situation at the southern border, the provisioning and defence of the border castles virtually used up all of the kingdom's revenues. Attempts at mobilising the population against the Ottomans in a crusade, in 1514, turned into a peasant war, the 'crusaders' blaming the lords for abandoning them to the pagans. Szapolyai rescued the country by defeating the 'holy host of the poor' and executing its leader, George Székely-Dózsa, on a throne of flames.

Even though a number of able and conscientious barons and their servitors did their best to keep the southern defences intact, the country could not face serious confrontation. The royal army was too small and too late to relieve Belgrade, when, in 1521, after the king had inexplicably refused to renew the truce, Sultan Süleyman the Magnificent laid siege to this key fortress. With Belgrade in Ottoman hands the country would be defenceless whenever the sultan chose to attack again. Calls for help went out in all directions, but because of previous diplomatic blunders and general European disinterest they yielded little more than encouraging words.[5] On August 1526, the Hungarian army was routed on the field near Mohács: the king, most of his barons, almost all prelates and tens of thousands of nobles and soldiers died and the central parts of the kingdom were devastated. Even though Süleyman soon retreated to the Balkans, Hungary could not recover from the shock and the loss of its best men. Two kings were elected, John Szapolyai by one faction and Ferdinand of Habsburg by another. King John counted on Ottoman support, Ferdinand on Habsburg resources to reunite the country, but both failed. When Buda fell, twenty-five years later, the country came to be divided into three parts: the Habsburgs holding the west and north, the Ottomans the centre and Szapolyai's son, John Sigismund, becoming prince of a vassal state by the sultan's grace in Transylvania and eastern Hungary. After more than five hundred years of statehood, the independent kingdom of Hungary had ceased to exist.

[5] In the 1970s a passionate debate raged among Hungarian scholars – and the wider public – over the alternative policies the country could have pursued in the 1500s. Perjés (1989) showed that Hungary was on the very edge of the Ottoman army's radius of operation, even beyond it. He assumed, but without sufficient documentary support, that the kingdom's leaders could have accepted an offer to retain independence in return for co-operation with Ottoman designs towards the regions further west. The debate contributed to the clarification of many details of military and diplomatic history.

CHAPTER 28

THE KINGDOM OF POLAND AND THE GRAND DUCHY OF LITHUANIA, 1370–1506

Aleksander Gieysztor

TERRITORY, POPULATION, CLIMATE

Central and eastern Europe in the late Middle Ages was home to many ethnic, cultural, political and social systems. During the fourteenth and fifteenth centuries this region, whose character had been taking shape over a number of centuries, experienced an increase in settlement density, especially in the kingdom of Poland and certain areas of the grand duchy of Lithuania. Together with the growth in rural settlement there came a slow but steady advance in population.

Demographic estimates for the period before statistics merely represent orders of magnitude. About 1370, the kingdom of Poland had 2 million inhabitants with a population density of 8.6 persons per square kilometre. By contrast with western Europe, which was adversely affected demographically and economically by the Black Death, the outbreak of plague in Poland did not have the character of a catastrophe, as can be seen from the increase in internal developments and quite intensive colonisation of the fourteen and fifteenth centuries.

After the personal union of the kingdom and the grand duchy of Lithuania in 1385 and the annexation in 1466 of Royal Prussia and Warmia (Ermland) at the cost of the Teutonic Order, both the Polish and Lithuanian states governed by the Jagiellonian dynasty covered an area at least five times greater than Poland under her last Piast king, Casimir III the Great (1333–70). Poland–Lithuania now had an area of about 1,240,000 square kilometres. At the beginning of the sixteenth century the population was in the range of 7.5 million split more or less evenly, even though Lithuania was three times larger geographically than the kingdom and the Rus′ian territories of the Polish crown. Poland had fifteen inhabitants per square kilometre while the population of the grand duchy did not exceed five persons per square kilometre. The evidence of the economic indicator lends credence to a significant rise in

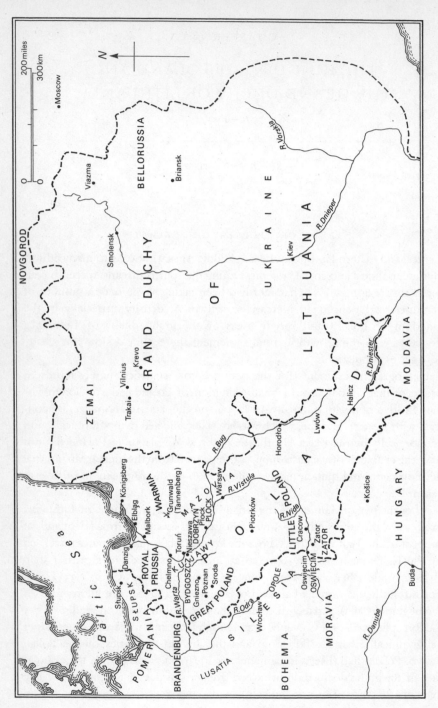

Map 18 Poland and Lithuania

population in fifteenth-century Poland, while the same was happening in the grand duchy of Lithuania, especially in her north-western territories.

Information on climatic fluctuations in this part of Europe at that time is so sparse that we may have to rely upon general European weather conditions in the fourteenth and fifteenth centuries, supplemented by the data of dendrochronology made available from excavations in Rus'. As we know from many places in Europe, the thirteenth century and the first half of the fourteenth underwent some cooling of the climate compared with the favourable conditions of preceding centuries. The probable improvement at the end of the century appears to have been only temporary; the fifteenth century again experienced severe climatic conditions, although these were much less harsh than the little ice age which struck from 1550 well into the seventeenth century. Various types of weather and regional variation certainly afflicted a wide band of central and eastern European territory. From the itinerary of Władysław II Jagiełło (Jogaila), king of Poland and grand duke of Lithuania, we may deduce that winter began early in November when the king drove in his sled for his progress around Lithuania which would last several months. There were still hoar frosts at the end of May and the king fell victim to one of these.

ANGEVIN GOVERNMENT

Casimir III (the Great) had no male heir, and so the royal line of Piast died with him in 1370. He provided for the transfer of the Polish crown after his death to his nephew, Louis of Anjou, king of Hungary. However, in his will he sought to secure the position of his grandson, Casimir of Słupsk (in Pomerania), by granting him significant territorial bequests, so that he might eventually succeed Louis, who also had only daughters to succeed him. Louis of Hungary did not mount the throne without incurring the opposition of the nobles of Great Poland (Polonia Maior) and Casimir of Słupsk. In this regard the terms of Casimir's will were soon undermined and the duke of Słupsk sought compensation for being passed over, accepting the duchies of Dobrzyń and Bydgoszcz. The late king's kinsman, Władysław the White, the rebel Piast duke of Kujawy, also pressed his claims to the crown.

The Angevin period lasted sixteen years, maintaining the unity of the kingdom of Poland and its administration. Louis strengthened the urban trade networks and the privileges of the towns (including full staple law (*ius stapuli*) for Cracow, which compelled merchants travelling through that town to put their goods up for sale there). But Louis did not rule Poland personally. His mother, Queen Elizabeth, sister of Casimir III, formed a regency and, after her death in 1380, another regency consisting of five nobles from Little Poland (Polonia Minor) led by Zawisza, bishop of Cracow, took over. Rus' of Halicz, which had been annexed to the Polish crown by Casimir III, was ruled by Duke Władysław of Opole, who attempted to strengthen the mission of the Catholic Church in south-west Rus' and to create a loyal nexus of local and immigrant knights.

The main problem facing the house of Anjou in Poland was how to secure the throne for Louis's daughters. Louis fostered the good will of the larger cities with his commercial policies. In 1374 he granted all the nobility and gentry of the kingdom a charter at Košice in Slovakia. This was an act of fundamental importance for the development of noble privileges. The king exonerated nobles from paying the plough tax as the *signum summi dominii* (service of two *grossi* per corn field (*laneus/lan*)). Depending on the quality of the soil, the *lan* covered 16–24 hectares cultivated by peasants on noble estates. Henceforth, whenever the king required additional revenues, he could impose them only with the agreement of the nobles. Shortly after this Louis was to grant similar privileges to the clergy.

The Angevin regime, in particular during the regency of the nobles from Little Poland, heightened the nobility's sense of its political value. After Louis's death in 1382 the nobility did not fully accept his wishes, refusing to consent to closer union with the Hungarian crown in the person of his daughter, Maria, who had been designated heir to the Polish throne and was engaged to Sigismund of Luxemburg, then margrave of Brandenburg. Two years of negotiations with the queen mother, Elizabeth of Bosnia, led to the accession of the younger daughter, ten-year-old Jadwiga (Hedwig) and her arrival in Cracow, where she was crowned king (*rex*) in 1384. The controlling oligarchs consulted the opposition in Great Poland which was itself divided by the internecine strife between supporters of the two powerful clans. They also took account of the other pretender to the throne, Siemowit III, duke of Mazovia. The lords of Cracow rejected Jadwiga's fiancé, the newly arrived William of Austria, and drove him out of the capital. They then turned their attention to the new partner in the international game in eastern Europe, the grand duchy of Lithuania. The web of motives which inclined them to turn to Lithuania included collaboration against a common enemy (the Teutonic Order), the need to settle affairs in southern Rus', where Lithuanian and Polish interests came into conflict, and the threat posed to both countries by the Black Sea Tatars.

LITHUANIA AND POLAND IN THE FOURTEENTH CENTURY

The Lithuanian state, which developed as a monarchy in the thirteenth century, had been consolidated by Grand Duke Gediminas (*c.* 1315–1342), and was to reach the peak of its political power as an independent state in the second half of the fourteenth century. Under the government of the sons of Gediminas, Grand Duke Algirdas and his ally, Prince Kestutis of Trakai, Lithuanian rulers continued to defend their lands against the attacks of the Teutonic Order, which was harrying the western borders of Lithuania in order to unite its lands in Prussia with the Letto-Estonian territories held by the Livonian branch of the Order.

While Lithuania was defending its northern and western borders from Catholic crusaders, it took over a wide expanse of territory which stretched from its own original ethnic domains in Aukštatija (Upper Lithuania) and Žemaitija (Lower, that is north-western, Lithuania) towards what became known later as Belorussia and Ukraine, as far as Smolensk, Briansk and the Black Sea steppes. Military successes strengthened the despotic authority of the grand duke. Whilst the Lithuanians, members of the Baltic family of Indo-European peoples, resisted Christianity despite repeated attempts to convert them to it, the Rus'ian population inhabiting the greater part of Lithuanian-controlled territory (not ethnic Lithuania but western Rus') had been Christians of the eastern rite for several centuries. In the fourteenth century the Lithuanian state used Rus'ian written culture in the ruler's chancery, but in order to preserve its political identity the Lithuanian nobility remained unwilling to convert to eastern Christianity, even though such a prospect was considered.

Jogaila (Jagiełło), son of Algirdas, became grand duke in 1377. Five years later he drove his uncle, Kestutis, from his domain and established himself as sole head of the grand duchy, taking power into his own hands. His first act was to seek an understanding with the Teutonic Order with which he concluded peace in 1382 at the unacceptable price of the surrender of Žemaitija. His second course of action was to effect a *rapprochement* with Moscow. In 1384 Jogaila sought a Muscovite alliance, arranged his marriage to the daughter of Dmitry Ivanovich Donskoi, and undertook to receive baptism in the eastern rite. However, these plans came to nought when a third way was offered him by the Polish nobility. This would involve Jogaila's baptism in the Latin rite, his marriage to Queen Jadwiga and his coronation as king of Poland. Before Lithuania's eyes spread the prospect of weakening the pressure from the Teutonic Order, initiating joint Lithuano-Polish efforts against the Tatars, and settling the disputed Lithuanian border in Galician Rus' which was occupied by Poland.

The personal union of the kingdom of Poland and the grand duchy of Lithuania was brought about by the Union of Krevo (1385). As patrimonial lord of Lithuania, when he became king of Poland Jogaila united his inheritance with Poland by the terms of this act. On the one hand the patrimonial and personal character of Jogaila's power contrasted with the Polish crown's established autonomy from the person of the king. On the other, Polish nobles who wished to interpret the Union as the annexation of Lithuania to the crown encountered resistance from the grand duke's kinsmen and counsellors who defended the separateness of the Lithuanian state.

Jogaila accepted baptism in the Latin rite in Cracow, taking the name of Władysław. As a young man of twenty-three or twenty-four, he married Jadwiga in 1386 when she was thirteen. The royal couple henceforth acted together in the most important political affairs. Jadwiga was a figure of uncommon beauty and education, a person of deep religious sentiment who was endowed with diplomatic talents that became apparent over the years. She died giving birth to her only daughter in 1399. Władysław II Jagiełło came to Cracow with the experience of government gained by his dynasty over several generations and, above all, with personal skills tested in politics and war. He was to occupy the Polish throne for forty-eight years.

The collective baptism of the Lithuanian population carried out in 1387 under the personal guidance of King Władysław began the conversion of the ethnically Lithuanian part of the grand duchy. At first there was compulsion from the authorities, followed by a feeling of obedience to ecclesiastical authority and of belonging to a wider Christendom. In 1387 a bishopric was established in Vilnius, a second following in Žemaitija in 1417. The numerical sparsity of the clergy, widely spread settlement and the powerful resistance put up by traditional culture meant that full acceptance of the new faith took several generations, embracing the upper social strata first. In addition to the Polish clergy, Lithuanian priests appeared early on. The leaders of the Lithuanian Church were educated at the University of Cracow which had been restored for this purpose, too, by Queen Jadwiga and King Władysław.

The resistance of members of the Lithuanian dynasty to the Polish interpretation of the Union of Krevo led to opposition formulated by the king's cousin, Vytautas (Vitold), son of Kestutis, who sought the support of the Teutonic Order. King Władysław, however, worked out a compromise between the Lithuanian and Polish positions. In 1392 he made Vytautas co-ruler of Lithuania, adopting for a few years the higher title of *dux supremus* while Vytautas was styled *magnus dux*. Over the years Grand Duke Vytautas became King Władysław's partner, but conducted his own domestic and foreign policies. He consolidated the grand duchy by removing several of his kinsmen from their own princely domains and turning them into grand-ducal governors. He maintained his Volynian borders, too, despite the actions of Polish nobles. Vytautas sought to make the Golden Horde his dependant, but in 1399, on the banks of the river Vorskla (which flows into the Dnieper), he suffered a defeat which fixed for three centuries the line of the Tatar threat to the southern borders of Lithuania and Poland. At the same time this setback illustrated the indispensability of the alliance of the two nations if they were to maintain their international position.

After the death of Queen Jadwiga, Władysław was acknowledged by the Polish nobility as king of Poland. This led to recognition of the equal political status of Lithuania and Poland by an act agreed by Władysław and Vytautas in 1401.

POLAND AND LITHUANIA IN CENTRAL EUROPEAN CONFLICTS

The danger posed to the two realms by the Teutonic Order lent a particular value to the Lithuano-Polish alliance. For a couple of decades the Order had pursued aggressive policies towards Lithuania whilst seeking a reconciliation with Poland, counting on the rivalry of the two neighbours. They united in the face of the threat posed to Poland by the alliance of the Order with Sigismund of Luxemburg who, as margrave of Brandenburg, stood between Great Poland and Danzig, and in the face of border conflicts on the river Notec. Lithuania could not accept the loss of Žemaitija forced upon Vytautas in 1398, and in 1409 it supported a Žemaitijan uprising against the Order.

Similarly, the Order decided upon a recourse to military methods. The Knights concluded an alliance with Sigismund of Luxemburg, now king of Hungary, his brother King Vaclav of Bohemia and the dukes of Western Pomerania. The 'Great War' of 1409–11 between Poland–Lithuania and the Order culminated in the battle of Grunwald (Tannenberg) in 1410. This, one of the greatest battles of the late Middle Ages (it involved some 60,000 men), ended with the defeat of the Order's forces. The grand master, Ulrich von Jungingen, and many Teutonic dignitaries were slain. But the peace settlement of 1411 satisfied only the war aims of Lithuania, which regained Žemaitija.

None the less the military and economic power of the Order was considerably weakened, to the advantage of the enhanced prestige of the allied peoples. From circles favouring church reform and from Jan Hus, who regarded the Order as an anachronism, there came letters of congratulations to King Władysław. A fresh act of union was drawn up in 1413 at Horodło on the river Bug, where forty-three Polish clans adopted a corresponding number of Lithuanian noble families, endowing them with Polish crests. King Władysław and Grand Duke Vytautas granted the Lithuanian nobles fiscal and legal privileges on the Polish model.

The Polish delegation to the Council of Constance began to play an active role there in 1415. Representatives from the recently converted Žemaitijans attended the Council as witnesses of the success of Władysław and Vytautas in carrying out their Catholic mission, while the metropolitan of Kiev attended as a representative from the grand duchy. The Poles were to come to the defence of Jan Hus. They presented the treatise of Paulus Vladimiri (of the University of Cracow) concerning papal and imperial power over the infidel. This canonist opposed conversion by the sword and defended the rights of pagans to own land, thereby provoking a bitter polemic with the supporters of the Teutonic Order. The Polish argument was backed by scholars from the University of Paris. Yet another war with the Order broke out in, but in 1422 the Knights were compelled to abandon Žemaitija once and for all. The Order's expansion in the Baltic region was contained, and Prussia and Livonia were separated from each other.

The Polish–Lithuanian federation now became the great power of central and eastern Europe. Following the outbreak of the Hussite War in Bohemia in 1420, Czech groups which supported ideas of national monarchy moderated by social policies endorsed the candidature of Władysław II Jagiełło as king of Bohemia. The king declined this proposal in the face of complications abroad and opposition at home from Polish nobles who were unwilling to support Hussite sympathies among the gentry. With the king's knowledge Vytautas received a similar offer, but he nominated Władysław's nephew, Prince Sigismund, son of Koributas, in his stead. Help for the Hussite rebellion was thwarted by the bishops and nobles headed by Zbigniew of Olesnica, bishop of Cracow, already a prominent political figure. The king had to recall Prince Sigismund and, in 1424, he was compelled to issue an edict against the Hussites and their allies. Nevertheless, in the following year Sigismund was to assume the role of king-elect and lent his support to the uprising of radical Hussite-Taborites in Silesia.

Following the birth of Crown Prince Władysław, whose mother was Władysław's fourth and last wife, Sophia, from the Lithuanian ducal family of Alseniskis, the king entered discussions with the nobility concerning the succession to the Polish crown. The king's son had an assured inheritance in Lithuania, for Vytautas had no heir, but in Poland the king had to secure his son's right to succeed him by granting privileges, in particular to the nobility, which circumscribed royal power. Of several charters which defined the legal status of the nobility over the course of centuries, the most important was the Privilege of Brest (in Kujawy) of 1425, known by its opening words as *Neminem captivabimus nisi iure victum*. This guaranteed that noble property would not be confiscated, nor would nobles be imprisoned, without due legal process.

After the death in 1430 of Vytautas, who had spread his influence on the Lithuano-Rus'ian border deep into Muscovy and had even considered accepting the royal crown which Sigismund of Luxemburg offered him, King Władysław placed the last of his living brothers, Švitrigaila, on the grand-ducal throne. He professed full independence from the kingdom of Poland, and allied himself with the Emperor Sigismund and the Teutonic Order which carried out a destructive raid on northern Poland. In 1432 Polish leaders managed to foment opposition to him in Lithuania which led to the fall of Švitrigaila's regime and the seizure of the grand-ducal throne by Vytautas's brother, Sigismund, son of Kestutis, who resumed the policy of union with Poland. A lasting achievement of Švitrigaila's brief reign was the granting of equal rights to Catholic and Orthodox boyars – until that time only Catholics had enjoyed such privileges.

THE REGENCY OF BISHOP ZBIGNIEW AND THE REIGN OF WŁADYSŁAW III

After the death of Władysław II Jagiełło in June 1434, his son, Władysław III, almost ten years old, succeeded to the throne with the agreement of the nobility. Government was carried out by a regency headed by a strong political individual, Zbigniew, bishop of Cracow, with a royal council still formed mainly of nobles from Little Poland. The opposition signified its dissatisfaction with the regency and made contact with the Bohemian Hussites. From that quarter there came, after the death of the Emperor Sigismund of Luxemburg in 1437, the proposal that Władysław II's younger son, Casimir, should take the Bohemian crown. The royal widow, Sophia, supported the plan but Zbigniew objected to it. Despite Polish attacks on Bohemia and Silesia, the Polish candidate lost to Albert of Habsburg. The bishop-regent helped Grand Duke Sigismund consolidate his position in Lithuania and defeat opposition from Švitrigaila. In Little Poland, Zbigniew fought the Hussite opposition led by Spytko of Melsztyn which enjoyed noble and even peasant support. In 1439 at the battle of Grotniki on the Nida the revolt was put down. Spytko was slain and denounced as an enemy of the country.

After the assassination of Grand Duke Sigismund at the hands of his boyars in 1440, the young Casimir, then thirteen years old, was sent to Lithuania in Władysław III's name as royal lieutenant. The Lithuanian nobles immediately acclaimed him as grand duke and renounced the personal union with the Polish crown. Without abandoning hope of renewing the Lithuanian alliance, the Polish nobles sought compensation in a union with Hungary.

In 1439, following the death of Albert of Habsburg who had been king of Bohemia and Hungary for a short time, the Hungarian nobles, in the face of the Turkish threat, turned to the court of Cracow and offered the crown of St Stephen to Władysław III and, despite pro-Habsburg opposition exhibited by certain magnates, he was crowned in Buda in 1440. The young king set about defending his realm against the Turks, aided by a coalition established by Pope Eugenius IV. In 1443 victories were won in Bulgaria and a useful peace concluded which, in the following year, provoked the Holy See to insist on the preparation of a new expedition aimed at reaching Constantinople. But the Venetian fleet failed to prevent a Turkish attack coming across the Bosphorus, and in 1444 the twenty-year-old Władysław III, along with many Polish and Hungarian knights and the papal legate, were killed at the battle of Varna. This defeat sealed the fate of the Byzantine Empire and the Balkan Slavs. The Ottoman threat now moved ever closer to central Europe. However, neither in Poland nor in Lithuania, where domestic problems predominated, was the importance of the role played by Władysław in the resistance against the Turks fully appreciated.

RESTORATION OF CROWN LANDS: POLAND AND LITHUANIA UNDER CASIMIR IV

Because of the initial uncertainty regarding the fate of Władysław, and also because of disputes between Polish and Lithuanian nobles, the practical accession of Casimir IV to the Polish throne was to take two years. The new king proved himself a consummate politician. He managed to secure the throne whilst acknowledging the equality of his two realms in a 'fraternal union' under his control. In Poland he faced the opposition of magnates headed by Bishop Zbigniew, but he was helped by the 'young barons of the kingdom' who had been summoned from Great Poland to lend support to the government of the king and his council. In the early years of his reign he also sought support from the cities. The king and the royal party successfully opposed the financial demands of the papal *curia* and countered clerical opposition to the royal nomination of bishops. The death of Cardinal Zbigniew in 1455 led to the defeat of the opposition from Little Poland. At the same time Casimir somewhat belatedly confirmed the privileges granted to the nobility by his predecessors, and then established his position in the kingdom with regard to the constitutional nature of the crown. Moreover, by granting separate privileges for several territories in Nieszawa at the beginning of the decisive war with the Teutonic Order, Casimir ensured that no new taxes could be raised or military levies called without the agreement of conventions of nobles known as land diets. He thus opened the way for the creation of parliamentary forms of consultation between the king and the privileged classes.

In Lithuania Casimir reigned with wide authority but not despotic power. He won the support of the Lithuanian lords with a charter granted in Vilnius in 1447 which endowed the boyars of the grand duchy with the same rights as those enjoyed by the Polish nobles, including individual freedoms, the right to hold their own courts and to trial by their peers, and the exemption of subject boyars from tribute for grand-ducal matters. He confirmed Lithuania's borders as they had been during Vytautas's reign and promised to give government offices only to Lithuanians. The border dispute between Lithuania and Poland was settled with a compromise: the grand duchy retained Volyn', and the kingdom kept Podolia. The war with Moscow was halted for a time by the peace of 1449. This was a turning-point which ended Lithuanian expansion into Rus'; a brief period of equilibrium ensued, after which Muscovite expansion began in earnest.

In Prussia and Pomerania the Teutonic *Ordensstaat* was undergoing a period of internal crisis. Wealthy cities such as Danzig, Torun (Thorn) and Elbląg (Elbing), with their German-speaking populations, opposed fiscal exploitation at the hands of the Order. Similarly the Order's vassals of knightly rank, whether they spoke German or Polish, combined to found the Lizard League (*Eidechsengesellschaft*). After 1440 the Prussian estates, the knights and the towns-folk joined together in the Prussian Union which, as representative of political society, conducted negotiations, mainly in matters of taxation, with the Order's grand master. The repression of the Union at the hands of the Order provoked a revolt. In 1454 Casimir IV received a rebel delegation led by Hans von Baisen and, invoking the rights of the crown, he promulgated the incorporation of Prussia into the kingdom. A Thirteen Years War then erupted, to be waged without Lithuanian assistance. International opinion did not favour the abolition of the Teutonic Order, and Popes Calixtus III and, after him, Pius II intervened by placing Poland under an interdict which the people and clergy promptly ignored. The war ended in 1466 with the Peace of Torun. Danzig and Pomerania, which had been lost to the Order in 1308, and the western part of Prussia, including Elbląg and Malbork (Marienburg), were ceded to the kingdom of Poland to be known henceforth as Royal Prussia. The Order's power was restricted to the remainder of Prussia, excluding Warmia (Ermland) which was held by the local bishop as a vassal of the Polish king. The grand master of the Order transferred his capital from the castle in Malbork to Königsberg and swore allegiance to the Polish king whom he acknowledged as the Order's sovereign.

In addition to this considerable restitution of crown lands, a little earlier Poland had made some territorial acquisitions on the Silesian border which were important because of their proximity to Cracow. In 1457 the king gained the duchy of Oświęcim and sovereignty over the duchy of Zator which would become a crown possession in 1497. The crown also received a part of the vassal duchy of Mazovia following the extinction of certain branches of the Mazovian Piasts (in 1462 and 1476).

THE JAGIELLONIAN DYNASTY IN CENTRAL AND EASTERN EUROPE

In the second half of his reign, Casimir IV's intention was to weave a network of alliances based on the several branches of the Jagiellonian dynasty. In spite of the possibilities then opening up, he did not seek further restitution of Silesian lands to the Polish crown; rather he devoted every effort to place his sons born of Elizabeth of Austria (the daughter of Emperor Albert II) on the thrones of Bohemia, Hungary, Poland and Lithuania. In this he was successful.

In Bohemian affairs Casimir IV did not allow himself to be drawn into the Catholic coalition against King George of Poděbrady; rather, he attempted to mediate between him, the emperor and King Mátyás Corvinus of Hungary. George agreed to recognise Casimir's eldest son, Vladislav, as his heir to the Bohemian throne. After George's death, the Bohemian Diet duly elected Vladislav in 1471, although Mátyás Corvinus managed to establish himself in Silesia, Lusatia and Moravia. The conflict with the king of Hungary found its expression in military and diplomatic disputes. Mátyás's death in 1490 opened the way for Vladislav to mount the Hungarian throne; with the aid of Hungarian magnates, he supplanted his younger brother, Jan Olbracht, the favourite of the gentry, who was compensated for his loss with the governorship of Silesia.

Thus the Jagiellonian dynasty took control of a vast expanse of central and eastern Europe from the borders with Moscow and the Baltic to the Black Sea and the Adriatic coastlands. Yet Casimir IV's diplomatic successes aroused no enthusiasm in Poland or Lithuania, since they brought no immediate advantages. The Habsburgs were to gather in the fruit of the king's labour in the following generation. The authority that Casimir IV created through the successes of the first decades of his reign was undermined by the onerous and, in noble eyes, unsuccessful military campaigns fought for dynastic interests. Important problems concerning the reform of the military and fiscal systems remained unsolved.

Casimir IV rarely visited Lithuania, but he did not yield to the demands of the Lithuanian nobles for the establishment of a lieutenancy there. At that time there was a growth in the expansion of Moscow which snatched Novgorod from the Lithuanian sphere of influence (1471) and followed a policy of gathering Rus'ian lands under its control at the expense of Lithuania. Casimir IV spent four years in Lithuania, entrusting the government of the kingdom to his second son, Casimir (later canonised), for two years. The king survived an attempt made on his life by Rus'ian princes with the connivance of the grand duke's vassals, two of whom were sentenced by the grand-ducal council and beheaded. The counter-offensive against Moscow, which had captured several border duchies and inspired Tatar invasions of the southern regions, was unsuccessful.

In 1475 the Turks took over the Genoese colony of Kaffa, on the northern coast of the Black Sea, a major centre of oriental trade, and in 1484 they seized Kilia (at the mouth of the Danube) and Akkerman (at the mouth of the

Dnestr), which belonged to Moldavia. In this situation Stephen, prince (voivode) of Moldavia, renewed his allegiance to the Polish crown, following the example of his predecessors. The immediate threat from the Turks and the Tatars was henceforth to become a constant feature of Lithuanian and Polish foreign policy.

KINGS JAN OLBRACHT AND ALEXANDER

After the death of Casimir IV in 1492 the Lithuanian lords elected his son, Alexander, as grand duke in accordance with his father's wishes. Casimir had bequeathed the Polish crown to his eldest son, Jan Olbracht. The personal union was suspended during Jan Olbracht's reign, although, like his grand-father, he used the title of *supremus dux* in Lithuania. He formed a plan for an anti-Turkish coalition which, instead of dealing with the Turkish threat, led to conflict with the Moldavian prince, Stephen, and defeat at his hands. An agree-ment was struck with the Turks which was to last many years. The king's success was the incorporation of the duchy of Plock in Mazovia into the Polish crown. In domestic affairs he relied on the support of the parliamentary chamber of deputies against the magnates of the royal council or senate. The short reign of Jan Olbracht provoked a counter-attack from the magnates during the reign of his brother Alexander (from 1501 onwards).

Alexander's reign in Lithuania opened with the loss of Viaz'ma to Ivan III which led to a speedy strengthening of the alliance with Poland. The war with Moscow (1500–3) brought Lithuania losses beyond the Dnieper and the begin-ning of the division of Belorussian and Ukrainian lands between Lithuania and Muscovy. After his election to the Polish throne, Alexander was compelled to consent to a change in the form of government which henceforth placed deci-sions of the highest importance for the state in the hands of the full council known, since the sixteenth century, as the senate. The government of the oli-garchy, which had control during the king's absence on campaign against Moscow, provoked widespread opposition among the gentry. Relying on the advice of his chancellor, Jan Laski, the king renewed his collaboration with the chamber of deputies and introduced genuine fiscal and administrative reforms, including the law *Nihil novi* (1505) which forbade the promulgation of new laws without the consent of the senators and the deputies of the region. This opened the way for a *monarchia mixta* on the Polish model with strong participation by the gentry. On Alexander's death in 1506 the throne passed to his 'only heir and successor' in both Jagiellonian states, the last of the brothers, Zygmunt I (Sigismund) 'the Old'.

THE POLISH ESTATES AND THE MONARCHY

In the fourteenth and fifteenth centuries the Polish kingdom assumed the form of a monarchy of privileged estates, whose rights stemmed from privileges granted to the nobles and gentry as a body and to the clergy as a whole. However, the towns did not enjoy any such uniform representation since royal privileges were bestowed on them individually. Similarly, villages were granted separate privileges for each village.

The *Corona Regni Poloniae* was perceived as an institution separate from the person of the king, replacing what previously had been a patrimonial concept of royal or ducal power. Outside those areas under royal government, the crown held some lands in vassalage and was believed to have rights to others which had once belonged to it. In a period of interregnum or when no male heir existed, the crown was represented by the estates, with the nobility and gentry, the privileged classes, occupying first place. The Polish crown exercised a sense of sovereignty which was expressed in theory by the principle that the king is emperor in his own realm (*rex imperator in regno suo*) and, in practice, by the indivisible and inalienable nature of its territory. From the thirteenth century the emblem of the kingdom had been a white eagle on a red field; from the restoration of the kingdom in 1295 the eagle had worn a crown on its head.

From the death of Louis of Hungary in 1382 royal power in Poland was based on the principle not of heredity but of election which, in the fifteenth century, limited candidacy to members of the Jagiellonian dynasty. At his coronation the king issued a general confirmation of the privileges enjoyed by the estates. Royal power extended widely in the administration of the kingdom which was regulated with the help of central palace officers (the marshal, the chancellor, the treasurer and others). In the provinces, the king had his lieutenants, *starosta*, often called the 'royal arm' (*brachium regale*) who were responsible for administration, taxation, justice in criminal matters and policing. The king was the highest judge and commander in chief of the army. He conducted foreign policy whilst domestic affairs were run by both the king and the royal council, comprising the highest dignitaries of the crown, certain officials and the bishops. The full council, or senate as it came to be known in the early sixteenth century, numbered about seventy members, of whom the king often convened only a number.

The ancient duchies incorporated into the kingdom survived as palatinates whose dignitaries were appointed by the king for life. These men retained some of their legal rights, but they lost their former powers as keepers of castles, while retaining the right to a place on the royal council. The holders of other ancient territorial offices preserved certain of their powers as local judges, but their titles were, above all, more an expression of their holders' rank among the nobility.

Each estate had its own judicature. The nobility had local courts in particular areas which acted on the principles of common law, besides adjudicating also in non-litigious matters such as the registering of property and credit transactions. The castle courts, under the control of the *starostas*, were important especially in criminal cases. In the course of the fifteenth century the courts of the gentry and the *starostas* alike ceased hearing cases from the peasantry. Church courts judged cases involving canon law, and acted with the gentry in cases connected with spiritual matters such as heresy, marital problems and wills containing religious bequests. The urban judiciary acted in certain towns; in cases of appeal the king summoned a high court for Little Poland in Cracow castle. The village judicature lost its right of appeal beyond the village lord who could only be indicted before the local court for miscarriage of justice.

The genesis of Polish parliamentarism may be traced from the *colloquia* or meetings of the nobles and gentry which, in the thirteenth and fourteenth centuries, had been summoned by local lords in various regions of the country to deal with political matters and to fulfil their judicial functions. At the end of the fourteenth century these became more frequent in two forms. For the whole kingdom there was the *sejm* (general assembly) or *conventio magna* dominated by the magnates of the royal council, whilst in the provinces, in Great Poland or (separately) in Little Poland, there were *conventiones generales* (provincial assemblies). The privileges granted by Casimir IV to the gentry in 1454 strengthened the hand of the third rank of the system of representation for the estates, the *sejmiki* (land diets) or *conventiones particulares* which numbered eighteen by the end of the fifteenth century. Local dignitaries and regional gentry took part in these. The king summoned them to approve additional royal taxation and to agree to the general mobilisation. The *sejmiki* pronounced on interpretations of the common law and elected two plenipotentiary deputies to attend assemblies summoned from all over the province or the kingdom. At the accession of Jan Olbracht, the *sejm* of the whole kingdom became the chief parliamentary form as provincial sessions were summoned less and less frequently. The Piotrkow *sejm* (1493) was the first two-chamber *sejm* to consist of the royal council (called the senate shortly afterwards) and the chamber of deputies, formed by local representatives. Urban leaders were also invited to attend in an advisory capacity. The *sejm* was soon to witness political conflict between and within its chambers.

THE NOBILITY AND GENTRY, PEASANTS, TOWNS, CHURCHES AND THE JEWS

The social influence of the aristocracy in the fourteenth century had been favoured by its clan structure which united, under a common crest and clan/family name, a lord, his kin and client knightly families. Noble privileges embraced the whole of the clan and its members and hence, despite attempts to regulate it with laws, the nobility was not divided into upper and lower castes. Despite the great differences in property-owning between the lords, the middling and the poorer gentry, the noble estate was a single body in the fifteenth century. It was, too, a large estate; in the sixteenth century (for which estimated figures are available) it may have amounted to 8 or 10 per cent of the population. The whole nobility enjoyed full allodial ownership of the land; there was no system of fiefs. The duty of loyalty to the king and crown of the kingdom of Poland bound it together.

Urban and agricultural reform in the thirteenth century had followed the model of German law (*ius teutonicum*) founded on the strength of ducal privileges granted to towns and villages in the face of immigrant colonists and the large number of native settlers who had come to live within the jurisdiction of that law. This law had local variations such as the *ius Culmense* (in Chelmno, Prussia) and the *ius Sredense*, named after the town of Sroda (Neumarkt) in Silesia. The towns were governed by the *wojt* (*Vogt, advocatus*) whose position was hereditary. His power had often been superseded in the fourteenth century by the town council, formed from the higher ranks of the urban mercantile patriciate (which produced the burgomaster), along with some representation from the commons (*communitas*), mainly the artisans who also grouped themselves into guilds. Towns paid additional taxes, every one of which was originally imposed with consent; however, from the mid-fifteenth century, the *sejmiki* and *sejms* did not seek agreement, but imposed taxes on towns and noble properties alike.

Despite the growth of commerce and local exchange, and the participation of large towns in the trade which linked western, central and north-eastern Europe, and regardless of a significant rise in local artisan production and means of credit, only a handful of towns such as Danzig, Cracow, Poznań and Lwów had populations which could be counted in tens of thousands. On the other hand, the network of smaller towns was dense and rivalled those of central European countries. However, the lack of representation prevented the towns of the kingdom from taking their place in a wider political life.

The position of villagers was varied. In the fifteenth century the majority lived under German law with local variations. The village paid the lord of the manor rent in coin, corn and modest services in labour dues. Custom regulated the right of a peasant to leave his village; the whole village could remove the lord if he raped the wife or daughter of a peasant, if he were excommunicated or if there were demands on the village to pay his debts. The headman of the village (*soltys*) inherited his status, held a greater parcel of land than the other villagers and had charge of the village court. In the fifteenth century lords of the manor tended to buy up the headships to increase the size of the manorial farm with the lands of the *sołtys* or the peasants. This led to peasants working on a lord's farm one day a week for each *lan* (*laneus, mansus*) of 16–24 hectares owned by them. In the fifteenth century monasteries led the way towards raising grain production for the new and expanding markets across the Baltic into western Europe. In the fourteenth century a vigorous new settlement of villages had spread into the wooded foothills of Little Poland. In the following century Polish settlers appeared in the western parts of Halicz, and immigrants came from Mazovia to Podlasie and as far as the lake district in Prussia, which thenceforth became known as Mazury. Together with these a sufficiently intensive form of agriculture was introduced: the three-field system and livestock breeding.

The Catholic Church organised its dioceses within two metropolitan sees: one had had its centre in Gniezno since AD 1000, and included the two Lithuanian sees; the other was based first in Halicz (1367–1414) and later in Lwów. The archbishop of Gniezno (bearing the title of primate from 1417) led the whole episcopate, crowned the king and occupied the first place in the royal council, which he did not cede even to the bishop of Cracow, Zbigniew, the first Polish cardinal. Together the two ecclesiastical provinces contained seventeen sees; the jurisdiction of Gniezno stretched into Wrocław (Breslau), whilst Lwów had jurisdiction over a diocese in Moldavia. Church property (owned by bishops, chapters, religious orders and the parishes) made up about 12 per cent of cultivated land. The nobles fought to change the tithe system and demanded the payment of taxation on ecclesiastical property. In Rus' the Orthodox Church enjoyed complete toleration. After the collapse of the short-lived Orthodox metropolitan see of Halicz (1370), the bishops of this province were placed under the jurisdiction of Kiev, where a metropolitan, with authority over nine sees, was established in 1458 for the Orthodox in Poland and Lithuania. The colonies of Armenian merchants had their own church and cathedral in Lwów after 1356; the attempt to unite the Orthodox and Roman Churches at the Council of Florence in 1439 did not involve the Polish Armenians. However, the idea of uniting the Orthodox and Roman Churches was supported by some of the Rus'ian prelates and the kings of Poland. Although an Orthodox metropolitan (Isidore of Kiev) took part in the Council of Ferrara–Florence (1439), no formal union between the Churches came of it.

The fourteenth and fifteenth centuries are marked by the further mass influx of Jews, the Yiddish-speaking Ashkenazim, from German-speaking lands. Thirteenth-century ducal privileges and those issued by the kings in the fourteenth and fifteenth centuries assured the Jews of a separate estate with their own autonomous organisation in particular towns, freedom of religion and judicial rights along with protection of their persons and the right to trade. Despite attempts in some towns to restrict or banish the Jewish population, Jewish rights were preserved in their entirety.

THE LITHUANIAN MONARCHY

State and political institutions evolved with increasing speed in the grand duchy of Lithuania throughout the fourteenth and fifteenth centuries. In the fourteenth century the power of the grand duke was based on inheritance, in the sense that he gained it by being the son of his father generally acknowledged as most fit to rule. The members of the dynasty had the right to be endowed with their hereditary lands under the grand duke's lordship. In the areas which were directly subject to him, the grand duke was absolute ruler and governed personally as leader and judge, although he received help from his court and his lieutenants in particular territories. In regions granted as duchies to members of the dynasty, or in those duchies where Rus'ian princes were installed, the duke was likewise an absolute ruler.

The boyar class comprised knights owing military service. It occupied lands distributed by the grand duke or regional duke which were heritable in the male line but subject to confiscation at the ruler's will. The population of boyar villages owed tribute and service to the grand duke on his lands or to the dukes on theirs. Apart from the free population of serfs subject to the boyars, there were also slaves, particularly enslaved prisoners of war.

In the fifteenth century privileges, which sometimes reflected the influence of Polish law issued by the grand dukes both for the grand duchy as a whole and for particular lands within it, helped to achieve new models of social relationships and institutions. There can be no doubt that the granting of such privileges resulted in the creation of a social structure more widely differentiated than before. In the course of the century, certainly by the time of the death of Vytautas, individual princes lost their lands to the grand duke who conferred them on a more limited basis. These princes were transformed from regional rulers into members of the upper class in which they joined the boyars who were termed lords and who formed a strong, propertied group. They were leaders with their own banners, and stood responsible only to the grand duke as judge. The remaining mass of boyars created a gentry differentiated by property. While a section of the gentry enjoyed the privileges granted to the boyarlords (inherited property, no punishment without trial, the consolidation of tax and personal dues), there were also boyars of the second rank who were subject to a prince or lords.

The peasant population consisted of those born as slaves who, as household servants, were deprived of all rights even when settled on manors and lands, and of serfs, who did have a legal identity, although they were bound to the soil. At the same time a considerable number of freemen enjoyed personal freedom but lacked property rights.

The towns in Lithuanian Rus' maintained their old structures, having a free population with differentiation between the richer denizens, who owed cavalry service, and the rest. In legal matters the towns were dependent on the grand-ducal or ducal lieutenants and their judiciary. From the end of the fourteenth century, with ducal agreement, a few towns (Vilnius and Trakai) came under German law: but there were still only a few of these in the fifteenth century. The network of towns with either local or German law became very rare. This is typical of eastern Europe, but contrasts with the situation in central and Baltic Europe.

Jews appeared in Lithuania by 1388, and more came in the next century to occupy urban settlements. They received three local charters from Grand Duke Vytautas (1388–9) which were confirmed as general privileges by King and Grand Duke Sigismund in 1507. The small number of Tatar military settlements on the territory of the grand duchy (from the second half of the fourteenth century) enjoyed full recognition of their Islamic confessional allegiance. In Vytautas's day, a small group of Karaites arrived in Lithuania to practise Judaism without Rabbinical or Talmudic teachings.

From 1440, when the Lithuanian lords elected Prince Casimir as their ruler, the office of grand duke became elective, although always limited to descendants of Władysław II Jagiełło. The grand duke exercised his authority with the help of court dignitaries of whom the chancellor (from 1458 always palatine of Vilnius at the same time) exercised wide authority in domestic and foreign affairs. Lieutenants controlled provincial administration and eventually, under Polish influence, these came to be called *starostas*, holding full financial and judicial powers. From 1413 onwards there were two voivodships, or palatinates: Vilnius and Trakai, with another centred on Kiev after 1471, along with the castellanies of Vilnius and Trakai. At the district (*powiat*) level the leaders were the standard bearers, that is gentry captains summoned to regional mobilisation.

Political society was constituted by the grand-ducal council. This included bishops, court and provincial officials, in total several dozen persons. Alongside this council was a more prescribed or secret council consisting of a handful of lords. These were advisory bodies with great political power which, from the mid-fifteenth century, were consulted regarding the levying of taxes. The summons of the grand-ducal council in 1492, directing each province to send ten or more representatives to the election of the new grand duke, led to the establishment of a Lithuanian *sejm*. However, like that of the land diets, the full development of the *sejm* was to occur in the sixteenth century.

FOURTEENTH- AND FIFTEENTH-CENTURY CULTURE

In particular after 1400, life at the courts of the king and leading secular and religious officers, as in the large towns of the kingdom of Poland, came close to the level of that of other central European countries at the end of the Middle Ages. Court celebrations and entertainments, tournaments, feasts and ostentatious decoration contrasted, as they did everywhere, even in the major towns, with the squalor and the poverty found in many towns. The higher nobility lived in contact with the urban patriciate and eagerly adopted foreign customs imported into the country or encountered on journeys abroad. None the less, there were regional variations. Silesia and Little Poland were the leaders in cultural matters; then came Royal Prussia, Great Poland and Mazovia. In the south-east, the new developments spread unevenly. In Lithuania, which still belonged culturally to eastern Europe, the first wave of westernisation was to affect the princes, nobles and the Catholic elements of the population in particular.

From the mid-fourteenth century Poland developed a network of cathedral, parish and town schools. This was to affect both the numbers of those who pursued studies in order to enter the Church and others, often sons of the nobility and townspeople, who did so with the aim of working in local courts and chanceries. Such schools also prepared men for university study in Italy (especially Bologna), France and at Prague.

The University of Cracow, the second after Prague to be established in central Europe, had been founded by Casimir III in 1364 on the Bolognese model to concentrate on law as a subject necessary to the administration of Church and state. Renewed by a foundation charter of Władysław II Jagiełło in 1400, the university came under the influence of Paris and established a faculty of theology. Maintaining contact with other universities, it influenced neighbouring lands, especially Lithuania. In philosophy, it tended towards nominalism and taught ethics and politics, spread conciliar doctrine within the Polish Church and maintained religious orthodoxy. From among the theologians, Matthew of Cracow and Iacobus de Paradiso stand out, while the lawyer Stanislaw de Scarbimiria developed the doctrine of the just war (1411). The school of astronomy led by Adalbert of Brudzewo and others produced the university's most famous alumnus, Nicholas Copernicus, who studied there between 1492 and 1496.

The study of literature and Italian humanism reached the university later in the century. Gregory of Sanok, archbishop of Lwów (d. 1471), patronised writers seeking new literary forms and secular subject matter. About 1470 a new circle grew up in Cracow around Filippo Buonaccorsi-Callimachus, and at the end of the century the 'Sodalitas litteraria Vistulana' was formed by Conrad

Celtis. Latin remained the major form of literary expression in many areas. In history, Jan Długosz (Longinus), canon of Cracow, teacher of the royal children and a diplomat, composed his *Annales seu cronicae inclyti regni Poloniae*, an extensive account of Polish history from the beginning to 1480, written in the style of Livy. The Polish language was used for biblical translations, statutes of common law and both religious and secular poetry. The first presses appeared in Cracow in 1473/5; the first Polish-language book was printed in Wrocław in 1475, and the first Cyrillic book was produced in Cracow in 1491.

The fine arts were represented by guilds of painters, sculptors and goldsmiths patronised by the royal and magnate courts, the Church and the towns. Gothic style common throughout central Europe had three provincial artistic centres: Silesia, Little Poland and Prussia which influenced one another, the kingdom and the grand duchy. The spread of western European art in the age of the Romanesque had reached the Vistula; in the Gothic period western influence spread as far as Vilnius and Lwów. From the other direction, Rus'ian art of the Novgorod and Volyn' schools reached Cracow and Lublin as a result of the personal 'ecumenism' of Władysław III and Casimir IV.

The nations within the Jagiellonian state, open to cultural interchange, were held together by loyalty to the kingdom or the grand duchy. Such was the legacy bequeathed to the age which followed.

CHAPTER 29

RUSSIA

Nancy Shields Kollmann

'RUSSIA' is the state descended from the grand principality that coalesced around Moscow in the fourteenth century and began the historical continuum that extended to the Russian Empire (1725–1917), the Soviet Union (1917–91) and modern Russia. The fifteenth century was one of the most significant, and underappreciated, centuries in Russian history. At the century's beginning the grand principality of Muscovy stretched from Mozhaisk (about 100 miles to Moscow's west) eastward to the Suzdal'-Nizhnii Novgorod grand principality (subject in part to Moscow since 1392), from Riazan' in the south-east to the northern forests of Beloozero, Vologda and Ustiug. But its power was more tenuous than this geographical expanse would suggest. Moscow's hold in the north and in Suzdal' was superficial; surrounding Moscow lay myriad principalities ranging from the weak Rostov and Iaroslavl' to the more potent grand principalities of Riazan' and Tver'. Powerful rivals included the city republics of Novgorod and Pskov, not forgetting the grand duchy of Lithuania. Yet by the end of the century Moscow had achieved clear dominance in this area often called north-east Rus' (in reference to the Kiev Rus' state that flourished from the tenth to the twelfth centuries and bequeathed to Muscovy some important heritages). The key to Moscow's success lay in the means, both institutional and symbolic, that it devised to consolidate its authority and to exploit and mobilise social resources. Those means of governance and ideological constructions endured for at least the next two centuries, and resonated beyond.

Sources for fifteenth-century Russia are by no means abundant, but in some areas, such as politics and diplomacy, they are remarkably rich. Chronicles flourished, with codices being compiled in the grand duchy (Smolensk), Ukraine, Moscow, Tver', Rostov, Vologda, Perm, Novgorod and Pskov. Jan Długosz's history reflects on the grand duchy; travellers to the grand duchy and the north-east offer interesting accounts (Gilbert de Lannoy, Josafo Barbaro,

Map 19   Russia

Ambrogio Contarini and others). Treaties survive from Novgorod, Pskov, Moscow, Tver' and the grand duchy with neighbouring powers and appanage kinsmen. Muscovite princely wills also survive. For social and economic history, extant sources are much weaker. Secular and ecclesiastical lawcodes from the Kiev era (the Nomocanon, or *Kormchaia kniga*; the Just Measure, or *Meriolo pravednoe*; the Charters of Vladimir and Iaroslav; the Russian Law, or *Russkaia pravda*) continued to be copied, edited and applied in the grand duchy, Novgorod and the north-east. Codifications of law and judicial procedure also appear: Pskov, 1397; the grand duchy, 1468; Novgorod, the 1470s; Moscow, 1497. The Lithuanian state chancellery records, collected in the 'Metrika', are rich, while for Muscovy only military muster rolls and some diplomatic records were produced at court. For north-east Rus', there survive documents of land transfer, wills, genealogies, some litigation over land, a few Novgorod and Tver' cadastres and a charter of local government (to Beloozero, 1488). Finally, saints' lives offer details of daily life.

The chronicle of Muscovy's regional expansion and geopolitical interaction displays vividly Moscow's successes. The dynamics of geopolitics in this century were structured by Moscow's rivalry with the grand duchy of Lithuania. The Kipchak khanate (or so-called Golden Horde) – westernmost outpost of the Mongol Empire, populated primarily by Tatars – had disintegrated by the early decades of the century and its splinter groups played only supporting roles in the regional balance of power: the khanate of Kazan' existed by the 1440s, producing a khanate in Kasimov in 1452 that generally acted as a Muscovite pawn; the Crimean khanate was controlled by the Girey clan by 1443; the Great Horde on the lower Volga coalesced in the wake of the destruction of Sarai by Timur (Tamerlane) in the first years of the century. The arenas of geopolitics focused on the region's two spheres of commercial activity, the Baltic and the Volga. From the mid-fifteenth century the Baltic witnessed a trading boom that lasted until the early seventeenth. It focused on grain exports from the Polish, Ukrainian and Belarus'an hinterlands, shipped at Stettin, Danzig, Königsberg and Memel. Ports and trade centres farther north – the Livonian towns of Riga, Dorpat (Tartu) and Reval (Tallinn), as well as Novgorod and Pskov – continued to export forest products, primarily furs and wax. A prominent casualty of the heated competition on the Baltic was the Hanseatic League, whose monopoly on Baltic trade disintegrated from the pressure of various forces: national governments anxious to capture income from the Hansa towns; the competition of Dutch, English, southern German and Swedish merchants; and a breakdown of discipline within the League itself. By the second half of the century Novgorod's economy also declined precipitously. Novgorod became embroiled in self-destructive conflicts with the Hansa; it suffered from competition in Pskov, Smolensk, Polotsk, Moscow and Kazan' (which was taking over the middle Volga and Kama basin from the Volga Bulgar khanate, which had been decimated by the collapse of the Mongol Empire at the end of the fourteenth century); Novgorod's trade empire proved to be inflexible, for it remained based on squirrel fur when European demand shifted to luxury fur by mid-century.

The Baltic trade enhanced inland routes extending from Moscow and Tver' westward to Novgorod and Pskov or to centres in the grand duchy such as Velikie Luki, Toropets, Vitebsk and Polotsk (both on the western Dvina), Smolensk and Vilnius. With trade on the Volga river eclipsed by Tatar strife, the Dnieper returned to its Kievan-era glory. Towns of the grand duchy on the Dnieper route, such as Chernihiv (on the Desna), Smolensk, Pereiaslav and Kiev (all on the Dnieper), Turov (on the Pripet) and Volodymyr in Volhynia flourished, while north-east Rus' merchants developed trade routes through Kolomna and Riazan' (on the Oka) to the upper Oka basin and on to the head-waters of the Desna, Dnieper and Don, and across the steppe to the Black Sea. The transit of goods to and from Europe and the east – once traversing the Mongol 'silk road' across the steppe through an axis at the Caspian Sea – now pivoted around the Black Sea. Genoese colonies at Soldaia (Sudak, Surozh) and Kaffa not only received annual expeditions of northern merchants from towns in the grand duchy and north-east Rus', but sent their own merchants (Italians, Tatars, Greeks, Armenians, Jews) in return. The Crimean Horde's trading centres at Ochakov and Perekop also prospered, even after Turkish conquest in 1475. It is thus no coincidence that the principal objects of contention between the grand duchy and Moscow lay on these routes: Novgorod, Pskov, Tver', Smolensk and the upper Oka basin.

The rivalry between the grand duchy and Moscow simmered throughout the first half of the century. In the first third of the century the towering figure of Grand Duke Vytautas (1382–1430) overshadowed the relationship. Driven by a desire to assert his control from the Vistula to the Volga and to safeguard the integrity of the grand duchy in its dynastic union with Poland (1385), Vytautas was the most important political figure of his generation in eastern Europe. Having failed in the first when defeated by the Great Horde at the Vorskla river in 1399, he none the less succeeded in the second goal through the Union of Horodło (1413). By virtue of the marriage, in 1391, of his daughter, Sofiia, to Grand Prince Vasilii I Dmitrievich (1389–1425) and Vasilii I's naming him guardian of his underage son, Vytautas exerted influence in Moscow. He refrained from taking over Muscovy in 1425 when the ten-year-old Vasilii II (1425–62) inherited the throne. Instead, in the late 1420s Vytautas acted on other fronts, pursuing campaigns against Pskov (1426) and Novgorod (1428) and securing treaties of subordination from the still independent princes of Pronsk, Riazan' and Tver'. In 1429 Vytautas agreed to accept a king's crown from the Holy Roman Emperor, but he died in 1430 while the crown was *en route*, blocked from reaching him by Vytautas's anxious rivals in Poland, the Papacy and the Teutonic and Livonian Orders.

Vytautas's death set off a succession struggle in the grand duchy which prevented it from playing an active role in north-east Rus' politics. In the 1430s and 1440s the grand principality of Moscow was similarly embroiled, the issues being dynastic succession and regional tensions. When the deaths of Vytautas and of Metropolitan Fotii (1431) deprived Vasilii II of effective patronage and mediators, the young ruler's uncle, Iurii of Galich (with a capital at Zvenigorod), challenged him for the throne. Since early in the fourteenth century the Daniilovich dynasty had been practising *de facto* primogeniture (despite traditions of collateral succession in the Riurikide dynasty from which it stemmed), because heirs were few and mortality high. Prince Iurii's claim threatened in the main the boyar clans, who had flourished under the predictability of linear succession; support for the young heir was therefore strong. The dynastic struggles flared for almost twenty years, in two phases. Prince Iurii won the Kremlin briefly in 1434, but died later that year. His son, Vasilii Kosoi, continued the challenge, but was blinded in 1435, temporarily ending the hostilities. These were renewed in 1445, when the defeat and temporary capture of Vasilii II by the Kazan' Tatars opened opportunity for Prince Iurii's second son, Dmitrii Shemiaka. Shemiaka seized the Kremlin and Vasilii II in 1446, blinding him in retaliation for Kosoi's mutilation. The war ended later that year with the expulsion of Shemiaka from the Kremlin and a victory for Vasilii II, his boyars and the principles of linear succession and central control.

The failure of the opposition can be attributed to its incoherence. The most consistent supporters of the Galich princes were trading centres of the upper Volga and northern territories rich in furs: Kostroma, Galich, Vologda, Beloozero and the city republic of Viatka (with its capital at Khlynov). Prince Ivan of Mozhaisk, whose lands approached the border with the grand duchy, also threw in his lot, as did Suzdal'-Nizhnii Novgorod. Although an in-law of Prince Iurii, the Lithuanian Grand Duke Švitrigaila (1430–2) was too embroiled in his own struggles for the throne in the grand duchy to help; disarray among the Tatars prevented them from playing a consistent role. Novgorod and Tver' feared Moscow too much to mount effective opposition. Novgorod tried to play both sides by sheltering both Vasilii II and Prince Vasilii Kosoi in 1434, but by the 1440s it openly supported Prince Dmitrii Shemiaka, offering him sanctuary in 1446. He died there in 1453, poisoned perhaps on Vasilii II's orders. Tver' initially supported the opposition, but in 1446 allied with Vasilii II, affirming the alliance with the betrothal of the future Ivan III (1462–1505) to Grand Prince Mikhail's daughter, Mariia. Finally, in 1449 the grand duchy agreed not to intervene, and renounced its designs on Novgorod and Tver'. Thus, the opposition to Vasilii II was diffuse and tentative.

One loser in the dynastic war was the Moscow Daniilovich dynasty itself, since the principle of linear succession proved to be costly. Ivan III forbade and delayed the marriages of several of his brothers, so that Iurii and Andrei the Younger died unmarried, Andrei of Uglich was arrested in 1491 with his two sons and died in captivity, and Boris of Volok Lamskii lived in constant tension with Ivan III. The majority of Vasilii II's remaining kinsmen were persecuted after the dynastic war: two descendants of Dmitrii Shemiaka and Ivan of Mozhaisk, who had fled to the grand duchy in the 1440s, were enticed back to Muscovy in 1500 and one, Shemiaka's grandson, was arrested with his son in 1523 (both died in prison). The loyal Prince Vasilii Iaroslavich of Borovsk was also arrested with most of his sons in 1456 and died soon thereafter. This stringent policy continued until Ivan IV (1533–84) was left with no direct or collateral male kin and the dynasty died out with his last surviving son, Fedor, in 1598.

There were two clear winners in the struggle, of which one was the Moscow boyar elite. That body's origins can be traced to the late fourteenth century in a core of families that founded hereditarily privileged military clans whose senior members had the hereditary right to serve as boyars.[1] That dignity gave them access to power, status, land and other largesse from the grand prince. Surviving the dynastic war, this core retained pre-eminence into the sixteenth century. The second victor in the dynastic war was the grand principality of Moscow itself. In the 1450s and 1460s Moscow consolidated its control of the remaining independent north-east Rus' principalities: Riazan', through complex marital connections from 1456 to 1521; Iaroslavl', in 1463; and Rostov Velikii, in 1463 and 1474. From the 1460s Moscow embarked on a concerted military and missionary effort to consolidate control on lands where Muscovite authority had been claimed since the 1360s: Vychegda Perm' and Perm Velikaia on the upper Kama. By the 1489 conquest of Viatka and that of the Iugra and Voguly tribes of the Urals in 1499, Moscow came to dominate these fur-rich lands.

The defeats of Novgorod and Tver' constituted Moscow's greatest achievements in the wake of the dynastic war. Novgorod held obstinately throughout the fifteenth century to a myopic foreign policy, the product of its ruling boyar oligarchy. Reforms from the first third of the fifteenth century increased the collective mayoralty (*posadnichestvo*) from six to eighteen; the number rose to twenty-four and eventually to thirty-four by the end of the century. The council of lords (*sovet gospod*, composed of all current

---

[1] Kollmann (1987), pp. 55–120.

and past mayors and thousandmen, chaired by the archbishop), became larger still (fifty or sixty members), representing almost all of the city's boyar families. This was a decisive turn to oligarchy, marking the mayoralty's transformation from a political office to a corporate estate, symbolised by the use on coins of an image modelled on the seal of oligarchic Venice.[2] After these reforms the famed town council (*veche*) of Novgorod became a rubber stamp.

Recognising the rising power of Moscow, Novgorod enlisted Lithuanian and Suzdal′ (Shuiskii) princes as defenders of the town and developed ever stronger pro-Lithuanian parties (although some groups advocated compromise with Moscow). After Shemiaka's death in 1453 in Novgorod, Moscow attacked the city and exacted harsh retribution. By the Treaty of Iazhelbitsy, Moscow ostensibly agreed to maintain Novgorodian 'tradition' (*starina, poshlina*), but restricted political associations, exacted a huge fine, claimed territory in the Beloozero lands and, worst of all, imposed the grand prince's court as highest court of appeal. In 1471, still defiant, the boyars of Novgorod agreed to accept Casimir, king of Poland and grand duke of Lithuania, as their sovereign. This apostasy prompted Moscow to mount a coalition with Tver′ and Pskov against Novgorod; failing to receive help from Casimir, Novgorod fell in a bloody defeat at the Shelon′ river. The Treaty of Korostyn′ reaffirmed the Iazhelbitsy terms, claimed Vologda and Volok Lamskii, forbade Novgorod to consort with the grand duchy and forced the city to issue a new judicial charter in Ivan III's name.

It has been persuasively argued that Moscow's goals in Novgorod were merely to establish a loyal government; it was the intransigence of the pro-Lithuanian factions which drove Ivan III to more radical measures.[3] In 1478, after an abortive military campaign, Novgorod capitulated. Ivan III took over its hinterland, dismantled the urban government, installed Moscow vicegerents (*namestniki*) and, over the next decade, exiled hundreds of Novgorod merchant, boyar and lesser landholding families to lands in central Muscovy, confiscating all boyar-owned property, almost all of the archbishop's lands and about three-quarters of monastic estates, about 80 per cent of seignorial properties in all. On about half of these, Moscow introduced conditional land tenure (*pomest′e*). The northern Dvina lands and most of the Obonezhskaia fifth were not distributed as *pomestiia* because their land was inhospitable for farming and too sparsely settled. The rest were reserved for the grand prince and tax-paying communes. Finally, Ivan III summarily closed down the German Hansa neighbourhood in Novgorod in 1494 for twenty years, giving

[2] Ianin (1962), pp. 232–366.   [3] Bernadskii (1961), pp. 200–313.

preferential treatment to his newly founded (1492) fortress and trade depot at Ivangorod on the Gulf of Finland.

Clearly, both lack of military preparedness and political mismanagement played a role in Novgorod's defeat. It had failed to make effective alliances or to compromise with Moscow. Its intransigence is well characterised by Archbishop Evfimii (1429–58). Under him three major chronicle codices and five lesser redactions were compiled, providing an alternative vision to Muscovite all-Rus' compendia. In 1436 he initiated cults associated with the victory of the Novgorodians against the Suzdalians in 1169 (an allegory for Novgorod's rivalry with Moscow), a victory commemorated in icons and in tales and saints' lives, the latter commissioned from the Serbian writer, Pakhomii Logofet. In 1439 Evfimii also canonised nine Novgorod arch-bishops and several eleventh- and twelfth-century princes, all revered for espousing Novgorodian liberties. The most spectacular of the anti-Muscovite Novgorodian compositions of the fifteenth century was the legendary 'Tale of the White Cowl', which linked Novgorod with Byzantium and Kiev Rus' as the recipient of the white cowl, given by the Roman Emperor Constantine the Great to Pope Sylvester, and miraculously transported from Rome to Constantinople and then to Novgorod as emblem of the city's claim to univer-sal political authority.[4]

Archbishop Evfimii also evoked Novgorod's past in architecture, rebuilding several churches according to their original twelfth-century designs. At the same time, Novgorodian icon painting reached a zenith, continuing traditions of austere composition and subject matter, bright palette and emotional direct-ness. Other realms of culture flourished: the Novgorodian Archbishop Gennadii (1484–1504) assembled translators and writers to make the first full Slav translation of the Bible, and to compose polemics against Moscow's pre-tensions on Novgorodian church property and ecclesiastical autonomy, as well as against the Judaisers. This group of free-thinkers in Novgorod and Moscow was accused of Jewish practices and anti-Trinitarianism, but their full beliefs are difficult to ascertain due to a paucity of non-tendentious sources. In the climate of oligarchy, Archbishop Evfimii's activities had no galvanising effect on the populace. Rather, they epitomised the stubborn wilfulness of Novgorod's boyars, who met every victorious Muscovite embassy in 1456, 1471 and 1478 with proposals based on thirteenth-century treaties that pre-served 'tradition' and restricted princely authority to a minimum.

As Muscovy subjugated Novgorod, tensions continued between the grand duchy and Moscow. King/Grand Duke Casimir allied with the Great Horde in the late 1460s; in consequence Moscow turned to the Crimean khanate, an

---

[4] Labunka (1978).

alliance that endured until 1512. Expecting Lithuanian aid that never came, the Great Horde mounted a major campaign against Moscow in 1480, but was easily pushed back, presaging its final conquest by Moscow in 1502. The 'stand on the Ugra river' was immortalised beyond all real significance by Bishop Vassian Rylo of Rostov Velikii in the late fifteenth century and has come to signify the 'throwing off of the Mongol yoke',[5] although effective authority of the Kipchak khanate over north-east Rus' had already disintegrated in the first half of the century.

Disappointed that his earlier alliances with Moscow had not yielded territorial gain in Novgorod, Grand Prince Mikhail Borisovich of Tver' allied with Casimir in 1483, securing the pact by marrying one of Casimir's kinswomen. Ivan III responded by conquering Tver' in 1485. Since the fourteenth century Tver' had remained an ambitious and powerful centre. Its striking school of icon painting testifies to the city's cultural achievements, paralleled by its rulers' ambitions. Tver' Grand Prince Boris Aleksandrovich (1425–61) sponsored building projects; under him in 1455 an ambitious chronicle was compiled that placed Tver' at the centre of Christian history; it would be followed by another in 1534. He commissioned panegyrics to three ancestors locally venerated as saints for their historical greatness and enmity with Moscow. In a panegyric written sometime before 1453 by the elder Foma, Grand Prince Boris Aleksandrovich himself was exalted as 'tsar' and 'sovereign' (*gosudar'*), titles which implied universal authority.[6] In the first decades after conquest, Moscow accorded Tver' special respect: it was awarded as a 'grand principality' to Ivan III's heir, and its administrative structure remained largely intact for a generation.[7] Some members of its elite were welcomed into the Moscow elite, and no wholesale deportations took place. Tver''s landed cavalrymen became a local gentry, a policy that in the long run marginalised them politically, but which at the time may have been a concession to Tverian traditions.

Meanwhile, Moscow and the grand duchy engaged in repeated border skirmishes in the 1480s to 1490s. Upper Oka princes increasingly shifted allegiance to Moscow from the grand duchy, arguing that they had suffered discrimination because of their Orthodox religion. At the death of King/Grand Duke Casimir in 1492, the grand duchy accepted peace conditions advantageous to Moscow, cementing the arrangement with the marriage of Ivan III's daughter Elena to Grand Duke Alexander in 1495. By 1500 Ivan III, in alliance with the Crimea and Denmark (which was seeking gains in Livonia), launched war against the grand duchy and its allies, the Livonian Order and the Great Horde. That conflict ended in 1503 with no lasting territorial changes, but it initiated a

---

[5] *Pamiatniki literatury drevnei Rusi. Vtoraia polovina XV veka*, pp. 514–37.

[6] Likhachev (ed.), 'Inoka Fomy "Slovo pokhval'noe o blagovernom velikom kniaze Borise Aleksandroviche"'; Lur'e (1939).   [7] Floria (1975).

century of nearly continual war, alternating with shaky armistices, between Moscow and the grand duchy.

Completing its aims of territorial expansion initiated in the fifteenth century, Moscow conquered and annexed Pskov in 1510. Pskov had continued to follow a Novgorodian political path, expanding its collective mayoralty to six or seven mayors and maintaining an exclusive council of lords dominated by fewer than ten families. The city flourished, particularly as its trading partners, the three Livonian towns, rose to dominate Baltic trade. Pskov's vibrant architecture and icon painting testify to its prosperity. Throughout the fifteenth century Pskov developed close ties with Moscow and in 1510 the city compromised to avoid a full-scale conquest. Only secular, not ecclesiastical, land was confiscated. Nevertheless, Pskov's town council and mayoralty were dismantled, 300 families were exiled to Moscow, while many others were dispossessed and Muscovite vicegerents assumed control in the city.

Because the harsh climate of north-east Rus' imposed limits on productivity and population growth, a discussion of its environment will serve as appropriate background to a discussion of governance. Three fundamental features shaped the physical environment, the first being northern latitude. Moscow, at 55° 45′ north latitude, is farther north than London and all major American and Canadian cities save those of Alaska. Among major cities in the British Isles, only Edinburgh and Glasgow are marginally farther north, but their climates are moderated by ocean currents. No natural obstacles prevent cold Arctic air from sweeping across the flat lands of north-east Rus', which constitute an extension of the European plain. A third formative feature is lakes and rivers that, with portages, form an intricate transportation network from the Baltic to the Black and Caspian Seas. Major north- or south-flowing rivers are the Dnieper, Don, middle and lower Volga, northern Dvina and Kama; east- or west-flowing waterways include the Niemen and western Dvina, upper Volga, Moskva, Kliaz'ma and Oka Rivers. Soil and vegetation proceed south in belts of increasing fertility. Covering virtually all the Novgorod lands is the coniferous forest, or taiga. Covering Belarus' and Muscovy, and north to Novgorod, is a belt of mixed evergreen and deciduous vegetation with brown podzolic soil; south of Moscow runs a very narrow belt of broad-leaf deciduous trees with slightly better grey forest soil. Marsh and fen are common throughout. There is one very significant patch of fertile loess soil around Vladimir and Suzdal'. Temperatures in Moscow average about −10 degrees C (13.5 degrees F) in January; the growing season is only five months per year at Moscow, with snow cover for at least five months and limited precipitation. The relative weakness, then, of soil, heat and moisture produced subsistence farming.

Certain essential factors have been seen as leading to Moscow's spectacular rise. Attention has been drawn to its favourable geographical position; its dynasty's system of *de facto* primogeniture; the military and political support obtained from the Kipchak khanate and the financial benefits related thereto; and the effect of the metropolitan see being located in Moscow from 1325.[8] These factors are significant but, by themselves, insufficient to account for Moscow's success: Tver' and Novgorod enjoyed some of these same, or comparable, attributes and yet they still fell to Moscow. Russian scholars have traditionally explained Moscow's success in terms of an inevitable march of the Russian people towards unity under the banner of the Muscovite princes. But modern Russian nationalism weighs too heavily on this interpretation for it to be a satisfactory explanation. For additional insights into its success, one can look at Moscow's responses to the challenges of the fifteenth century. For example, Moscow capitalised on the vulnerabilities of its neighbours: as the Volga Bulgars and Novgorod weakened, so it pressed its expansion into the Novgorodian north, the Kama basin and the Urals; among Orthodox princes in the upper Oka area, it fomented anti-Catholic sentiment. More importantly, Moscow devised dynamic and effective means of governance that allowed it to consolidate its authority over human and natural resources.

Fifteenth-century Muscovite society and politics were grounded in personal relationships among family, community, clients and lords. The majority of the population was juridically free and lived in communes, either urban (*posady*) or rural (*volosti*). To the grand prince's tribute collectors (*dan'shchiki*), tax-paying (*tiaglye*) people paid the Mongol and princely tributes (the *vykhod* and *dan'*) in cash or kind. To his vicegerents in towns and district administrators in the countryside (*namestniki* and *volosteli*), tax payers rendered horses and services, paid sales taxes, customs duties and other small levies, and mustered for infantry service. To specialised officials, *putnye* boyars, tax payers paid goods in kind: furs, honey, wax, game; for urban fortification chiefs (*gorodchiki*), they repaired and fortified towns; they paid the upkeep (*korm*) of the prince's officials, whether resident or circuit; they were subject to the judicial authority of the vicegerent or district administrator for important crimes, although communes maintained jurisdiction over most civil issues.[9]

By and large peasants farmed their own closed fields, sowing rye, barley and oats, supplementing their diets with berries, nuts and mushrooms and small amounts of root vegetables, fish, meat and dairy products. Taxable people shared communal meadows, forests and ponds. They rarely achieved better than a three-to-one yield on their crops. Ruin was a constant threat from crop

[8] Kliuchevskii (1957), pp. 5–27.
[9] On tax obligations, see Veselovskii (1936), pp. 37–55; Gorskii (1966), pp. 162–261; Alekseev (1966), pp. 97–128; Blum (1969), pp. 101–5; Kashtanov (1988), pp. 59–91.

failure, epidemic, natural disaster and the ravages of war, accounting for the fact that a substantial minority of the peasant populace was dependent on landlords as renters, indentured servants or even as slaves. Although some became dependent when their communes were awarded by the prince to a lord, and some when they fell into arrears on debt obligations, most chose the status voluntarily because of advantageous terms, in return for military or fiscal protection or if their holdings were devastated by some natural disaster. Landlords as a rule enjoyed immunities on their lands: they and their people paid few taxes, tolls or services to the grand prince, with the exception of *dan'* and *vykhod*; landlords judged their own people independently of the prince's judicial network. Owners rarely maintained a large consolidated demesne; they exploited their holdings as 'upkeep' (*kormlenie*), just as princely officials exploited their subject populations.

The social stratum of landholders was large and various. It ranged from very small holders, such as peasants who had acquired a bit of land or families whose holdings had been reduced by partible inheritance, to wealthy princes, boyars, bishops and monasteries. The average owner was a smallholder: for example, two-thirds of over 1,600 Novgorod lay landholders recorded at the end of the fifteenth century held only 10 per cent of the land, while just twenty-seven men owned over one third of it.[10] Both men and women could acquire land; landownership did not require service, and some did not serve, judging by a Tver' cadastre of the 1530s in which many landholders were listed as serving no one. As a rule, lay landholders served princes or boyars, retaining the right to move to another lord without loss of land or other punishment. Many smallholders received their land as grants from such patrons and in return performed various services: some served in the military retinue of the boyar, prince, metropolitan or bishop (monasteries generally did not field military retinues); some were bailiffs and major-domos; some were specialised artisans and workers such as fishermen, falconers, fur collectors, dogkeepers, equerries, cooks and bakers.[11] The Tver' cadastre identifies about a third of its landholders as retainers of the bishops of Tver' or Riazan', of local monasteries, of large landholders or of princes who maintained some sovereign rights (the others served the Moscow grand prince or no one at all).[12] The most eminent of such dependants were the boyars, the grand prince's counsellors, who led his retinue (*dvor*) in war, served in major administrative positions and supported their own retinues on portions of their lands. Thus the army in any

[10] Blum (1969), p. 77.
[11] On dependent relations, see Eck (1933), pp. 185–254; Veselovskii (1926), pp. 14–22, (1936), pp. 56–68, and (1947), pp. 203–16, 231–43; Alekseev (1966), pp. 42–67; Blum (1969), pp. 70–105, 168–98; Pavlov-Sil'vanskii (1988), pp. 288–302, 395–425.
[12] Lappo (1893), pp. 226–31; Blum (1969), pp. 181–2.

of the principalities was comprised of privately maintained retinues loyal to lords who themselves stood in a hierarchy of personal loyalty from humble retainer to boyar and prince.

Administration was similarly grounded in personal relationships. Local officials were awarded their posts as sources of income by the local prince. The boyars who judged the prince's elite were themselves his dependants and servitors. Such a highly personalised governing structure functioned well in politically fragmented north-east Rus', but it could not offer rulers great wealth or military might. As long as land and service were not linked, as long as immunities were common, and as long as private retinues comprised the army, the ambitions of princes would be thwarted. Not surprisingly, the rise of Muscovy rested not only on the political victories described above, but also on administrative innovation.

Although chronologically not the first, the most prominent administrative measure was the expansion of the retinue (*dvor*) of the grand prince at the expense of those of private landlords, achieved by granting land in conditional tenure (*pomest'e*). The large-scale use of *pomest'e* began in Novgorod: over 1,300 *pomestiia* were assigned to men transferred from the centre, while the Novgorodian deportees received *pomestiia* in the centre (Moscow, Vladimir, Murom, Nizhnii Novgorod, Pereiaslavl' Zalesskii, Iur'ev Polskoi, Rostov Velikii, Kostroma, etc.). Such mass confiscations were exceptional. In other conquered territories, such as Viaz'ma (1494), Toropets (1499), Pskov (1510) and Smolensk (1514), confiscations took place on a lesser scale. Gradually over the sixteenth century, *pomest'e* grants – from court (*dvortsovye*) lands, confiscated appanages and free peasant communes – brought most available lands under conditional status.[13] It has been argued that the *pomest'e* system broke the back of the boyar elite by destroying its retinues and creating a new social force, the *pomeshchiki* (service landholders).[14] *Pomest'e* distribution in the late fifteenth and early sixteenth centuries, however, shows no strict delineation between holders of conditional and allodial (*votchina*) land. From the very beginning in Novgorod, *pomestiia* were granted to princes (mainly from Iaroslavl' and Rostov), to boyars and lesser non-princely families, and also to clients of such families (who constituted 20 per cent of *pomest'e* recipients in Novgorod). But the *pomest'e* system did not thereby destroy the practice of keeping private retinues. Not only did 'service princes' (who retained sovereign rights) and eminent boyars continue to maintain retinues into the sixteenth century, but so also did lesser holders. The structure of military service itself supported retinues by requiring that landholders bring to battle armed cavalrymen in pro-

---

[13] Bazilevich (1945); Veselovskii (1947), pp. 86–91; Zimin (1959); Alekseev (1966), pp. 129–67; Blum (1969), pp. 139–40.

[14] Zimin (1964 and 1970) and Kobrin (1985) pp. 90–135 summarise and criticise this position.

portion to the land they held, whether that land was allodial or conditional. By 1556, standards for such supplementary soldiers were set. Even the 1550 lawcode tacitly recognised private retinues by setting 'dishonour' payments for the dependants of boyars (*liudi*).[15]

Thus, the *pomest′e* system enriched and expanded the landholding elite as a whole; the idea of class struggle between *pomest′e* 'gentry' and *votchina* 'aristocracy' in this period has rightly been termed a 'myth'.[16] Rather, political groups focused on clans and their factions, formed by dependency, friendship and marriage. The *pomest′e* system was a brilliant strategy because it used rather than challenged the fundamental structuring principle of society – personal dependency. It co-opted the landed elite and oriented most ties of personal loyalty – previously intricately networked in individual relationships among princes, members of ecclesiastical hierarchies or boyars – towards the grand prince himself.

The *pomest′e* system complemented the transformation of local administration towards more private and local centres of control. As most tax-paying peasant communes were shifted to private jurisdiction, the traditional authority of landlords to police and judge their people provided the centre with a ready-made local administration. Vicegerents and district administrators gradually became superfluous, all the more so since they were prone to corruption. Their judicial autonomy was infringed by the requirement that representatives of the local populace and city administrators should oversee their courts.[17] Some of their fiscal authority was transferred during the period 1460s–1520s to city administrators (*gorodovye prikashchiki*), probably chosen from among local landholders. Their police and remaining fiscal authority were conclusively eliminated in the 'brigandage' and 'land' reforms of the late 1530s to 1550s, which transferred these duties to locally selected boards.[18] The grand prince's boyar courts, and later *prikaz* courts, handled the highest ranking social groups and cases of murder, arson, theft with material evidence, land disputes, false accusation, dishonour, brigandage and other high crimes. Similarly, from the late fifteenth century, the Kremlin government captured revenues increasingly being lost from the privatisation of peasant communes by narrowing fiscal immunities. New taxes were introduced: a fee in place of service for the postal network; taxes for the ransoming of war captives, for border and town fortifications, for new military units. Fiscal immunities were granted increas-

---

[15] *Rossiiskoe zakonodatel′stvo*, II, p. 101; *Zakonodatel′nye akty Russkogo gosudarstva vtoroi poloviny XVI–pervoi poloviny XVII veka*, no. 11.

[16] Zimin (1964), pp. 21–5; Kobrin (1985), pp. 199–218.

[17] *Rossiiskoe zakonodatel′stvo*, II (the 1488 Beloozero charter and the 1497 lawcode).

[18] *Pamiatniki russkogo prava*, IV; *Rossiiskoe zakonodatel′stvo*, II; *Zakonodatel′nye akty Russkogo gosudarstva vtoroi poloviny XVI–pervoi poloviny XVII veka*, nos. 11, 16.

ingly rarely from the mid-fifteenth century on, and were generally limited in time; from the 1480s to the middle of the sixteenth century virtually no charters of fiscal immunities were issued. Thus all peasants became liable for all the major taxes.

Legislation on the alienation of land issued under Ivan III and Vasilii III (1505–33) and affirmed in decrees between 1551 and 1572 pursued another goal implicit in the preceding reforms, that of turning local cavalrymen into regional corporations.[19] The inheritance laws limited the sphere of potential recipients of land through sale, gift or inheritance to kinsmen or in some cases to men of the same district, thus safeguarding the integrity of serving families and communities. Landholders were also forbidden to alienate property to the Church, and the right of women to own and dispose of land was curtailed, although these provisions had only limited success. In the integration of conquered territories, regional elite formation was also promoted: regional autonomies were widely tolerated (Tver', Beloozero); the grand prince's court (*dvortsovye*) lands in Tver', Novgorod, Riazan' and Dmitrov were administered through local major-domos (*dvoretskie*). Finally, the lawcodes of 1497 and 1550 reflect a limited centralising policy: only the familiar major crimes – murder, brigandage, theft with material evidence, verbal insult, false accusation, disputes over loans – are mentioned, as well as the proper registration of slaves and limitations on the mobility of peasants.[20] These last two social phenomena tended to drain the tax and military service base. Remaining crimes were implicitly left to landlords' and communal courts.

Just as it nurtured provincial 'corporations' of landholding cavalrymen, the Kremlin also cultivated a central elite. From the late fifteenth century it integrated newly arrived or newly elevated clans into the highest ranks of service, at the same time protecting the status of established boyar families by compiling muster rolls (*razriadnye knigi*) that named major commanders from 1375 (chronicle excerpts were used as evidence for the period until 1475). An apparently private genealogy listing the established Muscovite clans, mostly non-princely, was drawn up at the end of the century, followed by official editions in the 1540s and 1550s which added new families, mainly princely clans from north-east Rus' and some émigré lines from the grand duchy.[21] The goal of such official codifications was social stability, and the result was a consolidated elite representing Muscovy's newly acquired territories and newly structured military forces.

The court's willingness to integrate new clans and consolidate a central elite

---

[19] *Zakonadatel'nye akty Russkogo gosudarstva vtoroi poloviny XVI – pervoi poloviny XVII veka*, 5, 22, 29, 36, 37; Veselovskii (1947), pp. 91–9; Kobrin (1985), pp. 48–89. [20] *Rossiiskoe zakonodatel'stvo*, II.

[21] *Polnoe sobranie russkikh letopisei*, XXIV, pp. 227–34; Buganov (ed.), *Razriadnaia kniga 1475–1598 gg.*; Bychkova (ed.), *Novye rodoslovnye knigi XVI v.*; *Razriadnaia kniga 1475–1605 gg.*

can be seen in the changing composition of the grand prince's council of boyars. Under Ivan III the group numbered nine to thirteen, mostly from old non-princely families. Under Vasilii III the group ranged from five to twelve and included new families such as the Shuiskii princes from Suzdal' and the Bel'skii princes from the grand duchy. After Ivan IV's minority, from 1547 to about 1555, new clans from all sides of the conflict were brought into the boyar elite in a process of reconciliation. The number of boyars more than tripled, reaching about forty. The culmination of this process – perhaps not fully carried out – was the plan, announced in the 1550s, to create a central elite distinct from the provincial cavalrymen by resettling 1,000 elite families around Moscow.

The policies surveyed above generally avoided coercive measures in their pursuit of military preparedness, elite formation and regional integration. Yet the Kremlin did resort to force when expedient. An illustration is the gradual abrogation, from at least 1433 on, of the right of a landholder to choose his lord freely and to leave service without punishment. Disgrace (*opala*), accompanied by confiscation of property, was frequent, although usually short-lived; they served as tools of discipline, even terror, among the elite. Less draconian measures included surety guarantees (*poruchnye gramoty*) imposed on individuals suspected of divided loyalties, often obliging hundreds of others to pay indemnity should the man in question flee Muscovy.[22]

Limiting the peasants' ability to change masters was also a decisive step in creating a viable landed service elite. Limitations on peasant movement are noted sporadically beginning under Vasilii II and were fixed in the lawcode of 1497, although it is wise to caution against exaggerating the degree of peasant enserfment in the fifteenth century.[23] Such restrictions reflect increased competition for populated land and manpower, as do changes in agrarian life observed from the 1460s on. Landlords began replacing rent with labour demands, prompting peasants to seek new masters. Large landholders in the most populous areas (primarily the immediate environs of Moscow and Novgorod) consolidated their holdings and introduced three-field crop rotation (although some scholars claim that these trends started much earlier and were more widespread). Disputes between peasant communes and landlords over boundaries and possession rights multiplied. In sum, landlords gradually ceased regarding their holdings as autonomous sources of revenues and began to take more direct control.

The reign of Ivan III, then, was seminal in establishing institutions and policies that increased Moscow's armed might, that enhanced its ability to exploit

[22] Zimin (1964), p. 22; Kleimola (1977a) and (1997b); Alef (1983 and 1986); Dewey (1987).
[23] Zimin (1964), p. 22.

natural and human resources, and that integrated its disparate territories and populations. One should not exaggerate, however, the degree of centralisation achieved in the fifteenth or even sixteenth centuries. Muscovite grand princes tolerated divided sovereignty well into the sixteenth century: Ivan III, Vasilii III and Ivan IV all maintained appanage principalities for their sons and collateral kin (the Staritskii line), although they kept these princes on a tight rein. They allowed the so-called 'service princes' – men from the most eminent Gediminide or Riurikide lines – to keep some sovereignty well into the six-teenth century; they continued to grant fiscal and judicial immunities in the face of the policy restricting them; they tolerated boyar and princely retinues; they delegated local administrative, judicial and police authority to brigandage and land elders. However eclectic these policies seem to our modern eyes, they admirably enhanced Moscow's power, might and wealth.

Moscow's pursuit of its power was as single-minded in the realm of ideas as it was in the complex realm of land, administration and social engineering. Grounding the ideological construction of Muscovy was the metropolitanate, a symbolic centre and a propagator of centralising ideas. The very presence of the metropolitan's see exalted the grand principality. In 1448 the grand prince and local bishops themselves appointed Riazan' Bishop Iona as metropolitan of Moscow, or 'metropolitan of Kiev and all-Rus',' as the title read, without consulting Constantinople. When Iona died in 1461, his successor took the title simply of 'metropolitan of all Rus'' because a see including the grand duchy had been created in Kiev in 1458. Moscow finally broke with Constantinople in reaction to three issues: the abortive union of the Orthodox and Catholic Churches sanctioned in 1439 by some members of the Orthodox hierarchy, including Moscow's Isidore; the grand duchy's persistent campaign for a met-ropolitanate, most notably the appointment of Grigorii Tsamblak as metro-politan by a council of bishops from the grand duchy in 1414; and the Turkish conquest of Constantinople in 1453.

The metropolitan's court in the Kremlin became the centre of writings that exalted Moscow and established a pantheon of historical figures and associa-tions depicting Moscow as supreme regional ruler. A Moscow compendium of *c.* 1390 and its successor, the even more comprehensive Trinity chronicle, com-piled in 1408 at the metropolitan's court, exemplified his 'all-Rus'' responsibil-ities. The Trinity chronicle drew on sources from Tver', Nizhnii Novgorod, Novgorod, Rostov Velikii, Riazan', Smolensk and Moscow, and began with the Kievan primary chronicle, in its Vladimir-based Laurentian version, thus implicitly linking Moscow with the Kievan heritage.[24] Further 'all-Rus''

[24] Priselkov (ed.), *Troitskaia letopis'*.

Muscovite codices, all drawn up under the metropolitan's direction, followed in 1418, as well as in the 1430s or 1448 (the dating is disputed), while others followed at various stages of Moscow's battles with Novgorod (1456, 1472, 1477, 1479) and the grand duchy (1492, 1493–4, 1495).[25] At the same time, other political centres were also turning chronicle writing to their own purposes.[26] Novgorod and Tver' continued chronicle compilations,[27] Pskov produced a codex in the 1450s or 1460s, as the Vologda and Perm lands did in the late fifteenth century. The court of the bishops of Rostov was active throughout the century.[28] After Vytautas's death in 1430, a codex was compiled in Smolensk chronicling the Gediminide dynasty. The grand duchy's first claim to 'all-Rus'' authority came in the 1440s, when the episcopal workshop at Smolensk reworked a Muscovite all-Rus' codex. In the early sixteenth century the Gediminide and Smolensk chronicles were combined into a bolder claim of regional authority.[29]

The fifteenth century also saw the construction of pantheons of local heroes, secular and saintly. Panegyrics and canonisations in Tver' and Novgorod have been mentioned. In 1457 Evfimii of Suzdal', founder of Monastery of the Saviour, was venerated as a local saint, followed by two other semi-mythical Suzdal' personages. In Iaroslavl', in 1463, the revered thirteenth-century Prince Fedor Rostislavich and two of his sons were made saints; in 1474 several clerics from Rostov were also elevated. Most interesting were legends and cults, written after Moscow's conquest of Novgorod, depicting Moscow–Novgorod relations in a favourable light: one rewrote Pakhomii Logofet's Life of the twelfth-century Archbishop Ioann/Il'ia to make this fierce defender of Novgorod into a partisan of Moscow. Over the course of the fifteenth century Muscovite liturgical calendars greatly expanded the number of feasts by including local saints and revivals of cults from the Kievan era. In 1547 Moscow fully incorporated into the 'all-Rus'' hagiographical pan-

[25] *Polnoe sobranie russkikh letopisei*, V–VI, XVIII, XXV, XXVII and XXVIII; Priselkov (ed.), *Troitskaia letopis'*; Lur'e, 'K probleme svoda 1448 g.', 'Eshche raz o svode 1448 g.' and *Dve istorii Rusi XV veka*.

[26] Shakhmatov, *Razyskaniia o drevneishikh russkikh letopisnykh svodakh* and *Obozrenie russkikh letopisnykh svodov XIV–XVI vv.* ; Nasonov, 'Letopisnye pamiatniki Tverskogo kniazhestva' and *Istoriia russkogo letopisaniia XI–nachala XVIII veka*; Priselkov, *Istoriia russkogo letopisaniia XI–XV vv.*, 'Letopisanie Zapadnoi Ukrainy i Belorussii' and *Troitskaia letopis'*; Likhachev, *Russkie letopsi i ikh kul'turno-istoricheskoe znachenie*; Kuzmin, *Riazanskoe letopisanie*; Lur'e, *Obshcherusskie letopisi XIV–XV vv.* and *Dve istorii Rusi XV veka*; Murav'eva, *Letopisanie severo-vostochnoi Rusi kontsa XIII–nachala XV veka*.

[27] *Polnoe sobranie russkikh letopisei*, IV, pt 1, pt 2, fasc. 1–3, XVI, pts 1–2; Nasonov and Tikhomirov (eds.) *Novgorodskaia pervaia letopis' starshego i mladshego izvoclov*; Nasonov, 'Letopisnye pamiatniki Tverskogo kniazhestva'; Likhachev, *Russkie letopisi i ikh kul'turno-istoricheskoe znachenie*; Lur'e, *Obshcherusskie letopisi XIV–XV vv.*

[28] Nasonov, *Pskovskie letopisi*; *Polnoe sobranie russkikh letopisei*, XX, XXIII, XXIV and XXVI.

[29] *Polnoe sobranie russkikh letopisei*, XVI, XVII, XXXII and XXXV; Priselkov, 'Letopisanie Zapadnoi Ukrainy i Belorussii'.

theon most of the locally revered Novgorod, Iaroslavl', Rostov and Suzdal' saints, illustrating how effectively and single-mindedly the grand princes used non-coercive, symbolic tools to consolidate power.[30]

Moscow also took deliberate steps to build its own pantheon. Through the medium of a secular saint's life (dated by some to the 1390s, but more likely written in the late 1440s),[31] Dmitrii Donskoi was raised to the level of patron prince-saint of Moscow, although he was never officially canonised. In 1447/8 Metropolitan Iona presided over the canonisation of three or four key figures: Metropolitan Aleksii (1353–78, instrumental at Dmitrii Donskoi's court), Kirill of Beloozero, Sergii of Radonezh and perhaps Dmitrii Prilutskii (all of whom had founded influential monasteries in the fourteenth century). From the 1440s to the 1460s, Pakhomii Logofet composed lives, canons and liturgies in honour of some of these figures. He wrote a Life of Kirill of Beloozero, and reworked a Life of Aleksii written in 1447/8 and one of Sergii composed in the early fifteenth century by Epifanii 'the Wise'. Sergii began to be depicted in icons, becoming the central figure in an icon with scenes of his life by the end of the century; Dmitrii Prilutskii was also so honoured (an icon of him c. 1503, attributed to Dionisii, survives).

The cult of Metropolitan Peter (1308–26) is particularly interesting. It had been nurtured since his death in Moscow in 1326; by the end of the fourteenth century Metropolitan Kiprian (1375–1406) had re-edited Peter's Life; already in 1399 and in the early fifteenth century Peter was being depicted on ecclesiastical garments, and in the early to mid-fifteenth century he was depicted as the central figure on an icon. That icon may have been painted in Tver'. Peter's cult was widespread: churches were dedicated to him in Novgorod and Tver' in the fifteenth century; a mid-century icon cloth from Tver' depicts him and Metropolitan Aleksii alongside Saints Vladimir, Boris and Gleb. But by the late fifteenth century Peter was clearly co-opted by Moscow. A document of 1458 affirming Iona as the first independently selected metropolitan calls Peter a 'miracle-worker', and the 1479 Moscow codex under the year 1470 depicts Ivan III on the eve of a campaign to Novgorod making a prayerful procession to the graves of Peter, Aleksii and Iona, called 'miracle-workers'. When the Cathedral of the Dormition in the Kremlin was rebuilt between 1472 and 1479, Metropolitan Peter's remains were removed and replaced with great ceremony, commemorated by canons to Peter composed by Pakhomii Logofet. Similar pomp and honour attended Metropolitan Aleksii: a new church was built to house his remains in the monastery of the Miracles in 1431, and another in 1483; a new redaction of his Life was written in 1486. Sometime in the last

---

[30] Khoroshev (1986); Bushkovitch (1992), pp. 80–7.

[31] Salmina (1970); *Pamiatniki literatury drevnei Rusi. XIV–seredina XV veka*, pp. 208–29.

decades of the fifteenth or early sixteenth century, matching icons of Peter and Aleksii, with scenes from their lives, attributed to the workshop of Dionisii, were painted for the Cathedral of the Dormition in the Kremlin. Metropolitan Iona himself was canonised in 1472, expanding the cult of the 'Moscow miracle-workers' (in the late sixteenth century Metropolitan Filipp joined the group). These metropolitans were revered for their patronage of Moscow and its dynasty and, as has been pointed out,[32] for their loyalty to the Church as well. The choice of these saints was not casual: Peter first linked Moscow with the universal authority of the Church; Aleksii was associated with Dmitrii Donskoi, whose reign was being elevated into a founding moment of Russian history; while Iona marked Moscow's ecclesiastical independence.

Architecture joined literature and icons in embellishing Moscow. New stone palaces and churches for the metropolitans were built in 1450, 1473 and 1484. The Cathedral of the Dormition was rebuilt by Aristotele Rodolfi Fioravanti from 1475 to 1479, and that of the Annunciation by Pskov masters in 1482. The Kremlin walls and towers were redone in brick from 1485 to 1516 by Italian engineers. Several new buildings were erected: the Treasury in 1485 by Marco Ruffo, the Faceted Palace in 1487–91 by Ruffo and Pietro-Antonio Solari, and a stone grand-princely palace from 1499 to 1508 by an Italian architect named Alvisio. The Cathedral of the Archangel Michael was rebuilt from 1505 to 1508 by a second Alvisio ('Novyi'). Important monasteries also built new stone edifices in the Kremlin: the monastery of Simonov in 1458; that of Trinity and St Sergii in 1460 and 1482, and that of the Miracles in 1501–4. Boyars are recorded as constructing stone palaces or churches in their Kremlin courts in 1450, 1471, 1485 and 1486.

Such building gave opportunity for artistic decoration which could carry political themes or simply demonstrate Moscow's glory. The celebrated Russian artist, Dionisii, adorned the walls and iconostases of major buildings in the Kremlin and leading monasteries. From a political perspective, the frescoes done after 1509 (not by Dionisii's workshop) in the Cathedral of the Archangel Michael are interesting; they portray life-size images of each member of the grand-princely dynasty buried in that cathedral. The Cathedral of the Dormition, finally, became a repository of Moscow's past and future pretensions. Its iconostasis included revered icons such as the Vladimir Mother of God: a twelfth-century Byzantine work, it had been brought to Kiev in 1125, to Vladimir in 1155, to Moscow temporarily in 1395, and was now permanently installed in Moscow. Here, too, were located revered fourteenth-century icons: an image of the Saviour that had stood at Metropolitan Peter's grave, an icon of the Trinity, an image of the 'Saviour with the Fiery Eye'. Several newly

[32] Stökl (1981).

painted icons also adorned the cathedral, including the previously mentioned hagiographical icons of Peter and Aleksii. Finally, the cathedral was the repository of the graves of all the metropolitans of Moscow from Peter on (except Aleksii). Thus the Cathedral of the Dormition symbolically depicted God's blessing on Moscow, its antiquity and eminence and its ties to Constantinople, Kiev and Vladimir.

Moscow's cults of saints and architectural ensembles created a 'usable past' that claimed succession from the grand princes of Vladimir. The claim was implicit in the modelling of the Cathedral of the Dormition (1475) after its counterpart in Vladimir, and in the reverence accorded to the Vladimir Mother of God icon. It could also be seen in genealogical consciousness: the Trinity codex (1408) traced Prince Daniil of Moscow (c. 1276–1303) to Vsevolod 'Big Nest' (1176–1212) and Ivan Kalita (1325–40) to his son Iaroslav (1237–46). The codex often dated to 1448 in the first chronicle of Sofiia began the genealogy of the Muscovite dynasty with the generation of Iurii Dolgorukii (1149–57). On the other hand, in the second half of the century, broader claims began to appear, claims that Moscow was the direct and exclusive descendant of the Kiev Rus' state, and that the Muscovite princes enjoyed universal political authority as 'emperor' (*tsar*), a title traditionally reserved for Byzantine emperors and Mongol khans.[33] The grand princes of Moscow used the title *gosudar vsei Rusi*, or 'sovereign of all Rus'', on coins and in treatises from the 1440s on, in relations with Novgorod in 1477 and in diplomacy. The grand duchy conceded the title in a treaty of 1494, even though Moscow had applied the 'all-Rus'' phrase to King/Grand Duke Casimir as recently as 1449.[34] In the last decades of the fifteenth century the Moscow court also adopted the double-head eagle as a symbol, according to one theory,[35] from the Habsburg model. In tales about the ecclesiastical council held at Ferrara/Florence in 1439, Vasilii II was frequently called tsar, and in reworkings of chronicle tales about Dmitrii Donskoi's victory over the Tatars in 1380 and in the panegyrical Life of Donskoi, explicit links between Moscow and Kiev Rus' were asserted. Dmitrii Donskoi was associated with Saints Vladimir (himself called a 'new Constantine'), Boris and Gleb; his rival, Mamai, was called 'a second Sviatopolk' (a Kievan prince reviled as traitor and killer of his brothers Boris and Gleb). Dmitrii Donskoi was called tsar, thus exceeding the limits of the Kiev Rus' analogy, and the Muscovite state was equated with the 'Russian land', a term in Kievan-era sources which referred to the Kievan heartland or to all the territory ruled by the Riurikide dynasty.[36] Clearly, the goal in these compositions was to discredit the grand duchy's claim on Rus' lands (Smolensk

[33] Gol'dberg (1969); Pelenski (1977) and (1983).   [34] Szeftel (1979).   [35] Alef (1966).
[36] *Pamiatniki literatury drevnei Rusi. XIV–seredina XV veka*, pp. 208–29.

and the upper Oka were Moscow's primary concern) by painting Moscow as the historically ordained 'gatherer of the Rus' lands' (this epithet was explicitly applied to Ivan Kalita in Dmitrii Donskoi's Life).

Moscow reached even beyond Kiev to classical Antiquity to assert its status, a step paralleling Renaissance-era historiography throughout Europe. Significantly, one available ecclesiastical example was not used. In 1492 Metropolitan Zosima had called Moscow the 'second Constantinople,' presaging the theory of 'Moscow, the Third Rome' of the early sixteenth-century monk, Filofei, which linked Moscow with Rome ecclesiastically. The significance of this has been exaggerated; it later became influential only in Muscovite Church circles, not in secular ideology and policy formation.[37] Rather, late fifteenth-century ideologues turned to a secular legend of classical heritage to legitimise their rule. The ideas were contained in the sixteenth-century 'Tale of the Princes of Vladimir', whose early redactions can be dated to the 1490s or the 1510s.[38] This composition traced the descent of the Moscow grand princes from the Roman Emperor, Caesar Augustus, and described the transfer of symbols of sovereignty – crown, mantle, gifts – from the Byzantine emperor to the Kievan Grand Prince Vladimir Monomakh (ruled 1113–25), whence they moved to the grand princes of Vladimir, and then Moscow. The tale was generally accompanied by a derogatory genealogy of the Gediminide dynasty of Lithuania, indicating clearly the geopolitical context in which the composition was intended to play a role. The choice of this particular version of the Byzantine inheritance is significant; Ivan III's marriage to Sophia Palaiologa, niece of the last Byzantine emperor, in 1472 provided a claim to universal political authority but, as has been pointed out,[39] that connection was sullied by the Palaiologan dynasty having presided over the fall of Constantinople in 1453.

All these efforts make clear the concerted desire in Moscow to construct a historical myth, a pantheon of national heroes and a contemporary image that would legitimise its power. One is struck by the diversity and dissonance of these discourses. Rome, Byzantium and Kiev are all proffered as historical antecedents, while many sources focus narrowly on Vladimir-Suzdal'. Heroes like Dmitrii Donskoi and Metropolitans Peter and Aleksii focus attention on the fourteenth century, a formative era for Moscow. The overt politicisation of these discourses, each striving to suit the needs of a particular conflict and of a broadened definition of Moscow's ambitions, should make us sceptical of the widely held assertion of direct historical continuity in Russian history from

[37] Gol'dberg (1969), (1975) and (1983); Goldfrank (1981); *Pamiatniki literatury drevnei Rusi. Konets XV–pervaia polovina XVI veka*, pp. 436–55.

[38] Zimin (1972b); *Pamiatniki literatury drevnei Rusi. Konets XV–pervaia polovina XVI veka*, pp. 422–35.

[39] Nitsche (1987).

Kiev to Moscow. Moscow was not the sole continuation of Kievan history nor a privileged bearer of 'Rus'' ethnic identity or national pride, although many generations of ideologues have so argued, and although Muscovy itself used such artifices as explanatory devices. Moscow's consolidation of power in the fifteenth century was structured by immediate circumstances and opportunities grounded in the patterns of international trade, geopolitics and regional development at the eastern extreme of the European plain.

CHAPTER 30

BYZANTIUM: THE ROMAN ORTHODOX WORLD, 1393–1492

Anthony Bryer

CHRONOLOGY AND DEFINITION

BYZANTINES were perhaps more concerned than most medieval people with the insecure business of measuring time and defining authority. There was not much they could do about either, but naming is a taming of the forces of nature and anarchy, and placed the humblest in relation to the stability of God. Byzantines called this order 'taxis'. They craved *taxis* all the more in the fifteenth-century *Anno Domini*, because for Orthodox Christians, who counted by the *Anno Mundi*, it was, quite simply, the end of the secular world. For subjects of either, or both, emperor and patriarch in Constantinople the New Rome, the world was created on 1 September 5508 BC. Gennadios II Scholarios, Sultan Mehemmed II's first patriarch after the fall of Constantinople to the Ottoman Turks on 29 May 1453, put matters in cosmic proportion by foretelling doomsday on 1 September 1492, the end of the seventh millennium AM. In 1393, the first year of the last century of the world, Patriarch Antonios IV (1389–97) had put matters in *taxis*. Grand Prince Vasilii I of Moscow (1389–1425) had complained that while there was a Church, there did not seem to be a credible emperor in Constantinople, to which the patriarch replied that 'it is not possible to have a Church without an emperor. Yea, even if, by the permission of God, the nations [i.e. the Turks] now encircle the government and residence of the emperor . . . he is still emperor and autocrat of the Romans – that is to say of all Christians.'[1]

The truth was that in 1393 the Ottoman Sultan Bayazid I, who had in 1389 won his throne and the vassalage of Serbia on the battlefield of Kosovo, annexed Bulgaria and was preparing to encircle the government and residence of the Emperor Manuel II Palaiologos (1391–1425) in Constantinople, a blockade which was only broken when the sultan was captured by Timur at Ankara in

---

[1] *Acta patriarchatus Constantinopolitani*, II pp. 190–1; cf. Obolensky (1971), pp. 264–6.

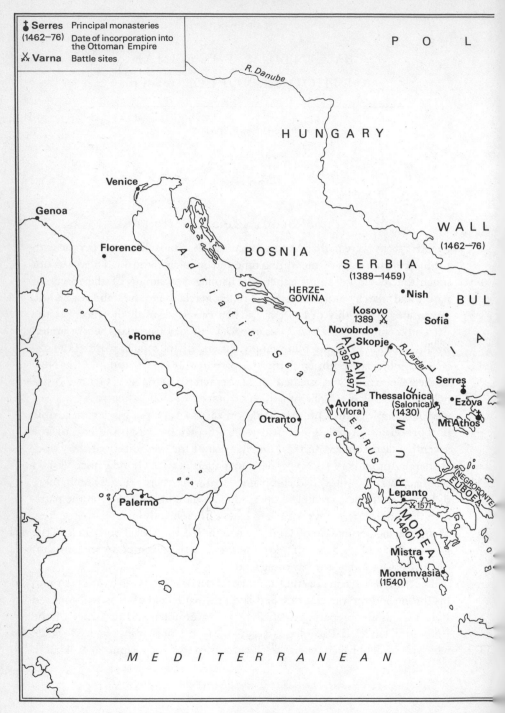

Map 20   The Roman Orthodox and Ottoman worlds in the fifteenth century

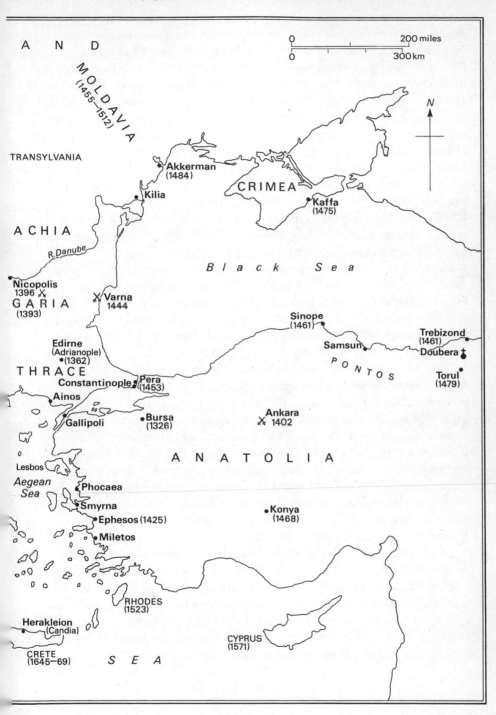

A   N   D

M O L D A V I A
(1455–1512)

TRANSYLVANIA

Akkerman
(1484)

Kilia

CRIMEA

Kaffa
(1475)

A C H I A

R. Danube

B l a c k   S e a

Nicopolis
1396 X
G A R I A
(1393)

X Varna
1444

Sinope
(1461)

Trebizond
(1461)

Samsun

Doubera †

P O N T O S

Edirne
(Adrianople)
(1362)

Torul
(1479)

T H R A C E

Constantinople Pera
(1453)

Ainos

Ankara
X 1402

Gallipoli

Bursa
(1326)

A N A T O L I A

Lesbos

*Aegean
Sea*

Phocaea

Smyrna

Konya
(1468)

Ephesos (1425)

Miletos

RHODES
(1523)

Herakleion
(Candia)

CYPRUS
(1571)

CRETE
(1645–69)   *S E A*

0   200 miles
0   300 km

N

1402.[2] The Mongols, however, soon left Anatolia, but not before reviving the nexus of emirates from which the Ottomans had sprung in what is now Turkey. Thrown into civil war until the emergence of Mehemmed I (1413–21), the Ottomans regrouped in their most recent Balkan conquests, giving Byzantium a half-century's respite. By 1453 the city was far from being a bulwark of the west against the hordes of Asia: indeed, the reverse. In secular terms the Ottoman state already ruled far more Orthodox Christians than did the Byzantine emperor. It was as a European ruler, based in the Balkans, that Sultan Mehemmed II (1444–6, 1451–81) finally took Constantinople as a preliminary to his conquest and reconquest of Anatolia, which occupied the rest of his reign.

The Ottomans were not a people but a dynasty; nor did their Muslim subjects then call themselves 'Turks'. Patriarch Antonios used the term 'nation' (Greek *ethnos*, Latin *natio*) pejoratively to describe such barbarians – but he did not call himself 'Greek' either, let alone 'Hellene', which meant an ancient pagan. He signed himself, in Greek, as 'Our Moderation, Antonios, elect of God, archbishop of Constantinople the New Rome, and ecumenical patriarch'. Today we call his flock 'Byzantines'. But this is as helpful as calling the French 'Lutetians', after the classical name of their capital in Paris. So far as Antonios was concerned, he and his flock were Christian subjects of the first Constantine's New Rome. Hence use is made of their own self-denominator of 'Roman Orthodox' to describe them in this chapter.

In the fifteenth century, 'Byzantines' still called themselves 'Romans' (Greek *Romaioi*), synonymous with 'Christians'; in Greek their Church was Catholic, or ecumenical. But Emperor John VIII Palaiologos (1425–48) had to appeal for support to an older Rome and another catholic Church against the encircling Ottomans. John would have been surprised to find himself described in the Latin version of the subsequent decree of the Union of the Churches as 'emperor of the Greeks', for he had actually subscribed to it in purple in Florence on 6 July 1439 as 'in Christ God faithful emperor and autocrat of the Romans' – his sprawling signature is in Greek.[3] But the emperor was emphatically Roman and his people soon confirmed their Orthodox identity too – by generally rejecting the Council of Florence.

This discussion of time and title may sound antiquarian today, but is vital to an understanding of the identity of the Roman Orthodox in the fifteenth century. It coincided roughly with the ninth century of the Muslim era, when it was the Ottomans who first named Byzantines for what they were: subjects of a Church which had survived an empire, called 'Rum', or Roman. The definition holds to this day, most vividly when a villager in north-eastern Turkey explains that 'This was Roman country; they spoke Christian here.'

² Matschke (1981), pp. 9–39.   ³ Gill (1961), p. 295; Buckton (1994), p. 220.

If this chapter were limited to the Byzantine Empire in the fifteenth century, it would be halved by the fall of Constantinople in 1453 which indeed resounded in the west, where historians have made that date one to remember, without quite explaining why. In truth, the change of municipal government in Constantinople was important, not so much in the west as to those whom it principally involved: the Roman Orthodox. The arrangements made between sultan and patriarch in 1454 may have been shadowy, but they introduced a new order, or *taxis*, which ensured the future of Roman Orthodox incorporated in later conquests of the Morea and the Pontos. Their internal politics still depended on who said what at Florence in 1439, but Roman Orthodox bonds which survived the conquest were older and simpler: those of patronage and *patris* – homeland.

This chapter therefore concentrates on the Roman Orthodox in the last century of their world: AM 6901–7000, or AD 1393–1492. It concentrates on four homelands, based on Salonica, Mistra, Constantinople and Trebizond. It must exclude other Orthodox, Greek-speaking or not, under Venetian, Hospitaller or local 'Latin' or 'Frankish' (mostly what would now be termed Italian) rule along the Adriatic coast, in the Aegean and (until 1523) the Dodecanese, or (until 1571) Cyprus. It excludes Albania (conquered from 1397 to 1497), Bulgaria (1393), Serbia (from 1389 to 1459) and Herzegovina and southern Bosnia (1463–5). It excludes the lands north of the Danube which emerged from the fourteenth century as posthumous Byzantine states (and were to adopt the very name of 'Romania'), being Wallachia (eventually incorporated as tributary from 1462 to 1476) and Moldavia (from 1455 to 1512). It must even exclude the peoples of the Crimea, whom Mehemmed II made tributary in 1475, turning the Black Sea into an Ottoman lake: Khazars, Armenians and Karaite Jews ruled by Crim-Tatar khans, Roman Orthodox princes of Gotthia and Genoese consuls in Kaffa.[4]

By the end of the century only two eastern Christian rulers survived wholly independent of the Ottoman Empire. Ethiopia had subscribed to the Union of Florence, but its Solomonic king, the *negus* Na'od (1478–1508) had an Orthodoxy of his own. Moscow had rejected Florence, so was Orthodox enough; Grand Prince Ivan III (1462–1505) had even married the niece of Constantine XI Palaiologos, last emperor in Constantinople (1449–53). But New Rome did not grant Russia its patriarchate until 1589, on the grounds that Old Rome had forfeited the title, and Moscow could enter the bottom of the list as Third Rome.[5]

At the end of the seventh millennium in Constantinople, Patriarch Maximos

[4] Vasiliev (1936) pp. 160–275; Ducellier (1981), pp. 323–653; Nicol (1984), pp. 157–216; Imber (1990), pp. 145–254.   [5] Jones and Monroe (1966), p. 57; Runciman (1968), pp. 320–37.

IV (1491–7) was spared the embarrassment which faces all who foretell a Day of Judgement which comes and goes without incident, for by AM 7000 most Roman Orthodox had adopted the western computation of AD 1492. Instead, he could say with more conviction than had his predecessor, Antonios, a century before, that while since 1453 it was demonstrably possible to have a Church without an emperor, it was now possible to have a Church with a sultan – indeed for Orthodox a sultan was preferable to a doge or pope. Patriarch Maximos urged the Republic of Venice to grant rights and freedom of worship to Roman Orthodox in the Ionian Islands which they enjoyed in the Ottoman Empire, while the Roman Orthodox Church in Cyprus had to wait until 1571 for the Ottoman conquest of the island to restore its autonomy.[6] Under Sultan Bayazid II in 1492, the identity, survival and even prosperity of the Roman Orthodox were more assured than they had seemed to be in 1393, when Bayazid I had threatened an emperor in Constantinople.

SALONICA AND ITS ARCHBISHOPS

The city of Salonica has many names: Greek Thessalonike, Roman Thessalonica, Slav Solun, Venetian Saloniccho, Turkish Selanik and Hebrew Slonki. For all these peoples it appeared to be the strategic or commercial key to the Balkans. The city stands close to where the Axios (Vardar) river is crossed by the Via Egnatia before it debouches into the Aegean Sea. The river, which rises deep in the Balkans, brought Slav traders to the annual fair of St Demetrios, patron of Salonica and (through their Salonican evangelists, Sts Cyril and Methodios) of all Slavs, each 26 October. The Egnatian highway runs from the Adriatic coast to Constantinople, so linking Old and New Rome at Salonica.

The Slavs found Salonica was a key which they could not turn. Even the most aggressive of Serbian tsars, Stefan Urosh IV, surnamed Dushan (1331–55), was unable to take the long-desired city of St Demetrios. By contrast its shallow harbour and October fair were not particularly attractive to Italian traders even when they were actually offered its key in 1423. By then Salonica had developed another reputation. As the second city of the Byzantine and (eventually) Ottoman Empire, its relationship with the capital in Constantinople was always uneasy. Even when ruled by a secondary member of the imperial family, it gained a local identity as a sort of city-state of its own, with a recognisable if inchoate local leadership, often headed by its archbishop.

The fourteenth-century urban and peasant uprisings of western Europe were paralleled in Byzantium. In western terms, revolutionary Salonica became

[6] Runciman (1968), p. 212.

a 'commune' from 1342 to 1350. In truth, its urban and artisanal mass was only just critical enough to claim local self-determination behind the great walls of the city, with a still shadowy political ideology called 'Zealot'. But Salonica did not forget those heady days. Its 'commune' was a hardly surprising response to outside pressures: civil war in Byzantium (1341–7), the Ottoman entry into Europe (1345–54) and the threat of Dushan (1345), all compounded by the Black Death (1347–8). Yet in Salonica these years are marked by some of the finest surviving late Byzantine decorated churches and by the career of the last great Father of the Roman Orthodox Church: St Gregory Palamas. Palamas was archbishop of Salonica from 1347 to 1359. His doctrines were confirmed by the Roman Orthodox Church in the next century and remain the vital spiritual ideology of the Slav Orthodox in particular. The essentially mystical theology of Palamas maintained that the unknowable essence of God could be approached by revelation rather than reason, and hence was in direct opposition to the Aristotelian scholasticism of the western Church. On the nearby monastic commune of Mount Athos, Palamism was given expression by Hesychasts – best described as 'Quietists' – whose spiritual connections with the political 'Zealots' were both obvious and obscure.[7]

The Ottomans first besieged Salonica from 1383 to 1387. Local leadership was divided between its governor, the future Emperor Manuel II Palaiologos, and its archbishop, Isidore Glabas (1380–4, 1386–96). Manuel told his subjects to defy the Turkish ultimatum. On St Demetrios's Day 1383 Glabas warned his flock to mend their ways, just as St Paul had twice written to the Thessalonians on hope, discipline and premature thoughts of the end of the world. Salonica duly fell in 1387. In 1393 the archbishop ventured back to his see. He found that the world there had not ended. Indeed, Ottoman occupation was more tolerable than Manuel had threatened. Sultan Bayazid had granted the citizens special favours and had left the infrastructure of Byzantine local government and its officers largely in place.[8]

The fact was that the Ottomans could do no other. Vastly outnumbered by the people they conquered, their problem was manpower: there were too few Muslims to go round, and of those too few Turks. The solution was obvious. While the conversion of an Orthodox Christian to Islam could be swift and relatively painless, it takes longer to turn a Roman into a Turk, which is a theme of this chapter. Yet there were short-cuts. In a sermon delivered in occupied Salonica in 1395 Archbishop Glabas was early to report on an expedient which may date from the first substantial Ottoman establishment in Europe, at Gallipoli in the Dardanelles in 1354. It is called *devshirme* ('recruitment') in Turkish and *paidomazoma* ('harvest of children') in Greek. This 'child levy' took

[7] Meyendorff (1964), pp. 13–115.   [8] Barker (1969), p. 53; Nicol (1993), p. 287; Vryonis (1956).

Christians for training in the Ottoman administration and, especially, in the 'new army' (Turkish *yeni cheri*; English janissary). Girls could aspire to the Harem. It was such converts who were the most eager for further conquest. Their advancement, especially after the battle of Ankara in 1402, led to tension with the old Anatolian Turkish leadership, which was to come to a head in 1453.

In the aftermath of Timur's victory at Ankara, Salonica reverted to Byzantium in 1403. Once again its archbishop provided characteristic leadership. Archbishop Symeon of Salonica (1416/17–29), urged his flock to keep firmly Roman and Orthodox. An ardent Hesychast, he sought to restore the identity of the city in the face of Venetian and Ottoman pressure. It was difficult to know who constituted the greater threat: the Turks, converts from Orthodoxy included, who were sent to chastise the Salonicans for their sins, or the Venetians who would infect them with the plague of heresy. From St Sophia, Constantinople, Symeon reintroduced a public liturgy to his own cathedral of St Sophia, in Salonica, and, as in Constantinople, regulated a twice-daily street procession of the protecting icon of the Mother of God called the Hodegetria. But in Constantinople Manuel II Palaiologos (1391–1425), by then aged seventy-three, was now more cautious. In 1423, unable to defend Salonica against the Ottomans, the emperor invited the Republic of Venice to do it for him. Archbishop Symeon tried to rally his Roman Orthodox by chastising them in the name of St Demetrios, on whose miraculous defences of the city in the past he wrote a great discourse in Venetian-occupied Salonica in 1427/8. Actually, the Venetians were initially welcomed as no great friends of the pope in Rome, but found the place expensive to defend and the Salonicans doing deals with the Turks. The end really came with Archbishop Symeon's death late in 1429, which meant that the Ottomans finally took a demoralised city on 29 March 1430. The Venetian captains had slipped away; the icon of the Hodegetria was smashed; and 7,000 Salonicans were taken captive.[9]

What happened next is partly revealed in Ottoman *tahrir defters*, tax and census registers. Short of manpower, the Ottomans correctly targeted cities such as Salonica, first to Islamicise, and then Turkicise. Outside the walls the overwhelmingly peasant population could await assimilation. Sultan Mehemmed II had a declared policy of demographic manipulation, today called 'ethnic cleansing', which has good Byzantine precedent. The Ottoman term was *sürgün* (forcible deportation and resettlement), which, along with *devshirme*, noted by Glabas, and natural erosion by conversion, should soon

---

[9] Dennis (1960); Darrouzès (ed.), 'Sainte-Sophie de Thessalonique d'après un rituel'; Symeon, *Politico-historical works*; Vryonis (1986).

have made Salonica the second Ottoman city of the Empire. But this did not happen. The place recovered slowly after 1430, within walls enclosing about 285 hectares, which in medieval Mediterranean terms could encompass a population of 30,000 or more.

In fact Salonica had an adult population of about 10,414 by 1478, which doubled to 20,331 in *c.* 1500 and only tripled to reach 29,220 by 1519. The precision of Ottoman registers is spurious (for it omits tax-evaders and tax-exempt), but the scale is reliable enough. Clearly, resettlement and conversion were belated. In 1478 the city had a Muslim population of 4,320, but its Christian (Roman Orthodox) element, with 6,094 souls, was still in an absolute majority with 59 per cent of households. By *c.* 1500 the Christian population had grown to 7,986 but, with 8,575, the Muslim population had doubled to reach, for the first and last time, a simple majority of 42 per cent of the inhabitants of Salonica. But about 1500 a third category was introduced, if incompletely recorded: 3,770 Jews. By 1519, 15,715 Jews were registered: 54 per cent of the population of Salonica, an absolute majority which they maintained until the semi-conversion of many to Islam with that of their false Messiah, Sabbatai Zavi (1625–76) after 1666.[10]

The conversion of the major city of the Balkans, from the staunchly Roman Orthodox see of Archbishops Palamas, Glabas and Symeon, first into a Muslim stronghold and then into the largest Jewish city in the world, all within the space of four decades, needs explanation. In the past, Byzantine emperors had in turn invited western Christian powers and Ottoman Turks to fight their wars against Orthodox Serbs and Bulgars for them, and regretted the expedient. Now the Ottoman state was faced with a greater, demographic, war. If Salonica could not be turned Turk, a third urban element could be introduced. Before 1430 there is evidence for a few Greek-speaking and Karaite Jews in the city, not even registered in 1478. But after their conquest of Granada in 1492, the Catholic sovereigns, Ferdinand and Isabel, expelled their Spanish (Sephardic) Jews, who spoke Ladino (or 'Latin'). Bayazid II welcomed them through Constantinople, largely to settle in Salonica. It was the greatest *sürgün* of all. Ottoman demographic strategy, if such it was, meant that Salonica did not have a Roman Orthodox majority again until after 1912, when it fell to Greece, once more to become a second city.[11]

THE MOREA, THE COUNCIL OF FLORENCE AND PLETHON

The history of the Morea is a late Byzantine success story, which also illustrates the dilemmas faced by Roman Orthodox leaders who were caught between the

---

[10] Lowry (1986b), pp. 327–32.   [11] Lowry (1986b), pp. 333–8; Dimitriades (1991).

west and the Ottomans in the fifteenth century. The medieval Morea was the ancient Peloponnese, the three-pronged peninsula of southern Greece, which had been conquered by the Franks in the aftermath of the Fourth Crusade of 1204. From 1262 it was steadily recovered by the Byzantines from the south, who shared it with the shrinking principality of Achaea, based on Andravida in the north-west, until the Latins were finally ejected in 1429. From 1349 the Morea was erected as an autonomous despotate, an appanage of Constantinople usually ruled, like Salonica, by a younger member of the imperial dynasty. The despots' capital was at Mistra, below a crusader castle which overlooks ancient Sparta and its plain. Unlike Salonica, Mistra was a new place, without strong-minded bishops. As the Frankish *Chronicle of the Morea* helpfully put it in 1249: 'And they named it Myzethras, for that was how they called it.'[12] The steep streets of Mistra, which cannot take wheeled traffic, still tumble past monastic enclosures, domed churches and balconied houses down to the only square and stabling, which is the courtyard of the despots' palace. Here on 6 January 1449 Despot Constantine (XI) Palaiologos was invested, but not crowned, as last Roman Orthodox emperor. As despot he had been a tributary of the Ottomans since 1447; as emperor he died in Constantinople on 29 May 1453, but it was not until 29 May 1460 that Mehemmed II took Mistra.[13]

The Morean economy was pastoral and transhumant in the highlands, with lowland agriculture, which included exports to Venice of Kalamata olives, along with silk and salt. Monemvasia gave its name to exports of malmsey wine and Corinth to currants. The archives of the despotate are largely lost, but it seems to have been run efficiently on late Byzantine fiscal and feudal lines, principally to finance its defence through agriculture.[14]

The peoples of the Morea were not as exotic as those of the Crimea, but since the seventh century had included Slav settlers. Despite evangelisation as Roman Orthodox from the tenth century, Slavs were still evident in Tsakonia, the wild east of the peninsula, while the Maniots in the south had a quite undeserved reputation as having been the last pagans in Byzantium. Frankish rulers had faced the same problems of manpower as would the Ottomans, who did not settle much either. The Franks left half-castes (*gasmouloi*), great castles, impeccable Cistercian monasteries and, in towns, now forlorn Gothic churches. But they did not take root as deep as other Latins in the Aegean and Ionian islands. In fact the most substantial demographic introduction in the Morea since the Slav was Albanian.

However called, Albanians had been moving south before the Ottomans used them to police the Balkans. The Greeks, Bulgars and Serbs had thrived

---

[12] Kalonaros (ed.), *Chronikon tou Moreos*, line 2990; Ilieva (1991); Lock (1994).
[13] Runciman (1980).   [14] Zakythinos (1975), II.

in the shade of the Byzantine Empire. The Albanians seized their turn under Ottoman patronage. They were eager, if sometimes casual, converts to Islam. For example, George, last Roman Orthodox mayor (*kephalē*) of Kanina (Vlora) in southern Albania, turned Turk in 1398, with the result that his family kept that office until 1943, incidentally supplying the Ottomans with thirty-one successive local *sandjakbeys*, 13 *beylerbeys* (of Rumelia, Anatolia and Syria), four field marshals (two Ottoman, one Egyptian, one Greek) and a grand vizier on the way. Muslim members of the Vlora family patronised local Roman Orthodox monasteries and died fighting the Latins at Rhodes (1522), Lepanto (1571) and Candia (Crete, 1668).[15] The Vlora dynasty, however, was unusual in keeping its identity: Ottoman policy was at best to pension off local ruling families.

Incomplete Ottoman registers show a growth of taxable population in the Morea from about 20,000 to 50,000 non-Muslim households between 1461 and 1512, figures surely too low even if shepherds could not be tracked down over a land mass of 20,000 square kilometres. Yet the indications are clear: the Latin and Muslim population was slight, and of the Orthodox over one third was Albanian.[16]

Fifteenth-century Mistra was, however, unmistakably not just Roman Orthodox, but 'Hellene' – in the person of Byzantium's last great original thinker: George Gemistos 'Plethon' (*c.* 1360–1452). A sort of neo-platonist, Plethon adopted his last name in allusion to Plato and probably inspired Cosimo de' Medici's foundation of a Platonic Academy in Florence. If there was a Byzantine 'Renaissance man', he was Plethon, a maverick who had already dabbled in turn with Zoroastrianism and Judaism (perhaps at the Ottoman court) and whose last autograph fragments of a *Book of Laws* exalt Zeus as supreme God. He was an awkward nonconformist to handle in Roman Orthodox Constantinople. It was perhaps for his own safety that Manuel II exiled him to Mistra *c.* 1410. But Plethon was soon addressing treatises to Emperor Manuel and to his son, Despot Theodore II Palaiologos (1407–43) on Platonic Republican lines, urging the division of the citizenry into three classes (of which the most important was its military) and the revival of ancient Hellenic virtues, not of identity of faith or ethnicity, but of patriotism. He had little time for monks, whose lands threatened to turn Byzantium into a monastic economy of almost Tibetan proportions. Such rhetoric may have been utopian, but Plethon held judicial office at Mistra and was rewarded with estates in the Morea. Perhaps on the principle that patriotism is more important than faith, Plethon was in his old age invited to represent the Roman Orthodox Church as a lay member of its delegation to what amounted to a

[15] Vlora (1973), II, pp. 271–7.   [16] Beldiceanu and Beldiceanu-Steinherr (1980), pp. 37–46.

theological summit conference with the western Church at Ferrara and
Florence in 1438–9.[17]

Like other conferences held under duress, the Council of Florence was soon
overtaken by military and political events. The crusade promised by Pope
Eugenius IV (1431–47) to save the Constantinople of John VIII Palaiologos
(1425–48) from the Ottomans, which the emperor sought in reward for Union,
got as far as the Bulgarian shore of the Black Sea, but came to grief at Varna in
1444. Ostensibly, however, the Council considered theological innovations and
terms developed in the western Church for which the Roman Orthodox had
no useful equivalent, or sometimes even definition: the addition of 'filioque' to
the creed; the notion of purgatory; and the question of unleavened bread –
matters which hardly bothered most Roman Orthodox unless they lived (as in
Crete or Cyprus) alongside westerners. But the essential issue was that of
authority, and the way that it had developed in Old and New Romes: the
primacy of the pope, archbishop of Old Rome and patriarch of the west, over
that of the ecumenical patriarch, archbishop of New Rome, to which the
Orthodox subscribed in 1439: they could at least agree to be 'Roman'. But
besides the Ottoman threat, the Orthodox delegation was under the additional
duress that the agenda and dialectical rules of the great debate were chosen by
western scholastics, who ran rings round them. For westerners the Union was a
matter of discipline: the reincorporation of the wayward Orthodox under the
authority of a single pope. But for the Roman Orthodox it touched their very
identity – hence the inclusion of pundits such as Plethon at the Council.[18]

Patriarch Michael III of Anchialos (1170–8) is first credited with identifying
the crux of the matter, when he told his emperor: 'Let the Muslim be my
material ruler, rather than the Latin my spiritual master. If I am subject to the
former, at least he will not force me to share his faith. But if I have to be united
in religion with the latter, under his control, I may have to separate myself from
God.'[19] His view was to be put more bluntly in words attributed to the Grand
Duke Luke Notaras on the eve of the fall of Constantinople in 1453: 'Better
the turban of the Turk than the tiara of the Latin [pope].'[20] Between 1439 and
1453 lines were drawn which were to dictate Roman Orthodox politics thereafter. Spiritual authority in the east had never been focused on a single see, as in
the west, but was in effect dispersed among the whole body of the faithful,
including the departed. While those alive soon made it clear that they did not
accept Union, the Byzantine government remained faithful to the expediency
of Florence until the bitter end. After 1453 there could be no going back – or
forward. What individual delegates did at Florence in 1439 is therefore vital to

[17] Woodhouse (1986).   [18] Gill (1961).
[19] Runciman (1955), p. 122; Magdalino (1993), pp. 292–3.
[20] Ducas, *Istoria turco-bizantina*, p. 329.

explaining not just their own fate, but that of the Roman Orthodox under the Ottomans.

The Roman Orthodox delegation which John VIII and his dying patriarch took to Florence was a fascinating final assembly of Byzantine intelligentsia, a network of patriotic, family and wandering scholarly contacts, in that order, which somehow survived later party politics. We have already met Plethon (who soon got bored), but to take the 'patriotic' link (from Greek *patris*, or sense of home), a remarkable number start with a connection with Trebizond in the Pontos. For instance the Aristotelian scholar George 'of Trebizond' (1395–*c.* 1472) was already a convinced Unionist and attended the Council as a lay member of the papal *curia*. His reaction to the events of 1453 was to invite Mehemmed II to convert to Rome, too, but he reported so fulsomely on the sultan, when they met in Constantinople in 1465, that he found himself in a papal prison. The family of John Eugenikos (1394–*c.* 1455) also came from Trebizond, on which he wrote patriotic encomia. He, however, left Florence before the end of the Council, to castigate the Union. Otherwise, most Roman Orthodox signed the decree of Union along with their emperor. Some recanted. Others, convinced by the argument at Florence, entered the western hierarchy itself.

However, Mark Eugenikos, brother of John and bishop of Ephesos (1437–45), refused to sign in 1439. A Palamite, but nevertheless pupil of Plethon, he was in 1456 canonised as a saint by Patriarch Gennadios II, who, as George Scholarios, had attended the Council, along with George Amiroutzes of Trebizond, as one of a remarkable trio of laymen. Bessarion of Trebizond, bishop of Nicaea (1437–9), had studied with Plethon and Amiroutzes and stayed on in Italy as a cardinal (1439–72). Gregory Mamme attended the Council as abbot of the great Constantinopolitan monastery of the Pantokrator, serving as ecumenical patriarch (Gregory III) between 1443 and 1450 when he returned west to be made titular Latin patriarch of Constantinople (1451–9). Isidore, from Monemvasia in the Morea, attended as Roman Orthodox bishop of Kiev and All Russia (1436–9). Also made a cardinal, he was sent to Moscow as papal legate to Grand Prince Vasilii II (1425–62), who promptly imprisoned him as a Unionist. Isidore persisted. He proclaimed the Union in Constantinople for Mamme on 12 December 1452, and escaped its fall to become Latin patriarch from 1459 to 1463 – to be succeeded in that office by none other than Bessarion.[21] In the face of so many lures and pressures it was *patris* that held this network together.

Plethon was the first to die, in his nineties, at home in his *patris* of Mistra on 26 June 1452. The last local decree of Constantine Palaiologos as despot was to

---

[21] Gill (1961) and (1964).

confirm Plethon's sons on his Laconic lands. But after 1453 Plethon's last work, the *Book of Laws*, was forwarded to Patriarch Gennadios, who could do no other than burn it. The book was not just heretical: it was plain pagan. In Mistra another of Plethon's circle had been the *despoina*, Cleope Malatesta, wife of the Despot Theodore III Palaiologos, younger brother of John VIII. In 1465 Sigismondo Pandolfo Malatesta (1417–68) penetrated Ottoman Mistra with a Venetian force, and retreated with the body of George Gemistos Plethon. He installed his remains in a sarcophagus in the south arcade of his extraordinary Malatesta Temple in Rimini, part-church, part-pantheon, with an epitaph to 'the greatest philosopher of his time'.[22]

MEHEMMED II AND GENNADIOS II SCHOLARIOS

There are two common views of the fall of Constantinople. The first is most vividly depicted in a painting presented to Queen Victoria in 1839 by a hero of the War of Independence of modern Greece from the Ottoman Turks, as a history lesson for the young queen. It shows Constantinople on the fateful day: 29 May 1453. Constantine XI had died a martyred emperor; his Latin allies are scuttling away by sea. Christian youths are rounded up in *devshirme*, to become janissaries who wield curved scimitars. The enthroned Sultan Mehemmed II supervises the placing of enormous yokes over the Roman Orthodox clergy and lay notables of Constantinople. A distinctly pagan-looking lady, person-ifying 'Hellas' disarmed, weeps under an olive tree. However, escaping to the highlands of the Morea are young braves in white Albanian kilts, ready to fight another day – which dawned in 1821.[23]

A second, revisionist, view of the event is in fact older than the schoolroom one. It is that, as heir of the Byzantine emperors, the conquering sultan created for his Roman Orthodox subjects a self-governing community, or *millet*, regu-lated by their patriarch, who now had greater political powers than he had ever enjoyed, especially over Slav Orthodox, and restored Constantinople as capital of the Roman Orthodox world. As late as 1798 Patriarch Anthimos of Jerusalem (1788–1808) explained that when the last emperors of Constantinople sold their Church to papal thraldom in 1439, it was through the particular favour of Heaven that the Ottoman Empire had been raised to protect the Greeks against heresy, as a safeguard against the politics of the western 'nations', and as champion of the Roman Orthodox Church.[24] No wonder the patriarch condemned the heroes of the Morea when they rose against their sultan in 1821.

[22] Runciman (1980), p. 117.   [23] Lidderdale (ed. and trans.), *Makriyannis*, pl. 1.
[24] Clogg, *The movement for Greek independence*, pp. 56–62.

However, what actually happened in 1453 is still obscured by the writing or rewriting of Roman Orthodox, Armenian or Jewish tradition two or three generations later. The non-Muslim peoples then claimed that the conqueror had treated them well. This suited the wishful thinking of all parties, Turkish included, and allows modern historians to assume that the arrangements which settled down a century later to have been in place from the start. Would that things were so tidy, and that sleeping myths could lie. Yet, it is worth looking again at what Sultan Mehemmed actually did, and ask who won or lost Constantinople on 29 May 1453. Even that is not a simple question. The Genoese were first off the mark. Three days later they got the sultan to confirm their privileges in Galata, opposite Constantinople. Dated 1 June 1453, this Turkish charter granted to the Latins is naturally written in Greek and preserved today in the British Museum. But no other community had a ready-made relationship to confirm, or has a document to record a status which had to begin anew through negotiation or accumulated custom.

Among losers, Constantine XI lost his life. He had supported not just Union with the Latins, but Mehemmed's rival, Orhan – in 1453 there were Turks, too, within Constantinople, if outnumbered by Orthodox outside the walls. The sultan's first action after the fall of the city should also give pause for thought. The fate of the emperor would have posed a tricky problem if Mehemmed had taken him alive. The sultan knew, however, what to do with his own prime minister, or grand vizier, Halil Djandarlıoghlu (1443–53), which was to put him to death. The Djandarlı family was of impeccable Anatolian Turkish descent. It had served the Ottoman dynasty since 1350, supplying its first and four other grand viziers. But Halil, described by both Muslims and Christians as 'friend of the Romans', had cautioned young Mehemmed against taking Constantinople. In 1453 the old Anatolian backwood beys, whom Timur had restored after 1402, and whom Halil represented, were among the losers.[25]

The ruling Orthodox dynasties lost, but a handful of secondary families, such as the Evrenos of Bithynia or the Vlora of Albania, which switched allegiance, remained influential under new masters. This period lasted only a generation or two, because their usefulness, to the Ottoman state as well as to their old co-religionists, receded by the end of the century. These decades (1453–92) were, however, vital to the new order, because first generation converts reached the highest ranks of the Ottoman army and government (which came almost to the same thing) before they forgot their origins. Unlike the Djandarlı beys, they were eager for conquest – of their native lands in particular. Like all converts, they tried harder and were typically patrons of new mosques and Islamic foundations in the Christian Balkans and the new capital.

[25] Buckton (1994), pp. 220–1; Frazee (1983), pp. 5–10; Ménage (1965).

Their inherited contacts in the Balkans and the Pontos assisted a relatively orderly transfer of power to Mehemmed II.[26]

An example is Mahmud pasha, a convert who served as the sultan's grand vizier from 1455 to 1474 and who successfully dealt with the surrender of the Serbian state in 1458 and of the empire of Trebizond in 1461, both after spirited campaigns. Yet both events were something of family affairs. Mahmud was born an Angelović, so the last prime ministers of Serbia and Trebizond, with whom he negotiated, happened to be, respectively, his brother and a cousin. The latter was none other than George Amiroutzes – the shadow of Florence fell over such Ottomans too.[27] After executing his own grand vizier in 1453, Mehemmed's next action was to look for a credible agent through whom to rule his Roman Orthodox subjects. Their emperor was dead. Their patriarch, Gregory III Mamme, had gone – quite literally – over to Rome. But Grand Duke Luke Notaras, the last Byzantine prime minister (1449–53), survived. He was outspokenly anti-Unionist, and Mehemmed seems to have turned to him. What exactly went wrong is obscured by mutual recriminations in later tradition, to do with sexual habits which may be acceptable in one culture, yet scandalous in another. Perhaps the reality is that Notaras would not convert to Islam. It would have lost his credibility not with Venice (where he had a good bank account) but with the Roman Orthodox, and therefore his usefulness to the sultan. Like Djandarlıoghlu, he and his sons were executed. It was only then, in January 1454, that Mehemmed looked to the religious institutions of his overwhelmingly non-Muslim subjects as a way of running them. With hindsight, this expedient seemed obvious, even predestined, but was not so at the time, when, despite the long experience of Islam in dealing with non-Muslim communities, such institutions did not then properly exist in the Ottoman state. In effect the Muslim sultan restored the ecumenical patriarchate, so setting a precedent for other community leaders whom the Ottomans brought under their eye in Constantinople: a chief *haham* for Jews (sometime between 1454 and 1492), and a new patriarch, or *katholikos*, for Armenians (sometime between 1461 and 1543), in addition to the privileges granted to western Christians on 1 June 1453, which survived for almost five centuries.[28]

The reconstitution of the see of Constantinople by the sultan is almost as obscure as its traditional foundation by St Andrew. But the evidence of his deed is enough. Mehemmed sought out and installed Gennadios II Scholarios (1454–6, 1462–3, 1464–5) as successor of the First-Called Apostle, and his own first patriarch. It was an inspired choice. Obviously, he could not trust a Unionist ally of the Papacy, a leading enemy of the Ottomans in the west. The

---

[26] Inalcik (1973), pp. 23–34; Imber (1990), p. 159.

[27] *Prosopographisches Lexikon der Palaiologenzeit* (1976–), I, pp. 75–6, no. 784.

[28] Braude (1982); Bardakjian (1982); Lewis (1984), pp. 126–36.

monk Gennadios had rallied the anti-Unionists of Constantinople, whose leadership he had inherited from his old teacher, Mark Eugenikos. A veteran of the Council of Florence, which he had attended under his lay name of George, Scholarios learned how to deal with the Unionists by adapting their own scholastic tools. Now, as patriarch, Gennadios proved adaptable to new facts of life – for example relaxing canon law to allow for the break-up of families and remarriage in the wake of the sack of the city. Even the title he adopted as patriarch was an innovation: 'the servant of the children of God, the humble Gennadios'. In complaining that his bishops were more trouble than the Turks, he recognised that to save the Roman Orthodox the patriarchate must become an Ottoman institution.[29]

Mehemmed was quite as remarkable as Gennadios. His stepmother was Orthodox. He wrote Greek and hung lamps before his collection of icons. He was a patron of Bellini and curious of all new things. Indeed old Turks complained that 'If you wish to stand in high honour on the sultan's threshold, you must be a Jew or a Persian or a Frank.'[30] Tradition has Mehemmed and Scholarios settling the future of the Roman Orthodox in *taxis*, a brave new order, and discussing higher theology in a side-chapel of the new patriarchal cathedral of the Pammakaristos. But happily unaware that they were describing what was later to be called a 'millet', or self-regulating community defined by religion, the fifty-year-old patriarch and twenty-two-year-old sultan appear to have felt their way, apparently making up the rules as they went along. The results are clear. It took a Turk to define a Greek adequately as the son of a Roman Orthodox. Mehemmed thereby ensured the survival of a hitherto endangered people, for the Roman Orthodox were thenceforth protected subjects of the sultan's patriarch. The patriarch was responsible to the sultan for regulating Roman Orthodox, by that definition, under canon law (including considerable fiscal franchise over his own flock), in return for privileges and immunities within the Ottoman state.[31]

It was in nobody's interest to question such a rosy tradition later. But it overlooks some harder realities of life in 1454, one of which was that Mehemmed II and his predecessors were primarily sultans of a militant Islamic state, however upstart. They took titles and epithets such as 'khan', 'shah', 'malik', 'shadow of God on earth' or, more contentiously, 'gazi' (or holy warrior against the infidel). Mehemmed II himself was styled 'ever victorious' and 'fatih' (or conqueror). As a pious ruler he founded mosques and charities, which often replaced churches and monasteries – the endowment of St Sophia in Constantinople alone, transferred from cathedral to mosque in 1456/7,

[29] Scholarios, *Œuvres complètes*, IV, p. 206; Turner (1964), pp. 365–72, and (1969).
[30] Babinger (1978), p. 508; Raby (1983).   [31] Pantazopoulos (1967); Kabrda (1969); Ursinus (1993).

numbered over 1,000 properties, including baths, butcheries and beer-shops.[32] The Ottoman state inherited from earlier Islamic practice long-established legal ways of dealing with *dhimmi*s – non-Muslims who, although protected, were unquestionably second-class subjects. Christians may have lived under their own canon law, but ultimately it was the *sharia*, or Islamic law, which was supreme.[33]

In turn Patriarch Gennadios may have been adroit in exploiting the position of the underdog, but in truth his encounters with Mehemmed in the Pammakaristos can hardly have been meetings of Renaissance minds. Judging by the patriarch's voluminous writings, he was deeply Roman and convention-ally Orthodox. His exposition of faith, prepared for the sultan, is uncompro-mising, even polemical. For him, both the Prophet and the pope were equivalents of the Great Beast of the Apocalypse. Gennadios had sharp views on the Armenians, too, and told the Jews that they laboured under an appalling delusion: it was in fact the Roman Orthodox who were the chosen people of God.[34]

The fifteenth-century Ottoman Empire reunited the Roman Orthodox as subjects of their patriarch in Constantinople. Yet it was not the Byzantine Empire in disguise. Even though Mehemmed resettled Constantinople as the centre of the Roman Orthodox world, he was even more effective in making it the capital of an Islamic empire. In 1453 the city was almost as depopulated as Salonica had been in 1430. The earliest surviving *defter* survey, dated 1477, which includes Constantinople proper (Istanbul) and the Frankish trading town of Galata (Pera) facing it over the Golden Horn, has been variously analysed. A total of 16,326 households were registered, making a population of over 80,000. Of these the absolute majority was already Muslim with 9,517 households. There were 5,162 Christian households, the majority (3,748) Roman Orthodox, which had been added to by resettlement (*sürgün*) from the Morea after 1460, Trebizond after 1461 and the Crimea after 1475 – the last two in quarters of their own. Besides 372 Armenian households and probably under-recorded Latins and gypsies, the final major element was Jewish, already with 1,647 households.[35]

Constantinople, and most of its communities, grew prodigiously in roughly the proportions set in 1477, reaching perhaps 200,000 by 1489 and certainly double that population in 1535. By 1489, at any rate, the curiously small regis-tered Roman Orthodox element had hardly grown. While Ottoman statistics can lie, more often they omit. The meetings of patriarch and sultan in the Pammakaristos were off the record, but the *defters* make one wonder if in 1454

[32] Inalcik (1969), p. 243.   [33] Cahen (1965).

[34] Scholarios, *Œuvres complètes*, III, p. 468; IV, pp. 211–31.

[35] Inalcik (1974), pp. 238–9; Lowry (1986b), pp. 323–6.

Gennadios did not get Mehemmed to exempt the refounded patriarchate, its dependants and properties, from the record too. For Gennadios it would only have been a temporary financial precaution – after all his prediction of the end of the world in 1492 is on record.[36]

ROMAN ORTHODOX BONDS AFTER 1453: THE PONTOS AND AMIROUTZES; MOUNT ATHOS AND MARA

Trebizond in the Pontos, the last Byzantine Empire to be conquered by Mehemmed II, is a final illustration of the bonds which still held the Roman Orthodox world together in the fifteenth century. The strongest tie was patronage; the most enduring *patris*. The Pontos, in north-eastern Anatolia, was a distinct *patris* to which its patrons, the Grand Komnenoi, emperors of Trebizond (1204–1461), added political identity. As separatist rulers, their legitimacy was all the more Roman Orthodox. Like the grand princes of Moscow, their obedience was to the patriarch, not the emperor, in Constantinople. The Grand Komnenos signed himself as 'faithful emperor and autocrat of All Anatolia, of the Iberians and Beyond' – which initially included the Crimea. This Black Sea coast was perhaps the most densely settled in the Byzantine world. By 1520–3 the population of central Pontos was registered at over 215,000 of whom 92 per cent were still Christian and 86 per cent Roman Orthodox, while the rest of Anatolia, about 5.7 million, was already 93 per cent Muslim.[37]

By contrast with the Pontos, the collapse of the Orthodox Church elsewhere in Anatolia after the Seljuk conquest from 1071 had been shockingly swift. It succumbed not so much to Islamic missionary zeal as to the loss of its economic base and the withdrawal of the patronage of its imperial officials – for whom all postings from Constantinople were colonial, whether the natives spoke Greek or not.[38] Only just in time to save the identity of such Roman Orthodox, Mehemmed had halted the structural disintegration of their Church by whatever settlement he made with Scholarios in 1454. The result was that ambitious and well-connected Roman Orthodox had an alternative to conversion thereafter. They could keep faith and enter patriarchal service. But without political independence the Church could only conserve the flock which paid for it, and was perilously dependent upon patrons. Without economic freedom its theological development was frozen at the point when the sultan recognised it: in authority anti-Unionist, in spirituality Palamite.

---

[36] Scholarios, *Œuvres complètes*, IV, pp. 511–12. [37] Bryer (1991), pp. 316–19.
[38] Vryonis (1971).

Although the patriarch was an essential officer of the Ottoman system, it was a fundamentally unequal alliance. Sultans supported the Church the better to use it – what had emperors done before them? But in the crucial period of conquest the Roman Orthodox found a patron who matched, like Mehemmed himself, that time of transition alone. She was Mara Branković (c. 1412–78), daughter of the last despot of Serbia by a sister of the last emperor of Trebizond. In 1435 Mara married Sultan Murad II (1421–51), father of Mehemmed II.[39]

The network of marriage alliances in which Mara enmeshed the Ottoman and Roman Orthodox dynasties arose from diplomatic expediency – if Serbia could come by dowry rather than conquest, so much the better. But Mara, never a mother, was a formidable widow. Above all she kept her faith, although she resisted a second marriage in 1451 – to her relative, Emperor Constantine XI Palaiologos. If she had agreed, the conquest of 1453 would have been even more of a family event than it was. The evidence, not just of tradition but of his acts, reveals how much the sultan revered his Christian stepmother. In 1459 he granted her both the cathedral of St Sophia in Salonica and the fief of Ezova, where she received ambassadors and held a sort of alternative Christian court until her death in 1478.[40] Ezova lies near the Strymon valley in eastern Macedonia between Serres and Mount Athos. Along with the Pontos it was one of the most prosperous areas of the late Byzantine world, where Mehemmed allowed some monasteries to keep their holdings and dependent peasants. The Strymon was dominated by the estates of the monasteries of Mount Athos (which Mara and her father endowed) and of the Prodromos on Mount Menoikeion, above Serres (where Patriarch Gennadios II Scholarios retired and is buried). Mehemmed II planned to pension off Mara's uncle, the Grand Komnenos David, in the same area after the fall of Trebizond in 1461.[41]

Mount Athos is a marble peak (3,345 metres high) at the tip of the northern of the three fingers of the Chalkidike peninsula which stretch into the Aegean Sea. It had been an eremitic and then monastic retreat from before the tenth century. Since St Gregory Palamas, its Hesychasts had made it an arbiter of spiritual authority among Roman and other Orthodox, countering that of the patriarchate itself. By the fifteenth century its outstations beyond Athos, estates and peasants (who outnumbered monks by over ten to one), were concentrated from Salonica to Serres, controlled islands such as Lemnos and spread as far as Trebizond. It was still to enter its most prosperous days under

---

[39] Ducas, *Istoria turco-bizantina*, pp. 257–89; Nicol (1994), pp. 110–19.
[40] Babinger (1978), pp. 163–4.
[41] *Prosopographisches Lexikon der Palaiologenzeit* (1976–), I, pp. 226–7, no. 12097; Zachariadou (1969); Lowry (1991).

the Ottomans, when it attracted the patronage of Danubian and Russian Orthodox rulers and pilgrims.[42]

In the late fifteenth century, Mara's Ezova in Macedonia was rivalled as a political and economic focus by an even more modest place on the other side of the Roman Orthodox world: the village of Doubera (Livera), 40 kilometres south of Trebizond in the Pontos. The 1515 *defter* registers a solidly Roman Orthodox population of only 333 souls (others were probably exempt), but reveals that it was also the *patris* of members of the Amiroutzes family. More significantly, in 1364 the Grand Komnenos Alexios III (also founder of an Athonite monastery) named Doubera as headquarters of the estates of his own nearby pilgrim monastery of Soumela, one of three in the Pontic interior which retained their privileges and tax exemptions after the fall of Trebizond in 1461, just as the Ottomans had favoured some of the monastic economies around Mara's Ezova.[43]

In 1461 Mahmud pasha sorted out terms of surrender of Trebizond with George Amiroutzes, after a tiresome campaign which left most of the Pontos itself unconquered. Sultan Mehemmed deported the Grand Komnenos David and his prime minister, Amiroutzes, as part of a *sürgün* to Constantinople. Thence Amiroutzes wrote to his old compatriot and fellow delegate at Florence, Bessarion, a vivid letter describing the fall of Trebizond – and asking for money to ransom his son and Bessarion's godson, Basil, who was in danger of forcible conversion to Islam. Amiroutzes was an anti-Unionist, but evidently not bothered that Bessarion was then a Latin cardinal. He appealed to closer bonds: shared connections of family and *patris*.[44] Had he already solicited Mahmud, who was surely better placed to help?

By 1463 Bessarion succeeded Isidore of Kiev as Latin patriarch. In the same year someone (the evidence that it was Amiroutzes is only circumstantial) denounced David to Mehemmed II. Refusing to apostasise, the imperial family of Trebizond died in gruesome circumstances. Apparently Mara could not, and Amiroutzes would not, intercede. Certainly Amiroutzes had shifted his allegiance to the sultan, for whom he prepared an exposition of Ptolemy's *Geography* with the assistance of his son – called Mehemmed. Was he Basil, who had converted after all? Most Roman Orthodox converted to Islam before culturally they turned Turk. But some of their leaders did it the other way round. Contrary to the poor view in which he is held in Greek tradition, George Amiroutzes himself does not seem to have bothered to convert. Apostasy would have denied him playing politics with the patriarchate, while at the sultan's court he could always use his cousin and ally, the grand vizier Mahmud pasha.[45]

[42] Bryer (1996).   [43] Lowry (1986a), p. 128.   [44] Migne (ed.), *Patrologia Graeca*, CXVI, cols. 723–8.
[45] Nicol (1994), pp. 120–5.

The year 1463 was even more eventful for the Roman Orthodox network. Patriarch Ioasaph I Kokkas (1459–63), who had succeeded Gennadios II Scholarios, denounced George Amiroutzes in turn – for his proposed big-amous marriage to the widow of the last Latin duke of Athens. Amiroutzes went ahead all the same. Tradition that he was an exasperating man was con-firmed dramatically on Easter Sunday 1463 when the affair drove Ioasaph to attempt suicide by leaping into the cistern below the Pammakaristos cathedral. Amiroutzes promptly moved in to manage patriarchal finances, using his son, Mehemmed, as intermediary with the sultan.[46] Behind a cloud of later tradition may be detected a characteristic trail of patronage and *patris* in the sequel.

By 1465 Mehemmed confirmed Amiroutzes's village of Doubera on the estates of Soumela as a monastic immunity. Soumela (and two other nearby mountain monasteries) constituted thereafter the only major economic counter to the Macedonian monastic lands protected by Mara, a rival patron.[47] In late 1466 Symeon 'of Trebizond' was presented as candidate for the patriar-chate, offering the sultan, for the first time, a bribe of office (called 'peshkesh'): 2,000 gold pieces. Monks do not commonly dispose of such sums, and Mehemmed had anyway dispossessed the monasteries of Trebizond city itself. By elimination, this points to Soumela as Symeon's monastery and brings us back to his sponsor. To put it bluntly, did Amiroutzes use the resources and connections of Doubera to buy the patriarchate for his candidate?

One consequence is certain. By offering a *peshkesh* bribe in 1466, there was no going back. By their own account, the Roman Orthodox initiated an auction of their own leadership, which spread to other offices and was to spiral for over three centuries. This was the self-imposed cost of protection of a Church by an Islamic state, largely borne by the faithful, whose principal contact with their patriarchate was to raise *peshkesh* and obey canon law. The only beneficiary was the Ottoman treasury. Sultans were not much concerned as to who was patriarch, so long as he was not Unionist or sponsored by Ottoman commer-cial or political rivals – which was to come in the seventeenth century, when French Jesuits and Dutch Calvinists competed to buy a whole Church.[48]

The short-term result was that in 1467 a Serbian party and Mara outbid Symeon with her own candidate. The Pontic party ran Symeon again. During his second term of office in 1472, Symeon swiftly deposed Bishop Pankratios of Trebizond who was implicated in a Turkman attempt to restore a Grand Komnenos in Trebizond – presumably under pressure from Amiroutzes who had known all parties involved since 1458, and now knew where his loyalties lay. Seven times the patriarchate went back and forth until in 1482 Symeon

[46] Bryer (1986), pp. 81–6.   [47] Nicol (1994), pp. 110–19.
[48] Runciman (1968), pp. 193–200, 259–88; Kresten (1970).

finally raised a record *peshkesh* for a third period of office, ousting an opponent of Amiroutzes's marriage of 1463. In 1484 Symeon at last held a synod which repudiated the Union of Florence of 1439.[49]

Patriarch Symeon nevertheless left unfinished business when he died in office in 1486. His death raised the perennial question of whom political funds belong to, for he had neglected to make a will. Who were his heirs? The leaders of the network which had held the Roman Orthodox world together had now died: Mahmud pasha (after 1474), Mara (1478), Mehemmed II himself (1481); and of the veterans of Florence, Isidore (1463), Bessarion (1472), Scholarios (*c.* 1472) and Amiroutzes himself (*c.* 1475).

Patriarch Niphon II (1486–8) was the first successful candidate of new patrons. They were Danubian princes, now Ottoman tributaries, who were to support the monasteries of Athos and the Pontos, too. However, Niphon was unable to claim Symeon's intestate fortune, which was confiscated by Iskender, treasurer of the new sultan, Bayazid II (1481–1512). But the network which reached back to Doubera still held: Iskender was yet another son of George Amiroutzes.[50]

'Patris' may be even stronger than patronage, and certainly faith, for Doubera village now had even greater aspirations – to empire. In 1479 the future Sultan Bayazid II took the last independent corner of the Roman Orthodox world, which was the rocky principality of Torul, south of Trebizond and Soumela, and for wife Maria, who converted and who, as Gulbahar *hatun*, held court in Trebizond where she died in 1505/6. Bayazid's son, the future Sultan Selim I (1512–20), was governor of Trebizond from 1489 to 1512, when he wrote in Greek to Venice as 'emperor of the Pontos and despot of Trebizond'. Selim confirmed the privileges of Soumela monastery. In turn his son, the future Sultan Süleyman (1520–66), was brought up in Trebizond, presumably by Maria-Gulbahar, from 1494/5.[51]

Maria is a more shadowy figure than Mara of Ezova, but the surest fact about her is vital: her birthplace, or *patris*, was none other than Doubera. The village itself escaped registration until 1515 and Ottoman *defters* are not designed to record any connections she may have had with the families of Amiroutzes, or of Patriarch Symeon, or even Bessarion. But it is a small place. Like Mara of Ezova, Maria of Doubera was probably only the stepmother of a sultan, who have many wives, or rather none at all. But in Trebizond Selim gave Gulbahar a marble tomb and in 1514 a mosque fit for an empress.[52]

The fate of the other inhabitants of Trebizond is a final reflection of that of the Roman Orthodox. Compared with its hinterland, the city was never popu-

[49] Chrysanthos (1933), pp. 531–41; Laurent (1968).
[50] *Prosopographisches Lexikon der Palaiologenzeit* (1976–), I, pp. 76–7, nos. 787–8.
[51] Chrysanthos (1933), p. 519.   [52] Bryer and Winfield (1985), I, pp. 197, 200.

lous – in 1436 about 4,000 souls. After its conquest it grew to 6,711 in 1486, 7,017 in 1523, 6,100 in 1553 and reached 10,575 in 1583 – figures about a third of the size of Salonica which also reflect the relative efficiency of Ottoman registrars and omit exempt groups. But the composition is revealing. After 1461 Mehemmed had instigated a *sürgün*, deporting the Christian leadership and importing Muslims (including recent Albanian converts), with the result that by *c.* 1486 Trebizond was 19 per cent Muslim and 81 per cent Christian (mostly Roman Orthodox). But the Christian population actually grew there-after, both in numbers and proportion (86 per cent) during the years of Selim's governorship, Süleyman's youth and Gulbahar's widowhood, when the Ottoman state should have been tightening its hold on the place. Trebizond was in danger of becoming totally Christian again, and, unlike the case of Salonica, Jews were not settled to break the demographic problem. There was a second *sürgün*. In 1553 the Christian : Muslim ratio was 53 : 47 per cent, but by 1583 had turned tables to 46 : 54 per cent. The critical point seems to have been when a Christian element had shrunk to about 55 per cent, when whole par-ishes (which paid a fixed levy) converted in landslides, leaving faithful individu-als unable to afford the balance. Most revealing is that by 1583, 43 per cent of the Muslims of Trebizond are identifiable as first or second generation con-verts. In other words the population of the city, whatever its faith, was then still almost 70 per cent native Pontic: people who kept to their *patris*.[53]

'Conversion' is used here as a convenient term, and indeed is technically understood in both Orthodoxy and Islam, with the difference that under _sharia_ law conversion or reconversion out of Islam met the penalty of death – in the Ottoman Empire until 1839. From the fifteenth century there were a number of attested Orthodox martyrs to their faith. Converts to Islam did not find immediate acceptance either. But, following Ottoman registrars, we can only record Roman Orthodox by civil status. The spiritual cost of the compromises to which the Church and individual faithful were driven in order to survive cannot be recorded, any more than what happened in the countryside. Here, monasteries such as Mara's in Macedonia and Maria's in the Pontos could offer secular as well as spiritual salvation. With the loss of such patrons elsewhere it may not have been too painful to slip in and out of unofficial Islam and Orthodoxy within a common peasant culture and local cults of *patris*.

By the reign of Sultan Sulayman I (1520–66) most Roman Orthodox who were going to convert to Islam had done so. In the west, Süleyman is called 'the Magnificent', but in the Ottoman Empire he is rightly named 'the Law-giver'. He regularised the local and customary laws inherited by the swift conquests of Constantinople, the Morea, Macedonia and the Pontos, under which most

[53] Lowry (1981).

Roman Orthodox had continued to live for a century after the fall of Constantinople in 1453, beyond even Gennadios Scholarios's prediction of the end of the world in 1492. The politics of the Union of Florence in 1439 could not be forgotten even after 1484. There were to be new patrons in Romania and Russia, but *patris* may have been the most enduring bond of all. Take, once more, the Soumelan village of Doubera, a steep place hidden in the Pontic undergrowth. After much lobbying the patriarchate created a final diocese in 1863, as influential as it was tiny. The parish church of Doubera became the cathedral of Rhodopolis. Today it is the mosque of Yazlik, a wholly Muslim Turkish village. But its titular bishop wields great influence – especially in Australia, where every second Greek claims to have come from Doubera. Surely this was the home of George Amiroutzes.[54]

[54] Bryer and Winfield (1985), I, p. 281; Bryer (1991), pp. 323–5; Balivet (1994).

CHAPTER 31

THE LATIN EAST

Anthony Luttrell

THE Latin communities in the east were composed predominantly of minority groups of westerners settled, permanently or temporarily, in the eastern Mediterranean, largely in consequence of earlier movements of Latin expansion. These developments were closely connected to the crusades which had conquered Jerusalem and Constantinople together with territories and islands in Greece, in the Aegean and on the Asiatic mainland. Some of these outposts were still in Latin hands in 1400, though the Ottoman Turks had by then secured considerable areas of Anatolia and the Balkans while the Mamluk regime, based on Cairo, was governing in Egypt and in what had before 1291 been Latin Syria. This presence in the east, whether in places under direct western rule, in Latin communities established in Greek lands, or in other Christian or infidel parts, comprised three varying and often overlapping classes: indigenous Latin settlers born and bred in the Levant; long-term expatriates in commercial, administrative, military or ecclesiastical posts; and merchants, sailors, mercenaries, missionaries, pilgrims and others stationed or travelling in the east for shorter periods.

The cosmopolitan world of scattered Levantine ports and islands was united by its seas, by its shipping and by the extensive trade which the Latins moved across them. This milieu was at the mercy of winds and currents, while much of the region was cold and snowy in winter. Lengthy and dangerous sea journeys took the westerners to the coastal termini supplied by the overland caravans arriving from the Asiatic east. The larger islands were mini-continents on which the quality of life could compare with that of the western Mediterranean mainlands, but the small islands were bleak, depopulated and miserable, without towns and amenities. These islands, all situated in a Greek-speaking area formerly within Byzantium, were dominated by small groups of Latins. Whether the administration was conducted by a monarchy as in Lusignan Cyprus, a metropolitan power as on Venetian Crete, a local Italian oligarchy as on Genoese Chios or a Latin military order as on Hospitaller Rhodes,

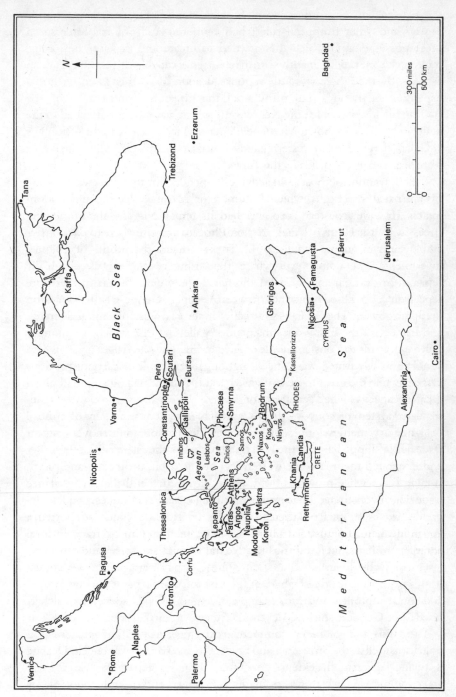

N

Tana

Kaffa

Black Sea

Varna

Nicopolis

Pera
Constantinople•Scutari
Gallipoli• •Bursa

Thessalonica

Ragusa

Venice

Rome•
Naples•

Otranto

Corfu

Palermo

Lepanto
Patras•Athens
Argos•
Nauplia•
Modon• Mistra
Koron•

Imbros
Aegean
Sea
Lesbos•
Chios•
Samos

Phocaea•
Smyrna•

Naxos•
Kos•
Nisyros•

Bodrum•

Kastellorizzo

RHODES

Ghcrigos•

Khania•
Candia•
Rethymnon•
CRETE

Famagusta•
Nicosia•
CYPRUS

Trebizond

Erzerum

Ankara•

Baghdad•

Jerusalem•

Beirut•

Cairo•

Alexandria•

Mediterranean Sea

Map 21 The Latin east

300 miles
500 km

the patterns of government were broadly similar. The Italian mercantile powers and other European rulers had economic and political interests in these possessions in which they needed to create and develop substantial multi-racial but predominantly Christian societies capable of resisting Turkish assaults. By 1400 there was little serious question of further Latin territorial expansion in the area, but throughout the fifteenth century most of the Aegean islands, except for the Negroponte which was virtually attached to the mainland and for Lesbos and its dependencies which lay close to the Ottomans at Gallipoli, remained in western hands. It was on the mainland that the Latins were over-run and expelled by the Turks.

Latin Levantine outposts and activities depended for their survival upon an overall naval superiority which Ottoman or Mamluk fleets could seldom match. However, western seapower had its limitations and the continuing necessity for the Latins of Ainos, Naxos, Phocaea and elsewhere to pay considerable sums as annual tribute to the Turks reduced the profits of colonial investment; and almost everywhere this tributary status was eventually replaced by outright annexation. Latin naval predominance was furthermore repeatedly jeopardised by clashes between Venetian, Genoese and lesser Latin maritime powers. The Catalans were active in the east as merchants and pirates, and from 1422 the Florentines maintained galleys at Pisa which occasionally sailed eastwards to Constantinople or Alexandria. The oared light galley, which could be heavily armed, was a speedy fighting unit capable of carrying precious cargoes while the great merchant galley and the round sailing ship had much greater capacity. The Venetians organised their galleys through a state-regulated system of convoys, the *mude*, which gave them a measure of control over military matters, prices, sailing dates, destinations and movements of trade. Latin shipping linked the Levantine harbours and islands to one another and integrated them into the western economic orbit, protecting and provisioning them while moving both their local produce and the long-distance trade which constituted their prime importance. Earlier conquests and settlements had developed estates and sources of revenue which supported a Levantine Latin population. There was a regional system of trade in local agrarian products, but it was the lucrative traffic in Asiatic spices and other luxuries which chiefly sustained western interest in the Levant. There were direct routes from Chios and elsewhere in the east to Atlantic ports such as Bruges and Southampton; in 1401, for example, thirty-four Genoese merchants chartered three Genoese ships at Alexandria for a voyage to Flanders.

The nature and volume of commercial exchanges naturally affected western policies as well as the prosperity and politics of the Latin Levant itself. Despite its political diversity, the extensive area from the Crimea to the Red Sea formed an economic zone which was primarily agricultural and often technologically backward, so that it became increasingly an underdeveloped region in which the Latins could dump their western industrial products. The Latin east exported its grain, wines, currants, honey, wax, cheese and other agrarian produce. Sweet red Cretan malmsey was much appreciated in the west, and mastic from the island of Chios, alum from the mines of Phocaea and sugar from the plantations of Cyprus were especially valuable. A considerable local cabotage was carried in small vessels, many of them Greek. By the fifteenth century the Asiatic spice trade had largely shifted to Alexandria but caravans travelled overland from Tabriz via Erzerum and from Baghdad through Syria to Bursa in north-west Anatolia where Genoese, Venetians and Florentines went as traders. Constantinople remained a centre for local, regional and trans-continental exchanges. The Black Sea, essentially an extension of the Aegean, retained some importance. Venetians and Genoese traded at Trebizond, Sansun and Sinope on the Pontic coast; they purchased waxes and skins in Bulgaria, and brought furs, fish, cereals and timber from Kaffa in the Crimea, and slaves from Tana in the Sea of Azov, part of the trade in slaves and wood moving along a north–south route to Mamluk Egypt. From the west came manufactured articles in metal, glass, paper and above all Italian, Flemish, Catalan, French and English woollen cloth.

At Constantinople the Venetians had their own quarter with two churches, twenty-five houses and various storehouses directed by a bailli who was a government official with wide jurisdiction. The Genoese had an important colony at Pera across the Golden Horn which operated as a useful observation post. Both these Italian powers had secured extremely lucrative customs exemptions from the emperor. The ledgers of a merchant such as Giacomo Badoer, a Venetian trading at Constantinople from 1436 to 1440, recorded a variety of affairs including commissions on purchases, sales and shipments, and it showed the importance of his Black Sea and Egyptian operations. In Egypt plague, depopulation, agrarian crises, technological stagnation and governmental interference interacted to produce a serious decline in textile production. Enormous payments of Venetian coin drained precious metal supplies from Europe into Syria and Egypt. The Venetian ducat became common currency in the Levant and even in India and beyond; in 1442 the Florentines had to counterfeit ducats for their Egyptian trade. Large profits were made from pepper, cinnamon, brazil wood and other luxuries arriving from India and south-east Asia through the Persian Gulf and the Red Sea, while the Venetians in particular carried pilgrims to Jerusalem and brought back Syrian cotton. Some westerners, such as the Cretan merchant Emmanuele Piloti at Cairo, spent years within the Mamluk domains acquiring, and sub-sequently reporting to the west, extremely shrewd perceptions of economic and political realities there. Latin notaries and local interpreters served visiting merchants at Beirut, Alexandria and elsewhere but western piracy and eastern extortions often led to tense relations with the Mamluks. The financier Jacques Coeur, who was based on Montpellier, himself went to purchase spices at Damascus in 1432 and subsequently he exported French copper and silver to the east. The southern Levant trade was not a Venetian monopoly but Venice increasingly assumed the predominant role in it after about 1410, while the hitherto considerable presence of Genoese, Catalans and other westerners diminished. After 1422 Sultan Barsbay responded to western exploitation of Egypt's weaknesses by using his control of Jidda to regulate and lower protection costs imposed in the Red Sea. He then sought to establish a pepper monopoly in Egypt and to double the sale price to the Venetians; in 1436 the Venetian consul was expelled from Alexandria and western merchants withdrew to Rhodes, but patient diplomacy eventually restored the Venetians' position.

Latin–Mamluk relations occasionally deteriorated into outright war. A Cypriot crusade had inflicted terrible long-term destruction on Alexandria in 1365, and in 1402 a Genoese fleet under the French Marshal, Jean de Boucicault, was prevented by bad weather from attacking Egypt but instead raided the Syrian coasts while also attacking Venetian property at Beirut. In 1403 the Hospitallers at Rhodes attempted, unsuccessfully, to establish a treaty with the Mamluk sultan which would have given them commercial advantages and a quasi-monopoly of the pilgrim trade. The Mamluks' seapower was not wholly negligible and in 1426 Sultan Barsbay invaded Cyprus, took King Janus to Cairo and reduced the kingdom to tributary status, but Mamluk attacks on Rhodes were beaten off between 1440 and 1444 and an equilibrium re-established. The last Cypriot mainland possession at Ghorigos on the southern Anatolian coast fell to the emir of Karaman, despite Hospitaller intervention from Rhodes, in 1448. Cyprus was debilitated by endless internal conflicts, the balance changing only in 1473 when the Venetians effectively secured command there; in 1489 Caterina Cornaro, the Venetian widow of the last Lusignan ruler, made the island over to Venice.

Maritime interests interacted with continental developments. Ottoman expansion in both Anatolia and the Balkans provoked a major Franco-Hungarian crusade which was crushed at Nicopolis on the Danube by the Sultan Bayazid and his Serbian vassals in 1396; John of Nevers, future duke of Burgundy, was taken prisoner to Bursa in Anatolia. The west lamented this overwhelming disaster which, however, may well have saved Constantinople from the Turks. Then, while the Emperor Manuel II was travelling as far as London on a largely ineffectual fund-raising tour, his capital was reprieved once again when the great Mongol conqueror Timur defeated Bayazid near Ankara on 28 July 1402. Timur advanced towards Constantinople, took

Smyrna castle from the Hospitallers of Rhodes and restored various Anatolian emirs to the lands from which Bayazid had ousted them; he then withdrew to Samarkand, leaving the devastated Ottoman domains divided by fratricidal conflicts between Bayazid's three sons. Timur had no fleet, yet the Venetian and Genoese captains greedily sacrificed the opportunity of crippling Ottoman power when they ferried many fleeing Turks across the waters from Asia into safety in Europe; the Latins then concluded with two of Bayazid's sons separate treaties designed to oppose Timur and to secure western commercial advantages. The westerners had already come to envisage a Turkish power as an integral part of the Levantine establishment. The Ottomans were enabled to reconstitute their shattered regime and, after about 1420, to recommence their Balkan and Anatolian expansion.

The west had political and religious concerns in the Levant. Christian opposition to the Ottomans in the Adriatic and the Balkans, which culminated in the unsuccessful Varna crusade of 1444, did not involve the Latins on a large scale, though a Venetian fleet sailed to the Dardanelles to collaborate in it. The long-delayed bartering of aid for Byzantium in return for Greek recognition of Roman religious supremacy was belatedly agreed after much theological haggling at the Councils held at Ferrara and Florence in 1438 and 1439. Alfonso V, king in Aragon, Naples and Sicily, had grandiose but unrealisable claims and aspirations in Byzantium and the east; in 1450 he acquired the strategic offshore islet of Kastellorizzo between Rhodes and Cyprus and defended it with a new castle. The Venetians defeated a large Ottoman fleet off the Gallipoli peninsula in 1416; they acquired Thessalonica in 1423 but lost it in 1430; they made a peace with the Ottomans in 1430 and then blockaded Genoese Chios. The Latin powers did not oppose the Turks consistently and they afforded little aid to Constantinople where small groups of Venetians, Genoese and other Latins fought valiantly in the final siege of 1453; other western help set out too late.

Forms of colonisation varied, but throughout much of the east the Latins were largely restricted to the coastal cities which were their centres of long-distance communication and commercial interchange. Huddled within town walls for solidarity as well as for safety, the western expatriates remained a largely separate governing class which dominated and often exploited an indigenous and mainly rural populace. On the Greek mainland the Latin principality of Achaea, conquered after the crusade of 1204, lay closest to the west, yet it was in full disintegration by 1400 when its Navarrese ruler Pedro de San Superan controlled only portions of the western Peloponnese. The weakness of its Neapolitan overlords and its own internal conflicts had delivered Latin Achaea and Glarentsa, its principal city, into the hands of an obscure group of predominantly Navarrese mercenaries who could not prevent repeated raids by

Ottoman armies advancing overland. The ancient Latin baronage was reduced to a few insecure families and the archbishop of Patras; Athens remained under the government of the Florentine family of Acciaiuoli until 1456. Centurione II Zaccaria, formerly baron of Arkadia, became prince of Achaea in 1404 and prolonged the principality's existence until 1430 when the Greeks under Thomas Palaiologos, despot of Mistra, secured control over almost the entire peninsula. Effective resistance to the Turks came only from the Venetians whose concern for their long-distance trade forced them to defend their vital naval bases at Coron and Modon in the south-west, and to reverse their policy of avoiding the expenses and complications of occupying and administering extended mainland positions. Venice acquired direct control of Corfu in 1386; of Nauplia, and also of Tinos and Mykonos, in 1390; of Argos in 1394; and of Lepanto in 1407. Western predominance on the mainland had evaporated. The old *Assizes de Romanie*, the feudal lawcode of Latin Greece, remained in effect, in Venetian translation, only in Negroponte, certain Aegean islands and Corfu. The Latin Chronicle of the Morea was never extended beyond 1377, and when the Neapolitan family of Tocco, who were despots of Epirus from 1418 to 1449, produced a chronicle it was in Greek verse. Only on Cyprus and Crete was a western chronicle tradition maintained.

The westerners were notably more successful on the islands. Cyprus, in Latin hands since 1191, had been an adjunct of the western establishment in Syria from which its nobility and governmental institutions fundamentally derived; in fact its Latin rulers continued to be crowned as kings of Jerusalem. Cyprus was a large and prosperous island where the inhabitants, though mainly Greek in speech and religion, remained surprisingly loyal to the Frankish dynasty. It derived much wealth from the trans-shipment of oriental trade, but the dynasty was weakened by its members' personal deficiencies, by an unruly nobility and by Genoese predominance in the principal port at Famagusta. Cyprus was increasingly exploited as an Italian colony, especially after the Genoese reinforced their hold on Famagusta in 1402/3 and pressured the crown into paying the very considerable sums it owed them. In 1426 the Mamluks captured King Janus in battle at Kherotikia, and his ransom and the tribute imposed on the kingdom further weakened the royal government. Decades of complicated quarrels ensued. Janus's son, John II, died in 1458; the latter's daughter, Charlotte, became queen but was defeated in 1464 by her half-brother, John II's illegitimate son who became king as James II. In 1460 James II even called in an Egyptian fleet. He died in 1473 as did his baby son James III in 1474, leaving as titular ruler James's widow, the Venetian Caterina Cornaro. In 1489 she formally handed Cyprus, in effect a Venetian protectorate since 1473, to Venice, a transfer requiring the formal consent of the Egyptian sultan as the island's overlord.

As elsewhere, the Latins on Cyprus reserved political power and fiscal advantages to themselves, maintaining a social distance from the Greeks which was rooted in religion and culture. The Roman Church, both secular and regular, served to bolster and institutionalise the Latins' collective identity and solidarity. Theoretically, the Greeks were not schismatical orthodox but uniates under Roman jurisdiction. A Latin nobility of perhaps a hundred families held small hereditary estates from which its incomes largely derived, and its male members were normally knights who were royal lieges and members of the ancient high court of Cyprus. The small ruling class was largely born locally, but it received a continuing influx of western merchants, mercenaries and others who acquired estates and titles through service, purchase or marriage. Some Catalans, Syrians and others, including a very few Greeks, entered this nobility during the fifteenth century. The government functioned through a royal council and an administrative and financial office, the *secrète*. After 1489 the Venetians ruled in Cyprus through a bailli appointed in Venice; they curtailed the nobility and replaced the high court with urban councils to which non-nobles were admitted, while Venetian subjects acquired lands, offices, incomes and, in certain cases, noble titles. By offering advantageous terms to settlers, including some from Corfu and the Peloponnese, Venice successfully repopulated towns and villages, transforming Cyprus into a genuine colony which it exploited but to which it brought security and prosperity, with cotton gradually replacing the island's sugar which was unable to compete with the cheaper sugar from the Atlantic islands.

Crete, acquired by the Venetians after 1204, was never self-governing. Instead, its Italian settlers were strictly controlled by a metropolitan machine regulated through a *duca*, or doge, of Candia and through other officials who were often appointed and directed from Venice, the *procuratores et sindici ad partes Levantis*. This Latin administration and its strongly established Roman Church made Crete the most considerable of western colonies and a notable centre of Latin culture. Northern Italian settlers had been installed as *feudatarii* who held property from the state and owed military service to it, and there were local councils with limited powers. With its agrarian produce, its slave traffic and its harbours at Khania, Rethymnon and Candia, the modern Herakleion, Crete was the hub of Venice's Levantine empire. Interference from Venice often proved clumsy, with written instructions frequently taking months to arrive; the Latin settlers themselves were angered when the central government taxed them heavily for defensive expenditures made partly in the interests of the metropolitan mercantile class. There was less antagonism between Latins and Greeks in the fifteenth century as intermarriage and proximity eroded barriers, as Greeks were employed in government service and as indigenous Cretans sat on local councils and were sent as envoys to Venice, but after 1439 there were rebellions and conspiracies, imprisonments and expulsions, provoked by the issue of Greek acceptance of Roman religious supremacy. Crete remained prosperous so that the area under cultivation was extended and the population rose; it continued to send wine, oil and above all much grain to the other colonies as well as to Venice. Though the Constantinople and Black Sea trade declined after 1453, Crete retained its importance as a vital stage on the routes to Cyprus and Alexandria.

The Genoese, with no single major colony, controlled a string of Levantine trading stations with a looser and more flexible system of bureaucratic direction and metropolitan defence than the centralised rigidity of Venice. Pera apart, their chief Aegean base and entrepot was the offshore island of Chios which was valuable for its mastic and the alum of nearby Phocaea. Chios had been acquired in 1346 through a pact made by a *mahona*, a joint-stock company financed by individual Genoese but supported by their metropolitan government. That was how colonial positions were occupied and maintained; after 1453 Genoa's state bank, the Casa di San Giorgio, directly administered its Black Sea colonies. In 1400 there were on Chios some 10,000 Greeks and perhaps 2,000 Latins, the latter largely resident in the city except for a few soldiers controlling outlying forts and towers. Such outposts had relatively small Latin communities; at Venetian Coron there were only eighty Latins in 1401. Agriculture on Chios was left to the Greeks. There were some mixed marriages, usually involving Greek women. The indigenous elite did retain certain of its privileges and there were Greek notaries, bankers and shippers, some of them responsible for the grain supply. A *podestà*, chosen in Genoa after the government had presented a list of names to the *mahonesi*, governed Chios with a council of Latins. The *mahona* exercised a monopoly on alum, mastic and salt, and generally maintained fair relations and an element of co-existence based on a community of interest with the leading Greeks. In 1480 Laonikos Chalkokandyles described the Genoese as behaving 'with the greatest moderation'. Further north, four successive generations of the Genoese family of Gattilusio, which had acquired Lesbos in 1355, apparently married Byzantine princesses; they also ruled Imbros, Samothrake and other places. The Gattilusio maintained their family contacts in Genoa but were really Byzantine dependants who spoke Greek, favoured the Byzantine Church and avoided conflict with the Turks who, however, ousted them between 1455 and 1462.

After 1204 Rhodes and its dependent islands had remained largely Greek until occupied by the military-religious order of the Hospital of St John between 1306 and 1310. There too the Latins came relatively late and made a pact giving the Greeks religious and other guarantees. They imported settlers, Greeks as well as Latins, and provided security and prosperity. The Hospitallers relied upon the resources of the European priories and commanderies which were in a sense their colonies, while Rhodes was their centre and headquarters which, technically, they held from no superior but the pope. The brethren's continuing function, the very justification for their existence, was the holy war against the infidel, and on losing Smyrna to Timur in 1402 they established a new mainland outpost in the isolated castle which they built during 1407/8 at Bodrum on the coast just north of Kos, thus creating a haven for Christian slaves escaping from the Turks. As the Ottomans secured a permanent hold in Anatolia, Rhodes became increasingly isolated and defensive. Its small navy faced the Turks at sea; its harbour developed into an ever more secure and important western entrepot which sheltered Catalan and other pirates as well as a cosmopolitan merchant community. For example, in an act drawn up in 1417 by a Venetian priest, who acted as notary with Catalan and Cretan witnesses, a Provençal inhabitant of Rhodes empowered a merchant from Ancona and another from Genoa to recover his credits abroad. That profits could be made was demonstrated by Niccolò Tron, elected doge at Venice in 1471, who had become rich during fifteen years spent as a merchant at Rhodes. Licensed privateering, the official *corso*, also brought in significant earnings. The city's defences were continually strengthened. Mamluk attacks were resisted between 1440 and 1444, but Turkish pressures on the outlying islands grew stronger after 1453 and culminated in the great Ottoman siege successfully resisted by the Master, Pierre d'Aubusson, in 1480. After 1482 the Hospitallers were secured against the Ottoman sultan through their custody of his brother Djem who eventually died in Italy in 1495. Though a moderately prosperous Greek business class developed there, Rhodes had no Greek nobility and there were very few hereditary Latin landholders to exploit a peasantry much of which was virtually free. The Hospital, paternalistic and restrained over matters of religion, was not seriously resented by the Greeks, who fought bravely to resist the Turks in 1480.

Western society was itself affected by its overseas activities. Particularly in Venice and Genoa, family and business groupings jockeyed for position in the special offices and committees which manipulated Levantine policies and appointments. Influence derived from eastern wealth and possessions was exerted at home by a new 'colonial' class as well as by established metropolitan families such as the Cornaro of Venice or the many Genoese clans with members established in eastern outposts. The Genoese were numerous on Rhodes and Cyprus as well as at Pera and on the other eastern Aegean islands close to the Anatolian coast. Venice sought to protect Crete and its other colonies, and it firmly superintended the petty Latin lords of the western Aegean islands who were Venetian citizens. The most important of these were the Crispi family which ruled Naxos as dukes of the Archipelago. In theory they were vassals of the princes of the Morea whose lawcode, the *Assizes de*

Romanie, did apply in their islands, but in practice appeals could be made to Venetian courts. In about 1400 Naxos was a base for Catalan and Basque pirates; its Latin settlers were relatively humble men who owed military service as galley oarsmen. Merchants from Barcelona, Florence, Ancona, Ragusa and other places without colonies of their own traded throughout the east, travelling on shipping of other powers. The Catalans, once strong on Rhodes and Cyprus, largely disappeared from the Levant after the 1460s.

There were numerous small Aegean islands which lacked water, fuel, communications, administration and even human contact, and were constantly at the mercy of drought, bad weather, Latin pirates and Turkish razzias; some had very small populations while others had none. The more than 100 isles in the Cyclades covered just over 2,000 square kilometres, of which 15 per cent was arable; only twenty of these islands were still inhabited in 1420. By 1500 about a fifth of the population on the Cyclades followed the Latin rite but many of these were Greeks. Some smaller islands, such as Amorgos and Nisyros, had Latin rulers but very few Latin inhabitants. Others received occasional Latin visits when ships were blown ashore or wrecked on them, and such visitors reported on the appalling conditions of the Greek islanders. Early in the fifteenth century Giovanni Quirini moved families from Tinos and Mykonos to settle them on his island of Stampalia, while the Gozzadini lord of Kythnos repopulated his island. Kastellorizzo, between Rhodes and Cyprus, had a Latin garrison but only a few permanent inhabitants who worked the saltings there. The economies of these small islands were precarious, though some had special exports, such as stone from Paros or sulphur from Nisyros, or they sent fruit and vegetables to markets on larger islands nearby.

No ethnic group could escape a range of natural disasters and other difficulties. Travellers often had trouble finding ships and many suffered terrifying storms, piracy and shipwreck. In about 1420 Cristoforo Buondelmonti was saved after seven days on an islet near Samos where he had prematurely scratched on a rock, in Latin significantly: 'Here the priest Cristophorus died of terrible hunger.' Plague was recurrent almost everywhere. Earthquakes caused enormous destruction throughout the region; that at Rhodes in 1481 was said to have done more damage than the Turkish siege of the previous year, while another at Kos in 1493 provoked emergency measures at Rhodes to send food, medicines, doctors, planks and other supplies, and above all to ensure the defence of those places where the walls had collapsed. Pirates, whether Latin, Greek or Turkish, took slaves, devastated coastal zones and pushed up commercial insurance costs. Disruption was widespread, and attacks on shipping and merchandise provoked reprisals and prolonged litigation. No one was ever safe at sea.

*

In the face of Ottoman advances, the Latin east shrank considerably during the fifteenth century, yet its society became more cohesive and its internal economies and the oriental trade made it more prosperous. The Latins' advantages depended on effective Italian-style governmental systems and on comparatively reasonable arrangements with their Greek subjects as well as on their advantages at sea. No single power could entirely dominate the area with a fleet of galleys since these could stay on station at sea for only a limited time, but the Latins maintained their general naval predominance over the developing Ottoman fleet. Galleys and oarsmen were particularly costly, and defence was a major expenditure for the Venetians. Shipping was mostly built in the west but the larger eastern ports were equipped for repairs and refitting. Land defences consisted of coastal watch-towers and inland castles to which the population could retreat from danger; fire signals sent warnings from one island to another. Fortresses and large ports had Latin garrisons, and the Hospital's mercenaries in the garrison of Bodrum castle actually formed a corporation of *socii* with its own written statutes. However, stone was cheaper than manpower and throughout the Latin east fortifications grew lower, broader and stronger as cannon became increasingly powerful. Thus the Rhodes of 1400 with its comparatively thin curtain and tallish projecting towers was transformed into a fortress protected by low, thick walls and an extensive system of barbicans and bastions which just resisted Ottoman bombardments and assaults in 1480 and almost did so again in 1522. Domestic and ecclesiastical building was mostly in a Mediterranean Gothic style with some major monuments, such as the cathedral at Nicosia, the great hospital begun at Rhodes in 1440, and a number of abbeys in the Morea, on Cyprus and elsewhere. Latin churches often had frescoes and panel paintings, sometimes in the western manner and occasionally, as on Crete and Rhodes, in an eclectic blend of Latin and Greek styles.

The Latins were established predominantly in urban coastal centres and, except on Cyprus and Rhodes, they were mostly Italians. Western commerce stimulated an astonishing development of harbour towns such as Famagusta, Rhodes and Chios in which moles, arsenals, pontoons, warehouses, churches and public buildings proliferated. In these outposts Latin minorities shared western Mediterranean ways of life, customs and culture, spoke romance tongues, and were governed under Italianate town statutes and the regulations of the Roman Church. They retained essential command of political power. Small groups of Syrians, Jews, Armenians and others sometimes occupied intermediate positions, but if Greek elites were occasionally granted a limited measure of power and responsibility, they were not fused with the Latin settler class; Greek resistance was often passive and cultural. A *modus vivendi* with a class of urban Greeks took a variety of forms. On Cyprus, and marginally on

Rhodes, there were arrangements involving fiefs and military service, but in the Morea this 'feudal' structure had effectively collapsed by 1400. Elsewhere, government was centralised, especially in areas under Venetian rule which were administered by metropolitan officials appointed usually for two years and subject to rigorous accounting controls; justice and taxation belonged to the government, though taxes were often farmed out. Levantine westerners, termed *latini* and *franchi*, were legally free; even in the fifteenth century many Greeks remained *paroikoi* or *villani*, that is subjects or serfs of very varying status who were broadly subject to a range of taxes and obligations which often derived from Byzantine practice. Many Latins, and even others, were entitled *civis* or *burgensis*, or they were described as *habitator* which implied temporary residence; thus, for example, some men were citizens of Genoa or of its Ligurian riviera, while other Genoese subjects were simply inhabitants of Genoese Chios or Pera who enjoyed a certain fiscal or juridical status. The authorities naturally tended to resent those Greeks, Syrians and others, who escaped their jurisdiction by acquiring some form of western citizenship.

Religious differences remained profound. Many Latin churchmen in the Levant had been born in the west, and the bishops, canons and other higher clergy who held the richer benefices were often absentees; ordinary priests were few, even for the relatively scanty Latin congregations. The formal machinery of cathedral and parish operated mainly in the towns, while in the countryside Latins sometimes spoke Greek and worshipped in Greek churches. The Latin Church held ecclesiastical property, mainly confiscated from the Greek Church, and it raised tithes. Though compelled by circumstances to a notional subjection to the Roman pope, the Greeks firmly maintained their own rite and language which characterised their fundamental resistance to Latinisation; thus as late as 1435 and 1445 two inscriptions commissioned by Greek priests for small Cretan churches mentioned the Byzantine Emperor John VIII Palaiologos in their dating clause. On the smaller islands the Latin bishop was frequently elsewhere, leaving a Greek *protopapas*, technically a delegate of the bishop who appointed him, to administer the Greek Church and its possessions according to Greek law and to represent the Greek population. In 1439 the Council at Florence approved a form of union but outside Latin domains that agreement had little effect in the east. Latin convents were scattered throughout the east, but the Dominicans and Franciscans at Pera, Jerusalem and elsewhere aimed to serve Latin minorities or to take missionary work into Asia rather than to convert Greeks. Venetian Tana, essentially a fortified counter at the mouth of the Don, was devastated in 1395 and on subsequent occasions. By the fifteenth century the disintegration of the Mongol empire with its secure road system had greatly reduced the penetration of western merchants and missionaries beyond the Mediterranean shores and had cut off contacts with the far east. Venetian merchants increasingly concentrated on Alexandria and the Genoese looked to the Atlantic.

Latin crusading enthusiasm undoubtedly survived, but it was often diverted to holy wars in the Balkans or in the west. Jerusalem itself retained a powerful spiritual attraction for men and women; pilgrimage there offered spiritual rewards and relics as well as travel, escape, adventure. In Cairo, pilgrims occasionally found westerners from as far away as Germany and Denmark who were stranded there as Mamluk soldiers. Many pilgrims sailed from Venice in well-regulated excursions; the land journey from the Syrian ports and visits to the holy places were managed by the Franciscans who also provided hospices. Accounts such as that of Felix Faber, who extended the standard itinerary to visit Mount Sinai and Cairo, helped to preserve the western consciousness of the east. An extensive literature of chronicles, poetic laments and reports on Levantine events and disasters was encouraged by the spread of printing, while a keen, if distorted, literary interest in the Turks circulated information on their religion, their government and, especially, their armies. The medallion of the young Mehemmed II made for the Burgundian noble Jehan Trieaudet or Gentile Bellini's portrait of the same sultan constituted visual equivalents; in 1480 Bellini also decorated Mehemmed's palace at Constantinople with erotic scenes. The Latins developed a respect for the Turks which went back at least to Jean de Boucicault's three-month stay at the court of Sultan Murad in 1388 when he offered to fight for the Ottoman sultan against an infidel enemy, just as Chaucer's fictitious knight served one Anatolian Muslim emir against another.

Western interests were also stimulated by humanist concerns for Antiquity, by the teaching of Greek in Italy and eventually by printed editions of classical texts. Thus in about 1420 the Florentine priest Cristoforo Buondelmonti spent several years continuing his Greek studies on Rhodes and purchasing classical manuscripts in the east; his *Liber Insularum Archipelagi* was widely copied in the west, its maps forming the basis of a long-lasting cartographical tradition. Buondelmonti described many classical remains, recounting his efforts to use shipping tackle to raise a fallen statue of Apollo on Delos and Jacomo Crispi's attempt to measure the depth of the crater at Santorini. His major successor as Hellenic traveller, Ciriaco of Ancona, was more scientific in his copying of sculptures and inscriptions; he reported how Crusino Summaripa, the Latin lord of Paros, excavated marble statues there. By the end of the century Isabella d'Este of Mantua was employing collectors to send ancient sculptures to Italy where such importations played a significant role in artistic developments. The Hospitallers burned many ancient marbles for lime but they also decorated the walls of their castle at Bodrum, the ancient Halikarnassos, with classical reliefs dug up from the Mausoleum.

Not only did a Greco-Latin culture thrive on Crete but Greek émigrés, estimated at 4,000 by 1478, made Venice a centre of Byzantine civilisation and had a profound effect on western intellectual life. The larger islands had their own schools, but men had to go west, often to Padua, for university study; the Greek Franciscan Peter Philargos, who was elected pope as Alexander V at Pisa in 1409, had degrees from Oxford and Paris. Latins sometimes knew Greek but only rarely Turkish. A petition of 1510 on Rhodes which called for a schoolmaster to teach both Latin and Greek to Latin and Greek boys, rich and poor, was signed in one script or the other by leading Rhodians, both Latin and Greek. Scholars from Constantinople and elsewhere reached Crete and their manuscripts were copied there. Students and bureaucrats took cultural inter-change back and forth so that western poetic themes inspired Cretan literature; icons, furniture and other items were exported westwards. In Cyprus Leontios Machairas and Georgios Bustron produced chronicles of Latin rule in Greek. The Valencian Joannot Martorell set much of his romance *Tirant lo Blanch* in the Latin east, about which he was quite well informed. Yet in reality many westerners were not at home in the Levant. In a copy of the Latin lawcode, the *Assizes de Romanie*, a homesick chancery clerk wrote 'Oh, when shall I go to the land of Venice' ('O, quando andar nella tiera di Venexia').

Constantinople fell to Mehemmed II on 28 May 1453, the Straits and the Black Sea passing under Ottoman control. The Genoese at Pera maintained an ambiguous neutrality during the siege but survived only as a Latin community under Turkish control, while in 1454 the Venetians made a treaty which allowed them a colony and commercial privileges in Constantinople. The Aegean Latins, in the Rhodian islands for example, felt the new Turkish threat almost immediately, and in 1461 Trebizond and the Greek towns along the Pontic coast were taken. The Latins lacked firm undivided leadership. Pope Pius II's schemes for an eastern crusade under his personal command collapsed in 1460, but from 1463 Venice fought the long and enormously expensive war of Negroponte in defence of its colonial positions, making initial conquests in the Morea, campaigning on the Aegean and the coasts of Cilicia, and negotiating or collaborating with the Karaman Turks and others. One effective ally, the Albanian Skanderbeg, died in 1468 and the fall of Negroponte in 1470 was a major loss. In the Black Sea, Venetian Tana and Genoese Kaffa were taken by the Turks in 1475. The Turks advanced overland to within sight of Venice. Peace in 1479 brought the further loss of Argos in the Peloponnese and of Scutari in Albania; the Venetians were forced to pay 10,000 ducats a year for the right to trade in Ottoman territories but thereafter their remaining northern Levantine colonies did prosper. The Turks turned elsewhere; in 1480 they tem-porarily took Otranto in Apulia but were repulsed at Rhodes. Ottoman advances continued yet the Latin islands were increasing their wealth and population, especially in the case of Cyprus which the Venetians transformed into a prospering colony on their route to Alexandria. The Hospitallers exploited their custody of the sultan's brother, Djem, to conduct an ambiguous policy of co-existence designed to exploit the position of Rhodes on trade routes running both east–west and north–south. They balanced their island's agrarian deficit through trade in Anatolia and investment in a carefully regulated and limited quota of piratical aggression.

The Latin strategic position in the Aegean inevitably worsened after 1453. No Venetian galley set out for the Black Sea thereafter and none for Constantinople between 1453 and 1479. The Venetians switched their operations southwards, retaining Crete, acquiring Cyprus and securing enormous profits at Alexandria where they were able to exploit Mamluk fears of the Ottomans. Genoa and Florence lacked the economic hinterlands necessary to provide a spice market on the scale of that enjoyed by Venice, and they could scarcely muster the precious metal available to the Venetians or match the organised tenacity of Venice's regulation of its shipping and merchants. The Genoese kept Chios but lost Famagusta, Pera and the Black Sea outposts. As they successfully concentrated their activities in the western Mediterranean and the Atlantic, the volume of their eastern trade fell sharply. Venice's mainland expansion which began in 1405 did not undermine its Levantine colonies; it could still mobilise the determination and resources necessary for the major Turkish war which opened in 1463. The Venetians' annual investment in Egypt and Syria probably reached over 600,000 ducats by 1500, while that of Genoa in the southern Levant perhaps averaged only about 75,000 ducats. The dramatic rise of pepper prices in 1499 was due not to the arrival of news that the Portuguese had reached India but to a new Venetian–Ottoman war in which the Turks disrupted the Venetians' Levantine communication network by taking Lepanto in 1499 and then Modon and Coron in the south-west Peloponnese in 1500.

European discoveries in the Atlantic and Pacific were to reduce the importance of the Levant to western Europe but, as the fifteenth century closed, the Latins were maintaining themselves on almost all the islands, having created on them societies and economies which were able to survive if afforded adequate military protection. The novel interaction of Mediterranean and more universal affairs was accompanied by the collapse of the Mamluk regime when the Ottomans took Cairo in 1517 and then advanced across north Africa. In the Levant the Turks normally expelled Latin settlers while reaching accommodations with the Greeks, but western merchants, pilgrims and others continued to trade and travel in the Levant as the Ottomans captured Rhodes in 1522, Chios in 1566, Cyprus in 1571 and Crete, following lengthy resistance, in 1669; Corfu was never taken.

CHAPTER 32

THE OTTOMAN WORLD

Elizabeth Zachariadou

THE AFTERMATH OF THE BATTLE OF ANKARA

During the first half of the fifteenth century Europe, although shaken by the Great Schism and deeply divided by wars, had one obvious enemy: the Ottoman Turk, who professed a different religion and, for this reason, was not just an enemy but the enemy of Christ and of the Cross. This fact did not prevent a Christian state from pursuing commercial relations with the Turks, or even from appealing to them for help against another Christian state. However, in religious propaganda and political theory it was the Turk who was labelled as the eternal foe.

The process of Ottoman expansion was halted by the Anatolian campaign of the Mongol *khan*, Timur. The Christians had watched his movements with great interest at least since 1394, when his troops began to press the eastern frontier of the Ottoman lands. The whole Christian world felt deep relief when the Mongol army dissolved the Ottoman state by crushing Sultan Bayazid I's troops near Ankara and taking him prisoner (1402). Timur, with his army, stayed in Anatolia for approximately one year after his victory. Towns and countryside were laid waste and the population, Muslim and non-Muslim, was mercilessly massacred by the Mongols. Crowds from Anatolia swarmed into the Balkans to save their lives and Constantinople was thronged with refugees. Nevertheless, the Byzantines kept celebrating the victory of Timur as if he were sent by God to liberate their besieged capital and to allow their state to grow and survive. Western Europeans, liberated from the danger of the Ottoman threat, tried to confirm their old commercial privileges in the Levant, but they did not proceed openly to further destruction of Ottoman power because conflicts among them were soon to break out.

The Ottoman Empire disintegrated in Anatolia as the various Turkish states, which had been annexed by the Ottomans, were restored by Timur to their previous lords (emirs). Once again Anatolia became a mosaic of small states: the emirate of Sarukhan having Manisa as its capital; the emirate of Germiyan, in the alum-producing region of Kütahya; the emirate of Aydin with the important towns of Smyrna and Ayasoluk (Ephesus); the emirate of Menteshe in the fertile plain of the Meander, with Balat (Miletus) as its capital; the emirate of Isfendiyar in the copper-producing region of Sinope. This last, which maintained frequent relations with the states situated on the northern Black Sea coast and in the mouth of the Danube, would play an important role in further political developments. In the European provinces (Rumelia) the Ottomans very soon recovered and started defending their possessions.

The earlier situation explains these developments. The Ottoman state, which had originated in Bithynia and had Bursa as its capital, represented a most important difference from the other Turkish emirates which had emerged in Anatolia after the collapse of the Seldjuks (*c.* 1300). From 1354 onwards, it expanded into the Balkans by conquering Byzantine and Slav territories and a second, European capital, Edirne (Adrianople), was created. The conquest in Europe, accomplished in the name of holy war (*djihad*) against the infidel, which was dictated by the Koran and constituted the official ideology of the state, attributed wealth and prestige to the sultans, who then turned to the east and, after negotiations or war, were gradually able to annex the other Turkish states and transform them into provinces (*sandjak*s) of their realm.[1]

Only the emirate of Karaman resisted successfully. The house of Karaman, like that of Osman, claimed affiliation with the Seldjuk sultans of Anatolia, because both houses wished to appear as their legitimate successors. The Karamanoglus possessed the Seldjuk capital, Konya (Ikonion), and carried out holy war against the neighbouring Christian kingdom of Cilician Armenia until the latter vanished in 1375; they also maintained political contacts with the Mamluks of Egypt and Syria, and commercial relations with the Franks of Cyprus. By the end of the fourteenth century Karaman was in a weak position resulting from Ottoman pressure, but it recovered after the invasion of Timur, who favoured it particularly.

The situation was different in Rumelia, the land where holy war was carried out against the Christians. In addition to the provinces of the state and the territories ruled by the sultan's Christian vassals, there were the domains of the lords of the marches, the *udj bey*s, that is the semi-independent military commanders entrusted by the sultan with conquest. Those among them who had long been established in Rumelia possessed redoubtable power. The most representative *udj bey* of those years is Evrenos, lord of the region around Thessalonica. Another enterprising *udj bey* of the time was Pasha-Yigit, established in Skopia. The presence of the *udj bey* resulted in the efficient military organisation of Rumelia which was not affected by the defeat at Ankara.

---

[1] Wittek (1938b), especially pp. 33–51; Inalcik (1973), pp. 9–11.

Although some Christian vassals of the sultan tried to take advantage of the situation, the Ottomans were able to keep them under control. Furthermore, Turkish military manpower in Rumelia was to be reinforced after the defeat. Bayazid's elder son, Süleyman, had abandoned the battlefield of Ankara when a Mongol victory became evident, and marched westwards to the Straits. He was accompanied by his father's vizier, Ali Djandarlı, descendant of a noble family whose members took over the vizierate in a hereditary way. Fearing the Mongols, numerous cadres of the Ottoman state and whole contingents of the army managed to cross the Straits, in spite of a Christian plan, disregarded by greedy Genoese and Venetian sailors, that no Turk should be transported to the European side.

Three sons of Bayazid, Süleyman, Mehemmed and Isa, staked an immediate claim to leadership over the Ottomans after their father's defeat. The Christian states, particularly the Byzantines, the Venetians and the Wallachians, tried to secure maximum advantage from the division of the Ottomans by supporting one prince against the others. Among the Turks, the idea that there was a family singled out by God to rule over them was deeply rooted. For the Ottomans, this was the family of Osman, only one of whose members was destined to become sultan. This conviction resulted in the custom of fratricide according to which a new sultan had to put to death his brothers or any other possible candidate to the throne. The custom, attested to exist in the middle of the fourteenth century, was to become a law, officially decreed by Mehemmed II after the fall of Constantinople.[2] However, in the crucial period following the battle of Ankara, this conviction contributed considerably to the reunification of the Ottoman state. It is remarkable that none of the *udj beys* or high officials disputed the throne or tried to establish his own rule. The only separatist movement, that of Djüneyd in the region of Smyrna, took place under the cover of members of the sultanic family.

Despite the strong position of the Ottomans in Rumelia, Süleyman, established in Edirne, yet afraid of a possible crossing of the Mongol army, began to solicit the Byzantine emperor and the other Christian powers of the Levant for peace. He knew, furthermore, that he would have to fight his brothers, particularly Mehemmed, for the throne. Rumours had certainly reached him that Mehemmed, established in the region of Amasya, where he had resided before the Mongol invasion, recognised Timur as his overlord.

After fairly long negotiations Süleyman concluded a peace treaty with the Christian powers of Romania, namely the Byzantine emperor, the Knights Hospitallers of Rhodes, Venice, Genoa and the duke of Naxos; the ruler of Serbia and the marquis of Bodonitza were also included (February 1403).

---

[2] Lewis (1968), pp. 66–7; Babinger (1978), pp. 65–6; Wittek (1938a), p. 23.

According to the main clauses of the treaty, the Byzantines took back an important territory in Thrace extending from the Propontis up to the Black Sea, as well as Thessalonica with its region; furthermore, they were exempted from all tributes formerly paid to the sultan. The Genoese colonies of the Levant and the duke of Naxos were also exempted from tributes. The Venetians resumed all their territories which had been conquered by the Ottomans in the past, and were granted a few new ones. The Hospitallers of Rhodes were to receive Salona in the Gulf of Corinth. Apart from these concessions, and other minor ones, made to each party separately, Süleyman reconfirmed old commercial privileges and guaranteed the safe-conduct of trade within his lands. Evrenos and other Turkish notables were very displeased at Süleyman's concessions to the Christians.[3] In some cases, the Turkish authorities openly displayed their disapproval of the treaty: when Byzantine officials went to take over Thessalonica, they met with the resistance of the Turks who rallied on the citadel and occupied it for a while until they received new orders to surrender.[4]

DYNASTIC AND SOCIAL STRIFE

The defeat at Ankara opened a period of political instability combined with social strife. Until 1413 there were sometimes two, sometimes three Ottoman states in conflict with one another. This period is known as the interregnum (*fetret devri*). Dynastic clashes and social upheaval were to continue within the Ottoman Empire until 1425.

After the conclusion of the treaty and the evacuation of Anatolia by the Mongol army, Süleyman, aiming at sole supremacy over the Ottomans, focused his attention on his two rival brothers. With this end in view, he crossed into Anatolia. It is not clear whom he entrusted with the administration of Rumelia since his vizier, Ali Djandarlı, accompanied him. In all likelihood Rumelia was left in the hands of the *udj beys*. The territory, whose economy had originally been geared to war and conquest, was now confronted with serious problems resulting from the peace, the more so as the number of warriors assembled there had increased with the arrival of those fleeing before the Mongols. However, peaceful relations on the whole were maintained with the neighbouring Christian states, including Hungary which, since the 1360s, had constituted the only real menace to the Ottomans in the Balkans. Furthermore, the Hungarians began to control the production and distribution of metals in central Europe.[5] In Bayazid I's days King Sigismund of Hungary caused trouble by exerting influence upon several Balkan states. His

---

[3] Dennis (1967), p. 82.   [4] Symeon, *Politico-historical works*, p. 44.   [5] Stromer (1981), pp. 13–26.

purpose was to expand his realm from the Black Sea to the Adriatic coast. Nevertheless, his projects regarding the Dalmatian ports caused anxiety to Venice, which avoided an alliance with him against the Turks. Furthermore, during the years following the battle of Ankara, Sigismund was entangled in dynastic strife against his rival, Ladislas of Naples. On the other hand, Ottoman relations with the Venetians, who had occupied some ports in Albania and in Greece, provoked limited military action, the Turks retaliating by harassing Venetian territories and inflicting damage upon Venetian merchants. A new treaty negotiated by Süleyman ended the dispute, the Venetians agreeing to pay annual tribute to him for their new possessions.[6]

In Anatolia Süleyman was first able to eliminate his brother Isa. Early in 1404 he occupied the old capital, Bursa, and the important town of Ankara. He then annexed the Black Sea coast between Herakleia and Samsun, as well as the region of Smyrna, where he obliged Djüneyd to recognise his overlordship. After Timur's death (1405) the Mongol grasp over Anatolia weakened, and Süleyman was free to turn against his other brother, Mehemmed. The latter, established in a predominantly Turkish milieu, extended his rule from Amasya up to Sivas and consolidated his position by maintaining good relations with the Karamanoglu and with the neighbouring nomadic populations. By marrying the daughter of Dhulkadir, the emir of Elbistan, he obtained access to important military manpower deriving from the tribes of that region. He alone proceeded to assume the title of sultan.[7] A few clashes between the two Ottoman princes came to nothing, and Mehemmed decided to transfer operations to Rumelia.

The instrument of his plans was a fourth brother, Musa, whom he despatched to Rumelia in 1409 with the help of the Isfendiyaroglu. The Byzantine emperor, the Venetians, the Serb ruler and, above all, the Wallachian voivode, Mircea, watching Süleyman's strong position with anxiety, were ready to support Musa.[8] Mircea received him in his territories and helped him to make preparations against Süleyman. When the latter was obliged to return to Rumelia in 1410, Mehemmed easily became the lord of the whole of Ottoman Anatolia. After a series of military operations, Musa emerged victorious, while Süleyman lost his life in February 1411.

At the beginning Musa, established in Edirne, governed the European provinces as a vassal of his brother, Mehemmed, who had moved to Bursa. When still fighting against Süleyman, Musa repudiated promises made to the Christian lords who had supported him, and revived the spirit of the holy war. Thus he won the support of the military who had long refrained from raiding

---

[6] Zachariadou (1983b), pp. 292–5.   [7] Wittek (1938a), pp. 25–8.
[8] Symeon, *Politico-historical works*, p. 48; *Byzantinischen Kleinchroniken*, I, p. 97.

Christian territories. He soon launched attacks on all directions and besieged Thessalonica and Constantinople.

Alarmed, the Christian lords turned to Mehemmed. Several high Ottoman officials, who had been connected with Süleyman's administration and, for this reason, had been persecuted by Musa, also joined Mehemmed, and a new struggle for sole supremacy over the Ottoman state began in 1412. For a while, Musa's position appeared strong, but defections to Mehemmed's side increased while the Byzantine emperor also offered him his help. Musa was finally defeated near Sofia and killed in 1413. The period of the interregnum was now ended, Mehemmed becoming the sultan of a reunited state and being generally recognised as his father's legitimate successor. Official Ottoman tradition would never consider Süleyman and Musa as real sultans.

Mehemmed, well aware that his territories had been devastated by the civil wars and that the unity of his state was only fragile, adopted a policy of peace towards the Christians. His intention was facilitated by the hostility prevailing among his main enemies, Venice and Hungary. Having insured peace in Rumelia, the sultan consolidated his position in Anatolia by defeating the Karamanoglu, who, profiting from the civil war, had besieged Bursa. He also put a temporary end to the separatist movement of Djüneyd in Smyrna, whom he sent to Nicopolis as an *udj bey* of the Danube frontier.

The Christian enemies of the Ottoman state tried to divide it once again, and a new pretender to the Ottoman throne appeared on the scene with the help of the Byzantines, the Wallachians and the Venetians, who now had established contacts with the emir of Karaman. He was Mustafa, who passed into history as the 'false' one (*düzme*) because Mehemmed's milieu claimed that he was not Bayazid I's son at all, but simply an impostor. Like Musa, Mustafa, with the help of the voivode Mircea, set off from Wallachia. Djüneyd joined him, abandoning his post at Nikopolis. Soon both were defeated by Mehemmed's troops near Thessalonica and compelled to take refuge with the Byzantines (1416).

It was now becoming apparent that the internal strife which had shaken the Ottoman state for more than a decade was not only a dynastic strife but was also connected with deep social problems. A revolution broke out under the spiritual leadership of the theologian and mystic, Sheyh Bedr ed-din, who had been Musa's judge of the army (*kaziasker*).[9] The popular masses, especially in the region of Aydin, participated wholeheartedly in the movement which was also supported by some Greek Orthodox monks. The rebels preached common ownership of fields and cattle, farm implements, food and clothing; also fraternisation with the Christians because, according to them, communion

[9] Werner (1985), pp. 217–33.

with the Christian faith was the only way to ensure the salvation of the soul. This last point suggests that the aim of the revolt was possibly a state based on a new religion deriving from both Islam and Christianity.

These doctrines certainly originated from the continuous political change and the religious confusion which went on for a long period in the Turkish territories. The political change, at first due to the existence of several Turkish states and the resulting strife among them, was exacerbated by Timur's occupation of Anatolia, while the disruptive civil wars made the lower classes poorer and therefore more ready to demand social change. The problem of the religious confusion was more complicated. Islam was certainly the religion of the conquerors, and the ruling group preached the principle of holy war, on which expansion was based. Nevertheless, this religion remained unorthodox in Anatolia. Beside the administrative authorities who were usually traditional Muslims and often theologians (*ulema*), there existed the nomads who had been recently and superficially Islamised so that they preserved their pagan or shamanistic beliefs. A few of the nomadic tribes were Christian causing additional confusion.[10] Dervishes often visited the newly conquered territories to preach Islam, but they largely belonged to sectarian and mystical circles, preferring to move away from central Islamic lands in order to diffuse their kind of faith with greater freedom. On the other hand, the subjugated Christian population of Anatolia had a long religious and cultural tradition, and for this reason was able to exercise considerable and varied influence upon the new masters. In the newly conquered Balkans, the Turks were in the minority. Mixed marriages were usual as large numbers of warriors from all over the Islamic world were attracted to the Turkish territories, situated between the Christian and the Muslim lands, to carry out holy war. These warriors had to find their women among their enemies, often among the prisoners. Sheyh Bedr ed-din himself was the son of a Muslim judge, established in Rumelia since the very early years of the conquest, and of the daughter of the Byzantine governor of a provincial town, who had been taken prisoner. Mixed marriages certainly meant a certain religious confusion among families which was to affect the whole of society. The situation was underlined at the end of the fourteenth century by a Muslim preacher in Bursa who said that Jesus was not inferior to the prophet Muhammad; also by the great mystical poet, Yunus Emre, who wrote that his soul at one moment prayed in a mosque and at another moment read the gospel in a church.[11]

Bedr ed-din's movement shook the foundations of the Ottoman state as it propagated fraternisation with the Christians, an ideal quite contrary to that of

[10] Beldiceanu-Steinherr (1991), pp. 21–73.
[11] Wittek (1938a), p. 31; Gölpinarlı (1965), p. 156; Mélikoff (1993), pp. 135–44.

the holy war. It also threatened the Greek Orthodox Church which, enjoying the protection of the sultans, had its place insured under Ottoman domination.[12] The revolution was therefore suppressed through military operations followed by a bloody massacre of men, women and children organised by Mehemmed I. Bedr ed-din himself was hanged in Serres. Nevertheless, an order of dervishes, the Torlak, professing that Jesus was God, survived.[13]

Mehemmed I had overcome the deep crisis, but his position became even weaker as the Venetians profited from the situation by destroying the Ottoman fleet at Kallipolis (May 1416). The sultan now revised his former policy of peace towards the Christians. In 1417 he launched a large-scale punitive campaign against Wallachian territories and reduced the voivode, Mircea, to the status of a tribute-paying vassal. Another Ottoman army marched to Albania and conquered the strategically important port of Avlona at the entrance to the Adriatic, and, in the following year, the strong fortress of Argyrokastron. Mehemmed then undertook a new expedition against the Danubian territories which was also crowned by diplomatic success when he managed to isolate King Sigismund of Hungary from two of his allies, Władysław of Poland and Vytautas (Vitold), the grand duke of Lithuania (1420).[14]

Mehemmed I died in May 1421 and he was succeeded by his son, Murad II. Dynastic strife, however, resumed. The Byzantines, aiming once again at the division of the Ottomans, set against Murad the pretender *Düzme* Mustafa and Djüneyd, both of whom had been in their hands since 1416. Their effort failed as Adorno, the Genoese *podestà* of Phocaea, put his fleet at the disposal of Murad II, who crossed to Thrace and eliminated Mustafa. The sultan also retaliated against the Byzantines by attacking their territories and especially by besieging Constantinople in the summer of 1422. The Byzantines then attempted to compel him to abandon the siege by supporting another pretender, his young brother, Mustafa, acclaimed sultan in Nicaea. However, Murad defeated him and put him to death.

The civil wars gave the opportunity to the Turkish emirs to move against the Ottomans. The Isfendiyaroglu invaded the territories of Sangarios, while the Karamanoglu tried to seize the important harbour of Antalya. The sultan was able to overcome these troubles, too. Djüneyd once again strove to establish his own state in Smyrna in collaboration with a new pretender, *Düzme* Mustafa's young son. In 1424 the sultan concluded a treaty with the Byzantines and another one with the Hungarians. Peace in the Balkans enabled him to overcome this pretender, too, and he despatched troops to Aydin who exterminated Djüneyd and his whole family. The region of Aydin, as well as the

---

[12] Zachariadou (1990–1).   [13] Spandugnino, *Dela origine deli Imperatori Ottomani*, pp. 247–8.
[14] Manfroni (1902); Papacostea (1976); Zachariadou (1983a).

neighbouring emirate of Menteshe, was then annexed to the Ottoman lands. About that time the region of Samsun, on the Black Sea, was also annexed. Murad II, having emerged victorious from these dynastic wars, probably wanted to have the restoration of his rule over Asia Minor publicly recognised, and he invited representatives of the Byzantine emperor, the Wallachian voivode, the Serb ruler and other Christian lords to Ephesus that year (1425).[15]

THE ORGANISATION OF THE STATE

A Muslim ruler's subjects were distinguished between the faithful and the unbelievers. The latter, in Ottoman territories, were the Christians and the Jews, who were allowed to live under the protection of the sultan as *dhimmi*s, having the obligation to pay two special taxes, namely the poll tax (*djizye*) and a land tax (*kharadj*).

About 1430, the Ottoman state had sixteen provinces (*sandjak*s) in Anatolia and twelve in Rumelia.[16] Most of the territories were distributed as *timars* to cavalrymen (*sipahi*). A *timar* was a parcel of land, with its cultivators, granted by the state to provide a livelihood to its holder, who had to appear whenever summoned by the sultan for a campaign. There were *timars* of higher and of lower revenue demanding greater or smaller obligations from their holders. The cadastre (*defter*) of a land census (*tahrir*), made in Albania in the year 1432, has been preserved, and gives a fairly clear picture of the *timar* system. The smaller *sandjak*s offered up to 1,000 horsemen, while the larger ones provided up to 6,000. In addition to the regular cavalry deriving from the provinces, there was the light cavalry of the raiders (*akindji*) in the service of the *udj-bey*s, which comprised nomads (*yürük*) as well as Christians (*martolos* and *voynuk*).[17]

The sultan also had his personal army, the janissaries (*yeniçeri*). In this matter the Ottomans followed an old Oriental custom going back to the Abbassid Khalifs, whereby the ruler's army was composed of soldiers who, being slaves, were his personal property (*kapu kulu*). In Murad's court there resided a body of 3,000 janissaries, mainly Albanians, Greeks, Bulgarians, Serbs, Bosnians and others.[18] In the early years of the Ottoman state these men were taken from the young prisoners captured in raids or in war, as the Islamic sacred law allotted one fifth (*pendjik*) of the booty, including captives, to the ruler. Later, perhaps in Murad II's years, periodical levies (*devshirme*) of the sons of the *dhimmi*s were made. This institution, reducing the *dhimmi*s to the status of slaves, was con-

---

[15] Ducas, *Historia Byzantina*, p. 196; Basso (1994), pp. 63–79, 285–9.
[16] Zachariadou (1987).   [17] *Hicrî 835 Sûret-i Defter-i Sancak-i Arvanid*; Beldiceanu (1980).
[18] *Ordo portae*, p. 6.

trary to the sacred law, but it was a source of special power for the sultan, as the youths, uprooted from their natural milieu, were wholly dependent on his person, considering him as their own father. The boys, once recruited, were given a training aimed at their Islamisation and Turkification. The most promising were taken into the palace as pages, others into the sultan's body-guard, others, still, into the army. The highest posts of the Empire became open to them with increasing frequency. The *udj-bey*s of Rumelia, such as Evrenos and Turakhan, the son of Pasha-Yigit, also had their own private armies of slaves within their domains.

Christian authors commented ironically on the sultans who used to frater-nise with individuals of very low origin, sons of shepherds and farmers. On the other hand, high Ottoman dignitaries were proud of their humble origins and praised the sultans who wisely recruited both officials and leaders and those who would act as exemplars of Islam from among the lowest levels of peasant society.[19]

In Anatolia, the sultan received military aid from his four Turkish vassals, the Karamanoglu, the Isfendiyaroglu, the Dhulkadiroglu and the lord of Alanya. In Rumelia there were also the sultan's Christian vassals who governed their territories under the obligation of paying an annual tribute to him, and of offering military aid or some other kind of service. Under this conventional rule Serbia, the Morea, the island of Lesbos, Ainos, Phocaea and several other territories were administered by their Christian lords. According to an old Oriental custom, adopted early by the Ottomans, they were obliged to appear in front of the sultan at fixed intervals to bring their tribute and presents. The sultan responded by offering a robe of honour (*khilat*). Several vassals, espe-cially from Albania and Epirus, had sons who stayed in the palace as hostages, having the opportunity of an apprenticeship with the Ottoman way of life, so that some of them embraced Islam. Such was the case of George, the son of the Albanian lord, Kastriotes, who became better known by his Muslim name, Iskender (Skender bey), given to him at the Ottoman court: later, he would become famous for his resistance to the Turks in his own country. Daughters of vassals were also kept in the Harem, as wives of the sultan. Murad II's Harem included the daughter of his Turkish vassal, Isfendiyaroglu, and the famous Mara, daughter of the Serb lord, Branković. These ladies were also part of the ruling system as they played the role of intermediaries between the sultan and their fathers' courts.

The sultanic family was the only one in Ottoman society for which descent by blood, and even then only on the male side, counted. From the fifteenth

[19] Ducas, *Historia Byzantina*, pp. 130, 137–8; Ménage (1966); Beldiceanu-Steinherr (1969); Demetriades (1993).

century, in particular, most sultans were born of slave, non-Turkish mothers. The imperial household, which constituted the summit of Ottoman society, thus comprised two sections: the sultan's personal servants and bodyguards, and the sultan's Harem, in both of which individuals of non-Turkish origin were to be found.

Agriculture, constituting the basis of the Ottoman economy and the financial support of the army, was closely connected to the *timar* system. In theory, the land belonged to the state which exercised strong control over the peasants (*reaya*). Most of them lived in lands granted as *timars* by the sultan and were obliged to pay the tithe (*ashr*) and other taxes to the *timar*-holder. The peasant possessed only the right of usufruct, which was inherited by his sons. There were also lands which belonged to individuals in full property (*mülk*), and also extensive lands dedicated to charitable institutions (*vakf*).[20]

WAR-MONGERS VERSUS MODERATES

Murad II was generally described as a ruler who preferred peace to war. Commenting on him, the Byzantine historian, Ducas, remarked that he cared for the benefit of the common people and had sympathy for his poor subjects, whether Muslims or *dhimmi*s. Not seeking the complete destruction of a defeated nation, Murad used to negotiate a treaty with the enemy, as soon as the latter sought peace.[21] The terms were usually to accept the enemy as a vassal who continued to rule over his own territory. In following this policy, Murad enjoyed the support of a group of high officials who wanted a state modelled according to Islamic tradition, such as Egypt or Persia, and having an economy based on trade, crafts and agriculture. The leader of this group was the vizier, Halil Djandarlı, also known by the nickname 'companion of the infidel' (*giaur ortaği*),[22] a name clearly invented by his belligerent opponents. On the other hand, Murad's milieu included persons strongly in favour of the ideal of holy war or the policy of conquest. Another of his viziers, Fazlullah, was a notorious war-monger, criticising the sultan for showing benevolent tolerance towards the infidel instead of treating them according to God's will by using his sword.[23]

The moderate party was encouraged by important economic development achieved during the years of relative peace preceding and following Murad II's accession. Trade began to thrive and several Ottoman cities, such as Bursa, with its important silk market,[24] expanded considerably. Venetian, Genoese and Ragusan merchants frequented Ottoman territories, while relations estab-

---

[20] Inalcik (1993).   [21] Ducas, *Historia Byzantina*, p. 228.
[22] Ducas, *Historia Byzantina*, p. 251.   [23] Ducas, *Historia Byzantina*, p. 208.
[24] Inalcik (1960) and (1970b), p. 211.

lished between the sultan and the duke of Milan opened new trade outlets to Italy. The townspeople prospered. When Ottoman troops besieged Constantinople, they were accompanied by numerous merchants, including money changers and perfume and shoe sellers, who had come from Turkish towns to buy items which would be pillaged by the soldiers.[25]

In 1427 an old-time vassal, the *knez* of Serbia, Stephan Lazarević, died. Both Ottomans and Hungarians intervened in Serbia, and a long period of war between the two states began. King Sigismund of Hungary, determined to fight the Turk, was encouraged by the Venetians. The latter occupied Thessalonica in 1423 but, unable to defend it against frequent Turkish raids, they therefore proposed joint action to the king. Together they sought allies in the east by making contacts with the lord of Mesopotamia, Osman Karayülük, and the emir of Karaman, both of whom enjoyed the support of Timur's successor, Shahrukh, established in Herat. In spite of this the Ottomans were to expel the Venetians from Thessalonica in 1430. In the same year they peacefully annexed the important cities of Yanina and Arta, possessions of the short-lived petty dynasty of the Tocco. The conflict with the Karamanoglu and Karayülük was more serious as their patron, Shahrukh, exercised pressure upon the sultan by demanding the yearly tribute imposed by Timur after the battle of Ankara. Murad convinced him that he should be exempted because he carried out holy war. Once, when ambassadors of Shahrukh visited Edirne, they were shown Hungarian prisoners and were offered 300 of them as a gift to their lord.[26]

In 1437 the Ottomans again took the offensive in the Balkans: Sigismund of Hungary died, while Fazlullah took over the office of vizier[27] and the war party strengthened its position. The Byzantine emperor, in an effort to save his crumbling state, decided to participate in the Council of Ferrara aimed at the union of the Greek Orthodox with the Roman Church. He met with the strong disapproval of the sultan who was afraid of the possibility of a crusade. When the Byzantine emperor finally sailed to Italy, Murad was incited by his high officials to proceed to an attack against Constantinople, but he was dissuaded by Halil Djandarlı.[28]

Unable to expel the Hungarians from Belgrade, the Ottomans were compensated by the conquest of the important silver mines of Novobrdo in 1439, and two years later they captured the town as well. The war continued, their opponents being led by a promising military commander, János Hunyadi, voivode of Transylvania. Pope Eugenius IV began to preach the crusade

[25] Cananus, *Narratio*, p. 464.
[26] Tardy (1978), pp. 12–36; Konstantin Mihailović, *Memoirs of a janissary*, p. 59; Jorga, *Notes et extraits*, pp. 25–30. [27] Ménage (1976), pp. 576–7.
[28] Sylvestre Syropoulos, *Les 'memoires' du grand ecclésiarque*, p. 182; Sphrantzes Georgios, *Memorii*, p. 60.

shortly after the signing of the Union of the Churches (1439), in spite of its outright rejection by the Byzantine people. The crusaders marched under the orders of Hunyadi and of the young king of Poland and Hungary, while the Karamanoglu raided the Ottoman territories in Anatolia. The sultan confronted the Christian army between Niš and Sofia in full winter. He was defeated and obliged to conclude a ten-year peace with the Christians (Treaty of Edirne–Szegedin 1444).

According to Islamic judicial principles, a truce with the infidel should not last for more than four months or, at the most, one year. Only if the Muslim party really needed to recover might a truce be made for ten years. It may be assumed that the sultan was in a difficult position, and the war party in his court highly critical. On the other hand, the sultan's vassals began to revolt, especially in Albania, the Morea and the territories of Karaman. Murad imposed order but, immediately afterwards, he announced his abdication in favour of his son, Mehemmed, then a youth twelve years old. Murad probably took this decision because he had failed in the war and lacked the support of all his high military officials. Signs of social unrest were also visible: in Edirne, a Muslim holy man, preaching heretical views, was sentenced to death, together with his followers.

On the other hand, the Christians overestimated the victories over the Turks, and a few weeks after the treaty they launched a new crusade. Murad took the lead of the army and crushed the Christians at the battle of Varna in which the young king, Władysław, was killed (10 November 1444). A couple of years later Murad II was brought back to the throne after a *coup d'état* organised by Halıl Djandarlı. He continued the struggle against Hunyadi, whom he defeated once again at Kosovo (1448), while his fleet threatened Constantinople and unsuccessfully attacked Kelli, at the mouth of the Danube.[29] He finally died in 1451.

THE FALL OF CONSTANTINOPLE AND THE AGE OF EXPANSION

When in February 1451 Mehemmed II ascended the throne for the second time, the situation was ripe for the final collapse of the Byzantine state. Constantinople being his prime target, the young sultan carefully avoided any clash with the Christian world. A huge Ottoman army surrounded the underpopulated Byzantine capital in the first days of April 1453, and Mehemmed himself, with his janissaries, encamped not far from the city walls. Heavy bombardment was carried out day and night by technically advanced cannons. Even more advanced engineering techniques were used to drag seventy-two boats over land from the Bosporus to the Golden Horn. On 29 May

---

[29] *Byzantinischen Kleinchroniken,* I, p. 99; Cazacu and Nasturel (1978).

Constantinople fell. An old dream of the Muslim world thus became a reality, and the church of St Sophia was converted into a mosque. The Ottoman Empire became the successor of the Byzantine.

An agreement on oath between the sultan and his army had preceded the final assault: the city was to be given over to sack by the soldiers. This meant that moveable property, including human beings, would belong to the soldiers, buildings and land to the sultan. Accordingly, the soldiers pillaged everything in the city and took all the inhabitants prisoners to sell them as slaves or to claim ransoms. Within the city neither man, nor animal, nor bird was heard to cry out or utter a voice the day after its fall.[30]

The sultan immediately took care of the repopulation and reorganisation of the city by inviting his dignitaries to settle, by liberating prisoners and establishing them in it, by calling back old Constantinopolitans who had moved to other places before the final siege and, mainly, by largely applying the Ottoman method of compulsory deportation: groups of inhabitants from other towns (*sürgün*) were obliged to settle in Constantinople. These were chosen from among merchants and craftsmen living in urban centres; most of them were *dhimmi*s. The sultan encouraged the new inhabitants by offering them houses and exemption from taxes. Another important measure for the repopulation of the city was the re-establishment of religious authorities. According to old Islamic principles, the sultan first named a patriarch of the Greek Orthodox community: he chose the openly anti-papal Gennadios Scholarios for this post. There followed the nomination of the learned Moshe Kapsali as rabbi, and finally that of Joachim as patriarch of the Armenians.[31]

Shortly after the conquest of Constantinople, Mehemmed ordered the execution of Halıl Djandarlı: the war party, with the sultan at its head, assumed all power, while the moderate one seemed to have disappeared. A long period of war began with the Ottoman state governed by those devoted to the idea of territorial expansion, of military glory or simply booty. Mehemmed was continuously on campaign or, as his biographer, Tursun Beg, put it: 'it was one of the Sultan's happy customs that if he achieved an easy conquest in one year, he would strive, if sufficient time remained, to add yet another victory to it'. The warlike spirit of the sultan's milieu is described by a Slav soldier resident for several years in his court, presumably as a janissary. On one occasion, Mehemmed, having heard that the pope's troops were marching against his territories, summoned his high officials to inform them about the danger and take counsel with them. They told him: 'Fortunate lord, march upon them in their lands; it is better than if you waited for them at home.'[32]

---

[30] Ducas, *Historia Byzantina*, p. 302.   [31] Inalcik (1969–70); Braude (1982).
[32] Imber (1990), p. 181; Konstantin Mihailović, *Memoirs of a janissary*, p. 145.

Mehemmed II judged that the existence of vassals was no longer useful and he transformed their domains into Ottoman provinces. The Gattilusi were expelled from Ainos and Lesbos (1454–62); the Branković family lost Serbia (1459); the Palaiologoi were removed from the Morea (1460); the Grand Komnenoi were compelled to surrender Trebizond (1461). Some among his ex-vassals, for instance the Grand Komnenoi and descendants of the Branković and of the Palaiologoi, were granted revenues from land by the sultan, usually in the Strymon region. Members of the old Christian aristocratic families living in the former vassal territories were often allowed to stay, some of them as *timar*-holders.

The Hungarians remained the most serious enemy of the Ottomans in Europe, as they continued to exercise influence upon the lesser Balkan states. Mehemmed II was unable to expel them from Belgrade, but he subjugated Bosnia (1463) and Herzegovina (1466), and carried out devastating campaigns against Wallachia (1462) and Moldavia (1476). Skender bey resisted for some years in Albania, but, after repeated military operations and his death (1468), this country also became Ottoman territory. Between 1463 and 1479 Mehemmed II fought against the Venetians, who fiercely defended their possessions in the Morea and in Albania, but lost the island of Euboia (Negroponte). He also fought against the Genoese, and expelled them from their possessions in the Crimea (1475). Finally, in 1480, he despatched an army which landed in southern Italy and occupied Otranto. On the other side, in Anatolia, he put an end to the emirate of Karaman (1475). His great foe in the east was Uzun-Hasan, the lord of the Akkoyunlu, who ruled over Persia, Mesopotamia and Armenia. Uzun-Hasan controlled important parts of the caravan routes connecting central Asia with Anatolia and possessed focal points of trade, such as the town of Erzindjan. Therefore, serious conflict of interests existed between him and the Ottoman sultan. Furthermore, the Akkoyunlu lord became more dangerous by establishing good relations with the pope and the Venetians. He was finally badly defeated by the Ottomans at Otluk Beli in 1473.

The historian Tursun bey never hid the fact that Ottoman troops were sometimes displeased by the arduous annual campaigns which they had to undertake. When, in full winter, Mehemmed began preparations for the campaign against Ainos, the janissaries resented the orders. When, in 1458, he ordered a campaign against the Morea, officers and soldiers showed signs of discontent at the excessively intense military activity. His vizier was obliged to remind them that the sultan had been chosen ruler by God in order to carry out holy war, and that world conquest could not be accomplished without sacrifice.[33]

---

[33] Inalcik and Murphey (1978), pp. 37, 43.

Despite devotion to war and its resulting preoccupations, Mehemmed and his milieu did not remain indifferent to the currents of the Renaissance flourishing among his enemies. Several humanists and artists visited the sultan's court, Gentile Bellini, who painted his portrait (see plate 24), being the most famous. The taste for Renaissance art was also developed among the sultan's subjects, as is attested by a few surviving monuments of the time.[34]

The excessively warlike policy of the sultan exhausted the economy of his lands. To finance his military operations he was obliged to increase customs fees and some of the taxes paid by the peasants, and to impose new taxes upon the inhabitants of Istanbul. He repeatedly debased the silver coinage: the silver coin (*akçe*) was devalued by approximately 30 per cent during his reign. In order to increase and reward his cavalry troops properly, he confiscated land properties belonging to charitable institutions (*vakf*) or to individuals (*mülk*), and distributed them as *timars*. This measure provoked the enmity of some influential families of landowners and especially that of the people of religion (*ehl-i din*), that is, the *ulema*, the *sheyh*s and dervishes, who controlled the *vakf*. The latter were already displeased because the sultan, in an effort to curtail non-military expenses, had abolished the gifts customarily distributed to them.[35]

AN EFFORT TOWARDS MERCANTILISM

Mehemmed II, faithful to his warlike ideas, finally died in 1481 on his way to a campaign directed against unidentified enemies who could have been the Mamluks. His death was followed by a civil war between his sons, Bayazid and Djem. The former emerged victorious and Djem took refuge with the Knights Hospitallers at Rhodes. Later, he was taken to western Europe, where several Christian powers were eager to use him as an instrument in their last effort to divide the Ottoman state. He died in Naples in February 1495.[36] Up to that date the duty of holy war was neglected, because Bayazid II did not take the risk of launching military operations which could involve Christian states.[37] In 1481 Otranto was abandoned.

New ideals now replaced the ideal of the holy war. Bayazid was described by contemporary authors as being different from his father, that is, as a pious monarch loving justice and respecting the holy law (*sharia*), while his father had largely made use of secular or customary law (*örf*). Bayazid was considered as being sent by God to consolidate Ottoman rule in the large territories conquered by his ancestors, and to organise them according to Islamic tradition. For these qualities, Bayazid was given the surname *veli* (saint) by the dervishes

---

[34] Mpouras (1973). See plate 24.   [35] Inalcik (1973), p. 35; cf. Beldiceanu (1965).
[36] Lefort (1981), pp. 5–13; Shai Har-El (1995), pp. 105–12, 115–16.
[37] See, however, Shai Har-El (1995).

who supported him in his struggle against Djem, and who were later rewarded with the restoration of their *vakfs*. Together with the tendency towards the consolidation and organisation of the Ottoman territories, there appeared another, a desire for knowledge of the Ottoman past, or, in modern terminology, a quest for an Ottoman identity. The sultan invited authors to write the history of the Ottoman dynasty and many of them responded so that several histories of the Ottomans were composed at that time.[38]

However, war could not be fully avoided. In 1484, the sultan took the field in a region where his grandfather and his ever-victorious father had previously failed. He conquered Kelli and Akkerman, two very important harbour cities on the Black Sea, frequented by European merchants, especially Genoese. The sultan himself was fully aware of the economic and strategic importance of his conquests, as appears from a letter addressed to the Ragusans in which he described Kelli as the key and the gate to Moldavia, Hungary and the Danubian regions, and Akkerman as the key and the gate to Poland, Russia and the land of the Tatars.[39]

After Djem's death, riots among the janissaries in Istanbul indicated that the army needed action. Yet, because the Turkish navy had long been inferior to that of many Christian states, Bayazid gave priority to the construction of a fleet. Venetian reports, composed with anxiety, give important information about shipbuilding as well as about the activities of Turkish corsairs in the Aegean Sea and beyond it.[40] In 1499, a war against Venice broke out and the Ottoman navy, which included several hundred galleys, defeated its enemy on several occasions. In the first year of the war, Bayazid conquered Lepanto, situated in the Gulf of Corinth, and he immediately ordered the construction of two castles in the vicinity, Rio and Antirio, to control the entrance to the inner part of the Gulf. In the following year, he deprived the Venetians of Modon and Koron, 'the two eyes' of the Signoria, and in the following one the Ottomans conquered Durazzo, a port constituting the primary point of departure for travellers and caravans moving inland, along the ancient Via Egnatia, to Adrianople and Constantinople.

Bayazid's conquests, although territorially limited, were highly important. The conquest of Kelli and Akkerman meant the last phase in the effort to close the Black Sea to westerners, while the conquest of the Venetian ports, on the outskirts of the Ottoman lands, established an economic unity and removed enemy outposts. Furthermore, the revenue of the state was increased considerably through the collection of the important customs fees paid in all these ports. It is obvious that Bayazid's targets were exclusively ports and not the

[38] Inalcik (1962), pp. 164–5.

[39] *Acta et diplomata Ragusina*, I, pt 2, pp. 757–8; Papacostea (1978), pp. 234–41.

[40] Kissling (1988), pp. 207–15; Fisher (1948), pp. 42–4, 52–5, 78–9.

conquest of land to be distributed as *timar*s to his soldiers. He did not try to take advantage of the serious rivalries then dividing his traditional enemies, such as Hungary, Poland or Moldavia; rather he chose to fight Venice.

The acquisition of ports certainly pleased the merchant class. During the long period of peace, from 1481 to 1495, merchants, Muslims or *dhimmi*s, were able to do good business and, consequently, to acquire power as a class. New perspectives were opened as the Black Sea became almost an Ottoman preserve. Foreigners in general were discouraged from sailing beyond the Bosphorus, and only merchants from central Europe, visiting the Ottoman Empire, sometimes came upon the Black Sea regions in the course of their travels. The highly lucrative Black Sea trade thus passed mainly into the hands of the sultan's subjects.[41] The merchant class was also strengthened by the arrival of large numbers of European Jews during the second half of the fifteenth century, especially after their expulsion from Spain in 1492.[42] The Ottoman administration, knowing that the newcomers were experienced in trade and banking, with connections in Europe and north Africa, favoured their establishment, so that many Jewish communities emerged in the principal ports of the Empire. One may therefore wonder whether Bayazid's policies were planned specifically to please the merchant class, or were even carried out under pressure of that class. An anonymous Greek author of the early sixteenth century remarked that in Bayazid's time everybody made money and spent it. As the author was a *dhimmi*, we are permitted to assume that he had businessmen in mind.[43]

Shortly after 1500 social strife began in Anatolia with the strong participation of the nomads, who revolted under a religious cover, the *kızılbaş* movement.[44] That revolt has been understood as a reaction to the centralising tendency of Bayazid's administration. However, it could also be connected with the rise of the merchant class. The nomads, when moving from one place to another, often disturbed the Anatolian land routes and sometimes controlled parts of them. They collected tolls from travellers and caravans. These activities inevitably brought them into confrontation with the merchants, who wished for a greater measure of law and order.

The new tendency emerging during Bayazid days was to be crystallised in the days of Selim I, if we judge from the words of a high dignitary and scholar, Kemal pashazade: 'My Sultan, you dwell in a city whose benefactor is the sea. If the sea is not safe, no ships will come, and if no ship comes, Istanbul perishes.'[45] They are in strong contrast with the words of Murad II's vizier, Fazlullah, or Mehemmed II's high officials who recommended the complete

---

[41] Kellenbenz (1967); Inalcik (1979).   [42] Inalcik (1969).   [43] *Ecthesis Chronica*, p. 55.
[44] Mélikoff (1975); Roemer (1990).   [45] Lewis (1961), p. 25 n. 7.

destruction of the infidel. The sultan was not incited to march against enemies abroad but to protect commercial vessels, belonging to both Ottomans and infidels, coming from over the sea. The inspiration clearly came from a mercantilist and not from an imperialist milieu. Nevertheless, while Ottoman policy was orientated towards trade and navigation, the world was changing rapidly. The Portuguese, having discovered new sea routes, appeared in the Red Sea, and the first signs of the decline of the Levantine trade soon became visible.[46] The Ottomans were then to revert once more to a policy of war and conquest.

[46] Özbaran (1994), pp. 89–97, 119–21.

CHAPTER 33

CONCLUSION

Christopher Allmand

'EUROPE is only as wide as a short summer night.' Thus Heinrich Böll could describe her breadth, from Russia in the east to the Atlantic seaboard in the west, in terms of a brief period of darkness. In contrast to the whole breadth and depth of the globe, small she might be. But her history was far from uniform. The attentive reader will have remarked that, for all the similarities between the histories of Europe's numerous countries and the generalisations made by contributors to the first parts of this volume, the many differences noted have shown a continent of great variety.

As a major part of its inheritance, fifteenth-century Europe had accepted a considerable diversity of political systems. Furthermore, there had long existed an eagerness, now given greater actuality by the need to resolve the fundamental problem regarding authority created by the Great Schism, to discuss the nature and sources of authority, and how best it should be translated into legitimate and effective power. The system of rule by one, monarchy or principality, dominated much of Europe, particularly in its western parts.[1] Yet other systems existed. One was that by which the Swiss Confederation was ruled, while another controlled the affairs of Venice. In Bohemia, there was a strong movement towards a wider form of popular participation in decision making in matters concerning society, something from which the Church, ruled by the pope (himself a kind of monarch), was not immune. Representation worked in some countries (England) but not in others (France). Some favoured it both out of principle and because it was thought to lead to more effective rule. One who taught this was Sir John Fortescue, whose criticisms of the French king's *dominium regale* was based on the fact that the consent implied in his English counterpart's *dominium politicum et regale* was conducive to a better relationship between ruler and ruled. The historian, it is clear, should not think of representative assemblies as being of only a single kind.

---

[1] On this, see Burns (1992).

Indeed, it is argued, there were three, even four kinds of representative organisations in late medieval Europe, all representing different elements in the social order from which they were historically descended, all aiming to do rather different things. It is from the study of the functions of each form of such organisation that we can best understand its true nature, and thus judge the level of success of its achievement. Those who see assemblies as necessarily created to meet the political needs and demands of princes should think again.[2] Corporate power could be exercised for purposes which were not political, because that had never been the intention in every case.

The diversity of European experience at the end of the Middle Ages could also be seen in the changing role played by nobilities, now increasingly national, in a rapidly altering world. How did this class (or classes) react to developments going on around it? What part, for instance, did nobilities play in the politics of their respective countries, and how far did 'ascendant' monarchies depend upon, and make use of, their support? There was certainly much variety of experience in this matter. How did this group, so varied in composition, background and tradition, react in different regions (even countries) to the changes occurring to its status? As the traditional fighting caste, how did the aristocracy adjust to developments taking place in the organisation and fighting of war?[3] What had become of chivalry by 1500? Was it still something real, or was it mainly a show fit for the entertainment of court or public? And what of those attempting to achieve nobility, the new men who, having made their fortunes or reputations in trade or in the courts of law, sought to achieve social promotion, constituting, in some sense, a challenge to the older, military nobility? What is clear is that neither the problems, nor the solutions developed to resolve them, were uniform, their variety providing a further example of the diversity of experience of one group of people who, in spite of differences of nationality, saw themselves as sharing a common gentility, the vital hallmark of true *noblesse*.[4]

In matters of religion much of the emphasis was on a world in which the lay believer was becoming significantly more important, the institutional Church and its clergy less so. In the long term, such a decline in appreciation of the Church's sacramental life and teaching was likely to have more far-reaching effects than did heresy, whose manifestations were more readily perceived and counteracted. Yet it would be wrong to claim that the religion of the late Middle Ages, with its emphasis on personal devotion and its interest in the teachings of recluses (female as well as male), meant that the institutional Church no longer had the influence once claimed for it. The preaching of acts of piety and charity, the emphasis on penance, self-denial, prayer to the Virgin

---

[2] See above, ch. 2.   [3] See above, ch. 8.   [4] See above, ch. 4.

and to the saints, the growing appreciation by the individual of the Incarnation of God made man in the person of Christ, whose life, passion and death were a fecund source of devotional inspiration for artists and those who patronised them, constituted positive aspects of religious practice and thought in fifteenth-century Europe.[5] The development of the manuscript book – in particular the book of hours – and, by the end of the century, of the printed prayer book met the growing demands of a world becoming more literate and better educated. Not surprisingly, when genuine calls for reform came (as they did), their source was often the laity seeking higher standards of morality and religious practice from all Christians. Likewise, it was a sign of the times that, as members of princely delegations, better educated laymen should have taken some part in the proceedings of the councils of the Church. The movement towards giving the laity a greater role in the Church's affairs began at least a century before the Reformation occurred.

Such developments were encouraged and made possible by two factors. One was the growth of a better educated laity. The increase in the number of educational institutions, schools as well as universities, may be linked to the story of the layman's growing role in society. Urban schools and charitable foundations helped to form the young. Opportunities for the educated to make careers outside the Church were becoming more numerous.[6] It was increasingly the secular world, and its demands, which were to inspire the foundation of numerous new universities (and, at Oxford and Cambridge, a number of new colleges and other foundations) whose general purpose was not only to enhance the honour of God and the defence of the faith (the religious element underlining the foundation of universities, often the inspiration of a bishop, should not be forgotten) but also to help in the advancement of that more elusive ideal, 'le bien et prouffit de la chose publique'.[7] This could be furthered in a number of ways. The creation of an educated class to promote good government was one of them.

Closely linked to education as a means of advancing the layman's position in society was the invention of printing, which appeared in the second half of the century. It is easy to claim that this development, whose practical effect was to be so great, was the most long-lasting single advance made in fifteenth-century Europe.[8] However, it is as well to recall that contemporary opinion was not at one regarding the benefits and advantages of printing. Yet, in spite of such scepticism, it was soon to help in all forms of education, by encouraging learning and giving Europe 'research centres of scholarship',[9] and allowing writers to enter controversy and argue their opinions in forms which could then be

---

[5] See above, ch. 10: Oakley (1979).   [6] See above, ch. 11; Reinhard (1996).

[7] Armstrong (1995), p. 17, referring to the founding of a university at Dole.

[8] See above, ch. 14; Eisenstein (1968).   [9] The phrase is that of Gilmore (1952), p. 264.

circulated. Princely courts soon seized upon the opportunities being offered. The texts of new laws could now be publicised in print. As men had been accustomed in time of war to listen to exhortatory propaganda from the pulpit, so now printing could be turned to educating the people about the issues of their day and increasing their awareness of the world around them. Erasmus was not alone in taking up the chance which the new technology gave him. The debates of the sixteenth century, the very form of the Reformation itself, might have been different without the development of the press.

The economic history of Europe was affected by famine and even more by war, although it is claimed that war did not have as ruinous an effect on international trade as might be expected.[10] The worst sufferers were the vulnerable rural communities which took their time to recover (since recovery involved rebuilding, the reintroduction of marginalised lands into the economy, and investment of scarce financial resources in tools, as well as a determination on the part of populations to recreate their societies), but much was achieved in the years of relative peace of the second half of the century. Historians are broadly agreed that populations began to increase and the sources of wealth were regenerated mainly in the century's third quarter, although the revival was not always general (France and Portugal were among the countries which did see this happen during these years; England, on the other hand, saw little change during that same period).

The decline in population had had less effect on towns which, although in many instances less prosperous than they had been, found their power extended as they came to dominate both their hinterlands and, in the case of important towns, the smaller ones within their economic orbit, a development which obliged such urban communities to take action to protect the activities of their merchants. Ports had a good future before them, in particular if they were involved in northern Europe's trade with the eastern Mediterranean which dealt mainly in luxury goods, for which a strong demand existed in an age which witnessed a rising standard of living.[11]

Towns had social as well as economic roles to play.[12] In many parts of Europe, above all in Italy and the Low Countries, they had a cultural vocation to fulfil. This could take on a number of forms. Many towns saw themselves as the providers of education, chiefly in the form of schools, in some cases of universities as well. The large urban corporations, or guilds, acted as artistic patrons, whose demands attracted artists to work for them or their members. In some parts of Europe, in Germany and, in particular, in Italy, cities encouraged the study of their history as one means of securing political prestige in an increasingly competitive world; the present could be enhanced by men's aware-

---

[10] See above, p. 159. [11] See above, ch. 31. [12] See above, ch. 6.

ness of the past. Likewise, the tradition of providing communal entertainment on feast days (a tradition which some rulers gratefully took up as a means of enhancing their own prestige) led to the writing of plays and the creation of pageants in which both religion and chivalry played a notable part.[13] The early history of printing, too, was often associated with towns. By 1469 Venice had already become the adopted home of the German printer, Johannes de Spira, an early association which was to make Venice, with its wide network of commercial links stretching to all points of the compass, a natural centre for printers to set up their workshops.[14]

Change was having an effect upon the traditional elites. The military nobility, as we have seen, was seeing far-reaching changes pass before it. The public's esteem of the soldier, the artistic evidence would suggest, was at least an ambiguous one.[15] New kinds of elites were appearing. With the development of technology, the technician began to rise in the world to enjoy a good standard of living as well as the favour and patronage of princes. It is clear, too, that a new view of the artist was emerging. This was promoted by the writing of the lives of artists, such as that of Brunelleschi composed by Manetti. It was also furthered by the enhanced role played in the public gaze by artists who competed against one another to secure public commissions. The artists' places of work, their ateliers, also played a part in educating the layman in artistic values and techniques, so that ordinary citizens acquired a better understanding of artists and their work. In this way these drew attention to themselves and to their contribution to society, earning both public praise and criticism in the process.[16]

A major theme, principally of the fourth part in the present *History*, has been the emphasis, however variable, placed upon the development of the state and the growth of government which accompanied it.[17] The rise of the state, which historians of recent years have traced back to the thirteenth century, took on different forms and emerged at different tempi in different parts of Europe. Everywhere it was to involve, in some way or other, a development of central control over a variety of aspects of life: religious, economic, military and cultural. Royal intervention in England against the subversive activities of the Lollard heretics in the century's early years, and the establishment, by royal request in 1478, of the Inquisition in Castile, originally to deal with converted Jews who renounced their Christianity, were both instances of the growth of

---

[13] See, most recently, Clough (1990) and Gunn (1990).   [14] Armstrong (1990), p. 2.
[15] Hale (1990).   [16] See above, ch. 15.
[17] See, for example, Autrand (1986); Bulst and Genet (1988); Coulet and Genet (1990); Genet (1990); Genet and Vincent (1986); Reinhard (1996); Rucquoi (1988); *Culture et idéologie* (1985); *Théologie et droit* (1991).

an important trend, that of the extension of secular authority over matters which, not long before, might have been regarded as the preserve of ecclesiastical authority. In the socio-economic sphere, the significance of the political poem *The Libelle of Englyshe polycye* (*c.* 1436) lay largely in the author's urgings that the government of the day should take action to improve the future of England's commercial and fishing communities which were being harmed by foreigners;[18] while France, in the decades following the ending of the war with England, would witness royal intervention in the movement of populations and in the attempt to create favourable conditions for economic recovery through manufacture and the regulation of trade. The development of taxation, already advanced in many territories by 1400, was now becoming a marked feature of life over the whole of Europe. This was so particularly in those countries involved in long wars requiring the financial support which only the state, which alone had the authority and the means of raising taxes, could provide.[19] What distinguished war in the fifteenth century from, say, war in the thirteenth was not so much the techniques used as the ability of the growing state to sustain the different forms of effort which war now required. Another, albeit very different, form of intervention could be observed in the encouragement given to printers by granting them a 'privilege', or monopoly of the production and sale of a particular book for a specified period of time after publication. Begun in Germany in 1479 as an agreement between a bishop and a printer anxious to secure the monopoly of providing breviaries for the diocesan clergy, the practice was taken up by the duke of Milan to promote a book in praise of the Sforza family, before spreading to other countries in the early sixteenth century. Originally an encouragement to enterprise, in different times the process could become a way of controlling the works which came off the presses.[20]

The appreciation of how an educated class could help further the interests of states encouraged rulers not only to help found schools and universities, but also to influence the appointments of teachers and the creation of syllabuses. Humanism, with the contribution which it might make to the educational, administrative and political requirements of a country (the mastery of the Latin language which a humanist *orator*, or ambassador, might use to express his master's ideas and intentions), was widely appreciated outside Italy.[21] And with education went the importance of the printed word which lay behind the development of a better educated and more widely informed public. The translation into vernacular languages of texts from the ancient world, and the production of a wide variety of handbooks on how (for example) to rule, fight,

---

[18] Holmes (1961).   [19] Genet and Le Mené (1987).   [20] Armstrong (1990), ch. 1.
[21] Queller (1967).

pray, preach or hunt constituted typical products of the late Middle Ages. Every encouragement should be given, through self-education and the acquisition of knowledge, to the fulfilment of that human potential in which the humanists believed so strongly.

The history of state development was not simply the history of institutions. Individual rulers, and therefore the power of the office which they exercised, lay at the centre of that growth. Yet, to place proper emphasis upon the role played by the monarchies of Europe is not to return to an old-fashioned form of history 'about kings and queens'. On the contrary, it is to give the monarchical office the attention which is its due. As one writer has recently put it, European monarchy consolidated its power during this century.[22] In some kingdoms it did so by pursuing a policy founded on the complementary supports of legitimacy and dynasticism.[23] In France (where the royal cause in the conflict against England was the legitimate succession to the throne enhanced by an appeal to a growing sense of dynasticism), in Portugal (where the Avis dynasty brought a sense of continuity and stability to the country)[24] and in England (where there were four challenges to the succession between 1399 and 1485) legitimacy, expressed in the principle of obedience to the 'natural lord', lay at the base of monarchical stability.[25] Not surprisingly, legitimacy embodied in dynasticism was emphasised by political propagandists, who stressed the age of a country's monarchy (the older, the better) and the long centuries of continuous rule which it had given. Dynasticism was also important in another way. The case of the duchy of Burgundy demonstrates how it might cement the formation of a largely artificial state by emphasising loyalty to the (Valois ducal) dynasty as the force uniting a number of diverse territories (some acquired by force of arms) which shared neither the focal point, language, history nor customs which might otherwise have kept them together.[26] Significantly, it became common to present a dynasty in the form of a family tree; the political claim being made was clear enough to all who saw it.

In spite of difficulties and some loss of power (to the nobility in eastern Europe, for example)[27] 'as the fifteenth century proceeded, the momentum of monarchy noticeably increased',[28] no sign of this being more effective than the increasingly frequent use made of the symbolic closed 'imperial' crown to demonstrate and underline the independence of the ruler and his firm control of his people. Thus reassured and, at least in theory, immune from deposition (although Pope Paul II formally deposed King George of Poděbrady for heresy in 1466) rulers could assume increasingly 'absolute' powers, particularly

---

[22] Burns (1992), p. 150.   [23] Burns (1992), ch. 3.   [24] See above, ch. 24(c).
[25] Genet (1995), pp. 103–6. For Burgundy, see Armstrong (1995), pp. 8–9.
[26] Armstrong (1995), pp. 6–9.   [27] See above, ch. 27.
[28] Hay (1957b), p. 6; Burns (1992), p. 148.

in the kingdoms and principalities of western Europe. This was the case under Alfonso in the kingdom of Naples; it was so, too, in France under Louis XI, as it was under in Castile and Aragon under the 'Catholic Kings'. Yet, in some cases, absolutism was softened by a more paternalistic form of rule: the obligations of rulers towards their people were emphasised by the dukes of Burgundy,[29] while both João I of Portugal and Louis XII of France were to be accorded the title of 'father of the people' by their subjects.[30]

Yet even the father must have sufficient power to rule (*regere*) firmly and effectively.[31] The use of the comparative approach can tell us much about how rulers built up these powers. Some governed by personality, by centring power around themselves. In England, the rule of Edward IV is regarded as having been very 'personal'; by contrast, Henry VII, his successor but one, relied more on institutions,[32] perhaps unwittingly helping to usher in the age when, some decades later, a form of 'revolution in government' would be introduced. Portugal witnessed the growth of royal power through the control, exercised in the kings' name, over the institutions of sovereignty, and the claim to sole authority to act for the general good against particular interests. The traditional role of the crown as legislator still won general consent.[33] In France, among the most 'advanced' of the monarchies, royal power was made effective by using the nobility both to exercise royal authority in the regions and to act as 'go-between' between the king and the localities, thus usurping the traditional, but never well-developed, role of the estates.[34] Strong links between kings and those who worked in their service became extremely important. In England, France and Scotland, for instance, bonds – which could take the form of membership of chivalric or princely orders – formed an increasingly important way of achieving clientage or dependence. Princely courts, always important, were to be accorded an increasingly significant role in the exercise of power and, in the case of monarchies and principalities, in the management of the developing state. Already centres of patronage where, in difficult times, men sought the offices which would lead, as in France, to the creation of a new nobility, *de robe*, they became centres of magnificence and of ceremony much of it, both north and south of the Alps, inspired by chivalry. In a world in which not all countries (such as Scotland and Savoy)[35] had well-established and fixed capitals, the courts of itinerant kings and princes acted as both ceremonial and political alternatives, in effect as centres of power where the decisions affecting the state were taken.

[29] Armstrong (1995), pp. 9–11.
[30] 'Pai dos portugueses' (above, p. 629); 'pater patriae' (above, p. 429).
[31] Burns (1992), p. 154.   [32] See above, ch. 21(b).   [33] Burns (1992), p. 155.
[34] Something like this was happening in England, too. See Watts (1996).
[35] For Scotland, see above, ch. 22(b); for Savoy, see Rosie (1989).

Significantly, the political vocabulary of the time was being adapted both to take account of and to encourage the perceived development of the state. By the fifteenth century the term *respublica*, having come to mean first the people working together for a common end and then a synonym for the political community itself, now assumed yet another sense, with the emphasis placed on a particular political society admitting no superior and allowing no corporate rival within its jurisdiction, ruled by an 'emperor' wearing a closed crown. Such a development was likely to lead to the growth of self-awareness among individual states, deliberately cultivated and encouraged by princely and royal courts.[36] This, too, would have the effect of furthering the divisions within society, something which became very clear to Pope Pius II when his failure to present a united response to the Ottoman threat at the Congress of Mantua in 1459 led him to recognise how much authority his office had lost and how far the interests and ambitions of individual states had become more important than the defence of Christendom.[37] With the outbreak of the wars in Italy at the end of the century the process would take another step forward.

Europe was a continent whose constituent parts were now finding their feet, often painfully. Bohemia was divided by both religious belief and practice as well as by racial background and social thought.[38] After the murder of Louis of Orleans in 1407, France, already long at war with England, inflicted upon herself the painful debate concerning tyrannicide,[39] thereby making the century's early years truly 'le temps des divisions'.[40] It was, in some measure, the need to find a response to those divisions which encouraged greater emphasis to be placed upon 'Europe', with its timely appeal to society's sense of a corporate history, in the face of the growing Turkish threat from without and divisions from within. Helped by the humanists, the word 'Christianity' would very slowly be replaced by 'Europe' which, by the fifteenth century, was coming to be used with increasing frequency and marked emotional content. Significantly, it was the humanist, Aeneas Sylvius Piccolomini, the future Pope Pius II, who would introduce the word 'European', meaning Christian, into the Latin language of his day.[41]

Implied in this new word was a sense of unity among Christians. What was lacking, however, was peace. Men and women wrote about what it could do to society;[42] in the early 1450s peace came to both France and Italy; in Castile, Germany, Scandinavia, Italy, above all in the Swiss Confederation, leagues were formed to create and preserve peace and the social order; and in 1464, a peace plan to encompass the whole of Europe was produced in the name of King

---

[36] Mager (1991).   [37] Housley (1992), pp. 105–7.   [38] See above, ch. 18.   [39] Guenée (1992).
[40] Allmand and Armstrong (1982), p. 11 and n. 66.   [41] Hay (1957a), pp. 73, 85–8, 95, 101.
[42] Allmand (1988), p. 154.

George of Poděbrady of Bohemia.[43] In the early years of the new century the cry for peace would be taken up by Erasmus and his fellow humanists.[44] Would their prayers ever be answered? Were the ambitions of the great monarchies, as well as those of smaller princedoms, truly compatible with lasting peace? Was there not something in the latest understanding of the word *respublica* which made it unlikely that the secular authority could live together with an independent Church? Could the peace of the late century be a reality? Or, as seemed more likely, was it simply the lull preceding the return to years of division which would shape the Christian Europe of the future?

[43] *Universal Peace Organization* (1964); Heymann (1965), ch. 13. [44] Adams (1962).

APPENDIX: GENEALOGICAL TABLES

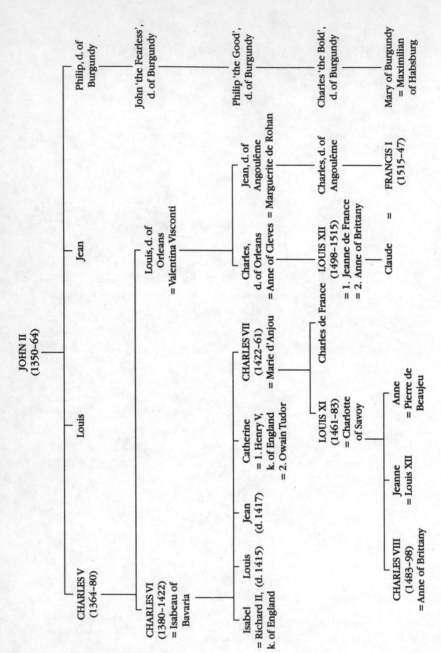

Table 1 The French succession (including the dukes of Burgundy)

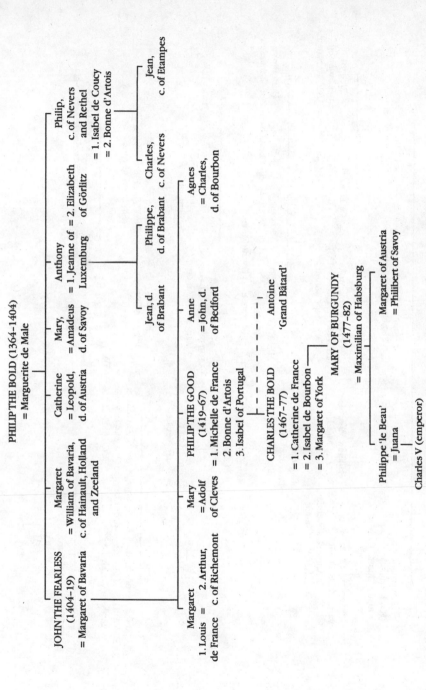

PHILIP THE BOLD (1364–1404)
= Marguerite de Male

JOHN THE FEARLESS
(1404–19)
= Margaret of Bavaria

Margaret
= William of Bavaria,
c. of Hainault, Holland
and Zeeland

Catherine
= Leopold,
d. of Austria

Mary,
= Amadeus
d. of Savoy

Anthony
= 1. Jeanne of = 2. Elizabeth
Luxemburg   of Görlitz

Philip,
c. of Nevers
and Rethel
= 1. Isabel de Coucy
= 2. Bonne d'Artois

Jean,
c. of Etampes

Margaret
1. Louis =   2. Arthur,
de France c. of Richemont

Mary
= Adolf
of Cleves

Jean, d.
of Brabant

Philippe,
d. of Brabant

Charles,
c. of Nevers

Agnes
= Charles,
d. of Bourbon

PHILIP THE GOOD
(1419–67)
= 1. Michelle de France
= 2. Bonne d'Artois
= 3. Isabel of Portugal

Anne
= John, d.
of Bedford

CHARLES THE BOLD
(1467–77)
= 1. Catherine de France
= 2. Isabel de Bourbon
= 3. Margaret of York

Antoine
'Grand Bâtard'

MARY OF BURGUNDY
(1477–82)
= Maximilian of Habsburg

Philippe 'le Beau'
= Juana

Margaret of Austria
= Philibert of Savoy

Charles V (emperor)

Table 2   The Valois house of Burgundy

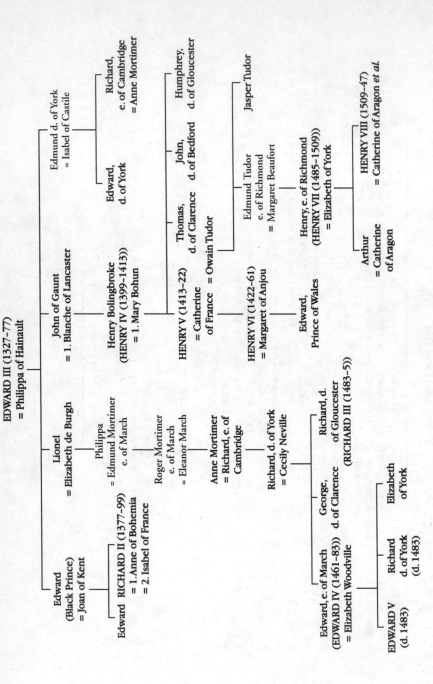

Table 3   The English succession

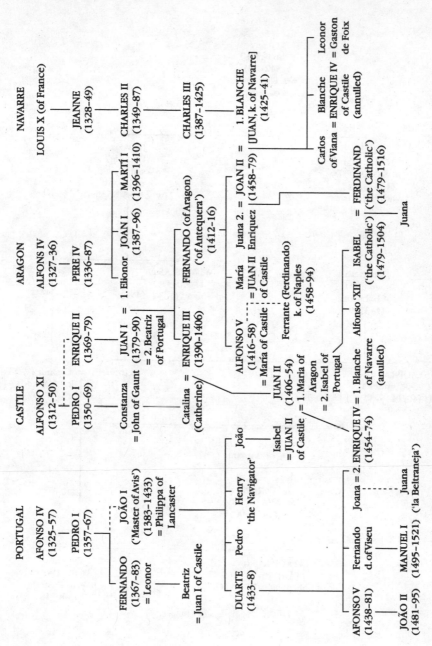

Table 4   The rulers of the Iberian kingdoms

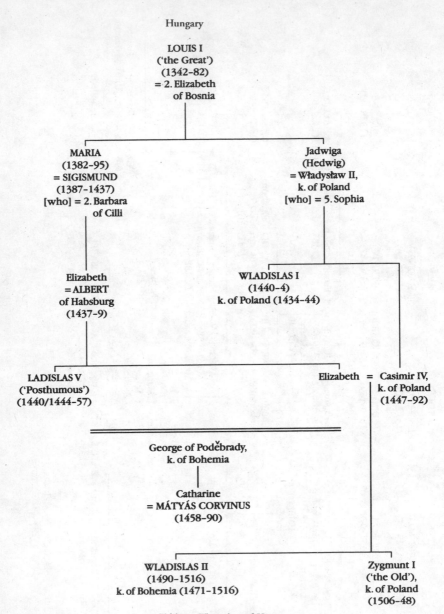

Hungary

LOUIS I
('the Great')
(1342–82)
= 2. Elizabeth
of Bosnia

MARIA
(1382–95)
= SIGISMUND
(1387–1437)
[who] = 2. Barbara
of Cilli

Jadwiga
(Hedwig)
= Władysław II,
k. of Poland
[who] = 5. Sophia

Elizabeth
= ALBERT
of Habsburg
(1437–9)

WLADISLAS I
(1440–4)
k. of Poland (1434–44)

LADISLAS V
('Posthumous')
(1440/1444–57)

Elizabeth = Casimir IV,
k. of Poland
(1447–92)

George of Poděbrady,
k. of Bohemia

Catharine
= MÁTYÁS CORVINUS
(1458–90)

WLADISLAS II
(1490–1516)
k. of Bohemia (1471–1516)

Zygmunt I
('the Old'),
k. of Poland
(1506–48)

Table 5   The rulers of Hungary

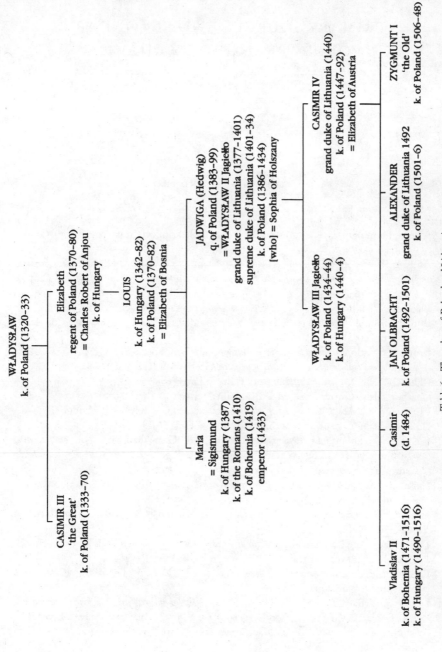

WŁADYSŁAW
k. of Poland (1320–33)

CASIMIR III
'the Great'
k. of Poland (1333–70)

Elizabeth
regent of Poland (1370–80)
= Charles Robert of Anjou
k. of Hungary

LOUIS
k. of Hungary (1342–82)
k. of Poland (1370–82)
= Elizabeth of Bosnia

Maria
= Sigismund
k. of Hungary (1387)
k. of the Romans (1410)
k. of Bohemia (1419)
emperor (1433)

JADWIGA (Hedwig)
q. of Poland (1383–99)
= WŁADYSŁAW II Jagiełło
grand duke of Lithuania (1377–1401)
supreme duke of Lithuania (1401–34)
k. of Poland (1386–1434)
[who] = Sophia of Holszany

WŁADYSŁAW III Jagiełło
k. of Poland (1434–44)
k. of Hungary (1440–4)

CASIMIR IV
grand duke of Lithuania (1440)
k. of Poland (1447–92)
= Elizabeth of Austria

Vladislav II
k. of Bohemia (1471–1516)
k. of Hungary (1490–1516)

Casimir
(d. 1484)

JAN OLBRACHT
k. of Poland (1492–1501)

ALEXANDER
grand duke of Lithuania 1492
k. of Poland (1501–6)

ZYGMUNT I
'the Old'
k. of Poland (1506–48)

Table 6   The rulers of Poland and Lithuania

PRIMARY SOURCES AND SECONDARY
WORKS ARRANGED BY CHAPTER

1 POLITICS: THEORY AND PRACTICE

Primary

Alberti, Leon Battista, *Momo o del principe*, ed. N. Balestrini, R. Consolo and A. Di Grado, Genoa (1986)

Andlau, Peter von, *De Imperio Romano-Germanico libri duo*, ed. J. Hürbin, *Zeitschrift der Savigny Stiftung für Rechtsgeschichte, Germanistische Abteilung* 12 (1891), pp. 34–103; 13 (1892), pp. 163–219

Baldus de Ubaldis, *Consiliorum sive responsorium volumen tertium*, Venice (1575)

Bonet, Honoré, *The tree of battles of Honoré Bonet*, ed. and trans. G.W. Coopland, Liverpool (1949)

Bruni, Leonardo, *Laudatio Florentinae urbis*, extracts in T. Klette, *Beiträge zur Geschichte und Literatur des Italianischen Gelehrtenrenaissance*, Greifswald (1889), II, pp. 84–105

Chartier, Alain, *Le livre de l'espérance*, ed. F. Rouy, Paris (1989)

Chartier, Alain, *Œuvres latines*, ed. P. Bourgain-Hemeryck, Paris (1977)

Chartier, Alain, *The poetical works of Alain Chartier*, ed. J.C. Laidlaw, Cambridge (1974)

Chartier, Alain, *Le quadrilogue invectif*, ed. E. Droz, Paris (1923)

Cusanus, Nicholaus, *De concordantia catholica*, ed. G. Kallen, in *Opera omnia*, XIV, Hamburg (1959); English trans. and ed. P.E. Sigmund, *The Catholic concordance*, Cambridge (1991)

Cusanus, Nicolaus, *Orationes*, in *Deutsche Reichstagsakten*, Göttingen (1957), XV:2, pp. 639–46, 874–6; XVI:2, pp. 407–32, 539–43

Decembrio, Pier Candido, 'Il De laudibus Mediolanensis urbis panegyricus', ed. G. Petraglione, *Archivio storico Lombardo* 4th series 8 (1907), pp. 5–45

Decembrio, Pier Candido, *Vita Philippi Mariae III Ligurum ducis*, ed. A. Butti and G. Petraglione, Rerum Italicarum Scriptores, 20:1, Bologna (1925–58)

Eiximenis, Francesc, *El regiment de la cosa publica*, ed. P.D. de Molins de Rei, Els Nostres Clássics, 13, Barcelona (1927)

Fitzralph, Richard, *De pauperie salvatoris*, bks I–IV in *Iohannis Wyclif De dominio divino*, ed. R.L. Poole, Wyclif Society, London (1890), pp. 257–476; bks V–VII in R.O. Brock, 'An edition of Richard Fitzralph's "De pauperie salvatoris" books V, VI and VII', dissertation, University of Colorado (1954)

Fortescue, Sir John, *De laudibus legum Anglie*, ed. S.B. Chrimes, Cambridge (1942)

Fortescue, Sir John, *The governance of England*, ed. C. Plummer, Oxford (1885); also in M.L. Kekewich, C. Richmond, A.F. Sutton, L. Visser-Fuchs and J.L. Watts (eds.), *The politics of fifteenth-century England. John Vale's book*, Stroud (1995), pp. 226–50

Fortescue, Sir John, *Opusculum de natura legis nature et de ejus censura in successione regnorum suprema*, ed. Lord Clermont, in *The works of Sir John Fortescue*, London (1869), II, pp. 63–184

Four English political tracts of the later Middle Ages, ed. J.-P. Genet, RHS, London (1977)

Gerson, Jean, *Œuvres complètes de Jean Gerson*, ed. P. Glorieux, VII, Paris (1968)

Gerson, Jean, *Opera omnia*, IV, Antwerp (1706)

Hoccleve, Thomas, *The regement of princes*, ed. F.J. Furnivall, EETS, extra series, 72, London (1897)

Hus, Jan, *Magistri Johannis Hus tractatus de ecclesia*, ed. S.H. Thomson, Boulder (1956)

Juvénal des Ursins, Jean, *Ecrits politiques*, ed. P.S. Lewis, 3 vols., SHF, Paris (1985–93)

Masselin, Jean, *Journal des états généraux tenus à Tours*, ed. A. Bernier, Collection des Documents Inédits, Paris (1835)

Mena, Juan de, *El laberinto de fortuna*, ed. R. Fouché-Delbosc, Mâcon (1904)

Monte, Piero da, *De potestate romani pontificis et generalis concilii*, ed. J.T. de Rocaberti, *Bibliotheca maxima pontificia*, Rome (1698), XVIII, pp. 100–37

L'ordonnance cabochienne, ed. A. Coville, Paris (1891)

Piccolomini, Aeneas Sylvius, *Epistola de ortu et auctoritate imperii romani*, in G. Kallen, *Aeneas Sylvius Piccolomini als Publizist in der 'Epistola de ortu et auctoritate imperii romani'*, Cologne (1939), pp. 50–100

Pisan, Christine de, *Le livre de la mutacion de fortune par Christine de Pisan*, ed. S. Solente, Paris (1959)

Pisan, Christine de, *Le livre du corps de policie*, ed. R.H. Lucas, Geneva (1967)

Rotuli parliamentorum, 6 vols., London (1767–77)

Le songe du vergier, ed. M. Schnerb-Lièvre, 2 vols., Paris (1982)

Torquemada, Juan de, *Oratio synodalis de primatu*, ed. E. Canda, Rome (1954)

Viterbo, James of, *De regimine Christiano*, ed. H.X. Arquillière, in *Le plus ancien traité de l'église. Jacques de Viterbo, 'De regimine Christiano'*, Paris (1926)

Wyclif, John, *De dominio divino*, ed. R.L. Poole, Wyclif Society, London (1890)

Wyclif, John, *De potestate papae*, ed. J. Loserth, Wyclif Society, London (1907)

Wyclif, John, *De veritate sacrae scripturae*, ed. R. Buddensieg, 3 vols., Wyclif Society, London (1905–7)

Wyclif, John, *Tractatus de civili dominio liber primus*, ed. R.L. Poole and J. Loserth, 3 vols., Wyclif Society, London (1890–1904)

Wyclif, John, *Tractatus de officio regis*, ed. A.W. Pollard and C. Sayle, 3 vols., Wyclif Society, London (1887)

Secondary works

Angermeier, H. (1984), *Die Reichsreform 1410–1455. Die Staatsproblematik in Deutschland zwischen Mittelalter und Gegenwart*, Munich

Arabeyre, P. (1990), 'Un prélat languedocien au milieu du XVe siècle: Bernard de Rosier, archevêque de Toulouse (1400–1475)', *Journal des savants*: 291–326

Arasse, D. (1985), 'L'art et l'illustration du pouvoir', in *Culture et idéologie* (1985), pp. 231–44

Ascheri, M. (1971), *Saggi sul diplovatazio*, Milan

Barbey, J. (1983), *La fonction royale. Essence et légitimité, d'après les 'Tractatus' de Jean de Terrevermeille*, Paris

Baron, H. (1966), *The crisis of the early Italian Renaissance. Civic humanism and republican liberty in an age of classicism and tyranny*, Princeton

Baron, H. (1968), *From Petrarch to Leonardo Bruni*, Chicago

Beaune, C. (1985), *Naissance de la nation France*, Paris; English trans., *The birth of an ideology. Myths and symbols of nation in late medieval France*, Berkeley (1991)

Belch, S.F. (1965), *Paulus Vladimiri and his doctrine concerning international law and politics*, The Hague

Black, A.J. (1970), *Monarchy and community. Political ideas in the later conciliar controversy, 1430–1450*, Cambridge

Black, A.J. (1992), *Political thought in Europe, 1250–1450*, Cambridge

Blockmans, W.P. (1985), 'Breuk of continuïteit? De Vlaamse privilegiën van 1477 in het licht van het staatsvormingsproces', in W.P. Blockmans (ed.), *Le privilêge général et les privilêges régionaux de Marie de Bourgogne pour les Pays-Bas, 1477*, Heule, pp. 97–125

Blockmans, W.P. (1993), 'Les origines des états modernes en Europe, XIIIe–XVIIIe siècles: état de la question et perspectives', in W.P. Blockmans and J.-P. Genet (eds.), *Visions sur le développement des états européens. Théories et historiographies de l'état moderne*, Rome, pp. 1–14

Bonney, R. (ed.) (1995), *Economic systems and state finance*, Oxford

Bulst, N. and Genet, J.-P. (eds.) (1988), *La ville, la bourgeoisie et la genèse de l'état moderne (XIIe–XVIIIe siècles)*, Paris

Burns, J.H. (1985), 'Fortescue and the political theory of *dominium*', *HJ* 28: 777–97

Burns, J.H. (1992), *Lordship, kingship and empire. The idea of monarchy, 1400–1525*, Oxford

Burns, J.H. (ed.) (1988), *The Cambridge history of medieval political thought*, Cambridge

Burns, J.H. and Goldie, M. (eds.) (1991), *The Cambridge history of political thought*, Cambridge

Canning, J.P. (1983), 'Ideas of the state in the thirteenth and fourteenth-century commentators on Roman law', *TRHS* 5th series 23: 1–27

Canning, J.P. (1987), *The political thought of Baldus of Ubaldis*, Cambridge

Carlyle, R.W. and A.J. (1903–36), *A history of medieval political theory in the west*, 6 vols., Edinburgh and London

Chrimes, S.B. (1936), *English constitutional ideas in the XVth century*, Cambridge

Coing, H. (ed.) (1973 and 1976), *Handbuch der Quellen und Literatur der neueren Europäischen Privatrechtsgeschichte*, I and II, Munich

Coleman, J. (1981), *English literature in history, 1350–1400. Medieval readers and writers*, London

Coleman, J. (1988), 'Property and poverty', in Burns (1988), pp. 607–48

Congar, Y. (1970), *L'église. De Saint Augustin à l'époque moderne*, Paris

Contamine, P. (1980), *La guerre au moyen âge*, Paris; English trans., *War in the Middle Ages*, Oxford (1984)

Contamine, P. (1989), *L'état et les aristocraties (France, Angleterre, Ecosse), XIIe–XVIIe siècle*, Paris

Contamine, P. (1992), *Histoire militaire de la France, des origines à 1715*, Paris

Coulet, N. (1977), 'Les entrées solennelles en Provence au XIVe siècle. Aperçus nouveaux sur les entrées royales françaises au bas moyen âge', *Ethnologie française* 7: 63–82

Coulet, N. and Genet, J.-P. (eds.) (1990), *L'état moderne. Le droit, l'espace et les formes de l'état*, Paris

Courtenay, W.J. (1971), 'Covenant and causality in Pierre d'Ailly', *Speculum* 46: 95–119

Culture et idéologie dans la genèse de l'état moderne (1985), Collection de l'Ecole Française de Rome, 82, Rome

Daly, L.J. (1962), *The political theory of John Wyclif*, Chicago

Di Camillo, O. (1976), *El humanismo castellano del siglo XV*, Valencia

Doe, N. (1990), *Fundamental authority in late medieval English law*, Cambridge

Dolezalek, G., Nörr, K.W. and Blell, C. (1973), 'Die Rechtsprechnungssammlungen der mittelalterlichen Rota', in Coing (1973), pp. 849–56

Farr, W. (1974), *John Wyclif as legal reformer*, Leiden

Finzi, C. (1991), 'Il principe e l'obbedienza. I primi scritti politici di Giovanni Pontano', in *Théologie et droit* (1991), pp. 263–79

Flüeler, C. (1992a), 'Die Rezeption der "Politica" des Aristoteles im 13 und 14 Jahrhundert', in Miethke (1992), pp. 127–38

Flüeler, C. (1992b), *Rezeption und Interpretation der Aristotelischen Politica im späten Mittelalter*, Cologne

Garin, E. (1988), *Renaissance humanism. Studies in philosophy and poetics*, New York

Gauvard, C. (1973), 'Christine de Pisan a-t-elle eu une pensée politique?', *RH* 250: 417–30

Genest, J.F. (1992), *Prédétermination et liberté créée à Oxford au XIVe siècle*, Paris

Genet, J.-P. (1990), 'L'état moderne: un modèle opératoire?', in J.-P. Genet (ed.), *L'état moderne. Genèse, bilans et perspectives*, Paris, pp. 261–81

Genet, J.-P. (1991), *Le monde au moyen âge. Espaces, pouvoirs, civilisations*, Paris

Genet, J.-P. (1992), 'Which state rises?', *Historical Research* 45: 119–33

Genet, J.-P. and Le Mené, M. (eds.) (1987), *Genèse de l'état moderne. Prélèvement et redistribution*, Paris

Gewirth, A. (1961), 'Philosophy and political thought in the fourteenth century', in F. Utley (ed.), *The forward movement of the fourteenth century*, Columbus

Gilmore, M.P. (1941), *Argument from Roman law in political thought, 1200–1600*, Cambridge, Mass.

Gouron, A. and Rigaudière, A. (eds) (1988), *Renaissance du pouvoir législatif et genèse de l'état*, Montpellier

Guenée, B. (1987), *Entre l'église et l'état. Quatre vies de prélats français à la fin du moyen âge (XIIIe–XV siècle)*, Paris; English trans., *Between Church and state. The lives of four French prelates in the late Middle Ages*, Chicago and London (1991)

Guenée, B. (1991), *L'occident aux XIVe et XVe siècles. Les états*, 4th edn, Paris; English trans., *States and rulers in later medieval Europe*, Oxford (1985)

Guenée, B. (1992), *Un meurtre, une société. L'assassinat du duc d'Orléans 23 novembre 1407*, Paris

Guenée, B. and Lehoux, F. (1968), *Les entrées royales françaises de 1328 à 1515*, Paris

Haller, J. (1941), *Piero da Monte. Ein Gelehrter und päpstlicher Beamter des 15 Jahrhundert: seine Briefsammlung*, Rome

Hanley, S. (1983), *The lit de justice of the kings of France. Constitutional ideology in legend, ritual and discourse*, Princeton

Hay, D. (1968), *Europe. The emergence of an idea*, 2nd edn, Edinburgh

Hazeltine, H.D. (1942), 'The age of Littleton and Fortescue', in Fortescue, *De laudibus legum Anglie*, pp. ix–liii

Hendrix, S.H. (1976), 'In quest of the *vera ecclesia*: the crises of late medieval ecclesiology', *Viator* 7: 347–78

Heymann, F.G. (1965), *George of Bohemia, king of heretics*, Princeton

Housley, N. (1992), *The later crusades, 1272–1580. From Lyons to Alcazar*, Oxford

Hudson, A. (1988), *The premature Reformation. Wycliffite texts and Lollard history*, Oxford

Ianziti, G. (1988), *Humanistic historiography under the Sforzas*, Oxford

Isenmann, E. (1990), 'Les caractéristiques constitutionnelles du Saint Empire Romain de Nation Germanique au XVe siècle', in Coulet and Genet (1990), pp. 143–66

Jackson, R. (1984), *Vivat rex. Histoire des sacres et couronnements en France, 1364–1825*, Strasburg; English trans., *Vive le roi. A history of the French coronation from Charles V to Charles X*, Chapel Hill and London (1984)

Justice, S. (1994), *Writing and rebellion. England in 1381*, Berkeley

Kaeuper, R.W. (1988), *War, justice and public order. England and France in the later Middle Ages*, Oxford

Kaminsky, H. (1963), 'Wyclifism as an ideology of revolution', *Church History* 32: 57–74

Kaminsky, H. (1964), 'Peter Chelciky: treatises on Christianity and social order', *Studies in Medieval and Renaissance History* 1: 107–79

Kantorowicz, E.H. (1957), *The king's two bodies*, Princeton

Kenny, A. (1985), *Wyclif*, Oxford

Kisch, G. (1970), *Consilia. Eine Bibliographie der juristischen Konsiliensammlungen*, Basle

Klapisch-Zuber, C. (1985), 'Rituels publics et pouvoirs d'état', in *Culture et idéologie* (1985), pp. 135–44

Krynen, J. (1981), *Idéal du prince et pouvoir royal en France à la fin du moyen âge (1380–1440). Essai sur la littérature politique du temps*, Paris

Krynen, J. (1991), 'Les légistes "Idiots politiques". Sur l'hostilité des théologiens à l'égard des juristes, en France, au temps de Charles V', in *Théologie et droit* (1991), pp. 171–98

Krynen, J. (1993), *L'empire du roi. Idées et croyances politiques en France XIIIe–XVe siècle*, Paris

Krynen, J. and Rigaudière, A. (eds.) (1992), *Droits savants et pratiques françaises du pouvoir (XIe–XVe siècles)*, Bordeaux

Lagarde, G. de (1956–70), *La naissance de l'esprit laïque au moyen âge*, 5 vols., 3rd edn, Paris and Louvain

Leff, G. (1957), *Bradwardine and the Pelagians*, Cambridge

Leff, G. (1968), *Paris and Oxford Universities in the thirteenth and fourteenth centuries*, London

Leff, G. (1976), *The dissolution of the medieval outlook*, New York

Lewis, P. (1993), *Ecrits politiques de Jean Juvénal des Ursins, III: La vie et l'œuvre*, SHF, Paris

Lida de Malkiel, M.R. (1950), *Juan de Mena, poeta del prerenacimiento español*, Mexico

McFarlane, K.B. (1952), *John Wycliffe and the beginnings of English non-conformity*, London

McFarlane, K.B. (1972), *Lancastrian kings and Lollard knights*, Oxford

McGrade, A. (1974), *The political thought of William of Ockham*, Cambridge

McIllwain, C.H. (1932), *The growth of political thought in the west*, New York

McReady, W.D. (1975), 'Papalists and antipapalists: aspects of the Church/State controversy in the later Middle Ages', *Viator* 6: 241–73

Maffei, D. (1964), *La donazione di Costantino nei giuristi medievali*, Milan
Maffei, D. (1966), *Gli inizi dell'umanesimo giuridico*, Milan
Mager, W. (1984), 'Republik', in O. Brunner, W. Conze and R. Koselleck (eds.), *Geschichtliche Grundbegriffe. Historisches Lexikon zur politisch-sozialen Sprache in Deutschland*, Stuttgart, V, pp. 549–651
Mager, W. (1968), *Zur Entstehung des moderne Staatsbegriffs*, Mainz and Wiesbaden
Mager, W. (1991), '*Res publica* chez les juristes, théologiens et philosophes à la fin du moyen âge', in *Théologie et droit* (1991), pp. 229–39
Messler, G. (1973), *Das Weltfriedensmanifest König Georgs von Podiebrad. Ein Beitrag zur diplomatie des 15 Jahrhunderts*, Kirnbach
Miethke, J. (1969), *Ockhams Weg zur Sozialphilosophie*, Berlin
Miethke, J. (1982), 'Die Traktate *De potestate papae* – ein typus politiktheoretischer Literatur im späteren Mittelalter', in R. Bultot and L. Génicot (eds.), *Les genres littéraires dans les sources théologiques et philosophiques médiévales*, Louvain, pp. 198–211
Miethke, J. (1991a), 'Kaiser und Papst im Spätmittelalter: Die Traktate *De potestate papae*', in H.G. Lieber (ed.), *Politische Theorien von der Antike bis zur Gegenwart*, Bonn, pp. 94–121
Miethke, J. (1991b), 'The concept of liberty in William of Ockham', in *Théologie et droit* (1991), pp. 89–100
Miethke, J. (ed.) (1992), *Das publikum politischer Theorie im 14 Jahrhundert*, Munich
Mohr, G.H. (1958), *Unitas Christiana. Studien zur Gesellschaftsidee des Nikolaus von Kues*, Trier
Muir, E. (1981), *Civic ritual in Renaissance Venice*, Princeton
Oakley, F. (1964), *The political thought of Pierre d'Ailly*, Yale
Oakley, F. (1981), 'Natural law, the *Corpus mysticum*, and consent in conciliar thought from John of Paris to Mathias Ugonis', *Speculum* 56: 786–810
Oberman, H.A. (1956), *Archbishop Thomas Bradwardine. A fourteenth-century Augustinian*, Utrecht
Ourliac, P. and Gilles, H. (1971), *La période post-classique (1378–1500), I: La problématique de l'époque. Les sources*, Histoire du Droit et des Institutions de l'Eglise, 13, Paris
Ozment, S. (1980), *The age of reform 1250–1550. An intellectual and religious history of late medieval and Reformation Europe*, New Haven and London
Pagden, A. (ed.) (1987), *The languages of political theory in early modern Europe*, Cambridge
Pannenberg, W. (1954), *Die Prädestinationslehre des Duns Skotus*, Göttingen
Paradisi, B. (1973), 'Il pensiero politico dei giuristi medievali', in L. Firpo (ed.), *Storia delle idee politiche, economiche e sociale*, Turin, II, pp. 575–618
Pascoe, L.B. (1973), *Jean Gerson. Principles of church reform*, Leiden
Pastoureau, M. (n.d.), *Couleurs, images, symboles. Etudes d'histoire et d'anthropologie*, Paris
Quillet, J. (1970), *La philosophie politique de Marsile de Padoue*, Paris
Quillet, J. (1977), *La philosophie politique du Songe du Vergier (1378). Sources doctrinales*, Paris
Rabil, A. (ed.) (1988), *Renaissance humanism. Foundations, forms and legacy*, I, Philadelphia
Reynolds, S. (1984), *Kingdoms and communities in western Europe*, Oxford
Riesenberg, P.N. (1962), 'The consilia literature: a prospectus', *Manuscripta* 6: 3–22
Robson, J.A. (1961), *Wyclif and the Oxford schools*, Oxford
Rouy, F. (1980), *L'esthétique du traité moral d'après les œuvres d'Alain Chartier*, Geneva
Rubin, M. (1991), *Corpus Christi. The Eucharist in late medieval culture*, Cambridge

Rubinstein, N. (1979), 'Le dottrine politiche nel rinascimento', in N. Rubinstein (ed.), *Il Rinascimento. Interpretazioni e problemi*, Rome and Bari, pp. 183–237

Rubinstein, N. (1987), 'The history of the word *politicus* in early modern Europe', in Pagden (1987), pp. 41–56

Rubinstein, N. (1991), 'Italian political thought, 1450–1530', in Burns and Goldie (1991), pp. 30–65

Schmitt, C. (1987), 'Le traité du cardinal Jean de Torquemada sur la pauvreté evangélique', *Archivum fratrum praedicatorum* 57: 103–44

Sigmund, P.E. (1963), *Nicholas of Cusa and medieval political thought*, Cambridge, Mass.

Singer, B. (1981), *Die Fürstenspiegel in Deutschland im Zeitalter des Humanismus und der Reformation*, Munich

Skinner, Q. (1978), *The foundations of modern political thought*, 2 vols., Cambridge

Spinka, M. (1966), *John Hus' concept of the Church*, Princeton

Stürner, W. (1987), *Peccatum und Potestas. Der Sündenfall und die Entstehung der herrscherlichen Gewalt im mittelalterlichen Staatsdenken*, Sigmaringen

Théologie et droit dans la science politique de l'état moderne (1991), Collection de l'Ecole Française de Rome, 147, Rome

Thomson, J.A.F. (1965), *The later Lollards 1414–1520*, Oxford

Thomson, W.R. (1983), *The Latin writings of John Wyclif*, Toronto

Tierney, B. (1972), *Origins of papal infallibility, 1150–1350. A study on the concepts of infallibility, sovereignty and tradition in the Middle Ages*, Leiden

Tierney, B. and Linehan, P.A. (eds.) (1980), *Authority and power. Studies in medieval law and government presented to Walter Ullmann on his seventieth birthday*, Cambridge

Tilly, C. (1990), *Coercion, capital and European states A.D. 900–1990*, New York

Trexler, R.C. (1980), *Public life in Renaissance Florence*, New York

Ullmann, W. (1961), *Principles of government and politics in the Middle Ages*, London

Ullmann, W. (1974), 'Die Bulle Unam Sanctam: Rückblick und Ausblick', *Römische Historischen Mitteilungen* 16: 45–58

Ullmann, W. (1975), *Medieval political thought*, Harmondsworth

Uyttebrouck, A. (1992), 'La cour de Brabant sous les ducs de la branche cadette de Bourgogne-Valois, 1406–1430', in *Actes des journées internationales Claus Sluter, 1990*, Dijon, pp. 311–35

Vale, M.G.A. (1974), *Charles VII*, London

Vanderjagt, A. (1981), *'Qui sa vertu anoblist'. Le concept de noblesse et de chose publique dans la pensée politique bourguignonne*, Groningen

Vanecek, V. (ed.) (1966), *Cultus pacis. Etudes et documents du 'Symposium Pragense Cultus Pacis 1464–1964'*, Prague

Vignaux, P. (1934), *Justification et prédestination au XIVe siècle. Duns Scot, Pierre d'Auriole, Guillaume d'Occam, Grégoire de Rimini*, Paris

Von der Heydte, F. (1952), *Die Geburtstunde des souveränen Staates*, Regensburg

Wahl, J.A. (1977), 'Baldus de Ubaldis and the foundations of the nation-state', *Manuscripta* 21: 80–96

Walravens, C.J.H. (1971), *Alain Chartier. Etudes biographiques*, Amsterdam

Walsh, K. (1981), *A fourteenth-century scholar and primate. Richard Fitzralph in Oxford, Avignon and Armagh*, Oxford

Walther, H.G. (1976), *Imperiales Königtum, Konziliarismus und Volkssouveränität. Studien zu den Grenzen des mittelalterlichen Souveränitätsgedankens*, Munich

Watanabe, M. (1963), *The political ideas of Nicholas of Cusa, with special reference to his 'De concordantia catholica'*, Geneva

Widmer, B. (1963), *Enea Silvio Piccolomini in der sittlichen und politischen Entscheidung*, Basle

Wilcox, D.J. (1969), *The development of Florentine humanist historiography in the fifteenth century*, Cambridge, Mass.

Wilks, M. (1964), *The problem of sovereignty in the later Middle Ages. The papal monarchy with Augustinus Triumphus and the publicists*, Cambridge

Witt, R.G. (1988), 'Medieval Italian culture and the origins of humanism', in Rabil (1988), I, pp. 29–70

Wolf, A. (1973), 'Die Gesetzgebung der entstehenden Territorialstaaten', in Coing (1973), pp. 517–800

Woolf, C.N.S. (1913), *Bartolus of Sassoferrata. His position in the history of medieval political thought*, Cambridge

2 REPRESENTATION (SINCE THE THIRTEENTH CENTURY)

Primary sources

Blockmans, W.P., 'Autocratie ou polyarchie? La lutte pour le pouvoir politique en Flandre de 1482 à 1492, d'après des documents inédits', *Bulletin de la Commission royale d'histoire* 140 (1974), pp. 257–368

Blockmans, W.P., Prevenier, W. and Zoete, A. (eds.), *Handelingen van de Leden en van de Staten van Vlaanderen (1384–1506)*, 9 vols., Brussels (1959–96)

Cuvelier, J., Dhondt, J. and Doehaerd, R. (eds.), *Actes des états généraux des anciens Pays-Bas, 1427–1477*, Brussels (1948)

Galbert of Bruges, *De multro, traditione et occisione glorioso Karoli comitis Flandriarum*, ed. J. Rider, Turnhout (1994)

Gorski, K., Biskup, M. and Janosz-Biskupowa, I. (eds.), *Akta Stanow Prus Krolewskich (1479–1526)*, 8 vols., Torun, Warsaw and Poznań (1955–95)

Graffart, A. and Uyttebouck, A., 'Quelques documents inédits concernant l'accession de la maison de Bourgogne au duché de Brabant (1395–1404)', *Bulletin de la Commission royale d'histoire* 137 (1971), pp. 57–137

Prevenier, W. and Smit, J.G. (eds.), *Bronnen voor de geschiedenis van de dagvaarten van Staten en steden van Holland voor 1544. Deel I: 1276–1433*, 2 vols., The Hague (1987–91)

Richardson, H.G. and Sayles, G.O. (eds.), *Rotuli parliamentorum Angliae hactenus inediti, 1279–1373*, London (1935)

Rotuli parliamentorum, 6 vols., London (1767–77)

Töppen, M. (ed.), *Acten der Ständetage Preussens unter der Herrschaft des Deutschen Ordens*, 5 vols., Leipzig (1874–86)

Secondary works

Bak, J.M. (1973), *Königtum und Stände in Ungarn im 14.–16. Jahrhundert*, Wiesbaden

Benl, R. (1992), 'Anfänge und Entwicklung des Ständewesens im spätmittelalterlichen Pommern', in Boockmann (1992b), pp. 121–35

Berthold, B. (1980), 'Städte und Reichsreform in der ersten Hälfte des 15. Jahrhunderts', in Töpfer (1980b), pp. 59–112

Bierbrauer, P. (1991), 'Die Ausbildung bäuerlicher Landschaften im Raum der Eidgenossenschaft', *Parliaments, Estates & Representation* 11: 91–102

Biskup, M. (1980), 'Die Rolle der Städte in der Ständevertretung des Königreichs Polen, einschließlich des Ordensstaates Preußen im 14./15. Jahrhundert', in Töpfer (1980b), pp. 163–94

Biskup, M. (1992), 'Die Stände im Preußen Königlichen Anteils 1466–1526', in Boockmann (1992b), pp. 83–99

Bisson, T.N. (1964), *Assemblies and representation in Languedoc in the thirteenth century*, Princeton

Bisson, T.N. (1977), 'A general court of Aragon (Daroca, February 1228)', *EHR* 92: 107–24

Bisson, T.N. (1986), *The medieval crown of Aragon*, Oxford

Blickle, P. (1986), 'Communalism, parliamentarism, republicanism', *Parliaments, Estates & Representation* 6: 1–13

Blickle, P. (ed.) 1997, *Resistance, representation and community*, Oxford.

Blockmans, W.P. (1973), 'La participation des sujets flamands à la politique monétaire des ducs de Bourgogne (1384–1500)', *Revue belge de numismatique* 119: 103–34

Blockmans, W.P. (1978a), *De volksvertegenwoordiging in Vlaanderen in de overgang van middeleeuwen naar nieuwe tijden (1384–1506)*, Brussels

Blockmans, W.P. (1978b), 'A typology of representative institutions in late medieval Europe', *JMedH* 4: 189–215

Blockmans, W.P. (1986), 'Vertretungssysteme im niederländischen Raum im Spätmittelalter', in K. Fritze, E. Müller-Mertens and J. Schildhauer (eds.), *Der Ost- und Nordseeraum*, Hansische Studien, 7, Weimar, pp. 180–9

Blockmans, W.P. (1992), 'From a typology of representation towards the localisation of power centres', in H.W. Blom, W.P. Blockmans and H. de Schepper (eds.), *Bicameralism*, The Hague, pp. 41–50

Blockmans, W.P. (1994), 'Voracious states and obstructing cities: an aspect of state formation in preindustrial Europe', in C. Tilly and W.P. Blockmans (eds.), *Cities & the rise of states in Europe, A.D. 1000 to 1800*, Boulder, pp. 218–50

Bonis, G. (1965), 'The Hungarian feudal diet (13th–18th centuries)', in *Gouvernés et gouvernants* (1965–6), XXV, pp. 287–307

Boockmann, H. (1988), 'Geschäfte und Geschäftigkeit auf dem Reichstag im späten Mittelalter', *HZ* 246: 297–325

Boockmann, H. (1992a), 'Bemerkungen zur frühen Geschichte ständischer Vertretungen in Preußen', in Boockmann (1992b), pp. 39–51

Boockmann, H. (ed.) (1992b), *Die Anfänge der ständischen Vertretungen in Preußen und seinen Nachbarländern*, Munich

Bos-Rops, J.A.M.Y. (1993), *Graven op zoek naar geld. De inkomsten van de graven van Holland en Zeeland, 1389–1433*, Hilversum

Bulst, N. (1987), 'Die französischen General- und Provinzialstände im 15. Jahrhundert. Zum Problem nationaler Integration und Desintegration', in F. Seibt and W. Eberhard (eds.), *Europa 1500. Integrationsprozesse im Widerstreit: Staaten, Regionen, Personenverbände, Christenheit*, Stuttgart, pp. 313–29

Bulst, N. (1992), *Die französischen Generalstände von 1468 und 1484. Prosopographische Untersuchungen zu den Delegierten*, Beihefte der Francia, 26, Sigmaringen

Bütikofer, N. (1991), 'Konfliktregulierung auf den Eidgenössischen Tagsatzungen des 15. und 16. Jahrhunderts', *Parliaments, Estates & Representation* 11: 103–15

Carsten, F.L. (1959), *Princes and parliaments in Germany, from the fifteenth to the eighteenth century*, Oxford

Chittolini, G. (1986), 'Su alcuni aspetti dello stato di Federico', in G. Cerboni Baiardi, G. Chittolini and P. Floriani (eds.), *Federico da Montefeltro. Lo stato, le arti, la cultura*, 3 vols., Rome, I, pp. 61–102

Comparato, V.I. (1980), 'Il controllo del contado a Perugia nella prima metà del Quattrocento. Capitani, vicari e contadini tra 1428 e 1450', *Forme e tecniche del potere nella città (secoli XIV–XVII)*, Annali della Facoltà di Scienze Politiche, 16, Perugia, pp. 147–90

D'Agostino, G. (1979), *Parlamento e società nel regno di Napoli, secoli XV–XVII*, Naples

Davies, R.G. and Denton, J.H. (eds.) (1981), *The English parliament in the Middle Ages*, Manchester

Dhondt, J. (1950), '"Ordres" ou "puissances". L'exemple des états de Flandre', *Annales ESC* 5: 289–305; repr. in Dhondt (1977), pp. 25–49

Dhondt, J. (1966), 'Les assemblées d'états en Belgique avant 1795', in *Gouvernés et gouvernants* (1965–6), XXIV, pp. 325–400; repr. in Dhondt (1977), pp. 179–247

Dhondt, J. (1977), *Estates or Powers. Essays in the parliamentary history of the southern Netherlands from the XIIth to the XVIIIth century*, Anciens Pays et Assemblées d'Etats, 69, Heule

Dumont, F. and Timbal, P.C. (1966), 'Gouvernés et gouvernants en France. Périodes du moyen âge et du XVIe siècle', in *Gouvernés et gouvernants* (1965–6), XXIV, pp. 181–233

Eberhard, W. (1987), 'Interessengegensätze und Landesgemeinde: die böhmischen Stände im nachrevolutionären Stabilisierungskonflikt', in F. Seibt and W. Eberhard (eds.), *Europa 1500*, Stuttgart, pp. 330–48

Edwards, J.G. (1957), *The Commons in medieval English parliaments*, London

Engel, E. (1980), 'Frühe ständische Aktivitäten des Städtebürgertums im Reich und in den Territorien bis zur Mitte des 14. Jahrhunderts', in Töpfer (1980b), pp. 13–58

Estepa Diez, C. (1988a), 'Curia y cortes en el reino de León', in *Las cortes de Castilla y León en la edad media*, Valladolid, pp. 23–103

Estepa Diez, C. (1988b), 'Las cortes del reino de León', in *El reino de León en la alta edad media*, I, León, pp. 181–282

Estepa Diez, C. (1990), 'La curia de León en 1188 y los orígines de las cortes', in *Las cortes de Castilla y León 1188–1988*, I, Valladolid, pp. 19–39

Fasoli, G. (1965), 'Gouvernants et gouvernés dans les communes italiennes, du XIe au XIIIe siècle', in *Gouvernés et gouvernants* (1965–6), XXV, pp. 47–86

Fernandez Albaladejo, P. and Pardos Martinez, J.A. (1988), 'Castilla, territorio sin cortes (siglos XV–XVII)', *Revista de las cortes generales* 15: 113–208

Folz, R. (1965), 'Les assemblées d'états dans les principautés allemandes (fin XIIIe–début XVIe siècle)', in *Gouvernés et gouvernants* (1965–6), XXV, pp. 163–91

Foreville, R. (1966), 'Gouvernés et gouvernants en Angleterre, des origines Anglo-Saxonnes à la mort d'Edouard Ier (1307)', in *Gouvernés et gouvernants* (1965–6), XXIV, pp. 127–63

Fryde, E.B. and Miller, E. (1970), *Historical studies of the English parliament*, 2 vols., Cambridge

Gorski, K. (1966), 'Die Anfänge des Ständewesens in Nord- und Ostmitteleuropa im Mittelalter', *Anciens pays et assemblées d'états* 40: 43–59

Gorski, K. (1975), 'Institutions représentatives et émancipation de la noblesse. Pour une typologie des assemblées d'états au XVe siècle', *Studies Presented to the International Commission for the History of Representative and Parliamentary Institutions* 52: 133–47

Gouvernés et gouvernants (1965–6) (*Recueils de la Société Jean Bodin, XXIV and XXV*), Brussels

Harris, G.L. (1966), 'Parliamentary taxation and the origins of appropriation of supply in England, 1207–1340', in *Gouvernés et gouvernants* (1965–6), XXIV, pp. 165–79

Heinig, P.J. (1990), 'Reichstag und Reichstagakten am Ende des Mittelalters', *Zeitschrift für Historische Forschung* 17: 419–28

Heinrich, G. (1992), 'Die "Freien Herren" und das Land. Markgrafenherrschaft und landständische Einflußnahme in Brandenburg während des Spätmittelalters', in Boockmann (1992b), pp. 137–50

Hintze, O. (1930), 'Typologie der ständischen Verfassungen des Abendlandes', *HZ* 141: 229–48; repr. in G. Oestreich (ed.), *Gesammelte Abhandlungen*, I, Gottingen (1962)

Hintze, O. (1931), 'Weltgeschichtliche Bedingungen der Representativverfassung', *HZ* 143: 1–47; repr. in G. Oestreich (ed.), *Gesammelte Abhandlungen*, I, Göttingen (1962); English trans. in F. Gilbert (ed.), *The historical essays of Otto Hintze*, New York and Oxford (1975)

Holenstein, A. (1990), 'Konsens und Widerstand. Städtische Obrigkeit und landschaftliche Partizipation im städtischen Territorium Bern (15.–16. Jahrhundert)', *Parliaments, Estates & Representation* 10: 3–27

Holenstein, A. (1991), *Die Huldigung der Untertanen. Rechtskultur und Herrschaftsordnung (800–1800)*, Stuttgart

Holt, J.C. (1965), *Magna Carta*, Cambridge

Kejr, J. (1980), 'Zur Entstehung des städtischen Standes im hussitischen Böhmen', in Töpfer (1980b), pp. 195–214

Kejr, J. (1992), 'Anfänge der ständischen Verfassung in Böhmen', in Boockmann (1992b), pp. 177–217

Kerhervé, J. (1987), *L'état breton aux 14e et 15e siècles. Les ducs, l'argent et les hommes*, 2 vols., Paris

Klueting, H. (1990), 'Las asambleas territoriales de Alemania', in *Las cortes de Castilla y León 1188–1988*, II, Valladolid, pp. 149–70

Koenigsberger, H.G. (1971), *Estates and revolutions. Essays in early modern European history*, Ithaca and London

Koenigsberger, H.G. (1977), 'Dominium regale or Dominium politicum et regale? Monarchies and parliaments in early modern Europe', in K. Bosl and K. Möckl (eds.), *Der moderne Parlamentarismus und seine Grundlagen in der ständischen Representation*, Berlin, pp. 43–68; repr. in his *Politicians and virtuosi. Essays in early modern history*, London (1986), pp. 1–25

Koenigsberger, H.G. (1978), 'The Italian parliaments from their origins to the end of the 18th century', *Journal of Italian History* 1: 18–49; repr. in his *Politicians and virtuosi. Essays in early modern history*, London (1986), pp. 27–61

Koenigsberger, H.G. (1983), 'Formen und Tendenzen des europäischen Ständewesens im 16. und 17. Jahrhundert', in P. Baumgart (ed.), *Ständetum und Staatsbildung in Brandenburg-Preussen*, Berlin, pp. 19–31

Koenigsberger, H.G. (1985), 'Fürst und Generalstaaten. Maximilian I. in den Niederlanden (1477–1493)', *HZ* 242: 557–79

Kokken, H. (1991), *Steden en Staten. Dagvaarten van steden en Staten van Holland onder Maria van Bourgondië en het eerste regentschap van Maximiliaan van Oostenrijk (1477–1494)*, The Hague

Krüger, K. (1983), 'Die ständischen Verfassungen in Skandinavien in der frühen Neuzeit. Modelle einer europäischen Typologie?', *Zeitschrift für Historische Forschung* 10: 129–48

Kubinyi, A. (1980), 'Zur Frage der Vertretung der Städte im ungarischen Reichstag bis 1526', in Töpfer (1980b), pp. 215–46

Lönnroth, E. (1989), 'Regional and national representation. The problems of communication in olden times', in N. Stjernquist (ed.), *The Swedish riksdag in an international perspective*, Stockholm, pp. 88–95

Major, J.R. (1960a), *Representative government in early modern France*, Madison

Major, J.R. (1960b), *Deputies to the estates general in Renaissance France*, Madison

Major, J.R. (1980), *Representative government in early modern France*, New Haven and London

Mallek, J. (1992), 'Die Ständerepräsentation im Deutschordensstaat (1466–1525) und im Herzogtum Preußen (1525–1566/68)', in Boockmann (1992b), pp. 101–15

Marongiu, A. (1949), *L'istituto parlamentare in Italia dalle origini al 1500*, Rome

Marongiu, A. (1962), *Il parlamento in Italia nel medio evo e nell'età moderna*, Milan

Marongiu, A. (1968), *Medieval parliaments. A comparative study*, London

McKisack, M. (1932), *The parliamentary representation of the English boroughs during the Middle Ages*, Oxford; repr. 1962

Monahan, A.P. (1987), *Consent, coercion and limit. The medieval origins of parliamentary democracy*, Leiden

Moraw, P. (1980), 'Versuch über die Entstehung des Reichstags', in H. Weber (ed.), *Politische Ordnungen und soziale Kräfte im alten Reich*, Wiesbaden, pp. 1–36

Moraw, P. (1992), 'Zu Stand und Perspektiven der Ständeforschung im spätmittelalterlichen Reich', in Boockmann (1992b), pp. 1–33

Moraw, P. (1994), 'Cities and citizenry as factors of state formation in the Roman-German empire of the late Middle Ages', in C. Tilly and W.P. Blockmans (eds.), *Cities and the rise of states in Europe, A.D. 1000–1800*, Boulder, pp. 100–27

Moraw, P. (1995), 'Die Funktion von Einungen und Bünden im spätmittelalterlichen Reich', in V. Press (ed.), *Alternativen zur Reichsverfassung in der frühen Neuzeit?*, Munich, pp. 1–21

Mundy, J.H. (1954), *Liberty and political power in Toulouse 1050–1230*, New York

Myers, A.R. (1961), 'The English parliament and the French estates-general in the Middle Ages', *Studies Presented to the International Commission for the History of Representative and Parliamentary Institutions* 24: 139–53

Neitmann, K. (1992), 'Die Landesordnungen des Deutschen Ordens in Preußen im Spannungsfeld zwischen Landesherrschaft und Ständen', in Boockmann (1992b), pp. 59–81

O'Callaghan, J.F. (1989), *The cortes of Castile–León 1188–1350*, Philadelphia

Ormrod, W.M. (1991), 'The crown and the English economy, 1290–1348', in B.M.S. Campbell (ed.), *Before the Black Death*, Manchester, pp. 149–83

Piskorski, W. (1930), *Las cortes de Castilla en el período de tránsito de la edad media a la moderna (1188–1520)*, trans. C. Sanchez Albornoz, Barcelona; repr. 1977

Powicke, F.M. and Fryde, E.B. (1961), *Handbook of British chronology*, 2nd edn, London

Prevenier, W. (1965), 'Les états de Flandre depuis les origines jusqu'en 1790', *Anciens pays et assemblées d'états* 33: 15–59

Procter, E.S. (1980), *Curia and cortes in Leon and Castile, 1072–1295*, Cambridge; trans. as *Curia y cortes en Castilla y León 1072–1295*, Madrid (1988)

Quillet, J. (1988), 'Community, counsel and representation', in J.H. Burns (ed.), *The Cambridge history of medieval political thought*, Cambridge, pp. 520–72

Rawcliffe, C. (1990), 'The place of the Commons in medieval English parliaments', in *Las cortes de Castilla y Leon 1188–1988*, II, Valladolid, pp. 15–35

Richard, J. (1966), 'Les états de Bourgogne', in *Gouvernés et gouvernants* (1965–6), XXIV, pp. 299–324

Roskell, J.S. (1954), *The Commons in the parliament of 1422*, Manchester

Roskell, J.S. (1965), *The Commons and their speakers in English parliaments*, Manchester

Roskell, J.S., Clark, L. and Rawcliffe, C. (1992), *The history of parliament. The House of Commons 1386–1421*, 4 vols., Stroud

Russocki, S. (1975), 'Typologie des assemblées pré-représentatives en Europe', *Studies Presented to the International Commission for the History of Representative and Parliamentary Institutions* 52: 27–38

Russocki, S. (1983), 'Die mittelalterlichen Stände als Kategorie der Gesellschaftsschichtung', *Acta Poloniae historica* 48: 5–36

Russocki, S. (1992), 'Gesellschaft und Ständestaat im Polen des ausgehenden Mittelalters', in Boockmann (1992b), pp. 169–76

Samsonowicz, H. (1992), 'Die Stände in Polen', in Boockmann (1992b), pp. 159–67

Schück, H. (1987), 'Sweden's early parliamentary institutions from the thirteenth century to 1611', in M.F. Metcalf (ed.), *The rikstag. A history of the Swedish parliament*, Stockholm, pp. 5–60

Sicard, G. (1990), 'Les états généraux de la France Capétienne', in *Las cortes de Castilla y León 1188–1988*, II, Valladolid, pp. 57–100

Smahel, F. (1992), 'Das böhmische Ständewesen im hussitischen Zeitalter: Machtfrage, Glaubensspaltung und strukturelle Umwandlungen', in Boockmann (1992b), pp. 219–46

Soule, C. (1968), *Les états généraux de France (1302–1789)*, Heule

Soule, C. (1990), 'Les états particuliers de France', in *Las cortes de Castilla y León 1188–1988*, II, Valladolid, pp. 101–19

Töpfer, B. (1980a), 'Die Rolle von Städtebünden bei der Ausbildung der Ständeverfassung in den Fürstentümern Lüttich und Brabant', in Töpfer (1980b), pp. 113–54

Töpfer, B. (ed.) (1980b), *Städte und Ständestaat. Zur Rolle der Städte bei der Entwicklung der Ständeverfassung in europäischen Staaten vom 13. bis zum 15. Jahrhundert*, Berlin

Uyttebrouck, A. (1975), *Le gouvernement du duché de Brabant au bas moyen âge (1355–1430)*, 2 vols., Brussels

Valdeón Baruque, J. (1930), 'Las cortes medievales castellano-leonesas en la historiografía reciente', in Piskorski (1977), pp. v–xxxv

Van den Hoven van Genderen, B. (1987), *Het Kapittel-Generaal en de Staten van het Nedersticht in de 15e eeuw*, Zutphen

Van Uytven, R. (1966), 'Standenprivilegies en -beden in Brabant onder Jan I (1290–1293)', *Revue belge de philologie et d'histoire* 44: 413–56

Van Uytven, R. (1985), '1477 in Brabant', in W.P. Blockmans (ed.), *Le privilège général et les privilèges régionaux de Marie de Bourgogne pour les Pays-Bas, 1477*, Anciens Pays et Assemblées d'Etats, 80, Kortrijk and Heule, pp. 253–371

Van Uytven, R. and Blockmans, W. (1969), 'Constitutions and their application in the Netherlands during the Middle Ages', *Revue belge de philologie et d'histoire* 47: 399–424

Van Werveke, H. (1958), 'Das Wesen der flandrischen Hansen', *Hansische Geschichtsblätter* 76: 7–20; repr. in his *Miscellanea mediaevalia*, Ghent (1968), pp. 88–103

Waley, D.P. (1969), *The Italian city-republics*, London

Wedgwood, J.C. (ed.) (1936–8), *History of parliament, 1439–1509*, 2 vols., London

Wellens, R. (1974), *Les états généraux des Pays-Bas des origines à la fin du règne de Philippe le Beau (1464–1506)*, Heule

Wernicke, H. (1986), 'Städtehanse und Stände im Norden des Deutschen Reiches zum Ausgang des Spätmittelalters', in K. Fritze, E. Müller-Mertens and J. Schildhauer (eds.), *Der Ost- und Nordseeraum*, Hansische Studien, 7, Weimar, pp. 190–208

Wolf, A. (1990), 'La Dieta Imperial de Alemania', in *Las cortes de Castilla y León 1188–1988*, II, Valladolid, pp. 125–48

Wyffels, C. (1967), 'Contribution à l'histoire monétaire de Flandre au XIIIe siècle', *Revue belge de philologie et d'histoire* 45: 1113–41

3 POPES AND COUNCILS

Primary sources

d'Ailly, Pierre, 'Tractatus de ecclesiastica potestate', in L. Dupin (ed.), *Gersonii opera*, II, Antwerp (1706), pp. 925–60

Almain, Jacob, 'De auctoritate ecclesie et conciliorum generalium adversus Thomam de Vio' [Cajetan], in L. Dupin (ed.), *Gersonii opera*, II, Antwerp (1706), pp. 977–1012

Cajetan, Thomas de Vio, 'De comparatione auctoritatis papae et concilii', in J. Rocaberti (ed.), *Biblioteca maxima pontifica*, XIX, Rome (1599), pp. 466–92; also edited by V.M.J. Pollet, Rome (1936)

Concilium Florentinum, ed. Pontifical Institute of Oriental Studies, 11 vols., Rome (1940–77)

Cusanus, Nicholaus, *De concordantia catholica*, ed. G. Kallen in *Opera omnia*, XIV, Hamburg (1959); English trans. and ed. P.E. Sigmund, *The Catholic concordance*, Cambridge (1991)

Cusanus, Nicholaus, 'Epistola ad Rodericum', in *Nicolai Cusani opera*, Basle (1565), pp. 825–9

Decius, Philippus, *Super decretalibus*, Lyons (1551)

Deutsche Reichstagsakten, Historische Kommission bei der Bayerischen Akademie der Wissenschaften, XIV–XVII, Stuttgart and Göttingen (1935–63)

Finke, H. *et al.* (eds.), *Acta concilii Constantiensis*, 4 vols., Münster (1896–1928)

Gerson, Jean, *L'œuvre ecclésiologique*, in *Œuvres complètes de Jean Gerson*, ed. P. Glorieux, VI, Tournai (1965)

Haller, J. *et al.* (eds.), *Concilium Basiliense*, 8 vols., Basle (1896–1936)

Hardt, H. von der (ed.), *Magnum oecumenicum Constantiense concilium*, 6 vols., Frankfurt and Leipzig (1697–1700)

Mansi, J.D. (ed.), *Sacrorum conciliorum nova et amplissima collectio*, XXVI–XXXII, Venice, Paris and Leipzig (1784–1901)

Mercati, A. (ed.), *Raccolta dei concordati*, I, Vatican City (1954)

Monte, Piero da, *Briefsammlung*, ed. J. Haller, Bibliothek der deutschen Institut in Rom, 19, Rome (1941)

More, Thomas, *Correspondence*, ed. E.F. Rogers, Princeton (1974)

Niem, Dietrich von, 'De modis uniendi ac reformandi ecclesiam in concilio generali', in Hardt (ed.), *Magnum oecumenicum Constantiense concilium*, I, pp. 68–141; English trans. in Cameron (1952), pp. 226–348; abridged version in M. Spinka (ed.), *Advocates of reform from Wyclif to Erasmus*, London (1953), pp. 149–74

Palacký, F. *et al.* (eds.), *Monumenta conciliorum generalium seculi XV*, 4 vols., Vienna and Basle (1857–1935)

Piccolomini, Aeneas Sylvius [Pius II], *De rebus Basiliae gestis*, in C. Fea (ed.), *Pius II . . . a calumniis vindicatus*, Rome (1823)

Raynaldus, O. (ed.), *Annales ecclesiastici*, vols. XXVII–XXIX, Rome and Bari (1874–6)

Rickel, Denis, 'De auctoritate summi pontificis et generalis concilii', in Denis Rickel, *Opera omnia*, XXXVI, Tournai (1908), pp. 525–674

Sandaeus, Felinus, *Commentaria ad quinque libros decretalium*, 4 vols., Lyons (1555)

Sangiorgio, Johannes Antonius, *Commentaria super toto decreto*, Paris (1497)

Segovia, Juan de, 'Amplificatio disputationis', in Palacký *et al.* (eds.), *Monumenta conciliorum generalium seculi XV*, III, pp. 695–941

Segovia, Juan de, 'Tractatus super presidentia in concilio Basiliensi', ed. P. Ladner, *Zeitschrift für schweizerische Kirchengeschichte* 62 (1968), pp. 31–113

Torquemada [Turrecremata], Juan de, *Commentarium super toto decreto*, I, Venice (1578)

Torquemada [Turrecremata], Juan de, *Summa de ecclesia*, Venice (1561)

Tudeschi, Nicholas de [Panormitanus], *Super primo-quinto decretalium*, 4 vols., Lyons (1534)

Vincke, J. (ed.), 'Acta concilii Pisani', *Römische Quartalschrift* 46 (1938), pp. 81–331

Zabarella, Francesco, 'Tractatus de schismate', in S. Schardius, *De jurisdictione, auctoritate et praeeminentia imperii ac potestate ecclesiastica*, Basle (1566), pp. 688–711

Secondary works

Bäumer, R. (1971), *Nachwirkungen des Konziliaren Gedankens in der Theologie und Kanonistik des frühen 16. Jahrhunderts*, Münster

Black, A. (1970), *Monarchy and community. Political ideas in the later conciliar controversy, 1430–1450*, Cambridge

Black, A. (1979), *Council and commune. The conciliar movement and the fifteenth-century heritage*, London

Brandmüller, W. (1968), *Das Konzil von Pavia–Siena, 1423–1424*, 2 vols., Münster

Brosse, O. de la (1965), *Le pape et le concile. La comparaison de leurs pouvoirs à la veille de la Réforme*, Paris

Cameron, J.K. (1952), 'Conciliarism in theory and practice, from the outbreak of the Schism till the end of the Council of Constance', dissertation, University of Hartford, Conn.

Delaruelle, E. *et al.* (eds.) (1962–4), *L'église au temps du grand schisme et de la crise conciliaire (1378–1449)*, 2 vols., Paris

Franzen, A. and Müller, W. (eds.) (1964), *Das Konzil von Konstanz. Beiträge zu seiner Geschichte und Theologie*, Freiburg

Gill, J. (1959), *The Council of Florence*, Cambridge

Haller, J. (1903), *Papstum und Kirchenreform*, I, Berlin

Hefele, C.J. and Hergenröther, J. (1912–17), *Histoire des conciles*, vols. V–VIII, Paris

Helmrath, J. (1987), *Das Basler Konzil. Forschungsstand und Probleme*, Cologne and Vienna

Inalcik, H. (1973), *The Ottoman Empire. The classical age, 1300–1600*, London

Izbicki, T. (1981), *Protector of the faith. Cardinal Johannes Turrecremata and the defense of the institutional Church*, Baltimore, Md.

Jedin, H. (1957), *A history of the Council of Trent*, I: *The struggle for the Council*, London

Landi, A. (1985), *Il papa deposto (Pisa 1409). L'idea conciliare nel grande scisma*, Turin

Martin, V. (1939), *Les origines du gallicanisme*, II, Paris

Oakley, F. (1962), 'On the road from Constance to 1688', *Journal of British Studies* 1: 1–32

Oakley, F. (1964a), *The political thought of Pierre d'Ailly. The voluntarist tradition*, London and New Haven, Conn.

Oakley, F. (1964b), 'Almain and Major: conciliar theory on the eve of the Reformation', *AHR* 70: 673–90

Pascoe, L.B. (1973), *Jean Gerson. Principles of Church reform*, Leiden

Pérouse, G. (1905), *Le Cardinal Aleman, président du concile de Bâle, et la fin du grand schisme*, Paris

Sieben, H.J. (1983), *Traktate und Theorien zum Konzil vom Beginn des grossen Schismas bis zum Vorabend der Reformation 1378–1521*, Frankfurter Theologische Studien, 30, Frankfurt

Sigmund, P. (1963), *Nicholas of Cusa and medieval political thought*, Cambridge, Mass.

Southern, R.W. (1962), *Western views of Islam in the Middle Ages*, Cambridge, Mass.

Stieber, J.W. (1978), *Pope Eugenius IV, the Council of Basle, and the secular and ecclesiastical authorities in the Empire. The conflict over supreme authority and power in the Church*, Leiden

Tierney, B. (1955), *Foundations of the conciliar theory. The contribution of the medieval canonists from Gratian to the Great Schism*, Cambridge

Valois, N. (1909), *Le pape et le concile 1378–1450. La crise religieuse du XVe siècle*, 2 vols., Paris

Werminghoff, A. (1910), *Nationalkirchliche Bestrebungen im deutschen Mittelalter*, Kirchenrechtliche Abhandlungen, 61, Stuttgart

4 THE EUROPEAN NOBILITY

Primary sources

Charny, Geoffroi de, *Le livre de chevalerie*, in *Œuvres de Froissart*, ed. Kervyn de Lettenhove, *Chroniques*, I: *Introduction, IIe et IIIe parties*, Brussels (1873), pp. 463–533

Commynes, Philippe de, *Mémoires*, ed. J. Calmette and G. Durville, 3 vols., Paris (1924–5)

Lull, Ramon, *Llibre de l'orde de cavvaleria*, Barcelona (1980)

Lull, Ramon, *The buke of the order of knyghthood, translated from the French by Sir Gilbert Hay*, ed. B. Botfield, Edinburgh (1847)

Lull, Ramon, *The book of the ordre of chyualry, translated and printed by William Caxton from a French version of Ramón Lull's 'Le libre del orde de cauayleria'*, ed. A.T.P. Byles, EETS, original series, 168, London (1926)

Machiavelli, Niccolò, *The chief works and others*, trans. A. Gilbert, I, Durham, N.C. (1965)

Pisan, Christine de, *L'art de chevalerie selon Végèce*, Antoine Verard, Paris (1488)

Pisan, Christine de, *The book of fayttes of armes and of chyualrye, translated and printed by William Caxton*, ed. A.T.P. Byles, EETS, original series, 189, London (1932)

Pisan, Christine de, *Le livre du corps de policie*, ed. R.H. Lucas, Geneva (1967)

Vanderjagt, A., *'Qui sa vertu anoblist'. The concepts of 'noblesse' and 'chose publicque' in Burgundian political thought*, Groningen (1981) (this includes fifteenth-century French translations of Giovanni Aurispa, Buonaccorso da Montemagno and Diego de Valera)

Secondary works

Adelige Sachkultur des Spätmittelalters. Internationaler Kongress Krems an der Donau 22. bis 25. September 1980 (1982), Veröffentlichungen des Instituts für mittelalterliche Realienkunde Österreichs, 5, Österreichische Akademie der Wissenschaften. Philosophisch-Historische Klasse, Sitzungsberichte, 400. Band, Vienna

Andermann, K. (1982), *Studien zur Geschichte des pfälzischen Niederadels im späten Mittelalter. Ein vergleichen Untersuchung an ausgewählte Beispielen*, Speyer

Armstrong, C.A.J. (1983), 'Had the Burgundian government a policy for the nobility?', in C.A.J. Armstrong, *England, France and Burgundy in the fifteenth century*, London, pp. 213–36

Autrand, F. (1979), 'L'image de la noblesse en France à la fin du moyen âge. Tradition et nouveauté', *Comptes rendus de l'Académie des inscriptions et belles-lettres*: 340–54

Autrand, F. (1990), 'Noblesse ancienne et nouvelle noblesse dans le service de l'état en France. Les tensions du début du XIVᵉ siècle', in *Gerarchie economiche e gerarchie sociali, secc. XIII–XVIII. Atti della dodicesima settimana di studi, Prato, 1980*, Florence, pp. 611–32

Bak, J.M. (1973), *Königtum und Stände in Ungarn im 14.–16. Jahrhundert*, Wiesbaden

Bardach, J. (1965), 'Gouvernants et gouvernés en Pologne au moyen âge et aux temps modernes', *Anciens pays et assemblées d'états* 36: 255–8

Baum, H.-P. (1986), 'Soziale Schichtung im Mainfränkischen Niederadel um 1400', *Zeitschrift für historische Forschung* 13: 129–48

Beceiro Pita, I. (1990), *Parentes, poder y mentalidad. La nobleza castellana (XIIᵒ–XVᵒ)*, Madrid

Beceiro Pita, I. (1991), 'Doléances et ligues de la noblesse dans la Castille de la fin du moyen âge (1420–1464)', in A. Rucquoi (ed.), *Genèse médiévale de l'Espagne moderne. Du refus à la révolte: les résistances*, Nice, pp. 107–26

Bonis, G. (1965), 'The Hungarian feudal diet (13th–18th centuries)', *Anciens pays et assemblées d'états*, 36: 287–307

Boulton, A.J.D. (1987), *The knights of the crown. The monarchical orders of knighthood in later medieval Europe, 1325–1520*, Woodbridge

Bresc, H. (1986), *Un monde méditerranéen. Economie et société en Sicile, 1300–1450*, 2 vols., Rome

Burleigh, M. (1984), *Prussian society and the Germanic Order. An aristocratic corporation in crisis, c. 1410–1466*, Cambridge

Bush, M.L. (1983–8), *The European nobility*, I: *Noble privilege*; II: *Rich nobles and poor nobles*, Manchester

Caron, M.-T. (1987), *La noblesse dans le duché de Bourgogne, 1315–1477*, Lille

Caron, M.-T. (1994), *Noblesse et pouvoir royal en France, XIII*–*XVI*ᵉ *siècle*, Paris.

Carpenter, C. (1980), 'The Beauchamp affinity. A study of bastard feudalism at work', *EHR* 95: 514–32

I ceti dirigenti nella Toscana del Quattrocento (1987), Impruneta

Charbonnier, P. (1980), *Une autre France. La seigneurie rurale en Basse-Auvergne du XIV*ᵉ *au XVI*ᵉ *siècle*, 2 vols., Clermont-Ferrand

Chittolini, G. (1979a), *La formazione dello stato regionale e le istituzioni del contado, secc. XIV e XV*, Turin

Chittolini, G. (ed.) (1979b), *La crisi degli ordinamenti comunali e le origini dello stato del Rinascimento*, Bologna

Contamine, P. (1981), *La France aux XIV*ᵉ *et XV*ᵉ *siècles. Hommes, mentalités, guerre et paix*, London

Contamine, P. (1984), 'La noblesse et les villes dans la France de la fin du moyen âge', *Bullettino dell'Istituto storico italiano per il medioevo e archivio muratoriano (Roma)* 91: 467–89

Contamine, P. (ed.) (1976), *La noblesse au moyen âge, XI*ᵉ–*XV*ᵉ *siècles. Essais à la mémoire de Robert Boutruche*, Paris

Contamine, P. (ed.) (1989), *L'état et les aristocraties, France, Angleterre, Ecosse, XII*ᵉ–*XVIIe siècle*, Paris

Contamine, P. (1997), *La noblesse au royaume de France de Philippe le Bel à Louis XII. Essai de synthèse*, Paris

Donati, C. (1988), *L'idea di nobiltà in Italia, sec. XIV–XVIII*, Rome and Bari

Dravasa, E. (1965), '*Vivre noblement*'. *Recherches sur la dérogeance de noblesse du XIV*ᵉ *au XVI*ᵉ *siècle*, Bordeaux

Dubois, H. (1981), 'Richesse et noblesse d'Odot Molain', *Mémoires de la Société pour l'histoire du droit et des institutions des anciens pays bourguignons, comtois et romands* 38: 143–58

Duncan, A.A.M. (1966), 'The early parliaments of Scotland', *SHR* 45: 36–58

Eberhard, W. (1991), 'The political system and the intellectual traditions of the Bohemian Ständestaat from the thirteenth to the sixteenth century', in R.J.H. Evans and T.V. Thomas (eds.), *Crown, Church and estates. Central European politics in the sixteenth and seventeenth centuries*, London, pp. 23–47

Favreau, R. (1960), 'La preuve de noblesse en Poitou au XVᵉ siècle', *Bulletin de la Société des antiquaires de l'ouest et des musées de Poitiers*. 618–22

Fédou, R. (1964), *Les hommes de loi lyonnais à la fin du moyen âge. Etude sur les origines de la classe de robe*, Lyons

Fédou, R. (1980), 'La noblesse en France à la fin du moyen âge (du milieu du XIVᵉ à la fin du XVᵉ siècle)', *Acta Universitatis Lodzensis* 71: 49–66

Ferraro, J.M. (1984), 'Proprietà terriera e potere nello stato veneto: la nobiltà bresciana del '400–'500', in G. Cracco and M. Knapton (eds.), *Dentro lo 'Stado italico'. Venezia e la Terraferma fra Quattro e Seicento*, Trent, pp. 159–82

Firpo, A.R. (1981), 'L'idéologie du lignage et les images de la famille dans les "Memorias" de Leonor Lopez de Cordoba (1400)', *MA* 87: 243–62

Fleckenstein, J. (ed.) (1985), *Das ritterliche Turnier im Mittelalter. Beiträge zu einer vergleichenden Formen- und Verhaltensgeschichte des Rittertums*, Göttingen

Folz, R. (1962–3), 'Les assemblées d'états dans les principautés allemandes (fin XIIIᵉ–début XVIᵉ siècles)', *Schweizer Beiträge zur allgemeine Geschichte* 20: 167–87

Fouquet, G. (1987), *Das Speyerer Domkapitel im späten Mittelalter (ca. 1350–1450). Adelige Freundschaft, fürstliche Patronage und päpstliche Klientel*, 2 vols., Mainz

Fügedi, E. (1986a), *Castles and society in medieval Hungary, 1000–1437*, Budapest

Fügedi, E. (1986b). *Kings, bishops, nobles and burghers in medieval Hungary*, London

Gasiorowski, A. (ed.) (1984), *The Polish nobility in the Middle Ages. Anthologies*, Wrocław, Warsaw, Danzig and Lodz

Gerbet, M.-C. (1977–9), 'La population noble dans le royaume de Castille vers 1500: la répartition géographique de ses différentes composantes', *Anales de historia antigua y medieval*: 78–99

Gerbet, M.-C. (1979), *La noblesse dans le royaume de Castille. Etude sur les structures sociales en Estrémadure de 1454 à 1516*, Paris

Gerbet, M.-C. (1994), *Les noblesses espagnoles au moyen âge, XIᵉ–XVᵉ siècle*, Paris

Giordanengo, G. (1970), 'Les roturiers possesseurs de fiefs nobles en Dauphiné aux XIVᵉ et XVᵉ siècles', *Cahiers d'histoire* 15: 319–34

Görner, R. (1987), *Raubritter. Untersuchungen zur Lage des spätmittelalterlichen Niederadels, besonders im südlichen Westfalen*, Münster

Gorsky, K. (1968), 'Les débuts de la représentation de la *communitas nobilium* dans les assemblées d'états de l'est européen', *Anciens pays et assemblées d'états* 47: 37–63

Griffiths, R.A. and Sherborne, J.W. (eds.) (1986), *Kings and nobles in the later Middle Ages. A tribute to Charles Ross*, New York

Harsgor, M. (1975), 'L'essor des bâtards nobles au XVᵉ siècle', *RH* 253: 319–54

Highfield, J.R.L. (1965), 'The Catholic kings and the titled nobility of Castile', in J.R. Hale, J.R.L. Highfield and B. Smalley (eds.), *Europe in the late Middle Ages*, London, pp. 358–85

Hohendahl, P. and Lotzeler, P.-M. (eds.) (1979), *Legitimationskrisen des deutschen Adels 1200–1900*, Stuttgart

Homem, A.L. de C. (1990), *Portugal nos finais da idade media. Estado, instituiçoès, sociedade politica*, Lisbon

Jones, M. (1981), 'The Breton nobility and their masters from the Civil War of 1341–64 to the late fifteenth century', in J.R.L. Highfield and R. Jeffs (eds.), *The crown and local communities in England and France in the fifteenth century*, Gloucester, pp. 51–71

Jones, M. (ed.) (1986), *Gentry and lesser nobility in late medieval Europe*, Gloucester and New York

Jones, P. (1978), 'Economia e società nell'Italia medievale: la leggenda della borghesia', in *Storia d'Italia Einaudi, annali*, I: *Dal feudalesimo al capitalismo*, Turin, pp. 187–372

Keen, M.H. (1985), *Some late medieval views on nobility*, The Creighton Lecture, London

Keen, M.H. (1990), *English society in the later Middle Ages, 1348–1500*, London

Klassen, J.M. (1978), *The nobility and the making of the Hussite revolution*, New York

Köhn, R. (1985), 'Die Einkommensquellen des Adels im ausgehenden Mittelalter, illustriert an südwestdeutschen Beispielen', *Schriften des Vereins für Geschichte des Bodensee* 103: 33–61

Ladewig Petersen, E. (1974), 'Monarchy and nobility in Norway in the period around 1500', *Mediaeval Scandinavia*, 7: 126–55

Lewis, P.S. (1968), *Later medieval France. The polity*, London and New York

Litwin, H. (1986), 'The Polish magnates, 1454–1648. The shaping of an estate', *Acta Poloniae historica* 53: 63–92

Lönnroth, E. (1958), 'Representative assemblies of mediaeval Sweden', *Etudes présentées à la Commission internationale pour l'histoire des assemblées d'états* 18: 123–31

Lorcin, M.-T. (1981), 'Veuve noble et veuve paysanne en Lyonnais d'après les testaments des XIVe et XVe siècles', *Annales de démographie historique*: 273–87

Luzzati, M. (1977), 'Familles nobles et familles marchandes à Pise et en Toscane dans le bas moyen âge', in G. Duby and J. Le Goff (eds.), *Famille et parenté dans l'Occident médiéval*, Rome, pp. 275–96

McFarlane, K.B. (1973), *The nobility of later medieval England*, Oxford

Marongiu, A. (1962), *Il parlamento in Italia nel medio evo e nell'età moderna*, Milan

Marongiu, A. (1968), *Medieval parliaments. A comparative study*, London

Mertes, K. (1988), *The English noble household, 1250–1600*, Oxford

Mitre Fernandez, M. (1968), *Evolucion de la nobleza en Castilla bajo Enrique III (1396–1406)*, Valladolid

Morgan, D.A.L. (1986), 'The individual style of the English gentleman', in Jones (1986), pp. 15–35

Mornet, E. (1983), 'Le voyage d'études des jeunes nobles danois du XIVe siècle à la Réforme', *Journal des savants*: 298–318

Mornet, E. (1988), 'Age et pouvoir dans la noblesse danoise (vers 1360–vers 1570)', *Journal des savants*: 119–54

Morsel, J. (1988), 'Crise? Quelle crise? Remarques à propos de la prétendue crise de la noblesse allemande à la fin du moyen age', *Sources* 14: 17–42

Moxo, S. de (1969), 'De la nobleza vieja a la nobleza nueva. La transformacion nobiliaria castellana en la baja Edad Media', *Cuadernos de historia* 3: 1–210

La noblesse de l'Europe méridionale du moyen âge: accès et renouvellement. Actes du colloque Paris, 14–15 janvier 1988 (1989), Arquivos do Centro Cultural Português, XXVI, Fondation Calouste Gulbenkian, Lisbon and Paris

Nortier, M. (1960), 'Maintenues de noblesse de 1473 à 1528', *Cahiers Léopold Delisle* 9: 5–27

Oexle, G.O. and Paravicini, W. (eds.), *Nobilitas, Funktion und Repräsentation des Adels in Alteuropa*, Göttingen

Orme, N. (1984), *From childhood to chivalry. The education of the English kings and aristocracy 1066–1530*, London and New York

Paravicini, W. (1975), *Guy de Brimeu. Der burgundische Staat und seine adlige Führungsschicht unter Karl dem Kühnen*, Bonn

Paravicini, W. (1977), 'Soziale Schichtung und soziale Mobilität am Hof der Herzöge von Burgund', *Francia* 5: 127–82

Paravicini, W. (1980), 'Expansion et intégration. La noblesse des Pays-Bas à la cour de Philippe le Bon', *Bijdragen en mededelingen betreffende de geschiedenis der Nederlanden* 95: 298–314

Paravicini, W. (1989–95), *Die Preussenreisen des europäischen Adels*, I and II, Sigmaringen

Pascoe, L.B. (1976), 'Nobility and ecclesiastical office in fifteenth-century Lyons', *Mediaeval Studies* 38: 313–31

Payling, S. (1991), *Political society in Lancastrian England. The greater gentry of Nottinghamshire*, Oxford

Perroy, E. (1962), 'Social mobility among the French *noblesse* in the later Middle Ages', *P&P* 21: 25–38

Perroy, E. (1976), *Les familles nobles du Forez au XIIIe siècle, essai de filiation*, 2 vols., Saint-Etienne and Montbrison

Peyvel, P. (1980–1), 'Le budget d'une famille noble à l'aube du XVe siècle: l'exemple des Rochefort en Forez', *Cahiers d'histoire* 25: 19–72

Polivka, N. (1985), 'The Bohemian lesser nobility at the turn of the 14th and 15th century (on the status of the lesser nobility in Bohemian society on the eve of the Hussite revolution)', *Historia* 25: 121–75

Press, V. (1980), 'Führungsgruppen in der deutschen Gesellschaft im Übergang zur Neuzeit um 1500', in H.H. Hoffmann and G. Franz (eds.), *Deutsche Führungsschichte in der Neuzeit. Eine Zwischenbilanz*, Boppard, pp. 29–77

Pugh, T.B. (1972), 'The magnates, knights and gentry', in S.B. Chrimes, C.D. Ross and R.A. Griffiths (eds.), *Fifteenth-century England 1399–1509. Studies in politics and society*, Manchester, pp. 86–128

Quintanilla, M.C. (1990a), 'Les confédérations de nobles et les *bandos* dans le royaume de Castille au bas moyen âge', *JMedH* 16: 165–79

Quintanilla, M.C. (1990b), 'Historiografia de un elite de poder: la nobleza castellana bajomedievale', *Hispania* 175: 719–36

Quintanilla Raso, M.R. (1982), 'Estructuras sociales y familiares y papel politico de la nobleza cordobesa (siglos XIV y XV)', in *En la Espagña medieval*, III: *Estudios en memoria del Professor D. Salvador de Moxo*, Madrid, pp. 331–52

Rapp, F. (1989), *Les origines médiévales de l'Allemagne moderne. De Charles IV à Charles Quint (1346–1519)*, Paris

Richard, J. (1960), 'Erection en dignité de terres bourguignonnes (XIVe et XVe siècles)', *Mémoires de la Société pour l'histoire du droit et des institutions des anciens pays bourguignons, comtois et romands*: 25–41

Rösener, W. (1982), 'Zur Problematik des spätmittelalterliche Raubrittertums', in H. Maurer and H. Patze (eds.), *Festschrift für Berent Schwineköper zu seinem siebzigsten Geburtstag*, Sigmaringen, pp. 469–88

Rosenthal, J.T. (1976), *Nobles and noble life 1295–1500*, London and New York

Rosenthal, J.T. (1984), 'Aristocratic marriage and the English peerage, 1350–1500: social institution and personal bond', *JMedH* 10: 181–94

Rosenthal, J.T. (1987), 'Other victims: peeresses as war widows, 1450–1500', *History* 72: 213–30

Rössler, H. (ed.) (1965), *Deutsches Adel, 1430–1555*, Darmstadt

Rucquoi, A. (1984), 'Noblesse urbaine en Castille (XIIIe–XVe siècle)', in *Les pays de la Méditerranée occidentale au moyen âge. Actes du CVI^e congrès national des Sociétés Savantes, Perpignan, 1981. Philologie et histoire jusqu'à 1610*, Paris, pp. 35–47

Rucquoi, A. (1990), 'Genèse médiévale de l'Europe moderne: du pouvoir et de la nation (1250–1516)', in *Genèse de l'état moderne, bilans et perspectives*, Paris, pp. 17–32

Russell Major, J. (1987), '"Bastard feudalism" and the kiss: changing social mores in late medieval and early modern France', *Journal of Interdisciplinary History* 17: 509–35

Russocki, S. (1979), 'Structures politiques dans l'Europe des Jagellon', *Acta Poloniae historica* 39: 101–42

Ryder, A. (1976), *The kingdom of Naples under Alfonso the Magnanimous. The making of a modern state*, Oxford

Sander, J. (1985), 'Der Adel am Hof König Ruprechts (1400–1410)', *Jahrbuch für west-deutsche Landesgeschichte* 11: 97–120

Seibt, F. (1966), 'Die Zeit der Luxemburger und der hussitischen Revolution, 1306 bis 1471', in K. Bosl (ed.), *Handbuch der Geschichte der böhmischen Länder*, 1, pt 2, Stuttgart, pp. 349–568

Stringer, K.J. (ed.) (1985), *Essays on the nobility of medieval Scotland*, Edinburgh

Trautz, F. (1977), 'Noblesse allemande et noblesse anglaise. Quelques points de comparaison', in G. Duby and J. Le Goff (eds.), *Famille et parenté dans l'occident médiéval*, Rome, pp. 63–81

Valdivieso, I. del Val (1982), 'Reaccion de la nobleza vizcaina ante la crisis bajomedieval', in *En la España medieval*, III: *Estudios en memoria del Profesor D. Salvador de Moxo*, Madrid, pp. 695–704

Vale, M.G.A. (1976), *Piety, charity and literacy among the Yorkist gentry, 1370–1480*, York

Vale, M.G.A. (1981), *War and chivalry. Warfare and aristocratic culture in England, France and Burgundy*, London

Ventura, A. (1964), *Nobiltà e popolo nella società veneta del '400 e '500*, Bari

Wagner, A.R. (1956), *Heralds and heraldry in the Middle Ages. An inquiry into the growth of the armorial function of the heralds*, Oxford

Wagner, A.R. (1967), *Heralds of England. A history of the office and College of Arms*, London

Willard, C.W. (1967), 'The concept of true nobility at the Burgundian court', *Studies in the Renaissance* 14: 33–48

Wood, J.B. (1980), *The nobility of the election of Bayeux, 1463–1666. Continuity through change*, Princeton

Wright, S.M. (1983), *The Derbyshire gentry in the fifteenth century*, Derbyshire Record Society, 8, Chesterfield

5 RURAL EUROPE

Secondary works

Abel, W. (1955), *Die Wüstungen des ausgehenden Mittelalters*, 2nd edn, Stuttgart

Abel, W. (1980), *Agricultural fluctuations in Europe. From the thirteenth to the twentieth centuries*, London (originally published as *Agrarkrisen und Agrarkonjunktur*, 3rd edn, Hamburg (1978)).

L'approvisionnement des villes de l'Europe occidentale au moyen âge et aux temps modernes (1985), Centre Culturel de l'Abbaye de Flaran, 5e Journées d'Histoire, Auch

Astill, G.G. and Grant, A. (eds.) (1988), *The countryside of medieval England*, Oxford

Aston, T.H. and Philpin, C.H.E. (eds.) (1985), *The Brenner debate*, Cambridge

Aymard, M. and Bresc, H. (1975), 'Nourritures et consommation en Sicile entre XIVe et XVIIIe siècle', *Annales ESC* 30: 592–9

Bailey, M. (1989), *A marginal economy? East Anglian Breckland in the later Middle Ages*, Cambridge

Baratier, E. (1961), *La démographie provençale du XIIIe au XVIe siècle*, Paris

Beresford, M.W. and Hurst, J.G. (1971), *Deserted medieval villages*, London

Biraben, J.-N. (1975), *Les hommes et la peste en France et dans les pays européens et méditerranéens*, Paris

Blanchard, I. (1986), 'The continental European cattle trade, 1400–1600', *EconHR* 2nd series 39: 427–60

Blickle, P. (1975), 'The economic, social and political background of the 12 articles of the Swabian peasants of 1525', *Journal of Peasant Studies* 3: 63–75

Blockmans, W.P. (1980), 'The social and economic effects of the plague in the Low Countries', *Revue belge de philologie et d'histoire* 58: 833–63

Blum, J. (1957), 'The rise of serfdom in eastern Europe', *AHR* 62: 807–36

Bois, G. (1984), *The crisis of feudalism. Economy and society in eastern Normandy, c. 1300–1550*, Cambridge (originally published as *Crise du féodalisme*, Paris (1976))

Boutruche, R. (1947), *La crise d'une société. Seigneurs et paysans du Bordelais pendant la Guerre de Cent Ans*, Paris

Brown, J.C. (1982), *In the shadow of Florence. Provincial society in Renaissance Pescia*, Oxford

Campbell, B.M.S. and Overton, M. (eds.) (1991), *Land, labour and livestock: historical studies in European agricultural productivity*, Manchester

Les communautés villageoises en Europe occidentale du moyen âge aux temps modernes (1984), Centre Culturel de l'Abbaye de Flaran, 4e Journées d'Histoire, Auch

D'Archimbaud, G.D. (1980), *Les fouilles de Rougiers. Contribution à l'archéologie de l'habitat rural médiéval en pays méditerranéen*, Paris

Day, J. (1975), 'Malthus démenti? Sous-peuplement chronique et calamités démographiques en Sardaigne au bas moyen-âge', *Annales ESC* 30: 684–702

De Vries, J. (1974), *The Dutch rural economy in the Golden Age, 1500–1700*, London

Derville, A. (1987), 'Dîmes, rendements du blé et révolution agricole dans le nord de la France au moyen âge', *Annales ESC* 42: 1411–32

Dufourcq, Ch.E and Gautier-Dalché, J. (1976), *Histoire économique et sociale de l'Espagne chrétienne au moyen âge*, Paris

Dupâquier, J. (ed.) (1988), *Histoire de la population française*, I, Paris

Dyer, C. (1989), *Standards of living in the later Middle Ages. Social change in England c. 1200–1520*, Cambridge

Epstein, S.R. (1991), 'Cities, regions and the late medieval crisis: Sicily and Tuscany compared', *P&P* 130: 3–50

Epstein, S.R. (1992), *An island for itself. Economic development and social change in late medieval Sicily*, Cambridge

Fourquin, G. (1964), *Les campagnes de la région Parisienne à la fin du moyen âge*, Paris

Freedman, P. (1991), *The origins of peasant servitude in medieval Catalonia*, Cambridge

Genicot, L. (1966), 'Crisis: from the Middle Ages to modern times', in M.M. Postan (ed.), *The Cambridge economic history of Europe*, I, 2nd edn, Cambridge, pp. 660–741

Genicot, L. (1990), *Rural communities in the medieval west*, Baltimore

Gissel, S. *et al.* (1981), *Desertion and land colonization in the Nordic countries, c. 1300–1600*, Stockholm

Glick, T.F. (1970), *Irrigation and society in medieval Valencia*, Cambridge, Mass.

Harvey, P.D.A. (1984), *The peasant land market in medieval England*, Oxford

Hatcher, J. (1977), *Plague, population and the English economy, 1348–1530*, London

Heers, J. (1990), *L'occident aux XIVe et XVe siècles*, 5th edn, Paris

Herlihy, D. (1965), 'Population, plague and social change in rural Pistoia, 1201–1430', *EconHR* 2nd series 18: 225–44

Herlihy, D. (1967), *Medieval and Renaissance Pistoia*, New Haven and London

Herlihy, D. and Klapisch-Zuber, C. (1978), *Les Toscans et leur familles*, Paris; trans. as *Tuscans and their families*, London (1985)

Hilton, R.H. (1973), *Bondmen made free*, London

Hilton, R.H. (1975), *The English peasantry in the later Middle Ages*, Oxford

Hoffman, R.C. (1989), *Land, liberties and lordship in a later medieval countryside. Agrarian structures and change in the duchy of Wrocław*, Philadelphia

Hoppenbrouwers, P.C.M. (1992), 'Een Middeleeuwse Samenleving. Het Land van Heusden (ca. 1360–ca. 1515)', *Afdeling Agrarische Geschiedenis Landbouwhogeschool, Bijdragen* 32: 1–997

Jones, P.J. (1968), 'From manor to Mezzaddria: a Tuscan case study in the medieval origins of modern agrarian society', in N. Rubinstein (ed.), *Florentine studies*, London, pp. 193–241

Klapisch, C. and Demonet, M. (1972), '"A uno pane e uno vino". La famille rurale Toscane au début du XVe siècle', *Annales ESC* 27: 873–901

Lamb, H.H. (1977), *Climate, present, past and future*, II: *Climatic history and the future*, London

Langdon, J.L. (1986), *Horses, oxen, and technological innovation*, Cambridge

Lartigaut, J. (1978), *Les campagnes du Quercy après la Guerre de Cent Ans (vers 1440–vers 1500)*, Toulouse

Laube, A. (1975), 'Precursors of the peasant war: "Bundschuh" and "Armer Konrad" – popular movements on the eve of the Reformation', *Journal of Peasant Studies* 3: 49–53

Le Roy Ladurie, E. (1969), *Les paysans de Languedoc*, Paris

Le Roy Ladurie, E. (1972), *Times of feast, times of famine*, London

Le Roy Ladurie, E. (1974), 'L'histoire immobile', *Annales ESC* 29: 673–92

Le Roy Ladurie, E. (1978), 'En haute Normandie: Malthus ou Marx', *Annales ESC* 33: 115–24

Leguai, A. (1982), 'Les révoltes rurales dans le royaume de France, du milieu du XIVe siècle à la fin du XVe', *MA* 88: 49–76

Lewis, P.S. (1971), *The recovery of France in the fifteenth century*, London

Lorcin, M.-T. (1974), *Les campagnes de la région Lyonnaise aux XIVe et XVe siècles*, Lyons

Mackay, A. (1972), 'Popular movements and pogroms in fifteenth-century Castile', *P&P* 55: 33–67

Mayhew, A. (1973), *Rural settlement and farming in Germany*, London

Mazzi, M.S. and Raveggi, S. (1983), *Gli uomini e le cose nelle campagne fiorentine del quattrocento*, Florence

Menjot, D. (1984), 'Notes sur le marché de l'alimentation et la consommation alimentaire à Murcie à la fin du moyen âge', in D. Menjot (ed.), *Manger et boire au moyen âge*, Nice, I, 199–210

Miller, E. (1991), *Agrarian history of England and Wales*, III: *1350–1500*, Cambridge

Mollat, M. (1986), *The poor in the Middle Ages*, New Haven

Neveux, H. (1975), 'Déclin et reprise: la fluctuation biséculaire', in G. Duby and A. Wallon (eds.), *Histoire de la France rurale*, Paris, II, pp. 15–173

Neveux, H. (1980), *Vie et déclin d'une structure économique*, Paris

Orrman, E. (1981), 'The progress of settlement in Finland during the late Middle Ages', *Scandinavian Economic History Review* 29: 129–43

Poos, L.R. (1991), *A rural society after the Black Death. Essex 1350–1525*, Cambridge

Postan, M.M. (1952), 'The trade of medieval Europe: the north', in M. Postan and E.E. Rich (eds.), *The Cambridge economic history of Europe*, II, Cambridge, pp. 119–256

Postan, M.M. (1966), 'Medieval agrarian society in its prime. England', in M.M. Postan (ed.), *The Cambridge economic history of Europe*, I, 2nd edn, Cambridge, pp. 548–632

Rösener, W. (1992), *Peasants in the Middle Ages*, Oxford (originally published as *Bauern im Mittelalter*, Munich (1985))

Scott, T. (1986), *Freiburg and the Breisgau*, Oxford

Scribner, R. and Benecke, G. (1979), *The German peasant war of 1525 – new viewpoints*, London

Sivery, G. (1990), *Terroirs et communautés rurales dans l'Europe occidentale au moyen âge*, Lille

Smith, R. (1988), 'Human resources', in Astill and Grant (1988), pp. 188–212

Stouff, L. (1970), *Ravitaillement et alimentation en Provence aux XIVe et XVe siècles*, Paris

Tits-Dieuaide, M.-J. (1975), *La formation des prix céréaliers en Brabant et en Flandre au XVe siècle*, Brussels

Toch, M. (1991), 'Ethics, emotion and self-interest: rural Bavaria in the later Middle Ages', *JMedH* 17: 135–47

Van der Wee, H. (1963), 'Typologie des crises et changements de structure aux Pays-Bas (XVe–XVIe siècles)', *Annales ESC* 18: 209–25

Van der Wee, H. and Van Cauwenberghe, E. (eds.) (1978), *Productivity of land and agricultural innovation in the Low Countries (1250–1800)*, Louvain

Verhulst, A. (1990), *Précis d'histoire rurale de la Belgique*, Brussels

Vicens Vives, J. (1964), *An economic history of Spain*, Princeton

Villages désertés et histoire économique, XIe–XVIIIe siècle (1965), Paris

Wettinger, G. (1982), 'Agriculture in Malta in the later Middle Ages', in M. Buhagier (ed.), *Proceedings of history week, 1981*, Malta, pp. 1–48

Wunder, H. (1983), 'Serfdom in later medieval and early modern Germany', in T.H. Aston, P. Coss, Christopher Dyer and Joan Thirsk (eds.), *Social relations and ideas*, Cambridge, pp. 249–72

6 URBAN EUROPE

Primary sources

Les affaires de Jacques Coeur. Journal du procureur Dauvet, ed. M. Mollat, 2 vols., Paris (1952–3)

Alberti, Leon Battista, *I primi tre libri della famiglia*, ed. F.C. Pellegrini and R. Spongano, Florence (1946)

Brant, Sebastian, *Narrenschiff*, ed. K. Goedeke, Leipzig (1872)

Bruni, Leonardo, *Historiarum florentini populi libri xii*, ed. E. Santini, Rome (1942)

Calendar of the letter-books of the city of London (A–L), ed. R.R. Sharpe, 11 vols., London (1899–1912)

The Chronicle of Novgorod, 1016–1471, trans. R. Michell and N. Forbes, with contributions by C.R. Beazley and A.A. Shakhmatov, RHS, London (1914)

Die Chroniken der deutschen Städte vom 14. bis ins 16. Jahrhundert, Historische Kommission bei der Bayerischen Akademie der Wissenschaften, Leipzig (1862–　)

Les entrées royales françaises de 1328 à 1515, ed. B. Guenée and F. Lehoux, Paris (1968)

The Great Chronicle of London, ed. A.H. Thomas and I.D. Thornley, London (1938)

Guicciardini, Francesco, *Ricordi, diari, memorie*, ed. M. Spinelli, Rome (1981)

Guida generale degli Archivi di Stato Italiani, ed. P. Carucci *et al.*, Rome (1981–　)

Hanserecesse, series I (1256–1430), ed. W. Junghans and K. Koppmann, 8 vols., Leipzig (1870–97); series II (1431–76), ed. G. von der Ropp, 7 vols., Leipzig (1876–92)

Hansiches Urkundenbuch, ed. K. Hohlbaum, K. Kunze and W. Stein, 11 vols., Halle and Leipzig (1876–1939)

Itinéraire d'Anselmo Adorno en Terre Sainte, 1470–71, ed. J. Heers and G. de Groer, Paris (1978)

Journal d'un bourgeois de Paris, 1405–1449, ed. C. Beaune, Paris (1990); English trans. J. Shirley, *A Parisian journal, 1405–1449*, Oxford (1968)

Machiavelli, Niccolò, *Florentine histories*, trans. L.F. Banfield and H.C. Mansfield, Jr, Princeton (1988)

Les miracles de Notre Dame, ed. G. Paris and U. Robert, 8 vols., Paris (1876–93)

Palmieri, Matteo, *Della vita civile*, ed. F. Battaglia, Bologna (1944)

Recueil de documents relatifs à l'industrie drapière en Flandres, ed. G. Espinas and H. Pirenne, 4 vols., Paris (1906–24)

Savonarola, Girolamo, *Œuvres spirituelles choisies*, ed. E.C. Bayonne, Paris (1980)

The travels of Leo of Rozmital, 1465–67, ed. M. Letts, Hakluyt Society, 2nd series, 108, London (1957)

Villon, François, *Poésies complètes*, ed. C. Thiry, Paris (1991)

Secondary works

General

Abulafia, D., Franklin, M. and Rubin, M. (eds.) (1992), *Church and city, 1000–1500. Essays in honour of Christopher Brooke*, Cambridge

Ashtor, E. (1989), 'The factors of technological and industrial progress in the later Middle Ages', *Journal of European Economic History* 18: 7–36

Barel, Y. (1977), *La ville médiévale. Système social, système urbain*, Grenoble

Bautier, R.-H. (1971), *The economic development of medieval Europe*, trans. H. Karolyi, London

Beresford, M. (1967), *New towns of the Middle Ages. Town plantation in England, Wales and Gascony*, London

Bertelli, S. (1978), *Il potere oligarchico nello stato-città medievale*, Florence

Black, A. (1984), *Guilds and civil society in European political thought from the twelfth century to the present*, Cambridge

Cambridge economic history of medieval Europe, The (1952, 1963), II: *Trade and industry in the Middle Ages*, ed. M.M. Postan and E.E. Rich; III: *Economic organization and policies in the Middle Ages*, ed. M.M. Postan, E.E. Rich and E. Miller, Cambridge

Chédeville, A., Le Goff, J. and Rossiaud, J. (1980), *La ville médiévale. Des Carolingiens à la Renaissance* (*Histoire de la France urbaine*, II), Paris

Cipolla, C.M. (1964), 'Economic depression of the Renaissance?', *EconHR* 2nd series 16: 519–24

Clarke, M.V. (1926), *The medieval city state. An essay on tyranny and federation in the later Middle Ages*, Cambridge

Contamine, P., Bompaire, M., Lebecq, S. and Sarrazin, J.-L. (1993), *L'économie médiévale*, Paris

Day, J. (1978), 'The great bullion famine of the fifteenth century', *P&P* 79: 3–54

Day, J. (1987), *The medieval market economy*, Oxford

Denecke, D. and Shaw, G. (eds.) (1988), *Urban historical geography. Recent progress in Britain and Germany*, Cambridge

De Roover, R. (1953), *L'évolution de la lettre de change. XIVe–XVIIIe siècles*, Paris

De Roover, R. (1974), *Business, banking and economic thought in late medieval and early modern Europe. Selected studies*, ed. J. Kirshner, Chicago and London

Eco, U. (1986), *Travels in hyperreality*, trans W. Weaver, London

Edwards, J. (1994), *The Jews in western Europe, 1400–1600*, Manchester

Ennen, E. (1979), *Die europäische Stadt des Mittelalters*, Göttingen

Epstein, S.A. (1991), *Wage labor and guilds in medieval Europe*, Chapel Hill

Epstein, S.R. (1994), 'Regional fairs, institutional innovation and economic growth in late medieval Europe', *EconHR* 2nd series 47: 459–82

Goetz, H.-W. (1986), *Leben im Mittelalter*, Munich

Gurevich, A. (1988), *Medieval popular culture. Problems of belief and perception*, Cambridge

Haase, C. (ed.) (1969–73), *Die Stadt des Mittelalters*, 3 vols., Darmstadt

Hanawalt, B.A. (ed.) (1986), *Women and work in pre-industrial Europe*, Bloomington, Ind.

Hanawalt, B.A. and Reyerson, K.L. (eds.) (1994), *City and spectacle in medieval Europe*, Minneapolis

Harte, N.B. and Ponting, K.G. (eds.) (1983), *Cloth and clothing in medieval Europe. Essays in memory of Professor E.M. Carus-Wilson*, London

Heers, J. (1966), *L'occident au XIVe et XVe siècles. Aspects économiques et sociaux*, 2nd edn, Paris

Heers, J. (1977), *Family clans in the Middle Ages. A study of political and social structures in urban areas*, Amsterdam

Heers, J. (1990), *La ville au moyen âge*, Paris

Herlihy, D. (1985), *Medieval households*, Cambridge, Mass.

Herlihy, D. (1990), *Opera muliebria. Women and work in medieval Europe*, New York

Hilton, R.H. (1992), *English and French towns in feudal society. A comparative study*, Cambridge

Hohenberg, P.M. and Lees, L.H. (1985), *The making of urban Europe, 1000–1950*, Cambridge, Mass.

Holmes, G.A. (1990), *The first age of the western city*, Inaugural Lecture, University of Oxford, 1989, Oxford

Howell, M.C. (1986), *Women, production and patriarchy in late medieval cities*, Chicago

Le Goff, J. (1980), *Time, work and culture in the Middle Ages*, trans. A. Goldhammer, Chicago

Lopez, R.S. (1952), 'Hard times and investment in culture', in K.H. Dannenfeldt (ed.), *The Renaissance: medieval or modern?*, New York, pp. 50–61

Lopez, R.S. (1986), *The shape of medieval monetary history. Collected studies*, London

Lopez, R.S. and Miskimin, H.A. (1962), 'The economic depression of the Renaissance', *EconHR* 2nd series 14: 408–26

Miskimin, H. (1975), *The economy of early Renaissance Europe, 1300–1460*, Cambridge

Miskimin, H. (1977), *The economy of late Renaissance Europe, 1460–1600*, Cambridge

Miskimin, H., Herlihy, D. and Udovitch, A.L. (eds.) (1977), *The medieval city. Essays written in honor of Robert S. Lopez*, New Haven, Conn.

Mollat, M. (1986), *The poor in the Middle Ages. An essay in social history*, New Haven, Conn.

Mols, R. (1954–6), *Introduction à la démographie historique des villes d'Europe du XIVe au XVIII siècles*, 3 vols., Gembloux and Louvain

Mols, R. (1974), 'Population in Europe, 1500–1700', in C. Cipolla (ed.), *Fontana economic history of Europe*, II: *The sixteenth and seventeenth centuries*, London

Pounds, N.J.G. (1994), *An economic history of medieval Europe*, 2nd edn, London
Rausch, W. (ed.) (1974), *Die Stadt am Ausgang des Mittelalters*, Linz
Rörig, F. (1967), *The medieval town*, trans. D. Bryant, London
Rosenthal, J.T. (ed.) (1990), *Medieval women and the sources of medieval history*, Athens, Ga.
Russell, J.C. (1972), *Medieval regions and their cities*, Newton Abbot
Saalman, H. (1968), *Medieval cities*, New York
Sprandel, R. (1969), 'La production du fer au moyen âge', *Annales ESC* 24: 305–21
Spufford, P. (1988), *Money and its use in medieval Europe*, Cambridge
Unger, R. (1980), *The ship in the medieval economy, 600–1600*, Toronto
Van der Wee, H. (ed.) (1988), *The rise and decline of urban industries in Italy and the Low Countries. Late Middle Ages – early modern times*, Louvain
Wolff, P. (1977), *Guide international d'histoire urbaine*, I: *Europe*, Commission Internationale pour l'Histoire des Villes, Paris

•

Cities and towns in Italy

Ady, C.M. (1955), *Lorenzo dei Medici and Renaissance Italy*, London
Barker, J.R. (1988), *Death in the community. Memorialization and the communities in an Italian commune in the late Middle Ages*, Atlanta
Baron, H. (1955), *The crisis of the early Italian Renaissance*, 2 vols., Princeton
Becker, M.B. (1967–8) *Florence in transition*, 2 vols., Baltimore
Bratchel, M.E. (1995), *Lucca, 1430–1494*, Oxford
Brown, J. (1989), 'Prosperity or hard times in Renaissance Italy?', *RQ* 42: 761–80
Brown, J. (ed.) (1995), *Language and images of Renaissance Italy*, Oxford
Brucker, G.A. (1969), *Renaissance Florence*, New York
Burckhardt, J. (1929), *The civilization of the Renaissance in Italy*, trans. S.G.C. Middlemore, London
Chambers, D.S. (1970), *The imperial age of Venice, 1380–1580*, London
Clarke, P.C. (1991), *The Soderini and the Medici. Power and patronage in fifteenth-century Florence*, Oxford
Cohn, S.K., Jr (1980), *The laboring classes in Renaissance Florence*, New York
Cristiani, E. (1962), *Nobiltà e popolo nel comune di Pisa*, Naples
Day, J. (1964), *Les douanes de Gênes, 1376–77*, 2 vols., Paris
Dean, T. (1987), *Land and power in late medieval Ferrara. The rule of the Este, 1350–1450*, Cambridge
Dean, T. and Wickham, C. (eds.) (1990), *City and countryside in late medieval and Renaissance Italy. Essays presented to Philip Jones*, London
De Roover, R. (1963), *The rise and decline of the Medici Bank*, Cambridge, Mass.
Epstein, S.R. (1992), *An island for itself. Economic development and social change in late medieval Sicily*, Cambridge
Epstein, S.R. (1993), 'Town and country: economy and institutions in late medieval Italy', *EconHR* 2nd series 46: 453–77
Fiumi, E. (1961), *Storia economica e sociale di San Gimignano*, Florence
Goldthwaite, R.A. (1968), *Private wealth in Renaissance Florence. A study of four families*, Princeton
Goldthwaite, R.A. (1980), *The building of Renaissance Florence. An economic and social history*, Baltimore

Goldthwaite, R.A. (1993), *Wealth and the demand for art in Italy, 1300–1600*, Baltimore

Gutkind, C.S. (1938), *Cosimo de' Medici. Pater patriae, 1389–1464*, Oxford

Hale, J.R. (1965), 'The development of the bastion, 1440–1534', in J.R. Hale, J.R.L. Highfield and B. Smalley (eds.), *Europe in the late Middle Ages*, London

Hale, J.R. (1977), *Florence and the Medici. The pattern of control*, London

Hay, D. (1966), *The Italian Renaissance in its historical background*, Cambridge

Hay, D. and Law, J. (1989), *Italy in the age of the Renaissance*, London

Heers, J. (1961), *Gênes au XVe siècle. Activité économique et problèmes sociaux*, Paris

Heers, J. (ed.) (1985), *Fortifications, portes de villes, places publiques, dans le monde méditerranéen*, Paris

Henderson, J. (1994), *Piety and charity in late medieval Florence*, Oxford

Herlihy, D. (1958), *Pisa in the early Renaissance. A study of urban growth*, New Haven, Conn.

Herlihy, D. (1967), *Medieval and Renaissance Pistoia. The social history of an Italian town*, New Haven and London

Herlihy, D. (1980), *Cities and society in medieval Italy*, London

Herlihy, D. and Klapisch-Zuber, C. (1978), *Les Toscans et leur familles. Une étude du catasto florentin de 1427*, Paris

Herlihy, D., Lopez, R.S. and Slessarev, V. (eds.) (1967), *Economy, society and government in medieval Italy. Essays in memory of Robert L. Reynolds*, Kent, Ohio

Holmes, G.A. (1969), *The Florentine Enlightenment, 1400–1500*, London

Holmes, G.A. (1973), 'The emergence of an urban Enlightenment at Florence, *c.* 1250–1450', *TRHS* 5th series 23: 111–34

Holmes, G.A. (1986), *Florence, Rome and the origins of the Renaissance*, Oxford

Holmes, G.A. (ed.) (1995), *Art and politics in Renaissance Italy*, Oxford

Hook, J. (1979), *Siena. A city and its history*, London

Ilardi, V. (1993), 'Renaissance Florence: the optical centre of the world', *Journal of European Economic History* 22: 507–41

Jones, P.J. (1965), 'Communes and despots: the city state in late medieval Italy', *TRHS* 5th series 15: 71–96

Kent, D. (1978), *The rise of the Medici faction in Florence, 1426–1434*, Oxford

Klapisch-Zuber, C. (1985), *Women, family and ritual in Renaissance Italy*, Chicago

Lane, F.C. (1934), *Venetian ships and shipbuilding of the Renaissance*, Baltimore

Lane, F.C. (1944), *Andrea Barbarigo, merchant of Venice, 1418–1449*, Baltimore

Lane, F.C. (1966), *Venice and history. Collected papers*, Baltimore

Lane, F.C. (1987), *Studies in Venetian social and economic history*, Baltimore

Lane, F.C. and Mueller, R.C. (1985), *Money and banking in medieval and Renaissance Venice*, Baltimore

Law, J.E. (1981), '"Super differentiis agitatis Venetiis inter districtuales et civitatem": Venezia, Verona e il Contado nel "1400"', *Archivio Veneto* 5th series 116: 5–32

Law, J.E. (1992), 'The Venetian mainland state in the fifteenth century', *TRHS* 6th series 2: 153–74

Luzzato, G. (1961a), *Storia economica di Venezia dall' XI al XVI secolo*, Venice

Luzzato, G. (1961b), *An economic history of Italy from the fall of the Roman Empire to the beginning of the sixteenth century*, trans. P. Jones, London

Mack, C.R. (1987), *Pienza. The creation of a Renaissance city*, Ithaca, N.Y.

Mallett, M.E. (1967), *The Florentine galleys in the fifteenth century*, Oxford

Martines, L. (1980), *Power and imagination. City states in Renaissance Italy*, London

Mazzaoui, M. (1981), *The Italian cotton industry in the later Middle Ages*, Cambridge

Mesquita, D.M.B. de (1965), 'The place of despotism in Italian politics', in J.R. Hale, J.R.L. Highfield and B. Smalley (eds.) *Europe in the late Middle Ages*, London

Molho, A. (1994), *Marriage alliance in late medieval Florence*, Cambridge, Mass.

Muir, E. (1981), *Civic ritual in Renaissance Florence*, Princeton

Mundy, J.H. (1989), 'In praise of Italy: the Italian Republics', *Speculum* 64: 815–34

Preyer, B. (1981), 'The Rucellai Palace', in *Giovanni Rucellai ed il suo zibaldone*, II: *A Florentine merchant and his palace*, London

Queller, D. (1986), *The Venetian patriciate. Reality versus myth*, Urbana and Chicago

Ramsey, P. (1982), *Rome in the Renaissance. The city and the myth*, Binghampton, N.Y.

Renouard, Y. (1949), *Les hommes d'affaires Italiens au moyen âge*, Paris

Rubinstein, N. (1966), *The government of Florence under the Medici (1434 to 1494)*, Oxford

Rubinstein, N. (1995), *The Palazzo Vecchio, 1298–1532*, Oxford

Rubinstein, N. (ed.) (1968), *Florentine studies. Politics and society in Renaissance Florence*, London

Ruggiero, G. (1980), *Violence in early Renaissance Florence*, New Brunswick

Sapori, A. (1946), *Studi di storia economica medievale*, 2nd edn, Florence

Sapori, A. (1970), *The Italian merchant in the Middle Ages*, New York

Schevill, F. (1963), *Medieval and Renaissance Florence*, 2 vols., New York

Stinger, R.L. (1985), *The Renaissance in Rome*, Bloomington, Ind.

Trexler, R.C. (1980), *Public life in Renaissance Florence*, New York

Waley, D. (1952), *Mediaeval Orvieto*, Cambridge

Waley, D. (1969), *The Italian city-republics*, London

Waley, D. (1985), *Late medieval Europe from St Louis to Luther*, 2nd edn, London

Woodward, W.H. (1897), *Vittorino da Feltre and other humanist educators*, 2nd edn, London

France and the Iberian peninsula

Baratier, E. (1967), *La démographie provençale du XIIIe au XIVe siècle*, Paris

Bois, G. (1984), *The crisis of feudalism. Economy and society in eastern Normandy*, Cambridge

Boutruche, R. (ed.) (1966), *Histoire de Bordeaux de 1453 à 1715*, Bordeaux

Carande, R. (1972), *Sevilla, fortaleza y mercado*, Seville

Carrère, C. (1967), *Barcelona, centre économique à l'époque des difficultés. 1380–1462*, 2 vols., Paris

Chevalier, B. (1975), *Tours, ville royale 1356–1520. Origine et développement d'une capitale à la fin du moyen âge*, Louvain and Paris

Chevalier, B. (1982), *Les bonnes villes de France aux XIVe et XVe siècles*, Paris

Collantes de Téran Sànchez, A. (1984), *Sevilla en la baja edad media. La ciudad y sus hombres*, 2nd edn, Seville

Constable, O.R. (1994), *Trade and traders in Muslim Spain. The commercial realignment of the Iberian peninsula, 900–1500*, Cambridge

Del Treppo, M. (1968), *I mercanti catalani e l'espansione della corona d'Aragona nel secolo XV*, Naples

Desportes, P. (1979), *Reims et les rémois aux XIIIe et XIVe siècles*, Paris

Díez, C. Estepa (ed.) (1984), *Burgos en la edad media*, Valladolid

Duby, G. (ed.) (1980), *Histoire de la France urbaine*, II: *La ville médiévale*, Paris

Edwards, J. (1982), *Christian Cordoba. The city and its region in the late Middle Ages*, Cambridge

Edwards, J. (1988), 'Religious faith and doubt in late medieval Spain: Soria *circa* 1450–1500', *P&P* 120: 3–25

Favier, J. (1973), 'La place d'affaires de Paris au XVe siècle', *Annales ESC* 28: 1245–79

Favier, J. (1974), *Paris au XVe siècle. Nouvelle histoire de Paris, 1380–1500*, Paris

Favreau, R. (1978), *La ville de Poitiers à la fin du moyen âge. Une capitale régionale*, 2 vols., Poitiers

Fournial, E. (1967), *Les villes et l'économie d'échange en Forez aux XIIIe et XIVe siècles*, Paris

Geremek, B. (1986), *Le salariat dans l'artisanat Parisien aux XIIIe–XVe siècles*, Paris

Geremek, B. (1987), *The margins of society in late medieval Paris*, trans. J. Birrell, Cambridge

Hébert, M. (1979), *Tarascon aux XIV et XV siècles. Histoire d'une communauté urbaine provençale*, Aix-en-Provence

Heers, J. (1957), 'Le royaume de Grenade et la politique marchande de Gênes en occident au XVe siècle', *MA* 63: 87–121

Hillgarth, J. (1976–8), *The Spanish kingdoms, 1250–1516*, 2 vols., Oxford

Humbert, F. (1961), *Les finances municipales de Dijon du milieu du XIVe siècle à 1477*, Paris

Mackay, A. (1981), *Money, prices and politics in fifteenth-century Castile*, London

Marques, A.H. de O. (1964), *A sociedade medieval Portuguesa*, Lisbon

Marques, A.H. de O. (1972), *A history of Portugal*, 2 vols., New York

Miskimin, H.A. (1984), *Money and power in fifteenth-century France*, New Haven

Mollat, M. (1952), *Le commerce maritime normand à la fin du moyen âge. Etude d'histoire économique et sociale*, Paris

Mollat, M. (ed.) (1979), *Histoire de Rouen*, Toulouse

O'Callaghan, J.F. (1975), *A history of medieval Spain*, Ithaca

Otis, L.L. (1985), *Prostitution in medieval society. The history of an urban institution in the Languedoc*, Chicago

Petit-Dutaillis, C. (1947), *Les communes françaises. Caractères et évolution des origines au XVIIIe siècle*, Paris

Rucquoi, A. (1987), *Valladolid en la edad media*, Valladolid

Stouff, L. (1970), *Ravitaillement et alimentation en Provence aux XIVe et XVe siècles*, Paris

Stouff, L. (1986), *Arles à la fin du moyen âge*, Aix-en-Provence

Torres Balbàs, L. (1987), 'La edad media', in L. Torres Balbàs and G. y Bellido (eds.), *Resumen histórico del urbanismo en España*, Madrid

Vicens Vives, J. (1957), *Historia social y económica de España y América*, II: *Patriciado urbano, reges católicos, descubrimento de América*, Barcelona

Vicens Vives, J. and Oller, J.N. (1969), *An economic history of Spain*, Princeton

Wolff, P. (1954), *Commerces et marchands de Toulouse (vers 1350–vers 1450)*, Paris

Wolff, P. (1978), 'Les luttes sociales dans les villes du midi Français, XIIIe–XVe siècles', in P. Wolff (ed.), *Regards sur le midi médiéval*, Paris, pp. 77–89

Wolff, P. (ed.), (1974), *Histoire de Toulouse*, Toulouse

The British Isles and the Netherlands

Barron, C.M. and Sutton, A.F. (eds.) (1994), *Medieval London widows, 1300–1500*, London

Bartlett, J.N. (1959–60), 'The expansion and decline of York in the later Middle Ages', *EconHR* 2nd series 12: 17–33

Beresford, M. and Finberg, H.P.R. (1973), *English medieval boroughs. A handlist*, Newton Abbot

Blair, J. and Ramsay, N. (eds.) (1991), *English medieval industries. Craftsmen, techniques, products*, London

Bonney, M. (1990), *Lordship and the urban community. Durham and its overlords, 1350–1540*, Cambridge

Brand, H. (1992), 'Urban policy or personal government: the involvement of the urban élite in the economy of Leiden at the end of the Middle Ages', in H. Diederiks, P. Hohenberg and M. Wagenaar (eds.), *Economic policy in Europe since the late Middle Ages. The visible hand and the fortune of cities*, Leicester, pp. 17–34

Britnell, R.H. (1986), *Growth and decline in Colchester, 1300–1525*, Cambridge

Britnell, R.H. (1993), *The commercialisation of English society 1000–1500*, Cambridge

Brulez, W. (1990), 'Brugge en Antwerpen in de 15th en 16th eeuw: een tegenstelling?', *Tijdschrift voor Geschiedenis* 73: 15–37

Butcher, A.F. (1979), 'Rent and the urban economy: Oxford and Canterbury in the later Middle Ages', *Southern History* 1: 11–43

De Roover, R. (1948), *Money, banking and credit in medieval Bruges: Italian merchant-bankers, Lombards and money-changers. A study in the history of banking*, Cambridge, Mass.

De Roover, R. (1968), *The Bruges money market around 1400*, Brussels

Dobson, R.B. (1977), 'Urban decline in late medieval England', *TRHS* 5th series 27: 1–22

Dobson, R.B. (1983), 'Cathedral chapters and cathedral cities: York, Durham and Carlisle in the fifteenth century', *Northern History* 19: 15–44

Espinas, G. (1913), *La vie urbaine de Douai*, 3 vols., Paris

Espinas, G. (1923), *La draperie dans la Flandre française au moyen âge*, 2 vols., Paris

Espinas, G. (1933), *Les origines du capitalisme*, I: *Sire Jehan Boinebroke, patricien et drapier Douaissien*, Lille

Ewan, E. (1990), *Townlife in fourteenth-century Scotland*, Edinburgh

Goldberg, P.J.P. (1986), 'Female labour, service and marriage in northern towns during the Middle Ages', *Northern History* 22: 18–38

Goldberg, P.J.P. (1992), *Women, work and life cycle in a medieval economy. Women in York and Yorkshire, c. 1300–1520*, Oxford

Graham, B.J. (1977), 'The towns of medieval Ireland', in R.A. Butlin (ed.), *The development of the Irish town*, London and Totowa

Graham, B.J. (1986–7), 'Urbanization in medieval Ireland', *Journal of Urban History* 13: 169–96

Grant, I.F. (1930), *The social and economic development of Scotland before 1603*, Edinburgh

Griffiths, R.A. (ed.) (1978) *Boroughs of medieval Wales*, Cardiff

Hanawalt, B.A. (1993), *Growing up in medieval London. The experience of childhood in history*, New York

Hill, F. (1965), *Medieval Lincoln*, Cambridge

Hilton, R.H. and Aston, T.H. (eds.) (1984), *The English rising of 1381*, Cambridge

Keene, D. (1985), *Survey of medieval Winchester*, 2 vols., Oxford

Kowaleski, M. (1988), 'The history of urban families in medieval England', *JMedH* 14: 47–63

Laurent, H. (1935), *Un grand commerce d'exploitation au moyen âge. La draperie des Pays-Bas, en France et dans les pays méditerranéens*, Paris

Lestocquoy, J. (1952), *Les villes de Flandres et d'Italie sous le gouvernement des patriciens (XIe–XVe siècles)*, Paris

Lynch, M., Spearman, M. and Stell, G. (eds.) (1988), *The Scottish medieval town*, Edinburgh

McKisack, M. (1932), *The parliamentary representation of the English boroughs during the Middle Ages*, Oxford

Marquant, R. (1940), *La vie économique à Lille sous Philippe le Bon*, Paris

Munro, J.H.A. (1972), *Wool, cloth and gold. The struggle for bullion in Anglo-Burgundian trade, 1340–1478*, Toronto

Munro, J.H.A. (1994), *Textiles, towns and trade. Essays in the economic history of late-medieval England and the Low Countries*, Toronto

Murray, J.M. (1986), 'The failure of corporation: notaries public in medieval Bruges', *JMedH* 12: 155–66

Murray, J.M. (1988), 'Family, marriage and moneychanging in medieval Bruges', *JMedH* 14: 115–25

Nicholas, D. (1985), *The domestic life of a medieval city. Women, children and the family in four-teenth-century Ghent*, Lincoln, Nebr.

Nicholas, D. (1987), *The metamorphosis of a medieval city. Ghent in the age of the Arteveldes, 1302–1390*, Lincoln, Nebr.

Nicholas, D. (1992), *Medieval Flanders*, London

Phythian-Adams, C. (1979), *The desolation of a city. Coventry and the urban crisis of the late Middle Ages*, Cambridge

Platt, C. (1973), *Medieval Southampton. The port and the trading community*, London

Reynolds, S. (1977), *An introduction to the history of medieval English towns*, Oxford

Sortor, M. (1993), 'Saint-Omer and its textile trades in the late Middle Ages: a contribu-tion to the proto-industrialization debate', *AHR* 98: 1475–99

Stone, L. (1955), *Sculpture in Britain. The Middle Ages*, Harmondsworth

Summerson, H. (1993), *Medieval Carlisle. The city and the borders from the late eleventh to the mid-sixteenth century*, Stroud

Swanson, H. (1987), *Medieval artisans. An urban class in late medieval England*, Oxford

Swanson, H. (1988), 'The illusion of economic structure: craft guilds in late medieval English towns', *P&P* 121: 29–48

Tait, J. (1936), *The medieval English borough. Studies on its origins and constitutional history*, Manchester

Thompson, A.H. (1947), *The English clergy and their organization in the later Middle Ages*, Oxford

Thomson, J.A.F. (ed.) (1988), *Towns and townspeople in the fifteenth century*, Gloucester

Thrupp, S. (1948), *The merchant class of medieval London*, Chicago

Torrie, E.P.D. (1990), *Medieval Dundee*, Abertay

Toussaert, J. (1960), *Le sentiment religieux en Flandre à la fin du moyen âge*, Paris

Van Houtte, J.A. (1952), 'Bruges et Anvers, marchés "nationaux" ou "internationaux" du XIVe au XVe siècle', *Revue du nord* 34: 89–108

Van Houtte, J.A. (1966), 'The rise and decline of the market of Bruges', *EconHR* 2nd series 19: 29–47

Van Houtte, J.A. (1967), *Bruges. Essai d'histoire urbaine*, Brussels

Van Houtte, J.A. (1977), *An economic history of the Low Countries, 800–1800*, New York

Van der Wee, H. (1963), *The growth of the Antwerp market and the European economy*, 3 vols., The Hague

Van der Wee, H. (1972), *Historische Aspecten van de economische groei*, Antwerp and Utrecht

Van Werveke, H. (1947), *Gent. Schets van een sociale geschiedenis*, Ghent

The German Reich, Scandinavia and eastern Europe

Barth, R. (1976), *Argumentation und Selbstverständnis der Bürgeropposition in städtischen Auseinandersetzungen des Spätmittelalters. Lübeck, 1403–08; Braunschweig, 1374–76; Mainz, 1444–46; Köln, 1396–1400*, 2nd edn, Cologne

Bonjour, E., Offler, H.S. & Potter, G.R. (1952), *A short history of Switzerland*, Oxford

Brady, T.A. (1985), *Turning Swiss. Cities and empire, 1450–1550*, Cambridge

Carsten, F.L. (1943), 'Medieval democracy in the Brandenburg towns and its defeat in the fifteenth century', *TRHS* 4th series 25: 73–91

Carsten, F.L. (1954), *The origins of Prussia*, Cambridge

Carsten, F.L. (1959), *Princes and parliaments in Germany from the fifteenth to the eighteenth century*, Oxford

Christiansen, E. (1980), *The northern crusades. The Baltic and the Catholic frontier, 1100–1525*, London

Dollinger, P. (1970), *The German Hansa*, London

Dopsch, H. and Spatzenegger, H. (eds.) (1981–91), *Geschichte Salzburgs. Stadt und Land*, 2 vols., Salzburg

Du Boulay, F.R.H. (1981), 'The German town chroniclers', in R.H.C. Davis and J.M. Wallace-Hadrill (eds.), *The writing of history in the Middle Ages. Essays presented to Richard William Southern*, Oxford, pp. 445–69

Du Boulay, F.R.H. (1983), *Germany in the later Middle Ages*, London

Fennell, J. (1968), *The emergence of Moscow*, London

Forstreuter, K. (1955), *Preussen und Russland*, Göttingen

Franz, D. (ed.) (1967), *Quellen zur Geschichte des deutschen Bauernstandes*, I, Berlin

Fritze, K. (1976), *Bürger und Bauer zur Hansezeit*, Weimar

Gerevich, L. (1990), *Towns in medieval Hungary*, Boulder, Colo.

Haase, C. (ed.) (1978), *Die Stadt des Mittelalters*, 3 vols., Darmstadt

Heckscher, E.F. (1954), *An economic history of Sweden*, Cambridge, Mass.

Heymann, F.G. (1954), 'The role of towns in the Bohemia of the later Middle Ages', *Cahiers d'histoire mondial* 2: 326–46

Isenmann, E. (1988), *Die Deutsche Stadt im Spätmittelalter, 1250–1500. Staatgestalt, Recht, Stadtregiment, Kirche, Gesellschaft, Wirtschaft*, Stuttgart

Klutchevsky, V.O. (1931), *History of Russia*, I, trans. C.J. Hogarth, London

Krekić, B. (ed.) (1987), *Urban society of eastern Europe in premodern times*, Berkeley

Lenk, W. (1966), *Das Nürnberger Fastnachtspiel des 15 Jahrhunderts*, Berlin

Ligers, J. (1946), *Histoire des villes de Lettonie et d'Esthonie*, Paris

Malowist, M. (1959–60), 'The economic and social development of the Baltic countries from the fifteenth to the seventeenth centuries', *EconHR* 2nd series 12: 177–89

Maschke, E. (1967), 'Die Unterschichten der mittelalterlichen Städte Deutschlands', in

E. Maschke and J. Sydow (eds.), *Gesellschaftliche Unterschichten in den Südest Deutschen Städten*, Stuttgart, pp. 1–74

Miller, D.A. (1969), *Imperial Constantinople*, London

Molenda, D. (1976), 'Mining towns in central-eastern Europe in feudal times', *Acta Poloniae historica* 34: 165–88

Nedkvitne, A. (1983), *Utenrikshandelen fra det vestafjelske Norge, 1100–1600*, Bergen

Olsen, O. (ed.) (1988–91), *Danmarkshistorie*, 16 vols., Copenhagen

Onasch, K. (1969), *Gross-Nowgorod*, Vienna and Munich

Planitz, H. (1980), *Die Deutsche Stadt im Mittelalter, von der Römerzeit bis zu den Zunftkämpfen*, 5th edn, Vienna

Rady, M.C. (1985), *Medieval Buda. A study of municipal government and jurisdiction in the kingdom of Hungary*, Boulder, Colo.

Rausch, W. (ed.) (1974), *Die Stadt am Ausgang des Mittelalters*, Linz

Rotz, R.A. (1976), 'Investigating urban uprisings with examples from Hanseatic towns, 1374–1416', in W.C. Jordan, B. McNab, and T.F. Ruiz (eds.), *Order and innovation in the Middle Ages: essays in honour of Joseph R. Strayer*, Princeton, pp. 215–33, 483–94

Rowell, S. (1995), *Lithuania ascending*, Cambridge

Rudwin, M.J. (1919), 'The origin of German Carnival comedy', *Journal of English and German Philology* 18: 402–54

Sawyer, B. and P. (1993), *Medieval Scandinavia. From conversion to Reformation, circa 800–1500*, Minneapolis and London

Schildauer, J. (1988), *The Hansa. History and culture*, trans. K. Vanovitch, London

Schönberg, G. (1879), *Finanzverhältnisse der Stadt Basel im XIV und XV Jahrhundert*, Tübingen

Sedlar, J.M. (ed.) (1994), *East central Europe in the Middle Ages, 1000–1500*, Seattle and London

Spalding, K. (1973), *Holland und die Hanse im 15 Jahrhundert*, Weimar

Strauss, G. (1966), *Nuremberg in the sixteenth century*, London

Stromer, W. von (1981), 'Commercial policy and economic conjuncture in Nuremberg at the close of the Middle Ages: a model of economic policy', *Journal of European Economic History* 10: 119–29

Sugar, P.F., Hanák, P. and Frank, T. (eds.) (1990), *A history of Hungary*, Bloomington, Ind.

Van Loewe, K. (1973), 'Commerce and agriculture in Lithuania, 1400–1600', *EconHR* 2nd series 26: 23–37

Vernadsky, G. (1959), *Russia at the dawn of the modern age*, New Haven, Conn.

7 COMMERCE AND TRADE

Primary sources

Carus-Wilson, E.M. (ed.), *The overseas trade of Bristol in the later Middle Ages*, Bristol Record Society, 7, Bristol (1937)

Childs, W.R. (ed.), *The customs accounts of Hull 1453–1490*, Yorkshire Archaeological Society Record Series, 144, Leeds (1986)

Cobb, H. (ed.), *The overseas trade of London. Exchequer customs accounts 1480–1*, London Record Society, 27, London (1990)

Diplomatarium Islandicum, ed. J. Sigurthsson *et al.*, Copenhagen (1857ff)
Diplomatarium Norvegicum, ed. C.C.A. Lange, C.R. Unger *et al.*, 19 vols. Oslo (1847–1919)
Doehaerd, R. (ed.), *Etudes anversoises. Documents sur le commerce international à Anvers 1488–1514*, 3 vols., Paris (1962)
Doehaerd, R. and Kerremans, C. (eds.), *Les relations commerciales entre Gênes, la Belgique, et l'Outremont d'après les archives notariales génoises 1400–1440*, Brussels (1952)
Ducaunnes-Duval, M.G. (ed.), 'Registre de la comptabilité de Bordeaux 1482–3', *Archives historiques du département de la Gironde* 50 (1915), pp. 1–166
Gilliodts van Severen, L. (ed.), *Cartulaire de l'ancien consulat d'Espagne à Bruges. Recueil de documents concernant le commerce maritime et l'intérieur, le droit des gens public et privé et l'histoire économique de la Flandre. Première partie. 1280–1550*, Bruges (1901–2)
Gilliodts van Severen, L. (ed.), *Cartulaire de l'ancienne estaple de Bruges. Recueil de documents concernant le commerce intérieur et maritime, les relations internationales et l'histoire économique de cette ville*, 2 vols., Bruges (1903–6)
Gras, N.S.B. (ed.), *The early English customs system*, Cambridge, Mass. (1918)
Hanham, A. (ed.), *The Cely letters 1472–1488*, EETS, original series, 273, Oxford (1975)
Hanserecesse (Die Recesse und andere Akten der Hansetäge), 1256–1430, ed. K. Koppmann, 8 vols., Leipzig (1870–97)
Hanserecesse 1431–76, ed. G. von der Ropp, 7 vols., Leipzig (1876–92)
Hanserecesse 1476–1530, ed. D. Schäfer and F. Techen, 9 vols., Leipzig and Munich (1881–1913)
Hansisches Urkundenbuch, ed. K. Hölbaum, K. Kunze and W. Stein, Verein für Hansische Geschichte, 11 vols., Halle and Leipzig (1876–1907)
The libelle of Englyshe polycye. A poem on the use of sea-power 1436, ed. G. Warner, Oxford (1926)
Lopez, R.S. and Raymond, I. (eds), *Medieval trade in the Mediterranean world*. New York (1995)
Melis, F. (ed.), *Documenti per la storia economica dei secoli XIII–XVI*, Florence (1972)
Mollat, M. (ed.), *Les affaires de Jacques Coeur. Journal du procureur Dauvet*, 2 vols., Paris (1952–3)
Mollat, M. (ed.), *Comptabilité du port de Dieppe au XVe siècle*, Paris (1951)
Ruddock, A.A. and Reddaway, T.F. (eds.), 'The accounts of John Balsall, purser of the *Trinity of Bristol* 1480–1', *Camden Miscellany XXIII*, RHS, London (1969)
Smit, H.J. (ed.), *Bronnen tot de geschiedenis van den Handel met England, Schotland en Ierland*, 4 vols., Rijks Geschiedkundige Publicatien, 65, 66, 86, 91, The Hague (1928–50)
Sneller, Z.W. and Unger, W.S. (eds.), *Bronnen tot de geschiedenis van den Handel met Frankrijk*, Rijks Geschiedkundige Publicatien, 70, The Hague (1930)
Stieda, W. (ed.), *Hildebrand Veckinchusen. Briefwechsel eines deutschen Kaufmanns im 15 Jahrhundert*, Leipzig (1921)
Torre, A. and E.A. de la (eds.), *Cuentas de Gonzalo de Baeza, tesorero de Isabel la Católica, 1477–1504*, Consejo Superior de Investigaciónes Cientificas, Patronato M. Menendez Pelayo, Biblioteca 'Reyes Católicos', Documentos y Textos, 5–6, Madrid (1955–6)

Secondary works

Asaert, G. (1973), *De Antwerpse Scheepvaart in de XVe eeuw* (1394–1480), Brussels
Asaert, G. (1979), 'Antwerp ships in English harbours in the fifteenth century', *Acta historiae Neerlandicae* 12: 29–47

Ashtor, E. (1983), *Levant trade in the later Middle Ages*, Princeton

Balard, M. (1978), *La Romanie génoise (XIIe–début XVe siècle)*, Rome and Genoa

Bang, N.E. (1906–32), *Tabeller over Skibsfart og Varentransport gennem Øresund 1497–1660*, 2 vols., Leipzig

Baratier, E. and Reynaud, F. (1951), *Histoire du commerce de Marseille de 1291–1480*, Paris

Bautier, R.-H. (1960, 1964), 'Notes sur le commerce du fer en Europe occidentale du XIIe au XVIe siècle', *Revue d'histoire de la sidérurgie* 1: 7–35; 4: 35–61

Bautier, R.-H. (1971), *The economic development of medieval Europe*, London

Bernard, J. (1968), *Navires et gens de mer à Bordeaux*, 3 vols., Paris

Bolton, J.L. (1980), *The medieval English economy*, London

Bridbury, A.R. (1955), *England and the salt trade in the later Middle Ages*, Oxford

Bridbury, A.R. (1962), *Economic growth. England in the later Middle Ages*, London

Bridbury, A.R. (1982), *Medieval English clothmaking. An economic survey*, London

Brulez, W. (1973), 'Bruges and Antwerp in the 15th and 16th centuries: an antithesis?', *Acta historiae Neerlandicae* 6: 1–26

Carrère, C. (1953), 'Le droit d'ancrage et le mouvement du port de Barcelone au milieu du XVe siècle', *Estudios de historia moderna* 3: 67–156

Carrère, C. (1967), *Barcelone. Centre économique à l'époque des difficultés, 1380–1462*, 2 vols., Paris

Carter, F.C. (1994), *Trade and development in Poland. An economic geography of Cracow, from its origins to 1795*, Cambridge

Carus-Wilson, E.M. and Coleman, O. (1967), *England's export trade 1275–1547*, Oxford

Casado Alonso, H. (1994), 'El comercio internacional burgalés en los siglos XV y XVI', *Actas del Simposio internacional 'El Consulado de Burgos'*, Burgos, pp. 173–247

Caster, G. (1962), *Le commerce du pastel et de l'épicerie à Toulouse*, Toulouse

Childs, W.R. (1978), *Anglo-Castilian trade in the later Middle Ages*, Manchester

Childs, W.R. (1981), 'England's iron trade in the fifteenth century', *EconHR* 2nd series 34: 25–47

Childs, W.R. (1992), 'Anglo-Portuguese trade in the fifteenth century', *TRHS* 6th series 2: 195–219

Christenson, E. (1957), 'Scandinavia and the advance of the Hanseatics', *Scandinavian Economic Review* 5: 89–117

Cipolla, C., Lopez, R.S. and Miskimin, H.A. (1963–4), 'The economic depression of the Renaissance?', *EconHR* 2nd series 16: 519–29

Craeybeckx, J. (1958), *Un grand commerce d'importation. Les vins de France aux anciens Pays Bas XIIIe–XVIe siècles*, Paris

Davis, R. (1976), 'The rise of Antwerp and its English connection 1406–1510', in D.C. Coleman and A.H. John (eds.), *Trade, government and economy in pre-industrial England*, London, pp. 2–20

Day, J. (1987), *The medieval market economy*, Oxford

De Gryse, R. (1951), 'De Vlaamse Haringvisserij in de XVe eeuw', *Annales de la Société d'émulation de Bruges* 88: 116–33

De Roover, R. (1948), *Money, banking and credit in mediaeval Bruges. Italian merchant-bankers, Lombards and moneychangers*, Cambridge, Mass.

De Roover, R. (1959), 'La balance commerciale entre les Pays Bas et l'Italie au XVe siècle', *Revue belge de philologie et d'histoire* 37: 375–86

De Roover, R. (1963), *The rise and decline of the Medici Bank 1397–1494*, Cambridge, Mass.

De Roover, R. (1968), *The Bruges money market around 1400*, Brussels

Delort, R. (1978), *Le commerce des fourrures en occident à la fin du moyen âge (vers 1300–vers 1450)*, Rome

Dollinger, P. (1989), *Die Hanse*, 4th edn, Stuttgart; 1st edn trans. D. Ault and S.H. Steinberg, *The German Hansa*, London (1970)

Edler de Roover, F. (1966), 'Andrea Banchi, Florentine silk manufacturer and merchant in the fifteenth century', *Studies in Medieval and Renaissance History* 3: 221–85

Epstein, S. (1992), *An island for itself. Economic development and social change in late medieval Sicily*, Cambridge

Fernández-Armesto, F. (1987), *Before Columbus. Exploration and colonisation from the Mediterranean to the Atlantic 1229–1492*, London

Fernández-Armesto, F. (1992), *Columbus*, Oxford

Ferreira Priegue, E. (1988), *Galicia en el comercio marítimo medieval*, Santiago de Compostella

Fudge, J. (1995), *Cargoes, embargoes and emissaries. The commercial and political interaction of England and the German Hanse 1450–1510*, Toronto

Gade, J.A. (1951), *The Hanseatic control of Norwegian commerce during the late Middle Ages*, Leiden

Garcia de Cortazar, J.A. (1966), *Vizcaya en el siglo XV*, Bilbao

Gelsinger, B.E. (1981), *Icelandic enterprise. Commerce and economy in the Middle Ages*, Columbia, S.C.

Guiral-Hadziiossif (1986), *Valence. Port mediterranéen au XVe siècle*, Paris

Hale, J. (1977), *Florence and the Medici*, London

Hanham, A. (1985) *The Celys and their world*, Cambridge

Hatcher, J. (1973), *English tin production and trade before 1550*, Oxford

Heers, J. (1955), 'Le commerce des basques en Mediterranée au XVe siècle', *Bulletin hispanique* 57: 292–324

Heers, J. (1957), 'Le royaume de Grenade et la politique marchande de Gênes en occident au XVe siècle', *MA* 63: 87–121

Heers, J. (1961), *Gênes au XV siècle*, Paris

Heers, J. (1966), *L'occident aux XIVe et XVe siècles. Aspects économiques et sociaux*, Paris

Heers, J. (1979), *Société et économie à Gênes (XIV–XV siècles)*, London

Heers, M.L. (1954), 'Les gênois et le commerce de l'alun à la fin du moyen âge', *Revue d'histoire économique et sociale* 32: 31–53

Herlihy, D. (1958), *Pisa in the early Renaissance*, New Haven

Hutchinson, G. (1994), *Medieval ships and shipping*, London

Iradiel Murugarren, P. (1974), *Evolución de la industria textil castellana en los siglos XII–XVI*, Salamanca

James, M.K. (1971), *Studies in the medieval wine trade*, Oxford

Jenks, S. (1992), *England, Die Hanse und Preussen. Handel und Diplomatie 1377–1474*, 3 vols., Cologne and Vienna

Kerling, N.J.M. (1954), *Commercial relations of Holland and Zeeland with England from the late thirteenth century to the close of the Middle Ages*, Leiden

Lane, F.C. (1944), *Andrea Barbarigo, merchant of Venice, 1418–1449*, Baltimore

Lane, F.C. (1966), *Venice and history. The collected papers of F.C. Lane*, Baltimore

Lane, F.C. (1973), *Venice. A maritime republic*, Baltimore

Lane, F.C. and Müller, R.C. (1985), *Money and banking in medieval and Renaissance Venice*, Baltimore

Livermore, H.V. (1954), 'The "privileges of an Englishman in the kingdoms and dominions of Portugal"', *Atlante* 2: 57–77

Lloyd, T.H. (1977), *The English wool trade in the Middle Ages*, Cambridge

Lloyd, T.H. (1991), *England and the German Hanse 1157–1611. A study of their trade and commercial diplomacy*, Cambridge

Lopez, R.S. (1956), 'The evolution of land transport in the Middle Ages', *P&P* 9: 17–29

Lopez, R.S. (1964), 'Market expansion: the case of Genoa', *Journal of Economic History* 24: 445–64

Lopez, R.S. and Miskimin, H.A. (1961–2), 'The economic depression of the Renaissance?', *EconHR* 2nd series 14: 408–26

Lopez, R.S., Miskimin, H.A. and Udovitch, A. (1970), 'England to Egypt, 1350–1500: long-term trends and long-distance trade', in M.A. Cook (ed.), *Studies in the economic history of the Middle East*, Oxford, pp. 93–128

Luzzatto, M. (1961), *An economic history of Italy to the beginning of the XVIth century*, London

MacKay, A. (1981), *Money, prices and politics in fifteenth century Castile*, London

Magalhães-Godinho, V. (1969), *L'économie de l'empire portugais aux XVe et XVIe siècles*, Paris

Mallett, M.E. (1967), *The Florentine galleys in the fifteenth century*, Oxford

Malowist, M. (1966), 'The problem of the inequality of economic development in Europe in the later Middle Ages', *EconHR* 2nd series 19: 15–28

Marques, A.H. de O. (1959a), *Hansa e Portugal na idade media*, Lisbon

Marques, A.H. de O. (1959b), 'Navigation entre la Prusse et le Portugal au début du XVe siècle', *Vierteljahrschrift für Sozial- und Wirtschaftsgeschichte* 46: 477–90

Marques, A.H. de O. (1962), 'Notas para a história da feitoria portuguesa na Flandres, no século XV', in *Studi in onore di A. Fanfani* II, Milan, pp. 437–76

Mazzoui, M. (1981), *The Italian cotton industry in the later Middle Ages*, Cambridge

Mollat, M. (1951), *Le commerce maritime normand à la fin du moyen âge*, Paris

Mollat, M. (1988), *Jacques Coeur ou l'esprit d'entreprise au XVe siècle*, Paris

Munro, J. (1972), *Wool, cloth and gold. The struggle for bullion in Anglo-Burgundian trade 1340–1478*, Toronto

Munro, J. (1988), 'Deflation and the petty coinage problem in the late-medieval economy: the case of Flanders, 1334–1484', *Explorations in Economic History* 25: 387–423

Nicholas, D. (1992), *Medieval Flanders*, London

Nightingale, P. (1995), *A medieval mercantile community. The Grocers' Company and the politics and trade of London, 1000–1485*, London and New Haven

Phillips, J.R.S. (1988), *The medieval expansion of Europe*, Oxford

Phillips, W.D., Jnr, and Phillips, C.R. (1992), *The worlds of Christopher Columbus*, Cambridge

Postan, M.M. and Miller, E. (eds.) (1987), *The Cambridge economic history of Europe*, II: *Trade and industry in the Middle Ages*, 2nd edn, Cambridge

Postan, M.M. and Power, E. (eds.) (1933), *Studies in English trade in the fifteenth century*, London

Postan, M.M., Rich, E.E., and Miller, E. (eds.) (1963), *The Cambridge economic history of Europe*, III: *Economic organization and policies in the Middle Ages*, Cambridge

Rau, V. (1957), 'A family of Italian merchants in Portugal in the fifteenth century: the Lomellini', in *Studi in onore di A. Sapori*, I, Milan, pp. 715–26

Rau, V. and Macedo, J. de (1962), *O açucar da Madeira nos fins do século XV*, Funchal

Renouard, Y. (1965), *Histoire de Bordeaux*, III: *Bordeaux sous les rois d'Angleterre*, Bordeaux

Renouard, Y. (1968), *Les hommes d'affaires italiens du moyen âge*, revised edn, Paris

Ruddock, A.A. (1951), *Italian merchants and shipping in Southampton*, Southampton

Sapori, A. (1952), *Le marchand italien au moyen âge*, Paris

Scammell, G.V. (1981), *The world encompassed. The first European maritime empires, c. 800–1650*, London

Schnyder, W. (1973), *Handel und Verkehr über die Pässe in Mittelalter*, Zurich

Sprandel, R. (1968), *Das Eisengewerbe im Mittelalter*, Stuttgart

Spufford, P. (1988), *Money and its use in medieval Europe*, Cambridge

Stromer, W. von (1970), 'Nuremberg in the international economies of the Middle Ages', *Business History Review* 44: 210–25

Thielemans, M.R. (1967), *Bourgogne et Angleterre. Relations politiques et économiques entre les Pays-Bas bourguignons et l'Angleterre, 1435–1467*, Brussels

Thiriet, F. (1959), *La Romanie vénitienne au moyen âge. Le développement et l'exploitation du domaine colonial vénitien (XIIe–XVe siècles)*, Paris

Thorsteinsson, B. (1970), *Enska öldin í sögu íslendinga*, Reykjavik

Touchard, H. (1967), *Le commerce maritime breton à la fin du moyen âge*, Paris

Unger, R. (1980), *The ship in the medieval economy 600–1600*, London and Montreal

Van Houtte, J. (1952), 'Bruges et Anvers, marchés "nationaux" ou "internationaux" du XIVe au XVIe siècle', *Revue du nord* 34: 89–108

Van Houtte, J. (1966), 'The rise and decline of the market of Bruges', *EconHR* 2nd series 19: 29–47

Van der Wee, H. (1963), *The growth of the Antwerp market and the European economy*, 3 vols., The Hague

Van Werveke, H. (1944), *Bruges et Anvers. Huit siècles de commerce flamand*, Brussels

Veale, E.M. (1966), *The English fur trade in the later Middle Ages*, Oxford

Verlinden, C. (1957), 'La colonie italienne de Lisbonne et le développement de l'économie métropolitaine et coloniale portugaise', in *Studi in onore di A. Sapori*, I, Milan, pp. 615–28

Watson, W.B. (1961), 'The structure of the Florentine galley trade with England and Flanders in the fifteenth century', *Revue belge de philologie et d'histoire* 39: 1073–91

Watson, W.B. (1962), 'The structure of the Florentine galley trade with England and Flanders in the fifteenth century', *Revue belge de philologie et d'histoire* 40: 317–47

Watson, W.B. (1967), 'Catalans in the markets of northern Europe during the fifteenth century', in *Homenaje a Jaime Vicens Vives*, II, Barcelona, pp. 785–813

Wolffe, P. (1954), *Commerces et marchands de Toulouse, 1350–1450*, Paris

8 WAR

Primary sources

Alberti, Leon Battista, *De re aedificatoria, libri X (c.* 1452), Florence (1485)

Barnard, F.P. (ed.), *The essential portions of Nicholas Upton's De studio militari, before 1446, translated by John Blount, Fellow of All Souls (c. 1500)*, Oxford (1931)

Bayley, C.C. (ed.), *War and society in Renaissance Florence. The De militia of Leonardo Bruni*, Toronto (1961)

Bonet, Honoré, *L'arbre des batailles*, ed. E. Nys, Brussels and Leipzig (1883); English trans. and ed. G.W. Coopland, *The tree of battles of Honoré Bonet*, Liverpool (1949)

Bueil, Jean de, *Le Jouvencel*, ed. C. Favre and L. Lecestre, 2 vols., SHF, Paris (1887–9)

Chartier, Alain, *Le quadrilogue invectif*, ed. E. Droz, 2nd edn, Paris (1950)

Commynes, Philippe de, *Mémoires*, ed. J. Calmette and G. Durville, 3 vols., Paris (1924–5)

Contamine, P., 'L'art de la guerre selon Philippe de Clèves, seigneur de Ravenstein (1456–1528): innovation ou tradition?', *Bijdragen en mededelingen betreffende de geschiedenis de Nederlanden* 95 (1980), pp. 363–76

Contamine, P., 'Les traités de guerre, de chasse, de blason, et de chevalerie', in *Grundriss der romanischen Literaturen des Mittelalters, Volume VIII/1 (La littérature française aux XIVe et XVe siècles)*, Heidelberg (1988), pp. 346–67

Contamine, P., 'The war literature of the late Middle Ages: the treatises of Robert de Balsac and Béraud Stuart', in Allmand (1976), pp. 102–21; repr. in Contamine (1981), ch. 3

Coopland, G.W., 'Le Jouvencel (revisited)', *Symposium* 5, no. 2 (1951), pp. 137–86

Le débat des hérauts d'armes de France et d'Angleterre, ed. L. Pannier, SATF, Paris (1877)

Díez de Games, G., *El Victorial, crónica de Don Pero Niño, conde de Buelna, por su alférez, Gutierre Díez de Games*, ed. J. de Mata Carriazo, Madrid (1940), English trans. J. Evans, *The unconquered knight. A chronicle of the deeds of Don Pero Niño, count of Buelna, by his standard bearer, Gutierre Diaz de Gamez (1431–1449)*, London (1928)

Fourquevaux, le Sieur de, *Instructions sur le faict de la guerre*, ed. G. Dickinson, London (1954)

Frontinus, Sextus Julius, *The stratagems*, trans. C.E. Bennett, Loeb Classical Library, Cambridge, Mass., and London (1969)

Jones, M. and Walker, S., 'Private indentures for life service in peace and war, 1278–1476', in *Camden Miscellany XXXII*, RHS, London (1994)

Kyeser, Conrad (aus Eichstätt), *Bellifortis*, ed. G. Quarg, 2 vols., Düsseldorf (1967)

The libelle of Englyshe polycye. A poem on the use of sea-power 1436, ed. G. Warner, Oxford (1926)

Lull, Ramon, *The book of the ordre of chyualry, translated and printed by William Caxton from a French version of Ramón Lull's 'Le libre del orde de cauayleria'*, ed. A.T.P. Byles, EETS, original series, 168, London (1926)

Meun, Jean de, *L'art de chevalerie. Traduction du De re militari de Végèce*, ed. U. Robert, SATF, Paris (1897)

Pisan, Christine de, *The book of fayttes of armes and of chyaulrye, translated and printed by William Caxton*, ed. A.T.P. Byles, EETS, original series, 189, London (1932)

Pons, N. (ed.), *'L'honneur de la couronne de France'. Quatre libelles contre les Anglais (v.1418–v.1429)*, SHF, Paris (1990)

Stuart, Bérault, seigneur d'Aubigny, *Traité sur l'art de la guerre*, ed. E. de Comminges, International Archives of the History of Ideas, 85, The Hague (1976)

Vegetius, Flavius Renatus, *De re militari*: with Frontinus, *Stratagematicon*; Modestus, *De re militari*; Aelianus, *De instruendis aciebus*; Onosander, *De optimo imperatore eiusque officio*, Rome (1494)

The earliest English translation of Vegetius' De re militari, ed. G. Lester, Heidelberg (1988)

Vegetius, *Epitoma rei militaris*, ed. A. Önnerfors, Stuttgart and Leipzig (1995)

Vegetius, *Epitome of military science*, trans. N.P. Milner, 2nd rev. edn, Liverpool (1996)

Weiss, R., 'The adventures of a first edition of Valturio's *De re militari*', in *Studi di bibliografia e di storia in onore di Tammaro de Marinis*, IV, Verona (1964), pp. 297–304

Secondary works

Allmand, C.T. (1988), *The Hundred Years War. England and France at war, c. 1300–c. 1450*, Cambridge

Allmand, C.T. (1991), 'Changing views of the soldier in late medieval France', in Contamine, Giry-Deloison and Keen (1991), pp. 171–88

Allmand, C.T. (1992a), 'Intelligence in the Hundred Years War', in K. Neilson and B.J.C. McKercher (eds.), *Go spy the land. Military intelligence in history*, Westport, Conn., and London, pp. 31–47

Allmand, C.T. (1992b), *Henry V*, London; rev. edn New Haven and London (1997)

Allmand, C.T. (1995), 'New weapons, new tactics, 1300–1500', in Parker (1995b), pp. 92–105

Allmand, C.T. (ed.) (1976), *War, literature, and politics in the late Middle Ages. Essays in honour of G.W. Coopland*, Liverpool

Anglo, S. (1988), 'Machiavelli as a military authority. Some early sources', in P. Denley and C. Elam (eds.), *Florence and Italy. Renaissance studies in honour of Nicolai Rubinstein*, London, pp. 321–34

Anglo, S. (ed.) (1990), *Chivalry in the Renaissance*, Woodbridge

Bak, J.M. and Király, B.K. (eds.) (1982), *From Hunyadi to Rakocki. War and society in late medieval and early modern Hungary*, Brooklyn, N.Y.

Barnes, J. (1982), 'The just war', in N. Kretzmann, A. Kenny and J. Pinborg (eds.), *The Cambridge history of later medieval philosophy*, Cambridge, pp. 771–84

Bartusis, M.C. (1992), *The late Byzantine army. Arms and society, 1204–1453*, Philadelphia

Bean, R. (1973), 'War and the birth of the nation state', *Journal of Economic History* 33: 203–21

Blanchard, J. (1989), 'Ecrire la guerre au XVe siècle', *Le moyen français* 24–5: 7–21

Blanchard, J. (1996), *Commynes l'européen. L'invention du politique*, Geneva

Borosy, A. (1982), 'The *Militia Portalis* in Hungary before 1526', in Bak and Király (1982), pp. 63–80

Bossuat, A. (1936), *Perrinet Gressart et François de Surienne, agents de l'Angleterre*, Paris

Bossuat, A. (1951a), 'Les prisonniers de guerre au XVe siècle: la rançon de Guillaume, seigneur de Chateauvillain', *AB* 23: 7–35

Bossuat, A. (1951b), 'Les prisonniers de guerre au XVe siècle: la rançon de Jean, seigneur de Rodemack', *Annales de l'est* 5th series 3: 145–62

Bossuat, A. (1954), 'Le rétablissement de la paix sociale sous le règne de Charles VII', *MA* 60: 137–62; English trans. in Lewis (1971), pp. 60–81

Brusten, C. (1953), *L'armée bourguignonne de 1465 à 1468*, Brussels

Caldwell, D.H. (1981), 'Royal patronage of arms and armour-making in fifteenth and sixteenth-century Scotland', in D.H. Caldwell (ed.), *Scottish weapons and fortifications, 1100–1800*, Edinburgh, pp. 72–93

Cauchies, J.-M. (ed.) (1986), *Art de la guerre, technologie et tactique en Europe occidentale à la fin du moyen âge et à la Renaissance*, Publications du Centre Européen d'Études Bourguignonnes XIVe–XVIe siècles, no. 26, Basle

Chambers, D., Clough, C.H. and Mallett, M.E. (eds.) (1993), *War, culture and society in Renaissance Venice. Essays in honour of John Hale*, London and Rio Grande, Ohio

Champion, P. (1906), *Guillaume de Flavy, capitaine de Compiègne*, Paris

Chevalier, B. and Contamine, P. (eds.) (1985), *La France de la fin du XVe siècle. Renouveau et apogée*, Paris

Cinq-centième anniversaire de la bataille de Nancy (1477) (1979), Actes du colloque de Nancy, 1977, Nancy

Cipolla, C.M. (1965), *Guns and sails in the early phase of European expansion (1400–1700)*, London

Clough, C.H. (1993), 'Love and war in the Veneto: Luigi da Porto and the true story of *Giulietta e Romeo*', in Chambers, Clough and Mallett (1993), pp. 99–127

Clough, C.H. (1995), 'The Romagna campaign of 1494: a significant military encounter', in D. Abulafia (ed.), *The French descent into Renaissance Italy, 1494–95. Antecedents and effects*, Aldershot, pp. 191–215

Clough, C.H. (ed.) (1976), *Cultural aspects of the Italian Renaissance. Essays in honour of Paul Oskar Kristeller*, Manchester and New York

Contamine, P. (1964), 'L'artillerie royale française à la veille des guerres d'Italie', *Annales de Bretagne* 71: 221–61

Contamine, P. (1970), 'Les armées française et anglaise à l'époque de Jeanne d'Arc', *Revue des sociétés savantes de Haute-Normandie. Lettres et sciences humaines* 57: 7–33

Contamine, P. (1971), 'The French nobility and the war', in K. A. Fowler (ed.), *The Hundred Years War*, London, pp. 135–62

Contamine, P. (1972), *Guerre, état et société à la fin du moyen âge. Etudes sur les armées des rois de France, 1337–1494*, Paris and The Hague

Contamine, P. (1976), 'Points de vue sur la chevalerie en France à la fin du moyen âge', *Francia* 4: 255–85; repr. in Contamine (1981), ch. 11

Contamine, P. (1978a), 'Guerre, fiscalité royale et économie en France (deuxième moitié du XVe siècle)', in M. Flinn (ed.), *Proceedings of the seventeenth international economic congress*, Edinburgh, II, pp. 266–73

Contamine, P. (1978b), 'Consommation et demande militaire en France et en Angleterre, XIIIe–XVe siècles', in *Domanda e consumi. Livelli e strutture (nei secoli XIII–XVIII)*, Atti della Sesta Settimana di Studio, 1974, Istituto Internazionale di Storia Economica F. Datini, Prato, Florence, pp. 409–28

Contamine, P. (1978c), 'Rançons et butins dans la Normandie anglaise (1424–1444)', in *Actes du 101e congrès des Sociétés savantes, Lille, 1976. Section de philologie et d'histoire jusqu'à 1610*, Paris, pp. 241–70; repr. in Contamine (1981), ch. 8

Contamine, P. (1979), 'L'idée de guerre à la fin du moyen âge: aspects juridiques et éthiques', *Comptes-rendus de l'académie des inscriptions et belles-lettres*, pp. 70–86; repr. in Contamine (1981), ch. 13

Contamine, P. (1981), *La France aux XIVe et XVe siècles. Hommes, mentalités, guerre et paix*, London

Contamine, P. (1984a), 'Les industries de guerre dans la France de la Renaissance: l'exemple de l'artillerie', *RH* 271: 249–80

Contamine, P. (1984b), *War in the Middle Ages*, Oxford

Contamine, P. (1987), 'Structures militaires de la France et de l'Angleterre au milieu du XVe siècle', in R. Schneider (ed.), *Das spätmittelalterliche Königtum in Europäischen Vergleich*, Sigmaringen, pp. 319–34

Contamine, P. (1989), 'Naissance de l'infantrie française (milieu XVe–milieu XVIe siècle)', in *Quatrième centenaire de la bataille de Coutras*, Pau, pp. 63–88

Contamine, P. (ed.) (1992), *Histoire militaire de la France, I: Des origines à 1715*, Paris

Contamine, P., Giry-Deloison, C. and Keen, M. (eds.) (1991), *Guerre et société en France, en Angleterre et en Bourgogne, XIVe–XVe siècle*, Lille

Corfis, I.A. and Wolfe, M. (eds.) (1995), *The medieval city under siege*, Woodbridge

Cruickshank, C.G. (1969), *Army royal. Henry VIII's invasion of France, 1513*, Oxford

Curry, A.E. (1979), 'The first English standing army? Military organization in Lancastrian Normandy, 1420–1450', in C. Ross (ed.), *Patronage, pedigree and power in later medieval England*, Gloucester and Totowa, pp. 193–214

Curry, A.E. (1982), 'L'effet de la libération de la ville d'Orléans sur l'armée anglaise: les problèmes de l'organisation militaire en Normandie de 1429 à 1435', in *Jeanne d'Arc, une époque, un rayonnement*, Paris, pp. 95–106

Curry, A.E. (1987), 'The impact of war and occupation on urban life in Normandy, 1417–1450', *French History* 1: 157–81

Curry, A.E. (1992), 'The nationality of men-at-arms serving in English armies in Normandy and the *pays de conquête*, 1415–1450: a preliminary survey', *Reading Medieval Studies* 18: 135–63

Curry, A. and Hughes, M. (1994), *Arms, armies and fortifications in the Hundred Years War*, Woodbridge and Rochester, N.Y.

Cuttino, G.P. (1985), *English medieval diplomacy*, Bloomington

De Vries, K.R. (1992), *Medieval military technology*, Peterborough, Ont., and Lewiston, N.Y.

De Vries, K.R. (1995), 'The impact of gunpowder weaponry on siege warfare in the Hundred Years War', in Corfis and Wolfe (1995), pp. 227–44

Del Treppo, M. (1973), 'Gli aspetti organizzativi, economici e sociali di una compagnia di ventura', *Rivista storica Italiana* 85: 253–75

Delbrück, H. (1982), *History of the art of war, within the framework of political history*, III: *The Middle Ages*, Westport and London

Dickinson, J.G. (1955), *The congress of Arras, 1435. A study in medieval diplomacy*, Oxford

Downing, B.M. (1992), *The military revolution and political change. Origins of democracy and autocracy in early modern Europe*, Princeton

Eltis, D. (1989), 'Towns and defence in late medieval Germany', *Nottingham Medieval Studies* 33: 91–103

Engel, P. (1982), 'János Hunyadi: the decisive years of his career, 1440–1444', in Bak and Király (1982), pp. 103–23

Finó, J.F. (1974), 'L'artillerie en France à la fin du moyen âge', *Gladius* 12: 13–31

Fowler, K.A. (ed.) (1971), *The Hundred Years War*, London

Fügedi, E. (1982), 'The *Militia Portalis* in Hungary before 1526', in Bak and Király (1982), pp. 63–80

500-Jahr-Feier der Schlacht bei Murten: Kolloquiumsakten/ 5e centenaire de la bataille de Morat: actes du colloque (1976), Freiburg and Berne

Gaier, C. (1973), *L'industrie et le commerce des armes dans les principautés belges du XIIIe à la fin du XVe siècle*, Paris

Gaier, C. (1978), 'L'invincibilité anglaise et le grand arc de la guerre de Cent Ans: un mythe tenace', *Tijdschrift voor geschiedenis* 91: 379–85

Gilbert, F. (1941), 'Machiavelli: the renaissance of the art of war', in E.M. Earle, *Makers of modern strategy*, Princeton, pp. 3–25

Gille, B. (1964), *Les ingénieurs de la Renaissance*, Paris

Goodman, A.E. (1981), *The Wars of the Roses. Military activity and English society, 1452–97*, London

Goodman, A.E. and Tuck, A. (eds.) (1991), *Wars and border societies in the Middle Ages*, London

Guenée, B. (1985), *States and rulers in later medieval Europe*, Oxford

Guilmartin, J.F., Jr (1974), *Gunpowder and galleys. Changing technology and Mediterranean warfare at sea in the sixteenth century*, Cambridge

Hale, J.R. (1957), 'International relations in the west: diplomacy and war', in G.R. Potter (ed.), *New Cambridge modern history*, I: *The Renaissance, 1493–1520*, Cambridge, pp. 259–91

Hale, J.R. (1960), 'War and public opinion in Renaissance Italy', in E.F. Jacob (ed.), *Italian Renaissance studies*, London, pp. 94–122; repr. in Hale (1983), pp. 359–87

Hale, J.R. (1962), 'War and public opinion in the fifteenth and sixteenth centuries', *P&P* 22: 18–33

Hale, J.R. (1965a), 'The early development of the bastion: an Italian chronology *c.* 1450–*c.* 1534', in J.R. Hale, J.R.L. Highfield and B. Smalley (eds.), *Europe in the late Middle Ages*, London, pp. 466–94. Reprinted in Hale (1983), pp. 1–29

Hale, J.R. (1965b), 'Gunpowder and the Renaissance: an essay in the history of ideas', in C.H. Carter (ed.), *From the Renaissance to the Counter-Reformation. Essays in honor of Garret Mattingly*, New York and London, pp. 113–44; repr. in Hale (1983), pp. 389–420

Hale, J.R. (1976), 'The military education of the officer class in early modern Europe', in Clough (1976), pp. 440–61; repr. in Hale (1983), pp. 225–46

Hale, J.R. (1977), *Renaissance fortification. Art or engineering?*, London

Hale, J.R. (1983), *Renaissance war studies*, London

Hale, J.R. (1985), *War and society in Renaissance Europe, 1450–1620*, London

Hale, J.R. (1986), 'Soldiers in the religious art of the Renaissance', *BJRULM* 69: 166–94

Hale, J.R. (1988), 'A humanistic visual aid. The military diagram in the Renaissance', *Renaissance Studies* 2: 280–98

Hale, J.R. (1990), *Artists and warfare in the Renaissance*, New Haven and London

Hall, B.S. (1995), 'The changing face of siege warfare: technology and tactics in transition', in Corfis and Wolfe (1995), pp. 257–75

Held, J. (1977), 'Military reform in early fifteenth-century Hungary', *East European Quarterly* 11: 129–39

Held, J. (1982), 'Peasants in arms, 1437–1438 & 1456', in Bak and Király (1982), pp. 81–101

Henneman, J.B. (1978), 'The military class and the French monarchy in the late Middle Ages', *AHR* 83: 946–65

Heymann, F.G. (1955), *John Zizka and the Hussite revolution*, Princeton

Hicks, M.A. (1986), 'Counting the cost of war: the Moleyns ransom and the Hungerford land-sales, 1453–87', *Southern History* 8: 11–35

Holmer, P.L. (1977), 'Studies in the military organization of the Yorkist kings', PhD dissertation, University of Minnesota

Huizinga, J. (1924), *The waning of the Middle Ages*, London

Jones, M.C.E. (1985), 'L'armée bretonne 1449–1491: Structures et carrières', in Chevalier and Contamine (1985), pp. 147–65; repr. in M.C.E. Jones, *The creation of Brittany. A late medieval state*, London (1988), pp. 351–69

Jones, M.K. (1986), 'Henry VII, Lady Margaret Beaufort and the Orléans ransom', in R.A. Griffiths and J. Sherborne (eds.), *Kings and nobles in the later Middle Ages. A tribute to Charles Ross*, Gloucester, pp. 254–73

Kantorowicz, E. (1951), '*Pro patria mori* in medieval political thought', *AHR* 56: 472–92

Keegan, J. (1978), *The face of battle*, Harmondsworth

Keegan, J. (1994), *A brief history of warfare – past, present, future*, Southampton

Keen, M.H. (1965), *The laws of war in the late Middle Ages*, London and Toronto

Keen, M.H. (1984), *Chivalry*, New Haven and London

Keen, M.H. (1995), 'Richard II's ordinances of war of 1385', in R.E. Archer and S. Walker (eds.), *Rulers and ruled in late medieval England. Essays presented to Gerald Harriss*, London and Rio Grande, pp. 33–48

Keen, M.H. (1996), *Nobles, knights and men-at arms in the Middle Ages*, London and Rio Grande, Ohio

Keep, J.L. (1985), *Soldiers of the Tsar. Army and society in Russia, 1462–1874*, Oxford

Knecht, R.J. (1994), *Renaissance warrior and patron. The reign of Francis I*, Cambridge

Ladero Quesada, M.A. (1964), *Milicia y economia en la guerra de Granada. El cerco de Baza*, Valladolid

Ladero Quesada, M.A. (1989), 'La organización militar de la corona de Castilla en la baja edad media', in *Castillos medievales del reino de León*, Madrid, pp. 11–34

Lewis, P.S. (1965), 'War propaganda and historiography in fifteenth-century France and England', *TRHS* 5th series 15: 1–21

Lewis, P.S. (1971), *The recovery of France in the fifteenth century*, London and New York

Lomax, D.W. (1980), 'A medieval recruiting-poster', in *Estudis històrics i documents dels Arxius de Protocols*, Collegi Notarial de Barcelona, Barcelona

Lot, F. (1946), *L'art militaire et les armées au moyen âge en Europe et dans le proche-orient*, Paris

Lourie, E. (1966), 'A society organized for war: medieval Spain', *P&P* 35: 54–76

Macdonald, I.I. (1948), *Don Fernando de Antequera*, Oxford

McFarlane, K.B. (1963), 'A business-partnership in war and administration, 1421–1445', *EHR* 78: 151–74

MacKay, A. (1977), *Spain in the Middle Ages. From frontier to empire, 1000–1500*, London

McNeill, W.H. (1983), *The pursuit of power. Technology, armed force and society since A.D. 1000*, Oxford

Mallett, M.E. (1967), *The Florentine galleys in the fifteenth century*, Oxford

Mallett, M.E. (1973), 'Venice and its *condottieri*', in J.R. Hale (ed.), *Renaissance Venice*, London, pp. 121–45

Mallett, M.E. (1974), *Mercenaries and their masters. Warfare in Renaissance Italy*, London

Mallett, M.E. (1976), 'Some notes on a fifteenth-century *condottiere* and his library: Count Antonio da Marsciano', in Clough (1976), pp. 202–15

Mallett, M.E. (1981), 'Diplomacy and war in later fifteenth-century Italy', *PBA* 67: 267–88

Mallett, M.E. (1992), 'Diplomacy and war in later fifteenth-century Italy', in G.C. Garfagnini (ed.), *Lorenzo de'Medici Studi*, Florence, pp. 233–56

Mallett, M.E. (1993), 'Venice and the war of Ferrara, 1482–84', in Chambers, Clough and Mallett (1993), pp. 57–72

Mallett, M.E. (1995), 'Siegecraft in late fifteenth-century Italy', in Corfis and Wolfe (1995), pp. 245–55

Mallett, M.E. (1994), 'The art of war', in T.A. Brady, H.A. Oberman and J.D. Tracy (eds.), *Handbook of European history, 1400–1600. Late Middle Ages, Renaissance and Reformation*, I, Leiden, New York and Cologne, pp. 535–62

Mallett, M.E. and Hale, J.R. (1984), *The military organization of a Renaissance state. Venice, c. 1400–1617*, Cambridge

Miskimin, H.A. (1984), *Money and power in fifteenth-century France*, New Haven and London

Mulryne, J.R. and Shewring, M. (eds.) (1989), *War, literature and the arts in sixteenth-century Europe*, Basingstoke and London

Nef, J.U. (1950), *War and human progress*, London

Newhall, R.A. (1924), *The English conquest of Normandy, 1416–1424*, New Haven

Newhall, R.A. (1940), *Muster and review. A problem of English military administration 1420–1440*, Cambridge, Mass.

Oman, C. (1924), *A history of the art of war in the Middle Ages*, 2nd edn, London

Oman, C. (1936), 'The art of war in the fifteenth century', in C.W. Prévité-Orton and Z.N. Brooke (eds.), *Cambridge medieval history*, VIII, pp. 646–59

O'Neil, B.H. St J. (1960), *Castles and cannon. A study of early artillery fortifications in England*, Oxford

Parker, G. (1988), *The military revolution. Military innovation and the rise of the west, 1500–1800*, Cambridge

Parker, G. (1995a), 'The gunpowder revolution, 1300–1500', in Parker (1995b), pp. 106–17

Parker, G. (ed.) (1995b), *The Cambridge illustrated history of warfare. The triumph of the west*, Cambridge

Paviot, J. (1995), *La politique navale des ducs de Bourgogne, 1384–1482*, Lille

Pégeot, P. (1991), 'L'armement des ruraux et des bourgeois à la fin du moyen âge. L'exemple de la région de Montbéliard', in Contamine, Giry-Deloison and Keen (1991), pp. 237–60

Pepper, S. and Adams, N. (1986), *Firearms and fortifications. Military architecture and siege warfare in sixteenth-century Siena*, Chicago and London

Phillpotts, C. (1984), 'The French battle plan during the Agincourt campaign', *EHR* 99: 59–66

Pieri, P. (1952), *Il Rinascimento e la crisi militare italiana*, Milan

Pieri, P. (1963), 'Sur les dimensions de l'histoire militaire', *Annales ESC* 18: 625–38

Pons, N. (1982), 'La propagande de guerre française avant l'apparition de Jeanne d'Arc', *Journal des savants*: 191–214

Pons, N. (1991), 'La guerre de Cent Ans vue par quelques polémistes français du XVe siècle', in Contamine, Giry-Deloison and Keen (1991), pp. 143–69

Powicke, M. (1969), 'Lancastrian captains', in T.A. Sandquist and M. Powicke (eds.), *Essays in medieval history presented to B. Wilkinson*, Toronto, pp. 371–82

Powicke, M. (1971), 'The English aristocracy and the war', in K.A. Fowler (ed.), *The Hundred Years War*, London, pp. 122–34

Pryor, J.H. (1988), *Geography, technology, and war. Studies in the maritime history of the Mediterranean, 649–1571*, Cambridge

Queller, D.E. (1967), *The office of ambassador in the Middle Ages*, Princeton

Quicherat, J. (1879), *Rodrigue de Villandrando, l'un des combattants pour l'indépendance française au quinzième siècle*, Paris

Rázsó, G. (1982), 'The mercenary army of King Matthias Corvinus', in Bak and Király (1982), pp. 125–40

Richmond, C.F. (1964), 'The keeping of the seas during the Hundred Years War: 1422–1440', *History* 49: 283–98

Richmond, C.F. (1967), 'English naval power in the fifteenth century', *History* 52: 1–15

Richmond, C.F. (1971), 'The war at sea', in Fowler (1971), pp. 96–121

Rogers, C.J. (1993), 'The military revolutions of the Hundred Years War', *Journal of Military History* 57: 241–78

Rose, S. (1982), *The navy of the Lancastrian kings. Accounts and inventories of William Soper, keeper of the king's ships, 1422–1427*, London

Rowe, B.J.H. (1931), 'Discipline in the Norman garrisons under Bedford, 1422–35', *EHR* 46: 194–208

Russell, F.H. (1975), *The just war in the Middle Ages*, Cambridge

Russell, J.G. (1986), *Peacemaking in the Renaissance*, London

Russell, J.G. (1996), *Diplomats at work. Three Renaissance studies*, Stroud

Ryder, A. (1976), *The kingdom of Naples under Alfonso the Magnanimous. The making of a modern state*, Oxford

Ryder, A. (1984), 'Cloth and credit: Aragonese war finance in the mid fifteenth century', *War and Society* 2: 1–21

Sablonier, R. (1979), 'Etats et structures militaires dans la confédération [suisse] autour des années 1480', in *Cinq-centième anniversaire de la bataille de Nancy* (1979), pp. 429–77

Salamagne, A. (1993), 'L'attaque des places fortes au XVe siècle à travers l'exemple des guerres anglo- et franco-bourguignonnes', *RH* 289: 65–113

Scattergood, V.J. (1971), *Politics and poetry in the fifteenth century*, London

Simms, K. (1975), 'Warfare in the medieval Gaelic lordships', *The Irish Sword* 12: 98–108

Solon, P.D. (1972), 'Popular response to standing military forces in fifteenth-century France', *Studies in the Renaissance* 19: 78–111

Sommé, M. (1986), 'L'artillerie et la guerre de frontière dans le nord de la France de 1477 à 1482', in Cauchies (1986), pp. 57–70

Sommé, M. (1991), 'L'armée bourguignonne au siège de Calais de 1436', in Contamine, Giry-Deloison and Keen (1991), pp. 197–219

Stewart, P. (1969), 'The soldier, the bureaucrat and fiscal records in the army of Ferdinand and Isabella', *Hispanic American Historical Review* 49: 281–92

Vale, M.G.A. (1976), 'New techniques and old ideals: the impact of artillery on war and chivalry at the end of the Hundred Years War', in Allmand (1976), pp. 57–72

Vale, M.G.A. (1981), *War and chivalry. Warfare and aristocratic culture in England, France and Burgundy at the end of the Middle Ages*, London

Vale, M.G.A. (1982), 'Warfare and the life of the French and Burgundian nobility in the late Middle Ages', in *Adelige Sachkultur des Spätmittelalters. Internationaler Kongress Krems an der Donau, 22. bis 25. September 1980*, Österreichische Akademie der Wissenschaften, Vienna, pp. 169–84

Vaughan, R. (1973), *Charles the Bold. The last Valois duke of Burgundy*, London

Vaughan, R. (1975), *Valois Burgundy*, London

White, L., Jr (1962), *Medieval technology and social change*, Oxford

Winkler, A.L. (1982), 'The Swiss and war: the impact of society on the Swiss military in the fourteenth and fifteenth centuries', PhD dissertation, Brigham Young University

Wood, N. (1967), 'Frontinus as a possible source for Machiavelli's method', *JHI* 28: 243–8

9 EXPLORATION AND DISCOVERY

Primary sources

Bracciolini, Poggio, *De varietate fortunae*, ed. O. Merisalo, Helsinki (1993)

Calendar of state papers. Spanish, 1485–1509, London (1862)

The Cosmographia of Martin Waldseemuller in facsimile, followed by the four voyages of Amerigo Vespucci, ed. C.G. Herbermann, New York (1969)

Díez de Games, G., *El victorial, crónica de Don Pero Niño, conde de Buelna, por su alférez, Gutierre Díez de Games*, ed. J. de Mata Carriazo, Madrid (1940)

Fuchs, W. (ed.), *The Mongol atlas of China by Chu Ssû pen and the Kuang yü-t'u*, Peiping (1946)

The Geography of Strabo, ed. H.L. Jones, 8 vols., London (1917–33)

Ibn Majid, *Arab navigation in the Indian Ocean before the coming of the Portuguese*, ed. G.R. Tibbetts, London (1981)

Kamal, Y., *Monumenta cartographica Africae et Aegypti*, 5 vols. in 16 parts, Cairo (1926–51)

Las Casas, B. de, *Historia de las Indias*, ed. A. Millares Carló, 3 vols., Mexico and Buenos Aires (1951)

Libro de Alexandre, ed. J. Cañas, Madrid (1988)

El libro de Marco Polo anotado por Cristóbal Colón, ed. J. Gil, Madrid (1987)

Lull, Ramon, *Libre de Evast e Blanquerna*, ed. S. Galmés, 4 vols., Barcelona (1935–54)

Ma Huan, *The overall survey of the ocean's shores, 1433*, ed. J.V.G. Mills, Cambridge (1970)

Mandeville, Sir John, *Travels: texts and translations*, ed. M. Letts, 2 vols., Cambridge (1953)

Marco Polo, *Le divisament dou monde. Il milione nelle redazione toscane e franco-italiana*, ed. G. Ronchi, Milan (1982)

Mauro, *Il mapamondo di Fra Mauro*, ed. T. Gasparrini Leporace, Venice (1956)

Monumenta Henricina, ed. A. Brásio *et al.*, 15 vols., Lisbon (1960–75)

Pacheco Pereira, D., *Esmeraldo de situ orbis*, ed. G.H.T. Kimble, London (1943)

Petrarch, F., *Le familiari*, ed. V. Rossi, 4 vols., Florence (1933)

Portugaliae monumenta cartographica, ed. A. Cortesão and A. Teixeira da Mota, 6 vols., Lisbon (1960)

The Prester John of the Indies. A true narrative of the lands of Prester John, being the narrative of the Portuguese embassy to Ethiopia in 1520, written by Fr. Francisco Alvares, ed. C.F. Beckingham and G.W.B. Huntingford, 2 vols., Cambridge (1961)

Ptolemy, Claudius, *Geographia*, 3 vols. in 2, Leipzig (1898)
Ptolemy, Claudius, *The Geography*, ed. E.L. Stevenson, New York (1932)
Smith, Adam, *The wealth of nations*, London (1937)
Varela, C. (ed.), *Cristóbal Colón. Textos y documentos completos*, Madrid (1984)
Worcestre, William, *Itineraries*, ed. J.H. Harvey, Oxford (1969)
Ymago mundi de Pierre d'Ailly, ed. E. Buron, 3 vols., Paris (1930)
Zurara, Gomes Eannes de, *Crónica da tomada de Ceuta*, ed. R. Brasil, Lisbon (1992)
Zurara, Gomes Eannes de, *Crónica dos feitos notáveis que se passaram na conquista da Guiné por mandado do infante Dom Henrique*, ed. T. de Sousa Soares, 2 vols., Lisbon (1978–81)

Secondary works

Adam, P. (1966), 'Navigation primitive et navigation astronomique', *VIe colloque international d'histoire maritime, Paris*, pp. 91–110
Axelson, E. (1973), *Congo to Cape. Early Portuguese explorers*, New York
Bartlett, R. (1993), *The making of Europe. Conquest, colonisation and cultural change*, London
Bartlett, R. and MacKay, A. (1989), *Medieval frontier societies*, Oxford
Beazeley, C.R. (1897–1906), *The dawn of modern geography*, 3 vols., London
Beckingham, C.F. (1980), 'The quest for Prester John', *BJRL* 62: 291–310
Benito Ruano, E. (1978), *San Borondón, octava isla canaria*, Valladolid
Boxer, C.R. (1969), *The Portuguese seaborne empire, 1415–1825*, London
Braudel, F. (1985), *Civilization and capitalism, fifteenth to eighteenth centuries*, III: *The perspectives of the world*, London
Campbell, T. (1987), 'Portolan charts from the late thirteenth century to 1500', in J.B. Harley and D. Woodward (eds.), *The history of cartography*, I: *Cartography in prehistoric, ancient and medieval Europe and the Mediterranean*, Chicago
Chaunu, P. (1959–60), *Séville et l'Atlantique, 1504–1650, partie interprétative*, 4 vols., Paris
Chaunu, P. (1969), *L'expansion européenne du XIIIe au XVe siècle*, Paris
Cortesao, A. (1969–70), *História da cartografia portuguesa*, 2 vols., Coimbra
Cortesao, A. (1975), 'A carta náutica de 1424', in *Esparsos*, 3 vols., Coimbra, III, pp. 1–211
Diffie, B.W. and Winius, G.D. (1977), *Foundations of the Portuguese empire, 1415–1580*, Minneapolis and Oxford
Fernández-Armesto, F. (1986), 'Atlantic exploration before Columbus; the evidence of maps', *Renaissance and Modern Studies* 30: 12–34
Fernández-Armesto, F. (1987), *Before Columbus. Exploration and colonisation from the Mediterranean to the Atlantic*, Basingstoke and Philadelphia
Fernández-Armesto, F. (1991a), *Columbus*, Oxford and New York
Fernández-Armesto, F. (1991b), *The Times atlas of world exploration*, London and New York
Finlay, R. (1991), 'The treasure ships of Zheng He: Chinese maritime imperialism in the age of discovery', *Terrae incognitae* 23: 1–12
Flint, V.I.J. (1992), *The imaginative landscape of Christopher Columbus*, Princeton and Oxford
Focus Martin Behaim (1992), ed. J.K.W. Willers, Nuremberg
Fuchs, W. (1953), 'Was South Africa already known in the XIIIth century?', *Imago mundi* 10: 50–6
Gil, J. and Varela, C. (1984), *Cartas de particulares a Colón y relaciones coetáneas*, Madrid

Greenblatt, S.J. (1991), *Marvellous possessions. The wonder of the New World*, Oxford

Grosjean, G. (1978), *Mapamundi. The Catalan atlas of the year 1375*, Zurich

Harley, J.B. and Woodward, D. (eds.) (1987), *The history of cartography*, 1: *Cartography in prehistoric, ancient and medieval Europe and the Mediterranean*, Chicago

Harvey, P.D.A. (1980), *Topographical maps, symbols, pictures and surveys*, Oxford

Hyde, J.K. (1982), 'Real and imaginary journeys in the later Middle Ages', *BJRULM* 65: 125–47

Keen, M. (1984), *Chivalry*, New Haven and London

Kimble, G.H.T. (1938), *Geography in the Middle Ages*, London

Kraus, H. (1955), *Catalogue no. 55*, New York

La Roncière, C. de (1924–7), *La découverte de l'Afrique au moyen âge. Cartographes et explorateurs*, Mémoires de la Société Royale de Géographie d'Egypte, 5, 6 and 13, Cairo

Laguarda Trías, R. (1974), *El enigma de las latitudes de Colón*, Valladolid

McGrath, P. (1978), 'Bristol and America, 1480–1631', in K.R. Andrews, N.P. Canny and P.E.H. Hair (eds.), *The westward enterprise*, Liverpool

Magalhães Godinho, V. de (1962), *A economia dos descobrimentos henriquinos*, Lisbon

Magalhães Godinho, V. de (1981–84), *Os descobrimentos e a história mundial*, 4 vols., Lisbon

Magnaghi, A. (1924), *Amerigo Vespucci*, 2 vols., Milan

Mauny, R. (1960), *Les navigations médiévales sur les côtes sahariennes*, Lisbon

Mollat du Jourdin, M. and La Roncière, M. de (1984), *Sea charts of the early explorers*, London

Morison, S.E. (1971), *The European discovery of America. The northern voyages, A.D. 500–1600*, New York

Morison, S.E. (1974), *The European discovery of America. The southern voyages, 1492–1616*, Oxford and New York

Navarro González, A. (1962), *El mar en la literatura medieval castellana*, La Laguna

Nebenzahl, K. (1990), *Maps from the age of discovery. Columbus to Mercator*, London and New York

Needham, J. *et al.* (1961–   ), *Science and civilisation in China*, Cambridge

Norwich, O.I. (1983), *Maps of Africa*, Johannesburg

O'Gorman, E. (1976), *La idea del descubrimiento de América*, Mexico

Parry, J.H. (1981), *The discovery of the sea*, Berkeley and Los Angeles

Phillips, J.R.S. (1988), *The medieval expansion of Europe*, Oxford

Phillips, W.D. and C.R. (1992), *The worlds of Christopher Columbus*, Cambridge and New York

Quinn, D.B. (1974), *England and the discovery of America, 1481–1620*, New York

Rosa Olivera, L. de la (1972), 'Francisco de Riberol y la colonia genovesa en Canarias', *Anuario de estudios atlánticos* 18: 61–198

Rumeu de Armas, A. (1955), *España en el Africa atlántica*, 2 vols., Madrid

Rumeu de Armas, A. (1975), *La conquista de Tenerife*, Santa Cruz de Tenerife

Rumeu de Armas, A. (1986), *El obispado de Telde, misioneros mallorquines y catalanes en el Atlántico*, Telde and Madrid

Russell, P.E. (1979), *O infante Dom Henrique e as ilhas Canarias*, Lisbon

Russell, P.E. (1984), *Prince Henry the Navigator. The rise and fall of a culture hero*, Oxford

Russell, P.E. (1986), 'White kings on black kings: Rui de Pina and the problem of black African sovereignty', in *Medieval and Renaissance studies in honour of Robert Brian Tate*, ed. I. Michael and R.A. Cardwell, Oxford, pp. 151–63

Russell-Wood, A.J.R. (1982), *The black man in slavery and freedom in colonial Brazil*, London and Basingstoke

Snow, P. (1988), *The star raft. China's encounter with Africa*, London

Taylor, E.G.R. (1928), 'Pactolus: river of gold', *Scottish Geographical Magazine* 44: 129–44

Taylor, E.G.R. (1956a), 'A letter dated 1577 from Mercator to John Dee', *Imago mundi* 13: 56–68

Taylor, E.G.R. (1956b), *The haven-finding art*, London

Unger, R.W. (1980), *The ship in the medieval economy, 600–1600*, London

Unger, R.W. (1991), *Medieval technology. Images of Noah the Shipbuilder*, New Brunswick, N.J.

Varela, C. (1992), *Cristóbal Colón. Retrato de un hombre*, Madrid

Verlinden, C. (1962), 'Un précurseur de Colomb: le flamand Ferdinand van Olmen (1487)', in *Revista portuguesa de história. Homenagem ao Prof. Dr. Damiao Peres*, Coimbra, pp. 453–66; repr. in English trans. in Verlinden (1970), pp. 181–95

Verlinden, C. (1966), *Les origines de la civilisation atlantique*, Paris

Verlinden, C. (1970), *The beginnings of modern colonization*, Ithaca, N.Y.

Verlinden, C. (1978), 'La découverte des archipels de la "Mediterranée atlantique" (Canaries, Madères, Açores) et la navigation astronomique primitive', *Revista portuguesa de história* 16: 124–39

Vietor, A.O. (1962), 'A pre-Columbian map of the world, *c.* 1489', *Yale University Library Gazette* 37: 8–12

Vigneras, L.A. (1976), *The discovery of South America and the Andalusian voyages*, Chicago

Yule Oldham, H. (1895), 'A pre-Columbian discovery of America', *Geographical Journal*, 5: 221–339

10 RELIGIOUS BELIEF AND PRACTICE

Secondary works

Adam, P. (1964), *La vie paroissiale en France au XIVe siècle*, Paris

Aston, M. (1984), *Lollards and reformers. Images and literacy in late medieval religion*, London

L'attesa dell'età nuova nella spiritualità della fine del medioevo (1962), Convegno del Centro Sulla Spiritualità Medievale, Todi

Axters, S. (1950), *Geschiedenis van de vroomheid in de Nederlande*, Antwerp

Baschet, J. (1993), *Les jugements de l'au-delà. Les représentations de l'enfer en France et en Italie*, Rome

Bastard-Fournié, M. (1973), 'Mentalités religieuses aux confins du Toulousain et de l'Albigeois à la fin du moyen âge', *AM* 85: 267–87

Binz, L. (1977), *Vie religieuse et réforme ecclésiastique dans le diocèse de Genève pendant le grand schisme et la crise conciliaire 1378–1450*, I, Mémoires et Documents Publiés par la Société d'Histoire et d'Archéologie de Genève, 46, Geneva

Blench, J.W. (1964), *Preaching in England in the later XVth and XVIth centuries*, London

Boockmann, H. (ed.) (1994), *Kirche und Gesellschaft im Heiligen Römischen Reich des 15. und 16. Jahrhunderts*, Göttingen

Brentano, R. (1994), *A new world in a small place. Church and religion in the diocese of Rieti (1188–1378)*, Berkeley, Los Angeles and London

Brown, C.F. and Smithers, G.V. (eds.) (1952), *Religious lyrics of the XIVth century*, Oxford

Brown, D.C. (1987), *Pastor and laity in the theology of Jean Gerson*, Cambridge

Cauchies, J.-M. (1989), *La dévotion moderne dans les pays bourguignons et rhénans, des origines à la fin du XVIe siècle*, Basle

Chiffoleau, J. (1980), *La comptabilité de l'au-delà*, Rome

Cognet, L. (1965), *Introduction aux mystiques rhéno-flamands*, Paris and Tournai

Cohn, N. (1957), *The pursuit of the millennium. Revolutionary millenarianism and mystical anarchists of the Middle Ages*, London

Coletti, V. (1987), *L'éloquence de la chaire*, Paris

Danet, A. (1973), *Le marteau des sorcières*, Paris

De Vooght, P. (1960), *L'hérésie de Jean Hus*, Louvain

Delaruelle, E. (1975), *La piété populaire au moyen âge*, Turin

Delumeau, J. (1991), *L'aveu et le pardon. Les difficultés de la confession (XIIIe–XVIII siècles)*, Paris

Delumeau, J. (1992–5), *Une histoire du paradis*, I: *Le jardin des délices*; II: *Mille ans de bonheur*, Paris

Dinzelbacher, P. and Bauer, D.R. (1988), *Religiöse Frauenbewegungen und mystische Frömmigkeit*, Cologne and Vienna

Eglise et vie religieuse en France au début de la Renaissance (1991), Colloque de Tours, 1991, Revue d'histoire de l'église de France

Elm, K. (1989), *Reformbemühungen und Observanzbestrebungen im spätmittelalterlichen Ordenswesen*, Berlin

Encadrement religieux des fidèles au moyen âge et jusqu'au concile de Trente (1985). Actes du 109e Congrès des Sociétés Savantes, Dijon, 1984, Paris

Epiney-Burgard, G. (1970), *Gérard Grote (1340–1384) et les débuts de la dévotion moderne*, Veröffentlichungen des Instituts fur europäische Geschichte, Mainz, 54, Wiesbaden

Faire croire. Modalités de la diffusion et de la réception des messages religieux du XIIe au XVe siècle (1981), Rome

Filthaut, E. (1961), *Johannes Tauler. Gedenkschrift zum 600 Geburtstag*, Essen

Filthaut, E. (1966), *Seuse. Studien zum 600 Geburtstag*, Cologne

Finucane, R.C. (1977), *Miracles and pilgrims. Popular beliefs in medieval England*, London

Francescanesimo e il teatro medievale. Atti del convegno di studi di San Miniato, 1982 (1984), Castelfiorentino

Gardiner, F.C. (1971), *The pilgrimage of desire. A study of theme and genre in medieval literature*, Leiden

Genicot, L. (1958), *La spiritualité médiévale*, Paris

Georges, A. (1971), *Le pèlerinage de Compostelle en Belgique et dans le nord de la France*, Brussels

Gieysztor, A. (1979), 'Xe–XVe siècles. La religion populaire en Pologne et en Bohème', in J. Delumeau (ed.), *Histoire vécue du peuple chrétien*, Toulouse, I, pp. 315–34

Godin, A. (1971), *Spiritualité franciscaine en Flandre au XVIe siècle. L'homéliaire de Jean Vitrier. Texte, étude thématique et sémantique*, Geneva

Grion, A. (1953), *Santa Caterina da Siena, dottrina e fonti*, Marcelliana

Hall, D.J. (1965), *English mediaeval pilgrimage*, London

Herbers, L. and Plötz, R. (1993), *Spiritualität des pilgerns*, Tübingen

Huizinga, J. (1955), *The waning of the Middle Ages*, Harmondsworth

Hyma, A. (1950), *The Brethren of the Common Life*, Grand Rapids

Jordan, W.K. (1960), *The charities of London, 1480–1660. The aspirations and the achievements of the urban society*, London

Jordan, W.K. (1961), *The charities of rural England. The aspirations and the achievements of the rural society*, London

La Roncière, C.-M. (1979), 'Dans la campagne florentine au XIVe siècle. Les communautés chrétiennes et leurs curés', in J. Delumeau, *Histoire vécue du peuple chrétien*, Toulouse, I, pp. 281–314

Lebrun, F. (1988), *Du christianisme flamboyant à l'aube des Lumières (XIVe–XVIIIe siècle*, Histoire de la France Religieuse, 2, Paris

Leclercq, J., Vandenbroucke, F. and Bouyer, L. (eds.) (1961), *La spiritualité du moyen âge*, Paris

Leff, G. (1967), *Heresy in the later Middle Ages*, 2 vols., Manchester

Lemaitre, N. (1988), *Le Rouergue flamboyant. Le clergé et les fidèles du diocèse de Rodez (1418–1563)*, Paris

Lobrichon, G. (1994), *La religion des laïcs en Occident (XIe–XIVe siècles)*, Paris

Lopez, E. (1994), *Culture et sainteté. Colette de Corbie (1381–1447)*, Saint-Etienne

Lorcin, M.-T. (1981), *Vivre et mourir en Lyonnais au moyen âge*, Lyons

Manselli, R. (1975), *La religion populaire au moyen âge. Problèmes de méthode et d'histoire*, Conférences Albert-le-Grand, Montreal

Martin, H. (1979), 'La prédication des masses au XVe siècle. Facteurs et limites d'une réussite', in J. Delumeau (ed.), *Histoire vécue du peuple chrétien*, Toulouse, II, pp. 9–42

Martin, H. (1988), *Le métier de prédicateur en France septentrionale à la fin du moyen âge*, Paris

Michaud-Quantin, P. (1962), *Somme de casuistique et manuels de confession au moyen âge (XIIe–XVIe siècles)*, Louvain and Lille

Moeller, B. (1965), 'Frömmigkeit in Deutschland um 1500', *Archiv für Reformationsgeschichte* 56: 5–30; trans. as 'Piety in Germany around 1500', in S.E. Ozment (ed.), *The Reformation in medieval perspective*, Chicago (1971), pp. 50–75, and as 'Religious life in Germany on the eve of the Reformation', in G. Strauss (ed.), *Pre-Reformation Germany*, New York and London (1972), pp. 13–42

Mollat, M. (1978), *Les pauvres au moyen âge*, Paris

Mollat, M. and Vauchez, A. (1990), *Un temps d'épreuves (1274–1449)*, Histoire du Christianisme, 6, Paris

La mort au moyen âge (1977), Colloque de l'Association des Historiens Médiévistes Français, 1975, Strasburg

Mourin, L. (1952), *Jean Gerson, prédicateur français*, Bruges

Oakley, F. (1979), *The western Church in the later Middle Ages*, Ithaca and London

Oberman, H.A. (1963), *The harvest of medieval theology*, Cambridge, Mass.

Owst, G.R. (1926), *Preaching in medieval England. An introduction to sermon manuscripts (1350–1450)*, Cambridge

Paravy, P. (1993), *De la chrétienté romaine à la Réforme en Dauphiné*, 2 vols., Rome

Post, R. (1968), *The Modern Devotion*, Leiden

Preger, W. (1874–93), *Geschichte der deutschen Mystik im mittelalter*, 3 vols., Leipzig

Prière au moyen âge (1982), Cahiers du CUERMA, Aix-en-Provence

Rapp, F. (1979), 'Christianisme et vie quotidienne dans les pays germaniques au XVe siècle. L'empreinte du sacré sur le temps', in J. Delumeau (ed.), *Histoire vécue du peuple chrétien*, Toulouse, I, pp. 335–64

Réau, L. (1955–9), *Iconographie de l'art chrétien*, 6 vols., Paris

Les religieuses dans le cloître et dans le monde (1994), Actes du Colloque de Poitiers, 1988, Saint-Etienne

Renaudin, P. (1957), *Mystiques anglais*, Paris

Rézeau, P. (1983), *Les prières aux saints en français à la fin du moyen âge*, Geneva

Rosenfeld, H. (1954), *Der mittelalterliche Totentanz*, Munster

Rosenthal, J.T. (1972), *The purchase of paradise. Gifts, giving, and the aristocracy 1307–1485*, London and Toronto

Rudolf, R. (1959), *Ars moriendi*, Cologne

Ruh, K. (1964), *Altdeutsche und altniederländische Mystik*, Darmstadt

Rusconi, R. (1979), *L'attenta della fine. Crisi della società, profezia ed Apocalisse in Italia al tempo del grande scisma d'occidente (1378–1417)*, Rome

Russell, J.B. (1972), *Witchcraft in the Middle Ages*, Ithaca and London

Schreiber, G. (1959), *Die vierzehn Nothelfer in Volksfrömmigkeit und Sakralkultur*, Innsbruck

Schreiner, K. (ed.) (1992), *Laïenfrömmigkeit im späten Mittelalter*, Munich

Smahel, F. (1985), *La révolution hussite, une anomalie historique*, Paris

Sumption, J. (1975), *Pilgrimage. An image of medieval religion*, London

Thomson, J.A.F. (1965), *The later Lollards, 1414–1520*, Oxford

Van der Wansem, C. (1958), *Het outstaan ende geschiedenis der Broederschap van het Gemene Leven tot 1400*, Louvain

Van Zyl, T.P. (1963), *Gerard Groote, ascetic and reformer*, Washington

Varanini, G.M. (ed.) (1990), *Vescovi e diocesi in Italia del XIV alla metà del XVI secolo*, 2 vols., Rome

Vauchez, A. (1981), *La sainteté en occident aux derniers siècles du moyen âge (1198–1431). Recherches sur les mentalités religieuses médiévales*, Rome

Vauchez, A. (1987), *Les laïcs au moyen âge. Pratiques et expériences religieuses*, Paris

Vincent, C. (1988), *Des charités bien ordonnées. Les confréries normandes de la fin du XIIIe siècle au début du XVIe siècle*, Paris

Whiting, R. (1989), *The blind devotion of the people. Popular religion and the English Reformation*, Cambridge

11 SCHOOLS AND UNIVERSITIES

Primary sources

This list represents only a selection of the publications of primary sources concerning the main European universities in the fifteenth century

Bulario de la Universidad de Salamanca, ed. V. Beltan de Heredia, 3 vols., Salamanca (1966–7)

Cartulario de la Universidad de Salamanca, ed. V. Beltran de Heredia, 6 vols., Salamanca (1970–3)

Chartularium Studii Bononiensis. Documenti per la storia dell'università di Bologna dalle origini fino al secolo XV, 15 vols., Bologna (1909–88)

Chartularium Universitatis Parisiensis, ed. H. Denifle and E. Châtelain, 4 vols., Paris (1889–97), and *Auctarium chartularii universitatis Parisiensis*, ed. H. Denifle and E. Châtelain, 6 vols., Paris (1894–1964)

Chartularium Universitatis Portugalensis, 9 vols., and 3 vols. of *Auctarium*, ed. A. Moreira de Sà, Lisbon, 1966–89

Gerson, Jean, *Œuvres complètes*, 10 vols., ed. P. Glorieux, Paris (1960–73)

Le livre des prieurs de Sorbonne (1431–1485), ed. R. Marichal, Paris (1987)

Monumenti della Università di Padova, ed. A. Gloria, 2 vols., Venice and Padua (1885–8)

Statuta Antiqua Universitatis Oxoniensis, ed. S. Gibson, Oxford (1931)

Les statuts et privilèges des universités françaises depuis leur fondation jusqu'en 1789, ed. M. Fournier, 4 vols., Paris (1890–4)

Secondary works

General works

Baldwin, J.W. and Goldthwaite, R.A. (eds.) (1972), *Universities in politics. Case studies from the late Middle Ages and early modern period*, Baltimore and London

Brizzi, G.P. and J. Verger (eds.) (1990, 1993, 1994), *Le università dell'Europa*, I: *La nascità delle università*; IV: *Gli uomini e i luoghi – secoli XII–XVIII*; V: *Le scuole e i maestri – il medio-evo*, Cinisello Balsamo

Cobban, A.B. (1975), *The medieval universities. Their development and organization*, London

Fried, J. (ed.) (1986), *Schulen und Studium im sozialen Wandel des hohen und späten Mittelalters*, Vorträge und Forschungen, XXX, Sigmaringen

Gabriel, A.L. (1969), *Garlandia. Studies in the history of the mediaeval universities*, Notre Dame and Frankfurt am Main

Gabriel, A.L. (ed.) (1977), *The economic frame of the mediaeval university*, Texts and Studies in the History of Mediaeval Education, XV, Notre Dame

Garin, E. (1957), *L'educazione in Europa, 1400–1600*, Bari

Grafton, A. and Jardine, L. (1986), *From humanism to the humanities. Education and the liberal arts in fifteenth- and sixteenth-century Europe*, London

History of universities (one annual issue since 1981)

IJsewijn, J. and Paquet, J. (eds.) (1978), *Les universités à la fin du moyen âge*, Publ. de l'Institut d'Etudes Médiévales, 2nd series, 2, Louvain; also published as J. IJsewijn and J. Paquet (eds.) *Universities in the late Middle Ages*, Mediaevalia Lovanensia, 1st series, 6, Louvain (1978)

Keil, G., Moeller, B. and Trusen (1987), W., *Der Humanismus und die oberen Fakultäten*, Mitteilung der Kommission für Humanismusforschung, XIV, Weinheim

Kenny, A., Kretzmann, N. and Pinborg, J. (eds.) (1982), *The Cambridge history of later medieval philosophy*, Cambridge

Kibre, P. (1948), *The nations in the mediaeval universities*, Cambridge, Mass.

Kibre, P. (1961), *Scholarly privileges in the Middle Ages. The rights, privileges, and immunities of scholars and universities at Bologna, Padua, Paris, and Oxford*, London

Le Goff, J. (1985), *Les intellectuels au moyen âge*, 2nd edn, Paris

Paquet, J. (1992), *Les matricules universitaires*, Typologie des Sources du Moyen Age Occidental, 65, Turnhout

Patschovsky, A. and Rabe, H. (eds.) (1994), *Die Universität in Alteuropa*, Konstanz

Piltz, A. (1981), *The world of medieval learning* (English trans.), Oxford

Rashdall, H. (1936), *The universities of Europe in the Middle Ages*, new edn by F.M. Powicke and A.B. Emden, 3 vols., London

Ridder-Symoens, H. de (ed.) (1992), *A history of the university in Europe*, I: *Universities in the Middle Ages*, Cambridge

Swanson, R.N. (1979), *Universities, academics and the Great Schism*, Cambridge Studies in Medieval Life and Thought, 3rd series, 12, Cambridge

Università e società nei secoli XII–XVI (1982), Pistoia

Les universités européennes du quatorzième au dix-huitième siècle. Aspects et problèmes (1967), Geneva

Verger, J. (1973), *Les universités au moyen âge*, Paris

Zimmermann, A. (ed.) (1974), *Antiqui und Moderni. Traditionsbewusstsein im späten Mittelalter*, Miscellanea Mediaevalia, IX, Berlin and New York.

Empire, northern and central Europe

Fuchs, C. (1995), '*Dives, Pauper, Nobilis, Magister, Frater, Clericus*'. *Sozialgeschichtliche Untersuchungen über Heidelberger Universitätsbesucher des Spätmittelalters (1386–1450)*, Education and Society in the Middle Ages and the Renaissance, 5, Leiden

Gabriel, A.L. (1969), *The mediaeval universities of Pécs and Pozsony*, Notre Dame and Frankfurt am Main

Kaminsky, H. (1972), 'The University of Prague in the Hussite revolution: the role of the masters', in Baldwin and Goldthwaite (1972), pp. 79–106

Meuthen, E. (1988), *Kölner Universitätsgeschichte*, I: *Die alte Universität*, Cologne and Vienna

Miner, J.N. (1987), 'Change and continuity in the schools of later medieval Nuremberg', *Catholic Historical Review* 72: 1–22

Mornet, E. (1983), 'Le voyage d'études des jeunes nobles danois du XIVᵉ siècle à la Réforme', *Journal des savants*: 287–318

Paquet, J. (1958), *Salaires et prébendes des professeurs de l'université de Louvain au XVᵉ siècle*, Léopoldville

Post, R.R. (1968), *The Modern Devotion. Confrontation with Reformation and humanism*, Leiden

Ridder-Symoens, H. de (1981), 'Milieu social, études universitaires et carrière de conseillers au Conseil de Brabant (1430–1600)', in *Liber amicorum Jan Buntinx*, Symbolae Fac. Litt. et Philos. Lovaniensis, series A, 10, Ghent, pp. 257–302

Schwinges, R.C. (1986), *Deutsche Universitätsbesucher im 14. und 15. Jahrhundert. Studien zur Sozialgeschichte des alten Reiches*, Stuttgart

Die Universität zu Prag (1986), Schriften der Sudetendeutschen Akademie der Wissenschaften und Künste, 7, Munich

England

Aston, T.H. (1979), 'Oxford's medieval alumni', *P&P* 74: 3–40

Aston, T.H., Duncan, G.D. and Evans, T.A.R. (1980), 'The medieval alumni of the University of Cambridge', *P&P* 86: 9–86

Catto, J.I. and Evans, R. (eds.) (1992), *The history of the University of Oxford*, II: *Late medieval Oxford*, Oxford

Cobban, A.B. (1988), *The medieval English universities: Oxford and Cambridge to c. 1500*, Berkeley and Los Angeles

Gabriel, A.L. (1974), *Summary bibliography of the history of Great Britain and Ireland up to 1800 covering publications between 1900 and 1968*, Texts and Studies in the History of Mediaeval Education, XIV, Notre Dame

Leader, D.R. (1988), *A history of the University of Cambridge*, I: *The University to 1546*, Cambridge

Lytle, G.F. (1978), 'The social origins of Oxford students in the late Middle Ages: New College, *c.* 1380–*c.* 1510', in Ijsewijn and Paquet (1978), pp. 426–54

Orme, N. (1973), *English schools in the Middle Ages*, London

Orme, N. (1976), *Education in the west of England. Cornwall, Devon, Dorset, Gloucestershire, Somerset, Wiltshire*, Exeter

Rosenthal, J. (1970), 'The training of an elite group. English bishops in the fifteenth century', *Trans. of the American Philosophical Society* new series 60/5: 5–54

France

Allmand, C.T. (1983), *Lancastrian Normandy*, Oxford, ch. 4

Favier, J. (1974), *Nouvelle histoire de Paris. Paris au XVe siècle*, Paris, pp. 68–79 and 199–235

Gabriel, A.L. (1992), *The Paris studium. Robert of Sorbonne and his legacy. Interuniversity exchange between the German, Cracow, Louvain Universities and that of Paris in the late medieval and humanistic period. Selected studies*, Texts and Studies in the History of Mediaeval Education, XIX, Notre Dame and Frankfurt am Main

Guenée, S. (1978–81), *Bibliographie de l'histoire des universités françaises des origines à la Révolution*, 2 vols., Paris

Guilbert, S. (1982), 'Les écoles rurales en Champagne au XVe siècle: enseignement et promotion sociale', in *Les entrées dans la vie. Initiations et apprentissages*, Nancy, pp. 127–47

Jacquart, D. (1981), *Le milieu médical en France du XIIe au XV siècle*, Geneva

Jones, M. (1978), 'Education in Brittany during the later Middle Ages', *Nottingham Medieval Studies* 22: 58–77

Millet, H. (1982), *Les chanoines du chapitre cathédral de Laon, 1272–1412*, Paris and Rome

Roux, S. (1992), *La rive gauche des escholiers (XVe siècle)*, Paris

Roy, L. (1994), 'L'université de Caen aux XVe et XVIe siècles. Histoire politique et sociale', 2 vols., PhD dissertation, University of Montréal

Tanaka, M. (1990), *La nation anglo-allemande de l'Université de Paris à la fin du moyen âge*, Paris

Verger, J. (1976a), 'Les universités françaises au XVe siècle: crise et tentatives de réforme', *Cahiers d'histoire* 21: 43–66

Verger, J. (1976b), 'Noblesse et savoir: étudiants nobles aux universités d'Avignon, Cahors, Montpellier et Toulouse (fin du XIVe siècle)', in P. Contamine (ed.), *La noblesse au moyen âge. XIe–XVe siècles. Essais à la mémoire de Robert Boutruche*, Paris, pp. 289–313

Verger, J. (1977), 'Le coût des grades: droits et frais d'examen dans les universités du Midi de la France an moyen âge', in Gabriel (1977), pp. 19–36

Verger, J. (1986a), 'Prosopographie et cursus universitaires', in N. Bulst and J.-P. Genet (eds.), *Medieval lives and the historian. Studies in medieval prosopography*, Kalamazoo, pp. 313–32

Verger, J. (ed.) (1986b), *Histoire des universités en France*, Toulouse

Verger, J. (1994), 'Les universités du midi de la France à la fin du moyen âge (début du XIVe s. – milieu du XVe s.)', Thèse d'Etat, University of Paris-Sorbonne

Verger, J. (1995a), 'Les institutions universitaires françaises au moyen âge: origines, modèles, évolution', in A. Romano (ed.), *Università in Europa. Le istituzioni universitarie dal medio evo ai nostri giorni–strutture, organizzazione, funzionamento*, Soveria Mannelli and Messina, pp. 61–79

Verger, J. (1995b), *Les universités françaises au moyen âge*, Education and Society in the Middle Ages and the Renaissance, 7, Leiden

Italy

Adorni, G. (1992), 'L'archivio dell'università di Roma', in *Roma e lo studium urbis. Spazio urbano e cultura dal Quattro al Seicento*, Rome, pp. 388–430

Bertanza, E. and Dalla Santa, G. (1907), *Maestri, scuole e scolari in Venezia fino al 1500*, Venice; repr. 1993

Castelli, P. (ed.) (1991), *La Rinascità del sapere. Libri e maestri dello studio ferrarese*, Venice

Ermini, G. (1971), *Storia dell'università di Perugia*, 2 vols., Florence

Gargan, L. (1971), *Lo studio teologico e la biblioteca dei Domenicani a Padova nel Tre e Quattrocento*, Padua

Grendler, P.F. (1989), *Schooling in Renaissance Italy. Literacy and Learning, 1300–1600*, Baltimore and London

Minnucci, G. and Kosuta, L., *Lo studio di Siena nei secoli XIV–XVI. Documenti e notizie biographiche*, Orbis Academicus, III, Milan

Nasalli Rocca, E. (1930), 'Il cardinale Bessarione legato pontificio in Bologna', *Atti e memorie della Reale Deputazione di storia patria per le prov. di Romagna* 4th series 40: 36–9

Ortalli, G. (1993), *Scuole, maestri e istruzione di base tra medioevo e Rinascimento. Il caso veneziano*, Venice

Quaderni per la storia dell'università di Padova (one annual issue since 1968)

Verde, A.F. (1973–85), *Lo studio fiorentino, 1473–1503. Documenti e ricerche*, 4 vols., Florence

Zanetti, D. (1962), 'A l'université de Pavie au XVe siècle: les salaires des professeurs', *Annales ESC* 17: 421–33

Spain

Ajo Gonzalez de Rapariegos y Sainz de Zuñiga, C.M. (1957–77), *Historia de las universidades hispanicas. Origenes y desarrollo desde su aparicion a nuestros dias*, 11 vols., Madrid

Estudios sobre los origenes de las universidades españolas (1988), Valladolid

Fernández Alvarez, F., Robles Carcedo, L. and Rodríguez San Pedro, L.E. (eds.) (1989–90), *La universidad de Salamanca*, 3 vols., Salamanca

12 HUMANISM

The list is confined to works directly cited or referred to in ch. 12; bibliographies more comprehensive than that provided here may be found in A. Rabil (ed.), *Renaissance humanism: foundations, forms, and legacy*, Philadelphia (1988), III, pp. 531–656, which is especially useful for indications of sources in English translation; and in *The Cambridge history of Renaissance philosophy*, ed. C.B. Schmitt *et al.*, Cambridge (1988), pp. 842–930.

Primary sources

Accolti, Benedetto, *De bello a christianis contra barbaros gesto*, in *Recueil des historiens des croisades. Historiens occidentaux*, Paris (1895), V, pp. 529–620

Accolti, Benedetto, *Dialogus [de praestantia virorum sui aevi]*, G. Galletti (ed.), *Philippi Villani liber de civitatis Florentiae famosis civibus*, Florence (1848), pp. 105–28

Alberti, Leon Battista, *Momus o del principe*, ed. G. Martini, Bologna (1942)

Alberti, Leon Battista, *Opera inedita et pauca separatim impressa*, ed. G. Mancini, Florence (1890)

Alberti, Leon Battista, *Opere volgari*, ed. C. Grayson, 3 vols., Bari (1960–73)

Alexandre de Villedieu, *Das Doctrinale des Alexander de Villa-Dei*, ed. D. Reichling, Berlin (1893)

Barzizza, Gasparino, *Opera*, ed. G.A. Furietto, Rome (1723)

Biondo, Flavio, *Historiarum ab inclinato Romano imperio decades III*, in his *De Roma triumphante...*, Basle (1531)

Biondo, Flavio, *Scritti inediti e rari*, ed. B. Nogara, Rome (1927)

Bracciolini, Poggio, *Lettere*, ed. H. Harth, 3 vols., Florence (1984–7)

Bracciolini, Poggio, *Opera*, Basle (1538)

Bruni, Leonardo, *Epistolarum libri VIII*, ed. L. Mehus, 2 vols., Florence (1741)

Bruni, Leonardo, *Historiarum florentini populi libri XII*, in *Rerum italicarum scriptores*, new series, 19, pt 3, ed. Emilio Santini, Città di Castello (1914)

Bruni, Leonardo, *Humanistisch-philosophische Schriften*, ed. H. Baron, Leipzig and Berlin (1928)

Bruni, Leonardo, *Laudatio florentinae urbis*, ed. H. Baron, in his *From Petrarch to Leonardo Bruni*, Chicago (1968), pp. 232–63

Bruni, Leonardo, *Oratio in funere Nannis Strozae*, in E. Baluze and G. Mansi (eds.), *Miscellanea novo ordine digesta...*, 4 vols., Lucca (1761–4), IV, pp. 2–7

Calco, Tristano, *Historiae patriae*, in J.G. Graevius, *Thesaurus antiquitatum et historiarum Italiae*, II, pt 1, Leiden (1704)

Cavalcanti, G., *Istorie fiorentine*, ed. G. di Pino, Milan (1944)

Cortesi, Paolo, *De hominibus doctis*, ed. G. Ferraù, Messina (1977)

Dante Alighieri, *De vulgari eloquentia*, in his *Opere minori*, II, ed. P.V. Mengaldo, B. Nardi, A. Furgoni, G. Brugnoli, E. Cecchini and F. Mazzoni, Milan and Naples (1979)

Evrard de Béthune, *Graecismus*, ed. J. Wrobel, Wratislav (1887)

Facio, Bartolomeo, *De humanae vitae felicitate. De excellentia ac praestantia hominis*, in F. Sandeus, *De regibus Siciliae et Apuliae*, Hanau (1611)

Filelfo, Francesco, *Epistolarum familiarium libri XXXVII*, Venice (1502)

Garin, E. (ed.), *Il pensiero pedagogico dello Umanesimo*, Florence (1958)

Garin, E. (ed.), *Prosatori latini del Quattrocento*, Milan (1952)

Gellius, Aulus, *The Attic nights of Aulus Gellius*, trans. J.C. Rolfe, 3 vols., Cambridge, Mass., and London (1927–61)

George of Trebizond, *Rhetoricorum libri quinque*, Venice (1470)

Guarino Veronese, *Epistolario*, ed. R. Sabbadini, 3 vols., Venice (1915–19)

Guicciardini, Francesco, *Storia d'Italia*, ed. C. Panigada, Bari (1929)

Innocent III, *De miseria humane conditionis*, ed. M. Maccarrone, Lugano (1955)

Lefèvre d'Etaples, Jacques, *The prefatory epistles of Jacques Lefèvre d'Etaples and related texts*, ed. E.F. Rice, Jr, New York (1972)

Machiavelli, Niccolò, *Il principe e Discorsi*, ed. S. Bertelli, Milan (1960)

Manetti, Giannozzo, *De dignitate et excellentia hominis*, ed. E.R. Leonard, Padua (1975)

Petrarch, Francesco, *Prose*, ed. G. Martellotti, P.G. Ricci, E. Carrara and E. Bianchi, Milan and Naples (1955)

Pico della Mirandola, Giovanni, *De hominis dignitate*, ed. E. Garin, Florence (1942)

Poliziano, Angelo, *Prose volgari inedite e poesie latine e greche edite e inedite*, ed. I. Del Lungo, Florence (1867)

Pontano, Giovanni, *I dialoghi*, ed. C. Previtera, Florence (1943)

Rinuccini, Alamanno, *Lettere ed orazioni*, ed. V.R. Giustiniani, Florence (1953)

Ross, J.B. and McLaughlin, M.M. (eds.), *The portable Renaissance reader*, New York (1953)

Salutati, Coluccio, *Epistolario*, ed. F. Novati, 4 vols., Rome (1891–1905)

Salutati, Coluccio, *Il trattato 'De tyranno' e lettere scelte*, ed. F. Ercole, Bologna (1942)

Scala, Bartolomeo, *Historia Florentinorum*, ed. J. Oligerus, Rome (1677)

Solerti, A. (ed.), *Le vite di Dante, Petrarca e Boccaccio, scritte fino al secolo XVI*, Milan (1904)

Traversari, Ambrogio, *Epistolae*, ed. P. Caneto and L. Mehus, Florence (1759)

Valla, Lorenzo, *Collatio Novi Testamenti*, ed. A. Perosa, Florence (1970)

Valla, Lorenzo, *De vero falsoque bono*, ed. M. Lorch, Bari (1970)

Valla, Lorenzo, *De libero arbitrio*, ed. M. Anfossi, Florence (1934)

Valla, Lorenzo, *Elegantiarum latinae linguae libri sex*, in his *Opera*, Basle (1540)

Valla, Lorenzo, *In Latinam Novi Testamenti interpretationem ex collatione Graecorum exemplarium Adnotationes apprime utiles*, ed. D. Erasmus, Paris (1505)

Vergerio, Pier Paolo, *De ingenuis moribus et liberalibus adolescentiae studiis*, ed. C. Miani, Atti e memorie della Società istriana di archeologia e storia patria, new series, 20–1 (1972–3), pp. 183–251

Vespasiano da Bisticci, *Le vite*, ed. A. Greco, Florence (1970–6)

Secondary works

Akkerman, F. and Vanderjagt, A.J. (eds.) (1988), *Rodolphus Agricola Phrisius, 1444–1485*, Leiden

Alessio, G.C. (1986), 'Le istituzioni scolastiche e l'insegnamento', in *Aspetti della letteratura latina nel secolo XIII: Atti del primo Convegno internazionale di studi dell'Associazione per il medioevo e l'umanesimo latini*, Perugia and Florence, pp. 3–28

Avesani, R. (1965), 'Il primo ritmo per la morte del grammatico Ambrogio e il cosiddetto "Liber catonianus"', *Studi medievali* 3rd series 6: 455–88

Avensani, R. (1967), *Quattro miscellanee medioevali e umanistiche*, Rome

Baron, H. (1938), 'Franciscan poverty and civic wealth as factors in the rise of humanistic thought', *Speculum* 13: 1–37

Baron, H. (1958), 'Moot problems of Renaissance interpretation: an answer to Wallace K. Ferguson', *JHI* 19: 26–34

Baron, H. (1966), *The crisis of the early Italian Renaissance. Civic humanism and republican liberty in an age of classicism and tyranny*, Princeton (rev. edn in 1 vol.; first published, 1955, in 2 vols.)

Bentley, J.H. (1983), *Humanists and holy writ: New Testament scholarship in the Renaissance*, Princeton

Bernstein, E. (1983), *German humanism*, Boston

Berschin, W. (1988), *Greek letters and the Latin Middle Ages: from Jerome to Nicholas of Cusa*, Washington

Billanovich, G. (1951), 'Petrarch and the textual tradition of Livy', *JWCI* 14: 137–208

Black, R. (1981), 'Benedetto Accolti and the beginnings of humanist historiography', *EHR* 96: 36–58

Black, R. (1985), *Benedetto Accolti and the Florentine Renaissance*, Cambridge

Black, R. (1986), 'The political thought of the Florentine chancellors', *HZ* 29: 991–1003

Black, R. (1987), 'The new laws of history', *Renaissance Studies* 1: 126–56

Black, R. (1990), 'Machiavelli, servant of the Florentine Republic', in Bock, Skinner and Viroli (1990), pp. 71–99

Black, R. (1991a), 'An unknown thirteenth-century manuscript of *Ianua*', in I. Wood and G.A. Loud (eds.), *Church and chronicle in the Middle Ages. Essays presented to John Taylor*, London, pp. 101–15

Black, R. (1991b), 'The curriculum of Italian elementary and grammar schools, 1350–1500', in D.R. Kelley and R.H. Popkin (eds.), *The shapes of knowledge from the Renaissance to the Enlightenment*, Dordrecht, pp. 137–63

Black, R. (1991c), 'Italian Renaissance education: changing perspectives and continuing controversies', *JHI* 52: 315–34

Black, R. (1991d), 'Reply to Paul Grendler', *JHI* 52: 519–520

Black, R. (1992), 'Florence', in R. Porter and M. Teich, *The Renaissance in national context*, Cambridge, pp. 21–41

Black, R. (1995), 'The Donation of Constantine: a new source for the concept of the Renaissance?', in A. Brown (ed.), *Language and images of the Renaissance*, Oxford, pp. 51–85

Black, R. (1996), 'Cicero in the curriculum of Italian Renaissance grammar schools', *Ciceroniana* 9: 105–20

Black, R. (1997), 'The vernacular and the teaching of Latin in the thirteenth and fourteenth centuries', forthcoming in *Studi medievali*

Black, R. (forthcoming), *Humanism and education in Renaissance society. Tradition and innovation in Tuscan schools, 1200–1500*, Cambridge

Black, R. and Pomaro, G. (forthcoming), *Boethius at school in medieval and Renaissance Florence*, Florence

Bock, G., Skinner, Q. and Viroli, M. (1990), *Machiavelli and republicanism*, Cambridge

Breen, Q. (1952), 'Giovanni Pico della Mirandola on the conflict of philosophy and rhetoric', *JHI* 13: 384–412

Brown, A. (1986), 'Platonism in fifteenth-century Florence and its contribution to early modern political thought', *JModH* 58: 383–413

Brucker, G. (1977), *The civic world of early Renaissance Florence*, Princeton

Brucker, G. (1979), 'Humanism, politics and the social order in early Renaissance Florence', in S. Bertelli *et al.* (eds.), *Florence and Venice. Comparisons and relations*, Florence, I, pp. 3–11

Buck, A. (1960), 'Die Rangstellung des Menschen in der Renaissance: dignitas et miseria hominis', *Archiv für Kulturgeschichte* 42: 61–75

Burckhardt, J. (1990), *The civilization of the Renaissance in Italy*, trans. S. Middlemore, introduction by P. Burke, notes by P. Murray, London (first published 1860)

Burdach, K. (1893), *Vom Mittelalter zur Reformation*, Halle

Burdach, K. (1910), 'Sinn und Ursprung der Worte Renaissance und Reformation', *Sitzungsberichte der Königlichpreussischen Akademie der Wissenschaften*, 594–646

Burdach, K. (1913), *Rienzo und die geistige Wandlung seiner Zeit*, Erste Hälfte (=*Briefwechsel des Cola di Rienzo*, ed. K. Burdach and P. Piur, Erster Teil=K. Burdach, *Von Mittelalter zur Reformation. Forschungen zur Geschichte der deutschen Bildung*, Zweiter Band), Berlin

Burke, P. (1969), *The Renaissance sense of the past*, London

Cameron, J.K. (1990), 'Humanism in the Low Countries', in Goodman and Mackay (1990), pp. 137–63

Cammelli, G. (1941–54), *I dotti bizantini e le origini dell'umanesimo*, 3 vols., Florence

Camporeale, S. (1972), *Lorenzo Valla: umanesimo e teologia*, Florence

Cassirer, E. (1963), *The individual and the cosmos in Renaissance philosophy*, Oxford (first published 1926)

Cobban, A.B. (1988), *The medieval English universities: Oxford and Cambridge to c. 1500*, Aldershot

Cochrane, E. (1981), *Historians and historiography in the Italian Renaissance*, Chicago

Croce, B. (1941), *History as the story of liberty*, London

D'Amico, J.F. (1988), 'Humanism and pre-Reformation theology', in Rabil (1988), III, pp. 349–79

Davis, C.T. (1974), 'Ptolemy of Lucca and the Roman Republic', *Proceedings of the American Philosophical Society* 118: 30–50

de la Mare, A. (1973), *The handwriting of Italian humanists*, I, i, Oxford

De Rosa, D. (1980), *Coluccio Salutati. Il cancelliere e il pensatore politico*, Florence

De Sanctis, F. (1930), *History of Italian literature*, 2 vols., introduction by B. Croce, New York (first published 1870–1)

Ferguson, W.K. (1948), *The Renaissance in historical thought*, Boston

Field, A. (1988), *The origins of the Platonic Academy of Florence*, Princeton

Fubini, R. (1968), 'Biondo Flavio', in *DBI*, Rome, X, pp. 536–59

Fueter, E. (1911), *Geschichte der neueren Historiographie*, Munich and Berlin

Gadol, J. (1969), *Leon Battista Alberti. Universal man of the early Renaissance*, Chicago

Garin, E. (1938), 'La "dignitas hominis" e la letteratura patristica', *La rinascita* 1: 102–46

Garin, E. (1953), *L'educazione umanistica in Italia*, Bari

Garin, E. (1954), 'Donato Acciaiuoli cittadino fiorentino', in his *Medioevo e Rinascimento*, Bari

Garin, E. (1957), *L'educazione in Europa (1400–1600)*, Bari

Garin, E. (1958), 'Platonici bizantini e platonici italiani: I. Nuove indagini sul Pletone', in his *Studi sul Platonismo medievale*, Florence, pp. 155–90

Garin, E. (1961), *La cultura filosofica del rinascimento italiano*, Florence

Garin, E. (1965), *Italian humanism*, tr. P. Munz, Oxford (first published 1947)

Garin, E. (1967), 'Guarino Veronese e la cultura a Ferrara', in his *Ritratti di umanisti*, Florence, pp. 69–106

Garin, E. (1969), *Science and civic life in the Italian Renaissance*, Garden City, N.Y.

Garin, E. (1975), 'La rinascita di Plotino', in E. Garin, *Rinascite e rivoluzioni. Movimenti culturali dal XIV al XVIII secolo*, Bari, pp. 89–129

Geanakopolos, D.J. (1966), *Byzantine east and Latin west*, Oxford

Geanakopolos, D.J. (1988), 'Italian humanism and Byzantine émigré scholars', in Rabil (1988), I, pp. 350–81

Gebhart, E. (1879), *Les origines de la Renaissance en Italie*, Paris

Gentile, G. (1912), *I problemi della scolastica e il pensiero italiano*, Bari

Gentile, G. (1931), 'La concezione humanistica del mondo', *Nuova antologia* 257: 307–17

Gentile, G. (1968), *Il pensiero italiano del Rinascimento*, in his *Opere*, xiv, Florence

Gleason, J.B. (1989), *John Colet*, Berkeley

Goetz, W. (1907), 'Mittelalter und Renaissance', *HZ* 98: 30–54

Goetz, W. (1914), 'Renaissance und Antike', *HZ* 113: 237–59

Gombrich, E.H. (1967), 'From the revival of letters to the reform of the arts: Niccolò Niccoli and Filippo Brunelleschi', in D. Fraser *et al.* (eds.) *Essays in the history of art presented to Rudolf Wittkower*, London, pp. 71–82

Gombrich, E.H. (1969), *In search of cultural history*, Oxford; repr. in his *Ideals and idols. Essays on values in history and in art*, Oxford (1979), pp. 24–59

Goodman, A.E. and MacKay, A. (eds.) (1990), *The impact of humanism on western Europe*, London

Grafton, A. (1977), 'On the scholarship of Poliziano and its context', *JWCI* 40: 150–88

Grafton, A. and Jardine, L. (1986), *From humanism to the humanities. Education and the liberal arts in fifteenth- and sixteenth-century Europe*, London

Gray, H.H. (1963), 'Renaissance humanism: the pursuit of eloquence', *JHI* 24: 497–514

Grendler, P. (1989), *Schooling in Renaissance Italy. Literacy and learning, 1300–1600*, Baltimore

Gundersheimer, W.L. (ed.) (1969), *French humanism, 1470–1600*, London

Hankins, J. (1990), *Plato in the Renaissance*, 2 vols., Leiden

Heath, T. (1971), 'Logical grammar, grammatical logic, and humanism in three German universities', *Studies in the Renaissance* 18: 9–64

Hoffmeister, G. (ed.) (1977), *The Renaissance and Reformation in Germany. An introduction*, New York

Holmes, G. (1969), *The Florentine Enlightenment*, London

Huizinga, J. (1990), *The waning of the Middle Ages*, London (first published 1924)

Hyma, A. (1965), *The Christian Renaissance. A history of the 'Devotio Moderna'*, 2nd edn, Hamden, Conn.

Ijsewijn, J. (1975), 'The coming of humanism to the Low Countries', in Oberman and Brady (1975), pp. 193–301

Karant-Nunn, S. (1990), 'Alas, a lack: trends in the historiography of pre-university education in early modern Germany', *RQ* 43: 788–98

Kelley, D.R. (1988), 'Humanism and history', in Rabil (1988), iii, pp. 237–70

Kohl, B.G. (1992), 'The changing concept of the *studia humanitatis* in the early Renaissance', *Renaissance Studies* 6: 185–209

Kraye, J. (1988), 'Moral philosophy', in C. Schmitt *et al.* (eds.), *The Cambridge history of Renaissance philosophy*, Cambridge, pp. 303–86

Kristeller, P.O. (1956), *Studies in Renaissance thought and letters*, i, Rome

Kristeller, P.O. (1961), 'Changing views of the intellectual history of the Renaissance since Jacob Burckhardt', in T. Helton (ed.), *The Renaissance. A reconsideration of the theories and interpretations of the age*, Madison, Wis., pp. 27–52

Kristeller, P.O. (1963–97), *Iter italicum. A finding list of uncatalogued or incompletely catalogued humanistic manuscripts of the Renaissance in Italian and other libraries*, 6 vols., Leiden and London

Kristeller, P.O. (1964), *Eight philosophers of the Italian Renaissance*, Stanford

Kristeller, P.O. (1965), 'The moral thought of Renaissance humanism', in his *Renaissance Thought*, II: *Papers on humanism and the arts*, New York, pp. 20–68

Kristeller, P.O. (1979a), *Renaissance thought and its sources*, ed. M. Mooney, New York

Kristeller, P.O. (1979b), 'Humanism and scholasticism in the Italian Renaissance', in Kristeller (1979a), pp. 85–105

Kristeller, P.O. (1984), 'Vita attiva e vita contemplativa in un brano inedito di Bornio da Sala e in San Tommaso d'Aquino', in *Essere e libertà. Studi in onore di Cornelio Fabro*, Perugia, pp. 211–24

Kristeller, P.O. (1985), 'The active and the contemplative life in Renaissance humanism', in B. Vickers (ed.), *Arbeit Musse Meditation. Betrachtungen zur Vita Activa und Vita Contemplativa*, Zurich, pp. 133–52

Lawrance, J.N.H. (1990), 'Humanism in the Iberian peninsula', in Goodman and Mackay (1990), pp. 220–58

Leader, D.R. (1988), *A history of the University of Cambridge*, I: *The University to 1546*, ed. C.N.L. Brooke, Cambridge

Levi, A.H.T. (ed.) (1970), *Humanism in France at the end of the Middle Ages and in the early Renaissance*, Manchester

Lorch, M. (1988), 'Lorenzo Valla', in Rabil (1988), I, pp. 332–49

McConica, J. (ed.) (1986), *The history of the University of Oxford*, III: *The Collegiate University*, ed. T.H. Aston, Oxford

Mack, P. (1993), *Renaissance argument. Valla and Agricola in the traditions of rhetoric and dialectic*, Leiden

Marchesi, C. (1910), 'Due grammatici latini del medio evo', *Bullettino della società filologica romana* 12: 19–56

Mestwerdt, P. (1917), *Die Anfänge des Erasmus. Humanismus und 'Devotio Moderna'*, Leipzig

Monfasani, J. (1988), 'Humanism and rhetoric', in Rabil (1988), III, pp. 171–235

Monfasani, J. (1990), 'Lorenzo Valla and Rudolph Agricola', *Journal of the History of Philosophy* 28: 181–200

Müntz, E. (1889–95), *Histoire de l'art pendant la Renaissance*, 3 vols., Paris

Najemy, J. (1982), *Corporatism and consensus in Florentine electoral politics, 1280–1400*, Chapel Hill, N.C.

Nauert, C.G., Jr (1973), 'The clash of humanists and scholastics: an approach to pre-Reformation controversies', *Sixteenth Century Journal* 4: 1–18

Nauert, C.G., Jr (1986), 'The humanist challenge to medieval German culture', *Daphnis: Zeitschrift für mittlere deutsche Literatur* 15: 277–306

Nauert, C.G., Jr (1990), 'Humanist infiltration into the academic world: some studies of northern universities', *RQ* 43: 799–812

Nauert, C.G., Jr (1995), *Humanism and the culture of Renaissance Europe*, Cambridge

Oberman, H.A. and Brady, T.A., Jr (eds.) (1975), *Itinerarium italicum. The profile of the Italian Renaissance in the mirror of its European transformations*, Leiden

Ong, W.J. (1958), *Ramus, method, and the decay of dialogue*, Cambridge, Mass.

Overfield, J.H. (1984), *Humanism and scholasticism in late medieval Germany*, Princeton

Panofsky, E. (1939), *Studies in iconology*, Oxford

Percival, W.K. (1972), 'The historical sources of Guarino's *Regulae grammaticales*: a reconsideration of Sabbadini's evidence', in G. Tarugi (ed.), *Civiltà dell'umanesimo*, Florence, pp. 263–84

Percival, W.K. (1975), 'The grammatical tradition and the rise of the vernaculars', in T.A. Sebeok (ed.), *Current trends in linguistics*, XIII: *Historiography of linguistics*, The Hague, pp. 231–75

Percival, W.K. (1976), 'Renaissance grammar: rebellion or evolution?', in G. Tarugi (ed.), *Interrogativi dell'umanesimo*, Florence, II, pp. 73–90

Percival, W.K. (1978), 'Textual problems in the Latin grammar of Guarino Veronese', *Res publica litterarum* 1: 241–54

Percival, W.K. (1981), 'The place of the Rudimenta grammatices in the history of Latin grammar', *Res publica litterarum* 4: 233–64

Percival, W.K. (1988), 'Renaissance grammar', in Rabil (1988), III, pp. 67–83

Phillips, M.M. (1949), *Erasmus and the northern Renaissance*, London

Post, R.R. (1968), *The Modern Devotion. Confrontation with Reformation and humanism*, Leiden

Rabil, A., Jr (ed.) (1988), *Renaissance humanism. Foundations, forms and legacy*, 3 vols., Philadelphia

Renan, E. (1884), 'St François d'Assise', in his *Nouvelles études d'histoire religieuse*, Paris, pp. 323–51

Renaudet, A. (1953), *Préréforme et humanisme à Paris pendant les premières guerres d'Italie (1494–1517)*, 2nd edn, Paris

Ricciardi, R. (1990), 'Pietro del Riccio Baldi (Crinitus Petrus)', in *DBI*, Rome, XXXVIII, pp. 265–8

Rice, E.F. (1958), *The Renaissance idea of wisdom*, Cambridge, Mass.

Rizzo, S. (1986), 'Il latino nell'Umanesimo', in A.A. Rosa (ed.), *Letteratura italiana*, V: *Le questioni*, Turin, pp. 379–408

Rizzo, S. (1990), 'Petrarca, il latino e il volgare', *Quaderni petrarcheschi* 7: 7–40

Rizzo, S. and De Nonno, M. (1997), 'In margine a una recente edizione di versi grammaticali del Valla', in *Filologia umanistica. Per Gianvito Resta*, Padua, pp. 1583–630

Rubinstein, N. (1982), 'Political theories in the Renaissance', in A. Chastel *et al.*, *The Renaissance. Essays in interpretation*, London, pp. 153–200

Sabbadini, R. (1905–14), *Le scoperte dei codici latini e greci ne' secoli XIV e XV*, 2 vols., Florence

Santini, E. (1910), 'Leonardo Bruni Aretino e i suoi "Historiarum Florentini populi libri xii"', *Annali della R. Scuola Normale Superiore di Pisa*, Filosofia e filologia, 22, pp. 1–174

Schmitt, C.T. (1983), *Aristotle and the Renaissance*, Cambridge, Mass.

Schmitt, W.O. (1969), 'Die Ianua (Donatus) – ein Beitrag zur lateinischen Schulgrammatik des Mittelalters und der Renaissance', *Beiträge zur Inkunabelkunde*, Dritte Folge, 4, pp. 43–80

Seigel, J.E. (1969), 'The teaching of Argyropoulos and the rhetoric of the first humanists', in T.K. Rabb and J.E. Seigel (eds.), *Action and conviction in early modern Europe*, Princeton

Sforza, G. (1884), 'La patria, la famiglia ed la giovinezza di papa Niccolò V', *Atti della Reale Accademia Lucchese di Scienze, Lettere ed Arti* 23: 1–400

Simone, F. (1969), *The French Renaissance. Medieval tradition and Italian influence in shaping the Renaissance in France*, London

Skinner, Q. (1978), *The foundations of modern political thought*, I: *The Renaissance*, Cambridge

Skinner, Q. (1990), 'Machiavelli's *Discorsi* and the pre-humanist origins of republican ideas', in Bock, Skinner and Viroli (1990), pp. 121–41

Smalley, B. (1960), *English friars and Antiquity in the early fourteenth century*, Oxford

Smalley, B. (1974), *Historians in the Middle Ages*, London

Spaventa, B. (1867), *Rinascimento, riforma, controriforma*, Naples

Spaventa, B. (1908), *La filosofia italiana nelle sue relazioni con la filosofia europea*, Bari

Spitz, L.W. (1957), *Conrad Celtis, the German arch-humanist*, Cambridge, Mass.

Spitz, L.W. (1963), *The religious Renaissance of the German humanists*, Cambridge, Mass.

Spitz, L.W. (1975), 'The course of German humanism', in Oberman and Brady (1975), pp. 371–436

Spitz, L.W. (1988), 'Humanism and the Protestant Reformation', in Rabil (1988), III, pp. 380–411

Stephens, J.N. (1986), 'Machiavelli's *Prince* and the Florentine revolution of 1512', *Italian Studies* 41: 45–61

Strauss, G. (ed.) (1972), *Pre-Reformation Germany*, London

Symonds, J.A. (1875–86), *Renaissance in Italy*, 7 vols., London

Taine, H. (1866), *Philosophie de l'art en Italie*, Paris

Tavoni, M. (1984), *Latino, grammatica, volgare. Storia di una questione umanistica*, Padua

Thode, H. (1885), *Franz von Assisi und die Anfänge der Kunst der Renaissance in Italien*, Berlin

Thomson, I. (1966), 'Manuel Chrysoloras and the early Italian Renaissance', *Greek, Roman and Byzantine Studies* 7: 63–82

Trinkaus, C. (1940), *Adversity's noblemen*, New York

Trinkaus, C. (1970), *In our image and likeness. Humanity and divinity in Italian humanist thought*, 2 vols., London

Trinkaus, C. (1983), *The scope of Renaissance humanism*, Ann Arbor

Trinkaus, C. (1988), 'Humanism and scholastic theology', in Rabil (1988), III, pp. 327–48

Ullman, B.L. (1955), *Studies in the Italian Renaissance*, Rome

Ullman, B.L. (1960), *The origin and development of humanistic script*, Rome

Ullman, B.L. and Stadter, P.A. (1972), *The public library of Renaissance Florence. Niccolò Niccoli, Cosimo de' Medici and San Marco*, Padua

Vasoli, C. (1988), 'The Renaissance concept of philosophy', in C. Schmitt *et al.* (eds.), *The Cambridge history of Renaissance philosophy*, Cambridge, pp. 57–74

Villari, P. (1877–82), *Niccolò Machiavelli e i suoi tempi*, 2 vols., Florence

Walker, D.P. (1972), *The ancient theology. Studies in Christian Platonism from the fifteenth to the eighteenth century*, London

Weiss, R. (1941), *Humanism in England during the fifteenth century*, Oxford

Weiss, R. (1969a), 'The dawn of humanism in Italy', *BIHR* 42: 1–16 (first published 1947)

Weiss, R. (1969b), *The Renaissance discovery of classical Antiquity*, Oxford

Witt, R.G. (1971), 'The rebirth of the concept of republican liberty in Italy', in A. Molho and J.A. Tedeschi (eds.), *Renaissance studies in honor of Hans Baron*, Florence, pp. 173–99

Witt, R.G. (1976), *Coluccio Salutati and his public letters*, Geneva

Witt, R.G. (1982), 'Medieval *Ars dictaminis* and the beginnings of humanism: a new construction of the problem', *RQ* 35: 1–35

Witt, R.G. (1983), *Hercules at the crossroads. The life, works, and thought of Coluccio Salutati*, Durham, N.C.

Witt, R.G. (1988), 'Medieval Italian culture and the origins of humanism as a stylistic ideal', in Rabil (1988), I, pp. 29–70

Yates, F. (1964), *Giordano Bruno and the Hermetic tradition*, London

13 MANUSCRIPTS AND BOOKS

Secondary works

Backhouse, J. (1979), *The illuminated manuscript*, Oxford

Blake, N.F. (1976), *Caxton. England's first publisher*, London

Bühler, C. (1960), *The fifteenth-century book. The scribes, the painters, the decorators*, Philadelphia

Clair, C. (1976), *A history of European printing*, London

Clough, C.H. (1973), 'Federigo da Montefeltro's patronage of the arts, 1468–1482', *JWCI* 36: 129–44

Clough, C.H. (1981), *The duchy of Urbino in the Renaissance*, London

Delaissé, L.M.J. (1968), *A century of Dutch manuscript illumination*, Berkeley

Delaissé, L.M.J. *et al.* (1959), *La miniature flamande. Le mécénat de Philippe le Bon*, Brussels

Du Boulay, F.R.H. (1983), *Germany in the later Middle Ages*, London

Garzelli, A. and de la Mare, A.C. (1985), *Miniatura fiorentina del Rinascimento, 1440–1525*, Florence

Goodman, A. and MacKay, A. (1990), *The impact of humanism on western Europe*, London

Harthan, J. (1977), *Books of hours and their owners*, Oxford

Ijsewijn, J. (1975), 'The coming of humanism to the Low Countries', in H.A. Oberman and T.A. Brady (eds.), *Itinerarium italicum. The profile of the Italian Renaissance in the mirror of its European transformations*, Leiden

Kempers, B. (1992), *Painting, power and patronage. The rise of the professional artist in Renaissance Italy*, London

Kempis, Thomas (1906), *The chronicle of the canons regular of Mount St Agnes*, trans. J.P. Arthur, London

Thomas à Kempis et la dévotion moderne (1971) (exhib. catal.), Brussels

Le livre illustré en occident (exhib. catal., Bibliothèque Royale), Brussels

Lemaire, C. and de Schryver, A. (1981), *Vlaamse kunst op perkament* (exhib. catal.) Bruges

Marrow, J.H. *et al.* (1989), *The golden age of Dutch manuscript painting*, Stuttgart and Zurich

Martens, M.P.J. *et al.* (1992), *Lodewijk van Gruuthuse. Mecenas en Europees Diplomat, ca. 1427–1492*, Bruges

Painter, G.D. (1962), *Catalogue of books printed in the XVth century now in the British Museum*, London

Post, R.R. (1968), *The Modern Devotion. Confrontation with Reformation and humanism*, Leiden

14 THE BEGINNING OF PRINTING

Secondary works

Amelung, P. (1979), *Der Frühdruck im deutschen Südwesten, 1473–1500*, I, Ulm and Stuttgart

Armstrong, L. (1981), *Renaissance miniature painters & classical imagery. The master of the Putti and his Venetian workshop*, London

Basanoff, A. (1965), *Itinerario della carta dall'oriente all'occidente e sua diffusione in Europa*, Milan

Bibliothèque Royale Albert Ier (1973), *Le cinquième centenaire de l'imprimerie dans les Pays-Bas*, Brussels

Bühler, C.F. (1958), *The university and the press in fifteenth-century Bologna*, Notre Dame, Ind.

Bühler, C.F. (1960), *The fifteenth-century book. The scribes, the printers, the decorators*, Philadelphia

Bussi, G.A. (1978), *Prefazioni alle edizioni di Sweynheym e Pannartz, prototipografi Romani*, ed. M. Miglio, Milan

Campbell, Tony (1987), *The earliest printed maps, 1472–1500*, London

Carter, H. (1969), *A view of early typography up to about 1600*, Oxford

Catalogue of books printed in the XVth century now in the British Museum (1908–85), pts 1–10, 12, London

Corsten, S. and Fuchs, R.W. (eds.) (1988–93), *Der Buchdruck im 15. Jahrhundert: eine Bibliographie*, 2 vols., Stuttgart

de la Mare, A.C. and Hellinga, L. (1978), 'The first book printed in Oxford; the Expositio Symboli of Rufinus', *Transactions of the Cambridge Bibliographical Society* 7: 184–244

Eisenstein, E.L. (1979), *The printing press as an agent of change. Communications and cultural transformations in early-modern Europe*, 2 vols., Cambridge

Eisenstein, E.L. (1983), *The printing revolution in early modern Europe*, Cambridge

Febvre, L. and Martin, H.-J. (1971), *L'apparition du livre*, 2nd edn, Paris; trans. as *The coming of the book. The impact of printing, 1450–1800* (1976), London

Fuhrmann, O.W. (1940), *Gutenberg and the Strasbourg documents of 1439*, New York

Geldner, F. (1968–70), *Die deutschen Inkunabeldrukker. Ein Handbuch der deutschen Buchdrukker des XV. Jahrhunderts nach Druckorten*, I, II, Stuttgart

Gesamtkatalog der Wiegendrucke (1925–   ), Leipzig and New York

Goff, F.R. (1973), *Incunabula in American libraries. A third census of fifteenth-century books recorded in North American collections*, New York

Goldschmidt, E.P. (1928), *Gothic & Renaissance book-bindings*, 2 vols., London

Goldschmidt, E.P. (1943), *Medieval texts and their first appearance in print*, Supplement to the Bibliographical Society Transactions, 16, London

Haebler, K. (1925), *Handbuch der Inkunabelkunde*, Leipzig; trans. as *The study of incunabula*, New York (1933)

Hellinga, L. (1982), *Caxton in focus. The beginning of printing in England*, London

Hellinga, L. and Goldfinch, J. (eds.) (1987), *Bibliography and the study of 15th-century civilisation*, London

Hellinga, L. and Härtel, H. (eds.) (1981), *Buch und Text im 15. Jahrhundert. Book and text in the fifteenth century*, Wolfenbütteler Abhandlungen zur Renaissanceforschung, 2, Hamburg

Hellinga, W. and L. (1966), *The fifteenth-century printing types of the Low Countries*, 2 vols., Amsterdam

Hind, A.M. (1935), *An introduction to a history of woodcut, with a detailed survey of work done in the fifteenth century*, 2 vols., London

Hindman, S. (ed.) (1991), *Printing the written word. The social history of books, circa 1450–1520*, Ithaca

Hindman, S. and Farquhar, J.D. (1977), *Pen to press. Illustrated manuscripts and printed books*, College Park, Md.

Hirsch, R. (1967), *Printing, selling and reading, 1450–1550*, Wiesbaden

Ing, J. (1988), *Johann Gutenberg and his Bible: A historical study*, New York

Ivins, W.M., Jr (1953), *Prints and visual communication*, London

Kenney, E.J. (1974), *The classical text. Aspects of editing in the age of the printed book*, Berkeley

Lehmann-Haupt, H. (1950), *Peter Schoeffer of Gernsheim and Mainz*, Rochester, N.Y.

Lowry, M. (1979), *The world of Aldus Manutius. Business and scholarship in Renaissance Venice*, Oxford

Lowry, M. (1991), *Nicholas Jenson and the rise of Venetian publishing in Renaissance Europe*, Oxford

Martin, H.-J. and Chartier, R. (eds.) (1982), *Histoire de l'édition française*, I: *Le livre conquérant, du moyen âge au milieu du XVIIe siècle*, Paris

Papers presented to the Caxton international congress, 1976 (1975–6), *Journal of the Printing Historical Society*, 11

Pollard, G. and Ehrman, A. (1965), *The distribution of books by catalogue from the invention of printing to A.D. 1800*, Cambridge

Reynolds, L.D. and Wilson, N.G. (1991), *Scribes and scholars. A guide to the transmission of Greek and Latin literature*, 3rd edn, Oxford

Rouse, M.A. and R. (1988), *Cartolai, illuminators, and printers in fifteenth-century Italy: the evidence of the Ripoli press*, Los Angeles

Schmidt, W. and Schmidt-Künsemüller, F.-A. (eds.) (1979), *Johannes Gutenbergs 42 zeilige Bibel. Kommentarband zur Faksimile-Ausgabe*, Munich

Scholderer, V. (1966), *Fifty essays in fifteenth- and sixteenth-century bibliography*, Amsterdam

Trapp, J.B. (ed.) (1983), *Manuscripts in the fifty years after the invention of printing*, London

Updike, D.B. (1952), *Printing types: their history, forms and use*, 2nd edn, Cambridge, Mass.

Vernet, A. (ed.) (1989), *Histoire des bibliothèques françaises. Les bibliothèques médiévales, du VIe siècle à 1500*, Paris

Wilson, A. (1976), *The making of the Nuremberg Chronicle*, Amsterdam

15 ARCHITECTURE AND PAINTING

Secondary works

General works

Baxandall, M. (1974), *Painting and experience in fifteenth-century Italy*, Oxford

Bialostocki, J. (1972), *Spätmittelalter und Beginnende Neuzeit*, Propyläen Kunstgeschichte, 7, Berlin

Burckhardt, J. (1990), *The civilization of the Renaissance in Italy*, Harmondsworth

Circa 1492. Art in the age of exploration (1991), exhibition catalogue, National Gallery of Art, Washington, New Haven and London

Dunkerton, J., Foister, S., Gordon, D. and Penny, N. (1991), *Giotto to Dürer. Early Renaissance painting in the National Gallery*, New Haven and London

Huizinga, J. (1955), *The waning of the Middle Ages*, Harmondsworth
Levey, M. (1967), *The early Renaissance*, Harmondsworth
Panofsky, E. (1970), *Renaissance and renascences in western art*, London
Wackernagel, M. (1981), *The world of the Florentine artists*, Princeton

Flanders and the north

Campbell, L. (1979), *Rogier van der Weyden*, London
Dhanens, E. (1980), *Hubert and Jan van Eyck*, Antwerp
Harbison, C. (1991), *The play of realism*, London
Müller, T. (1968), *Sculpture in Germany, the Netherlands, France and Spain, 1400–1500*, Harmondsworth
Panofsky, E. (1953), *Early Netherlandish painting*, 2 vols., Cambridge, Mass.
Seidel, L. (1993), *Jan van Eyck's Arnolfini portrait. Stories of an icon*, Cambridge

Italy

Baxandall, M. (1971), *Giotto and the orators*, Oxford
Goldthwaite, R. (1980), *The building of Renaissance Florence*, Baltimore
Heydrenreich, L.H. and Lotz, W. (1974), *Architecture in Italy 1400–1600*, Harmondsworth
Pope-Hennessy, J. (1971), *Italian Renaissance sculpture*, London
Saalman, H. (1980), *The cupola of S. Maria del Fiore*, London
Welch, E.S. (1995), *Art and authority in Renaissance Milan*, Yale
White, J. (1987), *The birth and rebirth of pictorial space*, Cambridge, Mass.

Memorials

Campbell, L. (1990), *Renaissance portraits*, New Haven and London
Seymour, C. (1966), *Sculpture in Italy 1400–1500*, Harmondsworth

Secular pleasures

Brown, C.M. (1976), '"Lo insaciabile desiderio nostro de cose antique" – new documents for Isabella d'Este's collection of antiquities', in C.H. Clough (ed.), *Cultural aspects of the Italian Renaissance. Essays in honour of Paul Oskar Kristeller*, Manchester and New York

see also Dunkerton *et al.* (1991); Heydrenreich and Lotz (1974); and Wackernagel (1981)

Sacred imagery

Baxandall, M. (1980), *The limewood sculptures of southern Germany*, New Haven and London
Gothic and Renaissance art in Nuremberg, 1300–1550 (1986), exhibition catalogue, Metropolitan Museum of Art, New York
Hood, W. (1993), *Fra Angelico at San Marco*, Yale
Humbrey, P. and Kemp, M. (eds.) (1991), *The altarpiece in the Renaissance*, Cambridge

Ringbom, S. (1983), *Icon to narrative. The rise of the dramatic close-up in fifteenth-century devotional painting*, Doornspijk

Van Os, H.W. (1984–90), *Siennese alterpieces 1215–1450. Form, content and function*, I and II, Groningen

see also Baxandall (1974); Dunkerton *et al.* (1981), and Müller (1968)

Nature into art

Clark, K. (1969), *Piero della Francesca*, London

Hills, P. (1987), *The light of early Italian painting*, New Haven and London

Kemp, M. (1989), *Leonardo da Vinci. The marvellous works of nature and man*, London

Martindale, A. (1972), *The rise of the artist in the Middle Ages and the early Renaissance*, London

Wittkower, R. (1973), *Architectural principles in the age of humanism*, London

Antiquity

Gombrich, E.H. (1985), *Symbolic images*, Oxford

Lightbown, R. (1978), *Botticelli*, 2 vols., London; revised edn in one volume (1989)

Lightbown, R. (1986), *Mantegna*, Oxford

Weiss, R. (1969), *The Renaissance discovery of classical Antiquity*, Oxford

Wind, E. (1958), *Pagan mysteries of the Renaissance*, London

see also Panofsky (1970)

16 MUSIC

Editions of music and theory treatises

Boethius, Anicius Manlius Severinus, *Fundamentals of music*, trans. C.M. Bower, ed. C.V. Palisca, New Haven (1989)

Corpus mensurabilis musicae (series in progress), various places (1951–   )

Corpus scriptorum de musica (series in progress), various places (1950–   )

Coussemaker, Edmond de (ed.) (1864), *Scriptorum de musica medii aevi*, 4 vols., Paris (1864–76); repr. Hildesheim (1963)

Early English church music (series in progress), London (1963–   )

Josquin Des Prés, *Werken*, ed. A. Smijers *et al.*, Amsterdam (1921–   )

Musica Britannica (series in progress), London (1951–   )

Ockeghem, Johannes, *Collected works*, I and II, ed. D. Plamenac, 2nd edn, New York (1959–66), and III, ed. R. Wexler, Philadelphia (1992)

Secondary works

Armstrong, C.A.J. (1983), 'L'échange culturel entre les cours d'Angleterre et de Bourgogne à l'époque de Charles le Téméraire', in C.A.J. Armstrong, *England, France and Burgundy in the fifteenth century*, London, pp. 403–17

Bent, M. (1981), *Dunstaple*, Oxford Studies of Composers, London

Boorman, S. (ed.) (1983), *Studies in the performance of late mediaeval music*, Cambridge

Bowers, R. (1975a), 'Choral institutions within the English Church. Their constitution and development, 1340–1500', PhD dissertation, University of East Anglia

Bowers, R. (1975b), 'Some observations on the life and career of Lionel Power', *Proceedings of the Royal Musical Association* 102: 103–27

Bowles, E.A. (1954), '*Haut et bas*: the grouping of musical instruments in the Middle Ages', *Musica disciplina* 8: 115–40

Bowles, E.A. (1959), 'The role of musical instruments in medieval sacred drama', *Musical Quarterly* 45: 67–84

Bowles, E.A. (1961), 'Musical instruments in civic processions during the Middle Ages', *Acta musicologica* 33: 147–61

Bukofzer, M. (1950), *Studies in medieval and Renaissance music*, New York

Carpenter, N.C. (1958), *Music in the medieval and Renaissance universities*, Norman, Okla.

Carter, H.H. (1961), *A dictionary of Middle English musical terms*, Indiana University Humanities Series, 45, Bloomington

Cazeaux, I. (1975), *French music in the fifteenth and sixteenth centuries*, New York

Census catalogue of manuscript sources of polyphonic music, 1400–1550 (1979–88), 5 vols., Illinois University Archives for Renaissance Manuscripts Studies, Renaissance Manuscript Studies, I, Stuttgart

Eckhardt, C.D. (ed.) (1980), *Essays in the numerical criticism of medieval literature*, London

Fallows, D. (1987a), *Dufay*, rev. edn, Master Musicians Series, London

Fallows, D. (1987b), 'The *contenance angloise*: English influence on continental composers of the fifteenth century', *Renaissance Studies* 1: 189–208; repr. in Fallows (1996)

Fallows, D. (1996), *Songs and musicians in the fifteenth century*, Aldershot

Fenlon, I. (ed.) (1981), *Music in medieval and early modern Europe*, Cambridge

Fenlon, I. (ed.) (1989), *The Renaissance*, Man and Music, 2, London

Gallo, F.A. (1985), *Music of the Middle Ages*, II, trans. K. Eales, Cambridge

Greene, G. (1977), 'The schools of minstrelsy and the choir-school tradition', *Studies in Music (University of Western Ontario)* 2: 31–40

Greene, R.L. (1977), *The early English carols*, 2nd edn, Oxford

Gushee, L.A. (1973), 'Questions of genre in medieval treatises on music', in W. Arlt *et al.* (eds.), *Gattungen der Musik in Einzeldarstellungen, Gedenkschrift Leo Schrade* (Erste Folge), Berne, pp. 365–433

Hamm, C. (1962), 'Manuscript structure in the Dufay era', *Acta musicologica* 34: 166–84

Harrison, F. Ll. (1963), *Music in medieval Britain*, 2nd edn, London

Hoppin, R. (1978), *Medieval music*, New York

Hughes, A. (1980), *Medieval music – the sixth liberal art*, rev. edn, Toronto

Hughes, Dom A. and Abraham, G. (eds.) (1960), *Ars nova and the Renaissance (1300–1540)*, New Oxford History of Music, 3, Oxford

Knighton, T. and Fallows, D. (eds.) (1992), *Companion to medieval and Renaissance music*, London

Lockwood, L. (1984), *Music in Renaissance Ferrara 1400–1505*, Oxford

McKinnon, J. (ed.) (1990), *Antiquity and the Middle Ages*, Man and Music, 1, London

The New Grove dictionary of music and musicians (1980), ed. S. Sadie, 20 vols., London

Palisca, C.V. (1985), *Humanism in Italian Renaissance musical thought*, New Haven

Peck, R.A. (1980), 'Number as cosmic language', in Eckhardt (1980), pp. 15–64

Perkins, L.L. (1984), 'Musical patronage at the royal court of France under Charles VII and Louis XI (1422–83)', *Journal of the American Musicological Society* 37: 507–66

Pirotta, N. (1984), *Music and culture in Italy from the Middle Ages to the Baroque*, Cambridge, Mass.

Planchart, A.E. (1988), 'Guillaume Du Fay's benefices and his relationship to the court of Burgundy', *Early Music History* 8: 117–71

Polk, K. (1987), 'Instrumental music in the urban centres of Renaissance Germany', *Early Music History* 7: 159–86

Southworth, J. (1989), *The English medieval minstrel*, Woodbridge

Sternfeld, F.W. (ed.) (1973), *Music from the Middle Ages to the Renaissance (A history of Western music, I)*, London

Stevens, J.E. (1979), *Music and poetry in the early Tudor court*, rev. edn, London

Strohm, R. (1981), 'European politics, and the distribution of music in the early fifteenth century', *Early Music History* 1: 305–23

Strohm, R. (1990), *Music in late medieval Bruges*, rev. edn, Oxford

Strohm, R. (1993), *The rise of European music, 1380–1500*, Cambridge

Strunk, O. (1950), *Source readings in music history*, New York

Trowell, B. (1978), 'Proportion in the music of Dunstable', *Proceedings of the Royal Musical Association* 105: 100–41

Ward, T.R. (1990), 'Music and music theory in the universities of central Europe during the fifteenth century', in Pompilio *et al.* (eds.), *Trasmissione e recezione delle forme di cultura musicale, Atti del XIV Congresso della Società Internazionale di Musicologia*, Turin, pp. 49–57

Wathey, A. (1989), *Music in the royal and noble households in late medieval England. Studies of sources and patronage*, New York

Wright, C. (1989), *Music and ceremony at Notre Dame of Paris, 500–1500*, Cambridge

17 GERMANY AND THE EMPIRE

Secondary works

Angermeier, H. (1966), *Königtum und Landfriede im deutschen Spätmittelalter*, Munich

Angermeier, H. (1984), *Die Reichsreform, 1410–1555. Die Staatsproblematik in Deutschland zwischen Mittelalter und Gegenwart*, Munich

Battenberg, F. (1981), *Beiträge zur höchsten Gerichtsbarkeit im Reich im 15. Jahrhundert*, Quellen und Forschungen zur höchsten Gerichtsbarkeit im alten Reich, 11, Cologne and Vienna

Benecke, G. (1982), *Maximilian I, 1459–1519. An analytical biography*, London

Blickle, P. (1973), *Landschaften im Alten Reich. Die staatliche Funktion des gemeinen Mannes in Oberdeutschland*, Munich

Blickle, P. (1989), *Studien zur geschichtlichen Bedeutung des deutschen Bauernstandes*, Quellen und Forschungen zur Agrargeschichte, 35, Stuttgart

Boockmann, H. (1987), *Stauferzeit und spätes Mittelalter. Deutschland 1125–1517 (Das Reich und die Deutschen, VII)*, Berlin

Boockmann, H. (1989), *Der Deutsche Orden. Zwölf Kapitel aus seiner Geschichte*, 3rd edn, Munich

Borchardt, F.L. (1971), *German Antiquity in Renaissance myth*, Baltimore, Md., and London

Brady, T.A., Jr, (1981), *Turning Swiss. Cities and Empire, 1450–1550*, Cambridge

Burleigh, M. (1984), *Prussian society and the German Order. An aristocratic corporation in crisis, c. 1410–1466*, Cambridge

Carsten, F.L. (1959), *Princes and parliaments in Germany from the fifteenth to the eighteenth century*, Oxford

Cohn, H.J. (1965), *The government of the Rhine Palatinate in the fifteenth century*, Oxford; repr. Aldershot and Brookfield, Vt. (1992)

Dickens, A.G. (1974), *The German nation and Martin Luther*, London

Dohna, L. Graf zu (1960), *Reformatio Sigismundi. Beiträge zum Verständnis einer Reformationsschrift des fünfzehnten Jahrhunderts*, Veröffentlichungen des Max-Planck-Instituts für Geschichte, 4, Göttingen

Dollinger, P. (1970), *The German Hansa*, London

Dralle, L. (1975), *Der Staat des Deutschen Ordens in Preußen nach dem II. Thorner Frieden. Untersuchungen zur ökonomischen und ständepolitischen Geschichte Altpreußens zwischen 1466 und 1497*, Frankfurter Historische Abhandlungen, 9, Wiesbaden

Du Boulay, F.R.H. (1983), *Germany in the later Middle Ages*, London

Duggan, L.G. (1978), *Bishop and chapter. The governance of the bishopric of Speyer to 1552*, Studies Presented to the International Commission for the History of Representative and Parliamentary Institutions, 62, New Brunswick, N.J.

Ehlers, J. (ed.) (1989), *Ansätze und Diskontinuität deutscher Nationsbildung im Mittelalter*, Nationes. Historische und philologische Untersuchungen zur Entstehung der europäischen Nationen im Mittelalter, 8, Sigmaringen

Fahlbusch, F.B. (1983), *Städte und Königtum im frühen 15. Jahrhundert. Ein Beitrag zur Geschichte Sigmunds von Luxemburg*, Städteforschung. Veröffentlichungen des Instituts für vergleichende Städteforschung in Münster, series A 17, Cologne and Vienna

Grüneisen, H. (1961), 'Die westlichen Reichsstände in der Auseinandersetzung zwischen dem Reich, Burgund und Frankreich bis 1473', *Rheinische Vierteljahrsblätter* 26: 22–77

Haller, B. (1965), *Kaiser Friedrich III. im Urteil der Zeitgenossen*, Vienna

Heinig, P.-J. (1982), 'Kaiser Friedrich III. und Hessen', *Hessisches Jahrbuch für Landesgeschichte* 32: 63–101

Heinig, P.-J. (1983), *Reichsstädte, Freie Städte und Königtum 1389–1450. Ein Beitrag zur deutschen Verfassungsgeschichte*, Veröffentlichungen des Instituts für Europäische Geschichte Mainz, Abteilung Universalgeschichte, 108, Wiesbaden

Heinig, P.-J. (1993), *Kaiser Friedrich III. (1440–1493) in seiner Zeit. Studien anläßlich des 500. Todestages am 19. August 1493/1993*, Forschungen zur Kaiser- und Papstgeschichte des Mittelalters, 12, Cologne, Weimar and Vienna

Hesslinger, H. (1970), *Die Anfänge des Schwäbischen Bundes. Ein Beitrag zur Geschichte des Einungswesens und der Reichsreform unter Kaiser Friedrich III.*, Forschungen zur Geschichte der Stadt Ulm, 9, Stuttgart

Hödl, G. (1978), *Albrecht II. Königtum, Reichsregierung und Reichsreform 1438–39*, Forschungen zur Kaiser- und Papstgeschichte des Mittelalters, 3, Cologne and Vienna

Hofacker, H.-G. (1980), *Die schwäbischen Reichslandvogteien im späten Mittelalter*, Spätmittelalter und Frühe Neuzeit. Tübinger Beiträge zur Geschichtsforschung, 8, Stuttgart

Isenmann, E. (1979), 'Reichsstadt und Reich an der Wende vom späten Mittelalter zur frühen Neuzeit', in J. Engel (ed.), *Mittel und Wege früher Verfassungspolitik. Kleine Schriften*, I, Spätmittelalter und Frühe Neuzeit. Tübinger Beiträge zur Geschichtsforschung, 9, Stuttgart, pp. 9–223

Isenmann, E. (1980), 'Reichsfinanzen und Reichssteuern im 15. Jahrhundert', *Zeitschrift für Historische Forschung* 7: 1–76, 129–218

Isenmann, E. (1988), *Die deutsche Stadt im Spätmittelalter: 1250–1500; Stadtgestalt, Recht, Stadtregiment, Kirche, Gesellschaft, Wirtschaft*, Stuttgart

Isenmann, E. (1990), 'Les caractéristiques constitutionnelles du Saint Empire Romain de Nation Germanique au XVe siècle', in N. Coulet and J.-P. Genet (eds.), *L'état moderne. Le droit, l'espace et les formes de l'état*, Paris, pp. 143–66

Jeserich, K.G.A., Pohl, H. and von Unruh, G.-C. (eds.) (1983), *Deutsche Verwaltungsgeschichte*, I: *Vom Spätmittelalter bis zum Ende des Reiches*, Stuttgart

Koller, H. (1987), 'Der Ausbau königlicher Macht im Reich des 15. Jahrhunderts', in R. Schneider (ed.), *Das spätmittelalterliche Königtum im europäischen Vergleich*, Vorträge und Forschungen, 32, Sigmaringen, pp. 425–64

Koller, H. (ed.) (1964), *Reformation Kaiser Siegmunds* (*Monumenta Germaniae Historica, Staatsschriften des späteren Mittelalters*, VI), Stuttgart

Krieger, K.F. (1979), *Die Lehnshoheit der deutschen Könige im Spätmittelalter (ca. 1200–1437)*, Untersuchungen zur deutschen Staats- und Rechtsgeschichte, Neue Folge, 23, Aalen

Krieger, K.F. (1992), *König, Reich und Reichsreform im Spätmittelalter* (*Enzyklopädie deutscher Geschichte*, XIV), Munich

Landwehr, G. (1967), *Die Verpfändung der deutschen Reichsstädte im Mittelalter*, Forschungen zur deutschen Rechtsgeschichte, 5, Cologne and Graz

Lauterbach, K.H. (1985), *Geschichtsverständnis, Zeitdidaxe und Reformgedanke an der Wende zum sechzehnten Jahrhundert. Das oberrheinische 'Büchli der hundert Capiteln' im Kontext des spätmittelalterlichen Reformbiblizismus*, Forschungen zur oberrheinischen Landesgeschichte, 33, Freiburg im Breisgau and Munich

Lauterbach, K.H. (1989), 'Der "Oberrheinische Revolutionär" und Mathias Wurm von Geudertheim. Neue Untersuchungen zur Verfasserfrage', *Deutsches Archiv für Erforschung des Mittelalters* 45: 109–72

Meuthen, E. (1984), *Das 15. Jahrhundert* (*Oldenbourg Grundriß der Geschichte*, IX), 2nd edn, Munich

Moraw, P. (1977), 'Fragen der deutschen Verfassungsgeschichte im späten Mittelalter. Bericht über ausgewählte Neuerscheinungen der Jahre 1969 bis 1974', *Zeitschrift für Historische Forschung* 4: 59–101

Moraw, P. (1979), 'Reichsstadt, Reich und Königtum im späten Mittelalter', *Zeitschrift für Historische Forschung* 6: 385–424

Moraw, P. (1984), 'Die Entfaltung der deutschen Territorien im 14. und 15. Jahrhundert', in *Landesherrliche Kanzleien im Spätmittelalter. Referate zum VI. Internationalen Kongreß für Diplomatik, München 1983*, I, Münchener Beiträge zur Mediävistik und Renaissance-Forschung, 35, Munich, pp. 61–108

Moraw, P. (1985), *Von offener Verfassung zu gestalteter Verdichtung. Das Reich im späten Mittelalter 1250 bis 1490* (*Propyläen Geschichte Deutschlands*, III), Frankfurt am Main and Berlin

Moraw, P. (1989), 'Cities and citizenry as factors of state formation in the Roman-German Empire of the late Middle Ages', *Theory and Society* 18: 631–62

Nehring, K. (1989), *Matthias Corvinus, Kaiser Friedrich III. und das Reich. Zum hunyadisch-*

habsburgischen Gegensatz im Donauraum, Südosteuropäische Arbeiten, 72, 2nd edn, Munich

Nonn, U. (1982), 'Heiliges Römisches Reich Deutscher Nation. Zum Nationen-Begriff im 15. Jahrhundert', _Zeitschrift für Historische Forschung_ 9: 129–42

Obenaus, H. (1961), _Recht und Verfassung der Gesellschaften mit St. Jörgenschild in Schwaben. Untersuchungen über Adel, Einung, Schiedsgericht und Fehde im 15. Jahrhundert_, Veröffentlichungen des Max-Planck-Instituts für Geschichte, 7, Göttingen

Press, V. (1980), 'Die Erblande und das Reich von Albrecht II. bis Karl VI. (1438–1740)', in R.A. Kann and F.E. Prinz (eds.), _Deutschland und Österreich. Ein bilaterales Geschichtsbuch_, Munich and Vienna, pp. 44–88

Rowan, S.W. (1977), 'The common penny (1495–99) as a source of German social and demographic history', _Central European History_ 10: 148–64

Rowan, S.W. (1980), 'Imperial taxes and German politics in the fifteenth century', _Central European History_ 13: 203–17

Schmid, P. (1988), _Der Gemeine Pfennig von 1495. Vorgeschichte und Entstehung, verfassungsgeschichtliche, politische und finanzielle Bedeutung_, Schriftenreihe der Historischen Kommission bei der Bayerischen Akademie der Wissenschaften, 34, Göttingen

Schmidt, H. (1958), _Die deutschen Städtechroniken als Spiegel des bürgerlichen Selbstverständnisses im Spätmittelalter_, Schriftenreihe der Historischen Kommission bei der Bayerischen Akademie der Wissenschaften, 3, Göttingen

Schmidt, G. (1984), _Der Städtetag in der Reichsverfassung. Eine Untersuchung zur korporativen Politik der freien und Reichsstädte in der ersten Hälfte des 16. Jahrhunderts_, Veröffentlichungen des Instituts für Europäische Geschichte Mainz, 113: Beiträge zur Sozial- und Verfassungsgeschichte des Alten Reiches, 5, Stuttgart

Schubert, E. (1975), 'Die Stellung der Kurfürsten in der spätmittelalterlichen Reichsverfassung', _Jahrbuch für westdeutsche Landesgeschichte_ 1: 97–128

Schubert, E. (1979), _König und Reich. Studien zur spätmittelalterlichen deutschen Verfassungsgeschichte_, Veröffentlichungen des Max-Planck-Instituts für Geschichte, 63, Göttingen

Schubert, E. (1992), _Einführung in die Grundprobleme der deutschen Geschichte im Spätmittelalter_, Darmstadt

Schulze, M. (1991), _Fürsten und Reformation. Geistliche Reformpolitik weltlicher Fürsten vor der Reformation_, Spätmittelalter und Reformation, Neue Folge, 2, Tübingen

Scribner, B. [R.W.] (ed.) (1995), _Germany. A new social and economic history_, 1, London, New York, Sydney and Auckland

Seibt, F. and Eberhard, W. (eds.) (1987), _Europa 1500. Integrationsprozesse im Widerstreit. Staaten, Regionen, Personenverbände_, Stuttgart

Sigmund, P.E. (ed.) (1991), _Nicholas of Cusa. The Catholic concordance_, Cambridge

Stieber, J.W. (1978), _Pope Eugenius IV, the Council of Basel and the secular and ecclesiastical authorities in the Empire. The conflict over supreme authority and power in the Church_, Studies in the History of Christian Thought, 13, Leiden

Strauss, G. (ed.) (1971), _Manifestations of discontent in Germany on the eve of the Reformation_, Bloomington, Ind., and London

Strauss, G. (ed.) (1972), _Pre-Reformation Germany_, London and Basingstoke

Thomas, H. (1983), _Deutsche Geschichte des Spätmittelalters 1250–1500_, Stuttgart, Berlin, Cologne and Mainz

Vann, J.A. and Rowan, S.W. (eds.) (1974), *The Old Reich. Essays on German political institutions, 1495–1806*, Studies Presented to the International Commission for the History of Representative and Parliamentary Institutions, 48, Brussels

Voigt, K. (1973), *Italienische Berichte aus dem spätmittelalterlichen Deutschland. Von Francesco Petrarca zu Andrea de' Franceschi, 1333–1492*, Kieler Historische Studien, 17, Stuttgart

Wefers, S. (1989), *Das politische System Kaiser Sigmunds*, Veröffentlichungen des Instituts für Europäische Geschichte Mainz, 138: Beiträge zur Sozial- und Verfassungsgeschichte des Alten Reiches, 5, Stuttgart

Wiesflecker, H. (1971–86), *Kaiser Maximilian I. Das Reich, Österreich und Europa an der Wende zur Neuzeit*, 5 vols., Munich and Vienna

Wiesflecker, H. (1991), *Maximilian I. Die Fundamente des habsburgischen Weltreiches*, Vienna and Munich

Wunder, H. (1986), *Die bäuerliche Gemeinde in Deutschland*, Göttingen

18 HUS, THE HUSSITES AND BOHEMIA

Primary sources

Daňhelka, J. (ed.), *Husitské skladby budyšínského rukopisu*, Prague (1952)

Hus, Jan, *De Ecclesia. The Church*, ed. and trans. D.S. Schaff, New York (1915)

Molnár, A. (ed.), 'Dcerka- O Poznání cěsty pravé k spasení', in *Mistr Jan Hus, Drobné spisy České*, Prague (1985)

Palacký, F. (ed.), *Archiv český čili staré písemné památky české i moravské*, I and III, Prague (1840, 1844)

Palacký, F. (ed.), *Documenta mag. Joannis Hus*, Prague (1869)

Palacký, F. (ed.), *Urkundliche Beiträge zur Geschichte des Hussitenkrieges in den Jahren 1419–1436*, 2 vols., Prague (1873)

Šimek, F. (ed.), *Staré letopisy české. Z vratislavského rukopisu*, Prague (1937)

Smctanka, E. (cd.), *Petra Chelčického. Postilla*, 2 vols., Prague (1900–3)

Spinka, M. (ed. and trans.), *The letters of John Hus*, Manchester (1972)

Thomson, S.H. (ed.), *Magistri Johannis Hus. Tractatus de Ecclesia*, Boulder (1956)

Secondary works

Bartoš, F.M. (1947), *Čechy v době Husově 1378–1415*, Prague

Bartoš, F.M. (1965–6), *Husitská revoluce*, 2 vols., Prague

Graus, F. (1949), *Chudina měská době předhusitské*, Prague

Graus, F. (1957), *Dějiny venkovského lidu v době předhusitské*, II, Prague

Graus, F. (1966), 'Die Bildung eines Nationalbewusstseins im mittelalterlichen Böhmen', *Historica* 13: 5–49

Heymann', F.G. (1954), 'The National Assembly of Čáslav', *Medievalia et humanistica*, 8: 32–55

Heymann, F.G. (1964), 'George of Poděbrady's plan for an international peace league', in M. Rechcigl (ed.), *The Czechoslovak contribution to world culture*, The Hague, London and Paris, pp. 224–44

Heymann, F.G. (1965), *George of Bohemia, king of heretics*, Princeton

Hlaváček, I. (1956), 'Husitské sněmy', *Sborník historický* 4: 71–109

Kalivoda, R. (1976), *Revolution und Ideologie; der Hussitismus*, Cologne and Vienna

Kaminsky, H. (1967), *A history of the Hussite revolution*, Berkeley

Kejř, J. (1984), *The Hussites*, Prague

Klassen, J. (1978), *The nobility and the making of the Hussite revolution*, New York

Macek, J. (1952–5), *Tábor v husitském revolučním hnutí*, 2 vols., Prague

Macek, J. (1955), 'Národnostní otázka v husitském revolučním hnutí', *Československý časopis historický* 3: 4–29

Maur, E. (1989), 'Příspěvek k demografické problemace předhusitských Čech', in *Acta Universitatis Carolinae – philosophica et historica*, I: *Studia historica*, 34: 7–71

Mezník, J. (1970), 'Národnostní složení předhusitské Prahy', *Sborník historický* 17: 5–30

Odložilík, O. (1965), *The Hussite king. Bohemia in European affairs, 1440–1471*, New Brunswick

Polívka, M. (1982), 'Mikuláš s Husi a nižší šlechta v počatcích husitiské revoluče', in *Rozpravy Československé Akademie Věd, Řada Společenskych Věd*, XCII, Prague, pp. 1–64

Polívka, M. (1985), 'The Bohemian lesser nobility at the turn of the 14th and 15th century', *Historica* 25: 121–75

Schwarz, E. (1965), *Volkstumsgeschichte der Sudetenländer. I Teil: Böhmen*, Munich

Sedlak, J. (1915), *M. Jan Hus*, Prague

Seibt, F. (1962), '*Communitas primogenitura*. Zur Prager Hegemonialpolitik in der hussitischen Revolution', in F. Seibt, *Hussiten Studien*, Munich, pp. 63–78

Seibt, F. (1965), *Hussitica. Zur Struktur einer Revolution*, Cologne and Graz

Šmahel, F. (1969, 1970), 'The idea of the "nation" in Hussite Bohemia', *Historica* 16: 143–247; 17: 93–197

Šmahel, F. (1985), *La révolution hussite, une anomalie historique*, Paris

Šmahel, F. (1988), *Dějiny Tábora, do roku 1421*, I, České Budějovice

Šmahel, F. (1990), *Dějiny Tábora, do roku 1452*, II, České Budějovice

Šmahel, F. (1993), *Husitská revoluce*, 4 vols., Prague

Spinka, M. (1966), *John Hus' concept of the Church*, Princeton

Thomson, S.H. (1941), 'Czech and German: action and interaction', *Journal of Central European Affairs* 1: 306–24

Tomek, V.V. (1899), *Dějepis města Prahy*, IV, Prague

Urbánek, R. (1957), 'Český mesianismus ve své době hrdinské', in R. Urbánek, *Z husitského věku*, Prague, pp. 7–28

Werner, E. (1991), *Jan Hus. Welt und Umwelt eines Praguer Frühreformators*, Weimar

19(a)   FRANCE AT THE END OF THE HUNDRED YEARS WAR (*c.* 1420–1461)

Secondary works

Allmand, C.T. (1976), 'The aftermath of war in fifteenth-century France', *History* 61: 344–57

Allmand, C.T. (1981), 'Local reaction to the French reconquest of Normandy: the case of Rouen', in J.R.L. Highfield and R. Jeffs (eds.), *The crown and local communities in England and France in the fifteenth century*, Gloucester, pp. 146–61

Allmand, C.T. (1983), *Lancastrian Normandy, 1415–1450. The history of a medieval occupation*, Oxford

Autrand, F. (1981), *Naissance d'un grand corps de l'état. Les gens du parlement de Paris, 1345–1454*, Paris

Blanchard, J. (ed.) (1995), *Représentation, pauvoir et royauté à la fin du moyen âge*, Paris

Boutruche, R. (1947), *La crise d'une société. Seigneurs et paysans du Bordelais pendant la guerre de Cent Ans*, Paris

Chevalier, B. and Contamine, P. (eds.) (1985), *La France de la fin du XVe siècle. Renouveau et apogée*, Paris

Contamine, P. (1978), 'Guerre, fiscalité royale et économie en France (deuxième moitié du XV siècle)', in M. Flinn (ed.), *Proceedings of the seventh international economic history congress*, 2 vols., Edinburgh, II, pp. 266–73

La 'France anglaise' au moyen âge (1988) (*Actes du 111e congrès national des Sociétés savantes (Poitiers, 1986). Section d'histoire médiévale et de philologie:* I), Paris

du Fresne de Beaucourt, G. (1881–91), *Histoire de Charles VII*, 6 vols., Paris

Gazzaniga, J.-L. (1976), *L'église du midi à la fin du règne de Charles VII (1444–1461)*, Paris

Harris, R. (1994), *Valois Guyenne. A study of politics, government and society in late medieval France*, Woodbridge and Rochester

Lartigaut, J. (1978), *Les campagnes du Quercy après la guerre de Cent Ans*. Toulouse

Lewis, P.S. (1965), 'War propaganda and historiography in fifteenth-century France and England', *TRHS* 5th series 15: 1–21

Lewis, P.S. (1985), *Essays in later medieval French history*, London and Ronceverte

Lewis, P.S. (ed.) (1971), *The recovery of France in the fifteenth century*, London and New York

La reconstruction après la guerre de Cent Ans (1981) (*Actes du 104e congrès national des Sociétés savantes (Bordeaux, 1979). Section de philologie et d'histoire jusqu'à 1610:* I), Paris

Vale, M.G.A. (1969), 'The last years of English Gascony, 1451–1453', *TRHS* 5th series, 19: 119–38

Vale, M.G.A. (1970), *English Gascony, 1399–1453*, Oxford

Vale, M.G.A. (1974), *Charles VII*, London

19(b) THE RECOVERY OF FRANCE, 1450–1520

Primary sources

Basin, Thomas, *Histoire de Louis XI*, ed. and trans. C. Samaran, 2 vols., Paris (1963–6)

Budé, Guillaume, *L'institution du prince*, in C. Bontems, L.-P. Raybaud and J.-P. Brancourt, *Le prince dans la France des XVIe et XVII siècles*, Paris (1965), pp. 77–143

Le débat des hérauts d'armes de France et d'Angleterre, ed. L. Pannier, SATF, Paris (1877)

Dispatches, with related documents, of Milanese ambassadors in France and Burgundy 1450–1483, ed. P.M. Kendall and V. Ilardi, 3 vols, Athens, Ohio (1970–81)

Lemaire de Belges, Jean, *[Oe]uvres*, ed. J. Stecher, 3 vols., Louvain (1882–5); repr. Geneva (1989)

Ordonnances des rois de France de la troisième race, 22 vols., Paris (1723–1849)

Ordonnances des rois de France. Règne de François I, 9 vols., Paris (1902–75)

Seyssel, Claude de, *La monarchie de France et deux autres fragments politiques*, ed. J. Poujol, Paris (1961); English trans. J.H. Hexter, *The monarchy of France*, New Haven (1981)

Van Caenegem, R.C. (ed.), *Les arrêts et jugés du Parlement de Paris sur appels flamands conservés dans les registres du Parlement (1454–1521)*, 2 vols., Brussels (1967–77)

La Vigne, André de, *Le voyage de Naples*, ed. A. Slerca, Milan (1981)

Secondary works

Abulafia, D. (ed.) (1995), *The French descent into Renaissance Italy. Antecedents and effects*, Aldershot

Allmand, C.T. (1976), 'The aftermath of war in fifteenth-century France', *History* 61: 344–57

Autrand, F. (1989), 'De l'Enfer au Purgatoire: la cour à travers quelques textes français du milieu du XIVe à la fin du XVe siècle', in P. Contamine (ed.), *L'état et les aristocraties (France, Angleterre, Ecosse), XIIe–XVII siècle*, Paris, pp. 51–78

Beaune, C. (1985), *Naissance de la nation France*, Paris; English trans. *The birth of an ideology. Myths and symbols of nation in late medieval France*, Berkeley (1991)

Bischoff, G. (1992), 'Maximilien Ier, roi des Romains, duc de Bourgogne et de Bretagne', in *1491, la Bretagne terre d'Europe* (1992), pp. 457–71

Bittmann, K. (1957), 'Die Zusammenkunft von Peronne. Ein Beitrag zur Kritik an den Memorien des Philippe de Commynes', *HZ* 184: 19–64

Bittmann, K. (1964), *Ludwig XI und Karl der Kühne. Die Memorien des Philippe de Commynes als historische Quelle*, Göttingen

Böhm, H. (1977), *'Gallica gloria'. Untersuchungen zum kulturellen Nationalgefühl in der älteren-französischen Neuzeit*, Freiburg

Bois, G. (1976), *Crise du féodalisme; économie rurale et démographie en Normandie orientale du début du 14e siècle au milieu du 16e siècle*, Paris; English trans. *The crisis of feudalism. Economy and society in eastern Normandy, c. 1300–1550*, Cambridge (1984)

Boone, M. (1992), 'D'un particularisme à l'autre: la Flandre et la Bretagne face à l'état centralisateur (XIVe–XVe siècle)', in *1491, la Bretagne, terre d'Europe* (1992), pp. 193–204

Bossuat, A. (1957), *Le bailliage royal de Montferrand (1425–1556)*, Paris

Bossuat, A. (1958), 'Les origines troyennes: leur rôle dans la littérature historique au XVe siècle', *AN* 8: 187–97

Bossuat, A. (1961), 'La formule "Le roi est empereur en son royaume". Son emploi au XVe siècle devant le parlement de Paris', *Revue historique de droit français et étranger* 4th series 39: 371–81; English trans. 'The maxim "The king is emperor in his kingdom": its use in the fifteenth century before the parlement of Paris', in Lewis (1971), pp. 185–95

Boudet, J.-P. (1987), 'Faveur, pouvoir et solidarités sous le règne de Louis XI: Olivier le Daim et son entourage', *Journal des savants*: 219–57

Boureau, A. (1988), *Le simple corps du roi. L'impossible sacralité des souverains français, XVe–XVIIIe siècle*, Paris

Boutruche, R. (ed.) (1966), *Bordeaux de 1453 à 1715* (*Histoire de Bordeaux*, ed. C. Higounet, IV), Bordeaux

1491, la Bretagne, terre d'Europe. Colloque international de Brest, 2–4 octobre 1991 (1992), ed. J. Kerhervé and T. Daniel, Brest and Quimper

Bridge, J.S. (1921–36), *A history of France from the death of Louis XI*, 5 vols., Oxford

Bulst, N. (1992), *Die französischen Generalstände von 1468 und 1484. Prosopographische Untersuchungen zu den Delegierten*, Sigmaringen

Calmette, J. and Déprez, E. (1937–9), *L'Europe occidentale de la fin du XIVe siècle aux guerres d'Italie* (*Histoire générale, Histoire du moyen âge*, ed. G. Glotz, VII, pts 1 and 2), Paris

Caron, M.-T. (1987), *La noblesse dans le duché de Bourgogne, 1315–1477*, Lille

Charbonnier, P. (1980), *Une autre France. La seigneurie en Basse-Auvergne du XIVe au XVIe siècle*, 2 vols., Clermont-Ferrand

Chaunu, P. and Gascon, R. (1977), *Histoire économique et sociale de la France*, 1, pt i: *De 1450 à 1660. L'état et la ville*, ed. F. Braudel, Paris

Chevalier, B. (1964), 'La politique de Louis XI à l'égard des bonnes villes: le cas de Tours', *MA* 70: 473–504; English trans. 'The policy of Louis XI towards the *bonnes villes*: the case of Tours', in Lewis (1971), pp. 265–93

Chevalier, B. (1975), *Tours, ville royale (1356–1520). Origine et développement d'une capitale à la fin du moyen âge*, Louvain and Paris

Chevalier, B. (1980), 'Gouverneurs et gouvernements en France entre 1450 et 1520', in F.K. Werner and W. Paravicini (eds.), *Histoire comparée de l'administration. 14e colloque franco-allemand, Tours, 1977*, Munich and Zurich, pp. 291–307

Chevalier, B. (1982), *Les bonnes villes de France du XIVe au XVIe siècle*, Paris

Chevalier, B. (1987a), 'Fiscalité municipale et fiscalité d'état en France du XIVe à la fin du XVIe siècle: deux systèmes liés et concurrents', in J.-P. Genet and M. Le Mené (eds.), *Genèse de l'état moderne. Prélèvement et redistribution*, Paris, pp. 137–51

Chevalier, B. (1987b), 'La réforme de la justice: utopie ou réalité (1440–1540)', in A. Stegmann (ed.), *Pouvoir et institutions en Europe au XVIe siècle*, Paris, pp. 237–47

Chevalier, B. (1988), 'L'état et les bonnes villes en France au temps de leur accord parfait (1450–1550)', in N. Bulst and J.-P. Genet (eds.), *La ville, la bourgeoisie et la genèse de l'état moderne (XII–XVIIIe siècles)*, Paris, pp. 71–85

Chevalier, B. (1994), 'France from Charles VII to Henry IV', in T.A. Brady, H.A. Oberman and J.D. Tracy (eds.), *Handbook of European history, 1400–1600, late Middle Ages, Renaissance and Reformation*, Leiden, New York and Cologne, pp. 370–401

Chevalier, B. (1995), 'Du droit d'imposer et de sa pratique. Finances et financiers du roi sous le règne de Charles VIII', in J. Blanchard (ed.), *Représentation, pouvoir et royauté à la fin du moyen âge*, Paris, pp. 33–47

Chevalier, B. and Contamine, P. (eds.) (1985), *La France de la fin du XVe siècle, renouveau et apogée; économie, pouvoirs, arts, culture et conscience nationales*, Paris

Cinq-centième anniversaire de la bataille de Nancy (1477) (1979), Actes du colloque organisé par l'Institut de Recherches Régionales en Sciences Sociales de l'Université de Nancy II, 1977, Nancy

Cinquième centenaire de la bataille de Morat. Actes du colloque 'Morat', avril 1976, Freiburg (1976)

Contamine, P. (1971), 'The French nobility and the war', in K.A. Fowler (ed.), *The Hundred Years War*, London, pp. 135–62; repr. in Contamine (1981)

Contamine, P. (1972), *Guerre, état et société à la fin du moyen âge*, Paris and The Hague

Contamine, P. (1977), 'Charles le Téméraire, fossoyeur et/ou fondateur de l'état bourguignon?', *Le Pays Lorrain* 58: 123–34

Contamine, P. (1978a), 'Un serviteur de Louis XI dans sa lutte contre Charles le Téméraire; Georges de la Tremoille, sire de Craon (vers 1437–1481)', *Annuaire-bulletin de la Société de l'histoire de France*, 1976–7, pp. 63–80; repr. in Contamine (1981)

Contamine, P. (1978b), 'Les fortifications urbaines en France à la fin du moyen âge: aspects financiers et économiques', *RH* 260: 23–47; repr. in Contamine (1981)

Contamine, P. (1981), *La France aux XIVe et XVe siècles. Hommes, mentalités, guerre et paix*, London

Contamine, P. (ed.) (1992), *Histoire militaire de la France*, I: *Des origines à 1715*, Paris

Coulet, N., Planche, A. and Robin, F. (eds.) (1982), *Le roi René. Le prince, le mécène, l'écrivain, le mythe*, Aix-en-Provence

Cuttler, S.H. (1982), *The law of treason and treason trials in later medieval France*, Cambridge

Daly, K. (1989), 'Mixing business with leisure: some French royal notaries and secre-taries and their histories of France, c. 1459–1509', in C.T. Allmand (ed.), *Power, culture, and religion in France c. 1350–c. 1550*, Woodbridge, pp. 99–115

Demurger, A. (1990), *Temps de crises, temps d'espoir, XIVe–XVe siècle*, Paris

Denis, A. (1979), *Charles VIII et les Italiens. Histoire et mythe*, Geneva and Paris

Derville, A. (1974), 'Pots-de-vin, cadeaux, racket, patronage. Essai sur les mécanismes de décision dans l'état bourguignon', *Revue du nord* 56: 341–64

Doucet, R. (1948), *Les institutions de la France au XVI siècle*, 2 vols., Paris

Dufournet, J. (1966), *La destruction des mythes dans les Mémoires de Philippe de Commynes*, Geneva

Dupâquier, J. (ed.) (1988), *Histoire de la population française*, I: *Des origines à la Renaissance*, Paris

Dupont-Ferrier, G. (1930–2), *Etudes sur les institutions financières de la France à la fin du moyen âge*, 2 vols., Paris

Dupont-Ferrier, G. (1942–58), *Gallia regia, ou état des officiers royaux des bailliages et sénéchaussées de 1328 à 1515*, 6 vols., Paris

Favier, J. (1974), *Nouvelle histoire de Paris. Paris au XVe siècle, 1380–1500*, Paris

Favier, J. (1978), 'Service du prince et service des administrés: les voies de la fortune et les chemins de l'opulence dans la France médiévale', in *Domanda e consumi. 6a Settimana di studio dell'Istituto intern. di storia economica, Prato, 1974*, Prato, pp. 237–46

Favier, J. (1984), *Les temps des principautés, de l'an mil à 1515*, Paris

Favreau, R. (1978), *La ville de Poitiers à la fin du moyen âge. Une capitale régionale*, 2 vols., Poitiers

Fédou, R. (1964), *Les hommes de loi lyonnais à la fin du moyen âge. Etude sur les origines de la classe de robe*, Paris

Gandilhon, R. (1941), *La politique économique de Louis XI*, Rennes

Gandilhon, R. (1944), 'L'unification des coutumes sous Louis XI', *RH* 194: 316–23

Gascon, R. (1956), 'Nationalisme économique et géographique des foires. La querelle des foires de Lyon, 1484–1494', *Cahiers d'histoire* 3: 253–87

Gaussin, P.-R. (1976), *Louis XI, un roi entre deux mondes*, Paris

Gaussin, P.-R. (1985), 'Les conseillers de Louis XI (1461–1483)', in Chevalier and Contamine (1985), pp. 105–34

Gazzaniga, J.-L. (1984), 'L'appel au concile dans la politique gallicane de la monarchie de Charles VII à Louis XII', *Bulletin de littérature ecclésiastique* 85: 111–29

Gazzaniga, J.-L. (1987), 'Les évêques de Louis XI', in *Eglise et pouvoir politique. Journées internationales d'histoire du droit, Angers, 1985*, pp. 151–66

Giesey, R.E. (1960a), 'The French estates and the *Corpus mysticum regni*', in *Album Helen Maud Cam*, I, Louvain and Paris, pp. 153–71

Giesey, R.E. (1960b), *The royal funeral ceremony in Renaissance France*, Geneva

Gilles, H. (1965), *Les états de Languedoc au XVe siècle*, Toulouse

Giry-Deloison, C. (1992), 'Henri VII et la Bretagne: aspects politiques et diploma-tiques', in *1491, la Bretagne, terre d'Europe* (1992), pp. 223–42

Grandson, 1476. Essai d'approche pluridisciplinaire d'une action militaire du XVe siècle (1976), ed. D. Reichel, Lausanne

Guenée, B. (1963), *Tribunaux et gens de justice dans le bailliage de Senlis à la fin du moyen âge (vers 1380 à 1500)*, Strasburg and Paris

Guenée, B. (1964), 'L'histoire de l'état en France à la fin du moyen âge, vue par les historiens français depuis cent ans', *RH* 232: 331–60; English trans. 'The history of the state in France at the end of the Middle Ages, as seen by French historians in the last hundred years', in Lewis (1971), pp. 324–52

Guenée, B. (1968), 'Espace et état dans la France du bas moyen âge', *Annales ESC* 23: 744–58

Guenée, B. (1971), *L'occident aux XIVe et XVe siècles. Les états*, Paris; English trans. *States and rulers in later medieval Europe* (1985), Oxford

Guéry, A. (1978), 'Les finances de la monarchie française sous l'ancien régime', *Annales ESC* 33: 216–39

Guy, J.A. (1986), 'The French king's council, 1483–1526', in R.A. Griffiths and J. Sherborne (eds.), *Kings and nobles in the late Middle Ages*, Gloucester, pp. 274–94

Harsgor, M. (1980), *Recherches sur le personnel du conseil du roi sous Charles VIII et Louis XII*, 4 vols., Lille and Paris

Higounet-Nadal, A. (1978), *Le Périgueux aux XIVe et XVe siècles; étude de démographie historique*, Bordeaux

Hocquet, J.-C. (1985), *Le sel et le pouvoir de l'an mil à la Révolution française*, Paris

Hocquet, J.-C. (1987), 'L'impôt du sel et l'état', in J.-C. Hocquet (ed.), *Le roi, le marchand et le sel*, Lille, pp. 27–49

Imbart de La Tour, P. (1948), *Les origines de la Réforme*, I, 2nd edn, Melun

Jackson, R.A. (1984), *Vivat rex. Histoire des sacres et couronnements en France*, Strasburg and Paris; English trans. *Vive le Roi! A history of the French coronation from Charles V to Charles X*, Chapel Hill and London (1984)

Jacquart, J. (1981), *François I*, Paris

Jones, M. (1982), '"Bons bretons et bons Francoys": the language and meaning of treason in later medieval France', *TRHS* 5th series 32: 91–112; repr. in M. Jones, *The creation of Brittany. A late medieval state*, London (1988), pp. 283–307

Kaeuper, R.W. (1988), *War, justice and public order. England and France in the later Middle Ages*, Oxford

Kantorowicz, E. (1957), *The king's two bodies. A study in mediaeval political theology*, Princeton

Kendall, P.M. (1971), *Louis XI, 'the universal spider'*, New York

Kerhervé, J. (1987), *L'état breton aux XIVe–XVe siècles. Les ducs, l'argent et les hommes*, 2 vols., Paris

Knecht, R.J. (1982), *Francis I*, Cambridge

Knecht, R.J. (1994), *Renaissance warrior and patron. The reign of Francis I*, Cambridge

Krynen, J. (1987), 'Le roi "très chrétien" et le rétablissement de la Pragmatique Sanction. Pour une explication idéologique du gallicanisme parlementaire et de la politique religieuse de Louis XI', in *Eglise et pouvoir politique. Journées internationales d'histoire du droit, Angers, 1985*, pp. 135–49

Krynen, J. (1989), '*Rex christianissimus*. A medieval theme at the roots of French absolutism', *History and Anthropology* 4: 79–95

Krynen, J. (1993), *L'empire du roi. Idées et croyances politiques en France, XIIIe–XVe siècle*, Paris

Labande-Mailfert, Y. (1954), 'Trois traités de paix, 1492–1493', *MA* 60: 379–401

Labande-Mailfert, Y. (1975), *Charles VIII et son milieu (1470–1498). La jeunesse au pouvoir*, Paris

Labande-Mailfert, Y. (1986), *Charles VIII. Le vouloir et la destinée*, Paris

Lapeyre, A. and Scheurer, R. (1978), *Les notaires et secrétaires du roi sous les règnes de Louis XI, Charles VIII et Louis XII (1461–1515). Notices personnelles et généalogiques*, 2 vols., Paris

Lartigaut, J. (1978), *Les campagnes du Quercy après la guerre de Cent Ans*, Toulouse

Le Roy Ladurie, E. (1966), *Les paysans du Languedoc*, Paris

Le Roy Ladurie, E. (1987), *Histoire de France. L'état royal, 1460–1610*, Paris; English trans. *The royal French state, 1460–1610*, Oxford (1994)

Le Roy Ladurie, E. and Morineau, M. (1977), *Histoire économique et sociale de la France*, I, pt ii: *De 1450 à 1660. Paysannerie et croissance*, ed. F. Braudel, Paris

Lecoq, A.-M. (1987), *Francois I imaginaire. Symbolique et politique à l'aube de la Renaissance française*, Paris

Leguai, A. (1947), *Dijon et Louis XI*, Dijon

Leguai, A. (1967a), 'Les "états princiers" en France à la fin du moyen âge', *Annali della fondazione italiana per la storia amministrativa* 4: 133–67

Leguai, A. (1967b), 'Emeutes et troubles d'origine fiscale pendant le règne de Louis XI', *MA* 73: 447–87

Leguai, A. (1973), 'Troubles et révoltes sous le règne de Louis XI: les résistances des particularismes', *RH* 249: 285–324

Leguai, A. (1977), 'La conquête de la Bourgogne par Louis XI', *AB* 49: 7–12

Leguai, A. (1981a), 'Les oppositions urbaines à Louis XI en Bourgogne et en Franche-Comté', *AB* 53: 31–7

Leguai, A. (1981b), 'The relations between the towns of Burgundy and the French crown in the fifteenth century', in J.R.L. Highfield and R. Jeffs (eds.), *The crown and local communities in England and France in the fifteenth century*, Gloucester, pp. 129–45

Leguay, J.-P. (1970), *Les comptes de miseurs de Rennes au XVe siècle*, Paris

Leguay, J.-P. (1981), *Un réseau urbain au moyen âge. Les villes du duché de Bretagne aux XIVe et XVe siècles*, Paris

Lesage, G. (1948), 'La circulation monétaire en France dans la seconde moitié du XVe siècle', *Annales ESC* 3: 304–16

Levi, A.H.T. (ed.) (1970), *Humanism in France at the end of the Middle Ages and in the early Renaissance*, New York and Manchester

Lewis, P.S. (1964), 'Decayed and non-feudalism in later medieval France', *BIHR* 37: 157–84; repr. in Lewis (1985b), pp. 41–68

Lewis, P.S. (1968), *Late medieval France. The polity*, London

Lewis, P.S. (1971), *The recovery of France in the fifteenth century*, London

Lewis, P.S. (1985a), 'Les pensionnaires de Louis XI', in Chevalier and Contamine (1985), pp. 167–81

Lewis, P.S. (1985b), *Essays in later medieval French history*, London

Lorcin, M.-T. (1974), *Les campagnes de la région lyonnaise aux XIVe et XVe siècles*, Lyons

Lot, F. and Fawtier, R. (1958), *Histoire des institutions françaises au moyen âge*, II: *Institutions royales*, Paris

Love, R.S. (1984), 'Contemporary and near-contemporary opinion of Louis XII, "père du peuple"', *Renaissance and Reformation* 20: 235–65

Major, J.R. (1960), *Representative institutions in Renaissance France, 1421–1559*, Madison

Major, J.R. (1962), 'The French Renaissance monarchy as seen through the estates-general', *Studies in the Renaissance* 9: 113–25

Major, J.R. (1964), 'The crown and the aristocracy in Renaissance France', *AHR* 69: 631–45

Major, J.R. (1980), *Representative government in early modern France*, London

Malettke, K. (1984), 'Zur Zeitgenössichen Verwendung der Termini *office* und *officiers*, vom XIV bis zum frühen XVI Jahrhundert in Frankreich', in *Amterhandel im Spätmittelalter und im XVI Jahrhundert*, Berlin, pp. 132–41

Mann, N. (1971), 'Humanisme et patriotisme en France au XVe siècle' *Cahiers de l'association internationale d'études françaises* 23: 59–84

Marchello-Nizia, C. (1979), *Histoire de la langue française aux XIVe et XVe siècles*, Paris

Michaud, H. (1977), 'Les institutions militaires des guerres d'Italie aux guerres de religion', *RH* 258: 29–43

Mieck, L. (1982), *Die Entstehung des modernen Frankreich (1450–1610). Strukturen, Institutionen, Entwicklungen*, Stuttgart

Miskimin, H.A. (1984), *Money and power in fifteenth-century France*, New Haven and London

Mollat, M. (1977), *Genèse médiévale de la France moderne, XIVe–XVe siècle*, Paris

Neveux, H. (1985), 'Reconstruction économique et rapports sociaux dans les campagnes françaises dans la seconde moitié du XVe siècle', in Chevalier and Contamine (1985), pp. 61–8

Olland, H. (1980), *La baronie de Choiseul à la fin du moyen âge (1485–1525)*, Nancy

Paravicini, W. (1985), 'Peur, pratiques, intelligences. Formes de l'opposition aristocratique à Louis XI d'après les interrogatoires du connétable de Saint-Pol', in Chevalier and Contamine (1985), pp. 183–96

Perroy, E. (1945), 'Feudalism or principalities in fifteenth-century France', *BIHR* 20: 181–5; repr. in E. Perroy, *Etudes d'histoire médiévale*, Paris (1979), pp. 177–81

Pocquet du Haut-Jussé, B.A. (1957), 'Les débuts du gouvernement de Charles VIII en Bretagne', *BEC* 115: 138–55

Pocquet du Haut-Jussé, B.A. (1961), 'Une idée politique de Louis XI: la sujétion éclipse la vassalité', *RH* 226: 383–98; English trans. 'A political concept of Louis XI: subjection instead of vassalage', in Lewis (1971), pp. 196–215

Potter, D. (1995), *A history of France. The emergence of a nation state*, Basingstoke

Poujol, J. (1958), 'Jean Ferrault on the king's privileges. A study of the medieval sources of Renaissance political theory in France', *Studies in the Renaissance* 5: 15–26

Quilliet, B. (1986), *Louis XII, père du peuple*, Paris

Rambert, G. (1951), *Histoire du commerce de Marseille*, III: *De 1480 à 1559*, Paris

La reconstruction après la guerre de Cent Ans (1981) (Actes du 104e congrès national des Sociétés savantes (Bordeaux, 1979). Section de philologie et d'histoire jusqu'à 1610: I), Paris

Rigaudière, A. (1982), *Saint-Flour, ville d'Auvergne au bas moyen âge. Etude d'histoire administrative et financière*, 2 vols., Paris

Rigaudière, A. (1985), 'Le financement des fortifications urbaines en France du milieu du XIVe siècle à la fin du XVe siècle', *RH* 273: 19–95

Rigaudière, A. (1993), 'Qu'est-ce qu'une bonne ville dans la France du moyen âge?', in A. Rigaudière (ed.), *Gouverner la ville au moyen âge*, Paris, pp. 53–112

Robin, F. (1985), *La cour d'Anjou-Provence. La vie artistique sous le règne de René d'Anjou*, Paris

'Le roi René: René, duc d'Anjou, de Bar et de Lorraine, roi de Sicile et de Jérusalem, roi d'Aragon, comte de Provence, 1409–1480' (1986), *Annales de l'Université d'Avignon* 1–2: 1–184

Scheller, R.-W. (1981–2), 'Imperial themes in art and literature of the early French Renaissance: the period of Charles VIII', *Simiolus* 12: 5–69

Scheller, R.-W. (1983), 'Ensigns of authority: French royal symbolism in the age of Louis XII', *Simiolus* 13: 75–141

Scheller, R.-W. (1985), 'Gallia cisalpina: Louis XII and Italy, 1499–1508', *Simiolus* 15: 5–61

Schmidt-Chazan, M. (1977), 'Histoire et sentiment national chez Robert Gaguin', in B. Guenée (ed.), *Le métier d'historien au moyen âge. Etudes sur l'historiographie médiévale*, Paris, pp. 223–300

Sciacca, E. (1975), *Le radici teoriche dell'assolutismo nel pensiero politico francese del primo cinquecento (1498–1519)*, Milan

Sciacca, E. (1983), 'Les états-généraux dans la pensée politique française du XVIe siècle (1484–1571)', in *Assemblee di Stati e Istituzioni rappresentative, Convegno internazionale Perugia, 1982*, pp. 73–84

Seguin, J.-P. (1961), *L'information en France de Louis XII à Henri II*, Geneva

Sherman, M. (1978), 'Pomp and circumstance; pageantry and propaganda in France during the reign of Louis XII, 1498–1515', *Sixteenth-Century Journal* 9: 13–32

Spooner, F.C. (1956), *L'économie mondiale et les frappes monétaires en France 1493–1680*, Paris

Stouff, L. (1986), *Arles à la fin du moyen âge*, Aix-en-Provence

Strayer, J.R. (1971), 'France: the Holy Land, the Chosen People, and the Most Christian King', in J.R. Stayer (ed.), *Medieval statecraft and the perspectives of history*, Princeton

Touchard, H. (1967), *Le commerce maritime breton à la fin du moyen âge*, Paris

Tucoo-Chala, P. (1961), *La vicomté de Béarn et le problème de la souveraineté, des origines à 1620*, Bordeaux

Vale, M.G.A. (1974), *Charles VII*, London

Vale, M.G.A. (1981), *War and chivalry. Warfare and aristocratic culture in England, France and Burgundy at the end of the Middle Ages*, London

Vaughan, R. (1970), *Philip the Good. The apogee of Burgundy*, London

Vaughan, R. (1973), *Charles the Bold. The last Valois duke of Burgundy*, London

Viala, A. (1953), *Le parlement de Toulouse et l'administration royale laïque (1420–1525 environ)*, 2 vols., Albi

Zeller, G. (1934), 'Les rois de France candidats à l'Empire: essai sur l'idéologie impériale en France', *RH* 173: 273–311, 497–534

Zeller, G. (1946), 'Procès à reviser? Louis XI, la noblesse, et la marchandise', *Annales ESC* 1: 331–41

20 BURGUNDY

Primary sources

Main literary sources

Chastellain, G., *Œuvres*, ed. J. Kervyn de Lettenhove, 8 vols., Brussels (1863–6)

Commynes, P. de, *Mémoires*, ed. J. Calmette and G. Durville, 3 vols., Paris (1924–5)

'La geste des ducs Phelippe et Jehan de Bourgongne', in J. Kervyn de Lettenhove (ed.), *Chroniques relatives à l'histoire de la Belgique sous la domination des ducs de Bourgogne*, II: *Textes français*, Brussels (1873), pp. 259–572

Journal d'un bourgeois de Paris, 1405–1449, ed. A. Tuetey, Paris (1881); English trans. J. Shirley, *A Parisian journal, 1405–1449*, Oxford (1968)

La Marche, O., *Mémoires*, ed. H. Beaune and J. d'Arbaumont, 4 vols., SHF, Paris (1883–8)

Lannoy, G. de., *Œuvres*, ed. C. Potvin, Louvain (1878)

Lefèvre de Saint-Rémy, J., *Chronique*, ed. F. Morand, 2 vols., SHF, Paris (1876–81)

'Le livre des trahisons de France', in J. Kervyn de Lettenhove (ed.), *Chroniques relatives à l'histoire de la Belgique sous la domination des ducs de Bourgogne*, II: *Textes français*, Brussels (1873), pp. 1–258

Molinet, J., *Chroniques*, ed. G. Doutrepont and O. Jodogne, 3 vols., Brussels (1935–7)

Monstrelet, E. de, *Chronique*, ed. L. Douët-d'Arcq, 6 vols., SHF, Paris (1857–62)

Le Pastoralet, ed. J. Blanchard, Paris (1983)

Other sources

Carteggi diplomatici fra Milano sforzesco e la Borgogna, ed. E. Sestan, 2 vols., Rome (1985–7)

Chartes de communes et d'affranchissement en Bourgogne, ed. J. Garnier, 4 vols., Dijon (1867–1918)

Comptes généraux de l'état bourguignon entre 1416 et 1420, ed. M. Mollat and R. Favreau, 5 vols., Paris (1965–76)

Dépêches des ambassadeurs milanais sur les campagnes de Charles le Hardi duc de Bourgogne de 1474 à 1477, ed. F. de Gingins-La Sarra, Paris and Geneva (1858)

Ordonnances de Philippe le Hardi, de Marguerite de Male et de Jean sans Peur, 1381–1419, I: *(1381–1393)*; II: *(1394–1405)*, ed. P. Bonenfant, J. Bartier and A. van Nieuwenhuysen, Brussels (1965, 1974)

Paravicini, W. (ed.), *Der Briefwechsel Karls des Kühnen (1433–1477)*, 2 vols., Frankfurt-am-Main (1995)

Paravicini, W. (ed.), 'Die Hofordnungen Philipps des Guten von Burgund', *Francia* 10 (1982), pp. 131–66; 11 (1983), pp. 257–301; 15 (1987), pp. 183–231

Pocquet du Haut-Jussé, B.-A. (ed.), *La France gouvernée par Jean sans Peur. Les dépenses du receveur général du royaume*, Paris (1959)

Secondary works

The dukes and the Burgundian state

Andt, E. (1924), *La chambre des comptes de Dijon à l'époque des ducs Valois*, I, Paris

Bartier, J. (1970), *Charles le Téméraire*, 2nd edn, Brussels

La bataille de Morat. Actes du colloque de Morat (1976) (1976), Fribourg and Berne

Bonenfant, P. (1945), *Philippe le Bon*, Brussels

Calmette, J. (1987), *Les grands ducs de Bourgogne*, 2nd edn, Paris

Cinq-centième anniversaire de la bataille de Nancy (1477) (1979) Actes du colloque organisé par l'Institut de Recherches Régionales en Sciences Sociales de l'Université de Nancy II, 1977, Nancy

Contamine P. (1992a), 'La Bourgogne au XVe siècle', in *Des pouvoirs en France, 1300–1500*, Paris, pp. 61–74

Contamine, P. (1992b), 'Charles le Téméraire, fossoyeur et/ou fondateur de l'état bourguignon', in *Des pouvoirs en France, 1300–1500*, Paris, pp. 87–98

Grandson 1476. Essai d'approche pluridisciplinaire d'une action militaire du XVe siècle (1976), Lausanne

Lacaze, Y. (1971), 'Le rôle des traditions dans la genèse d'un sentiment national au XVe siècle: la Bourgogne de Philippe le Bon', *BEC* 129: 303–85

Liège et Bourgogne. Actes du colloque de Liège (1968) (1972), Liège

Paravicini, W. (1976), *Karl der Kühne. Das Ende des Hauses Burgund*, Göttingen, Zurich and Frankfurt-am-Main

Vaughan, R. (1962), *Philip the Bold. The formation of the Burgundian state*, London

Vaughan, R. (1966), *John the Fearless. The growth of Burgundian power*, London

Vaughan, R. (1970), *Philip the Good. The apogee of Burgundy*, London

Vaughan, R. (1973), *Charles the Bold. The last Valois duke of Burgundy*, London

Vaughan, R. (1975), *Valois Burgundy*, London

The dukes and the civil war

Autrand, F. (1986), *Charles VI. La folie du roi*, Paris

Bonenfant, P. (1958), *Du meurtre de Montereau au traité de Troyes*, Brussels

Famiglietti, R.C. (1986), *Royal intrigue. Crisis at the court of Charles VI, 1392–1420*, New York

Guenée, B. (1992), *Un meurtre, une société. L'assassinat du duc d'Orléans, 23 novembre 1407*, Paris

Nordberg, M. (1964), *Les ducs et la royauté. Etudes sur la rivalité des ducs d'Orléans et de Bourgogne, 1392–1407*, Uppsala

Schnerb, B. (1988), *Les Armagnacs et les Bourguignons. La maudite guerre*, Paris

Regional studies

Fiétier, R. (ed.) (1977), *Histoire de la Franche-Comté*, Toulouse

Prevenier, W. and Blockmans, W. (1986), *The Burgundian Netherlands*, Cambridge

Richard, J. (ed.) (1978), *Histoire de la Bourgogne*, Toulouse

Institutions, finances and money

Billioud, J. (1922), *Les états de Bourgogne aux XIVe et XVe siècles*, Dijon

Cauchies, J.-M. (1982), *La législation princière pour le comté de Hainaut. Ducs de Bourgogne et premiers Habsbourg (1427–1506)*, Brussels

Cauchies, J.-M. (1995), 'Le droit et les institutions dans les anciens Pays-Bas sous Philippe le Bon (1419–1467). Essai de synthèse', *Cahiers de Clio* 123: 33–68

Dubois, H. (1987a), 'Caractères originaux (et moins originaux) de l'impôt du sel en Bourgogne à la fin du moyen âge', in J.-C. Hocquet (ed.), *Le roi, le marchand et le sel*, Lille, pp. 119–31

Dubois, H. (1987b), 'Naissance de la fiscalité dans un état princier au moyen âge: l'exemple de la Bourgogne', in J.-P. Genet and M. Le Mené (eds.), *Genèse de l'état moderne. Prélèvement et redistribution*, Paris, pp. 91–100

Dumas-Dubourg, F. (1988), *Le monnayage des ducs de Bourgogne*, Louvain-la-Neuve

Mollat, M. (1958), 'Recherches sur les finances des ducs Valois de Bourgogne', *RH* 219: 285–321

Prevenier, W. (1961), *De leden en de Staten van Vlaanderen (1384–1405)*, Brussels

Richard, J. (1957a), 'Le gouverneur de Bourgogne au temps des ducs Valois', *Mémoires de la Société pour l'histoire du droit et des institutions des anciens pays bourguignons, comtois et romands* 19: 101–12

Richard, J. (1957b), 'Les institutions ducales dans le duché de Bourgogne', in F. Lot and R. Fawtier (eds.), *Histoire des institutions françaises au moyen âge*, II: *Institutions seigneuriales*, Paris, pp. 209–47

Richard, J. (1966), 'Les états de Bourgogne', in *Recueils de la Société Jean Bodin*, 24: *Gouvernés et gouvernants*, Brussels, pp. 299–324

Spufford, P. (1970), *Monetary problems and policies in the Burgundian Netherlands 1433–1496*, Leiden

Van Nieuwenhuysen, A. (1984), *Les finances du duc de Bourgogne Philippe le Hardi (1384–1404). Economie et politique*, Brussels

Van Rompaey, J. (1967), *Het grafelijk baljuwsambt in Vlaanderen tijdens de Boergondische periode*, Brussels

Van Rompaey, J. (1973), *De Grote Raad van de hertogen van Boergondië en het Parlement van Mechelen*, Brussels

War and armies

Brusten, C. (1954), *L'armée bourguignonne de 1465 à 1468*, Brussels

Brusten, C. (1976), 'Les compagnies d'ordonnance dans l'armée bourguignonne', in *Grandson 1476* (1976), pp. 112–69

Brusten, C. (1979), 'La fin des compagnies d'ordonnance de Charles le Téméraire', in *Cinq-centième anniversaire . . . de Nancy* (1979), pp. 363–75

Garnier, J. (1895), *L'artillerie des ducs de Bourgogne d'après les documents conservés aux archives de la Côte d'Or*, Paris

Paviot, J. (1995), *La politique navale des ducs de Bourgogne, 1384–1482*, Lille

Schnerb, B. (1993), *Bulgnéville (1431). L'état bourguignon prend pied en Lorraine*, Paris

The court

Caron, M.-T. (1994), 'Une fête dans la ville en 1402: le mariage d'Antoine comte de Rethel à Arras', *Villes et sociétés urbaines au moyen âge. Hommage à M. le Professeur Jacques Heers*, Paris, pp. 173–83

Cartellieri, O. (1929), *The court of Burgundy*, London

De Smedt, R. (ed.) (1994), *Les chevaliers de l'ordre de la Toison d'Or*, Frankfurt am Main

Lafortune-Martel, A. (1984), *Fête noble en Bourgogne au XVe siècle. Le banquet du faisan (1454). Aspects politiques, sociaux et culturels*, Montreal and Paris

Paravicini, W. (1991), 'The court of the dukes of Burgundy. A model for Europe?', in R.G. Asch and A.M. Birke (eds.), *Princes, patronage and the nobility. The court at the beginning of the modern age, c. 1450–1650*, London and Oxford, pp. 69–102

Political society

Bartier, J. (1955), *Légistes et gens de finances au XVe siècle. Les conseillers des ducs de Bourgogne, Philippe le Bon et Charles le Téméraire*, Brussels

Berger, R. (1971), *Nicolas Rolin, Kanzler der Zeitenwende im Burgundisch-Französich Konflikt 1422–1461*, Freiburg

Caron, M.-T. (1987), *La noblesse dans le duché de Bourgogne, 1315–1477*, Lille

Kamp, H. (1993), *Memoria und Selbstdarstellung. Die Stiftungen des burgundischen Kanzlers Rolin*, Sigmaringen

Paravicini, W. (1975), *Guy de Brimeu. Der Burgundische Staat und seine adlige Führungsschicht unter Karl dem Kühnen*, Bonn

Towns, population and exchange

Arnould, M.-A. (1956), *Les dénombrements de foyers dans le comté de Hainaut (XIVe–XVIe siècles)*, Brussels

Bocquet, A. (1969), *Recherches sur la population rurale de l'Artois et du Boulonnais pendant la période bourguignonne (1384–1477)*, Arras

Clauzel, D. (1982), *Finances et politique à Lille pendant la période bourguignonne*, Dunkirk

Dollinger, P. (1970), *The German Hanse*, London

Dubois, H. (1976), *Les foires de Chalon et le commerce dans la vallée de la Saône à la fin du moyen âge (v. 1280–v. 1430)*, Paris

Dubois, H. (1978), 'Le Téméraire, les Suisses et le sel', *RH* 259: 309–33

Fourquin, G. (ed.) (1970), *Histoire de Lille*, I: *Des origines à l'avènement de Charles Quint*, Lille

Gras, P. (ed.) (1987), *Histoire de Dijon*, Toulouse

Humbert, F. (1961), *Les finances municipales de Dijon du milieu du XIVe siècle à 1477*, Paris

Laurent, H. (1935), *La draperie des Pays-Bas en France et dans les pays méditerranéens (XIIe–XVe s.)*, Paris

Sosson, J.-P. (1977), *Les travaux publics de la ville de Bruges XIVe–XVe siècles. Les matériaux. Les hommes*, Brussels

Thielemans, M.-R. (1966), *Bourgogne et Angleterre. Relations économiques entre les Pays-Bas bourguignons et l'Angleterre, 1435–1467*, Brussels

Viaux, D. (1988), *La vie paroissiale à Dijon à la fin du moyen âge*, Dijon

Patronage and artistic life

Actes des journées internationales Claus Sluter (1990) (1992), Dijon

Camp, P. (1990), *Les imageurs bourguignons de la fin du moyen âge*, Dijon

David, H. (1947), *Philippe le Hardi. Le train somptuaire d'un grand Valois*, Dijon

David, H. (1951), *Claus Sluter*, Paris

De Patoul, B. and Van Schoute, R. (eds.) (1994), *Les primitifs flamands et leur temps*, Louvain-la-Neuve

De Winter, P. (1985), *La bibliothèque de Philippe le Hardi, duc de Bourgogne (1363–1404)*, Paris

Devaux, J. (1996), *Jean Molinet, indiciaire bourguignon*, Paris

Dhaenens, E. (1980), *Hubert et Jan Van Eyck*, Antwerp

Doutrepont, G. (1909), *La littérature française à la cour des ducs de Bourgogne*, Paris

Lecat, J.P. (1986), *Le siècle de la Toison d'Or*, Paris

Marix, J. (1939), *Histoire de la musique et des musiciens de la cour de Bourgogne sous le règne de Philippe le Bon*, Strasburg

Martens, M. (1992), *Lodewijk van Gruuthuse. Mecenas en europees diplomaat, ca. 1427–1492* (exhibition catalogue), Bruges

Régnier-Bohler, D. (ed.) (1995), *Splendeurs de la cour de Bourgogne. Récits et chroniques*, Paris

21(a) LANCASTRIAN ENGLAND

Primary sources

The history of Lancastrian England is written from a wide range of different kinds of primary source materials. Extracts from a large representative selection of primary sources, translated into English, are collected together in *English historical documents, 1327–1485*, ed. A.R. Myers, London (1969).

The most important categories of primary sources are:

1. The records of the central institutions of royal government (including parliament, the law courts, exchequer and chancery), the great majority of which are to be found in the Public Record Office in London. The proceedings of parliament are published in *Rotuli parliamentorum*, 6 vols., London (1767–77).

2. The estate papers of noble and gentry families (including financial and estate accounts and manorial court rolls). For pioneering use of these sources, see McFarlane (1973).

3. Chronicles and narrative accounts of the period. For a detailed survey of fifteenth-century historical writing, see Gransden (1982), pp. 194–479.

4. Contemporary collections of gentry letters, of which the largest and most important is *Paston letters and papers of the fifteenth century*, ed. N. Davis, 2 vols., Oxford (1971–6).

5. Contemporary poems and songs: for a printed collection, see *Historical poems of the fourteenth and fifteenth centuries*, ed. R.H. Robbins, New York (1959).

Secondary works

Allmand, C.T. (1983), *Lancastrian Normandy, 1415–1450*, Oxford

Allmand, C.T. (1992), *Henry V*, London; rev. edn New Haven and London (1997)

Aston, M. (1960), 'Lollardy and sedition, 1381–1431', *P&P* 17: 1–44

Bean, J.M.W. (1959), 'Henry IV and the Percies', *History* 44: 212–27

Brown, A.L. (1972), 'The reign of Henry IV', in Chrimes *et al.* (1972), pp. 1–28

Carpenter, M.C. (1980), 'The Beauchamp affinity: a study of bastard feudalism at work', *EHR* 95: 515–32

Carpenter, M.C. (1992), *Locality and polity. A study of Warwickshire landed society, 1401–1499*, Cambridge

Chrimes, S.B. (1936), *English constitutional ideas in the fifteenth century*, Cambridge

Chrimes, S.B., Ross, C.D. and Griffiths, R.A. (eds.) (1972) *Fifteenth-century England 1399–1509*, Manchester

Goodman, A.E. (1981), *The Wars of the Roses. Military activity and English society 1452–97*, London

Gransden, A. (1982), *Historical writing in England*, II: *c. 1307 to the early sixteenth century*, London

Griffiths, R.A. (1981a), *The reign of King Henry the sixth. The exercise of royal authority 1422–1461*, London

Griffiths, R.A. (ed.) (1981b), *Patronage, the crown and the provinces*, Gloucester

Harriss, G.L. (1988), *Cardinal Beaufort*, Oxford

Harriss, G.L. (ed.) (1985), *Henry V. The practice of kingship*, Oxford

Harvey, I.M.W. (1991), *Jack Cade's rebellion of 1450*, Oxford

Jacob, E.F. (1961), *The fifteenth century*, Oxford

Johnson, P.A. (1988), *Duke Richard of York 1411–1460*, Oxford

Jones, M.K. (1981), 'John Beaufort, duke of Somerset and the French expedition of 1443', in Griffiths (1981b), pp. 79–102

Jones, M.K. (1989), 'Somerset, York and the Wars of the Roses', *EHR* 104: 285–307

Kingsford, C.L. (1913), *English historical literature in the fifteenth century*, Oxford

Kirby, J.L. (1970), *Henry IV of England*, London

McFarlane, K.B. (1972), *Lancastrian kings and Lollard knights*, Oxford

McFarlane, K.B. (1973), *The nobility of later medieval England*, Oxford

McFarlane, K.B. (1981), *England in the fifteenth century. Collected essays*, London

McNiven, P. (1987), *Heresy and politics in the reign of Henry IV*, Woodbridge

Newhall, R.A. (1924), *The English conquest of Normandy*, New Haven

Nicolas, N.H. (1827) *The battle of Agincourt*, London

Powell, E. (1989), *Kingship, law and society. Criminal justice in the reign of Henry V*, Oxford

Rogers, A.R. (1969), 'Henry IV, the Commons and taxation', *Medieval Studies* 31: 444–70

Roskell, J.S. (1965), *The Commons and their speakers in medieval English parliaments*, Manchester

Ross, C.D. (1975), *Edward IV*, London

Ross, C.D. (1976), *The Wars of the Roses*, London

Storey, R.L. (1966), *The end of the house of Lancaster*, London

Vale, M. (1970), *English Gascony*, Oxford

Vaughan, R. (1966), *John the Fearless*, London

Vaughan, R. (1970), *Philip the Good*, London

Watts, J.L. (1996), *Henry VI and the politics of kingship*, Cambridge

Wolffe, B.P. (1981), *Henry VI*, London

Wylie, J.H. (1884–98), *History of England under Henry the fourth*, 4 vols., London

Wylie, J.H. and Waugh, W.T. (1914–29), *The reign of Henry the fifth*, 3 vols., Cambridge

21(b) YORKIST AND EARLY TUDOR ENGLAND

Primary sources

'Chronicle of the rebellion in Lincolnshire, 1470', ed. J.G. Nichols, *Camden Miscellany I*, London (1837)

Crowland chronicle. Continuations 1459–1486, ed. N. Pronay and J. Cox, London (1986)

Fortescue, John, *The governance of England*, ed. C. Plummer, Oxford (1885)

Historie of the arrivall of Edward IV in England, ed. J. Bruce, Camden Society, original series, 1, London (1838)

Hughes, P.L. and Larkin, J.F. (eds.), *Tudor royal proclamations*, 1, New Haven and London (1964)

Mancini, Dominic, *The usurpation of Richard III*, ed. C.A.J. Armstrong, Oxford (1969)

Paston letters and papers of the fifteenth century, ed. N. Davis, 2 vols., Oxford (1971–6)

Warkworth, John, *A chronicle of the first thirteen years of the reign of King Edward the fourth*, ed. J.O. Halliwell, Camden Society, original series, 10, London (1839)

Secondary works

Anglo, S. (1969), *Spectacle, pageantry and early Tudor policy*, Oxford

Anglo, S. (ed.) (1990), *Chivalry in the Renaissance*, Woodbridge

Antonovics, A.V. (1986), 'Henry VII, king of England, "by the grace of Charles VIII of France"', in Griffiths and Sherborne (1986), pp. 169–84

Arthurson, I. (1987), 'The rising of 1497: a revolt of the peasantry?' in Rosenthal and Richmond (1987), pp. 1–18

Arthurson, I. (1994), *The Perkin Warbeck conspiracy, 1491–1499*, Gloucester

Bennett, M. (1987), *Lambert Simnel and the battle of Stoke*, Gloucester

Bennett, M. (1990), 'Henry VII and the northern rising of 1489', *EHR* 105: 34–59

Bernard, G. (1985), *The power of the early Tudor nobility: a study of the fourth and fifth earls of Shrewsbury*, Brighton

Bernard, G. (ed.) (1992), *The Tudor nobility*, Manchester

Cameron, A. (1974), 'The giving of livery and retaining in Henry VII's reign', *Renaissance and Modern Studies* 18: 17–35

Carpenter, C. (1986), 'The duke of Clarence and the midlands: a study in the interplay of local and national politics', *Midland History* 11: 23–48

Carpenter, C. (1992), *Locality and polity. A study of Warwickshire landed society, 1401–1499*, Cambridge

Chrimes, S.B. (1972), *Henry VII*, London

Condon, M. (1979), 'Ruling elites in the reign of Henry VII', in Ross (1979), pp. 109–42

Condon, M. (1990), 'From caitiff and villain to pater patriae: Reynold Bray and the profits of office', in Hicks (1990), pp. 137–68

Conway, A. (1932), *Henry VII's relations with Scotland and Ireland, 1485–98*, Cambridge

Davies, C.S.L. (1987), 'Bishop John Morton, the Holy See, and the accession of Henry VII', *EHR* 102: 2–30

Davies, C.S.L. (1990), 'Richard III, Brittany, and Henry Tudor', *Nottingham Medieval Studies* 37: 110–26

Griffiths, R.A. and Sherborne, J. (eds.) (1986), *Kings and nobles in the later Middle Ages. A tribute to Charles Ross*, Gloucester

Griffiths, R.A. and Thomas, R.S. (1985), *The making of the Tudor dynasty*, Gloucester

Gunn, S. (1990), 'Chivalry and the politics of the early Tudor court', in Anglo (1990), pp. 107–28

Gunn, S. (1993), 'The courtiers of Henry VII', *EHR* 108: 23–49

Gunn, S. (1995), *Early Tudor government, 1485–1558*, Basingstoke

Hanham, A. (1975), *Richard III and his early historians*, Oxford

Harriss, G.L. (1993), 'Political society and the growth of government in late medieval England', *P&P* 138: 28–57

Hicks, M.A. (1978), 'Dynastic change and northern society: the career of the fourth earl of Northumberland', *NH* 14: 78–107

Hicks, M.A. (1979), 'The changing role of the Wydevilles in Yorkist politics to 1483', in Ross (1979), pp. 60–86

Hicks, M.A. (1980), *False, fleeting, perjur'd Clarence. George, duke of Clarence, 1449–78*, Gloucester

Hicks, M.A. (1984a), 'Attainder, resumption and coercion 1461–1529', *Parliamentary History* 3: 15–31

Hicks, M.A. (1984b), 'Edward IV, the duke of Somerset and Lancastrian loyalism in the north', *NH* 20: 23–37

Hicks, M.A. (1986), 'The Yorkshire rebellion of 1489 reconsidered', *NH* 22: 39–62

Hicks, M.A. (ed.) (1990), *Profit, piety and the professions in later medieval England*, Gloucester

Holland, P. (1988), 'The Lincolnshire rebellion of March 1470', *EHR* 103: 849–69

Horrox, R.E. (1989), *Richard III. A study of service*, Cambridge

Horrox, R.E. (ed.) (1987), *Richard III and the north*, Hull

Horrox, R.E. (ed.) (1994), *Fifteenth-century attitudes. Perceptions of society in late medieval England*, Cambridge

Ives, E.W. (1968), 'Andrew Dymmock and the papers of Antony, Earl Rivers, 1482–3', *BIHR* 41: 216–29

Johnson, P.A. (1988), *Duke Richard of York*, Oxford

Jones, M.K. (1988), 'Sir William Stanley of Holt: politics and family allegiance in the late fifteenth century', *WHR* 14: 1–22

Jones, M.K. and Underwood, M.G. (1992), *The king's mother. Lady Margaret Beaufort, countess of Richmond and Derby*, Cambridge

Lander, J.R. (1961), 'Attainder and forfeiture, 1453–1509', *HJ* 4: 120–51

Lander, J.R. (1963), 'Marriage and politics in the fifteenth century: the Nevills and the Wydevills', *BIHR* 36: 119–52

Lander, J.R. (1971), 'Bonds, coercion and fear: Henry VII and the peerage', in Rowe and Stockdale (1971), pp. 328–67

Lowe, D. (1981), 'Patronage and politics: Edward IV, the Wydevilles and the council of the prince of Wales, 1471–83', *BBCS* 29: 545–73

Morgan, D.A.L. (1973), 'The king's affinity in the polity of Yorkist England', *TRHS* 5th series 23: 1–25

Morgan, D.A.L. (1987), 'The house of policy: the political role of the late Plantagenet household', in Starkey (1987), pp. 25–70

Pollard, A.J. (1977), 'The tyranny of Richard III', *JMedH* 3: 147–65

Pollard, A.J. (1979), 'Lord Fitzhugh's rising in 1470', *BIHR* 52: 170–5

Pollard, A.J. (1986), 'St Cuthbert and the hog: Richard III and the county palatine of Durham', in Griffiths and Sherborne (1986), pp. 109–29

Pollard, A.J. (1990), *North-eastern England during the Wars of the Roses. Lay society, war and politics 1450–1500*, Oxford

Pollard, A.J. (ed.) (1984), *Property and politics. Essays in later medieval English history*, Gloucester

Pugh, T.B. (1992), 'Henry VII and the English nobility', in Bernard (1992), pp. 49–101

Rawcliffe, C. (1980), 'Henry VII and Edward duke of Buckingham: the repression of an "over-mighty subject"', *BIHR* 53: 114–18

Richmond, C.F. (1970), 'Fauconberg's Kentish rising of May 1471', *EHR* 85: 673–92

Rosenthal, J.T. and Richmond, C.F. (eds.) (1987), *People, politics and community in the later Middle Ages*, Gloucester

Ross, C.D. (1974), *Edward IV*, London

Ross, C.D. (1981), *Richard III*, London

Ross, C.D. (ed.) (1979), *Patronage, pedigree and power in late medieval England*, Gloucester

Rowe, J.G. and Stockdale, W.H. (eds.) (1971), *Florilegium historiale. Essays presented to Wallace K. Ferguson*, Toronto

Rowney, I. (1984), 'Resources and retaining in Yorkist England: William Lord Hastings and the honour of Tutbury', in Pollard (1984), pp. 139–55

Scofield, C. (1923), *The life and reign of Edward the fourth*, 2 vols., London

Starkey, D. (ed.) (1987), *The English court. From the Wars of the Roses to the Civil War*, London

Thompson, B. (ed.) (1995), *The reign of Henry VII*, Stamford

Watts, J. (1996), *Henry VI and the politics of kingship*, Cambridge

Weightman, C. (1989), *Margaret of York, duchess of Burgundy, 1446–1503*, Gloucester

Williams, C.H. (1928), 'The rebellion of Humphrey Stafford in 1486', *EHR* 43: 181–9

Wolffe, B.P. (1971), *The royal demesne in English history*, London

Wood, C.T. (1975), 'The deposition of Edward V', *Traditio* 31: 247–86

22(a)   IRELAND

Primary sources

'John Benet's chronicle for the years 1400 to 1462', ed. G.L. and M.A. Harriss, *Camden Miscellany XXIV*, RHS, London (1972)

Chronicque de la traison et mort de Richard Deux, roi Dengleterre, ed. B. Williams, London (1846)

An English chronicle of the reigns of Richard II, Henry IV, Henry V and Henry VI written before 1471, ed. J.S. Davies, Camden Society, original series, 64, London (1856)

Harris, W., 'The voyage of Sir Richard Edgecombe into Ireland in the year 1488', in *Hibernica*, 2 vols., Dublin (1747–50), I, pp. 59–77

Henry of Marlborough, *Chronicle of Ireland*, trans. James Ware, in *Historie of Ireland*, J. Ware (ed.), Dublin (1633); repr. in J. Ware (ed.), *Ancient Irish histories. The workes of Spenser, Campion, Hanmer, and Marleburrough*, Dublin (1809); repr. Port Washington and London (1970), II, pp. 1–32

The libelle of Englyshe polycye. A poem on the use of sea-power 1436, ed. G. Warner, Oxford (1926)

Poems on marcher lords, ed. A. O'Sullivan and P. O'Riain, Irish Texts Society, 53, Dublin (1987)

The register of John Swayne, archbishop of Armagh and primate of Ireland, 1418–1439, ed. D.A. Chart, Belfast (1935)

A roll of the proceedings of the king's council in Ireland . . . 1392–93, ed. J. Graves, RS, London (1877)

Rotuli parliamentorum, 6 vols., London (1767–77)

State papers . . . Henry VIII, 11 vols., Record Commission, London (1830–52)

Statute rolls of the parliament of Ireland . . . reign of King Edward the fourth, ed. H.F. Berry and J.F. Morrissey, 2 vols., Dublin (1914–39)

Statute rolls of the parliament of Ireland. Reign of King Henry the sixth, ed. H.F. Berry, Dublin (1910)

Statutes and ordinances and acts of the parliament of Ireland. King John to Henry V, ed. H.F. Berry, Dublin (1907)

The statutes of the realm, 11 vols. in 12, Record Commission, London (1810–28)

Ypodigma Neustriae a Thoma Walsingham, ed. H.T. Riley, RS, London (1876)

Secondary works

Betham, Sir W. (1830), *Dignities, feudal and parliamentary and the constitutional legislature of the United Kingdom . . .*, Dublin and London

Carpenter, D.M. (1988), 'The pilgrim from Catalonia/Aragon; Ramon de Perellós 1397', in M. Haren and Y. de Pontfarcy (eds.), *The medieval pilgrimage to St Patrick's Purgatory*, Enniskillen, pp. 99–119

Conway, A. (1932), *Henry VII's relations with Scotland and Ireland 1485–1498*, Cambridge

Cosgrove, A. (1981), *Late medieval Ireland, 1370–1541*, Dublin

Cosgrove, A. (1983), 'Parliament and the Anglo-Irish community; the declaration of 1460', in A. Cosgrove and J.I. McGuire (eds.), *Parliament and community. Historical studies* XIV, Belfast

Cosgrove, A. (1985), 'Marriage in medieval Ireland', in A. Cosgrove (ed.), *Marriage in Ireland*, Dublin

Cosgrove, A. (1990), 'The writing of Irish medieval history', *IHS* 27: 97–112

Cosgrove, A. (ed.) (1987), *A new history of Ireland*, II: *Medieval Ireland 1169–1534*, Oxford

Curtis, E. (1932), 'Richard, duke of York, as viceroy of Ireland, 1447–60', *Journal of the Royal Society of Antiquaries of Ireland* 62: 158–86

Ellis, S.G. (1986a), *Reform and revival. English government in Ireland 1470–1534*, Woodbridge

Ellis, S.G. (1986b), 'Nationalist historiography and the English and Gaelic worlds in the late Middle Ages', *IHS* 25: 1–18

Empey, C.A. (1988), 'The Anglo-Norman community in Tipperary and Kilkenny in the Middle Ages; change and continuity', in G. Mac Niocaill and P.F. Wallace (eds.), *Keimelia. Studies in medieval archaeology and history in memory of Tom Delaney*, Galway, pp. 449–67

Frame, R. (1993), 'Les Engleys nées en Irlande: the English political identity in medieval Ireland', *TRHS* 6th series 3: 83–104

Gillingham, J. (1987), 'Images of Ireland 1170–1600; the origins of English imperialism', *History Today* 37(2): 16–22

Johnson, P.A. (1988), *Duke Richard of York 1411–1460*, Oxford

Lydon, J.F. (1972), *The lordship of Ireland in the Middle Ages*, Dublin and London

Lydon, J.F. (1973), *Ireland in the later Middle Ages*, Dublin

Lydon, J.F. (1979), 'The city of Waterford in the later Middle Ages', *Decies* 12: 5–15

Matthew, E. (1984), 'The financing of the lordship of Ireland under Henry V and Henry VI', in A.J. Pollard (ed.), *Property and politics. Essays in late medieval English history*, Gloucester, pp. 97–115

Moody, T.W., Martin, F.X., and Byrne, F.J. (eds.) (1984), *A new history of Ireland*, IX: *Maps, genealogies, lists*, Oxford

Murphy, B. (1967), 'The status of the native Irish after 1331', *Irish Jurist* 2: 116–38

O'Neill, T. (1987), *Merchants and mariners in medieval Ireland*, Dublin

O'Sullivan, H. (1989), 'The march of south-east Ulster in the fifteenth and sixteenth centuries: a period of change', in R. Gillespie and H. O'Sullivan (eds.), *The borderlands, essays on the history of the Ulster–Leinster border*, Belfast, pp. 55–74

Otway-Ruthven, A.J. (1968), *A history of medieval Ireland*, London; 2nd edn, London and New York, 1980

Richardson, H.G. and Sayles, G.O. (1952), *The Irish parliament in the Middle Ages*, Philadelphia and London; 2nd edn, 1964

Simms, K. (1989a), 'Bards and barons; the Anglo-Irish aristocracy and the native culture', in R. Bartlett and A. Mackay (eds.), *Medieval frontier societies*, Oxford

Simms, K. (1989b), 'The Norman invasion and the Gaelic recovery', in R. Foster (ed.), *The Oxford illustrated history of Ireland*, Oxford, pp. 53–103

Stalley, R. (1988), 'Sailing to Santiago: the medieval pilgrimage to Santiago de Compostela and its artistic influence on Ireland', in J. Bradley (ed.), *Settlement and society in medieval Ireland*, Kilkenny, pp. 397–420

Watt, J.A. (1956), 'Negotiations between Edward II and John XXII concerning Ireland', *IHS* 10: 1–20

Watt, J.A. (1970), *The Church and the two nations in medieval Ireland*, Cambridge

Watt, J.A. (1972), *The Church in medieval Ireland*, Dublin

Watt, J.A. (1989), 'The Church and the two nations in late medieval Armagh', in W.J. Sheils and D. Ward (eds.), *The Churches, Ireland and the Irish*, Studies in Church History 25, Oxford, pp. 37–54

Wood, H. (1928), 'Two chief governors of Ireland at the same time', *Journal of the Royal Society of Antiquaries of Ireland* 58: 156–7

Wylie, J.H. and Waugh, W.T. (1929), *Henry V*, III, Cambridge

22(b) SCOTLAND: 1406–1513

Primary sources

Acts of the parliaments of Scotland, ed. T. Thomson and C. Innes, 12 vols., Edinburgh (1814–75)

Barbour, John, *The Bruce*, ed. M.P. McDiarmid and J.A.C. Stevenson, STS, 4th series, 12, 13 and 15, Edinburgh (1980–5)

Calendar of state papers and manuscripts existing in the archives and collections of Milan, I, ed. A.B. Hinds, London (1912)

The exchequer rolls of Scotland, ed. J. Stuart *et al.*, 23 vols., Edinburgh (1878–1908)

Hary's Wallace, ed. M.P. McDiarmid, STS, 4th series, 4 and 5, Edinburgh (1968–9)

Liber Pluscardensis, ed. F.J.H. Skene, 2 vols., Edinburgh (1877–80)

Lindsay, Sir David, 'The testament of the Papyngo', in *The works of Sir David Lyndsay of the Mount*, I, ed. D. Hamer, STS, Edinburgh (1931)

Registrum magni sigilli regum Scottorum, ed. J.M. Thomson *et al.*, 11 vols., Edinburgh (1882–1914)

Scotichronicon by Walter Bower, ed. D.E.R. Watt, VIII, bks 15 and 16, Edinburgh (1987)

Wyntoun, Andrew of, *The Orygynale Cronykil of Scotland*, ed. D. Laing, 2 vols., Edinburgh (1872–9)

Secondary works

Balfour, P.J. (ed.), (1904–14), *The Scots peerage*, 9 vols., Edinburgh

Barrow, G.W.S. (1979), 'The idea of freedom in late medieval Scotland', *Innes Review* 30: 16–34

Bassett, S. (ed.), (1989), *The origins of Anglo-Saxon kingdoms*, Leicester

Bawcutt, P. (1976), *Gavin Douglas*, Edinburgh

Bawcutt, P. (1992), *Dunbar the makar*, Oxford

Brown, A.L. (1978), 'The Scottish "establishment" in the later fifteenth century', *Juridical Review* 23: 89–105

Brown, J.M. (ed.), (1977), *Scottish society in the fifteenth century*, London

Brown, M.H. (1992), '"That old serpent and ancient of evil days": Walter earl of Atholl and the death of James I', *SHR* 71: 23–45

Brown, M.H. (1994a), *James I*, Edinburgh

Brown, M.H. (1994b), 'Scotland tamed? Kings and magnates in late medieval Scotland: a review of recent work', *Innes Review* 45: 120–46

Burns, J.H. (1962), *Scottish churchmen and the Council of Basle*, Glasgow

Burns, J.H. (1963), 'The conciliarist tradition in Scotland', *SHR* 42: 89–104

Burns, J.H. (1990), 'John Ireland: theology and public affairs in the late fifteenth century', *Innes Review* 41: 151–81

Caldwell, D.H. (ed.) (1981), *Scottish weapons and fortifications, 1100–1800*, Edinburgh

Charles-Edwards, T. (1989), 'Early medieval kingships in the British Isles', in Basset (1989), pp. 28–39

Cowan, I.B. (1967), *The parishes of medieval Scotland*, STS, Edinburgh

Cowan, I.B. (1982), *The Scottish Reformation*, London, chs. 1–3

Dodgshon, R.A. (1981), *Land and society in early Scotland*, Oxford

Dunbar, J.G. (1978), *The architecture of Scotland*, London

Duncan, A.A.M. (1976), *James I, 1424–37*, occasional paper, University of Glasgow

Dunlop, A.I. (1950), *The life and times of James Kennedy, bishop of St Andrews*, Edinburgh

Grant, A. (1976), 'Earls and earldoms in late medieval Scotland, c. 1310–1460' in J. Bossy and P. Rupp (eds.), *Essays presented to Michael Roberts*, Belfast, pp. 24–40

Grant, A. (1978), 'The development of the Scottish peerage', *SHR* 57: 1–27

Grant, A. (1981), 'The revolt of the lord of the Isles and the death of the earl of Douglas', *SHR* 60: 169–74

Grant, A. (1984), *Independence and nationhood. Scotland, 1306–1470*, New History of Scotland, 3, London

Grant, I.F. (1930), *Social and economic developments of Scotland before 1603*, Edinburgh

Kinsley, J. (1958), *The poems of William Dunbar*, Oxford

Leyser, K. (1979), *Rule and conflict in an early medieval society*, London

Lyall, R.J. (1976), 'Politics and poetry in fifteenth- and sixteenth-century Scotland', *Scottish Literary Journal* 3: 5–29

Lyall, R.J. (1989), 'Books and book owners in fifteenth-century Scotland', in J. Griffiths and D. Pearsall (eds.), *Book production and publishing in Britain 1375–1475*, Cambridge, pp. 239–56

Lynch, M., Spearman, M. and Stell, G. (eds.) (1988), *The Scottish medieval town*, Edinburgh

Macdougall, N. (1982), *James III. A political study*, Edinburgh

Macdougall, N. (1989), *James IV*, Edinburgh

Macdougall, N. (ed.) (1983), *Church, politics and society. Scotland 1408–1929*, Edinburgh

Macfarlane, L.J. (1969), 'The primacy of the Scottish Church, 1472–1521', *Innes Review* 20: 111–29

Macfarlane, L.J. (1985), *William Elphinstone and the kingdom of Scotland, 1431–1514*, Aberdeen

McGladdery, C. (1992), *James II*, Edinburgh

MacQueen, J. (1967), *Robert Henryson*, Oxford

McRoberts, D. (1968), 'The Scottish Church and nationalism in the fifteenth century', *Innes Review* 19: 3–14

Mapstone, S. (1989), 'A mirror for a divine prince: John Ireland and the four daughters of God', in J.D. McClure and M.R.G. Spiller (eds.), *Bryght lanternis. Essays on the language and literature of medieval and Renaissance Scotland*, Aberdeen, pp. 308–23

Mapstone, S. (1991), 'Was there a court literature in fifteenth-century Scotland?', *Studies in Scottish Literature* 26: 410–21

Mason, R. (1987a), 'Kingship, tyranny and the right to resist in fifteenth-century Scotland', *SHR* 66: 125–51

Mason, R. (ed.), (1987b), *Scotland and England 1286–1815*, Edinburgh

Mason, R. and Macdougall, N. (eds.) (1992), *People and power in Scotland. Essays presented to T.C. Smout*, Edinburgh

Nicholson, R. (1973), 'Feudal developments in late medieval Scotland', *Juridical Review* 18: 1–21

Nicholson, R. (1974), *Scotland. The later Middle Ages*, Edinburgh History of Scotland, Edinburgh

Rait, R.S. (1924), *The parliaments of Scotland*, Glasgow

Sellar, D. (1989), 'Celtic law and Scots law: survival and integration', *Scottish Studies* 29: 1–27

Stewart, I.H. (1966), *The Scottish coinage*, London

Stringer, K.J. (ed.) (1985), *Essays on the nobility of medieval Scotland*, Edinburgh

Thomson, J.A.F. (1968), 'Innocent VIII and the Scottish Church', *Innes Review* 19: 23–31

Webster, B. (1975), *Scotland from the eleventh century to 1603*, London

Wormald, J. (1980), 'Bloodfeud, kindred and government in early modern Scotland', *P&P* 87: 54–97

Wormald, J. (1981), *Court, kirk and community. Scotland, 1470–1625*, New History of Scotland, 4, London

Wormald, J. (1985), *Lords and men in Scotland. Bonds of manrent, 1442–1603*, Edinburgh

Wormald, J. (1986), 'Lords and lairds in fifteenth-century Scotland: nobles and gentry?', in M. Jones (ed.), *Gentry and lesser nobility in late medieval Europe*, Gloucester and New York, pp. 181–200

Wormald, J. (ed.) (1991), *Scotland revisited*, London

22(C) WALES

Primary sources

Cywyddau Iolo Goch ac Eraill, ed. H. Lewis, T. Roberts and I. Williams, 2nd edn, Cardiff (1937)

Gwaith Guto'r Glyn, ed. I. Williams and J. Llywelyn Williams, 2nd edn, Cardiff (1961)

Gwaith Lewis Glyn Cothi, ed. D. Johnston, Cardiff (1994)

The history of the Gwydir family, written by Sir John Wynn, knight and bart., ed. J. Ballinger, Cardiff (1927)

Owen, George, *The description of Penbrokshire*, ed. H. Owen, 3 vols., London (1892–1906)

Pugh, T.B., '"The indenture for the Marches" between Henry VII and Edward Stafford (1477–1521), duke of Buckingham', *EHR* 71 (1956), pp. 436–9

Pugh, T.B. (ed.), *The Marcher lordships of south Wales, 1415–1536. Select documents*, Cardiff (1963)

Registrum vulgariter nuncupatum The record of Caernarvon, ed. H. Ellis, London (1838)

The statutes of Wales, ed. I. Bowen, London (1908)

Secondary works

Carr, A.D. (1966–8), 'Sir Lewis John: a medieval London Welshman', *BBCS* 22: 260–70

Carr, A.D. (1968–9), 'Welshmen and the Hundred Years War', *WHR* 4: 21–46

Carr, A.D. (1979), 'The making of the Mostyns: the genesis of a landed family', *THSC*: 137–57

Carr, A.D. (1982), *Medieval Anglesey*, Llangefni

Carr, A.D. (1990–91), 'Gwilym ap Gruffydd and the rise of the Penrhyn estate', *WHR* 15: 1–20

Carr, A.D. (1995), *Medieval Wales*, London

Chrimes, S.B. (1972), *Henry VII*, London

Davies, R.R. (1966), 'The twilight of Welsh law', *History* 51: 143–64

Davies, R.R. (1969), 'The survival of the blood-feud in medieval Wales', *History* 154: 338–57

Davies, R.R. (1987), *Conquest, coexistence and change. Wales 1063–1415*, Oxford

Davies, R.R. (1995), *The revolt of Owain Glyn Dŵr*, Oxford

Evans, H.T. (1915), *Wales and the Wars of the Roses*, Cambridge

Griffiths, R.A. (1962), 'Royal government in the southern counties of the Principality of Wales, 1422–85', PhD dissertation, University of Bristol

Griffiths, R.A. (1964), 'Gruffydd ap Nicholas and the rise of the house of Dinefwr', *NLWJ* 13: 256–68

Griffiths, R.A. (1964–5), 'Gruffydd ap Nicholas and the fall of the house of Lancaster', *WHR* 2: 213–31

Griffiths, R.A. (1966), 'Gentlemen and rebels in later medieval Cardiganshire', *Ceredigion* 5: 143–67

Griffiths, R.A. (1972a), *The Principality of Wales in the later Middle Ages. The structure and personnel of government, I: South Wales, 1277–1536*, Cardiff

Griffiths, R.A. (1972b), 'Wales and the Marches', in S.B. Chrimes, C.D. Ross and R.A. Griffiths (eds.), *Fifteenth-century England, 1399–1509. Studies in politics and society*, Manchester, pp. 145–72

Griffiths, R.A. (1974), 'Patronage, politics and the principality of Wales, 1413–1461', in H. Hearder and H.R. Loyn (eds.), *British government and administration. Studies presented to S.B. Chrimes*, Cardiff, pp. 69–86

Griffiths, R.A. (1976–7), 'Richard, duke of York and the royal household in Wales, 1449–50', *WHR* 8: 14–25

Griffiths, R.A. (1993), *Sir Rhys ap Thomas and his family. A study in the Wars of the Roses and early Tudor politics*, Cardiff

Griffiths, R.A. (ed.) (1978), *Boroughs of medieval Wales*, Cardiff

Griffiths, R.A. and Thomas, R.S. (1985), *The making of the Tudor dynasty*, Gloucester

Gunn, S.J. (1984–5), 'The regime of Charles, duke of Suffolk, in north Wales and the reform of Welsh government, 1509–25', *WHR* 12: 461–94

Jack, R.I. (1980–1), 'The cloth industry in medieval Wales', *WHR* 10: 443–60

Jarman, A.O.H. and Hughes, G.R. (eds.) (1979), *A guide to Welsh literature*, II, Swansea

Jones, D.C. (1961), 'The Bulkeleys of Beaumaris, 1440–1547', *Transactions of the Anglesey Antiquarian Society and Field Club*: 1–20

Jones, G.E. (1984), *Modern Wales. A concise history, 1485–1979*, Cambridge

Jones, J.G. (1974), 'Government and the Welsh community: the north-east borderland in the fifteenth century', in H. Hearder and H.R. Loyn (eds.), *British government and administration. Studies presented to S.B. Chrimes*, Cardiff, pp. 55–68

Jones, M.K. (1988–9), 'Sir William Stanley of Holt: politics and family allegiance in the late fifteenth century', *WHR* 14: 1–22

Jones, W.G. (1917–18), 'Welsh nationalism and Henry Tudor', *THSC*: 1–59

Lewis, E.A. (1903), 'The development of industry and commerce in Wales during the Middle Ages', *TRHS* 2nd series 17: 121–75

Lowe, D.E. (1976–8), 'The council of the prince of Wales and the decline of the Herbert family during the second reign of Edward IV (1471–1483)', *BBCS* 27: 278–97

Morgan, C.L. (1985), 'Prophecy and Welsh nationhood in the fifteenth century', *THSC*: 9–25

Pierce, T. Jones (1972a), 'Some tendencies in the agrarian history of Caernarvonshire in the later Middle Ages', in J.B. Smith (ed.), *Medieval Welsh society. Selected essays by T. Jones Pierce*, Cardiff, pp. 39–60

Pierce, T. Jones (1972b), 'The law of Wales: the last phase', in J.B. Smith (ed.), *Medieval Welsh society. Selected essays by T. Jones Pierce*, Cardiff, pp. 369–89

Pugh, T.B. (ed.) (1971), *Glamorgan County History*, III: *The Middle Ages*, Cardiff

Roberts, G. (1963), 'Wales and England: antipathy and sympathy, 1282–1485', *WHR* 1: 375–96

Smith, J.B. (1965–6), 'The regulation of the frontier of Meirionnydd in the fifteenth century', *Journal of the Merioneth Historical and Record Society* 5: 105–11

Smith, J.B. (1966–7), 'Crown and community in the principality of north Wales in the reign of Henry Tudor', *WHR* 3: 145–71

Smith, J.B. (1966–8), 'The last phase of the Glyn Dŵr rebellion', *BBCS* 22: 250–60

Thomas, D.H. (1968), 'The Herberts of Raglan as supporters of the house of York in the second half of the fifteenth century', MA dissertation, University of Wales (Cardiff)

Thomas, R.S. (1971), 'The political career, estates and "connection" of Jasper Tudor', PhD dissertation, University of Wales (Swansea)

Walker, D. (1990), *Medieval Wales*, Cambridge

Williams, G. (1974), 'Prophecy, poetry and politics in medieval and Tudor Wales', in H. Hearder and H.R. Loyn (eds.), *British government and administration. Studies presented to S.B. Chrimes*, Cardiff, pp. 104–16

Williams, G. (1976), *The Welsh Church from Conquest to Reformation*, 2nd edn, Cardiff

Williams, G. (1985), *Harri Tudur a Chymru / Henry Tudor and Wales*, Cardiff (bilingual)

Williams, G. (1987), *Recovery, reorientation and Reformation. Wales c. 1415–1642*, Oxford

Williams, Gruffydd A. (1986), 'The bardic road to Bosworth: a Welsh view of Henry Tudor', *THSC*: 7–31

Williams, Gwyn A. (1959), 'Owain Glyn Dŵr', in A.J. Roderick (ed.), *Wales through the ages*, I, Llandybie

23(a) THE NORTHERN ITALIAN STATES

Secondary works

General works

Aymard, M. (1991), 'La fragilità di un'economia avanzata: l'Italia e le trasformazioni dell'economia', in Ruggiero Romano (ed.), *Storia dell'economia italiana*, II: *L'età moderna. Verso la crisi*, Turin, pp. 5–137

Baron, H. (1966), *The crisis of the early Italian Renaissance*, rev. edn, Princeton

Baron, H. (1988), *In search of Florentine civic humanism. Essays on the transition from medieval to modern thought*, 2 vols., Princeton

Bellotti, B. (1923), *La vita di Bartolomeo Colleoni*, Bergamo

Bertelli, S. *et al.* (1979), *Florence and Venice. Comparisons and relations*, I, Florence

Bertelli, S. *et al.* (1985), *Italian Renaissance courts*, Milan

Brown, J.C. (1989), 'Prosperity or hard times in Renaissance Italy?', *RQ* 42: 761–80

Bueno de Mesquita, D.M. (1970), 'The place of despotism in Italian politics', in J.R. Hale *et al.* (eds.), *Europe in the late Middle Ages*, London, pp. 301–31

Capitani, O. *et al.* (1981), *Comuni e signorie. Istituzioni, società e lotte per l'egemonia*, UTET Storia d'Italia, IV, Turin

Cherubini, G. *et al.* (1988), *Storia della società italiana*, VIII: *I secoli del primato italiano – il Quattrocento*, Milan

Chittolini, G. (1979), *La formazione dello stato regionale e le istituzioni del contado*, Turin

Cipolla, C.M. (1963), 'The economic depression of the Renaissance', *EconHR* 15: 519–24

Cracco, G. *et al.* (1987), *Comuni e signorie nell'Italia nordorientale e centrale. Veneto, Emilia-Romagna, Toscana*, UTET Storia d'Italia, VII, i, Turin

Fasano Guarini, E. (1983), 'Gli stati dell'Italia centro-settentrionale fra Quattro e Cinquecento: continuità e trasformazioni', *Società e storia* 6: 617–39

Fubini, R. (1994), *Italia Quattrocentesca. Politica e diplomazia nell' età di Lorenzo il Magnifico*, Milan

Hay, D. and Law, J. (1989), *Italy in the age of the Renaissance, 1380–1530*, London and New York

Ilardi, V. (1986), *Studies in Italian Renaissance diplomatic history*, Aldershot and Brookfield, Vt.

Jones, P.J. (1965), 'Communes and despots. The city state in late medieval Italy', *TRHS* 5th series 15: 71–96

Lopez, R.S. (1953), 'Hard times and investment in culture', in W.K. Ferguson *et al.*, *The Renaissance. A symposium*, New York, pp. 29–54

Lopez, R.S. and Miskimin, H.A. (1962), 'The economic depression of the Renaissance', *EconHR* 14: 408–26

Luzzatto, G. (1961), *An economic history of Italy*, trans. P.J. Jones, London
Mallett, M.E. (1974), *Mercenaries and their masters. Warfare in Renaissance Italy*, London
Martines, L. (1979), *Power and imagination. City states in Renaissance Italy*, London
Mattingly, G. (1955), *Renaissance diplomacy*, London
Nada Patroni, A.M. and Airaldi, G. (1986), *Comuni e signorie nell'Italia settentrionale. Il Piemonte e la Liguria*, UTET Storia d'Italia, V, Turin
Pieri, P. (1952), *Il Rinascimento e la crisi militare italiana*, Turin
Pillinini, G. (1970), *Il sistema degli stati italiani, 1454–94*, Venice
Romano, R. and Vivanti, C. (eds.) (1972–4), *Einaudi storia d'Italia*, I and II, Turin
Rossi, P. (ed.) (1977), *Il Rinascimento nelle corti padane. Società e cultura*, Bari
Seigel, J.E. (1966), 'Civic humanism or Ciceronian rhetoric?', *P&P* 34: 3–48
Simeoni, L. (1950), *Le signorie*, 2 vols., Milan
Smyth, C.H. and Garfagnini, G.C. (eds.) (1989), *Florence and Milan. Comparisons and relations*, I, Florence
Valeri, N. (1969), *L'Italia nell'età dei principati dal 1343 al 1516*, rev. edn, Milan

Florence and the Florentine state

Ady, C.M. (1955), *Lorenzo de' Medici and Renaissance Italy*, London
Ames-Lewis, F. (ed.) (1992), *Cosimo 'il Vecchio' de' Medici*, Oxford
Bizocchi, R. (1987), *Chiesa e potere nella Toscana del Quattrocento*, Bologna
Brown, A. (1979), *Bartolomeo Scala, chancellor of Florence*, Princeton
Brown, A. (1992), *The Medici in Florence. The exercise and language of power*, Florence
Brown, J.C. (1982), *In the shadow of Florence. Provincial society in Renaissance Pescia*, New York and Oxford
Brucker, G.A. (1969), *Renaissance Florence*, New York
Brucker, G.A. (1977), *The civic world of early Renaissance Florence*, Princeton
Centro Italiano di studi e d'arte, Pistoia (1979), *Egemonia fiorentina ed autonomie locali nella Toscana nord-occidentale del primo Rinascimento*, Pistoia
Conti, E. (1984), *L'imposte dirette a Firenze nel Quattrocento (1427–94)*, Rome
De Roover, R. (1963), *The rise and decline of the Medici bank*, Cambridge, Mass.
Denley, P. and Elam, C. (eds.) (1988), *Florence and Italy. Renaissance studies in honour of Nicolai Rubinstein*, London
Garfagnini, G.C. (ed.) (1992), *Lorenzo de' Medici. Studi*, Florence
Garfagnini, G.C. (ed.) (1994), *Lorenzo il Magnifico e il suo mondo*, Florence
Goldthwaite, R.A. (1968), *Private wealth in Renaissance Florence*, Princeton
Goldthwaite, R.A. (1980), *The building of Renaissance Florence*, Baltimore and London
Gutkind, C.S. (1938), *Cosimo de' Medici: pater patriae (1389–1464)*, Oxford
Hale, J.R. (1977), *Florence and the Medici. The pattern of control*, London
Herlihy, D. and Klapisch-Zuber, C. (1985), *Tuscans and their families. A study of the Florentine catasto of 1427*, New Haven and London
Holmes, G. (1969), *The Florentine Enlightenment, 1400–1450*, London
Hook, J. (1984), *Lorenzo de' Medici*, London
Kent, D. (1978), *The rise of the Medici. Faction in Florence, 1426–34*, Oxford
Kent, F.W. (1977), *Household and lineage in Renaissance Florence*, Princeton
Mallett, M.E. (1967), *The Florentine galleys in the fifteenth century*, Oxford
Martines, L. (1963), *The social world of the Florentine humanists*, London

Medici, Lorenzo de' (1977–   ), *Lettere*, general ed. N. Rubinstein, 6 vols., Florence
Molho, A. (1971), *Florentine public finances in the early Renaissance, 1400–1433*, Cambridge, Mass.
Pinto, G. (1982), *La Toscana nel tardo medioevo*, Florence
Rubinstein, N. (1966), *The government of Florence under the Medici*, London
Rubinstein, N. (ed.) (1968), *Florentine studies*, London
Trexler, R. (1980), *Public life in Renaissance Florence*, London

Venice and the terraferma *state*

Cessi, R. (1944–6), *Storia della repubblica di Venezia*, 2 vols., Milan and Messina
Chambers, D.S. (1970), *The imperial age of Venice*, London
Chambers, D.S. and Pullan, B. (eds.) (1992), *Venice. A documentary history, 1450–1630*, Oxford
Cini, Fondazione (1957), *La civiltà veneziana del Quattrocento*, Florence
Cozzi, G. and Knapton, M. (1986), *Storia della repubblica di Venezia dalla guerra di Chioggia alla riconquista della Terraferma*, UTET Storia d'Italia, XII, i, Turin
Cracco, G. and Knapton, M. (1983), *Dentro lo 'Stado Italico': Venezia e la Terraferma fra Quattrocento e Seicento*, Trent
Finlay, R. (1980), *Politics in Renaissance Venice*, London
Grubb, J.S. (1988), *Firstborn of Venice. Vicenza in the early Renaissance state*, Baltimore and London
Hale, J.R. (ed.) (1974), *Renaissance Venice*, London
King, M.L. (1986), *Venetian humanism in the age of patrician dominance*, Princeton
Labalme, P.H. (1969), *Bernardo Giustinian, a Venetian of the Quattrocento*, Rome
Lane, F.C. (1966), *Venice and history*, Baltimore
Lane, F.C. (1973), *Venice, a maritime republic*, Baltimore and London
Lane, F.C. (1987), *Studies in Venetian social and economic history*, ed. B.G. Kohl and R.C. Mueller, London
Lane, F.C. and Mueller, R.C. (1985), *Money and banking in medieval and Renaissance Venice*, I, Baltimore and London
Law, J. (1992), 'The Venetian mainland state in the fifteenth century', *TRHS* 6th series 2: 153–74
Logan, O. (1972), *Culture and society in Venice, 1470–1700. The Renaissance and its heritage*, London
Lowry, M.J.C. (1979), *The world of Aldus Manutius*, Oxford
Luzzatto, G. (1961), *Storia economica di Venezia dall'XI al XVI secolo*, Venice
Mallett, M.E. and Hale, J.R. (1984), *The military organisation of a Renaissance state. Venice, c. 1400 to 1617*, Cambridge
Maranini, G. (1931), *La costituzione di Venezia dopo la serrata del Maggior Consiglio*, 2 vols., Venice
Muir, E. (1981), *Civic ritual in Renaissance Venice*, Princeton
Queller, D. (1986), *The Venetian patriciate. Reality versus myth*, Chicago
Romanin, S. (1912–25), *Storia documentata di Venezia*, 2nd edn, 10 vols., Venice
Romano, D. (1987), *Patricians and popolani. The social foundations of the Venetian Renaissance state*, Baltimore and London

Varanini, G.M. (1980), *Il distretto veronese nel Quattrocento*, Verona

Ventura, A. (1964), *Nobiltà e popolo nella società veneta del '400 e '500*, Bari

Viggiano, A. (1993), *Governanti e governati. Legittimità del potere ed esercizio dell'autorità sovrana nello stato veneto della prima età moderna*, Treviso

Duchy of Milan

Ady, C.M. (1907), *A history of Milan under the Sforza*, London

Barbieri, G. (1938), *Economia e politica nel ducato visconteo-sforzesco*, Milan

Blastenbrei, P. (1987), *Die Sforza und ihr Heer*, Heidelberg

Bueno de Mesquita, D.M. (1941), *Giangaleazzo Visconti*, Cambridge

Catalano, F. (1986), *Ludovico il Moro*, Milan

Cerioni, L. (1970), *La diplomazia Sforzesca nella seconda metà del Quattrocento e i suoi cifrari segreti*, 2 vols., Rome

Cognasso, F. (1966), *I Visconti*, Varese

Frangioni, L. (1987), 'La politica economica del dominio di Milano nei secc. XV–XVI', *Nuova rivista storica* 71: 253–68

Kendall, P.M. and Ilardi, V. (1970–81), *Dispatches with related documents of Milanese ambassadors in France and Burgundy*, 3 vols., Athens, Ohio

Mainoni, P., 'Lo stato milanese dei Visconti e degli Sforza', in Cherubini *et al.* (1988), pp. 169–201

Malaguzzi Valeri, F. (1913–23), *La corte di Ludovico il Moro. La vita privata e l'arte a Milano nella seconda metà del Quattrocento*, Milan

Milano nell' età di Ludovico il Moro (1983), 2 vols., Archivio Storico Civico, Milan

Santoro, C. (1977), *Gli Sforza*, Varese

Gli Sforza a Milano e in Lombardia, e i loro rapporti con gli stati italiani ed europei (1450–1535) (1982), Atti del convegno internazionale, Milano, maggio 1981, Milan

Soldi Rondinini, G. (1984), *Saggi di storia e storiografia visconteo-sforzeschi*, Bologna

Treccani degli Alfieri, Fondazione (1955–6), *Storia di Milano*, VI and VII, Milan

The smaller states

Ady, C.M. (1937), *The Bentivoglio of Bologna*, Oxford

Ascheri, M. (1985), *Siena nel Rinascimento. Istituzioni e sistema politica*, Siena

Bratchel, M.E. (1995), *Lucca, 1430–94. The reconstruction of an Italian city-republic*, Oxford

Cognasso, F. (1981), *I Savoia*, Varese

Coniglio, G. (1967), *I Gonzaga*, Varese

Coniglio, G. and Mazzoldi, L. (1958), *Mantova. La storia*, I, Mantua

Cusin, F. (1937), *Il confine orientale d'Italia nella politica europea del XIV e XV secolo*, Milan

Dean, T. (1987), *Land and power in late medieval Ferrara. The rule of the Este, 1350–1450*, Cambridge

Gundersheimer, W.L. (1973), *Ferrara. The style of a Renaissance despotism*, Princeton

Heers, J. (1971), *Gênes au XVe siècle*, Paris

Liecht, P.S. (1955), *Studi di storia friulana*, Udine

Mozzarelli, C. (1979), *Lo stato gonzaghesco. Mantova del 1382 al 1707*, UTET Storia d'Italia, XVII, Turin

Pandiani, E. (1952), *La vita della repubblica di Genova,* Genoa

Tommasoli, W. (1968), *Momenti e figure della politica dell'equilibrio. Federico da Montefeltro e l'impresa di Rimini,* Urbino

Treccani degli Alfieri, G. (1963), *Storia di Brescia,* II, Brescia

23(b) THE PAPAL STATES AND THE KINGDOM OF NAPLES

Secondary works

Abulafia, D. (1990), 'The crown and the economy under Ferrante I of Naples (1458–94)', in T. Dean and C. Wickham (eds.), *City and countryside in late medieval and Renaissance Italy,* London and Ronceverte, pp. 125–46

Abulafia, D. (ed.) (1995), *The French descent into Renaissance Italy, 1494–95. Antecedents and effects,* Aldershot

Ady, C.M. (1913), *Pius II,* London

Ady, C.M. (1937), *The Bentivoglio of Bologna,* London

Ametller y Vinyas, J. (1903–28), *Alfonso V de Aragón en Italia y la crisis religiosa del siglo XV,* 3 vols., Gerona and San Feliu de Guixols

Atlas, A. (1985), *Music at the Aragonese court of Naples,* Cambridge

Beloch, K.J. (1937–65), *Bevölkerungsgeschichte Italiens,* Berlin and Leipzig

Bentley, J.H. (1987), *Politics and culture in Renaissance Naples,* Princeton

Black, C.F. (1970), 'The Baglioni as tyrants of Perugia, 1488–1540', *EHR* 85: 245–81

Brezzi, P. and Panizza Lorch, M. (1984), *Umanesimo a Roma nel Quattrocento,* Rome and New York

Burchard, J. (1910), *The diary of John Burchard of Strasburg AD 1483–1506,* I, *1483–1492,* trans. A.H. Mathew, London

Caravale, M. and Caracciolo, A. (1978), *Lo stato pontificio da Martino V a Pio IX,* Turin

Clough, C.H. (1984–5), 'Federigo da Montefeltro: the good Christian prince', *BJRULM* 67: 293–348

Cole, A. (1995), *The art of the Italian Renaissance courts,* London

Croce, B. (1970), *History of the kingdom of Naples,* trans. F. Frenaye, Chicago

D'Amico, J.F. (1988), 'Humanism in Rome', in A. Rabil (ed.), *Renaissance humanism,* I, Philadelphia, pp. 264–95

Dean, T. (1988), *Land and power in medieval Ferrara. The rule of the Este, 1350–1450,* Cambridge

Del Treppo, M. (1972), *I mercanti catalani e l'espansione della corona aragonese nel secolo XV,* Naples

Delumeau, J. (1962), *L'alun de Rome,* Paris

Faraglia, N.F. (1904), *Storia della regina Giovanna II d'Angiò,* Lanciano

Faraglia, N.F. (1908), *Storia della lotta tra Alfonso V e Renato d'Angiò,* Lanciano

Filangieri de Candida, R. (1964), *Castel Nuovo, reggia angioina ed aragonese in Napoli,* Naples

Gentile, P. (1909), *La politica interna di Alfonso V d'Aragona nel regno di Napoli dal 1443 al 1450,* Montecassino

Ghirarducci, C. (n.d.), *Della historia di Bologna,* ed. A. Sorbelli, Rerum Italicarum Scriptores, n.s., Città di Castello

Gregorovius, F. (1898–1900), *History of the city of Rome in the Middle Ages,* VI, pt 2, VII, pt 1, trans. A. Hamilton, London

Grohmann, A. (1969), *Le fiere del regno di Napoli in età aragonese*, Naples

Gundersheimer, W.L. (1973), *Ferrara. The style of a Renaissance despotism*, Princeton

Hay, D. (1977), *The Church in Italy in the fifteenth century*, Cambridge

Hay, D. and Law, J. (1989), *Italy in the age of the Renaissance, 1380–1530*, London

Heers, J. (1986), *A la cour pontificale au temps des Borgia et des Médicis, 1420–1520*, Paris

Hersey, G.L. (1973), *The Aragonese arch at Naples*, New Haven

Infessura, S. (1890), *Diario della città di Roma di Stefano Infessura scribasenato*, ed. O. Tommasini, Rome

Jones, P.J. (1974), *The Malatesta of Rimini and the papal state*, Cambridge

Lecoy de la Marche, A. (1875), *Le Roi René*, Paris

Leone, A. (1983), *Profili economici della Campania aragonese*, Naples

Lulvès, J. (1909), 'Päpstliche wahlkapitulationen', *Quellen und Forschungen aus italienischen archiven* 12: 212–35

Marinis, T. de (1947–53), *La biblioteca napoletana dei re d'Aragona*, Milan

Messer, A. (1912), *Le codice aragonese*, Paris

Miglio, M. (1975), *Storiografia pontificia del quattrocento*, Bologna

Mollat, G. (1951), 'Contribution à l'histoire du sacré collège de Clément V à Eugène IV', *Revue d'histoire ecclésiastique* 46: 22–112

Notar Giacomo (1945), *Cronica di Napoli*, ed. P. Garzilli, Naples

Nunziante, E. (1898), *I primi anni di Ferdinando d'Aragona e l'invasione di Giovanni d'Angiò (1458–1464)*, Naples

Palermino, R.J. (1980), 'The Roman Academy', *Archivum historiae pontificiae*, 18: 117–56

Paltroni, P. (1966), *Commentari della vita e gesti dell'Illustrissimo Federico, duca d'Urbino*, ed. W. Tommasoli, Urbino

Partner, P. (1958), *The papal state under Martin V. The administration and government of the temporal power in the early fifteenth century*, London

Partner, P. (1960), 'The "budget" of the Roman Church in the Renaissance period', in E.F. Jacob (ed.), *Italian Renaissance studies*, London, pp. 256–78

Partner, P. (1972), *The lands of St. Peter. The papal state in the Middle Ages and the early Renaissance*, London

Partner, P. (1990), *The pope's men. The papal civil service in the Renaissance*, Oxford

Partner, P. (1991), 'The papal state: 1417–1600', in M. Greengrass (ed.), *Conquest and coalescence. The shaping of the state in early modern Europe*, London, pp. 25–47

Pastor, L. von (1891–1911), *The history of the popes from the close of the Middle Ages*, I–V, trans. F.I. Antrobus and R. Kerr, London

Petrone, P. di Lello (1910), *La Mesticanza*, ed. F. Isoldi, Rerum Italicarum Scriptores, n.s., Bologna

Pius II (1984), *Commentarii rerum memorabilium*, ed. L. Totaro, Milan

Pillinini, G. (1970), *Il sistema degli stati Italiani, 1454–1494*, Venice

Pontieri, E. (1963), *La Calabria a metà del secolo XV e le rivolte di Antonio Centelles*, Naples

Pontieri, E. (1969), *Ferrante d'Aragona re di Napoli*, Naples

Pontieri, E. (1975), *Alfonso il Magnanimo, re di Napoli 1435–1458*, Naples

Pontieri, E. (1979), *Il comune dell'Aquila nel declino del medioevo*, L'Aquila

Porzio, D. (1964), *La congiura dei baroni contra il re Ferdinando il primo*, ed. E. Pontieri, Naples

Prodi, P. (1988), *Papal prince – one body and two souls. The papal monarchy in early modern Europe*, Cambridge

Pullan, B. (1973), *A history of early Renaissance Italy*, London

Re, N. del (1970), *La curia romana*, Rome

Ryder, A. (1965), 'The evolution of imperial government in Naples under Alfonso V of Aragon', in J. Hale, R. Highfield and B. Smalley (eds.), *Europe in the late Middle Ages*, London, pp. 332–57

Ryder, A. (1976), *The kingdom of Naples under Alfonso the Magnanimous*, Oxford

Ryder, A. (1990), *Alfonso the Magnanimous, king of Aragon, Naples and Sicily, 1396–1458*, Oxford

Santoro, M. (1988), 'Humanism in Naples', in A. Rabil (ed.), *Renaissance humanism*, I, Philadelphia, pp. 296–331

Schiappoli, I. (1940–1), 'La marina degli Aragonesi di Napoli', *Archivio storico per le provinci napoletane* 65: 7–65; 66: 7–36

Società Editrice Storia di Napoli (1969–74), *Storia di Napoli*, III and IV, Naples

Thomson, J.A.F. (1980), *Popes and princes, 1417–1517. Politics and polity in the late medieval Church*, London

Trinchera, F. (1866–72), *Codice aragonese*, Naples

Volterra, Jacopo Gherardi da (Volterrano) (1904), *Il diario romano*, ed. E. Carusi, Rerum Italicarum Scriptores, n.s., Città di Castello

Westfall, C.W. (1974), *In this most perfect paradise. Alberti, Nicholas V and the invention of conscious urban planning in Rome, 1447–55*, University Park, Pa.

24(a) ARAGON

Primary sources

Belluga, Pere, *Speculum principum*, Venice (1580)

Cortes de los antiguos reinos de Aragón, Valencia y Principado de Cataluña, 27 vols., Real Academia de la Historia, Madrid (1896–1922)

Eiximenis, Francesc, *El regiment de la cosa pública*, ed. P. Daniel de Molins de Rei, Els nostres clàssics, 13, Barcelona (1927)

Parlaments a les corts catalans, ed. R. Albert and J. Gassiot, Els nostres clàssics, 19–20, Barcelona (1950)

Turell, Gabriel, *Recort*, ed. E. Bagué, Els nostres clàssics, 67, Barcelona (1950)

Zurita, Jerónimo, *Anales de la corona de Aragón*, ed. A. Canellas López, 9 vols., Saragossa (1967–85)

Secondary works

General works

Bisson, T.N. (1986), *The medieval crown of Aragon. A short history*, Oxford

Dualde Serrano, M. and Camarena Mahiques, J. (1971), *El compromiso de Caspe*, Valencia

Elias de Tejada, F. (1963–5), *Historia del pensamiento político catalán*, I: *La Cataluña clásica*; II: *Mallorca y Menorca clásicas*; III: *La Valencia clásica*, Seville

Hillgarth, J.N. (1976–8), *The Spanish kingdoms, 1250–1516*, 2 vols., Oxford

Lalinde Abadía, J. (1979), *La corona de Aragón en el Mediterráneo medieval (1229–1479)*, Saragossa

Menéndez Pidal, R. (1964), 'El Compromiso de Caspe, autodeterminación de un pueblo (1410–12)', in *Historia de España*, ed. R. Menéndez Pidal, XV, Madrid, pp. ix–clxiv

Soldevila, F. (1971), *El Compromís de Casp (Resposta al Sr. Menéndez Pidal)*, 2nd edn, Barcelona

Suárez Fernández, L. (1969), *La España de los reyes católicos (1474–1516) (Historia de España*, ed. R. Menéndez Pidal, XVII*)*, 2 vols., Madrid

Suárez Fernández, L. (1980), *Los Trastámara y la unidad española (1369–1517) (Historia general de España y América*, ed. L. Suárez Fernández, V), Madrid

Suárez Fernández, L., Canellas López, A. and Vicens Vives, J. (1964), *Los Trastámaras de Castilla y Aragón en el siglo XV (Historia de España*, ed. R. Menéndez Pidal, XV), Madrid

Vicens Vives, J. (1956), *Els Trastàmares*, Barcelona

Vilar, P. (1956–9) 'Le déclin catalan du bas moyen âge. Hypothèses sur sa chronologie', *Estudios de historia moderna* 6: 1–68

Regional studies

Catalonia

Batlle Gallart, C. (1988), *L'expansió baix-medieval (segles XIII–XV) (Història de Catalunya*, ed. P. Vidal, III), Barcelona

Martínez Ferrando, E. (1936), *Pere de Portugal 'rei dels Catalans' vist a través dels registres de la seva cancelleria*, Barcelona

Martínez Ferrando, E. (1966), *Baixa edat mitjana (segles XII–XV) (Història dels Catalans*, ed. F. Soldevila, III), Barcelona

Salrach, J.M. and Duran, E. (1982), *Història dels països catalans. Dels orígens a 1714*, Barcelona

Soldevila, F. (1962), *Història de Catalunya*, 2nd edn, 3 vols., Barcelona

Aragon

Lacarra, J.M. (1972), *Aragón en el pasado*, Madrid

Sarasa Sánchez, E. (1986), *Aragón en el reinado de Fernando I (1412–16)*, Saragossa

Valencia

Belenguer Cebrià, E. (1976), *València en la crisi del segle XV*, Barcelona

Belenguer Cebrià, E. (ed.) (1989), *Història del país valencià, de la conquista a la federació hispànica*, Barcelona

Sicily

Bresc, H. (1986), *Un monde méditerranéen. Economie et société en Sicile, 1300–1450*, Palermo and Rome

Corrao, P. (1991), *Governare un regno. Potere, società e istituzioni in Sicilia fra Trecento e Quattrocento*, Naples

D'Alessandro, V. (1989), *La Sicilia dal Vespro all'unità d'Italia (Storia d'Italia*, ed. G. Galasso, XVI), Turin

Individual rulers

Boscolo, A. (1954), *La politica italiana di Ferdinando I d'Aragona*, Cagliari

Boscolo, A. (1962), *La politica italiana di Martino il Vecchio, re d'Aragona*, Padua

Ryder, A. (1990), *Alfonso the Magnanimous, king of Aragon, Naples and Sicily, 1396–1458*, Oxford

Vicens Vives, J. (1936–7), *Ferran II i la ciutat de Barcelona (1479–1516)*, 3 vols. Barcelona

Vicens Vives, J. (1952), *Fernando el Católico, príncipe de Aragón, rey de Sicilia*, Madrid

Vicens Vives, J. (1953), *Juan II de Aragón (1398–1479). Monarquía y revolución en la España del siglo XV*, Barcelona

Vicens Vives, J. (1962), *Historia crítica de la vida y reinado de Fernando II de Aragón*, Saragossa

Institutions

Les corts a Catalunya (1991), Actes del congrés d'història institucional, Barcelona, 1988, Barcelona

Cruselles, E. (1989), *El maestre racional de Valencia. Función política y desarollo administrativo del oficio público en el siglo XV*, Valencia

Lalinde Abadía, J. (1963), *La gubernación general de la corona de Aragón*, Madrid and Saragossa

Lalinde Abadía, J. (1978), 'Los parlamentos y demas instituciones representativas', in *Relazioni, IX Congresso di storia della corona d'Aragona*, Naples, pp. 103–79

Lalinde Abadía, J. (1980), 'El pactismo en los reinos de Aragón y de Valencia', in *El pactismo en la historia de España*, Madrid, pp. 113–39

Sánchez Aragonés, L.M. (1994), *Cortes, monarquía y ciudades en Aragón durante el reinado de Alfonso el Magnánimo (1416–1458)*, Saragossa

Sánchez Aragonés, L.M. (ed.) (1993), *Estudios sobre renta, fiscalidad y finanzas en la Cataluña bajomedieval*, Barcelona

Sesma Muñoz, J.A. (1976), 'Las generalidades del reino de Aragón. Su organización a mediados del siglo XV', *Anuario de historia del derecho español* 46: 393–467

Sesma Muñoz, J.A. (1977), *La diputación del reino de Aragón en la época de Fernando II (1479–1516)*, Saragossa

Sevillano Colóm, F. (1965), 'Cancillerías de Fernando I de Antequera y de Alfonso V el Magnánimo', *Anuario de historia del derecho español* 35: 169–216

Udina Martorell, F. (1978), 'La organización político-administrativa de la corona de Aragón de 1416 a 1516', in *Relazioni, IX Congresso di storia della corona d'Aragona*, Naples, pp. 49–83

Vallet de Goytisolo, J. (1980), 'Valor jurídico de las leyes paccionadas en el Principado de Cataluña', in *El pactismo en la historia de España*, Madrid, pp. 75–110

Economy and society

Batlle Gallart, C. (1973), *La crisis social y económica de Barcelona a mediados del siglo XV*, 2 vols., Barcelona

Bonassie, P. (1975), *La organización del trabajo en Barcelona a fines del siglo XV*, Barcelona

Carrère, C. (1967), *Barcelone, centre économique à l'époque des difficultés, 1380–1462*, 2 vols., Paris and The Hague

Del Treppo, M. (1972), *I mercanti catalani e l'espansione della corona d'Aragona nel secolo XV*, 2nd edn, Naples; trans. *Els mercaders catalans i l'expansió de la corona catalano-aragonesa*, Barcelona (1976)

Freedman, P.H. (1988), *Assaig d'història de la pagesia catalana (segles XI–XV)*, Barcelona

Furió, A. (ed.) (1985), *València un mercat medieval*, Valencia

Guiral-Hadziiossif, J. (1986), *Valence, port méditerranéen au XV siècle (1410–1525)*, Paris

Hamilton, E.J. (1936), *Money, prices and wages in Valencia, Aragon and Navarre, 1351–1500*, Cambridge, Mass.

Küchler, W. (1983), *Die Finanzen der krone Aragon während des 15 Jahrhunderts. Alfons V und Johann II*, Münster and Westfalen

Manca, C. (1966), *Aspetti dell'espansione economica catalano-aragonese nel Mediterraneo occidentale. Il commercio internazionale del sale*, Milan

Santamaria Arandez, A. (1966), *Aportación al estudio de la economia de Valencia durante el siglo XV*, Valencia

Sarasa Sánchez, E. (1979), 'La condición social de los vassallos de señorio en Aragón durante el siglo XV: criterios de identidad', *Aragón en la edad media* 2: 203–44

Sesma Muñoz, J.A. (1979), 'Trayectoria económica de la hacienda del reino de Aragón en el siglo XV', *Aragón en la edad media* 2: 171–201

Sobrequés i Vidal, S. and Sobrequés i Callicó, J. (1973), *La guerra civil catalana del segle XV. Estudis sobre la crisi social i econòmica de la Baixa Edat Mitjana*, 2 vols., Barcelona

Usher, A.P. (1943), *The early history of deposit banking in Mediterranean Europe*, Cambridge, Mass.

Vicens Vives, J. (1945), *Historia de los remensas en el siglo XV*, Barcelona

24(b) CASTILE AND NAVARRE

Primary sources

Chacón, Gonzalo, *Crónica de don Alvaro de Luna*, ed. J. de Mata Carriazo, Madrid (1940)

Díez de Games, *El Victorial, crónica de Don Pero Niño, conde de Buelna, por su alférez Gutierre Díez de Games*, ed. J. de Mata Carriazo, Madrid (1940)

Galíndez de Carvajál, Lorenzo, *Anales breves del reinado de los reyes católicos D. Fernando y Doña Isabel de gloriosa memoria*, in C. Rossel (ed.), *Crónicas de los reyes de Castilla*, III, Biblioteca de autores españoles, 70, Real Academia Española, Madrid (1953)

Historia de los hechos del marqués de Cádiz (1443–1488), Colección de documentos inéditos para la historia de España, 106, Madrid (1893)

Perez de Guzmán, Fernán, *Generaciones ye semblanzas*, ed. R.B. Tate, London (1965)

The travels of Leo of Rozmital through Germany, Flanders, England, France, Spain, Portugal and Italy, trans. and ed. M. Letts, Hakluyt Society, second series 108, Cambridge (1957)

Secondary works

General

García de Cortazar, J.A. (1973), *La época medieval*, Madrid

Hillgarth, J.N. (1976–8), *The Spanish kingdoms, 1250–1516*, 2 vols., Oxford

Iradiel, P., Moreta, S. and Sarasa, E. (1989), *Historia medieval de la España cristiana*, Madrid
Lacarra, J.M. (1972–3), *Historia política del reino de Navarra en la edad media*, 3 vols., Pamplona
Leroy, B. (1985), *Navarre au moyen âge*, Paris
Lewis, A.R. and McGann, T.F. (1963), *The New World looks at its history*, Austin
MacKay, A. (1977), *Spain in the Middle Ages*, London
O'Callaghan, J.F. (1975), *A history of medieval Spain*, London
Valdeón Baruque, J. (1968), *El reino de Castilla en la edad media*, Bilbao

Regional

Arié, R. (1973), *L'Espagne musulmane au temps des Nasrides (1239–1492)*, Paris
Benito Ruano, E. (1961), *Toledo en el siglo XV*, Madrid
García de Cortazar, J.A. (1966), *Vizcaya en el siglo XV*, Bilbao
Ladero Quesada, M.A. (1969), *Granada. Historia de un pais islámico (1232–1571)*, Madrid
Ladero Quesada, M.A. (1975), *Andalucía en el siglo XV. Estudios de historia politica*, Madrid
Lopes de Coca Castañer, J.E. (1977), *La tierra de Málaga a fines del siglo XV*, Granada
Torres Fontes, J. (1973), *Don Pedro Fajardo, adelantado mayor de Murcia*, Madrid

Particular aspects

Azcona, T. de (1964), *Isabel la Católica. Estudio crítico de su vida y su reinado*, Madrid
MacKay, A. (1985), 'Ritual and propaganda in fifteenth-century Castile', *P&P* 107: 3–43
Philips, W.D. (1978), *Enrique IV and the crisis of fifteenth-century Castile*, Cambridge, Mass.
Round, N. (1986), *The greatest man uncrowned. A study of the fall of Don Alvaro de Luna*, London
Russell, P.E. (1955), *The English intervention in Spain and Portugal in the time of Edward III and Richard II*, Oxford
Suárez Fernández, L. (1959), *Navegación y comercio en el golfo de Vizcaya*, Madrid
Suárez Fernández, L. (1975), *Nobleza y monarquía*, 2nd edn, Valladolid
Vicens Vives, J. (1953), *Juan II de Aragón (1398–1479)*, Barcelona

Institutions

Bermúdez Aznar, A. (1974), *El corregidor en Castilla durante la baja edad media (1348–1474)*, Murcia
Las cortes de Castilla y León en la edad media (1988), 3 vols., Valladolid
García de Valdeavellano, L. (1970), *Curso de historia de las instituciones españolas. De los origines al final de la edad media*, Madrid
González Alonso, B. (1970), *El corregidor castellano (1348–1808)*, Madrid
González Alonso, B. (1981), *Sobre el estado y la administración de la corona en Castilla en el siglo XV*, Madrid
Ladero Quesada, M.A. (1973), *La hacienda real de Castilla en el siglo XV*, La Laguna
Ladero Quesada, M.A. (1982), *El siglo XV en Castilla. Fuentes de renta y política fiscal*, Barcelona
Ladero Quesada, M.A. (1993), *Fiscalidad y poder real en Castilla (1252–1369)*, Madrid

Pérez Bustamante, R. (1976), *El gobierno y la administración territorial de Castilla (1270–1474)*, 2 vols., Madrid

Piskorski, W. (1977), *Las cortes de Castilla en el período de tránsito de la edad media a la moderna (1188–1520)*, Barcelona

Economy and society

Asenjo González, M. (1986), *Segovia. La ciudad y su tierra a fines del medioevo*, Segovia

Baer, Y. (1966), *A history of the Jews in Christian Spain*, 2 vols., Philadelphia

Bandas y querellas dinásticas en España al final de la edad media (1991), Biblioteca Española, Paris

Beinart, H. (1981), *Conversos on trial. The Inquisition in Ciudad Real*, Jerusalem

Benito Ruano, E. (1961), *Toledo en el siglo XV*, Madrid

Bernal, A.M., Collantes de Terán, A. and García-Baquero, A. (1978), 'Sevilla: de los gremios a la industrialización', *Estudios de historia social* 5–6: 7–307

Bishko, C.J. (1963), 'The Castilian as plainsman. The medieval ranching frontier in La Mancha and Extremadura', in A.R. Lewis and T.F. McGann (eds.), *The New World looks at its history*, Austin

Borrero Fernández, M. (1983), *El mundo rural sevillano en el siglo XV. Aljarafe y Ribera*, Seville

Cabrera Muñoz, E. (1977), *El condado de Belalcázar, 1444–1518*, Cordoba

Cabrillana, N. (1968), 'La crisis del siglo XIV en Castilla: la Peste Negra en el obispado de Palencia', *Hispania* 109: 245–58

Cabrillana, N. (1969), 'Salamanca en el siglo XV: nobles y campesinos', *Cuadernos de historia. Anexos de Hispania* 3: 255–95

Carrasco, J. (1973), *La población de Navarra en el siglo XIV*, Pamplona

Casado, H. (1988), *Señores, mercaderes y campesinos. La comarca de Burgos a fines de la edad media*, Valladolid

Chacón-Jiménez, F. (1979), *Murcia en la centuria del Quinientos*, Murcia

Childs, W.R. (1978), *Anglo-Castilian trade in the later Middle Ages*, Manchester

Collantes de Terán, A. (1976), 'Le latifundium sévillan aux XIVe et XVe siècles', *Mélanges de la Casa de Vélazquez* 12: 101–25

Collantes de Terán, A. (1977a), *Sevilla en la baja edad media. La ciudad y sus hombres*, Seville

Collantes de Terán, A. (1977b), 'Nuevas poblaciones del siglo XV en el reino de Sevilla', *Cuadernos de historia* 7: 283–336

Estcpa, C., Ruiz, T., Bonachía, J.A. and Casado, H. (1984), *Burgos en la edad media*, Burgos

García de Cortazar, J.A. (1966), *Vizcaya en el siglo XV. Aspectos económicos y sociales*, Bilbao

Gerbet, M.-C. (1972), 'Les guerres et l'accès à la noblesse en Espagne de 1456 à 1592', *Mélanges de la Casa de Velázquez* 7: 295–326

Gerbet, M.-C. (1977–9), 'La population noble dans le royaume de Castille vers 1500', *Anales de historia antigua y medieval* 3: 78–99

Gerbet, M.-C. (1979), *La noblesse dans le royaume de Castille. Etude sur ses structures en Estrémadure de 1454 à 1516*, Paris

González Jiménez, M. (1973), *El concejo de Carmona a fines de la edad media*, Seville

Gutierrez Nieto, J.I. (1977), 'Semántica del término Comunidad antes de 1520: las asociaciones juramentadas de defensa', *Hispania* 136: 319–67

Hamilton, E.J. (1936), *Money, prices and wages in Valencia, Aragon and Navarre, 1351–1500*, Cambridge, Mass.

Iradiel, P. (1974), *Evolución de la industria textil castellana en los siglos XIII–XVI*, Salamanca

Kamen, H. (1965), *The Spanish Inquisition*, London

Klein, J. (1920), *The Mesta*, Cambridge, Mass.

MacKay, A. (1972), 'Popular movements and pogroms in fifteenth-century Castile', *P&P* 55: 33–67

MacKay, A. (1981), *Money, prices and politics in fifteenth-century Castile*, London

MacKay, A. (1986), 'The lesser nobility in the kingdom of Castile', in M. Jones (ed.), *Gentry and lesser nobility in later medieval Europe*, Gloucester and New York, pp. 159–80

MacKay, A. (1990), 'Faction and civil strife in late medieval Castilian towns', *BJRULM* 72: 119–31

MacKay, A. and McKendrick, G. (1986), 'The crowd in theatre and the crowd in history: Fuenteovejuna', *Renaissance Drama* n.s. 17: 125–47

Martínez Moro, J. (1977), *La renta feudal en la Castilla del siglo XV. Los Stúñigas*, Valladolid

Milhou, A. (1983), *Colón y su mentalidad mesiánica en el ambiente franciscanista español*, Valladolid

Netanyahu, B. (1966), *The marranos of Spain from the late fourteenth to the early sixteenth century*, New York

Phillips, J.R.S. (1988), *The medieval expansion of Europe*, Oxford

Ponsot, P. (1980), 'Un cas de croissance démographique précoce: la Basse-Andalousie au XVe et au début du XVIe siècle', *Annales de démographie historique* 4: 143–53

Prosperi, A. (1992), 'New Heaven and New Earth; prophecy and propaganda at the time of the discovery and conquest of the Americas', in M. Reeves (ed.), *Prophetic Rome in the high Renaissance period*, Oxford

Quintanilla, M.C. (1979), *Nobleza y señoríos en el reino de Córdoba. La casa de Aguilar (siglos XIV y XV)*, Cordoba

Rucquoi, A. (1987), *Valladolid en la edad media*, 2 vols., Valladolid

Suárez Fernández, L. (1980), *Judíos españoles en la edad media*, Madrid

The cultural context

Black, A. (1970), *Monarchy and community. Political ideas in the later conciliar controversy*, Cambridge

Black, A. (1992), *Political thought in Europe, 1250–1450*, Cambridge

Burns, J.H. (1992), *Lordship, kingship and empire, 1400–1525*, Oxford

Deyermond, A.D. (1971), *The Middle Ages*, London and New York

Gilman, S. (1972), *The Spain of Fernando de Rojas. The intellectual and social landscape of 'La Celestina'*, Princeton

Lawrance, J.N.H. (1990), 'Humanism in the Iberian peninsula', in A. Goodman and A. MacKay (eds.), *The impact of humanism on western Europe*, London and New York

Round, N.G. (1962), 'Renaissance culture and its opponents in fifteenth-century Castile', *Modern Language Review* 57: 204–15

Russell, P.E. (1978), *Temas de 'La Celestina' y otros estudios del 'Cid' al 'Quijote'*, Barcelona

Tate, R.B. (1970), *Ensayos sobre la historiografía peninsular del siglo XV*, Madrid

Tate, R.B. (1977), 'Political allegory in fifteenth-century Spain', *Journal of Hispanic Philology* 1: 169–86

24(c) PORTUGAL

Secondary works

Coelho, M.H. de C. and Magalhães, J.R. (1986), *O poder concelhio (das origens às cortes constituintes)*, Coimbra

Godinho, V.M. (1962), *A economia dos descobrimentos henriquinos*, Lisbon

Godinho, V.M. (1990), *Mito e mercadoria, utopia e prática de navegar (séculos XIII–XVIII*, Lisbon

Gonçalves, I. (1964), *Pedidos e empréstimos públicos em Portugal durante a idade média*, Lisbon

Hespanha, A.M. (1982), *História das instituições (Épocas medieval e moderna)*, Coimbra

Homem, A.L.C. (1990), *O desembargo régio (1320–1433)*, Oporto

Livro dos conselhos de el-rei D. Duarte (1982), ed. J.J. Alves Dias, Lisbon

Marques, A.H. de O. (1986), *Portugal na crise dos séculos XIV e XV (Nova história de Portugal*, ed. J. Serrão and A.H. de O. Marques, IV), Lisbon

Marques, J. (1988), *A arquidiocese de Braga no século XV*, Lisbon

Mattoso, J. (1985), *Identificaçao de um país. (Ensaio sobre as origens de Portugal, 1096–1325)*, 2 vols., Lisbon

Moreno, H.C.B. (1979), *A batalha de Alfarrobeira*, 2 vols., Coimbra

Resende, Garcia de (1973), *Crónica de D. Joao II e miscelânea*, Lisbon

Sousa, A. de (1982), 'As cortes de Leiria-Santarém de 1433', *Estudos medievais* 2: 71–224

Sousa, A. de (1983), 'Conflitos entre o bispo e a câmara do Porto nos meados do século XV', *Boletim cultural da câmara municipal do Porto* 2nd series 1: 9–103

Sousa, A. de (1984), 'A morte de D. João I (um tema de propaganda dinástica)', in *Lucerna*, Número de homenagem a D. Domingos de Pinho Brandão, pp. 417–87

Sousa, A. de (1985), 'O discurso político dos concelhos nas cortes de 1385', *Revista da faculdade de Letras [Oporto]: história* 2nd series 2: 9–44

Sousa, A. de (1989a), 'O parlamento na época de D. João II', *Actas do congresso internacional Bartolomeu Dias e a sua época*, I, Oporto, pp. 231–61

Sousa, A. de (1989b), 'A estratégia política dos municípios no reinado de D. João II', *Revista da faculdade de Letras [Oporto]: história* 2nd series 6: 137–74

Sousa, A. de (1990), *As cortes medievais portuguesas (1385–1480)*, 2 vols., Oporto

Sousa, A. de (1993), 'A monarquia feudal (1325–1480)', in J. Mattoso (ed.), *História de Portugal*, II, Lisbon, pp. 310–556

Zurara, Gomes Eancs de (1978), *Crónica do conde D. Duarte de Meneses*, ed. L. King, Lisbon

25 THE SWISS CONFEDERATION

Secondary works

Ammann, H. (1955), 'Das schweizerische Städtewesen des Mittelalters in seiner wirtschaftlichen und sozialen Ausprägung', in *Recueils de la Société Jean Bodin*, VII: *La ville*, Brussels, pp. 483–529

Andenmatten, B. and De Raemy, D. (eds.) (1990), *La maison de Savoie en pays de Vaud*, Lausanne

Baum, W. (1993), *Die Habsburger in den Vorlanden, 1386–1486. Krise und Höhepunkt der habsburgischen Machtstellung in Schwaben am Ausgang des Mittelalters*, Vienna

Baum, W. (1994), *Reichs- und Territorialgewalt (1273–1437). Königtum, Haus Oesterreich und Schweizer Eidgenossen im späten Mittelalter*, Vienna

Berger, H. (1978), *Der Alte Zürichkrieg im Rahmen der europäischen Politik. Ein Beitrag zur 'Aussenpolitik' Zürichs in der ersten Hälfte des 15. Jahrhunderts*, Zurich

Bergier, J.-F. (1990), *Die Wirtschaftsgeschichte der Schweiz, Von den Anfängen bis zur Gegenwart*, Zurich

Bibliographie der Schweizergeschichte (1913–), ed. Schweizerische Landesbibliothek, Berne and Zurich

Bickel, A. (1978), *Die Herren von Hallwil im Mittelalter, Beitrag zur schwäbisch–schweizerischen Adelsgeschichte*, Aarau

Bickel, A. (1982), *Willisau. Geschichte von Stadt und Umland bis 1500*, 2 vols., Lucerne

Bierbrauer, P. (1991), *Freiheit und Gemeinde im Berner Oberland 1300–1700*, Berne

Black, A. (1979), *Council and commune. The conciliar movement and the fifteenth-century heritage*, London

Blickle, P. (1973), *Landschaften im Alten Reich. Die staatliche Funktion des gemeinen Mannes in Oberdeutschland*, Munich

Blickle, P. (1981), *Deutsche Untertanen. Ein Widerspruch*, Munich

Blickle, P. (1985), *Gemeindereformation. Die Menschen des 16. Jahrhunderts auf dem Weg zum Heil*, Munich

Blickle, P. (1990), 'Friede und Verfassung, Voraussetzungen und Folgen der Eidgenossenschaft von 1291', in *Innerschweiz und frühe Eidgenossenschaft. Jubiläumsschrift 700 Jahre Eidgenossenschaft*, I: *Verfassung, Kirche, Kunst*, ed. Historischer Verein der Fünf Orte, Olten, pp. 13–202

Bodmer, J.-P. (1976), *Chroniken und Chronisten im Spätmittelalter*, Berne

Brady, T.A., Jr (1985), *Turning Swiss. Cities and Empire, 1450–1550*, Cambridge

Brändli, P.J. (1986), 'Mittelalterliche Grenzstreitigkeiten im Alpenraum', *Mitteilungen des historischen Vereins des Kantons Schwyz* 78: 19–188

Bundi, M. (1982), *Zur Besiedlungs- und Wirtschaftsgeschichte Graubündens im Mittelalter*, Chur

Castelnuovo, G. (1994), *Seigneurs et lignages dans le pays de Vaud. Du royaume de Bourgogne à l'arrivée des Savoie*, Lausanne

Chiesi, G. (1988), *Bellinzona ducale. Ceto dirigente e politica finanziaria nel Quattrocento*, Bellinzona

Contamine, P. (1984), *War in the Middle Ages*, Oxford

De Capitani, F. (1982), *Adel, Bürger und Zünfte im Bern des 15. Jahrhunderts*, Berne

Dierauer, J. (1907–20), *Geschichte der Schweizerischen Eidgenossenschaft*, 5 vols., Gotha

Dietrich, C. (1985), *Die Stadt Zürich und ihre Landgemeinden während der Bauernunruhen von 1489 und 1525*, Frankfurt am Main and Zurich

Dubuis, P. (1990), *Une économie alpine à la fin du moyen âge. Orsières, l'Entremont et les régions voisines, 1250–1500*, 2 vols., Sion

Dürr, E. (1933), *Die Politik der Eidgenossen im XIV. und XV. Jahrhundert. Eidgenössische Grossmachtpolitik im Zeitalter der Mailänderkriege*, Berne

Durrer, R. (1917–21), *Bruder Klaus. Die ältesten Quellen über den seligen Nikolaus von Flüe, sein Leben und seinen Einfluss*, 2 vols., Sarnen

Esch, A. (1988), 'Alltag der Entscheidung. Berns Weg in den Burgunderkrieg', *Berner Zeitschrift für Geschichte und Heimatkunde* 50: 3–64

Esch, A. (1990), 'Mit Schweizer Söldnern auf dem Marsch nach Italien. Das Erlebnis der Mailänderkriege 1510–1515 nach bernischen Akten', *Quellen und Forschungen aus italienischen Archiven und Bibliotheken* 70: 348–440

Feller, R. and Bonjour, E. (1962), *Geschichtsschreibung der Schweiz*, I: *Vom Spätmittelalter zur Neuzeit*, Basle

Gasser, A. (1930), *Entstehung und Ausbildung der Landeshoheit im Gebiete der Schweizerischen Eidgenossenschaft. Ein Beitrag zur Verfassungsgeschichte des deutschen Mittelalters*, Aarau

Gasser, A. (1932), *Die territoriale Entwicklung der schweizerischen Eidgenossenschaft, 1291–1797*, Aarau

Gasser, A. (1973), 'Ewige Richtung und Burgunderkriege. Zur Klärung einer alten Streitfrage', *Schweizerische Zeitschrift für Geschichte* 23: 697–749

Geschichte der Schweiz und der Schweizer / Nouvelle histoire de la Suisse et des suisses / Nuova Storia della Svizzera e degli svizzeri (1986), ed. B. Mesmer, J.-C. Favez and R. Broggini, I, 2nd edn, Basle

Geschichte des Kantons Zürich, I: *Frühzeit bis Spätmittelalter* (1995), Zurich

Gilomen, H.-J. (1982), 'Die städtische Schuld Berns und der Basler Rentenmarkt im 15. Jahrhundert', *Basler Zeitschrift für Geschichte und Altertumskunde* 82: 5–69

Gössi, A. (1978), 'Die Verwaltung der Stadt Luzern und ihr Schriftgut im späten 14. Jahrhundert', in *Luzern 1178–1978. Beiträge zur Geschichte der Stadt*, Lucerne, pp. 171–97

Guenée, B. (1971), *L'Occident aux XIVe et XVe siècles. Les états*, Paris; English trans., *States and rulers in later medieval Europe* (1985), Oxford

Handbuch der Schweizer Geschichte (1980), ed. H. Helbling *et al.*, I, 2nd edn, Zurich

Head, R.C. (1995), *Early modern democracy in the Grisons. Social order and political language in a Swiss mountain canton, 1470–1620*, Cambridge

Helmrath, J. (1987), *Das Basler Konzil, 1431–1449. Forschungsstand und Probleme*, Cologne

Helvetica Sacra (1972–), Berne

Historischer Atlas der Schweiz (1958), ed. H. Ammann and K. Schib, 2nd edn, Aarau

Holenstein, A. (1991), *Die Huldigung der Untertanen. Rechtskultur und Herrschaftsordnung (800–1800)*, Stuttgart and New York

Im Hof, U. (1974), *Geschichte der Schweiz*, Stuttgart

Innerschweiz und Frühe Eidgenossenschaft. Jubiläumsschrift 700 Jahre Eidgenossenschaft (1990), ed. Historischer Verein der Fünf Orte, 2 vols., Olten

Köppel, C. (1986), 'Wirtschaftliche Reorganisation in einer geistlichen Grundherrschaft als Prozess regionaler Integration am Beispiel des Fraumünsters in Zürich (1418–1525)', in F. Seibt and W. Eberhardt (eds.), *Europa 1500. Integrationsprozess im Widerstreit. Staaten, Regionen, Personenverbände, Christenheit*, Stuttgart, pp. 247–61

Körner, M. (1981), *Luzerner Staatsfinanzen 1415–1798. Strukturen, Wachstum, Konjunkturen*, Lucerne

Lutz, E.C. (1990), *Spiritualis fornicatio. Heinrich Wittenwiler, seine Welt und sein 'Ring'*, Sigmaringen

Marchal, G.P. (1986), *Sempach 1386. Von den Anfängen des Territorialstaates Luzern. Beiträge zur Frühgeschichte des Kantons Luzern*, Basle

Marchal, G.P. (1987a), 'Die Antwort der Bauern. Elemente und Schichtungen des eidgenössischen Geschichtsbewusstseins am Ausgang des Mittelalters', in H. Patze (ed.), *Geschichtsschreibung und Geschichtsbewusstsein im Spätmittelalter*, Sigmaringen, pp. 757–90

Marchal, G.P. (1987b), 'Die Schweiz von den Anfängen bis 1499', in F. Seibt (ed.), *Europa im Hoch- und Spätmittelalter*, Stuttgart, pp. 533–45

Marchal, G.P. (1990), 'Die "Alten Eidgenossen" im Wandel der Zeiten. Das Bild der frühen Eidgenossen im Traditionsbewusstsein und in der Identitätsvorstellung der Schweizer vom 15. bis in 20. Jahrhundert', in *Innerschweiz und frühe Eidgenossenschaft. Jubiläumsschrift 700 Jahre Eidgenossenschaft*, II: *Gesellschaft, Alltag, Geschichtsbild*, ed. Historischer Verein der Fünf Orte, Olten, pp. 307–403

Marchal, G.P. (1991), 'Die schweizerische Geschichtsforschung und die österreichische Herrschaft: Ergebnisse und Fragen', in P. Rück (ed.), *Die Eidgenossen und ihre Nachbarn im Deutschen Reich des Mittelalters*, Marburg an der Lahn, pp. 15–36

Marchal, G.P. (1992), 'Das Mittelalter und die nationale Geschichtsschreibung der Schweiz', in S. Burghartz *et al.* (eds.), *Spannungen und Widersprüche. Gedenkschrift für František Graus*, Sigmaringen, pp. 91–108

Maurer, H. (1991), *Schweizer und Schwaben. Ihre Begegnung und ihr Auseinanderleben am Bodensee im Spätmittelalter*, Constance

Meier, B. and Sauerländer, D. (1995), *Das Surbtal im Spätmittelalter. Kulturlandschaft und Gesellschaft einer ländlichen Region 1250 bis 1550*, Aarau

Meyer, W. (1990), 'Siedlung und Alltag. Die mittelalterliche Innerschweiz aus der Sicht des Archäologen', in *Innerschweiz und frühe Eidgenossenschaft. Jubiläumsschrift 700 Jahre Eidgenossenschaft*, II: *Gesellschaft, Alltag, Geschichtsbild*, ed. Historischer Verein der Fünf Orte, Olten, pp. 235–305

Mommsen, K. (1985), *Eidgenossen, Kaiser und Reich. Studien zur Stellung der Eidgenossenschaft innerhalb des heiligen römischen Reiches*, Basle

Morard, N. (1982), 'Auf der Höhe der Macht (1394–1536)', in *Geschichte der Schweiz und der Schweizer*, I, pp. 211–352

Moraw, P. (1986), 'Reich, König und Eidgenossen im späten Mittelalter', *Jahrbuch der Historischen Gesellschaft Luzern* 4: 15–33

Niederstätter, A. (1995), *Der alte Zürichkrieg. Studien zum österreichisch–eidgenössischen Konflikt, sowie zur Politik König Friedrichs III. in den Jahren 1440 bis 1446*, Vienna, Cologne and Weimar

Ochsenbein, P. (1979), 'Beten "mit zertanen armen" – ein alteidgenössischer Brauch', *Schweizerisches Archiv für Volkskunde* 75: 129–72

Oechsli, W. (1891), *Die Anfänge der Schweizerischen Eidgenossenschaft. Zur Säkularfeier des ersten Bundes vom 1. August 1291*, Zurich

Othenin-Girard, M. (1994), *Ländliche Lebensweise und Lebensformen im Spätmittelalter. Eine wirtschafts- und sozialgeschichtliche Untersuchung der nordwestschweizerischen Herrschaft Farnsburg*, Basle

Paravicini, W. and Kruse, H. (eds.) (1995), *Der Briefwechsel Karls des Kühnen (1433–1477)*, 2 vols., Frankfurt am Main and Berlin

Peyer, H.C. (1975), 'Wollgewerbe, Viehzucht, Solddienst und Bevölkerungs-entwicklung in Stadt und Landschaft Freiburg i. Ue. vom 14. bis 16. Jahrhundert', in H. Kellenbenz (ed.), *Agrarische Nebengewerbe und Formen der Reagrarisierung im Spätmittelalter und 19./20. Jahrhundert*, Stuttgart, pp. 79–95

Peyer, H.C. (1976), 'Die Anfänge der schweizerischen Aristokratien', in K. Messmer and P. Hoppe (eds.), *Luzerner Patriziat. Sozial- und wirtschaftsgeschichtliche Studien zur Entstehung und Entwicklung im 16. und 17. Jahrhundert*, Lucerne, pp. 1–28

Peyer, H.C. (1978), *Verfassungsgeschichte der alten Schweiz*, Zurich

Peyer, H.C. (1980), 'Die Entstehung der Eidgenossenschaft', in *Handbuch der Schweizer Geschichte*, I, pp. 161–238

Peyer, H.C. (1981), 'Die Schweizer Wirtschaft im Umbruch in der zweiten Hälfte des 15. Jahrhunderts', in F. Elsener *et al.* (eds.), *500 Jahre Stanser Verkommnis; Beiträge zu einem Zeitbild*, Stans, pp. 59–70

Peyer, H.C. (1982), 'Die wirtschaftliche Bedeutung der fremden Dienste für die Schweiz vom 15. zum 18. Jahrhundert', in H.C. Peyer, *Könige, Stadt und Kapital; Aufsätze zur Wirtschafts- und Sozialgeschichte des Mittelalters*, ed. L. Schmugge, R. Sablonier and K. Wanner, Zurich, pp. 219–31

Rippmann, D. (1990), *Bauern und Städter. Stadt-Land-Beziehung im 15. Jahrhundert; Das Beispiel Basel, unter besonderer Berücksichtigung der Nahmarktbeziehungen und der sozialen Verhältnisse im Umland*, Basle

Robinson, P. (1995), *Die Fürstabtei St. Gallen und ihr Territorium 1463–1529*, St Gallen

Rogger, D. (1989), *Obwaldner Landwirtschaft im Spätmittelalter*, Sarnen

Romer, H. (1995), *Herrschaft, Reislauf und Verbotspolitik. Beobachtungen zum rechtlichen Alltag der Zürcher Solddienstbekämpfung im 16. Jahrhundert*, Zurich

Rück, P. (ed.) (1991), *Die Eidgenossen und ihre Nachbarn im Deutschen Reich des Mittelalters*, Marburg an der Lahn

Sablonier, R. (1979a), *Adel im Wandel. Eine Untersuchung zur sozialen Situation des ostschweizerischen Adels um 1300*, Göttingen

Sablonier, R. (1979b), 'Etat et structures militaires dans la Confédération autour des années 1480', in *Cinq-centième anniversaire de la Bataille de Nancy (1477)*, Actes du colloque organisé par l'Institut de Recherches Regionales en Sciences Sociales de l'Université de Nancy II, 1977, Nancy

Sablonier, R. (1982), 'Zur wirtschaftlichen Situation des Adels im Spätmittelalter', in *Adelige Sachkultur des Spätmittelalters*, Internationaler Kongress Krems an der Donau, 1980, Vienna, pp. 9–34

Sablonier, R. (1985a), 'Rittertum, Adel und Kriegswesen im Spätmittelalter', in J. Fleckenstein (ed.), *Das ritterliche Turnier im Mittelalter. Beiträge zu einer vergleichenden Formen- und Verhaltensgeschichte des Rittertums*, Göttingen, pp. 532–67

Sablonier, R. (1985b), 'Die Burgunderkriege und die europäische Politik', in A. Schmid (ed.), *Die grosse Burgunder Chronik des Diebold Schilling von Bern, 'Zärcher Schilling'. Kommentar zur Faksimile-Ausgabe der Handschrift Ms A5 der Zentralbibliothek Zürich*, Lucerne, pp. 39–49

Sablonier, R. (1990), 'Innerschweizer Gesellschaft im 14. Jahrhundert: Sozialstruktur und Wirtschaft', in *Innerschweiz und frühe Eidgenossenschaft. Jubiläumsschrift 700 Jahre Eidgenossenschaft*, II: *Gesellschaft, Alltag, Geschichtsbild*, ed. Historischer Verein der Fünf Orte, Olten, pp. 9–23

Sablonier, R. (1994), 'Die Grafen von Rapperswil: Kontroversen, neue Perspektiven und ein Ausblick auf die "Gründungszeit" der Eidgenossenschaft um 1300', *Der Geschichtsfreund* 147: 5–44

Schaufelberger, W. (1966), *Der alte Schweizer und sein Krieg. Studien zur Kriegführung vornehmlich im 15. Jahrhundert*, 2nd edn, Zurich

Schaufelberger, W. (1980), 'Spätmittelalter', in *Handbuch der Schweizer Geschichte*, I, pp. 238–388

Schlumpf, V. (1969), *Die frumen edlen puren*. Untersuchung zum Stilzusammenhang zwischen den historischen Volksliedern der Alten Eidgenossenschaft und der deutschen Heldenepik, Zurich

Schmid, R. (1995), *Reden, rufen, Zeichen setzen. Politisches Handeln während des Berner Twingherrenstreits 1469–1471*, Zurich

Schnyder, W. (1925), *Die Bevölkerung der Stadt und Landschaft Zürich vom 14. bis 17. Jahrhundert. Eine methodologische Studie*, Zurich

Schorer, C. (1989), 'Berner Ämterbefragungen. Untertanenrepräsentation und -Mentalität im ausgehenden Mittelalter', *Berner Zeitschrift für Geschichte und Heimatkunde* 51: 217–53

Sieber-Lehmann, C. (1995), *Spätmittelalterlicher Nationalismus. Die Burgunderkriege am Oberrhein und in der Eidgenossenschaft*, Göttingen

Siegrist, J.J. (1952), 'Beiträge zur Verfassungs- und Wirtschaftsgeschichte der Herrschaft Hallwil', *Argovia* 64: 5–523

Sonderegger, S. (1987), 'Wirtschaftliche Regionalisierung in der spätmittelalterlichen Nordostschweiz. Am Beispiel der Wirtschaftsführung des Heiliggeistspitals St. Gallen', *Schriften des Vereins für Geschichte des Bodensees und seiner Umgebung* 105: 19–37

Sonderegger, S. (1994), *Landwirtschaftliche Entwicklung in der spätmittelalterlichen Nordostschweiz. Eine Untersuchung ausgehend von den wirtschaftlichen Aktivitäten des Heiliggeist-Spitals St. Gallen*, St Gallen

Stettler, B. (1979), 'Habsburg und die Eidgenossenschaft um die Mitte des 14. Jahrhunderts', *Schweizerische Zeitschrift für Geschichte* 29: 750–64

Stettler, B. (1985), 'Der Sempacher Brief von 1393 – ein verkanntes Dokument aus der älteren Schweizergeschichte', *Schweizerische Zeitschrift für Geschichte* 35: 1–20

Stettler, B. (1988), 'Landfriedenswahrung in schwieriger Zeit – Zürichs äussere Politik zu Beginn des 15. Jahrhunderts', *Schweizerische Zeitschrift für Geschichte* 38: 45–61

Suter, B. (1977), *Arnold von Winkelried, der Heros von Sempach. Die Ruhmesgeschichte eines Nationalhelden*, Stans

Tremp, E. (1990), 'Buchhaltung des Jenseits. Das Buss- und Ablasswesen in der Innerschweiz im späteren Mittelalter', *Der Geschichtsfreund* 143: 103–44

Vaughan, R. (1973), *Charles the Bold. The last Valois duke of Burgundy*, London

Vismara, G., Cavanna, A. and Vismara, P. (1990), *Ticino medievale. Storia di una terra lombarda*, Locarno

Wackernagel, H.G. (1956), *Altes Volkstum der Schweiz. Gesammelte Schriften zur historischen Volkskunde*, Basle

Walder, E. (1983), 'Das torechte Leben von 1477 in der bernischen Politik 1477 bis 1481', *Berner Zeitschrift für Geschichte und Heimatkunde* 45: 73–134

Walder, E. (1994), *Das Stanser Verkommnis. Ein Kapitel eidgenössischer Geschichte*, Stans

Weishaupt, M. (1992), *Bauern, Hirten und 'frume edle puren'. Bauern- und Bauernstaatsideologie in der spätmittelalterlichen Eidgenossenschaft und der nationalen Geschichtsschreibung der Schweiz*, Basle

Zahnd, U.M. (1979), *Die Bildungsverhältnisse in den bernischen Ratsgeschlechtern im ausgehenden Mittelalter. Verbreitung, Charakter und Funktion der Bildung in der politischen Führungsschicht einer spätmittelalterlichen Stadt*, Berne

Zangger, A. (1987), 'Zur Verwaltung der St. Galler Klosterherrschaft unter Abt Ulrich

Rösch', in W. Vogler (ed.), *Ulrich Rösch, St. Galler Fürstabt und Landesherr. Beiträge zu seinem Wirken und seiner Zeit*, St Gallen, pp. 151–78
Zehnder, L. (1976), *Volkskundliches in der älteren schweizerischen Chronistik*, Basle

26 THE STATES OF SCANDINAVIA, C. 1390–C. 1536

Primary sources

Aktstykker vedrørende Erik of Pommerns afsættelse som konge af Danmark, ed. A. Hude, Copenhagen (1897; repr. 1971)
Den danske rigslovgivning 1397–1513, ed. Å. Andersen, Copenhagen (1989)
Den danske rigslovgivning 1513–1523, ed. Å. Andersen, Copenhagen (1991)

Secondary works

Note: *(D)=Danish; (N)=Norwegian; (S)=Swedish*

Ahnlund, N. (1944), 'Till diskussionen om 1400-talets svenska riksmöten', *Historisk Tidskrift* (S) 64: 1–28
Albrectsen, E. (1981), *Herredømmet over Sønderjylland 1375–1404. Studier over Hertugdømmets lensforhold og indre opbygning på dronning Margrethes tid*, Copenhagen
Aldener, G. (1946–8), 'Kronologiska synspunkter på Amund Sigurdsson Bolts uppror', *Historisk Tidskrift* (N) 34: 407–22
Anderson, I. (1960), *Sveriges historia*, 5th edn, Stockholm
Anthoni, E. (1955), 'Drottning Margaretas frälseräfst i Finland', *Historisk Tidskrift för Finland* 40: 1–31
Arup, E. (1902–4), 'Den finansielle side af erhvervelsen af hertugdømmerne 1460–1487', *Historisk Tidskrift* (D) 7 (4): 317–88, 399–489
Authen Blom, G. (ed.), (1977) *Urbaniseringsprosessen i norden I*, Oslo, Bergen and Tromsø
Benedictow, O.J. (1974), 'Knut Alvsson og hans vei till opprør', *Historisk Tidskrift* (N) 53: 122–47
Benedictow, O.J. (1977), *Norges historie*, V: *1448–1536*, Oslo
Bergsland, K. (1970), 'Om middelalderens Finnmarker', *Historisk Tidskrift* (N) 49: 365–409
Bergström, R. (1943), *Studier till den stora krisen i nordens historia 1517–1523*, Uppsala
Beyer, M. (1975), 'Den norske tronfølgeutviklingen 1319–1450', *Historisk Tidskrift* (N) 54: 181–224
Bruun, H. (1932–4), 'Var udstederne af Opsigelsesbrevet af 23. Juni 1439 alle Rigsraader?', *Historisk Tidskrift* (D) 10 (2): 84–92
Bruun, H. (1960–2), 'Biskop Jens Andersen (Lodehat) som oppositionsfører', *Historisk Tidskrift* (D) 11 (6): 427–66
Bruun, H. (1960–2), 'Kalundborgvidissen 1425 af Kalmarunionsbrevet 1397', *Historisk Tidskrift* (D) 11 (6): 521–73
Carlsson, G. (1915), *Hemming Gadh. En statsman och prelat från Sturetiden. Biografisk studie*, Uppsala

Carlsson, G. (1938), 'König Erich der Pommer und sein baltischer Imperialismus', *Baltische Studien*, Neue Folge, 40: 1–17

Carlsson, G. (1941), *Sveriges historia. Senare Medeltiden*, I: *Tidsskedet 1389–1448*, Stockholm

Carlsson, G. (1949a), 'Svante Nilssons Finlandsexpedition 1504 och Sören Norby', *Historisk Tidskrift* (S) 69: 41–50

Carlsson, G. (1949b), 'Några problem i Sturetidens historia', *Historisk Tidskrift* (S) 69: 229–53

Carlsson, G. (1955), *Kalmar recess 1483*, Historiskt Arkiv, III, Stockholm

Christensen, A.E. (1951–2), 'Erik af Pommerns danske kongemagt', *Scandia* 21: 44–60

Christensen, A.E. (1980), *Kalmarunionen og nordisk politik 1319–1439*, Copenhagen

Christensen, H. (1983), *Len og magt i Danmark 1439–1481*, Aarhus

Dahlerup, T. (1989), *Danmarks historie*, VI: *De fire stænder, 1400–1500*, Copenhagen

Enemark, P. (1957–8), 'Den økonomiske baggrund for de første oldenborgske kongers udenrigspolitik', *Jyske Samlinger Ny rk.* 4: 1–20

Enemark, P. (1982), 'Christian I og forholdet til Sverige 1448–1454', *Historie. Jyske Samlinger Ny rk.* 14: 440–92

Erslev, K. (1882), *Dronning Margrethe og Kalmarunionens grundlæggelse*, Copenhagen

Erslev, K. (1901), *Erik af Pommern, hans kamp for Sønderjylland og Kalmarunionens opløsning*, Copenhagen

Etting, V. (1986), *Margrete den Første*, Copenhagen

Friedland, K. (1991), *Die Hanse*, Stuttgart, Berlin and Cologne

Fritze, K. (1964), 'Dänemark und die hansische-holländische Konkurrenz in der Ostsee zu Beginn des 15. Jahrhunderts', *Wissenschaftliche Zeitschrift der Universität Greifswald*, Gesellschaftswissenschaftliche Reihe 13: 79–87

Fyllingsnes, F. (1990), *Undergongen til dei norrøne bygdene på Grønland i seinmellomalderen: eit forskningshistorisk oversyn*, Oslo

Gissel, S., Jutikkala, E., Österberg, E., Sandnes, J. and Teitsson, B. (1981), *Desertion and land colonisation in the Nordic countries c. 1300–1600. Comparative report from the Scandinavian research project on deserted farms and villages*, Det Nordiske Ødegårdsprojekt Publikation, 11, Stockholm

Gjerset, K. (1924), *History of Iceland*, New York

Gregersen, H.V. (1981), *Slesvig og Holsten før 1830*, Copenhagen

Hamre, L. (1946–8), 'Omkring stadfestingen av sættergjerden i 1458', *Historisk Tidsskrift* (N) 34: 205–19

Hoffmann, E. (1990), *Geschichte Schleswig-Holsteins*, IV, pt 2: *Spätmittelalter und Reformationszeit*, Neumünster

Hørby, K. (1989) *Danmarks historie*, V: *Velstands krise og tusind baghold, 1250–1400*, Copenhagen

Hørby, K. and Venge, M. (1980), *Danmarks historie, II, pt I: 1340–1559*, Copenhagen

Imsen, S. (1972), *Arv. Annammelse. Valg. En studie i norsk tronfølgerett i tidsrommet 1319–1450*, Oslo

Imsen, S. and Sandnes, J. (1977), *Norges historie*, IV: *1319–1448*, Oslo

Jutikkala, E. and Pirinen, K. (1978), *Histoire de la Finlande*, Neuchâtel

Keller, C. (1989), *The eastern settlement reconsidered. Some analyses of Norse medieval Greenland*, Oslo

Kjersgaard, E. (1970), *Danmarks historie*, IV: *1241–1448*, Copenhagen

Kjersgaard, E. and Hvidtfeldt, J. (1970), *Danmarks historie*, V: *1448–1533*, Copenhagen

Koht, H. (1956), *Dronning Margareta og Kalmarunionen*, Kriseår i norsk historie, 5, Oslo

Kongemagt og Samfund i Middelalderen. Festskrift til Erik Ulsig på 60-årsdagen 13 februar 1988 (1988), ed. P. Enemark *et al.*, Aarhus

Kraft, S. (1944), *Sveriges historia. Senare Medeltiden*, II: *Tidsskedet 1448–1520*, Stockholm

Kraft, S. (1971), *Tre senmedeltida godsorganisationer*, Skånsk senmedeltid och renässans, 9, Lund

Kumlien, K. (1953), *Sverige och hanseaterna. Studier i svensk politik och utrikeshandel*, Kungl. Vitterhets-, historie- och antikvitetsakademiens handlingar, Stockholm

Linton, M. (1971), *Drottning Margareta. Fullmäktig fru och rätt husbonde. Studier i Kalmarunionens förhistoria*, Studica Historia Gothoburgensia, XII, Stockholm

Linton, M. (1973), 'De ekonomiska förutsättningarna för drottning Margaretas politiska program', *Scandia* 39: 39–63

Lönnroth, E. (1938), 'Slaget på Brunkeberg och dess förhistoria', *Scandia* 11: 159–213

Lönnroth, E. (1969), *Sverige och Kalmarunionen 1397–1457*, 2nd edn, Studia Historica Gothoburgensia, X, Göteborg

Losman, B. (1970), *Norden och reformkonsilierna 1408–1449*, Studia Historica Gothoburgensia, XI, Göteborg

Losman, B. (1972), 'Drottning Margaretas ekonomi och donationspolitik', *Scandia* 38: 26–58

Lund, N. and Hørby, K. (1980), *Dansk socialhistorie*, II: *Samfundet i vikingetic og middelalder 800–1500*, Copenhagen

Lundbak, H. (1985), '. . . *Såfremt som vi skulle være deres lydige borgere'. Rådene i København og Malmø 1516–1536 og deres politiske virksomhed i det feudale samfund*, Odense

Mare Balticum. Beiträge zur Geschichte des Ostseeraums in Mittelalter und Neuzeit. Festschrift zum 65. Geburtstag von Erich Hoffmann (1992), ed. W. Paravicini *et al.*, Kieler Historische Studien, 36, Sigmaringen

Marmøy, R. (1963), *Vårt folks historie*, IV: *Gjennom Bølgedalen, 1387–1660*, Oslo

Middelalderstudier. Tilegnede Aksel E. Christensen på tresårsdagen 11 september 1966 (1966), ed. T.E. Chistiansen *et al.*, Copenhagen

Niitemaa, V. (1960), *Der Kaiser und die nordische Union bis zu den Burgunderkriegen*, Annales Academiae Scientiarum Fennicae, ser. B, CXVI, Helsinki

Den nordiske adel i senmiddelalderen. Struktur, funktioner og internordiske relationer (1971), Copenhagen

Olesen, J.E. (1980), *Rigsråd. Kongemagt. Union. Studier over det danske rigsråd og den nordiske kongemagts politik 1434–1449*, Aarhus

Olsson, G. (1946), 'Freden i Köpenhamn 1509', *Studier tillägnade Curt Weibull*, Göteborg, 313–35

Olsson, G. (1947), *Stat och kyrka i Sverige vid medeltidens slut*, Göteborg

Olsson, G. (1950), 'Sverige och Danmark 1501–1508', *Scandia* 20: 38–87

Olsson, G. (1953), 'Sverige och landet vid Göta älvs mynning under medeltiden', Göteborg Högskolas Årsskrift, 59, pt 3, Göteborg

Palme, S.U. (1949), *Riksföreståndarvalet 1512. Studier i nordisk politik og svensk statsrätt 1470–1523*, Uppsala Universitets Årsskrift 1949, 7, Uppsala

Palme, S.U. (1950a), 'Till den statsrättliga tolkningen av 1397 års acta', *Scandia* 20: 88–97

Palme, S.U. (1950b), *Sten Sture den äldre*, Stockholm

Pasternak, J. (1960), 'Erik af Pommern og købstadsforordningen af 1422, 15. februar', *Scandia* 26: 329–42

Petersen, E.L. (1968–9), 'Henrik Krummedige og Norge. Studier over Danmarks forhold til Norge 1523–1533', *Historisk Tidsskrift* (D) 12 (3): 1–82

Petersen, E.L. (1972), 'Frederik I, Tyge Krabbe og Vincens Lunge. Studier over den danske regerings norske politik 1525–30', *Historisk Tidsskrift* (N) 51: 101–49

Petersen, E.L. (1974), 'Monarchy and nobility in Norway in the period around 1500', *Mediaeval Scandinavia* 7: 126–55

Petersen, E.L. (1980), *Dansk socialhistorie, III: Fra standssamfund til rangssamfund 1500–1700*, Copenhagen

Poulsen, B. (1990), 'Slesvig før delingen i 1490. Et bidrag til senmiddelalderens finans-forvaltning', *Historisk Tidsskrift* (D) [15 (5)] 90: 38–63

Profiler i nordisk senmiddelalder og renaissance. Festskrift til Poul Enemark. På tresårsdagen 13 april 1983 (1983), ed. S.E. Green Pedersen *et al.*, Arusia-Historiske Skrifter, II, Aarhus

Rebas, H. (1976), *Infiltration och handel. Studier i senmedeltida nordisk Baltikumpolitik, I: Tiden omkring 1440–1479*, Göteborg

Rebas, H. (1977), 'Högadlig intressepolitik, slaget på S:t Jørgensbjerg och Köpenhamnstraktaterna År 1441', *Scandia* 43: 136–84

Riis, T. (1988), 'La Baltique et le monde baltique au XVe siècle', *Critica storica*, 25: 713–28

Riis, T. (1989), *Should auld acquaintance be forgot . . . Scottish–Danish relations c. 1450–1707*, 2 vols., Odense

Riis, T. (ed.) (1995), *Studien zur Geschichte des Ostseeraumes im 15. Jahrhundert*, Odense

Rosén, J. (1950), 'Drottning Margaretas svenska räfst', *Scandia* 20: 169–246

Rosén, J. (1969), *Svensk historia, I: Tiden före 1718*, 3rd edn, Stockholm

Sällström, Å.M. (1951), *Aristokrati och hierarki i det medeltida Sverige, I: Studier kring Kalmarmötet år 1397*, Lund

Schandt, R.H. (1975), 'The Gotland campaign of the Teutonic knights, 1398–1408', *Journal of Baltic Studies* 6: 247–58

Schreiner, J. (1934–6), 'Norges overgang fra arverike til valgrike', *Historisk Tidsskrift* (N) 30: 312–31

Schreiner, J. (1935), *Hanseatene og Norges nedgang*, Oslo

Schreiner, J. (1941), *Hanseatene og Norge i det 16. århundre*, Oslo

Schreiner, J. (1948), *Pest og prisfall i senmiddelalderen. Et problem i norsk historie*, Avhandlinger utgitt av Det Norske Videnskaps-Akademi i Oslo, II, Historisk-filosofisk klasse 1948, no. 1, Oslo

Schreiner, J. (1952), 'Hærmakt og riksstyre', *Historisk Tidsskrift* (N) 36: 99–139

Schreiner, J. (1956), 'Hyllingsbrevene fra 1389', *Historisk Tidsskrift* (N) 37: 333–46

Sjöberg, E. (1966–7), 'Odenseprivilegiet af 1527', *Historisk Tidsskrift* (D) 12 (2): 337–62

Skyum-Nielsen, N. (1955–7), 'Ærkekonge og ærkebiskop. Nye træk i dansk kirkehisto-rie 1376–1536', *Scandia* 23: 1–101

Skyum-Nielsen, N. (1964), *Blodbadet i Stockholm og dets juridiske maskering*, Copenhagen

Sundström, H. (1974), 'Bebyggelseutvecklingen i Övre Norrland under senmedelti-den', *Scandia* 40: 192–205

Tuck, A. (1972), 'Some evidence for Anglo-Scandinavian relations at the end of the fourteenth century', *Mediaeval Scandinavia* 5: 75–88

Venge, M. (1972), *Christian 2.s fald. Spillet om magten i Danmark januar–februar 1523*, Odense

Venge, M. (1977), *'Når vinden føjer sig . . .' Spillet om magten i Danmark marts-december 1523*, Odense

Werlich, R.-G (1989), 'Königtum und Städte in Dänemark, 1340–1439', dissertation, University of Greifswald

Westergaard, W. (1932), 'The Hansa towns and Scandinavia on the eve of Swedish independence', *JModH* 4: 349–60

Westergaard, W. (1937), 'Denmark, Russia, and the Swedish revolution, 1480–1503', *Slavonic Review* 16: 129–40

Westin, G.T. (1948–49), 'Striden kring riksföreståndarvalen 1512', *Scandia* 19: 214–65

Westin, G.T. (1958), *Riksföreståndaren och makten. Politiska utvecklingslinier i Sverige 1512–1517*, Skrifter utgivna av K. Vetenskapssocieteten i Lund, 52, Lund

Westin, G.T. (1971), *Maktkamp i senmedeltidens Sverige: uppsatser och studier*, Stockholm

Wie Andersen, L. *et al.* (1975), *Uppsala-Overenskomsten 1520: Magtstruktur og magtkamp i Sverige, januar–oktober 1520*, Odense

Wieselgren, G. (1949), *Sten Sture d. Y. och Gustav Trolle*, Lund

Wittendorff, A. (1989), *Danmarks historie*, VII: *På Guds og Herskabs nåde, 1500–1600*, Copenhagen

Würtz Sørensen, J. (1983), *Bondeoprør i Danmark 1438–1441*, Odense

Yrwing, H. (1958), 'Lybeck, de nordiska rikena och konungavalet i Strängnäs 1523', *Scandia* 24: 194–254

Yrwing, H. (1966), 'Frän riksföreståndarvalet 1470 till slaget vid Brunkeberg', *Scandia* 32: 124–68

Yrwing, H. (1968), 'Sten Sture, Ivar Axelsson och unionsfrågan 1471–1484', *Scandia* 34: 100–63

Yrwing, H. (1970), 'Ivar Axelssons fall', *Scandia* 36: 17–45

Yrwing, H. (1979), 'Baltisk intressepolitik och den nordjydska bonderesningen 1441', *Scandia* 45: 205–22

Yrwing, H. (1986), 'Kampen om Östersjömarknaderna under 1500-talets första decennier', *Scandia* 52: 5–38

27 HUNGARY: CROWN AND ESTATES

Primary sources

Bonfini, Antonius, *Rerum ungaricarum decades*, ed. I. Fógel, L. Juhász, B. Iványi, 4 vols., Budapest (1941–62)

Decreta regni Hungariae. Gesetze und Verordnungen Ungarns 1301–1457, ed. F. Döry, G. Bónis and V. Bácskai, Budapest (1976)

Decreta regni Hungariae. Gesetze und Verordnungen Ungarns 1458–1490, ed. F. Döry, G. Bónis, G. Érszegi and S. Teke, Budapest (1989)

The laws of medieval Hungary. Decreta regni mediævalis Hungariæ, III, 1301–1457, ed. and trans. J.M. Bak, P. Engel and J.R. Sweeney, Salt Lake City (1992)

The laws of medieval Hungary. Decreta regni mediævalis Hungariæ, II, 1458–90, ed. and trans. J.M. Bak, L.S. Domonkos and P.B. Harvey, Los Angeles (1995)

Monumenta rusticorum in Hungaria rebellium anno MDXIV, coll. A. Fekete-Nagy, ed. V. Kenéz, L. Solymosi and G. Érszegi, Budapest (1979)

Thurócz, Johannes de, *Chronica Hungarorum*, ed. E. Galántai, J. Kristó and E. Mályusz, 2 vols. in 3, Budapest (1985–8)

Vitéz de Zredna, Johannes, *Opera quæ supersunt*, ed. I. Boronkai, Budapest (1980)

Zsigmondkori oklevéltár (Calendar for the age of Sigismund), ed. E. Mályusz, 2 vols. in 3 (to 1411 so far), Budapest (1954–)

Secondary works

Bak, J.M. (1973), *Königtum und Stände in Ungarn im 14.–16. Jh.*, Wiesbaden

Bak, J.M. (1987), 'Monarchie im Wellental: Materielle Grundlagen des ungarischen Königtums im fünfzehnten Jahrhundert', in R. Schneider (ed.), *Das spätmittelalterliche Königtum im europäischen Vergleich*, Sigmaringen, Vorträge und Forschungen, 32, pp. 347–84

Bak, J.M. (1991), 'The Hungary of Matthias Corvinus', *Bohemia: A Journal for Central European History* 31: 339–49

Bak, J.M. and Király, B.K. (eds.) (1982), *From Hunyadi to Rakocki. War and society in late medieval and early modern Hungary*, Brooklyn, N.Y.

Bernath, M. (ed.) (1980), *Historische Bücherkunde Südosteuropa*, I, 2, Munich, pp. 755–1227

Birnbaum, M.D. (1981), *Janus Pannonius. Poet and politician*, Zagreb

Bónis, G. (1965a), 'The Hungarian feudal diet: 13th to 18th centuries', in *Recueils de la Société Jean Bodin*, XXV: *Gouvernés et gouvernants*, Brussels

Bónis, G. (1965b), 'Ständisches Finanzwesen in Ungarn im frühen 16. Jahrhundert', in *Nouvelles études historiques publiées à l'occasion du XIIe Congrès international des sciences historiques*, Budapest, I, pp. 83–103

Csapodi, C. and Csapodi-Gárdonyi, K. (1982), *Bibliotheca Corviniana*, Budapest

Fine, J.V.A. (1987), *The late medieval Balkans. A critical survey from the late twelfth century to the Ottoman conquest*, Ann Arbor

Fügedi, E. (1986a), *Castle and society in medieval Hungary (1000–1437)*, Budapest

Fügedi, E. (1986b), *Kings, bishops, nobles and burghers in medieval Hungary*, ed. J.M. Bak, London

Held, J. (1977), 'Military reform in early fifteenth-century Hungary', *East European Quarterly* 11: 129–39

Klaniczay, T. and Jankovics, J. (eds.) (1994), *Matthias Corvinus and the humanism in central Europe*, Budapest

Kubinyi, A. (1977), 'Die Wahlkapitulationen Wladislaws II. in Ungarn', in R. Vierhaus (ed.), *Herrschaftsverträge, Wahlkapitulationen, Fundamentalgesetze*, Göttingen

Kubinyi, A. (1991), 'Stände und Staat in Ungarn in der zweiten Hälfte des 15. Jh.s', *Bohemia: A Journal for Central European History* 31: 312–25

Mályusz, E. (1965), 'Les débuts du vote de la taxe par les ordres dans la Hongrie féodale', in *Nouvelles études historiques publiées à l'occasion du XIIe Congrès international des sciences historiques*, Budapest, I, pp. 55–82

Mályusz, E. (1990), *Kaiser Sigismund in Ungarn 1387–1437*, trans. A. Szmodits, Budapest

Marosi, E. (1991) 'Die "Corvinische Renaissance" in Mitteleuropa', *Bohemia: A Journal for Central European History* 31: 326–38

Nehring, K. (1989), *Matthias Corvinus, Kaiser Friedrich III. und das Reich. Zum hunyadisch-habsburgischen Gegensatz im Donauraum*, 2nd rev. edn, Munich

Perjés, G. (1989) *The fall of the medieval kingdom of Hungary. Mohács 1526–Buda 1541*, Boulder and Highland Lakes

Rady, M. (1985), *Medieval Buda. A study in municipal government and jurisdiction in the kingdom of Hungary*, Boulder

Rázsó, G. (ed.) (1990), *Hunyadi Mátyás*, Budapest

Russocki, S. (1979), 'Structures politiques dans l'Europe des Jagellon', *Acta Poloniae historica* 39: 101–42

Schallaburg -'82. Matthias Corvinus und die Renaissance in Ungarn (1982), Katalog des Niederösterreichischen Landesmuseum, 118, Vienna

Sugar, P.F. and Hanák, P. (eds.) (1990), *A history of Hungary*, Bloomington and Indianapolis, pp. 54–82

Szakály, F. (1979), 'Phases of Turco-Hungarian warfare before the battle of Mohács (1365–1526)', *Acta Orientalia Academiæ Scientiarum Hungaricæ* 23: 65–111

28 THE KINGDOM OF POLAND AND THE GRAND DUCHY OF LITHUANIA, 1370–1506

Secondary works

General books and syntheses

Bardach, J. and Kaczmarczyk, Z. (1964–6), *Historia państwa i prawa*, 2 vols., Warsaw

The Cambridge history of Poland (1950), ed. W.T. Reddaway, I, Cambridge

Dabrowski, J. (1926), 'Dzieje Polski średniowiecznej, 1333–1506', *Dzieje Polski Średniowiecznej*, Cracow

Halecki, O. (1983), *A history of Poland*, ed. A. Polonsky, London

Historia Polski (1964), ed. Institute of History, Polish Academy of Sciences, 4th edn, I–III, Warsaw

Kieniewicz, S. (ed.) (1975), *History of Poland*, 2nd edn, Warsaw

Kumor, B. and Obertyński, Z. (eds.) (1974), *Historia kosciola w Polsce*, I, Poznań

Polski slownik biograficzny (1936–) 33 vols., Cracow

Poland and Lithuania

Bardach, J. (1988), *O dawnej i niedawnej Litwie*, Poznań

Biskup, M. (1967), *Wojna Trzynastoletnia z Zakonem Krzyżackim*, Warsaw

Biskup, M. and Górski, K. (1987), *Kazimierz Jagiellonczyk. Zbiór studiów o Polsce drugiej połowy XV w.*, Warsaw

Biskup, M. and Labuda, G. (1986), *Dzieje Zakonu Krzyżackiego w Prusach*, Danzig

Bloockman, H. (1981), *Der Deutsche Orden. Zwölf Kapitel aus seiner Geschichte*, Munich

Ekdahl, S. (1982), *Die Schlacht bei Tannenberg 1410. Quellenskritische Untersuchungen*, I, Berlin

Gasiorowski, A. (ed.) (1984), *The Polish nobility in the Middle Ages*, Wrocław

Gieysztor, A. (ed.) (1972), *Polska dzielnicowa i zjednoczona. Panstwo, Spoleczeństwo, Kultura*, Warsaw

Halecki, O. (1919–20), *Dzieje Unii jagiellońskiej*, 2 vols., Cracow

Halecki, O. (1991), *Jadwiga of Anjou and the rise of east central Europe*, ed. T.V. Gromada, Boulder

Kłoczowski, J. (1984), *Europa słowiańska XIV–XV w.*, Warsaw

Krzyżaniakowa, J. and Ochmański, J. (1990), *Władysław II Jagiełło*, Wrocław

Kuczyński, S.K. (1987), *Wielka wojna z Zakonem Krzyżackim w latach 1410–1411*, 5th edn, Warsaw

Łowmiański, H. (1983), *Studia nad dziejami Wielkiego Księstwa Litewskiego*, Poznań

Ludwig, M. (1983), *Tendenzen und Erfolge der modernen polnischen spätmittelalterlichen Forschung unter besonderer Berücksichtigung der Stadtgeschichte*, Berlin

Nadolski, A. (1990), *Grunwald. Problemy wybrane*, Olsztyń

Ochmanski, J. (1986), *Dawna Litwa. Studia historyczne*, Olsztyń

29 RUSSIA

Primary sources

Chronicles

Kuzmin, A.G., *Riazanskoe letopisanie*, Moscow (1965)

Likhachev, D.S., *Russkie letopisi i ikh kul'turno-istoricheskoe znachenie*, Moscow and Leningrad (1947)

Lur'e, I.S., *Dve istorii Rusi XV veka*, St Petersburg (1994)

Lur'e, I.S., 'Eshche raz o svode 1448 g. i Novgorodskoi Karamzinskoi letopisi', *Trudy Otdela drevnerusskoi literatury* 32 (1977), pp. 199–218

Lur'e, I.S., *Obshcherusskie letopisi XIV–XV vv.*, Leningrad (1976)

Lur'e, I.S., 'K probleme svoda 1448 g.', *Trudy Otdela drevnerusskoi literatury* 24 (1969), pp. 142–6

Murav'eva, L.L., *Letopisanie severo-vostochnoi Rusi kontsa XIII–nachala XV veka*, Moscow (1983)

Nasonov, A.N., *Istoriia russkogo letopisaniia XI–nachala XVIII veka*, Moscow (1969)

Nasonov, A.N., 'Letopisnye pamiatniki Tverskogo kniazhestva', *Izvestiia Akademii nauk SSSR. Seriia 7: Otdelenie gumanitarnykh nauk*, nos. 9–10 (1930), pp. 709–73

Nasonov, A.N., *Pskovskie letopisi*, 2 fascs., Moscow and Leningrad (1941–55)

Priselkov, M.D., *Istoriia russkogo letopisaniia XV–XV vv.*, Leningrad 1940)

Priselkov, M.D., 'Letopisanie Zapadnoi Ukrainy i Belorussii', *Uchenye zapiski Leningradskogo gosudarstvennogo universiteta. Seriia istoricheskikh nauk* 7, no. 67 (1940), pp. 5–24

Shakhmatov, A.A., *Obozrenie russkikh letopisnykh svodov XIV–XVI vv.*, Moscow and Leningrad (1938)

Shakhmatov, A.A., *Razyskaniia o drevneishikh russkikh letopisnykh svodakh*, St Petersburg (1908)

Zimin, A.A., *Russkie letopisi i khronografy kontsa XV–XVI vv. Uchebnoe posobie*, Moscow (1960)

Other selected sources

Akty feodal'nogo zemlevladeniia i khoziaistva XIV–XVI vekov, 3 vols., Moscow (1951–61)

Akty istoricheskie, I (1841), 5 vols., St Petersburg (1841–2); *Dopolneniia k Aktam istoricheskim*, 12 vols., St Petersburg (1846–72)

Akty istoricheskie, otn. k Rosii, izvlechennye iz inostrannykh arkhivov i bibliotek . . . A. K. Turgenevym, 3 vols., St Petersburg (1841–8); *Dopolneniia k Aktam istoricheskim . . . Turgenevym*, St Petersburg (1848)

Akty iuridicheskie, St Petersburg (1838)

Akty, otnosiashchiesia do iuridicheskogo byta drevnei Rossii, 3 vols., St Petersburg (1857–84)

Akty, otnosiashchiesia k istorii Iuzhnoi i Zapadnoi Rossii, 15 vols., St Petersburg (1846–92)

Akty, otnosiashchiesia k istorii Zapadnoi Rossii, I–II (1846–8), 5 vols., St Petersburg (1846–53)

Akty, sobrannye v bibliotekakh i arkhivakh Rossiiskoi imperii Arkheograficheskoiu ekspeditsieiu . . ., 4 vols., St Petersburg (1836)

Akty sotsial'no-ekonomicheskoi istorii severo-vostochnoi Rusi kontsa XIV–nachala XVI v., 3 vols., Moscow (1952–64)

Akty sotsial'no-ekonomicheskoi istorii severo-vostochnoi Rusi kontsa XIV–nachala XVI v.. Akty Solovetskogo monastyria, 1479–1571 gg., Leningrad (1988)

Beneshevich, V.N. (ed.), *Drevnerusskaia slavianskaia kormchaia XIV titulov bez tolkovanii*, St Petersburg (1906)

Buganov, V.I. (ed.), *Razriadnaia kniga 1475–1598 gg.*, Moscow (1966)

Bychkova, M.E. (ed.), *Novye rodoslovnye knigi XVI v.*, in *Redkie istochniki po istorii Rossii*, II Moscow (1977)

Dukhovnye i dogovornye gramoty velikikh i udel'nykh kniazei XIV–XVI vv., Moscow and Leningrad (1950)

Gramoty Velikogo Novgoroda i Pskova, Moscow (1949)

Kalachov, N.V. (ed.), *Pistsovye knigi Moskovskogo gosudarstva XVI v.*, I, pts 1–2, St Petersburg (1872–7)

Likhachev, N.P. (ed.), 'Inoka Fomy "Slovo pokhval'noe o blagovernom velikom kniaze Borise Aleksandroviche"', in *Pamiatniki drevnei pis'mennosti i iskusstva*, CLXVIII, St Petersburg (1908), pp. i–lx, 1–55

Nasonov, A.N. (ed.), *Pskovskie letopisi*, 2 fascs., Moscow (1941–51)

Nasonov, A.N. and Tikhomirov, M.N. (eds.) *Novgorodskaia pervaia letopis' starshego i mladshego izvodov*, Moscow and Leningrad (1950)

Novgorodskie pistsovye knigi, izdannye Arkheograficheskoiu kommissieiu, 6 vols., St Petersburg (1859–1915)

Pamiatniki diplomaticheskikh snoshenii drevnei Rossii s derzhavami inostrannymi, I (1851), 10 vols., St Petersburg (1851–71)

Pamiatniki literatury drevnei Rusi. XIV–seredina XV veka, Moscow (1981)

Pamiatniki literatury drevnei Rusi. Konets XV – pervaia polovina XVI veka, Moscow (1984)

Pamiatniki literatury drevnei Rusi. Vtoraia polovina XV veka, Moscow (1982)

Pamiatniki russkogo prava, I (1952), II (1953), III (1955), IV (1956), 8 vols., Moscow (1952–63)

Pamiatniki russkoi pis'mennosti XV–XVI vv. Riazanskii krai, Moscow (1978)

Polnoe sobranie russkikh letopisei, 38 vols. to date, St Petersburg and Moscow (1841–)

Priselkov, M.D. (ed.), *Troitskaia letopis'. Rekonstruktsiia teksta*, Moscow (1950)
Razriadnaia kniga 1475–1605 gg., 4 vols., in 10 pts to date, Moscow (1977–   )
Rossiiskoe zakonodatel'stvo X–XX vekov v deviati tomakh, 1 (1984), II (1985), 9 vols., Moscow
    (1984–94)
Russkii feodal'nyi arkhiv XIV – pervoi treti XVI veka, Moscow (1986)
Sbornik Imp. Russkogo istoricheskogo obshchestva, XXXV (1882), XLI (1884), LIII (1885), LIX
    (1887), LXXI (1892), XCV (1895), 148 vols., St Petersburg and Petrograd (1866–1918)
Sobranie gosudarstvennykh gramot i dogovorov, I–II (1813–19), 5 vols., Moscow (1813–94)
Storozhev, V.N. (ed.), *Pistsovye knigi Riazanskogo kraia XVI–XVII vv.*, 1 vol. in 3 pts,
    Riazan' (1898–1904)
Tikhomirov, M.N. (ed.), *Zakon sudnyi liudem kratkoi redaktsii*, Moscow (1961)
Tikhomirov, M.N. and L.V. Milov (eds.), *Merilo pravednoe*, Moscow (1961)
Zakonodatel'nye akty Russkogo gosudarstva vtoroi poloviny XVI – pervoi poloviny XVII veka,
    Leningrad (1986)
Zakonodatel'nye akty Velikogo kniazhestva litovskogo XV–XVI vv., Leningrad (1936)

Secondary works

Political chronicles

Alef, G. (1983), *Rulers and nobles in fifteenth-century Muscovy*, London
Alef, G. (1986), *The origins of Muscovite autocracy. The age of Ivan III*, in *Forschungen zur ost-
    europäischen Geschichte* 39
Bazilevich, K. V. (1952), *Vneshniaia politika russkogo tsentralizovannogo gosudarstva. Vtoraia
    polovina XV v.*, Moscow
Bernadskii, V.N. (1961), *Novgorod i novgorodskaia zemlia v XV veke*, Moscow and
    Leningrad
Birnbaum, H. (1981), *Lord Novgorod the Great*, I, Columbus
Bychkova, M.E. (1975), *Rodoslovnye knigi XVI–XVII vv. kak istoricheskii istochnik*,
    Moscow
Cherepnin, L.V. (1948–51), *Russkie feodal'nye arkhivy XIV–XV vekov*, 2 vols., Moscow
    and Leningrad
Cherepnin, L.V. (1960), *Obrazovanie russkogo tsentralizovannogo gosudarstva v 14–15 vv.*,
    Moscow
Croskey, R.M. (1987), *Muscovite diplomatic practice in the reign of Ivan III*, New York and
    London
Crummey, R.O. (1987), *The formation of Muscovy, 1304–1613*, London and New York
Dollinger, P. (1970), *The German Hansa*, London
Fennell, J.L.I. (1963), *Ivan the Great of Moscow*, London
Floria, B.N. (1975), 'O putiakh politicheskoi tsentralizatsii Russkogo gosudarstva (na
    primere Tverskoi zemli)', in *Obshchestvo i gosudarstvo feodal'noi Rusi*, Moscow, pp.
    281–90
Gnevushev, A.M. (1915), *Ocherki ekononomicheskoi i sotsial'noi zhizni sel'skogo naseleniia
    Novgorodskoi oblasti posle prisoedineniia Novgoroda k Moskve*, I, Kiev
Ianin, V.L. (1962), *Novgorodskie posadniki*, Moscow
Ianin, V.L. (1970), *Aktovye pechati drevnei Rusi X–XV vv.*, Moscow
Ianin, V.L. (1981), *Novgorodskaia feodal'naia votchina*, Moscow

Istoriia Moskvy (1952–9), 6 vols. in 7 pts, Moscow

Kafengauz, B.B. (1969), *Drevnii Pskov. Ocherki po istorii feodal'noi respubliki*, Moscow

Kashtanov, S.M. (1967), *Sotsial'no-politicheskaia istoriia Rossii kontsa XV–pervoi poloviny XVI v.*, Moscow

Kashtanov, S.M. (1988), *Finansy srednevekovoi Rusi*, Moscow

Kazakova, N.A. (1975), *Russko-livonskie i russko-ganzeiskie otnosheniia. Konets XIV–nachalo XVI v.*, Leningrad

Khoroshev, A.S. (1980), *Tserkov' v sotsial'no-politicheskoi sisteme novgorodskoi feodal'noi respubliki*, Moscow

Kliuchevskii, V.O. (1957), *Kurs russkoi istorii*, in *Sochineniia*, II, 8 vols., Moscow, 1956–9

Kobrin, V.B. (1985), *Vlast' i sobstvennost' v srednevekovoi Rossii (XV–XVI vv)*, Moscow

Kolankowski, L. (1930), *Dzieje wielkiego księstwa litewskiego za Jagiełłonów*, Warsaw

Langer, L. (1984), 'The *Posadnichestvo* of Pskov: some aspects of urban administration in medieval Russia', *Slavic Review* 43: 46–62

Lur'e, I.S. (1939), 'Rol' Tveri v sozdanii Russkogo natsional'nogo gosudarstva', *Uchenye zapiski Leningradskogo gosudarstvennogo universiteta. Seriia istoricheskikh nauk* 36: 75–92

Martin, J. (1983), 'Muscovy's northeastern expansion: the context and a cause', *Cahiers du monde russe et soviétique* 24: 459–70

Martin, J. (1995), *Medieval Russia, 980–1584*, Cambridge

Maslennikova, N.N. (1955), *Prisoedinenie Pskova k russkomu tsentralizovannomu gosudarstvu*, Leningrad

Nitsche, P. (1972), *Grossfurst und Thronfolger. Die Nachfolgepolitik der Moskauer Herrscher bis zum Ende des Rjurikidenhauses*, Cologne

Nosov, N.E. (1957), *Ocherki po istorii mestnogo upravleniia russkogo gosudarstva pervoi poloviny XVI v.*, Moscow

Ocherki istorii SSSR. Period feodalizma IX–XV vv. (1953), ed. B.D. Grekov *et al.*, 2 pts, Moscow

Presniakov, A.E. (1918a), *Moskovskoe tsarstvo*, Petrograd

Presniakov, A.E. (1918b), *Obrazovanie velikorusskogo gosudarstva*, Petrograd

Russ, H. (1975), *Adel und adelsoppositionen im Moskauer Staat*, Wiesbaden

Thompson, M.W. (1967), *Novgorod the Great*, New York

Tikhomirov, M.N. (1957), *Srednevekovaia Moskva v XIV–XV vekakh*, Moscow

Tikhomirov, M.N. (1966), *Srednevekovaia Rossiia na mezhdunarodnykh putiakh (XI–XV vv)*, Moscow

Vernadsky, G. (1959), *Russia at the dawn of the modern age*, New Haven and London

Zimin, A.A. (1960), *Reformy Ivana Groznogo*, Moscow

Zimin, A.A. (1972a), *Rossiia na poroge novogo vremeni*, Moscow

Zimin, A.A. (1982), *Rossiia na rubezhe XV–XVI stoletii*, Moscow

Zimin, A.A. (1988), *Formirovanie boiarskoi aristokratii v Rossii vo vtoroi polovine XV–pervoi treti XVI v.*, Moscow

Zimin, A.A. (1991), *Vitiaz' na raspute*, Moscow

Culture and ideology

Alef, G. (1966), 'The adoption of the Muscovite two-headed eagle: a discordant view', *Speculum* 41: 1–12

Andreyev, Nikolay (1977), 'Literature in the Muscovite period (1300–1700)', in R. Auty and D. Obolensky, *An introduction to Russian language and literature*, Cambridge, pp. 90–110

Birnbaum, H. (1977), 'Lord Novgorod the Great: its place in medieval culture', *Viator* 8: 215–54

Borisov, N.S. (1986), *Russkaia tserkov' v politicheskoi bor'be XIV–XV vekov*, Moscow

Budovnits, I.U. (1947), *Russkaia publitsistika XVI veka*, Moscow and Leningrad

Bushkovitch, P. (1992), *Religion and society in Russia. The sixteenth and seventeenth centuries*, New York

D'iakonov, M.A. (1889), *Vlast' moskovskikh gosudarei. Ocherki iz istorii politicheskikh idei drevnei Rusi do kontsa XVI veka*, St Petersburg

Fedotov, G.P. (1966), *The Russian religious mind*, II: *The Middle Ages. The thirteenth to the fifteenth centuries*, Cambridge, Mass.

Gol'dberg, A.L. (1969), 'U istokov moskovskikh istoriko-politicheskikh idei XV v.', *Trudy Otdela drevnerusskoi literatury* 24: 147–50

Gol'dberg, A.L. (1975), 'Istoriko-politicheskie idei russkoi knizhnosti XV–XVII vekov', *Istoriia SSSR* 5: 60–77

Gol'dberg, A.L. (1983), 'Ideia "Moskva-tretii Rim" v tsikle sochinenii pervoi poloviny XVI v.', *Trudy Otdela drevnerusskoi literatury* 37: 139–49

Goldfrank, D.M. (1981), 'Moscow, the third Rome', in *Modern encyclopedia of Russian and Soviet history*, XXIII, pp. 118–21

Golubinskii, E.E. (1901–10), *Istoriia russkoi tserkvi*, 2 vols., in 4 pts, Moscow

Halperin, C. (1976), 'The Russian land and the Russian tsar: the emergence of Muscovite ideology, 1380–1408', *Forschungen zur osteuropäischen Geschichte* 23: 7–103

Karger, M.K. (1973), *Novgorod the Great. Architectural guidebook*, Moscow

Kartashev, A.V. (1959), *Ocherki po istorii russkoi tserkvi*, 2 vols., Paris

Kazakova, N.A. and Lur'e, I.S. (1955), *Antifeodal'nye ereticheskie dvizheniia na Rusi XIV–nachala XVI veka*, Moscow and Leningrad

Khoroshev, A.S. (1986), *Politicheskaia istoriia russkoi kanonizatsii (XI–XVI vv.)*, Moscow

Labunka, M. (1978), 'The legend of the Novgorodian white cowl', PhD dissertation, Columbia University

Lazarev, V.N. (1966), *Old Russian murals and mosaics from the XI to the XVI century*, London

Lazarev, V.N. (1976), *Novgorodskaia ikonopis'*, 2nd edn, Moscow

Lazarev, V.N. (1980), *Moskovskaia shkola ikonopisi*, Moscow

Levin, E. (1983), 'The role and status of women in medieval Novgorod', PhD dissertation, Indiana University

Likhachev, D.S. (1958), *Chelovek v literature drevnei Rusi*, Leningrad

Likhachev, D.S. (1967), *Poetika drevnerusskoi literatury*, Leningrad

Likhachev, D.S. (1973), *Razvitie russkoi literatury X–XVII vekov. Epokhi i stili*, Leningrad

Likhachev, D.S. (1987), *Velikii put'. Stanovlenie russkoi literatury, XI–XVII vekov*, Moscow

Lur'e, I.S. (1939), 'Rol' Tveri v sozdanii russkogo natsional'nogo gosudarstva', *Uchenye zapiski Leningradskogo gosudarstvennogo universiteta* 36: 85–109

Lur'e, I.S. (1960), *Ideologicheskaia bor'ba v russkoi publitsistike kontsa XV–nachala XVI veka*, Moscow and Leningrad

Makarii, Metropolitan of Moscow (1857–87), *Istoriia russkoi tserkvi*, 12 vols., St Petersburg

Nitsche, P. (1987), 'Translatio imperii? Beobachtungen zum historischen

Selbstverständnis im Moskauer Zartum um die Mitte des 16. Jahrhunderts', *Jahrbücher für Geschichte Osteuropas* 35: 321–38

Ocherki russkoi kul'tury XIII–XV vekov (1969), 2 pts, Moscow

Pautkin, A.A. (1989), 'Kharakteristika lichnosti v letopis'nykh kniazheskikh nekrologakh', in *Germenevtika drevnerusskoi literatury. XI–XVI veka*, Moscow, pp. 231–46

Pelenski, J. (1977), 'The origins of the official Muscovite claim to the "Kievan inheritance"', *Harvard Ukrainian Studies* 1: 29–52

Pelenski, J. (1983), 'The emergence of the Muscovite claims to the Byzantine–Kievan "imperial inheritance"', *Harvard Ukrainian Studies* 7: 520–31

Philipp, W. (1970), 'Die gedankliche Begründung der Moskauer Autokratie bei ihrer Entstehung (1458–1522)', *Forschungen zur osteuropäischen Geschichte* 15: 59–118

Philipp, W. (1983), 'Die religiöse Begründung der altrussischen Haupstadt', *Forschungen zur osteuropäischen Geschichte* 33: 227–38

Rowland, D. (1979), 'The problem of advice in Muscovite tales about the Time of Troubles', *Russian History* 6: 259–83

Salmina, M.A. (1966), '"Letopisnaia povest" o Kulikovskoi bitve i "Zadonshchina"', in *'Slovo o polku Igoreve' i pamiatniki Kulikovskogo tsikla. K voprosu o vremeni napisaniia 'Slova'*, Moscow and Leningrad, pp. 344–84·

Salmina, M.A. (1970), 'Slovo o zhitii i o prestavlenii velikogo kniazia Dmitriia Ivanovicha, tsaria Rus'kogo', *Trudy Otdela drevnerusskoi literatury* 25: 81–104

Salmina, M.A. (1974), 'K voprosu o datirovke "Skazaniia o Mamaevom poboishche"', *Trudy Otdela drevnerusskoi literatury* 29: 98–124

Salmina, M.A. (1977), 'Eschche raz o datirovke "Letopisnoi povesti" o Kulikovskoi bitve', *Trudy Otdela drevnerusskoi literatury* 32: 3–39

Slovar' knizhnikov i knizhnosti drevnei Rusi, I–II (1987–9), 3 vols. in 5 pts, Leningrad

Smirnova, E.E. (1989), *Moscow icons*, Oxford

Sobolevskii, A.I. (1899), *Zapadnoe vliianie na literaturu moskovskoi Rusi XV–XVII vekov*, St Petersburg

Stökl, G. (1981), 'Staat und Kirche im Moskauer Russland. Die vier Moskauer Wundertäter', *Jahrbücher für Geschichte Osteuropas* 29: 481–93

Szeftel, M. (1979), 'The title of the Muscovite monarch up to the end of the seventeenth century', *Canadian–American Slavic Studies* 13 nos. 1–2: 59–81

Tikhomirov, M.N. (1968), *Russkaia kul'tura X–XVIII vekov*, Moscow

Tikhomirov, N.I. and Ivanov, V.N. (1967), *Moskovskii kreml'. Istoriia arkhitektury*, Moscow

Val'denberg, V. (1916), *Drevnerusskie ucheniia o predalakh tsarskoi vlasti*, Petrograd

Zimin, A.A. (1972b), 'Antichnye motivy v russkoi publitsistike kontsa XV v.', in *Feodal'naia Rossiia vo vsemirnom istoricheskom protsesse*, Moscow, pp. 128–38

Governance

Abramovich, G.V. (1975), 'Pomestnaia sistema i pomestnoe khoziaistvo v Rossii v poslednei chetverti XV i XVI v.', doctoral dissertation, Leningrad

Bardach, J. (1970), *Studia z ustroju prawa Wielkiego księstwa litewskiego XIV–XVII w.*, Warsaw

Bazilevich, K.V. (1945), 'Novgorodskie pomeshchiki iz posluzhil'tsev v kontse XV v.', *Istoricheskie zapiski* 14: 62–80

Blum, J. (1969), *Lord and peasant in Russia from the ninth to the nineteenth century*, New York

Cherepnin, L.V. (1940), 'Iz istorii drevnerusskikh feodal'nykh otnoshenii XIV–XVI vv.', *Istoricheskie zapiski* 9: 31–78

Chernov, A.V. (1954), *Vooruzhennye sily Russkogo gosudarstva v XV–XVII vv.*, Moscow

Dewey, H.W. (1987), 'Political *Poruka* in Muscovite Rus'', *Russian Review* 46: 117–34

D'iakonov, M.A. (1908), *Ocherki obshchestvennogo i gosudarstvennogo stroia drevnei Rusi*, 2nd edn, St Petersburg

Eck, A. (1933), *Le moyen âge russe*, Paris

Floria, B.N. (1972), 'Evoliutsiia podatnogo immuniteta svetskikh feodalov Rossii vo vtoroi polovine XV–pervoi polovine XVI v.', *Istoriia SSSR* 1: 48–71

Gorskii, A.D. (1982), 'O votchinnom sude na Rusi v XIV–XV vv.', in *Rossiia na putiakh tsentralizatsii. Sbornik statei*, Moscow, pp. 25–35

Halbach, U. (1985), *Der russische Fürstenhof vor dem 16. Jahrhundert*, Stuttgart

Hammond, V.E. (1987), 'The history of the Novgorodian *pomest'e*: 1480–1550', PhD dissertation, University of Illinois at Champaign-Urbana

Howes, R.C. (trans. and ed.) (1967), *The testaments of the grand princes of Moscow*, Ithaca

Ivina, L.I. (1979), *Krupnaia votchina severo-vostochnoi Rusi kontsa XIV–pervoi poloviny XVI v.*, Leningrad

Kaiser, D.H. (1980), *The growth of the law in medieval Russia*, Princeton

Keep, J. (1985), *Soldiers of the tsar. Army and society in Russia, 1462–1874*, Oxford

Kleimola, A.M. (1977a), 'The Muscovite autocracy at work: the use of disgrace as an instrument of control', in W.E. Butler (ed.), *Russian law. Historical and political perspectives*, Leiden, pp. 29–50

Kleimola, A.M. (1977b), 'The changing face of the Muscovite aristocracy: the sixteenth century. Sources of weakness', *Jahrbücher für Geschichte Osteuropas* 25: 481–93

Kleimola, A.M. (1979), 'Up through servitude: the changing condition of the Muscovite elite in the sixteenth and seventeenth centuries', *Russian History* 6: 210–29

Kliuchevskii, V.O. (1919), *Boiarskaia duma drevnei Rusi*, 5th edn, St Petersburg

Kliuchevskii, V.O. (1959), *Istoriia soslovii v Rossii*, in *Sochineniia v vos'mi tomakh*, VI, Moscow, pp. 276–463

Kobrin, V.B. (1985), *Vlast' i sobstvennost' v srednevekovoi Rossii (XV–XVI vv.)*, Moscow

Kollmann, N.S. (1987), *Kinship and politics. The making of the Muscovite political system, 1345–1547*, Stanford

Kotliarov, A.N. (1980), 'O boiarskikh posluzhil'tsakh kak istochnike sluzhilogo dvoriantsva (do serediny XVI v.)', in *Russkoe tsentralizovannoe gosudarstvo*, Moscow, pp. 44–7

Lappo, I.I. (1893), *Tverskii uezd v XVI veke*, Moscow

Limonov, I.A. (1987), *Vladimiro-Suzdal'skaia Rus'. Ocherki sotsial'no-politicheskoi istorii*, Moscow

Pavlov-Sil'vanskii, N.P. (1988), *Feodalizm v Rossii*, Moscow

Philipp, W. (1980), 'Zur Frage nach der Existenz altrussischer Stände', *Forschungen zur osteuropäischen Geschichte* 27: 64–76

Rozhdestvenskii, S.V. (1897), *Sluzhiloe zemlevladenie v Moskovskom gosudarstve XVI v.*, St Petersburg

Sergeevich, V.I. (1887), 'Vol'nye i nevol'nye slugi moskovskikh gosudarei', *Nabliudatel'* 6: 58–89

Sergeevich, V.I. (1904), *Lektsii i issledovaniia po drevnei istorii russkogo prava*, 3rd edn, St Petersburg

Szeftel, M. (1965), 'Aspects of feudalism in Russian history', in R. Coulborn (ed.), *Feudalism in history*, Hamden, Conn., pp. 167–82

Vernadsky, G. (1939), 'Feudalism in Russia,' *Speculum* 14: 300–23

Veselovskii, S.B. (1926), *K voprosu o proiskhozhdenii votchinnogo rezhima*, Moscow

Veselovskii, S.B. (1936), *Selo i derevnia v severo-vostochnoi Rusi XIV–XVI vv.*, Moscow and Leningrad

Veselovskii, S.B. (1947), *Feodal'noe zemlevladenie v severo-vostochnoi Rusi*, 1 vol. in 2 pts, Moscow and Leningrad

Veselovskii, S.B. (1969), *Issledovaniia po istorii klassa sluzhilykh zemlevladel'tsev*, Moscow

Vladimirskii-Budanov, M.F. (1909), *Obzor istorii russkogo prava*, 6th edn, St Petersburg

Zimin, A.A. (1959), 'Iz istorii pomestnogo zemlevladeniia na Rusi', *Voprosy istorii* 11: 130–42

Zimin, A.A. (1964), 'O politicheskikh predposylkakh vozniknoveniia russkogo absoliutizma', *Absoliutizm v Rossii (XVI–XVIII vv.)*, Moscow, pp. 18–49

Zimin, A.A. (1970), 'V.I. Lenin o "moskovskom tsarstve" i cherty feodal'noi razdroblennosti v politicheskom stroe Rossii XVI veka', in *Aktual'nye problemy istorii Rossii epokhi feodalizma. Sbornik statei*, Moscow, pp. 270–93

Zimin, A.A. (1973), *Kholopy na Rusi (s drevneishikh vremen do kontsa XV v.)*, Moscow

Trade and agrarian life

Alekseev, I.G. (1966), *Agrarnaia i sotsial'naia istoriia severo-vostochnoi Rusi XV–XVII vv.. Pereiaslavskii uezd*, Moscow and Leningrad

Bater, J.H. and French, R.A. (eds.) (1983), *Studies in Russian historical geography*, 2 vols., London

Budovnits, I.U. (1966), *Monastyri na Rusi i bor'ba s nimi krest'ian v XIV–XVI v.*, Moscow

Cherepnin, L.V. and Nazarov, V.D. (1986), 'Krest'ianstvo na Rusi v seredine XII–kontse XV v.', in *Istoriia krest'ianstva v Evrope*, II: *Epokha feodalizma*, Moscow, pp. 250–86

Danilova, L.V. (1955), *Ocherki po istorii zemlevladenii i khoziaistva v Novgorodskoi zemle v XIV–XV vv.*, Moscow

Gorskii, A.D. (1966), *Ocherki ekonomicheskogo polozheniia krest'ian severo-vostochnoi Rusi XIV–XV vv.*, Moscow

Gorskii, A.D. (1974), *Bor'ba krest'ian za zemliu na Rusi v XV–nachala XVI veka*, Moscow

Grekov, B.D. (1952–4), *Krest'iane na Rusi s drevneishikh vremen do XVII veka*, 2 vols., 2nd edn, Moscow

Kazakova, N.A. (1945), *Rus' i Pribaltika. IX–XVII vv.*, Leningrad

Kazakova, N.A. (1975), *Russko-livonskie i russko-ganzeiskie otnosheniia: Konets XIV–nachalo XVI v.*, Leningrad

Khoroshkevich, A.L. (1963), *Torgovlia Velikogo Novgoroda s Pribaltikoi i Zapadnoi Evropoi v XIV–XV vekakh*, Moscow

Khoroshkevich, A.L. (1980), *Russkoe gosudarstvo v sisteme mezhdunarodnykh otnoshenii kontsa XV–nachala XVI v.*, Moscow

Kochin, G.E. (1965), *Sel'skoe khoziaistvo na Rusi v period obrazovaniia Russkogo tsentralizo-vannogo gosudarstva konets XIII–nachalo XVI v.*, Moscow and Leningrad

Kolycheva, E.I. (1971), *Kholopstvo i krepostnichestvo (konets XV–XVI v.)*, Moscow

Martin, J. (1975), 'Les uškujniki de Novgorod: marchands ou pirates?', *Cahiers du monde russe et soviétique* 16: 5–18

Martin, J. (1986), *Treasure of the land of darkness. The fur trade and its significance for medieval Russia*, Cambridge

Sakharov, A.M. (1959), *Goroda severo-vostochnoi Rusi XIV–XV vekov*, Moscow

Shapiro, A.L. (1971), *Agrarnaia istoriia severo-zapada Rossii. Vtoraia polovina XV–nachala XVI veka*, Leningrad

Shapiro, A.L. (1977), *Problemy sotsial'no-ekonomicheskoi istorii Rusi XIV–XVI vv.*, Leningrad

Shapiro, A.L. (1987), *Russkoe krestianstvo pered zakreposhcheniem XIV–XVI vv.*, Leningrad

Smirnov, P.P. (1947–8), *Posadskie liudi i ikh klassovaia bor'ba do serediny XVII v.*, 2 vols., Moscow and Leningrad

Smith, R.E.F. (1966), 'Medieval agrarian society in its prime: Russia', in M.M. Postan (ed.), *The Cambridge economic history of Europe*, I, Cambridge, pp. 507–47

Smith, R.E.F. (1977), *Peasant farming in Muscovy*, Cambridge

Syroechkovskii, V.E. (1936), *Gosti surozhanie*, Moscow and Leningrad

30 BYZANTIUM: THE ROMAN ORTHODOX WORLD, 1393–1492

Primary sources

Acta patriarchatus Constantinopolitani, in F. Miklosich and I. Müller (eds.), *Acta et diplomata Graeca medii aevi*, II, Vienna (1862)

Clogg, R. (ed. and trans.), *The movement for Greek independence 1770–1821. A collection of documents*, London (1976)

Darrouzès, J. (ed.), 'Sainte-Sophie de Thessalonique d'après un rituel', *Revue des études Byzantines*, 34 (1976), pp. 45–78

Ducas, *Istoria turco-bizantina (1341–1462)* ed. V. Grecu, Bucharest (1958)

Kalonaros, P.P. (ed.), *Chronikon tou Moreos*, Athens (1940)

Lidderdale, H.A. (ed. and trans.), *Makriyannis. The memoirs of General Makriyannis, 1797–1864*, Oxford (1966)

Migne, J.P. (ed.), *Patrologia Graeca*, CXVI, Paris (1866)

Scholarios, George, *Œuvres complètes*, ed. L. Petit, X.A. Siderides and M. Jugie, I–VIII, Paris (1928–36)

Symeon, archbishop of Thessalonika, *Politico-historical works (1416/17 to 1429)*, ed. D. Balfour, Wiener Byzantinistische Studien, XIII, Vienna (1979)

Secondary works

Babinger, F. (1978), *Mehmed the Conqueror and his time*, New Jersey

Balivet, M. (1994), *Romanie Byzantine et pays de Rûm Turc. Histoire d'un espace d'imbrication gréco-Turque*, Istanbul

Bardakjian, K.B. (1982), in Braude and Lewis (1982), I, pp. 89–100

Barker, J.W. (1969), *Manuel II Palaeologus (1391–1425)*, New Brunswick

Beldiceanu, N. and Beldiceanu-Steinherr, I. (1980), 'Recherches sur la Morée', *Südöst-Forschungen* 39: 17–74

Braude, B. (1982), 'Foundation myths of the *millet* system', in Braude and Lewis (1982), I, pp. 69–88

Braude, B. and Lewis, B. (eds.) (1982), *Christians and Jews in the Ottoman Empire*, I–II, New York and London

Bryer, A. (1986), 'Continuity and change in Trebizond's Matzouka/Maçuka valley', in Bryer and Lowry (1986), pp. 51–96

Bryer, A. (1991), 'The Pontic Greeks before the diaspora', *Journal of Refugee Studies* 4: 315–34

Bryer, A. (ed.) (1996), *Mount Athos and Byzantine monasticism*, London

Bryer, A. and Lowry, H. (eds.) (1986), *Continuity and change in late Byzantine and early Ottoman society*, Birmingham and Washington, DC

Bryer, A. and Ursinus, M. (eds.) (1991), *Manzikert to Lepanto. The Byzantine world and the Turks, 1071–1571, Byzantinische Forschungen*, 16, Amsterdam

Bryer, A. and Winfield, D. (1985), *The Byzantine monuments and topography of the Pontos*, I–II, Washington, DC

Buckton, D. (ed.) (1994), *Byzantium. Treasures of Byzantine art and culture from British collections*, London

Cahen, C. (1965), 'Dhimma', in *Encyclopaedia of Islam*, II, pp. 227–31

Chrysanthos [Philippides, Metropolitan of Trebizond] (1933), 'He ekklesia Trapezountos', *Archeion Pontou* 4–5: 1–904

Dennis, G.T. (1960), *The reign of Manuel II Palaeologus in Thessalonica, 1382–1387*, Rome

Dimitriades, V. (1991), 'Byzantine and Ottoman Thessaloniki', in Bryer and Ursinus (1991), pp. 265–9

Ducellier, A. (1981), *La façade maritime de l'Albanie au moyen âge*, Thessalonika

Encyclopaedia of Islam, I–, (1960–), Leiden

Frazee, C.A. (1983), *Catholics and sultans*, Cambridge

Gill, J. (1961), *The Council of Florence*, Cambridge

Gill, J. (1964), *Personalities of the Council of Florence*, Oxford

Ilieva, A. (1991), *Frankish Morea (1205–1262). Socio-cultural interaction between the Franks and the local population*, Athens

Imber, C. (1990), *The Ottoman Empire 1300–1481*, Istanbul

Inalcik, H. (1969), 'The policy of Mehmed II toward the Greek population of Istanbul and the Byzantine buildings of the city', *DOP* 23: 229–49

Inalcik, H. (1973), *The Ottoman Empire. The classical age, 1300–1600*, London

Inalcik, H. (1974), 'Istanbul', in *Encyclopaedia of Islam*, IV, pp. 224–48

Jones, A.H.M. and Monroe, E. (1966), *A history of Ethiopia*, Oxford

Kabrda, J. (1969), *Le système fiscale de l'église Orthodoxe dans l'empire Ottoman*, Brno

Kresten, O. (1970), *Das Patriarchat von Konstantinopel im Ausgehenden 16. Jahrhundert*, Vienna

Laurent, V. (1968), 'Les premiers patriarches de Constantinople sous domination Turque (1454–1476)', *Revue des études Byzantines* 26: 229–63

Lewis, B. (1984), *The Jews of Islam*, London

Lock, P. (1994), *The Franks in the Aegean, 1204–1500*, London and New York

Lowry, H.W. (1981), *Trabzon Şehrinin Islamaşma ve Türkleşmesi 1461–1583*, Istanbul

Lowry, H.W. (1986a), 'Privilege and property in Ottoman Maçuka during the opening decades of the *Tourkokratia*', in Bryer and Lowry (1986), pp. 97–128

Lowry, H.W. (1986b), '"From lesser wars to the mightiest war"; the Ottoman conquest and the transformation of Byzantine urban centers in the fifteenth century', in Bryer and Lowry (1986), pp. 321–38

Lowry, H.W. (1991), 'The fate of Byzantine monastic properties under the Ottomans: examples from Mount Athos, Limnos and Trabzon', in Bryer and Ursinus (1991), pp. 275–312

Magdalino, P. (1993), *The empire of Manuel I Komnenos, 1143–1180*, Cambridge

Matschke, K.P. (1981), *Die Schlacht bei Ankara und das Schicksal von Byzanz*, Weimar

Ménage, V. (1965), 'Djandar', in *Encyclopaedia of Islam*, II, pp. 444–5

Meyendorff, J. (1964), *A study of Gregory Palamas*, London

Nicol, D.M. (1984), *The despotate of Epiros, 1267–1479*, Cambridge

Nicol, D.M. (1993), *The last centuries of Byzantium, 1261–1453*, Cambridge

Nicol, D.M. (1994), *The Byzantine lady. Ten portraits, 1250–1500*, Cambridge

Obolensky, D. (1971), *The Byzantine Commonwealth. Eastern Europe, 500–1453*, London

Pantazopoulos, N.J. (1967), *Church and law in the Balkan peninsula during the Ottoman rule*, Thessalonike

Prosopographisches Lexikon der Palaiologenzeit, ed. E. Trapp, I– (1976–   ), Vienna

Raby, J. (1983), 'Mehmed the conqueror's Greek scriptorium', *DOP* 37: 15–34

Runciman, S. (1955), *The eastern schism*, Oxford

Runciman, S. (1965), *The fall of Constantinople: 1453*, Cambridge

Runciman, S. (1968), *The Great Church in captivity. A study of the patriarchate of Constantinople from the eve of the Turkish conquest to the Greek war of independence*, Cambridge

Runciman, S. (1980), *Mistra. Byzantine capital of the Peloponnese*, London

Turner, C.J.G. (1964), 'Pages from late Byzantine philosophy of history', *BZ* 57: 345–73

Turner, C.J.G. (1969), 'The career of George-Gennadius Scholarios', *Byzantion* 39: 420–55

Ursinus, M.O.H. (1993), 'Millet', in *Encyclopaedia of Islam*, VI, pp. 61–4

Vasiliev, A.A. (1936), *The Goths in the Crimea*, Cambridge, Mass.

Vlora, E. (1973), *Lebenserinnerungen*, II, Munich

Vryonis, S. (1956), 'Isidore Glabas and the Turkish "Devshirme"', *Speculum*, 31: 433–43

Vryonis, S. (1971), *The decline of medieval Hellenism in Asia Minor and the process of Islamization from the eleventh through the fifteenth century*, Los Angeles

Vryonis, S. (1986), 'The Ottoman conquest of Thessaloniki in 1430', in Bryer and Lowry (1986), pp. 281–321

Woodhouse, C.M. (1986), *George Gemistos Plethon. The last of the Hellenes*, Oxford

Zachariadou, E. (1969), 'Early Ottoman documents of the Prodromos monastery (Serres)', *Südöst-Forschungen* 28: 1–12

Zakythinos, D.A. (1975), *Le despotat grec de Morée*, ed. C. Maltézou, I–II, London

31 THE LATIN EAST

Secondary works

Andrews, K. (1953), *Castles of the Morea*, Princeton

Arbel, B., Hamilton, B. and Jacoby, D. (eds.) (1989), *Latins and Greeks in the eastern Mediterranean*, London

Argenti, P. (1958), *The occupation of Chios by the Genoese and their administration of the island: 1346–1566*, 3 vols., Cambridge

Ashtor, E. (1978), *Studies on the Levantine trade in the Middle Ages*, London

Ashtor, E. (1983), *Levantine trade in the later Middle Ages*, Princeton

Ashtor, E. (1986), *East–west trade in the medieval Mediterranean*, London

Ashtor, E. (1992), *Technology, industry and trade. The Levant versus Europe, 1250–1500*, London

Balard, M. (1978), *La Romanie génoise (XIIe–début du XIVe siècle)*, 2 vols., Bibliothèque des Ecoles Françaises d'Athènes et de Rome, 235, Rome

Balard, M. (1989), *La Mer Noire et la Romanie génoise: XIIIe–XVe siècles*, London

Balard, M. (ed.) (1989), *Etat et colonisation au moyen âge et à la Renaissance*, Lyons

Balard, M. and Ducellier, A. (eds.) (1995), *Coloniser au moyen âge*, Paris

Barker, J. (1969), *Manuel II Palaeologus (1391–1425). A study in late Byzantine statesmanship*, New Brunswick

Beck, H.-G., Manoussacas, M. and Pertusi, A. (eds.) (1977), *Venezia centro di mediazione tra oriente e occidente (secoli XV–XVI). Aspetti e problemi*, 2 vols., Florence

Bertelè, T. and Dorini, U. (1956), *Il libro dei conti (Constantinopoli 1436–1440) di Giacomo Badoer*, Rome

Bodnar, E. and Mitchell, C. (1976), *Cyriacus of Ancona's journeys in the Propontis and the northern Aegean*, Philadelphia

Bon, A. (1969), *La Morée franque. Recherches historiques, topographiques et archéologiques sur la Principauté d'Achaïe (1205–1403)*, Bibliothèque des Ecoles Françaises d'Athènes et de Rome, 213, Paris

Bryer, A. and Lowry, H. (eds.) (1986), *Continuity and change in late Byzantine and early Ottoman society*, Birmingham and Washington DC

Cardini, F. (ed.) (1982), *Toscana e terrasanta nel medioevo*, Florence

Cook, M. (ed.) (1970), *Studies in the economic history of the Middle East from the rise of Islam to the present day*, London

Coruni, S. and Donati, L. (1989), *L'Istituto veneto e la missione cretese di Giuseppe Gerola. Collezione fotografica 1900–1902*, Venice

Del Treppo, M. (1972), *I mercanti catalani e l'espansione della corona d'Aragona nel secolo XV*, 2nd edn, Naples

Delaville le Roulx, J. (1913), *Les Hospitaliers à Rhodes jusqu'à la mort de Philibert de Naillac: 1310–1421*, Paris

Ducellier, A. (1981), *La façade maritime de l'Albanie au moyen âge. Durazzo et Valona du XIe au XVe siècle*, Thessalonika

Enlart, C. (1987), *Gothic art and the Renaissance in Cyprus*, rev. edn, London

Fedalto, G. (1973–81), *La chiesa latina in oriente*, 3 vols. (I: 2nd edn), Verona

Frazee, C. (1988), *The island princes of Greece. The dukes of the archipelago*, Amsterdam

Gabriel, A. (1921–3), *La cité de Rhodes* MCCCX–MDXXII, 2 vols., Paris

Geanakopolos, D. (1966), *Byzantine east and Latin west. Two worlds of Christendom in the Middle Ages – studies in ecclesiastical and cultural history*, Oxford

Geanakopolos, D. (1976), *Interaction of the 'sibling' Byzantine and western cultures in the Middle Ages and the Italian Renaissance: 330–1600*, New Haven

Gerola, G. (1905–32), *Monumenti veneti nell'isola di Creta*, 4 vols., Venice

Gill, J. (1959), *The Council of Florence*, Cambridge

Heyd, G. (1885), *Histoire du commerce du Levant au moyen âge*, 2 vols., Leipzig

Hill, G. (1948), *A history of Cyprus*, II–III, Cambridge

Holton, D. (ed.) (1991), *Literature and society in Renaissance Crete*, Cambridge

Housley, N. (1992), *The later crusades 1274–1580. From Lyons to Alcazar*, Oxford

Hussey, J. (ed.) (1966), *The Cambridge medieval history*, IV: *The Byzantine Empire*, pt 1, Cambridge

Jacoby, D. (1971), *La féodalité en Grèce médiévale. Les 'Assises de Romanie' – sources, applications et diffusion*, Paris and The Hague

Jacoby, D. (1979), *Recherches sur la Méditerranée orientale du XIIe au Xve siècle. Peuples, sociétés, économies*, London

Jacoby, D. (1989), *Studies on the crusader states and on Venetian expansion*, London

Karpov, S. (1986), *Imperio di Trebisonda, Venezia, Genova et Roma: 1204–1461*, Rome

Kollias, E. (1988), *The city of Rhodes and the palace of the grand master*, Athens

Krekić, B. (1961), *Dubrovnik (Raguse) et le Levant au moyen âge*, Paris

Krekić, B. (1980), *Dubrovnik, Italy and the Balkans in the late Middle Ages*, London

Lane, F. (1966), *Venice and history. The collected papers of Frederic C. Lane*, Baltimore

Lane, F. (1987), *Studies in Venetian social and economic history*, London

Legrand, E. (ed.) (1892), *Description des îles de l'archipel par Christophe Buondelmonti*, Paris

Lock, P. (1995), *The Franks and the Aegean: 1204–1500*, London

Lopez, R. and Raymond, I. (1955), *Medieval trade in the Mediterranean world*, Records of Civilization: Sources and Studies, 52, New York

Luttrell, A. (1978), *The Hospitallers in Cyprus, Rhodes, Greece and the west: 1291–1440*, London

Luttrell, A. (1982), *Latin Greece, the Hospitallers and the crusades: 1291–1440*, London

Luttrell, A. (1986), *The later history of the Maussolleion and its utilization in the Hospitaller castle of Bodrum*, The Maussolleion at Halikarnassos: Reports of the Danish Archaeological Expedition to Bodrum, 2, Aarhus

Luttrell, A. (1992), *The Hospitallers of Rhodes and their Mediterranean world*, Aldershot

Mas-Latrie, L. de (1852–61), *Histoire de l'île de Chypre sous le règne des princes de la maison de Lusignan*, 3 vols., Paris

Metcalf, D. (1983), *Coinage of the crusades and the Latin east in the Ashmolean Museum*, London

Miller, W. (1908), *The Latins in the Levant. A history of Frankish Greece (1205–1566)*, London

Miller, W. (1921), *Essays on the Latin Orient*, Cambridge

Müller-Wiener, W. (1966), *Castles of the crusaders*, London

Nicol, D. (1984), *The despotate of Epirus: 1267–1479*, Cambridge

Nicol, D. (1988), *Byzantium and Venice: A study in diplomatic and cultural relations*, Cambridge

Oikonomidès, N. (1979), *Hommes d'affaires grecs et latins à Constantinople (XIII–XVe siècles)*, Montreal and Paris

Pertusi, A. (ed.) (1966), *Venezia e l'oriente fra tardo medioevo e Rinascimento*, Civiltà Europea e Civiltà Veneziana: Aspetti e Problemi, 4, Florence

Pertusi, A. (ed.) (1973), *Venezia e il Levante fino al secolo XV*, Florence

Pistarino, G. (1990), *Genovesi d'oriente*, Civico Istituto Colombiano: Studi e Testi, 14, Genoa

Poleggi, E. (ed.) (1989), *Città portuali del Mediterraneo. Storia e archaeologia*, Genoa

Prescott, H. (1954), *Jerusalem journey. Pilgrimage to the Holy Land in the fifteenth century*, London

Ragosta, R. (ed.) (1981), *Le genti del mare mediterraneo*, Biblioteca di Storia Economica, 5, Naples

Richard, J. (1962a), *Chypre sous les Lusignans. Documents chypriotes des archives du Vatican (XIVe et XVe siècles)*, Bibliothèque Archéologique et Historique, 73, Paris

Richard, J. (1962b), *Les relations entre l'occident et l'orient au moyen âge*, London

Richard, J. (1977), *La papauté et les missions d'orient au moyen âge (XIIIe–XVe siècles)*, Collection de l'Ecole Française de Rome, 33, Rome

Richard, J. (1983a), *Croisés, missionaires et voyageurs. Perspectives orientales du monde latin médiéval*, London

Richard, J. (1983b), *Le livre des remembrances de la secrète du royaume de Chypre: 1468–1469*, Sources et Etudes de l'Histoire de Chypre, 10, Nicosia

Richard, J. (1992), *Croisades et états latins d'orient. Points de vue et documents*, London

Riley-Smith, J. (ed.) (1991), *The atlas of the crusades*, London

Runciman, S. (1965), *The fall of Constantinople: 1453*, Cambridge

Schlumberger, G. (1878), *Numismatique de l'orient latin*, Paris

Schwoebel, R. (1967), *The shadow of the crescent. The Renaissance image of the Turk (1453–1517)*, Nieuwkoop

Settis, S. (ed.) (1986), *Memoria dell'antico nell'arte italiana*, III, Turin

Setton, K. (1975a), *Catalan domination of Athens: 1311–1388*, rev. edn, London

Setton, K. (1975b), *Los Catalanes en Grecia*, Barcelona

Setton, K. (1978), *The Papacy and the Levant (1204–1571)*, II: *The fifteenth century*, Memoirs of the American Philosophical Society, 127, Philadelphia

Setton, K. (ed.) (1975–89), *A history of the crusades*, III–VI, Madison, Wis.

Slot, B. (1982), *Archipelagus Turbatus. Les Cyclades entre colonisation latine et occupation ottomane, c. 1500–1718*, 2 vols., Leiden

Smith, A. (1962), *The architecture of Chios*, London

Sommi-Picenardi, G. (1900), *Itinéraire d'un chevalier de Saint-Jean de Jérusalem dans l'île de Rhodes*, Lille

Stylianou, A. and J. (1985), *The painted churches of Cyprus. Treasures of Byzantine art*, London

Thiriet, F. (1975), *La Romanie vénitienne au moyen-âge. Le développement et l'exploitation du domaine colonial vénitien (XIIe–XVe siècles)*, Bibliothèque des Ecoles Françaises d'Athènes et de Rome, 193, Paris

Thiriet, F. (1977), *Etudes sur la Romanie gréco-vénitienne (Xe–XVe siècles)*, London

Topping, P. (1977), *Studies on Latin Greece A.D. 1205–1715*, London

Tyerman, C. (1988), *England and the crusades 1095–1588*, Chicago

Vatin, N. (1994), *L'ordre de Saint-Jean-de-Jérusalem, l'empire Ottoman et la Méditerranée orientale entre les deux sièges de Rhodes: 1480–1522*, Paris

Verlinden, C. (1977), *L'Esclavage dans l'Europe médiévale*, II, Ghent
Zachariadou, E. (1983), *Trade and crusade. Venetian Crete and the emirates of Mentesche and Aydin (1300–1415)*, Venice
Zakythinos, D. (1975), *Le despotat grec de Morée*, 2 vols., rev. edn, London

32   THE OTTOMAN WORLD

Primary sources

Acta et diplomata Ragusina, ed. J. Radonić, 2 vols. in 3 pts, Belgrade (1934–5)
Die Byzantinischen Kleinchroniken, ed. P. Schreiner, *Corpus fontium historiae Byzantinae, series Vindobonensis*, I–III, Vienna (1975–9)
Cananus, *Narratio*, ed. I. Bekkerus, *Georgius Phrantzes, Ioannes Cananus, Ioannes Anagnostes*, Bonn (1838), pp. 457–79
Ducas Michaelis Ducae nepotis, *Historia Byzantina*, ed. I. Bekkerus, Bonn (1834)
Ecthesis chronica et chronicon Athenarium, ed. S.P. Lambros, London (1902)
Hicrî 835 Sûret-i Defter-i Sancak-i Arvanid, ed. H. Inalcik, Ankara (1954)
Jorga, N., *Notes et extraits pour servir à l'histoire des croisades au XVe siècle*, 4th series, Bucharest (1915)
Konstantin, Mihailović, *Memoirs of a janissary*, trans. B. Stolz, historical commentary and notes by S. Soucek, Michigan Slavic Publications, Ann Arbor (1975)
Ordo portae, description Grecque de la porte et de l'armée du Sultan Mehmed II, ed. Ş. Baştav, Magyar-Görög Tanulmányok, 27, Budapest (1947)
Spandugnino, *Dela origine deli Imperatori Ottomani*, ed. C.N. Sathas, *Documents inédits relatifs à l'histoire de la Grèce au moyen âge*, IX, Paris (1890), pp. 138–261
Sphrantzes Georgios, *Memorii 1401–1477*, ed. V. Grecu, Bucharest (1966)
Sylvestre Syropoulos, *Les 'mémoires' du grand ecclésiarque de l'église de Constantinople Sylvestre Syropoulos sur le concile de Florence (1438–1439)*, ed. V. Laurent, Paris (1971)
Symeon, archbishop of Thessalonika, *Politico-historical works (1416/17 to 1429)*, ed. D. Balfour, Wiener Byzantinistiche Studien, XIII, Vienna (1979)

Secondary works

Babinger, F. (1978), *Mehmed the Conqueror and his time*, trans. R. Manheim, ed. W.C. Hickman, Princeton
Basso, E. (1994), *Genova. Un impero sul mare*, Consiglio Nazionale delle Ricerche, Istituto sui Rapporti Italo-Iberici, 20, Cagliari
Beldiceanu, N. (1965), 'Recherches sur la reforme foncière Mehmed II', *Acta historica* 4: 27–39
Beldiceanu, N. (1980), *Le timar dans l'empire Ottoman (début du XIVe–début XVIe siècle)*, Wiesbaden
Beldiceanu-Steinherr, I. (1969), 'En marge d'un acte concernant le pengyek et les aqıngı', *Revue des études islamiques* 37: 21–47
Beldiceanu-Steinherr, I. (1991), 'Les Bektaši à la lumière des recensements ottomans (XVe–XVIe siècles)', *Wiener Zeitschrift für die Kunde des Morgenlandes* 81:21–79
Braude, B. (1982), 'Foundation myths in the millet system', in B. Braude and B. Lewis

(eds.), *Christians and Jews in the Ottoman Empire. The functioning of a plural society*, I: *The central lands*, London and New York, pp. 69–88

Cazacu, M. and Nasturel, P.S. (1978), 'Une démonstration navale des Turcs devant Constantinople et la bataille de Kilia (1448)', *Journal des savants*: 197–210

Christensen, S. (1987), 'European-Ottoman military acculturation in the late Middle Ages', in B.P. McGuire (ed.), *War and peace in the Middle Ages*, Copenhagen, pp. 227–51

Demetriades, V. (1993), 'Some thoughts on the origins of the Devshirme', in E. Zachariadou (ed.), *The Ottoman emirate (1300–1389)*, Halcyon Days in Crete I, a Symposium held in Rethymnon 11–13 January 1991, Rethymnon, pp. 23–33

Dennis, G. (1967), 'The Byzantine–Turkish treaty of 1403', *Orientalia Christiana periodica* 33: 72–88

Fisher, S.N. (1948), *The foreign relations of Turkey, 1481–1512*, Urbana

Gölpınarlı, A. (1965), *Yunus Emre Risalat al Nushiyya ve Divan*, Istanbul

Imber, C. (1990), *The Ottoman Empire 1300–1481*, Istanbul

Inalcik, H. (1960), 'Bursa and the commerce of the Levant', *Journal of Economic and Social History of the Orient* 3: 131–47

Inalcik, H. (1962), 'The rise of Ottoman historiography', in B. Lewis and P.M. Holt (eds.), *Historians of the Middle East*, London, pp. 152–67

Inalcik, H. (1969), 'Capital formation in the Ottoman Empire', *Journal of Economic History* 19: 121–2

Inalcik, H. (1969–70), 'The policy of Mehmed II toward the Greek population of Istanbul and the Byzantine buildings of the city', *DOP* 23/4: 231–49

Inalcik, H. (1970a), *The Cambridge history of Islam*, I: *The central Islamic lands*, Cambridge, pp. 295–353

Inalcik, H. (1970b), 'The Ottoman economic mind and aspects of the Ottoman economy', in M. Cook (ed.), *Studies on the economic history of the Middle East*, London, pp. 207–18

Inalcik, H. (1973), *The Ottoman Empire. The classical age 1300–1600*, London

Inalcik, H. (1979), 'The question of the closing of the Black Sea under the Ottomans', in *'Black Sea' Birmingham, 18–20 March 1978, Archeion Pontou* 35: 74–110

Inalcik, H. (1993), 'Village, peasant and empire', in *The Middle East and the Balkans under the Ottoman Empire. Essays on economy and society*, Indiana University Turkish Studies and Turkish Ministry of Culture Joint Series, 9, Bloomington, pp. 137–60

Inalcik, H. and Murphey, R. (1978), *The history of Mehmed the Conqueror by Tursun beg*, Minneapolis and Chicago

Kellenbenz, H. (1967), 'Handelsverbindungen zwischen Mitteleuropa und Istanbul über Venedig in der ersten Hälfte des 16. Jahrhunderts' *Studi Veneziani* 9: 194–9

Kissling, H.J. (1988), 'Betrachtungen über die Flottenpolitik Sultan Bâjezids (1481–1512)', in *Dissertationes Orientales et Balcanicae Collectae* II, Munich, pp. 207–15

Lefort, J. (1981), *Documents grecs dans les archives de Topkapi Sarayi, contribution à l'histoire de Cem Sultan*, Ankara

Lewis, B. (1961), *The emergence of modern Turkey*, London

Lewis, B. (1968), 'The Mongols, the Turks and the Muslim polity', *TRHS* 5th series 18: 49–68

Manfroni, C. (1902), 'La battaglia di Gallipoli e la politica Veneto-turca (1381–1420)', *Ateneo Veneto* 25: 3–34, 129–69

Mélikoff, I. (1975), 'Le problème kızılbaş', *Turcica* 6: 49–67

Mélikoff, I. (1993), 'L'origine sociale des premiers Ottomans', in E. Zachariadou (ed.), *The Ottoman emirate (1300–1389)*, Halcyon Days in Crete I, a Symposium held in Rethymnon 11–13 January 1991, Rethymnon, pp. 135–44

Ménage, V.L. (1966), 'Some notes on the devshirme', *Bulletin of the School of Oriental and African Studies* 29: 64–78

Ménage, V.L. (1976), 'The "annals of Murad II"', *Bulletin of the School of Oriental and African Studies* 39: 569–84

Mpouras, C. (1973), 'Τὸ ἐπιτύμβιο τοῦ Λουκᾶ Σπαντουνῆ στὴ βασιλικὴ τοῦ ἁγίου Δημητρίου Θεσσαλονίκης', *Epistemonike Epeteris tes Polytechnikes Scholes Thessalonikes* 6: 3–63

Özbaran, S. (1994), *The Ottoman response to European expansion*, Analecta Isisiana, XII, Istanbul

Papacostea, S. (1976), 'Kilia et la politique orientale de Sigismond de Luxembourg', *Revue Roumaine d'histoire* 15: 421–36

Papacostea, S. (1978), 'Die politischen Voraussetzungen für die Wirtschaftliche Vorherrschaft des osmanischen Reiches im Schwarzmeergebiet (1453–1484)', *Münchner Zeitschrift für Balkankunde* 1: 217–45

Roemer, H.R. (1990), 'The Qızılbash Turcomans: founders and victims of the Safavid theocracy', in M.M. Mazzaoui and Vera B. Moreen (eds.), *Intellectual studies in Islam. Essays written in honor of Martin B. Dickson*, Salt Lake City, pp. 27–39

Shai Har-El (1995), *Struggle for domination in the Middle East. The Ottoman–Mamluk War*, Leiden, New York and Cologne

Stromer, W. von (1981), 'Die Struktur von Produktion und Verteilung von Bunt- und Edelmetallen an der Wende vom Mittelalter zur Neuzeit und ihre bestimmenden Faktoren', in H. Kellenbenz (ed.), *Precious metals in the age of expansion. Papers of the XIVth International Congress of the Historical Sciences, 1975*, Beiträge zur Wirtschaftsgeschichte, 2, Stuttgart, pp. 13–26

Tardy, L. (1978), *Beyond the Ottoman Empire*, Studia Uralo-Altaica, 13, Szeged

Werner, E. (1985), *Die Geburt einer Grossmacht – Die Osmanen. Forschungen zur Mittelalterlichen Geschichte 32*, 4th edn, Weimar

Wittek, P. (1938a), 'De la defaite d'Ankara à la prise de Constantinople', *Revue des études islamiques* 12: 1–34

Wittek, P. (1938b), *The rise of the Ottoman Empire*, London

Zachariadou, E.A. (1983a), 'Ottoman diplomacy and the Danube frontier (1420–1424)', in *Okeanos. Essays presented to Ihor Sevcenko, Harvard Ukrainian Studies* 13: 680–90

Zachariadou, E.A. (1983b), 'Süleyman çelebi in Rumili and the Ottoman chronicles', *Der Islam* 60: 268–96

Zachariadou, E.A. (1987), 'Lauro Quirini and the Turkish Sandjaks (ca. 1430)', in *Raiyyet Rüsûmu. Essays presented to Halil Inalcik, Journal of Turkish Studies* 11: 239–47

Zachariadou, E.A. (1990–1), 'The neomartyr's message', *Bulletin of the Centre for Asia Minor Studies* 8: 51–63

CONCLUSION

Secondary works

Adams, R.P. (1962), *The better part of valor. More, Erasmus, Colet and Vives on humanism, war, and peace, 1496–1535*, Seattle

Allmand, C.T. (1988), *The Hundred Years War. England and France at war, c. 1300–c. 1450*, Cambridge

Allmand, C.T. and Armstrong, C.A.J. (eds.) (1982), *English suits before the parlement of Paris, 1420–1436*, RHS, London

Anglo, S. (ed.) (1990), *Chivalry in the Renaissance*, Woodbridge

Armstrong, C.A.J. (1995), 'Les ducs de Bourgogne, interprètes de la pensée politique du 15e siècle', *AB* 67: 5–34

Armstrong, E. (1990), *Before copyright. The French book-privilege system, 1498–1526*, Cambridge

Autrand, F. (ed.) (1986), *Prosopographie et genèse de l'état moderne*, Collection de l'Ecole Normale Supérieure de Jeunes Filles, 30, Paris

Blanchard, J. (1996), *Commynes l'Européen. L'invention du politique*, Geneva

Blockmans, W.P. and Genet, J.-P. (eds.) (1993), *Visions sur le développement des états européens. Théories et historiographies de l'état moderne*, Rome

Bulst, N. and Genet, J.-P. (eds.) (1988), *La ville, la bourgeoisie et la genèse de l'état moderne (XIIe–XVIIIe siècles)*, Paris

Burns, J.H. (1992), *Lordship, kingship and empire. The idea of monarchy, 1400–1525*, Oxford

Clough, C.H. (1990), 'Chivalry and magnificence in the golden age of the Italian Renaissance', in Anglo (1990), pp. 25–47

La conscience européenne au XVe et au XVI siècle (1982), Collection de l'Ecole Normale Supérieure de Jeunes Filles, 22, Paris

Contamine, P. (ed.) (1989), *L'état et les aristocraties (France, Angleterre, Ecosse), XIIe–XVIIe siècle*, Paris

Coulet, N. and Genet, J.-P. (eds.) (1990), *L'état moderne. Le droit, l'espace et les formes de l'état*, Paris

Culture et idéologie dans la genèse de l'état moderne (1985), Collection de l'Ecole Française de Rome, 82, Rome

Eisenstein, E.L. (1968), 'Some conjectures about the impact of printing on western society and thought', *JModH* 40: 1–56

Genet, J.-P. (1995), 'La monarchie anglaise: une image brouillée', in J. Blanchard (ed.), *Représentation, pouvoir et royauté à la fin du moyen âge*, Paris, pp. 93–107

Genet, J.-P. (ed.) (1990), *L'état moderne: genèse. Bilans et perspectives*, Paris

Genet, J.-P. and Le Mené, M. (1987), *Genèse de l'état moderne. Prélèvement et redistribution*, Paris

Genet, J.-P. and Vincent, B. (eds.), (1986), *L'état et l'église dans la genèse de l'état moderne*, Collection de la Casa de Velazquez, 1, Madrid

Gilmore, M.P. (1952), *The world of humanism, 1453–1517*, New York

Goldsmith, J.L. (1995, 1996), 'The crisis of the late Middle Ages: the case of France', *French History* 9: 417–50; 10: 162

Guenée, B. (1985), *States and rulers in late medieval Europe*, Oxford

Guenée, B. (1992), *Un meurtre, une société. L'assassinat du duc d'Orléans, 23 novembre 1407*, Paris

Gunn, S. (1990), 'Chivalry and the politics of the early Tudor court', in Anglo (1990), pp. 107–28

Hale, J.R. (1957), 'International relations in the west: diplomacy and war', in Potter (1957), pp. 259–91

Hale, J.R. (1971), *Renaissance Europe 1480–1520*, London

Hale, J.R. (1990), *Artists and warfare in the Renaissance*, New Haven and London

Harriss, G.L. (ed.) (1993), *Henry V: The practice of kingship*, Stroud

Hay, D. (1957a), *Europe. The emergence of an idea*, Edinburgh

Hay, D. (1957b), 'Introduction', in Potter (1957), pp. 1–19

Heymann, F. (1965), *George of Bohemia*, Princeton

Holmes, G.A. (1961), 'The "Libel of English policy"', *EHR* 76: 193–216

Housley, N. (1992), *The later crusades. From Lyons to Alcazar, 1274–1580*, Oxford

Mager, W. (1991), 'Res publica chez les juristes, théologiens et philosophes à la fin du moyen âge: sur l'élaboration d'une notion-clé de la théorie politique moderne', in *Théologie et droit* (1991), pp. 229–39

Oakley, F. (1979), *The western Church in the later Middle Ages*, Ithaca and London

Potter, G.R. (ed.) (1957), *The new Cambridge modern history*, I: *The Renaissance, 1493–1520*, Cambridge

Prévité-Orton, C.W. and Brooke, Z.N. (eds.) (1936), *The Cambridge medieval history*, VIII: *The close of the Middle Ages*, Cambridge

Queller, D.E. (1967), *The office of ambassador in the Middle Ages*, Princeton

Reinhard, W. (ed.) (1996), *Power elites and state building*, Oxford

Rosie, A. (1989), '"Morisques" and "Momeryes": aspects of court entertainment at the court of Savoy in the fifteenth century', in C.T. Allmand (ed.) (1989), *Power, culture, and religion in France, c. 1350–c. 1550*, Woodbridge, pp. 57–74

Rucquoi, A. (ed.) (1988), *Realidad e imagines del poder. España a fines de la edad media*, Valladolid

Théologie et droit dans la science politique de l'état moderne (1991), Collection de l'Ecole Française de Rome, 147, Rome

The universal peace organization of King George of Bohemia. A fifteenth-century plan for world peace 1462/1464 (1964), London

Watts, J.L. (1996), *Henry VI and the politics of kingship*, Cambridge

INDEX